Dear Reader

With the aim of giving a maximum amount of information in a limited number of pages Michelin has adopted a system of symbols which is today known the world over.

Failing this system the present publication would run to six volumes.

Judge for yourselves by comparing the descriptive text below with the equivalent extract from the Guide in symbol form.

🏨 ✿✿ **Europa** (Helder) Ⓜ ⑄, 𝒫 21 32 43, ≤ valley, 🍴 « Flowered garden » – ✻ ☎ 🚗, 🖭
March-October — **M** *(closed Monday)* 240/410 — 🍴 45 — **35 rm** 385/680 — ½ P 420/530.
Spec. Gratin de queues d'écrevisses, Volaille de Bresse aux morilles, Soufflé au chocolat. **Wines.** St Véran, Chiroubles.

A very comfortable hotel where you will enjoy a pleasant stay and be tempted to prolong your visit.

The excellence of the cuisine, which is personally supervised by the proprietor Mr Helder, is worth a detour.

The hotel in its quiet secluded setting away from the built-up-area offers every modern amenity.

To reserve phone 21 32 43.

The hotel affords a fine view of the valley ; in good weather it is possible to eat out of doors. The hotel is enhanced by an attractive flowered garden.

Smoking is not allowed in certain areas of the establishment.

Direct dialling telephone in room.

Parking facilities, under cover, are available to hotel guests.

The hotel accepts payment by American Express credit card.

The establishment is open from March to October but the restaurant closes every Monday.

The set meal prices range from 240 F for the lowest to 410 F for the highest.

The cost of continental breakfast served in the bedroom is 45 F.

35 bedroomed hotel. The charges vary from 385 F for a single to 680 F for the best twin bedded room.

Prices for half-board range in high season from 420 to 530 F.

Included for the gourmet are some culinary specialities, recommended by the hotelier : Gratin de queues d'écrevisses, Volaille de Bresse aux morilles, Soufflé au chocolat. In addition to the best quality wines you will find many of the local wines worth sampling : St Véran, Chiroubles.

This demonstration clearly shows that each entry contains a great deal of information. The symbols are easily learnt and to know them will enable you to understand the Guide and to choose those establishments that you require.

CONTENTS

DISTANCES BY ROAD

(in kilometres)

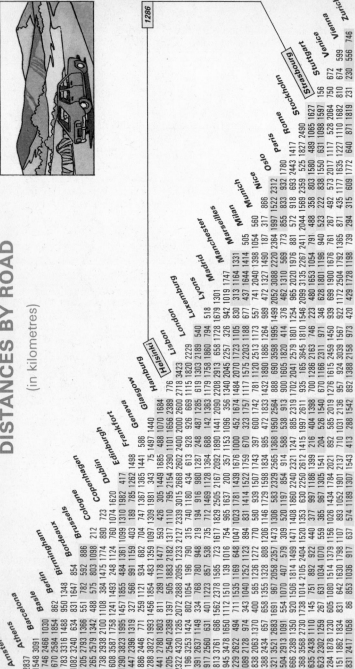

AIR LINKS (in hours)

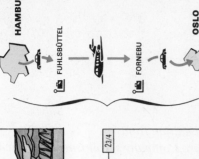

HAMBURG · FUHLSBÜTTEL · FORNEBU · OSLO

31/2 not daily

Cities (diagonal labels):
Amsterdam, Athens, Barcelona, Basle, Berlin, Birmingham, Bordeaux, Brussels, Cologne, Copenhagen, Dublin, Edinburgh, Frankfort, Geneva, Glasgow, Hamburg, Helsinki, Lisbon, London, Luxemburg, Lyons, Madrid, Manchester, Marseilles, Milan, Munich, Nice, Oslo, Paris, Rome, Stockholm, Strasbourg, Stuttgart, Venice, Vienna, Zürich

This revised edition from
Michelin Tyre Company's Tourism Department
offers you a selection of
hotels and restaurants in the main European cities.
The latter have been chosen for
their business or tourist interest.

In addition the guide indicates establishments,
located in other towns,
renowned for the excellence of their cuisine.

We hope that the guide will help you
with your choice of a hotel or restaurant
and prove useful for your sightseeing.
Have an enjoyable stay.

Signs and symbols

HOTELS AND RESTAURANTS

CATEGORY, STANDARD OF COMFORT

Luxury in the traditional style	🏰🏰🏰	XXXXX
Top class comfort	🏰🏰	XXXX
Very comfortable	🏰	XXX
Comfortable	🏠	XX
Quite comfortable	🏠	X
In its class, hotel with modern amenities	M	

ATMOSPHERE AND SETTING

Pleasant hotels	🏰🏰 ... 🏠
Pleasant restaurants	XXXXX ... X
Particularly attractive feature	« Park »
Very quiet or quiet secluded hotel	🐾
Quiet hotel	🐾
Exceptional view — Panoramic view	⩽ sea, ❋
Interesting or extensive view	⩽

CUISINE

Exceptional cuisine in the country, worth a special journey	✿✿✿
Excellent cooking : worth a detour	✿✿
A very good restaurant in its category	✿
Other recommended carefully prepared meals	M

HOTEL FACILITIES

🛗 📺	Lift (elevator) — Television in room
⌇✗⌇	Non-smoking areas
▤	Air conditioning
☎	Telephone in room : direct dialling for outside calls
📞	Telephone in room : outside calls connected by operator
✗ ⊥ ▨	Hotel tennis court(s) — Outdoor or indoor swimming pool
⊜ ♨	Sauna — Exercise room
☞ ♠	Garden — Beach with bathing facilities
☝	Meals served in garden or on terrace
⊛ Ⓟ	Garage — Car park
♿	Bedrooms accessible to disabled people
🏛	Equipped conference hall
✗	Dogs are not allowed
without rest.	The hotel has no restaurant

PRICES

These prices are given in the currency of the country in question. Valid for 1991 the rates shown should only vary if the cost of living changes to any great extent.

Meals

M 75/130 — Set meal prices

M a la carte
110/180 — " a la carte " meals

b.i. — House wine included

Hotels

30 rm 185/300 — Lowest price for a comfortable single and highest price for the best double room

½ P — SB — Half board — Short Break

Breakfast

⊐ 25 — Price of breakfast

Bb — Breakfast with choice from buffet

Service and taxes

Except in Greece, Portugal and Spain, prices shown are inclusive, that is to say service and V.A.T. included. In U.K. and Ireland, **s** = service only included, **t** = V.A.T. only included. In Italy, when not included, a percentage for service is shown after the meal prices.

SIGHTS

Worth a journey	★★★
Worth a detour	★★
Interesting	★

TOWN PLANS

Main conventional signs

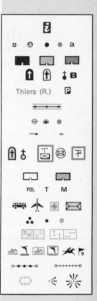

Tourist Information Centre..

Hotel, restaurant – Reference letter on the town plan ....

Place of interest and its main entrance ⎱
Interesting church or chapel .... ⎰ Reference letter on the town plan ..

Shopping street – Public car park ....

Tram ....

Underground station ....

One-way street ....

Church or chapel – Poste restante, telegraph – Telephone ....

Public buildings located by letters :

Police (in large towns police headquarters) – Theatre – Museum ....

Coach station – Airport – Hospital – Covered market ....

Ruins – Monument, statue – Fountain ....

Garden, park, wood – Cemetery, Jewish cemetery ....

Outdoor or indoor swimming pool – Racecourse – Golf course ....

Cable-car – Funicular ....

Sports ground, stadium – View – Panorama..............................

Names shown on the street plans are in the language of the country to conform to local signposting.

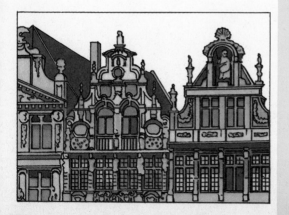

Avec cette nouvelle édition,
les Services de Tourisme du Pneu Michelin
vous proposent une sélection
d'hôtels et restaurants
des principales villes d'Europe,
choisies en raison de leur vocation internationale
sur le plan des affaires et du tourisme.

Vous y trouverez également les grandes tables
situées hors de ces grandes villes.

Nous vous souhaitons d'agréables séjours
et espérons que ce guide vous aidera utilement
pour le choix d'un hôtel,
d'une bonne table
et pour la visite des principales curiosités.

Signes et symboles

HOTELS ET RESTAURANTS

CLASSE ET CONFORT

Grand luxe et tradition	🏨	XXXXX
Grand confort	🏨	XXXX
Très confortable	🏨	XXX
Bon confort	🏨	XX
Assez confortable	🏠	X
Dans sa catégorie, hôtel d'équipement moderne	M	

L'AGRÉMENT

Hôtels agréables	🏨 ... 🏠
Restaurants agréables	XXXXX ... X
Élément particulièrement agréable	« Park »
Hôtel très tranquille, ou isolé et tranquille	🐾
Hôtel tranquille	🐾
Vue exceptionnelle, panorama	⩽ sea, ☀
Vue intéressante ou étendue	⩽

LA TABLE

Une des meilleures tables du pays, vaut le voyage	✸✸✸
Table excellente, mérite un détour	✸✸
Une très bonne table dans sa catégorie	✸
Autre table soignée	M

L'INSTALLATION

🛗 📺	Ascenseur, Télévision dans la chambre
🚭	Non-fumeurs
▤	Air conditionné
☎	Téléphone dans la chambre direct avec l'extérieur
🕾	Téléphone dans la chambre relié par standard
✂ ⊥ ◰	Tennis — Piscine : de plein air ou couverte
⊆s 𝄕	Sauna — Salle de remise en forme
🜨 ⚓s	Jardin — Plage aménagée
☂	Repas servis au jardin ou en terrasse
🚗 Ⓟ	Garage — Parc à voitures
♿	Chambres accessibles aux handicapés physiques
⚐	L'hôtel reçoit les séminaires
🐕	Accès interdit aux chiens
without rest.	L'hôtel n'a pas de restaurant

LES PRIX

Les prix sont indiqués dans la monnaie du pays. Établis pour l'année 1991, ils ne doivent être modifiés que si le coût de la vie subit des variations importantes.

Au restaurant

M 75/130	Prix des repas à prix fixes
M a la carte 110/180	Prix des repas à la carte
b.i.	Boisson comprise

A l'hôtel

30 rm 185/300	Prix minimum pour une chambre d'une personne et maximum pour la plus belle chambre occupée par deux personnes
½ P — SB	Demi-pension — "Short Break" (forfait 2 nuits et dîners)

Petit déjeuner

⊡ 25	Prix du petit déjeuner.
Bb	Petit déjeuner buffet

Service et taxes

A l'exception de la Grèce, du Portugal et de l'Espagne, les prix indiqués sont nets. Au Royaume Uni et en Irlande, s = service compris, t = T.V.A. comprise. En Italie, le service est parfois compté en supplément aux prix des repas. Ex. : (16%).

LES CURIOSITÉS

Vaut le voyage
Mérite un détour
Intéressante

LES PLANS

Principaux signes conventionnels

Information touristique . . . .

Hôtel, restaurant — Lettre les repérant sur le plan . . . .

Monument intéressant et entrée principale ⎫
Église ou chapelle intéressante . . . . ⎬ Lettre les repérant sur le plan . . . . . .

Rue commerçante — Parc de stationnement public . . . .

Tramway . . . .

Station de métro . . . .

Sens unique . . . .

Église ou chapelle — Poste restante, télégraphe — Téléphone . . . .

Édifices publics repérés par des lettres :

Police (dans les grandes villes commissariat central) — Théâtre — Musée . . . .

Gare routière — Aéroport — Hôpital — Marché couvert . . . .

Ruines — Monument, statue — Fontaine . . . .

Jardin, parc, bois — Cimetière, cimetière israélite . . . .

Piscine de plein air, couverte — Hippodrome — Golf . . . .

Téléphérique — Funiculaire . . . .

Stade — Vue — Panorama . . . .

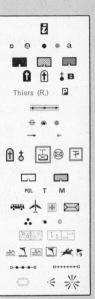

*Les indications portées sur les plans sont dans la langue
du pays, en conformité avec la dénomination locale.*

Mit dieser Neuauflage
präsentieren Ihnen die Michelin-Touristikabteilungen
eine Auswahl von Hotels und Restaurants
in europäischen Hauptstädten
von internationaler Bedeutung
für Geschäftsreisende und Touristen.

Besonders gute Restaurants in der näheren Umgebung
dieser Städte wurden ebenfalls aufgenommen.

Wir wünschen einen angenehmen Aufenthalt
und hoffen, daß Ihnen dieser Führer
bei der Wahl eines Hotels, eines Restaurants
und beim Besuch der Hauptsehenswürdigkeiten
gute Dienste leisten wird.

Zeichen und Symbole

HOTELS UND RESTAURANTS

KLASSENEINTEILUNG UND KOMFORT

Großer Luxus und Tradition	🏰	XXXXX
Großer Komfort	🏛	XXXX
Sehr komfortabel	🏛	XXX
Mit gutem Komfort	🏠	XX
Mit ausreichendem Komfort	🏠	X
Moderne Einrichtung	M	

ANNEHMLICHKEITEN

Angenehme Hotels	🏰 ... 🏠
Angenehme Restaurants	XXXXX ... X
Besondere Annehmlichkeit	« Park »
Sehr ruhiges oder abgelegenes und ruhiges Hotel	🕊
Ruhiges Hotel	🕊
Reizvolle Aussicht, Rundblick	≤ sea, ✳
Interessante oder weite Sicht	≤

KÜCHE

Eine der besten Küchen des Landes : eine Reise wert	✿✿✿
Eine hervorragende Küche : verdient einen Umweg	✿✿
Eine sehr gute Küche : verdient Ihre besondere Beachtung	✿
Andere sorgfältig zubereitete Mahlzeiten	M

19

EINRICHTUNG

⬍ TV	Fahrstuhl — Fernsehen im Zimmer
⳽⤫	Nichtraucher
▤	Klimaanlage
☎	Zimmertelefon mit direkter Außenverbindung
☏	Zimmertelefon mit Außenverbindung über Telefonzentrale
✂ ⳴ ⛱	Tennis — Freibad — Hallenbad
⏛s ⼋	Sauna — Fitneß Center
⛵ ⵑ⚓	Garten — Strandbad
⛩	Garten-, Terrassenrestaurant
⬅🚗 Ⓟ	Garage — Parkplatz
♿	Für Körperbehinderte leicht zugängliche Zimmer
⚎	Konferenzraum
🐕̸	Das Mitführen von Hunden ist unerwünscht
without rest	Hotel ohne Restaurant

DIE PREISE

Die Preise sind in der jeweiligen Landeswährung angegeben. Sie gelten für das Jahr 1991 und können nur geändert werden, wenn die Lebenshaltungskosten starke Veränderungen erfahren.

Im Restaurant

M 75/130	Feste Menupreise
M a la carte 110/180	Mahlzeiten "a la carte "
b.i.	Getränke inbegriffen

Im Hotel

30 rm 185/300	Mindestpreis für ein Einzelzimmer und Höchstpreis für das schönste Doppelzimmer für zwei Personen
½ P - SB	Halbpension — "Short Break" : Pauschale für 2 Nächte (Halbpension)

Frühstück

⊊25	Preis des Frühstücks
Bb	Frühstücksbuffet

Bedienungsgeld und Gebühren

Mit Ausnahme von Griechenland, Portugal und Spanien sind die angegebenen Preise Inklusivpreise. In den Kapiteln über Großbritannien und Irland bedeutet s = Bedienungsgeld inbegriffen, t = MWSt inbegriffen. In Italien wird für die Bedienung gelegentlich ein Zuschlag zum Preis der Mahlzeit erhoben.

SEHENSWÜRDIGKEITEN

Eine Reise wert
Verdient einen Umweg
Sehenswert

STADTPLÄNE

Erklärung der wichtigsten Zeichen

Informationsstelle . . . .

Hotel, Restaurant – Referenzbuchstabe auf dem Plan . . . .

Sehenswertes Gebäude mit Haupteingang ⎫
Sehenswerte Kirche oder Kapelle . . . . ⎬ Referenzbuchstabe auf dem Plan . . .
⎭

Einkaufsstraße – Öffentlicher Parkplatz, Parkhaus

Straßenbahn . . . .

U-Bahnstation . . . .

Einbahnstraße . . . .

Kirche oder Kapelle – Postlagernde Sendungen, Telegraph – Telefon . . . .

Öffentliche Gebäude, durch Buchstaben gekennzeichnet :

Polizei (in größeren Städten Polizeipräsidium) – Theater – Museum . . . .

Autobusbahnhof – Flughafen – Krankenhaus – Markthalle . . . .

Ruine – Denkmal, Statue – Brunnen . . . .

Garten, Park, Wald – Friedhof, Jüd. Friedhof . . . .

Freibad – Hallenbad – Pferderennbahn – Golfplatz und Lochzahl . . . .

Seilschwebebahn – Standseilbahn . . . .

Sportplatz – Aussicht – Rundblick . . . .

Die Angaben auf den Stadtplänen erfolgen, übereinstimmend mit der örtlichen Beschilderung, in der Landessprache.

この改訂版ガイドブックはミシュラン・タイヤ社観光部
がおとどけするものです。

ビジネスに、観光に、国際的な拠点ヨーロッパ主要都市
が誇る自慢のホテルとレストランを、そして郊外にたた
ずむ名うてのレストランをあわせて、御紹介いたします。

このガイドブックが、より快適なホテル、味わい深いレ
ストランやあこがれの地と出逢うきっかけとなり、皆さ
まの旅をより素晴らしいものにするお手伝いができれ
ば幸いです。

記号
と
シンボルマーク

ホテルとレストラン

等級と快適さ

豪華で伝統的様式
トップクラス
たいへん快適
快適
かなり快適
等級内での近代的設備のホテル

居心地

居心地よいホテル
居心地よいレストラン
特に魅力的な特徴
大変静かなホテル又は人里離れた静かなホテル
静かなホテル
見晴らしがよい展望(例:海)、パノラマ
素晴らしい風景

料理

最上の料理、出かける価値あり
素晴らしい料理、寄り道の価値あり
等級内では大変おいしい料理
その他の心のこもった料理

設備

🛗 📺	エレベーター、室内テレビ
🚭	非喫煙室
▤	空調設備
☎	室内に電話あり、外線直通
☏	室内に電話あり、外線は交換台経由
✄ 🏊 🏊	テニスコート。屋外プール。屋内プール。
≦ₛ ⑂	サウナ。トレーニングルーム。
🛥 ⚓	くつろげる庭。整備された海水浴場
🍴	食事が庭またはテラスでできる
🚗 Ⓟ	駐車場、パーキング。
🦽	体の不自由な方のための設備あり
🏛	会議又は研修会の出来るホテル
🐕̸	犬の連れ込みおことわり
without rest.	レストランの無いホテル

料金

料金は1991年のその国の貨幣単位で示してありますが、物価の変動などで変わる場合もあります。

レストラン

M 75/130

定食、ア・ラ・カルトそれぞれの最低料金と最高料金。

M a la carte
110/180

b.i.

飲物付

ホテル

30 rm 185/300

一人部屋の最低料金と二人部屋の最高料金。

½ P – SB

一食付き宿泊。「ショート・ブレイク」（二泊＋二夕食）。

朝食

🍴 25

朝食代

Bb

朝食はビュッフェ形式

サービス料と税金

ギリシャ、ポルトガル、スペイン以外の国に関しては正価料金。英国及びアイルランドでは、s.：サービス料込み、t.：付加価値税込み、を意味する。イタリアでは、サービス料が料金に加算されることがある。例：(16%)

名　所

出かける価値あり・・

立ち寄る価値あり・・

興味深い・・・

★★★
★★
★

地　図

主な記号

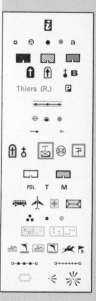

ツーリストインフォメーション・・・・・・・・・・・・・・・・・・・・・・・・・・・・・・・・

ホテル・レストラン——地図上での目印番号・・・・・・・・・

興味深い歴史的建造物と、その中央入口 ｝ 地図上での
興味深い教会または聖堂 目印番号

商店街——公共駐車場・・・・・・・・・・・・・・・・・・・・・・・・・・・・・・・・・・・・

路面電車・・

地下鉄駅・・・

一方通行路・・

教会または聖堂——局留郵便、電報——電話・・・・・・・・・

公共建造物、記号は下記の通り・・・・・・・・・・・・・・・・・・・・・・・・・・・・

警察(大都市では、中央警察署)——劇場——美術館、博物館・・・・・

長距離バス発着所——空港——病院——屋内市場・・・・・

遺跡——歴史的建造物、像——泉・・・・・・・・・・・・・・・・・・・・・・・・・

庭園、公園、森林——墓地——ユダヤ教の墓地・・・・・・・・・

屋外プール、屋内プール——競馬場——ゴルフ場・・・・・・・・・

ロープウェイ——ケーブルカー・・・・・・・・・・・・・・・・・・・・・・・・・・・

スタジアム——風景——パノラマ・・・・・・・・・・・・・・・・・・・・・・・・・・

地図上の名称は、地方の標識に合わせてその国の言葉で表記されて
います。

Austria
Österreich

Vienna
Salzburg

PRACTICAL INFORMATION

LOCAL CURRENCY

Austrian Schilling ; 100 S = 9.43 US $ (Jan. 91)

TOURIST INFORMATION

In Vienna : Österreich-Information, 1040 Wien, Margaretenstr. 1, ℘ (0222) 5 87 20 00
Niederösterreich-Information, 1010 Wien, Heidenschuß 2, ℘ (0222) 5 33 31 14

In Salzburg : Landesverkehrsamt, Sigmund-Haffner-Gasse 16, ℘ (0662) 80 42 23 27

AIRLINES

AUSTRIAN AIRLINES : 1010 Wien, Kärtner Ring 18, ℘ (0222) 7 17 99
AIR FRANCE : 1010 Wien, Kärntner Str. 49, ℘ (0222) 5 14 19
BRITISH AIRWAYS : 1010 Wien, Kärntner Ring 10, ℘ (0222) 65 76 91
DEUTSCHE LUFTHANSA : 1015 Wien, Kärtner Str. 42, ℘ (0222) 5 88 36
JAPAN AIRLINES : Kärntner Ring 14, ℘ (0222) 505 57 38
PAN AM : 1010 Wien, Kärntner Ring 5, ℘ (0222) 5 12 66 46

FOREIGN EXCHANGE

Hotels, restaurants and shops do not always accept foreign currencies and it is wise,
therefore, to change money and cheques at the banks and exchange offices which
are found in the larger stations, airports and at the frontier.

SHOPPING and BANK HOURS

Shops are open from 9am to 6pm, but often close for a lunch break. They are closed
Saturday afternoon, Sunday and Bank Holidays (except the shops in railway stations).

Branch offices of banks are open from Monday to Friday between 8am and 12.30pm
(in Salzburg 12am) and from 1.30pm to 3pm (in Salzburg 2pm to 4.30pm), Thursday to
5.30pm (only in Vienna).

In the index of street names those printed in red are where the principal shops are
found.

BREAKDOWN SERVICE

ÖAMTC : See addresses in the text of Vienna and Salzburg

ARBÖ : in Vienna : Mariahilfer Str. 180, ℘ (0222) 85 35 35
in Salzburg : Münchner Bundesstr. 9, ℘ (0662) 3 36 01

In Austria the ÖAMTC (emergency number ℘ 120) and the ARBÖ (emergency number
℘ 123) make a special point of assisting foreign motorists. They have motor patrols
covering main roads.

TIPPING

Service is generally included in hotel and restaurant bills. But in Austria, it is usual to
give more than the expected tip in hotels, restaurants and cafés. Taxi-drivers, porters,
barbers and theatre attendants also expect tips.

SPEED LIMITS

The speed limit in built up areas (indicated by place name signs at the beginning and
end of such areas) is 50 km/h - 31 mph ; on motorways 130 km/h - 80 mph and on all
other roads 100 km/h - 62 mph.

SEAT BELTS

The wearing of seat belts in Austria is compulsory for drivers and passengers.

VIENNA

SIGHTS

HOFBURG★★★ FGY

Imperial Palace of the Habsburgs (Kaiserpalast der Habsburger) : Swiss Court – Royal Chapel – Amalienhof – Stallburg – Leopold Wing – Ballhausplatz – Imperial Chancellery – Spanish Riding School – Neue Burg – Josefsplatz – Michaelerplatz – In der Burg – Capuchins Crypt – Church of the Augustinians. Art Collections : Imperial Treasury★★★ – Imperial Apartments★★ – Austrian National Library (Great Hall★) – Collection of Court Porcelain and Silver★★ – Collection of Arms and Armour★★ – Collection of Old Musical Instruments★ – Albertina (Dürer Collection★) – Museum of Ephesian Sculpture (Reliefs of Ephesus★★).

BUILDINGS AND MONUMENTS

St Stephen's Cathedral★★ (Stephansdom) GY – Schönbrunn★★ (Apartments★★★, Park★★, Coach Room★) AS – Upper and Lower Belvedere★★ (Oberes und Unteres Belvedere) (Terraced Gardens and Art Collections★) HZ and DV – Opera★ (Staatsoper)★ GY – Church of St Charles★ (Karlskirche) GZ – Church of St Michael (Michaeler Kirche) GY – Church of the Minor Friars (Minoritenkirche) FY – Church of the Teutonic Order (Deutschordenskirche) (Altarpiece★, Treasure★) GY E – Church of the Jesuits (Jesuitenkirche) HY H – Church of Our Lady of the River Bank (Maria am Gestade) GX – Church of the Faithful Virgin (Maria Treu) AS F – Mozart Memorial (Mozart-Gedenkstätte) GY F – Dreimäderlhaus FX W.

STREETS, PLACES, PARKS

Kärntner Straße GY – Graben (Plague Column) GY – Am Hof (Column to the Virgin) GY – Herrengasse★ GY – Maria-Theresien-Platz FY – Prater★ (Giant Whell, ≤★) BR – Oberlaapark★ BS – Heldenplatz FY – Burggarten GY – Volksgarten FY – Rathausplatz FY.

IMPORTANT MUSEUMS (Hofburg and Belvedere see above)

Museum of Fine Arts★★★ (Kunsthistorisches Museum) FY – Historical Museum of the City of Vienna★★ (Historisches Museum der Stadt Wien) GZ M6 – Austrian Folklore Museum★★ (Österreichisches Museum für Volkskunde) CU M7 – Gallery of Painting and Fine Arts★ (Gemäldegalerie der Akademie der Bildenden Künste) GZ M9 – Natural History Museum★ (Naturhistorisches Museum) FY M1 – Birthplace of Schubert (Schubert-Museum) CT M16 – Austrian Museum of Applied Arts★ (Österreichisches Museum für angewandte Kunst) HY M10.

EXCURSIONS

Danube Tower★★ (Donauturm) BR – Leopoldsberg ≤★★ AR – Kahlenberg ≤★ AR – Klosterneuburg Abbey (Stift Klosterneuburg) (Altarpiece by Nicolas of Verdun★) AR – Grinzing AR – Baden★ AS – Vienna Woods★ (Wienerwald) AS.

VIENNA **(WIEN)** Austria 𝟗𝟖𝟕 ⑩, 𝟒𝟐𝟔 ⑫ – pop. 1 500 000 – alt. 156 m. – ✆ 01.

🛄 Freudenau 65a, ℰ 2 18 95 64 – 🚃 Wien-Schwechat by ③, ℰ 77 70 and 5 05 57 57, Air Terminal, at Stadtpark (HY) ℰ 72 35 34 – 🚗 – ℰ 56 50 29 89 and 56 50 56 85.

Exhibition Centre, Messeplatz 1, ℰ 9 31 52 40.

🛈 Tourist-Information, 🖂 A-1010, Kärtner Str. 38, ℰ 513 88 92 – ÖAMTC, 🖂 A-1010, Schubertring 1, ℰ 71 19 90, Fax 7 13 18 07.

Budapest 208 ④ – München 435 ⑦ – Praha 292 ① – Salzburg 292 ⑦ – Zagreb 362 ⑥.

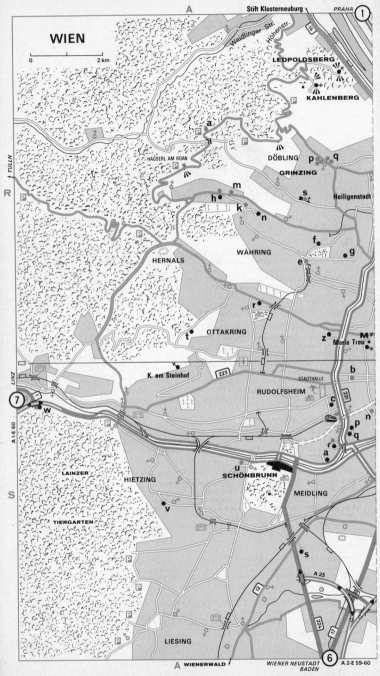

WIEN

0   2 km

Stift Klosterneuburg   PRAHA   ①

A

LEOPOLDSBERG

KAHLENBERG

Weidlinger Str.   Höhenstr.

a   P

P

DÖBLING   p   q

HÄUSERL AM ROAN   GRINZING

s   Heiligenstadt

m   h   k   n   f   g

WÄHRING   e

HERNALS

r   z   M7

t   OTTAKRING   Maria Treu

K. am Steinhof   223   STADTHALLE   b

RUDOLFSHEIM   221   c

p   n

7   q

w   a   r   a

u   SCHÖNBRUNN

LAINZER   HIETZING   MEIDLING

v

TIERGARTEN   s

A 23

12   224

LIESING   17

WIENERWALD   WIENER NEUSTADT   6
BADEN   A 2-E 59-60

TULLN   R   S

LINZ   A 1-E 60

30

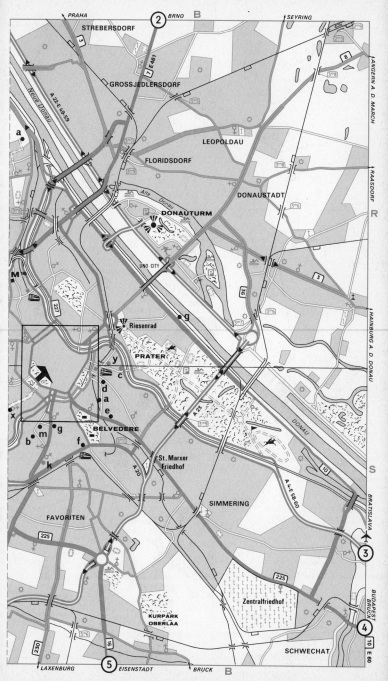

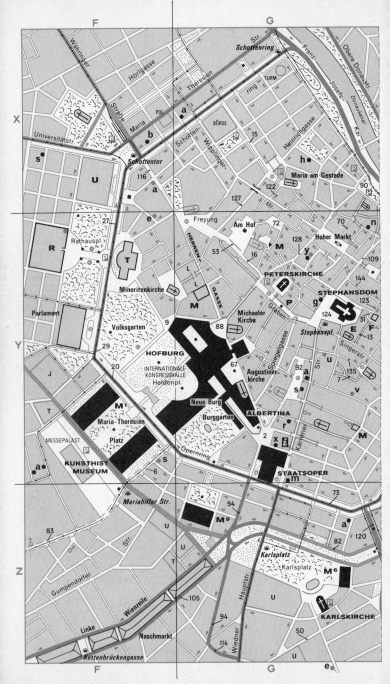

WIEN

Babenbergestr.	FY	6
Graben	GY	
Kärntner Straße	GY	
Landstraßer Hauptstr.	HY	76
Mariahilfer Str.	FZ	83
Rotenturmstraße	GY	109
Stephansplatz	GY	124
Tuchlauben	GY	128
Wollzeile	GY	144
Albertinaplatz	GY	2
Ballgasse	GY	7
Ballhausplatz	FY	9
Bäckerstr.	HY	10
Blutgasse	GY	13
Börsegasse	GX	15
Bognergasse	GY	16
Burgring	FY	20
Dr. Karl Lueger Platz	HY	26
Dr. Karl Lueger Ring	FY	27
Dr. Renner Ring	FY	29
Domgasse	GY	31
Dominikanerbastei	HY	32
Essiggasse	HY	40
Gußhausstr.	GZ	50
Heidenschuß	GY	53
Heiligenkreuzerhof	HY	54
Invalidenstr.	HY	63
Josefsplatz	GY	67
Judengasse	GY	70
Judenplatz	GY	72
Kärtner Ring	GZ	73
Leopoldsgasse	HX	79
Lothringerstr.	GZ	82
Marienbrücke	HX	85
Marxergasse	HY	86
Michaelerplatz	GY	88
Morzinplatz	GX	90
Neuer Markt	GY	92
Operngasse	GZ	94
Postgasse	HY	97
Prinz Eugen Str.	HZ	99
Rechte Wienzeile	GZ	105
Rennweg	HZ	107
Rosenbursenstr.	HY	108
Schönlaterngasse	HY	110
Schleifmühlgasse	GZ	114
Schottengasse	FX	116
Schubertring	HY	118
Schwarzenbergplatz	GZ	120
Schwedenbrücke	HX	121
Strobelgasse	GY	122
Sonnenfelsgasse	HY	125
Tiefer Graben	GX	127
Vordere Zollamtsstr.	HY	132
Weihburggasse	GY	135
Weiskirchnerstr.	HY	137

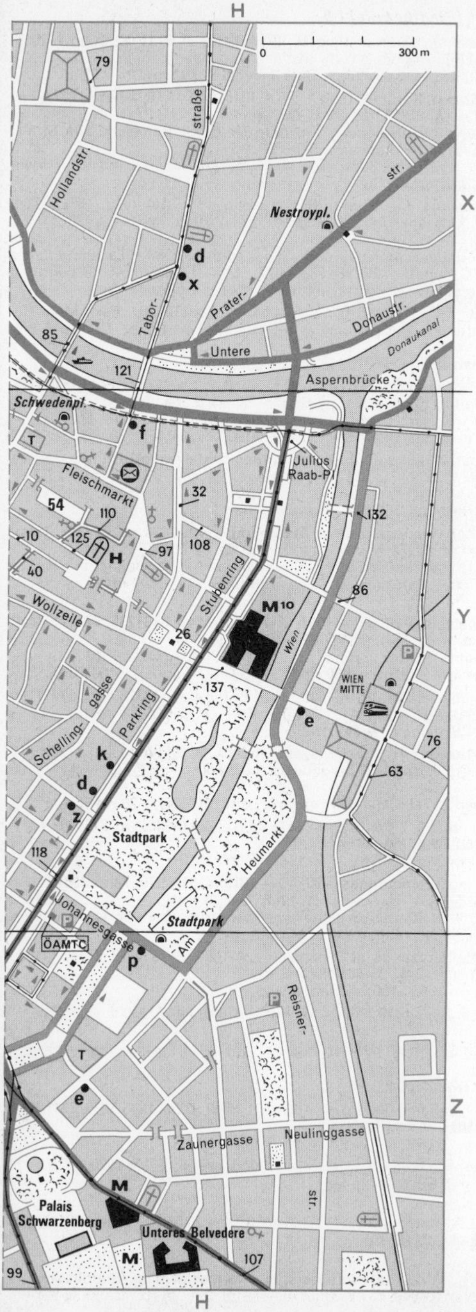

Write us...

If you have any comments on the contents of this guide.

Your praise as well as your criticisms will receive careful consideration and, with your assistance, we will be able to add to our stock of information and, where necessary, amend our judgments.

Thank you in advance !

Town Centre, city districts (Stadtbezirke) 1-9 :

🏨🏨 **Imperial** (converted 19C palace), Kärntner Ring 16, ⊠ A-1015, ℰ 50 11 00, Telex 112630, Fax 50110410 − 📳 ⇔ rm 🗏 📺 − 🕍 25/200. ⅏ rest   GZ **a**
Restaurants : **Zur Majestät** (booking essential) − **Café Imperial** − **152 rm** Bb − 22 appart.

🏨🏨 ⊕ **Bristol - Restaurant Korso**, Kärntner Ring 1, ⊠ A-1015, ℰ 5 16 16, Telex 112477, Fax 51516550 − 📳 ⇔ rm 🗏 📺 − 🕍 25/150. ⅍ ⓪ ᴇ 𝖵𝖨𝖲𝖠. ⅏ rest   GYZ **m**
M (closed Saturday lunch and 8 to 25 August) a la carte 395/825 − **Rôtisserie Sirk M** a la carte 320/550 − **144 rm** 3050/5100 − 13 appart. 7800/8800
Spec. Marinierter Kalbskopf mit Ingwer und Balsamessig. Gebratene Seeforelle auf Petersilienschaum. Soufflierter Scheiterhaufen mit Calvadosäpfeln.

🏨🏨 ⊕ **Plaza Wien - Restaurant La Scala**, Schottenring 11, ⊠ A-1010, ℰ 31 39 00, Telex 135859, Fax 31390160, Massage, 🔽, 🚅 − 📳 ⇔ rm 🗏 📺 🕭 ⇔ − 🕍 25/200. ⅍ ⓪ ᴇ 𝖵𝖨𝖲𝖠. ⅏ rest   GX **a**
M (closed lunch Saturday, Sunday and Bank Holidays) a la carte 490/880 − **Le Jardin** (lunch only) **M** a la carte approx. 300 (buffet) − **250 rm** 3350/4600 Bb − 37 appart. 5450/25500
Spec. Meeresfrüchte im Nudelteig, Medaillons vom Kalb La Scala, Waldbeeren in Blätterkrokant.

🏨🏨 **Sacher**, Philharmonikerstr. 4, ⊠ A-1010, ℰ 5 14 56, Telex 112520, Fax 51457810, « Collection of valuable furniture and paintings » − 📳 ⇔ rm 🗏 📺 🕭 ⅍ ⓪ ᴇ 𝖵𝖨𝖲𝖠 ⅏ rest   GY **x**
M a la carte 365/695 − **124 rm** 1550/4500 Bb − 3 appart. 9000/13500.

🏨🏨 **Vienna Marriott Hotel**, Parkring 12a, ⊠ A-1010, ℰ 51 51 80, Telex 112249, Fax 515186736, Massage, 🚅, 🔽 − 📳 ⇔ rm 🗏 📺 🕭 ⇔ − 🕍 25/400. ⅍ ⓪ ᴇ 𝖵𝖨𝖲𝖠 ⅏ rest   HY **d**
Restaurants : **Symphonika** (dinner only, closed Sunday) **M** a la carte 500/790 − **Parkring-Restaurant M** a la carte 325/690 − **304 rm** 2550/4100 − 7 appart. 5200/11900.

🏨🏨 **Penta Hotel** (former imperial riding school with modern hotel wing), Ungargasse 60, ⊠ A-1030, ℰ 71 17 50, Telex 112529, Fax 7117590, Massage, 🚅, 🔽 − 📳 ⇔ rm 📺 🕭 ⅍ ⓪ ᴇ 𝖵𝖨𝖲𝖠   BS **a**
M a la carte 255/545 − **342 rm** 1450/2500 Bb − 3 appart. 6000.

🏨🏨 **Vienna Hilton**, Landstraßer Hauptstr. 2 (near Stadtpark), ⊠ A-1030, ℰ 7 17 00, Telex 136799, Fax 7130691 − 📳 ⇔ rm 🗏 📺 🕭 ⇔ − 🕍 25/700. ⅍ ⓪ ᴇ 𝖵𝖨𝖲𝖠 ⅏ rest   HY **e**
Restaurants : **Prinz Eugen** (closed lunch Saturday, Sunday and Bank Holidays) (booking essential) **M** a la carte 400/760 − **Café am Park M** a la carte 300/500 − **603 rm** 2810/3580 Bb − 25 appart. 8440/24500.

🏨🏨 **Intercontinental**, Johannesgasse 28, ⊠ A-1037, ℰ 71 12 20, Telex 131235, Fax 7134489, 🚅 − 📳 ⇔ rm 🗏 📺 🕭 ⇔ − 🕍 25/1000. ⅍ ⓪ ᴇ 𝖵𝖨𝖲𝖠 ⅏ rest   HZ **p**
Restaurants : **Vier Jahreszeiten** (closed Saturday lunch and Sunday dinner) **M** a la carte 355/750 − **Brasserie M** a la carte 260/510 − **500 rm** 2250/3600 − 44 appart. 5100/7800.

🏨🏨 **Scandic Crown Hotel**, Handelskai 269, ⊠ A-1020, ℰ 2 17 77, Telex 133318, Fax 21777199, 🌴, Massage, 🔽, 🏊 (heated), ⅍ − 📳 ⇔ rm 🗏 📺 🕭 🅿 − 🕍 25/300. ⅏ rest   BR **g**
Restaurants : **Scandirama** − **Symphony** − **367 rm** Bb.

🏨🏨 **Hotel im Palais Schwarzenberg**, Schwarzenbergplatz 9, ⊠ A-1030, ℰ 78 45 15, Telex 136124, Fax 784714, « Converted 1727 baroque palace, park » − 📳 📺 🅿 − 🕍 25/200. ⅍ ᴇ 𝖵𝖨𝖲𝖠   HZ
M (booking essential) (closed 24 February - 4 March) a la carte 510/880 − **38 rm** 3630/12260.

🏨 **Hotel de France**, Schottenring 3, ⊠ A-1010, ℰ 34 35 40, Telex 114360, Fax 315969, 🚅 − 📳 🗏 rest 📺 − 🕍 25/120. ⅍ ⓪ ᴇ 𝖵𝖨𝖲𝖠. ⅏ rest   FX **b**
M a la carte 250/385 − **218 rm** 2400/3600 Bb − 10 appart. 4000/5000.

🏨 **SAS-Palais-Hotel**, Parkring/Weihburggasse 32, ⊠ A-1010, ℰ 51 51 70, Telex 136127, Fax 5122216, 🚅 − 📳 ⇔ rm 🗏 📺 🕭 − 🕍 25/100. ⅍ ⓪ ᴇ 𝖵𝖨𝖲𝖠. ⅏ rest   HY **z**
M (closed 2 to 6 January, 4 to 10 February and lunch Saturday and Sunday) a la carte 410/610 − **165 rm** 2540/5240 Bb − 8 appart. 5800/7800.

🏨 **Biedermeier**, Landstraßer Hauptstr. 28 (at Sünnhof), ⊠ A-1030, ℰ 75 55 75, Telex 111039, Fax 755575503, 🌴 − 📳 📺 ⇔ − 🕍 25/50. ⅍ ⓪ ᴇ 𝖵𝖨𝖲𝖠   BS **d**
M a la carte 245/420 − **204 rm** 1850/2150 − 18 appart. 4600/4900.

🏨 **Ambassador**, Neuer Markt 5, ⊠ A-1010, ℰ 5 14 66, Telex 111906, Fax 5132999 − 📳 📺   GY **s**
107 rm Bb.

🏨 **Europa**, Neuer Markt 3, ⊠ A-1015, ℰ 51 59 40, Telex 112292, Fax 5138138 − 📳 🗏 📺 ☎ − 🕍 25/50. ⅍ ⓪ ᴇ. ⅏ rest   GY **a**
M a la carte 330/490 − **102 rm** 1380/2400 Bb.

🏨 **City-Central** without rest, Taborstr. 8a, ⊠ A-1020, ℰ 21 10 50, Telex 134570, Fax 21105140 − 📳 📺 ☎ 🕭 🅿. ⅍ ⓪ ᴇ 𝖵𝖨𝖲𝖠   HX **x**
58 rm 1360/1780 Bb.

🏨 **K. u. K. Hotel Maria Theresia** without rest, Kirchberggasse 6, ⊠ A-1070, ℰ 5 21 23, Telex 111530, Fax 5212370 − 📳 📺 ☎ ⇔ − 🕍 25/50   FY **a**
123 rm Bb.

🏨 **Rathauspark** without rest, Rathausstr. 17, ⊠ A-1010, ℰ 4 23 66 10, Telex 112817, Fax 423661761 − 📳 📺 ☎ − 🕍 40. ⅍ ⓪ 𝖵𝖨𝖲𝖠   FX **s**
117 rm 1190/2190 Bb.

🏨 **K u. K Palais Hotel** without rest (modern hotel in a former palace), Rudolfsplatz 11, ⊠ A-1010, ℰ 5 33 13 53, Telex 134049, Fax 533135370 − 📳 📺 ☎ − 🕍 50. ⅍ ⓪ ᴇ 𝖵𝖨𝖲𝖠   GX **h**
66 rm 1390/1790 Bb.

🏨 **Alba Hotel Palace**, Margaretenstr. 92, ⊠ A-1050, ℰ 55 46 86, Telex 114321, Fax 55468686,
🛄 – 📳 ▤ 📺 🕿 🛋 – 🔥 25/130. 🝙 ⓞ ⴹ 𝘝𝘐𝘚𝘈. ⁂ rest   BS **b**
M a la carte 245/450 – **117 rm** 1250/1690 Bb.

🏨 **Stefanie**, Taborstr. 12, ⊠ A-1020, ℰ 21 15 00, Telex 134589, Fax 21150160, 🏤 – 📳 📺 🕿
🛋 – 🔥 25/200. 🝙 ⓞ ⴹ 𝘝𝘐𝘚𝘈   HX **d**
M 180/300 (lunch) and a la carte 220/400 – **130 rm** 1180/1880 Bb.

🏨 **Amadeus** without rest, Wildpretmarkt 5, ⊠ A-1010, ℰ 63 87 38, Telex 111102, Fax
63873838 – 📳 📺 🕿. 🝙 ⓞ ⴹ 𝘝𝘐𝘚𝘈   GY **y**
closed 22 to 28 December – **30 rm** 1010/1830 Bb.

🏨 **Pullman Hotel Belvedere**, Am Heumarkt 35, ⊠ A-1030, ℰ 7 52 53 50, Telex 111822, Fax
752535844 – 📳 📺 🕿 🛋 – 🔥 30. 🝙 ⓞ ⴹ 𝘝𝘐𝘚𝘈. ⁂ rest   HZ **e**
M a la carte 185/300 – **211 rm** 1240/2700 Bb.

🏨 **Alba-Accadia**, Margaretenstr. 53, ⊠ A-1050, ℰ 5 88 50, Telex 113264, Fax 58850899 – 📳
📺 🕿 🛋. 🝙 ⓞ ⴹ 𝘝𝘐𝘚𝘈   BS **m**
M a la carte 210/425 – **104 rm** 1190/2600 Bb.

🏨 **Capricorno** without rest, Schwedenplatz 3, ⊠ A-1010, ℰ 53 33 10 40, Telex 115266, Fax
53376714 – 📳 📺 🕿 🛋 🅿. 🝙 ⴹ 𝘝𝘐𝘚𝘈   HY **f**
46 rm 1060/1780 Bb.

🏨 **President**, Wallgasse 23, ⊠ A-1060, ℰ 5 99 90, Telex 112523, Fax 567646 – 📳 ▤ 📺 🕿 🛋
– 🔥 50   AS **q**
77 rm Bb.

🏨 **Astoria**, Führichgasse 1, ⊠ A-1015, ℰ 51 57 70, Telex 112856, Fax 5157782 – 📳 ▤ rest 📺
🕿. 🝙 ⴹ 𝘝𝘐𝘚𝘈   GY **r**
M a la carte 305/500 – **108 rm** 1200/3200 Bb.

🏨 **Kummer**, Mariahilfer Str. 71a, ⊠ A-1061, ℰ 5 88 95, Telex 111417, Fax 5878133 – 📳 ⁂ rm
📺 🕿. 🝙 ⓞ ⴹ 𝘝𝘐𝘚𝘈   BS **x**
M a la carte 240/350 – **106 rm** 1200/2050 Bb.

🏨 **Erzherzog Rainer**, Wiedner Hauptstr. 27, ⊠ A-1041, ℰ 50 11 10, Telex 132329, Fax
50111350 – 📳 ▤ rest 📺 🕿 – 🔥 50. 🝙 ⓞ ⴹ 𝘝𝘐𝘚𝘈   BS **g**
M a la carte 285/455 – **84 rm** 1020/2000 Bb.

🏨 **Mercure**, Fleischmarkt 1a, ⊠ A-1010, ℰ 53 46 00, Telex 112048, Fax 53460232 – 📳 ⁂ rm
▤ 📺 🕿 ऴ. 🝙 ⴹ 𝘝𝘐𝘚𝘈   GY **n**
M a la carte 200/385 – **155 rm** 1340/1760 Bb.

🏨 **Am Parkring**, Parkring 12, ⊠ A-1015, ℰ 5 14 80, Telex 113420, Fax 5148040 – 📳 ▤ 📺 🕿 🛋
🛋. 🝙 ⓞ ⴹ 𝘝𝘐𝘚𝘈. ⁂   HY **k**
M (closed Sunday dinner) a la carte 275/445 – **64 rm** 1460/1980 Bb – 3 appart. 2400.

🏨 **Am Stephansplatz**, Stephansplatz 9, ⊠ A-1010, ℰ 53 40 50, Telex 114334, Fax 53405711
– 📳 ▤ rest 📺 🕿. 🝙 ⴹ 𝘝𝘐𝘚𝘈 – (accepted by the hotel only)   GY **g**
M a la carte 230/375 – **62 rm** 1260/1920 Bb.

🏨 **Prinz Eugen**, Wiedner Gürtel 14, ⊠ A-1040, ℰ 5 05 17 41, Telex 132483, Fax 5055308 – 📳
⁂ rm 📺 🕿. 🝙 ⓞ ⴹ 𝘝𝘐𝘚𝘈   BS **f**
M (also diet) a la carte 235/380 – **110 rm** 1560/2500 Bb.

🏨 **Ibis**, Mariahilfer Gürtel 22, ⊠ A-1060, ℰ 56 56 26, Telex 133833, Fax 564368 – 📳 ▤ 📺 🕿
ऴ 🛋 – 🔥 25/180   AS **p**
341 rm Bb.

🏨 **Hungaria**, Rennweg 51, ⊠ A-1030, ℰ 7 13 25 21, Telex 131797, Fax 755930 – 📳 📺 🕿
🛋. 🝙 ⴹ 𝘝𝘐𝘚𝘈   BS **e**
M a la carte 210/380 ऴ – **168 rm** 1150/2550 Bb.

XXXX ✪✪ **Steirereck**, Rasumofskygasse 2 / Ecke Weißgerberlände, ⊠ A-1030, ℰ 7 13 31 68,
Fax 7135168 – 𝘝𝘐𝘚𝘈   BS **c**
closed Saturday, Sunday and Bank Holidays – **M** (remarkable wine-list, visit of the
wine-cellar possible) (booking essential) a la carte 450/705
Spec. Kalbskopfnödel mit Flußkrebsen, Wildentenbrust auf getrüffeltem Mangoldgemüse, Das Wiener
Kaffee-Dessert.

XXX **Zu den drei Husaren**, Weihburggasse 4, ⊠ A-1010, ℰ 5 12 10 92, Fax 512109218 – 🝙
ⓞ ⴹ 𝘝𝘐𝘚𝘈   GY **u**
closed mid July - mid August and 24 to 28 December – **M** a la carte 420/780.

XXX ✪ **Gottfried**, Untere Viaduktgasse 45/Marxergasse, ⊠ A-1030, ℰ 7 13 82 56, Fax
713355130, remarkable wine list – 🝙 𝘝𝘐𝘚𝘈   BRS **y**
closed Saturday lunch and Bank Holidays, May - September closed Saturday and Sunday –
M (booking essential) 330/510 (lunch) and a la carte 470/715
Spec. Carpaccio vom Rinderfilet mit Kresse und Trüffeleierspeise, Ravioli von Steingarnelen, Flugentenbrust in
Apfel-Majoran-Sauce mit Krautroulade und Grammelknödeln.

XXX **Hauswirth**, Otto-Bauer-Gasse 20, ⊠ A-1060, ℰ 5 87 12 61, Fax 5860419 – 🝙 ⓞ 𝘝𝘐𝘚𝘈
closed Sunday, Bank Holidays and 24 March - 1 April – **M** a la carte 340/565.   AS **n**

XXX **Steirer Stub'n**, Wiedner Hauptstr. 111, ⊠ A-1050, ℰ 55 43 49, Fax 550888 – 🝙 ⓞ ⴹ
𝘝𝘐𝘚𝘈   BS **k**
closed Sunday and Bank Holidays – **M** (booking essential) a la carte 270/450.

XXX **Grotta Azzurra** (Italian rest.), Babenberger Str. 5, ⊠ A-1010, 𝒫 5 86 10 44, Fax 5879465
– 🖾 ⓘ **E** 𝘝𝘐𝘚𝘈   FY s
closed Sunday and mid July - mid August – **M** 275/325 (lunch) and a la carte 350/490.

XXX **Kupferdachl**, Schottengasse 7 (entrance Mölker Bastei), ⊠ A-1010, 𝒫 63 93 81, Fax
5354042 – 🖾 ⓘ **E** 𝘝𝘐𝘚𝘈   FX a
closed Saturday lunch, Sunday and 25 July - 11 August – **M** a la carte 325/530.

XX **Schubertstüberln**, Schreyvogelgasse 4, ⊠ A-1010, 𝒫 63 71 87, Fax 5353546, 🛱 – 🖾
ⓘ **E** 𝘝𝘐𝘚𝘈   FXY e
closed Saturday, Sunday, Easter, Whitsuntide and 24 December - 2 January – **M** a la carte
275/555.

XX **Steinerne Eule**, Halbgasse 30, ⊠ A-1070, 𝒫 93 22 50, 🛱 – **E**   AS b
closed Sunday and Monday – **M** a la carte 360/630.

XX **Zum Kuckuck**, Himmelpfortgasse 15, ⊠ A-1010, 𝒫 5 12 84 70 – **E**   GY v
closed Saturday and Sunday – **M** a la carte 340/520.

XX **Wiener Rathauskeller** (vaults with murals), Rathausplatz 1, ⊠ A-1010, 𝒫 4 21 21 90, Fax
42121927 – 🖾 ⓘ **E** 𝘝𝘐𝘚𝘈   FY R
closed Sunday and Bank Holidays – **M** a la carte 205/380 ⅃.

XX **Salut**, Wildpretmarkt 3, ⊠ A-1010, 𝒫 5 33 13 22 – 🖾 ⓘ **E** 𝘝𝘐𝘚𝘈   GY y
closed Sunday, Bank Holidays and 6 to 27 August – **M** a la carte 320/425.

X Das Restaurant, Argentinierstr. 26, ⊠ A-1040, 𝒫 5 05 40 37   GZ e

X **Leupold**, Schottengasse 7, ⊠ A-1010, 𝒫 63 93 81 – 🖾 ⓘ **E** 𝘝𝘐𝘚𝘈   FX a
closed Saturday lunch, Sunday, Bank Holidays and 25 July - 11 August – **M** a la carte
205/440.

City districts (Stadtbezirke) 12 - 15 :

🏨 **Ramada Hotel**, Ullmannstr. 71, ⊠ A-1150, 𝒫 8 50 40, Telex 112206, Fax 8504100, ≘, 🖳
– 🛗 ⋘ rm ▤ 𝘵𝘷 ⋯ – 🔥 25/200. 🖾 ⓘ **E** 𝘝𝘐𝘚𝘈 . 🛠 rest   AS a
Restaurants : **Orangerie M** a la carte 255/530 – **Allegro M** (buffet lunch only) 300, a la carte
255/530 (dinner) – **309 rm** 1700/2150 Bb – 3 appart. 4400.

🏨 **Garten Hotel Altmannsdorf** ⌂, Hoffingergasse 26, ⊠ A-1120, 𝒫 8 04 75 27,
Telex 135327, Fax 804752751, 🛱, Park, ≘ – 🛗 𝘵𝘷 ⋯ – 🔥 25/100. 🖾 ⓘ **E** 𝘝𝘐𝘚𝘈   AS s
closed 23 to 29 December – **M** a la carte 255/415 – **41 rm** 1020/1700 Bb.

🏨 **Austrotel**, Felberstr. 4, ⊠ A-1150, 𝒫 98 11 10, Telex 115181, Fax 98111930, ≘ – 🛗 𝘵𝘷
& ⋯ – 🔥 25/260. 🖾 ⓘ **E** 𝘝𝘐𝘚𝘈   AS c
M a la carte 230/440 – **254 rm** 1400/2500 Bb.

🏨 **Reither**, Graumanngasse 16, ⊠ A-1150, 𝒫 85 61 65, Telex 136430, Fax 855244, ≘, 🖳 –
🛗 𝘵𝘷 🕿 ⋯. 🖾 ⓘ **E** 𝘝𝘐𝘚𝘈. 🛠 rest   AS r
closed February, 15 to 31 July and 22 to 27 December – **M** *(dinner only, closed Saturday,
Sunday and Bank Holidays)* a la carte 190/360 ⅃ – **50 rm** 950/1450 Bb.

🏠 **Arabella - Hotel Jagdschloß** without rest, Jagdschloßgasse 79, ⊠ A-1130,
𝒫 8 04 35 08, 𝕷 (heated), 🛱 – 🛗 𝘵𝘷 🕿 ⋯   AS v
closed 3 January - 19 February – **48 rm** 720/1900 Bb.

XX **Altwienerhof** with rm, Herklotzgasse 6, ⊠ A-1150, 𝒫 83 71 45, Fax 85982532, « Winter
garden, court terrace » – 🛗 𝘵𝘷 🕿   AS r
M *(closed Saturday lunch, Sunday, Bank Holidays and 1 to 20 January)* a la carte 445/695 –
20 rm 490/1800 Bb.

XX **Hietzinger Bräu**, Auhofstr. 1, ⊠ A-1130, 𝒫 87 77 70 87, Fax 877708722   AS u
closed mid July - mid August and 24 to 27 December – **M** *(mainly boiled beef dishes)* a la
carte 295/465.

City districts (Stadtbezirke) 16-19 :

🏨 **Modul**, Peter-Jordan-Str. 78, ⊠ A-1190, 𝒫 47 66 00, Telex 116736, Fax 47660117 – 🛗 ▤
𝘵𝘷 ⋯ Ⓟ – 🔥 25/100. 🖾 ⓘ **E** 𝘝𝘐𝘚𝘈   AR f
M *(closed Saturday and Sunday)* a la carte 315/550 – **43 rm** 1300/2200 Bb – 10 appart.
2900.

🏨 **Clima Villenhotel** ⌂, Nussberggasse 2c, ⊠ A-1190, 𝒫 37 15 16, Telex 115670, Fax
371392, « Rest. Bockkeller, vaulted cellar with Tyrolian farmhouse furniture, dinner only,
closed Sunday », ≘, 𝕷, 🖳, 🛱 – 🛗 𝘵𝘷 🕿 ⋯ Ⓟ – 🔥 25/70. 🖾 ⓘ **E** 𝘝𝘐𝘚𝘈   BR a
M a la carte 285/380 – **30 rm** 1550/1990 Bb.

🏨 **Schloß Wilhelminenberg** ⌂, Savoyenstr. 2, ⊠ A-1160, 𝒫 45 85 03, Telex 132008, Fax
454876, « Terrace with ≤ Vienna, Park » – 🛗 🕿 Ⓟ – 🔥 30/120. 🖾 ⓘ **E** 𝘝𝘐𝘚𝘈   AR t
M a la carte 140/340 – **90 rm** 640/1535 Bb.

🏨 **Maté** (with guest-house), Ottakringer Str. 34, ⊠ A-1170, 𝒫 4 04 55, Telex 115485, Fax
40455888, ≘, 🖳 – 🛗 ▤ rest 𝘵𝘷 🕿 ⋯ Ⓟ. 🖾 ⓘ **E** 𝘝𝘐𝘚𝘈   AR z
M a la carte 225/445 ⅃ – **172 rm** 920/2000 Bb.

🏨 **Gartenhotel Glanzing** ⌂, without rest, Glanzinggasse 23, ⊠ A-1190, 𝒫 47 04 27 20,
Telex 75211307, Fax 470427214, ≘ – 🛗 𝘵𝘷 🕿 ⋯   AR n
20 rm 1180/2200 Bb.

🏨 Cottage without rest, Hasenauerstr. 12, ⊠ A-1190, 𝒫 31 25 71, Telex 134146, Fax 31257110,
🛱 – 🛗 𝘵𝘷 🕿 – **23 rm** Bb.   AR g

🏠 **Jäger** without rest, Hernalser Hauptstr. 187, ⊠ A-1170, 𝒫 46 66 20, Fax 4666208 – 📶 📺
🕿 E *VISA*   AR **r**
18 rm 960/1200.

🏠 **Schild** without rest, Neustift am Walde 97, ⊠ A-1190, 𝒫 4 42 19 10, Fax 44219153, 🚗 –
📶 📺 🕿 👆 ⌂   AR **h**
33 rm 750/1140 Bb.

XX **Fischerhaus**, an der Höhenstraße, ⊠ A-1190, 𝒫 44 13 20, Fax 443533, 🏠 – 🅿   AR **a**
closed January, February, Sunday dinner and Monday – **M** a la carte 335/535.

XX **Eckel**, Sieveringer Str. 46, ⊠ A-1190, 𝒫 32 32 18, Fax 326660, 🏠, (remarkable wine-list)
– 🔾   AR **s**
closed Sunday, Monday, 13 to 28 August and 22 December - 13 January – **M** a la carte
210/525 👗.

XX **Sailer**, Gersthofer Str. 14, ⊠ A-1180, 𝒫 47 21 21, Fax 4721214, 🏠, « Kellerstuben »
closed Sunday and Bank Holidays – **M** 200 (lunch) and a la carte 260/430.   AR **e**

XX **Kirchenstöckl**, Himmelstr. 4, ⊠ A-1190, 𝒫 32 15 71, Fax 32571322, self-grown wines only
– 🔾 E *VISA*   AR **p**
dinner only, closed Sunday and July - August – **M** a la carte 200/425.

X **Römischer Kaiser**, Neustift am Walde 2, ⊠ A-1190, 𝒫 44 11 04, « Terraced garden with
≤ Vienna »   AR **k**

Heurigen and Buschen-Schänken (wine gardens) – (mostly self-service, hot and cold
dishes from buffet, prices according to weight of chosen meals, therefore not shown
below. Buschen-Schänken sell their own wines only) :.

X **Oppolzer**, Himmelstr. 22, ⊠ A-1190, 𝒫 32 24 16, « Garden » – 📠 🔾 E *VISA*   AR **p**
dinner only, closed Monday and 2 weeks February – **M** (buffet).

X **Altes Preßhaus**, Cobenzlgasse 15, ⊠ A-1190, 𝒫 32 23 93, Telex 132211, Fax 32234285,
🏠, « Old vaulted wine cellar » – 📠 🔾 E *VISA*   AR **p**
dinner only, closed until 4 p.m. and 5 January - 28 February – **M** (buffet).

X **Wolff**, Rathstr. 44, ⊠ A-1190, 𝒫 44 23 35, « Terraced garden »   AR **m**

X **Fuhrgassl Huber** (Wine-garden with Viennese Schrammelmusik), Neustift am Walde 68,
⊠ A-1190, 𝒫 44 14 05, « Court-terrace »   AR **h**
dinner only – **M** (buffet) 👗.

X **Grinzinger Hauermandl**, Cobenzlgasse 20, ⊠ A-1190, 𝒫 3 22 04 44, Fax 32147122, 🏠 –
📠 🔾 E *VISA*   AR **q**
dinner only, closed Sunday – **M** a la carte 185/335.

X **Grinzinger Weinbottich**, Cobenzlgasse 28, ⊠ A-1190, 𝒫 32 42 37, Fax 32571322, « Shady
garden » – 🔾 E *VISA*   AR **q**
dinner only, closed Monday – **M** a la carte 165/325.

at Auhof motorway station W : 8 km :

🏨 **Novotel Wien-West**, Wientalstraße, ⊠ A-1140, 𝒫 (0222) 9 72 54 20, Telex 135584, Fax
974140, 🏠, 🏊 (heated), 🚗 – 📶 ⇔ rm 📺 🕿 👆 🅿 – 🔏 25/300. 📠 🔾 E *VISA*   AS **w**
M a la carte 205/330 – **115 rm** 1045/2420 Bb.

at Vösendorf A-2334 S : 11 km by ⑥ or A 2 AS :

🏛 **City-Club-Hotel**, Parkallee 2 (Shopping City Süd), 𝒫 (0222) 69 35 35, Telex 132281, Fax
693317, 5 restaurants and recreation-centre in a separate building – 📶 ▤ 📺 🅿 – 🔏 25/280.
📠 🔾 E *VISA*
M a la carte 215/425 – **471 rm** 2080/2570 Bb – 20 appart. 3680/6000.

🏨 Novotel Wien-Süd, Nordring 4 (Shopping City Süd), 𝒫 (0222) 6 92 60 10, Telex 134793, Fax
694859, 🏠, 🏊 (heated) – 📶 ▤ rest 📺 🕿 👆 🅿 – 🔏 25/250
102 rm Bb.

at Schwechat-Mannswörth A-2323 SE : 15 km by ④ and B 9 :

🏠 Reinisch (with guest-house, 📶), Mannswörther Str. 76, 𝒫 (0222) 77 72 90, Fax 773890, 🏠
– 📺 🕿 🅿
66 rm Bb.

at Vienna-Schwechat airport ③ : 20 km :

🏨 Novotel Wien Airport, ⊠ A-1300 Schwechat, 𝒫 (0222) 77 66 66, Telex 111566, Fax 773239,
🏠, 🍴, 🏊 (heated) – 📶 ▤ 📺 🕿 👆 🅿 – 🔏 25/300
183 rm Bb.

XX Le Gourmet, airport (2. floor, 📶), ⊠ A-1300 Schwechat, 𝒫 (0222) 77 70 26 72, ≤

at Groß-Enzersdorf A-2301 E : 16 km, by B 3 BR :

🏨 **Am Sachsengang**, Schloßhofer Str. 60 (B 3), 𝒫 (02249) 2 90 10, Telex 136236, Fax 2905,
« Terrace », Massage, 🍴, 🏊, 🚗 – 📺 🕿 🅿 – 🔏 25/120. 📠 🔾 E *VISA* – (accepted by
the hotel only)
closed 21 to 28 December – **M** a la carte 280/455 – **54 rm** 700/1100 Bb -(annex with 50 rm
summer 1991).

See : ⩽ ** on the town (from the Mönchsberg) Y K — Hohensalzburg ** X, Z : ⩽ ** (from the Kuenburg Bastion), ❋ ** (from the Reck Tower), Museum (Burgmuseum)★ Z **M3** — St. Peter's Churchyard (Petersfriedhof) ** Z — St. Peter's Church (Stiftskirche St. Peter) ** Z — Residenz ** Z — Natural History Museum (Haus der Natur) ** Y **M2** — Franciscan's Church (Franziskanerkirche)★ Z **A** — Getreidegasse★ Y — Mirabell Gardens (Mirabellgarten)★ V — Hettwer Bastei★ : ⩽★ Y — Mozart's Birthplace (Mozarts Geburtshaus) Y **D**.

Envir. : Road to the Gaisberg (Gaisbergstraße) ** (⩽★) by ① — Untersberg★ by ② : 10 km (with ⓖ) — Mondsee★ ① : 28 km (by motorway A 1).

⛳ Salzburg-Wals, Schloß Klessheim, 𝒫 85 08 51 ; ⛳ Hof (① : 20 km), 𝒫 (06229) 23 90 ; ⛳ St. Lorenz (① : 29 km), 𝒫 (06232) 38 35.

✈ Innsbrucker Bundesstr. 95 (by ③), 𝒫 85 12 23 - City Ait Terminal, Südtiroler Platz (Autobus Station) V — 🚌 𝒫 71 54 14 22.

Exhibition Centre (Messegelände), Linke Glanzeile 65, 𝒫 3 45 66.

🛈 Tourist Information, Mozartplatz 5, 𝒫 84 75 68.

ÖAMTC, Alpenstr. 102 (by ②), 𝒫 2 05 01, Fax 2050145.

Wien 292 ① — Innsbruck 177 ③ — München 140 ③.

SALZBURG

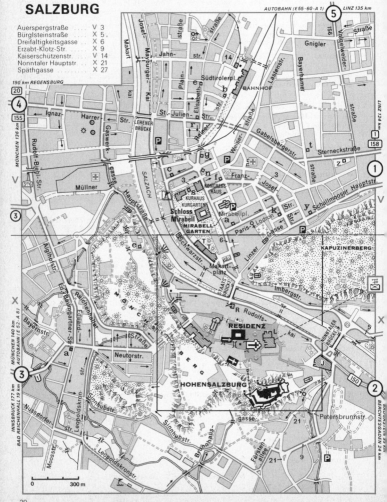

SALZBURG

0   200 m

Salzburg Sheraton Hotel, Auerspergstr. 4, ℰ 79 32 10, Telex 632518, Fax 881776, « Terrace in spa gardens », entrance to the spa facilities – 🛗 ⇙ rm 🗏 📺 & 🚗 – 🛗 25/150. 🖭 ⓪ 🗲 𝗩𝗜𝗦𝗔 ⅗ rest   V s
Restaurants : **Mirabell** – **Bistro** – **165 rm** Bb – 9 appart.

Österreichischer Hof, Schwarzstr. 5, ℰ 7 25 41, Telex 633590, Fax 7525514, « Salzach-side setting, terrace with ⩽ old town and castle » – 🛗 🗏 📺 🚗 – 🛗 25/70. 🖭 ⓪ 🗲 𝗩𝗜𝗦𝗔   Y b
Restaurants : **Zirbelzimmer M** a la carte 390/560 – **Salzach-Grill M** a la carte 320/490 – **119 rm** 2050/4200 – 3 appart. 11500.

Bristol, Makartplatz 4, ℰ 7 35 57, Telex 633337, Fax 735576 – 🛗 🗏 rest 📺 – 🛗 80. 🖭 ⓪ 🗲 𝗩𝗜𝗦𝗔 ⅗ rest   Y a
closed 10 January - 21 March – **M** 270 (lunch) and la carte 420/620 – **75 rm** 2250/5200 Bb – 10 appart. 6900/8000.

Schloß Mönchstein ⑤, Am Mönchsberg 26, ℰ 8 48 55 50, Telex 632080, Fax 848559, ⩽ Salzburg and environs, 🍽, « Small castle with elegant, stylish furnishings, wedding chapel, park », 🍽, ⅙ – 🛗 📺 🅿 – 🛗 40. 🖭 ⓪ 🗲 𝗩𝗜𝗦𝗔 ⅗ rest   X e
M a la carte 450/910 – **17 rm** 2000/6500.

Goldener Hirsch, Getreidegasse 37, ℰ 84 85 11, Telex 632967, Fax 848517845, « 15C Patrician house, tastefully furnished » – 🛗 ⇙ rm 🗏 rest 📺 – 🛗 40/70   Y e
71 rm – 3 appart.

Rosenberger, Bessarabierstr. 94, ℰ 3 55 46, Telex 3622405, Fax 3951095, ⇐ – 🛗 ⇙ rm 📺 & 🚗 🅿 – 🛗 25/360. 🖭 ⓪ 🗲 𝗩𝗜𝗦𝗔   by ④
M a la carte 210/380 🍷 – **120 rm** 910/1500 Bb.

Dorint-Hotel, Sterneckstr. 20, ℰ 88 20 31, Telex 631075, Fax 8820319, ⇐ – 🛗 ⇙ rm 🗏 rest 📺 & 🚗 – 🛗 25/300   V z
140 rm Bb.

Mercure, Bayerhamerstr. 14, ℰ 88 14 38, Telex 632341, Fax 71111411, 🍽, entrance to the sports and tennis centre – 🛗 ⇙ rm 📺 & 🚗 🅿 – 🛗 25/300. 🖭 ⓪ 🗲 𝗩𝗜𝗦𝗔   V t
M a la carte 260/440 – **121 rm** 1700/1980 Bb.

🏨 **Theater-Hotel**, Schallmooser Hauptstr. 13, ℰ 8 81 68 10, Telex 632319, 🍸, Massage, ⓢ
— 📞 🛏 🅿 ⇔ — 🔬 40. 🆎 ⓞ 🅴 *VISA* ⚶ rest V y
M a la carte 205/395 — **58 rm** 1500/2180 Bb — 11 appart. 2880.

🏨 **Carlton** without rest, Markus-Sittikus-Str. 3, ℰ 88 21 91, Fax 7478447, ⓢ — 📞 ❖ 📺 ☎
🅿 🆎 ⓞ 🅴 *VISA* V c
40 rm 1400/1990 Bb — 12 appart. 2200/2700.

🏨 **Novotel Salzburg City**, Franz-Josef-Str. 26, ℰ 88 20 41, Telex 632886, Fax 74240 — 📞 📺 ☎
🕭 ⇔ 🅿 — 🔬 25/140 — **140 rm** V k

🏨 **Winkler**, Franz-Josef-Str. 7, ℰ 7 35 13, Telex 633961, Fax 72176, 🍸 — 📞 ❖ rm 📺 ☎
📞 40. 🆎 ⓞ 🅴 *VISA* V f
M a la carte 255/460 — **103 rm** 1200/3260 Bb.

🏨 **Pitter**, Rainerstr. 6, ℰ 7 85 71, Telex 633532, Fax 7857190, 🍸 — 📞 📺 ☎ — 🔬 25/150. 🆎
ⓞ 🅴 *VISA* V n
M a la carte 205/390 ⅋ — **200 rm** 740/2350 Bb.

🏨 **Europa**, Rainerstr. 31, ℰ 73 39 10, Telex 633424, Fax 732958, rest. on the 14th floor with
≤ Salzburg and environs — 📞 ▤ rest 📺 ☎ 🅿 — 🔬 25/80. 🆎 ⓞ 🅴 *VISA* ⚶ rest V b
M a la carte 280/400 — **104 rm** 930/1900 Bb.

🏨 **Austrotel**, Mirabellplatz 8, ℰ 88 16 88, Telex 632361, Fax 881687 — 📞 📺 ☎ 🕭 — 🔬 45
73 rm Bb. V a

🏨 **Schaffenrath**, Alpenstr. 115, ℰ 2 31 53, Telex 633207, Fax 29314, 🍸, Massage, ⓢ — 📞
📺 ☎ 🅿 — 🔬 25/100. 🆎 ⓞ 🅴 *VISA* by ②
M a la carte 193/400 — **50 rm** 890/2900 Bb.

🏨 **Kasererhof**, Alpenstr. 6, ℰ 2 12 65, Telex 633477, Fax 28376, 🍸, 🐎 — 📞 📺 ☎ 🅿 🆎 🅴
VISA — closed February — **M** (closed Saturday and Sunday) a la carte 250/540 — **51 rm**
1260/3015 Bb — 6 appart. 3620/4520 by ②

🏨 **Hohenstauffen** without rest, Elisabethstr. 19, ℰ 7 21 93, Fax 7219251 — 📞 📺 ☎ ⇔ 🆎
🅿 🅴 *VISA* V e
27 rm 720/1520.

🏠 **Stieglbräu** (Brewery-inn), Rainerstr. 14, ℰ 7 76 92(hotel) 7 76 94(rest.), Telex 633671, Fax
7769271, 🍸 — 📞 📺 ☎ 🅿 — 🔬 25. 🆎 ⓞ 🅴 *VISA* V g
M a la carte 216/400 — **50 rm** 850/2000 Bb.

🏠 **Fuggerhof** without rest, Eberhard-Fugger-Str. 9, ℰ 2 04 79/6 41 29 00, Telex 632533, Fax
64129040, ≤, ⓢ, 🐎 — 📞 📺 ☎ 🅿. ⚶ by Bürglsteinstr. X
closed 20 December - 20 January — **20 rm** 950/2200.

🏠 **Zum Hirschen**, St.-Julien-Str. 21, ℰ 73 14 10, Telex 632691, Fax 7314158, 🍸, Massage, ⓢ
— 📞 📺 ☎ 🅿 — 🔬 25/50. ⚶ rest — **80 rm** V r

🏠 **Elefant** 🦢, Sigmund-Haffner-Gasse 4, ℰ 84 33 97, Telex 632725 — 📞 📺 ☎. 🆎 ⓞ 🅴 *VISA*
M (closed Tuesday and 1 to 25 November) a la carte 170/360 — **38 rm** 650/1800 Bb. Y f

🏠 **Weiße Taube** 🦢 without rest, Kaigasse 9, ℰ 84 24 04, Telex 633065, Fax 84178350 — 📞
☎. 🆎 ⓞ 🅴 *VISA*. ⚶ Z r
33 rm 750/1600.

✕✕ **Café Winkler** (modern café-rest. with casino), Mönchsberg 32 (access by 📞, 19 A.S.),
ℰ 8 41 21 50, Fax 84525830, ≤ Salzburg, 🍸 — 🔬 25/120. 🆎 ⓞ 🅴 *VISA* Y
closed Monday September - July — **M** 310 (lunch) and a la carte 390/570.

✕✕ Riedenburg, Neutorstr. 31, ℰ 84 92 64, 🍸 — 🅿 X a

✕✕ **K u. K Restaurant am Waagplatz**, Waagplatz 2 (1st floor), ℰ 84 21 56, Fax 84215770, 🍸,
« Medieval dinner with period performance in the Freysauff-Keller (by arrangement) »
(booking essential) ⅋. Z h

✕✕ **Mozart**, Getreidegasse 22 (1st floor, 📞), ℰ 84 37 46, Fax 846852 — 🆎 ⓞ 🅴 *VISA* Y t
closed Thursday, Friday lunch and 22 May - 16 June — **M** (booking essential) a la carte
340/505.

✕✕ Zum Mohren, Judengasse 9, ℰ 84 23 87 — ⚶ — (booking essential). Y g

at Salzburg-Aigen A-5026 by Bürglsteinstr. X :

🏠 **Doktorwirt**, Glaser Str. 9, ℰ 2 29 73, Telex 632938, 🍸, ⓢ, 🏊 (heated), 🐎 — 📺 ☎ 🅿.
🆎 ⓞ 🅴 *VISA*. ⚶ rest
closed 10 to 25 February and 20 October - November — **M** (closed Monday) a la carte
180/370 ⅋ — **39 rm** 700/1400.

✕ **Gasthof Schloß Aigen**, Schwarzenbergpromenade 37, ℰ 2 12 84, 🍸 — 🅿. 🆎 ⓞ 🅴
VISA — closed Thursday and Wednesday — **M** a la carte 170/400 ⅋.

at Salzburg-Liefering A-5020 by ④ :

🏨 **Brandstätter**, Münchner Bundesstr. 69, ℰ 34 53 50, Fax 3453590, 🍸, ⓢ, 🔲, 🐎 — 📞 📺
☎ 🅿 🔬 40. 🆎 ⓞ 🅴 *VISA*
closed 23 to 27 December — **M** (booking essential, closed 4 to 18 January) a la carte 240/555
⅋ — **36 rm** 660/1950.

at Salzburg-Maria Plain A-5101 by Plainstr. V :

🏠 **Maria Plain** 🦢 (17C inn), Plainbergweg 33, ℰ 5 07 01, Telex 632801, Fax 507119, « Garden
with ≤ » — 📞 📺 ☎ ⇔ 🅿 — 🔬 40 — **30 rm** Bb — 3 appart.

at Salzburg-Parsch A-5020 by Bürglsteinstr. X :

🏰 **Fondachhof** 🦢, Gaisbergstr. 46, 🖉 64 13 31, Telex 632519, Fax 641576, ≼, « 18C manor house in a park », 🚗, ⌛, ⌱ (heated), 🛁 – 🔟 📺 🕾 ⇔ ❢ – 🔬 25. 🆎 ⓪ 🖪 𝘝𝘐𝘚𝘈. ⁂ rest
20 March - October – (rest. for residents only) – **28 rm** 1100/3300 – 4 appart. 3200/5200.

🏠 **Villa Pace** 🦢, Sonnleitenweg 9, 🖉 64 15 01, Telex 631141, Fax 64150122, ≼ town and Hohensalzburg, 🚗, ⌱ (heated), 🛁 – 🔟 🕾 ⇔ ❢. ⁂ rest
(booking essential) – **12 rm**.

on the Heuberg NE : 3 km by ① – alt. 565 m :

🏠 **Schöne Aussicht** 🦢, ✉ A-5023 Salzburg, 🖉 (0662) 64 06 08, Telex 631153, Fax 6406902, « Garden with ≼ Salzburg and Alps », 🚗, ⌱ (heated), 🛁, ⁂ – 🔟 🕾 ❢ – 🔬 40. 🆎 ⓪ 🖪 𝘝𝘐𝘚𝘈.
closed 7 January - March – **M** *(closed Sunday)* a la carte 252/530 – **30 rm** 950/1800 Bb.

on the Gaisberg by ① :

🏰 **Kobenzl** 🦢, Gaisberg 11, alt. 750 m, ✉ A-5020 Salzburg, 🖉 (0662) 64 15 10, Telex 633833, Fax 64223871, 🏛, « Beautiful panoramic location with ≼ Salzburg and Alps », Massage, 🚗, 🛁, 🛁 – 🔟 ⇔ ❢ – 🔬 40. 🆎 ⓪ 𝘝𝘐𝘚𝘈. ⁂ rest
mid March - October – **M** a la carte 350/560 – **35 rm** 1450/5550 Bb – 4 appart. 5900/6500.

🏠 **Die Gersberg Alm** 🦢, Gaisberg 37, alt. alt. 800 m, ✉ A-5020 Salzburg, 🖉 (0662) 64 12 57, Fax 64125780, 🏛, 🚗 – 🔟 🕾 ❢ – 🔬 25/60. ⁂ – **42 rm** Bb.

🏠 **Berghotel Zistel-Alm** 🦢, Gaisberg 16, alt. 1 001 m, ✉ A-5026 Salzburg-Aigen, 🖉 (0662) 64 10 67, Fax 20104200, ≼ Alps, 🏛, 🚗, 🛁 – 🕾 ⇔ ❢. 🆎 ⓪ 🖪 𝘝𝘐𝘚𝘈. ⁂ rest
closed 26 October - 20 December – **M** a la carte 170/450 ⅊ – **24 rm** 390/1400.

at Anif A-5081 ② : 7 km – ☼ 06246 :

🏠 **Point Hotel**, Berchtesgadener Str.364, 🖉 42 56, Telex 631003, Fax 4256443, 🏛, Massage, 🚗, ⌱ (heated), 🚗, ⁂ (covered court) – ▐≸ 🔟 🕾 ❢ – 🔬 25/100
62 rm Bb.

🏠 **Friesacher** (with guest-house Aniferhof), 🖉 20 75, Telex 632943, Fax 207549, 🏛, 🚗, 🚗, ⁂ – ▐≸ 🔟 🕾 ❢ – 🔬 25. ⓪ 🖪
closed 2 to 22 January – **M** *(closed Wednesday)* a la carte 185/380 ⅊ – **70 rm** 680/1380 Bb.

🏠 **Hubertushof, Neu Anif 4** (near motorway exit Salzburg Süd), 🖉 24 78, Telex 632684, Fax 421768, 🏛 – ▐≸ 🔟 🕾 ❢ – 🔬 25/60 – **70 rm** Bb.

🏠 **Romantik-Hotel Schloßwirt** (17C inn with Biedermeier furniture), Halleiner Bundesstr. 22, 🖉 21 75, Telex 631169, Fax 217580, ⌀, 🚗 – ▐≸ 🕾 ⇔ ❢. 🆎 ⓪ 🖪 𝘝𝘐𝘚𝘈
closed February – **M** a la carte 280/440 – **32 rm** 850/1700 Bb.

at Hof A-5322 ① : 20 km :

🏰 **Schloß Fuschl** 🦢 (former 15C hunting seat with 3 guest-houses), 🖉 (06229) 2 25 30, Telex 633454, Fax 2253531, ≼, 🏛, Massage, 🚗, 🛁, 🎣, 🚗, ⁂ – ▐≸ 🔟 ⇔ ❢ – 🔬 25/100. 🆎 ⓪ 🖪 𝘝𝘐𝘚𝘈. ⁂ rest
M 400 (lunch) and a la carte 500/720 – **84 rm** 1500/3400 Bb – 5 appart. 4800/5800.

🏠 **Jagdhof am Fuschlsee** (former 18C farm-house with guest-house), 🖉 (06229) 2 37 10, Telex 633454, Fax 2253531, ≼, 🏛, « Hunting museum », 🚗, 🛁, 🚗 – 🔟 🕾 ❢ – 🔬 25/180. 🆎 ⓪ 🖪 𝘝𝘐𝘚𝘈. ⁂ rest
M a la carte 210/380 ⅊ – **50 rm** 600/1350 Bb.

at Fuschl am See A-5330 ① : 26 km :

🏰 **Parkhotel Waldhof** 🦢, Seepromenade, 🖉 (06226) 2 64, Telex 632487, Fax 644, ≼, 🏛, Massage, 🚗, 🛁, 🎣, 🚗, ⁂ – 🔟 🕾 ❢. ⁂ rest
closed 10 January - March – **M** a la carte 250/450 – **67 rm** 650/1790 Bb.

✗✗ **Brunnwirt**, 🖉 (06226) 2 36, 🏛 – ❢ 🆎 ⓪ 🖪 𝘝𝘐𝘚𝘈. ⁂
dinner only except during the festival, closed Sunday and 7 to 25 January – **M** *(booking essential)* a la carte 370/700.

at the Mondsee ① : 28 km (by motorway A 1) – ☼ 06232 :

🏰 **Seehof** 🦢, (SE : 7 km), ✉ A-5311 Loibichl, 🖉 2 55 00, Fax 255051, ≼, 🏛, Massage, 🚗, 🎣, ⁂ – 🔟 ❢
10 March - 25 September – **M** a la carte 320/580 – **31 rm** 1800/3300 Bb – 10 appart. 3300/4000 – ½ P 1480/2600.

🏠 ❀ **Weißes Kreuz**, Herzog-Odilo-Str. 25, ✉ A-5310 Mondsee, 🖉 22 54, Fax 225434, 🏛 – ▐≸ 🕾 ⇔ ❢. 🆎
closed 12 November - 12 December – **M** *(remarkable wine-list, booking essential)* (closed Wednesday, November - April also Tuesday) 260/695 a la carte 374/590 – **10 rm** 500/1200
Spec. Ganslsuppe mit Schinkenknöderl (Oct.- May). Mondsee-Zander auf Eierschwammerlcreme, Marillenblätterteig mit Himbeerschaum.

✗✗✗ ❀ **Landhaus Eschlböck-Plomberg** with rm, (S : 5 km), ✉ A-5310 St. Lorenz - Plomberg, 🖉 35 72, Fax 316620, ≼, 🏛, 🚗, 🛁 – 🔟 🕾 ⇔ ❢. ⓪ 🖪
M *(booking essential)* (closed 3 weeks January and Monday September - May) a la carte 380/670 – **12 rm** 750/2600
Spec. Pasteten und Terrinen, Lachsforelle mit Selleriebutter, Marillengratin mit Vanilleparfait.

Benelux

Belgium

Brussels
Antwerp
Bruges
Liège

Grand Duchy of Luxemburg

Luxemburg

Netherlands

Amsterdam
The Hague
Rotterdam

PRACTICAL INFORMATION

LOCAL CURRENCY

Belgian Franc : 100 F = 3.21 US $ (Jan. 91) can also be used in Luxemburg
Dutch Florin : 100 Fl. = 58.78 US $ (Jan. 91)

TOURIST INFORMATION

Telephone numbers and addresses of Tourist Offices are given in the text of each city under 🛈.

FOREIGN EXCHANGE

In Belgium, banks close at 3.30pm and weekends ; **in the Netherlands,** banks close at 5.00pm and weekends, Schiphol Airport exchange offices open daily from 6.30am to 11.30pm.

TRANSPORT

Taxis : may be hailed in the street, at taxi ranks or called by telephone.
Bus, tramway : practical for long and short distances and good for sightseeing.

POSTAL SERVICES

Post offices open Monday to Friday from 9am to 5pm in Benelux.

SHOPPING

Shops and boutiques are generally open from 9am to 7pm in Belgium and Luxemburg, and from 9am to 6pm in the Netherlands. The main shopping areas are :
in Brussels : Rue Neuve, Porte de Namur, Avenue Louise - Also Brussels antique market on Saturday from 9am to 3pm, and Sunday from 9am to 1pm (around place du Grand-Sablon) - Flower market (Grand-Place) on Sunday morning.
in Antwerp : Bird Market : Sunday from 8.30am to 1pm - Antwerp diamond quarter.
in Bruges : Calashes on the Market Place for shopping and town sightseeing.
in Amsterdam : Kalverstraat, Leidsestraat, Nieuwendijk, P.C. Hoofstraat and Utrechtsestraat. Second-hand goods and antiques. Amsterdam Flea Market (near Waterlooplein).
in Den Haag : Hoogstraat, Korte Poten, Paleispromenade, De Passage and Spuistraat.
in Rotterdam : Binnenweg, Hoogstraat, Karel Doormanstraat, Lijnbaan and Stadhuisplein.

BREAKDOWN SERVICE

24 hour assistance :
Belgium : TCB, Brussels ☎ (0 2) 233 22 22 — VTB-VAB, Antwerp ☎ (0 3) 253-63 63 — RACB, Brussels ☎ (0 2) 736 59 59.
Luxemburg : ACL ☎ 45 00 45.
Netherlands : ANWB, The Hague ☎ (0 70) 314 71 47.

TIPPING

In Benelux, prices include service and taxes.

SPEED LIMITS

In Belgium and Luxemburg, the maximum speed limits are 120 km/h-74 mph on motorways and dual carriageways, 90 km/h-56 mph on all other roads and 60 km/h-37 mph in built-up areas. In the Netherlands, 100/120 km/h-62/74 mph on motorways and "autowegen", 80 km/h-50 mph on other roads and 50 km/h-31 mph in built-up areas.

SEAT BELTS

In each country, the wearing of seat belts is compulsory.

BRUSSELS

BRUSSELS **(BRUXELLES - BRUSSEL) 1000** Brabant **213** ⑱ and **409** ⑬ − Pop. 970 346 agglomeration − ⊙ 0 2.

⛳ ⛳ at Tervuren by ⑥ : 13 km, Château de Ravenstein ✆ (0 2) 767 58 01, ⛳ at Melsbroek NE : 15 km, Steenwagenstraat 11 ✆ (0 2) 751 82 05 − ⛳ at Anderlecht, Zone Sportive de la Pede, Drève Olympique 1 ✆ (0 2) 521 16 87 − ⛳ at Watermael-Boitsfort, chaussée de la Hulpe 53a ✆ (0 2) 672 22 22 − ⛳ at Overijse by ⑦ : 14 km, Gemslaan 35 ✆ (0 2) 687 50 30 − ⛳ at Itterbeek by ⑪ : 9 km, J.M. van Lierdelaan 28 b ✆ (0 2) 569 69 81.

✈ **National** NE : 12 km ✆ 722 31 11 − **Air Terminal** : Air Terminus, r. du Cardinal Mercier 35 LZ ✆ 511 90 30.

🚕 ✆ 2186050 ext. 4106.

🛈 Town Hall (Hôtel de Ville), Grand'Place, ⊠ 1000 ✆ 513 89 40 − Tourist Association of the Province, r. Marché-aux-Herbes 61, ⊠ 1000 ✆ 513 07 50.

Paris 308 ⑨ − Amsterdam 204 ① − Düsseldorf 222 ⑤ − Lille 116 ⑫ − Luxembourg 219 ⑦.

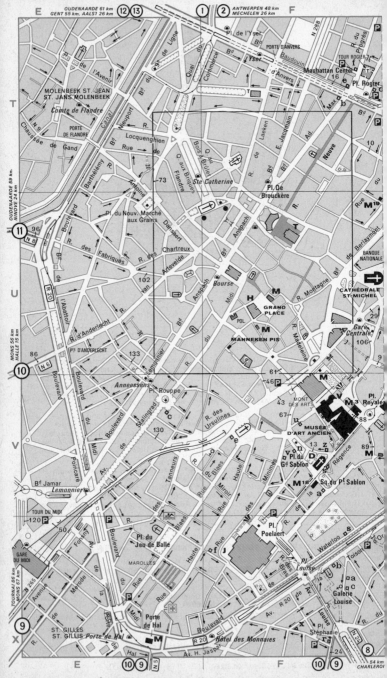

Room prices are subject to the addition of a local tax of 6%

BRUXELLES (BRUSSEL)

🏨 **SAS Royal**, r. Fossé-aux-Loups 47, ⊠ 1000, 𝒞 219 28 28, Telex 22202, Fax 219 62 62, « Patio with vestige of 12C Brussels enclosure wall », ⥩ – 🛗 ⁂ rm 🔲 📺 ☎ & 🚗 – 🔬 25-400. 🆎 ① 🅴 𝘝𝘐𝘚𝘈. ⋇ rest   LY **c**
M see rest. **Sea Grill** below – **Atrium** a la carte 750/1400 – **248 rm** ⇌ 8900/10500.

🏨 **Pullman Astoria**, r. Royale 103, ⊠ 1000, 𝒞 217 62 90, Telex 25040, Fax 217 11 50, « Early 20C residence » – 🛗 ▤ rest 📺 ☎ – 🔬 25-200. 🆎 ① 🅴 𝘝𝘐𝘚𝘈. ⋇ rest   GTU **b**
M Palais Royal *(closed Saturday lunch)* a la carte 1700/2300 – ⇌ 580 – **125 rm** 4850/7200 – ½ P 6720/7570.

🏨 **Métropole**, pl. de Brouckère 31, ⊠ 1000, 𝒞 217 23 00, Telex 21234, Fax 218 02 20, « Late 19C hall and lounges », ⥩ – 🛗 ▤ rest 📺 ☎ – 🔬 25-600. 🆎 ① 🅴 𝘝𝘐𝘚𝘈. ⋇ rest   LY **r**
M L'Alban Chambon *(closed Saturday, Sunday and Bank Holidays)* 1300/1950 – **400 rm** ⇌ 4900/7800.

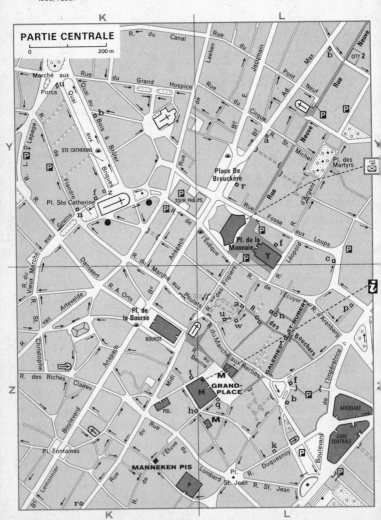

🏨 **Bedford**, r. Midi 135, ✉ 1000, ℰ 512 78 40, Telex 24059, Fax 514 17 59 – 🛗 ▤ rest 📺 ☎
   🍸 – 🔒 25-200. ◼ ⓪ E 𝘝𝘐𝘚𝘈. 🛠️   KZ **r**
   M a la carte 1100/1500 – **275 rm** ⚏ 4400/7200 – ½ P 3600/5250.

🏨 **Jolly Atlanta**, bd A.-Max 7, ✉ 1000, ℰ 217 01 20, Telex 21475, Fax 217 37 58 – 🛗 ▤ rest
📺 ☎ 🍸 – 🔒 50. ◼ ⓪ E 𝘝𝘐𝘚𝘈. 🛠️ rest   LY **t**
   M *(closed Saturday, Sunday and August)* 1200/2300 – **244 rm** ⚏ 7100/7700.

🏨 **Président Centre** without rest., r. Royale 160, ✉ 1000, ℰ 219 00 65, Telex 26784, Fax
218 09 10 – 🛗 ▤ 📺 ☎ 🍸. ◼ ⓪ E 𝘝𝘐𝘚𝘈   GU **a**
   73 rm ⚏ 4900/5900.

🏨 **Arenberg**, r. d'Assaut 15, ✉ 1000, ℰ 511 07 70, Telex 25660, Fax 514 19 76 – 🛗 🍸⟨⟩ rm 📺
☎ – 🔒 50-90. ◼ ⓪ E 𝘝𝘐𝘚𝘈   LZ **p**
   M a la carte 900/1400 – **155 rm** ⚏ 4600/5200.

🏨 **Chambord** without rest., r. Namur 82, ✉ 1000, ℰ 513 41 19, Telex 20373, Fax 514 08 47 –
🛗 📺 ☎ – 🔒 25. ◼ ⓪ E 𝘝𝘐𝘚𝘈. 🛠️   GV **v**
   70 rm ⚏ 3295/4575.

🏨 **Sabina** without rest., r. Nord 78, ✉ 1000, ℰ 218 26 37, Fax 219 32 39 – 🛗 ☎   GU **e**
   24 rm ⚏ 900/1550.

XXXX ❀ **Sea Grill** - (at H. SAS Royal), r. Fossé-aux-Loups 47, ✉ 1000, ℰ 219 28 28, Telex 22202,
Fax 219 62 62, Seafood – ▤. 🄿. ◼ ⓪ E 𝘝𝘐𝘚𝘈   LY **c**
   closed Sunday, Bank Holidays and 19 July-20 August – **M** a la carte 1950/2650
   Spec. Langoustines à la vapeur d'algues, Gravlax sauce moutarde, Turbot rôti, béarnaise de homard.

XXX ❀❀❀ **Comme Chez Soi** (Wynants), pl. Rouppe 23, ✉ 1000, ℰ 512 29 21, Fax 511 80 52,
« Belle Epoque atmosphere in an Horta decor » – ▤. 🄿. ◼ ⓪ E   EV **c**
   closed Sunday, Monday, July and Christmas-New Year – **M** (booking essential) a la carte
   2100/2750
   Spec. Filets de sole, mousseline au Riesling et aux crevettes grises, Faisan au céléri-rave et aux marrons
   (15 October-December), Émincé de mangues chaudes voilé de frangipane.

XXX **Astrid ''Chez Pierrot''**, r. Presse 21, ✉ 1000, ℰ 217 38 31, Fax 217 38 31 – ◼ ⓪ E 𝘝𝘐𝘚𝘈
   closed Sunday, 1 week Easter and 15 July-15 August – **M** 800/1600.   GU **d**

XX **Roma**, r. Princes 12, ✉ 1000, ℰ 218 34 30, Italian cuisine – ▤. ◼ ⓪ E 𝘝𝘐𝘚𝘈. 🛠️   LY **f**
   closed Saturday lunch and Sunday – **M** 1700.

Quartier de l'Europe

🏨 **Europa**, r. Loi 107, ✉ 1040, ℰ 230 13 33, Telex 25121, Fax 230 36 82, 🍸⟨⟩ – 🛗 🍸⟨⟩ rm ▤ 📺
☎ 🄿 – 🔒 25-400. ◼ ⓪ E 𝘝𝘐𝘚𝘈. 🛠️ rm   HV **s**
   M Les Continents 1500/2200 – ⚏ 500 – **240 rm** 7000/9000.

🏨 **Archimède** without rest., r. Archimède 22, ✉ 1040, ℰ 231 09 09, Telex 20420, Fax 230 33 71
– 🛗 📺 ☎ 🄿 ◼ ⓪ E 𝘝𝘐𝘚𝘈   HU **y**
   56 rm ⚏ 5600/5800.

🏨 **Euro-flat** without rest., bd Charlemagne 50, ✉ 1040, ℰ 230 00 10, Telex 21120, Fax
230 36 83, 🍸⟨⟩ – 🛗 📺 ☎ – 🔒 25. ◼ ⓪ E 𝘝𝘐𝘚𝘈. 🛠️   HU **p**
   135 rm ⚏ 5200/6300.

🏨 **City Garden** 🛠️ without rest., with suites, r. Joseph II 59, ✉ 1040, ℰ 230 09 45, Telex
63570, Fax 230 64 37 – 🛗 🍸⟨⟩ 📺 ☎. ◼ ⓪ E 𝘝𝘐𝘚𝘈. 🛠️   GU **r**
   95 rm ⚏ 4300/5800.

🏨 **Alfa Chelton** without rest., r. Véronèse 48, ✉ 1040, ℰ 735 20 32, Telex 64253, Fax 735 07 66
– 🛗 📺 ☎ – **48 rm**.

XX **Villa de Bruselas**, r. Archimède 65, ✉ 1040, ℰ 735 60 90, 🌳, Partly Spanish cuisine –
◼ ⓪ E 𝘝𝘐𝘚𝘈   HU **e**
   closed Saturday lunch, Sunday, Bank Holidays and August – **M** a la carte 1300/2100.

X **Le Gigotin**, r. Stevin 102, ✉ 1040, ℰ 230 30 91, 🌳 – ◼ ⓪ E 𝘝𝘐𝘚𝘈   HU **n**
   closed Saturday, Sunday and August – **M** a la carte 900/1400.

X **La Maison Suisse**, r. Philippe le Bon 2, ✉ 1040, ℰ 230 43 41, Swiss specialities – 🄿. ◼
⓪ E 𝘝𝘐𝘚𝘈 – *closed Saturday lunch, Sunday, Monday dinner, Bank Holidays, 15 August-1
September and 22 December-4 January* – **M** a la carte approx. 1500   HU **a**

Quartier Grand'Place (Ilot Sacré)

🏨 **Royal Windsor**, r. Duquesnoy 5, ✉ 1000, ℰ 511 42 15, Telex 62905, Fax 511 60 04 – 🛗
🍸⟨⟩ rm ▤ 📺 ☎ 🍸 – 🔒 25-250. ◼ ⓪ E 𝘝𝘐𝘚𝘈   LZ **k**
   M Les 4 Saisons *(closed 21 July-21 August)* a la carte 1600/2900 – **280 rm** ⚏ 8250/11500.

🏨 **Amigo**, r. Amigo 1, ✉ 1000, ℰ 511 59 10, Telex 21618, Fax 513 52 77, « Various art collection » – 🛗 ▤ rest 📺 ☎ 🍸 🍸 – 🔒 25-90. ◼ ⓪ E 𝘝𝘐𝘚𝘈. 🛠️ rest   KZ **h**
   M a la carte 1100/1700 – **183 rm** ⚏ 6250/7700.

🏨 **Novotel Grand'Place**, r. Marché-aux-Herbes 120, ✉ 1000, ℰ 514 33 33, Telex 20377, Fax
511 77 23 – 🛗 🍸⟨⟩ rm 📺 ☎. ◼ ⓪ E 𝘝𝘐𝘚𝘈   LZ **b**
   M (open until midnight) a la carte 900/1400 – ⚏ 460 – **136 rm** 4720/4900.

🏨 **Arlequin** without rest., r. Fourche 17, ✉ 1000, ℰ 514 16 15, Telex 65608, Fax 514 18 25 – 🛗
📺 ☎. ◼ ⓪ E 𝘝𝘐𝘚𝘈 – **60 rm** ⚏ 1600/2200.   LZ **w**

🏨 **Ibis**, r. Marché-aux-Herbes 100, ✉ 1000, ℰ 514 40 40, Telex 25490, Fax 514 50 67 – 🛗
🍸⟨⟩ rest ▤ rest ☎ 🍸 – 🔒 25-130. ◼ ⓪ E 𝘝𝘐𝘚𝘈   LZ **f**
   M a la carte approx. 900 – **170 rm** ⚏ 3370/3850.

XXXX ۞ **La Maison du Cygne,** Grand'Place 9, ⊠ 1000, 🖉 511 82 44, Fax 514 31 48, « Former 17C guildhouse » – ℗ AE ① E VISA
          LZ **q**
closed Saturday lunch, Sunday, 3 weeks August and Christmas-New Year – **M** a la carte 2150/2800
Spec. Salade tiède de langoustines, Turbot braisé au thym, Dos d'agneau ''Cygne''.

XX **La Tête d'Or,** r. Tête d'Or 9, ⊠ 1000, 🖉 511 02 01, « Ancient Brussels residence » – AE ① E VISA
          KZ **t**
closed Saturday and Sunday – **M** a la carte 1500/2000.

XX **La Table d'Or,** r. Fourche 50, ⊠ 1000, 🖉 217 47 00, Fax 219 91 01, Open until 11 p.m. – AE ① E VISA ⁜
          LZ **a**
closed Saturday lunch, Sunday and 20 July-10 August – **M** 1565/1965.

XX **La Porte du Japon,** r. Fourche 9, ⊠ 1000, 🖉 511 15 11, Japanese cuisine, open until 11 p.m. – ▤ AE ① E VISA
          LZ **u**
closed Monday – **M** a la carte 1100/2350.

XX **Aux Armes de Bruxelles,** r. Bouchers 13, ⊠ 1000, 🖉 511 55 98, Fax 514 33 81, Brussels atmosphere, open until 11 p.m. – ▤ AE ① E VISA
          LZ **c**
closed Monday and June – **M** 895/1645.

X **L'Ogenblik,** Galerie des Princes 1, ⊠ 1000, 🖉 511 61 51, Open until midnight – AE ① E VISA – *closed Sunday* – **M** a la carte 1500/2100.
          LZ **n**

X **Taverne du Passage,** Galerie de la Reine 30, ⊠ 1000, 🖉 512 37 31, Fax 511 08 82, Brussels atmosphere, open until midnight – AE ① E VISA
          LZ **r**
closed Wednesday and Thursday in June and July – **M** a la carte 750/1500.

X **Rôtiss. Vincent,** r. Dominicains 8, ⊠ 1000, 🖉 511 23 03, Brussels atmosphere, « Frescos in ceramic tiles » – ▤ AE ① E VISA
          LZ **n**
closed August – **M** 895.

Quartier Ste-Catherine (Marché-aux-Poissons)

XX **La Sirène d'Or,** pl. Ste-Catherine 1a, ⊠ 1000, 🖉 513 51 98, Fax 502 13 05, Seafood – ▤. AE ① E VISA
          KY **n**
closed Sunday, Monday, 1 to 23 July and 23 December-2 January – **M** a la carte 1600/2200.

XX ۞ **François,** quai aux Briques 2, ⊠ 1000, 🖉 511 60 89, Fax 512 06 57, Seafood – ⁜≈ ▤. AE ① E VISA
          KY **z**
closed Monday and June – **M** a la carte 1400/2400
Spec. Salade ou tomate aux crevettes épluchées du jour, Anguille au vert, Plateau royal de fruits de mer (October-15 March).

XX ۞ **La Belle Maraîchère** (Devreker), pl. Ste-Catherine 11, ⊠ 1000, 🖉 512 97 59, Fax 513 76 91, Seafood – ▤ ℗ AE ① E VISA
          KY **f**
closed Wednesday and Thursday – **M** a la carte 1400/2200
Spec. Soupe de poissons, Fricassée de homard aux petits légumes, Turbot grillé sauce béarnaise.

XX **Au Cheval Marin,** Marché-aux-Porcs 25, ⊠ 1000, 🖉 513 02 87, « Ancient decor » – ℗ AE ① E VISA
          KY **u**
closed Sunday and 1 week August – **M** 900/1750.

X **La Marie Joseph,** quai au Bois-à-Brûler 47, ⊠ 1000, 🖉 218 05 96, Seafood, open until 11 p.m. – AE ① E VISA
          KY **b**
closed Monday – **M** a la carte 1200/1900.

Quartier des Sablons

XXX ۞۞ **L'Écailler du Palais Royal** (Basso), r. Bodenbroek 18, ⊠ 1000, 🖉 512 87 51, Seafood – AE ① E VISA
          FV **z**
closed Sunday, Bank Holidays and 29 July-August – **M** a la carte 2350/2850
Spec. St-Jacques meunières, julienne de chicons (October-April), Barbue aux deux céleris et jus de veau giroflé, Homard au Sauvignon.

XXX **En Provence ''Chez Marius'',** pl. du Petit Sablon 1, ⊠ 1000, 🖉 511 12 08, Fax 512 27 89 – AE ① E VISA ⁜
          FV **s**
closed Sunday – **M** 1300/1950.

XX **Les Brigittines,** pl. de la Chapelle 5, ⊠ 1000, 🖉 512 68 91, Fax 512 41 30, 🍴, « Belle Epoque atmosphere » – AE ① E VISA
          FV **e**
closed Saturday lunch, Sunday and August – **M** a la carte 1300/2350.

XX ۞ **Trente rue de la Paille** (Martiny), r. Paille 30 (transfer planned), ⊠ 1000, 🖉 512 07 15, Fax 514 23 33, Open until 11.30 p.m. – AE ① E VISA
          FV **u**
closed Saturday, Sunday, Bank Holidays, 29 June-July and 21 December-1 January – **M** a la carte 1700/2400
Spec. Foie gras de canard aux pommes, poires et Porto, Rouget-barbet rôti au romarin, Gratin de fraises.

XX **Au Duc d'Arenberg,** pl. du Petit Sablon 9, ⊠ 1000, 🖉 511 14 75, « Collection of modern paintings » – AE ① E VISA
          FV **a**
closed Sunday, Bank Holidays and last week December – **M** 1950/2450.

X **L'Herbe Rouge,** r. Minimes 34, ⊠ 1000, 🖉 512 48 34, Open until 11.30 p.m. – AE ① E VISA – *closed Saturday lunch and Sunday* – **M** a la carte 1700/2300.
          FV **v**

X **Au Vieux Saint-Martin,** pl. du Grand Sablon 38, ⊠ 1000, 🖉 512 64 76, Pub-rest., open until midnight
          FV **n**
M a la carte 1100/1700.

Quartier Palais de Justice

🏰 **Hilton International,** bd de Waterloo 38, ⊠ 1000, ℰ 513 88 77, Telex 22744, Fax 513 72 33, 🚗 – 🛗 ⇔ rm 🗏 📺 🕿 🕭 ⇔ – 🔬 50-500. 🖭 ① E 𝗩𝗜𝗦𝗔. ⫻ FX **s**
M see rest. **Maison du Bœuf** below – **Plein Ciel 27th floor** ≤ town (closed Saturday and 15 July-20 August) (lunch only) 950/1550 – **Café d'Egmont** a la carte 1000/1500 – 立 750 –
454 rm 8600/13300.

🍽🍽🍽🍽 **Maison du Bœuf** - (at H. Hilton), 1st floor, bd de Waterloo 38, ⊠ 1000, ℰ 513 88 77, Telex 22744, Fax 513 72 33, ≤ – 🗏 🅿. 🖭 ① E 𝗩𝗜𝗦𝗔. ⫻ FX **s**
M a la carte 1700/2500.

🍽 ⊛ **Au Beurre Blanc** (Hella), r. Faucon 2a, ⊠ 1000, ℰ 513 01 11 – 🖭 ① E 𝗩𝗜𝗦𝗔 FX **f**
closed Saturday, Sunday, 2 weeks Easter, 15 August-3 September and 25 December-4 January
– **M** a la carte 1600/2100
Spec. Suprême de baisin à la crème de bacon et noisettes (mid October-end December), Assiette du pêcheur au beurre blanc, Ris et rognon de veau au jus de truffes.

Quartier Avenue Louise (see also at Ixelles)

🏰 **Mayfair,** av. Louise 381, ⊠ 1050, ℰ 649 98 00, Telex 24821, Fax 640 17 64, « Opulent decor » – 🛗 ⇔ rm 🗏 📺 🕿 ⇔ – 🔬 30. 🖭 ① E 𝗩𝗜𝗦𝗔. ⫻ rest
M a la carte 1700/2200 – 立 500 – **99 rm** 8000/9500.

🏰 **Stéphanie,** av. Louise 91, ⊠ 1050, ℰ 539 02 40, Telex 25558, Fax 538 03 07, 🔲 – 🛗 ⇔ 🗏 rest 📺 🕿 ⇔ – 🔬 50-200. 🖭 ① E 𝗩𝗜𝗦𝗔. ⫻ rest
M L'Avenue Louise (closed Saturday, Sunday lunch, 27 July-25 August and 21 to 31 December) a la carte 1400/2000 – **142 rm** 立 6950/8250.

🏰 **Brussels President** without rest., av. Louise 315, ⊠ 1050, ℰ 640 24 15, Telex 25075, Fax 647 34 63 – 🛗 📺 🕿. 🖭 ① E 𝗩𝗜𝗦𝗔. ⫻
38 rm 立 4250/4700.

🏰 **Alfa Louise** without rest., r. Blanche 4, ⊠ 1050, ℰ 537 92 10, Telex 62434, Fax 537 00 18 –
🛗 📺 🕿 ⇔ – 🔬 30. 🖭 ① E 𝗩𝗜𝗦𝗔
83 rm 立 3950/4550.

🏰 **L'Agenda** without rest., r. Florence 6, ⊠ 1050, ℰ 539 00 31, Telex 63947, Fax 539 00 63 –
🛗 📺 🕿 ⇔. 🖭 ① E 𝗩𝗜𝗦𝗔
立 300 – **38 rm** 2750/3050.

🍽🍽 **Tagawa,** av. Louise 279, ⊠ 1050, ℰ 640 50 95, Japanese cuisine – 🗏 🅿. 🖭 ① E 𝗩𝗜𝗦𝗔. ⫻
closed Saturday lunch and Sunday – **M** 855/3255.

Quartier Bois de la Cambre

🍽🍽🍽🍽🍽 ⊛⊛ **Villa Lorraine** (Van de Casserie), av. du Vivier d'Oie 75, ⊠ 1180, ℰ 374 31 63, 🌣 –
🅿. 🖭 ① E 𝗩𝗜𝗦𝗔
closed Sunday and 1 to 30 July – **M** a la carte 2350/3300
Spec. Petit rouget et artichaut en vinaigrette, Escalopes de ris de veau au Meursault, Chaud-froid de saumon et noix de St-Jacques (October-April).

🍽🍽🍽 ⊛ **La Truffe Noire,** bd de la Cambre 12, ⊠ 1050, ℰ 640 44 22, Fax 647 97 04 – 🖭 ① E 𝗩𝗜𝗦𝗔
closed Saturday lunch, Sunday, 1 week Easter, last 2 weeks August and late December –
M a la carte 2550/3300
Spec. Carpaccio aux truffes, Risotto de homard au basilic, St-Pierre aux poireaux et truffes.

Quartier Atomium (Centenaire - Trade Mart)

🍽🍽🍽 **Le Centenaire,** av. J. Sobieski 84, ⊠ 1020, ℰ 478 66 23 – 🖭 ① E 𝗩𝗜𝗦𝗔
closed Sunday, Monday, July and Christmas-New Year – **M** a la carte 1200/1800.

🍽🍽 ⊛ **Les Baguettes Impériales** (Mme Ma), av. J. Sobieski 70, ⊠ 1020, ℰ 479 67 32, 🌣, Vietnamese cuisine, « Exotic decor » – 🖭
closed Tuesday, Sunday dinner, Easter and August – **M** a la carte 2000/2400.
Spec. Crêpes croustillantes au homard, Langoustines caramélisées aux poivres, Magret d'oie à la moutarde de mangue.

🍽 **Adrienne Atomium,** Parc Expositions, ⊠ 1020, ℰ 478 30 00, ≤, Buffets – 🖭 ① E 𝗩𝗜𝗦𝗔
closed Sunday and Bank Holidays – **M** 690.

Quartier Gare du Nord (Botanique)

🏰 **Sheraton Towers,** pl. Rogier 3, ⊠ 1210, ℰ 219 34 00, Telex 26887, Fax 218 66 18, 🚗, 🔲
– 🛗 ⇔ rm 🗏 📺 🕿 ⇔ – 🔬 25-1500. 🖭 ① E 𝗩𝗜𝗦𝗔. ⫻ FT **e**
M Comtes de Flandre (closed Saturday and Sunday) a la carte 1700/2500 – 立 595 –
504 rm 9500/12900.

🏰 **President World Trade Center,** bd E. Jacqmain 180, ⊠ 1210, ℰ 217 20 20, Telex 21066, Fax 218 84 02, 🚗 – 🛗 ⇔ rm 📺 🕿 ⇔ – 🔬 25-350. 🖭 ① E 𝗩𝗜𝗦𝗔. ⫻
M (closed Saturday, Sunday and July-August) a la carte 950/2200 – **305 rm** 立 7000/7500.

🏰 **Le Dome,** bd du Jardin Botanique 13, ⊠ 1000, ℰ 218 06 80, Telex 61317, Fax 218 41 12 –
🛗 📺 🕿 – 🔬 25-100. 🖭 ① E 𝗩𝗜𝗦𝗔. ⫻ rest FT **b**
M (closed Sunday, Monday dinner and Bank Holidays) 980/1200 – **77 rm** 立 5100/6500.

🏰 **Président Nord** without rest., bd A. Max 107, ⊠ 1000, ℰ 219 00 60, Telex 61417, Fax 218 12 69 – 🛗 📺 🕿. 🖭 ① E 𝗩𝗜𝗦𝗔 LY **b**
63 rm 立 3800/4650.

ANDERLECHT

🏨 **Le Prince de Liège,** chaussée de Ninove 664, ⊠ 1080, ℰ 522 16 00, Fax 520 81 85 – 🛗 📺
🕿 🚐 – 🔏 25. 🖭 ⓞ 🗲 𝘝𝘐𝘚𝘈
M *(closed Sunday dinner and 8 July-4 August)* 750/1250 – **21 rm** 🖙 1950/2550.

XXX **Saint-Guidon** 2nd floor, av. Théo Verbeeck 2 (in the Constant Vanden Stock stadium),
⊠ 1070, ℰ 520 55 36, Fax 520 07 40 – ⓟ – 🔏 25-400. ⓞ 🗲 𝘝𝘐𝘚𝘈
*closed July, Christmas-New Year, Saturday, Sunday, first league match days and Bank
Holidays* – **M** (lunch only) a la carte 1700/2300.

XX **La Réserve,** chaussée de Ninove 675, ⊠ 1080, ℰ 522 26 53, 佘 – 🖭 ⓞ 🗲 𝘝𝘐𝘚𝘈
closed Monday, Tuesday, Saturday lunch and 17 July-7 August – **M** a la carte 1200/1900.

X **La Paix** r. Ropsy-Chaudron 49 (opposite slaughterhouse), ⊠ 1070, ℰ 523 09 58, Pub-rest.
– 🖭 🗲 𝘝𝘐𝘚𝘈
closed Saturday and Sunday – **M** (lunch only) a la carte 800/1000.

AUDERGHEM (OUDERGEM)

XX ⬡ **La Grignotière** (Chanson), chaussée de Wavre 2041, ⊠ 1160, ℰ 672 81 85 – 🖭 ⓞ 🗲
𝘝𝘐𝘚𝘈
closed Sunday, Monday and Bank Holidays – **M** 1800/2300.
Spec. Brouillade de langoustines, Ris de veau au four farci de cuisses de grenouilles, Gibiers (15 October-
10 January).

XX **L'Abbaye de Rouge Cloître,** r. Rouge Cloître 8, ⊠ 1160, ℰ 672 45 25, ≼, 佘, « On
forest border » – ⓟ – 🔏 25-55. 🖭 ⓞ 🗲 𝘝𝘐𝘚𝘈
closed Saturday, Sunday and 21 December-6 January – **M** a la carte 1000/1700.

X **New Asia,** chaussée de Wavre 1240, ⊠ 1160, ℰ 660 62 06, Chinese cuisine – ⤢, 🖭 ⓞ
🗲 𝘝𝘐𝘚𝘈, ⅏
closed Monday and last 2 weeks July – **M** a la carte approx. 800.

ETTERBEEK

XX **La Fontaine de Jade,** av. de Tervuren 5, ⊠ 1040, ℰ 736 32 10, Chinese cuisine – 🖭 ⓞ
🗲 𝘝𝘐𝘚𝘈
closed Tuesday and 31 July-27 August – **M** a la carte approx. 1100.

X **Harry's Place,** r. Bataves 65, ⊠ 1040, ℰ 735 09 00 – 🖭 ⓞ 🗲 𝘝𝘐𝘚𝘈
*closed Thursday dinner, Saturday lunch, Sunday, Bank Holidays, mid July-mid August and
Christmas-New Year* – **M** a la carte approx. 1300.

X **Le Pavillon d'Été,** av. de Tervuren 107, ⊠ 1040, ℰ 732 03 59, Fax 732 10 56, Pub-rest.,
open until midnight – 🖭 ⓞ 🗲 𝘝𝘐𝘚𝘈
closed Sunday, Monday and 20 July-5 August – **M** a la carte 1100/1700.

EVERE

🏨 **Belson** without rest., chaussée de Louvain 805, ⊠ 1140, ℰ 735 00 00, Telex 64921, Fax
735 60 43 – 🛗 ⤢ 📺 🕿 ⓟ – 🔏 25. 🖭 ⓞ 🗲 𝘝𝘐𝘚𝘈
🖙 555 – **87 rm** 6050.

🏨 **Mercure,** av. J. Bordet 74, ⊠ 1140, ℰ 242 53 35, Telex 65460, Fax 245 05 95, 佘 – 🛗
⤢ rm ▤ rest 📺 🕿 ⅂ 🚐 – 🔏 30-60. 🖭 ⓞ 🗲 𝘝𝘐𝘚𝘈
M *(closed lunch Saturday and Sunday)* a la carte 1000/1800 – 🖙 450 – **120 rm** 3350/5100.

XX **Le Citron Vert,** av. H. Conscience 242, ⊠ 1140, ℰ 241 12 57, Fax 242 70 05, Open until
11 p.m. – 🖭 ⓞ 🗲 𝘝𝘐𝘚𝘈
closed Monday dinner, Tuesday and 29 July-27 August – **M** 750.

FOREST (VORST)

XXX **Le Chouan,** av. Brugmann 100, ⊠ 1060, ℰ 344 09 99, Seafood – ▤. 🖭 ⓞ 🗲 𝘝𝘐𝘚𝘈
closed Saturday lunch, Sunday dinner and July – **M** a la carte 1400/2300.

XX **L'Abel Abbaye,** pl. Saint-Denis 9, ⊠ 1190, ℰ 332 11 59, ≼, 佘 – ⓟ. 🖭 ⓞ 🗲 𝘝𝘐𝘚𝘈
closed Sunday dinner, Monday and August – **M** 795.

GANSHOREN

XXX ⬡⬡⬡ **Bruneau,** av. Broustin 73, ⊠ 1080, ℰ 427 69 78, Fax 425 97 26 – 🖭 ⓞ 🗲 𝘝𝘐𝘚𝘈
*closed holiday Thursdays, Tuesday dinner, Wednesday, mid June-mid July and Christmas-
New Year* – **M** a la carte 2500/3300.
Spec. Panaché des 3 foies d'oie, Poêlée de langoustines aux lentilles, Côte d'agneau à la persillade truffée.

XXX ⬡⬡ **Claude Dupont,** av. Vital Riethuisen 46, ⊠ 1080, ℰ 427 54 50, Fax 426 65 40 – 🖭 ⓞ
🗲 𝘝𝘐𝘚𝘈
closed Monday, Tuesday and 8 July-14 August – **M** a la carte 1600/2700.
Spec. Marinière de saumon et loup de mer à la crème de caviar, Aiguillettes de canard colvert au cidre et
reinettes (September-10 February), Baluchon de raie et de homard au vinaigre balsamique.

XX **Cambrils** 1st floor, av. Charles-Quint 365, ⊠ 1080, ℰ 465 35 82, 佘 – ▤. 🖭 ⓞ 🗲 𝘝𝘐𝘚𝘈
closed Monday, Monday dinner and 15 July-16 August – **M** 780/950.

XX **San Daniele,** av. Charles-Quint 6, ⊠ 1080, ℰ 426 79 23, Italian cuisine – 🖭 ⓞ 🗲 𝘝𝘐𝘚𝘈
closed Sunday, Bank Holidays and 15 July-15 August – **M** a la carte 900/1700.

IXELLES (ELSENE)

🏨 **Leopold,** r. Luxembourg 35, ⊠ 1040, ℰ 511 18 28, Telex 62804, Fax 514 19 39, ⇔ – 🕼
⇔ rm 📺 ☎ ⟷ – 🛦 25-50. 🕮 ⑩ 🗲 𝐕𝐈𝐒𝐀. ⅙ rm   GV **u**
M *(closed Saturday lunch and Sunday)* 850/2100 – **33 rm** � 3000/4100.

XXX **Aub. de Boendael,** square du Vieux Tilleul 12, ⊠ 1050, ℰ 672 70 55, Grill, Rustic – ▤ 🅟.
🕮 ⑩ 🗲 𝐕𝐈𝐒𝐀
closed Saturday, Sunday, Bank Holidays, first 3 weeks August and Christmas-New Year – **M**
a la carte 1500/2500.

XX **Les Foudres,** r. Eugène Cattoir 14, ⊠ 1050, ℰ 647 36 36, 😚, « Former wine cellar » –
🅟. 🕮 ⑩ 🗲 𝐕𝐈𝐒𝐀
closed Saturday lunch and Sunday – **M** 850/1200.

XX **Le Chalet Rose,** av. du Bois de la Cambre 49, ⊠ 1050, ℰ 672 78 64, Fax 660 59 88, 😚 –
🅟. 🕮 ⑩ 🗲 𝐕𝐈𝐒𝐀
closed Saturday lunch, Sunday, Bank Holidays and 1 week Easter – **M** a la carte 1600/2400.

X **La Pagode d'Or,** chaussée de Boondael 332, ⊠ 1050, ℰ 649 06 56, 😚, Vietnamese
cuisine, open until 11 p.m. – 🕮 ⑩ 🗲 𝐕𝐈𝐒𝐀. ⅙
M a la carte 900/1400.

Quartier Bascule

🏨 **Forum** without rest., av. du Haut-Pont 2, ⊠ 1060, ℰ 343 01 00, Telex 62311, Fax 347 00 54
– 🕼 📺 ☎ ⟷ – 🛦 80. 🕮 ⑩ 🗲 𝐕𝐈𝐒𝐀
78 rm � 3500/4100.

XX **La Mosaïque,** r. Forestière 23, ⊠ 1050, ℰ 649 02 35, Fax 647 11 49 – 🕮 ⑩ 🗲 𝐕𝐈𝐒𝐀
closed Saturday lunch and Sunday – **M** a la carte 2400.

XX **La Charlotte aux Pommes,** pl. du Châtelain 40, ⊠ 1050, ℰ 640 53 88 – 🕮 ⑩ 🗲
𝐕𝐈𝐒𝐀
closed Saturday, Sunday, mid August-mid September and carnival – **M** a la carte 1600/2050.

XX **La Thaïlande,** av. Legrand 29, ⊠ 1050, ℰ 640 24 62, 😚, Thaï cuisine – 🕮 ⑩ 🗲 𝐕𝐈𝐒𝐀
closed Sunday – **M** a la carte 900/1200.

Quartier Avenue Louise (see also at Bruxelles)

🏨 **Sofitel,** av. de la Toison d'Or 40, ⊠ 1060, ℰ 514 22 00, Telex 63547, Fax 514 57 44 – 🕼
⇔ rm ▤ 📺 ☎ – 🛦 25-120. 🕮 ⑩ 🗲 𝐕𝐈𝐒𝐀   FX **b**
M a la carte 1200/2000 – ⊆ 525 – **171 rm** 6200.

🏨 **Argus** without rest., r. Capitaine Crespel 6, ⊠ 1050, ℰ 514 07 70, Telex 29393, Fax 514 12 22
– 🕼 📺 ☎. 🕮 ⑩ 🗲 𝐕𝐈𝐒𝐀   FX **a**
41 rm ⊆ 2650/2950.

XX **Le Criterion,** av. de la Toison d'Or 7, ⊠ 1060, ℰ 512 37 68, Pub-rest., open until midnight
– 🕮 ⑩ 🗲 𝐕𝐈𝐒𝐀. ⅙   GX **p**
M a la carte 1100/1800.

X **Shogun,** r. Capitaine Crespel 10, ⊠ 1050, ℰ 512 83 19, 😚, Japanese cuisine, teppan-yaki,
open until 11 p.m. – 🕮 ⑩ 🗲 𝐕𝐈𝐒𝐀   FX **c**
closed Saturday lunch, Sunday and mid July-mid August – **M** a la carte 1000/1400.

JETTE

XX ❀ **Le Sermon** (Kobs), av. Jacques Sermon 91, ⊠ 1090, ℰ 426 89 35, Fax 426 70 90 – 🕮 🗲
𝐕𝐈𝐒𝐀
closed Sunday, Monday and 25 June-July – **M** a la carte approx. 1800
Spec. Moules au Champagne (August-March), Sole "Sermon", Caneton aux pommes et poivre vert.

XX **Rôtiss. Le Vieux Pannenhuis,** r. Léopold-Ier 317, ⊠ 1090, ℰ 425 83 73, 😚, « 17C inn »
– ▤. 🕮 ⑩ 🗲 𝐕𝐈𝐒𝐀
closed Saturday lunch, Sunday and July – **M** 875.

MOLENBEEK-ST-JEAN (SINT-JANS-MOLENBEEK)

XXX **Le Béarnais,** bd Louis Mettewie 318, ⊠ 1080, ℰ 523 11 51 – ▤. 🕮 ⑩ 🗲 𝐕𝐈𝐒𝐀
closed Sunday and Monday dinner – **M** a la carte 1400/1900.

ST-GILLES (SINT-GILLIS)

🏨 **Ramada,** chaussée de Charleroi 38, ⊠ 1060, ℰ 539 30 00, Telex 25539, Fax 538 90 14 – 🕼
⇔ rm ▤ 📺 ☎ ⟷ – 🛦 25-170. 🕮 ⑩ 🗲 𝐕𝐈𝐒𝐀. ⅙ rest
M a la carte 1100/1500 – ⊆ 550 – **195 rm** 6000/7000.

🏨 **Delta,** chaussée de Charleroi 17, ⊠ 1060, ℰ 539 01 60, Telex 63225, Fax 537 90 11 – 🕼
▤ rest 📺 ☎ ⟷ – 🛦 60-100. 🕮 ⑩ 🗲 𝐕𝐈𝐒𝐀. ⅙ rest   FX **r**
M a la carte 750/1050 – **246 rm** ⊆ 4500/5100.

🏨 **Manos** without rest., chaussée de Charleroi 102, ⊠ 1060, ℰ 537 96 82, Telex 65369, Fax
539 36 55 – 🕼 📺 ☎. 🕮 ⑩ 🗲 𝐕𝐈𝐒𝐀
⊆ 390 – **38 rm** 3375/3675.

🏠 **La Cascade** without rest., r. Source 14, ✉ 1060, ✆ 538 88 30, Telex 26637, Fax 538 92 79 –
📺 🗺 ☎ ⇔ 🅿 – 🛠 50. 🆎 ⑩ 🗉 *VISA*. ✵
40 rm ⊇ 2830/3520.

🏠 **Diplomat** without rest., r. Jean Stas 32, ✉ 1060, ✆ 537 42 50, Telex 61012, Fax 539 33 79 –
📺 📺 ☎ 🆎 ⑩ 🗉 *VISA*   FX **x**
68 rm ⊇ 4500/5100.

XX **L'Auvergne**, r. Aqueduc 61, ✉ 1050, ✆ 537 31 25, Rustic – ✵⇔ 🆎 ⑩ 🗉 *VISA*
    closed Sunday, Monday, 15 July-15 August and 20 to 31 December – **M** 875.

XX **Le Fronton Basque**, chaussée de Waterloo 361, ✉ 1060, ✆ 537 21 18, Oyster bar and
    seafood – 🆎 ⑩ 🗉 *VISA*
    M a la carte 1000/2600.

XX **Palatino**, r. Aqueduc 7, ✉ 1050, ✆ 538 64 15, Partly Italian cuisine – 🍽 🆎 ⑩ 🗉 *VISA*. ✵
    M a la carte 1100/1400.

X **Le Forcado**, chaussée de Charleroi 192, ✉ 1060, ✆ 537 92 20, �, Portuguese cuisine –
    🆎 ⑩ 🗉 *VISA*
    closed Sunday, Bank Holidays, August and carnival week – **M** a la carte 900/1400.

ST-JOSSE-TEN-NOODE (SINT-JOOST-TEN-NODE)

🏰 **Scandic Crown**, r. Royale 250, ✉ 1210, ✆ 220 66 11, Telex 61871, Fax 217 84 44, 🚡 – 📺
    ✵⇔ rm 🍽 📺 ☎ ⇔ – 🛠 30-500. 🆎 ⑩ 🗉 *VISA*. ✵ rest   GT **r**
    M *(closed Saturday and mid July-mid August)* a la carte 1800/2400 – **302 rm** ⊇ 7300/8000.

🏠 **New Siru**, pl. Rogier 1, ✉ 1210, ✆ 217 75 80 and 217 83 08 (rest.), Telex 21722, Fax
    218 33 03, « Every room decorated by a contemporary Belgian artist, collection of early
    cutlery in the restaurant » – 📺 🍽 rest 📺 ☎ 🅿 – 🛠 70. 🆎 ⑩ 🗉 *VISA*   FT **f**
    M Le Couvert 1000/1450 – **101 rm** ⊇ 4900/5200 – ½ P 2600/3250.

🏠 **Albert Premier** without rest., pl. Rogier 20, ✉ 1210, ✆ 217 21 25, Telex 27111, Fax 217 93 31
    – 📺 📺 ☎ & – 🛠 25-70. 🆎 ⑩ 🗉 *VISA*   FT **d**
    285 rm ⊇ 2750/3250.

XX **De Ultieme Hallucinatie**, r. Royale 316, ✉ 1210, ✆ 217 06 14, Fax 217 72 40, « Art
    Nouveau interior » – 🆎 ⑩ 🗉 *VISA*. ✵   GT **u**
    closed Saturday lunch, Sunday, and 20 July-16 August – **M** 950/2000.

SCHAERBEEK (SCHAARBEEK)

XX **Den Botaniek**, r. Royale 328, ✉ 1210, ✆ 218 48 38, Fax 218 41 95, « 1900 decor, garden »
    – 🆎 ⑩ 🗉 *VISA*   GT **n**
    *closed Saturday lunch, Sunday, Bank Holidays, last 2 weeks September and Christmas-New
    Year* – **M** a la carte 1650/2600.

Quartier Meiser

🏠 **Lambermont** without rest., bd Lambermont 322, ✉ 1030, ✆ 242 55 95, Telex 62220, Fax
    242 55 95 – 📺 📺 ☎. 🆎 ⑩ 🗉 *VISA*
    42 rm ⊇ 2700/3100.

XX **Philippe Riesen** 1st floor, bd Aug. Reyers 163, ✉ 1040, ✆ 736 41 38 – 🆎 ⑩ 🗉 *VISA*
    closed Saturday, Sunday, Bank Holidays and Christmas-New Year – **M** 950/1650.

UCCLE (UKKEL)

🏠 **County House**, square des Héros 2, ✉ 1180, ✆ 375 44 20, Telex 22392, Fax 375 31 22 – 📺
    🍽 rest 📺 ☎ ⇔ 🅿 – 🛠 25-80. 🆎 ⑩ 🗉 *VISA*. ✵ rest
    M 750/1600 – **96 rm** ⊇ 4600.

XXX ❀ **L'Orangeraie** (Beyls), av. Winston Churchill 81, ✉ 1180, ✆ 345 71 47, Fax 375 74 23 –
    🆎 ⑩ 🗉 *VISA*
    closed Saturday lunch, Sunday and 20 July-15 August – **M** a la carte 2700/3250
    Spec. Mousse de bécasses (15 October-15 February), Saumon et foie d'oie en feuille de vigne, Dos de turbot
    aux aubergines.

XX ❀ **Villa d'Este**, r. Etoile 142, ✉ 1180, ✆ 377 86 46, �, « Terrace » – 🅿. 🆎 ⑩ *VISA*
    closed Sunday dinner, Monday, July and late December – **M** a la carte 1650/2300
    Spec. Sole farcie aux poireaux, Cassolette de petits gris au chou vert, sauce cerfeuil (Winter), Coquelet à la
    moutarde de Meaux.

XX **Les Frères Romano**, av. de Fré 182, ✉ 1180, ✆ 374 70 98, � – 🆎 ⑩ 🗉 *VISA*. ✵
    closed 3 weeks August, Sunday and Bank Holidays except Christmas-New Year – **M** a la
    carte 1500/2200.

XX **A'mbriana**, r. Edith Cavell 151, ✉ 1180, ✆ 375 01 56, Italian cuisine – 🆎 🗉 *VISA*
    closed Tuesday, Saturday lunch and August – **M** a la carte 950/1500.

XX **L'Éléphant Bleu**, chaussée de Waterloo 1120, ✉ 1180, ✆ 374 49 62, Fax 375 44 68, Thaï
    cuisine, « Exotic decor » – 🍽. 🆎 ⑩ 🗉 *VISA*
    closed Saturday lunch, 25 December and early January – **M** a la carte 1100/1900.

X **Brasseries Georges**, av. Winston Churchill 257, ✉ 1180, ✆ 347 21 00, Fax 344 02 45, �,
    Open until midnight – 🍽. 🆎 ⑩ 🗉 *VISA*
    closed Sunday – **M** a la carte 900/1500.

X **De Hoef**, r. Edith Cavell 218, ✉ 1180, ✆ 374 34 17, �, Grill, 17C inn – 🆎 ⑩ 🗉 *VISA*
    M 625.

WATERMAEL-BOITSFORT (WATERMAAL-BOSVOORDE)

XX **Host. Des 3 Tilleuls** 🕭 with rm, Berensheide 8, ✉ 1170, 𝒫 672 30 14, Fax 673 65 52, 🏤
– 📺 🕿, ⒜ ⓞ ∈ 𝓥𝓘𝓢𝓐, 🛇 rm
M *(closed Sunday and 15 July-15 August)* a la carte 1600/2500 – **7 rm** 🖙 2350/3900.

XX **Le Canard Sauvage,** chaussée de La Hulpe 194, ✉ 1170, 𝒫 673 09 75, Fax 675 21 45 – ⒜
ⓞ ∈ 𝓥𝓘𝓢𝓐
closed Saturday lunch, Sunday dinner and 15 July-20 August – **M** a la carte 1000/1800.

XX **Nouveau Chez Nous,** r. Middelbourg 28, ✉ 1170, 𝒫 673 53 93, Fax 673 53 93 – ⒜ ⓞ ∈
𝓥𝓘𝓢𝓐 – *closed Sunday dinner, Monday and 5 to 28 August* – **M** a la carte 800/1500.

XX **Samambaïa,** r. Philippe Dewolfs 7, ✉ 1170, 𝒫 672 87 20, Fax 675 20 74, Brazilian cuisine
– ⒜ ⓞ ∈
closed Sunday, Monday and 23 July-21 August – **M** a la carte 1000/1300.

XX **Les Rives du Gange,** av. de la Fauconnerie 1, ✉ 1170, 𝒫 672 16 01, Telex 62661, Fax
672 43 30, Indian cuisine – ⒜ ⓞ ∈ 𝓥𝓘𝓢𝓐
M a la carte 1300/1900.

WOLUWÉ-ST-LAMBERT (SINT-LAMBRECHTS-WOLUWE)

XXX ❀ **Mon Manège à Toi,** r. Neerveld 1, ✉ 1200, 𝒫 770 02 38, Fax 762 95 80, « Flowered
garden » – ⒫ ⒜ ⓞ ∈ 𝓥𝓘𝓢𝓐 🛇
closed Saturday, Sunday, Bank Holidays, 7 to 31 July and 23 December-1 January – **M** a la
carte 2200/3000
Spec. Terrine de foie d'oie et homard, Fricassée de homard aux fruits de la passion, Pigeonneau farci, sauce à
la cannelle (mid February-mid August).

XXX **Lindekemale,** av. J.F. Debecker 6, ✉ 1200, 𝒫 770 90 57, 🏤, « 15C watermill » – ⒫, ⒜
∈ 𝓥𝓘𝓢𝓐
closed Saturday, Sunday, Bank Holidays and August – **M** a la carte 1800/2300.

XX **Le Relais de la Woluwe,** av. Georges Henri 1, ✉ 1200, 𝒫 762 66 36, Fax 762 18 55, 🏤,
« Terrace and garden » – ⒜ ⓞ ∈ 𝓥𝓘𝓢𝓐, 🛇
closed Saturday lunch, Sunday, Bank Holidays, 1 week Easter and Christmas-New Year –
M a la carte 1500/2000.

WOLUWÉ-ST-PIERRE (SINT-PIETERS-WOLUWE)

XXX ❀ **Des 3 Couleurs** (Tourneur), av. de Tervuren 453, ✉ 1150, 𝒫 770 33 21, 🏤, « Terrace »
closed 2 to 16 April, September and Monday, Tuesday except Bank Holidays – **M** a la carte
1600/2100
Spec. Croustillant de cervelle aux câpres, Saumon "Liliane", Râble de lièvre poivrade (mid October-mid January).

XX **Médicis,** av. de l'Escrime 124, ✉ 1150, 𝒫 782 07 11, Fax 782 19 24, 🏤 – ⒜ ⓞ ∈ 𝓥𝓘𝓢𝓐
closed Saturday lunch – **M** 1050/1580.

BRUSSELS ENVIRONS

at Diegem Brussels-Zaventem motorway Diegem exit Ⓒ Machelen pop. 11 220 – ✉ 1831
Diegem – ⬢ 0 2 :

🏨 **Holiday Inn,** Holidaystraat 7, 𝒫 720 58 65, Telex 24285, Fax 720 41 45, ⇕s, 🏊, 🛇 – 🛗
🛇⇖ rm 🗏 📺 🕿 ⒫ – 🕭 25-500. ⒜ ⓞ ∈ 𝓥𝓘𝓢𝓐, 🛇 rest
M a la carte 1100/1700 – 🖙 550 – **309 rm** 7000/8000.

🏨 **Sofitel Airport,** Bessenveldstraat 15, 𝒫 725 11 60, Telex 26595, Fax 721 43 45, 🏤, ⇕s, 🏊
– 🛇⇖ rm 🗏 📺 🕿 ⒫ – 🕭 25-500. ⒜ ⓞ ∈ 𝓥𝓘𝓢𝓐
M a la carte 1600/2200 – 🖙 525 – **125 rm** 5450.

🏨 **Novotel Airport,** Olmenstraat, 𝒫 725 30 50, Telex 26751, Fax 721 39 58, 🏤, 🏊 – 🛗
🛇⇖ rm 🗏 📺 🕿 ⒫ – 🕭 25-250. ⒜ ⓞ ∈ 𝓥𝓘𝓢𝓐, 🛇 rest
M (open until midnight) a la carte 900/1500 – 🖙 435 – **209 rm** 4250/4470.

🏨 **Fimotel Airport,** Berkenlaan 5, 𝒫 725 33 80, Telex 20906, Fax 725 38 10, 🏤 – 🛗 📺 🕿 ᴧ
⒫ – 🕭 25-200. ⒜ ⓞ ∈ 𝓥𝓘𝓢𝓐, 🛇 rest
M 615 – **79 rm** 🖙 3200/3700.

XX **Diegemhof,** Calenbergstraat 51, 𝒫 720 11 34, 🏤 – ⒜ ⓞ ∈ 𝓥𝓘𝓢𝓐, 🛇
closed Saturday and Sunday – **M** a la carte 1350/1900.

at Dilbeek by ⑪ : 7 km – pop. 36 291 – ✉ 1700 Dilbeek – ⬢ 0 2 :

🏨 **Relais Delbeccha** 🕭, Bodegemstraat 180, 𝒫 569 44 30, Fax 569 75 30, 🏤, ⇕s, 🏊, 🚗 –
📺 🕿 ⒫ – 🕭 30-100. ⒜ ⓞ ∈ 𝓥𝓘𝓢𝓐, 🛇 rest
M 1650 – 🖙 300 – **14 rm** 3400/4800.

XX **Host. d'Arconati** 🕭 with rm, d'Arconatistraat 77, 𝒫 569 35 15, Fax 569 35 04, 🏤, « Flowered garden » – 📺 🕿 ⇔ ⒫ – 🕭 60. ⒜ ∈
closed February – **M** *(closed Sunday dinner, Monday and Tuesday)* a la carte 1200/1600 –
6 rm 🖙 1500/2500.

at Dworp (Tourneppe) by ⑨ : 16 km Ⓒ Beersel pop. 21 418 – ✉ 1653 Dworp – ⬢ 0 2 :

🏨 **Kasteel Gravenhof** 🕭 without rest., Alsembergsesteenweg 94, 𝒫 380 44 99, Fax
380 40 60, « Wooded environment », 🚗 – 🛗 📺 🕿 ⒫ – 🕭 25-120. ⒜ ∈ 𝓥𝓘𝓢𝓐, 🛇
🖙 375 – **24 rm** 3750.

at Groot-Bijgaarden Ⓒ Dilbeek pop. 36 291 – ⊠ 1702 Groot-Bijgaarden – ✪ 0 2 :

XXXXX ✿✿ **De Bijgaarden,** I. Van Beverenstraat 20 (near castle), ℰ 466 44 85, Fax 463 08 11, ≤, 斎 – 亜 ⓞ Ε 𝖵𝖨𝖲𝖠
closed Saturday lunch, Sunday, 1 to 8 April and 15 August-4 September – **M** a la carte 2150/3950
Spec. Tuile de truffes et crème de bacon aux lentilles, St-Pierre au poivre, sauce diable, Poire confite à la liqueur de mandarines et épices.

XXX ✿ **Michel** (Coppens), Schepen Gossetlaan 31, ℰ 466 65 91, Fax 466 90 07, 斎 – ⓟ ⓞ Ε 𝖵𝖨𝖲𝖠
closed Sunday, Monday and August – **M** a la carte 1850/2400
Spec. Gratin de homard à la mirepoix, Poêlée de champignons des bois au foie d'oie (April-November), Mille-feuille aux fraises des bois.

at Hoeilaart – pop. 9 029 – ⊠ 1560 Hoeilaart – ✪ 0 2 :

XXXXX ✿✿✿ **Romeyer,** Groenendaalsesteenweg 109 (at Groenendaal), ℰ 657 05 81, Fax 657 27 73, « ≤ garden and private lake » – ⓟ 亜 ⓞ Ε 𝖵𝖨𝖲𝖠
closed 1 to 18 August, February, Sunday dinner and Monday – **M** a la carte 2450/3450
Spec. Sole aux muscats (September), Boudin de homard sauce homardine, Queues d'écrevisses "à ma façon".

XXX **Aloyse Kloos,** Terhulpsesteenweg 2 (at Groenendaal), ℰ 657 37 37, 斎 – ⓟ 亜 ⓞ Ε 𝖵𝖨𝖲𝖠
closed Sunday dinner, Monday, 19 March-8 April and mid August-mid September – **M** 1450/2300.

at Huizingen by ⑨ : 12 km Ⓒ Beersel pop. 21 418 – ⊠ 1654 Huizingen – ✪ 0 2 :

XX **Terborght,** Oud Dorp 16 (near E 19), ℰ 380 10 10, Fax 380 10 97, « Rustic interior » – ⓟ. 亜 ⓞ Ε 𝖵𝖨𝖲𝖠. ✼
closed dinner Sunday and Tuesday, Monday, 22 July-8 August and 11 to 25 February – **M** 1450.

at Kobbegem by ⑬ : 11 km Ⓒ Asse pop. 26 586 – ⊠ 1730 Kobbegem – ✪ 0 2 :

XXX **Chalet Rose,** Brusselsesteenweg 331, ℰ 452 60 41, Fax 452 60 41, 斎 – ⓟ. 亜 ⓞ Ε 𝖵𝖨𝖲𝖠
closed Sunday dinner and Monday – **M** 1250/1750.

XXX **De Plezanten Hof,** Broekstraat 2, ℰ 452 89 39 – 亜 ⓞ Ε 𝖵𝖨𝖲𝖠
closed dinner Tuesday and Sunday, Wesdnesday, 22 July-14 August and 1 week February – **M** a la carte 1550/2200.

at Machelen – pop. 11 220 – ⊠ 1830 Machelen – ✪ 0 2 :

XXX ✿ **André D'Haese,** Heirbaan 210, ℰ 252 50 72, Fax 252 50 72, « Modern decor » – ⓟ. 亜 ⓞ Ε 𝖵𝖨𝖲𝖠. ✼
closed Saturday lunch, Sunday and 7 to 28 July – **M** a la carte 1600/2400
Spec. Hure de lapereau, Soupe de homard au pistou, Ris de veau braisé à brun et à blanc.

at Meise by ① : 14 km – pop. 16 325 – ⊠ 1860 Meise – ✪ 0 2 :

XX **Aub. Napoléon,** Bouchoutlaan 1, ℰ 269 30 78 – ⓟ. 亜 ⓞ Ε 𝖵𝖨𝖲𝖠
closed August – **M** a la carte 1500/2250.

XX **Koen Van Loven,** Brusselsesteenweg 11, ℰ 270 05 77 – ⓟ. 亜 ⓞ Ε 𝖵𝖨𝖲𝖠. ✼
closed Sunday dinner and Monday – **M** a la carte 1700/2300.

at Overijse by ⑦ : 16 km – pop. 21 635 – ⊠ 3090 Overijse – ✪ 0 2 :

XXXX ✿✿ **Barbizon** (Deluc), Welriekendedreef 95 (at Jezus-Eik), ℰ 657 04 62, Fax 657 40 66, 斎, « Terrace and garden » – ⓟ 亜 ⓞ Ε 𝖵𝖨𝖲𝖠
closed Tuesday, Wednesday, 16 July-7 August and February – **M** a la carte 1800/3000
Spec. Homard en chemise, beurre "Barbizon", Raviolis de saumon au coulis de langoustines, Escalope de foie d'oie aux mangues et muscats.

X **Istas,** Brusselsesteenweg 652 (NW : 2 km at Jezus-Eik), ℰ 657 05 11, 斎, Pub-rest. – ⓟ
closed Wednesday, Thursday and August – **M** a la carte 750/1100.

at Schepdaal by ⑪ : 12 km Ⓒ Dilbeek pop. 36 291 – ⊠ 1703 Schepdaal – ✪ 0 2 :

🏠 **Lien Zana** without rest., Ninoofsesteenweg 209, ℰ 569 65 25, Telex 26937, Fax 569 64 64, ⌿ – 🛗 📺 ☎ ⓟ – 🔏 25. 亜 ⓞ Ε 𝖵𝖨𝖲𝖠
closed 23 December-2 January – **19 rm** ⊑ 2200/2800.

at Sint-Genesius-Rode (Rhode-St-Genèse) by ⑥ : 13 km – pop. 17 370 – ⊠ 1640 Sint-Genesius-Rode – ✪ 0 2 :

🏠 **Aub. de Waterloo** without rest., chaussée de Waterloo 212, ℰ 358 35 80, Telex 24042, Fax 358 38 06 – 🛗 📺 ☎ ⓟ – 🔏 25-80. 亜 ⓞ Ε 𝖵𝖨𝖲𝖠
89 rm ⊑ 3960/5300.

at Strombeek-Bever Ⓒ Grimbergen pop. 31 351 – ⊠ 1853 Strombeek-Bever – ✪ 0 2 :

XX **Le Val Joli,** Leestbeekstraat 16, ℰ 460 65 43, Fax 460 04 00, 斎, « Terrace and garden » – ⓟ 亜 ⓞ 𝖵𝖨𝖲𝖠
closed Monday, Tuesday and first 3 weeks October – **M** 780/990.

at Vlezenbeek by ⑩ : 11 km Ⓒ Sint-Pieters-Leeuw pop. 28 516 – ✉ 1602 Vlezenbeek – ☼ 0 2 :

XX **Philippe Verbaeys,** Dorp 49, ℰ 569 05 25, Fax 569 05 25, 😤 – Ⓞ ⅇ ꟻꟾ𝚂𝙰
closed Sunday, Monday, 30 March-15 April and 21 July-12 August – **M** 750/1150.

X **Aub. Le St-Esprit,** Postweg 250 (road to the castle of Gaasbeek), ℰ 532 42 18 – 🜇 Ⓞ ꟻꟾ𝚂𝙰
closed Sunday dinner, Monday, September and first 2 weeks March – **M** a la carte 1250/2150.

at Wemmel – pop. 13 465 – ✉ 1780 Wemmel – ☼ 0 2 :

XX **Parkhof,** Parklaan 7, ℰ 460 42 89, 😤, « Terrace » – ℗. 🜇 Ⓞⅇ ꟻꟾ𝚂𝙰
closed Wednesday dinner, Thursday, 1 week Easter and late August-early September – **M** 1000/1700.

at Wezembeek-Oppem by ⑤ : 11 km – pop. 12 122 – ✉ 1970 Wezembeek-Op. – ☼ 0 2 :

XXX **L'Aub. Saint-Pierre,** Sint-Pietersplein 8, ℰ 731 21 79 – 🜇 Ⓞ ⅇ ꟻꟾ𝚂𝙰
closed Saturday lunch, Sunday, Bank Holidays, 13 July-19 August and 21 December-3 January
– **M** a la carte 1600/2100.

at Zaventem – pop. 25 601 – ✉ 1930 Zaventem – ☼ 0 2 :

🏨 **Sheraton Airport,** at airport (NE by A 201), ℰ 725 10 00, Telex 27085, Fax 725 11 55 – 🛗
🌊 rm 🖭 📺 ☎ & ℗ – 🔬 25-520. 🜇 Ⓞⅇ ꟻꟾ𝚂𝙰 🍴 rest
M Concorde a la carte 1450/2200 – 🍽 625 – **290 rm** 7000/8300.

XX ✿ **Stockmansmolen** 1st floor, H. Henneaulaan 164, ℰ 725 34 34, « Former watermill » –
℗ 🜇 Ⓞⅇ ꟻꟾ𝚂𝙰 🍴
closed Saturday and Sunday – **M** a la carte 1750/2400
Spec. Papillote de saumon à l'étuvée de légumes, Pigeonneau grillé aux épices, "Tout au fruits de la passion".

Berlare 9290 Oost-Vlaanderen ❷❶❸ ⑤ and ❹❶❾ ③ – pop. 12 629 – ☼ 0 52 – 38 km.

XXX ✿✿ **'t Laurierblad** (Van Cauteren), Dorp 4, ℰ 42 48 01, Telex 29356, Fax 42 59 97 – ℗. Ⓞ
ⅇ ꟻꟾ𝚂𝙰 – *closed Monday, Tuesday, 12 August-8 September and 23 December-2 January* –
M a la carte 1750/2800
Spec. Gnocchi de pommes de terre et homard, Agneau au gingembre en croûte feuilletée, Fondant de ris et tête de veau aux truffes.

Genval 1322 Brabant Ⓒ Rixensart pop. 20 191 ❷❶❸ ⑱ and ❹❶❾ ⑱ – ☼ 0 2 – 21 km.

XXXX ✿✿ **Le Trèfle à 4** (Haquin) - (at H. Château du Lac), av. du Lac 87, ℰ 654 07 98, Fax
653 62 00, ≤ lake and wooded environment – ℗. 🜇 Ⓞⅇ ꟻꟾ𝚂𝙰
closed Monday, Tuesday and 7 January-8 February – **M** a la carte 2200/3250
Spec. Poêlée de langoustines, buisson de légumes et herbes frites, Viennoise de turbotin et beurre blanc, Pigeonneau en bécasse.

ANTWERP (ANTWERPEN) 2000 ❷❶❷ ⑮ and ❹❶❾ ④ – pop. 476 044 – ☼ 0 3.

See : Old Antwerp*** : Cathedral*** and Market Square* (Grote Markt) FY – Rubens' House**
(Rubenshuis) GZ – Butchers' House* (Vleeshuis) : Musical instruments* FY D – Interior* of the
St. James' church (St-Jacobskerk) GY – The port*** (Haven) ⚓ FY – Zoo** (Dierentuin) EU –
St. Charles Borromeo's Church* (St-Carolus-Borromeuskerk) GY – St. Paul's Church (St-Pauluskerk) : interior* and wood-carving* FY.

Museums : Royal Art Gallery*** (Koninklijk Museum voor Schone Kunsten) CV – Plantin-
Moretus*** (ancient printing-office) FZ – Mayer Van den Bergh** (Brueghel) GZ – Maritime
"Steen"* (Nationaal Scheepvaartmuseum Steen) FY M¹ – Rockox House* (Rockoxhuis) GY M²
– Open-air Museum of Sculpture Middelheim* (Openluchtmuseum voor Beeldhouwkunst) –
Museum of Photography* – Ethnographic Museum* FY M¹⁰.

🏌🏌 at Kapellen by ② : 22 km, G. Capiaulei 2 ℰ (0 3) 666 84 56 - 🏌 at Aartselaar by ⑩ : 10 km,
Kasteel Cleydael ℰ (0 3) 887 00 79 - 🏌 at Wommelgem by ⑥ : 9 km, Uilenbaan 15 ℰ (0 3)
353 02 92 - 🏌🏌 at Broechem by ⑥ : 12 km, Bossenstein Kasteel ℰ (0 3) 485 64 46.

🛈 Grote Markt 15 ℰ 232 01 03 – Koningin Astridplein (Pavilion) ℰ 233 05 70 – Tourist association of the
province, Karel Oomsstraat 11, ✉ 2018, ℰ 216 28 10.

Brussels 48 ⑩ – Amsterdam 159 ④ – Luxemburg 261 ⑱ – Rotterdam 103 ④.

Plans on following pages

Room prices are subject to the addition of a local tax of 6%

Town Centre

🏨 **Alfa De Keyser,** De Keyserlei 66, ✉ 2018, ℰ 234 01 35, Telex 34219, Fax 232 39 70, ⛱,
🔲 – 🛗 🌊 rm 🖭 📺 ☎ – 🔬 25-120. 🜇 Ⓞⅇ ꟻꟾ𝚂𝙰 🍴   EU **b**
M a la carte 1300/1700 – **117 rm** 🍽 5790/7000 – ½ P 6500/7000.

🏨 **Pullman Park,** Desguinlei 94, ✉ 2018, ℰ 216 48 00, Telex 33368, Fax 216 47 12, ⛱ – 🛗
🌊 rm 🖭 📺 ☎ ⇄ – 🔬 25-450. 🜇 Ⓞⅇ ꟻꟾ𝚂𝙰 🍴 rest
M Tiffany's *(closed Saturday dinner)* a la carte 1600/2300 – **216 rm** 🍽 4200/8200.

🏨 **Carlton,** Quinten Matsijslei 25, ✉ 2018, ℰ 231 15 15, Telex 31072, Fax 225 30 90, ≤ – 🛗
🌊 rm 🖭 📺 ☎ ⇄ – 🔬 30-100. 🜇 Ⓞⅇ ꟻꟾ𝚂𝙰   DV **v**
M *(closed 1 to 21 August)* a la carte 1100/1700 – **127 rm** 🍽 4350/5150.

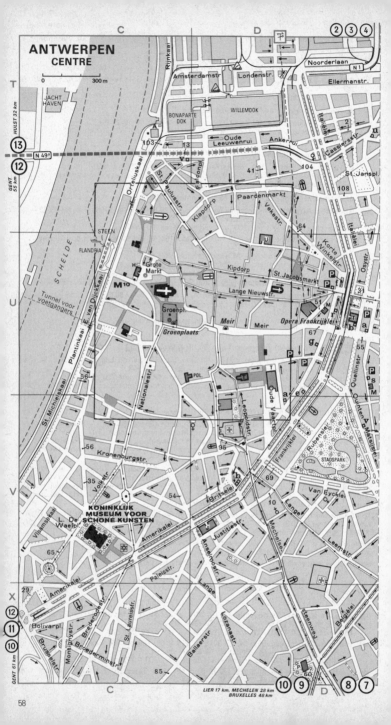

STREET INDEX TO ANTWERPEN TOWN PLANS

Continued on next page

59

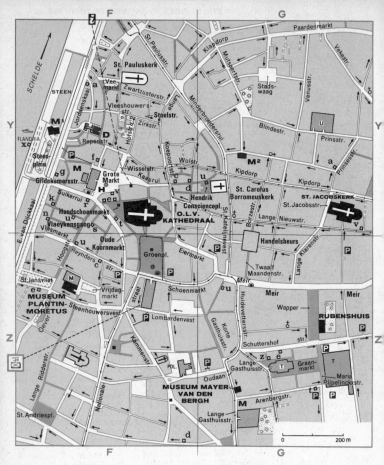

STREET INDEX TO ANTWERPEN TOWN PLANS (Concluded)

🏨 **Plaza** without rest., Charlottalei 43, ✉ 2018, 𝓟 218 92 40, Telex 31531, Fax 218 88 23 – 🔟 🖩 ☎ 🚗, 🖭 ⑩ 🗲 *VISA*.   EV **v**
76 rm ⟺ 3600/5200.

🏨 **Alfa Empire** without rest., Appelmansstraat 31, ✉ 2018, 𝓟 231 47 55, Telex 33909, Fax 233 40 60 – 🛗 ✂ 🖿 🔟 ☎. 🖭 ⑩ 🗲 *VISA*   DU **s**
70 rm ⟺ 4650/5700.

🏨 **Alfa Congress**, Plantin en Moretuslei 136, ✉ 2018, 𝓟 235 30 00, Telex 31959, Fax 235 52 31 – 🛗 ✂ rm 🔟 ☎ 🚗 🅟 – 🏌 30-70. 🖭 ⑩ 🗲 *VISA*. ℅ rest   EV **s**
M *(closed Saturday, Sunday, Bank Holidays and 22 December-2 January)* a la carte 1200/1500 – **66 rm** ⟺ 3550/4000.

🏨 **Firean** ⟿ without rest., Karel Oomsstraat 6, ✉ 2018, 𝓟 237 02 60, Telex 26937, Fax 238 11 68, « Ancient residence in typical Art-Deco style » – 🛗 🔟 ☎ 🚗. 🖭 ⑩ 🗲 *VISA*. ℅
closed 29 July-19 August and 21 December-6 January – **12 rm** ⟺ 2975/3600.

🏨 **Residence** without rest., St-Jacobsmarkt 85, 𝓟 232 76 75, Telex 35768, Fax 233 73 28 – 🛗 🔟 ☎ 🚗. 🖭 ⑩ 🗲 *VISA*. ℅   DU **f**
⟺ 300 – **19 rm** 3000/5000.

🏨 **Antwerp Tower** without rest. with 11 apartments in annex, Van Ertbornstraat 10, ✉ 2018, 𝓟 234 01 20, Telex 34478, Fax 233 39 43 – 🛗 🔟 📺 🚗. 🖭 ⑩ 🗲 *VISA*. ℅   DU **b**
39 rm ⟺ 2900/3500.

XXX **Fouquets** 1st floor, De Keyserlei 17, ✉ 2018, 𝓟 233 97 42, Fax 226 16 88, 🍴, Open until 11.30 p.m. – 🖩. 🖭 ⑩ 🗲 *VISA*   DU **a**
closed 15 July-24 August – **M** 950.

XXX **Loncin**, Markgravelei 127, 𝓟 248 29 89, Fax 248 29 89, Open until midnight – 🖩. ⑩ *VISA* ℅
closed lunch Saturday and Sunday, Tuesday and Wednesday – **M** a la carte 1900/2300.

XX **Vateli**, Kipdorpvest 50, 𝓟 233 17 81, Classic – 🖩 🅟. 🖭 ⑩ 🗲 *VISA*   DU **g**
closed Sunday, Monday, Bank Holidays, 4 weeks July and Christmas-New Year – **M** 1150/2300.

XX **Philippe Grootaert**, Frankrijklei 106, 𝓟 233 84 06, Fax 231 74 49, « Contemporary decor » – 🖭 ⑩ 🗲 *VISA*   DU **e**
closed Saturday lunch, Sunday, last 2 weeks July, Christmas and New Year – **M** 1475/2500.

XX **Sawadee**, 1st floor, Britselei 16, 𝓟 233 08 59, Telex 71068, Fax 231 37 59, Thaï cuisine, « Ancient mansion » – 🖭 ⑩ 🗲 *VISA*. ℅   DV **b**
closed Tuesday and August – **M** a la carte 1000/1300.

XX **De Poterne**, Desguinlei 186, ✉ 2018, 𝓟 238 28 24 – 🖭 ⑩ 🗲
closed Saturday, Sunday, Bank Holidays, 21 July-15 August and 24 December-2 January – **M** a la carte 1650/2150.

XX **Liang's Garden**, Markgravelei 141, ✉ 2018, 𝓟 237 22 22, Chinese cuisine – 🖩. 🖭 ⑩ 🗲 *VISA* ℅
closed Sunday and 5 to 21 August – **M** a la carte 950/1950.

XX **De Barbarie**, Van Breestraat 4, ✉ 2018, 𝓟 232 81 98, 🍴 – 🖭 ⑩ 🗲 *VISA*   DV **b**
closed Sunday, Monday and first 3 weeks September – **M** a la carte 1650/2300.

XX **Blue Phoenix**, Frankrijklei 14, 𝓟 233 33 77, Chinese cuisine – 🖩. 🖭 🗲 *VISA*. ℅   DU **r**
closed Monday and August – **M** 750/1500.

X ❀ **De Zeste** (Garnich R.), Lange Dijkstraat 36, ✉ 2008, 𝓟 233 45 49 – 🖩. 🖭 ⑩ 🗲 *VISA*
closed Saturday lunch, Sunday, Monday, 3 weeks August, Christmas and New Year – **M** (booking essential) a la carte 1450/2100   DT **u**
Spec. St-Jacques aux poireaux, Filets de sole aux truffes, Rognon de veau aux échalotes.

X **Milano,** Statiestraat 15, ✉ 2018, 𝓟 232 67 43, Partly Italian cuisine, open until 2 a.m. – 🖩. 🖭 ⑩ 🗲 *VISA*   EU **q**
M a la carte 800/2150.

Old Antwerp

🏨 **De Rosier** ⟿ without rest., Rosier 23, 𝓟 225 01 40, Telex 33697, Fax 231 41 11, « Former 17C residential house », �〰, 🔲, �── – 🛗 🔟 ☎ 🚗. 🖭 ⑩ 🗲 *VISA*   FZ **d**
closed Christmas and New Year – ⟺ 600 – **10 rm** 6890/15900.

🏨 **Alfa Theater,** Arenbergstraat 30, 𝓟 231 17 20, Telex 33910, Fax 233 88 58 – 🛗 ✂ rm 🖩 rest 🔟 ☎ – 🏌 25. 🖭 ⑩ 🗲 *VISA*. ℅   GZ **t**
M *(closed Saturday, Sunday and Bank Holidays)* a la carte approx. 1400 – **83 rm** ⟺ 4100/6400 – ½ P 3195/3820.

🏨 **Villa Mozart,** Handschoenmarkt 3, 𝓟 231 30 31, Fax 231 56 85, 🍴, �〰 – 🛗 🔟 ☎ – 🏌 25. 🖭 ⑩ 🗲 *VISA*   FY **e**
M (open until 11 p.m.) a la carte 1500/2050 – **25 rm** ⟺ 5500/8500 – ½ P 4050/5200.

🏨 **Prinse** ⟿ without rest., Keizerstraat 63, 𝓟 226 40 50, Fax 225 11 48 – 🛗 🖿 🔟 ☎ 🚗. 🏌 25-120. 🖭 ⑩ 🗲 *VISA*. ℅   GY **a**
30 rm ⟺ 3000/5000.

🏠 **Antigone** without rest., Jordaenskaai 11, ☎ 231 66 77, Fax 231 37 74 – 🛗 📺 ☎. 🖭 ⓞ **E**
VISA ⚗️　　　　　　　　　　　　　　　　　　　　　　　　　　　FY **a**
17 rm 🛏 3500.

🏠 **Arcade** without rest., Meistraat 39 (Theaterplein), ☎ 231 88 30, Telex 31104, Fax 234 29 21
– 🛗 📺 ☎ 🖧 – 🚪 75. 🖭 **E VISA**　　　　　　　　　　　　　　　　　DV **a**
150 rm 🛏 2700/3000.

XXXX ✿✿ 🖂 **Sir Anthony Van Dijck** (Paesbrugghe), Oude Koornmarkt 16 (Vlaeykensgang),
🖂 231 61 70, Fax 225 11 69, « Situated in a 16C lane » – 🖭 ⓞ **E VISA** ⚗️　　FY **s**
closed Saturday, Sunday and 16 to 20 April, 30 July-17 August, 24 to 31 December – **M** a la
carte 1900/2500
Spec. Blanc de poularde farci aux foie gras et truffes, Matelote de filets de sole aux artichauts et champignons.

XXX ✿✿ **La Pérouse**, Steenplein (pontoon), ☎ 231 31 51, Telex 35529, Fax 231 31 02, ⩍,
« Anchored vessel » – ☰ ⓟ. 🖭 ⓞ **E VISA** ⚗️　　　　　　　　　　　　　　FY **x**
15 September-15 May except Sunday, Monday and Bank Holidays – **M** a la carte 2300/3600
Spec. St-Jacques au verjus, Lasagne de langoustines et piments doux à la crème aigre, Fondant de ris de veau
au jus de truffes.

XXX **St. Jacob in Galicië**, Braderijstraat 16, ☎ 225 19 31, Fax 234 31 66, « In a 16C house
complex » – 🖭 ⓞ **E VISA**　　　　　　　　　　　　　　　　　　　　　　FY **f**
closed Saturday lunch, Sunday, Bank Holidays, 16 July-6 August and 23 to 26 December –
M a la carte 1600/2600.

XXX **Den Gulden Greffoen**, Hoogstraat 37, ☎ 231 50 46, Fax 233 20 39, « In a 15C house » –
☰. 🖭 ⓞ **E VISA** ⚗️　　　　　　　　　　　　　　　　　　　　　　　　FZ **u**
closed Saturday lunch and Sunday – **M** a la carte 1900/2800.

XXX **La Rade**, 1st floor, Van Dijckkaai 8, ☎ 233 37 37, Fax 233 49 63, « Former 19C freemason's
lodge » – 🖭 ⓞ **E VISA** ⚗️　　　　　　　　　　　　　　　　　　　　　　FY **g**
closed 8 to 28 July, carnival week, Saturday lunch, Sunday and Bank Holidays – **M** a la carte
2150/2700.

XXX ✿ **'t Fornuis** (Segers), Reyndersstraat 24, ☎ 233 62 70, « 17C house, rustic interior » – 🖭
ⓞ **E VISA**. ⚗️　　　　　　　　　　　　　　　　　　　　　　　　　　FZ **c**
closed Saturday, Sunday, last 3 weeks August and Christmas-New Year – **M** a la carte
2000/2500
Spec. Sole à la rhubarbe, Escalope de saumon au miel.

XX **Petrus**, Kelderstraat 1, ☎ 225 27 34 – ☰. 🖭 ⓞ **E VISA**　　　　　　　　GZ **z**
closed Saturday lunch, Sunday dinner, Monday, 3 weeks July and carnival week – **M** a la
carte 1500/1900.

XX **Neuze Neuze** Wijngaardstraat 19, ☎ 232 57 83, Fax 225 27 38 – 🖭 ⓞ **E VISA**. ⚗️　FY **d**
closed Sunday, Bank Holidays, 24 March-2 April and 21 July-8 August – **M** a la carte
1650/2000.

XX **De Kerselaar**, Grote Pieter Potstraat 22, ☎ 233 59 69, Fax 233 11 49 – 🖭 ⓞ **E VISA**　FY **n**
closed lunch Saturday and Monday, Sunday, 1 to 22 July and 23 to 30 December – **M** a la
carte 1700/2200.

XX **'t Silveren Claverblat**, Grote Pieter Potstraat 16, ☎ 231 33 88 – 🖭 ⓞ **E VISA**. ⚗️　FY **k**
closed Tuesday, Saturday lunch, first 2 weeks September and late February-early March –
M 1950.

XX **De Koperen Ketel**, Wiegstraat 5, ☎ 233 12 74 – 🖭 ⓞ **E VISA**. ⚗️　　　　　GZ **u**
closed Saturday lunch, Sunday and Bank Holidays – **M** a la carte 1100/1700.

XX **P. Preud'homme**, Suikerrui 28, ☎ 233 42 00, Open until 11 p.m. – ☰. 🖭 ⓞ **E VISA**. ⚗️
closed February and Tuesday October-June – **M** a la carte 1300/2000.　　　FY **r**

XX **De Gulden Beer**, Grote Markt 14, ☎ 226 08 41, 🍽️, Partly Italian cuisine, open until
11 p.m. – ☰. 🖭 ⓞ **E VISA**　　　　　　　　　　　　　　　　　　　　　FY **v**
M a la carte 1050/1900.

XX **De Manie**, H. Conscienceplein 3, ☎ 232 64 38 – 🖭 ⓞ **E VISA**. ⚗️　　　　　GY **w**
closed 1 to 14 April, 1 to 14 September, Wednesday and Sunday – **M** a la carte 1300/1800.

XX **Corum**, Wijngaardstraat 5, ☎ 234 02 89 – ☰. 🖭 ⓞ **E VISA**. ⚗️　　　　　　FY **e**
closed Saturday lunch, Sunday, Monday, July, Christmas and New Year – **M** a la carte
1700/2450.

XX **VIP Diners**, Lange Nieuwstraat 95, ☎ 233 13 17 – 🖭 ⓞ **E VISA**　　　　　GY **v**
closed Saturday lunch, Sunday, Bank Holidays, 2 weeks Easter and last 2 weeks July –
M 1380/1560.

XX **Het Nieuwe Palinghuis**, Sint-Jansvliet 14, ☎ 231 74 45, Seafood – ☰. 🖭 ⓞ **E VISA**
closed Monday, Tuesday and June – **M** a la carte 1200/2450.　　　　　　FZ **e**

XX **De Drie Koningen**, Brouwersvliet 30, ☎ 231 16 42 – 🖭 ⓞ **E VISA**. ⚗️　　　　CT **v**
closed Saturday lunch and Sunday – **M** 950/1600.

XX **Fourchette**, Schuttershofstraat 28, ☎ 231 33 35 – 🖭 ⓞ **E VISA**　　　　　GZ **e**
closed Saturday lunch, Sunday, Monday, late July-early August and carnival – **M** a la carte
1200/1500.

XX ✿ **De Matelote** (Garnich D.), Haarstraat 9, ☎ 231 32 07, Seafood – 🖭 ⓞ **E VISA**　FY **w**
closed lunch Saturday and Monday, Sunday and July – **M** a la carte 1500/2600.
Spec. Bouillon de crustacés et coquillages, Lotte meunière à la moutarde et au chou, St-Pierre aux olives
noires.

✗ **In de Schaduw van de Kathedraal,** Handschoenmarkt 17, ℰ 232 40 14, 佘, Mussels in
season – 歴 ① E 𝓥𝓘𝓢𝓐
FY **e**
closed Monday October-May, Tuesday and February – **M** a la carte 1100/1800.

✗ **Rooden Hoed,** Oude Koornmarkt 25, ℰ 233 28 44, Mussels in season, Antwerp atmosphere – 歴. 彩
FY **t**
closed Wednesday, Thursday, 11 June-11 July and carnival – **M** (dinner only) a la carte
1100/1800.

Suburbs

North – ⊠ 2030 :

🏨 **Novotel,** Luithagen-Haven 6, ℰ 542 03 20, Telex 32488, Fax 541 70 93, ⊒, 彩 – 劇 ⅙⊨ rm
🔟 ☎ & ❷ – 🔬 25-200. 歴 ① E 𝓥𝓘𝓢𝓐. 彩 rest
M (open until midnight) a la carte 800/1300 – ⊊ 375 – **119 rm** 3000/3600.

South – ⊠ 2020 :

🏨 **Holiday Inn Crowne Plaza,** G. Legrellelaan 10, ℰ 237 29 00, Telex 33843, Fax 216 02 96
– 劇 🎬 🔟 彩 ⇦ ❷ – 🔬 25-750. 歴 ① E 𝓥𝓘𝓢𝓐
M (open until 11 p.m.) a la carte 900/2000 – **254 rm** ⊊ 5400/6850.

at Borgerhout – ⊠ 2140 Borgerhout – ✪ 0 3 :

🏨 **Scandic Crown,** Luitenant Lippenslaan 66, ℰ 235 91 91, Telex 34479, Fax 235 08 96, 佘,
⊒ – 劇 ⅙⊨ rm 🎬 🔟 ☎ ❷ – 🔬 25-100. 歴 ① E 𝓥𝓘𝓢𝓐
M a la carte 900/1300 – **203 rm** ⊊ 4200/5400 – ½ P 4675/6000.

at Deurne – ⊠ 2100 Deurne – ✪ 0 3 :

✗✗ **Périgord,** Turnhoutsebaan 273, ℰ 325 52 00 – ❷. 歴 ① E 𝓥𝓘𝓢𝓐. 彩
closed Tuesday dinner, Wednesday, Saturday lunch, July and 1 week February – **M** 1195.

at Ekeren – ⊠ 2180 Ekeren – ✪ 0 3 :

✗✗ ❀ **Hof de Bist** (Mme Vercammen), Veltwijcklaan 258, ℰ 664 61 30 – ❷. 歴 ① E
closed Sunday, Monday and August – **M** (booking essential) a la carte 1900/2250
Spec. Foie d'oie maison à la salade d'haricots, Selle d'agneau à l'estragon, Homard poêlé et champignons au
vinaigre balsamique.

at Merksem – ⊠ 2170 Merksem – ✪ 0 3 :

✗✗✗ **Maritime,** Bredabaan 978, ℰ 646 22 23, Fax 646 22 71, 佘, Seafood – ❷. 歴 ① E 𝓥𝓘𝓢𝓐
closed Sunday – **M** a la carte 1450/2200.

at Wilrijk – ⊠ 2610 Wilrijk – ✪ 0 3 :

✗✗ **Schans XV,** Moerelei 155, ℰ 828 45 64, Fax 828 93 29, 佘, « Early 20C redoubt » – ⅙⊨
❷. 歴 ① E 𝓥𝓘𝓢𝓐. 彩
*closed Thursday dinner, Saturday lunch, Sunday, Bank Holidays, 2 weeks August, 2 weeks
February and after 8.30 p.m.* – **M** a la carte 1700/2500.

✗✗ **Bistrot,** Doornstraat 186, ℰ 829 17 29 – 歴 ① E 𝓥𝓘𝓢𝓐
closed Monday, Tuesday, Saturday lunch and late July-early August – **M** a la carte 1000/2000.

Environs

at Aartselaar : by ⑩ : 10 km – pop. 13 543 – ⊠ 2630 Aartselaar – ✪ 0 3 :

✗✗✗✗ **Host. Kasteelhoeve Groeninghe** with rm, Kontichsesteenweg 78, ℰ 457 95 86, Fax
458 13 68, ≼, 佘, « Restored Flemish farm, country atmosphere », 鈴 – 🔟 ☎ ❷ –
🔬 25-120. 歴 ① E 𝓥𝓘𝓢𝓐. 彩
closed 14 to 31 July, 22 December-6 January, Sunday and Bank Holidays – **M** a la carte
1750/2700 – ⊊ 500 – **7 rm** 3900/6000.

✗✗✗ **Lindenbos,** Boomsesteenweg 139, ℰ 888 09 65, Fax 844 47 58, « Converted castle with
park and lake » – ❷. 歴 ① E 𝓥𝓘𝓢𝓐. 彩
closed Monday and August – **M** a la carte 1800/2400.

✗✗ **Buerstede,** Antwerpsesteenweg 27, ℰ 887 45 67, 佘 – ⅙⊨ ❷. 歴 ① E 𝓥𝓘𝓢𝓐. 彩
closed Saturday lunch, Sunday and last 2 weeks July – **M** a la carte 1750/2250.

at Brasschaat : by ② and ③ : 11 km – pop. 33 618 – ⊠ 2930 Brasschaat – ✪ 0 3 :

✗✗✗ ❀ **Het Villasdal** (Van Raes), Kapelsesteenweg 480, ℰ 664 58 21, Fax 605 08 42, 佘 – ❷.
歴 ① E 𝓥𝓘𝓢𝓐 – *closed Saturday lunch, Sunday dinner, Monday, 16 July-6 August and last
week January-first week February* – **M** a la carte 1900/2400
Spec. Langoustines grillées et salade à l'huile de truffes et vinaigre balsamique, Sole farcie aux jeunes
poireaux, pétoncles et safran, Ris et rognon de veau à l'estragon.

✗✗✗ **Halewijn,** Donksesteenweg 212 (Ekeren-Donk), ℰ 647 20 10, 佘 – ① E 𝓥𝓘𝓢𝓐
closed Monday – **M** 1000/1650.

at Kapellen : by ② : 15,5 km – pop. 23 269 – ⊠ 2950 Kapellen – ✪ 0 3 :

✗✗✗ ❀ **De Bellefleur** (Buytaert), Antwerpsesteenweg 253, ℰ 664 67 19, 佘, « Winter garden »
– ❷. 歴 ① E 𝓥𝓘𝓢𝓐
closed Sunday, July and 2 weeks February – **M** a la carte 1900/2500
Spec. Kari de langoustines au gingembre, Porcelet rôti au malt Whisky, Soufflé chaud au chocolat amer et aux
poires.

at Kontich : by ⑧ : 12 km – pop. 18 475 – ✉ 2550 Kontich – ☎ 0 3 :

XXX **Carême,** Koningin Astridlaan 114, ☎ 457 63 04, Fax 457 93 02 – Ⓟ. AE ⓓ E VISA
closed Saturday lunch, Sunday and July – **M** 1250/1950.

XXX **Alexander's,** Mechelsesteenweg 318, ☎ 457 26 31 – Ⓟ. AE ⓓ E VISA. ✻
closed Sunday dinner, Monday and July – **M** 1595.

at Schoten 10 km – pop. 30 824 – ✉ 2900 Schoten – ☎ 0 3 :

XXX **Uilenspiegel,** Brechtsebaan 277, ☎ 651 61 45, 🏖, « Terrace and garden » – Ⓟ. AE E VISA
closed Saturday lunch, Sunday dinner and Monday – **M** 1350/1790. on N 115

XXX **Kleine Barreel,** Bredabaan 1147, ☎ 645 85 84, Fax 313 73 12 – ▤ Ⓟ. AE ⓓ E VISA. ✻
M a la carte 1500/2150.

XX **De Witte Raaf,** Horstebaan 97, ☎ 658 86 64, 🏖 – Ⓟ. AE ⓓ E VISA
closed Tuesday dinner, Wednesday, 19 August-5 September and 1 to 8 January – **M** a la carte 1100/2000.

at Wijnegem by ⑤ : 10 km – pop. 8 252 – ✉ 2110 Wijnegem – ☎ 0 3 :

XXX **Ter Vennen,** Merksemsebaan 278, ☎ 326 20 60, 🏖, « Small farmhouse with elegant interior » – Ⓟ. AE ⓓ E VISA. ✻
closed Sunday – **M** a la carte 1600/2400.

Kruiningen Zeeland (Netherlands) C Riemerswaal pop. 19 345 **212** ⑬⑭ and **408** ⑯ – ☎ 0 1130 – 56 km.

XXX ✿✿ **Inter Scaldes** (Mme Boudeling) (new hotel in annex), Zandweg 2 (W : 1 km), ✉ 4416 NA, ☎ 17 53, Fax 17 63, 🏖, « Terrace-veranda overlooking flowered garden » – Ⓟ. AE ⓓ E VISA
closed Monday, Tuesday and January – **M** a la carte 115/179
Spec. Homard fumé, sauce au caviar, Huîtres de Zélande en gelée (15 September-April), Turbot en robe de truffes et son beurre.

Oisterwijk Noord-Brabant (Netherlands) **212** ⑦ and **408** ⑱ – pop. 18 177 – ☎ 0 4242 – 88 km.

XXXXX ✿✿ **De Swaen** (Spijkers) with rm, De Lind 47, ✉ 5061 HT, ☎ 1 90 06, Telex 52617, Fax 8 58 60, « Terrace and flowered garden » – |♦| ▤ TV ☎ – 🏛 25 or more. AE ⓓ E VISA. ✻
closed 8 to 21 July and 31 December – **M** a la carte 140/180 – **18 rm** ☐ 225/275
Spec. Salades "De Swaen", Coquelet à la vapeur de truffes, Turbot à l'infusion de persil.

BRUGES (BRUGGE) 8000 West-Vlaanderen 213 ③ and 409 ② – pop. 117 857 agglomeration – ☎ 0 50.

See : Trips on the canals*** (Boottocht) CY E – Historic centre and canals*** – Procession of the Holy Blood*** – Market square** (Markt) : Belfry and Halles*** (Belfort-Hallen) CY F – Market-town** (Burg) CY D – Beguinage** (Begijnhof) CZ – Basilica of the Holy Blood* CY A – Church of Our Lady* (O.L. Vrouwekerk) : tower**, statue of the Madonna**, tombstone of Mary of Burgundy** CZ S – Rosery quay (Rozenhoedkaai) ≤** CY – Dijver ≤** CZ – St. Boniface bridge (Bonifaciusbrug) : site** CZ – Chimney of the "Brugse Vrije" in the Court of Justice (Gerechtshof) CY B.

Museums : Groeninge*** (Stedelijk Museum voor Schone Kunsten) CZ – Memling*** (St. John's Hospital) CZ – Gruuthuse* CZ M1 – Brangwyn* (Brangwynmuseum) CZ M4.

Envir. : Zedelgem : baptismal font* in the St. Lawrence's church by ⑥ : 10,5 km.

⛳ at Damme NE : 7 km, Doornstraat 16 ☎ (0 50) 33 35 72.

ℹ Burg 11 ☎ 44 86 86 – Tourist association of the province, Kasteel Tillegem ✉ 8200 ☎ 38 02 96.

Brussels 96 ③ – Ghent 45 ③ – Lille 72 ⑪ – Ostend 28 ⑤.

Plans on following pages

Pullman, Boeveriestraat 2, ☎ 34 09 71, Telex 81369, Fax 34 40 53, 🏊, 🏋, 🌳 – |♦| ⇆ rm ▤ TV ☎ ♿ Ⓟ – 🏛 35-200. AE ⓓ E VISA. ✻ rest CZ **a**
M 950/2150 – **155 rm** ☐ 4200/5200.

De Tuilerieën without rest., Dijver 7, ☎ 34 36 91, Fax 34 04 00, ≤, 🏊, 🏋 – |♦| TV ☎ Ⓟ – 🏛 45. AE ⓓ E VISA CYZ **p**
25 rm ☐ 5100/10250.

Oud Huis Amsterdam ⛯, Spiegelrei 3, ☎ 34 18 10, Telex 83121, Fax 33 88 91, ≤, « 17C residence, former Dutch trading post » – |♦| TV ☎ Ⓟ – 🏛 25. AE ⓓ E VISA. ✻ CY **w**
M see rest. **'t Bourgoensche Cruyce** below, 1 km by shuttle service – **22 rm** ☐ 3500/6000.

De Orangerie ⛯ without rest., Karthuizerinnenstraat 10, ☎ 34 16 49, Telex 82443, Fax 33 30 16, « Canalside ancient residence » – |♦| TV ☎ Ⓟ. AE ⓓ E VISA CY **y**
18 rm ☐ 5100/8250.

de' Medici ⛯ without rest., Potterierei 15, ☎ 33 98 33, Telex 82227, Fax 33 07 64, 🌳 – |♦| TV ☎ Ⓟ – 🏛 35. AE ⓓ E VISA. ✻ DX **b**
28 rm ☐ 4000/4500.

Academie, Wijngaardstraat 7, ☎ 33 22 66, Fax 33 21 66 – |♦| ▤ rest TV ☎ 🚗 – 🏛 30-300. AE ⓓ E VISA. ✻ CZ **k**
M *(closed Monday)* 395/1695 – **34 rm** ☐ 2700/2950 – ½ P 2175.

🏨 **Karos** without rest., Hoefijzerlaan 37, ℰ 34 14 48, Telex 82377, Fax 34 00 91, ☎s, 🔲 – 🛗 🗐
🔟 ☎ 🕭 🅿. 🕮 E 𝕍𝕀𝕊𝔸
60 rm ⊐ 2690/4560.
BY r

🏨 **Novotel Centrum**, Katelijnestraat 65b, ℰ 33 75 33, Telex 81799, Fax 33 65 56, ⅃, 🞵 – 🛗
❄⟐ rm ▤ 🔟 ☎ 🕭 – 🔏 50-400. 🕮 ⓞ E 𝕍𝕀𝕊𝔸. 🞅 rest
CZ v
M (open until midnight) a la carte 850/1450 – ⊐ 400 – **126 rm** 3460/4150.

🏨 **Parkhotel** without rest., Vrijdagmarkt 5, ℰ 33 33 64, Telex 81686, Fax 33 47 63 – 🛗 🔟 ☎
⟐ – 🔏 25-115. 🕮 ⓞ E 𝕍𝕀𝕊𝔸
CZ g
56 rm ⊐ 2700/3500.

🏨 **Portinari** ⌂ without rest., 't Zand 15, ℰ 34 10 34, Telex 82400, Fax 34 41 80 – 🛗 🔟 ☎ 🕭
🅿 – 🔏 80. 🕮 ⓞ E 𝕍𝕀𝕊𝔸
CZ x
37 rm ⊐ 2500/4500.

🏨 **Alfa Dante** without rest., Coupure 29, ℰ 34 01 94, Telex 81452, Fax 34 35 39, ≼ – 🛗 🔟 ☎
– 🔏 25-60. 🕮 ⓞ E 𝕍𝕀𝕊𝔸. 🞅
DY e
22 rm ⊐ 3750/5250.

🏨 **Die Swaene** ⌂, Steenhouwersdijk 1, ℰ 34 27 98, Telex 82446, Fax 33 66 74, ≼, « Stylish
furnishing » – 🛗 🔟 ☎ – 🔏 30. 🕮 ⓞ E 𝕍𝕀𝕊𝔸
CY g
M (closed Wednesday, Thursday lunch, 3 to 17 July and 2 weeks January) a la carte 1700/2800
– **24 rm** ⊐ 3500/4950 – ½ P 2450/4575.

🏨 **Pandhotel** ⌂ without rest., Pandreitje 16, ℰ 34 06 66, Telex 81018, Fax 34 05 56 – 🛗 🔟
☎. 🕮 ⓞ E 𝕍𝕀𝕊𝔸
CY u
24 rm ⊐ 2950/5500.

🏨 **De Castillion**, Heilige Geeststraat 1, ℰ 34 30 01, Telex 83252, Fax 33 94 75, ☎s – 🔟 ☎ 🅿
– 🔏 50. 🕮 ⓞ E 𝕍𝕀𝕊𝔸. 🞅 rest
CZ w
M 925/1895 – **20 rm** ⊐ 3650/5800 – ½ P 2925/5175.

🏨 **Prinsenhof** ⌂ without rest., Ontvangersstraat 9, ℰ 34 26 90, Telex 81315, Fax 34 23 21 –
🛗 🔟 ☎ 🕭 🅿. 🕮 ⓞ E 𝕍𝕀𝕊𝔸
CY c
16 rm ⊐ 3000/4000.

🏨 **Bryghia** without rest., Oosterlingenplein 4, ℰ 33 80 59, Fax 34 14 30 – 🛗 🔟 ☎. 🕮 ⓞ E
𝕍𝕀𝕊𝔸
CY f
18 rm ⊐ 2600/3500.

🏨 **Adornes** without rest., St-Annarei 26, ℰ 34 13 36, Fax 34 20 85, ≼, « Period vaulted cellars »
– 🛗 🔟 ☎. 🕮 E 𝕍𝕀𝕊𝔸
DY r
closed 2 January-13 February – **20 rm** ⊐ 2100/3200.

🏨 **Aragon** without rest., Naaldenstraat 24, ℰ 33 35 33, Telex 81593, Fax 34 28 05 – 🛗 🔟 ☎
⟐. 🕮 ⓞ E 𝕍𝕀𝕊𝔸
CY t
18 rm ⊐ 2500/3250.

🏨 **Biskajer** ⌂ without rest., Biskajersplein 4, ℰ 34 15 06, Telex 81874, Fax 34 39 11 – 🛗 🔟
☎. 🕮 ⓞ E 𝕍𝕀𝕊𝔸
CY j
17 rm ⊐ 2700/3400.

🏨 **Ter Duinen** without rest., Langerei 52, ℰ 33 04 37, Fax 34 42 16 – 🛗 🔟 ☎. 🕮 ⓞ E 𝕍𝕀𝕊𝔸
🞅
CX a
18 rm ⊐ 2000/3300.

🏨 **Azalea** without rest., Wulfhagestraat 43, ℰ 33 14 78, Telex 81282, Fax 33 97 00, ☎s – 🔟 ☎
🕭 ⟐. 🕮 ⓞ E 𝕍𝕀𝕊𝔸
CY p
25 rm ⊐ 2600/4200.

🏨 **Europ** ⌂ without rest., Augustijnenrei 18, ℰ 33 79 75, Telex 82490, Fax 34 52 66 – 🛗 🔟 ☎
⟐ – 🔏 30. 🕮 ⓞ E 𝕍𝕀𝕊𝔸. 🞅
CY b
10 March-15 November – **31 rm** ⊐ 2580/3840.

🏨 **Ter Brughe** without rest., Oost-Gistelhof 2, ℰ 34 03 24, Telex 82265 – 🔟 ☎. 🕮 ⓞ E 𝕍𝕀𝕊𝔸
closed January – **24 rm** ⊐ 2650/4200.
CY d

🏨 **Erasmus**, Wollestraat 35, ℰ 33 57 81, Fax 34 36 30, « Terrace ≼ inner courtyard (classified
historic monument) » – 🛗 🔟 ☎ ⟐. 🕮 ⓞ E 𝕍𝕀𝕊𝔸
CY a
closed 15 January-15 February – **M** (closed Tuesday) a la carte approx. 900 – **10 rm**
⊐ 3000/4500.

🏨 **Boudewijn I** ⌂, 't Zand 21, ℰ 33 69 62, Telex 81163, Fax 34 44 57 – 🛗 🔟 ☎ – 🔏 25. 🕮
ⓞ E 𝕍𝕀𝕊𝔸
CZ t
closed 15 to 31 January – **M** (closed Tuesday) 550/850 – **11 rm** ⊐ 1850/3500 – ½ P 2300/2400.

🏨 **Bourgoensch Hof** without rest., Wollestraat 39, ℰ 33 16 45, Telex 26937, Fax 34 36 54, ≼
canals and ancient Flemish houses – 🛗 🔟 ⟐. 🞅
CY a
15 March-15 November and weekends in winter – **11 rm** ⊐ 2250/5000.

🏨 **Albert I** without rest., Koning Albertlaan 2, ℰ 34 09 30 – 🔟 ☎. 🕮 ⓞ E 𝕍𝕀𝕊𝔸. 🞅
CZ h
11 rm ⊐ 2200/2450.

🏨 🛞 **Maraboe** (De Smedt), Hoefijzerlaan 9, ℰ 33 81 55, Fax 33 29 28 – 🔟 ☎. 🕮 ⓞ E 𝕍𝕀𝕊𝔸
closed 5 to 26 March and 27 November-1 December – **M** (closed Sunday dinner and
Monday except Bank Holidays) (booking essential) a la carte 1500/2000 – **8 rm** ⊐ 1700/2200
– ½ P 2030/2680
CZ d
Spec. Homard au four aux herbes de tortue, Suprême de pigeonneau et estouffade de légumes, Paupiettes de
sole aux épinards, sauce mousseline.

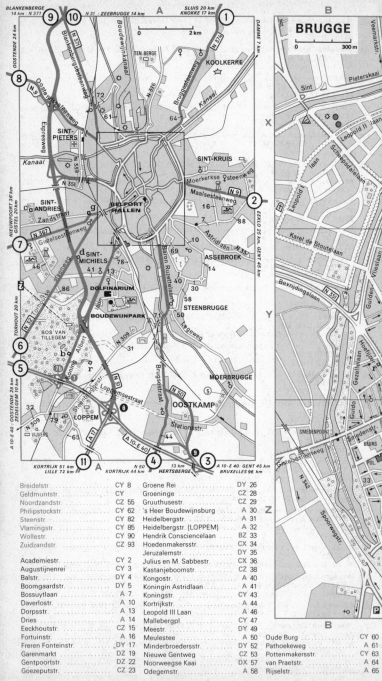

BRUGGE

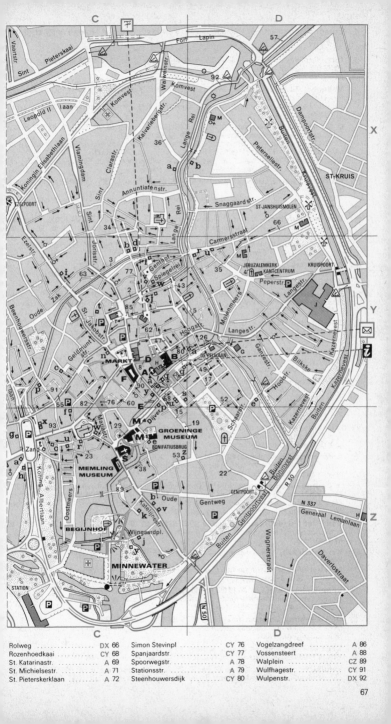

🏠 **Egmond** ⑤ without rest., Minnewater 15, 𝄜 34 14 45, « Garden setting » – 📺 ☎ 🅿. 🖭
⓪ Ɛ 𝒱𝒾𝒮𝒜   CZ **y**
March-November – **9 rm** 🖙 2500/3100.

🏠 **Ibis**, Katelijnestraat 65a, 𝄜 33 75 75, Telex 81313, Fax 33 64 19 – 📳 📺 ☎ ⅙ – 🔄 30. 🖭
⓪ Ɛ 𝒱𝒾𝒮𝒜. ⅙ rest   CZ **b**
M 650/850 – **127 rm** 🖙 2700/3100.

XXX **Vasquez**, Zilverstraat 38, 𝄜 34 08 45, Telex 83245, Fax 33 52 41, 🎴, « 15C residence,
flowered inner courtyard » – 🖭 ⓪ Ɛ 𝒱𝒾𝒮𝒜   CZ **f**
closed Wednesday, Thursday lunch, 14 to 31 July and 2 weeks February – **M** a la carte
2100/2800.

XXX ❀ **De Snippe** (Huysentruyt) ⑤ with rm, Nieuwe Gentweg 53, 𝄜 33 70 70, Fax 33 76 62,
« 18C house with wall paintings » – 📳 📺 ☎ 🅿 🖭 ⓪ Ɛ 𝒱𝒾𝒮𝒜   CZ **z**
closed 3 weeks carnival – **M** *(closed Sunday and Monday lunch except Bank Holidays)* a la
carte 2000/2600 – **12 rm** *(closed Sunday out of season)* 🖙 3750/6000
Spec. Poêlée d'huîtres de Zélande aux mangues et truffes (September-March). St-Jacques en écailles de
céleri-rave (October-March). Bar en croûte de sel, sauce aux poivres.

XXX **De Witte Poorte**, Jan Van Eyckplein 6, 𝄜 33 08 83, Telex 82232, « Vaulted dining room,
garden » – 🖭 ⓪ Ɛ 𝒱𝒾𝒮𝒜   CY **v**
closed Sunday and Monday except Bank Holidays, 2 weeks July and 2 weeks January – **M** a la
carte 1800/2500.

XXX **Duc de Bourgogne** with rm, Huidenvettersplein 12, 𝄜 33 20 38, Fax 34 40 37, ≼ canals,
« Rustic decor and wall paintings of late medieval style » – 📺 rest 📺 ☎. 🖭 ⓪ Ɛ
𝒱𝒾𝒮𝒜   CY **q**
closed 2 weeks July and 3 weeks January – **M** *(closed Monday and Tuesday lunch)* a la
carte approx. 1800 – **9 rm** 🖙 2950/4250.

XXX **Den Braamberg**, Pandreitje 11, 𝄜 33 73 70, Fax 33 99 73 – 🖭 ⓪ Ɛ 𝒱𝒾𝒮𝒜   CY **u**
closed Sunday dinner, Thursday, 15 to 30 August and 1 to 15 January – **M** a la carte
1750/2200.

XXX **Huyze Die Maene** 1st floor, Markt 17, 𝄜 33 39 59, Fax 33 44 60 – 🖭 ⓪ Ɛ 𝒱𝒾𝒮𝒜   CY **n**
closed Tuesday dinner, Wednesday, last week June-first 2 weeks July and 2 weeks February
– **M** a la carte 1600/2400.

XXX **Den Gouden Harynck**, Groeninge 25, 𝄜 33 76 37, Fax 34 42 70 – 🅿. 🖭 ⓪ Ɛ 𝒱𝒾𝒮𝒜   CZ **e**
closed Sunday, Monday, 1 week March, last week July and last week December – **M** a la
carte 1100/2100.

XXX **'t Pandreitje**, Pandreitje 6, 𝄜 33 11 90, Fax 34 00 70 – 🖭 ⓪ Ɛ 𝒱𝒾𝒮𝒜   CDY **s**
closed Wednesday, Sunday, 1 to 19 July, 28 October-3 November and 7 to 20 February –
M a la carte 1950/2900.

XX ❀❀ **De Karmeliet** (Van Hecke), Jeruzalemstraat 1, 𝄜 33 82 59 – 🖭 ⓪ Ɛ 𝒱𝒾𝒮𝒜. ⅙   DY **u**
closed Sunday dinner, Monday, first 2 weeks September and 2 weeks February – **M** a la
carte 2000/2700
Spec. Escargots en papillote fine de pomme de terre et herbettes. Raviolis à la vanille, pommes confites en
chaud-froid, Pigeon de Bresse farci de truffes (mid February-mid September).

XX ❀ **Hermitage** (Dryepondt), Ezelstraat 18, 𝄜 34 41 73 – 🖭 ⓪ Ɛ 𝒱𝒾𝒮𝒜   CY **i**
closed Wednesday, Sunday, July and August – **M** (booking essential) a la carte 1800/2300
Spec. Suprême de turbot à l'effiloché de poireaux. Ris de veau au Vin Jaune. Sole ''Belle Meunière''.

XX **Ambrosius**, Arsenaalstraat 53, 𝄜 34 41 57, 🎴, « Rustic » – 𝒱𝒾𝒮𝒜. ⅙   CZ **j**
closed Monday, Tuesday, first 2 weeks September and first 2 weeks February – **M** (dinner
only except Sunday) 1750.

XX **'t Bourgoensche Cruyce** - (at H. Oud Huis Amsterdam), Wollestraat 41, 𝄜 33 79 26,
Telex 83121, Fax 33 88 91, ≼ canals and ancient Flemish houses – 🖭 Ɛ 𝒱𝒾𝒮𝒜. ⅙   CY **a**
*closed Tuesday May-October, Sunday and Monday lunch October-May, first 2 weeks
November and February* – **M** a la carte 2000/2850.

XX **René Van Puyenbroeck**, 't Zand 13, 𝄜 33 30 35 – 🖭 ⓪ Ɛ 𝒱𝒾𝒮𝒜   CZ **x**
closed Sunday dinner, Monday, first 3 weeks July, 1 week November and 1 week March –
M 1150/1650.

XX **Kardinaalshof**, Sint-Salvatorkerkhof 14, 𝄜 34 16 91, Fax 34 20 62, Seafood – 🖭 ⓪ Ɛ
𝒱𝒾𝒮𝒜   CZ **r**
*closed Wednesday, Saturday lunch, last week November-first week December and first week
January* – **M** a la carte 1350/1900.

XX **Spinola**, Spinolarei 1, 𝄜 34 17 85, Fax 39 12 01, « Rustic » – 🖭 ⓪ Ɛ 𝒱𝒾𝒮𝒜   CY **j**
closed Sunday and Monday lunch except Bank Holidays and 25 December-1 January – **M** a
la carte 900/1400.

XX **De Lotteburg**, Goezeputstraat 43, 𝄜 33 75 35, 🎴 – 🖭 ⓪ Ɛ 𝒱𝒾𝒮𝒜   CZ **u**
closed Monday and Tuesday except Bank Holidays, 1 week carnival and 22 July-8 August –
M a la carte 1200/1700.

X **Chez Olivier**, Meestraat 9, 𝄜 33 36 59, ≼   DY **a**
closed Wednesday, Thursday, Friday lunch and 12 to 22 November – **M** 1300/2100.

X **Tanuki**, Noordstraat 3, 𝄜 31 75 12, Fax 31 75 12, Japanese cuisine. Ɛ 𝒱𝒾𝒮𝒜. ⅙   CZ **k**
closed Monday and Tuesday except Bank Holidays – **M** a la carte 750/1100.

South – ✉ 8200 – ✿ 0 50 :

🏨 **Novotel Zuid**, Chartreuseweg 20, ℰ 38 28 51, Telex 81507, Fax 38 79 03, ⚞, ☒, ⟿ – ﹟
✗⟩ rm 🗏 rest 📺 ☎ ᕫ 🅿 – ⚠ 25-230, ⯀ ⦾ 🇪 *VISA*   A r
M (open until midnight) à la carte 900/1400 – ☐ 375 – **101 rm** 2950/3700.

✕✕✕ ⊛ **Weinebrugge** (Galens), Koning Albertlaan 242, ℰ 38 44 40 – 🅿, ⯀ 🇪   A b
closed Sunday dinner November-March, Wednesday, Thursday, last week June, 2 weeks
September and 2 weeks January – **M** à la carte approx. 3500
Spec. Saumon d'Écosse aux langoustines, Picasso de homard, Feuillantine à la mousse framboisée.

South-West – ✉ 8200 – ✿ 0 50 :

🏨 **Pannenhuis** 🦢, Zandstraat 2, ℰ 31 19 07, Telex 82345, Fax 31 77 66, ≤, ⚞, « Terrace and
garden » – 📺 ☎ ᕫ 🅿 – ⚠ 25. ⯀ ⦾ 🇪 *VISA*, ⅏ rest   A g
M *(closed Tuesday dinner except September, Wednesday, 1 to 15 July and 15 January-*
1 February) à la carte 1200/1900 – **20 rm** *(closed 15 January-1 February)* ☐ 2600/4900 –
½ P 3250/3950.

✕✕✕ **Ter Heyde** 🦢 with rm, Torhoutsesteenweg 620 (by ⑥ : 8 km on N 32), ℰ 38 38 58, ⚞,
« Stately home in extensive grounds » – ☞ ⬤ 🅿 ⯀ 🇪 *VISA* ⅏
closed Wednesday dinner, Thursday and January – **M** à la carte 2100/2700 – **5 rm** ☐
2300/3600.

✕✕ **Vossenburg** 🦢 with rm, Zandstraat 272 (Coude Ceucen), ℰ 31 70 26, ≤, « Converted
castle in a park » – 📺 ⬤ 🅿 ⯀ 🇪 *VISA*. ⅏   A c
closed 18 February-7 March – **M** *(closed Monday dinner and Tuesday)* 950/1500 – **7 rm**
☐ 4150.

at Hertsberge by ④ : 12,5 km 🅲 Oostkamp pop. 20 171 – ✉ 8020 Hertsberge – ✿ 0 50 :

✕✕✕ **Manderley**, Kruisstraat 13, ℰ 27 80 51, ⚞, « Terrace and garden » – 🅿, ⯀ ⦾ 🇪 *VISA*
closed Sunday dinner, Monday and last 3 weeks January – **M** à la carte 1500/2250.

at Ruddervoorde by ④ : 12 km 🅲 Oostkamp pop. 20 171 – ✉ 8020 Ruddervoorde –
✿ 0 50 :

✕✕✕ **Host. Leegendael** 🦢 with rm, Kortrijkstraat 486 (N 50), ℰ 27 76 99, Fax 27 58 80, « Ancient
residence, country atmosphere » – 📺 ⬤ 🅿 ⯀ ⦾ 🇪 *VISA*
closed last 2 weeks August-first week September and carnival – **M** *(closed Wednesday and*
Sunday dinner) à la carte 1500/2000 – **7 rm** ☐ 1750/2550.

at Sint-Kruis by ② : 6 km 🅲 Bruges – ✉ 8310 Sint-Kruis – ✿ 0 50 :

✕✕✕ **Jonkman**, Maalsesteenweg 438, ℰ 36 07 67, Fax 35 76 96, ⚞, « Terrace » – 🅿, ⯀ ⦾ 🇪
VISA – *closed Thursday dinner, Sunday, 1 to 8 April, last week June and 1 to 15 October* – **M**
à la carte 1650/2100.

at Waardamme by ④ : 11 km 🅲 Oostkamp pop. 20 171 – ✉ 8020 Waardamme – ✿ 0 50 :

✕✕✕ **Ter Talinge**, Rooiveldstraat 46, ℰ 27 90 61, « Terrace » – 🅿. ⯀ 🇪 *VISA*
closed Wednesday dinner, Thursday, 26 August-6 September and 20 February-6 March –
M à la carte 1100/1600.

at Zedelgem by ⑥ : 10,5 km – pop. 19 865 – ✉ 8210 Zedelgem – ✿ 0 50 :

🏨 **Zuidwege** without rest., Torhoutsesteenweg 126, ℰ 20 13 39 – 📺 ☎ 🅿. ⯀ ⦾ 🇪 *VISA*. ⅏
closed 25 December-4 January – **17 rm** ☐ 1500/2200.

✕✕ **Ter Leepe**, Torhoutsesteenweg 168, ℰ 20 01 97 – 🅿. ⯀ ⦾ 🇪 *VISA*
closed Wednesday dinner, Sunday, 16 July-2 August and 1 to 12 February – **M** à la carte
1200/1600.

Gent 9000 Oost-Vlaanderen 🔢 ④ and 🔢 ③ – pop. 232 620 – ✿ 0 91 – 45 km.

South :

✕✕✕ ⊛⊛ **Apicius** (Slawinsky), Maurice Maeterlinckstraat 8, ℰ 22 46 00, « Garden » – ⯀ ⦾ 🇪
VISA. ⅏ – *closed Saturday lunch, Sunday, 1 week Easter and 21 July-15 August* – **M** à la
carte 2200/4000
Spec. Barbue aux copeaux de thon, Roulade de bœuf, Macaronade de glace au chocolat.

Kortrijk 8500 West-Vlaanderen 🔢 ⑮ and 🔢 ⑪ – pop. 76 314 – ✿ 0 56 – 51 km.

✕✕✕ ⊛⊛ **Filip Bogaert**, Minister Tacklaan 5, ℰ 20 30 34, Fax 20 30 75, « Late 19C residential
house » – 🅿 ⯀ ⦾ 🇪 *VISA*
closed dinner Wednesday and Sunday and 2 weeks August – **M** à la carte 2300/3200
Spec. Bouchon de foie d'oie aux graines de pavot, Turbot rôti aux écailles de pommes nouvelles et truffes,
Perdreau rôti aux feuilles de vigne et chou vert (20 September-20 October).

Waregem 8790 West-Vlaanderen 🔢 ⑯ and 🔢 ⑪ – pop. 33 044 – ✿ 0 56 – 47 km.

✕✕✕ ⊛⊛ **'t Oud Konijntje** (Mme Desmedt), Bosstraat 53 (S : 2 km near E 17), ℰ 60 19 37,
Telex 86350, Fax 60 92 12, ⚞, « Flowered terrace » – 🅿. ⯀ ⦾ 🇪 *VISA*
closed dinner Thursday and Sunday, Friday, 22 July-13 August and 22 December-4 January
– **M** à la carte 1900/2500
Spec. Sole aux épinards et jus de viande, Raviolis de foie de canard et carpaccio de son magret, Ris de veau
aux langoustines et cerfeuil.

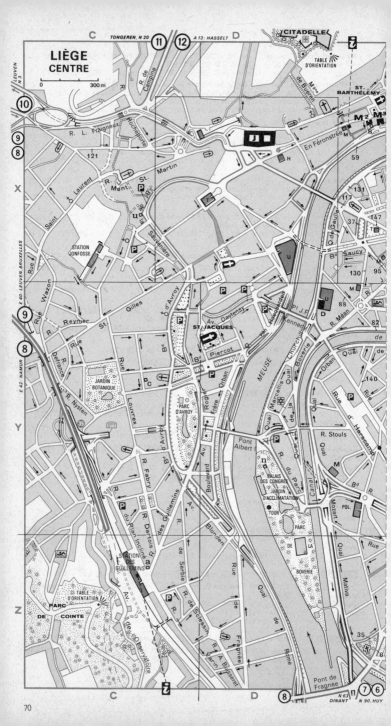

To obtain a general view of Benelux,

use the Michelin Map **987**

Germany - Austria - Benelux

(1 in: 16 miles)

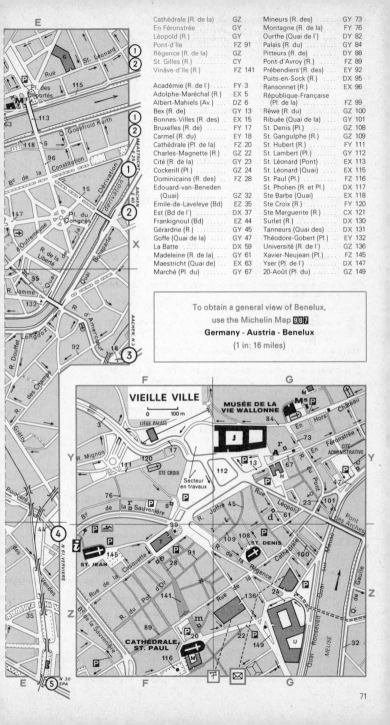

LIÈGE 4000 ❷❶❸ ㉒ and ❹❶❾ ⑮ – pop. 200 312 – 🕭 0 41.

See : Old town★★ – Baptismal font★★★ of St. Bartholomew's church DX – Citadel ≤★★ DX – Treasury★★ of St. Paul's Cathedral FZ – Palace of the Prince-Bishops★ : court of honour★★ GY J – The Perron★ (market cross) GY A – Aquarium★ DY D – St. James church★ DY – Cointe Park ≤★ CZ – Altarpiece★ in the St. Denis church GZ – Church of St. John : statues★ in wood of the Calvary FZ.

Museums : Life in Wallonia★★ GY – Curtius★ : evangelistary★★★, glassware Museum : collection★ EX M¹ – Ansembourg★ DX M² – Arms★ DX M³ – Religious and Roman Art Museum★ GY M⁵.

Envir. : Baptismal font★ in the church★ of St. Severin-en-Condroz by ⑥ : 23 km.

🏌 at Ougrée by ⑥ : 7 km, rte du Condroz 541 ℰ (0 41) 36 20 21 - 🏌 at Gomzé-Andoumont by ⑤ : 17 km, r. Gomzé 30 ℰ (0 41) 60 92 07.

✈ ℰ 42 52 14.

🛈 En Féronstrée 92 ℰ 22 24 56 and Gare des Guillemins ℰ 52 44 19 – Tourist association of the province, bd de la Sauvenière 77 ℰ 22 42 10.

Brussels 97 ⑨ – Amsterdam 242 ① – Antwerp 119 ⑫ – Köln 122 ② – Luxemburg 159 ⑤.

Plans on preceding pages

Room prices are subject to the addition of a local tax of 6 %

🏨 **Ramada,** bd Sauvenière 100, ℰ 22 49 10, Telex 41896, Fax 22 39 83 – 🛗 ≤ rm 🔳 🔲 ☎
   ⟵ – ⚖ 25-100. 🔲 ⓞ 🛤 🗾   CX **u**
M a la carte 1100/1600 – 🍽 495 – **105 rm** 4500/5500.

🏨 **Holiday Inn,** Esplanade de l'Europe 2, ⊠ 4020, ℰ 42 60 20, Telex 41156, Fax 43 48 10, ≤, ⩲, 🔲, 🔳 ≤ rm 🔳 🔲 ☎ ৬ ⟵ – ⚖ 40. 🔲 ⓞ 🛤 🗾 ℛ rest   DY **n**
M Ile de Meuse a la carte 1000/1600 – **219 rm** 🍽 4900/6200.

🏠 **Univers** without rest., r. Guillemins 116, ℰ 52 26 50, Telex 42424, Fax 52 16 53 – 🛗 ☎ –
   ⚖ 25-80. 🔲 ⓞ 🛤 🗾   CZ **a**
🍽 295 – **49 rm** 1600/1950.

🏠 **Le Cygne d'Argent,** r. Beeckman 49, ℰ 23 70 01, Telex 42617, Fax 22 49 66 – 🛗 🔲 ☎
   ⟵ 🔲 ⓞ 🛤 🗾   CY **c**
M *(closed Friday, Saturday and Sunday)* (dinner for residents only) – 🍽 240 – **22 rm**
1600/2220 – ½ P 1670/1940.

XXX **Vieux Liège,** quai Goffe 41, ℰ 23 77 48, « 16C house » – 🔳 🔲 ⓞ 🛤 🗾   GY **c**
closed Wednesday dinner, Sunday, Bank Holidays, mid July-mid August and 1 week Easter
– **M** a la carte 1800/2200.

XXX **La Ripaille** 1st floor, Ilot St-Georges 5, ℰ 22 16 56 – 🛤 🔲 🛤 🗾   DX **s**
closed Saturday lunch, Sunday and mid July-mid August – **M** a la carte 1000/1600.

XXX **L'Héliport,** bd Frère-Orban, ℰ 52 13 21, ≤, 🌴 – 🅿. 🛤 🔲 🛤 🗾   DY **q**
closed Sunday, Monday dinner and last 3 weeks July – **M** 1295/1695.

XX **As Ouhès,** pl. Marché 21, ℰ 23 32 25 – 🛤 🔲 ⓞ 🛤 🗾   GY **r**
closed Saturday lunch, Sunday and last 3 weeks July – **M** a la carte 750/1250.

XX **L'Ecailler,** r. Dominicains 26, ℰ 22 17 49, Seafood – 🔳 🛤 🔲 ⓞ 🛤 🗾   FZ **e**
M a la carte 1200/1900.

XX **Y-Sing,** bd Sauvenière 50, ℰ 23 35 78, Chinese cuisine – 🛤 🔲 ⓞ 🛤 🗾   FY **r**
closed Wednesday except Bank Holidays and 16 to 31 August – **M** (dinner only) 500/850.

X **Max,** pl. de la République Française 12, ℰ 22 08 59 – 🛤 🔲 ⓞ 🛤 🗾   FY **s**
M a la carte 900/1500.

X **Le Shanghai** 1st floor, Galeries Cathédrale 104, ℰ 22 22 63, Fax 23 00 50, Chinese cuisine
– 🔳. 🛤 🔲 ⓞ 🛤 🗾   FZ **m**
closed Tuesday and 18 August-12 September – **M** a la carte 750/1100.

X **Lalo's Bar,** r. Madeleine 18, ℰ 23 22 57, Italian cuisine – 🛤 🔲 🛤 🗾 ℛ   GY **d**
closed Saturday lunch, Sunday and Bank Holidays – **M** 750/990.

at Ans – pop. 27 031 – ⊠ 4430 Ans – 🕭 0 41 :

XX **La Fontaine de Jade,** r. Yser 321, ℰ 46 49 72, Chinese cuisine, open until 11 p.m. – 🔳
🛤 🔲 ⓞ 🛤 🗾 ℛ
closed Monday except Bank Holidays and mid August-early September – **M** a la carte
750/1100.

X **Le Marguerite,** r. Walthère Jamar 171, ℰ 26 43 46 – 🛤 🔲 ⓞ 🛤 🗾
closed Saturday lunch, Sunday, Monday, 1 week Easter, 15 July-15 August and 23 December-2 January – **M** a la carte approx. 1300.

at Argenteau by ① : 13 km © Visé pop. 16 998 – ⊠ 4601 Argenteau – 🕭 0 41 :

X **Le Tourne Bride,** chaussée d'Argenteau 42, ℰ 79 17 11 – 🅿. 🛤 🔲 ⓞ 🛤 🗾
closed Sunday, Bank Holidays and August – **M** a la carte 1200/2000.

à Chênée © Liège – ⊠ 4032 Chênée – 🕭 0 41 :

XX **Le Gourmet,** r. Large 91, ℰ 65 87 97, 🌴 – 🛤 🔲 ⓞ 🛤 🗾
closed Wednesday, Saturday lunch and 15 to 31 July – **M** a la carte 1100/1500.

XX **Le Vieux Chênée,** r. Gravier 45, ℰ 67 00 92 – 🛤 🔲 ⓞ 🛤 🗾
closed Thursday, 3 weeks July and 1 week end January – **M** a la carte 900/1300.

à Engis by N 617 direction Namur – pop. 5 714 – ✉ 4480 Engis – ☎ 0 41 :

XX **La Ciboulette,** quai Herten 11, ✆ 75 19 65, 🏠 – AE ⓞ E VISA
closed Saturday lunch, dinner Sunday, Monday and Wednesday – **M** a la carte approx. 1300.

at Hermalle-sous-Argenteau by ① : 14 km Ⓒ Oupeye pop. 23 220 – ✉ 4681 Hermalle-sous-Argenteau – ☎ 0 41 :

XXX **Au Comte de Mercy,** r. Tilleul 5, ✆ 79 35 35, 🏠, « Rustic » – Ⓟ – 🏟 25 or more. AE ⓞ E VISA. ✻
closed Sunday, Monday, 3 days after Easter, July and 1 to 10 January – **M** a la carte 1250/2100.

at Herstal – pop. 36 919 – ✉ 4040 Herstal – ☎ 0 41 :

🏨 **Post House** ⛰, r. Hurbise (by motorway E 40 exit 34), ✆ 64 64 00, Telex 41103, Fax 48 06 90, 🏊 – |‡| ▤ rest 📺 ☎ Ⓟ – 🏟 25-60. AE ⓞ E VISA
M 990 – **94 rm** ☕ 3560/4640.

at Ivoz-Ramet Ⓒ Flémalle pop. 26 967 – ✉ 4400 Ivoz-Ramet – ☎ 0 41 :

X **Chez Cha-Cha,** pl. François Gérard 10, ✆ 37 18 43, 🏠, Grill – Ⓟ. AE E VISA
closed dinner Monday and Tuesday, Saturday lunch and Sunday – **M** a la carte 750/1200.

at Neuville-en-Condroz by ⑥ : 18 km Ⓒ Neupré pop. 8 471 – ✉ 4121 Neuville-en-Condroz – ☎ 0 41 :

XXXX ✿✿ **Chêne Madame** (Tilkin), av. de la Chevauchée 70 (in Rognacs wood SE : 2 km), ✆ 71 41 27, Fax 71 29 43 – Ⓟ. AE ⓞ E VISA. ✻
closed Monday, dinner Sunday and Thursday, August and 23 December-4 January – **M** a la carte 2000/2800
Spec. Crêpe de homard au fenouil, Agneau de lait en croûte (February-July), Gibiers en saison.

at Rotheux-Rimière by ⑥ : 16 km Ⓒ Neupré pop. 8 471 – ✉ 4120 Rotheux-Rimière – ☎ 0 41 :

X **Au Vieux Chêne,** r. Bonry 146 (near N 63), ✆ 71 46 51 – Ⓟ. AE ⓞ E VISA. ✻
closed Wednesday, dinner Monday and Tuesday, August and 2 weeks Christmas-New Year – **M** a la carte 800/1500.

at Tilff S : 12 km by N 633 Ⓒ Esneux pop. 11 867 – ✉ 4130 Tilff – ☎ 0 41 :

XXX **Casino** with rm, pl. Roi-Albert 3, ✆ 88 10 15, Fax 88 33 16 – ☎. ✻ rm
closed 15 December-15 January – **M** *(closed Monday)* a la carte 1300/2000 – **6 rm** ☕ 1600/2300.

Hasselt 3500 Limburg **213** ⑨ and **409** ⑥ – pop. 65 798 – ☎ 0 11 – 42 km.

at Stevoort by N 2 : 5 km to Kermt, then road on the left Ⓒ Hasselt – ✉ 3512 Stevoort – ☎ 0 11 :

🏨 ✿✿ **Scholteshof** (Souvereyns) ⛰, Kermtstraat 130, ✆ 25 02 02, Telex 39684, Fax 25 43 28, ≤, 🏠, « 18C farmhouse with English-style garden, country atmosphere », ✻ – 📺 ☎ Ⓟ – 🏟 25 or more. AE ⓞ E VISA
closed Wednesday, 15 July-1 August and 15 to 30 January – **M** a la carte 2750/3950 – ☕ 450 – **16 rm** 4000/14000
Spec. Couronne de coquilles, pommes grillées et truffes (October-April), Émulsion de langoustines à la vanille, Selle et côte d'agneau "Art Nouveau".

St-Vith 4780 Liège **214** ⑨ and **409** ⑯ – pop. 8 488 – ☎ 0 80 – 78 km.

XXX ✿✿ **Zur Post** (Pankert) with rm, Hauptstr. 39, ✆ 22 80 27 – 📺 ☎. AE E VISA. ✻
closed Sunday dinner and Monday except Bank Holidays, 1 to 12 July and January – **M** a la carte 2300/2950 – ☕ 350 – **8 rm** 1450/2400
Spec. Langoustines grillées aux graines de sésame, Assiette de poissons et crustacés au beurre de Champagne, Côtelettes de pigeonneau farcies et foie gras (February-September).

LUXEMBURG

SIGHTS

See : Site★★ – Old Luxemburg★★ DY – "Chemin de la Corniche"★★ and the rocks DY **29** – The Bock cliff ⩽★★, Bock Casemates★★ DY **A** – Place de la Constitution ⩽★★ DY **28** – Grand-Ducal Palace★ DY **K** – Our Lady's Cathedral (Notre Dame)★ DY **L** – Grand-Duchess Charlotte Bridge★ DY – Boulevard Victor Thorn ⩽★ DY **97**.

Museum : State (Musée de l'Etat)★★ DY **M**[1].

LUXEMBURG (LUXEMBOURG) 215 ⑤ and 409 ㉖ – pop. 78 250.

Senningerberg, near Airport ✆ 3 40 90.

Findel by ③ : 6 km ✆ 40 08 08 – **Air terminal** : pl. de la Gare ✆ 48 11 99.

pl. d'Armes. ✉ 2011. ✆ 2 28 09 and 2 75 65 – Air Terminal, pl. de la Gare ✆ 48 11 99 – Findel, Airport ✆ 40 08 08.

Amsterdam 391 ⑧ – Bonn 190 ③ – Bruxelles 219 ⑧.

Plan on next page

Luxembourg-Centre :

Le Royal, bd Royal 12, ✉ 2449, ✆ 4 16 16, Telex 2979, Fax 2 59 48, ≘, ☒ – |‡| ▤ TV ☎ ♿ ⇔ P – 🏛 25-400. AE ⓓ E VISA. ✻ rest — CY **e**
M **Le Relais Royal** *(closed Saturday lunch, Bank Holidays and 29 July-19 August)* 2250 – **170 rm** ☐ 6950/11600.

Cravat, bd Roosevelt 29, ✉ 2450, ✆ 2 19 75, Telex 2846, Fax 2 67 11 – |‡| TV ☎ – 🏛 70. AE ⓓ E VISA. ✻ rest — DY **a**
M a la carte 1000/2000 – **59 rm** ☐ 4900/5900.

Rix without rest., **bd Royal 20,** ✉ **2449,** ✆ **47 16 66, Telex 1234, Fax 2 75 35,** ≘ – |‡| TV ☎ P. ✻ – *closed 20 December-2 January* – **22 rm** ☐ 3210/4320. — CY **b**

XXXX **Clairefontaine,** pl. de Clairefontaine 9, ✉ 1341, ✆ 46 22 11, Fax 47 08 21 – ▤. AE ⓓ E VISA. ✻ – *closed Saturday lunch, Sunday, Bank Holidays, 15 July-7 August and carnival week* – **M** 2000/2680 — DY **v**

XXX ✿✿ **St-Michel** (Guillou) 1st floor, **r. Eau 32,** ✉ **1449,** ✆ **2 32 15, Fax 46 25 93,** « **Rustic** » – AE ⓓ E VISA — DY **e**
closed Saturday, Sunday, Bank Holidays, 24 July-26 August and 23 December-5 January – **M** (booking essential) a la carte 2000/3500
Spec. Consommé aux ravioles de foie d'oie, Cotriade de bar au jus de crustacés, Gratin de fruits exotiques.
Wines Pinot gris, Riesling.

XXX **La Cigogne,** r. Curé 24, ✉ 1368, ✆ 2 82 50, Fax 46 51 21 – ⓓ E VISA. ✻ — DY **r**
closed Saturday, Sunday, Bank Holidays and August – **M** a la carte 1800/2200.

XXX **Speltz,** r. Chimay 8, ✉ 1333, ✆ 47 49 50 – AE ⓓ E VISA — DY **n**
closed Saturday, Sunday, Bank Holidays, first week April, 27 July-11 August and last week December – **M** 1100/1450.

XX **Hemmen,** plateau du St-Esprit 5, ✉ 1475, ✆ 47 00 23, Fax 47 00 24, 余 – ▤. AE ⓓ E VISA
closed Sunday dinner and 1 week January – **M** a la carte 1900/2600. — DZ **s**

X **Brédewée,** r. Large/Corniche 9, ✉ 1917, ✆ 2 26 96, 余 – AE ⓓ E VISA — DY **u**
closed Sunday and first week January – **M** 1590/1980.

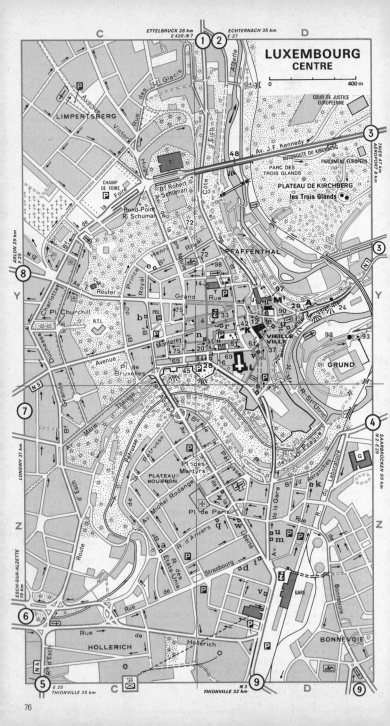

STREET INDEX TO LUXEMBOURG TOWN PLAN

Luxembourg-Station :

🏨 **Arcotel** without rest., av. Gare 43, ⊠ 1611, ℰ 49 40 01, Telex 3776 – 🛗 📺 ☎ ⑩ 🝗 𝑉𝐼𝑆𝐴
⋇
30 rm � 3200/3800.
DZ **u**

🏨 **Nobilis,** av. Gare 47, ⊠ 1611, ℰ 49 49 71, Telex 3212, Fax 40 31 01 – 🛗 🗏 📺 ☎ ⟵⟶
🝆 40. 🝗 ⑩ 🝗 𝑉𝐼𝑆𝐴
DZ **m**
M 750/1800 – � 340 – **43 rm** 2780/3365.

🏨 **President,** pl. Gare 32, ⊠ 1616, ℰ 48 61 61, Telex 1510, Fax 48 61 80 – 🛗 📺 ☎ – 🝆 40.
🝗 ⑩ 🝗 𝑉𝐼𝑆𝐴 ⋇ rest
DZ **v**
M *(closed Sunday, Bank Holidays and August)* (dinner only) 1200/1600 – **36 rm** � 3500/5800.

🏨 **Central Molitor,** av. Liberté 28, ⊠ 1930, ℰ 48 99 11, Telex 2613, Fax 48 33 82 – 🛗 📺
⟵⟶ 🝗 ⑩ 🝗 𝑉𝐼𝑆𝐴 ⋇ rest
DZ **x**
M *(closed Friday and 15 December-15 January)* 890 – **36 rm** � 3500/3800.

🏩 **Marco Polo** without rest., r. Fort Neipperg 27, ⊠ 2230, ℰ 404 88 01, Fax 40 48 84 – 🛗 📺
☎ ⟵⟶ 🝗 ⑩ 🝗 𝑉𝐼𝑆𝐴
DZ **k**
18 rm � 2500/3500.

🏩 **Aub. du Coin,** bd de la Pétrusse 2, ⊠ 2320, ℰ 40 21 01, Fax 40 36 66 – 🛗 📺 ☎. 🝗 𝑉𝐼𝑆𝐴
closed 15 December-15 January – **M** *(closed Sunday and Bank Holidays)* a la carte 1500/2100
CZ **a**
– **23 rm** � 2300/2800 – ½ P 2750/4500.

🏩 **Bristol** without rest., r. Strasbourg 11, ⊠ 2561, ℰ 48 58 29, Telex 2328, Fax 48 64 80 – 🛗
📺 ☎ ⟵⟶ 🝗 ⑩ 🝗 𝑉𝐼𝑆𝐴
DZ **d**
� 225 – **29 rm** 800/2200.

XXX **Cordial** 1st floor, pl. Paris 1, ⊠ 2314, ℰ 48 85 38 – 🝗 𝑉𝐼𝑆𝐴
DZ **w**
closed Friday, Saturday lunch, 15 July-10 August and carnival week – **M** a la carte 2250/3000.

XX **Italia** with rm, r. Anvers 15, ⊠ 1130, ℰ 48 66 26, Telex 3644, Fax 48 08 07, ⋈, Italian
cuisine – 📺 ☎. 🝗 𝑉𝐼𝑆𝐴
DZ **q**
M a la carte 950/1800 – **20 rm** � 2300/2700.

XX **La Bourgogne,** r. Strasbourg 1, ⊠ 2561, ℰ 49 49 65 – 🝗 🝗 𝑉𝐼𝑆𝐴
DZ **t**
closed Saturday lunch and Sunday – **M** 750/1500.

Airport by ③ : 8 km – ⊠ Luxembourg :

🏨 **Sheraton Aérogolf** ⋟, rte de Trèves, ⊠ 1019, ℰ 3 45 71, Telex 2662, Fax 3 42 17, ≼ – 🛗
⋇⟶ rm 🗏 📺 ☎ 🝉 – 🝆 120. 🝗 ⑩ 🝗 𝑉𝐼𝑆𝐴
M **Le Montgolfier** (open until 11.30 p.m.) a la carte 1200/2100 – � 500 – **146 rm** 6300/8200.

🏨 **Ibis,** rte de Trèves, ⊠ 2632, ℰ 43 88 01, Telex 60790, Fax 43 88 02, ≼ – 🛗 🗏 📺 ☎ 🝙 🝉 –
🝆 80. 🝗 ⑩ 🝗 𝑉𝐼𝑆𝐴
M a la carte 750/1300 – **120 rm** � 2500/3500 – ½ P 3250/3500.

XX **Le Grimpereau,** r. Cents 140, ⊠ 1319, ℰ 43 67 87 – 🝉. 🝗 𝑉𝐼𝑆𝐴 ⋇
*closed 25 to 30 March, 29 July-15 August, 28 October-3 November, Sunday dinner and
Monday* – **M** a la carte 1200/1900.

at Dommeldange – ⊠ Dommeldange :

🏨 **Intercontinental** ⋟, r. Jean Engling 12, ⊠ 1466, ℰ 4 37 81, Telex 3754, Fax 43 60 95, ≼,
⥱, – 🛗 ⋇⟶ rm 🗏 📺 ☎ 🝙 🝉 – 🝆 280. 🝗 ⑩ 🝗 𝑉𝐼𝑆𝐴 ⋇ rest
M *(closed lunch Saturday and Sunday and August)* a la carte approx. 2300 – � 530 –
344 rm 5300/8550.

🏨 **Parc,** rte d'Echternach – E 42, ⊠ 1453, ℰ 43 56 43, Telex 1418, Fax 43 69 03, ⥱, 🝟, 🝞,
⋇ – 🛗 🗏 rest 📺 🝙 🝉 – 🝆 25-1800. 🝗 ⑩ 🝗 𝑉𝐼𝑆𝐴
M a la carte 1400/1900 – **221 rm** � 2900/4000 – ½ P 2700/3500.

🏨 **Host. du Grünewald,** rte d'Echternach 10, ⊠ 1453, ℰ 43 18 82 and 42 03 14 (rest.), Telex
60543, Fax 42 06 46 – 🛗 🗏 rest 📺 ☎ 🝉. 🝗 ⑩ 🝗 𝑉𝐼𝑆𝐴 ⋇ rest
M *(closed Saturday lunch, Sunday, Bank Holidays except weekends and 3 weeks February)* a
la carte 1700/2600 – **28 rm** � 2900/4200.

at Hesperange – pop. 9 615 – ⊠ Hespérange :

XXX ❀ **L'Agath** (Steichen) with rm, rte de Thionville 274 (Howald), ⊠ 5884, ℰ 48 86 87, Fax 48 55 05, 🏤 – 🔟 ☎ 🅿, 🆎 ⓞ 🇪 𝘝𝘐𝘚𝘈
closed Sunday, Monday, 1 week Easter, mid July-1 August and Christmas-New Year – **M** a la carte 2200/2900 – **6 rm** 🖙 1600/3300
Spec. Raviolis de homard au coulis de langoustines, Petite pêche de poissons en bouillabaisse, Pigeon en "Bécasse". **Wines** Riesling.

Upland of Kirchberg – ⊠ Luxembourg :

🏨 **Pullman,** r. Fort Niedergrünewald 6, ⊠ 2226, ℰ 43 77 61, Telex 2751, Fax 43 86 58, 🏤, 🔲 – 🛗 ✗✗ rm 🗏 🔟 ☎ 👌 🅿 – 🔬 200. 🆎 ⓞ 🇪 𝘝𝘐𝘚𝘈, 🛠 rest
M **Les Trois Glands** *(closed Saturday lunch and August)* a la carte 1300/1600 – **260 rm** 🖙 4700/6500.

at the skating-rink of Kockelscheuer – ⊠ Luxembourg :

XXX ❀❀ **Patin d'Or** (Berring), r. Bettembourg 40, ⊠ 1899, ℰ 2 64 99, Fax 40 40 11 – 🗏 🅿. ⓞ 🇪 𝘝𝘐𝘚𝘈. 🛠
closed Saturday lunch, Sunday, Bank Holidays, 1 week Easter, 1 week Whitsuntide, late August-early September and 23 December-early January – **M** a la carte 2100/2800
Spec. Salade de homard au beurre de Sauternes, Blanc de turbot rôti à la mouginoise, Pied de porc farci aux truffes. **Wines** Pinot gris, Riesling.

Echternach 215 ③ and 409 ㉗ – pop. 4 194 – 35 km.

at Geyershof SW : 7 km by E 29 🄲 Consthum pop. 281 – ⊠ Echternach :

XXX ❀❀ **La Bergerie** (Phal), ⊠ 6251, ℰ 7 94 64, Fax 7 97 71, ≼, 🏤, « Country atmosphere, flowered surroundings » – 🅿 ⓞ 🇪 𝘝𝘐𝘚𝘈
closed Sunday dinner, Monday and 25 January-1 March – **M** a la carte 2350/3000
Spec. Bar rôti à l'aigre-doux aux épices, Salade de cailles aux choux confits et endives, Pêche rôtie au caramel et pistaches. **Wines** Pinot gris, Riesling Koëppchen.

AMSTERDAM

SIGHTS

See : Old Amsterdam★★★ : the canals★★★ (Grachten) : Singel ; Herengracht Cromhout Houses (Cromhouthuizen) ; Reguliersgracht ≤★ ; Keizersgracht – Boat trips★ (Rondvaart) – Beguine Convent★★ (Begijnhof) LY – Dam : pulpit★ in the New Church★ (Nieuwe Kerk) LXY – Flower market★ (Bloemenmarkt) LY – Rembrandt Square (Rembrandtsplein) MY – Thin Bridge★ (Magere Brug) MZ – Leeuwenburg House ≤★ MX – Artis★ (Zoological Garden) – Royal Palace★ (Koninklijk Paleis) LY **B**.

Museums : Rijksmuseum★★★ KZ – Vincent van Gogh National Museum★★★ (Rijksmuseum) – Municipal★★ (Stedelijk Museum) : Modern Art – Amsterdam Historical Museum★★ (Amsterdams Historisch Museum) LY – Madame Tussaud's★ : wax museum LY **M¹** – Amstelkring Museum "Our Dear Lord in the Attic" (Museum Amstelkring Ons'Lieve Heer op Solder) : clandestine chapel MX **M⁴** – Rembrandt's House★ (Rembrandthuis) : works by the master MY **M⁵** – Netherlands Maritime History Museum★ (Nederlands Scheepvaart Museum) – Tropical Museum★ (Tropenmuseum) – Allard Pierson★ : antiquities LY **M²** – Jewish Museum★ (Joods Historisch Museum) MY **M¹⁵**.

AMSTERDAM Noord-Holland 408 ⑩ ㉗ ㉘ – Pop. 694 680 – ✿ 0 20.

🐎 Zwarte Laantje 4 at Duivendrecht ✆ (0 20) 694 36 50.

✈ at Schiphol SW : 9,5 km ✆ (0 20) 601 09 66 (information) and 674 77 47 (reservations).

🚂 (Departure from 's-Hertogenbosch) ✆ 620 22 66 and 601 05 41 (Schiphol).

⚓ to Göteborg : Scandinavian Seaways Cie ✆ 611 66 15.

🛈 Stationsplein. ⊠ 1012 AB ✆ 626 64 44.

Bruxelles 204 – Düsseldorf 227 – Den Haag 60 – Luxembourg 419 – Rotterdam 76.

AMSTERDAM
CENTRE

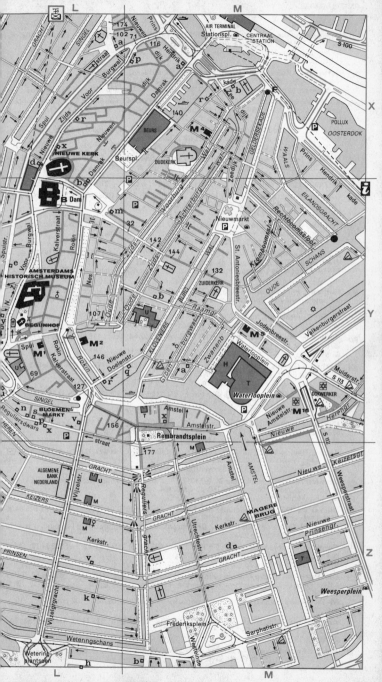

Centre

🏨🏨🏨 **Europe,** Nieuwe Doelenstraat 2, ⊠ 1012 CP, 𝒫 623 48 36, Telex 12081, Fax 624 29 62, ⇐,
⇔, 🖵 – |⧚| ⇔ 🆃🆅 ☎ 🅿 – 🔬 25-250. 🆀🅴 ⓞ 🅴 𝘝𝘐𝘚𝘈   LY   r
M see rest. **Excelsior** below – **Le Relais** a la carte 80/123 – ⌧ 29 – **91 rm** 375/750 –
½ P 325.

🏨🏨🏨 **Barbizon Palace,** Prins Hendrikkade 59, ⊠ 1012 AD, 𝒫 556 45 64, Telex 10187, Fax
624 33 53, ⇐ – |⧚| 🆅 🆃🆅 ☎ 🅿 – 🔬 25-210. 🆀🅴 ⓞ 🅴 𝘝𝘐𝘚𝘈   MX   b
M Vermeer (dinner only) a la carte 75/116 – ⌧ 30 – **268 rm** 440/520 – ½ P 336/388.

🏨🏨🏨 **Sonesta,** Kattengat 1, ⊠ 1012 SZ, 𝒫 621 22 23, Telex 17149, Fax 627 52 45, « Contemporary
art collection », ⇐ – |⧚| ⇔ 🆃🆅 ☎ 🅖 🔬 – 🔬 25-400. 🆀🅴 ⓞ 🅴 𝘝𝘐𝘚𝘈. ⅋ rest   LX   a
M a la carte 47/94 – ⌧ 30 – **425 rm** 355/415.

🏨🏨🏨 **Marriott,** Stadhouderskade 21, ⊠ 1054 ES, 𝒫 607 55 55, Telex 15087, Fax 607 55 11, ⇐ –
|⧚| 🆅 🆃🆅 ☎ 🅖 – 🔬 25-360. 🆀🅴 ⓞ 🅴 𝘝𝘐𝘚𝘈. ⅋ rest   JZ   p
M (dinner only) a la carte approx. 65 – ⌧ 33 – **395 rm** 425/500.

🏨🏨🏨 **Holiday Inn Crowne Plaza,** Nieuwe Zijds Voorburgwal 5, ⊠ 1012 RC, 𝒫 620 05 00,
Telex 15183, Fax 620 11 73, ⇐, 🖵 – |⧚| ⇔ rm 🆃🆅 ☎ & ⇔ – 🔬 25-260. 🆀🅴 ⓞ 🅴 𝘝𝘐𝘚𝘈.
⅋   MX   p
M 7-Seas (dinner only until 11 p.m.) a la carte 52/90 – ⌧ 28 – **270 rm** 325/525 – ½ P 390.

🏨🏨🏨 **SAS Royal** ⅌, Rusland 17, ⊠ 1012 CK, 𝒫 623 12 31, Telex 10365, Fax 520 82 00, ⇐ – |⧚|
⇔ rm 🆃🆅 ☎ & 🅖 – 🔬 25-180. 🆀🅴 ⓞ 🅴 𝘝𝘐𝘚𝘈. ⅋   MY   b
M a la carte 61/93 – **231 rm** ⌧ 435/485 – ½ P 298/332.

🏨🏨🏨 **Scandic Crown Victoria,** Damrak 1, ⊠ 1012 LG, 𝒫 623 42 55, Telex 16625, Fax 625 29 97,
⇐, 🖵 – |⧚| ⇔ rm 🆃🆅 rest 🆃🆅 ☎ & 🅖 – 🔬 25-250. 🆀🅴 ⓞ 🅴 𝘝𝘐𝘚𝘈. ⅋   MX   a
M a la carte 46/93 – ⌧ 33 – **321 rm** 230/375.

🏨🏨🏨 **Gd H. Krasnapolsky,** Dam 9, ⊠ 1012 JS, 𝒫 554 91 11, Telex 12262, Fax 622 86 07, ⇐ –
|⧚| ⇔ rm 🆃🆅 ☎ & 🅖 – 🔬 25-1500. 🆀🅴 ⓞ 🅴 𝘝𝘐𝘚𝘈. ⅋   LY   m
M Le Reflet d'Or (closed lunch Saturday and Sunday) a la carte 74/106 – **330 rm** ⌧
280/410.

🏨🏨🏨 **Pulitzer,** Prinsengracht 323, ⊠ 1016 GZ, 𝒫 523 52 35, Telex 16508, Fax 627 67 53, 🏛,
« Contemporary art collection », 🛳 – |⧚| ⇔ rm 🆃🆅 rest 🆃🆅 ☎ ⇔ – 🔬 25-160. 🆀🅴 ⓞ 🅴
𝘝𝘐𝘚𝘈   KY   r
M De Goudsbloem (closed 1 to 29 July, 1 to 6 January and lunch Saturday and Sunday)
(open until 11 p.m.) a la carte 73/108 – ⌧ 28 – **240 rm** 305/355.

🏨🏨 **Jolly Carlton,** Vijzelstraat 2, ⊠ 1017 HK, 𝒫 622 22 66, Telex 11670, Fax 626 61 83 – |⧚|
🆃🆅 rest 🆃🆅 ☎ 🅖 – 🔬 25-80. 🆀🅴 ⓞ 🅴 𝘝𝘐𝘚𝘈. ⅋ rest   LY   v
M a la carte 65/89 – ⌧ 35 – **219 rm** 280/500 – ½ P 268/478.

🏨🏨 **Barbizon Centre,** Stadhouderskade 7, ⊠ 1054 ES, 𝒫 685 13 51, Telex 12601, Fax 685 16 11,
⇐ – |⧚| 🆃🆅 ☎ ⇔ – 🔬 150. 🆀🅴 ⓞ 🅴 𝘝𝘐𝘚𝘈   JZ   c
M a la carte 67/107 – ⌧ 30 – **236 rm** 355/510 – ½ P 270/320.

🏨🏨 **American,** Leidsekade 97, ⊠ 1017 PN, 𝒫 624 53 22, Telex 12545, Fax 625 32 36, 🏛, ⇐ –
|⧚| 🆃🆅 ☎ – 🔬 80-200. 🆀🅴 ⓞ 🅴 𝘝𝘐𝘚𝘈   JKZ   v
M Café Américain a la carte 60/80 – ⌧ 29 – **188 rm** 310/435.

🏨🏨 **Capitool,** Nieuwe Zijds Voorburgwal 67, ⊠ 1012 RE, 𝒫 627 59 00, Telex 14494, Fax
623 89 32, ⇐ – |⧚| ⇔ rm 🆃🆅 ☎ & – 🔬 30-100. 🆀🅴 ⓞ 🅴 𝘝𝘐𝘚𝘈   LX   r
M (dinner only) a la carte 44/64 – **148 rm** ⌧ 245/290 – ½ P 218/285.

🏨🏨 **Ascot,** Damrak 95, ⊠ 1012 LP, 𝒫 626 00 66, Telex 16620, Fax 627 09 82 – |⧚| ⇔ rm 🆃🆅
☎ & – 🔬 25-70. 🆀🅴 ⓞ 🅴 𝘝𝘐𝘚𝘈. ⅋ rest   LY   b
M a la carte 60/88 – ⌧ 25 – **109 rm** 310/340 – ½ P 210/230.

🏨🏨 **Doelen,** Nieuwe Doelenstraat 24, ⊠ 1012 CP, 𝒫 622 07 22, Telex 14399, Fax 622 10 84, ⇐ –
|⧚| ⇔ rm 🆃🆅 rest 🆃🆅 ☎ – 🔬 25-150. 🆀🅴 ⓞ 🅴 𝘝𝘐𝘚𝘈   MY   q
M (dinner only) a la carte 58/80 – **85 rm** ⌧ 345.

🏨🏨 **Dikker en Thijs,** Prinsengracht 444, ⊠ 1017 KE, 𝒫 626 77 21, Telex 13161, Fax 625 89 86
– |⧚| 🆃🆅 ☎ ⇔ – 🔬 25. 🆀🅴 ⓞ 🅴 𝘝𝘐𝘚𝘈. ⅋ rest   KZ   s
M see rest. Dikker en Thijs below – **De Prinsenkelder** (dinner only until 11.30 p.m.) a la carte
57/101 – ⌧ 26 – **25 rm** 230/335.

🏨🏨 **Caransa,** Rembrandtsplein 19, ⊠ 1017 CT, 𝒫 622 94 55, Telex 13342, Fax 622 27 73, 🏛 –
|⧚| ⇔ rm 🆃🆅 ☎ – 🔬 30-150. 🆀🅴 ⓞ 🅴 𝘝𝘐𝘚𝘈   MY   x
M 41 – ⌧ 25 – **66 rm** 295/375.

🏨🏨 **Die Port van Cleve,** Nieuwe Zijds Voorburgwal 178, ⊠ 1012 SJ, 𝒫 624 48 60, Telex
13129, Fax 622 02 40, « Delft faiences in the restaurant » – |⧚| 🆃🆅 ☎ – 🔬 25-50. 🆀🅴 ⓞ 🅴
𝘝𝘐𝘚𝘈. ⅋   LX   d
M De Blauwe Parade (closed lunch Saturday and Sunday) 58/70 – **102 rm** ⌧ 165/310 –
½ P 235.

🏨 **Ambassade** without rest., Herengracht 341, ⊠ 1016 AZ, 𝒫 626 23 33, Telex 10158, Fax
624 53 21, ⇐ – |⧚| 🆃🆅 ☎. 🆀🅴 ⓞ 🅴 𝘝𝘐𝘚𝘈   KY   f
47 rm ⌧ 180/240.

🏨 **Arthur Frommer** without rest., Noorderstraat 46, ⊠ 1017 TV, 𝒫 622 03 28, Telex 14047,
Fax 620 32 08 – |⧚| 🆃🆅 ☎ 🅖. 🆀🅴 ⓞ 🅴 𝘝𝘐𝘚𝘈   LZ   k
⌧ 18 – **90 rm** 180/230.

🏠 **Rembrandt** without rest., Herengracht 255, ⊠ 1016 BJ, ℰ 622 17 27, Telex 15424, Fax 625 06 30 – 📱 😣⇔ 📺 ☎. 🕮 ⓞ 🗲 *VISA*
KY **p**
🖵 25 – **111 rm** 265/335.

🏠 **Estheréa** without rest., Singel 305, ⊠ 1012 WJ, ℰ 624 51 46, Telex 14019, Fax 623 90 01 –
📱 📺 ☎. 🕮 ⓞ 🗲 *VISA*. ⅏
KY **t**
75 rm 🖵 250/250.

🏠 **De Roode Leeuw,** Damrak 93, ⊠ 1012 LP, ℰ 624 03 96, Telex 10569, Fax 620 47 16 – 📱
≡ rest 📺 ☎ – 🔏 25-50. 🕮 ⓞ 🗲 *VISA*
LXY **b**
M 40 – **78 rm** 🖵 150/235 – ½ P 148/157.

🏠 **Owl** without rest., Roemer Visscherstraat 1, ⊠ 1054 EV, ℰ 618 94 84, Telex 13360, Fax 618 94 41 – 📱 📺 ☎. 🕮 🗲 *VISA*. ⅏
JZ **e**
34 rm 🖵 130/175.

🏠 **Nicolaas Witsen** without rest., Nicolaas Witsenstraat 6, ⊠ 1017 ZH, ℰ 626 65 46, Fax 620 51 13 – 📱 📺 ☎. 🕮 ⓞ 🗲 *VISA*. ⅏
MZ **b**
31 rm 🖵 100/185.

🏠 **Wiechmann** without rest., Prinsengracht 328, ⊠ 1016 HX, ℰ 626 33 21 – 📺 ☎
KY **s**
36 rm 🖵 135/200.

🏠 **Asterisk** without rest., Den Texstraat 16, ⊠ 1017 ZA, ℰ 626 23 96, Fax 638 27 90 – 📺 ☎.
🗲 *VISA*
LZ **h**
26 rm 🖵 55/169.

🏠🏠🏠🏠 **Dikker en Thijs** 1st floor, Prinsengracht 444, ⊠ 1017 KE, ℰ 626 77 21, Telex 13161, Fax 625 89 86 – 🕮 ⓞ 🗲 *VISA*. ⅏
KZ **s**
closed Sunday and 28 July-12 August – **M** (dinner only) 90/105.

🏠🏠🏠🏠 ✿ **Excelsior** - (at H. Europe), Nieuwe Doelenstraat 2, ⊠ 1012 CP, ℰ 623 48 36, Telex 12081, Fax 624 29 62, ≤, 🌱 – ≡. 🕮 ⓞ 🗲 *VISA*
LY **r**
closed Saturday lunch – **M** a la carte 105/145
Spec. Langoustines au curry et pommes à la crème, Feuillantine de turbot, Perdreau choucroute à la crème de foie d'oie (September-January).

🏠🏠🏠 **Martinn** 12th floor, De Ruyterkade 7 (harbour building), ⊠ 1013 AA, ℰ 625 62 77, Fax 638 56 29, ≤ – ≡ **P**. 🕮 ⓞ 🗲 *VISA*
closed Saturday and Sunday – **M** a la carte 60/87.

🏠🏠🏠 **Radèn Mas,** Stadhouderskade 6, ⊠ 1054 ES, ℰ 685 40 41, Fax 685 39 81, Indonesian cuisine, « Exotic decor » – ≡. 🕮 ⓞ 🗲 *VISA*
JZ **b**
closed lunch Saturday and Sunday – **M** a la carte 61/110.

🏠🏠 **Dynasty,** Reguliersdwarsstraat 30, ⊠ 1017 BM, ℰ 626 84 00, Fax 622 20 38, 🌱, Oriental cuisine – ≡. 🕮 ⓞ 🗲 *VISA*. ⅏
LY **p**
closed Tuesday – **M** (dinner only until 11 p.m.) a la carte 55/95.

🏠🏠 **'t Swarte Schaep** 1st floor, Korte Leidsedwarsstraat 24, ⊠ 1017 RC, ℰ 622 30 21, Fax 624 82 68, Open until 11 p.m., « 17C old Dutch interior » – ≡. 🕮 ⓞ 🗲 *VISA*
KZ **d**
closed 25, 26 and 31 December and 1 January – **M** a la carte 90/140.

🏠🏠 **Les Quatre Canetons,** Prinsengracht 1111, ⊠ 1017 JJ, ℰ 624 63 07, Fax 638 45 99 – 🕮 ⓞ 🗲 *VISA*
MZ **d**
closed Saturday lunch, Sunday, Easter, Whitsun and 31 December-1 January – **M** 83/105.

🏠🏠 **Tout Court,** Runstraat 13, ⊠ 1016 GJ, ℰ 625 86 37 – 🕮 ⓞ 🗲 *VISA*
KY **m**
closed Sunday, Monday and 23 July-18 August – **M** (dinner only until 11.30 p.m.) 50/70.

🏠🏠 **Sichuan Food,** Reguliersdwarsstraat 35, ⊠ 1017 BK, ℰ 626 93 27, Chinese cuisine – ≡.
🕮 ⓞ 🗲 *VISA*
LY **s**
closed Wednesday – **M** (dinner only until 11.30 p.m.) a la carte 55/85.

🏠🏠 **De Oesterbar,** Leidseplein 10, ⊠ 1017 PT, ℰ 623 29 88, Seafood, open until midnight –
≡. 🕮 ⓞ 🗲. ⅏
KZ **y**
M 40/80.

🏠🏠 **Treasure,** Nieuwe Zijds Voorburgwal 115, ⊠ 1012 RH, ℰ 623 40 61, Fax 645 39 17, Chinese cuisine – ≡. ⅏
LX **x**
M a la carte 40/73.

🏠🏠 **Manchurian,** Leidseplein 10a, ⊠ 1017 PT, ℰ 623 13 30, Fax 622 30 38, Oriental cuisine, open until 11 p.m. – ≡. 🕮 ⓞ 🗲 *VISA*. ⅏
KZ **y**
closed late December-early February – **M** a la carte 43/108.

🏠🏠 **Les Trois Neufs,** Prinsengracht 999, ⊠ 1017 KM, ℰ 622 90 44 – 🕮 ⓞ 🗲 *VISA*
LZ **v**
closed Monday, mid July-mid August and 27 December-2 January – **M** (dinner only) a la carte 55/76.

🏠🏠 **Le Pêcheur,** Reguliersdwarsstraat 32, ⊠ 1017 BM, ℰ 624 31 21, Fax 624 31 21, 🌱, Seafood, open until 11 p.m. – 🕮 ⓞ 🗲 *VISA*. ⅏
LY **x**
closed 25 and 31 December – **M** a la carte 69/86.

🏠🏠 **Lana Thai,** Warmoesstraat 10, ⊠ 1012 JD, ℰ 624 21 79, Thaï cuisine – 🕮 ⓞ 🗲 *VISA*. ⅏
MX **y**
M (dinner only) a la carte 53/88.

🏠🏠 **La Camargue,** Reguliersdwarsstraat 7, ⊠ 1017 BJ, ℰ 623 93 52, Open until 11 p.m. – ≡.
🕮 ⓞ 🗲 *VISA*. ⅏
LY **n**
closed 31 December and 1 January – **M** 50.

XX **Het Amsterdamse Wijnhuis,** Reguliersdwarsstraat 23, ✉ 1017 BJ, ℰ 623 42 59 – AE O E LY **n**
closed Saturday lunch, Sunday, Monday and last week December-first week January – **M** 50/68.

XX **Sea Palace,** Oosterdokskade 8, ✉ 1011 AE, ℰ 626 47 77, Telex 14693, Fax 620 42 66, Asian cuisine, « Floating restaurant with ≤ town » – AE O E VISA. ✻
M a la carte approx. 65.

XX ✿ **Christophe** (Royer), Leliegracht 46, ✉ 1015 DH, ℰ 625 08 07 – ▤. AE O E VISA KX **a**
closed 4 to 25 August, 31 December-2 January, Sunday and Monday – **M** (dinner only until 11 p.m.) a la carte 85/130
Spec. Nage de St-Jacques et crevettes à l'orange, Rougets grillés aux artichauts "barigoule", Pigeonneau à la marocaine.

XX **Edo,** Dam 9, ✉ 1012 SJ, ℰ 554 60 96, Fax 671 23 99, Chinese cuisine, teppan-yaki – AE O E VISA. ✻ LY **m**
M 55/100.

X **Le Provençal,** Weteringschans 91, ✉ 1017 RZ, ℰ 623 96 19 – ▤. AE O E VISA KZ **b**
M 55/80.

X **Tom Yam,** Staalstraat 22, ✉ 1011 JM, ℰ 622 95 33, Thaï cuisine – AE O E VISA MY **a**
closed Monday and 25 and 31 December – **M** (dinner only) a la carte 45/76.

X **Bistro La Forge,** Korte Leidsedwarsstraat 26, ✉ 1017 RC, ℰ 624 00 95 – AE O E VISA
closed 24, 31 December and 1 January – **M** (dinner only) 40/50. KZ **d**

X **Lucius,** Spuistraat 247, ✉ 1012 VP, ℰ 624 18 31, Fax 627 61 53, Seafood – AE O E VISA
closed 31 December – **M** (dinner only until 11 p.m.) a la carte 53/78. LY **e**

X **Haesje Claes,** Spuistraat 273, ✉ 1012 RV, ℰ 624 99 98, Fax 627 48 17, « Typical atmosphere » – AE O E VISA. ✻ LY **y**
closed lunch Sunday and Bank Holidays – **M** a la carte 40/60.

X **Kantjil,** Spuistraat 291, ✉ 1012 VS, ℰ 620 09 94, Fax 623 21 66, ☂, Pub-rest., Indonesian cuisine, open until 11 p.m. – ⇔. AE O E VISA. ✻ LY **y**
closed 4 May – **M** a la carte 40/57.

X **Oshima,** Prinsengracht 411, ✉ 1016 HM, ℰ 625 09 96, Japanese cuisine – AE O E VISA. ✻ KY **e**
closed Monday – **M** (dinner only) a la carte 40/64.

South and West Quarters

Okura, Ferdinand Bolstraat 333, ✉ 1072 LH, ℰ 678 71 11, Telex 16182, Fax 671 23 44, ≘s – |♣| ▤ TV ☎ ⇔ P – 🅰 25-600. AE O E VISA. ✻
M see rest. **Ciel Bleu** below – **Yamazato** (Japanese cuisine) 100/150 – ☕ 30 – **370 rm** 430/480.

Garden, Dijsselhofplantsoen 7, ✉ 1077 BJ, ℰ 664 21 21, Telex 15453, Fax 679 93 56 – |♣| ⇔ TV ☎ P – 🅰 25-150. AE O E VISA
M see rest. **De Kersentuin** below – ☕ 30 – **97 rm** 325/410.

Apollo, Apollolaan 2, ✉ 1077 BA, ℰ 673 59 22, Telex 14084, Fax 673 97 71, ☂, « Terrace with ≤ canal » – |♣| ⇔ rm TV ☎ P – 🅰 25-200. AE O E VISA. ✻ rest
M (open until 11 p.m.) a la carte 85/122 – ☕ 30 – **220 rm** 325/435 – ½ P 405/525.

Hilton, Apollolaan 138, ✉ 1077 BG, ℰ 678 07 80, Telex 11025, Fax 662 66 88 – |♣| ⇔ rm ▤ rest TV ☎ P – 🅰 25-325. AE O E VISA. ✻ rest
M a la carte 64/90 – ☕ 32 – **270 rm** 390/610.

Altea, Joan Muyskenweg 10, ✉ 1096 CJ, ℰ 685 81 81, Telex 13382, Fax 694 87 35, ≘s – |♣| ⇔ rm ▤ rest TV ☎ ♿ P – 🅰 25-500. AE O E VISA. ✻
M a la carte 49/78 – **178 rm** ☕ 195/225.

Novotel, Europaboulevard 10, ✉ 1083 AD, ℰ 541 11 23, Telex 13375, Fax 646 28 23 – |♣| ⇔ rm TV ☎ P – 🅰 25-300. AE O E VISA
M (open until midnight) a la carte 55/86 – ☕ 23 – **600 rm** 225/255 – ½ P 285.

Memphis without rest., De Lairessestraat 87, ✉ 1071 NX, ℰ 673 31 41, Telex 12450, Fax 673 73 12 – |♣| TV ☎ – 🅰 25-45. AE O E VISA
74 rm ☕ 280/340.

Cok Hotels, Koninginneweg 34, ✉ 1075 CZ, ℰ 664 61 11 – |♣| TV ☎ – 🅰 25-80. AE O E VISA
M a la carte approx. 50 – **159 rm** ☕ 140/190.

Toro ⛭ without rest., Koningslaan 64, ✉ 1075 AG, ℰ 673 72 23, Fax 675 00 31 – |♣| TV ☎. AE O E VISA
22 rm ☕ 145/180.

Jan Luyken without rest., Jan Luykenstraat 58, ✉ 1071 CS, ℰ 573 07 30, Telex 16254, Fax 676 38 41 – |♣| TV ☎ – 🅰 25-150. AE O E VISA. ✻ JZ **x**
63 rm ☕ 260/290.

Borgmann ⛭ without rest., Koningslaan 48, ✉ 1075 AE, ℰ 673 52 52, Fax 676 25 80 – |♣| TV ☎. AE O E VISA. ✻
15 rm ☕ 110/180.

🏨 **Apollofirst,** Apollolaan 123, ⊠ 1077 AP, 𝄐 673 03 33, Telex 13446, Fax 675 03 48, 🛋 – ▯
▤ rest 📺 ☎. 🄰🄴 ⓪ 🄴 *VISA*. 🛠 rest
M *(closed Sunday)* a la carte 55/89 – **40 rm** ⊏ 225/250.

🏨 **Delphi** without rest., Apollolaan 105, ⊠ 1077 AN, 𝄐 679 51 52, Telex 16659, Fax 675 29 41
– ▯ 📺 ☎. 🄰🄴 ⓪ 🄴 *VISA*
closed 24 December-2 January – **50 rm** ⊏ 150/250.

🏨 **Zandbergen** without rest., Willemsparkweg 205, ⊠ 1071 HB, 𝄐 676 93 21, Fax 676 18 60 –
📺 ☎. 🄰🄴 ⓪ 🄴 *VISA*
17 rm ⊏ 100/185.

🏨 **Bastion Zuid-West** without rest., Nachtwachtlaan 11, ⊠ 1058 EV, 𝄐 669 16 21, Fax
669 16 31 – 📺 ☎. 🄰🄴 ⓪ 🄴 *VISA*. 🛠
⊏ 13 – **40 rm** 89/105.

XXX ✿ **De Kersentuin** - (at H. Garden), Dijsselhofplantsoen 7, ⊠ 1077 BJ, 𝄐 664 21 21, Telex
15453, Fax 679 93 56 – ⓟ 🄰🄴 ⓪ 🄴 *VISA*. 🛠
closed Sunday lunch, Sunday, 31 December and 1 January – **M** a la carte 105/140
Spec. Escargots, fritots d'anguille et magret à la crème d'ail, Raviolis de truffes et carpaccio de canette au
romarin, Poularde de Malines en demi-deuil à la moutarde régionale.

XXX **Ciel Bleu** 23rd floor - (at H. Okura), Ferdinand Bolstraat 333, ⊠ 1072 LH, 𝄐 678 71 11,
Telex 16182, Fax 671 23 44, ≤ town – ▤ ⓟ. 🄰🄴 ⓪ 🄴 *VISA*. 🛠
M (dinner only until 11 p.m.) 75/95.

XXX **Parkrest. Rosarium,** Amstelpark 1, Europaboulevard, ⊠ 1083 HZ, 𝄐 644 40 85, Fax
646 60 04, 🛋, « Flowered park » – ⓟ 🄰🄴 ⓪ 🄴 *VISA*
closed Sunday – **M** a la carte 88/121.

XX ✿ **De Trechter** (de Wit), Hobbemakade 63, ⊠ 1071 XL, 𝄐 671 12 63 – 🄰🄴 ⓪ 🄴. 🛠
closed Sunday, Monday, Bank Holidays, 14 July-7 August and 31 December-15 January –
M (dinner only, booking essential) a la carte 94/116
Spec. Terrine d'anguille au vert aux tomates confites (April-Nov.), Terrine de foie gras d'oie, filet de bœuf et
persil, Côte de porc rôtie aux poireaux et à l'ail.

XX ✿ **Halvemaan,** Van Leyenberglaan 20 (Gijsbrecht van Aemstelpark), ⊠ 1082 GM,
𝄐 644 03 48, Fax 644 17 77, ≤, « Terrace with ≤ private lake » – ⓟ. 🄰🄴 ⓪ 🄴 *VISA*. 🛠
closed Saturday lunch, Sunday and 25 December-2 January – **M** a la carte 95/125
Spec. Salade de boudin noir, Sole vapeur aux gingembre, ail et oignons verts, Soupe froide de fruits rouges à
la menthe.

XX ✿ **De Graaf** 1st floor, Emmalaan 25, ⊠ 1075 AT, 𝄐 662 48 84, Fax 675 60 91 – 🄰🄴 ⓪ 🄴 *VISA*.
🛠
closed Sunday – **M** a la carte 86/123
Spec. Pâté de foie d'oie au ris de veau fumé, Canette rôtie au gingembre, Pâtisseries.

XX **Bartholdy,** Van Baerlestraat 35, ⊠ 1071 AP, 𝄐 662 26 55, 🛋 – ▤. 🄰🄴 🄴 *VISA*
M a la carte 67/106.

XX **Le Garage,** Ruysdaelstraat 54, ⊠ 1071 XE, 𝄐 679 71 76, Fax 662 22 49 – 🄰🄴 ⓪ 🄴 *VISA*
M 55/113.

XX **Vivaldi's,** Van Baerlestraat 49, ⊠ 1071 AP, 𝄐 679 88 88, 🛋 – 🄰🄴 ⓪ 🄴
closed Monday and 1 to 21 July – **M** (dinner only until 11 p.m.) a la carte 55/76.

XX **Beddington's,** Roelof Hartstraat 6, ⊠ 1071 VH, 𝄐 676 52 01 – 🄰🄴 ⓪ 🄴 *VISA*. 🛠
closed Sunday and lunch Saturday and Monday – **M** a la carte 64/83.

XX **Keyzer,** Van Baerlestraat 96, ⊠ 1071 BB, 𝄐 671 14 41, Fax 673 73 53 – 🄰🄴 ⓪ 🄴 *VISA*.
🛠
closed Sunday and Bank Holidays – **M** 55.

XX **Het Bosch,** Jollenpad 10 (by Amstelveenseweg), ⊠ 1081 KC, 𝄐 644 58 00, Fax 644 19 64,
≤, 🛋, « Lakeside setting terrace » – ▤ ⓟ. 🄰🄴 ⓪ 🄴 *VISA*. 🛠
closed Saturday lunch – **M** a la carte 68/103.

X **Ravel,** Gelderlandplein 2, ⊠ 1082 LA, 𝄐 644 16 43, Fax 642 86 84, Pub-rest. – ▤. 🄰🄴 ⓪ 🄴
VISA
closed Sunday lunch – **M** 55.

X **Brasserie Van Baerle,** Van Baerlestraat 158, ⊠ 1071 BG, 𝄐 679 15 32, 🛋, Pub-rest.,
open until 11 p.m. – 🄰🄴 ⓪ 🄴 *VISA*
closed Saturday and 25 December-1 January – **M** 53/70.

X **Oriënt,** Van Baerlestraat 21, ⊠ 1071 AN, 𝄐 673 49 58, Indonesian cuisine – ▤. 🄰🄴 ⓪ 🄴
                                                                                    JZ **q**
closed 27 to 31 December – **M** (dinner only) a la carte 40/73.

North

🏨 **Galaxy,** Distelkade 21, ⊠ 1031 XP, 𝄐 634 43 66, Telex 18607, Fax 636 03 45 – ▯ 📺 ☎ ⓟ
– 🛠 25-250. 🄰🄴 ⓪ 🄴 *VISA*
M *(closed lunch Saturday and Sunday)* a la carte 52/70 – **280 rm** ⊏ 195/230.

🏨 **Bastion Noord** without rest., Rode Kruisstraat 28 (by Nieuwe Purmerweg), ⊠ 1025 KN,
𝄐 632 31 31, Fax 634 44 96 – 📺 ☎ ⓟ. 🄰🄴 ⓪ 🄴 *VISA*. 🛠
⊏ 13 – **40 rm** 89/105.

Environs

at Schiphol (international airport) Ⓒ Haarlemmermeer pop. 93 427 – ❸ 0 20 :

🏨🏨 **Hilton International,** Herbergierstraat 1, ✉ 1118 ZK, ℰ 603 45 67, Telex 15186, Fax 648 09 17, 🚗, Ⓛ – ◫ ╳◟ rm 🗐 🗹 ☎ & Ⓟ – 🔏 25-110. ◭ ⓞ Ⓔ 𝘝𝘐𝘚𝘈. ⅝ rest
M a la carte 72/111 – ⇔ 31 – **275 rm** 395/570.

XX **Aviorama** 3rd floor, Sc`hipholweg 1, ✉ 1118 AA, ℰ 604 11 05, Fax 648 45 83, ⇐ – ▤. ◭
ⓞ Ⓔ 𝘝𝘐𝘚𝘈. ⅝
M a la carte 54/76.

by motorway The Hague (A 4) – ❸ 0 20 :

🏨🏨 **Pullman,** Oude Haagseweg 20, ✉ 1066 BW, ℰ 617 90 05, Telex 15524, Fax 615 90 27 – ⃻
╳◟ rm 🗐 rest 🗹 ☎ & Ⓟ – 🔏 25-250. ◭ ⓞ Ⓔ 𝘝𝘐𝘚𝘈. ⅝
M a la carte 53/79 – **151 rm** ⇔ 215/245 – ½ P 250/280.

🏨🏨 **Barbizon,** Kruisweg 495, ✉ 2132 NA Hoofddorp (15 km), ℰ (0 2503) 6 44 22, Telex 74546,
Fax (0 2503) 3 79 66, 🍴, 🚗 – ⃻ ╳◟ rm 🗐 🗹 ☎ & Ⓟ – 🔏 25-500. ◭ ⓞ Ⓔ 𝘝𝘐𝘚𝘈. ⅝
M *(closed lunch Saturday and Sunday)* a la carte approx. 85 – ⇔ 28 – **244 rm** 350/395 –
½ P 388.

🏨 **Ibis,** Schipholweg 181, ✉ 1171 PK Badhoevedorp, ℰ (0 2968) 9 12 34, Telex 16491, Fax
(0 2968) 9 23 67 – ⃻ 🗹 ☎ Ⓟ – 🔏 25-250. ◭ ⓞ Ⓔ 𝘝𝘐𝘚𝘈
M (open until 11 p.m.) a la carte 40/90 – ⇔ 20 – **508 rm** 155/200 – ½ P 185.

Amstelveen Noord-Holland 𝟰𝟬𝟴 ⑳ ㉗ – pop. 69 505 – ❸ 0 20 – 11 km.

XXX ❀ **Molen ''De Dikkert'',** Amsterdamseweg 104a, ✉ 1182 HG, ℰ 641 13 78, Fax 647 54 67,
« 17C windmill » – Ⓟ. ◭ ⓞ Ⓔ 𝘝𝘐𝘚𝘈
closed Saturday lunch, Sunday except Bank Holidays and last week July-first 2 weeks August
– **M** a la carte 108/137
Spec. Brandade glacée de turbot, Foie gras de canard braisé enrobé de chou, Râble de lièvre aux pruneaux
sauce poivrade (15 Oct.-Dec.).

Haarlem Noord-Holland 𝟰𝟬𝟴 ⑩ – pop. 149 198 – ❸ 0 23 – 24 km.

at Overveen W : 4 km Ⓒ Bloemendaal pop. 17 412 – ❸ 0 23 :

XXX ❀❀ **De Bokkedoorns,** Zeeweg 53, ✉ 2051 EB, ℰ 26 36 00, Fax 27 31 43, 🍴, « Terrace
with ⇐ dunes » – ▤ Ⓟ. ◭ ⓞ Ⓔ 𝘝𝘐𝘚𝘈
closed Monday, Saturday lunch, 5, 24 and 31 December-5 January – **M** a la carte 95/142
Spec. Panaché d'entrées maison, Ragoût de homard, jus aux herbes, Selle d'agneau, sauce de légumes au
curry.

Hoorn Noord-Holland 𝟰𝟬𝟴 ⑩⑪ – pop. 56 474 – ❸ 0 2290 – 43 km.

XX ❀❀ **De Oude Rosmolen** (Fonk), Duinsteeg 1, ✉ 4551 ER, ℰ 1 47 52, Fax 1 49 38 – ▤. ◭
ⓞ Ⓔ 𝘝𝘐𝘚𝘈. ⅝
closed Thursday, 18 August, 2 to 19 September and 27 December-2 January – **M** (dinner
only, booking essential) a la carte 96/128
Spec. Profiterolles à la mousse de foie gras, Pintadeau fondant, sauce fleurette truffée, Pâtisseries maison.

Zaandam Noord-Holland Ⓒ Zaanstad pop. 129 653 𝟰𝟬𝟴 ⑩ – ❸ 0 75 – 16 km.

XXX ❀ **De Hoop op d'Swarte Walvis,** Kalverringdijk 15 (Zaanse Schans), ✉ 1509 BT,
ℰ 16 55 40, Fax 16 24 76, 🍴, « 18C residence in a museum village » – ╳◟ Ⓟ. ◭ ⓞ Ⓔ
𝘝𝘐𝘚𝘈
closed 27 December-1 January, Saturday lunch January-March and Sunday – **M** a la carte
95/128
Spec. Navarin de homard à l'anis, Foie gras d'oie et suprêmes de cailles au miel, St-Jacques et ris de veau aux
gingembre et pommes.

The HAGUE (Den HAAG or 's-GRAVENHAGE) Zuid-Holland 𝟰𝟬𝟴 ⑨ – pop. 443 845 – ❸ 0 70.

See : Scheveningen★★ – Binnenhof★ : The Knights' Room★ (Ridderzaal) JV **A** – Hofvijver (Court
pool) ⇐★ JV – Lange Voorhout★ JV – Panorama Mesdag★ HV **B** – Madurodam★.

Museums : Mauritshuis★★★ JV **D** – Municipal★★ (Gemeentemuseum) – Mesdag★ HU **M²**.

⛳ at Wassenaar N : 4 km, Gr. Haesebroekseweg 22 ℰ (0 1751) 7 96 07 - ⛳ at Wassenaar, Hoge
klei 1 ℰ (0 1751) 1 78 46.

✈ Amsterdam-Schiphol NE : 37 km ℰ 364 80 30, (0 20) 601 09 66 (information) and (0 20)
674 77 47 (reservations) – Rotterdam-Zestienhoven SE : 17 km ℰ (0 10) 415 76 33 (information)
and 437 27 45, 415 54 30 (reservations).

🚂(departs from 's-Hertogenbosch) ℰ 347 16 81.

🅘 Kon. Julianaplein 30, ✉ 2595 AA, ℰ 354 62 00.

Amsterdam 55 – Brussels 182 – Rotterdam 24 – Delft 13.

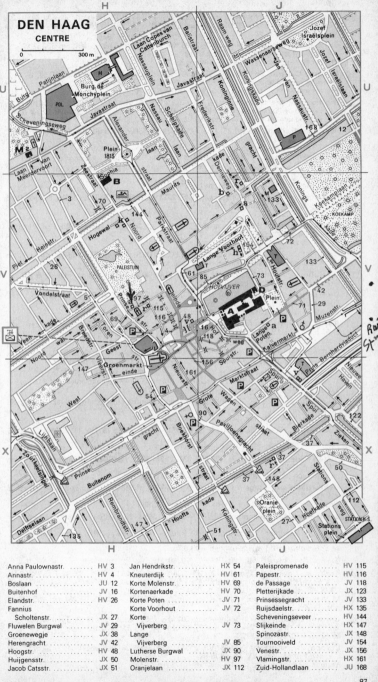

🏨🏨 **Des Indes,** Lange Voorhout 54, ⊠ 2514 EG, ℰ 363 29 32, Telex 31196, Fax 345 17 21, « Late 19C residence » – 🛗 ⁺⁺ rm 🗏 rest 📺 ☎ 🅿 – 🍴 250. 🆎 ⚫ 🅴 𝒱𝒾𝒮𝒜. ⚡ rest   JV **s**
M Le Restaurant a la carte 72/111 – ⌷ 33 – **77 rm** 360/460.

🏨🏨 **Sofitel,** Koningin Julianaplein 35, ⊠ 2595 AA, ℰ 381 49 01, Telex 34001, Fax 382 59 27 – 🛗 ⁺⁺ rm 🗏 🗏 📺 ☎ – 🍴 45-150. 🆎 ⚫ 🅴 𝒱𝒾𝒮𝒜
M a la carte approx. 90 – ⌷ 28 – **144 rm** 255/300.

🏨🏨 **Pullman Central,** Spui 180, ⊠ 2511 BW, ℰ 363 67 00, Telex 32000, Fax 363 93 98, ⩘ – 🛗 ⁺⁺ rm 🗏 rest 📺 ☎ ♿ 🅿 – 🍴 110. 🆎 ⚫ 🅴 𝒱𝒾𝒮𝒜   JX **v**
M a la carte 51/91 – **159 rm** ⌷ 220/260 – ½ P 255.

🏨🏨 **Promenade,** van Stolkweg 1, ⊠ 2585 JL, ℰ 352 51 61, Telex 31162, Fax 354 10 46, ⩗, « Collection of Dutch modern paintings » – 🛗 🗏 rest 📺 ☎ 🅿 – 🍴 125. 🆎 ⚫ 🅴 𝒱𝒾𝒮𝒜
M La Cigogne (closed Saturday and Sunday) a la carte 75/106 – ⌷ 30 – **101 rm** 275/300.

🏨🏨 ❀ **Corona,** Buitenhof 42, ⊠ 2513 AH, ℰ 363 79 30, Telex 31418, Fax 361 57 85 – 🛗 🗏 rest 📺 ☎ 🅿 – 🍴 100. 🆎 ⚫ 🅴 𝒱𝒾𝒮𝒜   HV **v**
M (closed last 2 weeks July) a la carte 100/140 – ⌷ 15 – **23 rm** 230/455 – ½ P 210/333
Spec. Côtelettes de saumon "Corona". Fricassée de ris de veau et petits gris aux truffes.

🏨🏨 **Bel Air,** Johan de Wittlaan 30, ⊠ 2517 JR, ℰ 350 20 21, Telex 31444, Fax 351 26 82, ⩗, 🖽 – 🛗 🗏 📺 ☎ 🅿 – 🍴 250. 🆎 ⚫ 🅴 𝒱𝒾𝒮𝒜
M a la carte 42/91 – ⌷ 20 – **350 rm** 190/240.

🏨🏨 **Parkhotel** without rest., Molenstraat 53, ⊠ 2513 BJ, ℰ 362 43 71, Telex 33005, Fax 361 45 25 – 🛗 🗏 rest 📺 ☎ 🅿 – 🍴 100. 🆎 ⚫ 🅴 𝒱𝒾𝒮𝒜   HV **a**
114 rm ⌷ 133/225.

🏨 **Paleis** without rest., Molenstraat 26, ⊠ 2513 BL, ℰ 362 46 21, Telex 34349, Fax 361 45 33, ⩘ – 🛗 📺 ☎ 🅿 – 🍴 100. 🆎 ⚫ 🅴 𝒱𝒾𝒮𝒜   HV **r**
⌷ 16 – **20 rm** 149/209.

XXX **Saur** 1st floor, Lange Voorhout 51, ⊠ 2514 EC, ℰ 346 33 44 – 🗏. 🆎 ⚫ 🅴 𝒱𝒾𝒮𝒜. ⚡   JV **h**
closed Sunday and Bank Holidays – **M** a la carte 82/133.

XXX **Da Roberto,** Noordeinde 196, ⊠ 2514 GS, ℰ 346 49 77, Italian cuisine – 🆎 ⚫ 🅴 𝒱𝒾𝒮𝒜. ⚡
closed Tuesday – **M** a la carte 72/93.   HV **k**

XXX **De Hoogwerf,** Zijdelaan 20 (by N 44), ⊠ 2594 BV, ℰ 347 55 14, Fax 381 95 96, �´, « 17C farmhouse, garden » – 🆎 ⚫ 🅴 𝒱𝒾𝒮𝒜
closed Monday and Bank Holidays except 25 and 26 December – **M** 75/88.

XXX **Royal Dynasty,** Noordeinde 123, ⊠ 2514 GG, ℰ 365 25 98, Asian cuisine, open until 11.30 p.m. – 🗏. 🆎 ⚫ 🅴 𝒱𝒾𝒮𝒜   HV **k**
closed Monday – **M** a la carte 52/75.

XX **La Grande Bouffe,** Maziestraat 10, ⊠ 2514 GT, ℰ 365 42 74 – 🆎 ⚫ 🅴 𝒱𝒾𝒮𝒜   HV **k**
closed lunch Saturday and Sunday, Monday and 22 July-15 August – **M** 60/80.

XX **Jean Martin,** Groenewegje 115, ⊠ 2515 LP, ℰ 380 28 95 – 🗏. 🆎 ⚫ 🅴 𝒱𝒾𝒮𝒜   JX **r**
closed Sunday, Monday and 22 December-1 January – **M** (dinner only until 11.30 p.m.) 50/83.

XX **Shirasagi,** Spui 170, ⊠ 2511 BW, ℰ 346 47 00, Japanese cuisine, teppan-yaki – 🗏 🅿. 🆎 ⚫ 🅴 𝒱𝒾𝒮𝒜. ⚡   JX **v**
closed lunch Saturday and Sunday – **M** 65/120.

XX **Aubergerie,** Nieuwe Schoolstraat 19, ⊠ 2514 HT, ℰ 364 80 70, Fax 360 73 38 – 🆎 ⚫ 🅴 𝒱𝒾𝒮𝒜   JV **b**
closed Tuesday – **M** (dinner only until 11 p.m.) 60/80.

XX **Radèn Ajoe,** Lange Poten 31, ⊠ 2511 CM, ℰ 364 56 13, Fax 364 45 92, Indonesian cuisine – 🆎 ⚫ 🅴 𝒱𝒾𝒮𝒜   JV **a**
closed lunch Saturday and Sunday – **M** a la carte 57/86.

X **Oesterbar-Saur,** Lange Voorhout 47, ⊠ 2514 EC, ℰ 346 25 65, Seafood – 🗏. 🆎 ⚫ 🅴 𝒱𝒾𝒮𝒜. ⚡   JV **h**
closed Sunday and Bank Holidays – **M** a la carte 67/98.

X **Les Ombrelles,** Hooistraat 4a, ⊠ 2514 BM, ℰ 365 87 89, Seafood, open until 11 p.m. – 🆎 ⚫ 🅴 𝒱𝒾𝒮𝒜   JV **r**
closed 24 December-2 January and lunch Saturday and Sunday – **M** a la carte 50/84.

at Scheveningen 🅲 's-Gravenhage – ❀ 0 70.

🛈 Gevers Deijnootweg 126, ⊠ 2586 BP, ℰ 354 62 00.

🏨🏨 **Kurhaus,** Gevers Deijnootplein 30, ⊠ 2586 CK, ℰ 352 00 52, Telex 33295, Fax 350 09 11, ⩗, « Former late 19C concert hall », ⩘, 🖽 – 🛗 ⁺⁺ rm 🗏 rest 📺 ☎ ♿ – 🍴 25-400. 🆎 ⚫ 🅴 𝒱𝒾𝒮𝒜. ⚡ rest
M Kandinsky (open until 11.30 p.m.) a la carte 92/131 – ⌷ 28 – **231 rm** 260/375 – ½ P 215/265.

🏨🏨 **Carlton Beach,** Gevers Deijnootweg 201, ⊠ 2586 HZ, ℰ 354 14 14, Telex 33687, Fax 352 00 20, ⩗, �´, ⩘, 🖽 – 🛗 🗏 rest 📺 ☎ 🅿 – 🍴 100. 🆎 ⚫ 🅴 𝒱𝒾𝒮𝒜
M 40/50 – **182 rm** ⌷ 205/285.

🏨🏨 **Europa,** Zwolsestraat 2, ⊠ 2587 VJ, ℰ 351 26 51, Telex 33138, Fax 350 64 73, ⩘, 🖽 – 🛗 ⁺⁺ rm 📺 ☎ 🅿 – 🍴 400. 🆎 ⚫ 🅴 𝒱𝒾𝒮𝒜
M (dinner only until 11 p.m.) 43 – ⌷ 26 – **173 rm** 200/285.

ᨆ **Flora Beach,** Gevers Deijnootweg 63, ⊠ 2586 BJ, 𝒫 354 33 00, Telex 32123, Fax 352 39 16, ⇌s – ⫷ TV ☎ P – ⚐ 80-100. ⚘ rest
M (dinner only) – **88 rm**.

ᨆ **Badhotel,** Gevers Deijnootweg 15, ⊠ 2586 BB, 𝒫 351 22 21, Telex 31592, Fax 355 58 70 –
⫷ TV ☎ P – ⚐ 40-100. ﹣ ① E VISA
M (dinner only) a la carte 41/68 – **92 rm** � 142/199 – ½ P 117/127.

XXX **Seinpost,** Zeekant 60, ⊠ 2586 AD, 𝒫 355 52 50, ≤, Seafood – ﹣ ① E
closed Thursday, lunch Saturday and Sunday, 24, 31 December and 1 January – **M** a la carte 54/108.

XXX **Radèn Mas,** Gevers Deijnootplein 125, ⊠ 2586 CR, 𝒫 354 54 32, Fax 354 54 32, Indonesian cuisine – ▤. ﹣ ① E VISA
closed lunch Saturday and Sunday – **M** a la carte 52/86.

XX **China Delight,** Dr Lelykade 118, ⊠ 2583 CN, 𝒫 355 54 50, Fax 354 66 52, Chinese cuisine, open until 11 p.m. – ▤. ① E VISA
M a la carte 47/72.

X **Ducdalf,** Dr Lelykade 5, ⊠ 2583 CL, 𝒫 355 76 92, ≤, 🍽, Seafood, Mussels in season –
P. ﹣ ① E VISA
closed 31 December and 1 January – **M** a la carte 40/89.

at Kijkduin : W : 4 km 🅒 's-Gravenhage – ✪ 0 70 :

ᨆ **Atlantic,** Deltaplein 200, ⊠ 2554 EJ, 𝒫 325 40 25, Telex 33399, Fax 368 67 21, ≤, 🍽, ⇌s,
▨ – ⫷ ⫸ rm TV ☎ P – ⚐ 25-150. ﹣ ① E VISA. ⚘ rest
M a la carte 68/98 – � 25 – **118 rm** 190/250 – ½ P 256/276.

ᨆ **Zeehaghe** without rest., Deltaplein 675, ⊠ 2554 GK, 𝒫 325 62 62, Telex 34186, Fax 325 40 69,
≤ – ⫷ ⫸ rm TV ☎ P – ⚐ 90. ﹣ ① E VISA
� 18 – **75 rm** 133/240.

at Leidschendam E : 6 km – pop. 32 628 – ✪ 0 70 :

ᨆ **Green Park,** Weigelia 22, ⊠ 2262 AB, 𝒫 320 92 80, Telex 33090, Fax 327 49 07, ≤, ⇌s – ⫷
⫸ rm ▤ rest TV ☎ P – ⚐ 350. ﹣ ① E VISA
M see rest Chagall below – **Brasserie The Greenery** (open until 11 p.m.) a la carte 41/62 –
� 27 – **96 rm** 210/240 – ½ P 259/310.

XXX ✿ **Chagall** - (at H. Green Park), Weigelia 20, ⊠ 2262 AB, 𝒫 327 69 10, Telex 33090, Fax 327 49 07, ≤ – ▤ P. ﹣ ① E VISA
closed Sunday and Monday – **M** a la carte 87/123
Spec. Carpaccio de turbot au pistou (April-October). Lotte panée au basilic en couronne de légumes. Ris de veau en beignets au soja.

XXX **Villa Rozenrust,** Veursestraatweg 104, ⊠ 2265 CG, 𝒫 327 74 60, Fax 327 50 62, 🍽 – P.
﹣ ① E VISA
closed Saturday lunch and Sunday – **M** a la carte 80/120.

at Voorburg E : 5 km – pop. 40 455 – ✪ 0 70 :

XXXX ✿ **Vreugd en Rust** (Savelberg) 🦢 with rm, Oosteinde 14, ⊠ 2271 EH, 𝒫 387 20 81, Fax 387 77 15, ≤, 🍽, « 17C residence with terrace in public park » – ⫷ ⫸ rm ▤ rest TV ☎ P
– ⚐ 35. ﹣ ① E VISA
M *(closed dinner 24 and 31 December)* a la carte 113/136 – **14 rm** � 200/495
Spec. Huîtres chaudes au safran et au caviar (September-April), Pigeon de Bresse à la sauge, Fromages régionaux sélectionnés.

XXX **Villa la Ruche,** Prinses Mariannelaan 71, ⊠ 2275 BB, 𝒫 386 01 10, Fax 386 50 64 – ▤. ﹣
① E VISA
closed lunch Saturday and Sunday – **M** a la carte 74/109.

at Wassenaar NE : 11 km – pop. 25 972 – ✪ 0 1751 :

ᨆ **Wassenaar,** Katwijkseweg 33 (N : 2 km), ⊠ 2242 PC, 𝒫 1 92 18, Telex 32087, Fax 7 64 81
– ⫷ TV ☎ P – ⚐ 50. ﹣ ① E VISA
M a la carte 49/79 – **57 rm** � 110/175 – ½ P 90/115.

XXXX ✿ **Aub. De Kieviet** 🦢 with rm, Stoeplaan 27, ⊠ 2243 CX, 𝒫 1 92 32, Fax 1 09 69, 🍽,
« Flowered terrace » – ⫷ ⫸ rm ▤ TV ☎ ♿ P – ⚐ 70. ﹣ ① E VISA
M a la carte 98/135 – ⊠welp 23 – **24 rm** 350/450 – ½ P 200/300
Spec. Turbotin vapeur aux nouilles noires et safran, Mosaïque de veau et bœuf aux artichauts, Chariot de desserts.

Michelin Green Guides in English

Austria	Italy	New York City
Canada	London	Portugal
England : The West Country	Mexico	Rome
Germany	Netherlands	Scotland
Greece	New England	Spain
		Switzerland

ROTTERDAM Zuid-Holland 🔢 ⑤ and 🔢 ㉔㉕ – pop. 576 232 – ۞ 0 10.

See : The harbour★★★ ⚓ KZ – Lijnbaan★ (Shopping centre) JKY – St. Laurence Church (Grote-of St. Laurenskerk) : interior★ KY D – Euromast★ (tower) (❄★★, ≼★) JZ.

Museums : Boymans-van Beuningen★★★ JZ – ''De Dubbele Palmboom''★ – Het Schielandshuis★ (History Museum) KY.

🏌 Kralingseweg 200 ℰ 452 76 46 - 🏌 at Rhoon SW : 11 km, Veerweg 2a ℰ (0 1890) 1 80 58.

🛫 Zestienhoven ℰ 415 76 33 (information) and 415 54 30, 437 27 45 (reservations).

🚇 (departs from 's-Hertogenbosch) ℰ 411 71 00.

🚢 Europoort to Kingston-upon-Hull : North Sea Ferries ℰ (0 1819) 5 55 55.

🛈 Coolsingel 67, 🖂 3012 AC, ℰ 06-34 03 40 65 and Central Station ℰ 413 60 06 – at Schiedam W : 6 km, Buitenhavenweg 9, 🖂 3113 BC, ℰ (0 10) 473 30 00.

Amsterdam 76 – The Hague 24 – Antwerp 103 – Brussels 149 – Utrecht 57.

Plan opposite

🏨 **Hilton International,** Weena 10, 🖂 3012 CM, ℰ 414 40 44, Telex 22666, Fax 411 88 84 – 🛗 ❄↔ rm 🖩 📺 🕭 ᴦ 🅿 – 🔬 250. 🆎 ① Ɛ 𝚅𝙸𝚂𝙰. ❄ rest   JKY **a**
M a la carte 48/80 – ⌧ 30 – **248 rm** 345/465.

🏨 **Parkhotel,** Westersingel 70, 🖂 3015 LB, ℰ 436 36 11, Telex 22020, Fax 436 36 11, 🍴 – 🛗 ❄↔ rm 🖩 📺 🕭 🅿 – 🔬 80. 🆎 ① Ɛ 𝚅𝙸𝚂𝙰   JZ **a**
M a la carte 57/86 – **154 rm** ⌧ 140/285.

🏨 **Rijnhotel,** Schouwburgplein 1, 🖂 3012 CK, ℰ 433 38 00, Telex 21640, Fax 414 54 82 – 🛗 📺 🕭 – 🔬 220. 🆎 ① Ɛ 𝚅𝙸𝚂𝙰. ❄ rest   JY **v**
M a la carte 48/69 – ⌧ 24 – **100 rm** 195/305.

🏨 **Atlanta,** Aert van Nesstraat 4, 🖂 3012 CA, ℰ 411 04 20, Fax 413 53 20 – 🛗 📺 🕭 🚗 🅿 – 🔬 80-400. 🆎 ① Ɛ 𝚅𝙸𝚂𝙰   KY **e**
M 40/75 – ⌧ 20 – **164 rm** 180/210.

🏨 **Savoy,** Hoogstraat 81, 🖂 3011 PJ, ℰ 413 92 80, Telex 21525, Fax 404 57 12 – 🛗 📺 🕭 🆎 ① Ɛ 𝚅𝙸𝚂𝙰   KY **n**
M (dinner only) a la carte 52/80 – ⌧ 21 – **94 rm** 140/160.

🏨 **Pax** without rest., Schiekade 658, 🖂 3032 AK, ℰ 466 33 44, Fax 467 52 78 – 🛗 📺 🕭 🅿 🆎 ① Ɛ 𝚅𝙸𝚂𝙰. ⚙   JY **m**
44 rm ⌧ 125/200.

🏨 **Scandia,** Willemsplein 1, 🖂 3016 DN, ℰ 413 47 90, Telex 21662, Fax 412 78 90, ≼ – 🛗 📺 🕭 – 🔬 70. 🆎 ① Ɛ 𝚅𝙸𝚂𝙰. ❄ rest   KZ **s**
M (closed Saturday and Sunday) 40/50 – ⌧ 20 – **49 rm** 125/195 – ½ P 140/210.

🏨 **Emma** without rest., Nieuwe Binnenweg 6, 🖂 3015 BA, ℰ 436 55 33, Telex 25320, Fax 436 76 58 – 🛗 📺 🚗 🅿. 🆎 ① Ɛ 𝚅𝙸𝚂𝙰   JZ **w**
26 rm ⌧ 120/155.

🏨 **Van Walsum,** Mathenesserlaan 199, 🖂 3014 HC, ℰ 436 32 75, Telex 20010, Fax 436 44 10 – 🛗 📺 🕭 🅿. 🆎 ① Ɛ 𝚅𝙸𝚂𝙰   JZ **e**
closed 20 December-2 January – **M** (residents only) – **26 rm** ⌧ 95/140 – ½ P 85/95.

🏨 **Zuiderparkhotel,** Dordtsestraatweg 285, 🖂 3083 AJ, ℰ 485 00 55, Telex 28755, Fax 485 63 04, 🍴 – 🛗 🍴 rest 📺 🕭 🅿. 🆎 ① Ɛ 𝚅𝙸𝚂𝙰 – 🔬 25-300. 🆎 ① Ɛ 𝚅𝙸𝚂𝙰
M a la carte 68/96 – ⌧ 19 – **113 rm** 150/205.

XXX ۞ **Parkheuvel (Helder),** Heuvellaan 21, 🖂 3016 GL, ℰ 436 05 30, Fax 436 71 40, ≼, 🌳, « Terrace » – 🅿. 🆎 ① Ɛ 𝚅𝙸𝚂𝙰   JZ **n**
closed Saturday lunch, Sunday and 27 December-2 January – **M** a la carte 95/140
Spec. ''Club Sandwich'' maison, Filet de barbue et queues de langoustines gratinées, Terrine de harengs nouveaux aux pommes de terre (June-August).

XXX **Le Coq d'Or** 1st floor, van Vollenhovenstraat 25, 🖂 3016 BG, ℰ 436 64 05, Fax 436 59 06, 🌳 – 🖩 🅿. 🆎 ① Ɛ 𝚅𝙸𝚂𝙰   KZ **a**
closed Saturday, Sunday, Bank Holidays and 24 December-1 January – **M** a la carte 80/115.

XXX **Old Dutch,** Rochussenstraat 20, 🖂 3015 EK, ℰ 436 03 44, Fax 436 78 26, 🌳, « Old Dutch interior » – 🖩 🅿. 🆎 ① Ɛ 𝚅𝙸𝚂𝙰   JZ **r**
closed Saturday, Sunday and Bank Holidays – **M** 63/78.

XXX **Radèn Mas** 1st floor, Kruiskade 72, 🖂 3012 EH, ℰ 411 72 44, Fax 411 97 11, Indonesian cuisine, « Exotic decor » – 🖩. 🆎 ① Ɛ 𝚅𝙸𝚂𝙰   JY **a**
closed lunch Saturday and Sunday – **M** a la carte 57/85.

XXX **World Trade Center** 23rd floor, Beursplein 37, 🖂 3011 AA, ℰ 405 44 65, Fax 412 01 11, ❄ city – 🛗 🖩 🅿. 🆎 ① Ɛ 𝚅𝙸𝚂𝙰. ❄   KY **x**
closed Saturday and Sunday – **M** a la carte 73/116.

XX **La Vilette,** Westblaak 160, 🖂 3012 KM, ℰ 414 86 92, Fax 452 15 13 – 🖩. 🆎 ① Ɛ 𝚅𝙸𝚂𝙰   JZ **t**
closed Saturday lunch, Sunday and Bank Holidays – **M** 55/100.

XX **Silhouet** Euromast tower (Entrance fee payable), Parkhaven 20, 🖂 3016 GM, ℰ 436 48 11, Fax 436 22 80, ❄ city and port – 🅿. 🆎 ① Ɛ 𝚅𝙸𝚂𝙰. ⚙   JZ
closed lunch Saturday and Sunday – **M** a la carte 70/98.

XX **Engels,** Stationsplein 45, 🖂 3013 AK, ℰ 411 95 50, Telex 26100, Fax 413 94 21, Open until 11 p.m., Multinational cuisines – 🖩. 🆎 ① Ɛ 𝚅𝙸𝚂𝙰   JY **v**
M a la carte 42/80.

ROTTERDAM
CENTRE

0   300 m

at Hillegersberg 🄲 Rotterdam – ✪ 0 10 :

XXX **Beau Rivage,** Weissenbruchlaan 149, ✉ 3054 LM, ℰ 418 40 40, Fax 418 64 65, ≼, 🍽, « Lakeside setting terrace » – 🅰🄴 ⓪ ⋿ 𝘝𝘐𝘚𝘈, ℅
closed lunch Saturday and Sunday and Bank Holidays – **M** a la carte 92/125.

at Kralingen 🄲 Rotterdam – ✪ 0 10 :

XXX **In den Rustwat,** Honingerdijk 96, ✉ 3062 NX, ℰ 413 41 10, Fax 404 85 40, « 16C house » – 🄴 🅿 🅰🄴 ⓪ ⋿,
closed Saturday, Sunday, Easter, Ascension Day, Whitsuntide and Christmas – **M** a la carte 69/101.

at Ommoord 🄲 Rotterdam – ✪ 0 10 :

XXX **Keizershof,** Martin Luther Kingweg 7, ✉ 3069 EW, ℰ 455 13 33 – 🅿 🅰🄴 ⓪ ⋿ 𝘝𝘐𝘚𝘈
M 40/90.

at Rhoon 🄲 Albrandswaard pop. 13 785 – ✪ 0 1890 :

XXX **Het Kasteel van Rhoon,** Dorpsdijk 63, ✉ 3161 KD, ℰ 1 88 84, Fax 1 24 18, ≼, 🍽, « In the dependency of the castle » – 🅿 🅰🄴 ⓪ ⋿ 𝘝𝘐𝘚𝘈
closed Saturday lunch, 25 and 26 December – **M** a la carte 70/108.

at Schiedam – pop. 69 438 – ✪ 0 10 :

🏨 **Novotel,** Hargalaan 2 (near A 20), ✉ 3118 JA, ℰ 471 33 22, Telex 22582, Fax 470 06 56, 🍽, 🏊 – 🛗 📺 ☎ ⅋ 🅿 – 🔬 200. 🅰🄴 ⓪ ⋿ 𝘝𝘐𝘚𝘈
M (open until midnight) 40/91 – ⌑ 20 – **138 rm** 180/195.

XXX **La Duchesse,** Maasboulevard 9, ✉ 3114 HB, ℰ 426 46 25, ≼ Nieuwe Maas (Meuse), 🍽 – 🄴 🅿 🅰🄴 ⓪ ⋿ 𝘝𝘐𝘚𝘈
closed Saturday lunch and Sunday – **M** 65/80.

XXX **Aub. Hosman Frères** 1st floor, Korte Dam 10, ✉ 3111 BG, ℰ 426 40 96, Telex 24207, Fax 473 00 08 – 🄴. 🅰🄴 ⓪ ⋿ 𝘝𝘐𝘚𝘈
closed Sunday, Monday and 16 to 29 July – **M** 60/99.

Europoort zone by ⑥ : 25 km – ✪ 0 1819 :

🏨 **De Beer Europoort,** Europaweg 210 (A 15), ✉ 3198 LD, ℰ 6 23 77, Telex 29979, Fax 6 29 23, ≼, 🍽, 🔲, 🏊 – 📺 ☎ ⅋ 🅿 – 🔬 25-250. 🅰🄴 ⓪ ⋿ 𝘝𝘐𝘚𝘈
M a la carte 46/89 – **78 rm** ⌑ 125/160 – ½ P 110/155.

Denmark
Danmark

Copenhagen

PRACTICAL INFORMATION

LOCAL CURRENCY

Danish Kroner : 100 D.Kr = 17.20 US $ (Jan. 91)

TOURIST INFORMATION

The telephone number and address of the Tourist Information office is given in the text under 🖪.

FOREIGN EXCHANGE

Banks are open between 9.30am and 4.00pm (6.00pm on Thursdays) on weekdays except Saturdays. The main banks in the centre of Copenhagen, the Central Station and the Airport have exchange facilities outside these hours.

MEALS

At lunchtime, follow the custom of the country and try the typical buffets of Scandinavian specialities.
At dinner, the a la carte and the menus will offer you more conventional cooking.

SHOPPING IN COPENHAGEN

Strøget (Department stores, exclusive shops, boutiques).
Kompagnistræde (Antiques).
See also in the index of street names, those printed in red are where the principal shops are found.

CAR HIRE

The international car hire companies have branches in Copenhagen - Your hotel porter should be able to give details and help you with your arrangements.

TIPPING

In Denmark, all hotels and restaurants include a service charge. As for the taxis, there is no extra charge to the amount shown on the meter.

SPEED LIMITS

The maximum permitted speed in cities is 50 km/h - 31mph, outside cities 80 km/h - 50mph and 100 km/h - 62mph on motorways.

SEAT BELTS

The wearing of seat belts is compulsory for drivers and all passengers except children under the age of 3 and taxi passengers.

COPENHAGEN

SIGHTS

See : Tivoli★★★ : May 1 to September 15 BZ – Harbour and Canal Tour★★★ (Kanaltur) : May to September 15 (Gammel Strand and Nyhavn) – Little Mermaid★★★ (Den Lille Havfrue) DX – Strøget★★ BCYZ – Nyhavn★★ DY – Amalienborg★★ : Changing of the Guard at noon DY – Rosenborg Castle★★ (Rosenborg Slot) CX Christiansborg Palace★★ (Christiansborg Slot) CZ – Old Stock Exchange★★ (Børsen) CZ – Round Tower★★ (Rundetårn) CY D Gråbrødretorv★ CY 28 – Gammel Strand CZ 26 – Marble Church★ (Marmorkirke) DY E – Royal Chapel and Naval Church★ (Holmen's Kirke) CZ B – King's Square★ (Kongens Nytorv) DY – Charlottenborg Palace★ (Charlottenborg Slot) DY F – Citadel★ (Kastellet) DX – Christianshavn★ DZ – Botanical Garden★ (Botanisk Have) BX – Frederiksberg Garden★ (Frederiksberg Have) AZ – Town Hall (Rådhus) : World Clock★ (Jens Olsen's Verdensur) BZ H. Breweries – Porcelain Factories.

Museums : Ny Carlsberg Glyptotek★★★ (Glyptoteket) BZ – National Museum★★ (Nationalmuseet) CZ – Royal Museum of Fine Arts★★ (Statens Museum for Kunst) CX – Thorvaldsen Museum★ CZ M1 – Royal Arsenal Museum★ (Tøjhusmuseet) CZ M2 – Royal Theatre Museum★ (Teaterhistorisk Museum) CZ M3 – Copenhagen City Museum★ (Bymuseet) AZ M4.

Outskirts : Open Air Museum★★ (Frilandsmuseet) NW : 12 km BX – Ordrupgaard Museum★ (Ordrupgaardsamlingen) N : 10 km CX – Dragør★ SW : 13 km DZ.

COPENHAGEN (KØBENHAVN) Danmark 985 Q 9 – pop. 622 000.

🏌 Dansk Golf Union 56 ✆ 33 13 12 21.

✈ Copenhagen/Kastrup SE : 10 km ✆ 31 54 17 01 – Air Terminal : main railway station.

🚂 Motorail for Southern Europe : ✆ 33 14 17 01.

🚉 Further information from the D S B, main railway station or tourist information centre (see below).

🛈 Danmarks Turistråd, H.C. Andersens Bould. 22 A - 1553 København.V ✆ 33 11 13 25.

Berlin 385 – Hamburg 305 – Oslo 583 – Stockholm 630.

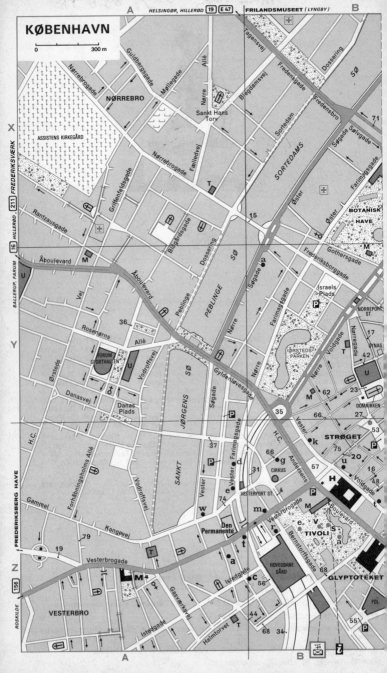

KØBENHAVN

0   300 m

HELSINGØR, HILLERØD 19 E 47   FRILANDSMUSEET (LYNGBY)

A   B

NØRREBRO

ASSISTENS KIRKEGÅRD

Sankt Hans Torv

FREDERIKSVÆRK   X

HILLERØD 211

BALLERUP, FARUM 16

Åboulevard

FORUM SPORTHALLEN

Danas Plads

SORTEDAMS SØ

BOTANISK HAVE

Israels Plads

NØRREPORT ST.

ØRSTEDS-PARKEN

PEBLINGE SØ

SANKT JØRGENS SØ

STRØGET

DOMKIRKEN

CIRKUS

VESTERPORT ST.

Den Permanente

FREDERIKSBERG HAVE

TIVOLI

GLYPTOTEKET

HOVEDBANE GÅRD

Vesterbrogade

VESTERBRO

ROSKILDE 156

Halmtorvet

96

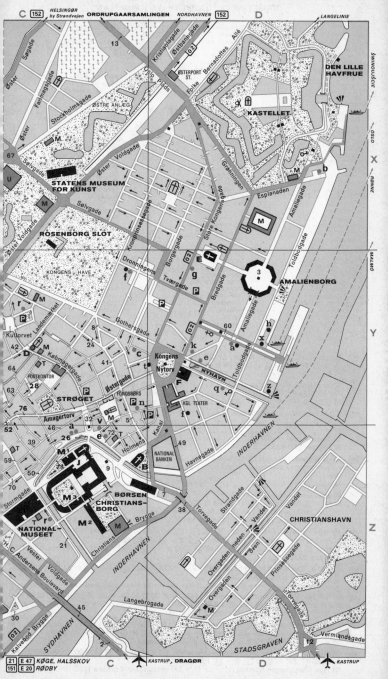

Angleterre, Kongens Nytorv 34, ✉ 1050 K, ℰ 33 12 00 95, Telex 15877, Fax 33 12 11 18 – 🕼 ☰ 📺 🖙 ⇔ – 🔏 250. 🌐 ⓞ 🗲 𝑉𝑆𝐴   CDY **t**
M 400/600 and a la carte – 😄 105 – **118 rm** 1650/2200, **12 suites** 2800/11500.

Sheraton - Copenhagen Ⓜ, 6 Vester Søgade, ✉ 1601 K, ℰ 33 14 35 35, Telex 27450, Fax 33 32 12 23, ≼, 🕿 – 🕼 ☰ rm 🕼 🖙 🖙 – 🔏 1 000. 🌐 ⓞ 🗲 𝑉𝑆𝐴   AZ **w**
M 500/600 and a la carte – **469 rm** 😄 2100/2400, **2 suites** 2600/10000.

SAS Scandinavia, Amager Boulevard 70, ✉ 2300 S, ℰ 33 11 23 24, Telex 31330, Fax 31 57 01 93, ≼ – Copenhagen, ≼ « Panoramic restaurant on 25th floor », ᵢ⁶ₔ, 🕿, 🔲, squash – 🕼 ⨝⨯ rm ☰ 📺 🖙 ⇔ 🖙 – 🔏 1 500. 🌐 by Amager Boulevard CZ
M Top of Town (closed Sunday) (dinner only) a la carte 179/340 – 😄 115 – **506 rm** 1500/2100, **36 suites** 5600/8200.

SAS Royal, Hammerichsgade 1, ✉ 1611 V, ℰ 33 14 14 12, Telex 27155, Fax 33 14 14 21, ≼, « Panoramic restaurant on 20th floor », 🕿 – 🕼 ⨝⨯ rm ☰ 📺 🖙 ⇔ 🖙 – 🔏 200. 🌐 ⓞ 🗲 𝑉𝑆𝐴   BZ **m**
M 195/440 and a la carte – 😄 115 – **264 rm** 1795/2395, **2 suites** 2495/12375.

Plaza, Bernstorffsgade 4, ✉ 1577 V, ℰ 33 14 92 62, Telex 15330, Fax 33 93 93 62, « Library bar » – 🕼 ☰ 📺 🖙 – 🔏 60. 🌐 🗲 𝑉𝑆𝐴   BZ **r**
closed 23 December -2 January – **M** Alexandra Newski (closed lunch May-mid August and Sunday) (Russian rest.) 216/316 and a la carte – 😄 95 – **87 rm** 1250/1850, **6 suites** 2600/5600.

Kong Frederik, Vester Voldgade 25, ✉ 1552 V, ℰ 33 12 59 02, Telex 19702, Fax 33 93 59 01, « Victorian pub, antiques » – 🕼 ☰ rm 📺 🖙 – 🔏 80. 🌐 🗲 𝑉𝑆𝐴 ⋈   BZ **k**
closed 21 December-2 January – **M** 220/390 and a la carte – 😄 95 – **107 rm** 1250/1750, **3 suites** 2000/6000.

Palace, Raadhuspladsen 57, ✉ 1550 V, ℰ 33 14 40 50, Telex 19693, Fax 33 14 52 79, 🕿 – 🕼 📺 🖙 – 🔏 50. 🌐 🗲 𝑉𝑆𝐴   BZ **u**
M (buffet lunch)/dinner a la carte 175/205 – **156 rm** 😄 1350/1600, **3 suites**.

Impérial, Vester Farimagsgade 9, ✉ 1606 V, ℰ 33 12 80 00, Telex 15556, Fax 33 93 80 31 – 🕼 ⨝⨯ rm 📺 🖙 ♿ – 🔏 100. 🌐 ⓞ 🗲 𝑉𝑆𝐴 ⋈   AZ **e**
M 230/275 and a la carte – **163 rm** 😄 1025/1290.

Copenhagen Admiral, Toldbodgade 24-28, ✉ 1253 K, ℰ 33 11 82 82, Telex 15941, Fax 33 32 55 42, ≼, « Former 18C warehouse », 🕿 – 🕼 📺 🖙 🖙 – 🔏 180. 🌐 🗲 𝑉𝑆𝐴   DY **h**
M a la carte 184/398 – 😄 82 – **363 rm** 765/990, **2 suites** 1125/1540.

Sophie Amalie Ⓜ, Sankt Annae Plads 21, ✉ 1250 K, ℰ 33 13 34 00, Telex 15815, Fax 33 32 55 42, 🕿 – 🕼 ☰ 📺 🖙 – 🔏 180. 🌐 🗲 𝑉𝑆𝐴   DY **x**
M (see Copenhagen Admiral H.) – 😄 82 – **130 rm** 825/990, **4 suites** 1125/1540.

🏠 **Neptun,** Sankt Annae Plads 18-20, ⊠ 1250 K, 𝒫 33 13 89 00, Telex 19554, Fax 33 14 12 50
– 🛗 🕎 🖭 🕿 – 🔬 60. 🖭 ⓓ ᴇ 𝐕𝐈𝐒𝐀   DY **a**
closed 21 December-2 January – **M** 190/300 and a la carte – **119 rm** ⊆ 870/1310, **10 suites**
1800.

🏠 **Kong Arthur** without rest., Nørre Søgade 11, ⊠ 1370 K, 𝒫 33 11 12 12, Telex 16512, Fax
33 32 61 30, ⇔ – 🛗 🕎 🕿 ⇔ 🅿. 🖭 ⓓ ᴇ 𝐕𝐈𝐒𝐀   BY **a**
90 rm ⊆ 825/1075, **1 suite** 1400/2700.

🏠 **Mayfair** without rest., Helgolandsgade 3-5, ⊠ 1653 V, 𝒫 31 31 48 01, Telex 27468, Fax
31 23 96 86 – 🛗 🕎 🖭. 🖭 ⓓ ᴇ 𝐕𝐈𝐒𝐀   AZ **a**
102 rm ⊆ 900/1500, **4 suites** 1900.

🏠 **Mercur,** Vester Farimagsgade 17, ⊠ 1625 V, 𝒫 33 12 57 11, Telex 19767, Fax 33 12 57 17,
🌂 – 🛗 🕎 🖭. 🖭 ⓓ ᴇ 𝐕𝐈𝐒𝐀   AZ **d**
M *(closed Sunday and Bank Holidays)* 108/178 and a la carte – **108 rm** ⊆ 995/1600, **1 suite**
1800.

🏠 **71 Nyhavn,** Nyhavn 71, ⊠ 1051 K, 𝒫 33 11 85 85, Telex 27558, Fax 33 93 15 85, ≼, « Former
warehouse » – 🛗 🕎 🕿. 🖭 ⓓ ᴇ 𝐕𝐈𝐒𝐀   DY **z**
M *(closed 24 to 26 December)* (buffet lunch) 168/dinner 285 and a la carte – ⊆ 85 – **76 rm**
1050/1750, **6 suites** 2250/2550.

🏠 **Grand,** Vesterbrogade 9a, ⊠ 1620 V, 𝒫 31 31 36 00, Telex 15343, Fax 31 31 33 50 – 🛗
🌂 rm 🕎 🕿 – 🔬 120   AZ **t**
147 rm.

🏠 **Scala - Copenhagen** Ⓜ without rest., Colbjørnsensgade 13, ⊠ 1652 V, 𝒫 31 22 11 00,
Fax 31 22 21 99 – 🕎 🕿 – 🔬 35. 🖭 ⓓ ᴇ 𝐕𝐈𝐒𝐀   ABZ **c**
131 rm ⊆ 850/1076, **3 suites** 1225.

🏠 **Ascot** without rest., Studiestraede 57, ⊠ 1554 V, 𝒫 33 12 60 00, Telex 15730, Fax 33 14 60 40
– 🛗 🕎 🕿 🅿. 🖭 ⓓ ᴇ 𝐕𝐈𝐒𝐀   BZ **g**
117rm ⊆ 650/1090, **3 suites** 990/2090.

🏠 **Opera** without rest., Tordenskjoldsgade 15, ⊠ 1055 K, 𝒫 33 12 15 19, Telex 15812, Fax
33 32 12 82 – 🛗 🕎 🕿. 🖭 ⓓ ᴇ 𝐕𝐈𝐒𝐀   DY **f**
closed 21 December-1 January – **85 rm** ⊆ 930/1330, **2 suites** 1630.

🏠 **Christian IV** Ⓜ without rest., Dronningens Tvaergade 45, ⊠ 1302 K, 𝒫 33 32 10 44, Fax
33 32 07 06 – 🛗 🕎 🕿. 🖭 ⓓ ᴇ 𝐕𝐈𝐒𝐀   CY **f**
42 rm ⊆ 850/1100.

🏠 **Danmark** without rest., Vester Voldgade 89, ⊠ 1552 V, 𝒫 33 11 48 06, Telex 15518, Fax
33 14 36 30 – 🛗 🕎 🕿 ⇔. 🖭 ⓓ ᴇ 𝐕𝐈𝐒𝐀   BZ **t**
closed 20 December-2 January – **49 rm** ⊆ 650/875, **2 suites** 1075/1250.

XXX ❀ **Kong Hans Kaelder,** Vingardsstraede 6, ⊠ 1070 K, 𝒫 33 11 68 68, Telex 50404,
« Vaulted Gothic cellar » – 🖭 ⓓ ᴇ 𝐕𝐈𝐒𝐀   CY **n**
closed Sunday, mid July-mid August, Christmas-New Year and Bank Holidays – **M** (booking
essential)(dinner only) 295/675 and a la carte 485/580
Spec. Foie gras poêlé au vinaigre de framboise, Homard « Tiger Lee ». Canard sauvage rôti sauce aux mûres
(saison).

XX ❀ **Nouvelle,** Gammel Strand 34 (1st floor), ⊠ 1202 K, 𝒫 33 13 50 18 – 🖭 ⓓ ᴇ 𝐕𝐈𝐒𝐀   CZ **a**
closed Sunday, last 2 weeks July, 22 December-6 January and Bank Holidays – **M** 225/385
and a la carte 338/438
Spec. Maize Pie with beluga caviar, Fricassée of sole with mussels and pear, Grilled Danish spring lamb with
wine leaves.

XX **Kommandanten,** NY Adelgade 7, ⊠ 1104 K, 𝒫 33 12 09 90, Fax 33 93 12 23, « 17C town
house, contemporary furnishings » – 🖭 ⓓ ᴇ 𝐕𝐈𝐒𝐀   CY **c**
closed lunch May-August, Saturday lunch, Sunday, Christmas-New Year and Bank Holidays
– **M** (booking essential) 230/450 and a la carte.

XX ❀ **Les Etoiles et une Rose,** Dronningens Tvaergade 43, ⊠ 1302 K, 𝒫 33 15 05 54, Fax
33 32 07 06. 🖭 ⓓ ᴇ 𝐕𝐈𝐒𝐀   CY **f**
closed Saturday lunch, Sunday and first 2 weeks January – **M** 176/495 and a la carte
Spec. Lightly salted sea trout with a scallop and lobster tartare, Lobster consomme with a japanese nori
seawead roll, Cutlets of Danish fallow deer with Perigord truffe and duck foie gras.

XX **Leonore Christine,** Nyhavn 9, ⊠ 1051 K, 𝒫 33 13 50 40 – 🖭 ⓓ ᴇ 𝐕𝐈𝐒𝐀   DY **e**
closed Sunday, 22 December-2 January and Bank Holidays – **M** 188/338 and a la carte.

XX **Krogs,** Gammel Strand 38, ⊠ 1202 K, 𝒫 33 15 89 15, Seafood – 🖭 ⓓ ᴇ 𝐕𝐈𝐒𝐀   CZ **a**
closed Sunday, 22 to 26 December and 31 December-4 January – **M** (dinner only) 385 and a
la carte.

XX **St. Gertruds Kloster,** 32 Hauser Plads, ⊠ 1127 K, 𝒫 33 14 66 30, Fax 33 93 93 65, « Part
14C monastery cellars » – ▤. 🖭 ⓓ ᴇ 𝐕𝐈𝐒𝐀   CY **r**
closed 27 May and Christmas-New Year – **M** (dinner only) 366/675 and a la carte.

X **Lille Laekkerbisken,** Gammel Strand 34 (ground floor), ⊠ 1202 K, 𝒫 33 32 04 00 – 🖭
ⓓ ᴇ 𝐕𝐈𝐒𝐀   CZ **a**
closed Sunday, last 2 weeks July, 22 December-6 January and Bank Holidays – **M** (lunch
only) a la carte 116/218.

X **Els,** Store Strandstraede 3, ⊠ 1255 K, 𝒫 33 14 13 41, Fax 33 91 15 00, « 19C murals » – 🖭
ⓓ ᴇ 𝐕𝐈𝐒𝐀   DY **k**
closed 24-25 December and 31 December-1 January – **M** 176/296.

✗ **Lumskebugten,** Esplanaden 21, ⊠ 1263 K, ✆ 33 15 60 29, 🍴, « Mid 19C café-pavilion »
– AE ⓘ E 𝑉𝐼𝑆𝐴   DX **b**
closed Saturday lunch, Sunday, Easter and Bank Holidays – **M** 190/485 and a la carte.

✗ **Den Gyldne Fortun,** Ved Stranden 18, ⊠ 1061 K, ✆ 33 12 20 11, Fax 33 93 35 11, Seafood
– AE ⓘ E 𝑉𝐼𝑆𝐴, ⅗   CZ **e**
*closed lunch Saturday and Sunday, 27 March-2 April, 9 May, 18 to 21 May and 22 December-2
January* – **M** 175/350 and a la carte.

✗ **Den Sorte Ravn,** Nyhavn 14, ⊠ 1051 K, ✆ 33 13 12 33 – AE ⓘ E 𝑉𝐼𝑆𝐴   DY **q**
closed 28 March-1 April, 18 to 20 May, Christmas and New Year – **M** 450 and a la carte.

in Tivoli : (Entrance fee payable)

✗✗✗ **Divan 2,** Vesterbrogade 3, ⊠ 1620 V, ✆ 33 12 51 51, Fax 33 91 08 82, ≤, 🍴, « Floral
decoration and terrace » –   BZ **a**
24 April-15 September – **M** 350/525 and a la carte.

✗✗✗ **Divan 1,** Vesterbrogade 3, ⊠ 1620 V, ✆ 33 11 42 42, Fax 33 11 74 07, ≤, 🍴, « Floral
decoration and terrace » – AE ⓘ E 𝑉𝐼𝑆𝐴   BZ **v**
24 April-16 September – **M** 210/395 and a la carte.

✗✗ **La Crevette,** Bernstorffsgade 5, ⊠ 1577 V, ✆ 33 14 68 47, Fax 33 14 60 06, ≤, 🍴, Seafood,
« Part mid 19C pavilion and terrace » – AE ⓘ E 𝑉𝐼𝑆𝐴   BZ **z**
23 April-16 September – **M** 250/350 and a la carte.

✗✗ **Belle Terrasse,** Vesterbrogade 3, ⊠ 1620 V, ✆ 33 12 11 36, Fax 33 15 00 31, ≤, 🍴,
« Floral decoration and terrace » – AE ⓘ E 𝑉𝐼𝑆𝐴   BZ **s**
25 April-16 September – **M** 275/475 and a la carte.

SMØRREBRØD.

The following list of simpler restaurants and cafés/bars
specialize in Danish open sandwiches and are generally
open 10.00am to 4.00pm.

✗ **Ida Davidsen,** St. Kongensgade 70, ⊠ 1264 K, ✆ 33 91 36 55 – ⓘ E   DY **g**
closed Saturday and Sunday – **M** approx. 95.

✗ **Slotskaelderen-Hos Gitte Kik,** Fortunstraede 4, ⊠ 1065 K, ✆ 33 11 15 37 – ⓘ E 𝑉𝐼𝑆𝐴
closed Monday and Sunday – **M** approx. 65.   CYZ **v**

✗ **Kanal Caféen,** Frederiksholms Kanal 18, ⊠ 1220 K, ✆ 33 11 57 70 – ⓘ E 𝑉𝐼𝑆𝐴   CZ **r**
closed Saturday and Sunday – **M** approx. 55.

✗ Sankt Annae, Sankt Annae Plads 12, ⊠ 1250 K, ✆ 33 12 54 97   DY **a**

at Klampenborg N : 12 km by Østbanegade-DX -on coast rd :

✗ **Den Gule Cottage,** Staunings Plaene, Strandvejen 506, ⊠ 2930, ✆ 31 64 06 91, ≤,
« Thatched cottage beside the sea » – ⓟ, AE ⓘ E 𝑉𝐼𝑆𝐴
M (booking essential) 195/410 and a la carte.

at Søllerød N : 16 km by Tagensvej – BX – Lyngbyvej and Road 19 – ⊠ 2840 Holte.

✗✗✗ ❀ **Søllerød Kro,** Søllerødvej 35, ⊠ 2840, ✆ 42 80 25 05, Fax 42 80 22 70, 🍴, « 17C thatched
inn, terrace » – ⓟ, AE ⓘ E 𝑉𝐼𝑆𝐴
closed 24 December – **M** 370/525 and a la carte 315/485
Spec. Sliced turbot on apples and salsify, gratinated with vanilla, Pot au feu with fillet of veal and lobster.
Liquorice delicacy with almond sorbet.

at Kastrup Airport SE : 10 km – ⊠ 2300 S.

🏨 **SAS Globetrotter,** Engvej 171, ⊠ 2300 S, NW : 2 ½ km ✆ 31 55 14 33, Telex 31222, Fax
31 55 81 45, ⌧, ☎ – 🛗 ✳ rm 📺 ☎ ⓟ – 🔒 350. AE ⓘ E 𝑉𝐼𝑆𝐴
M 188/358 and a la carte – **196 rm** ⌐ 1195/1795.   by Amager Boulevard   CZ

Finland
Suomi

Helsinki

PRACTICAL INFORMATION

LOCAL CURRENCY

Finnish Mark : 100 FIM = 27.43 $ (Jan. 91)

TOURIST INFORMATION

The Tourist Office is situated near the Market Square, Pohjoisesplanadi 19 ✆169 3757 and 174 088. Open from 15 May to 15 September, Monday to Friday 8.30am - 6pm, Saturday 8.30am - 1pm, and from 16 September to 14 May, Monday 8.30am - 4.30pm and Tuesday to Friday 8.30am - 4.00pm. Hotel bookings are possible from a reservation board situated in airport arrival lounge ; information also available free.

FOREIGN EXCHANGE

Banks are open between 9.15am and 4.15pm on weekdays only. Exchange office at the Railway Station open daily from 11.30am to 6pm and at Helsinki-Vantaa airport also daily between 6.30am and 11pm.

MEALS

At lunchtime, follow the custom of the country and try the typical buffets of Scandinavian specialities.
At dinner, the a la carte and the menus will offer you more conventional cooking.
A lot of city centre restaurants are closed for a few days over the Midsummer Day period.

SHOPPING IN HELSINKI

Furs, jewelry, china, glass and ceramics, Finnish handicraft and wood.
In the index of street names, those printed in red are where the principal shops are found. Your hotel porter will be able to help you and give you information.

THEATRE BOOKINGS

A ticket service - Lippupalvelu, Mannerheimintie 5, is selling tickets for cinema, concert and theatre performances - Telephone 643 043, open Mon-Fri 9am to 5pm, Sat. 9am to 2pm (except 24 June to 5 Aug.).

CAR HIRE

The international car hire companies have branches in Helsinki city and at Vantaa airport. Your hotel porter should be able to help you with your arrangements.

TIPPING

Service is normally included in hotel and restaurant bills - Doormen, baggage porters etc. are generally given a gratuity ; taxi drivers are usually not tipped.

SPEED LIMITS

The maximum permitted speed on motorways is 120 km/h - 74 mph (in winter 100 km/h - 62 mph), 80 km/h - 50 mph on other roads and 50 km/h - 31 mph in built-up areas.

SEAT BELTS

The wearing of seat belts in Finland is compulsory for drivers and for front and rear seat passengers.

HELSINKI

SIGHTS

See : Senate Square★★★ (Senaatintori) DY 53 : Lutheran Cathedral (Tuomiokirkko) DY, University Library (Yliopiston kirjasto) CY **B**, Senate House (Valtioneuvosto) DY **C**, Sederholm House DY **E** − Market Square★★ (Kauppatori) DY **26** : Uspensky Cathedral (Uspenskin katedraali) DY, Presidential Palace (Presidentinlinna) DY **F**, Havis Amanda Fountain DY **K** − Spa Park★ (Kaivopuisto) DZ ; Esplanade★★ (Eteläesplanadi CY **8**, Pohjoisesplanadi CY **43**) ; Aleksanterinkatu★ CDY **2** ; Atheneum Art Museum★★ (Ateneumintaidemuseo) CY **M¹** − Mannerheimintie★★ BCXY : Parliament House (Eduskuntatalo) BX, Rock Church (Temppeliaukion kirkko) BX, National Museum (Kansallismuseo) BX **M²**, Helsinki City Museum (Helsingin kaupunginmuseo) BX **M³**, Finlandia Hall (Finlandiatalo) BX − Sibelius Monument★★ (Sibeliuksen puisto) AX ; Stadium tower (Olympia-stadion) BX : view★★.

Sightseeing by sea : Fortress of Suomenlinna★★ ; Seurasaari Open-Air Museum★ (from Kauppatori) ; Helsinki zoo★ (Korkeasaari).

Entertainment : Helsinki Festival★★ (23 August to 9 September).

HELSINKI Finland ⑨⑧⑤ L 21 − Pop. 491 777 − ✪ 90.

▥ Tali Manor ✆ 550 235.

✈ Helsinki-Vantaa N : 19 km ✆ 818 51 - Finnair Head Office, Mannerheimintie 102 ✆ 818 83 60, Telex 124 404 - Air Terminal : Hotel Intercontinental, Mannerheimintie 46.

⛴ To Sweden, USSR and boat excursions : contact the City Tourist Office (see below) - Car Ferry : Silja Line - Finnjet Line ✆ 180 41.

🛈 City Tourist Office, Pohjoisesplanadi 19 ✆ 169 3757, Fax 655 783 − Automobile and Touring Club of Finland : Autoliitto ✆ 694 0022, Telex 124 839, Fax 693 25 78.

Lahti 103 − Tampere 176 − Turku 165.

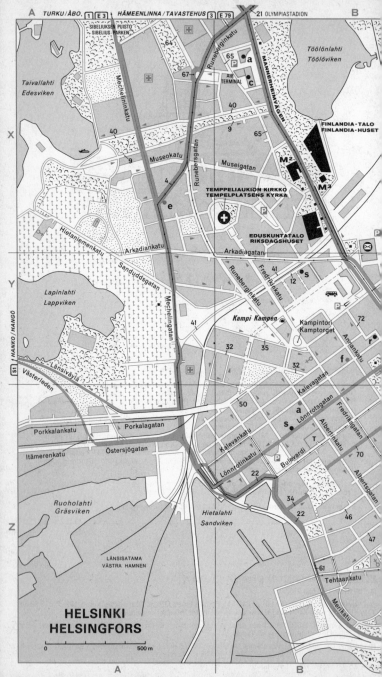

SIBELIUKSEN PUISTO
SIBELIUS-PARKEN

64

65 ● a

67

AIR
TERMINAL ● c

40

9

Runeberginkatu

Mannerheimintie
MANNERHEIMVÄGEN

Töölönlahti
Töölöviken

FINLANDIA-TALO
FINLANDIA-HUSET

Taivallahti
Edesviken

Mechelininkatu

Museokatu

40

Runebergsgatan

Museigatan

M²

M³

TEMPPELIAUKION KIRKKO
TEMPELPLATSENS KYRKA

EDUSKUNTATALO
RIKSDAGSHUSET

4

e

Hietaniemenkatu

Arkadiankatu

Sanduddsgatan

Mechelingatan

Arkadiagatan

Runeberginkatu

Fredrikinkatu

41

12 ● s

Lapinlahti
Lappviken

41

Kampi Kampen

Kampintori
Kamptorget

72

r ●

Amerikankatu

f

32

35

32

Länsiväylä

Västerleden

SI HANKO/HANGÖ

50

Kalevagatan

Kalevankatu

Lönnrotsgatan

a

s

Albertinkatu

Fredriksgatan

Porkkalankatu

Porkalagatan

Östersjögatan

22

Lönnrotinkatu

Bulevardi

70

Albertsgatan

Itämerenkatu

Ruoholahti
Gräsviken

Hietalahti
Sandviken

34

22

46

47

LÄNSISATAMA
VÄSTRA HAMNEN

61

Tehtaankatu

Merikatu

HELSINKI
HELSINGFORS

0   500 m

A   B

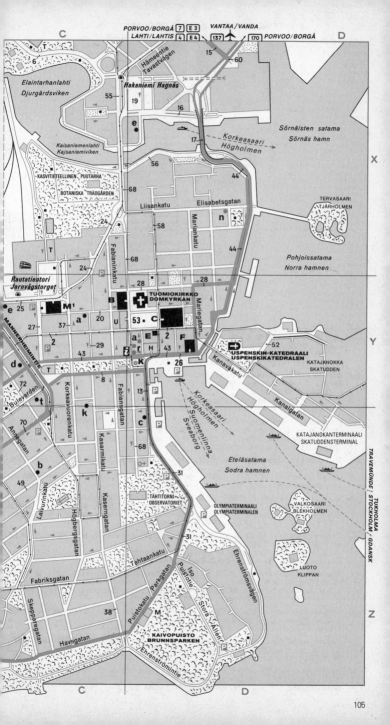

Inter-Continental, Mannerheimintie 46, 00260, ℰ 40551, Telex 122159, Fax 4055255, ☎s, ◯ – |♣| ⁂ rm ▤ ⊜ ☜ Ⓟ – 🏛 400. 🖭 ⓪ ☰ 𝚅𝙸𝚂𝙰   BX c
closed 1 to 28 July, 23 to 29 December and 24 to 28 February – **M** – **Galateia** (Seafood) *(closed Saturday and Sunday)* (dinner only) 350 and a la carte – **Brasserie** (buffet lunch)/dinner 180 and a la carte – **543 rm** ☲ 890/970, **12 suites** 2000/4000.

Strand Intercontinental, John Stenbergin Ranta 4, 00530, ℰ 39351, Telex 126202, Fax 761 362, ≼, « Contemporary decor, modern art collection », ☎s, ◯ – |♣| ⁂ rm ▤ ▥ ☎ ♿ – 🏛 320. 🖭 ⓪ 𝚅𝙸𝚂𝙰   DX e
closed Christmas – **M Atrium Plaza** a la carte 203/235 – **Pamir** *(closed Saturday, Sunday, Easter and July)* 170/420 and a la carte – **192 rm** ☲ 860/1030, **8 suites** 2100/4600.

Hesperia, Mannerheimintie 50, 00260, ℰ 43101, Telex 122117, Fax 4310995, ☎s, ◯ – |♣| ⁂ rm ▤ rest ▥ ☎ ♿ Ⓟ – 🏛 400. 🖭 ⓪ ☰ 𝚅𝙸𝚂𝙰   BX a
M – **Russian Room** *(closed Sunday and July)* (dinner only) 290 and a la carte – ☲ 40 – **379 rm** 780/1140, **4 suites** 1800/3600.

Ramada Presidentti, Eteläinen Rautatiekatu 4, 00100, ℰ 6911, Telex 121953, Fax 6947886, ☎s, ◯ – |♣| ⁂ rm ▤ rm ▥ ☎ ♿ – 🏛 400. 🖭 ⓪ ☰ 𝚅𝙸𝚂𝙰   BY s
closed Christmas – **M** *(closed Sunday lunch and Saturday)* 150/212 and a la carte – **495 rm** ☲ 800/950, **5 suites** 3000/3500.

Lord ⌖, Lönnrotinkatu 29, 00180, ℰ 680 1680, Fax 680 1315, « Part Jugendstil (Art Nouveau) building, fireplaces », ☎s – |♣| ⁂ rm ▤ ▥ ☎ ♿ ☜ – 🏛 170. 🖭 ⓪ ☰ 𝚅𝙸𝚂𝙰   BZ s
closed 22 to 26 December – **M** *(closed Saturday lunch, Sunday and 21 June-5 August)* 170/250 and a la carte – **35 rm** ☲ 620/750, **1 suite** 1000/1500.

Palace, Eteläranta 10, 00130, ℰ 134 561, Telex 121570, Fax 654 786, ☎s – |♣| ⁂ rm ▥ ☎ – 🏛 170. 🖭 ⓪ ☰ 𝚅𝙸𝚂𝙰   DZ c
closed Easter and Christmas – **M La Vista** 180/235 and a la carte – (see also rest. **Palace Gourmet** below) – **53 rm** ☲ 820/970, **6 suites** 1650/2450.

Klaus Kurki, Bulevardi 2, 00120, ℰ 618 911, Telex 121670, Fax 608 538, ☎s – |♣| ⁂ rm ▤ rm ▥ ☎. 🖭 ⓪ ☰ 𝚅𝙸𝚂𝙰. ⌖   CY t
closed 28 March-2 April and Christmas – **M** *(closed lunch Saturday and Sunday)* 140/170 and a la carte – ☲ 35 – **133 rm** ☲ 680/840, **2 suites** 1200.

Seurahuone without rest., Kaivokatu 12, 00100, ℰ 170 441, Telex 122234, Fax 664 170, ☎s – |♣| ⁂ ▥ ☎ – 🏛 70. 🖭 ⓪ ☰ 𝚅𝙸𝚂𝙰   CY e
118 rm ☲ 650/1100.

Arctia Hotel Marski, Mannerheimintie 10, 00100, ℰ 68061, Telex 121240, Fax 642 377, ☎s – |♣| ⁂ rm ▤ ▥ ☎ ☜ – 🏛 600. 🖭 ⓪ ☰ 𝚅𝙸𝚂𝙰   CY d
M 132 (lunch) and a la carte 117/170 – ☲ 30 – **157 rm** 750/820, **7 suites** 1800.

Pasila 🅼, Maistraatinportti 3, 00240, ℰ 148 841, Telex 125809, Fax 143 771, ☎s, squash – |♣| ⁂ rm ▤ ▥ ♿ ☜ Ⓟ – 🏛 80. 🖭 ⓪ ☰ 𝚅𝙸𝚂𝙰   N : 3 km by Mannerheimintie   BX
M 135/250 and a la carte – **252 rm** ☲ 510/650, **1 suite** 750/1300.

🏨 **Rivoli Jardin** Ⓜ ⚏ without rest., Kasarmikatu 40, 00130, 𝒫 177 880, Telex 125881, Fax 656 988, ⬧ – ▮ ✦ rm ▦ ☎ க. Ⅲ ⓞ Ε *VISA* ✦
CYZ **k**
closed 22 to 27 December – **53 rm** ⌷ 690/790. **1 suite** 1800.

🏨 **Helsinki** without rest., Hallituskatu 12, 00100, 𝒫 171 401, Telex 121022, Fax 176 014, ⬧ – ▮
✦ rm ☎ – க 30. ✦
CY **a**
129 rm.

🏨 **Torni,** Yrjönkatu 26, 00100, 𝒫 131 131, Telex 125153, Fax 1311361, ⬧ – ▮ ✦ rm ▦ ☎ –
க 30. Ⅲ ⓞ Ε *VISA* ✦
BY **r**
M – Ritarisali 200/450 and a la carte – **146 rm** ⌷ 660/950. **9 suites** 950.

🏨 **Aurora** without rest., Helsinginkatu 50, 00530, 𝒫 717 400, Telex 125643, Fax 714 240, ƒ෧.
⬧, ⟨⟩, squash – ▮ ✦ rm ▦ ☎ Ⓟ – க 80. Ⅲ ⓞ Ε *VISA*
70 rm ⌷ 430/630.
NE : 2 km by Helsinginkatu BX

🏠 **Anna** without rest., Annankatu 1, 00120, 𝒫 648 011, Telex 125514, Fax 602 664, ⬧ – ▮ ✦
▦ ☎. Ⅲ Ε *VISA* ✦
CZ **b**
closed Christmas-New Year – **59 rm** ⌷ 380/520. **1 suite** 800/900.

XXX **Havis Amanda,** Unioninkatu 23, 00170, 𝒫 666 882, Telex 121570, Fax 631 435, Seafood –
Ⅲ ⓞ Ε *VISA*
DY **r**
closed Sunday and Bank Holidays – **M** (booking essential) (restricted lunch) 180/330 and a la carte.

XXX **Palace Gourmet,** (at Palace H.), Eteläranta 10 (10th floor), 00130, 𝒫 134 561, Telex 121570, Fax 654 786, ⟨ harbour and city – ▤. Ⅲ ⓞ Ε *VISA*
DZ **c**
closed Saturday, Sunday, 4 weeks July and Bank Holidays – **M** 250/420 and dinner a la carte.

XXX **Alexander Nevski,** Pohjoisesplanadi 17, 00170, 𝒫 639 610, Group Telex 121570, Fax 631 435, Russian rest. – ▤. Ⅲ ⓞ Ε *VISA*
DY **r**
closed lunch in July and Sunday – **M** (restricted lunch)/dinner 360 and a la carte.

XXX ✿ **George,** Kalevankatu 17, 00100, 𝒫 647 662, Fax 603 787 – ▤. Ⅲ ⓞ Ε *VISA*
BY **f**
closed Saturday lunch, Sunday, Midsummer Day, July and Christmas – **M** (restricted lunch)/dinner 354 and a la carte 255/354
Spec. Warm beetroot timbale and ceps with lingonberry sauce, Wild duck cooked in an old fashioned way, Lapp cheese and cinnamon pudding with arctic cloudberry sauce.

XX **Svenska Klubben,** Maurinkatu 6, 00170, 𝒫 1354706, Fax 1354896, « Scottish style house »
– ▤
DX **n**

XX **Rivoli (Kala and Cheri),** Albertinkatu 38, 00180, 𝒫 643 455, « Nautical decor » – ▤. Ⅲ ⓞ Ε *VISA*
BZ **a**
closed Saturday lunch, Sunday, 29 March-1 April, 21 to 23 June, 24 to 26 December and Bank Holidays – **M** (restricted lunch)/dinner a la carte 145/233.

XX **Piekka,** Mannerheimintie 68, 00260, 𝒫 493 591, Fax 495 664, Finnish rest. – Ⅲ ⓞ Ε *VISA*
by Mannerheimintie BX
closed 28 March-1 April and 16 to 20 April – **M** (dinner only) a la carte 136/261.

XX **Amadeus,** Sofiankatu 4, 00170, 𝒫 626 676 – Ⅲ ⓞ Ε *VISA*
DY **a**
closed Saturday lunch, Sunday and Bank Holidays – **M** (restricted lunch)/dinner 330.

X **Troikka,** Caloniuksenkatu 3, 00100, 𝒫 445 229, Russian rest. – ▤. Ⅲ ⓞ Ε *VISA*
AX **e**
closed Saturday, Sunday, Easter and Christmas – **M** 200 and a la carte.

on 137 N : 15 km – ⊠ Vanta – ✿ 90 Helsinki :

🏨 **Airport Hotel Rantasipi** Ⓜ, Takamaantie 4, Box 53, 01510, 𝒫 87051, Telex 121812, Fax 822 846, ⬧, ⟨⟩ – ▮ ✦ rm ▦ ☎ க. Ⓟ – க 150. Ⅲ ⓞ Ε *VISA*
M 110 and dinner a la carte – **296 rm** ⌷ 640/730. **4 suites** 1200/1700.
by Helsinginkatu BX

France

Paris and Environs
Bordeaux
Cannes
Lyons
Marseilles
Monaco (Principality of)
Nice
Strasbourg
Valley of the Loire

PRACTICAL INFORMATION

LOCAL CURRENCY

French Franc : 100 F = 19.49 US $ (Jan. 91)

TOURIST INFORMATION IN PARIS

Paris "Welcome" Office (Office de Tourisme de Paris - Accueil de France) :
127 Champs-Élysées, 8th, ✆ 47 23 61 72, Telex 611984
American Express 11 Rue Scribe, 9th, ✆ 42 66 09 99

AIRLINES

T.W.A. : 101 Champs-Élysées, 8th, ✆ 47 20 62 11
PAN AM : 1 Rue Scribe, 9th, ✆ 42 66 45 45
BRITISH AIRWAYS : 91 Champs-Élysées, 8th, ✆ 47 78 14 14
AIR FRANCE : 119 Champs-Élysées, 8th, ✆ 45 35 61 61
AIR INTER : 1 Avenue Mar. Devaux, 91551 Paray-Vieille-Poste Cedex, ✆ 46 75 12 12
UTA : 3 Boulevard Malesherbes, 8th, ✆ 40 17 46 46

FOREIGN EXCHANGE OFFICES

Banks : close at 5pm and at weekends
Orly Airport : daily 6.30am to 11.30pm
Charles de Gaulle Airport : daily 6am to 11.30pm

TRANSPORT IN PARIS

Taxis : may be hailed in the street when showing the illuminated sign-available day
and night at taxi ranks or called by telephone.
Bus-Métro (subway) : for full details see the Michelin Plan de Paris no 11. The metro
is quicker but the bus is good for sightseeing and practical for short distances.

POSTAL SERVICES

Local post offices : open Mondays to Fridays 8am to 7pm ; Saturdays 8am to noon
General Post Office, 52 rue du Louvre, 1st : open 24 hours

SHOPPING IN PARIS

Department stores : Boulevard Haussmann, Rue de Rivoli and Rue de Sèvres
Exclusive shops and boutiques : Faubourg St-Honoré, Rue de la Paix and Rue Royale,
Avenue Montaigne.
Antiques and second-hand goods : Swiss Village (Avenue de la Motte Picquet),
Louvre des Antiquaires (Place du Palais Royal), Flea Market (Porte Clignancourt).

TIPPING

Service is generally included in hotel and restaurants bills. But you may choose to
leave more than the expected tip to the staff. Taxi-drivers, porters, barbers and
theatre or cinema attendants also expect a small gratuity.

BREAKDOWN SERVICE

Certain garages in central and outer Paris operate a 24 hour breakdown service. If you
breakdown the police are usually able to help by indicating the nearest one.

SPEED LIMITS

The maximum permitted speed in built up areas is 50 km/h - 31 mph ; on motorways
the speed limit is 130 km/h - 80 mph and 110 km/h - 68 mph on dual carriageways. On
all other roads 90 km/h - 56 mph.

SEAT BELTS

The wearing of seat belts is compulsory for drivers and passengers.

PARIS
and environs

PARIS 75 Maps : **10**, **11**, **12** and **14** G. Paris — ⊕ 1.

Population : Paris 2 176 243 ; Ile-de-France region : 9 878 500.
Altitude : Observatory : 60 m ; Place Concorde : 34 m
Air Terminals : Esplanade des Invalides, 7th, ✆ 43 23 97 10 — Palais des Congrès, Porte Maillot, 17th, ✆ 42 99 20 18
Paris' Airports : see Orly and Charles de Gaulle (Roissy)
Railways, motorail : information ✆ 45 82 50 50.

7

ARRONDISSEMENTS

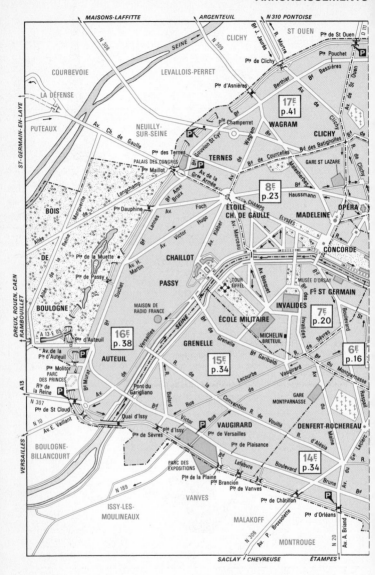

P Car park	_.._.._ Arrondissement boundary
	One-way street
Ring road (interchange: complete, partial)	

AND DISTRICTS

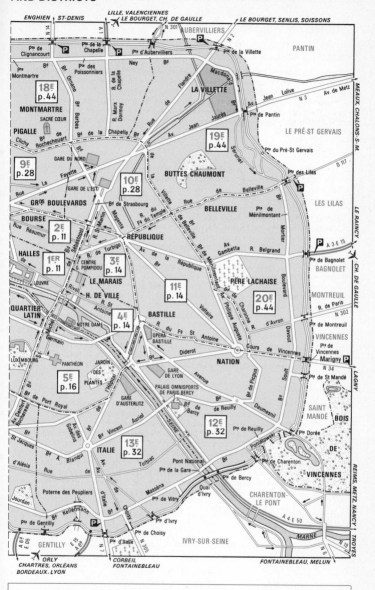

To find your way in the capital, use the **Michelin street plans of Paris**

10 sheet map, **12** sheet map with street index,

11 atlas with street index and practical information,

14 atlas with street index.

SIGHTS

STREETS – SQUARES – GARDENS

Champs-Élysées★★★ F 8, F 9, G 10 – Place de la Concorde★★★ (Obelisk of Luxor) G 11 – Tuileries Gardens★★ (Jardin des Tuileries) H 12 – Rue du Faubourg St-Honoré★★ G 11, G 12 – Avenue de l'Opéra★★ G 13 – Place Vendôme★★ G 12 – Place des Vosges★★ J 17 – Place du Tertre★★ D 14 – Botanical Gardens★★ (Jardin des Plantes) L 16 – Avenue Foch★ F 6, F 7 – Rue de Rivoli★ G 12 – Rue Mouffetard★ M 15 – Place de la Bastille (July Column : Colonne de Juillet) – Place de la République – Grands Boulevards F 13, F 14.

OLD QUARTERS

Cité★★★ (Ile St-Louis, The Quays) J 14, J 15 – Le Marais★★★ – Montmartre★★★ D 14 – Montagne Ste Geneviève★★ (Latin Quarter : Quartier Latin) K 14.

MAIN MONUMENTS

Louvre★★★ (Royal Palace : Palais des Rois de France★★★ ; Cour Carrée, Perrault's Colonnade, Embankment Façade : façade sur le quai, the "two arms" of the Louvre : les "bras" du Louvre, Carrousel Triumphal Arch : Arc de Triomphe du Carrousel, and The Pyramid.) H 13 – Notre Dame Cathedral★★★ K 15 – Sainte Chapelle★★★ J 14 – Arc de Triomphe★★★ F 8 (Place Charles de Gaulle) – Eiffel Tower★★★ (Tour Eiffel) J 7 – The Invalides★★★ (Dôme Church : Napoléon's tomb) J 10 – Palais Royal★★ H 13 – Madeleine★★ G 11 – Opera★★ F 12 – St. Germain l'Auxerrois Church★★ H 14 – Conciergerie★★ J 14 – Ecole Militaire★★ K 9 – Luxembourg★★ (Palace, gardens) KL 13 – Panthéon★★ L 14 – St. Séverin Church★★ K 14 – St. Germain des Prés Church★★ J 13 – St. Etienne du Mont Church★★ – St. Sulpice Church★★ K 13 – Hôtel de Lamoignon★★ J 16 – Hôtel Guénégaud★★ (Museum of the Chase) H 16 – Hôtel de Rohan★★ H 16 – Soubise Palace★★ (Historical Museum of France) H 16 – The Sacré Cœur Basilica★★ D 14 – Montparnasse Tower★★ LM 11 – Institute of France★ (Institut de France) J 13 – Radio France House★ (Maison de Radio France) – Palais des Congrès★ – St. Roch Church★ G 13 – Alexandre III Bridge★ (Pont Alexandre III) H 10 – Pont Neuf J 14 – Pont des Arts J 13.

MAIN MUSEUMS

Louvre★★★ : Frieze of the Archers, Seated Scribe, Vénus de Milo, Winged Victory of Samothrace, Nymphs of Jean Goujon, Mona Lisa : La Joconde, Regent diamond… H 13 – Orsay★★★ H 12 – Army Museum★★★ (The Invalides★★★) J 10 – Centre for Science and Industry★★★ (La Villette★★) BC 20 – Modern Art Museum★★★ (Georges Pompidou Centre★★) H 15 – Decorative Arts★★ H 13 – Hôtel de Cluny and its Museum★★ (The Lady and the Unicorn) K 14 – Rodin★★ (Hôtel de Biron) J 10 – Historical Museum of Paris★★ (Hôtel Carnavalet★) J 17 – Picasso★★ (Hôtel Salé) H 17 – Museum of French Monuments★★, Museum of Man★★, Maritime Museum★★ (Chaillot Palace) H 7 – Science Museum★★ (Palais de la Découverte★★) G 10 – National Technical Museum★★ (Conservatoire des Arts et Métiers★★) G 16.

K 14, G 10 : *Reference letters and numbers on the Michelin town plans* **10**, **11**, **12**, *or* **15**.

ALPHABETICAL LIST OF HOTELS AND RESTAURANTS

■ HOTELS, RESTAURANTS

Listed by districts and arrondissements

(List of Hotels and Restaurants in alphabetical order, see pp 5 to 8)

G 12 : These reference letters and numbers correspond to the squares on the Michelin **Map of Paris** n° **10**, **Paris Atlas** n° **11**, **Map with street index** n° **12** and **Map of Paris** n° **14**.

Consult any of the above publications when looking for a car park nearest to a listed establishment.

**Opéra, Palais-Royal,
Halles, Bourse.**
1st and 2nd arrondissements.
1st : ⊠ 75001
2nd : ⊠ 75002

Ritz ⑤, 15 pl. Vendôme (1st) ℰ 42 60 38 30, Telex 222262, Fax 42 60 23 71, ☆, « Attractive pool and luxurious fitness centre » – |創 🗏 🔟 ☎ ἀ – 益 30 - 80. 亞 ① Ε 𝒱𝒮𝒜. ⋘ rest   G 12
M see **Espadon** below – ⊑ 150 – **142 rm** 2750/3900, 45 apartments.

Meurice, 228 r. Rivoli (1st) ℰ 42 60 38 60, Telex 230673, Fax 49 27 94 97 – |創 ⇌ rm 🗏 🔟 ☎ ἀ – 益 40 - 100. 亞 ① Ε 𝒱𝒮𝒜. ⋘ rest   G 12
M 300 (lunch)/650 – ⊑ 120 – **148 rm** 1950/3200, 36 apartments.

Inter-Continental, 3 r. Castiglione (1st) ℰ 44 77 11 11, Telex 220114, Fax 44 77 14 60, ☆ – |創 ⇌ rm 🗏 🔟 ☎ ἀ – 益 500. 亞 ① Ε 𝒱𝒮𝒜. ⋘ rest   G 12
Café Tuileries (coffee shop) **M** 115 – **La Terrasse Fleurie M** 340/500 – ⊑ 150 – **424 rm** 1800/2400, 16 apartments.

Lotti, 7 r. Castiglione (1st) ℰ 42 60 37 34, Telex 240066, Fax 40 15 93 56 – |創 ⇌ rm 🗏 🔟 ☎ – 益 25. 亞 ① Ε 𝒱𝒮𝒜. ⋘ rest   G 12
M a la carte 280/490 – ⊑ 110 – **129 rm** 1500/3000.

Westminster, 13 r. Paix (2nd) ℰ 42 61 57 46, Telex 680035, Fax 42 60 30 66 – |創 ⇌ rm 🗏 rm 🔟 ☎ – 益 40. 亞 ① Ε 𝒱𝒮𝒜   G 12
M see **Le Céladon** below – ⊑ 100 – **84 rm** 1750/2250, 18 apartments.

du Louvre, pl. A. Malraux (1st) ℰ 42 61 56 01, Telex 220412, Fax 42 60 02 90 – |創 🗏 🔟 ☎ ἀ – 益 100. 亞 ① Ε 𝒱𝒮𝒜   H 13
Brasserie Le Louvre M 95/175 ἀ – ⊑ 85 – **200 rm** 980/1950.

Édouard VII et rest. le Delmonico, 39 av. Opéra (2nd) ℰ 42 61 56 90, Telex 680217, Fax 42 61 47 73 – |創 🗏 rest 🔟 ☎ – 益 45. 亞 ① Ε 𝒱𝒮𝒜   G 13
M *(closed August, Saturday, Sunday and Bank Holidays)* 220/400 – ⊑ 30 – **76 rm** 750/1020, 4 apartments 1800.

Normandy, 7 r. Échelle (1st) ℰ 42 60 30 21, Telex 213015, Fax 42 60 45 81 – |創 🔟 ☎ – 益 50. 亞 ① Ε 𝒱𝒮𝒜   H 13
L'Echelle *(closed Saturday and sunday)* **M** 180 and a la carte 160/280 – ⊑ 65 – **123 rm** 870/1420, 8 apartments 1600.

Cambon without rest, 3 r. Cambon (1st) ℰ 42 60 38 09, Telex 240814, Fax 42 60 30 59 – |創 🔟 ☎. 亞 ① Ε 𝒱𝒮𝒜   G 12
⊑ 65 – **43 rm** 830/1180.

Mayfair without rest, 3 r. Rouget-de-Lisle (1st) ℰ 42 60 38 14, Telex 240037, Fax 40 15 04 78 – |創 🔟 ☎. 亞 ① Ε 𝒱𝒮𝒜   G 12
⊑ 75 – **53 rm** 750/1460.

Novotel Paris Halles Ⓜ, 8 pl. M.-de-Navarre (1st) ℰ 42 21 31 31, Telex 216389, Fax 40 26 05 79, ☆ – |創 🗏 🔟 ☎ ἀ – 益 40 - 100. 亞 ① Ε 𝒱𝒮𝒜   H 14
M a la carte approx. 180 ἀ – ⊑ 55 – **280 rm** 750/1050, 5 apartments 1400.

Royal St Honoré without rest, 13 r. Alger (1st) ℰ 42 60 32 79, Telex 680429, Fax 42 61 21 49 – |創 🔟 ☎ – 益 25. 亞 ① Ε 𝒱𝒮𝒜   G 12
⊑ 45 – **71 rm** 670/870, 3 apartments 1550.

Castille, 37 r. Cambon (1st) ℰ 42 61 55 20, Telex 213505, Fax 40 15 97 64, ☆ – |創 🔟 ☎. 亞 ① Ε 𝒱𝒮𝒜   G 12
Relais Castille *(closed Saturday, Sunday and Bank Holidays)* **M** a la carte 140/210 – ⊑ 60 – **61 rm** 1450, 15 apartments.

🏠 **de Noailles** Ⓜ without rest, 9 r. Michodière (2nd) ℰ 47 42 92 90, Telex 290644, Fax 49 24 92 71 – 🛗 ☎ 🄴 𝒱𝐼𝑆𝐴
☑ 35 – **58 rm** 650/750. — G 13

🏠 **Favart** without rest, 5 r. Marivaux (2nd) ℰ 42 97 59 83, Telex 213126, Fax 40 15 95 58 – 🛗 📺 ☎ ぐ. 🄰🄴 🄴 𝒱𝐼𝑆𝐴
37 rm ☑ 500/600. — F 13

🏠 **François** without rest, 3 bd Montmartre (2nd) ℰ 42 33 51 53, Telex 211097, Fax 40 26 29 90 – 🛗 📺 🎁. 🄰🄴 ① 🄴 𝒱𝐼𝑆𝐴. ⚘
☑ 45 – **62 rm** 565/780, 7 apartments 795/930. — F 14

🏠 **Montana Tuileries** without rest, 12 r. St-Roch (1st) ℰ 42 60 35 10, Telex 214404, Fax 42 61 12 28 – 🛗 📺 ☎ 🄰🄴 ① 🄴 𝒱𝐼𝑆𝐴
☑ 45 – **25 rm** 660/920. — G 12

🏠 **Duminy Vendôme** without rest, 3 r. Mont-Thabor (1st) ℰ 42 60 32 80, Telex 213492, Fax 42 96 07 83 – 🛗 📺 ☎ – 🔥 30. 🄰🄴 🄴 𝒱𝐼𝑆𝐴
☑ 40 – **79 rm** 700/900. — G 12

🏠 **Molière** without rest, 21 r. Molière (1st) ℰ 42 96 22 01, Telex 213292, Fax 42 60 48 68 – 🛗 📺 ☎. 🄰🄴 ① 🄴 𝒱𝐼𝑆𝐴. ⚘
☑ 35 – **29 rm** 400/600, 3 apartments 1200. — G 13

🏠 **Lautrec Opéra** Ⓜ without rest, 8 r. d'Ambroise (2nd) ℰ 42 96 67 90, Telex 216502, Fax 42 96 06 83 – 🛗 📺 ☎ 🄰🄴 🄴 𝒱𝐼𝑆𝐴. ⚘
☑ 25 – **30 rm** 500/700. — F 13

🏠 **Baudelaire Opéra** Ⓜ without rest, 61 r. Ste Anne (2nd) ℰ 42 97 50 62, Telex 216116, Fax 42 86 85 85 – 🛗 📺 ☎ 🄰🄴 ① 🄴 𝒱𝐼𝑆𝐴
☑ 31 – **29 rm** 440/530, 5 duplex 650. — G 13

🏠 **Gd H. de Champagne** without rest, 17 r. J.-Lantier (1st) ℰ 42 36 60 00, Telex 215955, Fax 45 08 43 33 – 🛗 📺 ☎ 🄰🄴 ① 🄴 𝒱𝐼𝑆𝐴
☑ 50 – **40 rm** 510/550, 3 apartments 1070. — J 14

🏠 **Gaillon-Opéra** without rest, 9 r. Gaillon (2nd) ℰ 47 42 47 74, Telex 215716, Fax 47 42 01 23 – 🛗 📺 ☎ 🄰🄴 ① 🄴 𝒱𝐼𝑆𝐴
☑ 30 – **26 rm** 550/700. — G 13

🏠 **Britannique** without rest, 20 av. Victoria (1st) ℰ 42 33 74 59, Telex 230600, Fax 42 33 82 65 – 🛗 📺 ☎ 🄰🄴 ① 🄴 𝒱𝐼𝑆𝐴. ⚘
☑ 40 – **40 rm** 470/650. — J 14

🏠 **Ducs de Bourgogne** without rest, 19 r. Pont-Neuf (1st) ℰ 42 33 95 64, Telex 216367, Fax 40 39 01 25 – 🛗 📺 ☎ 🄰🄴 🄴 𝒱𝐼𝑆𝐴. ⚘
☑ 38 – **50 rm** 410/520. — H 14

🏠 **Louvre-Forum** without rest, 25 r. du Bouloi (1st) ℰ 42 36 54 19, Telex 240288, Fax 42 33 66 31 – 🛗 📺 ☎ 🄰🄴 🄴 𝒱𝐼𝑆𝐴
☑ 30 – **28 rm** 370/460. — H 14

🏠 **Ducs d'Anjou** without rest, 1 r. Ste-Opportune (1st) ℰ 42 36 92 24, Telex 218681, Fax 42 36 16 63 – 🛗 📺 ☎ 🄰🄴 ① 🄴 𝒱𝐼𝑆𝐴
☑ 38 – **38 rm** 360/530. — H 14

🏠 **Timhôtel Le Louvre** without rest, 4 r. Croix des Petits Champs (1st) ℰ 42 60 34 86, Telex 216405, Fax 42 60 10 39 – 🛗 📺 ☎ ぐ. 🄰🄴 ① 🄴 𝒱𝐼𝑆𝐴
☑ 40 – **56 rm** 365/475. — H 13

🏠 **Family** without rest, 35 r. Cambon (1st) ℰ 42 61 54 84 – 🛗 📺 ☎ ぐ. 🄰🄴 🄴 𝒱𝐼𝑆𝐴 — G 12
☑ 28 – **25 rm** 450/550.

XXXXX ✿✿ **Espadon** - Hôtel Ritz, 15 pl. Vendôme (1st) ℰ 42 60 38 30, Telex 220262, Fax 42 60 23 71, 🍽️ – 🗐 🄰🄴 ① 🄴 𝒱𝐼𝑆𝐴. ⚘ — G 12
M 330 (lunch) and a la carte 450/680
Spec. Petite salade ''Cendrillon''. Omble chevalier du lac Pavin (November-December), Ris de veau braisé.

XXXX ✿✿ **Grand Vefour**, 17 r. Beaujolais (1st) ℰ 42 96 56 27, Fax 42 86 80 71, « Pre-Revolutionary (late 18C) Café Style » – 🗐 🄰🄴 ① 🄴 𝒱𝐼𝑆𝐴. ⚘ — G 13
closed August, Saturday lunch and Sunday – **M** 305 (lunch) and a la carte 470/650
Spec. Croustillant de foie gras et artichaut confit, Sole au jus de moules, Noisettes d'agneau à la vinaigrette de basilic.

XXXX ✿✿ **Carré des Feuillants** (Dutournier), 14 r. Castiglione (1st) ℰ 42 86 82 82, Fax 42 86 07 71 – 🗐 🄰🄴 ① 🄴 𝒱𝐼𝑆𝐴 — G 12
closed Saturday (except dinner September-June) and Sunday – **M** 250 (lunch) and a la carte 400/550
Spec. Homard en gaspacho blanc, Saint-Jacques en fine croûte persillée, Perdreau rôti à la ventrèche croquante.

XXXX ✿ **Drouant**, pl. Gaillon (2nd) ℰ 42 65 15 16, Fax 49 24 02 15 – 🗐 🄰🄴 ① 🄴 𝒱𝐼𝑆𝐴 — G 13
M 290 (lunch) and a la carte 420/600 - **Café Drouant M** a la carte 240/350
Spec. Tian de rouget aux épinards et tomate acidulée, Pigeonneau rôti en croûte de pommes de terre, Macaron aux deux chocolats.

XXXX ✦✦ **Gérard Besson**, 5 r. Coq Héron (1st) ℰ 42 33 14 74, Fax 42 33 85 71 – 🗏 🖭 ⓞ 🗲 𝑉𝐼𝑆𝐴
closed 6 to 28 July, 21 December-5 January, Saturday and Sunday – **M** 250 (lunch) and a la carte 370/510   **H 14**
Spec. Champignons et truffes fraîches (season), Volailles de Bresse, Biscuit glacé à la framboise.

XXX ✦ **Mercure Galant**, 15 r. Petits-Champs (1st) ℰ 42 97 53 85 – 𝑉𝐼𝑆𝐴   **G 13**
closed Saturday lunch and Sunday – **M** 230 (lunch) and a la carte 330/450
Spec. Tournedos de saumon fumé, Coeur de Charolais à la moelle en papillote, Mille et une feuilles.

XXX ✦ **Le Céladon** - Hôtel Westminster, 15 r. Daunou (2nd) ℰ 42 61 57 46, Telex 680035, Fax 42 60 30 66 – 🗏 🖭 ⓞ 🗲 𝑉𝐼𝑆𝐴   **G 12**
closed August, Saturday, Sunday an Bank Holidays – **M** 300 and a la carte 400/510
Spec. Tartare de saumon à l'émulsion d'herbettes, Parmentier de homard, Noix de ris de veau grillé aux chicons.

XXX ✦ **Goumard**, 17 r. Duphot (1st) ℰ 42 60 36 07, Seafood, « Lovely azulejos panels » – 🗏 🖭 ⓞ 🗲 𝑉𝐼𝑆𝐴. ⌱   **G 12**
closed 30 April-13 May, 12 to 19 August, 24 December-6 January, Sunday and Monday – **M** a la carte 365/500
Spec. Poêlée de Saint-Jacques en aigre doux (October-May), Fricassée de moules aux girolles (June-December), Rougets à la "Catalane".

XXX ✦ **Pierre '' A la Fontaine Gaillon ''**, pl. Gaillon (2nd) ℰ 42 65 87 04, 🍽 – 🗏 🖭 ⓞ 🗲 𝑉𝐼𝑆𝐴
closed August, Saturday lunch and Sunday – **M** a la carte 190/360.   **G 13**

XXX **Chez Vong**, 10 r. Grande-Truanderie (1st) ℰ 40 39 99 89, Chinese and Vietnamese rest. – 🗏 🖭 ⓞ 🗲 𝑉𝐼𝑆𝐴
closed Sunday – **M** a la carte 175/320.   **H 15**

XXX **La Corbeille**, 154 r. Montmartre (2nd) ℰ 40 26 30 87 – ⌱ 🖭 🗲 𝑉𝐼𝑆𝐴   **G 14**
closed 1 to 15 August (except dinner September-February), Sunday and Bank Holidays – **M** 220/495.

XX **Pied de Cochon**, 6 r. Coquillière (1st) ℰ 42 36 11 75, Fax 45 08 48 90 – 🗏 🖭 ⓞ 𝑉𝐼𝑆𝐴   **H 14**
M a la carte 170/330.

XX ✦ **Chez Pauline**, 5 r. Villedo (1st) ℰ 42 96 20 70, Fax 49 27 99 89 – 🗏 🖭 🗲 𝑉𝐼𝑆𝐴   **G 13**
closed 27 July-20 August, 21 to 30 December, Saturday (except lunch October-April) and Sunday – **M** (🗏 1st floor) 190 (lunch) and a la carte 250/400
Spec. Salade tiède de tête de veau, Fricassée de filets de sole et queues de langoustines au Sauternes, Compote de lièvre à la royale (late Sept.-late Dec.)

XX ✦ **Pierre Au Palais Royal**, 10 r. Richelieu (1st) ℰ 42 96 09 17 – ⓞ 🗲 𝑉𝐼𝑆𝐴   **H 13**
closed August, Saturday, Sunday and Bank Holidays – **M** a la carte 225/410
Spec. Filets de maquereaux au cidre, Médaillon de lotte en papillote, Rognon de veau rôti à l'échalote confite.

XX **Saudade**, 34 r. Bourdonnais (1st) ℰ 42 36 30 71, Portuguese rest. – 🗏 🖭 ⓞ 🗲 𝑉𝐼𝑆𝐴. ⌱
closed August and Sunday – **M** a la carte 165/255.   **H 14**

XX **Capeline**, 18 r. Louvre (1st) ℰ 42 86 95 05 – 🗏 🖭 ⓞ 🗲 𝑉𝐼𝑆𝐴   **H 14**
closed 12 August-2 September, February Holidays, Saturday lunch and Sunday – **M** 220 b.i./320.

XX **Kinugawa**, 9 r. Mont-Thabor (1st) ℰ 42 60 65 07, Fax 42 60 45 21, Japanese rest. – 🗏 🖭 🗲 𝑉𝐼𝑆𝐴. ⌱   **G 12**
closed 24 December-7 January and Sunday – **M** a la carte 170/300.

XX ✦ **Pharamond**, 24 r. Grande-Truanderie (1st) ℰ 42 33 06 72 – 🖭 ⓞ 🗲 𝑉𝐼𝑆𝐴   **H 15**
closed 21 July-19 August, Monday lunch and Sunday – **M** a la carte 190/350
Spec. Saint-Jacques au cidre (15 October-May), Tripes à la mode de Caen, Aile de volaille au foie gras et chou.

XX **Escargot Montorgueil**, 38 r. Montorgueil (1st) ℰ 42 36 83 51, Fax 42 36 35 05, « Bistro 1830 decor » – 🖭 ⓞ 🗲 𝑉𝐼𝑆𝐴   **H 14**
closed 1 to 19 August and Monday – **M** 240 and a la carte 250/350.

XX ✦ **Pile ou Face**, 52bis r. N.-D.-des-Victoires (2nd) ℰ 42 33 64 33, Fax 42 36 61 09 – 🗏 🗲 𝑉𝐼𝑆𝐴
closed 22 July-25 August, 23 December-1 January, Saturday, Sunday and Bank Holidays – **M** a la carte 250/440   **G 14**
Spec. Escalope de foie gras au pain d'épices, Pigeonneau rôti à l'huile de truffe, Dessert au chocolat de Marianne.

XX **Bernard Chirent**, 28 r. Mont-Thabor (1st) ℰ 42 86 80 05 – 🗲 𝑉𝐼𝑆𝐴   **G 12**
closed Saturday lunch and Sunday – **M** 170 b.i. and a la carte 215/335.

XX **Pavillon Baltard**, 9 r. Coquillière (1st) ℰ 42 36 22 00, 🍽 – 🗏 🖭 ⓞ 🗲 𝑉𝐼𝑆𝐴   **H 14**
M 148 and a la carte 170/260 ⌱.

XX **Velloni**, 22 r. des Halles (1st) ℰ 42 21 12 50, Italian rest. – 🖭 ⓞ 🗲 𝑉𝐼𝑆𝐴. ⌱   **H 14**
closed August and Sunday – **M** a la carte 185/270.

XX **A la Grille St-Honoré**, 15 pl. Marché St-Honoré (1st) ℰ 42 61 00 93 – 🖭 ⓞ 🗲 𝑉𝐼𝑆𝐴   **G 13**
closed 4 to 20 August, 22 December-2 January, Sunday and Monday – **M** 180 and a la carte 225/400.

XX **Coup de coeur**, 19 r. St-Augustin (2nd) ℰ 47 03 45 70 – 🖭 ⓞ 🗲 𝑉𝐼𝑆𝐴   **G 13**
closed Saturday lunch and Sunday – **M** 125/160 b.i..

XX **Vaudeville**, 29 r. Vivienne (2nd) ℰ 40 20 04 62, Fax 49 27 08 78, brasserie – 🖭 ⓞ 🗲 𝑉𝐼𝑆𝐴
M a la carte 125/285 ⌱.   **FG 14**

XX **Chatelet Gourmand,** 13 r. Lavandières Ste-Opportune (1st) ✆ 40 26 45 00 – 🆎 ⓪ 🇪 🇻🇮🇸🇦 – *closed August, Saturday lunch, Sunday and Bank Holidays* – **M** 140/380.   J 14

XX **Le Grand Colbert,** 2 r. Vivienne (2nd) ✆ 42 86 87 88 – 🆎 ⓪ 🇪 🇻🇮🇸🇦   G 13
M a la carte 160/230 ⓵.

XX **Le Soufflé,** 36 r. Mont-Thabor (1st) ✆ 42 60 27 19 – 🍽. 🆎 ⓪ 🇪 🇻🇮🇸🇦   G 12
closed Sunday – **M** 190.

XX **Les Cartes Postales,** 7 r. Gomboust (1st) ✆ 42 61 02 93 – 🍽. 🇻🇮🇸🇦. 🛇   G 13
closed 29 July-17 August, Saturday lunch, Sunday and Bank Holidays – **M** (booking essential) 135/285.

XX **La Main à la Pâte,** 35 r. St-Honoré (1st) ✆ 45 08 85 73, Italian rest. – 🆎 🇪 🇻🇮🇸🇦   H 14
closed Sunday – **M** 160 and a la carte 195/270 ⓵.

XX **Chez Gabriel,** 123 r. St-Honoré (1st) ✆ 42 33 02 99 – 🆎 ⓪ 🇪 🇻🇮🇸🇦. 🛇   H 14
closed 12 July-20 August, 24 December-3 January, Sunday and Bank Holidays – **M** 145/235.

XX **Le Saint Amour,** 8 r. Port Mahon (2nd) ✆ 47 42 63 82 – 🍽. 🆎 ⓪ 🇪 🇻🇮🇸🇦   G 13
closed 13 July-5 August (except dinner 16 September-14 June), Sunday and Bank Holidays – **M** a la carte 210/345.

XX **Le Caveau du Palais,** 19 pl. Dauphine (1st) ✆ 43 26 04 28 – 🆎 🇪 🇻🇮🇸🇦   J 14
closed Saturday October-May and Sunday – **M** 190 b.i./250.

X ✿ **Aux Petits Pères '' Chez Yvonne ''** (Boutard), 8 r. N.-D.-des-Victoires (2nd) ✆ 42 60 91 73 – 🍽. 🆎 🇪 🇻🇮🇸🇦   G 14
closed August, Saturday, Sunday and Bank Holidays – **M** (booking essential) 158 and a la carte 175/300
Spec. Saint-Jacques à la provençale (October-April), Ris de veau à la ''Toulousaine'', Faisan aux choux (season).

X **Le Brin de Zinc... et Madame,** 50 r. Montorgueil (2nd) ✆ 42 21 10 80 – 🆎 🇻🇮🇸🇦   G 14
closed Saturday lunch and Sunday – **M** a la carte 200/280.

X **Chez Georges,** 1 r. Mail (2nd) ✆ 42 60 07 11 – 🍽   G 14
closed Sunday and Bank Holidays – **M** a la carte 185/315.

X **Bonne Fourchette,** 320 r. St-Honoré, in the backyard (1st) ✆ 42 60 45 27 – 🍽. ⓪ 🇪 🇻🇮🇸🇦   G 12
closed February Holidays, Saturday (except dinner 1 April-30 June and September-31 October) and Sunday lunch – **M** 110/160.

X **La Clef du Périgord,** 38 r. Croix des Petits Champs (1st) ✆ 40 20 06 46 – 🇪 🇻🇮🇸🇦   GH 14
closed 1 to 15 May, 12 to 25 August, Saturday lunch and Sunday – **M** 135/188 b.i..

X **Rond de Serviette,** 16 r. St-Augustin (2nd) ✆ 49 27 09 90 – 🍽 🇪 🇻🇮🇸🇦   G 13
closed Saturday (except dinner October-June) and Sunday – **M** a la carte 140/210.

X **Pasadena,** 7 r. du 29-Juillet (1st) ✆ 42 60 68 96 – 🆎 🇻🇮🇸🇦   G 12
closed August, Saturday dinner and Sunday – **M** 90/150 ⓵.

X **Cochon Doré,** 16 r. Thorel (2nd) ✆ 42 33 29 70 – 🍽. 🇪 🇻🇮🇸🇦   G 15
closed Monday – **M** 90/150.

X **Paul,** 15 pl. Dauphine (1st) ✆ 43 54 21 48 – 🇪 🇻🇮🇸🇦. 🛇   J 14
closed August, Tuesday October-May and Monday – **M** a la carte 170/280.

X **La Poule au Pot,** 9 r. Vauvilliers (1st) ✆ 42 36 32 96 – 🇪 🇻🇮🇸🇦   H 14
closed Monday – **M** (dinner only) a la carte 200/330.

Bastille, République, Hôtel de Ville.
3rd, 4th and 11th arrondissements.

    3rd : ✉ 75003
    4th : ✉ 75004
    11th : ✉ 75011

🏨 **Pavillon de la Reine** Ⓜ 🐾 without rest, 28 pl. Vosges (3rd) ✆ 42 77 96 40, Telex 216160, Fax 42 77 63 06 – 🛗 📺 ☎ ⓹ ⟷. 🆎 ⓪ 🇪 🇻🇮🇸🇦   J 17
⌖ 75 – **30 rm** 1080/1300, 23 apartments 1450/2500.

🏨 **Holiday Inn** Ⓜ, 10 pl. République (11th) ✆ 43 55 44 34, Telex 210651, Fax 47 00 32 34, 🍴 – 🛗 ≼⋗ rm 🍽 📺 ☎ ⓹ 🅿 – 🔺 200. 🆎 ⓪ 🇪 🇻🇮🇸🇦   G 17
Belle Époque *(closed 3 August-1 September and Sunday)* **M** 205 (lunch) and a la carte 240/360 – ⌖ 85 – **305 rm** 1100/1540, 7 apartments, 9 duplex.

🏨 **Jeu de Paume** Ⓜ without rest, 54 r. St-Louis-en-l'Ile (4th) ✆ 43 26 14 18, Telex 205160, « 17C tennis court » – 🛗 📺 ☎ – 🔺 30. 🆎 ⓪ 🇪 🇻🇮🇸🇦   K 16
⌖ 65 – **32 rm** 780/990, 8 duplex.

🏨 **Atlantide République** Ⓜ without rest, 114 bd Richard-Lenoir (11th) ✆ 43 38 29 29, Telex 216907, Fax 43 38 03 18 – 🛗 📺 ☎. 🆎 ⓪ 🇪 🇻🇮🇸🇦   H 18
⌖ 32 – **27 rm** 410/520.

🏨 **Beaubourg** Ⓜ without rest, 11 r. S. Le Franc (4th) ✆ 42 74 34 24, Telex 216100, Fax 42 78 68 11 – 🛗 📺 ☎. 🆎 ⓪ 🇪 🇻🇮🇸🇦. 🛇   H 15
⌖ 30 – **28 rm** 430/540.

🏨 **Méridional** Ⓜ without rest, 36 bd Richard-Lenoir (11th) ℰ 48 05 75 00, Telex 211324, Fax 43 57 42 85 – 📳 📺 ☎ ⒶⒺ ⓪ Ε 𝗩𝗜𝗦𝗔
⊆ 40 – **36 rm** 600. J 18

🏨 **Bretonnerie** Ⓜ without rest, 22 r. Ste-Croix-de-la-Bretonnerie (4th) ℰ 48 87 77 63, Fax 42 77 26 78 – 📳 📺 ☎ Ε 𝗩𝗜𝗦𝗔 ⋘
closed 26 July-25 August – ⊆ 38 – **30 rm** 480/680. J 16

🏨 **Lutèce** without rest, 65 r. St-Louis-en-l'Ile (4th) ℰ 43 26 23 52, Fax 43 29 60 25 – 📳 📺 ☎
⋘
⊆ 40 – **23 rm** 650/690. K 16

🏨 **Deux Iles** Ⓜ without rest, 59 r. St-Louis-en-l'Ile (4th) ℰ 43 26 13 35, Fax 43 29 60 25 – 📳 📺 ☎
⊆ 40 – **17 rm** 560/660. K 16

🏨 **Rivoli Notre Dame** without rest, 19 r. Bourg Tibourg (4th) ℰ 42 78 47 39, Telex 215314, Fax 40 29 07 00 – 📳 📺 ☎ ⒶⒺ ⓪ Ε 𝗩𝗜𝗦𝗔 ⋘
⊆ 30 – **31 rm** 480/570. J 16

🏨 **Bastille Spéria** Ⓜ without rest, 1 r. Bastille (4th) ℰ 42 72 04 01, Telex 214327, Fax 42 72 56 38 – 📳 📺 ☎ ⒶⒺ ⓪ Ε 𝗩𝗜𝗦𝗔
⊆ 35 – **42 rm** 460/520. J 17

🏨 **Vieux Saule** Ⓜ without rest, 6 r. Picardie (3rd) ℰ 42 72 01 14, Telex 216840, Fax 40 27 88 21
– 📳 📺 ☎ ⒶⒺ ⓪ Ε 𝗩𝗜𝗦𝗔 ⋘
⊆ 40 – **31 rm** 330/450. H 17

🏨 **Campaville** Ⓜ without rest, 9 r. Chemin Vert (11th) ℰ 43 38 58 08, Telex 218019, Fax 43 38 52 28 – 📳 📺 ☎ ⅙ 🅿 Ε 𝗩𝗜𝗦𝗔
⊆ 28 – **162 rm** 385. J 18

🏨 **Vieux Marais** without rest, 8 r. Plâtre (4th) ℰ 42 78 47 22, Fax 42 78 34 32 – 📳 📺 ☎ Ε 𝗩𝗜𝗦𝗔 ⋘
⊆ 30 – **30 rm** 325/510. H 16

🏨 **Nord et Est** without rest, 49 r. Malte (11th) ℰ 47 00 71 70, Fax 43 57 51 16 – 📳 📺 ☎ Ε 𝗩𝗜𝗦𝗔 ⋘
closed August and 24 December-2 January – ⊆ 30 – **45 rm** 290/320. G 17

🏨 **Paris Voltaire** Ⓜ without rest, 79 r. Sedaine (11th) ℰ 48 05 44 66, Telex 215401, Fax 48 07 87 96 – 📳 📺 ☎ ⒶⒺ ⓪ Ε 𝗩𝗜𝗦𝗔
closed 15 to 31 August – ⊆ 32 – **28 rm** 400/500. J 9

🏨 **Mondia** without rest, 22 r. Grd Prieuré (11th) ℰ 47 00 93 44, Fax 43 38 66 14 – 📳 📺 ☎ ⒶⒺ ⓪ Ε 𝗩𝗜𝗦𝗔
⊆ 25 – **23 rm** 290/320. G 17

🏨 **Place des Vosges** without rest, 12 r. Birague (4th) ℰ 42 72 60 46, Fax 42 72 02 64 – 📳 ☎ ⒶⒺ ⓪ Ε 𝗩𝗜𝗦𝗔
⊆ 30 – **16 rm** 260/380. J 17

XXXX ✿✿✿ **L'Ambroisie** (Pacaud), 9 pl. des Vosges (4th) ℰ 42 78 51 45 – Ε 𝗩𝗜𝗦𝗔 ⋘ J 17
closed 5 to 26 August, February Holidays, Sunday and Monday – **M** a la carte 550/700
Spec. Feuillantine de queues de langoustines aux graines de sésame, Queue de boeuf en crépine et turban de macaroni, Tarte fine sablée au cacao amer.

XXX **Ambassade d'Auvergne,** 22 r. Grenier St-Lazare (3rd) ℰ 42 72 31 22, Fax 42 78 85 47 –
⋡⋗ 📃 Ε 𝗩𝗜𝗦𝗔 H 15
closed 15 to 31 July – **M** a la carte 170/240.

XXX **Le Péché Mignon,** 5 r. Guillaume-Bertrand (11th) ℰ 43 57 02 51 – 📃 ⒶⒺ Ε 𝗩𝗜𝗦𝗔 H 19
closed 4 August-2 September, 1 to 9 March, Sunday and Monday – **M** a la carte 200/320.

XXX ✿ **Miravile** (Épié), 72 quai Hôtel de Ville (4th) ℰ 42 74 72 22 – 📃 Ε 𝗩𝗜𝗦𝗔 J 15
closed Saturday lunch and Sunday – **M** 280/400
Spec. Beignet de foie gras caramélisé au Porto, Lotte rôtie et salade d'herbes, Tournedos de pied de cochon aux truffes.

XXX **Le Domarais,** 53bis r. Francs-Bourgeois (4th) ℰ 42 74 54 17 – ⒶⒺ ⓪ Ε 𝗩𝗜𝗦𝗔 H 16
closed lunch Saturday, Sunday and Monday – **M** 240.

XX **Bofinger,** 5 r. Bastille (4th) ℰ 42 72 87 82, Fax 42 72 97 68, brasserie, « Belle Epoque decor » – ⒶⒺ ⓪ 𝗩𝗜𝗦𝗔 J 17
M 160 b.i. and a la carte 160/300 ⅃

XX ✿ **Benoît,** 20 r. St-Martin (4th) ℰ 42 72 25 76 J 15
closed August, Saturday and Sunday – **M** a la carte 300/400 ⅃
Spec. Ballotine de canard au foie gras, Cassoulet, Boeuf mode braisé à l'ancienne.

XX ✿ **A Sousceyrac** (Asfaux), 35 r. Faidherbe (11th) ℰ 43 71 65 30 – 📃 ⒶⒺ 𝗩𝗜𝗦𝗔 J 19
closed August, Saturday and Sunday – **M** a la carte 250/330
Spec. Foie gras frais en terrine, Ris de veau entier à l'étuvée, Lièvre à la royale (season).

XX **Repaire de Cartouche,** 8 bd Filles-du-Calvaire (11th) ℰ 47 00 25 86 – 🆎 ⓪ 𝑉𝐼𝑆𝐴   H 17
closed 1 to 25 August, Saturday lunch and Sunday – **M** 140 and a la carte 180/310.

XX **Franc Pinot,** 1 quai Bourbon (4th) ℰ 43 29 46 98, Fax 42 77 18 16, « Former wine cellar »
– 🆎 ⓪ 𝐄 𝑉𝐼𝑆𝐴   K 16
closed Sunday and Monday – **M** 150 (lunch) and a la carte 310/430.

XX **L'Aiguière,** 37bis r. Montreuil (11th) ℰ 43 72 42 32 – 🗏 🆎 ⓪ 𝐄 𝑉𝐼𝑆𝐴   K 20
closed Saturday lunch and Sunday – **M** 100 (lunch)/170 and a la carte 230/340.

XX **Coconnas,** 2bis pl. Vosges (4th) ℰ 42 78 58 16, 🌧 – 🆎 ⓪ 𝐄 𝑉𝐼𝑆𝐴   J 17
closed mid December-mid January, Monday and Tuesday – **M** a la carte 200/330.

XX **L'Alisier,** 26 r. Montmorency (3rd) ℰ 42 72 31 04 – 𝐄 𝑉𝐼𝑆𝐴. 🎇   H 16
closed August, Saturday lunch and Sunday – **M** 130/175.

XX **Wally,** 16 r. Le Regrattier (4th) ℰ 43 25 01 39, North African rest. – 🆎 ⓪ 𝐄 𝑉𝐼𝑆𝐴. 🎇   K 15
closed Sunday – **M** 290 b.i.

XX **Guirlande de Julie,** 25 pl. des Vosges (3rd) ℰ 48 87 94 07, 🌧 – 🗏 🆎 𝐄 𝑉𝐼𝑆𝐴   J 17
closed January, Monday and Tuesday – **M** 160.

XX **Les Amognes,** 243 r. Fg St-Antoine (11th) ℰ 43 72 73 05 – 𝐄 𝑉𝐼𝑆𝐴   K 20
closed 30 March-6 April, 12 to 31 August, 23 to 28 December, Sunday dinner and Monday –
M 140 and a la carte 180/275.

XX **Pyrénées Cévennes,** 106 r. Folie-Méricourt (11th) ℰ 43 57 33 78 – 𝐄 𝑉𝐼𝑆𝐴   G 17
closed August, Saturday, Sunday and Bank Holidays – **M** a la carte 180/370.

X **Au Gourmet de l'Isle,** 42 r. St-Louis-en-l'Ile (4th) ℰ 43 26 79 27 – 𝐄 𝑉𝐼𝑆𝐴   K 16
closed Monday and Thursday – **M** 110.

X **Le Monde des Chimères,** 69 r. St-Louis-en-l'Ile (4th) ℰ 43 54 45 27 – 𝑉𝐼𝑆𝐴   K 16
closed February Holidays, Sunday and Monday – **M** a la carte 230/320.

X **L'Oulette,** 38 r. Tournelles (4th) ℰ 42 71 43 33 – 𝐄 𝑉𝐼𝑆𝐴   J 17
closed 3 to 25 August, 21 to 29 December, Saturday and Sunday – **M** 130 (lunch)/150
(dinner).

X **Chez Fernand,** 17 r. Fontaine au Roi (11th) ℰ 43 57 46 25 – 𝑉𝐼𝑆𝐴   G 18
closed Sunday and Monday – **M** 120 (lunch) and a la carte 140/275.

Quartier Latin, Luxembourg,

Jardin des Plantes.

5th and 6th arrondissements.
   5th : ✉ 75005
   6th : ✉ 75006

🏨 **Lutétia** Ⓜ, 45 bd Raspail (6th) ℰ 45 44 38 10, Telex 270424, Fax 45 44 50 50 – 🛗 🗏 📺 ☎
– 🔼 700. 🆎 ⓪ 𝐄 𝑉𝐼𝑆𝐴   K 12
M see Le Paris below - Brasserie Lutétia **M** a la carte 170/305 ⅃ – ⇌ 85 – **258 rm** 950/1950,
27 apartments.

🏨 **Victoria Palace** ﹩, 6 r. Blaise-Desgoffe (6th) ℰ 45 44 38 16, Telex 270557, Fax 45 49 23 75
– 🛗 📺 ☎. 🆎 ⓪ 𝐄 𝑉𝐼𝑆𝐴. 🎇   L 11
M 145 – **110 rm** ⇌ 800/1300.

🏨 **Relais Christine** Ⓜ ﹩ without rest, 3 r. Christine (6th) ℰ 43 26 71 80, Telex 202606, Fax
43 26 89 38, « Fine setting » – 🛗 🗏 📺 ☎ ⇌ – 🔼 25. 🆎 ⓪ 𝐄 𝑉𝐼𝑆𝐴   J 14
⇌ 80 – **34 rm** 1200/1600, 17 duplex 1600/2200.

🏨 **Quality Inn** Ⓜ without rest, 92 r. Vaugirard (6th) ℰ 42 22 00 56, Telex 206900, Fax
42 22 05 39 – 🛗 ✖⇌ 🗏 📺 ☎ ⅙ ⇌ – 🔼 35. 🆎 ⓪ 𝐄 𝑉𝐼𝑆𝐴   L 12
⇌ 55 – **134 rm** 640/850.

🏨 **Sainte Beuve** Ⓜ without rest, 9 r. Ste Beuve (6th) ℰ 45 48 20 07, Telex 270182, Fax
45 48 67 52 – 🛗 📺 ☎. 🆎 𝐄 𝑉𝐼𝑆𝐴. 🎇   L 12
⇌ 70 – **22 rm** 650/1100.

🏨 **Littré** ﹩, 9 r. Littré (6th) ℰ 45 44 38 68, Telex 203852, Fax 45 44 88 13 – 🛗 📺 ☎ – 🔼 25.
🆎 ⓪ 𝐄 𝑉𝐼𝑆𝐴. 🎇   L 11
M 145 – **93 rm** ⇌ 680/925, 4 apartments 1300.

🏨 **La Villa** Ⓜ without rest, 29 r. Jacob (6th) ℰ 43 26 60 00, Telex 202437, Fax 46 34 63 63,
« Contemporary decor » – 🛗 🗏 📺 ☎ ⅙. 🆎 𝐄 𝑉𝐼𝑆𝐴. 🎇   J 13
⇌ 80 – **28 rm** 750/1100, 4 apartments.

🏨 **Latitudes St Germain** Ⓜ without rest, 7-11 r. St-Benoit (6th) ℰ 42 61 53 53, Telex 213531,
Fax 49 27 09 33 – 🛗 🗏 📺 ☎ ⅙. 🆎 ⓪ 𝐄 𝑉𝐼𝑆𝐴   J 13
⇌ 55 – **117 rm** 750/840.

🏨 **Abbaye St-Germain** ﹩ without rest, 10 r. Cassette (6th) ℰ 45 44 38 11 – 🛗 ☎. 🎇   K 12
44 rm ⇌ 730/1200, 4 duplex 1800.

🏨 **Madison H.** without rest, 143 bd St-Germain (6th) 🕾 43 29 72 50, Telex 201628, Fax 43 29 72 50 – 🛗 ▤ 📺 ☎. 🆎 ⓪ 🗲 𝘝𝘐𝘚𝘈

J 13

⊆ 50 – **55 rm** 600/1050.

🏨 **Saint-Grégoire** Ⓜ without rest, 43 r. Abbé Grégoire (6th) 🕾 45 48 23 23, Telex 205343, Fax 45 48 33 95 – 🛗 📺 ☎. 🆎 ⓪ 🗲 𝘝𝘐𝘚𝘈. ❄

L 12

⊆ 55 – **20 rm** 650/1100.

🏨 **Left Bank H.** Ⓜ without rest, 11 r. Ancienne Comédie (6th) 🕾 43 54 01 70, Telex 200502, Fax 43 26 17 14 – 🛗 ▤ 📺 ☎ ⅘. 🆎 ⓪ 🗲 𝘝𝘐𝘚𝘈. ❄

K 13

⊆ 25 – **31 rm** 725/850.

🏨 **Relais St Germain** without rest, 9 carrefour de l'Odéon (6th) 🕾 43 29 12 05, Telex 201889, Fax 46 33 45 30, « Fine setting » – 🛗 ▤ 📺 ☎. 🆎 ⓪ 🗲 𝘝𝘐𝘚𝘈

K 13

10 rm ⊆ 1160/1320.

🏨 **Angleterre** without rest, 44 r. Jacob (6th) 🕾 42 60 34 72, Fax 42 60 16 93 – 🛗 📺 ☎. 🆎 ⓪ 𝘝𝘐𝘚𝘈. ❄ – ⊆ 35 – **29 rm** 600/950.

J 13

🏨 **St-Germain-des-Prés** without rest, 36 r. Bonaparte (6th) 🕾 43 26 00 19, Telex 200409, Fax 40 46 83 63 – 🛗 📺 ☎. 🗲 𝘝𝘐𝘚𝘈. ❄

J 13

30 rm ⊆ 780/1200.

🏨 **Villa des Artistes** Ⓜ without rest, 9 r. Grande Chaumière (6th) 🕾 43 26 60 86, Telex 204080, Fax 43 54 73 70 – 🛗 📺 ☎. 🆎 ⓪ 🗲 𝘝𝘐𝘚𝘈

L 12

59 rm ⊆ 550/700.

🏨 **Ferrandi** without rest, 92 r. Cherche-Midi (6th) 🕾 42 22 97 40, Telex 205201, Fax 45 44 89 97 – 🛗 ☎. 🆎 ⓪ 🗲 𝘝𝘐𝘚𝘈

L 11

⊆ 50 – **41 rm** 385/850.

🏨 **St Christophe** Ⓜ without rest, 17 r. Lacépède (5th) 🕾 43 31 81 54, Telex 204304, Fax 43 31 12 54 – 🛗 📺 ☎ ⅘. 🆎 ⓪ 🗲 𝘝𝘐𝘚𝘈. ❄

L 15

⊆ 42 – **31 rm** 600/650.

🏨 **Panthéon** Ⓜ without rest, 19 pl. Panthéon (5th) 🕾 43 54 32 95, Telex 206435, Fax 43 26 64 65, ⇐ – 🛗 📺 ☎. 🆎 ⓪ 🗲 𝘝𝘐𝘚𝘈. ❄

L 14

⊆ 30 – **32 rm** 600/700.

🏨 **Grands Hommes** Ⓜ without rest, 17 pl. Panthéon (5th) 🕾 46 34 19 60, Telex 200185, Fax 43 26 67 32, ⇐ – 🛗 📺 ☎. 🆎 ⓪ 🗲 𝘝𝘐𝘚𝘈. ❄

L 14

⊆ 30 – **32 rm** 600/700.

🏨 **Jardin de Cluny** without rest, 9 r. Sommerard (5th) 🕾 43 54 22 66, Telex 206975, Fax 40 51 03 36 – 🛗 📺 ☎. 🆎 ⓪ 🗲 𝘝𝘐𝘚𝘈. ❄

K 14

40 rm ⊆ 480/650.

🏨 **Elysa Luxembourg** Ⓜ without rest, 6 r. Gay-Lussac (5th) 🕾 43 25 31 74, Telex 206881 – 🛗 📺 ☎. 🆎 ⓪ 🗲 𝘝𝘐𝘚𝘈

L 14

⊆ 35 – **30 rm** 450/660.

🏨 **Notre Dame** Ⓜ without rest, 1 quai St-Michel (5th) 🕾 43 54 20 43, Telex 206650, Fax 43 26 61 75, ⇐ – 🛗 📺 ☎. 🆎 ⓪ 🗲 𝘝𝘐𝘚𝘈. ❄

K 14

⊆ 35 – **23 rm** 470/770, 3 duplex 1050.

🏨 **Parc St-Séverin** Ⓜ without rest, 22 r. Parcheminerie (5th) 🕾 43 54 32 17, Telex 270905, Fax 43 54 70 71 – 🛗 📺 ☎. 🆎 ⓪ 🗲 𝘝𝘐𝘚𝘈. ❄

K 14

⊆ 45 – **27 rm** 400/1300.

🏨 **de Fleurie** without rest, 32 r. Grégoire de Tours (6th) 🕾 43 29 59 81, Telex 206153, Fax 43 29 68 44 – 🛗 📺 ☎. 🆎 ⓪ 🗲 𝘝𝘐𝘚𝘈. ❄

K 13

⊆ 45 – **29 rm** 550/950.

🏨 **Odéon H.,** without rest, 3 r. Odéon (6th) 🕾 43 25 90 67, Telex 202943, Fax 43 25 55 98 – 🛗 ▤ 📺 ☎. 🆎 ⓪ 🗲 𝘝𝘐𝘚𝘈. ❄

K 13

⊆ 40 – **34 rm** 650/850.

🏨 **Collège de France** Ⓜ without rest, 7 r. Thénard (5th) 🕾 43 26 78 36, Fax 46 34 58 29 – 🛗 📺 ☎. 🆎 ⓪. ❄

K 14

⊆ 30 – **29 rm** 450/500.

🏨 **des Saints-Pères** without rest, 65 r. Sts-Pères (6th) 🕾 45 44 50 00, Telex 205424, Fax 45 44 90 83 – 🛗 📺 ☎ ⅘. 🆎 𝘝𝘐𝘚𝘈. ❄

J 12

⊆ 45 – **34 rm** 400/1500, 3 apartments 1500.

🏨 **Trois Collèges** Ⓜ without rest, 16 r. Cujas (5th) 🕾 43 54 67 30, Telex 206034, Fax 46 34 02 99 – 🛗 📺 ☎. 🆎 ⓪ 🗲 𝘝𝘐𝘚𝘈. ❄

K 14

⊆ 35 – **44 rm** 290/510.

🏨 **Aramis St Germain** without rest, 124 r. Rennes (6th) 🕾 45 48 03 75, Telex 205098, Fax 45 44 99 29 – 🛗 📺 ☎. 🔐 40. 🆎 ⓪ 🗲 𝘝𝘐𝘚𝘈. ❄

L 12

⊆ 45 – **42 rm** 450/650.

🏨 **Jardin des Plantes** without rest, 5 r. Linné (5th) 🕾 47 07 06 20, Telex 203684, Fax 47 07 62 74 – 🛗 ☎. 🆎 ⓪ 🗲 𝘝𝘐𝘚𝘈

L 15

⊆ 35 – **33 rm** 340/590.

🏨 **De l'Odéon** without rest, 13 r. St-Sulpice (6th) 🕾 43 25 70 11, Telex 206731, Fax 43 29 97 34, « 16C setting » – 🛗 📺 ☎. 🆎 ⓪ 🗲 𝘝𝘐𝘚𝘈

K 13

⊆ 39 – **29 rm** 500/740.

🏨 **Avenir** without rest, 65 r. Madame (6th) 🕾 45 48 84 54, Telex 200428, Fax 45 49 26 80 – 🛗 📺 ☎. 🆎 ⓪ 🗲 𝘝𝘐𝘚𝘈. ❄

L 12

⊆ 30 – **35 rm** 400/510.

🏨 **Le Régent** without rest, 61 r. Dauphine (6th) ℰ 46 34 59 80, Telex 206257, Fax 40 51 05 07
– 🛗 📺 ♿ 💳, 🅰🅴 🕦 🖻 𝐕𝐈𝐒𝐀 J 13
☒ 40 – **25 rm** 550/750.

🏨 **Trianon Palace** without rest, 3 r. Vaugirard (6th) ℰ 43 29 88 10, Telex 202263, Fax 43 29 15 98
– 🛗 📺 ☎ 🅰🅴 🕦 🖻 𝐕𝐈𝐒𝐀 ⁂ K 14
☒ 41 – **110 rm** 535/635.

🏨 **Bréa** without rest, 14 r. Bréa (6th) ℰ 43 25 44 41, Telex 202053 – 🛗 📺 ☎ 🖻 𝐕𝐈𝐒𝐀 ⁂
☒ 40 – **23 rm** 510/650. L 12

🏨 **Select** without rest, 1pl. Sorbonne (5th) ℰ 46 34 14 80, Telex 201207, Fax 46 34 51 79 – 🛗
📺 ☎ 🅰🅴 🕦 🖻 𝐕𝐈𝐒𝐀 K 14
☒ 30 – **69 rm** 460/680.

🏨 **Rennes Montparnasse** without rest, 151bis r. Rennes (6th) ℰ 45 48 97 38, Telex 250048,
Fax 45 44 63 57 – 🛗 📺 ☎ 🅰🅴 🕦 🖻 𝐕𝐈𝐒𝐀 L 12
closed August – ☒ 37 – **41 rm** 430/570.

🏨 **Marronniers** without rest, 21 r. Jacob (6th) ℰ 43 25 30 60 – 🛗 ☎ ⁂ J 13
☒ 46 – **37 rm** 600/660.

🏨 **Terminus Montparnasse** without rest, 59 bd Montparnasse (6th) ℰ 45 48 99 10, Telex
202636, Fax 45 48 59 10 – 🛗 📺 ☎ 🅰🅴 🕦 🖻 𝐕𝐈𝐒𝐀 L 11
closed 29 July-26 August – ☒ 30 – **63 rm** 415/545.

🏨 **Pas-de-Calais** without rest, 59 r. Sts-Pères (6th) ℰ 45 48 78 74, Telex 270476, Fax
45 44 94 57 – 🛗 📺 ☎ 🖻 𝐕𝐈𝐒𝐀 J 12
41 rm ☒ 560/690.

🏨 **Delavigne** without rest, 1 r. Casimir-Delavigne (6th) ℰ 43 29 31 50, Telex 201579, Fax
43 29 78 56 – 🛗 📺 ☎ 🖻 𝐕𝐈𝐒𝐀 ⁂ K 13
☒ 35 – **34 rm** 410/620.

🏨 **Louis II** without rest, 2 r. St-Sulpice (6th) ℰ 46 33 13 80, Telex 206561, Fax 46 33 17 29 – 🛗
☎ 🅰🅴 🕦 🖻 𝐕𝐈𝐒𝐀 K 13
☒ 32 – **22 rm** 399/580.

🏨 **Agora St-Germain** without rest, 42 r. Bernardins (5th) ℰ 46 34 13 00, Telex 260881, Fax
46 34 75 05 – 🛗 📺 ☎ 🅰🅴 🕦 🖻 𝐕𝐈𝐒𝐀 ⁂ K 15
☒ 35 – **39 rm** 530/590.

🏨 **Nations** without rest, 54 r. Monge (5th) ℰ 43 26 45 24, Telex 200397, Fax 46 34 00 13 – 🛗
📺 ☎ 🅰🅴 🕦 🖻 𝐕𝐈𝐒𝐀 L 15
☒ 40 – **38 rm** 480/500.

🏨 **Gd H. Suez** without rest, 31 bd St-Michel (5th) ℰ 46 34 08 02, Telex 202019 – 🛗 📺 ☎ 🅰🅴
🕦 🖻 𝐕𝐈𝐒𝐀 ⁂ K 14
49 rm ☒ 300/450.

🏨 **La Sorbonne** without rest, 6 r. Victor Cousin (5th) ℰ 43 54 58 08, Telex 206373, Fax
40 51 05 18 – 🛗 📺 ☎ 🖻 𝐕𝐈𝐒𝐀 K 14
☒ 30 – **37 rm** 360/450.

🏨 **Albe** without rest, 1 r. Harpe (5th) ℰ 46 34 09 70, Telex 203328, Fax 40 46 85 70 – 🛗 📺 ☎
🅰🅴 🖻 𝐕𝐈𝐒𝐀 ⁂ K 14
☒ 30 – **43 rm** 397/515.

🏨 **Muséum** without rest, 9 r. Buffon (5th) ℰ 43 31 51 90 – 🛗 📺 ☎ 🖻 𝐕𝐈𝐒𝐀 L 16
☒ 25 – **24 rm** 250/350.

🏨 **Gd H. des Principautés Unies** without rest, 42 r. Vaugirard (6th) ℰ 46 34 11 80 – 🛗
kitchenette 📺 ☎ 🖻 𝐕𝐈𝐒𝐀 ⁂ K 13
closed August – ☒ 28 – **28 rm** 405/425.

XXXXX ✿✿✿ **Tour d'Argent** (Terrail), 15 quai Tournelle (5th) ℰ 43 54 23 31, « ≤ Notre Dame -
little museum showing the development of eating, utensils. In the cellar : an illustrated
history of wine » – 🅰🅴 🕦 𝐕𝐈𝐒𝐀 K 16
closed Monday – **M** 375 (lunch) and a la carte 650/860
Spec. Saint-Jacques poêlées au naturel et soufflé d'oursins, Canard du ''Centenaire'', Soufflé praliné à l'ancienne.

XXX ✿✿ **Jacques Cagna**, 14 r. Gds Augustins (6th) ℰ 43 26 49 39, Fax 43 54 54 48, « Old
Parisian house » – 🗐. 🅰🅴 🕦 🖻 𝐕𝐈𝐒𝐀 J 14
closed August, 21 December-2 January, Saturday and Sunday – **M** 260 (lunch) and a la
carte 460/650
Spec. Petits escargots en surprise, Goujonnettes de sole et rougets de roche en friture sauce béarnaise, Côte
de veau mijotée à l'ancienne.

XXX ✿ **Le Paris** - Hôtel Lutétia, 45 bd Raspail (6th) ℰ 45 48 74 34, Telex 270424, Fax 45 44 50 50
– 🗐. 🅰🅴 🕦 🖻 𝐕𝐈𝐒𝐀 K 12
closed August, Saturday and Sunday – **M** 280 (lunch) and a la carte 310/410
Spec. Salade de canette sauvage à la Cuberland (Sept.-Feb.), Timbale de petites nouilles aux Saint-Jacques
(Oct.-March), Navarin de carré d'agneau au Madère.

XXX ✿✿ **Relais Louis XIII**, 1 r. Pont de Lodi (6th) ℰ 43 26 75 96, Fax 42 89 05 78, « 16C cellar, fine furniture » – ■, 🅰🅴 ⓄD 🅴 𝑉𝐼𝑆𝐴 　　　　　　　　　　　　　　　　　　　　　　　J 14
　　closed 20 July-20 August, Monday lunch and Sunday – **M** 230 (lunch) and a la carte 355/575
　　Spec. Ravioli de langoustines à l'estragon, Panaché de poissons à l'oursinade, Trois filets mignons sauce "velours".

XXX **Lapérouse**, 51 quai Gds Augustins (6th) ℰ 43 26 68 04, Fax 43 26 99 39, « Belle Epoque decor » – ■, 🅰🅴 ⓄD 🅴 𝑉𝐼𝑆𝐴. ⠜　　　　　　　　　　　　　　　　　　　　　　J 14
　　closed August, Sunday dinner and Monday – **M** 190 (lunch) and a la carte 330/620.

XXX **Le Procope**, 13 r. Ancienne Comédie (6th) ℰ 43 26 99 20, Fax 43 54 16 86, « Former 18C literary café » – 🅰🅴 ⓄD 🅴 𝑉𝐼𝑆𝐴 – **M** a la carte 155/280 ⁂.　　　　　　　　　K 13

XX **Aub. des Deux Signes**, 46 r. Galande (5th) ℰ 43 25 46 56, « Medieval decor » – 🅰🅴 ⓄD 🅴 𝑉𝐼𝑆𝐴 – *closed August and Sunday* – **M** 140 (lunch)/220.　　　　　　　　　　K 14

XX ✿ **Au Pactole**, 44 bd St-Germain (5th) ℰ 46 33 31 31 – 🅰🅴 🅴 𝑉𝐼𝑆𝐴　　　　　　　K 15
　　closed Saturday lunch and Sunday – **M** 145/280.

XX ✿ **Dodin-Bouffant**, 25 r. F.-Sauton (5th) ℰ 43 25 25 14 – ■, ⓄD 🅴 𝑉𝐼𝑆𝐴　　　　K 15
　　closed 4 August-1 September, 21 December-3 January and Sunday – **M** 170 and a la carte 280/375
　　Spec. Assiette de champignons (season), Daube d'huîtres et pieds de porc, Gibier (season).

XX **Calvet**, 165 bd St-Germain (6th) ℰ 45 48 93 51 – ■, 🅰🅴 ⓄD 🅴 𝑉𝐼𝑆𝐴　　　　　J 12
　　closed August – **M** 129/185.

XX **Diapason**, 30 r. Bernardins (5th) ℰ 43 54 21 13 – 🅰🅴 ⓄD 🅴 𝑉𝐼𝑆𝐴　　　　　　　K 15
　　closed 1 to 15 August, Saturday lunch and Sunday – **M** 165 and a la carte 230/350.

XX **Quai de la Tournelle**, 25 quai de la Tournelle (5th) ℰ 46 34 07 78 – ■, 𝑉𝐼𝑆𝐴　　　K 15
　　closed Saturday lunch and Sunday – **M** 150 (lunch) and a la carte 270/390.

XX ✿ **Clavel**, 65 quai Tournelle (5th) ℰ 46 33 18 65 – ■, 🅴 𝑉𝐼𝑆𝐴　　　　　　　　K 15
　　closed 4 to 26 August, February Holidays, Sunday dinner and Monday – **M** 170 (lunch) and a la carte 280/400
　　Spec. Feuilleté de haddock aux poireaux, Tourte de canard au foie gras, Gâteau au chocolat noir "N'Gaïnde".

XX **Chat Grippé**, 87 r. d'Assas (6th) ℰ 43 54 70 00 – ■, 🅴 𝑉𝐼𝑆𝐴. ⠜　　　　　　　LM 13
　　closed August, Saturday lunch and Monday – **M** 220/315.

XX **La Truffière**, 4 r. Blainville (5th) ℰ 46 33 29 82 – ■, 🅰🅴 ⓄD 🅴 𝑉𝐼𝑆𝐴　　　　L 15
　　closed 5 to 19 August and Monday – **M** 95/300.

XX **La Petite Cour**, 8 r. Mabillon (6th) ℰ 43 26 52 26, 🍽 – 🅴 𝑉𝐼𝑆𝐴　　　　　　　K 13
　　M 158 (lunch) and a la carte 200/320.

XX **L'Arrosée**, 12 r. Guisarde (6th) ℰ 43 54 66 59 – 🅰🅴 ⓄD 🅴 𝑉𝐼𝑆𝐴　　　　　　K 13
　　closed 1 to 5 January and Sunday – **M** 145/210.

XX **La Marlotte**, 55 r. Cherche Midi (6th) ℰ 45 48 86 79 – 🅰🅴 ⓄD. ⠜　　　　　　　K 12
　　closed August, Saturday and Sunday – **M** 200 b.i./300 b.i..

XX **Marty**, 20 av. Gobelins (5th) ℰ 43 31 39 51 – 🅰🅴 ⓄD 🅴 𝑉𝐼𝑆𝐴　　　　　　　　M 15
　　M 149 b.i. and a la carte 170/310.

XX **La Foux**, 2 r. Clément (6th) ℰ 43 54 09 53 – ■, 🅰🅴 🅴 𝑉𝐼𝑆𝐴　　　　　　　　K 13
　　closed 23 December-2 January, Monday lunch and Sunday – **M** 150 (lunch) and a la carte 180/300.

XX **Yugaraj**, 14 r. Dauphine (6th) ℰ 43 26 44 91, Indian rest. – ■, 🅰🅴 ⓄD 𝑉𝐼𝑆𝐴. ⠜　J 14
　　closed Monday – **M** 196/230.

XX **Les Tuffeaux**, 11 r. Dupin (6th) ℰ 42 22 64 56 – 🅰🅴 🅴 𝑉𝐼𝑆𝐴　　　　　　　K 12
　　closed 1 to 23 August, Saturday lunch and Sunday – **M** 170 (lunch) and a la carte 210/300.

XX **Au Régent**, 97 r. Cherche Midi (6th) ℰ 42 22 32 44 – 🅰🅴 ⓄD 🅴 𝑉𝐼𝑆𝐴　　　　L 11
　　closed August, Sunday and Monday – **M** 125 and a la carte 190/230.

XX **Le Sybarite**, 6 r. Sabot (6th) ℰ 42 22 21 56 – ■, 🅰🅴 ⓄD 🅴 𝑉𝐼𝑆𝐴　　　　　K 12
　　closed Saturday lunch and Sunday – **M** 168 (lunch) and a la carte 200/290.

XX **Au Grilladin**, 13 r. Mézières (6th) ℰ 45 48 30 38 – 🅰🅴 𝑉𝐼𝑆𝐴　　　　　　　　K 12
　　closed 27 July-28 August, 22 December-2 January, Monday lunch and Sunday – **M** 146 and a la carte 150/300.

XX **Joséphine "Chez Dumonet"**, 117 r. Cherche Midi (6th) ℰ 45 48 52 40 – 🅴 𝑉𝐼𝑆𝐴　L 11
　　closed July, 20 to 29 December, Saturday and Sunday – **M** a la carte 210/330.

X **Rôtisserie du Beaujolais**, 19 quai Tournelle (5th) ℰ 43 54 17 47 – 𝑉𝐼𝑆𝐴　　　K 15
　　closed January and Monday – **M** a la carte 150/210.

X **Balzar**, 49 r. Écoles (5th) ℰ 43 54 13 67, brasserie – 🅰🅴 🅴 𝑉𝐼𝑆𝐴　　　　　K 14
　　closed August and 24 December-3 January – **M** a la carte 130/280.

X **Allard**, 41 r. St-André-des-Arts (6th) ℰ 43 26 48 23 – 🅰🅴 ⓄD 🅴 𝑉𝐼𝑆𝐴　　　　K 14
　　closed 31 July-4 September, 23 December-3 January, Saturday and Sunday – **M** a la carte 275/410.

X **Moissonnier**, 28 r. Fossés-St-Bernard (5th) ℰ 43 29 87 65 – 🅴 𝑉𝐼𝑆𝐴　　　　　K 15
　　closed August, Sunday dinner and Monday – **M** a la carte 160/280.

X ✿ **La Timonerie** (de Givenchy), 35 quai St-Michel (5th) ℰ 43 25 44 42 – ■, 𝑉𝐼𝑆𝐴　K 15
　　closed 24 February-11 March, Monday March-August, Saturday September-February and Sunday – **M** 120 and a la carte 225/370.
　　Spec. Patatou poitevin, Sandre rôti au chou et pommes de terre en vinaigrette, Tarte fine au chocolat.

※ **Chez Maître Paul,** 12 r. Monsieur-le-Prince (6th) ℰ 43 54 74 59 — 🅰🅴 ⊙ 🄴 𝘝𝘐𝘚𝘈 K 13
closed Saturday lunch and Sunday — **M** 165 and a la carte 150/250.

※ **Moulin à Vent''Chez Henri'',** 20 r. Fossés-St-Bernard (5th) ℰ 43 54 99 37 — 🄴 𝘝𝘐𝘚𝘈. ⅍
closed August, Sunday and Monday — **M** a la carte 220/330. K 15

※ **Le Palanquin,** 12 r. Princesse (6th) ℰ 43 29 77 66, Vietnamese rest. — 🄴 𝘝𝘐𝘚𝘈 K 13
closed 12 to 25 August and Sunday — **M** a la carte 130/220.

※ **La Vigneraie,** 16 r. Dragon (6th) ℰ 45 48 57 04 — 🅰🅴 ⊙ 🄴 𝘝𝘐𝘚𝘈 J 12
closed 11 to 18 August and Sunday lunch — **M** a la carte 170/280.

※ **La Cantine,** 245 bis r. St-Jacques (5th) ℰ 43 26 97 92 — 🄴 𝘝𝘐𝘚𝘈 L 14
closed Sunday — **M** 200/250.

Faubourg-St-Germain,
Invalides,
École Militaire.

7th arrondissement.
7th : ⊠ *75007*

🏨🏨 **Pont Royal et rest. Les Antiquaires,** 7 r. Montalembert ℰ 45 44 38 27, Telex 270113,
Fax 45 44 92 07 — 🛗 kitchenette 🔲 ☎ — 🔏 30. 🅰🅴 ⊙ 🄴 𝘝𝘐𝘚𝘈 ⅍ rest J 12
M *(closed August, 25 December-1 January and Sunday)* 160 and a la carte 200/315 — **73 rm**
⊠ 850/1550, 5 apartments 2800.

🏨🏨 **Duc de Saint Simon** Ⓜ without rest, 14 r. St-Simon ℰ 45 48 35 66, Telex 203277, Fax
45 48 68 25, « Tastefully furnished interior » — 🛗 📺 ☎. ⅍ J 11
⊠ 70 — **29 rm** 950/1400, 5 apartments 1900.

🏨🏨 **Cayré** Ⓜ without rest, 4 bd Raspail ℰ 45 44 38 88, Telex 270577, Fax 45 44 98 13 — 🛗 📺 ☎
— 🔏 30. 🅰🅴 ⊙ 🄴 𝘝𝘐𝘚𝘈 J 12
126 rm ⊠ 1150/1200.

🏨🏨 **La Bourdonnais,** 111 av. La Bourdonnais ℰ 47 05 45 42, Telex 201416, Fax 45 55 75 54 —
🛗 📺 ☎ ➿. ⊙ 🄴 𝘝𝘐𝘚𝘈. ⅍ rest J 9
M see rest. **La Cantine des Gourmets** below — **60 rm** ⊠ 420/580.

🏨 **Eiffel Park H.** Ⓜ without rest, 17 bis r. Amélie ℰ 45 55 10 01, Telex 202950, Fax 47 05 28 68
— 🛗 📺 ☎ ➿ — 🔏 40. 🅰🅴 ⊙ 🄴 𝘝𝘐𝘚𝘈. ⅍ J 9
⊠ 40 — **36 rm** 655/900.

🏨 **Université** without rest, 22 r. Université ℰ 42 61 09 39, Fax 42 60 40 84, « Fine furniture »
— 🛗 📺 ☎. ⅍ J 12
⊠ 45 — **28 rm** 500/900.

🏨 **Les Jardins d'Eiffel** Ⓜ without rest, 8 r. Amélie ℰ 47 05 46 21, Telex 206582, Fax
45 55 28 08 — 🛗 ↝ 📺 ☎ ➿. 🅰🅴 ⊙ 🄴 𝘝𝘐𝘚𝘈 H 9
⊠ 40 — **44 rm** 640/760.

🏨 **Élysées Maubourg** Ⓜ without rest, 35 bd La Tour-Maubourg ℰ 45 56 10 78, Telex
206227, Fax 47 05 65 08 — 🛗 📺 ☎. 🅰🅴 ⊙ 🄴 𝘝𝘐𝘚𝘈 H 10
⊠ 40 — **30 rm** 510/730.

🏨 **Beaugency** Ⓜ without rest, 21 r. Duvivier ℰ 47 05 01 63, Telex 201494, Fax 45 51 04 96 —
🛗 📺 ☎. 🅰🅴 ⊙ 🄴 𝘝𝘐𝘚𝘈 J 9
30 rm ⊠ 430/660.

🏨 **Verneuil-St-Germain** Ⓜ without rest, 8 r. Verneuil ℰ 42 60 82 14, Telex 211608, Fax
42 61 40 38 — 🛗 📺 ☎. 🅰🅴 ⊙ 🄴 𝘝𝘐𝘚𝘈 J 12
⊠ 40 — **26 rm** 640/670.

🏨 **Lenox Saint-Germain** without rest, 9 r. Université ℰ 42 96 10 95, Fax 42 61 52 83 — 🛗 📺
☎. 🅰🅴 ⊙ 🄴 𝘝𝘐𝘚𝘈. ⅍ J 12
⊠ 40 — **32 rm** 480/670.

🏨 **De Varenne** Ⓜ ⌂ without rest, 44 r. Bourgogne ℰ 45 51 45 55, Telex 205329, Fax
45 51 86 63 — 🛗 📺 ☎. 🅰🅴 🄴 𝘝𝘐𝘚𝘈 J 10
⊠ 35 — **24 rm** 430/580.

🏨 **Londres** without rest, 1 r. Augereau ℰ 45 51 63 02, Telex 206398, Fax 47 05 28 96 — 🛗 📺
☎. 🅰🅴 ⊙ 🄴 𝘝𝘐𝘚𝘈 J 8
⊠ 32 — **30 rm** 440/560.

🏨 **Suède** without rest, 31 r. Vaneau ℰ 47 05 00 08, Telex 200596, Fax 47 05 69 27 — 🛗 ☎. 🅰🅴 🄴
𝘝𝘐𝘚𝘈. ⅍ — ⊠ 40 — **40 rm** 505/780. K 11

🏨 **Bourgogne et Montana,** 3 r. Bourgogne ℰ 45 51 20 22, Telex 270854, Fax 45 56 11 98 —
🛗 🔲 rest 📺 ☎. 🅰🅴 ⊙ 🄴 𝘝𝘐𝘚𝘈 H 11
M *(closed August, Saturday and Sunday)* 160 and a la carte 170/280 ⅃ — **30 rm** ⊠ 500/720,
5 apartments 950.

🏨 **St-Germain** without rest, 88 r. Bac ℰ 45 48 62 92, Fax 45 48 26 89 — 🛗 📺 ☎. 🅰🅴 🄴 𝘝𝘐𝘚𝘈 J 11
⊠ 32 — **29 rm** 295/560.

🏨 **France** Ⓜ without rest, 102 bd La Tour-Maubourg ℘ 47 05 40 49, Telex 205020, Fax 45 56 96 78 – 🛗 📺 ☎ &. 🖭 ᴇ 𝘝𝘐𝘚𝘈
J 9
⊆ 30 – **60 rm** 300/430.

🏨 **Derby H.** without rest, 5 av. Duquesne ℘ 47 05 12 05, Telex 206236, Fax 47 05 43 43 – 🛗
📺 🖭 ᴇ 𝘝𝘐𝘚𝘈
J 9
⊆ 45 – **44 rm** 420/550.

🏨 **Saxe Résidence** 🌄 without rest, 9 villa Saxe ℘ 47 83 98 28, Telex 270139, Fax 47 83 85 47 – 🛗 📺 ☎ 🖭 ᴇ 𝘝𝘐𝘚𝘈 🎿
K 9
⊆ 30 – **51 rm** 520/550.

🏨 **Chomel** without rest, 15 r. Chomel ℘ 45 48 55 52, Telex 206522, Fax 45 48 89 76 – 🛗 📺 ☎.
🖭 ⓞ ᴇ 𝘝𝘐𝘚𝘈 🎿
K 12
⊆ 34 – **23 rm** 480/670.

🏨 **Lindbergh** without rest, 5 r. Chomel ℘ 45 48 35 53, Telex 201777, Fax 45 49 31 48 – 🛗 📺
☎. 🖭 ⓞ ᴇ 𝘝𝘐𝘚𝘈
K 12
⊆ 35 – **26 rm** 360/470.

🏨 **Bersoly's** without rest, 28 r. Lille ℘ 42 60 73 79, Telex 217505, Fax 49 27 05 55 – 🛗 📺 ☎.
🖭 ᴇ
J 13
closed 15 to 30 August – ⊆ 40 – **16 rm** 525/610.

🏨 **Tourville** without rest, 16 av. Tourville ℘ 47 05 52 15, Telex 250786, Fax 45 50 45 67 – 🛗 📺
☎. 🖭 ⓞ ᴇ 𝘝𝘐𝘚𝘈 🎿
J 9
⊆ 30 – **31 rm** 380/480.

🏨 **Solférino** without rest, 91 r. Lille ℘ 47 05 85 54, Telex 203865, Fax 45 55 51 16 – 🛗 ☎. ᴇ
𝘝𝘐𝘚𝘈 🎿
H 11
closed 23 December-3 January – ⊆ 30 – **33 rm** 219/552.

🏨 **L'Empereur** without rest, 2 r. Chevert ℘ 45 55 88 02, Fax 45 51 88 54 – 🛗 📺 ☎. ᴇ 𝘝𝘐𝘚𝘈   J 9
⊆ 32 – **34 rm** 365/400.

🏨 **Tour Eiffel** without rest, 17 r. Exposition ℘ 47 05 14 75 – 🛗 📺 ☎. ᴇ 𝘝𝘐𝘚𝘈
J 9
⊆ 22 – **22 rm** 320/400.

🏨 **Turenne** without rest, 20 av. Tourville ℘ 47 05 99 92, Telex 203407, Fax 45 56 06 04 – 🛗 ☎.
🖭 ⓞ ᴇ 𝘝𝘐𝘚𝘈
J 9
⊆ 27 – **34 rm** 280/480.

🏨 **Mars H.** without rest, 117 av. La Bourdonnais ℘ 47 05 42 30 – 🛗 ☎. ᴇ 𝘝𝘐𝘚𝘈 🎿
J 9
⊆ 30 – **24 rm** 160/350.

🏨 **Champ de Mars** without rest, 7 r. Champ de Mars ℘ 45 51 52 30 – 🛗 ☎. ᴇ 𝘝𝘐𝘚𝘈
J 9
closed 4 to 27 August – ⊆ 30 – **25 rm** 300/360.

🏨 **Résidence Orsay** without rest, 93 r. Lille ℘ 47 05 05 27 – 🛗 ☎. ᴇ 𝘝𝘐𝘚𝘈 🎿
H 11
closed August – ⊆ 28 – **32 rm** 190/380.

XXXX ❀ **Jules Verne,** Eiffel Tower : 2nd platform, lift in south leg ℘ 45 55 61 44, Telex 205789,
Fax 47 05 94 40, ≼ Paris – 🗐. 🖭 ⓞ ᴇ 𝘝𝘐𝘚𝘈 🎿
J 7
M 270 (lunch except weekends) and a la carte 400/580
Spec. Foie gras d'oie aux deux cuissons, Croustillant de turbot rôti à la julienne de légumes, Crème chocolat et
tuile à l'orange.

XXXX ❀❀ **Le Divellec,** 107 r. Université ℘ 45 51 91 96, Telex 270519, Fax 45 51 31 75, Seafood –
🗐. 🖭 ⓞ ᴇ 𝘝𝘐𝘚𝘈 🎿
H 10
closed 27 July-27 August, 23 December-2 January, Sunday and Monday – **M** 250 (lunch)
and a la carte 480/660
Spec. Mariné de Saint-Jacques au foie gras de canard poêlé, Lotte rôtie au safran et citron confit, Saint-Pierre
au fumet de pétoncles.

XXX ❀❀ **Duquesnoy,** 6 av. Bosquet ℘ 47 05 96 78 – 🗐. 🖭 ᴇ 𝘝𝘐𝘚𝘈
H 9
closed 1 to 18 August, Saturday lunch and Sunday – **M** 240 (lunch) and a la carte 340/620
Spec. Saint-Jacques fumées "minute", Pâté chaud de caille et foie gras, Feuillantines de riz "Impératrice".

XXX ❀❀ **L'Arpège** (Passard), 84 r. Varenne ℘ 45 51 20 02, Fax 47 05 09 06 – 🗐. 🖭 ⓞ ᴇ 𝘝𝘐𝘚𝘈
closed 26 July-20 August, Sunday lunch and Saturday – **M** 220 (lunch) and a la carte
450/700
J 10
Spec. Ris de veau à la truffe et châtaignes, Lotte aux épices et son farci de coquillages, Tomate farcie confite
au sirop vanillé.

XXX ❀ **La Cantine des Gourmets,** 113 av. La Bourdonnais ℘ 47 05 47 96 – 🗐. 🖭 ᴇ 𝘝𝘐𝘚𝘈   J 9
M 220 b.i. (lunch) and a la carte 310/480 🍸
Spec. Club-sandwich de pigeonneau aux truffes, Curry de langoustines, Risotto d'agneau aux girolles.

XXX ❀ **Regain** (Delaveyne), 135 r. St-Dominique ℘ 47 53 09 85, Fax 45 56 96 16 – 🗐. 🖭 ᴇ 𝘝𝘐𝘚𝘈
J 9
closed August, Saturday and Sunday – **M** 240 (lunch) and a la carte 275/415
Spec. Soupe de canard, Friandise de merlan "Pein ciel" au beurre nantais, Miroton de pommes de terre au foie
gras poêlé.

XXX **Chez les Anges,** 54 bd La Tour-Maubourg ✆ 47 05 89 86 – ▤. AE ◑ E VISA J 9
closed Sunday dinner – **M** 230 and a la carte 220/480.

XXX **La Flamberge,** 12 av. Rapp ✆ 47 05 91 37 – ▤. AE ◑ E VISA H 8
closed 1 to 9 May, 30 July-21 August and 24 December-2 January – **M** 190 (lunch) and a la carte 350/500.

XXX ✲ **La Boule d'Or,** 13 bd La Tour-Maubourg ✆ 47 05 50 18 – ▤. AE ◑ E VISA H 10
closed Saturday lunch and Monday – **M** 180 and a la carte 240/350
Spec. Terrine de foie frais de canard, Royal de poissons "Choisy", Soufflé chaud au citron.

XXX **Beato,** 8 r. Malar ✆ 47 05 94 27, Italian rest. – ▤. AE E VISA. ✻ H 9
closed August, Christmas-New Year, Sunday and Monday – **M** 230 b.i./300.

XXX **Focly,** 71 av. Suffren ✆ 47 83 27 12, Chinese and Thai rest. – ▤. AE VISA K 8
M 125 b.i. (lunch)/200 b.i.

XX ✲ **Ferme St-Simon** (Vandenhende), 6 r. St-Simon ✆ 45 48 35 74 – ▤. VISA J 11
closed 1 to 25 August, Saturday lunch and Sunday – **M** 195 (lunch) and a la carte 240/330
Spec. Carpaccio de poisson (summer), Foie de veau aux pommes épicées en feuilletage, Gâteau Suffren.

XX ✲ **Récamier** (Cantegrit), 4 r. Récamier ✆ 45 48 86 58, Fax 42 22 84 76, 龠 – ▤. ◑ E VISA
closed Sunday – **M** a la carte 300/430 K 12
Spec. Oeufs en meurette, Mousse de brochet sauce Nantua, Sauté de boeuf "Bourguignon".

XX **Au Quai d'Orsay,** 49 quai d'Orsay ✆ 45 51 58 58 – AE E VISA H 9
M 180 b.i. and a la carte 230/375.

XX **Le Petit Laurent,** 38 r. Varenne ✆ 45 48 79 64 – AE ◑ VISA J 11
closed 4 to 20 August, Saturday lunch and Sunday – **M** 175 and a la carte 210/300.

XX **Le Florence,** 22 r. Champ-de-Mars ✆ 45 51 52 69, Italian rest. – ▤. AE ◑ E VISA J 9
closed August, Sunday and Monday – **M** a la carte 200/300.

XX ✲ **Le Bellecour,** 22 r. Surcouf ✆ 45 51 46 93 – AE ◑ E VISA H 9
closed August, Saturday (except dinner 1 October-30 June) and Sunday – **M** 180 and a la carte 270/370
Spec. Langoustines rôties, Truffières de Saint-Jacques (December-March), Tarte aux pommes de terre renversées au foie gras.

XX **D'Chez Eux,** 2 av. Lowendal ✆ 47 05 52 55 – ▤. ◑ E VISA J 9
closed August and Sunday – **M** a la carte 235/360.

XX **Giulio Rebellato,** 20 r. Monttessuy ✆ 45 55 79 01, Italian rest. – ▤. AE E VISA. ✻ H 8
closed August, Saturday lunch and Sunday – **M** a la carte 230/360.

XX **Vert Bocage,** 96 bd La Tour-Maubourg ✆ 45 51 48 64 – ▤. AE ◑ E VISA J 9
closed Saturday and Sunday – **M** a la carte 240/350.

XX **Le Luz,** 4 r. Pierre-Leroux ✆ 43 06 99 39 – ▤. AE ◑ E VISA K 11
closed 25 August-2 September, Saturday lunch and Sunday – **M** 140 and a la carte 190/330.

XX **Aux Délices de Szechuen,** 40 av. Duquesne ✆ 43 06 22 55, 龠, Chinese rest. – ▤. AE VISA K 10
closed 29 July-26 August and Monday – **M** 95 (except Sunday) and a la carte 130 ♁.

XX **Le Club,** (Au Bon Marché) 38 r. Sèvres - 1st floor magasin 2 ✆ 45 48 95 25, Fax 45 49 27 99 – ▤. AE ◑ E VISA K 11
closed Sunday – **M** (lunch only) 149 ♁.

XX **Chez Ribe,** 15 av. Suffren ✆ 45 66 53 79 – AE ◑ E VISA J 7
closed August, Christmas-New Year, Saturday lunch and Sunday – **M** 158/168.

XX **Gildo,** 153 r. Grenelle ✆ 45 51 54 12, Fax 45 51 57 42, Italian rest. – ▤. E VISA J 9
closed August, Christmas Holidays, Monday lunch and Sunday – **M** a la carte 230/290.

XX **Tan Dinh,** 60 r. Verneuil ✆ 45 44 04 84, Vietnamese rest. J 12
closed August – **M** a la carte 240/300.

XX **Le Champ de Mars,** 17 av. La Motte-Picquet ✆ 47 05 57 99 – AE ◑ VISA J 9
closed 15 July-21 August, Tuesday dinner and Monday – **M** 110 and a la carte 160/270.

X ✲ **Vin sur Vin** (Vidal), 20 r. Monttessuy ✆ 47 05 14 20 – VISA H 8
closed 1 to 8 May, 11 to 26 August, 22 December-1 January – **M** a la carte 210/320
Spec. Saumon mariné façon "Saur", Colvert farci et sa potée de légumes (October-mid March), Imparfait à la nougatine.

X **Bistrot de Breteuil,** 3 pl. de Breteuil ✆ 45 67 07 27, 龠 – E VISA L 10
M 162 b.i.

X **Chez Collinot,** 1 r. P. Leroux ✆ 45 67 66 42 – E VISA K 11
closed August, Saturday (except dinner September-June), Sunday and Bank Holidays – **M** 115 and a la carte 155/265.

X **Nuit de St Jean,** 29 r. Surcouf ✆ 45 51 61 49 – AE ◑ E VISA. ✻ H 9
closed 1 to 9 May, 10 to 20 August, 23 December-6 January, Saturday lunch and Sunday – **M** 120.

X **Pantagruel,** 20 r. Exposition ✆ 45 51 79 96 – AE ◑ E VISA J 9
closed Saturday lunch – **M** a la carte 175/320.

X **La Calèche,** 8 r. Lille ✆ 42 60 24 76 – AE ◑ E VISA J 12
closed 5 August-2 September, 25 December-1 January, Saturday and Sunday – **M** 130/160.

X **Thoumieux,** 79 r. St Dominique ✆ 47 05 49 75, Telex 205635, Fax 47 05 36 96 – ▤. E VISA
M a la carte 110/210. H 9

Champs-Élysées, St-Lazare, Madeleine.

8th arrondissement.

8th : ✉ 75008

Plaza-Athénée, 25 av. Montaigne ☎ 47 23 78 33, Telex 650092, Fax 47 20 20 70 – ☎ – 30 - 100. AE ⓓ E VISA. ✗ rest G 9
M see **Régence and Relais Plaza** below – 105 – **215 rm** 2530/4390, 41 apartments.

Crillon, 10 pl. Concorde ☎ 42 65 24 24, Telex 290241, Fax 47 42 72 10 – rm ☎ – 30 - 60. AE ⓓ E VISA G 11
M see **Les Ambassadeurs** below - **L'Obélisque** ☎ 42 65 11 08 *(closed 28 July-25 August)* **M** 210 – 120 – **117 rm** 2100/3500, 46 apartments.

Bristol, 112 r. Fg St-Honoré ☎ 42 66 91 45, Telex 280961, Fax 42 66 68 68, – ☎ – 40 - 150. AE ⓓ E VISA. ✗ F 10
M see **Bristol** below – 120 – **152 rm** 2100/3100, 45 apartments.

George V, 31 av. George-V ☎ 47 23 54 00, Telex 650082, Fax 47 20 40 00, – rm ☎ – 600. AE ⓓ E VISA G 8
M see **Les Princes** and **Le Grill** below – 110 – **293 rm** 2590/3010, 58 apartments.

Royal Monceau, 37 av. Hoche ☎ 45 61 98 00, Telex 650361, Fax 45 63 28 93, « Pool and fitness centre » – ☎ – 30 - 300. AE ⓓ E VISA. ✗ E 8
Le Jardin M 270 (lunch) and a la carte 370/525 – **Le Carpaccio** *(closed August)* **M** 270 (lunch) and a la carte 280/475 – 125 – **180 rm** 1950/2650, 39 apartments.

Prince de Galles, 33 av. George-V ☎ 47 23 55 11, Telex 280627, Fax 47 20 96 92, – rm ☎ – 40 - 200. AE ⓓ E VISA. ✗ rm G 8
M (Sunday Brunch only 210) 215/265 – 95 – **141 rm** 1850/2250, 30 apartments.

Vernet M, 25 r. Vernet ☎ 47 23 43 10, Telex 290347, Fax 40 70 10 14 – ☎. AE ⓓ E VISA. ✗ rest F 8
M *(closed 1 to 23 August, Saturday and Sunday)* a la carte 300/450 – 90 – **54 rm** 1450/1800, 3 apartments.

San Régis M, 12 r. J. Goujon ☎ 43 59 41 90, Telex 643637, Fax 45 61 05 48, « Tasteful decor » – rm ☎. AE ⓓ E VISA. ✗ G 9
M a la carte 270/380 – 90 – **34 rm** 1250/2400, 10 apartments.

Balzac M, 6 r. Balzac ☎ 45 61 97 22, Telex 290298, Fax 42 25 24 82 – ☎. AE ⓓ E VISA. ✗ rm F 8
M see **Bice** below – 85 – **56 rm** 1460/1680, 14 apartments.

de Vigny M without rest, 9 r. Balzac ☎ 40 75 04 39, Telex 651822, Fax 40 75 05 81, « Tasteful decor » – ☎. AE ⓓ E VISA. ✗ F 8
90 – **25 rm** 1700/1900, 12 apartments.

La Trémoille, 14 r. La Trémoille ☎ 47 23 34 20, Telex 640344, Fax 40 70 01 08 – ☎. AE ⓓ E VISA G 9
M a la carte 210/300 – 80 – **96 rm** 1700/2650, 14 apartments 2520/2650.

Warwick M, 5 r. Berri ☎ 45 63 14 11, Telex 642295, Fax 45 63 75 81 – ☎ – 30 - 120. AE ⓓ E VISA F 9
M see **La Couronne** below – 100 – **144 rm** 1720/2700, 4 apartments.

Golden Tulip St-Honoré M, 220 r. Fg St-Honoré ☎ 49 53 03 03, Telex 650657, Fax 40 75 02 00, – kitchenette ☎ – 200. AE ⓓ E VISA. ✗ E 8
M 195/235 a la carte Saturday and Sunday – **52 rm** 1550/1750, 20 apartments.

Lancaster, 7 r. Berri ☎ 43 59 90 43, Telex 640991, Fax 42 89 22 71, – rm ☎. AE ⓓ E VISA. ✗ rest F 9
M 210 and a la carte 285/415 – 100 – **66 rm** 1800/2400, 9 apartments.

Pullman Windsor M, 14 r. Beaujon ☎ 45 63 04 04, Telex 650902, Fax 42 25 36 81 – ☎ – 130. AE ⓓ E VISA. ✗ rest F 8
M see **Le Clovis** below – 90 – **135 rm** 1150/1600, 11 apartments.

Relais Carré d'Or M, 46 av. George V ☎ 40 70 05 05, Telex 640561, Fax 47 23 30 90, – kitchenette ☎. AE ⓓ E VISA. ✗ F 8
M 220 and a la carte 225/365 – 100, 21 apartments 3350/15000.

Château Frontenac, 54 r. P.-Charron ✉ 75008 ☎ 47 23 55 85, Telex 644994, Fax 47 23 03 32 – ☎ – 30. ⓓ E VISA. ✗ rm G 9
M *(closed August, Saturday and Sunday)* a la carte 250/320 – 70 – **102 rm** 780/1350, 4 apartments 1350.

Bedford, 17 r. Arcade ☎ 42 66 22 32, Telex 290506, Fax 42 66 51 56 – ☎ – 80. E VISA. ✗ rest F 11
M *(closed 29 July-25 August, Saturday and Sunday)* a la carte 160/240 – **137 rm** 640/900, 10 apartments 1350/1650.

🏨🏨🏨 **Résidence du Roy** Ⓜ without rest, 8 r. François 1er ℰ 42 89 59 59, Telex 648452, Fax 40 74 07 92 — 🛗 kitchenette ▤ 📺 ☎ ௧, ⟷ – 🔏 25. 🖭 ⓞ Ε 𝗩𝗜𝗦𝗔
⟷ 60 – **5 rm** 890/970, 31 apartments 1145/1750.
G 9

🏨🏨🏨 **Claridge Bellman,** 37 r. François 1er ℰ 47 23 54 42, Telex 641150, Fax 47 23 08 84 — 🛗 ▤
📺 ☎. 🖭 ⓞ Ε 𝗩𝗜𝗦𝗔. ⸝⸜
M *(closed August, 23 December-1 January, Saturday and Sunday)* a la carte 230/350 ⅃ – ⟷
69 – **42 rm** 920/1250.
G 9

🏨🏨🏨 **Napoléon,** 40 av. Friedland ℰ 47 66 02 02, Telex 640609, Fax 47 66 82 33 — 🛗 📺 ☎·
🔏 130. 🖭 ⓞ Ε 𝗩𝗜𝗦𝗔
Napoléon Baumann ℰ 42 27 99 50 (Seafood) *(closed 1 to 21 August)* **M** a la carte 240/410 –
⟷ 60 – **70 rm** 1050/1450, 32 apartments.
F 8

🏨🏨🏨 **California** without rest, 16 r. Berri ℰ 43 59 93 00, Telex 644634, Fax 45 61 03 62 — 🛗 📺 ☎
– 🔏 40. 🖭 ⓞ Ε 𝗩𝗜𝗦𝗔
⟷ 82 – **174 rm** 995/1450, 3 apartments 2700.
F 9

🏨🏨 **Concorde-St-Lazare,** 108 r. St-Lazare ℰ 40 08 44 44, Telex 650442, Fax 42 93 01 20 — 🛗
▤ 📺 ☎ – 🔏 95. 🖭 Ε 𝗩𝗜𝗦𝗔
Café Terminus M 125/180 – ⟷ 82 – **314 rm** 1150/1950.
E 12

🏨🏨 **Queen Elizabeth,** 41 av. Pierre-1er-de-Serbie ℰ 47 20 80 56, Telex 641179, Fax 47 20 89 19
– 🛗 📺 ☎. 🔏 25 - 30. 🖭 ⓞ Ε 𝗩𝗜𝗦𝗔
M *(closed August, Saturday and Sunday)* (lunch only) 130 b.i./220 – ⟷ 80 – **49 rm** 1000/1500,
17 apartments 1700/2500.
G 8

🏨🏨 **Pullman St-Honoré** without rest, 15 r. Boissy d'Anglas ℰ 42 66 93 62, Telex 240366, Fax
42 66 14 98 — 🛗 ▤ 📺 ☎. 🖭 ⓞ Ε 𝗩𝗜𝗦𝗔
⟷ 85 – **104 rm** 680/900, 8 apartments 1400.
G 11

🏨🏨 **L'Horset Astor,** 11 r. Astorg ℰ 42 66 56 56, Telex 642737, Fax 42 65 18 37 — 🛗 ▤ rest 📺
☎ – 🔏 25. 🖭 ⓞ Ε 𝗩𝗜𝗦𝗔
M *(closed Saturday and Sunday)* 210 (lunch) and a la carte 240/380 – ⟷ 50 – **128 rm**
820/870.
F 11

🏨🏨 **Royal Alma** Ⓜ without rest, 35 r. Jean Goujon ℰ 42 25 83 30, Telex 641428, Fax 45 63 68 64
– 🛗 📺 ☎. 🖭 ⓞ Ε 𝗩𝗜𝗦𝗔. ⸝⸜
⟷ 80 – **68 rm** 900/1300, 8 apartments 1600/2500.
G 9

🏨🏨 **François 1er** Ⓜ, 7 r. Magellan ℰ 47 23 44 04, Telex 648880, Fax 47 23 93 43 — 🛗 ▤ 📺 ☎.
🖭 ⓞ Ε 𝗩𝗜𝗦𝗔
M 150/350 – ⟷ 85 – **36 rm** 1150/1280, 4 apartments 2060.
F 8

🏨🏨 **de l'Élysée** Ⓜ without rest, 12 r. Saussaies ℰ 42 65 29 25, Telex 281665, Fax 42 65 64 28 —
🛗 📺 ☎. 🖭 ⓞ Ε 𝗩𝗜𝗦𝗔. ⸝⸜ – ⟷ 50 – **32 rm** 480/880.
F 11

🏨🏨 **Elysées-Marignan,** 12 r. Marignan ℰ 43 59 58 61, Telex 644018, Fax 45 63 28 87 — 🛗 📺
☎ – 🔏 80. 🖭 ⓞ Ε 𝗩𝗜𝗦𝗔
M *(closed August, Saturday, Sunday and Bank Holidays)* a la carte 180/330 – ⟷ 60 – **79 rm**
1450, 22 apartments 1800/2400.
G 9

🏨🏨 **Élysées Ponthieu et résidence Le Cid** Ⓜ without rest, 24 r. Ponthieu ℰ 42 25 68 70,
Telex 640053, Fax 42 25 80 82 — 🛗 kitchenette ▤ 📺 ☎. 🖭 ⓞ Ε 𝗩𝗜𝗦𝗔
⟷ 40 – **92 rm** 720/1450, 6 apartments 1800/2400.
F 9

🏨🏨 **Royal H.** without rest, 33 av. Friedland ℰ 43 59 08 14, Telex 280965, Fax 45 63 69 92 — 🛗
📺 ☎. 🖭 ⓞ Ε 𝗩𝗜𝗦𝗔
⟷ 50 – **58 rm** 775/990.
F 8

🏨🏨 **Résidence Champs-Elysées** Ⓜ without rest, 92 r. La Boétie ℰ 43 59 96 15, Telex
650695, Fax 42 56 01 38 — 🛗 📺 ☎. ⓞ Ε 𝗩𝗜𝗦𝗔
⟷ 65 – **83 rm** 700/1100.
F 9

🏨🏨 **Résidence Monceau** Ⓜ without rest, 85 r. Rocher ℰ 45 22 75 11, Telex 280671, Fax
45 22 30 88 — 🛗 📺 ☎ ௧. 🖭 ⓞ Ε 𝗩𝗜𝗦𝗔. ⸝⸜
⟷ 30 – **50 rm** 560.
E 11

🏨🏨 **Concortel** without rest, 19 r. Pasquier ℰ 42 65 45 44, Telex 660228, Fax 42 65 18 33 — 🛗 📺
☎. 🖭 ⓞ Ε 𝗩𝗜𝗦𝗔 – ⟷ 35 – **44 rm** 520/680.
F 11

🏨🏨 **Résidence St-Honoré** without rest, 214 r. Fg-St-Honoré ℰ 42 25 26 27, Telex 640524, Fax
45 63 30 67 — 🛗 📺 ☎. 🖭 ⓞ Ε 𝗩𝗜𝗦𝗔
⟷ 35 – **91 rm** 740/950.
E 9

🏨🏨 **Powers** without rest, 52 r. François-1er ℰ 47 23 91 05, Telex 642051, Fax 49 52 04 63 — 🛗 📺
☎. 🖭 ⓞ Ε 𝗩𝗜𝗦𝗔. ⸝⸜
⟷ 50 – **53 rm** 630/950.
G 9

🏨🏨 **Castiglione,** 40 r. Fg-St-Honoré ℰ 42 65 07 50, Telex 240362, Fax 42 65 12 27 — 🛗 ▤ rest
📺 ☎ – 🔏 50. 🖭 ⓞ Ε 𝗩𝗜𝗦𝗔
M 160/200 – ⟷ 60 – **105 rm** 890/1390, 14 apartments.
G 11

🏨🏨 **Printemps et rest. Chez Martin,** 1 r. Isly ℰ 42 94 12 12, Telex 290744, Fax 42 94 05 02 —
🛗 📺 ☎ – 🔏 25 - 35. 🖭 𝗩𝗜𝗦𝗔
M *(closed 19 July-5 August, Saturday and Sunday)* 103 b.i./168 ⅃ – **67 rm** ⟷ 433/900.
F 12

🏨🏨 **New Roblin et rest. le Mazagran,** 6 r. Chauveau-Lagarde ℰ 42 65 57 00, Telex 640154,
Fax 42 65 19 49 — 🛗 ▤ 📺 ☎. 🖭 ⓞ Ε 𝗩𝗜𝗦𝗔. ⸝⸜ rest
M *(closed Saturday, Sunday and Bank Holidays)* 130/140 ⅃ – ⟷ 50 – **70 rm** 570/700, 7
apartments 1250/1350.
F 11

🏨 **West End** without rest, 7 r. Clément-Marot 🕾 47 20 30 78, Telex 611972, Fax 47 20 34 42 —
🛗 📺 🕾 . 🅰🅴 ⓪ 🄴 💳
⊏ 40 – **49 rm** 600/1400. G 9

🏨 **Lido** Ⓜ without rest, 4 passage Madeleine 🕾 42 66 27 37, Telex 281039, Fax 42 66 61 23 —
🛗 📺 🕾 . 🅰🅴 ⓪ 🄴 💳
⊏ 25 – **32 rm** 515/730. F 11

🏨 **Cordélia** Ⓜ without rest, 11 r. Greffulhe 🕾 42 65 42 40, Telex 281760, Fax 42 65 11 81 — 🛗
📺 🕾. 🅰🅴 ⓪ 🄴 💳
⊏ 45 – **30 rm** 600/650. F 11

🏨 **Franklin Roosevelt** without rest, 18 r. Clément-Marot 🕾 47 23 61 66, Telex 614797, Fax
47 20 44 30 — 🛗 📺 🕾. 🅰🅴 🄴 💳. ⋘
⊏ 40 – **45 rm** 640/750. G 9

🏨 **Colisée** without rest, 6 r. Colisée 🕾 43 59 95 25, Telex 643101, Fax 45 63 26 54 — 🛗 📺 🕾.
🅰🅴 ⓪ 🄴 💳
⊏ 30 – **44 rm** 465/660. F 9

🏨 **Rochambeau** without rest, 4 r. La Boétie 🕾 42 65 27 54, Telex 640030, Fax 42 66 03 81 — 🛗
📺 🕾. 🅰🅴 ⓪ 🄴 💳
50 rm ⊏ 650/880. F 11

🏨 **Atlantic** without rest, 44 r. Londres 🕾 43 87 45 40, Telex 650477, Fax 42 93 06 26 — 🛗 📺
🕾. 🅰🅴 🄴 💳. ⋘
⊏ 40 – **93 rm** 370/620. E 12

🏨 **L'Orangerie** Ⓜ without rest, 9 r. de Constantinople 🕾 45 22 07 51, Telex 650294, Fax
45 22 16 49 — 🛗 📺 🕾. 🅰🅴 ⓪ 🄴 💳. ⋘
⊏ 25 – **29 rm** 400/600. E 11

🏨 **St Augustin** without rest, 9 r. Roy 🕾 42 93 32 17, Telex 283919, Fax 42 93 19 34 — 🛗 📺 🕾.
🅰🅴 ⓪ 🄴 💳
⊏ 30 – **62 rm** 550/750. F 11

🏨 **Queen Mary** without rest, 9 r. Greffulhe 🕾 42 66 40 50, Telex 640419, Fax 42 66 94 92 — 🛗
📺 🕾. 🄴 💳. ⋘
⊏ 40 – **36 rm** 550/700. F 12

🏨 **Waldorf Florida** without rest, 12 bd Malesherbes 🕾 42 65 72 06, Telex 650557, Fax
40 07 10 45 — 🛗 📺 🕾. 🅰🅴 ⓪ 🄴 💳
44 rm ⊏ 640/830. F 11

🏨 **Résidence Saint-Philippe** without rest, 123 r. Fg-St-Honoré 🕾 43 59 86 99, Telex 650837
— 🛗 📺 🕾. 🅰🅴 🄴 💳. ⋘
⊏ 30 – **38 rm** 430/690. F 9-10

🏨 **Alison** Ⓜ without rest, 21 r. Surène 🕾 42 65 54 00, Telex 640435, Fax 42 65 08 17 — 🛗 📺
🕾. 🅰🅴 ⓪ 🄴 💳
⊏ 40 – **35 rm** 420/690. F 11

🏨 **Astoria** without rest, 42 r. Moscou 🕾 42 93 63 53, Telex 290061, Fax 42 93 30 30 — 🛗 📺 🕾.
🅰🅴 ⓪ 🄴 💳. ⋘
⊏ 30 – **82 rm** 550/790. D 11

🏨 **Bradford** without rest, 10 r. St-Philippe-du-Roule 🕾 43 59 24 20, Telex 648530, Fax
45 63 20 07 — 🛗 🕾. 🄴 💳. ⋘
46 rm ⊏ 570/700. F 9

🏨 **Lord Byron** without rest, 5 r. Chateaubriand 🕾 43 59 89 98, Telex 649662, Fax 42 89 46 04,
🌳 — 🛗 📺 🕾. 🄴 💳. ⋘
⊏ 50 – **31 rm** 595/850. F 9

🏨 **Rond-Point des Champs-Elysées** without rest, 10 r. Ponthieu 🕾 43 59 55 58, Telex
642386, Fax 45 63 99 75 — 🛗 📺 🕾. 🅰🅴 ⓪ 🄴 💳. ⋘
⊏ 30 – **44 rm** 450/780. F 10

🏨 **Élysées** without rest, 100 r. La Boétie 🕾 43 59 23 46, Telex 648572, Fax 42 56 33 80 — 🛗 📺
🕾. 🅰🅴 ⓪ 🄴 💳. ⋘
⊏ 25 – **29 rm** 405/550. F 9

🏨 **Angleterre-Champs-Élysées** without rest, 91 r. La Boétie 🕾 43 59 35 45, Telex 640317,
Fax 45 63 22 22 — 🛗 📺 🕾. 🅰🅴 ⓪ 🄴 💳
⊏ 30 – **40 rm** 420/545. F 9

🏨 **Plaza Haussmann** without rest, 177 bd Haussmann 🕾 45 63 93 83, Telex 643716, Fax
45 61 14 30 — 🛗 📺 🕾. 🅰🅴 ⓪ 🄴 💳
⊏ 25 – **41 rm** 485/640. F 9

🏩 **Charing Cross** Ⓜ without rest, 39 r. Pasquier 🕾 43 87 41 04, Telex 290681, Fax 42 93 70 45
— 🛗 📺 🕾. 🅰🅴 ⓪ 💳
31 rm ⊏ 365/479. F 11

🏩 **Ministère** without rest, 31 r. Surène 🕾 42 66 21 43, Fax 42 66 96 04 — 🛗 📺 🕾. 🅰🅴 🄴 💳
⊏ 30 – **28 rm** 300/540. F 11

🏩 **Lavoisier-Malesherbes** without rest, 21 r. Lavoisier 🕾 42 65 10 97, Telex 281801, Fax
42 65 02 43 — 🛗 📺 ☏. 🄴 💳. ⋘
⊏ 26 – **32 rm** 320/430. F 11

XXXXX ❀❀❀ **Lucas-Carton** (Senderens), 9 pl. Madeleine ℰ 42 65 22 90, Telex 281088, Fax
42 65 06 23, « 1900 Fine decor » – ▤. **E** *VISA*. ⅍   G 11
closed 3 to 25 August, 21 December-5 January, Saturday and Sunday – **M** 375 (lunch) and a
la carte 500/850
Spec. Langoustines sautées au beurre d'estragon, Dorade aux amandes et sa raviole de seiche à l'encre, Lapin
à la moutarde de Crémone.

XXXXX ❀❀❀ **Lasserre**, 17 av. F.-D.-Roosevelt ℰ 43 59 53 43, Fax 45 63 72 23, Open roof in fine
weather – ▤. **E** *VISA*. ⅍   G 10
closed 4 August-2 September, Monday lunch and Sunday – **M** a la carte 480/680
Spec. Morue fraîche gratinée aux artichauts confits, Pintadeau Richelieu, Sabayon de pruneaux et sorbet au
thé.

XXXXX ❀❀❀ **Taillevent** (Vrinat), 15 r. Lamennais ℰ 45 61 12 90 – ▤. **E** *VISA*. ⅍   F 9
closed 27 July-27 August, February Holidays, Saturday, Sunday and Bank Holidays – **M**
(booking essential) a la carte 500/700
Spec. Cervelas de fruits de mer, Noisettes d'agneau à la sauce aux herbes, Chaud-froid de fruits en gelée.

XXXXX ❀❀ **Les Ambassadeurs** - Hôtel Crillon, 10 pl. Concorde ℰ 42 65 11 12, Telex 290241, Fax
47 42 72 10, « 18C decor » – ▤. **AE** **①** **E** *VISA*. ⅍   G 11
M 310 (lunch) and a la carte 410/650
Spec. Gratin dauphinois de homard à la crème au caviar, Couscous de bar aux graines de sésame, Joues de
porcelet à la ficelle.

XXXXX ❀❀ **Laurent**, 41 av. Gabriel ℰ 42 25 00 39, « Pleasant terrace » – **AE** **①** **E** *VISA*. ⅍   G 11
closed Saturday lunch, Sunday and Bank Holidays – **M** 380 (lunch) and a la carte 480/790
Spec. Langoustines croustillantes et courgettes au citron confit, Agneau de trois façons, Les deux soufflés
Laurent.

XXXXX ❀ **Bristol**, 112 r. Fg St-Honoré ℰ 42 66 91 45, Telex 280961, Fax 42 66 68 68 – ▤. **AE** **①** **E**
VISA. ⅍ – **M** a la carte 475/650   F 10
Spec. Salade de langoustines et ragoût de tourteau à l'avocat, Escalope de turbot au Sauternes, Médaillon de
veau aux girolles.

XXXXX ❀ **Régence** - Hôtel Plaza Athénée, 25 av. Montaigne ℰ 47 23 78 33, Telex 650092, Fax
47 20 20 70, 😃 – ▤. **AE** **①** **E** *VISA*. ⅍   G 9
M a la carte 370/700
Spec. Soufflé de homard, Duo de langoustines et Saint-Jacques, Macaron Nélusko au sabayon de noisettes.

XXXXX **Ledoyen**, carré Champs-Élysées ℰ 47 42 23 23, Telex 282358, Fax 47 42 55 01, 😃 – **℗**.
AE **①** **E** *VISA*. ⅍   G 10
Le Guépard *(closed Sunday)* **M** 380 (lunch) and a la carte 520/720 – **Le Carré** *(closed Sunday)*
M a la carte 260/410 ⅃
Spec. Carpaccio de thon aux pétales d'ail frit, Saumon d'Ecosse en crépine de peau de sole, Selle d'agneau en
croûte d'épices.

XXXX ❀ **Élysée Lenôtre**, 10 av. Champs-Élysées ℰ 42 65 85 10, Fax 42 65 76 23, 😃 – 🕭 **℗**. **AE**
① *VISA* – Rez-de-Chaussée *(closed Saturday, Sunday and Bank Holidays)* **M** (lunch only)
330 – **1er étage** *(dinner only)* **M** a la carte 380/620   G 10
Spec. Poêlée de langoustines à la rémoulade de poireaux, Blanc de turbot rôti au jus de viande, Trois parfums
de macaron autour d'un savarin.

XXXX ❀ **Les Princes** - Hôtel George V, 31 av. George V ℰ 47 23 54 00, Telex 650082, Fax
47 20 40 00, 😃 – ▤. **AE** **①** **E** *VISA*   G 8
M 350 b.i. (lunch) and a la carte 390/630
Spec. Salade de tourteau en folie, Selle d'agneau rôtie à la noix de coco et ananas, Tarte aux poires et grains
de vanille.

XXXX ❀ **Chiberta**, 3 r. Arsène-Houssaye ℰ 45 63 77 90, Fax 45 62 85 08 – ▤. **AE** **①** **E** *VISA*   F 8
closed 31 July-28 August, Christmas-New Year, Saturday, Sunday and Bank Holidays – **M** a la
la carte 390/550
Spec. Sole au beurre et céleri, Canette rôtie confite à la bécassine, Tarte au chocolat glacé au miel d'acacia.

XXXX **Le Bacchus Gourmand**, 21 r. François 1er ℰ 47 20 15 83, Fax 40 70 12 74, 😃 – ▤. **AE** **①**
E *VISA*   G 9
closed August, Saturday and Sunday – **M** 290 (lunch) and a la carte 365/460.

XXXX **Lamazère**, 23 r. Ponthieu ℰ 43 59 66 66, Fax 42 25 69 97 – ▤. **AE** **①** **E** *VISA*. ⅍   F 9
closed 29 July-30 August and Sunday – **M** 270 (lunch) and a la carte 420/570.

XXXX ❀ **La Marée**, 1 r. Daru ℰ 43 80 20 00, Fax 48 88 04 04, Seafood – ▤. **AE** **①** *VISA*   E 8
closed 21 July-21 August, Saturday and Sunday – **M** a la carte 400/600
Spec. Bar à la vapeur d'algues et basilic, Petite marmite tropézienne, Râble de lièvre à la caladoise (October-
February).

XXXX **Fouquet's**, 99 av. Champs-Élysées ℰ 47 23 70 60, Telex 648227, Fax 47 20 08 69 – **AE**
① **E** *VISA*   F 8
Rez-de-Chaussée (grill) **M** 240 and a la carte 250/380 ⅃ – **1er étage** *(closed 15 July-20*
August and Sunday) **M** a la carte 280/400
Spec. Duo de foies de canard et d'oie, Sole au Champagne, Noisettes d'agneau rôties en croustade de
pommes de terre.

XXX **15 Montaigne Maison Blanche,** 15 av. Montaigne *✆* 47 23 55 99, Fax 47 20 09 56, 🏤 –
☰ 🄴 *VISA* G 9
M 150/290 (lunch) and a la carte 330/500.

XXX ✿ **La Couronne** - Hôtel Warwick, 5 r. Berri *✆* 45 63 78 49, Telex 642295, Fax 45 63 75 81 –
☰, 🄰🄴 🄾 🄴 *VISA* 🕸 F 9
closed 5 August-1 September, Sunday and Bank Holidays – **M** 250 and a la carte 320/430
Spec. Tartelette de noix de Saint-Jacques (season), Rôti de lotte au pistil de safran, Millefeuille d'avelines sur
lait d'amandes.

XXX **Le Marcande,** 52 r. Miromesnil *✆* 42 65 19 14, 🏤 – ☰. 🄰🄴 🄾 *VISA* F 10
closed 3 to 26 August, Saturday, Sunday and Bank Holidays – **M** 210 (lunch) and a la carte
310/430.

XXX ✿ **Le Clovis** - Hôtel Pullman Windsor, 4 r. B.-Albrecht *✆* 45 63 04 04, Telex 650902, Fax
42 35 36 81 – ☰ 🄰🄴 🄾 🄴 *VISA* F 8
closed 26 July-26 August, 20 December-2 January, Saturday, Sunday and Bank Holidays –
M 255 (lunch) and a la carte 320/410
Spec. Tartare de dorade rose et saumon mariné, Bar au dill cuit sur le sel au varech, Agneau au romarin et
crème de haricot.

XXX **Le 30 - Fauchon,** pl. Madeleine *✆* 47 42 56 58, Fax 47 42 83 75 – ☰. 🄰🄴 🄾 🄴 *VISA*. 🕸 F 12
closed Sunday – **M** a la carte 320/410.

XXX **Le Jardin Violet,** 19 r. Bayard *✆* 47 20 55 11, Chinese rest. – ☰. 🄰🄴 🄾 🄴 *VISA* G 9
M 150/350.

XXX ✿ **Copenhague,** 142 av. Champs-Élysées (1st floor) *✆* 43 59 20 41, Fax 42 25 83 10, Danish
rest. – ☰. 🄰🄴 🄾 🄴 *VISA*. 🕸 F 8
*closed 29 July-27 August, 1 to 7 January, Saturday lunch in summer, Sunday and Bank
Holidays* – **M** a la carte 260/420 - **Flora Danica M** a la carte 200/360
Spec. Saumon mariné à l'aneth, Mignon de renne aux mûres jaunes en aigre doux, Mandelrand avec sorbets et
fruits.

XXX **Alain Rayé,** 49 r. Colysée *✆* 42 25 66 76, Fax 42 56 29 97 – 🄰🄴 🄴 *VISA* F 10
closed Saturday lunch, Sunday and Bank Holidays – **M** 235/500.

XXX **Relais-Plaza** - Hôtel Plaza Athénée, 21 av. Montaigne *✆* 47 23 46 36, Telex 650092, Fax
47 20 20 70 – ☰. 🄰🄴 🄾 🄴 *VISA* 🕸 G 9
M 295 (dinner) and a la carte 325/580.

XXX **Le Grill** - Hôtel George V, 31 av. George V *✆* 47 23 54 00, Fax 47 30 04 49 – ☰. 🄰🄴 🄾 🄴
VISA G 8
M a la carte 200/370.

XXX **Yvan,** 1bis r. J. Mermoz *✆* 43 59 18 40, Fax 45 63 78 69 – ☰. 🄰🄴 🄾 🄴 *VISA* F-G 10
closed Saturday lunch and Sunday – **M** 158/278.

XXX **Les Géorgiques,** 36 av. George V *✆* 40 70 10 49 – ☰. 🄰🄴 🄾 🄴 *VISA*. 🕸 G 8
closed Saturday lunch and Sunday – **M** 180 (lunch) and a la carte 290/460.

XXX **Indra,** 10 r. Cdt-Rivière *✆* 43 59 46 40, Fax 42 89 90 18, Indian rest. – ☰. 🄰🄴 🄾 🄴 *VISA* F 9
closed Saturday lunch and Sunday – **M** 220/300.

XX **Baumann Marbeuf,** 15 r. Marbeuf *✆* 47 20 11 11, Fax 47 23 69 65 – 🕸 ☰. 🄰🄴 🄾 🄴 *VISA*
closed 10 to 20 August – **M** a la carte 150/280 🍴. G 9

XX **Fermette Marbeuf,** 5 r. Marbeuf *✆* 47 23 31 31, Fax 40 70 02 11, « 1900 decor with
genuine ceramics and leaded glass windows » – ☰. 🄰🄴 🄾 *VISA* G 9
M a la carte 200/330 🍴.

XX **Bice** - Hôtel Balzac, 6 r. Balzac *✆* 42 89 86 34, Fax 42 25 24 82, Italian rest. – ☰. 🄰🄴 🄾 🄴
VISA F 8
M a la carte 250/400.

XX **Chez Tante Louise,** 41 r. Boissy d'Anglas *✆* 42 65 06 85 – ☰. 🄰🄴 🄾 🄴 *VISA* F 11
closed August, Saturday and Sunday – **M** 190 and a la carte 230/420.

XX **Le Boeuf sur le Toit,** 34 r. Colisée *✆* 43 59 83 80, Fax 45 63 45 40, brasserie – ☰. 🄰🄴 🄾
🄴 *VISA* F 10
M a la carte 135/300 🍴.

XX **Androuët,** 41 r. Amsterdam *✆* 48 74 26 93, Telex 280466, Fax 49 95 02 54, Cheese specialities – ☰. 🄰🄴 🄾 🄴 *VISA*. 🕸 E 12
closed Sunday and Bank Holidays – **M** 190/250.

XX **Le Grenadin,** 46 r. Naples *✆* 45 63 28 92 – ☰. 🄴 *VISA* E 11
closed 8 to 14 July, 12 to 18 August, Christmas-New Year, Saturday and Sunday – **M**
200/350.

XX **Marius et Janette,** 4 av. George V *✆* 47 23 41 88, Fax 45 56 98 42, Seafood – ☰. 🄰🄴 🄴
VISA F 8
closed 22 December-1 January, Saturday and Sunday – **M** 250 b.i. and a la carte 320/550.

XX **Tong Yen,** 1bis r. J. Mermoz *✆* 42 25 04 23, Fax 45 63 51 57, Chinese rest. with Vietnamese
and Thai specialities – ☰. 🄰🄴 🄾 🄴 *VISA* F 10
closed 1 to 25 August – **M** a la carte 180/350.

XX **Le Drugstorien,** 1 av. Matignon (1st floor) *✆* 43 59 38 70, Telex 648566, Fax 45 61 90 66 –
☰. 🄰🄴 🄾 🄴 *VISA* G 10
M a la carte 170/300.

XX **L'Étoile Marocaine,** 56 r. Galilée ℘ 47 20 44 43, Morrocan rest. – ▤. AE ⓓ F 8
M 161/243.

XX **Le Lloyd's,** 23 r. Treilhard ℘ 45 63 21 23 – AE E VISA E 10
closed Saturday and Sunday – **M** a la carte 250/340.

XX **Chez Bosc,** 7 r. Richepanse ℘ 42 60 10 27 – AE ⓓ E VISA G 12
closed 15 July-15 August, Saturday lunch and Sunday – **M** 170 and a la carte 250/400.

XX **Daniel Météry,** 4 r. Arcade ℘ 42 65 53 13 – AE E VISA F 11
closed 11 to 18 August, Saturday lunch, Sunday and Bank Holidays – **M** 170 and a la carte 230/360.

XX **Chez Max,** 19 r. Castellane ℘ 42 65 33 81 – E VISA F 11
closed 31 July-1 September, Saturday, Sunday and Bank Holidays – **M** 180/250.

XX **Artois,** 13 r. Artois ℘ 42 25 01 10 – E VISA F 9
closed Saturday lunch and Sunday – **M** (booking essential) a la carte 200/280.

XX **Le Sarladais,** 2 r. Vienne ℘ 45 22 23 62 – ▤. E VISA E 11
closed August, Saturday lunch and Sunday – **M** 140 (dinner) and a la carte 180/280.

XX **Annapurna,** 32 r. Berri ℘ 45 63 91 56, Indian rest. – ▤. AE ⓓ VISA F 9
closed Saturday lunch and Sunday – **M** a la carte 160/300.

XX **Le Pichet,** 68 r. P. Charron ℘ 43 59 50 34 – ▤. AE ⓓ E VISA GF 9
closed 24 December-6 January, Saturday and Sunday – **M** a la carte 240/340.

XX **Stresa,** 7 r. Chambiges ℘ 47 23 51 62, Italian rest. – AE ⓓ G 9
closed 1 to 26 August, 20 December-4 January, Saturday dinner and Sunday – **M** a la carte 240/350.

X **Bistrot de Marius,** 6 av. George V ℘ 40 70 11 76, ⛱, Seafood – AE E VISA G 8
M a la carte 190/295 ♖.

X **La Petite Auberge,** 48 r. Moscou ℘ 43 87 91 84 – E VISA D 11
closed Saturday and Sunday – **M** 130 and a la carte 180/270.

X **Ferme des Mathurins,** 17 r. Vignon ℘ 42 66 46 39 – E VISA F 12
closed 1 August-2 September, Sunday and Bank Holidays – **M** 140/190.

X **Finzi,** 182 bd Haussmann ℘ 45 62 88 68, Italian rest. – ▤. E VISA F 8
closed Sunday lunch in August – **M** a la carte 155/270.

Opéra, Gare du Nord, Gare de l'Est, Grands Boulevards.

9th and 10th arrondissements.
9th : ✉ 75009
10th : ✉ 75010

Le Grand Hôtel, 2 r. Scribe (9th) ℘ 40 07 32 32, Telex 220875, Fax 42 66 12 51 – |‡| kitchenette ⇆ rm ▤ rm TV ☎ – ♟ 500. AE ⓓ E VISA. ✻ rest F 12
M see **Opéra-Café de la Paix, Relais Capucines-Café de la Paix** below – ☕ 135 – **470 rm** 1650/3200, 23 apartments.

Scribe M, 1 r. Scribe (9th) ℘ 47 42 03 40, Telex 214653, Fax 42 65 39 97 – |‡| ⇆ rm ▤ TV ☎ ♿ – ♟ 80. AE ⓓ E VISA. ✻ rest F 12
Le Jardin des Muses snack **M** a la carte approx. 160 ♖ – **Les Muses** *(closed August, Saturday, Sunday and Bank Holidays)* **M** 220 (lunch)/350 – ☕ 100 – **206 rm** 1450/2300, 11 apartments.

Ambassador, 16 bd Haussmann (9th) ℘ 42 46 92 63, Telex 650912, Fax 40 22 08 74 – |‡| ▤ TV ☎ – ♟ 120. AE ⓓ E VISA. ✻ rest F 13
M 230/350 – ☕ 100 – **300 rm** 1100/1800.

Commodore, 12 bd Haussmann (9th) ℘ 42 46 72 82, Telex 280601, Fax 47 70 23 81 – |‡| TV ☎ ♿. AE ⓓ E VISA F 13
M 220 (lunch) and a la carte 150/210 ♖ – ☕ 70 – **152 rm** 1700, 11 apartments.

Altéa Ronceray M without rest, 10 bd Montmartre (9th) ℘ 42 47 13 45, Telex 283906, Fax 42 47 13 63 – |‡| TV ☎ – ♟ 65. AE ⓓ E VISA F 14
☕ 59 – **117 rm** 650/750, 13 apartments 990/1190.

Brébant M, 32 bd Poissonnière (9th) ℘ 47 70 25 55, Telex 280127, Fax 42 46 65 70 – |‡| TV ☎ – ♟ 80. AE ⓓ E VISA F 14
M 85/140 – **122 rm** ☕ 675/820.

L'Horset Pavillon, 38 r. Échiquier (10th) ℘ 42 46 92 75, Telex 283905, Fax 42 47 03 97 – |‡| ▤ TV ☎. AE ⓓ E VISA. ✻ rest F 15
M *(closed Saturday and Sunday)* 130/250 – ☕ 45 – **92 rm** 620/700 – ½ P 525.

Cidotel Lafayette M without rest, 49 r. Lafayette (9th) ℘ 42 85 05 44, Telex 283025, Fax 49 95 06 60 – |‡| TV ☎. AE ⓓ E VISA F 14
☕ 40 – **75 rm** 800.

🏨🏨 **St-Pétersbourg** without rest, 33 r. Caumartin (9th) ℰ 42 66 60 38, Telex 680001, Fax
42 66 53 54 — 🕻 📺 ☎. 🆀 ① 🗲 𝘝𝘐𝘚𝘈
100 rm ⇌ 465/850.   F 12

🏨🏨 **Astra** Ⓜ without rest, 29 r. Caumartin (9th) ℰ 42 66 15 15, Telex 210408, Fax 42 66 98 05 —
🕻 ⬛ 📺 ☎. 🆀 ① 🗲 𝘝𝘐𝘚𝘈. ✻
⇌ 35 — **85 rm** 590/880.   F 15

🏨🏨 **Blanche Fontaine** Ⓜ ⤳ without rest, 34 r. Fontaine (9th) ℰ 45 26 72 32, Telex 660311,
Fax 42 81 05 52 — 🕻 📺 ☎ ⇦. 🆀 𝘝𝘐𝘚𝘈. ✻
⇌ 35 — **45 rm** 413/483, 4 apartments 660.   D 13

🏨🏨 **Paris Est** Ⓜ without rest, cour d'Honneur (10th) ℰ 42 05 00 33, Telex 217916, Fax 42 09 91 60
— 🕻 📺 ☎. 🆀 🗲 𝘝𝘐𝘚𝘈
⇌ 37 — **34 rm** 360/570.   E 16

🏨 **Opéra Cadet** Ⓜ without rest, 24 r. Cadet (9th) ℰ 48 24 05 26, Telex 282287, Fax 42 46 68 09
— 🕻 📺 ☎ & ⇦. 🆀 ① 🗲 𝘝𝘐𝘚𝘈
⇌ 40 — **90 rm** 650.   F 14

🏨 **Mercure Monty** Ⓜ, 5 r. Monthyon (9th) ℰ 47 70 26 10, Telex 660677, Fax 42 46 55 10 — 🕻
📺 ☎ — 🔬 50. 🆀 ① 🗲 𝘝𝘐𝘚𝘈
M *(closed Sunday)* 100/160 ⅃ — ⇌ 52 — **72 rm** 670.   F 14

🏨 **Gotty** Ⓜ without rest, 11 r. Trévise (9th) ℰ 47 70 12 90, Telex 660330 — 🕻 📺 ☎   F 14
44 rm

🏨 **Celte La Fayette** Ⓜ without rest, 25 r. Buffault (9th) ℰ 49 95 09 49, Telex 610611, Fax
49 95 01 88 — 🕻 📺 ☎ &. 🆀 ① 🗲 𝘝𝘐𝘚𝘈. ✻
⇌ 35 — **51 rm** 480/630.   E 14

🏨 **Libertel du Moulin** Ⓜ without rest, 39 r. Fontaine (9th) ℰ 42 81 93 25, Telex 660055, Fax
40 16 09 90 — 🕻 📺 ☎. 🆀 ① 🗲 𝘝𝘐𝘚𝘈. ✻
⇌ 40 — **50 rm** 505/565.   D 13

🏨 **Anjou-Lafayette** Ⓜ without rest, 4 r. Riboutté (9th) ℰ 42 46 83 44, Telex 281001, Fax
48 00 08 97 — 🕻 📺 ☎. 🆀 ① 🗲 𝘝𝘐𝘚𝘈
⇌ 30 — **39 rm** 450/650.   E 14

🏨 **Paix République** without rest, 2bis bd St Martin (10th) ℰ 42 08 96 95, Telex 680632, Fax
42 06 36 30 — 🕻 📺 ☎. 🆀 ① 🗲 𝘝𝘐𝘚𝘈. ✻
⇌ 35 — **45 rm** 480/850.   G 16

🏨 **Athènes** Ⓜ without rest, 21 r. Athènes (9th) ℰ 48 74 00 55, Telex 640715, Fax 42 81 04 75 —
🕻 📺 ☎. 🆀 🗲 𝘝𝘐𝘚𝘈. ✻
⇌ 35 — **36 rm** 475/555.   E 12

🏨 **La Tour d'Auvergne** without rest, 10 r. La Tour d'Auvergne (9th) ℰ 48 78 61 60, Telex
281604, Fax 49 95 99 00 — 🕻 ✻ 📺 ☎. 🆀 ① 🗲 𝘝𝘐𝘚𝘈. ✻
⇌ 30 — **25 rm** 500/650.   E 14

🏨 **Résidence du Pré** Ⓜ without rest, 15 r. P. Sémard (9th) ℰ 48 78 26 72, Telex 660549, Fax
40 23 98 28 — 🕻 📺 ☎. 🆀 🗲 𝘝𝘐𝘚𝘈. ✻
⇌ 25 — **40 rm** 365/405.   E 15

🏨 **Carlton's H.** without rest, 55 bd Rochechouart (9th) ℰ 42 81 91 00, Telex 640649, Fax
42 81 97 04 — 🕻 📺 ☎. 🆀 ① 🗲 𝘝𝘐𝘚𝘈
⇌ 45 — **103 rm** 530/720.   D 14

🏨 **Chamonix** Ⓜ without rest, 8 r. Hauteville (10th) ℰ 47 70 19 49, Telex 283177 — 🕻 📺 ☎. 🆀
① 🗲 𝘝𝘐𝘚𝘈
⇌ 35 — **34 rm** 500/630.   F 15

🏨 **Caumartin** Ⓜ without rest, 27 r. Caumartin (9th) ℰ 47 42 95 95, Telex 680702, Fax 47 42 88 19
— 🕻 📺 ☎. 🆀 ① 🗲 𝘝𝘐𝘚𝘈
⇌ 40 — **40 rm** 720.   F 12

🏨 **D'Estrées** Ⓜ ⤳ without rest, 2bis cité Pigalle (9th) ℰ 48 74 39 22, Telex 290609, Fax
42 25 81 95 — 🕻 📺 ☎. 🆀 ① 🗲 𝘝𝘐𝘚𝘈
⇌ 33 — **23 rm** 480/510.   E 13

🏨 **Du Pré** without rest, 10 r. P. Sémard (9th) ℰ 42 81 37 11, Telex 660549, Fax 40 23 98 28 — 🕻
📺 ☎. 🆀 🗲 𝘝𝘐𝘚𝘈. ✻
⇌ 30 — **41 rm** 365/450.   E 15

🏨 **Bergère** without rest, 34 r. Bergère (9th) ℰ 47 70 34 34, Telex 290668, Fax 47 70 36 36 — 🕻
📺 ☎. 🆀 ① 🗲 𝘝𝘐𝘚𝘈
⇌ 30 — **134 rm** 590/790.   F 14

🏨 **Morny** without rest, 4 r. Liège (9th) ℰ 42 85 47 92, Telex 660822, Fax 40 16 44 84 — 🕻 📺
☎. 🆀 ① 🗲 𝘝𝘐𝘚𝘈
41 rm ⇌ 475/760.   E 12

🏨 **Printania** without rest, 19 r. Château d'Eau (10th) ℰ 42 01 84 20, Telex 215425, Fax
42 39 55 12 — 🕻 📺 ☎. 🆀 ① 🗲 𝘝𝘐𝘚𝘈. ✻
⇌ 30 — **51 rm** 435/520.   F 16

🏨 **Corona** ⤳ without rest, 8 cité Bergère (9th) ℰ 47 70 52 96, Telex 281081, Fax 42 46 83 49 —
🕻 📺 ☎. 🆀 ① 🗲 𝘝𝘐𝘚𝘈
⇌ 35 — **56 rm** 470/680, 4 apartments 910.   F 14

🏛 **Florida** without rest, 7 r. Parme (9th) ℰ 48 74 47 09, Telex 640410, Fax 42 80 29 96 – 🛗 📺
🕿, 🅰🅴 ⓪ 🖻 𝑽𝑰𝑺𝑨, ⅋
D 12
🛏 30 – **31 rm** 460/760.

🏛 **Alane** without rest, 72 bd Magenta (10th) ℰ 40 35 83 30, Telex 214227 – 🛗 📺 🕿, 🅰🅴 ⓪ 🖻
𝑽𝑰𝑺𝑨
F 16
🛏 30 – **32 rm** 350/500.

🏛 **Baccarat** Ⓜ without rest, 19 r. Messageries (10th) ℰ 47 70 96 92, Telex 648895 – 🛗 📺 🕿,
🅰🅴 ⓪ 🖻 𝑽𝑰𝑺𝑨, ⅋
E 15
🛏 28 – **53 rm** 350/455.

🏛 **Capucines** without rest, 6 r. Godot de Mauroy (9th) ℰ 47 42 06 37, Telex 290046 – 🛗 🕿,
🖻 𝑽𝑰𝑺𝑨
F 12
🛏 25 – **46 rm** 300/410.

🏛 **Moris** Ⓜ without rest, 13 r. R.-Boulanger (10th) ℰ 42 06 27 53, Telex 212024, Fax 40 40 05 23
– 🛗 📺 🕿, 🅰🅴 ⓪ 🖻 𝑽𝑰𝑺𝑨, ⅋
G 16
🛏 35 – **48 rm** 460/540.

🏛 **Français** without rest, 13 r. 8-Mai 1945 (10th) ℰ 40 35 94 14, Telex 230431, Fax 40 35 55 40
– 🛗 📺 🕿, 🖻 𝑽𝑰𝑺𝑨
E 16
🛏 28 – **71 rm** 360/400.

🏛 **Caravelle** without rest, 68 r. Martyrs (9th) ℰ 48 78 43 31, Telex 649052, Fax 40 23 98 72 –
🛗 📺 📺 🕿, 🖻 𝑽𝑰𝑺𝑨
D 14
🛏 35 – **32 rm** 470/500.

🏛 **Modern' Est** without rest, 91 bd Strasbourg (10th) ℰ 40 37 77 20, Telex 375974, Fax
40 37 17 55 – 🛗 📺 🕿, 🖻 𝑽𝑰𝑺𝑨, ⅋
E 16
🛏 28 – **30 rm** 310/390.

🏛 **Hélios** without rest, 75 r. Victoire (9th) ℰ 48 74 28 64, Telex 283255, Fax 42 85 30 85 – 🛗 📺
🕿, 🅰🅴 ⓪ 🖻 𝑽𝑰𝑺𝑨
F 13
🛏 40 – **50 rm** 394/589.

🏛 **Gd H. Haussmann** without rest, 6 r. Helder (9th) ℰ 48 24 76 10, Telex 650018, Fax
48 00 97 18 – 🛗 📺 🕿, 🅰🅴 ⓪ 🖻 𝑽𝑰𝑺𝑨, ⅋
F 13
🛏 35 – **59 rm** 390/560.

🏛 **Royal Médoc** without rest, 14 r. Geoffroy Marie (9th) ℰ 47 70 37 33, Telex 660053, Fax
47 70 34 88 – 🛗 📺 🕿, 🅰🅴 ⓪ 🖻 𝑽𝑰𝑺𝑨
F 14
41 rm 🛏 530/680.

🏛 **London** without rest, 32 bd Italiens (9th) ℰ 48 24 54 64, Telex 642360, Fax 48 00 08 83 – 🛗
📺 🕿, 🅰🅴 🖻 𝑽𝑰𝑺𝑨, ⅋
F 13
🛏 21 – **49 rm** 344/540.

🏛 **Gare du Nord** without rest, 33 r. St-Quentin (10th) ℰ 48 78 02 92, Telex 642415, Fax
45 26 88 31 – 🛗 📺 🕿, 🅰🅴 🖻 𝑽𝑰𝑺𝑨, ⅋
E 16
🛏 30 – **48 rm** 350/480.

🏛 **Montréal** without rest, 23 r. Godot-de-Mauroy (9th) ℰ 42 65 99 54, Fax 49 24 07 33 – 🛗 📺
🕿, 🅰🅴 ⓪ 🖻 𝑽𝑰𝑺𝑨
F 12
closed August – 🛏 35 – **14 rm** 270/550, 5 apartments 550.

🏛 **Florence** without rest, 26 r. Mathurins (9th) ℰ 47 42 63 47, Telex 290085 – 🛗 📺 🕿, 🅰🅴 ⓪
🖻 𝑽𝑰𝑺𝑨
F 12
🛏 38 – **20 rm** 500/700.

🏛 **América** without rest, 15 r. Geoffroy Marie (9th) ℰ 48 24 09 02, Telex 280729 – 🛗 📺 🕿,
🅰🅴 ⓪ 🖻 𝑽𝑰𝑺𝑨, ⅋
F 14
🛏 25 – **37 rm** 250/480.

🏛 **Peyris** without rest, 10 r. Conservatoire (9th) ℰ 47 70 50 83 – 🛗 📺 🕿, 🖻 𝑽𝑰𝑺𝑨
F 14
🛏 25 – **50 rm** 350/460.

🏚 **Urbis Lafayette** without rest, 122 r. Lafayette (10th) ℰ 45 23 27 27, Telex 290272, Fax
42 46 73 79 – 🛗 📺 🕿, ⴕ, 🖻 𝑽𝑰𝑺𝑨
E 16
🛏 32 – **70 rm** 343/386.

🏚 **Gd H. Lafayette Buffault** without rest, 6 r. Buffault (9th) ℰ 47 70 70 96, Telex 642180 –
🛗 📺 🕿, 🅰🅴 🖻 𝑽𝑰𝑺𝑨
E 14
🛏 25 – **47 rm** 175/345.

🏚 **Riboutté-Lafayette** without rest, 5 r. Riboutté (9th) ℰ 47 70 62 36, Fax 48 00 91 50 – 🛗
📺 🕿, 🖻 𝑽𝑰𝑺𝑨
E 14
🛏 25 – **24 rm** 370/420.

🏚 **Résidence Magenta** without rest, 35 r. Y.-Toudic (10th) ℰ 42 40 17 72, Telex 216543, Fax
42 02 59 66 – 🛗 📺 🕿, 🅰🅴 🖻 𝑽𝑰𝑺𝑨, ⅋
F 17
🛏 28 – **32 rm** 290/450.

🏚 **Fénelon** without rest, 23 r. Buffault (9th) ℰ 48 78 32 18 – 🛗 📺 🕿, 🅰🅴 🖻 𝑽𝑰𝑺𝑨
E 14
39 rm 🛏 470/600.

Prices are given in local currency.
Valid for 1991 the rates shown should only vary
if the cost of living changes to any great extent.

XXXX ✿ **Rest. Opéra-Café de la Paix** - Le Grand Hôtel, pl. Opéra (9th) ☎ 40 07 30 10, Telex 220875, Fax 42 66 12 51, « Second Empire decor » – 🔲 AE ⍉ E VISA
F 12
closed August – **M** a la carte 380/460
Spec. Poêlée de petite pêche sur émincé de céleri, Blanc de turbot aux épices, Chaud-froid au cacao.

XXX **Charlot ''Roi des Coquillages''**, 12 pl. Clichy (9th) ☎ 48 74 49 64, Fax 40 16 11 00, Seafood – 🔲 AE ⍉ E VISA
D 12
M 250 b.i. (lunch) and a la carte 230/400.

XXX **Le Louis XIV**, 8 bd St-Denis (10th) ☎ 42 08 56 56 – AE ⍉ E VISA
G 15
1 September-31 May – **M** a la carte 225/425.

XX **Au Chateaubriant**, 23 r. Chabrol (10th) ☎ 48 24 58 94, Italian rest., Paintings Collection – 🔲 AE E VISA ⌘
E 15
closed August, Sunday and Monday – **M** a la carte 200/360.

XX **Chez Michel**, 10 r. Belzunce (10th) ☎ 48 78 44 14 – 🔲 AE ⍉ E VISA
E 15
closed 26 July-24 August, February Holidays, Friday and Saturday – **M** (booking essential) 170 (lunch) and a la carte 280/450.

XX ✿ **La Table d'Anvers** (Conticini), 2 pl. Anvers (9th) ☎ 48 78 35 21 – AE E VISA
D 14
closed 4 to 25 August, Saturday lunch and Sunday – **M** 250/450
Spec. Ruffian au homard, Selle d'agneau rôtie au romarin et abricots secs, Macaron au chocolat blanc.

XX **Brasserie Flo Printemps**, (Printemps de la Mode - 6e étage) 64 bd Haussman (9e) ☎ 42 82 58 81, Fax 45 26 31 24 – 🔲 AE E VISA
F 12
closed Sunday and Bank Holidays – **M** (lunch only) a la carte 150/220 ⌘.

XX **Relais Capucines-Café de la Paix** - Le Grand Hôtel, 12 bd Capucines (9th) ☎ 40 07 30 20, Telex 220875, Fax 42 66 12 51 – ⌘⌐ AE ⍉ E VISA
F 12
M 165 and a la carte 185/260 ⌘.

XX **Grand Café Capucines** (24 hr service), 4 bd Capucines (9th) ☎ 47 42 19 00, Fax 47 42 74 22, Early 20C decor – AE ⍉ E VISA
F 13
M a la carte 170/370 ⌘.

XX **Le New Port**, 79 r. Fg St-Denis (10th) ☎ 48 24 19 38, Seafood – AE E VISA
F 15
closed 29 July-19 August, Christmas-New Year, Saturday lunch and Sunday – **M** 89/140.

XX **Le Quercy**, 36 r. Condorcet (9th) ☎ 48 78 30 61 – AE ⍉ E VISA
E 14
closed August, Sunday and Bank Holidays – **M** 138 and a la carte 170/290.

XX **Bistrot Papillon**, 6 r. Papillon (9th) ☎ 47 70 90 03 – AE ⍉ E VISA
E 15
closed 23 March-7 April, 3 to 25 August, Saturday, Sunday and Bank Holidays – **M** 125 and a la carte 200/280.

XX **Julien**, 16 r. Fg St-Denis (10th) ☎ 47 70 12 06, Fax 42 47 00 65, Early 20C brasserie – 🔲 AE ⍉ E VISA
F 15
M a la carte 140/270 ⌘.

XX **Le Franche-Comté**, 2 bd Madeleine (Maison de la Franche-Comté) (9th) ☎ 49 24 99 09, Fax 49 24 96 56 – AE E VISA
F 12
closed Sunday and Bank Holidays – **M** 150 and a la carte 130/250 ⌘.

XX **Brasserie Flo**, 7 cour Petites-Écuries (10th) ☎ 47 70 13 59, Fax 42 47 00 80, 1900 setting – AE ⍉ E VISA
F 15
M a la carte 145/270 ⌘.

XX **Le Saintongeais**, 62 r. Fg Montmartre (9th) ☎ 42 80 39 92 – AE ⍉ E VISA
E 14
closed August, Saturday and Sunday – **M** a la carte 170/250.

XX **Petit Riche**, 25 r. Le Peletier (9th) ☎ 47 70 68 68, Fax 48 24 10 79, « Late 19C decor » – AE ⍉ E VISA
F 13
closed Sunday – **M** 180 b.i. and a la carte 170/290 ⌘.

XX **Comme Chez Soi**, 20 r. Lamartine (9th) ☎ 48 78 00 02 – AE ⍉ E VISA
E 14
closed August, Saturday and Sunday – **M** 170/220.

XX **Aux Deux Canards**, 8 r. Fg Poissonnière (10th) ☎ 47 70 03 23, restaurant for non-smokers – 🔲 AE ⍉ E VISA
F 15
closed 12 July-26 August, Saturday lunch and Sunday – **M** a la carte 170/300.

XX **Terminus Nord**, 23 r. Dunkerque (10th) ☎ 42 85 05 15, Fax 40 16 13 98, brasserie – AE ⍉ E VISA – **M** a la carte 140/270 ⌘.
E 16

XX **Pagoda**, 50 r. Provence (9th) ☎ 48 74 81 48, Chinese rest. – 🔲 VISA
F 13
closed Sunday – **M** 48 (except Saturday)/150.

XX **La P'tite Tonkinoise**, 56 r. Fg Poissonnière (10th) ☎ 42 46 85 98, Vietnamese rest. – E VISA – *closed 1 August-15 September, 22 December-5 January, Sunday and Monday* – **M** a la carte 130/200
F 15

X **Relais Beaujolais**, 3 r. Milton (9th) ☎ 48 78 77 91 – E VISA
E 14
closed August, Saturday and Sunday – **M** 130 (lunch) and a la carte 160/300.

X **Petit Batailley**, 26 r. Bergère (9th) ☎ 47 70 85 81 – AE ⍉ E VISA
F 14
closed August, 1 to 6 January, Saturday lunch, Sunday and Bank Holidays – **M** 100/205 ⌘.

X La Grille, 80 r. Fg Poissonnière (10th) ☎ 47 70 89 73
E 15

X **Chez Jean l'Auvergnat**, 52 r. Lamartine (9th) ☎ 48 78 62 73 – VISA
E 14
closed 10 to 30 August, Saturday 1 July-30 September and Sunday – **M** 130/200.

X **Bistro des Deux Théâtres**, 18 r. Blanche (9th) ☎ 45 26 41 43 – 🔲 E VISA
E 12
M 165 b.i.

Bastille, Gare de Lyon,
Place d'Italie,
Bois de Vincennes.
12th and 13th arrondissements.
12th : ⊠ 75012
13th : ⊠ 75013

🏨🏨 **Novotel Paris Bercy** Ⓜ, 86 r. Bercy (12th) ℰ 43 42 30 00, Telex 218332, Fax 43 45 30 60,
🍴 – 🛗 ▤ 📺 ☎ ♿ – 🔬 30 - 150. 🆎 ⑩ 🄴 ⚟
M a la carte approx. 150 ⅃ – ☲ 52 – **129 rm** 640/680.
M 19

🏨🏨 **Mercure Paris Bercy** Ⓜ, 6 bd Vincent Auriol (13th) ℰ 45 82 48 00, Telex 205010, Fax
45 82 19 16 – 🛗 ⤢ rm ▤ rest 📺 ☎ ♿ – 🔬 40. 🆎 ⑩ 🄴 ⚟
M 18
M *(closed 27 July-25 August, 25 December-2 January, Saturday, Sunday and Bank Holidays)*
a la carte approx. 200 – ☲ 50 – **89 rm** 500/700.

🏨🏨 **Équinoxe** Ⓜ without rest, 40 r. Le Brun (13th) ℰ 43 37 56 56, Telex 201476, Fax 45 35 52 42
– 🛗 📺 ☎ ⇦. 🆎 ⑩ 🄴 ⚟
N 15
☲ 30 – **49 rm** 450/590.

🏨🏨 **Paris-Lyon-Palace** without rest, 11 r. Lyon (12th) ℰ 43 07 29 49, Telex 213310, Fax
46 28 91 55 – 🛗 📺 ☎ – 🔬 150. 🆎 ⑩ 🄴 ⚟
L 18
☲ 35 – **128 rm** 460/480.

🏨🏨 **Mercure Paris XIII** Ⓜ without rest, 21 rue Tolbiac (13th) ℰ 45 84 61 61, Telex 250822, Fax
45 84 43 38 – 🛗 📺 ☎ ♿ 🄿 – 🔬 25. 🆎 ⑩ 🄴 ⚟
P 18
☲ 50 – **71 rm** 620.

🏨🏨 **Relais de Lyon** without rest, 64 r. Crozatier (12th) ℰ 43 44 22 50, Telex 216690, Fax
43 41 55 12 – 🛗 📺 ☎ ⇦. 🆎 ⑩ 🄴 ⚟. ⚞
K 19
☲ 30 – **34 rm** 400/483.

🏨 **Modern H. Lyon** without rest, 3 r. Parrot (12th) ℰ 43 43 41 52, Telex 230369, Fax 43 43 81 16
– 🛗 📺 ☎. 🆎 🄴 ⚟. ⚞
L 18
☲ 36 – **52 rm** 340/545.

🏨 **Média** Ⓜ without rest, 22 r. Reine Blanche (13th) ℰ 45 35 72 72, Telex 206702, Fax
45 35 52 42 – 🛗 📺 ☎ – 🔬 25. 🆎 ⑩ 🄴 ⚟
M 15
closed August – ☲ 30 – **19 rm** 450/480.

🏨 **Terminus-Lyon** without rest, 19 bd Diderot (12th) ℰ 43 43 24 03, Telex 230702, Fax
43 44 09 00 – 🛗 📺 ☎. 🆎 ⑩ 🄴 ⚟. ⚞
L 18
☲ 35 – **61 rm** 450/550.

🏨 **Slavia** without rest, 51 bd St-Marcel (13th) ℰ 43 37 81 25, Telex 205542, Fax 45 87 05 03 –
🛗 📺 ☎. 🆎 🄴 ⚟. ⚞
M 16
☲ 26 – **37 rm** 285/325, 6 apartments 385.

🏨 **Midi** without rest, 114 av. Daumesnil (12th) ℰ 43 07 72 03, Telex 215917, Fax 43 43 21 75 –
📺 ☎. 🆎 ⑩ 🄴 ⚟
L 20
☲ 30 – **36 rm** 340/420.

🏨 **Résidence Vert Galant** Ⓜ ⚘, 43 r. Croulebarbe (13th) ℰ 43 36 22 41, Telex 202371 –
📺 ☎ ♿. 🆎 ⑩ 🄴 ⚟. ⚞ rm
N 15
M see Étchegory below – ☲ 35 – **14 rm** 400/500.

🏨 **de Weha** without rest, 205 av. Choisy (13th) ℰ 45 86 06 06, Telex 206898, Fax 43 31 42 06 –
🛗 📺 ☎. 🆎 ⑩ 🄴 ⚟
P 16
☲ 32 – **34 rm** 490.

🏨 **Corail** without rest, 23 r. Lyon (12th) ℰ 43 43 23 54, Telex 212002, Fax 43 43 82 55 – 🛗 📺
☎. 🆎 ⑩ 🄴 ⚟
L 18
☲ 29 – **50 rm** 300/390.

🏨 **Claret,** 44 bd Bercy (12th) ℰ 46 28 41 31, Telex 217115, Fax 49 28 09 29 – 🛗 📺 ☎. 🆎 ⑩
🄴 ⚟ – **M** *(closed Saturday lunch and Sunday)* a la carte 90/150 ⅃ – ☲ 30 – **52 rm**
380/500
M 19

🏨 **Gd H. Gobelins** without rest, 57 bd St-Marcel (13th) ℰ 43 31 79 89 – 🛗 📺 ☎
M 16
☲ 25 – **45 rm** 220/330.

🏨 **Ibis Paris Bercy** Ⓜ, 77 rue Bercy (12th) ℰ 43 42 91 91, Telex 216391, Fax 43 42 34 79, 🍴
– 🛗 📺 ☎ ♿ – 🔬 25 - 180. 🆎 🄴 ⚟
M 19
M 70/90 ⅃ – ☲ 30 – **368 rm** 415/435.

🏨 **Marceau** without rest, 13 r. J. César (12th) ℰ 43 43 11 65, Telex 214006, Fax 43 41 67 70 –
🛗 📺 ☎. 🄴 ⚟. ⚞
K 17
closed mid July-mid August – ☲ 30 – **53 rm** 295/345.

🏨 **Des Trois Gares** without rest, 1 r. J. César (12th) ℰ 43 43 01 70, Telex 216392, Fax
43 41 36 58 – 🛗 📺 ☎. 🄴 ⚟. ⚞
K 17
☲ 25 – **36 rm** 200/360.

🏨 **Palym H.** without rest, 4 r. E.-Gilbert (12th) ℰ 43 43 24 48, Fax 43 41 69 47 – 🛗 📺 ⤢. 🄴
⚟. ⚞ – ☲ 30 – **51 rm** 270/350.
L 18

🏨 **Viator** without rest, 1 r. Parrot (12th) ℰ 43 43 11 00, Telex 216236, Fax 43 43 10 89 – 🛗 📺
☎. 🄴 ⚟. ⚞ – ☲ 30 – **45 rm** 290/340.
L 18

🏠 **Urbis Paris Tolbiac** without rest, 177 r. Tolbiac (13th) 🕿 45 80 16 60, Telex 200821, Fax
45 80 95 80 — 🛗 📺 🖚 ᴋ. 🖃 VISA   P 15
🛏 30 — **60 rm** 350/380.

🏠 **Résidence Les Gobelins** without rest, 9 r. Gobelins (13th) 🕿 47 07 26 90, Telex 206566,
Fax 43 31 44 05 — 🛗 📺 🕿. 🖭 ⓞ 🖃 VISA   N 15
🛏 30 — **32 rm** 300/400.

🏠 **Timhôtel** without rest, 22 r. Barrault (13th) 🕿 45 80 67 67, Telex 205461, Fax 45 89 36 93 —
🛗 📺 🕿. 🖭 🖃 VISA   P 15
🛏 40 — **73 rm** 355/382.

🏠 **Terrasses** without rest, 74 r. Glacière (13th) 🕿 47 07 73 70, Telex 203488 — 🛗 🕿. VISA ⬩   N 14
🛏 26 — **49 rm** 160/400.

🏠 **Jules César** without rest, 52 av. Ledru-Rollin (12th) 🕿 43 43 15 88, Telex 670945, Fax
43 43 53 60 — 🛗 📺 🕿. 🖃 VISA ⬩   K 18
🛏 25 — **48 rm** 290/310.

🏠 **Terminus et Sports** without rest, 96 cours Vincennes (12th) 🕿 43 43 97 93, Telex 217581
— 🛗 📺 🕿. 🖃 VISA ⬩   L 23
🛏 28 — **43 rm** 170/310.

🏠 **Nouvel H.** without rest, 24 av. Bel Air (12th) 🕿 43 43 01 81, Telex 240139, Fax 43 44 64 13,
🚗 — 📺 🕿. 🖭 ⓞ 🖃 VISA   L 21
🛏 37 — **28 rm** 220/520.

🏠 **Arts** without rest, 8 r. Coypel (13th) 🕿 47 07 76 32 — 🛗 🕿. 🖭 🖃 VISA   N 16
🛏 24 — **37 rm** 150/290.

XXXX **Fouquet's Bastille**, 130 r. Lyon (12th) 🕿 43 42 18 18, Fax 43 42 08 20 — 🍽. 🖭 ⓞ VISA ⬩
Rez-de-Chaussée M a la carte 180/370 — **1ᵉʳ étage** (closed Saturday lunch and Sunday) **M** a
la carte 400/400.   K 18

XXX ❀ **Au Pressoir** (Séguin), 257 av. Daumesnil (12th) 🕿 43 44 38 21, Fax 43 43 81 77 — 🍽. 🖃
VISA   M 22
closed August, February Holidays, Saturday and Sunday — **M** a la carte 300/420
Spec. Assiette de fruits de mer tièdes (October-March), Rondin de lotte au lard et pois cassés, Coeur de filet de
boeuf au coulis de truffes.

XXX **Train Bleu**, Gare de Lyon (12th) 🕿 43 43 38 39, Telex 240788, Fax 43 43 97 96, « Fine
murals recalling the journey from Paris to the Mediterranean » — 🖭 ⓞ 🖃 VISA   L 18
closed 1 July-30 September — **M** (1st floor) 200 b.i. (lunch) and a la carte 225/330.

XX ❀ **Au Trou Gascon**, 40 r. Taine (12th) 🕿 43 44 34 26 — 🖭 ⓞ 🖃 VISA   M 21
closed August, 28 December-5 January, Saturday and Sunday — **M** (booking essential) 200
and a la carte 200/440
Spec. Persillé d'anguille à la bohémienne, Petit pâté chaud de cèpes, Lièvre à la Royale (October-mid December).

XX **La Gourmandise**, 271 av. Daumesnil (12th) 🕿 43 43 94 41 — 🖭 VISA   M 22
closed 1 to 8 May, 5 to 25 August, Monday dinner, Saturday lunch and Sunday — **M** 180 and
a la carte 250/420.

XX **Au Petit Marguery**, 9 bd Port-Royal (13th) 🕿 43 31 58 59 — 🖭 ⓞ 🖃 VISA   M 15
closed August, 24 December-2 January, Sunday and Monday — **M** a la carte 230/370.

XX **Les Vieux Métiers de France**, 13 bd A. Blanqui (13th) 🕿 45 88 90 03 — 🍽. 🖭 ⓞ 🖃 VISA   P 15
closed Sunday and Monday — **M** 165/290.

XX **Le Luneau**, 5 r. Lyon (12th) 🕿 43 43 90 85 — 🖭 ⓞ 🖃 VISA   L 18
M 135 ⬩.

XX **La Flambée**, 4 r. Taine (12th) 🕿 43 43 21 80 — 🖭 ⓞ VISA   M 20
closed 1 to 20 August, 22 to 28 December, Sunday dinner and Saturday — **M** 110/275.

XX **La Frégate**, 30 av. Ledru-Rollin (12th) 🕿 43 43 90 32, Seafood — VISA   L 18
closed 1 to 20 August, Saturday and Sunday — **M** 190/280.

XX **Le Traversière**, 40 r. Traversière (12th) 🕿 43 44 02 10 — 🖭 ⓞ 🖃 VISA   K 18
closed August, Sunday dinner and Bank Holidays — **M** 150 and a la carte 180/320.

XX **La Sologne**, 164 av. Daumesnil (12th) 🕿 43 07 68 97 — 🖃 VISA   M 21
closed Saturday and Sunday — **M** 120/230.

XX **L'Escapade en Touraine**, 24 r. Traversière (12th) 🕿 43 43 14 96 — 🖭 🖃 VISA   L 18
closed 2 August-2 September, Saturday, Sunday and Bank Holidays — **M** 140 and a la carte
125/225.

X **Mange Tout**, 24 bd Bastille (12th) 🕿 43 43 95 15 — 🖭 🖃 VISA   K 17
closed 12 to 18 August and Sunday — **M** 98 and a la carte 150/240 ⬩.

X **Le Quincy**, 28 av. Ledru-Rollin (12th) 🕿 46 28 46 76   L 17
closed Saturday, Sunday, and Monday — **M** a la carte 185/350.

X **Etchegorry**, 41 r. Croulebarbe (13th) 🕿 43 31 63 05, Telex 202371 — 🖭 ⓞ 🖃 VISA   N 15
closed Sunday — **M** 130/190.

X **Le Rhône**, 40 bd Arago (13th) 🕿 47 07 33 57, 🌳 — 🖃 VISA   N 14
closed August, Saturday, Sunday and Bank Holidays — **M** 73 b.i./150.

X **Chez Françoise**, 12 r. Butte aux Cailles (13th) 🕿 45 80 12 02 — 🖭 ⓞ 🖃 VISA ⬩   P 15
closed 25 April-2 May, 4 August-1 September, Saturday lunch and Sunday — **M** 88/122 ⬩.

**Vaugirard,
Gare Montparnasse, Grenelle,
Denfert-Rochereau.**

14th and 15th arrondissements.
14th : ⊠ 75014
15th : ⊠ 75015

🏨🏨🏨 **Hilton** M, 18 av. Suffren (15th) 𝒫 42 73 92 00, Telex 200955, Fax 47 83 62 66, 🛖 – 🛗
🍴✕ rm 🗐 📺 ☎ 👌 – 🔬 40 - 350. 🆎 ⓞ 🗲 𝚅𝙸𝚂𝙰
Western M a la carte 220/380 – **La Terrasse M** a la carte 165/290 ↓ – ☲ 120 – **455 rm**
1450/2100, 36 apartments.

🏨🏨🏨 **Nikko** M, 61 quai Grenelle (15th) 𝒫 40 58 20 00, Telex 205811, Fax 45 75 42 35, ≤, ◲ – 🛗
🍴✕ rm 🗐 📺 ☎ 🅿 – 🔬 800. 🆎 ⓞ 🗲 𝚅𝙸𝚂𝙰
M see **Les Célébrités** below - **Brasserie Pont Mirabeau M** a la carte 180/300 – **Rest. japonais
Benkay M** a la carte 300/480 – ☲ 70 – **779 rm** 1160/2400. 7 apartments.

🏨🏨🏨 **Sofitel Paris Porte de Sèvres** M, 8 r. L.-Armand (15th) 𝒫 40 60 30 30, Telex 200432, Fax
45 57 04 22, ≤, indoor pool overlooking Paris – 🛗 🗐 ☎ 👌 ⇦ – 🔬 1 200. 🆎 ⓞ 🗲 𝚅𝙸𝚂𝙰 N 5
M see **Le Relais de Sèvres** below - **La Tonnelle** (brasserie) **M** 145 ↓ – ☲ 80 – **601 rm**
700/900, 14 apartments 1400/1800.

🏨🏨🏨 **Méridien Montparnasse** M, 19 r. Cdt-Mouchotte (14th) 𝒫 43 20 15 51, Telex 200135, Fax
43 20 61 03, ≤ – 🛗 🍴✕ rm 🗐 📺 ☎ 👌 – 🔬 1 400. 🆎 ⓞ 🗲 𝚅𝙸𝚂𝙰. 🕊️ M 11
Montparnasse 25 (closed August. Saturday. Sunday) **M** a la carte 275/435 – **Justine M** 185
and a la carte 170/325 – ☲ 96 – **915 rm** 1350/1650, 35 apartments.

🏨🏨🏨 **Pullman St-Jacques** M, 17 bd St-Jacques (14th) 𝒫 40 78 79 80, Telex 270740, Fax
45 88 43 93 – 🛗 🍴✕ 🗐 📺 ⇦ – 🔬 40 - 1 200. 🆎 ⓞ 🗲 𝚅𝙸𝚂𝙰 N 13-14
Brasserie Le Français (closed 24 to 31 December) **M** 172 – ☲ 70 – **797 rm** 1015/1360, 14
apartments 1700/2100.

🏨🏨 **Mercure Paris Vaugirard** M, porte de Versailles (15th) 𝒫 45 33 74 63, Telex 260844, Fax
48 28 22 11 – 🛗 🍴✕ rm 🗐 📺 👌 ⇦ – 🔬 120. 🆎 ⓞ 🗲 𝚅𝙸𝚂𝙰. 🕊️ rest N 7
M a la carte 210/300 – ☲ 54 – **91 rm** 970/1250.

🏨🏨 **Mercure Paris Montparnasse** M, 20 r. Gaîté (14th) 𝒫 43 35 28 28, Telex 201532, Fax
43 27 98 64 – 🛗 🗐 📺 👌 ⇦ – 🔬 100. 🆎 ⓞ 🗲 𝚅𝙸𝚂𝙰 M 11
Bistrot de la Gaîté M a la carte 140/210 – ☲ 58 – **177 rm** 830, 8 suites 1 000.

🏨🏨 **Adagio Paris Vaugirard** M, 253 r. Vaugirard (15th) 𝒫 40 45 10 00, Telex 250709, Fax
40 45 10 10 – 🛗 🍴✕ rm 🗐 📺 rest ⇦ – 🔬 400. 🆎 ⓞ 🗲 𝚅𝙸𝚂𝙰 M 9
Le Transatlantique M 110 – **Le Club** (closed July-August. Saturday and Sunday) **M** 250 –
☲ 65 – **185 rm** 830/930.

🏨🏨 **Lenox Montparnasse** M without rest, 15 r. Delambre (14th) 𝒫 43 35 34 50, Telex 260745,
Fax 43 20 46 64 – 🛗 ☎. 🆎 ⓞ 🗲 𝚅𝙸𝚂𝙰. 🕊️ M 12
☲ 40 – **52 rm** 460/890.

🏨🏨 **Orléans Palace H.** without rest, 185 bd Brune (14th) 𝒫 45 39 68 50, Telex 205490, Fax
45 43 65 64 – 🛗 ☎ – 🔬 35. 🆎 ⓞ 🗲 𝚅𝙸𝚂𝙰 R 11
☲ 35 – **92 rm** 410/520.

🏨🏨 **L'Aiglon** without rest, 232 bd Raspail (14th) 𝒫 43 20 82 42, Telex 206038, Fax 43 20 98 72 –
🛗 kitchenette ☎. 🆎 ⓞ 🗲 𝚅𝙸𝚂𝙰 M 12
☲ 32 – **38 rm** 400/600, 9 apartments 650/800.

🏨🏨 **Renoir** M without rest, 39 r. Montparnasse (14th) 𝒫 43 21 72 50, Telex 205436, Fax
43 21 68 72 – 🛗 📺 ☎. 🆎 ⓞ 🗲 𝚅𝙸𝚂𝙰. 🕊️ L 12
☲ 30 – **29 rm** 450/550.

🏨🏨 **Waldorf** M without rest, 17 r. Départ (14th) 𝒫 43 20 64 79, Telex 201677, Fax 43 35 17 52 –
🛗 🗐 ☎. 🆎 ⓞ 🗲 𝚅𝙸𝚂𝙰. 🕊️ L 11
☲ 32 – **30 rm** 470/680.

🏨 **Wallace** without rest, 89 r. Fondary (15th) 𝒫 45 78 83 30, Telex 205277, Fax 40 58 19 43 – 🛗
☎. 🆎 ⓞ 🗲 𝚅𝙸𝚂𝙰 L 8
☲ 35 – **35 rm** 450/500.

🏨 **Versailles** M without rest, 213 r. Croix Nivert (15th) 𝒫 48 28 48 66, Telex 200473, Fax
45 30 16 22 – 🛗 ☎. 🆎 ⓞ 🗲 𝚅𝙸𝚂𝙰 N 7
☲ 38 – **41 rm** 440/660.

🏨 **Arès** without rest, 7 r. Gén. de Larminat (15th) 𝒫 47 34 74 04, Telex 206083, Fax 47 34 48 56
– 🛗 📺 ☎. 🆎 ⓞ 🗲 𝚅𝙸𝚂𝙰. 🕊️ K 8
☲ 32 – **43 rm** 415/445.

🏨 **Mercure Paris XV** M without rest, 6 r. St-Lambert (15th) 𝒫 45 58 61 00, Telex 206936, Fax
45 54 10 43 – 🛗 📺 ☎ 👌 ⇦ – 🔬 35. 🆎 ⓞ 🗲 𝚅𝙸𝚂𝙰 M 7
☲ 50 – **56 rm** 590.

🏨 **Beaugrenelle St-Charles** M without rest, 82 r. St-Charles (15th) 𝒫 45 78 61 63, Telex
270263, Fax 45 79 04 38 – 🛗 📺 ☎. 🆎 ⓞ 🗲 𝚅𝙸𝚂𝙰 K 7
☲ 28 – **51 rm** 310/380.

🏨 **Alizé Grenelle** Ⓜ without rest, 87 av. É. Zola (15th) ℰ 45 78 08 22, Telex 250095, Fax 40 59 03 06 – 🔟 ☎. 🅰🅴 ⓪ 🄴 𝖵𝖨𝖲𝖠
L 7
⌑ 28 – **50 rm** 330/380.

🏨 **Capitol** Ⓜ without rest, 9 r. Viala (15th) ℰ 45 78 61 00, Telex 202881, Fax 45 79 32 51 – 🛗 🔲 🔟 ☎. 🅰🅴 ⓪ 🄴 𝖵𝖨𝖲𝖠
K 7
⌑ 45 – **42 rm** 500/540.

🏨 **Messidor** without rest, 330 r. Vaugirard (15th) ℰ 48 28 03 74, Telex 204606, Fax 48 28 75 17, 🚗 – 🛗 🔟 ☎. 🅰🅴 ⓪ 🄴 𝖵𝖨𝖲𝖠
M 8
⌑ 45 – **65 rm** 450/800, 7 apartments 650/800.

🏨 **Alésia Montparnasse** without rest, 84 r. R. Losserand (14th) ℰ 45 42 16 03, Telex 206629, Fax 45 42 11 60 – 🛗 ⇆ 🔟 ☎. 🅰🅴 ⓪ 🄴 𝖵𝖨𝖲𝖠
N 10
⌑ 35 – **45 rm** 380/420.

🏨 **Ibis Alésia** Ⓜ, 49 r. Plantes (14th) ℰ 40 44 50 51, Telex 206995, Fax 40 44 53 44 – 🛗 🔲 ☎ ♿ ⇔ – 🔺 150. 🅰🅴 🄴 𝖵𝖨𝖲𝖠
P 11
M 115/175 🍴 – ⌑ 35 – **264 rm** 420.

🏨 **Résidence St-Lambert** without rest, 5 r. E. Gibez (15th) ℰ 48 28 63 14, Telex 205459, Fax 45 33 45 50 – 🛗 🔟 ☎. 🅰🅴 ⓪ 🄴 𝖵𝖨𝖲𝖠
N 8
⌑ 32 – **48 rm** 390/530.

🏨 **Joigny** without rest, 8 r. St-Charles (15th) ℰ 45 79 33 35, Fax 45 79 40 84 – 🛗 🔟 ☎. 🅰🅴 ⓪ 🄴 𝖵𝖨𝖲𝖠 – ⌑ 40 – **36 rm** 450/500.
K 7

🏨 **Primavera** without rest, 147ter r. Alésia (14th) ℰ 45 42 06 37, Telex 206831, Fax 45 42 44 56 – 🛗 🔟 ☎ ♿. 🄴 𝖵𝖨𝖲𝖠 ✂
P 11
⌑ 30 – **70 rm** 380/540.

🏨 **Sophie Germain** without rest, 12 r. Sophie Germain (14th) ℰ 43 21 43 75, Telex 206720 – 🛗 🔟 ☎. 🅰🅴 ⓪ 🄴 𝖵𝖨𝖲𝖠 ✂
NP 12
⌑ 30 – **33 rm** 460/530.

🏨 **L'Orchidée** without rest, 65 r. l'Ouest (14th) ℰ 43 22 70 50, Telex 203026, Fax 42 79 97 46 – 🛗 🔟 ☎ ♿. 🅰🅴 𝖵𝖨𝖲𝖠 ✂
N 11
⌑ 35 – **40 rm** 450/690.

🏨 **L'Alligator** without rest, 39 r. Delambre (14th) ℰ 43 35 18 40, Telex 270545, Fax 43 35 30 71 – 🛗 🔟 ☎. 🅰🅴 🄴 𝖵𝖨𝖲𝖠 ✂
M 12
⌑ 40 – **35 rm** 395/600.

🏨 **Châtillon H.** without rest, 11 square Châtillon (14th) ℰ 45 42 31 17, Fax 45 42 72 09 – 🛗 🔟 ☎. 🄴 𝖵𝖨𝖲𝖠 ✂
P 11
⌑ 24 – **31 rm** 260/300.

🏨 **Tourisme** without rest, 66 av. La-Motte-Picquet (15th) ℰ 47 34 28 01, Telex 270568 – 🛗 🔟 ☎. 𝖵𝖨𝖲𝖠 ✂
K 8
⌑ 25 – **60 rm** 230/360.

🏨 **Bailli de Suffren** without rest, 149 av. Suffren (15th) ℰ 47 34 58 61, Telex 204854, Fax 45 67 75 82 – 🛗 🔟 ☎. 🅰🅴 🄴 𝖵𝖨𝖲𝖠
L 9
⌑ 40 – **25 rm** 470/560.

🏨 **Terminus Vaugirard** without rest, 403 r. Vaugirard (15th) ℰ 48 28 18 72, Telex 206562, Fax 48 28 56 34 – 🛗 🔟 ☎. 🄴 𝖵𝖨𝖲𝖠 ✂
N 7
closed 16 to 26 December – ⌑ 35 – **90 rm** 450/550.

🏨 **France** without rest, 46 r. Croix-Nivert (15th) ℰ 47 83 67 02, Fax 47 83 67 02 – 🛗 🔟 ☎. 🄴 𝖵𝖨𝖲𝖠 – ⌑ 32 – **30 rm** 350/470.
L 8

🏨 **Acropole** without rest, 199 bd Brune (14th) ℰ 45 39 64 17, Telex 203131, Fax 45 42 18 21 – 🛗 🔟 ☎. 🅰🅴 ⓪ 🄴 𝖵𝖨𝖲𝖠. ✂
R 12
⌑ 30 – **41 rm** 330/440.

🏨 **Cécil'H.** without rest, 47 r. Beaunier (14th) ℰ 45 40 93 53, Telex 206873 – 🛗 🔟 ☎. 🅰🅴 🄴 𝖵𝖨𝖲𝖠 ✂
R 12
⌑ 28 – **25 rm** 325/360.

🏨 **Agenor** without rest, 22 r. Cels (14th) ℰ 43 22 47 25, Telex 203994, Fax 42 79 94 01 – 🛗 🔟 ☎. 🅰🅴 🄴 𝖵𝖨𝖲𝖠. ✂
M 11
⌑ 28 – **19 rm** 330/420.

🏨 **Ariane Montparnasse** without rest, 35 r. Sablière (14th) ℰ 45 45 67 13, Telex 203554, Fax 45 45 39 49 – 🛗 🔟 ☎. 🅰🅴 ⓪ 🄴 𝖵𝖨𝖲𝖠
N 11
⌑ 30 – **30 rm** 340/400.

🏨 **Fondary** without rest, 30 r. Fondary (15th) ℰ 45 75 14 75, Telex 206761, Fax 45 75 84 42 – 🛗 🔟 ☎. 🅰🅴 🄴 𝖵𝖨𝖲𝖠
L 8
⌑ 36 – **20 rm** 330/395.

🏨 **Istria** without rest, 29 r. Campagne Première (14th) ℰ 43 20 91 82, Telex 203618, Fax 43 22 48 45 – 🛗 🔟 ☎. 🅰🅴 🄴 𝖵𝖨𝖲𝖠
M 12
⌑ 35 – **26 rm** 415/510.

🏨 **Pasteur** without rest, 33 r. Dr.-Roux (15th) ℰ 47 83 53 17, Fax 45 66 62 39 – 🛗 ☎. 🄴 𝖵𝖨𝖲𝖠
M 10
closed late July-late August – ⌑ 30 – **19 rm** 295/410.

🏨 **Friant** without rest, 8 r. Friant (14th) ℰ 45 42 71 91, Fax 45 42 04 67 – 🛗 🔟 ☎. 🄴 𝖵𝖨𝖲𝖠 ✂
P 11
⌑ 26 – **27 rm** 315/350.

🏨 **Sèvres-Montparnasse** without rest, 153 r. Vaugirard (14th) ℰ 47 34 56 75, Telex 206300, Fax 40 65 01 86 – 🛗 🔟 ☎. 🅰🅴 ⓪ 🄴 𝖵𝖨𝖲𝖠 ✂
L 10
⌑ 30 – **35 rm** 380/430.

XXXX ✿ **Les Célébrités** - Hôtel Nikko, 61 quai Grenelle (15th) ✆ 40 58 20 00, Telex 205811, Fax 45 75 42 35, ← – ▤. AE ⓓ E VISA K 6
M 230 (lunch) and a la carte 420/670
Spec. Salade de langoustines rôties, Blanc de turbot à la tomate et au basilic, Côte de veau de lait poêlée "Grand-Mère".

XXXX ✿ **Relais de Sèvres** - Hôtel Sofitel Paris, 8 r. L.-Armand (15th) ✆ 40 60 33 66, Telex 200432, Fax 45 57 04 22 – ▤. AE ⓓ E VISA N 5
closed August, 24 December-2 January, Saturday and Sunday – **M** 310 (lunch) and a la carte 280/400
Spec. Gratin de lentilles vertes au foie gras, Fricassée de sole à l'aigre doux, Aiguillette de boeuf à la moutarde à l'estragon.

XXX ✿ **Morot Gaudry,** 6 r. Cavalerie (15th) (8th floor) ✆ 45 67 06 85, Fax 45 67 55 72, ☂ – ▤. AE E VISA K 8
closed Saturday and Sunday – **M** 200 (lunch) and a la carte 310/430
Spec. Croustillant de langoustines (Sept.-June), Grenadin de veau aux écrevisses et croquette de pied de porc, Grouse à la ficelle (15 September-28 February).

XXX **Armes de Bretagne,** 108 av. Maine (14th) ✆ 43 20 29 50 – ▤. AE ⓓ E VISA N 11
closed August, Sunday dinner and Monday – **M** 200 and a la carte 250/430.

XXX **Pavillon Montsouris,** 20 r. Gazan (14th) ✆ 45 88 38 52, Fax 45 88 63 40, ←, ☂, « 1900 Pavilion beside the park » – Ⓟ. ⓓ E VISA. ✂ R 14
M 245.

XXX **Moniage Guillaume** with rm, 88 r. Tombe-Issoire (14th) ✆ 43 22 96 15, Fax 43 27 11 79 – TV ☎. AE ⓓ E VISA P 12
closed August and Sunday – **M** 195 b.i. (lunch) and a la carte 280/460 – ☕ 28 – **5 rm** 240/320.

XXX **Lous Landès,** 157 av. Maine (14th) ✆ 45 43 08 04 – ▤. AE ⓓ E VISA N 11
closed 5 to 24 August, Saturday lunch and Sunday – **M** a la carte 230/380.

XXX **Olympe,** 8 r. Nicolas Charlet (15th) ✆ 47 34 86 08 – ▤. AE ⓓ E VISA L 10
closed August, Saturday lunch, Sunday lunch and Monday – **M** a la carte 310/420.

XX **Lal Qila,** 88 av. É. Zola (15th) ✆ 45 75 68 40, Indian rest., « Original decor » – ▤. AE E VISA. ✂ L 7
closed Monday lunch and Sunday – **M** 185 and a la carte 140/205.

XX ✿ **Jacques Hébert,** 38 r. Sébastien Mercier (15th) ✆ 45 57 77 88 – E VISA L 5
closed 21 July-19 August, Sunday and Monday – **M** 170 and a la carte 250/440
Spec. Langoustines rôties au pamplemousse, Ris de veau à la crème de champignons, Délice ananas et pommes au Calvados.

XX **L'Aubergade,** 53 av. La Motte-Picquet (15th) ✆ 47 83 23 85, ☂ – E VISA J 9
closed 25 March-4 April, 29 July-29 August, 23 December-3 January, Sunday dinner and Monday – **M** 150 b.i. (lunch) and a la carte 220/330.

XX **La Chaumière des Gourmets,** 22 pl. Denfert-Rochereau (14th) ✆ 43 21 22 59 – VISA N 12
closed 30 March-7 April, 3 August-3 September, Saturday lunch and Sunday – **M** 240 and a la carte 270/375.

XX ✿ **Bistro 121,** 121 r. Convention (15th) ✆ 45 57 52 90 – AE ⓓ E VISA M 7
closed 14 July-15 August, 24 to 31 December, Sunday and Monday – **M** 240 and a la carte 290/435
Spec. Foie de canard chaud au verjus, Panaché de sole et homard aux langoustines, Poule au pot farcie quercynoise.

XX ✿ **Le Dôme,** 108 bd du Montparnasse (14th) ✆ 43 35 25 81, Fax 42 79 01 19, Seafood – ▤. AE ⓓ VISA LM 12
closed Monday – **M** a la carte 290/460
Spec. Pétales de Saint-Jacques crues aux truffes (December-March), Rouget à la "planche", Saint-Pierre aux légumes croquants.

XX **La Coupole,** 102 bd Montparnasse (14th) ✆ 43 20 14 20, Fax 43 35 46 14, « 1920 Parisian brasserie » – AE ⓓ E VISA L 12
M a la carte 150/250 ♖.

XX ✿ **Petite Bretonnière** (Lamaison), 2 r. Cadix (15th) ✆ 48 28 34 39 – VISA N 7
closed August, Saturday lunch and Sunday – **M** a la carte 270/370
Spec. Terrine de confits aux champignons, Magret de canard, Tourtière landaise.

XX **Yves Quintard,** 99 r. Blomet (15th) ✆ 42 50 22 27 – E VISA M 8
closed Saturday lunch and Sunday – **M** 150/300.

XX **Didier Délu,** 85 r. Leblanc (15th) ✆ 45 54 20 49 – AE ⓓ E VISA M 5
closed 10 to 18 August, 21 December-1 January, Saturday and Sunday – **M** 170 (lunch) and a la carte 235/330.

XX **L'Entre Siècle,** 29 av. Lowendal (15th) ✆ 47 83 51 22 – E VISA K 9
closed 4 August-1 September, Saturday lunch and Sunday – **M** 160 b.i. (lunch) and a la carte 230/330.

XX **Senteurs de Provence,** 295 r. Lecourbe (15th) ✆ 45 57 11 98, Seafood – AE ⓓ E VISA M 6
closed 4 to 25 August, 23 to 26 December, Sunday and Monday – **M** 175 and a la carte 190/320.

XX **Napoléon et Chaix,** 46 r. Balard (15th) ☏ 45 54 09 00 — 🔳 **E** 𝘝𝘐𝘚𝘈   M 5
closed August and Sunday – **M** a la carte 220/350.

XX **La Gauloise,** 59 av. La Motte-Picquet (15th) ☏ 47 34 11 64, 🏠 – 🆎 ⓄⒹ **E** 𝘝𝘐𝘚𝘈   K 8
closed Christmas-New Year, Saturday and Sunday – **M** a la carte 230/360.

XX **Monsieur Lapin,** 11 r. R. Losserand (14th) ☏ 43 20 21 39 – 🆎 **E** 𝘝𝘐𝘚𝘈   N 11
closed August, Saturday lunch and Monday – **M** 200 (lunch) and a la carte 250/400.

XX **Le Croquant,** 28 r. J. Maridor (15th) ☏ 45 58 50 83 – 🆎 ⓄⒹ **E** 𝘝𝘐𝘚𝘈   M 6
closed 1 to 13 May, Sunday and Monday – **M** a la carte 220/380.

XX **Le Copreaux,** 15 r. Copreaux (15th) ☏ 43 06 83 35 – **E** 𝘝𝘐𝘚𝘈   M 9
closed Saturday in August and Sunday – **M** 145/185.

XX **L'Étape,** 89 r. Convention (15th) ☏ 45 54 73 49 – **E** 𝘝𝘐𝘚𝘈   M 6
closed Christmas Holidays, Saturday (except dinner 16 September-30 June) and Sunday –
M 140 and a la carte 170/300.

XX **La Chaumière,** 54 av. F.-Faure (15th) ☏ 45 54 13 91 – 🆎 Ⓓ 𝘝𝘐𝘚𝘈   M 7
closed August, Monday dinner and Tuesday – **M** a la carte 180/280.

XX **La Giberne,** 42bis av. Suffren (15th) ☏ 47 34 82 18 – 🆎 ⓄⒹ **E** 𝘝𝘐𝘚𝘈   J 8
closed 27 July-25 August, Saturday lunch and Sunday – **M** 150/350.

XX **Le Clos Morillons,** 50 r. Morillons (15th) ☏ 48 28 04 37 – 𝘝𝘐𝘚𝘈   N 8
closed 1 to 21 August, February Holidays, Saturday lunch and Sunday – **M** 210 (lunch)/275.

XX **Filoche,** 34 r. Laos (15th) ☏ 45 66 44 60 – **E** 𝘝𝘐𝘚𝘈. 🛇   K 8
closed 20 July-21 August, 22 December-6 January, Saturday and Sunday – **M** a la carte
185/280.

XX **Les Vendanges,** 40 r. Friant (14th) ☏ 45 39 59 98 – **E** 𝘝𝘐𝘚𝘈   R 11
closed August, Saturday lunch, Sunday and Bank Holidays – **M** 140 and a la carte 170/250.

XX **Pierre Vedel,** 19 r. Duranton (15th) ☏ 45 58 43 17 – 𝘝𝘐𝘚𝘈. 🛇   M 6
closed 14 to 30 July, Christmas-New Year, Saturday – **M** a la carte 200/300.

XX **Mina Mahal,** 25 r. Cambronne (15th) ☏ 47 34 19 88, Indian rest. – 🔳 🆎 𝘝𝘐𝘚𝘈. 🛇   L 8
closed Monday lunch and Sunday – **M** 150/350.

XX ❀ **La Cagouille** (Allemandou), 10 pl. Constantin Brancusi (14th) ☏ 43 22 09 01, 🏠, Seafood
– **E** 𝘝𝘐𝘚𝘈   M 11
closed 5 to 12 May, 11 August-2 September, 29 December-7 January, Sunday and Monday –
M a la carte 280/420
Spec. Huîtres de Marennes, Céteaux frits, Effiloché de raie sauce gribiche.

X **Oh! Duo,** 54 av. E. Zola (15th) ☏ 45 77 28 82 – **E** 𝘝𝘐𝘚𝘈   L 6
closed August, Saturday and Sunday – **M** 122/130 🍷.

X **La Bonne Table,** 42 r. Friant (14th) ☏ 45 39 74 91 – **E** 𝘝𝘐𝘚𝘈   R 11
closed July, 24 December-4 January, Saturday and Sunday – **M** a la carte 180/300.

X **Trois Chevrons,** 148 av. F. Faure (15th) ☏ 45 54 12 26 – 𝘝𝘐𝘚𝘈   M 5
closed 13 to 20 August, 22 December-8 January, Saturday and Sunday – **M** a la carte
200/295 🍷.

X **La Datcha Lydie,** 7 r. Dupleix (15th) ☏ 45 66 67 77, Russian rest. – **E** 𝘝𝘐𝘚𝘈   K 8
closed 10 July-31 August and Wednesday – **M** 115 b.i. and a la carte 130/245.

X **Le Gastroquet,** 10 r. Desnouettes (15th) ☏ 48 28 60 91 – **E** 𝘝𝘐𝘚𝘈   N 7
closed 8 to 29 July, Saturday and Sunday – **M** 140.

X **Chez Pierre,** 117 r. Vaugirard (15th) ☏ 47 34 96 12 – 🔳 **E** 𝘝𝘐𝘚𝘈   L 11
closed 28 April-9 May, 3 July-26 August, Monday lunch, Saturday – **M** 110 (lunch only)/185.

X **L'Armoise,** 67 r. Entrepreneurs (15th) ☏ 45 79 03 31 – **E** 𝘝𝘐𝘚𝘈   L 7
closed 5 to 21 August, February Holidays, Saturday lunch and Sunday dinner – **M** 158
b.i./186.

X **Le Caroubier,** 8 av. Maine (15th) ☏ 45 48 14 38, North African rest. – 𝘝𝘐𝘚𝘈   L 11
closed 15 July-30 August, Sunday and Monday – **M** a la carte 120/185.

X **La Gitane,** 53bis av. La Motte-Picquet (15th) ☏ 47 34 62 92, 🏠 – **E** 𝘝𝘐𝘚𝘈   K 8
closed Saturday and Sunday – **M** a la carte 130/185.

X **Chez Yvette,** 46bis bd Montparnasse (15th) ☏ 42 22 45 54 – 𝘝𝘐𝘚𝘈   L 11
closed August, Saturday and Sunday – **M** a la carte 100/200.

X **Trois Horloges,** 73 r. Brancion (15th) ☏ 48 28 24 08, North African rest. – 🆎 Ⓓ 𝘝𝘐𝘚𝘈
🛇   N 9
closed 1 to 10 January, Tuesday lunch and Monday – **M** a la carte 150/220.

X **L'Amuse Bouche,** 186 r. Château (14th) ☏ 43 35 31 61 – 🆎 **E** 𝘝𝘐𝘚𝘈   N 11
closed 12 to 18 August, Saturday lunch and sunday – **M** (booking essential) 130 (lunch) and
a la carte 105/265.

X **Le Saint-Vincent,** 26 r. Croix-Nivert (15th) ☏ 47 34 14 94 – 🔳 **E** 𝘝𝘐𝘚𝘈. 🛇   L 8
closed Sunday – **M** a la carte 140/230 🍷.

X **Fellini,** 58 r. Croix-Nivert (15th) ☏ 45 77 40 77, italian rest. – **E** 𝘝𝘐𝘚𝘈. 🛇   L 8
closed August, Saturday lunch and Sunday – **M** a la carte 170/285.

Passy, Auteuil,
Bois de Boulogne,
Chaillot, Porte Maillot.

16th arrondissement.

🏨 **Park Avenue et Central Park** Ⓜ, 55 av. Poincaré ⊠ 75116 ℰ 45 53 44 60, Telex 643862, Fax 47 27 53 04, 🏤 – 🛗 kitchenette ▤ 📺 🕿 – 🔬 400. ⌶ ⓪ 🗲 𝘝𝘐𝘚𝘈   G 6
M *(closed Saturday, Sunday and Bank Holidays)* 190 and a la carte 240/370 – **99 rm**
⇌ 1250/1570, 13 apartments 1920/3120.

🏨 **Raphaël**, 17 av. Kléber ⊠ 75116 ℰ 45 02 16 00, Telex 610356, Fax 45 01 21 50, « Tasteful antiquated decor » – 🛗 📺 🕿 – 🔬 50. ⌶ ⓪ 🗲 𝘝𝘐𝘚𝘈   F 7
M 210 and a la carte 260/385 – ⇌ 90 – **87 rm** 1500/2500, 22 apartments.

🏨 **Baltimore** Ⓜ, 88bis av. Kléber ⊠ 75116 ℰ 45 53 83 33, Telex 611591, Fax 45 53 94 84 – 🛗 ▤ 📺 🕿 – 🔬 30 - 100. ⌶ ⓪ 🗲 𝘝𝘐𝘚𝘈. 🛠   G 7
L'Estournel *(closed August, Saturday and Sunday)* **M** 235 and a la carte 285/400 – **118 rm**
⇌ 1250/1510.

🏨 **Villa Maillot** Ⓜ without rest, 143 av. Malakoff ⊠ 75116 ℰ 45 01 25 22, Telex 649808, Fax 45 00 60 61 – 🛗 ▤ 📺 🕿 🕭, ⌶ ⓪ 🗲 𝘝𝘐𝘚𝘈   F 6
⇌ 90 – **39 rm** 1400/1600, 3 apartments 2300.

🏨 **Garden Elysée** Ⓜ ⑊, 12 r. St-Didier ⊠ 75116 ℰ 47 55 01 11, Telex 648157, Fax 47 27 79 24, 🏤 – 🛗 📺 🕿 🕭. ⌶ ⓪ 🗲 𝘝𝘐𝘚𝘈   G 7
M *(closed August, Saturday and Sunday)* 150/200 – ⇌ 70 – **48 rm** 1100/1520.

🏨 **Résidence Bassano** Ⓜ without rest, 15 r. Bassano ⊠ 75116 ℰ 47 23 78 23, Telex 649872, Fax 47 20 41 22 – 🛗 kitchenette ▤ 📺 🕿. ⌶ ⓪ 🗲 𝘝𝘐𝘚𝘈   G 8
⇌ 65 – **28 rm** 650/1050, 3 apartments 1950.

🏨 **Majestic** without rest, 29 r. Dumont d'Urville ⊠ 75116 ℰ 45 00 83 70, Telex 640034 – 🛗 ▤ 📺 🕿. ⌶ ⓪ 🗲 𝘝𝘐𝘚𝘈   F 7
⇌ 50 – **27 rm** 850/1100, 3 apartments 1700.

🏨 **Rond-Point de Longchamp** Ⓜ, 86 r. Longchamp ⊠ 75116 ℰ 45 05 13 63, Telex 640883, Fax 47 55 94 79 – 🛗 ▤ 📺 🕿 – 🔬 40. ⌶ ⓪ 🗲 𝘝𝘐𝘚𝘈   G 6
M (coffee shop) 110/210 – ⇌ 40 – **57 rm** 590/810.

🏨 **Alexander** without rest, 102 av. V. Hugo ⊠ 75116 ℰ 45 53 64 65, Telex 610373, Fax 45 53 12 51 – 🛗 📺 🕿. ⌶ ⓪ 🗲 𝘝𝘐𝘚𝘈. 🛠   G 6
⇌ 55 – **59 rm** 760/1035, 3 apartments 1870.

🏨 **Union H. Étoile** without rest, 44 r. Hamelin ⊠ 75116 ℰ 45 53 14 95, Telex 611394, Fax 47 55 94 79 – 🛗 kitchenette 📺 🕿. ⌶ ⓪ 🗲 𝘝𝘐𝘚𝘈   G 7
⇌ 38 – **29 rm** 600/720, 13 apartments 900/1050.

🏨 **Elysées Bassano** without rest, 24 r. Bassano ⊠ 75116 ℰ 47 20 49 03, Telex 611559, Fax 47 23 06 72 – 🛗 📺 🕿. ⌶ ⓪ 🗲 𝘝𝘐𝘚𝘈   G 8
⇌ 40 – **40 rm** 580/720.

🏨 **Victor Hugo** without rest, 19 r. Copernic ⊠ 75116 ℰ 45 53 76 01, Telex 630939, Fax 45 53 69 93 – 🛗 📺 🕿. ⌶ ⓪ 🗲 𝘝𝘐𝘚𝘈. 🛠   G 7
⇌ 40 – **75 rm** 550/685.

🏨 **Sévigné** without rest, 6 r. Belloy ⊠ 75116 ℰ 47 20 88 90, Telex 610219, Fax 40 70 98 73 – 🛗 📺 🕿. ⌶ ⓪ 🗲 𝘝𝘐𝘚𝘈   G 7
⇌ 40 – **30 rm** 580/680.

🏨 **Frémiet** without rest, 6 av. Frémiet ⊠ 75016 ℰ 45 24 52 06, Telex 630329, Fax 42 88 77 46 – 🛗 📺 🕿. ⌶ ⓪ 🗲 𝘝𝘐𝘚𝘈   J 6
⇌ 35 – **34 rm** 585/725.

🏨 **Floride Etoile** Ⓜ without rest, 14 r. St-Didier ⊠ 75116 ℰ 47 27 23 36, Telex 615087, Fax 47 27 79 24 – 🛗 📺 🕿 – 🔬 40. ⌶ ⓪ 🗲 𝘝𝘐𝘚𝘈. 🛠   G 7
⇌ 40 – **60 rm** 760/780.

🏨 **Massenet** without rest, 5bis r. Massenet ⊠ 75116 ℰ 45 24 43 03, Telex 640196, Fax 45 24 41 39 – 🛗 📺 🕿. ⌶ ⓪ 🗲 𝘝𝘐𝘚𝘈. 🛠   J 6
⇌ 30 – **41 rm** 415/665.

🏨 **Résidence Foch** without rest, 10 r. Marbeau ⊠ 75116 ℰ 45 00 46 50, Telex 630886, Fax 45 01 98 68 – 🛗 📺 🕿. ⌶ ⓪ 🗲 𝘝𝘐𝘚𝘈   F 6
⇌ 40 – **21 rm** 570/640, 4 apartments 900.

🏨 **Kléber** without rest, 7 r. Belloy ⊠ 75116 ℰ 47 23 80 22, Telex 612830, Fax 49 52 07 20 – 🛗 📺 🕿. ⌶ ⓪ 🗲 𝘝𝘐𝘚𝘈   G 7
⇌ 40 – **22 rm** 580/950.

🏨 **Murat** Ⓜ without rest, 119bis bd Murat ⊠ 75016 ℰ 46 51 12 32, Telex 648963, Fax 46 51 70 01 – 🛗 📺 🕿. ⌶ ⓪ 🗲 𝘝𝘐𝘚𝘈. 🛠   M 3
⇌ 45 – **28 rm** 600.

🏨 **Résidence Chambellan Morgane** Ⓜ without rest, 6 r. Keppler ⊠ 75116 ℰ 47 20 35 72, Telex 613682, Fax 47 20 95 69 – 🛗 📺 🕿. ⌶ ⓪ 🗲 𝘝𝘐𝘚𝘈. 🛠   GF 8
⇌ 40 – **20 rm** 540/810.

🏨 **Résidence Impériale** Ⓜ without rest, 155 av. Malakoff ⊠ 75116 ℰ 45 00 23 45, Telex 651158, Fax 45 01 88 82 – 🛗 🗏 📺 ☎. ⁂ⒶⒺⓄ ⒺⓋⁱˢᵃ
⊑ 30 – **37 rm** 590/790.　　　　　　　　　　　　　　　　　　　　　　　　　E 6

🏨 **Résidence Kléber** Ⓜ without rest, 97 r. Lauriston ⊠ 75016 ℰ 45 53 83 30, Telex 613106, Fax 47 55 92 52 – 🛗 📺 ☎. ⒶⒺⓄ Ⓔ Ⓥⁱˢᵃ　　　　　　　　　　　　　　　　G 7
⊑ 40 – **51 rm** 720.

🏨 **Étoile Maillot** without rest, 10 r. Bois de Boulogne (angle r. Duret) ⊠ 75116 ℰ 45 00 42 60, Telex 613936, Fax 45 00 55 89 – 🛗 📺 ☎. ⒶⒺⓄ Ⓔ Ⓥⁱˢᵃ　　　　　F 6
⊑ 40 – **27 rm** 510/670.

🏨 **Passy Eiffel** without rest, 10 r. Passy ⊠ 75016 ℰ 45 25 55 66, Telex 612753, Fax 42 88 89 88
– 🛗 ⁂ ☎. Ⓔ Ⓥⁱˢᵃ　　　　　　　　　　　　　　　　　　　　　　　　　J 6
⊑ 30 – **50 rm** 470/560.

🏨 **Résidence Marceau** without rest, 37 av. Marceau ⊠ 75116 ℰ 47 20 43 37, Telex 648509
– 🛗 📺 ☎. ⒶⒺ Ⓔ Ⓥⁱˢᵃ. ⁂　　　　　　　　　　　　　　　　　　　　　G 8
closed 5 to 24 August – ⊑ 30 – **30 rm** 500/600.

🏨 **Ambassade** without rest, 79 r. Lauriston ⊠ 75116 ℰ 45 53 41 15, Telex 613643, Fax 45 53 69 93 – 🛗 📺 ☎. ⒶⒺⓄ Ⓔ Ⓥⁱˢᵃ. ⁂　　　　　　　　　　　　　　G 7
⊑ 35 – **38 rm** 400/520.

🏨 **Beauséjour Ranelagh** without rest, 99 r. Ranelagh ⊠ 75016 ℰ 42 88 14 39, Telex 614072, Fax 40 50 81 21 – 🛗 📺 ☎. ⒶⒺ　　　　　　　　　　　　　　　　　　　J 4
⊑ 30 – **30 rm** 350/550.

🏨 **Longchamp** without rest, 68 r. Longchamp ⊠ 75116 ℰ 47 27 13 48, Telex 610342, Fax 47 55 68 26 – 🛗 📺 ☎. ⒶⒺ Ⓔ Ⓥⁱˢᵃ　　　　　　　　　　　　　　　G 6
⊑ 40 – **23 rm** 580/680.

🏨 **Hameau de Passy** Ⓜ ⋙ without rest, 48 r. Passy ⊠ 75016 ℰ 42 88 47 55, Telex 651469, Fax 42 30 83 72 – 🛗 📺 ☎. ⒶⒺ Ⓔ Ⓥⁱˢᵃ　　　　　　　　　　　　　J 5-6
32 rm ⊑ 440/500.

🏨 **Queen's H.** without rest, 4 r. Bastien Lepage ⊠ 75016 ℰ 42 88 89 85, Fax 40 50 67 52 – 🛗 ⁂ 📺 ☎. ⒶⒺ Ⓔ Ⓥⁱˢᵃ. ⁂　　　　　　　　　　　　　　　　　　　K 4
⊑ 35 – **22 rm** 260/520.

🏨 **Keppler** without rest, 12 r. Keppler ⊠ 75116 ℰ 47 20 65 05, Telex 640544, Fax 47 23 02 29
– 🛗 📺 ☎. ⒶⒺ Ⓔ Ⓥⁱˢᵃ. ⁂　　　　　　　　　　　　　　　　　　　　F 8
⊑ 24 – **49 rm** 355/360.

XXXX ⁕⁕ **Faugeron**, 52 r. Longchamp ⊠ 75116 ℰ 47 04 24 53, Fax 47 55 62 90 – 🗏. Ⓔ Ⓥⁱˢᵃ. ⁂
closed August, 23 December-2 January, Saturday and Sunday – **M** 310 (lunch) and a la carte 400/600　　　　　　　　　　　　　　　　　　　　　　　　　　　　　G 7
Spec. Grenouilles dorées et crème à la Plucheverte, Curry de jarret de veau au Sauternes, Pyramide de desserts.

XXXX ⁕⁕⁕ **Jamin** (Robuchon), 32 r. Longchamp ⊠ 75116 ℰ 47 27 12 27 – 🗏. Ⓥⁱˢᵃ　　G 7
closed 8 July-5 August, Saturday and Sunday – **M** (booking essential) a la carte 500/800
Spec. Salade de pommes, mâche et truffes "croque-au-sel" (Dec.-March), Oeuf mollet et crème céleri au fumet de truffes en gelée, Pintade et foie gras rôtis.

XXXX ⁕⁕ **Vivarois** (Peyrot), 192 av. V.-Hugo ⊠ 75116 ℰ 45 04 04 31 – 🗏. ⒶⒺⓄ Ⓔ Ⓥⁱˢᵃ　　G 5
closed August, Saturday, Sunday and Bank Holidays – **M** 350 b.i. (lunch) and a la carte 420/600
Spec. Fondant de légumes à la purée d'olives, Poissons au gré de la marée, Rissolettes de pieds d'agneau et ses artichauts "Provençale".

XXX ⁕ **Toit de Passy** (Jacquot), 94 av. P. Doumer (6th floor) ⊠ 75016 ℰ 45 24 55 37, Fax 45 20 94 57, 🌧 – 🗏 Ⓟ. ⒶⒺ Ⓔ Ⓥⁱˢᵃ　　　　　　　　　　　　　　HJ 5
closed 4 to 12/5, 10 to 18/8, 21/12-6/1, Saturday (except dinner 1/9-21/12), Sunday and Bank Holidays – **M** 265 (lunch) and a la carte 370/520
Spec. Foie gras froid poché au vin de Graves, Saint-Jacques grillées (October-March), Pigeonneau en croûte de sel.

XXX ⁕ **Tsé-Yang**, 25 av. Pierre 1ᵉʳ de Serbie ⊠ 75016 ℰ 47 20 68 02, Chinese rest., « Tasteful decor » – 🗏. ⒶⒺⓄ Ⓔ Ⓥⁱˢᵃ　　　　　　　　　　　　　　　　　G 8
M 175/275.

XXX **Sully d'Auteuil**, 78 r. Auteuil ⊠ 75016 ℰ 46 51 71 18 – 🗏. ⒶⒺ Ⓔ Ⓥⁱˢᵃ　　K 3
closed 5 to 25 August, Saturday lunch and Sunday – **M** a la carte 310/450.

XXX **Jean-Claude Ferrero**, 38 r. Vital ⊠ 75016 ℰ 45 04 42 42 – 🗏. ⒶⒺ Ⓔ Ⓥⁱˢᵃ　　H 5
closed 1 to 13/5, 15/8-2/9, Saturday (except dinner 11 November-30/4) Sunday and Bank Holidays – **M** 220 (lunch) and a la carte 260/475.

XXX **Le Petit Bedon**, 38 r. Pergolèse ⊠ 75116 ℰ 45 00 23 66, Fax 45 01 96 29 – 🗏. ⒶⒺⓄ Ⓔ Ⓥⁱˢᵃ　　　　　　　　　　　　　　　　　　　　　　　　　　F 6
closed 1 to 15 August, Saturday 1 May-31 August and Sunday – **M** 200 (lunch) and a la carte 320/520.

XXX ❀ **Patrick Lenôtre,** 28 r. Duret ⊠ 75116 ✆ 45 00 17 67, Fax 45 00 10 48 — ▤. ◪ ⓪ *VISA*
closed 1 to 19 August, Saturday lunch and Sunday – **M** 220 (lunch) and a la carte 240/460
   Spec. Saumon caramélisé au jus d'ail et soja, Pied de porc à la rouennaise, Canard aux deux cuissons.   F 6

XXX ❀ **Port Alma** (Canal), 10 av. New-York ⊠ 75116 ✆ 47 23 75 11 — ◪ ⓪ **E** *VISA*
closed August and Sunday – **M** 200 (lunch) and a la carte 240/400   H 8
   Spec. Salade de langoustines et coques, Fricassée de sole poêlée au foie gras, Soufflé au chocolat.

XXX **Le Pergolèse,** 40 r. Pergolèse ⊠ 75016 ✆ 45 00 21 40 — ◪ ⓪ **E** *VISA*   F 6
closed 3 to 25 August, 24 December-2 January, Saturday and Sunday – **M** a la carte
275/400.

XX ❀ **Relais d'Auteuil** (Pignol), 31 bd Murat ⊠ 75016 ✆ 46 51 09 54 — ◪ **E** *VISA*   L 3
closed August, Saturday lunch and Sunday – **M** 170 (lunch) and a la carte 290/440
   Spec. Amandine de foie gras frais, Madeleines au miel de bruyère avec glace miel et noix.

XX **Al Mounia,** 16 r. Magdebourg ⊠ 75116 ✆ 47 27 57 28, Moroccan rest. — ▤. ◪ **E** *VISA*
   ❀   G 7
   closed 14 July-31 August and Sunday – **M** a la carte 150/275.

XX **Giulio Rebellato,** 136 r. Pompe ⊠ 75116 ✆ 47 27 50 26, Italian rest. — ◪ **E** *VISA*. ❀   G 6
closed August, Christmas-New Year, Saturday lunch and Sunday – **M** a la carte 220/280.

XX ❀ **Fontaine d'Auteuil** (Grégoire), 35bis r. La Fontaine ✆ 42 88 04 47 — ⓪ **E** *VISA*   K 5
closed Saturday lunch and Sunday – **M** 160 (lunch) and a la carte 250/350 ⬙
   Spec. Salade de ris de veau aux aubergines, Aiguillettes de Saint-Pierre au piment doux et coriandre, Velours
au chocolat amer et griottes.

XX ❀ **Conti,** 72 r. Lauriston ⊠ 75116 ✆ 47 27 74 67 — ▤. ◪ ⓪ **E** *VISA*   G 7
closed 5 to 25 August, Saturday, Sunday and Bank Holidays – **M** 260 b.i. (lunch) and a la
carte 290/400
   Spec. Ravioli de champignons (June-October), Tagliatelles aux truffes blanches (October-December), Saltimbocca de soles.

XX **Villa Vinci,** 23 r. P. Valéry ⊠ 75116 ✆ 45 01 68 18, Italian rest. — ▤. **E** *VISA*. ❀   F 7
closed August, Saturday and Sunday – **M** 170 (lunch) and a la carte 220/360.

XX **Paul Chêne,** 123 r. Lauriston ⊠ 75116 ✆ 47 27 63 17 — ▤. ◪ ⓪ **E** *VISA*   G 6
closed 2 August-3 September, 21 December-1 January, Saturday and Sunday – **M** a la carte
260/455.

XX ❀ **La Petite Tour** (Israël), 11 r. Tour ⊠ 75116 ✆ 45 20 09 31 — ◪ ⓪ **E** *VISA*   H 6
closed August and Sunday – **M** a la carte 235/400
   Spec. Terrine de canard, Filets de sole à l'orange, Rognon de veau à la moutarde.

XX **Sous l'Olivier,** 15 r. Goethe ⊠ 75116 ✆ 47 20 84 81, ☂ — **E** *VISA*   G 8
closed Saturday, Sunday and Bank Holidays – **M** a la carte 210/325.

XX **Palais du Trocadéro,** 7 av. Eylau ⊠ 75016 ✆ 47 27 05 02, Chinese rest. — ▤. ◪ **E**
   VISA   H 6
   M a la carte 150/220.

XX **Le Gd Chinois,** 6 av. New York ⊠ 75116 ✆ 47 23 98 21, Chinese rest. — ◪ ⓪   H 8
closed 29 July-27 August and Monday – **M** a la carte 150/280.

XX **Marius,** 82 bd Murat ⊠ 75016 ✆ 46 51 67 80 — **E** *VISA*   M 2
closed August, Saturday lunch and Sunday – **M** a la carte 185/290.

X **Chez Géraud,** 31 r. Vital ⊠ 75016 ✆ 45 20 33 00, « Fine Longwy porcelain mural » — **E**
   VISA   H 5
   closed 31 July-1 September, Saturday and Sunday – **M** a la carte 180/300.

X **Brasserie de la Poste,** 54 r. Longchamp ⊠ 75116 ✆ 47 55 01 31, Fax 39 50 74 32 — **E**
   VISA   G 7
   M a la carte 140/210 ⬙.

X **Beaujolais d'Auteuil,** 99 bd Montmorency ⊠ 75016 ✆ 47 43 03 56 — ◪ **E** *VISA*   K 3
closed Saturday lunch and Sunday – **M** 105 b.i. and a la carte 160/240.

in the Bois de Boulogne :

XXXX ❀ **Pré Catelan,** rte de Suresnes ⊠ 75016 ✆ 45 24 55 58, Telex 614983, Fax 45 24 43 25,
   ☂, ☘ — ⓟ ◪ ⓪ **E** *VISA*   H 2
   closed February Holidays, Sunday dinner and Monday – **M** a la carte 420/620.
   Spec. Soufflé d'oursins (winter), Noisettes d'agneau à la truffe noire, Macarons glacés au coulis rouge.

XXXX ❀ **Grande Cascade,** allée de Longchamp (opposite the hippodrome) ⊠ 75016 ✆ 45 27
   33 51, Fax 42 88 99 06, ☂ — ⓟ ◪ ⓪ **E** *VISA*
   closed 20 December-20 January and dinner 1 November-15 April – **M** 270 (lunch) and a la
carte 400/600
   Spec. Délices des Landes aux salades tendres, Meunière de homard à la crème de cerfeuil, Rosette de filet de
boeuf au foie gras.

*If you would like a more complete selection of hotels and restaurants,
consult the **MICHELIN** Red Guides for the following countries :*

      Benelux, Deutschland, España Portugal, France,

        Great Britain and Ireland, and Italia,

all in annual editions.

Clichy, Ternes, Wagram.

17th arrondissement.
17th : ⊠ 75017

🏨 **Concorde La Fayette** Ⓜ, 3 pl. Gén.-Koenig 𝒫 40 68 50 68, Telex 650892, Fax 40 68 50 43, « 34th floor bar with ≤ Paris » – 🛗 🗏 📺 ☎ – 🏛 40. 🖭 ⓞ Ⅎ 𝑉𝐼𝑆𝐴 E 6
M see **Etoile d'Or** below - **L'Arc-en-Ciel M** 215/235 ⅊ – **Les Saisons** (coffee shop) **M** a la carte 170/240 ⅊ – ⊑ 85 – **935 rm** 1350/2100, 44 apartments.

🏨 **Méridien** Ⓜ, 81 bd Gouvion St Cyr 𝒫 40 68 34 34, Telex 651952, Fax 40 68 31 31 – 🛗 🗏 📺 ☎ – 🏛 50 - 800. 🖭 ⓞ Ⅎ 𝑉𝐼𝑆𝐴 E 6
M see **Clos de Longchamp** below - **Café l'Arlequin M** a la carte 170/275 – **Le Yamato** (Japanese rest.) *(closed Aug., 1 to 7 January, Sunday and Monday)* **M** carte 160 à 270 – **La Maison Beaujolaise** *(closed August, 23 to 29 December and Sunday)* **M** a la carte approx. 200 – ⊑ 89 – **989 rm** 1600/1850, 17 apartments.

🏨 **Splendid Etoile** without rest, 1bis av. Carnot 𝒫 43 80 14 56, Telex 280773, Fax 47 64 05 09 – 🛗 🗏 📺 ☎. ⓞ Ⅎ 𝑉𝐼𝑆𝐴. 🛠 F 7
closed August, Saturday and Sunday – ⊑ 65 – **50 rm** 780/1200, 7 apartments 1200.

🏨 **Regent's Garden** 🍃 without rest, 6 r. P.-Demours 𝒫 45 74 07 30, Telex 640127, Fax 40 55 01 42, « Garden » – 🛗 📺 ☎. 🖭 ⓞ Ⅎ 𝑉𝐼𝑆𝐴 E 7
⊑ 34 – **40 rm** 620/870.

🏨 **Pierre** Ⓜ without rest, 25 r. Th.-de-Banville 𝒫 47 63 76 69, Telex 643003, Fax 43 80 63 96 – 🛗 📺 ☎ 🖢. 🏛 30. 🖭 ⓞ Ⅎ 𝑉𝐼𝑆𝐴 D 8
⊑ 50 – **50 rm** 570/800.

🏨 **Balmoral** without rest, 6 r. Gén.-Lanrezac 𝒫 43 80 30 50, Telex 642435, Fax 43 80 51 56 – 🛗 📺 ☎. 🖭 ⓞ Ⅎ 𝑉𝐼𝑆𝐴 E 7
⊑ 35 – **57 rm** 500/650.

🏨 **Magellan** 🍃 without rest, 17 r. J.B.-Dumas 𝒫 45 72 44 51, Telex 644728, Fax 40 68 90 36, 🚗 – 🛗 📺 ☎. 🖭 Ⅎ 𝑉𝐼𝑆𝐴. 🛠 D 7
⊑ 25 – **75 rm** 460.

🏨 **Mercure** Ⓜ without rest, 27 av. Ternes 𝒫 47 66 49 18, Telex 650679, Fax 47 63 77 91 – 🛗 🗏 📺 ☎. 🖭 ⓞ Ⅎ 𝑉𝐼𝑆𝐴 E 8
⊑ 52 – **56 rm** 510/750.

🏨 **Résidence St-Ferdinand** Ⓜ without rest, 36 r. St-Ferdinand 𝒫 45 72 66 66, Telex 649565, Fax 45 74 12 92 – 🛗 🗏 📺 ☎. 🖭 ⓞ Ⅎ 𝑉𝐼𝑆𝐴 E 6-7
⊑ 35 – **42 rm** 620/790.

🏨 **Banville** without rest, 166 bd Berthier 𝒫 42 67 70 16, Telex 643025, Fax 44 40 42 77 – 🛗 📺 ☎. 🖭 Ⅎ 𝑉𝐼𝑆𝐴 D 8
⊑ 35 – **39 rm** 520/570.

🏨 **Mercédès** Ⓜ without rest, 128 av. Wagram 𝒫 42 27 77 82, Telex 644751, Fax 40 53 09 89 – 🛗 🗏 📺 ☎. 🖭 Ⅎ 𝑉𝐼𝑆𝐴 D 9
⊑ 48 – **35 rm** 600.

🏨 **De Neuville**, 3 r. Verniquet 𝒫 43 80 26 30, Telex 648822, Fax 43 80 38 55 – 🛗 📺 ☎. 🖭 ⓞ Ⅎ 𝑉𝐼𝑆𝐴 C 8
M *(closed August, Saturday and Sunday)* a la carte 150/220 ⅊ – ⊑ 38 – **28 rm** 540/630.

🏨 **Harvey** Ⓜ without rest, 7bis r. Débarcadère 𝒫 45 74 27 19, Telex 650855, Fax 40 68 03 56 – 🛗 📺 ☎. 🖭 ⓞ Ⅎ 𝑉𝐼𝑆𝐴 E 6
⊑ 30 – **32 rm** 450/640.

🏨 **Cheverny** Ⓜ without rest, 7 villa Berthier 𝒫 43 80 46 42, Telex 648848, Fax 47 63 26 62 – 🛗 📺 ☎. 🖭 ⓞ Ⅎ 𝑉𝐼𝑆𝐴 D 7
⊑ 35 – **50 rm** 455/535.

🏨 **Étoile Pereire** 🍃 without rest, 146 bd Péreire 𝒫 42 67 60 00, Fax 42 67 02 90 – 🛗 📺 ☎. 🖭 ⓞ Ⅎ 𝑉𝐼𝑆𝐴. 🛠 D 7
⊑ 50 – **21 rm** 460/650, 5 apartments 900.

🏨 **Royal Magda** without rest, 7 r. Troyon 𝒫 47 64 10 19, Telex 641068, Fax 47 64 02 12 – 🛗 📺 ☎. 🖭 ⓞ Ⅎ 𝑉𝐼𝑆𝐴 E 8
⊑ 35 – **26 rm** 530/590, 11 apartments 650/750.

🏨 **Belfast** without rest, 10 av. Carnot 𝒫 43 80 12 10, Telex 642777, Fax 43 80 34 93 – 🛗 📺 ☎. 🖭 ⓞ Ⅎ 𝑉𝐼𝑆𝐴 E 7
⊑ 38 – **54 rm** 535/695.

🏨 **Théâtre** without rest, 5 r. Chéroy 𝒫 43 87 21 48, Telex 281821 – 🛗 📺 ☎. 🖭 ⓞ Ⅎ 𝑉𝐼𝑆𝐴. 🛠 D 11
closed 2 to 23 August – ⊑ 28 – **20 rm** 440/490.

🏨 **Star H. Étoile** without rest, 18 r. Arc de Triomphe 𝒫 43 80 27 69, Telex 643569, Fax 40 54 94 84 – 🛗 📺 ☎. 🖭 ⓞ Ⅎ 𝑉𝐼𝑆𝐴 E 7
⊑ 36 – **62 rm** 465/650.

🏨 **Monceau** without rest, 7 r. Rennequin 𝒫 47 63 07 52, Telex 649094 – 🛗 📺 ☎. 🖭 Ⅎ 𝑉𝐼𝑆𝐴 E 8
⊑ 35 – **25 rm** 380/470.

🏨 **Étoile Park H.** without rest, 10 av. Mac Mahon 🖉 42 67 69 63, Telex 649266, Fax 43 80 18 99
— 📶 📺 ☎. 🅰🅴 ⓪ 🄴 𝒱𝐼𝒮𝒜   E 8
closed 23 December-2 January – 🖵 45 – **28 rm** 435/700.

🏨 **Monceau Étoile** without rest, 64 r. Levis 🖉 42 27 33 10, Telex 643170, Fax 42 27 59 58 — 📶
📺 ☎. 🄴 𝒱𝐼𝒮𝒜. 🕉   D 10
26 rm 🖵 470/550.

🏨 **Astor Élysées** without rest, 36 r. P. Demours 🖉 42 27 44 93, Telex 650078, Fax 40 53 91 34
— 📶 📺 ☎. 🄴 𝒱𝐼𝒮𝒜. 🕉   D 8
🖵 45 – **45 rm** 575/690.

🏨 **Empire H.** without rest, 3 r. Montenotte 🖉 43 80 14 55, Telex 643232, Fax 47 66 04 33 — 📶
📺 ☎. 🅰🅴 ⓪ 🄴 𝒱𝐼𝒮𝒜   E 8
🖵 – **49 rm** 380/630.

🏨 **Courcelles** without rest, 184 r. Courcelles 🖉 47 63 65 30, Telex 642252, Fax 46 22 49 44 —
📶 📺 ☎. 🅰🅴 ⓪ 🄴 𝒱𝐼𝒮𝒜   D 8
🖵 35 – **42 rm** 495/615.

🏨 **Palma** without rest, 46 r. Brunel 🖉 45 74 74 51, Telex 644183, Fax 45 74 40 90 — 📶 📺 ☎. 🄴
𝒱𝐼𝒮𝒜. 🕉   E 7
🖵 28 – **37 rm** 310/400.

🏨 **Acacias Étoile** without rest, 11 r. Acacias 🖉 43 80 60 22, Telex 643551, Fax 48 88 96 40 —
📶 📺 ☎. 🅰🅴 ⓪ 🄴 𝒱𝐼𝒮𝒜   E 7
🖵 33 – **37 rm** 440/560.

🏦 **Prima H.,** 167 r. Rome 🖉 46 22 21 09, Telex 642186, Fax 46 22 21 09 — 📶 🄴 rest 📺 ☎. 🅰🅴
⓪ 🄴 𝒱𝐼𝒮𝒜   C 10
M 95/150 🍴 – 🖵 25 – **30 rm** 280/350.

🏦 **Flaubert** without rest, 19 r. Rennequin 🖉 46 22 44 35, Telex 649689, Fax 43 80 32 34 — 📶 📺
☎. ⓪ 🄴 𝒱𝐼𝒮𝒜   D 8
🖵 30 – **36 rm** 360/600.

🏦 **Bel'Hôtel** without rest, 20 r. Pouchet 🖉 46 27 34 77, Telex 642396, 🌿 — 📶 📺 ☎. 🅰🅴 🄴 𝒱𝐼𝒮𝒜
closed August – 🖵 25 – **30 rm** 160/360.   B 11

🍴🍴🍴🍴 ⁂⁂ **Guy Savoy,** 18 r. Troyon 🖉 43 80 40 61, Fax 46 22 43 09 — 🔲. 🅰🅴 🄴 𝒱𝐼𝒮𝒜   E 8
closed Saturday (except dinner November-Easter) and Sunday – **M** a la carte 420/650
Spec. Huîtres en nage glacée, Crème légère de lentilles et langoustines, Pigeonneau "poché-grillé" et risotto
aux petits abats.

🍴🍴🍴🍴 ⁂⁂ **Michel Rostang,** 20 r. Rennequin 🖉 47 63 40 77, Telex 649629, Fax 47 63 82 75 — 🔲.
🅰🅴 🄴 𝒱𝐼𝒮𝒜   D 8
closed 1 to 15 August, Saturday (except dinner September-April) and Sunday – **M** 260
(lunch)/540 and a la carte
Spec. Tarte tiède croustillante de saumon cru, Galette chaude et dorée de cheveux d'ange, Canette de Bresse
au sang.

🍴🍴🍴🍴 ⁂⁂ **Le Clos Longchamp** - Hôtel Méridien, 81 bd Gouvion-St-Cyr (Pte Maillot) 🖉 40 68
30 40, Telex 290952, Fax 40 68 30 81 — 🔲. 🅰🅴 ⓪ 🄴 𝒱𝐼𝒮𝒜   E 6
closed 11 to 18 August and Sunday – **M** 240 (lunch) and a la carte 420/520
Spec. Suçarelles de grenouilles à la citronnelle (March-December), Marbré de foie de canard au Beaumes de
Venise, Rognon de veau en croûte au genièvre.

🍴🍴🍴🍴 ⁂ **Étoile d'Or** - Hôtel Concorde Lafayette, 3 pl. Gén.-Koenig 🖉 40 68 51 28, Fax 40 68 50 43 —
🔲. 🅰🅴 🄴 𝒱𝐼𝒮𝒜   E 6
closed 20 July-18 August, Saturday lunch and Sunday – **M** 260 (lunch) and a la carte
380/540
Spec. Dos de saumon en vessie, Suprême de pigeon rôti au gratin de macaroni, Timbale de chocolat au café.

🍴🍴🍴🍴 ⁂ **Manoir de Paris,** 6 r. P. Demours 🖉 45 72 25 25, Fax 45 74 80 98 — 🔲. 🅰🅴 ⓪ 🄴 𝒱𝐼𝒮𝒜 E 7
closed Saturday (except dinner September-June) and Sunday – **M** 290 (lunch) and a la carte
310/440
Spec. Salade tiède de coquillages et crustacés, Daurade au naturel et légumes fondants, Suprême de pintade
et jus à la sauge.

🍴🍴🍴 ⁂⁂ **Apicius** (Vigato), 122 av. Villiers 🖉 43 80 19 66, Fax 44 40 09 57 — 🔲. 🅰🅴 ⓪ 🄴 𝒱𝐼𝒮𝒜   D 8
closed August, Saturday and Sunday – **M** a la carte 400/500
Spec. Foie gras poêlé en aigre doux aux radis noirs confits, Pieds de porc en crépinette au persil et jus de
truffes, Grand dessert au chocolat amer.

🍴🍴🍴 ⁂⁂ **Amphyclès** (Groult), 78 av. Ternes 🖉 40 68 01 01, Fax 40 68 91 88 — 🔲. ⓪ 🄴 𝒱𝐼𝒮𝒜   E 7
closed 7 to 28 July, Saturday lunch and Sunday – **M** 220 (lunch) and a la carte 330/520
Spec. Gelée de pied de veau au fumet de truffe, Risotto à l'étuvée de homard, Canette à l'orange et à la
coriandre.

🍴🍴🍴 **Maître Corbeau,** 6 r. Armaillé 🖉 42 27 19 20 — 🔲. 🅰🅴 ⓪ 🄴 𝒱𝐼𝒮𝒜   E 7
closed 28 July-21 August, 1 to 11 March, Saturday lunch and Sunday – **M** 190/250 b.i.

XXX ❀ **Timgad** (Laasri), 21 r. Brunel 🕾 45 74 23 70, Telex 649239, Fax 45 75 11 16, Maghreb rest., « Moorish decor » – 🗏, 🖭 ⓞ 🗲 𝚅𝙸𝚂𝙰, ⅏
E 7
M 200/450
Spec. Pastilla, Couscous, Tajine.

XXX ❀ **Sormani** (Fayet), 4 r. Gén.-Lanrezac 🕾 43 80 13 91 – 🗏, 🗲 𝚅𝙸𝚂𝙰
E 7
closed 1 to 22 August, 22 December-2 January, 22 February-4 March, Saturday, Sunday and Bank Holidays – **M** a la carte 290/410
Spec. Assiette de légumes à la florentine (15/4-31/7), Soufflé au fromage et à la brandade de morue (30/9-31/3), Menu "truffes blanches" (15/10-15/12).

XXX ❀ **Faucher**, 123 av. Wagram 🕾 42 27 61 50, Fax 46 22 25 72, 🍴 – 🗲 𝚅𝙸𝚂𝙰
D 8
closed 12 to 18 August, Saturday lunch and Sunday – **M** 180 (lunch) and a la carte 220/350
Spec. Haddock aux lentilles, Ris de veau croustillant sur glace de Porto, Millefeuille aux trois chocolats.

XXX **Chez Augusta**, 98 r. Tocqueville 🕾 47 63 39 97, Fax 42 27 21 71, Seafood – 🗏, 🗲 𝚅𝙸𝚂𝙰
C 9
closed 10 to 26 August, Saturday lunch, Sunday and Bank Holidays – **M** a la carte 270/450.

XXX ❀ **Paul et France** (Romano), 27 av. Niel 🕾 47 63 04 24 – 🗏, 🖭 ⓞ 🗲 𝚅𝙸𝚂𝙰, ⅏
D 8
closed 14 July-15 August, Saturday and Sunday – **M** 250 b.i. (lunch) and a la carte 330/470
Spec. Ravioli de tourteau, Rougets au beurre d'anchois, Rognon de veau au jus de truffe.

XX **Le Madigan**, 22 r. Terrasse 🕾 42 27 31 51, Fax 42 67 70 29, 🍴 – 🖭 🗲 𝚅𝙸𝚂𝙰, ⅏ D 10
closed Saturday lunch, Sunday and Bank Holidays – **M** 170/230 ⌣.

XX ❀ **A l'Arcade** (Albistur), 18 r. Bayen 🕾 45 72 02 19 – 🗏, 🗲 𝚅𝙸𝚂𝙰
E 8
closed August, Saturday lunch and Sunday – **M** 190 and a la carte 260/390
Spec. Huîtres chaudes au Champagne (October-April), Paupiettes de sole et langoustines, Gibier (October-January).

XX **L'Introuvable**, 15 r. Arc de Triomphe 🕾 47 54 00 28 – 🖭 🗲 𝚅𝙸𝚂𝙰
E 7
closed August, Saturday lunch and Sunday – **M** 180 and a la carte 250/350.

XX ❀ **Le Petit Colombier** (Fournier), 42 r. Acacias 🕾 43 80 28 54, Fax 44 40 04 29 – 🗏, 🖭 🗲
𝚅𝙸𝚂𝙰
E 7
closed 28 July-19 August, Sunday lunch and Saturday – **M** 200 (lunch) and a la carte 255/415
Spec. Oeufs rôtis aux truffes (November-February), Filets de grouse aux baies de genièvre (September-January), Pigeonneau fermier à la croque au sel.

XX **Andrée Baumann**, 64 av. Ternes 🕾 45 74 16 66, Fax 45 72 44 32 – 🗏, 🖭 🗲 𝚅𝙸𝚂𝙰
E 7
M a la carte 180/330 ⌣.

XX **La Braisière**, 54 r. Cardinet 🕾 47 63 40 37, Fax 47 63 04 76 – 🖭 𝚅𝙸𝚂𝙰
D 9
closed August, Saturday and Sunday – **M** 165 and a la carte 220/320.

XX **Gourmand Candide**, 6 pl. Mar. Juin 🕾 43 80 01 41, 🍴 – 🖭 ⓞ 🗲 𝚅𝙸𝚂𝙰
D 8
closed August, Saturday (except dinner September-May) and Sunday – **M** a la carte 240/390.

XX **Billy Gourmand**, 20 r. Tocqueville 🕾 42 27 03 71 – 🗲 𝚅𝙸𝚂𝙰
D 10
closed 1 to 26 August, Saturday lunch and Sunday – **M** 240 b.i. and a la carte 205/345.

XX **La Soupière**, 154 av. Wagram 🕾 42 27 00 73 – 🗏, 🖭 🗲 𝚅𝙸𝚂𝙰
D 9
closed 10 to 18 August, Saturday lunch and Sunday – **M** 160/240.

XX **La Grosse Tartine**, 91 bd Gouvion St Cyr 🕾 45 74 02 77 – 🗏, 🖭 ⓞ 🗲 𝚅𝙸𝚂𝙰
E 6
M a la carte 190/340.

XX **Le Beudant**, 97 r. des Dames 🕾 43 87 11 20 – 🗏, 🗲 𝚅𝙸𝚂𝙰
D 11
closed 15 to 25 August, Saturday lunch and Sunday – **M** 140/285.

XX **La Coquille**, 6 r. Débarcadère 🕾 45 74 25 95 – 🗏, 🖭 ⓞ 🗲 𝚅𝙸𝚂𝙰
E 7
closed 28 July-3 September, 22 December-2 January, Sunday and Monday – **M** a la carte 250/350.

XX **Ballon des Ternes**, 103 av. Ternes 🕾 45 74 17 98 – 🖭 🗲 𝚅𝙸𝚂𝙰
E 6
M a la carte 180/280.

XX **Chez Laudrin**, 154 bd Péreire 🕾 43 80 87 40 – 🗏, 🖭 🗲 𝚅𝙸𝚂𝙰
D 7
closed 1 to 8 May, Saturday and Sunday – **M** a la carte 240/380.

XX **La Truite Vagabonde**, 17 r. Batignolles 🕾 43 87 77 80, 🍴 – 🖭 𝚅𝙸𝚂𝙰
D 11
closed Sunday dinner – **M** 220 b.i./300.

XX **La Petite Auberge**, 38 r. Laugier 🕾 47 63 85 51 – ⓞ 🗲 𝚅𝙸𝚂𝙰
D 7-8
closed 3 August-3 September, Sunday and Monday – **M** (booking essential) 175 (lunch) and a la carte 230/400.

XX **L'Écrevisse**, 212bis bd Péreire 🕾 45 72 17 60 – 🗏, 🖭 ⓞ 🗲 𝚅𝙸𝚂𝙰
E 6
closed Saturday lunch and Sunday – **M** a la carte 180/290.

XX **Chez Guyvonne**, 14 r. Thann 🕾 42 27 25 43 – 𝚅𝙸𝚂𝙰
D 10
closed 15 to 31 July, 20 December-6 January, Saturday, Sunday and Bank Holidays – **M** a la carte 250/325.

XX **Chez Georges**, 273 bd Péreire 🕾 45 74 31 00 – 🗲 𝚅𝙸𝚂𝙰, ⅏
E 6
closed August – **M** a la carte 200/300.

XX **Epicure 108**, 108 r. Cardinet 🕾 47 63 50 91 – 🗲 𝚅𝙸𝚂𝙰
D 10
closed Saturday lunch and Sunday – **M** 220/300.

XX **La Niçoise**, 4 r. P. Demours 🕾 45 74 42 41, Fax 45 74 80 98, Specialities of Nice – 🗏, 🖭
ⓞ 🗲 𝚅𝙸𝚂𝙰
E 7
closed Saturday lunch and Sunday – **M** a la carte 160/210.

XX **Le Gouberville,** 1 pl. Ch. Fillon ℰ 46 27 33 37, 🌣 – 𝚅𝙸𝚂𝙰   C 10-11
  closed 12 to 26 August, Sunday and Monday – **M** 135 and a la carte 185/310.

XX **Chez Léon,** 32 r. Legendre ℰ 42 27 06 82 – ⓞ 𝙴 𝚅𝙸𝚂𝙰   D 10
  closed 31 July-1 September, February Holidays, Saturday and Sunday – **M** 155 and a la
  carte 165/365.

XX **L'Écailler du Palais,** 101 av. Ternes ℰ 45 74 87 07, Seafood – ▤. 𝙰𝙴 ⓞ 𝙴 𝚅𝙸𝚂𝙰   E 6
  closed 5 to 25 August – **M** a la carte 230/365.

XX **Le Troyon,** 4 r. Troyon ℰ 43 80 57 02 – 𝙴 𝚅𝙸𝚂𝙰   E 8
  closed Saturday lunch and Sunday – **M** a la carte 160/240.

XX **La Toque,** 16 r. Tocqueville ℰ 42 27 97 75 – ▤. 𝚅𝙸𝚂𝙰   D 10
  closed 20 July-20 August, Christmas-New Year, Saturday and Sunday – **M** a la carte 190/280.

X **Bistrot de l'Étoile,** 75 av. Niel ℰ 42 27 88 44 – ▤. 𝙴 𝚅𝙸𝚂𝙰. ⚘   D 8
  closed Sunday – **M** a la carte 180/230.

X **Bistrot d'à Côté Villiers,** 16 av. Villiers ℰ 47 63 25 61 – 𝙰𝙴 𝚅𝙸𝚂𝙰   D 10
  closed 12 to 18 August, Saturday lunch and Sunday – **M** a la carte 170/235.

X **Le Distrait,** 150 bd Péreire ℰ 48 88 93 68 – ▤. 𝙴 𝚅𝙸𝚂𝙰   D 7
  closed 10 to 27 August, Saturday lunch, Sunday and Bank Holidays – **M** a la carte 170/240.

X **Bistrot d'à Côté Flaubert,** 10 r. G. Flaubert ℰ 42 67 05 81 – 𝙰𝙴 𝚅𝙸𝚂𝙰   D 8
  closed 12 to 18 August, Saturday lunch and Sunday – **M** a la carte 160/250.

X **Les Béatilles,** 127 r. Cardinet ℰ 42 27 95 64 – 𝙴 𝚅𝙸𝚂𝙰   D 10
  closed February Holidays, 29 July-19 August, Saturday lunch and Sunday – **M** 120 (lunch)
  and a la carte 220/330.

X ❀ **Mère Michel** (Gaillard), 5 r. Rennequin ℰ 47 63 59 80 – 𝙴 𝚅𝙸𝚂𝙰   E 8
  closed August, Saturday, Sunday and Bank Holidays – **M** (booking essential) a la carte
  240/330
  Spec. Cressonnette de foies de volaille au Xérès, Poissons au beurre blanc, Jambon aux mojettes vendéennes.

X **Le Champart,** 132 r. Cardinet ℰ 42 27 36 78 – 𝙰𝙴 𝚅𝙸𝚂𝙰   C 10
  closed August, February Holidays, Saturday lunch and Sunday – **M** 130 b.i. and a la carte
  150/230.

X **L'Oeuf à la Neige,** 16 r. Salneuve ℰ 47 63 45 43 – 𝙰𝙴 ⓞ 𝙴 𝚅𝙸𝚂𝙰   D 10
  closed 1 to 25 August, 25 December-1 January, Saturday lunch and Sunday – **M** 120 and a
  la carte 125/300.

X **Bistrot de l'Étoile,** 13 r. Troyon ℰ 42 67 25 95 – 𝙴 𝚅𝙸𝚂𝙰. ⚘   E 8
  closed Saturday lunch and Sunday – **M** a la carte 160/200.

Montmartre, La Villette,
Belleville.

18th, 19th and 20th arrondissements.
  18th : ✉ 75018
  19th : ✉ 75019
  20th : ✉ 75020

🏨🏨🏨 **Terrass'H.** Ⓜ, 12 r. J. de Maistre (18th) ℰ 46 06 72 85, Telex 280830, Fax 42 52 29 11 – 🛗
  ▤ rest 📺 ☎ – 🔬 30. 𝙰𝙴 ⓞ 𝙴 𝚅𝙸𝚂𝙰   C 13
  Le Guerlande *(closed 1 to 28 August)* **M** a la carte 240/365 – **L'Albaron M** a la carte 130/250
  ⅄ – ⌘ 60 – **88 rm** 760/990, 13 apartments 1260 – ½ P 615/685.

🏨🏨 **Mercure Paris Montmartre** Ⓜ without rest, 1 r. Caulaincourt (18th) ℰ 42 94 17 17, Telex
  640605, Fax 42 93 66 14 – 🛗 📺 ☎ ⅄ – 🔬 120. 𝙰𝙴 ⓞ 𝙴 𝚅𝙸𝚂𝙰   D 12
  ⌘ 60 – **308 rm** 790/840.

🏨 **Palma** Ⓜ without rest, 77 av. Gambetta (20th) ℰ 46 36 13 65, Telex 216056, Fax 46 36 03 27
  – 🛗 📺 ☎. 𝙰𝙴 𝙴 𝚅𝙸𝚂𝙰. ⚘   G 21
  ⌘ 25 – **32 rm** 300/350.

🏨 **Belgrand** Ⓜ without rest, 60 r. Belgrand (20th) ℰ 43 61 28 38, Telex 233620 – 🛗 📺 ☎. 𝙰𝙴
  ⓞ 𝙴 𝚅𝙸𝚂𝙰   G 22
  ⌘ 30 – **27 rm** 350/390.

🏨 **Regyn's Montmartre** without rest, 18 pl. Abbesses (18th) ℰ 42 54 45 21 – 🛗 📺 ☎. 𝙴
  𝚅𝙸𝚂𝙰   D 13
  ⌘ 30 – **22 rm** 310/380.

🏨 **Résidence Montmartre** without rest, 10 r. Burq (18th) ℰ 46 06 51 91, Telex 282779, Fax
  42 52 82 59 – 🛗 📺 ☎. 𝙰𝙴 ⓞ 𝙴 𝚅𝙸𝚂𝙰   D 13
  ⌘ 45 – **50 rm** 450/590.

🏨 **Super H.** without rest, 208 r. Pyrénées (20th) ℰ 46 36 97 48, Telex 215588, Fax 46 36 26 10
  – 🛗 📺 ☎. 𝙰𝙴 ⓞ 𝙴 𝚅𝙸𝚂𝙰   G 21
  closed August – ⌘ 26 – **28 rm** 245/410.

🏛 **Roma Sacré Coeur** Ⓜ without rest, 101 r. Caulaincourt (18th) ℘ 42 62 02 02, Telex
643492, Fax 42 54 34 92 — 🔄 📺 ☎ 🅰🅴 ⓞ 🖪 𝘝𝘪𝘴𝘢 C 14
⛢ 30 – **57 rm** 370/380.

🏛 **Eden H.** without rest, 90 r. Ordener (18th) ℘ 42 64 61 63, Telex 290504, Fax 42 64 11 43 — 🔄
📺 ☎ 🅰🅴 ⓞ 🖪 𝘝𝘪𝘴𝘢 ✆
⛢ 25 – **35 rm** 320/350. B 14

🏛 **Pyrénées Gambetta** without rest, 12 av. Père Lachaise (20th) ℘ 47 97 76 57, Telex 213533
— 🔄 📺 ☎ 🅰🅴 𝘝𝘪𝘴𝘢 H 21
⛢ 26 – **32 rm** 144/350.

🏛 **H. Le Laumière** without rest, 4 r. Petit (19th) ℘ 42 06 10 77, Telex 212688, Fax 42 06 72 50
— 🔄 📺 ☎ 🖪 𝘝𝘪𝘴𝘢 D 19
⛢ 27 – **54 rm** 195/330.

🏛 **Prima-Lepic** without rest, 29 r. Lepic (18th) ℘ 46 06 44 64, Telex 281162, Fax 46 06 66 11 —
🔄 📺 ☎ 🖪 𝘝𝘪𝘴𝘢 ✆ D 13
⛢ 32 – **38 rm** 260/500.

🏛 **Capucines Montmartre** without rest, 5 r. A.-Bruant (18th) ℘ 42 52 89 80, Telex 281648,
Fax 42 52 29 57 — 🔄 📺 ☎ 🅰🅴 ⓞ 🖪 𝘝𝘪𝘴𝘢 D 13
⛢ 30 – **29 rm** 270/350.

XXX ⊗ **Beauvilliers** (Carlier), 52 r. Lamarck (18th) ℘ 42 54 54 42, Fax 42 62 70 30, 🌺, « 1900
decor, terrace » — 🅰🅴 🖪 𝘝𝘪𝘴𝘢 ✆ C 14
closed 1 to 16 September, Monday lunch and Sunday — **M** 175 b.i. and a la carte 380/500
Spec. Ris de veau en aspic, Turbot au jus de jarret et christophines, Suprême de pintade en peau d'épices aux
moules.

XXX **Pavillon Puebla,** Parc Buttes-Chaumont, entrée : av. Bolivar, r. Botzaris (19th) ℘ 42 08
92 62, Fax 42 39 83 16, 🌺, « Pleasant situation in the park » — 🖪 𝘝𝘪𝘴𝘢 E 19
closed August, February, Sunday and Monday — **M** 230 and a la carte 290/410.

XXX ⊗ **Cochon d'Or,** 192 av. J.-Jaurès (19th) ℘ 42 45 46 46, Fax 42 40 43 90 — ▤ 🅰🅴 ⓞ 🖪 𝘝𝘪𝘴𝘢
M 230 and a la carte 220/490 C 20
Spec. Salade de tête de veau, Filets de sole "Yvonne Ayral", Grillade de boeuf "Cochon d'Or".

XXX **Charlot 1ᵉʳ "Merveilles des Mers",** 128bis bd Clichy (18th) ℘ 45 22 47 08, Fax
44 70 07 50, Seafood — 🅰🅴 ⓞ 🖪 𝘝𝘪𝘴𝘢 D 12
closed 15 June-31 July — **M** 200 (lunch) and a la carte 260/400.

XX **Le Clodenis,** 57 r. Caulaincourt (18th) ℘ 46 06 20 26 — 🖪 𝘝𝘪𝘴𝘢 ✆ C 13
closed Sunday (except lunch June-November) and Monday — **M** 180 (lunch) and a la carte
270/430.

XX **Deux Taureaux,** 206 av. J.-Jaurès (19th) ℘ 42 02 12 40 — 🅰🅴 ⓞ 🖪 𝘝𝘪𝘴𝘢 C 21
closed Saturday and Sunday — **M** a la carte 150/290.

XX **Au Clair de la Lune,** 9 r. Poulbot (18th) ℘ 42 58 97 03 — 🅰🅴 ⓞ 𝘝𝘪𝘴𝘢 D 14
closed Monday lunch and Sunday — **M** 195 and a la carte 225/370.

XX **Grandgousier,** 17 av. Rachel (18th) ℘ 43 87 66 12 — 🅰🅴 ⓞ 🖪 𝘝𝘪𝘴𝘢 D 12
closed 4 to 25 August, Saturday lunch, Sunday and Bank Holidays — **M** 145 and a la carte
205/270.

XX **La Chaumière,** 46 av. Secrétan (19th) ℘ 42 06 54 69 — 🅰🅴 ⓞ 🖪 𝘝𝘪𝘴𝘢 E 18
closed 5 to 18 August — **M** 133 b.i. and a la carte 180/320.

XX **Boeuf Couronné,** 188 av. J.-Jaurès (19th) ℘ 42 39 44 44 — 🅰🅴 ⓞ 🖪 𝘝𝘪𝘴𝘢 ⅄ C 20
closed Sunday — **M** a la carte 205/340 ⅄.

XX **Les Chants du Piano,** 10 r. Lambert (18th) ℘ 42 62 02 14, Fax 42 54 98 52 — 🅰🅴 ⓞ 🖪 𝘝𝘪𝘴𝘢
closed 26 to 31 August, Sunday dinner and Monday lunch — **M** 139/219. C 14

XX **Poulbot Gourmet,** 39 r. Lamarck (18th) ℘ 46 06 86 00 — 𝘝𝘪𝘴𝘢 C 14
closed Sunday — **M** a la carte 200/290.

X **Cottage Marcadet,** 160 r. Marcadet (18th) ℘ 42 57 71 22 — 🖪 𝘝𝘪𝘴𝘢 C 13
closed 30 April-15 May and January — **M** 185 b.i. and a la carte 210/300.

X **Marie-Louise,** 52 r. Championnet (18th) ℘ 46 06 86 55 — ⓞ 🖪 𝘝𝘪𝘴𝘢 B 15
closed late July-early September, Spring Holidays, Sunday, Monday and Bank Holidays — **M**
100 and a la carte 115/220.

X **Le Sancerre,** 13 av. Corentin Cariou (19th) ℘ 40 36 80 44 — 🅰🅴 ⓞ 🖪 𝘝𝘪𝘴𝘢 B 19
closed Saturday and Sunday — **M** a la carte 180/250.

X **Aucune Idée,** 2 pl. St-Blaise (20th) ℘ 40 09 70 67 — 𝘝𝘪𝘴𝘢 H 22
closed 1 to 21 August, Sunday dinner and Monday — **M** 95/195 ⅄.

Environs

K 11 : These reference letters and numbers correspond to the squares on the **Michelin plans of Parisian suburbs** nos **18**, **20**, **22**, **24**.

La Défense 92 Hauts-de-Seine **101** ⑭, **18** – ⊠ **92400** Courbevoie.
See : Quarter** : perspective* from the parvis.
Paris 9,5.

🏨🏨 **Sofitel Paris CNIT** Ⓜ ⤶, 2 pl. Défense ✆ 46 92 10 10, Telex 613782, Fax 46 92 10 50 – 📶 ⊱ rm 🗏 📺 ☎ & ⟚. 🅰🄴 ⓞ 🄴 𝘝𝘐𝘚𝘈   U-V 19
Les Communautés **M** a la carte 250/370 – � 85 – **141 rm** 1200/1600, 6 apartments 2350/3000.

🏨🏨 **Sofitel Paris La Défense** Ⓜ ⤶, 34 cours Michelet, par bd circulaire sortie Défense 4 ✆ 47 76 44 43, Telex 612189, Fax 47 73 72 74, 🛱 – 📶 ⊱ rm 🗏 📺 ☎ & ⟚ – 🔼 50. 🅰🄴 ⓞ 🄴 𝘝𝘐𝘚𝘈   V 20
Les 2 Arcs **M** 315 (lunch) except Sunday and a la carte 190/330 – ⊥ 85 – **149 rm** 1100.

🏨🏨 **Novotel Paris La Défense** Ⓜ, 2 bd Neuilly ✆ 47 78 16 68, Telex 630288, Fax 47 78 84 71, ≼ – 📶 🗏 📺 ☎ & – 🔼 25 - 150. 🅰🄴 ⓞ 🄴 𝘝𝘐𝘚𝘈   V 21
M a la carte approx. 150 🍷 – ⊥ 52 – **278 rm** 680/720.

🏨 **Ibis Paris La Défense** 🅰🄴, 4 bd Neuilly ✆ 47 78 15 60, Telex 611555, Fax 47 78 94 16 – 📶 🗏 📺 ☎ & – 🔼 120. 🄴 𝘝𝘐𝘚𝘈   V 21
M 75/95 🍷 – ⊥ 32 – **284 rm** 415/435.

🍴🍴🍴🍴 **Fouquet's Europe,** au CNIT, 2 pl. Défense, (5th floor) ✆ 46 92 28 04, Fax 46 92 28 16 – 🗏 🅰🄴 ⓞ 🄴 𝘝𝘐𝘚𝘈   V 19
closed Saturday dinner and Sunday – **M** a la carte 240/405 🍷.

Enghien-les-Bains 95880 Val-d'Oise **101** ⑤, **18** – pop. 9 739 h. alt. 50 – Spa (closed January) – Casino .
See : Lake* – Deuil-la-Barre : historiated capitals* in Notre-Dame Church, NE : 2 km.
🏌 of Domont Montmorency ✆ 39 91 07 50, N : 8 km.
🅸 Office de Tourisme 2 bd Cotte ✆ 34 12 41 15.
Paris 16.

🏨🏨 **Grand Hôtel** ⤶, 85 r. Gén.-de-Gaulle ✆ 34 12 80 00, Telex 607842, Fax 34 12 73 81, 🛱, « Attractive flowered garden » – 📶 🗏 📺 ☎ ⓟ – 🔼 35. 🅰🄴 ⓞ 🄴 𝘝𝘐𝘚𝘈. ❀ rest   K 25
M 160/220 – ⊥ 65 – **46 rm** 800/1100, 3 apartments 1300 – ½ P 580/670.

🍴🍴🍴🍴 ⊛⊛ **Duc d'Enghien,** au Casino ✆ 34 12 90 00, ≼ lake, 🛱 – 🗏. 🅰🄴 ⓞ 🄴 𝘝𝘐𝘚𝘈   J 25
closed August, 1 to 10 January, Sunday dinner and Monday – **M** 325 b.i. (lunch) and a la carte 460/610
Spec. Langoustines poêlées à la vanille et menthe fraîche, Bar poêlé sur sa croûte de pommes de terre, Moelleux au chocolat.

🍴🍴 **Aub. Landaise,** 32 bd d'Ormesson ✆ 34 12 78 36 – 🅰🄴 🄴 𝘝𝘐𝘚𝘈   J 26
closed August, Sunday dinner and Wednesday – **M** a la carte 170/240.

Maisons-Laffitte 78600 Yvelines **101** ⑬, **18** – pop. 22 892 h. alt. 40.
See : Château*.
Paris 21.

🍴🍴🍴 ⊛⊛ **Le Tastevin** (Blanchet), 9 av. Eglé ✆ 39 62 11 67, Fax 39 62 73 09, 🛱 – 🗏 🅰🄴 ⓞ 🄴 𝘝𝘐𝘚𝘈
closed 12 August-4 September, February Holidays, Monday dinner and Tuesday – **M** a la carte 440/440   M 11
Spec. Poêlée de queues de langoustines et salade d'herbes fraîches, Le meilleur du canard aux trois façons, Assiette du Maître chocolatier.

🍴🍴🍴 ⊛⊛ **Vieille Fontaine** (Clerc), 8 av. Gretry ✆ 39 62 01 78, 🛱, « Garden » – **M** 220 and a la carte 360/520   L 12
closed August, Sunday and Monday –
Spec. Saumon à la "Youpof" et rillettes d'olives, Terrine tiède de pieds de mouton aux champignons, Tian de Saint-Jacques (October-April).

🍴🍴 **Le Laffitte,** 5 av. St-Germain ✆ 39 62 01 53 – 🅰🄴 𝘝𝘐𝘚𝘈   M 11
closed August, Sunday dinner, Tuesday dinner and Wednesday – **M** a la carte 190/300.

Marne-la-Vallée 77206 S.-et-M. **101** ⑲
Paris 26.

SE : 6 km by interchange of Lagny A 4 – ⊠ **77090** Collégien :

🏨🏨 **Novotel** Ⓜ, ✆ 60 05 91 15, Telex 691990, Fax 64 80 48 37, 🛱, ⤳, 🛱 – 📶 🗏 ☎ & ⓟ – 🔼 130. 🅰🄴 ⓞ 🄴 𝘝𝘐𝘚𝘈
M a la carte approx. 150 🍷 – ⊥ 45 – **200 rm** 410/450.

Neuilly-sur-Seine 92200 Hauts-de-Seine 101 ⑮, 18 – pop. 64 450 h. alt. 36.

See : Bois de Boulogne★★ : Jardin d'acclimatation★, (Children's Amusement Park, Miniature Railway and Zoo in the Bois de Boulogne), Bagatelle★ (Park and – Garden) National Museum of Popular Art and Traditions★★ – Palais des Congrès★ : main conference hall★★, ≤★ from hotel Concorde-Lafayette.

Paris 8.

L'Hôtel International de Paris M without rest, 58 bd V.-Hugo ✆ 47 58 11 00, Telex 610971, Fax 47 58 75 52, – 🛗 ▤ TV ☎ P – 🏛 120. AE ⓓ E VISA V 23
☕ 70 – **318 rm** 880/1250, 3 apartments.

Paris Neuilly M without rest, 1 av. Madrid ✆ 47 47 14 67, Telex 613170, Fax 47 47 97 42 – 🛗 ▤ TV ☎. AE ⓓ E VISA W 21
☕ 48 – **74 rm** 680/740, 6 apartments 925.

Parc Neuilly without rest, 4 bd Parc ✆ 46 24 32 62, Telex 613689, Fax 46 40 77 31 – 🛗 TV ☎. E VISA U 22
☕ 34 – **71 rm** 265/420.

XXX ✿ **Jacqueline Fénix,** 42 av. Ch. de Gaulle ✆ 46 24 42 61 – ▤. AE E VISA W 23
closed August, 25 to 31 December, Saturday and Sunday – **M** (booking essential) a la carte 320/420
Spec. Vinaigrette de cresson et langoustines aux nouilles "grillotées", Dorade rose en marinade d'épices douces, Mosaïque de chocolat blanc.

XXX ✿ **Truffe Noire** (Jacquet), 2 pl. Parmentier ✆ 46 24 94 14, Fax 46 37 27 02 – VISA. ✱ W 23
closed 12 August-1 September, Saturday and Sunday – **M** 220 and a la carte 230/330
Spec. Foie gras de canard au Layon (October-April), Gratin de Saint-Jacques aux coquillages (October-April), Pavé de boeuf à la moelle.

XXX **Focly,** 79 av. Ch. de Gaulle ✆ 46 24 43 36, Chinese rest. – ▤. AE E VISA V 21
closed 12 to 25 August – **M** 100 (lunch) and a la carte 140/240.

XX **Jarrasse,** 4 av. Madrid ✆ 46 24 07 56 – AE ⓓ E VISA W 21
closed 5 July-3 September, Sunday dinner and Monday – **M** a la carte 260/445.

XX **San Valero,** 209 ter av. Ch. de Gaulle ✆ 46 24 07 87, Spanish rest. – AE ⓓ E VISA ✱ V 21
closed 23 December-3 January, Saturday lunch, Sunday and Bank Holidays – **M** 150 (except Saturday)/190.

X **Le Bistrot d'à Côté Neuilly,** 4 r. Boutard ✆ 47 45 34 55 – AE E VISA W 21
closed 12 to 18 August, Saturday lunch and Sunday – **M** a la carte 160/250.

X **La Catounière,** 4 r. Poissonniers ✆ 47 47 14 33 – ▤. VISA W 22
closed 28 April-12 May, August, Saturday lunch and Sunday – **M** 164 b.i..

Orly (Paris Airports) 94396 Val-de-Marne 101 ㉖, 24 – pop. 23 886 h. alt. 89.

✈ ✆ 49 75 15 15.

Paris 16.

Hilton Orly M, près aérogare ✆ 46 87 33 88, Telex 265971, Fax 49 78 06 75, ≤ – 🛗 ▤ TV ☎ ♿ P – 🏛 300. AE ⓓ E VISA AR 31
Le Café du Marché **M** a la carte 200/290 – ☕ 75 – **366 rm** 780/1500.

Altéa Paris Orly M, rte Fontainebleau - Z.I. Nord ✆ 46 87 23 37, Telex 204345, Fax 46 87 71 92 – 🛗 ▤ TV ☎ ♿ P – 🏛 30. AE ⓓ E VISA
M 125 b.i./155 b.i. 🧒 – ☕ 50 – **194 rm** 530/690.

Orly Airport South :

XX Le Grillardin, ✆ 46 87 24 25, Telex 204233, Fax 49 75 36 69, ≤ – ▤
M (lunch only).

Orly Airport West :

XXX **Maxim's,** ✉ 94546 ✆ 46 87 16 16, Fax 46 87 05 39, ≤ – ▤. AE ⓓ E VISA
M (lunch only) 300 and a la carte 310/440 - **Grill M** 240 b.i. and a la carte 220/390.

XX **Jardin d'Orly,** ✉ 94546 ✆ 46 87 16 16, Fax 46 87 05 39, ≤ – ▤. AE ⓓ VISA
closed August, Saturday and Sunday – **M** 180.

X **La Galerie,** ✉ 94546 ✆ 46 87 16 16, Fax 46 87 05 39, ≤ – ▤. AE ⓓ VISA
M a la carte 140/210.

When driving through towns use the plans in the ***Michelin Red Guide.*** *Features indicated include: throughroutes and by-passes, traffic junctions and major squares, new streets, car parks, pedestrian streets... All this information is revised annually.*

Roissy-en-France (Paris Airports) 95700 Val-d'Oise **101** ⑧ – pop. 2 512 h. alt. 85.
⤴ ✆ 48 62 22 80.
Paris 25.

at Roissy-Town :

🏨 **Altéa**, allée Verger ✆ 34 29 40 00, Telex 605205, Fax 34 29 00 18 – |≱| ⇆ rm 🖃 🕾 & 🅿 –
🏂 160. 🖭 ⓪ 🗲 *VISA*
Hermès *(closed 27/7-1/9, 25/12-4/1, Saturday, Sunday and Bank Holidays)* **M** 190 b.i./310 –
Brasserie M 80/155 – 🖵 58 – **198 rm** 450/890, 4 apartments 1120.

🏨 **Holiday Inn** 🖩, 1 allée Verger ✆ 34 29 30 00, Telex 605143, Fax 34 29 90 52 – |≱| ⇆ rm 🖃
🕥 🕾 🅿 – 🏂 250. 🖭 ⓪ 🗲 *VISA*
M 110/160 b.i. – 🖵 70 – **243 rm** 740/950.

🏩 **Ibis** 🖩, av. Raperie ✆ 34 29 34 34, Telex 699083, Fax 34 29 34 19 – |≱| 🖃 🕥 🕾 & 🅿 –
🏂 25 - 80. 🖭 🗲 *VISA*
M 90 ⅛ – 🖵 32 – **200 rm** 415/435.

in the airport area :

🏰 **Sofitel** 🖩, ✆ 48 62 23 23, Telex 230166, Fax 48 62 78 49, 🔲, ℀ – |≱| ⇆ rm 🖃 🕥 🕾 & 🅿
– 🏂 25 - 500. 🖭 ⓪ 🗲 *VISA*
Les Valois panoramic rest. *(closed lunch Saturday, Sunday, Bank Holidays)(dinner only in
August)* **M** 260/400 – **Le Jardin** (brasserie) (ground floor) **M** 139 – 🖵 65 – **344 rm** 720/820,
8 apartments 1300.

🏨 **Novotel** 🖩, ✆ 48 62 00 53, Telex 232397, Fax 48 62 00 11 – |≱| 🖃 🕥 🕾 & 🅿 – 🏂 70. 🖭
⓪ 🗲 *VISA*
M a la carte approx. 170 ⅛ – 🖵 50 – **199 rm** 620/670.

in the airport nr. 1 :

🕷🕷🕷🕷 **Maxim's**, ✆ 48 62 16 16, Telex 240270, Fax 48 62 45 96 – 🖃. 🖭 ⓪ 🗲 *VISA*
M (lunch only) 250 and a la carte 300/450.

🕷🕷 **Grill Maxim's**, ✆ 48 62 16 16, Telex 236356, Fax 48 62 45 96 – 🖭 ⓪ 🗲 *VISA*
M 220 b.i. and a la carte 180/300.

Rungis 94150 Val-de-Marne **101** ㉖, **24** – pop. 2 650 h. alt. 80.
Paris 13.

at Pondorly : Access : from Paris, Highway A 6 and take Orly Airport exit from outside of
Paris, A 6 and Rungis exit :

🏨 **Pullman Orly** 🖩, 20 av. Ch. Lindbergh ✉ 94656 ✆ 46 87 36 36, Telex 260738, Fax 46 87 08 48,
🏤, 🔟 – |≱| 🖃 🕥 🕾 & 🖚 🅿 – 🏂 25 - 250. 🖭 ⓪ 🗲 *VISA*   AN 30
La Rungisserie M 180 b.i./200 ⅛ – 🖵 75 – **204 rm** 600/915.

🏨 **Holiday Inn** 🖩, 4 av. Ch. Lindbergh ✉ 94656 ✆ 46 87 26 66, Telex 265803, Fax 45 60 91 25,
℀ – |≱| 🖃 🕥 🕾 & 🅿 – 🏂 50 - 200. 🖭 ⓪ 🗲 *VISA*   AR 31
M 115/165 – 🖵 70 – **168 rm** 795/995.

🏩 **Ibis** 🖩, 1 r. Mondétour ✉ 94656 ✆ 46 87 22 45, Telex 261173, Fax 46 87 84 72, 🏤 – |≱| 🕥
🕾 & 🅿 – 🏂 80. 🗲 *VISA*, ℀ rest   AM 53
M 90 ⅛ – 🖵 29 – **119 rm** 300.

St-Germain-en-Laye ⟨🚆⟩ 78100 Yvelines **101** ⑫, **18** – pop. 40 829 h. alt. 78.

See : Terrace⋆⋆ BY – English Garden⋆ BY – Castel⋆ BZ : Museum of National Antiqui-
ties⋆⋆ – Priory Museum⋆ AZ.

🖥🖥 ✆ 34 51 75 90 by ④ : 3 km ; 🖥🖥🖥 of Fourqueux ✆ 34 51 41 47 by r. de Mareil AZ.
🛈 Office Municipal de Tourisme 38 r. au Pain ✆ 34 51 05 12.
Paris 30 ③.

Plan opposite

🏰 **Pavillon Henri IV** 🦢, 21 r. Thiers ✆ 34 51 62 62, Telex 695822, Fax 39 73 93 73, ≤ Paris
and the River Seine, 🏤, 🐎 – |≱| 🕥 🕾 🅿 – 🏂 200. 🖭 ⓪ 🗲 *VISA*   BZ **s**
M 240 (lunch) and a la carte 300/450 – 🖵 50 – **39 rm** 500/1300, 3 apartments 1900 –
½ P 720/870.

to the NW by ① : 2,5 km on N 284 and rte des Mares – ✉ 78100 St-Germain-en-Laye :

🏨 **La Forestière** 🖩 🦢, 1 av. Prés.-Kennedy ✆ 39 73 36 60, Telex 696055, Fax 39 73 73 88, 🐎
– |≱| 🕾 🅿 – 🏂 30. 🗲 *VISA*
M see **Cazaudehore** below – 🖵 55 – **24 rm** 605/720, 6 apartments 820/895.

🕷🕷🕷 **Cazaudehore**, 1 av. Prés.-Kennedy ✆ 34 51 93 80, Fax 39 73 73 88, 🏤, « Flowered garden
in woods » – 🅿. 🗲 *VISA*
closed Monday except Bank Holidays – **M** a la carte 250/470.

ST-GERMAIN EN-LAYE

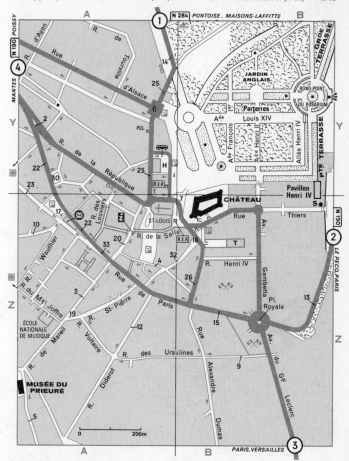

*The hotels have entered into certain undertakings
towards the readers of this Guide.
Make it plain that you have the most recent Guide.*

Versailles ℗ 78000 Yvelines 101 ②. 22 – pop. 95 240 h. alt. 132.

See : Castel★★★ Y – Gardens★★★ (fountain display★★★ (grandes eaux) and illuminated night performances★★★ (fêtes de nuit) in summer) – Ecuries Royales★ Y – The Trianons★★ – Lambinet Museum★ Y **M.**

🏌 Racing Club France (private) ℰ 39 50 59 41 by ③ : 2,5 km.

🛈 Office de Tourisme 7 r. Réservoirs ℰ 39 50 36 22.

Paris 22 ①.

VERSAILLES

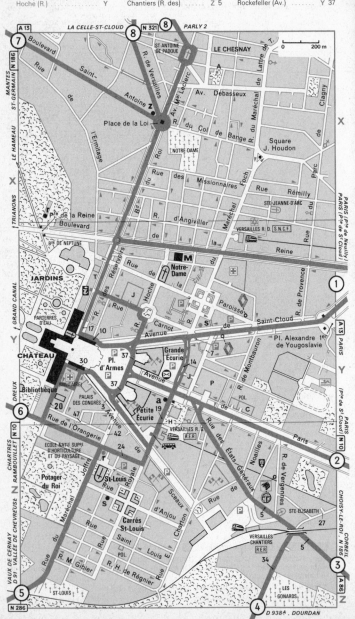

🏨🏨 **Trianon Palace** ⟪ (Due to refurbishment closed until the end of June), 1 bd Reine ℰ 30 84 38 00, Telex 698863, Fax 39 49 00 77, ⛲, park, « Pool and fitness centre », ✖ – 📱 📺 ☎ 🅿 – 🔏 80. 🆎 ⓞ 🄴 𝑉𝐼𝑆𝐴. ✖ rest   X r
M *(closed Sunday)* a la carte 410/570 – ⌲ 100 – **90 rm** 1500/2650, 33 apartments.

🏨🏨 **Pullman Place d'Armes** Ⓜ, 2 av. Paris ℰ 39 53 30 31, Telex 697042, Fax 39 53 87 20 – 📱
▤ 📺 ☎ ⅙ ⟷ – 🔏 150. 🆎 ⓞ 🄴 𝑉𝐼𝑆𝐴   Y a
M 185/320 – ⌲ 70 – **146 rm** 620/880, 6 apartments 1200.

🏨 **Novotel** Ⓜ, 4 bd St-Antoine at Le Chesnay ⌧ 78150 ℰ 39 54 96 96, Telex 689624, Fax
39 54 94 40 – 📱 ▤ 📺 ☎ ⅙ ⟷ – 🔏 25 - 150. 🆎 ⓞ 🄴 𝑉𝐼𝑆𝐴   X z
M a la carte approx. 150 ⅃ – ⌲ 47 – **105 rm** 490/520.

🏨 **Mercure** Ⓜ without rest, r. Marly-le-Roi at Le Chesnay, in front of Commercial Centre
Parly II ⌧ 78150 ℰ 39 55 11 41, Telex 695205, Fax 39 55 06 22 – 📱 ⟷ ▤ 📺 ☎ 🅿. 🆎 ⓞ 🄴
𝑉𝐼𝑆𝐴
⌲ 48 – **78 rm** 530.

🏠 **Résidence du Berry** Ⓜ without rest, 14 r. Anjou ℰ 39 49 07 07, Telex 689058, Fax
39 50 59 40 – 📱 📺 ☎. 🆎 ⓞ 🄴 𝑉𝐼𝑆𝐴   Z s
⌲ 35 – **38 rm** 340/410.

🏠 **Urbis** Ⓜ without rest, av. Dutartre at Le Chesnay, Commercial Centre Parly II ⌧ 78150
ℰ 39 63 37 93, Telex 689188, Fax 39 55 18 66 – 📱 ⟷ 📺 ☎ ⅙. 🄴 𝑉𝐼𝑆𝐴
⌲ 29 – **72 rm** 325/340.

XXX **Rescatore,** 27 av. St-Cloud ℰ 39 50 23 60, Seafood – ▤. 🆎 🄴 𝑉𝐼𝑆𝐴   Y s
closed Saturday lunch and Sunday – **M** 250/375.

XX **Potager du Roy,** 1 r. Mar.-Joffre ℰ 39 50 35 34, Fax 39 51 15 45 – ▤. 𝑉𝐼𝑆𝐴   Z r
closed Sunday and Monday – **M** 115/160.

and beyond...

Joigny 89300 Yonne 🗺 ④ – pop. 10 488 h. alt. 101.

See : Vierge au Sourire★ in St-Thibault's Church – Côte St-Jacques ≼★ 1,5 km by D 20.

🖪 Office de Tourisme quai H.-Ragobert ℰ 86 62 11 05.

Paris 146 – Auxerre 27 – Gien 74 – Montargis 59 – Sens 30 – Troyes 76.

🏨 ❀❀❀ **A la Côte St-Jacques** (Lorain) 🅜 ॐ, 14 fg Paris ℰ 86 62 09 70, Telex 801458, Fax 86 91 49 70, ≼, « Tasteful decor », 🔲, 🚗 – 🛊 🗐 rm 🆃🆅 ☎ & ⇔ 🅿 – 🔬 40. 🆀🆂 ① 🅴 𝖵𝖨𝖲𝖠
closed 6 January-6 February – **M** (Sunday booking essential) 300 (lunch only)/560 and a la
carte – 🖙 80 – **25 rm** 600/1700, 4 apartments 2450
Spec. Huîtres en petite terrine océane, Bar légèrement fumé à la crème de caviar, Abricots rôtis en couronne
sablée. **Wines** Chablis, Irancy.

Pontoise ⟨⟨⟩⟩ 95300 Val d'Oise 🗺 ⑤ – pop. 29 411 h. alt. 27.

🖪 Office de Tourisme 6 pl. Petit-Martroy ℰ (1) 30 38 24 45.

Paris 35 – Beauvais 55 – Dieppe 135 – Mantes-la-Jolie 39 – Rouen 91.

at Cormeilles-en-Vexin NW by D 915 – 🖂 95830 :

XXX ❀❀ **Relais Ste-Jeanne** (Cagna), on D 915 ℰ (1) 34 66 61 56, 🌉, « Garden » – 🅿. 🆀🆂 ①
𝖵𝖨𝖲𝖠
closed August, 20 to 27 December, February Holidays, Monday, lunch Sunday and Tuesday
– **M** 250/480 and a la carte
Spec. Coquilles St-Jacques à la crème d'ail et olives noires (Oct.-May), Pintade truffée aux tagliatelles de céleri,
Fondant au praliné "Mathilde de France".

Rheims ⟨⟨⟩⟩ 51100 Marne 🗺 ⑥ ⑯ – pop. 181 985 h. alt. 83.

See : Cathedral★★★ : tapestries★★ – St-Remi Basilica★★ : interior★★★ – Palais du Tau★★
– Champagne cellars★ – Place Royale★ – Porte Mars★ – Hôtel de la Salle★ – Foujita
Chapel★ – Library★ of Ancient College des Jésuites – St-Remi Museum★★ – Hôtel
le Vergeur Museum★ – St-Denis Museum★ – Historical centre of the French motor
industry★ – Envir. : Fort de la Pompelle : German helmets★ 9 km to the SE by N 44.

🏌 Rheims-Champagne ℰ 26 03 60 14 at Gueux ; to the NW by N 31-E 46 : 9,5 km.

🚗 ℰ 26 88 50 50.

🖪 Office de Tourisme and Accueil de France (Informations facilities and hotel reservations - not more
than 5 days in advance) 1 r. Jadart ℰ 26 88 37 89, Telex 830631 and 2 r. Guillaume-de-Machault
ℰ 26 47 25 69, Telex 840890 – - A.C. 7 bd Lundy ℰ 26 47 34 76.

Paris 143 – Bruxelles 214 – Châlons-sur-Marne 45 – Lille 199 – Luxembourg 232.

🏨 ❀❀❀ **Boyer "Les Crayères"** 🅜 ॐ, 64 bd Vasnier ℰ 26 82 80 80, Telex 830959, Fax
26 82 65 52, ≼, 🌉, « Elegant mansion in park », 💥 – 🛊 🗐 🆃🆅 ☎ 🅿 – 🔬 30. 🆀🆂 ① 🅴 𝖵𝖨𝖲𝖠
closed 23 December-13 January – **M** *(closed Tuesday lunch and Monday)* (booking essential)
a la carte 380/550 – 🖙 80 – **16 rm** 980/1590, 3 apartments 1790
Spec. Pastilla de pieds de porc aux truffes, Blanc de turbot en croustillant et purée d'artichaut truffée, Viennoise
de ris de veau au paprika. **Wines** Champagne.

Saulieu 21210 Côte-d'Or 🗺 ⑰ – pop. 3 183 h. alt. 514.

Paris 250 – Autun 41 – Avallon 39 – Beaune 77 – Clamecy 77 – Dijon 73.

🏨 ❀❀❀ **Côte d'Or** (Loiseau) 🅜 ॐ, 2 r. Argentine ℰ 80 64 07 66, Telex 350778, Fax 80 64 08 92,
« Tasteful inn », 🚗 – ᐊ᐀ rest 🆃🆅 ☎ 🅿. 🆀🆂 ① 🅴 𝖵𝖨𝖲𝖠
M 360/620 and a la carte – 🖙 80 – **12 rm** 260/600, 10 apartments
Spec. Grenouilles à la purée d'ail et jus de persil, Sandre rôti au vin rouge, Blanc de volaille et foie gras au jus
de truffes. **Wines** Savigny-les-Beaune, Chablis.

Vézelay 89450 Yonne 🗺 ⑮ – pop. 582 h. pilgrimage (22 July).

See : Ste-Madeleine Basilica★★★ : tower ✼★.

Envir. : Site★ of Pierre-Perthuis SE : 6 km.

🖪 Syndicat d'Initiative r. St-Pierre (April-1 November) ℰ 86 33 23 69.

Paris 217 – Auxerre 51 – Avallon 15 – Château-Chinon 60 – Clamecy 23.

at St-Père : SE : 3 km by D 957 – alt. 148 – 🖂 89450 – See : Church of N.-Dame★.

🏨 ❀❀❀ **L'Espérance** (Meneau) 🅜 ॐ, ℰ 86 33 20 45, Telex 800005, Fax 86 33 26 15, ≼, « Country
garden » – 🗐 rest 🆃🆅 ☎ 🅿. 🆀🆂 ① 🅴 𝖵𝖨𝖲𝖠
closed early January-early February – **M** *(closed Wednesday lunch and Tuesday except
Bank Holidays)* (booking essential) 300 (lunch)/550 and a la carte – 🖙 90 – **18 rm** 600/1200,
4 apartments
Spec. Soupe de raie aux herbes, Homard rissolé aux gousses d'ail, Pastilles d'agneau "Léonel". **Wines** Vézelay,
Chablis.

BORDEAUX P 33000 Gironde 🗺️ ⑨ – pop. 211 197 h. Greater Bordeaux 617 705 alt. 5.

See : Grand Théâtre★★ DX – Cathedral★ and Pey Berland Belfry★ DY **E** – Place de la Bourse★ EX – St-Michel Basilica★ EY **F** – Place du Parlement★ EX **66** – Church of N.-Dame★ DX D – Façade★ of Ste-Croix Church FZ **L** – Fountain★ of the Monument to the Girondins DX R – Great Bell★ (Grosse cloche) DZ **D** – Main Courtyard★ of the Town Hall (Hôtel-de-Ville) DY **H** – Balcony★ of the Cours Xavier Arnozan – Fine Arts Museum★★ (Musée des Beaux Arts) CDY **M1** Decorative Arts★ DY **M2** – The mint★ of Pessac (Etablissement monétaire de Pessac), of Aquitaine★ DY **M5.**

🏌️ Golf Bordelais ℰ 56 28 56 04, to the NW D109 : 4 km ; 🏌️ de Bordeaux Lac ℰ 56 50 92 72, to the N by D 2 : 10 km ; 🏌️🏌️ of Cameyrac ℰ 56 72 96 79, to the NE by N 89 : 18 km ; 🏌️🏌️🏌️ International of Bordeaux-Pessac ℰ 56 36 24 47 to the SW N 150.

✈️ of Bordeaux-Mérignac : Air France ℰ 56 34 32 32 to the W : 11 km – 🚗 ℰ 56 92 50 50.

🚩 Office de Tourisme and Accueil de France, (Information, exchange facilities and hotel reservations - not more than 5 days in advance) 12 cours 30-Juillet ℰ 56 44 28 41, Telex 570362 at the Gare St-Jean ℰ 56 91 64 70 and the airport, Arrivals Hall ℰ 52 34 39 39 – A.C. 8 pl. Quinconces ℰ 56 44 22 92 – Bordeaux wine Exhibition (Maison du vin de Bordeaux), 3 cours 30-Juillet (Information, wine-tasting - closed weekends from 16 Oct. to 14 May) – ℰ 56 00 22 66 DX z.

Paris 579 – Lyon 550 – Nantes 326 – Strasbourg 922 – Toulouse 245.

Plan on next page

🏰 **Burdigala** Ⓜ, 115 r. G. Bonnac ℰ 56 90 16 16, Telex 572981, Fax 56 93 15 06 – 🛗 ▤ 📺 ☎ ⟵ ⟶ – 🔺 100. ☒ ⓓ **E** 𝒱𝒾𝒮𝒜   CX **r**
M 130/320 – ⊑ 60 – **64 rm** 620/880, 7 duplex 1050.

🏰 **Pullman Mériadeck** Ⓜ, 5 r. R. Lateulade ℰ 56 56 43 43, Telex 540565, Fax 56 96 50 59 – 🛗 ▤ 📺 ☎ – 🔺 350. ☒ ⓓ **E** 𝒱𝒾𝒮𝒜. 🍽️ rest   CY **w**
Le Mériadeck **M** 130 b.i./190 b.i. – ⊑ 60 – **194 rm** 480/895.

🏨 **Alliance** Ⓜ, 30 r. de Tauzia ⊠ 33800 ℰ 56 92 21 21, Telex 573848, Fax 56 91 08 06, ☕ – ⊁⟵ rm ▤ 📺 ☎ ⟵ ⟶ – 🔺 80. ☒ **E** 𝒱𝒾𝒮𝒜   FZ **v**
M *(closed Sunday)* 80/120 – ⊑ 45 – **90 rm** 450/500 – ½ P 475.

🏨 **Novotel Mériadeck** Ⓜ, 45 cours Maréchal Juin ℰ 56 51 46 46, Telex 573749, Fax 56 98 25 56, ☕ – 🛗 📺 ☎ ⟵ ⟶ – 🔺 80. ☒ ⓓ **E** 𝒱𝒾𝒮𝒜   CY **m**
M a la carte approx. 120 – ⊑ 48 – **136 rm** 470/520.

🏨 **Normandie** without rest, 7 cours 30-Juillet ℰ 56 52 16 80, Telex 570481, Fax 56 51 68 91 – 🛗 📺 ☎. ☒ ⓓ **E** 𝒱𝒾𝒮𝒜   DX **z**
⊑ 34 – **100 rm** 260/470.

🏨 **Majestic** without rest, 2 r. Condé ℰ 56 52 60 44, Telex 572938, Fax 56 79 26 70 – 🛗 📺 ☎. ☒ ⓓ **E** 𝒱𝒾𝒮𝒜   DX **a**
⊑ 30 – **49 rm** 290/400.

🏨 **Gd H. Français** Ⓜ without rest, 12 r. Temple ℰ 56 48 10 35, Telex 550587, Fax 56 81 76 18 – 🛗 📺 ☎. ☒ ⓓ **E** 𝒱𝒾𝒮𝒜   DX **v**
⊑ 40 – **35 rm** 350/480.

🏨 **Royal St Jean** Ⓜ without rest, 15 r. Ch. Domercq ⊠ 33800 ℰ 56 91 72 16, Telex 570468, Fax 56 91 08 32 – 🛗 📺 ☎ ⚹. ☒ ⓓ **E** 𝒱𝒾𝒮𝒜   FZ **u**
⊑ 40 – **37 rm** 250/410.

🏨 **Ibis Mériadeck** Ⓜ, 35 cours Mar. Juin ℰ 56 90 10 33, Telex 572918, Fax 56 96 33 15 – 🛗 ▤ rm 📺 ☎ ⚹ 🅿 – 🔺 350. **E** 𝒱𝒾𝒮𝒜   CY **m**
M 80/160 ⅃ – ⊑ 320 – **210 rm** 290/350.

🏨 **Royal Médoc** without rest, 3 r. Sèze ℰ 56 81 72 42, Telex 571042, Fax 56 51 74 98 – 🛗 📺 ☎. ☒ ⓓ **E** 𝒱𝒾𝒮𝒜   DX **u**
⊑ 30 – **45 rm** 230/360.

🏨 **Relais Bleus** Ⓜ, 68 r. Tauzia ℰ 56 91 55 50, Telex 651422, Fax 56 91 08 41 – 🛗 📺 ☎ ⚹. ☒ ⓓ **E** 𝒱𝒾𝒮𝒜   FZ **b**
M 68/110 – ⊑ 32 – **89 rm** 260/350 – ½ P 195.

🏨 **Presse** Ⓜ without rest, 6 r. Porte Dijeaux ℰ 56 48 53 88, Telex 573259, Fax 56 01 05 82 – 🛗 📺 ☎. ☒ ⓓ **E** 𝒱𝒾𝒮𝒜   DX **k**
⊑ 28 – **30 rm** 195/330.

XXXX ⊛ **Le Chapon Fin** (Garcia), 5 r. Montesquieu ℰ 56 79 10 10, « Unusual 1900 Rococo decor » – ▤. ☒ ⓓ **E** 𝒱𝒾𝒮𝒜. 🍽️   DX **p**
closed Sunday and Monday – **M** 140/400
Spec. Gaspacho de homard (summer), Lamproie à la bordelaise, Tournedos "1900". Wines Premières Côtes de Bordeaux-Bouliac.

XXX ⊛ **Le Rouzic** (Gautier), 34 Cours du Chapeau Rouge ℰ 56 44 39 11 – ☒ ⓓ **E** 𝒱𝒾𝒮𝒜   DX **b**
closed Saturday lunch and Sunday – **M** 150 (lunch) and a la carte 290/450
Spec. Ravioles d'huîtres au curry, Lamproie à la bordelaise, Côtelettes d'agneau de Pauillac grillées à la tapenade. Wines Graves, Bordeaux Supérieur.

XXX ⊛ **La Chamade** (Carrère), 20 r. Piliers de Tutelle ℰ 56 48 13 74 – ▤. **E** 𝒱𝒾𝒮𝒜   DX **d**
closed Sunday lunch and Saturday 14 July-15 August – **M** 180/450
Spec. Escalope de foie gras de canard poêlée aux lardons de magret séché, Homard breton rôti, Rôti de filets de canette au farci de foie gras.

XXX ⊛ **Jean Ramet**, 7 pl. J. Jaurès ℰ 56 44 12 51 – ▤. **E** 𝒱𝒾𝒮𝒜   EX **u**
closed 29 April-5 May, 5 to 25 August, 29 December-5 January, Saturday and Sunday – **M** a la carte 250/400
Spec. Petite marmite d'écrevisses au Sauternes, Blanquette de veau à l'ancienne, Desserts de "Tante Dolly". Wines Moulis.

To go a long way quickly, use **Michelin Maps** at scale of 1 : 1 000 000.

164

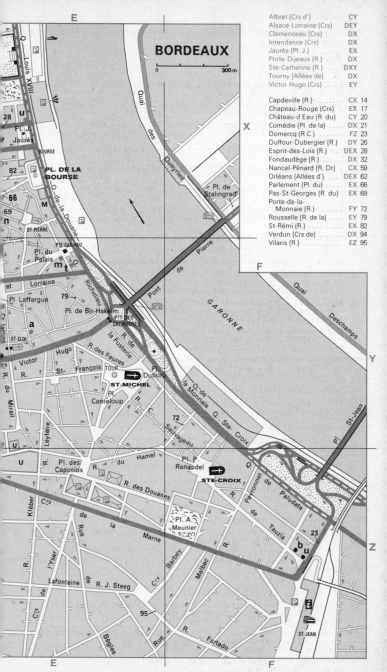

BORDEAUX

0   300 m

*Ensure that you have up to date **Michelin** maps in your car.*

165

XXX ✿ **Pavillon des Boulevards** (Franc), 120 r. Croix de Seguey ✆ 56 81 51 02, 🏞 – ▤. AE ⓓ E VISA
closed 29 April-12 May, 12 to 18 August, Saturday lunch, Sunday and Bank Holidays – **M** 200/320
Spec. Consommé de homard au cumin, Filets de rougets au lard, Chinoiserie de pigeonneau. **Wines** Premières Côtes de Bordeaux, Cadillac.

XXX **Le Cailhau,** 3 pl. Palais ✆ 56 81 79 91 – ▤. AE ⓓ E VISA. ✻ EY **m**
closed 29 July-19 August, Saturday lunch and Sunday – **M** 160/350.

XXX **Villa Carnot,** 335 bd Wilson ✉ 33200 ✆ 56 08 04 21, 🏞 – AE ⓓ E VISA. ✻
closed 1 to 20 September, Sunday and Monday – **M** 150/295.

XX ✿ **Le Vieux Bordeaux** (Bordage), 27 r. Buhan ✆ 56 52 94 36 – AE VISA EY **a**
closed 1 to 21 August, February Holidays, Saturday lunch, Sunday and Bank Holidays – **M** 130/230
Spec. Escalope de foie de canard à la pêche, Turbot en braisade de Sauternes, Cocotte de veau "Vieux Bordeaux".

XX **Les Provinces,** 41 r. St-Rémi ✆ 56 81 74 30, Fax 56 48 05 05 – AE ⓓ E VISA DX **t**
closed Sunday – **M** 70 b.i./250 b.i..

XX **Didier Gélineau,** 26 r. Pas St Georges ✆ 56 52 84 25 – ⓓ E VISA EX **n**
closed Sunday (except lunch 16 October-14 April) and Saturday lunch – **M** 89/230.

XX **Les Plaisirs d'Ausone,** 10 r. Ausone ✆ 56 79 30 30 – AE E VISA EY **t**
closed spring Holidays, 1 to 8 January, Monday lunch, Saturday lunch and Sunday – **M** 150 b.i./280.

XX **Le Buhan,** 28 r. Buhan ✆ 56 52 80 86 – E VISA EY **a**
closed Monday – **M** 130/220.

at Parc des Expositions : North of the town – ✉ **33000** Bordeaux :

🏨 **Sofitel Aquitania** Ⓜ, ✆ 56 50 83 80, Telex 570557, Fax 56 39 73 75, ≤, 🏊 – 🛗 ⇎ rm ▤ TV ☎ ♿ Ⓟ – 🏛 25 - 600. AE ⓓ E VISA
Le Flore **M** a la carte 140/220 – ☕ 65 – **204 rm** 545, 8 apartments.

🏨 **Mercure Pont d'Aquitaine** Ⓜ, ✆ 56 50 90 14, Telex 540097, Fax 56 50 23 95, 🏞, 🏊, 🎾 – 🛗 ⇎ rm ▤ TV ☎ ♿ Ⓟ – 🏛 80 - 120. AE ⓓ E VISA
M 98 🍷 – ☕ 45 – **100 rm** 530.

🏨 **Novotel-Bordeaux le Lac** Ⓜ, ✆ 56 50 99 70, Telex 570274, Fax 56 43 00 66, 🏞, 🏊 – 🛗 ⇎ rm ▤ TV ☎ ♿ Ⓟ – 🏛 350. AE ⓓ E VISA
M a la carte approx. 150 🍷 – ☕ 48 – **176 rm** 430/480.

🏨 **Mercure Bordeaux le Lac** Ⓜ, ✆ 56 50 90 30, Telex 540077, Fax 56 43 07 55, 🏞 – 🛗 ⇎ rm ▤ TV ☎ ♿ Ⓟ – 🏛 250. AE ⓓ E VISA
M 100/200 – ☕ 48 – **108 rm** 450/470.

at Carbon-Blanc NE : 8 km by ① – pop. 5 h. – ✉ **33560** :

XXX **Marc Demund,** av. Gardette ✆ 56 06 14 55, 🏞, park – Ⓟ. AE ⓓ E VISA
closed 14 to 26 August, Sunday dinner and Monday – **M** 150/330.

at Bouliac – ✉ **33270** :

🏨 ✿✿ **Le St-James** (Amat) Ⓜ 🐎, pl. C. Hosteins, near church ✆ 56 20 52 19, Telex 573001, Fax 56 20 92 58, ≤, 🏞, « Original contemporary decoration », 🌳 – TV ☎ Ⓟ. AE ⓓ VISA. ✻
M 250 b.i./420 and a la carte - **Le Bistroy M** a la carte approx. 150 – ☕ 70 – **18 rm** 750/1200 – ½ P 570/850
Spec. Fondant d'aubergines au cumin, Homard sauté aux pommes de terre, Civet de canard au fumet de cèpes. **Wines** Entre-Deux-Mers, Premières Côtes de Bordeaux.

to the W :

at Pessac : 9 km – pop. 50 h. – ✉ **33600** :

🏨 **La Réserve** Ⓜ 🐎, av. Bourgailh ✆ 56 07 13 28, Telex 560585, Fax 56 07 13 28, 🏞, « Park », 🏊, 🎾 – ☎ Ⓟ – 🏛 60. AE ⓓ E VISA
28 February-15 November – **M** 250/330 – ☕ 58 – **19 rm** 520/890 – ½ P 600/800.

🏨 **Royal Brion** without rest, 10 r. Pin Vert ✆ 56 45 07 72, Fax 56 46 13 75 – TV ☎ 🚗 Ⓟ. AE ⓓ E VISA
closed 2 to 20 January – ☕ 33 – **26 rm** 260/340.

at the airport : 11 km by D 106E – ✉ **33700** Mérignac :

🏨 **Novotel-Mérignac** Ⓜ, av. Kennedy ✆ 56 34 10 25, Telex 540320, Fax 56 55 99 64, 🏞, 🏊, 🌳 – ▤ TV ☎ ♿ Ⓟ – 🏛 25 - 200. AE ⓓ E VISA
M a la carte approx. 150 – ☕ 48 – **137 rm** 430/460.

🏨 **Le Patio** Ⓜ, av. J.-F. Kennedy at Mérignac ✆ 56 55 93 42, Telex 540183, Fax 56 47 64 94, 🏞, 🏊 – 🛗 ⇎ rm ▤ rest TV ☎ ♿ Ⓟ – 🏛 60. AE ⓓ E VISA
M 115/180 – ☕ 45 – **80 rm** 370/420 – ½ P 340/360.

🏨 **Fimotel** Ⓜ, 97 av. J.-F. Kennedy ✆ 56 34 33 08, Telex 541315, Fax 56 34 01 90, 🏞, 🏊 – 🛗 TV ☎ ♿ – 🏛 40. AE ⓓ E VISA
M 70/110 🍷 – ☕ 33 – **60 rm** 285/300 – ½ P 234.

Eugénie-les-Bains 40320 Landes 🔢 ① – pop. 408 h. alt. 90 – Spa (February-November).

Bordeaux 152.

🏨 ✿✿✿ **Les Prés d'Eugénie et le Couvent des Herbes** (Guérard) Ⓜ ⌂, 𝒫 58 05 06 07, Telex 540470, Fax 58 51 13 59, « 19C mansion, elegant decor, park », ⚊, ✵ – 🛗 📺 ☎ 🅿. ⚼ ⓪ 🖾 🆅🆂🅰. ✵

closed 2 December-14 February – **M** (low-calorie menu for residents only) - 260/350 and a la carte - **rest. Michel Guérard** (booking essential) **M** 420/560 and a la carte – ⌂ 90 – **28 rm** 1173/1380, 7 apartments 1564/1679

Spec. Langoustines grillées en mesclun paysan, Tourte chaude de canard au foie gras, Pain perdu d'autrefois. Wines Tursan blanc, Côtes de Gascogne.

Le Couvent des Herbes Ⓜ ⌂, « 18C Convent » – 📺 ☎ 🅿. ⚼ ⓪ 🖾 🆅🆂🅰. ✵ rest
closed 2 December-14 February – **M** see **Les Prés d'Eugénie** and **Michel Guérard** – ⌂ 90 – **5 rm** 1403/1610, 3 apartments 2070.

Grenade-sur-l'Adour 40270 Landes 🔢 ① – pop. 2 132 h. alt. 55.

Bordeaux 140.

✕✕✕ ✿✿ **Pain Adour et Fantaisie** (Oudill) with rm, 7 pl. Tilleuls 𝒫 58 45 18 80, Fax 58 45 16 57, ⌂, « Riverside terrace » – ▤ rm 📺 ☎ & 🅿. ⓪ 🖾 🆅🆂🅰. ✵ rm
closed 1 to 14 March, Monday September-June (except accommodation) and Sunday dinner except July-August – **M** 150/380 and a la carte – ⌂ 60 – **11 rm** 380/750
Spec. Tuile craquante de langoustines au curry, Agneau de lait à la mode de Chalosse (September-April). Vacherin glacé à l'herbe des troubadours. **Wines** Pacherenc du Vic Bilh, Madiran.

Langon ◁🆂🅿▷ 33210 Gironde 🗾 ② – pop. 6 308 h. alt. 22.

Bordeaux 47.

🏨 ✿✿ **Claude Darroze** Ⓜ, 95 cours Gén. Leclerc 𝒫 56 63 00 48, Fax 56 63 41 15, ⌂ – 📺 ☎ ❡ 🅿. ⚼ ⓪ 🖾 🆅🆂🅰. ✵ rm
closed 15 October-5 November and 5 to 25 January – **M** 185/460 and a la carte – ⌂ 55 – **16 rm** 300/400
Spec. Salade de petits artichauts aux queues de langoustines tièdes, Plateau de fruits de mer chauds, Foie de canard au vinaigre de Xérès. **Wines** Entre-Deux-Mers, Graves rouge.

Pons 17800 Char.-Mar. 🔢 ⑤ – pop. 5 364 h. alt. 20.

Bordeaux 96.

at Mosnac S : 11 km bye Bordeaux road and D 134 – ✉ 17800 :

🏨 ✿✿ **Moulin de Marcouze** (Bouchet) Ⓜ ⌂, 𝒫 46 70 46 16, Telex 793453, Fax 46 70 48 14, « Tasteful mansion on the banks of the River Seugne », ⚊ – ▤ 📺 ☎ & 🅿. ⚼ 🖾 🆅🆂🅰.
closed February, Wednesday lunch and Tuesday 15 September-30 June except Bank Holidays – **M** 180/400 and a la carte – ⌂ 65 – **10 rm** 490/650
Spec. Ravioli de petits gris, Gigot d'agneau de sept heures, Gratin de fruits.

CANNES 06400 Alpes-Mar. 🔢 ⑨. 🔢 ✿✿ – pop. 72 787 h. alt. 2 – Casinos Carlton Casino BYZ, Palm Beach X, Municipal BZ.

See : Site★★ - Sea-Front★★ : Boulevard★★ BCDZ – and Pointe de la Croisette★ X – ≤★ from the Mount Chevalier Tower AZ V – The Castre Museum★ (Musée de la Castre) AZ M – Super-Cannes observatory ✵★★★ E : 4 km X – Tour into the Hills★ (Chemin des Collines) NE : 4 km V – The Croix des Gardes X E ≤★ W : 5 km then 15 mn.

📑 Country-Club of Cannes-Mougins 𝒫 93 75 79 13 by ⑤ : 9 km ; 📑📑 Golf-Club of Cannes-Mandelieu 𝒫 93 49 55 39 by ② : 6,5 km ; 📑 Biot 𝒫 93 65 08 48 by ⑤ : 14 km ; 📑 Opio-Valbonne 𝒫 93 42 00 08 by ⑤ : 15 km ; 📑 Val Martin 𝒫 93 42 07 98 by ⑤ : 12 km by N 285, D 3 and D 103.

📧 Direction Générale du Tourisme et des Congrès and Accueil de France (Informations, exchange facilities and hotel reservations not more than 5 days in advance). espl. Prés. Georges-Pompidou 𝒫 93 39 01 01, Telex 470749 (Welcome Office 𝒫 93 39 24 53) and Railway Station 𝒫 93 71 19 77, Telex 470795 – A.C. 12bis r. L. Blanc 𝒫 93 39 38 94.

Paris 906 ⑤ – Aix-en-Provence 151 ⑤ – Grenoble 316 ⑤ – Marseille 163 ⑤ – Nice 32 ⑤ – Toulon 128 ⑤.

Plans on following pages

🏨 **Carlton Intercontinental**, 58 bd Croisette 𝒫 93 68 91 68, Telex 470720, Fax 93 38 20 90, ≤, 🏖, 🐎 – 🛗 ▤ 📺 ☎ & ⇔ – 🔒 30 - 250. ⚼ ⓪ 🖾 🆅🆂🅰. ✵ rest   CZ **e**
M see **La Côte** below – ⌂ 120 – **300 rm** 1900/3050, 28 apartments.

🏨 **Martinez**, 73 bd Croisette 𝒫 93 94 30 30, Telex 470708, Fax 93 39 67 82, ≤, ⌂, ⚊, 🐎 – 🛗 ▤ 📺 ☎ ❡ 🅿 – 🔒 60 - 1 000. ⚼ ⓪ 🖾 🆅🆂🅰.   DZ **N**
closed late November-early January – **M** see **La Palme d'Or** below - **L'Orangeraie M** 200 – ⌂ 90 – **417 rm** 1190/3090, 13 apartments.

🏨 **Majestic**, bd Croisette 𝒫 92 98 77 00, Telex 470787, Fax 93 38 97 90, ≤, ⌂, ⚊, 🐎, 🌴 – 🛗 ▤ 📺 ☎ & ⇔ – 🔒 400. ⚼ ⓪ 🖾 🆅🆂🅰.   BZ **N**
closed 1 to 19 December – **Le Sunset M** 230 – ⌂ 95 – **258 rm** 950/3250, 24 apartments – ½ P 860/1645.

CANNES - LE CANNET - VALLAURIS

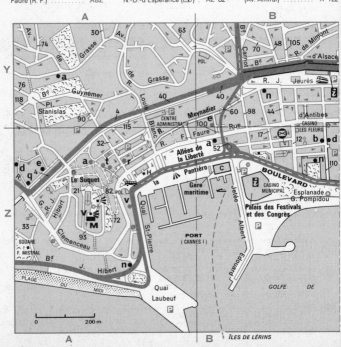

168

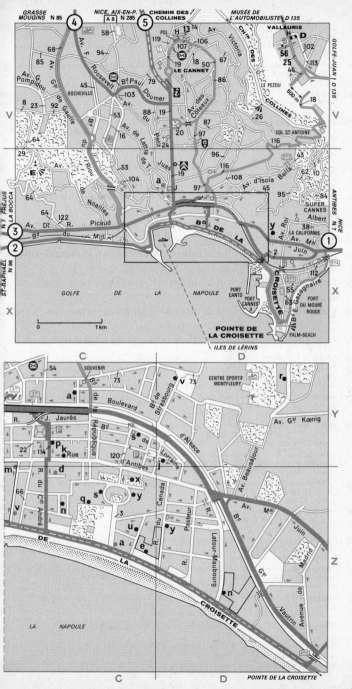

🏰 Gray d'Albion Ⓜ, 38 r. Serbes ℰ 93 68 54 54, Telex 470744, Fax 93 99 26 10, 🦽 – 🛗
`⟨⟩` rm 🗏 rm 📺 ☎ 🚾, – 🛗 30 - 200. 🖭 ⓞ 🗲 𝘝𝘐𝘚𝘈 BZ **d**
M see Royal Gray below – **Les 4 Saisons M** a la carte 180/240 – ⌂ 70 – **172 rm** 850/1500, 14
apartments.

🏰 Pullman Beach without rest, 13 r. Canada ℰ 93 94 50 50, Telex 470034, Fax 93 68 35 38, 🏊
– 🛗 🗏 📺 ☎ 🚾 ⟨⟩ – 🛗 30 - 60. 🖭 ⓞ 🗲 𝘝𝘐𝘚𝘈 DZ **y**
closed 20 November-26 December – ⌂ 75 – **94 rm** 770/1550.

🏰 Savoy Ⓜ, 5 r. F. Einessy ℰ 93 99 57 57, Telex 461873, Fax 93 68 25 59, 🍽, 🏊, 🦽 – 🛗 🗏
📺 ☎ 🚾, – 🛗 120. 🖭 ⓞ 🗲 𝘝𝘐𝘚𝘈 CZ **u**
M (closed February) 145 – ⌂ 65 – **96 rm** 490/1100, 5 apartments – ½ P 500/700.

🏰 Sofitel Méditerranée Ⓜ, 2 bd J. Hibert ℰ 93 99 22 75, Telex 470728, Fax 93 39 68 36, 🍽
« Roof top terrace with 🏊 and ≤ Cannes'sbay » – 🛗 `⟨⟩` rm 🗏 📺 ☎ ⟨⟩ – 🛗 150. 🖭
ⓞ 🗲 𝘝𝘐𝘚𝘈 AZ **n**
closed 18 November-19 December – **M** 155/205 – ⌂ 80 – **150 rm** 780/1230, 5 apartments
1800.

🏰 Grand Hôtel, 45 bd Croisette ℰ 93 38 15 45, Telex 470727, Fax 93 68 97 45, ≤, 🦽, 🌿 –
🛗 🗏 rm 📺 ☎ Ⓟ – 🛗 30. 🖭 🗲 𝘝𝘐𝘚𝘈. 🦷 rest CZ **q**
closed 1 December-1 December – **M** 175 – ⌂ 60 – **74 rm** 730/1460 – ½ P 690/960.

🏩 Cristal Ⓜ, 15 rd-pt Duboys d'Angers ℰ 93 39 45 45, Telex 470844, Fax 93 38 64 66, 🍽 – 🛗
🗏 📺 ☎ ⟨⟩. 🖭 ⓞ 🗲 𝘝𝘐𝘚𝘈 CZ **s**
M 135/300 – ⌂ 65 – **51 rm** 715/1650, 5 apartments 2000.

🏩 Novotel Ⓜ 🦘, 25 av. Beauséjour ℰ 93 68 91 50, Telex 470039, Fax 93 38 37 08, ≤, 🍽
« Garden », 🦶, 🏊, 🎾 – 🛗 🗏 📺 ☎ ⟨⟩ – 🛗 400. 🖭 ⓞ 🗲 𝘝𝘐𝘚𝘈 DY **i**
M 150/200 – ⌂ 55 – **181 rm** 850/1100.

🏩 Fouquet's Ⓜ without rest, 2 rd-pt Duboys d'Angers ℰ 93 38 75 81, Fax 93 39 92 93 – 🗏
📺 ☎ ⟨⟩. 🖭 ⓞ 🗲 𝘝𝘐𝘚𝘈 CZ **y**
closed 1 November-26 December – ⌂ 60 – **10 rm** 890/1200.

🏩 Splendid without rest, 4 r. F. Faure ℰ 93 99 53 11, Fax 93 99 55 02, ≤ – 🛗
kitchenette 🗏 📺 ☎. 🖭 ⓞ 🗲 𝘝𝘐𝘚𝘈 BZ **a**
63 rm ⌂ 550/930.

🏩 Victoria Ⓜ without rest, rd-pt Duboys d'Angers ℰ 93 99 36 36, Fax 93 38 03 91, 🏊 – 🛗 🗏
📺 ☎ ⟨⟩. 🖭 ⓞ 🗲 𝘝𝘐𝘚𝘈 🦷 CZ **x**
closed 10 November-20 December – ⌂ 40 – **25 rm** 650/1000.

🏨 Paris without rest, 34 bd Alsace ℰ 93 38 30 89, Telex 470995, Fax 93 39 04 61, 🏊, 🌿 – 🛗
📺 ☎ – 🛗 40. 🖭 ⓞ 🗲 𝘝𝘐𝘚𝘈. 🦷 CY **a**
closed 10 November-16 January – ⌂ 50 – **45 rm** 280/760, 5 apartments.

🏨 Embassy, 6 r. Bône ℰ 93 38 79 02, Telex 470081, Fax 93 99 07 98 – 🛗 🗏 📺 ☎. 🖭 ⓞ 🗲
𝘝𝘐𝘚𝘈 DY **j**
M (closed lunch Monday and Tuesday) 105 – ⌂ 35 – **60 rm** 430/700 – ½ P 362/460.

🏨 Abrial without rest, 24 bd Lorraine ℰ 93 38 78 82, Telex 470761, Fax 92 98 67 41 – 🛗 🗏 📺
☎ ⟨⟩ – 🛗 30. 🖭 ⓞ 🗲 𝘝𝘐𝘚𝘈 CY **s**
⌂ 42 – **50 rm** 542/580.

🏨 Host. de l'Olivier without rest, 5 r. Tambourinaires ℰ 93 39 53 28, Telex 970902, Fax
93 39 55 85, 🏊 – 📺 ☎ Ⓟ. 🖭 🗲 𝘝𝘐𝘚𝘈. 🦷 AZ **e**
closed 23 November-28 December – ⌂ 35 – **23 rm** 470/570.

🏨 Beau Séjour, 5 r. Fauvettes ℰ 93 39 63 00, Telex 470975, Fax 92 98 64 66, 🍽, 🏊, 🌿 – 🛗
🗏 rm 📺 ☎ ⟨⟩ – 🛗 30. 🖭 ⓞ 🗲 𝘝𝘐𝘚𝘈. 🦷 rest AZ **d**
closed 1 November-15 December – **M** 140 – **46 rm** ⌂ 600 – ½ P 460.

🏨 La Madone 🦘 without rest, 5 av. Justinia ℰ 93 43 57 87, Fax 93 43 22 79, 🌿 – kitchenette
📺 🦽. 🖭 ⓞ 🗲 𝘝𝘐𝘚𝘈 X **y**
⌂ 40 – **25 rm** 400/620.

🏨 Des Congrès et Festivals Ⓜ without rest, 12 r. Teisseire ℰ 93 39 13 81, Fax 93 39 56 28
– 🛗 🗏 📺 ☎. 🖭 ⓞ 🗲 𝘝𝘐𝘚𝘈 CY **p**
closed 1 November-20 January – ⌂ 35 – **20 rm** 420/590.

🏨 Ruc H. without rest, 15 bd Strasbourg ℰ 93 38 64 32, Telex 970033, Fax 93 39 54 18 – 🛗
`⟨⟩` 🗏 📺 ☎. 🖭 🗲 𝘝𝘐𝘚𝘈. 🦷 DY **v**
closed 25 November-24 December – ⌂ 30 – **30 rm** 270/710.

🏨 Château de la Tour 🦘, 10 av. Font-de-Veyre by ③ ✉ 06150 Cannes-La-Bocca ℰ 93 47
34 64, Telex 470906, Fax 93 47 86 61, 🏊 – 🛗 📺 ☎ Ⓟ. 🖭 ⓞ 🗲 𝘝𝘐𝘚𝘈. 🦷 rest
M (closed 15 December-25 December) 110 – ⌂ 35 – **42 rm** 520/680 – ½ P 405/485.

🏨 France without rest, 85 r. Antibes ℰ 93 39 23 34, Fax 93 68 53 43 – 🛗 🗏 📺 ☎. 🖭 ⓞ 🗲
𝘝𝘐𝘚𝘈 CY **k**
⌂ 30 – **34 rm** 250/390.

🏠 Cheval Blanc without rest, 3 r. Maupassant ℰ 93 39 88 60 – 📺 🦽. 🗲 𝘝𝘐𝘚𝘈 AY **a**
⌂ 25 – **16 rm** 190/260.

🏠 Roches Fleuries without rest, 2 r. Fauvettes ℰ 93 39 28 78, 🌿 – 🛗 🦽. 🦷 AZ **a**
closed 14 November-28 December – ⌂ 20 – **24 rm** 125/260.

🏠 Modern without rest, 11 r. Serbes ℰ 93 39 09 87 – 🛗 📺 ☎ BZ **b**
closed 4 November-28 December – ⌂ 25 – **19 rm** 220/550.

XXXXX ۞ **La Belle Otéro,** 58 bd Croisette, on the 7th floor of the Carlton hôtel ℰ 93 39 69 69, Fax 92 98 90 92 – ▤ 🝔 ⓞ ☰ 🝔 CZ **e**
closed 27 October-15 November, 10 February-15 March and Sunday 15 September-31 March – **M** (dinner only) a la carte 480/650
Spec. Poêlée de langoustines aux farcis de légumes, Pistou de langouste aux haricots ''cocos'' et macaroni, Poitrine de pigeonneau rôtie au miel de romarin.

XXXXX ۞ **La Côte** - Hôtel Carlton Intercontinental, 58 bd Croisette ℰ 93 68 91 68, Telex 470720, Fax 93 38 20 90, 霜 – ▤ 🝔 ⓞ ☰ 🝔 ❀ CZ **e**
closed mid November-mid December, Tuesday and Wednesday – **M** a la carte 310/700
Spec. Macédoine de cigale de Méditerranée, Anchoiade de loup et marinière de coquillages, Canette de Bresse rôtie en deux services. Wines Côtes de Provence.

XXXXX ۞۞ **La Palme d'Or** - Hôtel Martinez, 73 bd Croisette ℰ 92 98 30 18, Telex 470708, Fax 93 39 67 82, 霜 – ▤ 🝔 🅿 🝔 ⓞ ☰ 🝔 DZ **n**
closed late November-early January, Tuesday (except dinner 15 May-15 September) and Monday – **M** 290/500 and a la carte
Spec. Turbot en croustille de pommes de terre, Homard à la vapeur et ravigote au verjus, Coeur de pigeonneau en cocotte aux pignons. Wines Bellet.

XXXX ۞۞ **Royal Gray** - Hôtel Gray d'Albion, 6 r. Etats-Unis ℰ 93 99 04 59, Telex 470744, Fax 93 99 26 10, 霜, « Tasteful, contemporary decor » – ▤ 🝔 ⓞ ☰ 🝔 CYZ **m**
closed 1 February-6 March, Monday (except dinner in July and August) and Sunday – **M** 340/500 and a la carte
Spec. Ravioli de caviar au saumon fumé, Agneau rôti aux petits artichauts et févettes, Dentelle de réglisse et coulis de pêche. Wines Cadière d'Azur.

XXX ۞ **Poêle d'Or** (Leclerc), 23 r. États-Unis ℰ 93 39 77 65 – ▤ 🝔 ⓞ ☰ 🝔 CZ **v**
closed 4 to 12 March, 12 November to 13 December, Tuesday lunch and Monday – **M** (week ends : booking essential) 180/290
Spec. Escalope de turbot aux girolles (season), Pigeonneau rôti à la tapenade, Crème brûlée à la pistache. Wines Côtes de Provence, Bellet.

XXX **Le Festival,** 52 bd Croisette ℰ 93 38 04 81, Fax 93 38 13 82, 霜 – ▤ 🝔 ⓞ ☰ 🝔 CZ **a**
closed 18 November-26 December, Sunday dinner and Monday late December-Easter – **M** 185/210.

XXX **Gaston et Gastounette,** 7 quai St-Pierre ℰ 93 39 47 92, 霜 – 🝔 ⓞ ☰ 🝔 AZ **v**
closed 3 to 20 January – **M** a la carte 215/410.

XX **La Mirabelle,** 24 r. St Antoine ℰ 93 38 72 75 – ▤ 🝔 ☰ 🝔 AZ **a**
closed 15 November-5 December, 15 February-1 March and Tuesday – **M** (dinner only) 195/255.

XX **Le Mesclun,** 16 r. St Antoine ℰ 93 99 45 19 – ▤ 🝔 ⓞ ☰ 🝔 AZ **t**
closed 1 to 15 March, 1 to 20 December and Wednesday out of season – **M** (dinner only) 165.

XX **Relais des Semailles,** 9 r. St Antoine ℰ 93 39 22 32 – ☰ 🝔 AZ **t**
closed November, March and Sunday – **M** (dinner only) 210/320.

XX **St-Benoit,** 9 r. Bateguier ℰ 93 39 04 17 – 🝔 ☰ 🝔 CZ **n**
closed 15 November-15 December, Tuesday lunch and Monday – **M** 120/155.

XX **La Cigale,** 1 r. Florian ℰ 93 39 65 79 – ▤ 🝔 ⓞ ☰ 🝔 CZ **d**
closed November, Sunday dinner 1 December-30 April and Monday – **M** 92/140 🍷.

X **L'Olivier,** 5 r. Rouguière ℰ 93 39 91 63 – 🝔 ⓞ ☰ 🝔 BY **e**
closed 15 December-15 January and Monday – **M** 85/140.

X **Aux Bons Enfants,** 80 r. Meynadier – ❀ AZ **r**
closed August, 20 December-5 January, Saturday dinner out of season – **M** 80.

X **Côté Jardin,** 12 av. St Louis ℰ 93 38 60 28, 霜 – ▤ 🝔 ☰ 🝔 X **a**
closed early February-mid March, Monday (except dinner April-October) and Sunday – **M** 145 🍷.

Antibes 06600 Alpes-Mar. 🐙 ⑨. 🔢 ㉞㉟ – pop. 63 248 h. alt. 9 – Cannes 11.

N : 4 km quartier de la Brague – ✉ 06600 Antibes :

XXXX ۞۞ **La Bonne Auberge** (Rostang), ℰ 93 33 36 65, Telex 470989, Fax 93 33 48 52, 霜, « Provençal style dining room and flowered terrace » – ☰ 🝔 🅿 🝔 ☰ 🝔
closed 15 Nov.-15 Dec., Wednesday lunch in July and August, Monday (except dinner April-Sept. and Bank Holidays) – **M** 410/580 and a la carte
Spec. Salade de homard aux ravioles de chèvre, Minute de loup grillé au beurre de soja, Canard au sang. Wines Bandol.

Juan-les-Pins 06160 Alpes-Mar. 🐙 ⑨. 🔢 ㉞㉟ – alt. 2.
Cannes 9.

🏨 ۞۞ **Juana et rest. La Terrasse** ⌘, la Pinède, av. G. Gallice ℰ 93 61 08 70, Telex 470778, Fax 93 61 76 60, 霜, 🏊, 🍸 – 🛗 ▤ rm 🝔 🝔 ⇦ 🅿
Early March-late October – **M** (closed Wednesday except 8 to 20 May, 24 to 31 August and 20 to 27 October) (dinner only July and August) 450/550 and a la carte – 🍽 85 – **45 rm** 750/2300, 5 apartments
Spec. Daurade royale poêlée aux senteurs d'anis vert, Selle d'agneau des Alpes cuite en terre d'argile, Fraises des bois en délice de pistaches et chocolat. Wines Côtes de Provence.

Mougins 06250 Alpes-Mar. 84 ⑨. 195 ㉔㊳ – pop. 11 920 h. alt. 260.

Cannes 7.

XXXX ✿✿✿ **Moulin de Mougins** (Vergé) with rm, at Notre-Dame-de-Vie SE : 2,5 km by D 3 ℰ 93 75 78 24, Telex 970732, Fax 93 90 18 55, ⇱, « Converted 16C oil mill », 🐎 – 🗑 📺 🛏 🅿. 🆎 ⓞ 🇪 𝓥𝓘𝓢𝓐

closed 3 February-6 April – **M** *(closed Monday except dinner 15 July-31 August and Thursday lunch)* 650 and a la carte – ⊑ 75 – **5 rm** 900/1300

Spec. Poupeton de fleurs de courgettes aux truffes, Fricassée de homard en crème de Sauternes, Suprême de canard et son ballotin de cuisse aux olives. **Wines** Cassis, Côtes de Provence.

LYONS 🅿 69000 Rhône 74 ⑪⑫ – pop. 418 476 h. Greater Lyons 1 173 797 h. alt. 169.

See : Site★★★ – Old Lyons★★ (Vieux Lyon) BX : Hôtel Bullioud : loggia★★ B, St-Jean★ : Chancel★★, – rue St-Jean★ 92, Hôtel de Gadagne★ M1, Maison du Crible★ D, Lantern tower★ of St-Paul Church BV – Basilica of N.-D.-de-Fourvière ✲✲★★ from the observatory, ≼★ from the esplanade BX – Basilica of St-Martin d'Ainay : capitals★ BYZ – Montée de Garillan★ BX – St-Nizier : Virgin and Child★ CX – Tête d'Or Park★ rose garden★ (roseraie) – Place des Terreaux : fountain★ CV – Chaponost Aqueduct★ : ruins - Underground passageways (Traboules) – Punch and Judy Show (Théâtre de Guignol) BX N – Museums : Textile★★★ CZ M2, Gallo-Roman Civilization★★ (Claudian table★★★) BX M3, Fine Arts★★★ CV M4, – Decorative Arts★★ CZ M5, Printing and Banking★★ CX M6, Guimet Natural History★★ – Puppet★ BX M1, Historic★ : lapidary★ BX M1, Apothecary's Shop★ (Civil Hospitals) CY M8.

Envir. : Rochetaillée : Museum Henri Malartre★★ : 12 km.

🏌🏌 Villette d'Anthon ℰ 78 31 11 33 to the E : 21 km ; 🏌 Verger-Lyon at St-Symphorien-d'Ozon ℰ 78 02 24 20, to the S : 14 km ; 🏌🏌 Lyon-Chassieu at Chassieu ℰ 78 90 84 77, E : 12 km by D 29 ; 🏌🏌 Salvagny (private) at the Tour of Salvagny ℰ 78 48 83 60 ; jonction Lyon-West : 8 km.

✈ of Lyon-Satolas ℰ 72 22 72 21 to the E : 27 km.

🚗🚗 ℰ 78 92 50 50.

🛈 Office de Tourisme and Accueil de France (Informations, exchange facilities, hotel reservations - not more than 5 days in advance). pl. Bellecour ℰ 78 42 25 75, Telex 330032 and Centre d'Echange de Perrache – A.C. 7 r. Grolée ℰ 78 42 51 01.

Paris 461 – Bâle 401 – Bordeaux 550 – Genève 151 – Grenoble 104 – Marseille 312 – St-Étienne 59 – Strasbourg 480 – Torino 300.

Plan on following pages

Hôtels

Town Centre (Bellecour-Terreaux) :

🏨 **Sofitel** Ⓜ, 20 quai Gailleton ⊠ 69002 ℰ 72 41 20 20, Telex 330225, Fax 72 40 05 50, ≼ – 🛗 ⇲ rm 🗑 📺 ☎ ⇦ – 🔬 250. 🆎 ⓞ 🇪 𝓥𝓘𝓢𝓐. 🎸 rest   CY **k**
Les Trois Dômes (8th floor) **M** 235/310 – **Sofi Shop** (ground floor) **M** 88 🍷. enf. 39 – ⊑ 72 – **179 rm** 800/995.

🏨 **Gd Hôtel Concorde**, 11 r. Grolée ⊠ 69002 ℰ 72 40 45 45, Telex 330244, Fax 78 37 52 55 – 🛗 🗑 rm 🗑 📺 ☎ – 🔬 80. 🆎 ⓞ 🇪 𝓥𝓘𝓢𝓐. 🎸 rest   DX **e**
Le Fiorelle *(closed Sunday lunch)* **M** 98/180 🍷 – ⊑ 50 – **140 rm** 440/850.

🏨 **Royal**, 20 pl. Bellecour ⊠ 69002 ℰ 78 37 57 31, Telex 310785, Fax 78 37 01 36 – 🛗 🗑 rm 📺 ☎. 🆎 ⓞ 🇪 𝓥𝓘𝓢𝓐   CY **d**
M grill 85 🍷 – ⊑ 48 – **80 rm** 450/810.

🏨 **Gd H. des Beaux-Arts** without rest, 75 r. Prés. E. Herriot ⊠ 69002 ℰ 78 38 09 50, Telex 330442, Fax 78 42 19 19 – 🛗 ⇲ 🗑 📺 ☎ – 🔬 30. 🆎 ⓞ 🇪 𝓥𝓘𝓢𝓐   CX **t**
⊑ 45 – **79 rm** 305/525.

🏨 **Carlton** without rest, 4 r. Jussieu ⊠ 69002 ℰ 78 42 56 51, Telex 310787, Fax 78 42 10 71 – 🛗 🗑 📺 ☎. 🆎 ⓞ 🇪 𝓥𝓘𝓢𝓐   DX **f**
⊑ 45 – **83 rm** 380/560.

🏨 **La Résidence** without rest, 18 r. V. Hugo ⊠ 69002 ℰ 78 42 63 28, Telex 900950, Fax 78 42 85 76 – 🛗 🗑 📺 ☎ – 🔬 40. 🆎 ⓞ 🇪 𝓥𝓘𝓢𝓐   CY **s**
⊑ 28 – **65 rm** 240/270.

🏨 **Globe et Cécil** without rest, 21 r. Gasparin ⊠ 69002 ℰ 78 42 58 95, Telex 305184, Fax 72 41 99 06 – 🛗 🗑 📺 ☎ – 🔬 60. 🆎 ⓞ 🇪 𝓥𝓘𝓢𝓐   CY **b**
⊑ 41 – **65 rm** 270/375.

🏨 **Bellecordière** Ⓜ without rest, 18 r. Bellecordière ⊠ 69002 ℰ 78 42 27 78, Telex 301633 – 🛗 🗑 📺 ☎. 🆎 🇪 𝓥𝓘𝓢𝓐   CY **a**
⊑ 28 – **35 rm** 280/290.

Perrache :

🏨 **Pullman Perrache**, 12 cours Verdun ⊠ 69002 ℰ 78 37 58 11, Telex 330500, Fax 78 37 06 56, ⇱, 🐎 ⇲ rm 🗑 📺 ☎ – 🔬 100. 🆎 ⓞ 🇪 𝓥𝓘𝓢𝓐   BZ **a**
M 130/180 🍷 – ⊑ 72 – **124 rm** 410/690.

🏨 **Charlemagne** Ⓜ, 23 cours Charlemagne ⊠ 69002 ℰ 78 92 81 61, Telex 380401, Fax 78 42 94 84 – 🛗 🗑 📺 ☎ ⇦ 🅿 – 🔬 120. 🆎 ⓞ 🇪 𝓥𝓘𝓢𝓐   BZ **b**
M *(closed 3 August-2 September, Saturday and Sunday)* 110/150 – ⊑ 45 – **116 rm** 365/500.

Vieux-Lyon :

🏠🏠 **Cour des Loges** Ⓜ ♨, 6 r. Boeuf ✉ 69005 ℰ 78 42 75 75, Telex 330831, Fax 72 40 93 61, « Contemporary decor in houses of Old Lyons » – 🛗 📧 📺 ☎ ఉ ⟷ – 🔬 45. ⒶⒺ ⑩ Ε 𝘝𝘐𝘚𝘈 ⋙ rest
BX **n**
Tapas des Loges **M** 80/160 – ⚏ 90 – **53 rm** 1100/1500, 10 apartments 1900/2900.

🏠🏠 ✿ **Tour Rose** (Chavent) Ⓜ, 22 r. Boeuf ✉ 69005 ℰ 78 37 25 90, Fax 78 42 26 02, « 16C house, tasteful decor on the theme of silk », ☞ – 🛗 kitchenette 📧 📺 ☎ – 🔬 25. ⒶⒺ ⑩ Ε 𝘝𝘐𝘚𝘈
BX **e**
M *(closed 4 to 18 August and Sunday)* 320/520 – ⚏ 90 – **6 rm** 1650, 6 apartments 1650/2800, 4 duplex
Spec. Salade de pommes de terre à la crème de caviar, Saumon mi-cuit au fumoir, Foie chaud de canard et filet de rouget aux lentilles. **Wines** Viognier, Brouilly.

La Croix-Rousse (Bord de Saône) :

🏠🏠 **Lyon Métropole** Ⓜ, 85 quai J. Gillet ✉ 69004 ℰ 78 29 20 20, Telex 380198, Fax 78 39 99 20, 🏋, ⚛, ⚓, ✵ – 🛗 – 🛗 📧 📺 ☎ ఉ ⟷ ℗ – 🔬 350. ⒶⒺ ⑩ Ε 𝘝𝘐𝘚𝘈
Grill **M** a la carte approx. 150 – **Les Eaux Vives** ℰ 78 29 36 36 *(closed 22 December-2 January, Sunday and July-August Bank Holidays)* **M** 120/200 – ⚏ 48 – **119 rm** 440/535.

Les Brotteaux :

🏠🏠 **Roosevelt** without rest, 25 r. Bossuet ✉ 69006 ℰ 78 52 35 67, Telex 300295, Fax 78 52 39 82 – 🛗 kitchenette 📧 📺 ☎ ⟷ ℗ – 🔬 60. ⒶⒺ ⑩ Ε 𝘝𝘐𝘚𝘈
⚏ 45 – **87 rm** 380/550, 3 apartments 700.

🏠 **Olympique** without rest, 62 r. Garibaldi ✉ 69006 ℰ 78 89 48 04 – 🛗 📺 ☎. ⒶⒺ 𝘝𝘐𝘚𝘈
⚏ 23 – **23 rm** 205/245.

La Part-Dieu :

🏠🏠 **Holiday Inn Crowne Plaza** Ⓜ, 29 r. Bonnel ℰ 72 61 90 90, Telex 330703, Fax 72 61 17 54, ⅃₅ – 🛗 📧 📺 ☎ ఉ ⟷ – 🔬 30 - 300 – **154 rm**.

🏠🏠 **Pullman Part-Dieu** Ⓜ, 129 r. Servient (32nd floor) ✉ 69003 ℰ 78 62 94 12, Telex 380088, Fax 78 60 41 77, ≤ Lyons and Valley of the Rhône – 🛗 📧 📺 ☎ ⟷ – 🔬 300. ⒶⒺ ⑩ Ε 𝘝𝘐𝘚𝘈
L'Arc-en-Ciel *(closed 15 July-15 August and Sunday dinner)* **M** 195/360 – **La Ripaille** grill (ground floor) *(closed Sunday lunch and Saturday)* **M** 110 ⅃ – ⚏ 55 – **245 rm** 595/865.

🏠🏠 **Mercure** Ⓜ, 47 bd Vivier-Merle ✉ 69003 ℰ 72 34 18 12, Telex 306469, Fax 78 53 40 69 – 🛗 📧 📺 ☎ ఉ – 🔬 100. ⒶⒺ ⑩ Ε 𝘝𝘐𝘚𝘈
M 125/145 ⅃ – ⚏ 46 – **124 rm** 590.

🏠 **Créqui** Ⓜ without rest, 158 r. Créqui ✉ 69003 ℰ 78 60 20 47, Fax 78 62 21 12 – 🛗 📺 ☎. Ε 𝘝𝘐𝘚𝘈 – ⚏ 33 – **28 rm** 294/325.

🏠 **Ibis** Ⓜ, pl. Renaudel ✉ 69003 ℰ 78 95 42 11, Telex 310847, Fax 78 60 42 85, ☞ – 🛗 📧 📺 ☎ ఉ ⟷ – 🔬 30. Ε 𝘝𝘐𝘚𝘈
M 81/100 ⅃ – ⚏ 29 – **144 rm** 275/295.

La Guillotière :

🏠🏠 **Gd H. Helder et Institut** without rest, 38 r. Marseille ✉ 69007 ℰ 78 61 61 61, Telex 306411, Fax 78 61 61 00 – 🛗 📺 ☎. ⒶⒺ ⑩ Ε 𝘝𝘐𝘚𝘈
98 rm ⚏ 300/360.

🏠🏠 **Columbia** without rest, 8 pl. A. Briand ✉ 69003 ℰ 78 60 54 65, Telex 305551 – 🛗 📧 📺 ☎ ⟷. ⒶⒺ ⑩ Ε 𝘝𝘐𝘚𝘈
⚏ – **66 rm** 230/270.

🏠🏠 **Urbis Université** without rest, 51 r. Université ✉ 69007 ℰ 78 72 78 42, Telex 340455, Fax 78 69 24 36 – 🛗 📧 📺 ☎ ⟷. ⒶⒺ Ε 𝘝𝘐𝘚𝘈
⚏ – **53 rm** 270/320.

Gerland :

🏠🏠 **Mercure** Ⓜ, 70 av. Leclerc ✉ 69007 ℰ 78 58 68 53, Telex 305484, Fax 78 61 05 54, ☞, ⅃ – 🛗 📧 📺 ☎ ఉ ⟷ – 🔬 450. ⒶⒺ ⑩ Ε 𝘝𝘐𝘚𝘈
M 125/145 ⅃ – ⚏ 46 – **194 rm** 510.

🏠 **Ibis** Ⓜ, 68 av. Leclerc ✉ 69007 ℰ 78 58 30 70, Telex 305483 – 🛗 📺 ☎ ఉ ⟷ – 🔬 30. Ε 𝘝𝘐𝘚𝘈 – **M** 77 ⅃ – ⚏ 30 – **129 rm** 275/295.

Montchat-Monplaisir :

🏠🏠 **Altea Park**, 4 r. Prof. Calmette ✉ 69008 ℰ 78 74 11 20, Telex 380230, Fax 78 01 43 38, ☞ – 🛗 📧 📺 ☎ ⟷ – 🔬 25. ⒶⒺ ⑩ Ε 𝘝𝘐𝘚𝘈
le Patio **M** 70/145 ⅃ – ⚏ 45 – **72 rm** 355/395.

🏠 **Lacassagne** without rest, 245 av. Lacassagne ✉ 69003 ℰ 78 54 09 12 – 🛗 📧 📺 ☎. ⒶⒺ ⑩ Ε 𝘝𝘐𝘚𝘈 – ⚏ 25 – **40 rm** 170/260.

at Bron : – pop. 41 h. – ✉ 69500 :

🏠🏠 **Novotel** Ⓜ, av. J. Monnet ℰ 78 26 97 48, Telex 340781, Fax 78 26 45 12, ☞, ⅃, ☞ – 🛗 📧 📺 ☎ ఉ ℗ – 🔬 25 - 800. ⒶⒺ ⑩ Ε 𝘝𝘐𝘚𝘈
M a la carte approx. 150 ⅃ – ⚏ 45 – **191 rm** 400.

🏠 **Ibis** Ⓜ, 36 av. Doyen J. Lépine ℰ 78 54 31 34, Telex 380694, Fax 78 53 31 51 – 🛗 📺 ☎ ఉ – 🔬 60. Ε 𝘝𝘐𝘚𝘈
M 76 ⅃ – ⚏ 29 – **140 rm** 215/300.

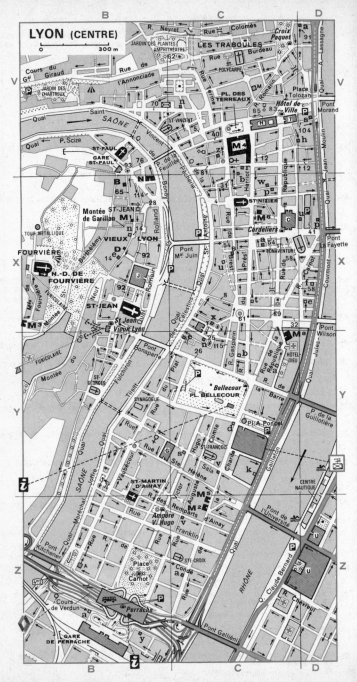

LYON (CENTRE)

0   300 m

Restaurants

XXXXX ✿✿✿ **Paul Bocuse,** bridge of Collonges N : 12 km by the banks of River Saône (D433, D51) ⊠ 69660 Collonges-au-Mont-d'Or 𝒫 78 22 01 40, Telex 375382, Fax 72 27 85 87, « Tasteful decor » – 🗏 ⊕. 🆎 ⓞ Ε 𝚅𝙸𝚂𝙰
  M 580/690 and a la carte
  Spec. Soupe aux truffes noires, Loup en croûte à la mousse de homard et sauce Choron, Volaille de Bresse en vessie. **Wines** Pouilly-Fuissé, Brouilly.

XXXX ✿✿ **Orsi,** 3 pl. Kléber ⊠ 69006 𝒫 78 89 57 68, Telex 305965, Fax 72 44 93 34, 🌧, « Elegant setting » – 🗏 🆎 Ε 𝚅𝙸𝚂𝙰
  closed Saturday in August and Sunday except lunch September-July – **M** 240 (lunch)/360 and a la carte
  Spec. Salade gourmande, Saint-Pierre aux poirettes croustillantes, Pigeonneau de Bresse aux gousses d'ail en chemise. **Wines** Saint-Amour, Saint-Véran.

XXXX **Roger Roucou ''Mère Guy''** (proposed bedrooms), 35 quai J. J. Rousseau ⊠ 69350 La Mulatière 𝒫 78 51 65 37, Telex 310241 – ⓟ 🆎 Ε 𝚅𝙸𝚂𝙰
  closed August, Sunday dinner and Monday – **M** 250 b.i./400.

XXX ✿✿ **Léon de Lyon** (Lacombe), 1 r. Pleney ⊠ 69001 𝒫 78 28 11 33, Telex 300134, Fax 78 39 89 05, « Typical local establishment » – 🗏. 🆎 Ε 𝚅𝙸𝚂𝙰 CVX **b**
  closed 28 July-20 August, Monday lunch and Sunday – **M** 240/430 and a la carte 🍴
  Spec. Poulet de Bresse aux écrevisses et petit gâteau de foies (July-Dec.), Ravioli à la lyonnaise (Dec.-April), Six desserts avec la praline de Saint-Genis. **Wines** Régnié, Saint-Véran.

XXX ✿ **Aub. de Fond-Rose** (Brunet), 23 quai Clemenceau ⊠ 69300 Caluire 𝒫 78 29 34 61, Fax 72 00 28 67, 🌧, « Garden » – ⓟ. 🆎 ⓞ Ε 𝚅𝙸𝚂𝙰
  closed Monday November-Easter, dinner Sunday and Bank Holidays – **M** 190/420
  Spec. Suprême de dorade au vin rouge (October-April), Filet de bar grillé au beurre de ciboulette, Volaille de Bresse à la broche (October-April). **Wines** Saint-Véran, Côte de Brouilly.

XXX ✿ **Bourillot,** 8 pl. Célestins ⊠ 69002 𝒫 78 37 38 64 – 🗏. 🆎 Ε 𝚅𝙸𝚂𝙰 CY **n**
  closed 29 June-29 July, 23 December-2 January, Sunday and Bank Holidays – **M** 210/400
  Spec. Quenelle de brochet au fumet de homard, Tournedos compoté aux truffes et morilles, Soufflé glacé au chocolat. **Wines** Coteaux du Lyonnais, Régnié.

XXX ✿ **Nandron,** 26 quai J. Moulin ⊠ 69002 𝒫 78 42 10 26, Fax 78 37 69 88 – 🗏. 🆎 ⓞ 𝚅𝙸𝚂𝙰
  closed 27 July-26 August, Friday dinner 1 May-31 July and Saturday – **M** 210/400 DX **p**
  Spec. Quenelle de brochet à la Nantua, Aile de volaille rôtie et farcie au foie gras, Soufflé chaud au chocolat et glace à la menthe. **Wines** Saint-Véran, Côte-Rôtie.

XXX ✿ **Mère Brazier,** 12 r. Royale ⊠ 69001 𝒫 78 28 15 49, « Typical local establishment » – 🆎 ⓞ Ε 𝚅𝙸𝚂𝙰 DV **a**
  closed 3 August-2 September, Saturday (except dinner from September-June) and Sunday – **M** 280/330
  Spec. Fond d'artichaut au foie gras, Quenelle au gratin, Volaille de Bresse Demi-Deuil. **Wines** Chiroubles, Saint-Joseph.

XXX ✿ **Fédora** (Judéaux), 249 r. M. Merieux ⊠ 69007 𝒫 78 69 46 26, Fax 72 73 38 80, 🌧 – 🆎 ⓞ Ε 𝚅𝙸𝚂𝙰
  closed 21 December-3 January, Saturday lunch, Sunday and Bank Holidays – **M** 160/260
  Spec. Foie gras frais de canard, Ragoût de homard et d'encornets, Raie à l'orange.

XXX ✿ **Le Quatre Saisons** (Bertoli), 15 r. Sully ⊠ 69006 𝒫 78 93 76 07 – 🗏. 🆎 ⓞ Ε 𝚅𝙸𝚂𝙰
  closed 1 to 15 August, Saturday lunch, Sunday – **M** 170/290
  Spec. Langoustines poêlées au thym, Pigeonneau truffé, Gibier (season). **Wines** Saint-Véran, Chiroubles.

XXX **Le Saint Alban,** 2 quai J. Moulin ⊠ 69001 ☎ 78 30 14 89 — ☰. **E** _VISA_ DV **s**
 closed 10 to 20 August, February Holidays, Saturday lunch, Sunday and Bank Holidays –
 M 140/270.

XXX **Les Fantasques,** 47 r. Bourse ⊠ 69002 ☎ 78 37 36 58 — ☰. **AE ① E** _VISA_ DX **u**
 closed 5 to 26 August and Sunday – **M** 200/350.

XXX ✿ **Henry** (Balladone), 27 r. Martinière ⊠ 69001 ☎ 78 28 26 08, « Mural paintings » — ☰.
 AE ① E _VISA_ CV **n**
 closed Monday except Bank Holidays – **M** 120/250 ⅃
 Spec. Dos de turbot rôti aux aromates, Fraise de veau mitonnée en cocotte, Salmis de palombe à l'ancienne
 (October-January). **Wines** Fleurie, Saint-Joseph.

XX **La Mère Vittet,** 26 cours Verdun ⊠ 69002 ☎ 78 37 20 17, Telex 305559, Fax 78 42 40 70 —
 ☰. **AE ① E** _VISA_ – **M** 150/355 ⅃ BZ **y**

XX **Le Nord,** 18 r. Neuve ⊠ 69002 ☎ 78 28 24 54 — ☰. _VISA_ CX **p**
 closed 12 to 18 August and Saturday – **M** 90/200.

XX ✿ **Le Passage,** 8 r. Plâtre ⊠ 69001 ☎ 78 28 11 16 — **AE ① E** _VISA_ CV **r**
 closed Saturday lunch, Sunday and Bank Holidays – **M** 230/290
 Spec. Ragoût de homard breton, Assiette chaude de coquillages et crustacés (September-January), Légumes
 nouveaux au sucre et truffes noires (Spring-Summer). **Wines** Saint-Joseph, Bugey.

XX ✿ **L'Alexandrin** (Alexanian), 83 r. Moncey ⊠ 69003 ☎ 72 61 15 69 — ☰. **E** _VISA_. ⚘
 closed 5 to 27 August, 24 December-2 January, Sunday and Monday – **M** 125/165
 Spec. Foie gras de canard aux chanterelles en terrine, Fleurs de courgette farcies à la mousse de rascasse,
 Croustillant de filet d'agneau au jus de paprika.

XX **Tante Alice,** 22 r. Remparts d'Ainay ⊠ 69002 ☎ 78 37 49 83 — ☰. **AE E** _VISA_ CZ **v**
 closed 26 July-26 August, 24 December-2 January, Friday dinner and Saturday – **M** 88/185.

XX **La Tassée,** 20 r. Charité ⊠ 69002 ☎ 78 37 02 35, Fax 72 40 05 91 — **AE ① E** _VISA_ CY **v**
 closed 24 December-2 January, Saturday and Sunday in July and August – **M** 115/250.

XX **Chez Gervais,** 42 r. P. Corneille ⊠ 69006 ☎ 78 52 19 13 — **AE ① E** _VISA_ – **M**
 closed July, Saturday (except dinner 1 October-30 April), Sunday and Bank Holidays – **M**
 130/250.

XX **La Voûte,** 11 pl. A. Gourju ⊠ 69002 ☎ 78 42 01 33 — ☰. **AE ① E** _VISA_ CY **e**
 closed 13 to 29 July and Sunday – **M** 98/160.

XX **Junet "Au Petit Col",** 68 r. Charité ⊠ 69002 ☎ 78 37 25 18 — ☰. **AE E** _VISA_ CZ **a**
 closed 5 to 15 August and Sunday dinner – **M** 140/350.

X ✿ **Chez Jean-François,** 2 pl. Célestins ⊠ 69002 ☎ 78 42 08 26 — **E** _VISA_ CX **x**
 closed 27 March-3 April, 20 July-19 August, Sunday and Bank Holidays – **M** 85/150 ⅃

X **Le Bistrot de Lyon,** 64 r. Mercière ⊠ 69002 ☎ 78 37 00 62, Fax 78 38 32 51, 余 — ☰. _VISA_
 M a la carte 180/235. CX **u**

X **La Pinte à Gones,** 59 r. Ney ⊠ 69006 ☎ 78 24 81 75 — **E** _VISA_
 closed August, 25 December-1 January, Saturday lunch, Sunday and Bank Holidays – **M**
 95/178.

 **Bouchons** : Regional specialities and wine tasting in a typical local atmosphere

X **Le Garet,** 7 r. Garet ⊠ 69001 ☎ 78 28 16 94 — **E** _VISA_ CDV **h**
 closed 20 July-20 August, Saturday and Sunday – **M** (booking essential) a la carte 105/
 160 ⅃

X **Chez Sylvain,** 4 r. Tupin ⊠ 69002 ☎ 78 42 11 98 CX **s**
 closed 1 to 21 August, Saturday and Sunday – **M** (booking essential) 76/89 a la carte dinner.

X **La Meunière,** 11 r. Neuve ⊠ 69002 ☎ 78 28 62 91 — **AE ① E** _VISA_ CX **w**
 closed 14 July-15 August, Sunday, Monday and Bank Holidays – **M** (booking essential)
 75/130.

X **Café du Jura,** 25 r. Tupin ⊠ 69002 ☎ 78 42 20 57 — **AE** _VISA_ CX **a**
 _closed 28 July-21 August, 25 December-1 January, Saturday (except dinner 1 October-30
 March) and Sunday_ – **M** (booking essential) a la carte 95/150 ⅃

X **Café des Fédérations,** 8 r. Major Martin ⊠ 69002 ☎ 78 28 26 00 — **AE** _VISA_ CV **z**
 closed August, 24 December-4 January, Saturday and Sunday – **M** (booking essential) 125.

Environs

to the NE :

 **at Rillieux-la-Pape** : 7 km by N 83 and N 84 – alt. 32 263 – ⊠ **69140** :

XXX ✿ **Larivoire** (Constantin), chemin des Iles ☎ 78 88 50 92, Fax 78 88 35 22, ≤, 余 — **P. E**
 VISA
 closed 27 August-5 September, 1 to 15 February, Monday dinner and Tuesday – **M** 190/380
 Spec. Oeufs en cocotte aux langoustines et morilles, Saumon laqué aux graines de sésame, Volaille de Bresse
 au vinaigre. **Wines** Pouilly-Loché, Chénas.

 **at Neyron** (01 Ain) by N 83 and N 84 : 14 km – ⊠ **01700** :

XXX ✿ **Le Saint Didier** (Champin), ☎ 78 55 28 72, 余 — **P. AE E** _VISA_
 closed 11 to 21 August, 26 December-21 January, Sunday dinner and Monday – **M** (booking
 essential) 175/350
 Spec. Profiteroles de foie gras sauce périgourdine, Étuvée de blanc de turbot au Champagne, Tournedos aux
 morilles.

at the airport of Satolas : 27 km by A 43 – ⊠ **69125** Lyon Satolas Airport :

🏨 **Sofitel** Ⓜ without rest, 3rd floor 🖉 72 22 71 61, Telex 380480, Fax 72 22 81 25, ≤ – 🛗 ▤ 📺
🕿 ◭ ① ☒ *VISA*
⌑ 60 – **120 rm** 580.

XXX La Gde Corbeille, 1st floor 🖉 72 22 71 76, Telex 306723, ≤ – ▤.

X Le Bouchon, 1st floor 🖉 72 22 71 99, Telex 306723 – ▤.

to the W :

Porte de Lyon - motorway junction A 6 N 6 Exit road signposted Limonest N : 10 km –
⊠ **69570** Dardilly ;

🏨 **Novotel Lyon-Nord** Ⓜ, 🖉 78 35 13 41, Telex 330962, Fax 78 35 08 45, 斎, ☇, 룾 – 🛗 ▤
📺 🕿 ⓟ – 🔏 150. ◭ ① ☒ *VISA*
M a la carte approx. 150 ⚘ – ⌑ 47 – **107 rm** 397/430.

🏨 **Mercure** Ⓜ, 🖉 78 35 28 05, Telex 330045, Fax 78 47 47 15, 斎, ☇, ℁ – 🛗 ⇐↦ rm ▤ rest
📺 🕿 ⓕ ⓟ – 🔏 30 - 250. ◭ ① ☒ *VISA*
M 105/120 ⚘ – ⌑ 48 – **175 rm** 455.

🏨 **Ibis Lyon Nord** Ⓜ, 🖉 78 66 02 20, Telex 305250, Fax 78 47 47 93, 斎, ☇, – 📺 🕿 ⓕ ⓟ –
🔏 30. ◭ ☒ *VISA*
M 100 ⚘ – ⌑ 29 – **69 rm** 280/300.

Chagny 71150 S.-et-L. 🖫🖫 ⑨ – pop. 5 604 h. alt. 216.
Lyon 143.

🏨 ❀❀❀ **Lameloise** Ⓜ, pl. d'Armes 🖉 85 87 08 85, Telex 801086, Fax 85 87 03 57, « Old
Burgundian house, tasteful decor » – 🛗 📺 🕿 ⇐↦. ◭ ☒ *VISA*
closed 18 December-23 January, Thursday lunch and Wednesday – **M** (booking essential) a
la carte 300/450 – ⌑ 75 – **20 rm** 320/850
Spec. Ravioli d'escargots dans leur bouillon d'ail doux, Pigeon de Bresse en vessie, Assiette du chocolatier.
Wines Chassagne-Montrachet rouge, Rully blanc.

Mionnay 01390 Ain 🖫🖫 ② – pop. 796 h. alt. 288.
Lyon 20.

XXXX ❀❀ **Alain Chapel** with rm, 🖉 78 91 82 02, Telex 305605, Fax 78 91 82 37, 斎, « Flowered
garden » – 📺 🕿 ⇐↦ ⓟ. ◭ ① ☒ *VISA*
closed January, Tuesday lunch and Monday – **M** 600/720 and a la carte – ⌑ 75 – **13 rm**
675/800
Spec. Bouillon de champignons en ''capuccino'', Salade de homard, Poulette de Bresse en vessie et sauce au
foie gras. **Wines** Mâcon-Clessé, Morgon.

Montrond-les-Bains 42210 Loire 🖫🖫 ⑱ – pop. 3 194 h. alt. 356.
Lyon 68.

🏨 ❀❀ **Host. La Poularde** (Etéocle), 🖉 77 54 40 06, Telex 307002, Fax 77 54 53 14, 룾 –
▤ rest 🕿 ⇐↦ – 🔏 40. ◭ ① ☒ *VISA*
closed 2 to 14 January, Monday dinner and Tuesday lunch (except Bank Holidays) –
M (Sunday : booking essential) 170/480 and a la carte – ⌑ 55 – **11 rm** 280/450, 3 duplex 750
Spec. Saumon mariné tiédi aux graines de sésame, Fricassée de poulette truffée, Gibier (season). **Wines**
Condrieu, Saint-Joseph.

Roanne ⬉ 42300 Loire 🖫🖫 ⑦ – pop. 49 638 h. alt. 279.
Lyon 86.

🏨 ❀❀❀ **Troisgros** Ⓜ, pl. Gare 🖉 77 71 66 97, Telex 307507, Fax 77 70 39 77, « Tasteful
contemporary decor », 룾 – 🛗 ▤ 📺 🕿 ⓟ. ◭ ☒ *VISA*
closed February Holidays, Wednesday lunch and Tuesday – **M** (booking essential) 460/560
and a la carte – ⌑ 90 – **15 rm** 650/1200, 6 duplex 1100/1800
Spec. Tête de veau à la tomate serrée, Sandre au vin de la Côte roannaise et à la moelle fumée, Jeu de
pommes. **Wines** Pouilly-Fuissé, Côte Roannaise.

St-Étienne Ⓟ 42000 Loire 🖫🖫 ⑲, 🖫🖫 ⑨ – pop. 206 087 h. alt. 517 – Lyon 59.

XXX ❀❀ **Pierre Gagnaire**, 3 r. G. Teissier 🖉 77 37 57 93, Fax 77 32 70 58 – ⇐↦. ◭ ① ☒ *VISA*
closed August, 2 to 18 February, Sunday and Monday – **M** 250/530 and a la carte
Spec. Attereaux de crêtes de coq et tourte de volaille à la marjolaine, Pigeon aux cosses de chocolat, Pain
d'épices et soufflé gentiane. **Wines** Crozes-Hermitage, Saint-Péray.

Valence Ⓟ 26000 Drôme 🖫🖫 ⑫ – pop. 68 157 h. alt. 123 – Lyon 100.

XXXX ❀❀❀ **Pic** with rm, 285 av. V. Hugo, Motorway exit sign-posted Valence-Sud 🖉 75 44 15 32,
斎, « Shaded garden » – 🛗 ▤ 📺 🕿 ⇐↦ ⓟ. ◭ ① ☒ *VISA*
closed August, February Holidays, Sunday dinner and Wednesday – **M** (Sunday : booking
essential) 450/550 and a la carte – ⌑ 80 – **4 rm** 550/1000
Spec. Galette de truffes et céleri au foie de canard, Filet de loup au caviar, Strate de boeuf au Cornas. **Wines**
Condrieu, Hermitage.

at Pont-de-l'Isère to the N by N 7 : 9 km – ⊠ 26600 :

✕✕✕ ❀❀ **Chabran** M with rm, N 7 ℰ 75 84 60 09, Telex 346333, Fax 75 84 59 65, 🍴 – 〜✕〜 rest
⬛ 📺 ☎ 🆎 ⓪ 🄴 *VISA*
closed 19 November-11 December, Sunday dinner and Monday except July-August –
M 210/430 and a la carte – 🍵 60 – **12 rm** 330/660
Spec. Salade de homard au museau de porc sauce soja. Dos de saumon aux senteurs drômoises. Selle
d'agneau rôtie à la gousse d'ail. **Wines** Crozes-Hermitage, Hermitage.

Vonnas 01540 Ain **74** ② – pop. 2 505 h. alt. 189.

Lyon 66.

🏨 ❀❀❀ **Georges Blanc** M ॐ, ℰ 74 50 00 10, Telex 380776, Fax 74 50 08 80, « Elegant inn
the banks of the Veyle, garden », ⊥, ✵ – 🛗 〜✕〜 rest ⬛ 📺 ☎ 🖙 🅿 🆎 ⓪ 🄴 *VISA*
closed 2 January-9 February – **M** *(closed Thursday (except dinner 15 June-15 September)
and Wednesday except Bank Holidays)* (booking essential) 380/580 and a la carte – 🍵 75
– **34 rm** 850/1500, 7 apartments 1600/3000
Spec. Crêpe parmentière au saumon et caviar. Soupe de haricots blancs aux truffes noires (Winter-Spring).
Poularde de Bresse aux gousses d'ail et foie gras. **Wines** Mâcon-Azé, Chiroubles.

MARSEILLES 🄿 13 B.-du-R. **84** ⑬ – pop. 878 689 h.

See : N.-D.-de-la-Garde Basilica ✵✲✲✲ EV – Old Port✲✲ DETU – Corniche Président-J.-F.-Ken-
nedy✲✲ – Modern Port✲✲ – Palais Longchamp✲ GS – St-Victor Basilica✲ : crypt✲✲ DU – Old
Major Cathedral✲ DS N – Pharo Parc 〜✲ DU – St-Laurent Belvedere 〜✲ DT E – Museum :
Grobet-labadié✲✲ GS M7, Cantini✲ : Marseilles and Moustiers pottery✲✲ (galerie de la Faïence
de Marseille et de Moustiers) FU – M5, Fine Arts✲ GS M8, Natural History Museum✲ GS M9 –
Mediterranean Archaeology✲ : collection of Egyptian antiquities✲✲ (Old Charity✲) DS M6, Roman
Docks DET M2 – Old Marseilles✲ DT M3.

Envir. : Corniche road✲✲ of Callelongue S : 13 km along the sea front.

Exc. : Château d'If✲✲ (✵✲✲✲) 1 h 30.

🛫 of Marseilles-Aix ℰ 42 24 20 41 to the N : 22 km ; 🛫 of Allauch-Marseille ℰ 91 05 20 60 :
jonction Marseille-East : 15 km ; by D 2 and D 4ᴬ.

✈ Marseilles-Marignane : Air France ℰ 42 78 21 00 to the N : 28 km.

🚗 ℰ 91 08 50 50.

🄱 Office de Tourisme 4 Canebière, 13001 ℰ 91 54 91 11, Telex 430402 and St-Charles railway Station
ℰ 91 50 59 18 - – A.C. 149 bd Rabatau, 13010 ℰ 91 78 83 00.

Paris 772 – Lyon 312 – Nice 188 – Torino 407 – Toulon 64 – Toulouse 398.

Plan on following pages

🏨 **Sofitel Vieux Port** M, 36 bd Ch. Livon ⊠ 13007 ℰ 91 52 90 19, Telex 401270, Fax
91 31 46 52, panoramic restaurant 〈 old port, ⊥ – 🛗 〜✕〜 rm ⬛ 📺 ☎ 🕭 🖙 – 🔬 180. 🆎
⓪ 🄴 *VISA* ⁣ DU n
les Trois Forts **M** 175/260 – 🍵 63 – **127 rm** 650/920, 3 apartments.

🏨 **Mercure-Centre** M, r. Neuve St-Martin ⊠ 13001 ℰ 91 39 20 00, Telex 401886, Fax
91 56 24 57 – 🛗 ⬛ 📺 ☎ 🖙 – 🔬 150. 🆎 ⓪ 🄴 *VISA* EST g
Oursinade *(closed August, Sunday and Bank Holidays)* **M** 195/270 – Oliveraie *(closed Saturday dinner)* **M** a la carte approx. 130 – 🍵 55 – **198 rm** 540/650.

🏨 **Pullman Beauvau** without rest, 4 r. Beauvau ⊠ 13001 ℰ 91 54 91 00, Telex 401778, Fax
91 54 15 76 – 🛗 ⬛ 📺 ☎ – 🔬 30. 🆎 ⓪ 🄴 *VISA* ET r
🍵 60 – **71 rm** 600/810.

🏨 **Novotel Marseille Centre** M, 3 bd Ch. Livon ⊠ 13007 ℰ 91 59 22 22, Telex 402937, Fax
91 31 15 48, 〈, 🍴, ⊥, 🖙 – 🔬 400. 🆎 ⓪ 🄴 *VISA* DU n
M a la carte approx. 130 ẞ – 🍵 45 – **93 rm** 470/530.

🏨 **New H. Bompard** ॐ without rest, 2 r. Flots Bleus ⊠ 13007 ℰ 91 52 10 93, Telex 400430,
Fax 91 31 02 14, 🐎 – 🛗 📺 ☎ 🅿 – 🔬 40. 🆎 ⓪ 🄴 *VISA*
🍵 42 – **47 rm** 295/360.

🏨 **St-Ferréol's** M without rest, 19 r. Pisançon ⊠ 13001 ℰ 91 33 12 21, Fax 91 54 29 97 – 🛗
⬛ 📺 ☎ 🆎 ⓪ 🄴 *VISA* FU h
closed 20 July-10 August – 🍵 35 – **19 rm** 243/356.

🏨 **New H. Sélect** M without rest, 4 allée Gambetta ⊠ 13001 ℰ 91 50 65 50, Telex 402175,
Fax 91 54 80 75 – 🛗 ⬛ 📺 ☎ – 🔬 25. 🆎 ⓪ 🄴 *VISA*. ✵ FS k
🍵 38 – **60 rm** 280/340.

🏨 **Alizé** M without rest, 7 quai Belges ⊠ 13001 ℰ 91 33 66 97, Fax 91 54 80 06, 〈 – 🛗 ⬛ 📺
☎ 🆎 ⓪ 🄴 *VISA* ETU b
🍵 28 – **35 rm** 273/396.

🏨 **New H. Astoria** without rest, 10 bd Garibaldi ⊠ 13001 ℰ 91 33 33 50, Fax 91 54 80 75 –
🛗 ⬛ 📺 ☎ 🆎 ⓪ 🄴 *VISA*. ✵ FT f
🍵 38 – **58 rm** 280/340.

🏨 **Castellane** without rest, 31 r. Rouet ⊠ 13006 ℰ 91 79 27 54, Telex 402326 – 🛗 📺 ☎
🆎 🄴 *VISA* GV f
🍵 32 – **55 rm** 343/375.

🏠 **Relais Bleus Préfecture** Ⓜ without rest, 13 r. Lafon ⊠ 13006 ℰ 91 33 34 34, Fax 91 54 10 59 – 🛗 📺 ☎ 🗄 ⇔ – 🛗 30. 🖭 ① Ɛ 𝘝𝘐𝘚𝘈
⊊ 32 – **83 rm** 265/350.
FU **w**

🏠 **Lutétia** without rest, 38 allées L. Gambetta ⊠ 13001 ℰ 91 50 81 78 – 🛗 📺 ☎. ① Ɛ 𝘝𝘐𝘚𝘈
⊊ 25 – **29 rm** 213/281.
FS **z**

XXX ❀ **Jambon de Parme,** 67 r. La Palud ⊠ 13006 ℰ 91 54 37 98 – ☰. 🖭 ① Ɛ 𝘝𝘐𝘚𝘈
FU **s**
closed 1 July-2 September, Sunday dinner and Monday – **M** a la carte 200/300
Spec. Rougets du Vallon des Auffes, Variétés de pâtes fraîches, Saltimbocca à la romaine. **Wines** Cassis, Bandol.

XXX **Patalain,** 49 r. Sainte ⊠ 13001 ℰ 91 55 02 78, Fax 91 54 15 29, « Elegant decor » – ☰. 🖭 ① Ɛ 𝘝𝘐𝘚𝘈
EU **f**
closed 14 July-5 September, Saturday lunch, Sunday and Bank Holidays – **M** 195/300.

XXX **La Ferme,** 23 r. Sainte ⊠ 13001 ℰ 91 33 21 12 – ☰. 🖭 ① Ɛ 𝘝𝘐𝘚𝘈
EU **m**
closed August, Saturday lunch, Sunday and Bank Holidays – **M** a la carte 250/310.

XXX **Les Échevins,** 44 r. Sainte ⊠ 13001 ℰ 91 33 08 08 – 🖭 ① Ɛ 𝘝𝘐𝘚𝘈
EU **x**
closed 14 July-15 August, Saturday lunch and Sunday – **M** 136/200.

XX **Michel Brasserie des Catalans,** 6 r. Catalans ⊠ 13007 ℰ 91 52 30 63, seafood – ☰. 🖭 Ɛ 𝘝𝘐𝘚𝘈
M a la carte 315/500.

XX **Brasserie New-York Vieux Port,** 7 quai Belges ⊠ 13001 ℰ 91 33 60 98, 🏠 – ☰
M a la carte 160/300 🍷.
ETU **e**

XX **Calypso,** 3 r. Catalans ⊠ 13007 ℰ 91 52 64 00, ≤, Seafood – 🖭 Ɛ 𝘝𝘐𝘚𝘈
closed Sunday dinner and Monday – **M** a la carte 250/300.

X **La Charpenterie,** 22 r. Paix ⊠ 13001 ℰ 91 54 22 89 – 🖭 ① Ɛ 𝘝𝘐𝘚𝘈
EU **d**
closed 16 July-16 August, Saturday lunch, Sunday and Bank Holidays – **M** 98/155.

at the Corniche :

🏨 **Concorde-Palm Beach** Ⓜ ⍋, 2 promenade Plage ⊠ 13008 ℰ 91 76 20 00, Telex 401894, Fax 91 77 37 83, ≤, 🏠, ⬧, 🦽 ◉ – 🛗 ☰ 📺 ☎ ⇔ ℗ – 🛗 450. 🖭 ① Ɛ 𝘝𝘐𝘚𝘈, 𝒮 rest
La Réserve M 160/215 – **Les Voiliers M** a la carte 120/185 🍷 – ⊊ 55 – **144 rm** 622/692.

🏨 ❀❀ **Le Petit Nice** (Passédat) Ⓜ ⍋, anse de Maldormé (turn at no 160 Corniche Kennedy) ⊠ 13007 ℰ 91 59 25 92, Telex 401565, Fax 91 59 28 08, 🏠, « Villas overlooking the sea, refined decor », ⬧ – 🛗 ☰ 📺 ☎ ℗. 🖭 ① Ɛ 𝘝𝘐𝘚𝘈
M (closed Sunday October-March except Bank Holidays) 390/590 and a la carte – ⊊ 90 –
15 rm 1000/1700 – ½ P 1610/2310
Spec. Compressé de Bouille-Abaisse port d'Orient, Loup de palangre, Gâteau de grenouilles au pied de porc. **Wines** Cassis, Palette.

XX **Peron,** 56 corniche Prés. Kennedy ⊠ 13007 ℰ 91 52 43 70, ≤ harbour entrance and château d'If – 🖭 ① Ɛ 𝘝𝘐𝘚𝘈
closed 1 to 8 May, January, Sunday dinner and Monday – **M** a la carte 180/300.

Les Baux-de-Provence 13 B.-du-R. 🟪🟪 ① – pop. 433 h. alt. 280 – ⊠ 13520 Maussane-les-Alpilles.

Marseilles 86.

in the Vallon :

XXXXX ❀❀ **Oustaù de Baumanière** (Thuilier) ⍋ with rm, ℰ 90 54 33 07, Telex 420203, Fax 90 54 40 46, ≤, « Tastefully decorated mansions, flowered terraces, ⬧, Riding club », 🖼
– ☰ rm 📺 ☎ ℗. 🖭 ① Ɛ 𝘝𝘐𝘚𝘈
closed 20 January-4 March, Thursday lunch and Wednesday 1 November-31 March – **M** 520/640 and a la carte – ⊊ 85 – **11 rm** 750/900, 13 apartments 1250 – ½ P 1120/1275
Spec. Pigeon farci au foie gras, Filets de rouget au basilic, Noisettes d'agneau Baumanière. **Wines** Coteaux des Baux, Gigondas.

XXX ❀ **La Cabro d'Or** Ⓜ ⍋ with rm, ℰ 90 54 33 21, Telex 401810, Fax 90 54 40 46, ≤, 🏠, « Shaded terraces, flowered garden, lake », ⬧, 🎾 – ☰ rm 📺 ☎ ℗ – 🛗 80. 🖭 ① Ɛ 𝘝𝘐𝘚𝘈
closed 12 November-21 December, Tuesday lunch and Monday 31 October-31 March –
M 290/360 – ⊊ 58 – **22 rm** 460/740 – ½ P 530/640
Spec. Salade à l'antiboise, Filets de sole aux écrevisses, Noisettes d'agneau Cabro d'Or. **Wines** Coteaux des Baux.

Carry-le-Rouet 13620 B.-du-R. 🟪🟪 ⑩ – pop. 4 570 h. alt. 4.

Marseilles 27 – Paris 956 – Menton 9 – Nice (by the Moyenne Corniche) 18 – San Remo 44.

XXXX ❀❀ **L'Escale** (Clor), ℰ 42 45 00 47, Fax 42 44 72 69, 🏠, « Terraces overlooking the Harbour, attractive view », 🖼 – 𝘝𝘐𝘚𝘈
Early February-early November and closed Monday (except dinner in July and August) and Sunday dinner – **M** (Sunday : booking essential) a la carte 350/470
Spec. Rougets de roche en nage de camoun et foie iodé, Dos de loup grillé aux épices, Homard rôti au beurre de corail. **Wines** Cassis, Coteaux d'Aix en Provence.

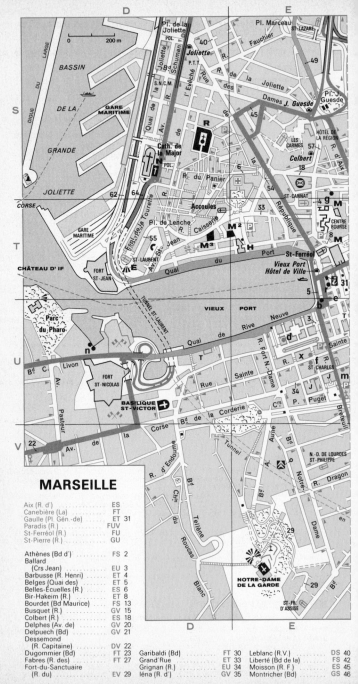

MARSEILLE

180

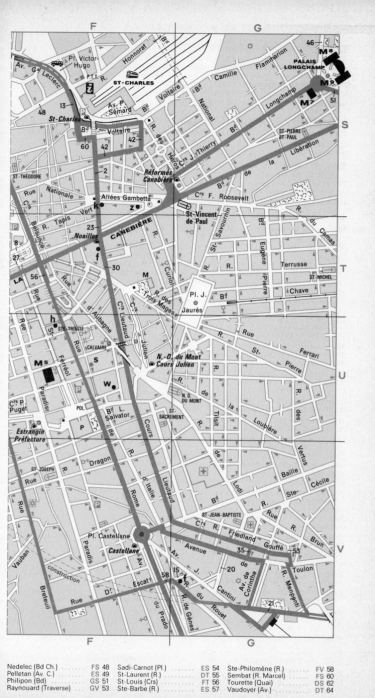

MONACO (Principality of) 🅱🅸 ⑩, 🅸🅾🅵 ㉗㉘ – pop. 30 000 h. alt. 65 – Casino .

Monaco Capital of the Principality – ⊠ **98000**.

See : Tropical Garden★★ (Jardin exotique) – ≤★ – Observatory Caves★ (Grotte de l'Observatoire) – St-Martin Gardens★ – Early paintings of the Nice School★★ in Cathedral – Recumbent Christ★ in the Misericord Chapel – Place du Palais★ – Prince's Palace★ – Museums : oceanographic★★ (aquarium)★, ≤★★ from the terrace), Prehistoric Anthropology★, Napoleon and Monaco History★.

Urban racing circuit – A. C. M. 23 bd Albert-1er ℰ 93 15 26 00, Telex 469003.

Monte-Carlo Fashionable resort of the Principality – Casinos Grand casino, Casino of Sporting Club, Casino Loews – **See** : Terrace★★ of the Grand casino – Museum of Dolls and Automata★.

🏌 Monte-Carlo Golf Club ℰ 93 41 09 11 to the S by N 7 : 11 km.

🛈 Direction Tourisme et Congrès, 2A bd Moulins ℰ 93 30 87 01, Telex 469760.

🏨🏨 **Paris**, pl. Casino ℰ 93 50 80 80, Telex 469925, Fax 93 25 59 17, ≤, 🍽, ☒, – 🛗 🖵 🔟 ☎ 🅿 – 🛎 50. 🆎 ⓞ 🆅🆂🅰. 🕸 rest
M see **Louis XV** and **Le Grill** below) - **Salle Empire** (14 June-28 September (dinner only) and 3 December-6 January) M a la carte 470/750 – ☷ 130 – **206 rm** 2200/2800, 40 apartments.

🏨🏨 **Hermitage**, square Beaumarchais ℰ 93 50 67 31, Telex 479432, Fax 93 50 47 12, ≤, 🍽, « Dining room in Baroque style », ☒ – 🛗 🖵 🔟 ☎ 🅿 – 🛎 80. 🆎 ⓞ 🆅🆂🅰. 🕸 rest
M 300/400 – ☷ 130 – **220 rm** 1800/2400, 22 apartments.

🏨🏨 **Métropole Palace** Ⓜ, 4 av. Madone ℰ 93 15 15 15, Telex 489836, Fax 93 25 24 44, ☒, 🌿 – 🛗 🖵 🔟 ☎ 🕭 ⟲ – 🛎 150. 🆎 ⓞ 🅴 🆅🆂🅰
M a la carte 150/250 🍴 – ☷ 95 – **100 rm** 1350/1900, 31 apartments.

🏨🏨 **Loews** Ⓜ, av. Spélugues ℰ 93 50 65 00, Telex 479435, Fax 93 30 01 57, ≤, 🍽, Casino and cabaret, 🎰, ☒ – 🛗 🖵 🔟 ☎ 🕭 ⟲ – 🛎 30 - 2 000. 🆎 ⓞ 🅴 🆅🆂🅰. 🕸 rest
Le Foie Gras (dinner only) M carte 450 à 650 – **L'Argentin** (dinner only) M 310 – **Le Pistou** (dinner only) M 215 /280 – **Café de la mer** M carte 160 à 280 – ☷ 110 – **600 rm** 1900/2200, 35 apartments.

🏨🏨 **Beach Plaza** Ⓜ, av. Princesse Grace, à la Plage du Larvotto ℰ 93 30 98 80, Telex 479617, Fax 93 50 23 14, ≤, 🍽, « Fashionable resort with good bathing facilities ☒, 🎰 » – 🛗 🖵 🔟 ☎ 🕭 ⟲ – 🛎 50 - 300. 🆎 ⓞ 🅴 🆅🆂🅰
Le Gratin M a la carte 270/400 – **Le Café-Terrasse** M a la carte 195/360 – ☷ 112 – **295 rm** 1940, 9 apartments.

🏨🏨 **Mirabeau** Ⓜ, 1 av. Princesse Grace ℰ 93 25 45 45, Telex 479413, Fax 93 50 84 85, ≤, ☒ – 🛗 🖵 rm 🔟 ☎ 🕭 ⟲ – 🛎 100. 🆎 ⓞ 🅴 🆅🆂🅰. 🕸 rest
M see **La Coupole** below – ☷ 130 – **99 rm** 1200/1900, 4 apartments 2500 – ½ P 1190/1340.

🏨 **Balmoral**, 12 av. Costa ℰ 93 50 62 37, Telex 479436, Fax 93 15 08 69, ≤ – 🛗 🖵 rm 🔟 ☎. 🆎 ⓞ 🅴 🆅🆂🅰. 🕸 – **M** snack (closed November, Sunday dinner, Monday and Bank Holidays) 80 – ☷ 45 – **77 rm** 350/700.

🏨 **Louvre** without rest, 16 bd Moulins ℰ 93 50 65 25, Telex 479645, Fax 93 30 23 68 – 🛗 🖵 🔟 ☎. 🆎 ⓞ 🅴 🆅🆂🅰. 🕸 – **35 rm** 524/778.

🏨 **Alexandra** without rest, 35 bd Princesse Charlotte ℰ 93 50 63 13, Telex 489286 – 🛗 🖵 🔟 ☎. 🆎 ⓞ 🅴 🆅🆂🅰. 🕸 – ☷ 44 – **55 rm** 450/670.

🍽🍽🍽🍽🍽 ۞۞۞ **Louis XV** – **Hôtel de Paris**, pl. Casino ℰ 93 50 80 80, Telex 469925, Fax 93 25 59 17, 🍽 – 🖵 🅿. 🆎 ⓞ 🅴 🆅🆂🅰
closed 26 November-25 December, 18 February-1 March, Tuesday and Wednesday except dinner from 26/6 to 28/8 – **M** 580/690 and a la carte
Spec. Légumes de printemps aux truffes (March-June), Pigeonneau cuit sur la braise (October-March), Fraises des bois et sorbet au mascarpone (April-July). **Wines** Bellet, Côtes de Provence.

🍽🍽🍽🍽 ۞ **Grill de l'Hôtel de Paris**, pl. Casino ℰ 93 50 80 80, Telex 469925, Fax 93 25 59 17, « Rooftop grill (open air) with ≤ over the Principality » – 🖵 🅿. 🆎 ⓞ 🆅🆂🅰
closed 3 to 22 December – **M** a la carte 450/680
Spec. Risotto à la fleur de courgette et pancetta, Rougets de roche en filets poêlés ''Niçoise'', Gourmandise au chocolat. **Wines** Bellet, Côtes de Provence Villars.

🍽🍽🍽 ۞ **La Coupole** – Hôtel Mirabeau, 1 av. Princesse Grace ℰ 93 25 45 45, Telex 479413, Fax 93 50 84 85, 🍽 – 🖵 🅿. 🆎 ⓞ 🅴 🆅🆂🅰
closed lunch in July and August – **M** 260/390
Spec. Gnocchi de fromage de chèvre frais, Dos de loup croustillant à la peau, Mignon de veau aux morilles.

🍽🍽🍽 **Giacomo**, av. Spélugues (126 galerie Métropole) ℰ 93 25 20 30, Fax 93 15 98 71, Italian cuisine – 🖵. 🆎 ⓞ 🅴 🆅🆂🅰 – **M** (booking essential) a la carte 330/600.

🍽🍽 **Le Saint Benoit**, 10 ter av. Costa ℰ 93 25 02 34, Fax 93 30 52 64, ≤ port and Monaco, 🍽 – 🖵. 🆎 ⓞ 🆅🆂🅰 – closed 8 December-6 January and Monday – **M** 155/220.

🍽 **Polpetta**, 6 av. Roqueville ℰ 93 50 67 84, Italian rest. – 🅴 🆅🆂🅰
closed 10 to 25 October, 20 February-15 March, Tuesday (except July and August) and Saturday lunch – **M** 140.

🍽 **Roger Vergé Café**, Galerie du Sporting d'Hiver ℰ 93 25 86 12 – 🖵. 🆎 ⓞ 🅴 🆅🆂🅰
closed Sunday – **M** 110/190.

at Monte-Carlo Beach (06 Alpes-Mar.) at 2,5 km – ⊠ **06190** Roquebrune-Cap-Martin :

🏨🏨 **Monte-Carlo Beach H.** Ⓜ ⟲, ℰ 93 78 21 40, Telex 462010, Fax 93 78 14 18, ≤ sea and Monaco, 🍽 – 🛗 🖵 rm 🔟 ☎ 🅿 – 🛎 30. 🆎 ⓞ 🅴 🆅🆂🅰. 🕸 rest
12 April-6 October – **M** a la carte 300/500 – ☷ 130 – **46 rm** 1950/2100.

NICE P 06000 Alpes-Mar. 84 ⑨⑩, 195 ㉖㉗ – pop. 338 486 h. alt. 5 – Casino Ruhl FZ.

See : Site** – Promenade des Anglais** EFZ – Old Nice* : Château ≤** JZ, Interior* of church of St-Martin-St-Augustin HY **D** – Balustraded staircase* of the Palais Lascaris HZ **K**, Interior* of Ste-Reparate Cathedral – HZ **L**, St-Jacques Church* HZ **N**, Decoration* of St-Giaume's Chapel HZ **R** – Mosaic* by Chagall in Law Faculty DZ **U** – Cimiez : Monastery* (Masterpieces** of the early Nice School in the church) HV **Q**, Roman Ruins* HV – Museums : Marc Chagall** GX, Matisse* HV **M2**, Fine Arts Museum** DZ **M**, Masséna* FZ **M1** – International Naive Style Museum* – Carnival*** (before Shrove Tuesday) – Mount Alban ≤** 5 km – Mount Boron ≤* 3 km – St-Pons Church* : 3 km.

Envir. : St-Michel Plateau ≤** 9,5 km.

Biot ✆ 93 65 08 48 : 22 km.

of Nice-Côte d'Azur ✆ 93 21 30 30 : 7 km.

✆ 93 87 50 50.

Office de Tourisme and Accueil de France (hotel reservations - not more than 7 days in advance) av. Thiers ✆ 93 87 07 07, Telex 460042 ; 5 av. Gustave-V ✆ 93 87 60 60 and Nice-Ferber near the Airport ✆ 93 83 32 64 – A.C. 9 r. Massenet ✆ 93 87 18 17.

Paris 931 – Cannes 32 – Genova 194 – Lyon 471 – Marseille 188 – Torino 220.

Plan on following pages

Négresco, 37 promenade des Anglais ✆ 93 88 39 51, Telex 460040, Fax 93 88 35 68, ≤, « Empire and Napoléon III furniture (16C and 18C) » – |‡| ▤ TV ☎ ♿ – 🔔 50 - 400. AE ⓓ E VISA FZ **k**
M see **Chantecler** below - **La Rotonde M** carte 190 à 280 – ☕ 100 – **130 rm** 1500/2200, 20 apartments.

Palais Maeterlinck M ⛰, Palais Maeterlinck, 6 km by lower loast Rd ✆ 93 56 21 12, Fax 93 26 39 91, ≤ sea, ⛱, 🏊, 🎾 – |‡| kitchenette ⇆ rm ▤ TV ☎ ♿ 🚗 P – 🔔 25. AE VISA. ✻
closed 6 January-12 February – **M** *(closed Saturday dinner and Monday)* 250/400 – ☕ 65 – **20 rm** 1500/3100, 6 apartments.

Sofitel M, 2-4 parvis de l'Europe ✆ 92 00 80 00, Telex 461800, Fax 93 26 27 00, 🏊 – |‡| ⇆ rm ▤ TV ☎ ♿ 🚗 – 🔔 60. AE ⓓ E VISA JX **t**
M a la carte 140/220 – ☕ 65 – **152 rm** 780.

Sofitel Splendid M, 50 bd V. Hugo ✆ 93 88 69 54, Telex 460938, Fax 93 87 02 46, ⛱, « 🏊 on 8th floor, ≤ Nice » – |‡| ⇆ rm ▤ TV ☎ – 🔔 30 - 100. AE ⓓ E VISA. ✻ rest FYZ **g**
M 125/160 – ☕ 70 – **116 rm** 650/990, 12 apartments 1100/1450 – ½ P 565/685.

Beach Régency M, 223 promenade des Anglais ✉ 06200 ✆ 93 37 17 17, Telex 461635, Fax 93 71 21 71, ⛱, « Rooftop swimming pool ≤ bay » – |‡| ▤ TV ☎ 🚗 – 🔔 400. AE ⓓ E VISA DZ **a**
Le Régency *(closed July and August)* **M** 160/175 – **La Piscine** grill *(open July and August)* **M** a la carte 250/350 – ☕ 75 – **320 rm** 830/1130, 12 apartments – ½ P 705/905.

Méridien M, 1 promenade des Anglais ✆ 93 82 25 25, Telex 470361, Fax 93 16 08 90, ⛱, « Rooftop swimming pool, ≤ bay » – |‡| ▤ TV ☎ ♿ – 🔔 400. AE ⓓ E VISA FZ **d**
La Terrasse M 190/240 – ☕ 85 – **314 rm** 1020/1680.

Beau Rivage M, 24 av. St-François-de-Paule ✉ 06300 ✆ 93 80 80 70, Telex 462708, Fax 93 80 55 77, 🎾 – |‡| ⇆ rm ▤ TV ☎ ♿ – 🔔 40. AE ⓓ E VISA GZ **y**
M *(closed Sunday)* a la carte 160/270 – ☕ 70 – **118 rm** 760/1000, 10 apartments 1600.

Élysée Palace M, 59 promenade des Anglais ✆ 93 86 06 06, Telex 970336, Fax 93 44 50 40, ≤, 🏊 – |‡| ⇆ rm ▤ TV ☎ ♿ 🚗 – 🔔 25. AE ⓓ E VISA. ✻ rest EZ **d**
M a la carte approx. 250 – ☕ 95 – **140 rm** 800/2750 – ½ P 580/620.

Pullman Nice M without rest, 28 av. Notre-Dame ✆ 93 80 30 24, Telex 470662, Fax 93 62 61 69, « Hanging garden on 2nd floor, 🏊 on 8th floor, ≤ » – |‡| ▤ TV ☎ – 🔔 25 - 120. AE ⓓ E VISA FXY **q**
☕ 58 – **200 rm** 535/980.

Plaza, 12 av. Verdun ✆ 93 87 80 41, Telex 460979, Fax 93 88 61 11, ≤, « Rooftop terrace » – |‡| ▤ TV ☎ – 🔔 30 - 550. AE ⓓ E VISA GZ **f**
M 120/180 – ☕ 70 – **183 rm** 600/1300, 10 apartments 1500/2500 – ½ P 550/800.

Westminster Concorde, 27 promenade des Anglais ✆ 93 88 29 44, Telex 460872, Fax 93 82 45 35, ≤, ⛱ – |‡| ▤ TV ☎ – 🔔 40 - 350. AE ⓓ E VISA. ✻ FZ **m**
Le Farniente M carte 210 à 390 – ☕ 70 – **105 rm** 700/1200.

West End, 31 promenade des Anglais ✆ 93 88 79 91, Telex 460879, Fax 93 88 85 07, ≤, ⛱ – |‡| ▤ TV ☎ – 🔔 150. AE ⓓ E VISA FZ **p**
M 140/250 – ☕ 50 – **130 rm** 450/1300, 3 apartments 1700 – ½ P 400/800.

La Pérouse ⛰, 11 quai Rauba-Capéu ✆ 93 62 34 63, Telex 461411, Fax 93 62 59 41, « ≤ Nice and promenade des Anglais », 🏊 – |‡| ▤ rm TV ☎ – 🔔 25. AE ⓓ E VISA HZ **k**
M *(15 March-30 September)* a la carte 160/260 – ☕ 70 – **65 rm** 545/1500.

Grand H. Aston M, 12 av. F. Faure ✆ 93 80 62 52, Telex 470290, Fax 93 80 40 02, « Roof top terrace » – |‡| ⇆ rm ▤ TV ☎ – 🔔 50 - 180. AE ⓓ E VISA. ✻ rest HZ **u**
Le Champagne *(closed 25 July-25 August, Saturday lunch and Sunday)* **M** 220/290 – ☕ 50 – **160 rm** 400/1000 – ½ P 550/850.

Altea Masséna M without rest, 58 r. Gioffredo ✆ 93 85 49 25, Telex 470192, Fax 93 62 43 27 – |‡| ▤ TV ☎. AE ⓓ E VISA GZ **k**
☕ 55 – **116 rm** 540/760.

NICE

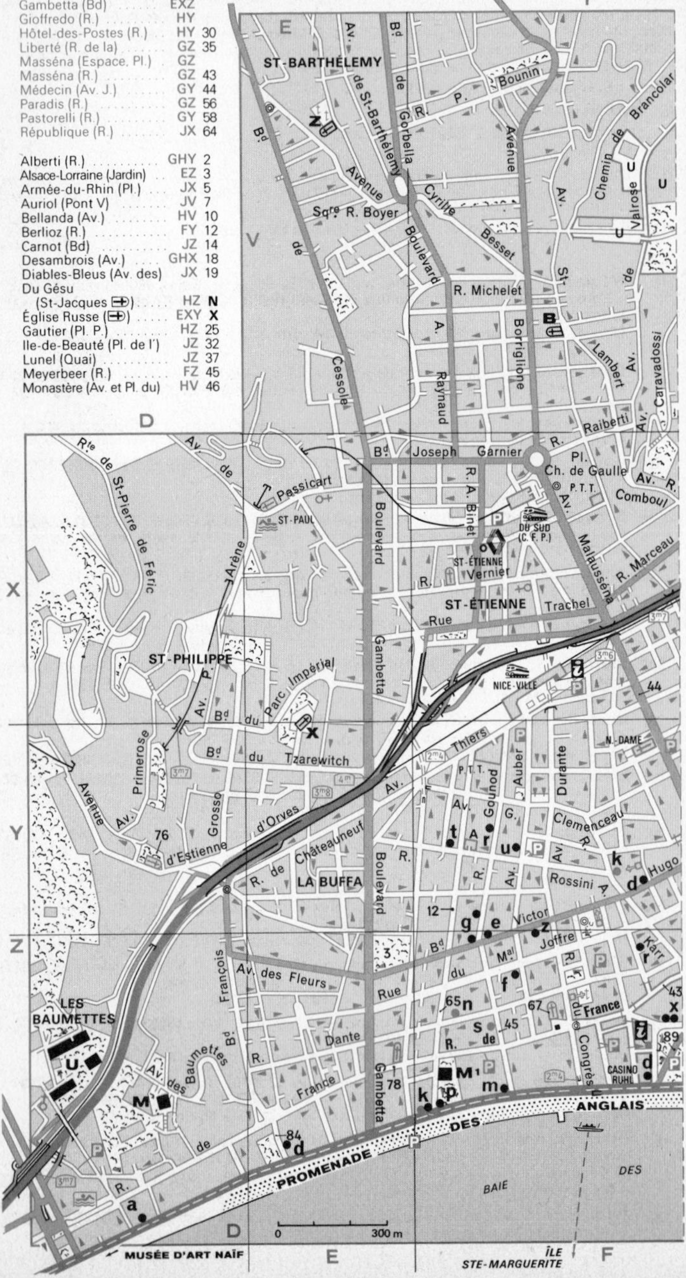

E
F
D
V
X
Y
Z
ST-BARTHÉLEMY
Bd de St-Barthélémy
Av. de St-Barthélemy
Bd de Gorbella
R. P. Bounin
Avenue
Cyrille
Besset
Chemin de Brancolar
Valrose
Av. St-Lambert
Sqre R. Boyer
Boulevard
R. Michelet
A. Raynaud
Borriglione
Cessole
Av. Caravadossi
Bd Joseph Garnier
R. Raiberti
Pl. Ch. de Gaulle
P.T.T.
Av. R. Comboul
Rte de St-Pierre de Féric
Av. de Pessicart
ST-PAUL
R. A. Binet
DU SUD (C. F. P.)
ST-ÉTIENNE
R. Vernier
Av. Malausséna
R. Marceau
Rue Trachel
Arène
Boulevard Gambetta
ST-PHILIPPE
Av. P.
Parc Impérial
Bd du Tzarewitch
NICE-VILLE
Av. Thiers
N.-DAME
Primerose
Avenue
Av. d'Estienne d'Orves
Grosso
R. de Châteauneuf
LA BUFFA
Av. Gounod
Auber
Durante
Av. G. Clemenceau
R. Rossini
Victor Hugo
Bd Mal Joffre
R. Karr
François
Av. des Fleurs
Rue du
Rue de France
Dante
Congrès
France
CASINO RUHL
LES BAUMETTES
Av. des Baumettes
Bd François
PROMENADE DES ANGLAIS
BAIE DES
0
300 m
MUSÉE D'ART NAÏF
ÎLE STE-MARGUERITE

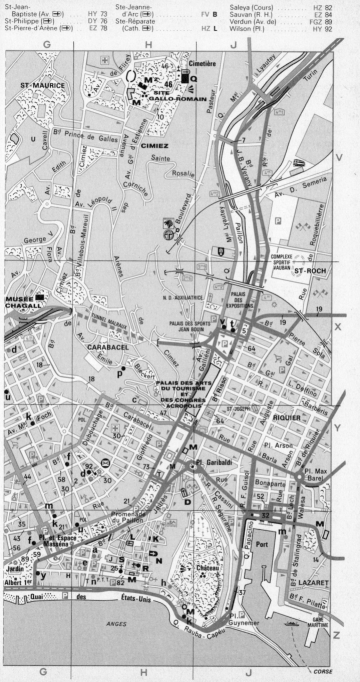

185

Novotel Ⓜ, 8-10 esplanade du Parvis de l'Europe ℰ 93 13 30 93, Telex 460243, Fax 93 13 09 04, 斎, ⊥ – 🛗 🗏 📺 ☎ ᵫ – 🔬 90. 🆎 ⓘ ᴇ 𝘝𝘐𝘚𝘈 JX **v**
M a la carte approx. 140 ⅜ – ☲ 46 – **173 rm** 495/560.

La Malmaison, 48 bd V. Hugo ℰ 93 87 62 56, Telex 470410, Fax 93 16 17 99, 斎 – 🛗 ⇔ rm 🗏 📺 ☎. 🆎 ⓘ ᴇ 𝘝𝘐𝘚𝘈. ℀ rest FYZ **e**
M (closed 2 July-1 August, Sunday dinner and Monday) 120/240 – ☲ 35 – **50 rm** 455/810 – ½ P 520/565.

Atlantic, 12 bd V. Hugo ℰ 93 88 40 15, Telex 460840, Fax 93 88 68 60 – 🛗 🗏 rm 📺 ☎ ℗ – 🔬 30 - 80. 🆎 ⓘ ᴇ 𝘝𝘐𝘚𝘈 FY **d**
M 110/120 – ☲ 50 – **123 rm** 600/900 – ½ P 970/1140.

Park, 6 av. de Suède ℰ 93 87 80 25, Telex 970176, Fax 93 82 29 27, ≼ – 🛗 🗏 📺 ☎ ᵫ– 🔬 100. 🆎 ⓘ ᴇ 𝘝𝘐𝘚𝘈 FZ **x**
Le Passage (closed Sunday) – ☲ 75 – **130 rm** 750/900.

Victoria without rest, 33 bd V. Hugo ℰ 93 88 39 60, Telex 461337, ℻ – 🛗 📺 ☎. 🆎 ⓘ ᴇ 𝘝𝘐𝘚𝘈 FYZ **z**
39 rm ☲ 510/590.

Ambassador without rest, 8 av. Suède ℰ 93 87 90 19, Telex 460025, Fax 93 82 14 90 – 🛗 🗏 📺 ☎ ᵫ. 🆎 ⓘ ᴇ 𝘝𝘐𝘚𝘈 FZ **x**
☲ 45 – **45 rm** 430/720.

Petit Palais Ⓜ ℀ without rest, 10 av. E. Bieckert ℰ 93 62 19 11, Telex 462233, ≼ Nice and sea – 🛗 📺 ☎. 🆎 ᴇ 𝘝𝘐𝘚𝘈 HX **p**
☲ 35 – **25 rm** 450/500.

Frantour Napoléon without rest, 6 r. Grimaldi ℰ 93 87 70 07, Telex 460949, Fax 93 16 17 80 – 🛗 🗏 📺 ☎. 🆎 ⓘ ᴇ 𝘝𝘐𝘚𝘈 FZ **r**
☲ 45 – **83 rm** 515/590.

Windsor, 11 r. Dalpozzo ℰ 93 88 59 35, Telex 970072, Fax 93 88 94 57, ⊥, ℻ – 🛗 📺 ☎. 🆎 ⓘ ᴇ 𝘝𝘐𝘚𝘈. ℀ rest FZ **f**
M (closed Sunday) a la carte approx. 180 – ☲ 25 – **60 rm** 375/590 – ½ P 375/435.

Lausanne without rest, 36 r. Rossini ℰ 93 88 85 94, Telex 461269, Fax 93 88 15 88 – 🛗 📺 ☎. 🆎 ⓘ ᴇ 𝘝𝘐𝘚𝘈 FY **t**
☲ 45 – **40 rm** 350/580.

Oasis Ⓜ ℀ without rest, 23 r. Gounod ℰ 93 88 12 29, Telex 462705, ℻ – 🛗 📺 ☎ ℗. 🆎 ⓘ ᴇ 𝘝𝘐𝘚𝘈 FY **r**
☲ 35 – **38 rm** 310/370.

Alexandra without rest, 41 r. Lamartine ℰ 93 62 14 43, Fax 93 62 30 34 – 🛗 📺 ☎. 🆎 ⓘ ᴇ 𝘝𝘐𝘚𝘈 GX **u**
☲ 35 – **53 rm** 325/400.

Gounod without rest, 3 r. Gounod ℰ 93 88 26 20, Telex 461705 – 🛗 🗏 📺 ☎ ⇦. 🆎 ⓘ ᴇ 𝘝𝘐𝘚𝘈 FYZ **g**
45 rm ☲ 440/560, 5 apartments 740.

Vendôme Ⓜ without rest, 26 r. Pastorelli ℰ 93 62 00 77, Telex 461762, Fax 93 13 40 78 – 🛗 🗏 📺 ☎ ℗. 🆎 ⓘ ᴇ 𝘝𝘐𝘚𝘈 GY **f**
☲ 30 – **57 rm** 470/600.

Trianon without rest, 15 av. Auber ℰ 93 88 30 69, Telex 970984, Fax 93 88 11 35 – 🛗 📺 ☎. 🆎 ⓘ ᴇ 𝘝𝘐𝘚𝘈 FY **u**
☲ 22 – **32 rm** 245/305.

Marbella without rest, 120 bd Carnot ⊠ 06300 ℰ 93 89 39 35, ≼ coastline – 📺 ☎. 🆎 ᴇ 𝘝𝘐𝘚𝘈. ℀
☲ 25 – **17 rm** 210/430.

XXXXX ✿✿ **Jacques Maximin**, 4 r. S. Guitry ℰ 93 80 70 10, Telex 462794, Fax 93 62 37 79, « Elegantly installed in a former theatre » – 🗏. 🆎 𝘝𝘐𝘚𝘈 GYZ **m**
M 350/700 and a la carte
Spec. Terrine d'ail doux à la gelée de poulet, Courgettes à la fleur et aux truffes, Tian d'agneau à la niçoise. Wines Bellet, Côtes de Provence.

XXXXX ✿ **Chantecler** - Hôtel Négresco, 37 promenade des Anglais ℰ 93 88 39 51, Telex 460040, Fax 93 88 35 68 – 🗏. 🆎 ⓘ ᴇ 𝘝𝘐𝘚𝘈 FZ **k**
closed mid November-mid December – **M** 390/550
Spec. Fenouil et anis à la crème et sarriette, Saint-Pierre au jus de ratatouille safrané, Filet de pageot aux câpres et tomates séchées. Wines Bellet.

XXX **Ane Rouge,** 7 quai Deux-Emmanuel ⊠ 06300 ℰ 93 89 49 63 – 🆎 ⓘ ᴇ 𝘝𝘐𝘚𝘈 JZ **m**
closed 20 July-1 September, Saturday, Sunday and Bank Holidays – **M** a la carte 350/470.

XXX ✿ **Florian** (Gillon), 22 r. A. Karr ℰ 93 88 86 60, Fax 93 87 31 98 – 🗏 ᴇ 𝘝𝘐𝘚𝘈 FY **k**
closed Saturday lunch, Sunday and lunch 20 June-1 September – **M** 220/320
Spec. Ravioles de daube à la niçoise, Côtes de pigeon ''Romanoff'', Noisettes de faon de biche en poivrade (1 September-15 January). Wines Bellet, Côtes de Provence.

XXX **L'Eridan**, 6 pl. Wilson ℰ 93 92 43 75, 斎 – 🗏. 🆎 ⓘ ᴇ 𝘝𝘐𝘚𝘈 HY **d**
closed 5 to 25 August, 22 to 29 December, Saturday lunch, Sunday and Bank Holidays – **M** 145/310.

XXX **La Toque Blanche**, 40 r. Buffa ℰ 93 88 38 18 – 🗏. ᴇ 𝘝𝘐𝘚𝘈 FZ **n**
closed 15 to 30 July, Sunday dinner and Monday – **M** (booking essential) 130/160.

XX **Les Dents de la Mer,** 2 r. St-François-de-Paule ⌧ 06300 𝒫 93 80 99 16, Seafood, « Unusual decor representing a submerged galleon » – 🍴. ⏇ ⓞ ⒠ 𝗩𝗜𝗦𝗔   HZ **n**
M 135/255.

XX **Boccaccio,** 7 r. Masséna 𝒫 93 87 71 76, Fax 93 82 09 06, Seafood – 🍴. ⏇ ⓞ ⒠ 𝗩𝗜𝗦𝗔   GZ **f**
M a la carte 240/360.

XX **Le Gd Pavois ''Chez Michel'',** 11 r. Meyerbeer 𝒫 93 88 77 42, Seafood – 🍴. ⒠ 𝗩𝗜𝗦𝗔
closed 1 July-15 August and Monday except bank holidays – **M** a la carte 200/320.   FZ **s**

XX **Los Caracolès,** 5 r. St-François-de-Paule ⌧ 06300 𝒫 93 80 98 23 – ⠤⇒ 🍴. ⒠ 𝗩𝗜𝗦𝗔   HZ **e**
closed 25 February-7 March, 8 July-12 August, Saturday lunch and Wednesday – **M** 180/220 ⅃.

XX **Don Camillo,** 5 r. Ponchettes ⌧ 06300 𝒫 93 85 67 95 – 🍴. ⒠ 𝗩𝗜𝗦𝗔   HZ **h**
closed August, Sunday and Monday – **M** 195/320.

X **Mireille,** 19 bd Raimbaldi 𝒫 93 85 27 23, One dish only : paella – 🍴. ⒠ 𝗩𝗜𝗦𝗔   GX **d**
closed 3 June-4 July, Monday and Tuesday except Bank Holidays – **M** a la carte approx. 130.

X **La Merenda,** 4 r. Terrasse ⌧ 06300, Specialities of Nice – 🍴   HZ **a**
closed August, Christmas-New Year, February, Saturday, Sunday and Monday – **M** a la carte approx. 160.

at the airport : 7 km – ⌧ 06200 Nice :

🏨 **Holiday Inn** Ⓜ, 179 bd R. Cassin 𝒫 93 83 91 92, Telex 970202, Fax 93 21 69 57, 🌡, 🟰 – 🛗
⠤⇒ rm 🍴 📺 ☎ ⅃ ⟷ – 🔏 150. ⏇ ⓞ ⒠ 𝗩𝗜𝗦𝗔. ⚸
M 95/160 – 🍵 78 – **150 rm** 825/925.

🏨 **Campanile** Ⓜ, 459 promenade des Anglais 𝒫 93 21 20 20, Telex 461640, Fax 93 83 83 96 –
🛗⏁ 📺 ☎ ⅃ ⟷ – 🔏 25 - 80. ⒠ 𝗩𝗜𝗦𝗔
M 82 b.i./110 b.i. – 🍵 27 – **170 rm** 345 – ½ P 283/311.

X **Grill Soleil d'Or,** 1st floor in Air Terminal 1 𝒫 93 21 36 14, Telex 970011, Fax 93 21 35 31, ⟨
– ⠤⇒ 🍴. ⏇ 𝗩𝗜𝗦𝗔
M a la carte 115/215 ⅃.

St-Martin-du-Var 06670 Alpes-Mar. 🅗🅗 ⑤. 🄸🄰🄵 ⑯ – pop. 1 528 h. alt. 122.
Nice 27.

XXXX ✿✿ **Jean-François Issautier,** S : 3 km on N 202 𝒫 93 08 10 65, Fax 93 29 19 73 – ℗. ⏇
ⓞ ⒠ 𝗩𝗜𝗦𝗔
closed 5 to 13 November, mid February-mid March, Sunday except lunch 1 September-30 June – **M** (booking essential) 240/400 and a la carte
Spec. Marinière de Saint-Pierre aux aromates, Petits "capouns" de langoustines au jus de truffes, Suprèmes de pigeonneau en potée de chou frisé. **Wines** Bellet blanc, Bandol.

STRASBOURG ℗ 67000 B.-Rhin 🅖🅒 ⑲ – pop. 252 264 h. Greater Strasbourg 409 161 alt. 140.

See : Cathedral★★★ : Astronomical clock★, ⠦★ CX - ⠦★ of rue Mercière CX 53 – Old City★★★
BCX : la Petite France★★ BX, Rue du Bain-aux-Plantes★★ BX **7**, Place de la Cathédrale★ CX **17**, –
Maison Kammerzell★ CX **e**, Château des Rohan★★ CX, Cour du Corbeau★ CX **18**, – Ponts couverts★
BX **B**, Place Kléber★ CV 53 – Barrage Vauban ⠦★★ BX **D** – Mausoleum★★ in St-Thomas Church
CX **E** – Hôtel de Ville★ CV **H** – Orangery★ – St-Pierre-le-Vieux Church : painted panels★,
scenes of the Passion of Christ★ BV – Boat trips on the Ill river and the canals★ CX – Museums :
Oeuvre N.-Dame★★★ CX **M1**, Château des Rohan (Museums★★) CX, Alsatian★ CX **M2** – Historical★
CX **M3** – Guided tours of the Port★ by boat – Palais de l'Europe★.

🏌🏌 Illkirch-Graffenstaden 𝒫 88 66 17 22 ; 🏌 of the Wantzenau at Wantzenau 𝒫 88 96 39 15 N :
by D 468 : 12 km.

⠦ of Strasbourg International : 𝒫 88 78 40 99, by D 392 : 12 km.

🚗 𝒫 88 22 50 50.

🄱 Officé de Tourisme and Accueil de France (Information and hotel reservations, not more than 5 days in advance), Palais des Congrès av. Schutzenberger 𝒫 88 37 67 68, Telex 870860 ; 10 pl. Gutenberg 𝒫 88 32 57 07 and pl. Gare 𝒫 88 32 51 49 - Welcome Office, Pont Europe (exchange facilities) 𝒫 88 61 39 23 – A.C. 5 av. Paix 𝒫 88 36 04 34.

Paris 489 – Bâle 145 – Bonn 360 – Bordeaux 922 – Frankfurt 218 – Karlsruhe 81 – Lille 545 – Luxembourg 223 – Lyon 480 – Stuttgart 157.

Plan on next page

🏨 **Hilton** Ⓜ, av. Herrenschmidt 𝒫 88 37 10 10, Telex 890363, Fax 88 36 83 27, 🌡 – 🛗
kitchenette ⠤⇒ rm 🍴 📺 ☎ ℗ – 🔏 30 - 350. ⏇ ⓞ ⒠ 𝗩𝗜𝗦𝗔
La Maison du Boeuf (closed 13 July-18 August, 20 February-9 March, Saturday and Sunday)
M a la carte 240/360 – **Le Jardin M** a la carte 145/225 ⅃ – 🍵 80 – **246 rm** 850/950,
5 apartments.

🏨 **Sofitel** Ⓜ, pl. St-Pierre-le-Jeune 𝒫 88 32 99 30, Telex 870894, Fax 88 32 60 67, 🌡, patio –
🛗 ⠤⇒ rm 🍴 📺 ☎ ⟷ – 🔏 120. ⏇ ⓞ ⒠ 𝗩𝗜𝗦𝗔   CV **s**
L'Alsace Gourmande 𝒫 88 75 11 10 **M** a la carte 145/230 ⅃ – 🍵 70 – **158 rm** 680/835, 5
apartments.

🏨 **Holiday Inn** Ⓜ, 20 pl. Bordeaux 𝒫 88 37 80 00, Telex 890515, Fax 88 37 07 04, 🌡, 🅕🅢, 🏊
– 🛗 ⠤⇒ rm 🍴 📺 ☎ ⅃ ℗ – 🔏 50 - 600. ⏇ ⓞ ⒠ 𝗩𝗜𝗦𝗔
La Louisiane M a la carte 170/270 ⅃ – 🍵 70 – **170 rm** 695/950.

STRASBOURG

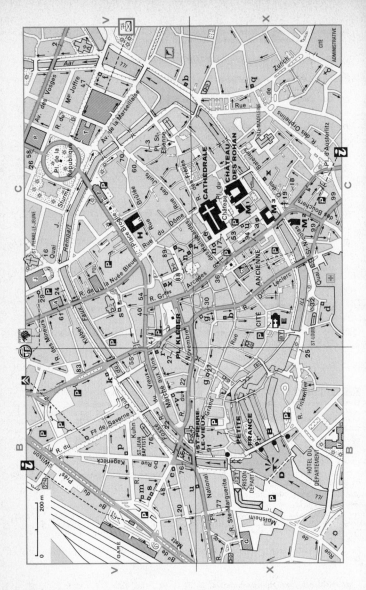

🏛 **Régent Contades** Ⓜ without rest, 8 av. Liberté ℰ 88 36 26 26, Telex 890641, Fax 88 37 13 70
– 📶 ▨ ▥ ☎ ♿, 🅰🅴 ⓞ 🅔 𝘝𝘐𝘚𝘈   CV **f**
closed Christmas-New Year – ☑ 60 – **46 rm** 700/1300.

🏛 **Terminus-Gruber**, 10 pl. Gare ℰ 88 32 87 00, Telex 870998, Fax 88 32 16 46 – 📶 ▨ ☎ ♿
– 🔬 60. 🅰🅴 ⓞ 🅔 𝘝𝘐𝘚𝘈   BV **m**
M *(closed 24 December-10 January)* 160 ♨ - **La Brasserie** Ⓜ 85 ♨ – ☑ 45 – **68 rm** 240/550.
10 apartments 550/650 – ½ P 470/620.

🏛 **Novotel** Ⓜ, quai Kléber ℰ 88 22 10 99, Telex 880700, Fax 88 22 20 92 – 📶 ▤ ▨ ☎ ♿ –
🔬 30 - 200. 🅰🅴 ⓞ 🅔 𝘝𝘐𝘚𝘈   BV **k**
M a la carte approx. 130 ♨ – ☑ 47 – **97 rm** 480/535.

🏛 **France** Ⓜ without rest, 20 r. Jeu des Enfants ℰ 88 32 37 12, Telex 890084, Fax 88 22 48 08
– 📶 ▨ ☎ ⇌ – 🔬 30. 🅰🅴 🅔 𝘝𝘐𝘚𝘈   BV **v**
☑ 31 – **66 rm** 385/545.

🏛 **Monopole-Métropole** without rest, 16 r. Kuhn ℰ 88 32 11 94, Telex 890366, Fax 88 32 82 55,
« Alsatian decor » – 📶 ▨ ☎ ⇌ – 🔬 30. 🅰🅴 ⓞ 🅔 𝘝𝘐𝘚𝘈   BV **p**
closed Christmas-New Year – ☑ 30 – **94 rm** 310/500.

🏛 **Gd Hôtel** without rest, 12 pl. Gare ℰ 88 32 46 90, Telex 870011, Fax 88 32 16 50 – 📶 ▨ ☎
♿, – 🔬 25. 🅰🅴 ⓞ 🅔 𝘝𝘐𝘚𝘈   BV **m**
☑ 40 – **90 rm** 400/480.

🏛 **des Rohan** Ⓜ without rest, 17 r. Maroquin ℰ 88 32 85 11, Telex 870047, Fax 88 75 65 37 –
📶 ▨ ▨ ☎ 𝘝𝘐𝘚𝘈   CX **u**
36 rm ☑ 280/570.

🏛 **Nouvel H. Maison Rouge** without rest, 4 r. Francs-Bourgeois ℰ 88 32 08 60, Telex
880130, Fax 88 22 43 73 – 📶 ▨ ☎ – 🔬 40. 🅰🅴 ⓞ 🅔 𝘝𝘐𝘚𝘈   CX **g**
☑ 50 – **140 rm** 350/500.

🏛 **Europe** without rest, 38 r. Fossé des Tanneurs ℰ 88 32 17 88, Telex 890220, Fax 88 75 65 45,
« Half timbered Alsatian house » – 📶 ▨ ☎ – 🔬 40. 🅔 𝘝𝘐𝘚𝘈   BX **g**
☑ 30 – **60 rm** 273/425.

🏨 **Cathédrale** Ⓜ without rest, 12 pl. Cathédrale ℰ 88 22 12 12, Telex 871054, Fax 88 23 28 00
– 📶 ▨ ☎ – 🔬 25. 🅰🅴 ⓞ 🅔 𝘝𝘐𝘚𝘈   CX **n**
☑ 42 – **32 rm** 390/650.

🏨 **La Dauphine** Ⓜ without rest, 30 r. 1ère Armée ℰ 88 36 26 61, Telex 880766, Fax 88 35 50 07
– 📶 ▨ ☎ ⇌. ⓞ 🅔 𝘝𝘐𝘚𝘈
closed 21 December-2 January – ☑ 35 – **45 rm** 360/400.

🏨 **Royal** Ⓜ without rest, 3 r. Maire Kuss ℰ 88 32 28 71, Telex 871067, Fax 88 23 05 39, ♨ – 📶
▨ ☎ – 🔬 40. 🅰🅴 🅔 𝘝𝘐𝘚𝘈. ⌘   BV **e**
☑ 39 – **52 rm** 295/425.

🏨 **Dragon** Ⓜ without rest, 2 r. Ecarlate ℰ 88 35 79 80, Telex 871102, Fax 88 25 78 95 – 📶 ▨
☎ ♿, 🅰🅴 ⓞ 🅔 𝘝𝘐𝘚𝘈. ⌘   CX **d**
☑ 45 – **30 rm** 380/510.

🏠 **Pax**, 24 r. Fg National ℰ 88 32 14 54, Telex 880506, Fax 88 32 01 16, 🌧 – 📶 ▨ ☎ –
🔬 25 - 100. 🅰🅴 🅔 𝘝𝘐𝘚𝘈   BVX **u**
closed Christmas-1 January – **M** *(closed Sunday November-March)* 84/160 ♨ – ☑ 30 –
119 rm 145/285.

🏠 **Continental** Ⓜ without rest, 14 r. Maire Kuss ℰ 88 22 28 07, Telex 880881, Fax 88 32 22 25
– 📶 ▨ ☎. 🅰🅴 ⓞ 🅔 𝘝𝘐𝘚𝘈   BV **s**
☑ 35 – **48 rm** 287/390.

🗙🗙🗙🗙🗙 ❀❀❀ **Le Crocodile** (Jung), 10 r. Outre ℰ 88 32 13 02, Fax 88 75 72 01 – ▤. 🅰🅴 ⓞ 🅔 𝘝𝘐𝘚𝘈
closed 7 July-5 August, 22 December-1 January, Sunday and Monday – **M** 360/580 and a la
carte   CV **x**
Spec. Foie d'oie poêlé à la brunoise confite. Feuilleté de ris de veau aux crêtes de coq. Selle de chevreuil
Saint-Hubert (June-January). **Wines** Riesling, Tokay-Pinot gris.

🗙🗙🗙🗙 ❀❀ **Buerehiesel** (Westermann), Set in the Orangery Park ℰ 88 61 62 24, Fax 88 61 32 00,
« Attractive Alsatian mansion in a park » – ▤. 🅿. 🅰🅴 ⓞ 🅔 𝘝𝘐𝘚𝘈
closed 7 to 22/8, 23/12-2/1, 18/2-4/3, Tuesday (except lunch 1/4-31/10) and Wednesday – **M**
260 (lunch)/480 and a la carte ♨
Spec. Schniederspaetle et cuisses de grenouilles poêlées au cerfeuil, Galette d'anguille aux pommes de terre
et chou blanc, Gourmandise au chocolat fondant. **Wines** Riesling, Tokay-Pinot gris.

🗙🗙🗙 **Valentin Sorg**, 6 pl. Homme de Fer (14th floor) ℰ 88 32 12 16, ≤ Strasbourg – ▤. 🅰🅴
🅔 𝘝𝘐𝘚𝘈   BV **r**
closed 12 to 29 August, February Holidays, Sunday dinner and Tuesday – **M** 150/400.

🗙🗙🗙 **Maison Kammerzell et H. Baumann** Ⓜ with rm, 16 pl. Cathédrale ℰ 88 32 42 14, Telex
891012, Fax 88 23 03 92, « Attractive 16C Alsatian house » – 📶 ▤ rm ▨ ☎. 🅰🅴 ⓞ 🅔 𝘝𝘐𝘚𝘈
M 180/250 ♨ – ☑ 48 – **9 rm** 420/630.   CX **e**

🗙🗙🗙 **Maison des Tanneurs dite ''Gerwerstub''**, 42 r. Bain aux Plantes ℰ 88 32 79 70, « Old
Alsatian house on the banks of the River Ill » – 🅰🅴 ⓞ 🅔 𝘝𝘐𝘚𝘈   BX **t**
closed 15 to 31 July, 22 December-22 January, Sunday and Monday – **M** a la carte 150/270.

🗙🗙🗙 **Zimmer**, 8 r. Temple Neuf ℰ 88 32 35 01, Fax 88 32 42 28 – 🅰🅴 ⓞ 🅔 𝘝𝘐𝘚𝘈   CV **y**
closed August, 1 to 6 January, Saturday lunch and Sunday – **M** 130/360.

XX **Buffet Gare,** pl. Gare 📞 88 32 68 28, Fax 88 32 88 34 — ▦ ◑ ▤ 𝘝𝘐𝘚𝘈   BV
L'Argentoratum **M** 85/135 ⅃ — L'Assiette **M** 63 ⅃.

XX **Bec Doré,** 8 quai Pêcheurs 📞 88 35 39 57 — ▤ 𝘝𝘐𝘚𝘈   CV **b**
closed spring Holidays, 1 to 21 August, Monday and Tuesday — **M** 140 ⅃.

XX **Estaminet Schloegel,** 19 r. Krutenau 📞 88 36 21 98 — ▤ 𝘝𝘐𝘚𝘈   CX **q**
closed 13 to 28 July, 24 December-6 January, Sunday and Monday — **M** 190/270 ⅃.

XX ✣ **Julien,** 22 quai Bateliers 📞 88 36 01 54 — ▦ ◑ ▤ 𝘝𝘐𝘚𝘈   CX **x**
closed 3 to 25 August, February Holidays, Saturday lunch and Sunday — **M** 190/290 ⅃
Spec. Blanc de Saint-Pierre aux aromates, Selle d'agneau en croûte de persil, Millefeuille au chocolat.

XX **Au Gourmet Sans Chiqué,** 15 r. Ste Barbe 📞 88 32 04 07 — ▤. ▦ ◑ ▤ 𝘝𝘐𝘚𝘈   CX **b**
closed 17 to 28 March, 11 to 29 August, Monday lunch and Sunday — **M** 180/300.

X **Ami Schutz,** 1 r. Ponts Couverts 📞 88 32 76 98, Fax 88 32 38 40, ⋧ — ↠. ▦ ◑ ▤   BX **r**
M 158 b.i./172 b.i.

Winstubs : Regional specialities and wine tasting in a typical Alsatian atmosphere :

X **Zum Strissel,** 5 pl. Gde Boucherie 📞 88 32 14 73, rustic decor — ▤. ▤ 𝘝𝘐𝘚𝘈   CX **a**
closed 10 to 31 July, February Holidays, Sunday and Monday — **M** 50/122 ⅃.

X **S'Burjerstuewel (Chez Yvonne),** 10 r. Sanglier 📞 88 32 84 15 — ▤ 𝘝𝘐𝘚𝘈   CVX **r**
closed 12 July-12 August and 22 December-2 January — **M** (booking essential) a la carte
120/180 ⅃.

X **Le Clou,** 3 r. Chaudron 📞 88 32 11 67 — ▤. ▤ 𝘝𝘐𝘚𝘈   CV **n**
closed 15 to 28 August, 31 December-7 January and Sunday — **M** (dinner only) a la carte
150/250.

at La Wantzenau : NE by D 468 : 12 km — pop. 4 h. — ✉ 67610 La Wantzenau :

🏨 **Hôtel Le Moulin** ▤ ⑊, S : 1,5 km by D 468 📞 88 96 27 83, Fax 88 96 68 32, ≤, « Ancient
watermill on a branch of the River III », ⋧ — ▥∣ ▥ ☎ ℗. ▦ ◑ ▤
closed 24 December-2 January — **M** see Au Moulin below — ⇌ 36 — **19 rm** 247/340.

🏠 **A la Gare** without rest, 32 r. Gare 📞 88 96 63 44 — ▥ ☎ ℗. ▤ 𝘝𝘐𝘚𝘈
closed 29 July-14 August — ⇌ 22 — **18 rm** 170/245.

XXX **A la Barrière,** 3 rte Strasbourg 📞 88 96 20 23, ⋧ — ℗. ▦ ◑ ▤ 𝘝𝘐𝘚𝘈
closed 6 to 27 August, February Holidays, Tuesday dinner and Wednesday — **M** (Sunday :
booking essential) 250 ⅃.

XXX **Relais de la Poste** ▤ with rm, 21 r. Gén. de Gaulle 📞 88 96 20 64, Fax 88 96 36 84, ⋧ —
▥∣ ▤ rest ▥ ☎ ⅋ ℗ — ▵ 25. ▦ ◑ ▤ 𝘝𝘐𝘚𝘈
closed 1 to 21 January — **M** *(closed Sunday dinner)* 250/350 ⅃ — ⇌ 45 — **19 rm** 250/350 —
½ P 420/480.

XXX **Zimmer,** 23 r. Héros 📞 88 96 62 08 — ▦ ◑ ▤ 𝘝𝘐𝘚𝘈
closed 14 July-7 August, 19 January-5 February, Sunday dinner and Monday — **M** 135/330 ⅃.

XX **Rest. Au Moulin** - Hôtel Au Moulin, S : 1,5 km by D 468 📞 88 96 20 01, Fax 88 96 68 32, ⋧,
« Flowered garden » — ↠ ▤ ▦ ◑ ▤ 𝘝𝘐𝘚𝘈
closed 27 June-22 July, 5 to 20 January, Sunday dinner, Bank Holidays dinner and Wednesday
— **M** 140/335 ⅃.

XX **Schaeffer,** 1 quai Bateliers 📞 88 96 20 29, ⋧ — ℗. ▦ ◑ ▤ 𝘝𝘐𝘚𝘈
closed 15 July-2 August, 24 December-7 January, Sunday dinner and Monday — **M** 130/
215 ⅃.

▨ **Colmar** ℗ 68000 H.-Rhin 🖪🖪 ⑲ — pop. 63 764 h. alt. 193.
Strasbourg 71.

XXXX ✣✣ **Schillinger,** 16 r. Stanislas 📞 89 41 43 17, Fax 89 24 28 87, « Fine decor » — ▤. ▦ ◑
▤ 𝘝𝘐𝘚𝘈
*closed 12 July-1 August, 25 February-4 March, Sunday dinner and Monday except Bank
Holidays* — **M** 250/450 and a la carte ⅃
Spec. Foie gras frais à la cuillère, Filet de sandre en grappe de raisin, Aiguillettes de canard au citron. **Wines**
Pinot blanc, Riesling.

▨ **Colroy-la-Roche** 67 B.-Rhin 🖪🖪 ⑧ — pop. 431 h. alt. 424 — ✉ 67420 Saales.
Strasbourg 62.

🏨 ✣✣ **Host. La Cheneaudière** ▤ ⑊, 📞 88 97 61 64, Telex 870438, Fax 88 47 21 73, ≤, ⋧,
« Fashionable country inn, garden », ⒑, ▦, ✼ — ▤ rest ▥ ☎ ℗. ▦ ◑ ▤ 𝘝𝘐𝘚𝘈
closed January and February — **M** 350/490 and a la carte — ⇌ 90 — **25 rm** 500/900,
6 apartments — ½ P 690/1000
Spec. Foie gras fumé, Ravioles de Munster au persil frit, Filet de chevreuil en strudel de chou vert (May-
December). **Wines** Riesling, Gewürztraminer.

When in a hurry use the **Michelin Main Road Maps :**

🖪🖪🖪 Europe, 🖪🖪🖪 Greece, 🖪🖪🖪 Germany, 🖪🖪🖪 Scandinavia-Finland,
🖪🖪🖪 Great Britain and Ireland, 🖪🖪🖪 Germany-Austria-Benelux, 🖪🖪🖪 Italy,
🖪🖪🖪 France, 🖪🖪🖪 Spain-Portugal and 🖪🖪🖪 Yugoslavia.

🏠 **Illhaeusern** 68 H.-Rhin **62** ⑲ – pop. 557 h. alt. 176 – ⊠ **68150** Ribeauvillé.
Strasbourg 60.

🏠 **La Clairière** Ⓜ ⤳ without rest, rte Guémar 🖉 89 71 80 80, Fax 89 71 86 22, ℀ – 🛗 📺 ☎
Ⓟ. **E** **VISA**
closed January and February – � 50 – **27 rm** 420/1050.

🅇🅇🅇🅇🅇 ✿✿✿ **Aub. de l'Ill** (Haeberlin), 🖉 89 71 83 23, Telex 871289, Fax 89 71 82 83, « Tasteful
decor, set on the banks of the River Ill, ≼ over flowered gardens » – ⤳ 🍽 **AE** ⓪ **E**
VISA
closed 1 to 7 July, February, Monday (except lunch in summer) and Tuesday – **M** (booking
essential) 400 (lunch)/600 and a la carte.
Spec. Truffe en croûte de pommes de terre, Filet d'esturgeon rôti sur lit de choucroute et ''misala'' à la crème
de caviar, Grande assiette de cochon de lait. **Wines** Riesling, Pinot blanc.

🏠 **Lembach** 67510 B.-Rhin **57** ⑲ – pop. 1 539 h. alt. 190.
Strasbourg 56.

🅇🅇🅇🅇 ✿✿ **Aub. Cheval Blanc** (Mischler), 🖉 88 94 41 86, Fax 88 94 20 74, 🌿 – Ⓟ **AE** **E** **VISA**
closed 8 to 26 July, 3 to 21 February, Monday and Tuesday – **M** 145/350 and a la carte.
Spec. Suprême de sandre au fumet de truffe, Médaillons de chevreuil à la moutarde (1 June-15 February),
Soupe de fruits rouges et crème brûlée à l'alisier. **Wines** Pinot Auxerrois.

🏠 **Marlenheim** 67520 B.-Rhin **62** ⑨ – pop. 2 822 h. alt. 184.
Strasbourg 20.

🅇🅇🅇 ✿✿ **Host. du Cerf** (Husser) with rm, 🖉 88 87 73 73, Fax 88 87 68 08, ☼, 🌿 – 📺 ☎ –
🛗 25. **AE** **E** **VISA**
closed February Holidays, Tuesday and Wednesday – **M** 325/450 and a la carte ⚒ – ⊏ 55 –
17 rm 450/550.
Spec. Presskopf de tête de veau poêlé en croustillant, Choucroute au cochon de lait et foie gras fumé,
Aumônières aux griottes et glace au fromage blanc. **Wines** Riesling, Pinot noir.

If you think you have been overcharged, let us know.
Where no rates are shown it is best to inquire terms in advance.

VALLEY OF THE LOIRE

🏠 **Tours** Ⓟ 37000 I.-et-L. **64** ⑮ – pop. 136 483 h. Greater Tours 251 320 alt. 48.

See : Cathedral quarter★★ : Cathedral★★ CY, Fine Arts Museum★★ CY M2, – Historial de
Touraine★ (château) CY, The Psalette★ CY F, Place Grégoire de Tours★ CY 20 – Old
Tours★★ : Place Plumereau★ AY , hôtel Gouin★ AY M4, rue Briçonnet★ AY 3 – St-Julien
quarter★ : Craft Guilds Museum★★ (Musée du Compagnonnage) BY M5, Beaune-Semblan-
çay Garden★ BY B, – St-Cosme Priory★ W : 3 km – Meslay Tithe Barn★ (Grange de
Meslay) N : 10 km.

🏌 of Touraine 🖉 47 53 20 28 ; domaine de la Touche at Ballan-Miré : 14 km ; 🏌 of Ardrée
🖉 47 56 77 38 : 14 km.

✈ of Tours-St-Symphorien : T.A.T 🖉 47 51 94 22 NE : 7 km.

🛈 Office de Tourisme and Accueil de France (Informations, exchange facilities and hotel reservations
- not more than 5 days in advance), pl. Mar. Leclerc (provisional address bd Heurteloup) 🖉 47 05 58 08,
Telex 750008 – Automobile Club de l'Ouest 4 pl. J. Jaurès 🖉 47 05 50 19.

Paris 234 – Angers 109 – Bordeaux 345 – Chartres 140 – Clermont-Ferrand 317 – Limoges 204 – Le Mans
82 – Orléans 112 – Rennes 236 – St-Étienne 426.

Plan on following pages

🏨 ✿✿ **Jean Bardet** Ⓜ ⤳, 57 r. Groison ⊠ 37100 🖉 47 41 41 11, Telex 752463, Fax 47 51 68 72,
« Park », ⌧, – 🔲 rest 📺 ☎ Ⓟ. **AE** ⓪ **E** **VISA**
closed 1 to 9 March – **M** *(closed Monday lunch April-October, Sunday dinner and Monday
October-April except Bank Holidays)* 250/620 and a la carte – ⊏ 95 – **10 rm** 550/1200,
5 apartments 1600
Spec. Saumon mi-fumé en harmonie, Pintadeau fermier truffé, Gésier de canard et homard rôti au coulis de vin
de Graves. **Wines** Vouvray, Chinon.

🏠 **Alliance** Ⓜ, 292 av. Grammont ⊠ 37200 🖉 47 28 00 80, Telex 750922, Fax 47 27 77 61, ≼,
☼, 🌿 – 🔲 🔲 📺 ☎ Ⓟ – 🛗 200. **AE** ⓪ **E** **VISA** ℀ rest
M a la carte 180/300 – ⊏ 55 – **119 rm** 440/515, 6 apartments.

🏠 **H. de Groison et rest. Jardin du Castel** Ⓜ ⤳, 10 r. Groison 🖉 47 41 94 40, Fax
47 51 50 28, ☼, « Former 18C mansion », 🌿 – 📺 ☎ ⇦. **AE** ⓪ **E** **VISA**
closed 8 January-5 February – **M** *(closed Saturday lunch and Wednesday)* 210/420 – ⊏ 65
– **10 rm** 480/710 – ½ P 550/670.

🏠 **Harmonie** Ⓜ, 15 r. F. Joliot-Curie 🖉 47 66 01 48, Telex 752587, Fax 47 61 66 38, ℀ – 🛗 📺
☎ ⚒ ⇦. **AE** **E** **VISA** ℀ rest
CZ **b**
M 99/150 – ⊏ 45 – **48 rm** 360/400, 6 apartments.

191

TOURS

The names of main shopping streets are indicated in red at the beginning of the list of streets.

Do not lose your way in Europe, use the Michelin *Main Road* *maps, scale : 1 inch : 16 miles.*

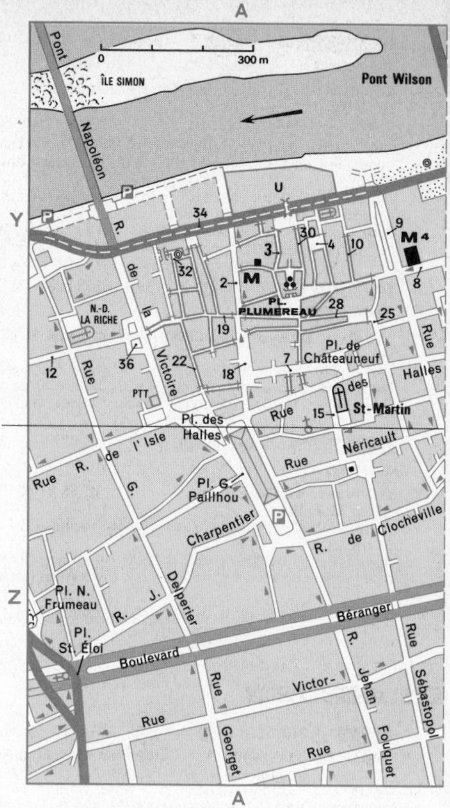

Royal M without rest, 65 av. Grammont ☎ 47 64 71 78, Telex 752006, Fax 47 05 84 62 – 40. AE E VISA.
34 – **50 rm** 292/344.

Univers et rest. La Touraine, 5 bd Heurteloup ☎ 47 05 37 12, Telex 751460, Fax 47 61 51 80 – 30. AE E VISA BZ **u**
M *(closed Saturday)* 170/200 – 45 – **89 rm** 400/690.

Bordeaux, 3 pl. Mar. Leclerc ☎ 47 05 40 32, Telex 750414, Fax 47 64 05 72 – AE E VISA BZ **t**
M 120/195 b.i. – 35 – **56 rm** 305/460 – ½ P 275/350.

Altéa M, 4 pl. Thiers ☎ 47 05 50 05, Telex 752740, Fax 47 20 22 07 – rest – 70. AE E VISA. rest
M a la carte 170/250 – 45 – **120 rm** 380/500 – ½ P 405/445.

Central H. without rest, 21 r. Berthelot ☎ 47 05 46 44, Telex 751173, Fax 47 66 10 26 – AE E VISA BY **k**
35 – **42 rm** 250/350.

Criden M without rest, 65 bd Heurteloup ☎ 47 20 81 14 – AE E VISA CZ **g**
34 – **33 rm** 273/337.

Mirabeau without rest, 89 bis bd Heurteloup ☎ 47 05 24 60, Fax 47 05 31 09 – AE E VISA CZ **e**
28 – **25 rm** 265/310.

Fimotel M, 247 r. Giraudeau ☎ 47 37 00 36, Fax 47 38 50 91 – – 40. AE E VISA
M 72/92 – 33 – **45 rm** 260/295, 3 apartments 350 – ½ P 210.

Arcade M, 1 r. G. Claude ☎ 47 61 44 44, Telex 751201, Fax 47 64 60 79 – – 30. AE E VISA
M *(closed Saturday and Sunday)* 65 b.i./85 – 35 – **139 rm** 275/325.

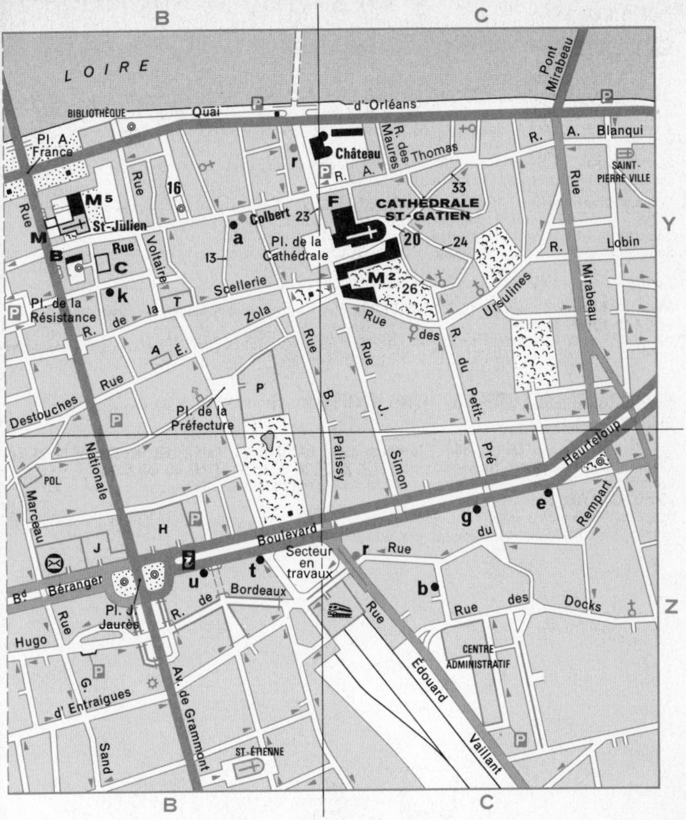

XXXX ✿✿ **Barrier,** 101 av. Tranchée ✉ 37100 ✆ 47 54 20 39, Fax 47 41 80 95 – ▤ **P**. **E** VISA
closed Sunday dinner – **M** 210/385 and a la carte
Spec. Matelote d'anguilles au Chinon et aux pruneaux, Jeune pigeon en vessie, Selle d'agneau avec son rognon. **Wines** Montlouis, Saint-Nicolas-de-Bourgueil.

XXX ✿ **La Roche Le Roy** (Couturier), 55 rte St Avertin ✉ 37200 ✆ 47 27 22 00, Fax 47 28 08 39, 斎 – **P**. AE **E** VISA
closed 8 to 20 August and Sunday – **M** 190/270
Spec. Dos de sandre rôti en meurette, Grenadin de lapereau au miel de romarin, Parfait café au sorbet cacao. **Wines** Chinon, Vouvray.

XX **Les Tuffeaux,** 19 r. Lavoisier ✆ 47 47 19 89 – ▤. **E** VISA — BY **r**
closed 14 to 30 July, Monday lunch and Sunday – **M** 150/200.

X **La Ruche,** 105 r. Colbert ✆ 47 66 69 83 – **E** VISA — BY **a**
closed 23 December-14 January, Monday lunch and Sunday – **M** 75/110.

at Rochecorbon NE : by N 152 – ✉ **37210** :

🏨 ✿ **Les Hautes Roches** Ⓜ 🐎, 86 quai Loire ✆ 47 52 88 88, Telex 300121, Fax 47 52 81 30, ≤, 斎, « Former troglodyte dwellings, elegantly installed » – |‡| TV ☎ **P**. AE **E** VISA
closed 17 February-12 March and 10 November-3 December – **M** *(closed Sunday dinner and Monday except Bank Holidays)* 150/250 – ☕ 60 – **11 rm** 895/1250 – ½ P 585/935
Spec. Dos de rouget à la lie de vin, Croustifondant de sole, Tarte fine aux pommes caramélisées. **Wines** Vouvray, Chinon.

Bracieux 41250 L.-et-Ch. 64 ⑱ – pop. 1 150 h. alt. 81 – Tours 81.

XXXX ✿✿ **Bernard Robin,** 1 av. Chambord ✆ 54 46 41 22, Fax 54 46 03 69, 斎 – **E** VISA
closed 23 December-30 January, Tuesday dinner and Wednesday – **M** (booking essential) 280/480 and a la carte
Spec. Salade de pigeon et homard, Dorade rôtie à la coriandre, Queue de boeuf en hachis Parmentier. **Wines** Cheverny, Chinon.

Montbazon 37250 I.-et-L. **64** ⑮ – pop. 3 011 h. alt. 71.

Tours 13.

🏰 ✿ **Château d'Artigny** ⊗, SW : 2 km by D 17 ℰ 47 26 24 24, Telex 750900, Fax 47 65 92 79, « Park, ≤ River Indre, riverside annex with 8 rm », ⍆, ✵ – 劇 ⅥV ☎ ℗ – 👜 80. **E** ₥₥
closed 1 December-11 January – **M** 260/380 – ⇋ 78 – **46 rm** 600/1260. 7 apartments 1420 – ½ P 630/1100
Spec. Poissons de Loire à notre façon, Noisettes d'agneau fermier du pays Lochois, Brochette aux trois fruits et sabayon au Vouvray moelleux. **Wines** Vouvray, Chinon.

XXXX ✿✿ **La Chancelière,** 1 pl. Marronniers ℰ 47 26 00 67, « Tasteful decor » – ▤. **E** ₥₥
closed 1 to 8 September, 17 February-9 March, Sunday (except lunch September-June) and Monday – **M** 280 (except Saturday dinner)/460 and a la carte
Spec. Ravioles d'huîtres au Champagne, Sauté de homard au lard. **Wines** Vouvray, Chinon.

to the W : 5 km by N 10, D 287 and D 87 – ✉ **37250** Montbazon :

XX **Moulin Fleuri** ⊗ with rm, ℰ 47 26 01 12, ≤, « Terrace overlooking the River Indre », ⋒ – ⅥV ☎ ℗ ⅍ **E** ₥₥
closed 15 to 30 October, 1 to 21 February and Monday except Bank Holidays – **M** a la carte 130/270 – ⇋ 36 – **12 rm** 155/295 – ½ P 225/315.

Romorantin-Lanthenay ⏛ 41200 L.-et-Ch. **64** ⑱ – pop. 18 187 h. alt. 88.

Tours 89.

🏰 ✿✿ **Gd H. Lion d'Or** Ⓜ, 69 r. Clemenceau ℰ 54 76 00 28, Telex 750990, Fax 54 88 24 87, « Tastefully decorated, flowered patio » – 劇 ⅥV ☎ ℥ ℗ – 👜 50. ⅍ ⱺ **E** ₥₥
closed early January-mid February – **M** (booking essential) 330/550 and a la carte – ⇋ 90 – **13 rm** 600/1700, 3 apartments 2000
Spec. Cuisses de grenouilles à la Rocambole, Langoustines rôties à la poudre d'épices douces, Pie de rhubarbe au gingembre (May-October). **Wines** Vouvray, Bourgueil.

Germany
Deutschland

PRACTICAL INFORMATION

LOCAL CURRENCY

Deutsche Mark : 100 DM = 66.33 US $ (Jan. 91)

TOURIST INFORMATION

Deutsche Zentrale für Tourismus (DZT)
Beethovenstr. 69, 6000 Frankfurt 1, ℘ 069/7 57 20, Telex 4189178
Fax 069/75 19 03

Hotel booking service
Allgemeine Deutsche Zimmerreservierung (ADZ)
Corneliusstr. 34, 6000 Frankfurt 1, ℘ 069/74 07 67
Telex 416666, Fax 069/75 10 56

AIRLINES

DEUTSCHE LUFTHANSA AG : Von-Gablenz-Str. 2, 5000 Köln 21, ℘ 0221/82 61
AIR CANADA : 6000 Frankfurt, Friedensstr. 7, ℘ 069/23 40 32
AIR FRANCE : 6000 Frankfurt, Friedensstr. 11, ℘ 069/2 56 63 20
AMERICAN AIRLINES : 6000 Frankfurt, Wiesenhüttenplatz 26, ℘ 069/2 56 01 11
BRITISH AIRWAYS : 1000 Berlin 15, Kurfürstendamm 178, ℘ 030/8 82 30 67
JAPAN AIRLINES : 6000 Frankfurt, Roßmarkt 15, ℘ 069/1 36 00
PAN AMERICAN : 6000 Frankfurt 75, Flughafen Terminal Mitte, ℘ 069/690 20 60
SABENA : 6000 Frankfurt, Roßmarkt 10, ℘ 069/29 90 06 94
SAS : 6000 Frankfurt, Schaumainkai 87, ℘ 069/63 39 31 29
TWA : 6000 Frankfurt 90, Hamburger Allee 2, ℘ 069/77 06 01

FOREIGN EXCHANGE

Is possible in banks, savings banks and at exchange offices.
Hours of opening from Monday to Friday 8.30am to 12.30pm and 2.30pm to 4pm
except Thursday 2.30pm to 6pm.

SHOPPING

In the index of street names, those printed in red are where the principal shops are
found.

BREAKDOWN SERVICE

ADAC : for the addresses see text of the towns mentioned
AvD : Lyoner Str. 16, 6000 Frankfurt 71-Niederrad, ℘ 069/6 60 60, Telex 41 12 37, Fax
069/660 62 10
In Germany the ADAC (emergency number 01308/19211), and the AvD (emergency
number 0130/99 09), make a special point of assisting foreign motorists. They have
motor patrols covering main roads.

TIPPING

In Germany, prices include service and taxes. You may choose to leave a tip if you
wish but there is no obligation to do so.

SPEED LIMITS

The speed limit, generally, in built up areas is 50 km/h - 31 mph and on all other roads
it is 100 km/h - 62mph. On motorways and dual carriageways, the recommended
speed limit is 130 km/h - 80 mph.

SEAT BELTS

The wearing of seat belts is compulsory for drivers and passengers.

BERLIN

SIGHTS

Kurfürstendamm★★ BDX and Memorial Church (Kaiser-Wilhelm-Gedächtniskirche) DEV – Brandenburg Gate★★ (Brandenburger Tor) NY – Zoological Park★★ (Zoologischer Garten, Aquarium) EV – Alexanderplatz★★ RSY – Television Tower★★ (Fernsehturm) RY – Olympia-Stadion★★ LS F – Botanical Gardens★★ (Botanischer Garten) MT – Wannsee★★ LT – Havel★ and Peacock Island★ (Pfaueninsel) LT – Unter den Linden★ NPY – Platz der Akademie★ PZ – Marx-Engels-Platz★ PY 70 – Karl-Marx-Allee★ SY – Nikolaiviertel★ RY – Neue Wache★ PY D – State Opera House★ (Deutsche Staatsoper) PY C – Soviet Memorial★ (Sowjetisches Ehrenmal) NS – Church of Maria Regina Martyrum★ (Maria-Regina-Martyrum-Kirche) BU D and Plötzensee Memorial (Gedenkstätte Plötzensee) DU – Radio Tower (🔭 ★) (Funkturm) AV.

MUSEUMS

Dahlem Museums★★★ (Museum Dahlem) (Painting Gallery★★, Ethnographic Museum★★) MT – Pergamon Museum★★★ PY M⁷ – Chateau of Charlottenburg★★ (Schloß Charlottenburg, at the Knobelsdorff-Wing: Painting Collection★★, Golden Gallery★★) BU – National Gallery★★ (Nationalgalerie) PY M⁸ – Arsenal★★ (Zeughaus) PY – Museum of Decorative Arts★ (Kunstgewerbemuseum) FV M² – Antique Museum★ (Antikenmuseum, ancient treasure★★★) BU M³ – Egyptian Museum★ (Ägyptisches Museum, bust of Queen Nefertiti★) BU M⁴ – National Gallery★ (Nationalgalerie) FV M⁶ – Bode-Museum★ PY M² – Altes Museum★ PY M³ – Chateau of Köpenick, Museum of Decorative Arts★ (Schloß Köpenick, Kunstgewerbemuseum) by Köpenicker Str. SZ.

BERLIN 987 ⑰⑱, 984 ⑮⑯ – Pop. 3 210 000 – alt. 40 m.

🛥 Berlin-Wannsee, Am Stölpchenweg, 𝒫 8 05 50 75.

✈ Tegel, 𝒫 4 11 01 and Schönefeld (S: 25 km), Interflug Ofice, Alexanderplatz 5 𝒫 2 10 91 81.

🚣 Berlin - Wannsee, 𝒫 31 04 33.

Exhibition Grounds (Messegelände) AV, 𝒫 3 03 81, Telex 182908.

🛈 Berlin Tourist-Information, Europa-Center (Budapester Straße), 𝒫 2 62 60 31, Telex 18 3356, Fax 21 23 25 20 ;

🛈 Berlin Information, at Television Tower (Fernsehturm) 1020 Berlin 𝒫 2 12 46 75.

ADAC, Berlin-Wilmersdorf, Bundesallee 29 (B 31). 𝒫 8 68 61, Telex 183513.

Frunkfurt/Oder 105 – Hamburg 289 – Hannover 288 – Leipzig 183 – Rostock 222.

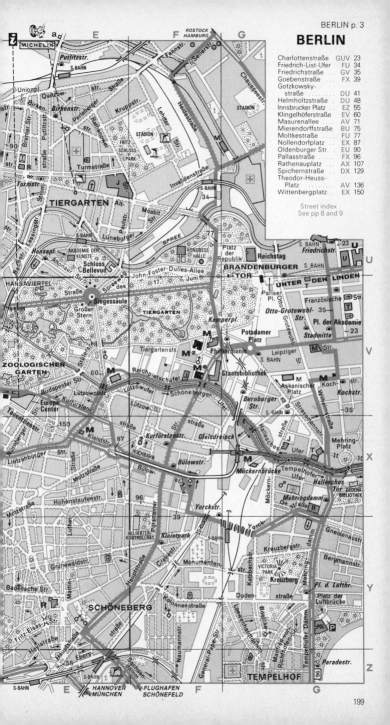

BERLIN

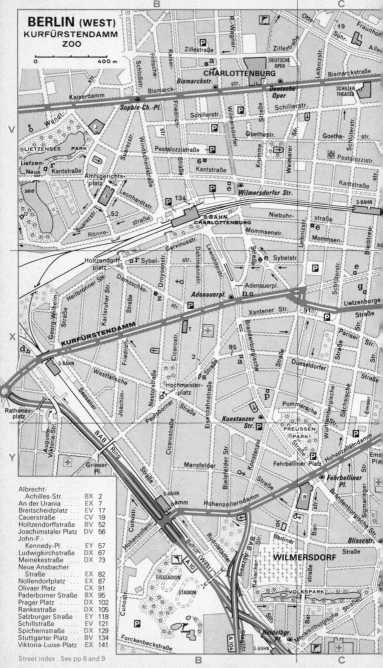

BERLIN (WEST)
KURFÜRSTENDAMM
ZOO

0   400 m

200

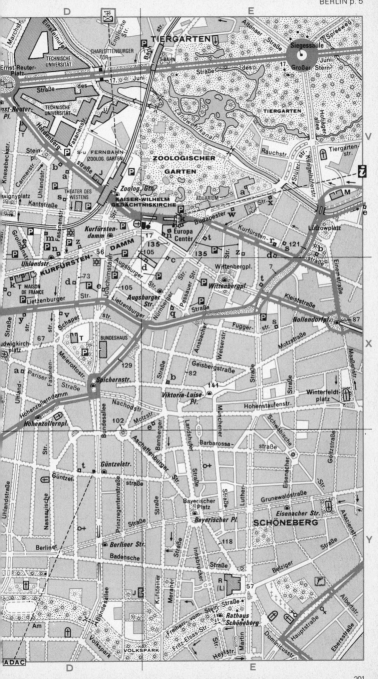

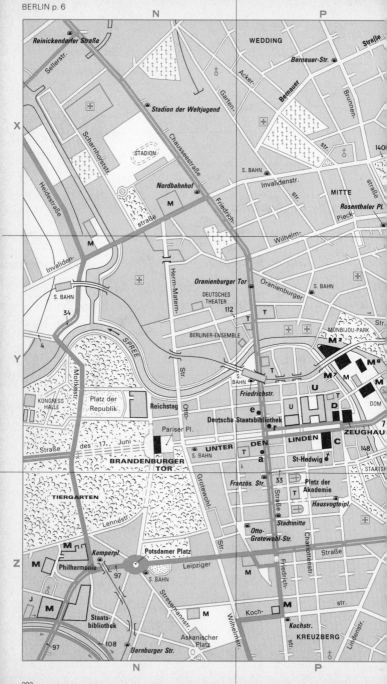

N

P

Reinickendorfer Straße

WEDDING

Straße

Berneuer-Str.

Sellerstr.

Acker-

Berneuer

Brunnen-

X

Stadion der Weltjugend

Scharnhorststr.

Chausseestraße

STADION

Garten-

str.

straße

140

Heidestraße

Nordbahnhof

Friedrich-

S. BAHN

Invalidenstr.

MITTE

Rosenthaler Pl.

straße

M

straße

Wilhelm-

Pieck-

Invaliden-

M

Oranienburger Tor

Oranienburger

S. BAHN

S. BAHN

Herm-Matern-

DEUTSCHES
THEATER

112

34

SPREE

Str.

T

MONBIJOU-PARK

4

BERLINER-ENSEMBLE

T

M 2

Motkestr.

S.
BAHN

T

M

M

Friedrichstr.

U

D

KONGRESS
HALLE

Platz der
Republik

Reichstag

Otto-

Friedrichstr.

U

T

DOM

DEN

ZEUGHAU

des

Pariser Pl.

Deutsche Staatsbibliothek

e

LINDEN

C

7

17.

Grotewohl-

UNTER

r

Straße

Juni

BRANDENBURGER
TOR

S. BAHN

T

a

St-Hedwig

148

STAATSI

TIERGARTEN

Lennéstr.

Französ. Str.

33

Platz der
Akademie

Charlottenstr.

Str.

Hausvogteipl.

Otto-
Grotewohl-Str.

Stadtmitte

M

M

Kemperpl.

Potsdamer Platz

Straße

Z

M

Philharmonie

97

Leipziger

Stresemannstr.

S. BAHN

M

Friedrich-

J

M

Staats-
bibliothek

Wilhelmstr.

M

str.

Koch-

Kochstr.

97

108

Bernburger Str.

Askanischer
Platz

KREUZBERG

Lindenstr.

N

P

BERLIN (OST)
UNTER DEN LINDEN

Street index :
See pp 8 and 9

Continued p. 9

Berlin - West

Town Centre : ⊠ 1000 - ☎ 030.

Bristol-Hotel Kempinski ⑤, Kurfürstendamm 27 (B 15), ℰ 88 43 40, Telex 185651, Fax 8836075, 佘, Massage, ⇔, ⌧ – 濠 ⇔ rm 圖 ⊡ ⟵ – 쓰 25/400. ⌸ ⓪ Ε 쪼 ⅏ Restaurants : **Kempinski-Grill** (closed Sunday) **M** a la carte 62/106 – **Kempinski-Restaurant** (closed Monday) **M** a la carte 49/81 – **Kempinski-Eck M** a la carte 33/50 – **325 rm** 355/ 480 Bb – 33 apart. 850/1250. DV **n**

Inter-Continental, Budapester Str. 2 (B 30), ℰ 2 60 20, Telex 184380, Fax 260280760, Massage, ⇔, ⌧ – 濠 圖 ⊡ ら ⟵ ℗ – 쓰 25/900. ⌸ ⓪ Ε 쪼 ⅏ rest EV **a** Restaurants (remarkable wine list) : **Zum Hugenotten M** a la carte 68/110 – **Buffet-Restaurant Brasserie M** 40(buffet) and a la carte 46/68 – **600 rm** 380/580 Bb – 70 apart. 700/2250.

Steigenberger Berlin, Los-Angeles-Platz 1 (B 30), ℰ 2 10 80, Telex 181444, Fax 2108117, 佘, Massage, ⇔, ⌧ – 濠 ⇔ rm 圖 ⊡ ら ⟵ – 쓰 25/600. ⌸ ⓪ Ε 쪼 EX **d** Restaurants : **Park-Restaurant** (dinner only, closed Monday) **M** a la carte 55/79 – **Berliner Stube M** a la carte 33/59 – **386 rm** 239/498 Bb – 11 apart. 648/1948.

Grand Hotel Esplanade (modern hotel with integrated collection of contemporary art), Lützowufer 15 (B 30), ℰ 26 10 11, Telex 185986, Fax 2629121, Massage, ⇔, ⌧ – 濠 ⇔ rm 圖 ⊡ ⟵ – 쓰 25/450. ⌸ ⓪ Ε 쪼 ⅏ rest EV **e** **M** (closed Sunday) a la carte 56/85 – **402 rm** 365/440 Bb – 33 apart. 585/1850.

Schweizerhof, Budapester Str. 21 (B 30), ℰ 2 69 60, Telex 185501, Fax 2696900, Massage, ⇔, ⌧ – 濠 ⇔ rm 圖 ⊡ ⟵ ℗ – 쓰 25/400. ⌸ ⓪ Ε 쪼 ⅏ rest EV **w** **M** 37 (lunch) and a la carte 55/81 – **430 rm** 380/580 Bb – 7 apart. 744/2544.

Palace - Restaurant La Réserve, Budapester Str. 42 (Europa-Centre) (B 30), ℰ 25 49 70, Telex 184825, Fax 2626577, free entrance to the thermal recreation centre – 濠 ⇔ rm 圖 ⊡ ⟵ ℗ – 쓰 25/400. ⌸ ⓪ Ε 쪼 ⅏ rest EV **k** **M** (dinner only) 95 and a la carte 56/70 – **258 rm** 252/594 Bb.

Berlin, Lützowplatz 17 (B 30), ℰ 2 60 50, Telex 184332, Fax 26052716, 佘, Massage, ⇔ – 濠 圖 ⊟ rest ⊡ ⟵ ℗ – 쓰 25/500. ⌸ ⓪ Ε 쪼 EV **b** **M** a la carte 38/88 – **470 rm** 275/470 Bb – 11 apart. 650/1550.

Savoy, Fasanenstr. 9 (B 12), ✆ 31 10 30, Telex 184292, Fax 31103333, roof garden terrace, – 30. AE E VISA. rest DV **s**
M a la carte 39/65 – **130 rm** 261/462 Bb – 8 apart. 642.

Ambassador, Bayreuther Str. 42 (B 30), ✆ 21 90 20, Telex 184259, Fax 21902380, Massage, – rm rest – 25/100. AE E VISA. rest EV **z**
Restaurants : **Conti-Fischstuben** *(dinner only, closed Sunday and Monday)* **M** 59/140 – **Schöneberger Krug M** a la carte 25/58 – **200 rm** 225/395 Bb.

Mondial, Kurfürstendamm 47 (B 15), ✆ 88 41 10, Telex 182839, Fax 8841150, Massage, – rest – 25/100. AE E VISA. rest CX **e**
M a la carte 36/72 – **75 rm** 170/380 Bb.

Alsterhof, Augsburger Str. 5 (B 30), ✆ 21 99 60, Telex 183484, Fax 243949, Massage, – AE E VISA. rest EX **q**
M a la carte 47/68 – **144 rm** 169/298 Bb.

Berlin Penta Hotel, Nürnberger Str. 65 (B 30), ✆ 21 00 78 19, Telex 182877, Fax 2132009, Massage, – rm – 25/120. AE E VISA. rest EV **t**
M a la carte 46/69 – **425 rm** 185/263 Bb.

President, An der Urania 16 (B 30), ✆ 21 90 30, Telex 184018, Fax 2141200, – – 25/120. rest EX **t**
M a la carte 38/77 – **132 rm** 195/285 Bb – 6 apart. 300/450.

Berlin Excelsior Hotel, Hardenbergstr. 14 (B 12), ✆ 3 19 90, Telex 184781, Fax 31992849 – rest – 25/120. AE E VISA. rest DV **b**
Restaurants : **Peacock M** 30 (lunch) and a la carte 43/75 – **Store House Grill M** a la carte 30/53 – **320 rm** 198/278 Bb – 3 apart. 575.

Art-Hotel Sorat without rest (modern hotel with exposition of contemporary art), Joachimstalerstr. 28 (B 15), ✆ 88 44 70, Fax 88447700 – . AE E VISA DX **e**
75 rm 195/255 Bb.

Am Zoo without rest, Kurfürstendamm 25 (B 15), ✆ 88 43 70, Telex 183835, Fax 88437714 – – 40 DV **z**
138 rm Bb.

Hecker's Deele, Grolmanstr. 35 (B 12), ✆ 8 89 00, Telex 184954, Fax 8890260 – rest . AE E VISA DV **e**
M a la carte 32/56 – **54 rm** 195/320 Bb.

Residenz - Restaurant Grand Cru, Meinekestr. 9 (B 15), ✆ 88 44 30, Telex 18 30 82, Fax 8824726 – . AE E VISA. rest DX **d**
M a la carte 50/76 – **85 rm** 184/250 Bb – 9 apart. 520.

Domus without rest, Uhlandstr. 49 (B 15), ✆ 88 20 41, Telex 185975, Fax 8820410 – . AE E VISA DX **a**
closed 24 December - 2 January – **72 rm** 110/200 Bb.

Sylter Hof, Kurfürstenstr. 116 (B 30), ✆ 2 12 00, Telex 183317, Fax 2142826 – – 25/200. AE E VISA. rest EV **d**
M a la carte 35/59 – **154 rm** 208/326 Bb – 16 apart. 536.

Kronprinz without rest (1894 restored house), Kronprinzendamm 1 (B 31), ✆ 89 60 30, Telex 181459, Fax 8931215 – – 30. AE E VISA BX **d**
53 rm 140/210 Bb.

Bremen without rest, Bleibtreustr. 25 (B 15), ✆ 8 81 40 76, Telex 184892, Fax 8824685 – . AE E VISA CX **g**
53 rm 210/310 Bb.

Hamburg, Landgrafenstr. 4 (B 30), ✆ 26 91 61, Telex 184974, Fax 2629394 – rm – 25/100. AE E VISA. rest EV **s**
M a la carte 35/62 – **240 rm** 179/260 Bb.

Castor, Fuggerstr. 8 (B 30), ✆ 21 30 30, Fax 21303160 – . AE E VISA EX **s**
M *(closed Saturday, Sunday, 1 to 20 January and July)* a la carte 32/54 – **78 rm** 148/205 Bb.

Arosa Parkschloß - Hotel, Lietzenburger Str. 79 (B 15), ✆ 88 00 50, Telex 183397, Fax 8824579, (heated) – – 40. AE E VISA DX **y**
M *(closed Sunday)* a la carte 45/76 – **90 rm** 160/290 Bb.

Kurfürstendamm am Adenauerplatz without rest, Kurfürstendamm 68 (B 15), ✆ 88 28 41, Telex 184630, Fax 8825528 – – 25/45. AE E VISA BX **n**
33 rm 88/230 Bb.

Berlin-Plaza, Knesebeckstr. 63 (B 15), ✆ 88 41 30, Telex 184181, Fax 88413754, – – 30. AE E VISA. DX **c**
M a la carte 25/42 – **131 rm** 158/220 Bb.

Astoria without rest, Fasanenstr. 2 (B 12), ✆ 3 12 40 67, Telex 181745, Fax 3125027 – . AE E VISA DV **a**
33 rm 169/230 Bb.

Remter without rest, Marburger Str. 17 (B 30), ✆ 24 60 61, Telex 183497, Fax 2138612 – . E VISA EVX **c**
33 rm 110/180 Bb.

Atrium-Hotel without rest, Motzstr. 87 (B 30), ✆ 24 40 57, Fax 8824593 – . E EX **e**
22 rm 85/130.

XXX **Ristorante Anselmo**, Damaschkestr. 17 (B 31), ℰ 3 23 30 94, Fax 3246228, « Modern Italian rest. » – ❄ BX z
closed Monday – **M** a la carte 58/76.

XX ✿ **Bamberger Reiter**, Regensburger Str. 7 (B 30), ℰ 24 42 82, Fax 2142348 – ❄ EX b
dinner only, closed Saturday, Sunday, 1 to 15 January and 4 to 27 August – **M** 96/145 and a la carte 78/105
Spec. Gänsestopfleber in Strudelteig, Taubenbrust in Spinatbiskuit, Erdbeerknödel mit Pralineneis.

XX **Mövenpick**, Europa-Centre (1st floor) (B 30), ℰ 2 62 70 77, Fax 2629486, ≼ – 🖭 ⓞ 🇪 𝕍𝕀𝕊𝔸
M a la carte 35/64. EV n

XX **Du Pont**, Budapester Str. 1 (B 30), ℰ 2 61 88 11, 👯 – 🖭 ⓞ 🇪 𝕍𝕀𝕊𝔸 EV x
closed Saturday lunch, Sunday, Bank Holidays and 24 December - 2 January – **M** a la carte 52/79.

XX **Daitokai** (Japanese rest.), Tauentzienstr. 9 (Europa Centre, 1st floor) (B 30), ℰ 2 61 80 99, Fax 2616036 – 🖭 🇪 𝕍𝕀𝕊𝔸 ❄
closed Monday – **M** a la carte 48/71. EV n

XX **Peppino** (Italian rest.), Fasanenstr. 65 (B 15), ℰ 8 83 67 22 – 🖭 🇪 𝕍𝕀𝕊𝔸 DX v
closed Monday and 4 weeks July - August – **M** a la carte 47/68.

XX **Ristorante Il Sorriso** (Italian rest.), Kurfürstenstr. 76 (B 30), ℰ 2 62 13 13, 👯 – 🖭 ⓞ 🇪 𝕍𝕀𝕊𝔸 ❄ EV r
closed Sunday – **M** *(booking essential for dinner)* a la carte 44/71.

X **Stachel** (Rest. bistro style), Giesebrechtstr. 3 (B 12), ℰ 8 82 36 29, 👯 – 🖭 🇪 𝕍𝕀𝕊𝔸 BX e
dinner only – **M** a la carte 42/60.

X **Kopenhagen** (Danish Smörrebröds), Kurfürstendamm 203 (B 15), ℰ 8 81 62 19 – 🗐 🖭 🇪 𝕍𝕀𝕊𝔸 DX k
M a la carte 35/60.

X **Friesenhof**, Uhlandstr. 185 (B 12), ℰ 8 83 60 79 – 🗐 🖭 🇪 𝕍𝕀𝕊𝔸 DV m
M a la carte 26/49.

X **Hongkong** (Chinese rest.), Kurfürstendamm 210 (2nd floor, 🛗) (B 15), ℰ 8 81 57 56 – 🖭 ⓞ 🇪 𝕍𝕀𝕊𝔸 DX T
M 14/22 (lunch)and a la carte 31/49.

at Berlin-Charlottenburg :

🏨 **Seehof** ⑤, Lietzensee-Ufer 11 (B 19), ℰ 32 00 20, Telex 182943, Fax 32002251, ≼, 👯, ⇔s, 🗐 – 🛗 🗐 rest 🖵 ⇦ – 🔬 25/50. 🖭 ⓞ 🇪 𝕍𝕀𝕊𝔸 ❄ rest BV r
M 29/45 (lunch)and a la carte 54/80 – **77 rm** 175/350 Bb.

🏨 **Kanthotel** without rest, Kantstr. 111 (B 12), ℰ 32 30 26, Telex 183330, Fax 3240952 – 🛗 🖵 ☎ 🅿 🖭 ⓞ 🇪 𝕍𝕀𝕊𝔸 BV e
55 rm 164/210 Bb.

🏨 **Schloßparkhotel** ⑤, Heubnerweg 2a (B 19), ℰ 3 22 40 61, Telex 183462, Fax 8919942, 🗐, 👯 – 🛗 🖵 ☎ 🅿 ❄ BU a
39 rm Bb.

🏨 **Kardell**, Gervinusstr. 24 (B 12), ℰ 3 24 10 66 – 🛗 🖵 ☎ 🅿 🖭 ⓞ 🇪 𝕍𝕀𝕊𝔸 BX r
M *(closed Saturday lunch)* a la carte 39/61 – **33 rm** 95/170 Bb.

🏨 **Am Studio** without rest, Kaiserdamm 80 (B 19), ℰ 30 20 81, Telex 182825, Fax 3019578 – 🛗 🖵 ☎ ⇦, 🖭 ⓞ 🇪 𝕍𝕀𝕊𝔸 AV c
80 rm 125/190 Bb.

🏨 **Ibis** without rest, Messedamm 10 (B 19), ℰ 30 39 30, Telex 182882, Fax 3019536 – 🛗 🖵 ☎ – 🔬 40 AV b
191 rm Bb.

XX ✿ **Ponte Vecchio** (Tuscan rest.), Spielhagenstr. 3 (B 10), ℰ 3 42 19 99 – ⓞ BV a
dinner only, closed Tuesday and 4 weeks July - August – **M** a la carte 55/74
Spec. Saltimbocca di rombo, Tortellini di ricotta alla salvia, Capretto al forno con fagiolini.

XX ✿ **Alt Luxemburg**, Pestalozzistr. 70 (B 12), ℰ 3 23 87 30 BV s
dinner only, closed Sunday, Monday, 3 weeks January and 3 weeks June - July – **M** 95 and a la carte 62/77.

XX **Ugo** (Italian rest.), Sophie-Charlotten-Str. 101 (B 19), ℰ 3 25 71 10 – 🖭 🇪 𝕍𝕀𝕊𝔸 BU s
dinner only, closed Monday and 8 to 29 July – **M** a la carte 61/72.

XX **Trio**, Klausenerplatz 14 (B 19), ℰ 3 21 77 82 BU e
dinner only, closed Wednesday and Thursday – **M** a la carte 44/80.

XX **Ristorante Mario** (Italian rest.), Leibnizstr. 43 (B 12), ℰ 3 24 35 16 CV e
M *(booking essential)*.

XX **Funkturm - Restaurant** (🛗, DM 2), Messedamm 22 (B 19), ℰ 30 38 29 96, ≼ Berlin – 🅿 🖭 ⓞ 🇪 𝕍𝕀𝕊𝔸 ❄ AV
M *(booking essential)* a la carte 47/75.

at Berlin-Dahlem by Hohenzollerndamm AZ :

🏨 **Forsthaus Paulsborn** ⑤, Am Grunewaldsee (B 33), ℰ 8 13 80 10, 👯 – 🖵 ☎ 🅿 **11 rm**.

XX **Alter Krug**, Königin-Luise-Str. 52 (B 33), ℰ 8 32 50 89, « Terrace » – 🅿 ⓞ 🇪 𝕍𝕀𝕊𝔸
closed Thursday – **M** a la carte 38/77.

at Berlin-Grunewald :

XXX **Hemingway's**, Hagenstr. 18 (B 33), ℰ 8 25 45 71, Fax 8266175 – 🖭 ⓞ 🅴 🆅🆂🅰. ❀
closed Saturday lunch – **M** *(booking essential)* a la carte 57/74.   by Bismarckallee   AY

XX **Chalet Corniche**, Königsallee 5b (B 33), ℰ 8 92 85 97, Fax 4328094, « Terrace on the bank
of the lake Halensee » – ⓟ. 🖭 ⓞ 🅴 🆅🆂🅰   AX   s
Monday to Saturday dinner only – **M** a la carte 53/83.

at Berlin-Nikolassee by Hohenzollerndamm   ABYZ :

XXX ✿ **Frühsammers Restaurant an der Rehwiese**, Matterhornstr. 101 (B 38), ℰ 8 03 27 20,
Fax 8033736, 🛱 – 🅴 🆅🆂🅰
dinner only, closed Sunday, 3 weeks January and 3 weeks July - August – **M** *(booking
essential)* 120/195
Spec. Wachtelbrüstchen mit Portweinsauce, Seezungenroulade mit beurre blanc, Apfelpfannküchle mit
Karamelsauce.

at Berlin-Reinickendorf by Sellerstr.   FU :

🏨 **Rheinsberg am See**, Finsterwalder Str. 64 (B 26), ℰ 4 02 10 02, Telex 185972, Fax 4035057,
« Lakeside garden terrace », Massage, ⇌, ⤫, ⬛, ⚐ – 🛗 🖭 ☎ ⓟ 🅴 🆅🆂🅰
M a la carte 40/71 – **80 rm** 145/260 Bb.

at Berlin-Siemensstadt by Siemensdamm   AU :

🏨 **Novotel**, Ohmstr. 4 (B 13), ℰ 38 10 61, Telex 181415, Fax 3819403, ⤫ (heated) – 🛗 ▤ rest
🖭 ☎ ♿ ⓟ – 🔏 25/200. 🖭 🅴 🆅🆂🅰
M a la carte 30/55 – **119 rm** 183/236 Bb – 5 apart. 266.

at Berlin-Steglitz by Hauptstr.   EYZ :

🏨 **Steglitz International**, Albrechtstr. 2 (B 41), ℰ 79 00 50, Telex 183545, Fax 79005550,
Massage, ⇌ – 🛗 🖭 ♿ ⇌ – 🔏 25/400. 🖭 ⓞ 🅴 🆅🆂🅰
M a la carte 41/62 – **212 rm** 180/270 Bb – 3 apart. 550.

🏨 **Ravenna Hotel** without rest, Grunewaldstr. 8 (B 41), ℰ 7 92 80 31, Telex 184310 – 🛗 ☎
⇌ ⓟ. 🖭 ⓞ 🅴 🆅🆂🅰
45 rm 125/250 Bb.

at Berlin-Tegel by Jakob-Kaiser-Platz   BU :

🏨 **Novotel Berlin Airport**, Kurt-Schumacher-Damm 202 (by airport approach) (B 51),
ℰ 4 10 60, Telex 181605, Fax 4106700, ⇌, ⤫ (heated) – 🛗 ▤ 🖭 ☎ ♿ ⓟ – 🔏 25/300. 🖭
🅴 🆅🆂🅰
M a la carte 36/57 – **187 rm** 175/220 Bb.

at Berlin-Waidmannslust by Sellerstr.   FU :

XXX ✿✿ **Rockendorf's Restaurant**, Düsterhauptstr. 1 (B 28), ℰ 4 02 30 99, Fax 4023000,
« Elegant installation » – ⓟ. 🖭 ⓞ 🅴 🆅🆂🅰
closed Monday, Tuesday, 3 weeks July - August and 22 December - 6 January – **M** *(booking
essential)* 85/190
Spec. Mousse von geräuchertem Seeteufel, Geschmortes Zicklein in Trüffeljus, Beerenmichel auf Vanillesauce
mit Pralineneis.

at Berlin-Wilmersdorf :

🏨 **Queens Hotel** without rest, Güntzelstr. 14 (B 31), ℰ 87 02 41, Telex 182948, Fax 8619326 –
🛗 ⇌⇌ rm 🖭 ☎ ⇌   DY   t
110 rm Bb.

🏨 **Pension Wittelsbach** without rest, Wittelsbacher Str. 22 (B 31), ℰ 87 63 45, Fax 8621532,
« Tasteful decor », ⚐ – 🛗 🖭 ☎ ♿ ⚶   BX   p
37 rm 70/240 Bb.

🏨 **Prinzregent** without rest, Prinzregentenstr. 47 (B 31), ℰ 8 53 80 51, Telex 185217, Fax
8547637 – 🛗 🖭 ☎ ⓟ. 🖭 🅴 🆅🆂🅰   DZ   s
35 rm 95/165.

🏨 **Franke**, Albrecht-Achilles-Str. 57 (B 31), ℰ 8 92 10 97, Telex 184857, Fax 8911639 – 🛗 ☎
ⓟ. 🖭 ⓞ 🅴 🆅🆂🅰   BX   s
M a la carte 25/42 – **67 rm** 110/180.

🏨 **Lichtburg**, Paderborner Str. 10 (B 15), ℰ 8 91 80 41, Telex 184208, Fax 8926106 – 🛗 ☎. 🖭
ⓞ 🅴 🆅🆂🅰   BX   a
M a la carte 25/38 – **62 rm** 100/180.

When driving through towns
*use the plans in the **Michelin Red Guide**.*
Features indicated include:
throughroutes and by-passes,
traffic junctions and major squares,
new streets, car parks, pedestrian streets...
All this information is revised annually.

Berlin - East ✉1020 — pop. 1 250 000 — ✪ 00372.

See : Sights see Berlin p. 1.

✈ Berlin-Schönefeld (S : 25 km) - Interflug-Stadtbüro, Alexanderplatz 5, ℘ 2 10 91 81.

🛈 Berlin Information, Am Fernsehturm, 1020 Berlin, ℘ 2 12 46 75.

🛈 Zentraler Touristenservice, Alexanderplatz 5, 1026 Berlin, ℘ 2 15 41 61.

🛈 Travel Service Interhotel, Unter den Linden 35, 1080 Berlin, ℘ 20 92 23 00, Telex 114770, Fax 2294098.

Plans on preceding pages

🏨 **Grand Hotel**, Friedrichstr. 158, ✉ 1080, ℘ 2 09 20, Telex 115189, Fax 2294095, 🍴, Massage,
⥱ — ⧫ 📺 & ⇔ — 🔥 25/100. 🆎 ➊ 🄴 𝗩𝗜𝗦𝗔   PY **a**
Restaurants : **Le Grand Silhouette** — **Goldene Gans** — **350 rm** Bb — 20 apart.

🏨 **Metropol**, Friedrichstr. 150, ✉ 1086, ℘ 2 20 40, Telex 114141, Fax 2204209, Massage, ⥱,
🔲 — ⧫ ▤ 📺 & ⇔ — 🔥 25/200. 🆎 ➊ 🄴 𝗩𝗜𝗦𝗔. % rest   PY **e**
M a la carte 38/86 — **340 rm** 230/365 Bb — 30 apart. 350/1200.

🏨 **Palasthotel**, Karl-Liebknecht-Str. 5, ℘ 24 10, Telex 115050, Fax 2127273, ⥱, 🔲 — ⧫ 📺
⇔ — 🔥 25/480. 🆎 ➊ 🄴 𝗩𝗜𝗦𝗔   RY **s**
600 rm Bb.

🏦 **Berliner-Congress-Center**, Märkisches Ufer 54, ✉ 1026, ℘ 2 70 05 31, Fax 3610740, ⥱
— ⧫ 📺 ⇔ — 🔥 25/100. 🆎 ➊ 🄴 𝗩𝗜𝗦𝗔. %   SZ **x**
M a la carte 16/28 — **110 rm** 150/200 — 12 apart. 350/450.

🏦 **Unter den Linden**, Unter den Linden 14, ✉ 1080, ℘ 2 20 03 11, Telex 112109 — ⧫ 📺 ☎. 🆎
➊ 🄴 𝗩𝗜𝗦𝗔   PY **r**
300 rm Bb.

🏦 **Berolina**, Karl-Marx-Allee 31, ℘ 2 10 95 41, Telex 114331 — ⧫ 📺 ☎ 🅿 — 🔥 25/60. 🆎 ➊
🄴 𝗩𝗜𝗦𝗔   SY **f**
344 rm — 11 apart.

🏦 **Stadt Berlin**, Alexanderplatz, ✉ 1026, ℘ 2 19 40, Telex 114111, ⥱ — ⧫ 📺 ☎ ⇔ —
🔥 25/400. 🆎 ➊ 🄴 𝗩𝗜𝗦𝗔   RY
880 rm — 60 apart..

XX **Ermeler Haus** (reconstructed 18 C Patrician house), Märkisches Ufer 10 (1st floor),
✉ 1026, ℘ 2 75 51 03 — %   RZ **c**
M a la carte 37/54.

XX **Ephraim - Palais**, Poststr. 16, ℘ 21 71 32 53 — %   RY **e**
M a la carte 30/51.

X **Am Marstall**, Marx-Engels-Forum 23, ℘ 21 71 32 13   RY **n**
closed dinner every 1st Monday of the month — **M** a la carte 27/51.

X **Zur letzten Instanz** (old Berlin inn from 1621), Waisenstr. 14, ℘ 2 12 55 28   RY **t**
closed Monday lunch — **M** *(booking essential)* a la carte 17/34.

at Berlin-Köpenick 1170 SE : 13 km by Köpenicker Landstraße NS :

X **Ratskeller Köpenick**, Alt Köpenick 21, ℘ (00372) 6 57 20 35
closed every fourth Wednesday of the month — **M** a la carte 21/34.

at Müggelsee SE : 15 km by Holzmarktstr. SZ :

🏦 **Seehotel Belvedere**, Müggelseedamm 288 (northern bank), ✉ 1170 Berlin-Köpenick-
Friedrichshagen, ℘ (00372) 6 45 56 82, ≤, « Lakeside terrace », ⥱ — 📺 ☎ 🅿 — 🔥 25/100.
%
M 47 and a la carte 23/42 — **32 rm** 145/190 Bb — 7 apart. 285.

🏦 **Müggelsee** ⋟, Am Müggelsee (southern bank), ✉ 1170 Berlin-Köpenick, ℘ (00372)
6 60 20, Fax 6602263, 🍴, Massage, ⥱ — 📺 ☎ 🅿 — 🔥 25/200. 🆎 ➊ 🄴 𝗩𝗜𝗦𝗔. %
M a la carte 35/64 — **174 rm** 104/210 Bb — 6 apart. 352.

at Peetzsee SE : 31 km by Holzmarktstr. SZ :

🏦 **Seegarten Grünheide** ⋟, Am Schlangenbuch 12, ✉ 1252 Grünheide, ℘ (0037357) 61 29,
⥱, 🐾, 🍴 — ⧫ 📺 ☎ & ⇔ 🅿 — 🔥 30. %
M a la carte 20/34 — **23 rm** 80/190.

Michelin Green Guides in English

Austria	Italy	New York City
Canada	London	Portugal
England : The West Country	Mexico	Rome
Germany	Netherlands	Scotland
Greece	New England	Spain
		Switzerland

COLOGNE (KÖLN) **5000.** Nordrhein-Westfalen 987 ㉓ ㉔, 412 D 14 – pop. 992 000 – alt. 65 m – ✿ 0221.

See : Cathedral (Dom)★★★ (Magi's Shrine★★★) DV – Roman-Germanic Museum (Römisch-Germanisches Museum)★★★ (Dionysos Mosaic) DV M1 – Wallraf-Richartz-Museum (14-16C pictures by Cologne Masters) and Museum Ludwig★★★ DV M3 – Schnütgen-Museum★★ (Madonnas of Cologne) DX M4 – St. Columbia (St. Kolumba)★ DX V – St. Alban the New (Neu St. Alban)★ – St. Maria of the Capitol (St. Maria im Kapitol) (wooden doors★★) DX D – Holy Apostles (St. Aposteln) (apse★) CX N – St. Severinus (St. Severin) (inside★) DY K – Rhine Park (Rheinpark)★.

🏌 Köln-Marienburg, Schillingsrotter Weg, ℰ 38 40 53 ; 🏌 Bergisch Gladbach-Refrath (E : 17 km), ℰ (02204) 6 31 14.

✈ Köln-Bonn at Wahn (SE : 17 km), ℰ (02203) 4 01.

🚗 ℰ 1 41 56 66.

Exhibition Centre (Messegelände), ℰ 82 11, Telex 8873426.

🛈 Tourist office (Verkehrsamt), Am Dom, ℰ 2 21 33 40, Telex 8883421, Fax 2213320.

ADAC, Luxemburger Str. 169, ℰ 47 27 47.

Düsseldorf 40 – Aachen 69 – Bonn 28 – Essen 68.

The reference (K 15) at the end of the address is the postal district : Köln 15

Plans on following pages

🏨🏨🏨 **Excelsior Hotel Ernst - Restaurant Hanse Stube**, Trankgasse 1 (K 1), ℰ 27 01, Telex 8882645, Fax 135150 – ▯ ≡ rest ☎ ▯ E ▥ ❀ rest   DV **a**
M a la carte 56/101 – **160 rm** 295/560 Bb – 20 apart. 950/1150.

🏨🏨🏨 **Dom-Hotel** ⌂, Domkloster 2a (K 1), ℰ 2 02 40, Telex 8882919, Fax 2024260, « Terrace with ≪ ≫ » – ▯ ☎ ▯ ⌂ – ⌂ 25/60. ▯ ⓞ E ▥ ❀ rest   DV **d**
M a la carte 60/106 – **126 rm** 311/572 Bb.

🏨🏨🏨 **Maritim**, Heumarkt 20 (K 1), ℰ 2 02 70, Telex 8886667, Fax 2027826, ≪, Massage, ☎, ▨ – ▯ ≪ rm ≡ ☎ ▯ ⌂ – ⌂ 25/1100. ▯ ⓞ E ▥   DX **m**
M a la carte 63/86 – **450 rm** 250/454 Bb – 28 apart.

🏨🏨🏨 **Ramada Renaissance Hotel**, Magnusstr. 20 (K 1), ℰ 2 03 40, Telex 8882221, Fax 2034777, ⌂, Massage, ☎, ▨ – ▯ ≪ rm ≡ ☎ ▯ ⌂ ⌂ – ⌂ 25/350. ▯ ⓞ E ▥ ❀ rest   CV **s**
Restaurants : **Raffael** *(closed Sunday)* **M** a la carte 52/89 – **Valentino M** a la carte 38/68 – **240 rm** 269/508 Bb – 9 apart.

🏨🏨🏨 **Inter-Continental**, Helenenstr. 14 (K 1), ℰ 22 80, Telex 8882162, Fax 2281301, Massage, ▨, ▨ – ▯ ☎ ▯ ⌂ ⌂ – ⌂ 25/1000. ▯ ⓞ E ▥ ❀ rest   CV **p**
M a la carte 59/90 – **290 rm** 279/498 Bb – 9 apart. 828/1648.

🏨🏨🏨 **Hotel im Wasserturm** ⌂, Kaygasse 2 (K 1), ℰ 2 00 80, Telex 8881109, Fax 2008888, « Modern hotel in a former water-tower », ☎ – ▯ ☎ ▯ ⌂. ▯ ⓞ E ▥ ❀ rest   DY **c**
M a la carte 59/90 – **90 rm** 326/502 Bb – 42 apart. 582/852.

🏨🏨🏨 **Holiday Inn Crowne Plaza**, Habsburger Ring 9 (K 1), ℰ 2 09 50, Telex 8886618, Fax 251206, Massage, ☎, ▨ – ▯ ≪ rm ≡ ☎ ▯ ⌂ ⌂ – ⌂ 25/300. ▯ ⓞ E
Restaurants : **Le Bouquet** *(closed Monday)* **M** a la carte 49/75 – **La Cave** *(closed Saturday and Sunday)* **M** a la carte 27/40 – **300 rm** 285/515 Bb – 3 apart. 810/1475.
by Hahnenstraße   CX

🏨🏨 **Consul**, Belfortstr. 9 (K 1), ℰ 7 72 10, Telex 8885242, Fax 7721259, Massage, ☎, ▨ – ▯ ≪ rm ≡ ☎ ▯ ⌂ ⌂ ☎ – ⌂ 25/200. ▯ ⓞ E ▥ ❀ rest   DU **v**
Restaurants : **Quirinal M** a la carte 45/74 – **Consülchen Pub M** a la carte 30/48 – **125 rm** 175/475 Bb.

🏨🏨 **Pullman-Hotel Mondial**, Kurt-Hackenberg-Platz 1 (K 1), ℰ 2 06 30, Telex 8881932, Fax 2063522, ⌂ – ▯ ≪ rm ☎ ▯ ⌂ ⌂ – ⌂ 25/250. ▯ ⓞ E ▥ ❀ rest   DV **f**
M 28/38 (lunch) and a la carte 56/82 – **204 rm** 182/316 Bb.

🏨🏨 **Senats Hotel**, Unter Goldschmied 9 (K 1), ℰ 2 06 20, Telex 8881765, Fax 247863 – ▯ ☎ – ⌂ 25/350. ▯ ⓞ E ▥ ❀ rest   DX **b**
closed 21 to 31 December – **M** *(closed Sunday dinner)* 25/35 (lunch) and a la carte 43/70 – **60 rm** 195/330 Bb.

🏨 **Dorint Hotel**, Friesenstr. 44 (K 1), ℰ 1 61 40, Telex 8881483, Fax 1614100 – ▯ ≪ rm ☎ ⌂ ⌂ – ⌂ 25/150. ▯ ⓞ E ▥ ❀ rest   CV **n**
M a la carte 40/67 – **103 rm** 229/520 Bb.

🏨 **Haus Lyskirchen**, Filzengraben 28 (K 1), ℰ 2 09 70, Telex 8885449, Fax 2097718, ☎, ▨ – ▯ ≡ rest ☎ ⌂ ⌂ ☎ – ⌂ 25/90. ▯ ⓞ E ▥   DY **u**
closed 23 December - 2 January – **M** *(closed Saturday lunch, Sunday and Bank Holidays)* a la carte 41/70 – **95 rm** 135/230 Bb.

🏨 **Altea Hotel Severinshof**, Severinstr. 199 (K 1), ℰ 2 01 30, Telex 8881852, Fax 2013666, ⌂, ☎ – ▯ ≪ rm ☎ ⌂ – ⌂ 25/80. ▯ ⓞ E ▥   DY **a**
M a la carte 40/71 – **253 rm** 168/276 Bb – 16 apart. 306/396.

🏨 **Coellner Hof**, Hansaring 100 (K 1), ℰ 12 20 75, Telex 8885264, Fax 135235 – ▯ ☎ ☎ ⌂ – ⌂ 30. ▯ ⓞ E ▥
M *(closed Friday dinner and Saturday)* a la carte 38/67 – **70 rm** 105/260 Bb.

🏨 **Viktoria** without rest, Worringer Str. 23 (K 1), 𝒫 72 04 76, Telex 8881979, Fax 727067 — |இ|
🔟 ☎ 🅿 ⅍ ⓐ 🅔 𝓥𝓘𝓢𝓐   by Konrad-Adenauer-Ufer DU
closed 24 December - 1 January — **47 rm** 145/420 Bb.

🏨 **Savoy** without rest, Turiner Str. 9 (K 1), 𝒫 12 04 66, Telex 8886360, Fax 120470, ⎓ — |இ|
⎓⟷ rm 🔟 ☎ ⅍ ⓐ 🅔 𝓥𝓘𝓢𝓐   DU s
closed 24 to 31 December — **85 rm** 145/400 Bb — 5 apart. 600.

🏨 **Europa Hotel am Dom**, Am Hof 38 (K 1), 𝒫 2 05 80, Telex 8881728, Fax 211021 — |இ| 🔟
☎ — ⚖ 30. ⅍ ⓐ 🅔 𝓥𝓘𝓢𝓐   DV z
M see rest. Ambiance am Dom — **90 rm** 149/349 Bb.

🏨 **Königshof** without rest, Richartzstr. 14 (K 1), 𝒫 23 45 83, Telex 8881318, Fax 238642 — |இ|
🔟 ☎ ⅍ ⓐ 🅔 𝓥𝓘𝓢𝓐   DV n
85 rm 105/395 Bb.

🏨 **Ascot-Hotel** without rest, Hohenzollernring 95 (K 1), 𝒫 52 10 76, Telex 8883018, Fax
521070 — |இ| 🔟 ☎. ⅍ ⓐ 🅔 𝓥𝓘𝓢𝓐. ⍟   CV a
closed 22 December - 1 January — **46 rm** 142/374 Bb.

🏨 **Kommerzhotel** without rest, Breslauer Platz (K 1), 𝒫 12 40 86, Fax 135927, ⎓ — |இ| 🔟
☎. ⅍ ⓐ 🅔 𝓥𝓘𝓢𝓐   DV r
77 rm 130/255 Bb.

🏨 **Am Augustinerplatz** without rest, Hohe Str. 30 (K 1), 𝒫 23 67 17, Fax 217533 — |இ| 🔟
☎. ⅍ ⓐ 🅔 𝓥𝓘𝓢𝓐   DX a
56 rm 105/295 Bb — 4 apart. 275/350.

🏨 **Lasthaus am Ring - Restaurant Charrue d'or**, Hohenzollernring 20 (K 1),
𝒫 21 04 85(Hotel) 21 76 10(Rest.), Telex 8882856 — |இ| 🔟 ☎ 🅿 — ⚖ 30   CX r
M *(closed Monday and June)* a la carte 50/90 — **52 rm** 98/265 Bb.

🏨 **Bristol** without rest (antique furniture), Kaiser-Wilhelm-Ring 48 (K 1), 𝒫 12 01 95,
Telex 8881146, Fax 131495 — |இ| 🔟 ☎. ⅍ ⓐ 🅔 𝓥𝓘𝓢𝓐   CU m
44 rm 125/350 Bb.

🏨 **Eden-Hotel** without rest, Am Hof 18 (K 1), 𝒫 23 61 23, Telex 8882889, Fax 246604 — |இ| 🔟
☎. ⅍ ⓐ 🅔 𝓥𝓘𝓢𝓐   DV w
closed 24 December - 3 January — **33 rm** 171/285 Bb — 4 apart.

🏨 **Residence** without rest, Alter Markt 55 (K 1), 𝒫 23 57 81, Telex 8885344, Fax 234140 — |இ|
🔟 ☎ ⅍ ⓐ 🅔 𝓥𝓘𝓢𝓐   DX c
60 rm 125/280 Bb — 3 apart. 380.

🏨 **Astor und Aparthotel** without rest, Friesenwall 68 (K 1), 𝒫 23 58 11, Telex 8886367, Fax
230490 — |இ| ⎓⟷ rm 🔟 ☎ 🅿. ⅍ ⓐ 🅔 𝓥𝓘𝓢𝓐   CX a
52 rm 134/450.

🏨 **Conti** without rest, Brüsseler Str. 40 (K 1), 𝒫 25 20 62, Telex 8881644, Fax 252107 — |இ| ☎
⎓⎓. ⅍ 🅔 𝓥𝓘𝓢𝓐   by Rudolfplatz CX
closed 13 December - 1 January — **43 rm** 90/220 Bb.

🏨 **Windsor** without rest, Von-Werth-Str. 36 (K 1), 𝒫 13 40 31 — |இ| 🔟 ☎   CU e
37 rm.

🏨 **Merian-Hotel** without rest, Allerheiligenstr. 1 (K 1), 𝒫 12 10 25, Telex 8883305, Fax 121029
— |இ| 🔟 ☎ ⎓⎓   DU c
closed 22 December - 4 January — **32 rm** 95/350 Bb.

🏨 **Ludwig** without rest, Brandenburger Str. 24 (K 1), 𝒫 16 05 40, Telex 8885326, Fax 137935
— |இ| 🔟 ☎ ⎓⎓. ⅍ ⓐ 🅔 𝓥𝓘𝓢𝓐 — **61 rm** 110/275 Bb.   DU x
closed 23 December - 1 January — **61 rm** 110/275 Bb.

𝗫𝗫𝗫𝗫 ❀ **Chez Alex**, Mühlengasse 1 (K 1), 𝒫 23 05 60 — ⓐ ⓐ 🅔 𝓥𝓘𝓢𝓐   DX k
closed Saturday lunch, Sunday and Bank Holidays — **M** *(booking essential)* a la carte 80/120
Spec. Ravioli d'escargots, Lasagne de homard, Magret de canard en croûte de poivre.

𝗫𝗫𝗫 ❀ **Rino Casati**, Ebertplatz 3 (K 1), 𝒫 72 11 08, Fax 728097 — ⓐ ⓐ 🅔 𝓥𝓘𝓢𝓐. ⍟   DU t
dinner only, closed July and Sunday except exhibitions — **M** *(booking essential)* a la carte
65/98
Spec. Hausgemachte Nudelgerichte, Gänsestopfleber in Torcolatoschaum, Lammcarré im Kartoffelmantel mit
zwei Saucen.

𝗫𝗫𝗫 **Die Bastei**, Konrad-Adenauer-Ufer 80 (K 1), 𝒫 12 28 25, Fax 138047, ≼ Rhein — ⓐ ⓐ 🅔
𝓥𝓘𝓢𝓐. ⍟   DU b
closed Saturday lunch — **M** a la carte 68/115.

𝗫𝗫𝗫 ❀ **Restaurant Bado - La poêle d'or**, Komödienstr. 52 (K 1), 𝒫 13 41 00 — ⓐ ⓐ 🅔 𝓥𝓘𝓢𝓐
*closed Sunday, Monday lunch, Bank Holidays, 3 weeks July - August and Christmas - New
Year* — **M** 45 (lunch) and a la carte 85/115 — **Bistro M** a la carte 32/44   DV c
Spec. Saumon fumée chaud sauce raifort, La dorade au thym, Le nougat glacé.

𝗫𝗫𝗫 **Börsen-Restaurant Maître**, Unter Sachsenhausen 10 (K 1), 𝒫 13 30 21, Fax 134264 —
▤ ⓐ ⓐ 🅔 𝓥𝓘𝓢𝓐. ⍟   CV r
closed Sunday and Bank Holidays — **M** 57/95 — **Börsenstube M** a la carte 31/72.

𝗫𝗫𝗫 **Ambiance am Dom** (at Europa-Hotel am Dom), Am Hof 38 (K 1), 𝒫 24 91 27 — ⓐ ⓐ 🅔
𝓥𝓘𝓢𝓐   DV z
closed Saturday lunch, Sunday, Bank Holidays and 3 weeks July - August — **M** 48 (lunch)
and a la carte 72/100.

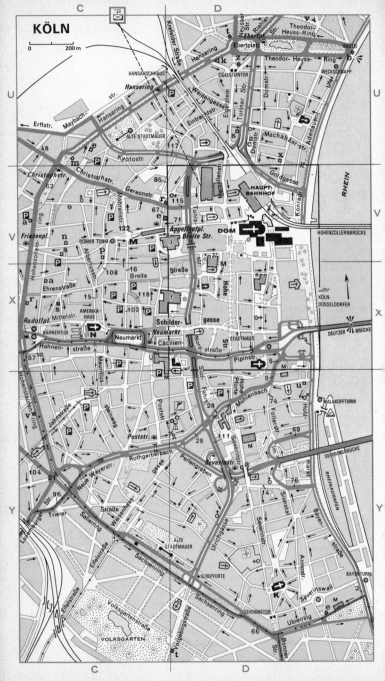

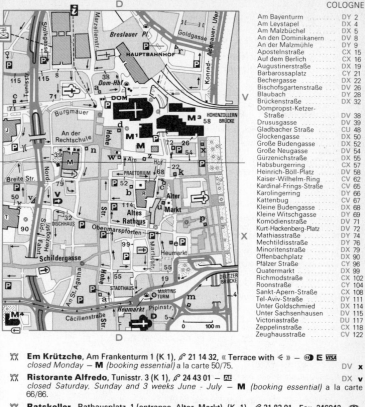

XX **Em Krützche**, Am Frankenturm 1 (K 1), ℰ 21 14 32, « Terrace with ≤ » – ⓐ Ε 𝖵𝖨𝖲𝖠
closed Monday – **M** (booking essential) a la carte 50/75. DV **x**

XX **Ristorante Alfredo**, Tunisstr. 3 (K 1), ℰ 24 43 01 – 𝖠Ε DX **v**
closed Saturday, Sunday and 3 weeks June - July – **M** (booking essential) a la carte 66/86.

XX **Ratskeller**, Rathausplatz 1 (entrance Alter Markt) (K 1), ℰ 21 83 01, Fax 246942, 🍽,
« Courtyard » – 🗐 ৬ 🔥 – 🛓 25/80. 𝖠Ε ⓐ Ε 𝖵𝖨𝖲𝖠 DX **u**
M a la carte 38/68.

XX Weinhaus im Walfisch (half-timbered building from the 17C), Salzgasse 13 (K 1), ℰ 21 95 75
DX **p**

XX **Soufflé**, Hohenstaufenring 53 (K 1), ℰ 21 20 22 – 𝖠Ε ⓐ Ε 𝖵𝖨𝖲𝖠 CY **v**
closed Saturday lunch, Sunday, Bank Holidays and 1 to 6 January – **M** a la carte 49/76.

XX **Restaurant Wack**, Benesisstr. 57 (K 1), ℰ 21 42 78 – Ε. 🦐 CX **s**
closed Saturday lunch and Sunday except exhibitions – **M** (booking essential) a la carte 61/81 – **Wackes** (dinner only) **M** a la carte 34/50.

XX **Daitokai** (Japanese rest.), Kattenbug 2 (K 1), ℰ 12 00 48, Fax 137503 – ▤. 𝖠Ε ⓐ Ε 𝖵𝖨𝖲𝖠
🦐 CV **e**
closed Sunday – **M** 32/38 (lunch) a la carte 48/74.

XX **De Donatis L'Osteria** (Italian rest.), Eigelstein 122 (entrace Greesbergstraße) (K 1),
ℰ 12 33 73 – ⓐ 𝖵𝖨𝖲𝖠 DU **z**
closed Saturday lunch, Wednesday and mid June - mid July – **M** a la carte 50/80.

X **Ballarin** (rest. in Bistro-style), Ubierring 35 (K 1), ℰ 32 61 33 – ⓐ DY **e**
dinner only, closed Sunday and Bank Holidays – **M** a la carte 60/75.

X **Ristorante Pan e vin**, Heumarkt 75 (K 1), ℰ 24 84 10 – 𝖠Ε Ε. 🦐 DX **e**
closed Monday except exhibitions – **M** a la carte 48/78.

X **La Baurie**, Vorgebirgstr. 35 (K 1), ℰ 38 61 49 – 𝖠Ε Ε 𝖵𝖨𝖲𝖠 DY **t**
closed Saturday lunch and Monday – **M** a la carte 61/82.

at Cologne 41-Braunsfeld by Rudolfplatz CX :

🏛 **Regent**, Melatengürtel 15, ℰ 5 49 90, Telex 8881824, Fax 5499998 – 🛉 ≒ rm 📺 ⓟ –
🛓 25/80. 𝖠Ε ⓐ Ε 𝖵𝖨𝖲𝖠
M (also vegetarian dishes) a la carte 28/70 – **168 rm** 187/416 Bb – 3 apart. 896.

at Cologne 21-Deutz by Deutzer Brücke DX :

🏨 **Hyatt Regency**, Kennedy-Ufer 2a, ℰ 8 28 12 34, Telex 887525, Fax 8281370, ≼, beer-garden, ≋s, 🖳 – 🛗 ½⇔ rm 🔲 📺 ℊ ⇔ 🅿 – 🔏 25/400. 🝿 ⑩ 🄴 𝗩𝗜𝗦𝗔
Restaurants : **Graugans** *(closed Saturday lunch and Sunday)* **M** a la carte 70/95 – **Glashaus**
M a la carte 40/55 – **307 rm** 308/591 Bb – 16 apart. 973/2646.

🏨 **Ilbertz** without rest, Mindener Str. 6, ℰ 88 20 49, Fax 883484, ≋s – 🛗 📺 ☎ ⇔. 🝿 ⑩
🄴 𝗩𝗜𝗦𝗔
30 rm 75/190 Bb.

ХХ **Der Messeturm**, Kennedy-Ufer (18th floor, 🛗), ℰ 88 10 08, Fax 811941, ≼ Cologne – 🔲
– 🔏 25. 🝿 ⑩ 🄴 𝗩𝗜𝗦𝗔 ℀
closed Saturday lunch – **M** a la carte 49/83.

at Cologne 30-Ehrenfeld by Rudolfplatz CX :

🏨 **Imperial**, Barthelstr. 93, ℰ 51 70 57, Telex 8883452, Fax 520993, ≋s – 🛗 📺 ☎ ⇔ 🅿. ⑩
🄴 𝗩𝗜𝗦𝗔
M *(dinner only)* a la carte 30/58 – **36 rm** 150/290 Bb.

ХХХ **Zum offenen Kamin**, Eichendorffstr. 25, ℰ 55 68 78 – 🝿 ⑩ 🄴 𝗩𝗜𝗦𝗔 by Erftstraße CU
closed Saturday lunch and Sunday except exhibitions – **M** 50 (lunch) and a la carte
64/90.

at Cologne 80-Holweide by Konrad-Adenauer-Ufer DU :

ХХХ **Isenburg**, Johann-Bensberg-Str. 49, ℰ 69 59 09, Fax 698703, 🍴 – 🅿. ⑩ 🄴 𝗩𝗜𝗦𝗔
closed Saturday lunch, Sunday, Monday, carnival, mid July - mid August and Christmas –
M *(booking essential)* a la carte 46/78.

at Cologne 50-Immendorf by Bonner Str. DY :

ХХ **Weinstuben Bitzerhof** with rm (1821 farmyard), Immendorfer Hauptstr. 21,
ℰ (02236) 6 19 21, 🍴, « Country house atmosphere » – 📺 ☎ ⇔. 🄴 ℀ rm
closed 4 weeks July - August – **M** a la carte 47/71 – **3 rm** 95/150.

at Cologne 41-Lindenthal by Rudolfplatz CX and B 264 :

🏨 **Queens Hotel**, Dürener Str. 287, ℰ 4 67 60, Telex 8882516, Fax 433765, « Garden with
🍴 » – 🛗 ½⇔ rm 🔲 rest 📺 ☎ ⇔ 🅿 – 🔏 25/600. 🝿 ⑩ 🄴 𝗩𝗜𝗦𝗔. ℀ rest
M 30 (lunch) and a la carte 48/83 – **147 rm** 199/343 Bb.

🏨 **Bremer**, Dürener Str. 225, ℰ 40 50 13, Telex 8882063, Fax 402034, ≋s, 🖳 – 🛗 🔲 rest 📺
☎ ⇔. 🝿 ⑩ 🄴 𝗩𝗜𝗦𝗔. ℀ rest
closed 28 March - 2 April and 23 December - 2 January – **M** *(booking essential)* a la carte
56/78 – **69 rm** 115/200.

ХХХ Rôtisserie zum Krieler Dom, Bachemer Str. 233 (entrance Krieler Straße), ℰ 43 29 43
M *(booking essential).*

at Cologne 51-Marienburg by Bonner Straße DY :

🏨 **Marienburger Bonotel**, Bonner Str. 478, ℰ 3 70 20, Telex 8881515, Fax 3702132, ≋s – 🛗
📺 ☎ ⇔ 🅿 – 🔏 25/100. 🝿 ⑩ 🄴 𝗩𝗜𝗦𝗔. ℀ rest
M a la carte 40/70 – **93 rm** 180/325 Bb – 4 apart.

ХХ **Marienburger Eule**, Bonner Str. 471, ℰ 38 15 78, Fax 343420 – 🝿 ⑩ 🄴 𝗩𝗜𝗦𝗔
closed lunch Saturday and Sunday – **M** a la carte 55/90.

at Cologne 40-Marsdorf by Rudolfplatz CX and B 264 :

🏨 Novotel Köln-West, Horbeller Str. 1, ℰ (02234) 51 40, Telex 8886355, Fax 514106, 🍴, ≋s,
🏊 (heated), 🖳 – 🛗 🔲 rest 📺 ☎ ℊ 🅿 – 🔏 25/300
199 rm Bb.

at Cologne 91-Merheim by Deutzer Brücke DX :

ХХХХ ✿✿ **Goldener Pflug**, Olpener Str. 421 (B 55), ℰ 89 55 09 – 🅿
closed Sunday, Bank Holidays and 3 weeks July - August – **M** 55 (lunch) and a la carte
106/156
Spec. Hummerragout mit Kerbel, Steinbutt mit Trüffeln, Nantaiser Ente (2 pers.).

at Cologne 41 - Müngersdorf by Rudolfplatz CX and B 55:

ХХХ **Landhaus Kuckuck**, Olympiaweg 2, ℰ 49 23 23, Fax 4972847, 🍴 – 🔏 25/100. 🝿 ⑩ 🄴
𝗩𝗜𝗦𝗔
closed Monday – **M** a la carte 50/78.

ХХ **Remise**, Wendelinstr. 48, ℰ 49 18 81, « Historic farm house » – 🅿. ⑩ 🄴 𝗩𝗜𝗦𝗔
closed Saturday lunch and Sunday – **M** *(booking essential)* a la carte 56/90.

at Cologne 90- Porz-Wahnheide SE : 17 km by A 59 :

🏨 **Holiday Inn**, Waldstr. 255, ℰ (02203) 56 10, Telex 8874665, Fax 5619, ≋s, 🖳, 🐎 – 🛗
½⇔ rm 🔲 📺 ☎ 🅿 – 🔏 25/90. 🝿 ⑩ 🄴 𝗩𝗜𝗦𝗔
M a la carte 42/75 – **113 rm** 252/364 Bb.

Wittlich 5560. Rheinland - Pfalz 987 ②③④. 412 D 17 — pop. 17 000 — alt. 155 m — ✆ 06571. Köln 130.

at Dreis 5561 SW : 8 km :

🏨 ✸✸ **Waldhotel Sonnora** ⚘, Auf dem Eichelfeld, ✆ (06578) 4 06, ≤, « Garden » – 📺 ☎ 🅿. 🄴. ✳
closed 7 January - 7 February — **M** *(booking essential, closed Tuesday lunch and Monday)* 85/105 and a la carte 66/90 — **20 rm** 60/120
Spec. Ravioli von Langustinen in Krustentiersauce, Loup de mer mit Kartoffelschuppen, Täubchen mit Trüffelsauce.

DRESDEN 8010. Sachsen 984 ②④. 987 ⑱ — pop. 500 000 — alt. 105 m — ✆ 003751.

See : Zwinger★★★ (Wall Pavilion★★, Nymphs' Bath★★, Porcelain Collection★★, National Mathematical-Physical Salon★★) AY — Semper Opera★★ AY — Former court church★★ (Hofkirche) BY — Palace (Schloß): royal houses★ (Fürstenzug), Long Passage★ (Langer Gang) BY — Albertinum: Picture Gallery Old Masters★★★ (Gemäldegalerie Alte Meister), Picture Gallery New Masters★★★ (Gemäldegalerie Neue Meister), Green Vault★★★ (Grünes Gewölbe) BY — Prager Straße★ ABZ — Museum of History of the town Dresden★ (Museum für Geschichte der Stadt Dresden) BY L — Church of the Cross★ (Kreuzkirche) BY — Japanese Palace★ (Japanisches Palais) ABX — Museum of Folk Art★ (Museum für Volkskunst) BX M 2 — Great Garden★ (Großer Garten) CDZ — Russian-Orthodox Church★ (Russisch-orthodoxe Kirche) (by Leningrader Str. BZ) — Brühl's Terrace ≤★ (Brühlsche Terrasse) BY.

Envir. : Schloß (palace) Moritzburg★ (NW : 14 km by Hansastr. BX) — Schloß (palace) Pillnitz★ (SE : 15 km by Bautzener Str. CX) — Saxon Swiss★★★ (Sächsische Schweiz): Bastei★★★, Festung (fortress) Königstein★★ ≤★★, Großsedlitz: Baroque Garden★.

✈ Dresden-Klotzsche (N : 13 km), Interflug City Office, Rampische Str. 2, ✆ 4 95 60 13.

🅱 Dresden-Information, Prager Str. 10, ✆ 4 95 50 25, Telex 26198.

Berlin 198 — Chemnitz 70 — Görlitz 98 — Leipzig 111 — Praha 152.

Plans on following pages

🏨 **Bellevue**, Köpckestr. 15, ⊠ 8060, ✆ 5 66 20, Telex 26162, Fax 55997, ≤, 🌁, « Court terraces », Massage, ⚖, 😌, 🔲 – 🛗 ⇆ rm 🗐 📺 ᴋ ⇔ 🅿 – 🔬 30/200. 🄰🄴 ⊙ 🄴 𝓥𝓘𝓢𝓐
  BX a
M a la carte 37/79 — **326 rm** 220/380 Bb — 6 apart. 500/950.

🏨 **Dresdner Hof**, An der Frauenkirche 5, ✆ 4 84 10, Telex 2488, Fax 4841700, 😌, 🔲 – 🛗 ⇆ rm 🗐 📺 ᴋ ⇔ 🅿 – 🔬 30/300. 🄰🄴 ⊙ 🄴 𝓥𝓘𝓢𝓐
  BY e
closed 11 to 14 January — **M** a la carte 34/79 — **333 rm** 240/435 Bb — 12 apart. 430/550.

🏨 **Newa**, Prager Straße, ✆ 4 96 71 12, Telex 26067, 🌁, 😌 – 🛗 📺 ☎. 🄰🄴 ⊙ 🄴 𝓥𝓘𝓢𝓐 BZ n
M a la carte 25/47 — **309 rm** 157/314 Bb.

🏨 **Lilienstein**, Prager Str. 15, ⊠ 8020, ✆ 4 85 60, Telex 26165 – 🛗 ☎. 🄰🄴 ⊙ 🄴 𝓥𝓘𝓢𝓐 BZ b
M a la carte 20/44 — **303 rm** 119/204 Bb — 9 appart. 218/245.

🏨 **Königstein**, Prager Str. 9, ✆ 4 85 60, Telex 26165, 😌 – 🛗 📺 ☎. 🄰🄴 ⊙ 🄴 𝓥𝓘𝓢𝓐 BZ d
M a la carte 20/40 — **295 rm** 115/205 Bb — 8 apart. 210/240.

🏨 **Motel Dresden** ⚘, Münzmeisterstr. 10, ⊠ 8020, ✆ 47 58 51, 🌁 – 📺 ☎ 🅿. 🄰🄴 ⊙ 🄴 𝓥𝓘𝓢𝓐
  by Leningrader Str. BZ
M a la carte 21/40 — **84 rm** 125/170 Bb.

🏨 **Astoria**, Ernst-Thälmann-Platz 1, ✆ 47 51 71, Telex 2442 – 🛗 📺 ☎ 🅿. 🄰🄴 ⊙ 🄴 𝓥𝓘𝓢𝓐
  by Parkstr. BZ
M a la carte 18/47 — **70 rm** 80/230 Bb.

XX **Opernrestaurant**, Theaterplatz 2 (1st floor), ✆ 4 84 25 00, 🌁 – 🄰🄴 ⊙ 🄴 𝓥𝓘𝓢𝓐 AY r
M a la carte 31/56.

XX **Blockhaus**, Neustädter Markt 19 (2nd floor), 🛗, ⊠ 8060, ✆ 54 41, ≤ – 🔬 30/200. 🄰🄴 ⊙ 🄴 𝓥𝓘𝓢𝓐 ✳ BX f
M a la carte 20/42.

XX **Kügelgenhaus** (18C historic building, early Romanticism Museum in Dresden), Straße der Befreiung 13, ⊠ 8060, ✆ 5 45 18, 🌁 – 🄰🄴 ⊙ 🄴 𝓥𝓘𝓢𝓐 BX h
M a la carte 16/33 ⏃.

X **Szeges**, Ernst-Thälmann-Str. 6 (1st floor), ✆ 4 95 13 71 – 🄰🄴 ⊙ 🄴 𝓥𝓘𝓢𝓐. ✳ BY p
M a la carte 18/49.

Pleasant hotels and restaurants
are shown in the Guide by a red sign. 🏨 … 🏠
Please send us the names
of any where you have enjoyed your stay. XXXXX … X
Your Michelin Guide will be even better.

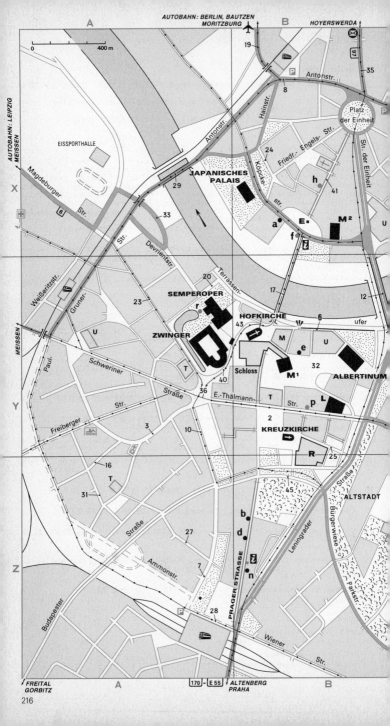

DRESDEN

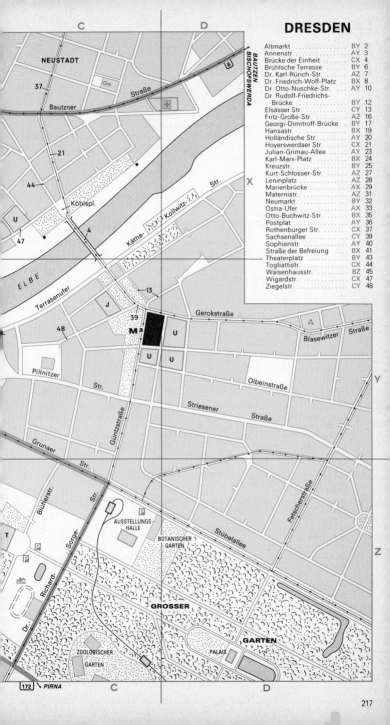

DÜSSELDORF 4000. 🆗 Nordrhein-Westfalen **987** ㉘ ㉔. **412** D 13 – pop. 570 000 – alt. 40 m
– ✪ 0211.

See : Königsallee★ – Hofgarten★ – Hetjensmuseum★ BX **M2** – Land Economic Museum
(Landesmuseum Volk u. Wirtschaft)★ BV **M1** – Goethemuseum★ CV **M3** – Thyssen building
(Thyssenhaus)★ CVX **E**.

Envir. : Chateau of Benrath (Schloß Benrath) (Park★) S : 10 km by Kölner Str. DXY

🏌 Ratingen-Hösel, NE : 16 km, ℘ (02102) 6 86 29 ; 🏌 Gut Rommeljans, NE : 12 km, ℘ (02102)
8 10 92 ; 🏌 D-Hubbelrath, E : 12 km, ℘ (02102) 7 21 78 ; 🏌 Düsseldorf-Hafen, ℘ (0211) 39 65 98.

✈ Düsseldorf-Lohausen (N : 8 km), ℘ 42 11.

🚗 ℘ 3 68 04 68.

Exhibition Centre (Messegelände), ℘ 4 56 01, Telex 8584853.

🅱 Tourist office, Konrad-Adenauer-Platz and Heinrich-Heine-Allee 24, ℘ 35 05 05, Telex 8587785, Fax 161071.
ADAC, Himmelgeister Str. 63, ℘ 3 10 93 33.

Amsterdam 225 – Essen 31 – Köln 40 – Rotterdam 237.

The reference (D 15) at the end of the address is the postal district : Düsseldorf 15

Plan on following pages

🏛🏛 **Breidenbacher Hof**, Heinrich-Heine-Allee 36 (D 1), ℘ 1 30 30, Telex 8582630, Fax 1303830,
⊜s – ❘≋❘ ❀⟷ rm 🔲 📺 ⟷ – ⚖ 25/90. ⚫ ⓞ ⓔ 🆅🆂🅰 ❀ rest   BX **a**
Restaurants : **Grill Royal** *(Saturday and Sunday dinner only)* **M** a la carte 72/99 –
Breidenbacher Eck M a la carte 47/72 – **Trader Vic's** *(dinner only)* **M** a la carte 49/63 –
135 rm 290/590 – 30 apart. 690/2600.

🏛🏛 **Steigenberger Parkhotel**, Corneliusplatz 1 (D 1), ℘ 86 51, Telex 8582331, Fax 131679,
❀ – ❘≋❘ ❀⟷ rm 📺 🅿 – ⚖ 25/250. ⚫ ⓞ ⓔ 🆅🆂🅰 ❀ rest   CX **p**
M a la carte 59/96 – **160 rm** 295/490 Bb – 12 apart. 650/1350.

🏛🏛 **Nikko**, Immermannstr. 41 (D 1), ℘ 83 40, Telex 8582080, Fax 161216, ❀, Massage, ⊜s, 🔲
– ❘≋❘ ❀⟷ rm 🔲 📺 ⟷ – ⚖ 25/500. ❀ rest   DX **a**
301 rm Bb – 16 apart..

🏛 **Holiday Inn**, Graf-Adolf-Platz 10 (D 1), ℘ 3 87 30, Telex 8586359, Fax 3873390, ⊜s, 🔲 –
❘≋❘ ❀⟷ rm 📺 🔲 ⟷ – ⚖ 25/80. ⚫ ⓞ ⓔ 🆅🆂🅰   CY **r**
M a la carte 49/68 – **177 rm** 317/467 Bb.

🏛 **Savoy**, Oststr. 128 (D 1), ℘ 36 03 36, Telex 8584215, Fax 356642, Massage, ⊜s, 🔲 – ❘≋❘
🔲 rest 📺 ⟷ 🅿 – ⚖ 25/100. ⚫ ⓞ ⓔ 🆅🆂🅰   CX **w**
M a la carte 43/74 – **130 rm** 185/362 Bb.

🏛 **Majestic - Restaurant La Grappa**, Cantadorstr. 4 (D 1), ℘ 36 70 30 (Hotel) 35 72 92
(Rest.), Telex 8584649, Fax 3670399, ⊜s – ❘≋❘ 📺 🕿 ♿ – ⚖ 40. ⚫ ⓞ ⓔ 🆅🆂🅰   DVX **b**
closed 22 December - 1 January – **M** *(Italian cooking)* (closed Sunday and Bank Holidays
except April/September) a la carte 58/82 – **52 rm** 170/410 Bb.

🏛 **Uebachs**, Leopoldstr. 5 (D 1), ℘ 36 05 66, Telex 8587620, Fax 358064 – ❘≋❘ 📺 ⟷ ⟷ –
⚖ 30. ⚫ ⓞ ⓔ 🆅🆂🅰 ❀ rest   DX **r**
M *(closed Sunday except exhibitions)* a la carte 45/73 – **82 rm** 147/310 Bb.

🏛 **Graf Adolf** 🗲, Stresemannplatz 1 (D 1), ℘ 3 55 40, Telex 8587844, Fax 354120, ⊜s – ❘≋❘
📺 🕿 ⟷ – ⚖ 25/120. ⚫ ⓞ ⓔ 🆅🆂🅰 ❀ rest   CX **e**
Restaurants : **Orangerie** – **Le Bistro** – **151 rm** 175/375 Bb – 9 apart. 350/450.

🏛 **Esplanade**, Fürstenplatz 17 (D 1), ℘ 37 50 10, Telex 8582970, Fax 374032, ⊜s, 🔲 – ❘≋❘ 📺
🕿 ⟷ – ⚖ 25/60. ⚫ ⓞ ⓔ 🆅🆂🅰   CY **s**
M a la carte 41/65 – **80 rm** 145/398 Bb.

🏛 **Grand Hotel** without rest, Varnhagenstr. 37 (D 1), ℘ 31 08 00, Telex 8584072, Fax 316667,
⊜s – ❘≋❘ ❀⟷ 📺 🕿 ♿ – ⚖ 30
70 rm Bb.

🏛 **Madison I** without rest, Graf-Adolf-Str. 94 (D 1), ℘ 1 68 50, Fax 1685328, 🛁, ⊜s, 🔲 – ❘≋❘
📺 🕿 ⟷ – ⚖ 25/100. ⚫ ⓞ ⓔ 🆅🆂🅰   DX **n**
95 rm 145/260 Bb.

🏛 **Madison II** without rest, Graf-Adolf-Str. 47 (D 1), ℘ 37 02 96, Fax 1685328 – ❘≋❘ 📺 🔲
⟷ ⚫ ⓞ ⓔ 🆅🆂🅰   CY **x**
closed 15 July - 14 August – **24 rm** 130/230 Bb.

🏛 **Hotel An der Kö** without rest, Talstr. 9 (D 1), ℘ 37 10 48, Fax 370835 – ❘≋❘ 🕿 🅿. ⚫ ⓞ ⓔ
🆅🆂🅰   CY **u**
40 rm 148/320 Bb.

🏛 **Monopol** without rest, Oststr. 135 (D 1), ℘ 8 42 08, Telex 8587770, Fax 328843 – ❘≋❘ ❀⟷ 📺
🕿. ⚫ ⓞ ⓔ 🆅🆂🅰   CX **b**
50 rm 195/270 Bb.

🏛 **Astoria** without rest, Jahnstr. 72 (D 1), ℘ 38 20 88, Telex 8581834, Fax 372089 – ❘≋❘ 📺 🕿
🅿. ⚫ ⓞ ⓔ 🆅🆂🅰 ❀   CY **b**
closed 20 December - 4 January – **25 rm** 115/280 Bb – 3 appart. 310.

🏛 **Concorde** without rest, Graf-Adolf-Str. 60 (D 1), ℘ 36 98 25, Telex 8588008, Fax 354606 –
❘≋❘ 📺 🕿. ⚫ ⓞ ⓔ 🆅🆂🅰   CY **f**
75 rm 130/305 Bb.

🏛 **Central** without rest, Luisenstr. 42 (D 1), ℘ 37 90 01, Telex 8582145, Fax 379094 – ❘≋❘ 📺
🕿. ⚫ ⓞ ⓔ 🆅🆂🅰   CY **v**
closed 20 December - 1 January – **75 rm** 170/450 Bb.

🏨 **Terminus** without rest, Am Wehrhahn 81 (D 1), ℘ 35 05 91, Telex 8586576, Fax 358350, 🚗,
🔲 – 📶 📺 ☎ – **44 rm** Bb.
DV **a**

🏨 **Ambassador** without rest, Harkortstr. 7 (D 1), ℘ 37 00 03, Telex 8586286, Fax 376702 – 📶
📺 ☎ 🅿. 🆎 ⑩ 🇪 𝒱𝐼𝑆𝐴
DY **a**
68 rm 102/200 Bb.

🏨 **Eden** without rest, Adersstr. 29 (D 1), ℘ 3 89 70, Telex 8582530, Fax 3897777 – 📶 ⇔ rm
📺 ☎ ⇔ – 🔬 25/100. 🆎 ⑩ 🇪 𝒱𝐼𝑆𝐴
CY **m**
130 rm 189/376 Bb.

🏨 **Bellevue** without rest, Luisenstr. 98 (D 1), ℘ 37 70 71, Fax 377076 – 📶 📺 ☎ ⇔ 🆎 ⑩
🇪 𝒱𝐼𝑆𝐴
CY **z**
closed 20 December - 5 January – **52 rm** 150/265 Bb.

🏨 **Lindenhof** without rest, Oststr. 124 (D 1), ℘ 36 09 63, Telex 8587012, Fax 162767 – 📶
☎. 🆎 ⑩ 🇪 𝒱𝐼𝑆𝐴
CX **u**
closed 3 weeks July - August and 24 December - 2 January – **43 rm** 120/230.

🏨 **Fürstenhof** without rest, Fürstenplatz 3 (D 1), ℘ 37 05 45, Telex 8586540, Fax 379062, 🚗
– 📶 ⇔ 📺 ☎. 🆎 ⑩ 🇪 𝒱𝐼𝑆𝐴
CY **e**
43 rm 205/280 Bb.

🏨 **Cristallo** without rest, Schadowplatz 7 (D 1), ℘ 8 45 25, Telex 8582119 – 📶 📺 ☎. 🆎 ⑩
🇪 𝒱𝐼𝑆𝐴 ⌘
CX **r**
closed 24 December - 1 January – **35 rm** 150/215.

🏨 **City** without rest, Bismarckstr. 73 (D 1), ℘ 36 50 23, Telex 8587362, Fax 365343 – 📶 📺 ☎.
🆎 ⑩ 🇪 𝒱𝐼𝑆𝐴
CX **d**
closed 23 December - 2 January – **54 rm** 120/260.

🏨 **Börsenhotel** without rest, Kreuzstr. 19a (D 1), ℘ 36 30 71, Telex 8587323, Fax 365338 – 📶
📺 ☎ – 🔬 80
CX **n**
76 rm Bb.

🏢 **Cornelius**, Corneliusstr. 82 (D 1), ℘ 38 20 55 (hotel) 37 64 74 (rest.), Telex 8587385, Fax
382050, 🚗 – 📶 📺 ☎ 🅿. 🆎 ⑩ 🇪 𝒱𝐼𝑆𝐴
CY **a**
closed 20 December - 7 January – **M** *(closed Saturday)* a la carte 32/52 – **48 rm** 130/
230 Bb.

🏢 **Prinz Anton** without rest, Karl-Anton-Str. 11 (D 1), ℘ 35 20 00, Telex 8588925, Fax 362010
– 📶 📺 ☎ ⇔. 🆎 ⑩ 🇪 𝒱𝐼𝑆𝐴
DX **c**
closed 23 December - 2 January – **42 rm** 95/350 Bb.

🏢 **Residenz** without rest, Worringer Str. 88 (D 1), ℘ 36 08 54, Telex 8587897, Fax 364676 –
📶 📺 ☎. 🆎 ⑩ 🇪 𝒱𝐼𝑆𝐴
DX **z**
34 rm 120/295 Bb.

🏢 **Schumacher** without rest, Worringer Str. 55 (D 1), ℘ 36 78 50, Telex 8586610, Fax 3678570,
🚗 – 📶 📺 ☎ ⇔. 🆎 ⑩ 🇪 𝒱𝐼𝑆𝐴
DX **e**
30 rm 120/230 Bb.

🏢 **Intercity-Hotel Ibis** without rest, Konrad-Adenauer-Platz 14 (D 1), ℘ 1 67 20,
Telex 8588913, Fax 1672101 – 📶 📺 ☎ ♿ – 🔬 35. 🆎 ⑩ 🇪 𝒱𝐼𝑆𝐴
DX **u**
166 rm 139/183 Bb.

XXX ❀ **Victorian**, Königstr. 3a (1st floor) (D 1), ℘ 32 02 22, Fax 131013 – 🍽. 🆎 ⑩ 🇪 𝒱𝐼𝑆𝐴. ⌘
closed Sunday and Bank Holidays – **M** *(booking essential)* 55 (lunch) and a la carte 65/95 –
Lounge *(closed Sunday and Bank Holidays mid July - August)* **M** a la carte 35/74
CX **e**
Spec. Entenleber mit grünem Pfeffer, Seehecht im Zitronensud pochiert, Kalbsniere in
Rotwein-Schalottenbutter.

XXX **La Scala** (Italian rest.), Königsallee 14 (1st floor) 📶 (D 1), ℘ 32 68 32 – 🆎 ⑩ 🇪 𝒱𝐼𝑆𝐴
closed 1 week Easter, 1 week Christmas and Sunday except dinner during exhibitions – **M** a
la carte 55/84.
CX **y**

XX **La Terrazza** (Italian rest.), Königsallee 30 (Kö-Centre, 2nd floor, 📶) (D 1), ℘ 32 75 40, Fax
320975 – 🆎 ⑩ 🇪 𝒱𝐼𝑆𝐴
CX **v**
closed Saturday, Sunday and Bank Holidays except exhibitions – **M** *(booking essential)* a la
carte 61/93.

XX **Mövenpick - Café des Artistes**, Königsallee 60 (Kö-Galerie) (D 1), ℘ 32 03 14, Fax 328058 –
🍽
CX **h**

XX **Tse Yang** (Chinese rest.), Immermannstr. 65 (Immermannhof) (D 1), ℘ 36 90 20 – 🆎 ⑩
🇪 𝒱𝐼𝑆𝐴
DX **v**
M a la carte 39/76.

XX **Weinhaus Tante Anna** (1593 former private chapel), Andreasstr. 2 (D 1), ℘ 13 11 63, Fax
132974, « Antique paintings and furniture » – 🆎 ⑩ 🇪 𝒱𝐼𝑆𝐴. ⌘
BX **c**
dinner only, closed Sunday except exhibitions – **M** *(booking essential)* a la carte 48/80.

XX **Daitokai** (Japanese rest.), Mutter-Ey-Str. 1 (D 1), ℘ 32 50 54, Fax 325056 – 🍽. 🆎 ⑩ 🇪
𝒱𝐼𝑆𝐴. ⌘
BX **z**
closed Sunday except exhibitions – **M** *(booking essential)* a la carte 48/74.

XX **Nippon Kan** (Japanese rest.), Immermannstr. 35 (D 1), ℘ 35 31 35, Fax 3613625 – 🆎 ⑩
🇪 𝒱𝐼𝑆𝐴. ⌘
CX **g**
M *(booking essential)* a la carte 34/76.

X **China-Sichuan-Restaurant**, Graf-Adolf-Platz 7 (1st floor) (D 1), ℘ 37 96 41
BY **s**
(booking essential).

When in Europe
never be without:
the Michelin Map no **920**
and
the Michelin Green Guides

Austria
England:
The West Country
Germany
Greece
Italy
London
Paris
Portugal
Rome
Scotland
Spain
Switzerland

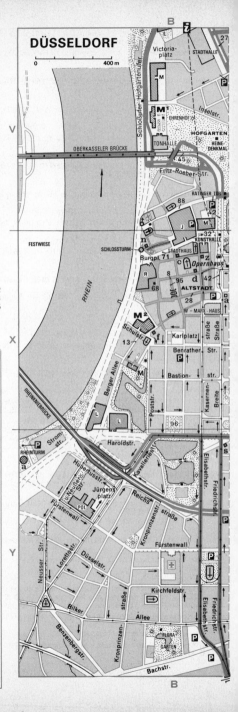

DÜSSELDORF

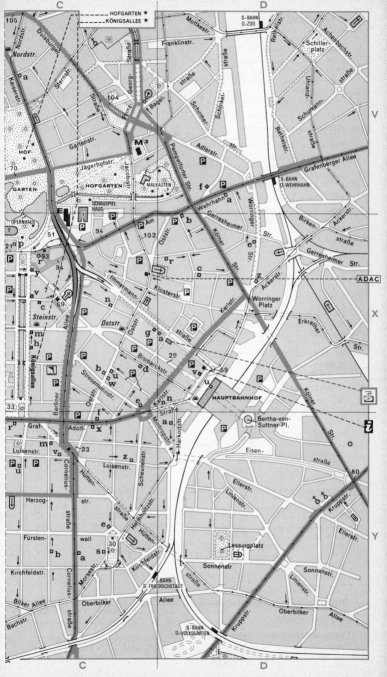

Brewery-inns :

✗ **Zum Schiffchen**, Hafenstr. 5 (D 1), 𝒫 13 24 22, Fax 134596 — 𝔸𝔼 ⓞ 𝐄 𝘝𝘐𝘚𝘈　　　BX **f**
closed Christmas - New Year, Sunday and Bank Holidays — **M** a la carte 31/58.

✗ Frankenheim, Wielandstr. 14 (D 1), 𝒫 35 14 47, beer garden　　　　　　　　　　DV **f**

✗ **Im Goldenen Ring**, Burgplatz 21 (D 1), 𝒫 13 31 61, Fax 324780, beer garden　　BX **n**
M a la carte 23/49.

✗ **Benrather Hof**, Steinstr. 1 (D 1), 𝒫 32 52 18, Fax 132957, �　　　　　　　　CX **m**
M a la carte 24/50.

✗ Im Goldenen Kessel, Bolker Str. 44 (D 1), 𝒫 32 60 07　　　　　　　　　　　　BX **d**

at Düsseldorf 13-Benrath by Kölner Str.DXY :

🏨 **Rheinterrasse**, Benrather Schloßufer 39, 𝒫 71 10 70, Telex 8582459, Fax 7110770,
« Terrace with ⩽ » — 📺 ☎ 𝐏 — 𝒜 25, 𝔸𝔼 ⓞ 𝐄 𝘝𝘐𝘚𝘈
M a la carte 52/73 — **42 rm** 110/245 Bb.

✗✗ **Lignano** (Italian rest.), Hildener Str. 43, 𝒫 71 19 36 — 𝔸𝔼 ⓞ 𝐄 𝘝𝘐𝘚𝘈, ⅌⅌
closed Saturday lunch, Sunday and 3 weeks July - August — **M** a la carte 55/78.

✗✗ **Pigage** (Italian rest.), Benrather Schloßallee 28, 𝒫 71 40 66 — ⓞ 𝐄 𝘝𝘐𝘚𝘈
closed Saturday lunch and Sunday except exhibitions — **M** a la carte 46/75.

at Düsseldorf 30-Derendorf by Prinz-Georg-Str. CV :

🏨 **Rhein Residence**, Kaiserswerther Str. 20, 𝒫 4 99 90, Massage, ⓢ — ▥ 📺
— 𝒜 30, 𝔸𝔼 ⓞ 𝐄 𝘝𝘐𝘚𝘈, ⅌⅌ rest　　　　　　　　　　by Duisburger Straße CV
M a la carte 40/52 — **126 rm** 228/361 Bb.

🏨 **Saga Excelsior** without rest, Kapellstr. 1, 𝒫 48 60 06, Telex 8584737, Fax 490242 — ▥ 📺
𝔸𝔼 ⓞ 𝐄 𝘝𝘐𝘚𝘈, ⅌⅌　　　　　　　　　　　　　　　　　　　　　　　　　CV **a**
65 rm 155/298.

🏨 **Michelangelo** without rest, Roßstr. 61, 𝒫 48 01 01, Telex 8588649, Fax 467742 — ▥ 📺 ☎
⇐⇒, 𝔸𝔼 ⓞ 𝐄 𝘝𝘐𝘚𝘈
closed 21 December - 1 January — **70 rm** 130/260 Bb.

🏨 **Consul** without rest, Kaiserswerther Str. 59, 𝒫 49 20 78, Telex 8584624, Fax 4982577 — ▥
📺 ☎ ⇐⇒, 𝔸𝔼 ⓞ 𝐄 𝘝𝘐𝘚𝘈
29 rm 127/220 Bb.

🏨 **Gildors Hotel** without rest (with guest house), Collenbachstr. 51, 𝒫 48 80 05,
Telex 8584418, Fax 446329 — ▥ 📺 ☎ ⇐⇒, 𝔸𝔼 ⓞ 𝐄 𝘝𝘐𝘚𝘈
closed Christmas - New Year — **50 rm** 145/265 Bb.

✗✗ Amalfi (Italian rest.), Ulmenstr. 122, 𝒫 43 38 09.

✗✗ **Gatto Verde** (Italian rest.), Rheinbabenstr. 5, 𝒫 46 18 17, � — 𝔸𝔼 ⓞ 𝐄 𝘝𝘐𝘚𝘈
closed Saturday lunch, Sunday, Monday and 6 to 31 August — **M** a la carte 47/71.

at Düsseldorf 13-Eller by Kölner Str. DXY :

🏨 **Novotel Düsseldorf Süd**, Am Schönenkamp 9, 𝒫 74 10 92, Telex 8584374, Fax 745512,
�, ⛱ (heated), ⇶ — ▥ ▤ 📺 ☎ ♿ 𝐏 — 𝒜 25/300, 𝔸𝔼 ⓞ 𝐄 𝘝𝘐𝘚𝘈
M a la carte 33/63 — **120 rm** 163/198 Bb.

at Düsseldorf 30-Golzheim by Fischerstr. BV :

🏨 **Inter-Continental**, Karl-Arnold-Platz 5, 𝒫 4 55 30, Telex 8584601, Fax 4553110, Massage,
ⓢ, ⛝ — ▥ ▤ 📺 ♿ ⇐⇒ 𝐏 — 𝒜 25/400, 𝔸𝔼 ⓞ 𝐄 𝘝𝘐𝘚𝘈, ⅌⅌ rest
Restaurants : **Les Continents** *(closed Saturday lunch, Sunday and 4 weeks July - August)*
M a la carte 82/108 — **Café de la Paix M** a la carte 45/80 — **310 rm** 274/582 Bb —
20 apart. 857/1332.

🏨 **Düsseldorf Hilton**, Georg-Glock-Str. 20, 𝒫 4 37 70, Telex 8584376, Fax 4377650, �, Ⅰ♿,
ⓢ, ⛝, ⇶ — ▥ ⅌⅌ rm ▤ 📺 ♿ 𝐏 — 𝒜 25/1500, 𝔸𝔼 ⓞ 𝐄 𝘝𝘐𝘚𝘈, ⅌⅌ rest
Restaurants : **San Francisco** *(dinner only, closed Monday and July)* **M** a la carte 67/98 —
Hofgarten M 32 (lunch buffet) a la carte 44/68 — **376 rm** 277/558 Bb — 9 apart. 853/1753.

🏨 **Golzheimer Krug** ⑤, Karl-Kleppe-Str. 20, 𝒫 43 44 53, Telex 8588919, Fax 453299, � —
📺 ☎ 𝐏 — 𝒜 25/80, 𝔸𝔼 ⓞ 𝐄 𝘝𝘐𝘚𝘈, ⅌⅌ rest
M *(closed Monday)* a la carte 37/72 — **32 rm** 145/450 Bb.

🏨 **Rheinpark** without rest, Bankstr. 13, 𝒫 49 91 86 — ⇐⇒ 𝐏, ⅌⅌
30 rm 60/130 Bb.

✗✗ **Fischer-Stuben-Mulfinger**, Rotterdamer Str. 15, 𝒫 43 26 12, « Garden terrace » — 𝔸𝔼
𝐄
closed Saturday — **M** (booking essential) a la carte 47/77.

✗✗ **Rosati** (Italian rest.), Felix-Klein-Str. 1, 𝒫 4 36 05 03, Fax 452963, � — 𝐏, 𝔸𝔼 ⓞ 𝐄 𝘝𝘐𝘚𝘈
closed Saturday lunch and Sunday — **M** (booking essential) a la carte 57/79 — **Rosati due**
M a la carte 30/49.

at Düsseldorf 12-Grafenberg by Grafenberger Allee DV :

🏨 **Rolandsburg** ⑤, Rennbahnstr. 2, 𝒫 61 00 90, Fax 6100943, �, « Modern hotel, elegant
installation », ⓢ, ⛝ — ▥ 📺 𝐏 — 𝒜 25/50, 𝔸𝔼 ⓞ 𝐄 𝘝𝘐𝘚𝘈
M a la carte 69/90 — **59 rm** 210/490 Bb.

at Düsseldorf 31-Kaiserswerth by Fischerstr. BV :

🏛 **Barbarossa** without rest, Niederrheinstr. 365 (B 8), 𝄐 40 27 19, Fax 400801 — |🛗| 🕿 🅿. 🆎 ① E 𝘝𝘐𝘚𝘈
33 rm 85/165 Bb.

🏛 **Haus Rittendorf** without rest, Friedrich-von-Spee-Str. 44, 𝄐 40 40 41 — 🕿 🅿
10 rm 78/150.

XXXX ✿✿✿ **Im Schiffchen** (French rest.), Kaiserswerther Markt 9 (1st floor), 𝄐 40 10 50, Fax 403667 — 🆎 ① E 𝘝𝘐𝘚𝘈. ✺
closed Sunday, Monday and Bank Holidays — **M** *(booking essential)* (see also **Restaurant Aalschokker** below) 144/189 and a la carte 112/146
Spec. Gänseleber-Maultasche auf Trüffel-Coulis, Brachfeldfrüchte in leichtem Knoblauchsud, Dentelle von weißem Ahrtal-Pfirsich (Saison).

XX ✿ **Aalschokker** (German cooking), Kaiserswerther Markt 9, 𝄐 40 39 48, Fax 403667 — 🆎 ① E 𝘝𝘐𝘚𝘈
closed Sunday, Monday and Bank Holidays — **M** *(booking essential)* 125 and a la carte 61/88
Spec. Maultaschen in Steinpilzbutter, Himmel und Erde mit Gänseleber, Zimtauflauf mit Dörrpflaumen.

at Düsseldorf 11-Lörick by Oberkasseler Brücke BV :

🏛🏛 **Fischerhaus** ⤾, Bonifatiusstr. 35, 𝄐 59 20 07, Telex 8584449 — 📺 🕿 🅿. 🆎 ① E 𝘝𝘐𝘚𝘈
M (see **Hummerstübchen** below) — **30 rm** 119/248 Bb.

XX ✿ **Hummerstübchen**, Bonifatiusstr. 35 (at Hotel Fischerhaus), 𝄐 59 44 02 — 🅿. 🆎 ① E 𝘝𝘐𝘚𝘈
closed Sunday, Monday and 3 weeks July - August — **M** *(booking essential)* a la carte 80/101
Spec. Gratin von Hummer auf Nudeln, Seeteufel mit Knoblauch in Beerenauslese, Lammrücken in der Rosmarinschwarte.

at Düsseldorf 30-Lohausen by Hofgartenufer BV :

🏛🏛 **Arabella Airport Hotel** ⤾, am Flughafen, 𝄐 4 17 30, Telex 8584612, Fax 4173707 — |🛗| ⇆ rm 🔲 🆎 ① E 𝘝𝘐𝘚𝘈 25/190. 🆎 ① E 𝘝𝘐𝘚𝘈
M 32 (lunch) and a la carte 41/63 — **200 rm** 161/384 Bb.

at Düsseldorf 30-Mörsenbroich by Rethelstr. DV :

🏛🏛🏛 **Ramada-Renaissance-Hotel**, Nördlicher Zubringer 6, 𝄐 6 21 60, Telex 172114001, Fax 6216666, 🎣, ⇆, 🔲 — |🛗| ⇆ rm ▣ 📺 🛗 ↔ ⇌ — 🅿 25/400. 🆎 ① E 𝘝𝘐𝘚𝘈. ✺ rest
M a la carte 62/83 — **245 rm** 321/512 Bb — 8 apart. 802/1402.

🏛 **Merkur** without rest, Mörsenbroicher Weg 49, 𝄐 63 40 31, Fax 622525 — 🕿 🅿. 🆎 ① E 𝘝𝘐𝘚𝘈
closed 23 to 31 December — **28 rm** 95/290 Bb.

at Düsseldorf 11-Oberkassel by Oberkasseler Brücke BV :

🏛🏛 **Ramada**, Am Seestern 16, 𝄐 59 10 47, Telex 8585575, Fax 593569, ⇆, 🔲 — |🛗| ⇆ rm ▣ 📺 🅿 — 🅿 25/200. 🆎 ① E 𝘝𝘐𝘚𝘈. ✺ rest
M a la carte 49/80 — **222 rm** 215/470 Bb — 6 apart. 800/1300.

🏛🏛 **Hanseat** without rest, Belsenstr. 6, 𝄐 57 50 69, Telex 8581997, Fax 589662, « Elegant furnishings » — 📺 🕿. 🆎 ① E 𝘝𝘐𝘚𝘈
39 rm 150/280 Bb.

XXX **De' Medici** (Italian rest.), Amboßstr. 3, 𝄐 59 41 51 — 🆎 ① E 𝘝𝘐𝘚𝘈
closed Saturday lunch, Sunday and Bank Holidays except exhibitions — **M** *(booking essential for dinner)* a la carte 47/72.

XX **Edo** (Japanese restaurants : Teppan, Robata and Tatami), Am Seestern 3, 𝄐 59 10 82, Fax 591394, « Japanese garden » — 🅿. 🆎 ① E 𝘝𝘐𝘚𝘈. ✺
closed Saturday lunch and Sunday except exhibitions — **M** a la carte 50/90.

at Düsseldorf 1-Unterbilk :

XXX **Savini**, Stromstr. 47, 𝄐 39 39 31, Fax 391719 — 🆎 ① E 𝘝𝘐𝘚𝘈 by Stromstr. BY
closed Sunday except exhibitions — **M** *(booking essential)* a la carte 65/90.

XX **Rheinturm Top 180** (revolving restaurant at 172 m), Stromstr. 20, 𝄐 84 85 80, Fax 325619, ✹ Düsseldorf and Rhein, (|🛗|, DM 4,50) — ▣ — 🅿 60. 🆎 ① E 𝘝𝘐𝘚𝘈. ✺ BY **a**
M a la carte 46/70.

at Meerbusch 1-Büderich 4005 by Oberkasseler Brücke BV — ✪ 02105/ 02132 :

XXX **Landhaus Mönchenwerth**, Niederlöricker Str. 56 (at the boat landing place), 𝄐 7 79 31, Fax 71899, ⬉, « Garden terrace » — 🅿. 🆎 ① E 𝘝𝘐𝘚𝘈. ✺
closed Sunday — **M** a la carte 51/80.

XXX **Landsknecht** with rm, Poststr. 70, 𝄐 59 47, Fax 10978 — 📺 🕿 🅿. 🆎 ① E 𝘝𝘐𝘚𝘈. ✺
M *(closed Saturday lunch September - June, Saturday July - August)* 48/100 — **8 rm** 95/260.

X **Lindenhof**, Dorfstr. 48, 𝄐 26 64
dinner only, closed Monday, 3 weeks July - August and 23 December - 4 January — **M** *(booking essential)* a la carte 35/60.

Essen 4300. Nordrhein-Westfalen 987 ⑭. 412 E 12 — pop. 620 000 — alt. 120 m — ✿ 0201 — Düsseldorf 31.

at Essen 18-Kettwig S : 11 km :

🏠 ✿✿ **Romantik-Hotel Résidence** ⬤, Auf der Forst 1, 𝒫 (02054) 89 11, Fax 82501 — 📺 ☎ 🅿 ⚿ ⓪ E 𝘝𝘐𝘚𝘈
closed 2 to 10 January and 9 to 27 July — **M** *(booking essential)* (dinner only, closed Sunday and Monday) a la carte 74/105 — **Benedikt** ✃⊃ *(opening see above)* **M** 105/170 — **18 rm** 165/450 Bb
Spec. Hummer auf Dicken Bohnen, Roulade von Lachs und Petersfisch, Quarkauflauf mit Zitrusfrüchten.

✗✗✗✗ ✿✿ **Ange d'or**, Ruhrtalstr. 326, 𝒫 (02054) 23 07, Fax 6343, 🌫 — 🅿 ⚿ ⓪ E 𝘝𝘐𝘚𝘈 🛇
dinner only, closed Sunday, Monday, 2 weeks Easter, mid July - early August, 1 week October and 20 December - 10 January — **M** *(booking essential)* 145 and a la carte 81/118
Spec. Steinbutt mit Meerrettichkruste auf Linsengemüse, Hummergerichte, Taube in Strudelteig.

Grevenbroich 4048. Nordrhein-Westfalen 987 ③. 412 C 13 — pop. 57 000 — alt. 60 m — ✿ 02181.

Düsseldorf 28.

✗✗✗✗ ✿✿ **Zur Traube** with rm, Bahnstr. 47, 𝒫 6 87 67, Telex 8517193, Fax 61122, remarkable winelist — 📺 ☎ ⇔ 🅿 ⚿ ⓪ E 𝘝𝘐𝘚𝘈 🛇
closed 23 December - 22 January, 24 March - 2 April and 14 to 30 July — **M** *(booking essential)* (closed Sunday and Monday) 128/158 and a la carte 75/113 — **6 rm** 190/490
Spec. Variationen von Langustinen, Crépinettes vom Täubchen, Nougatparfait im Baumkuchenmantel.

FRANKFURT AM MAIN 6000. Hessen 418 IJ 16, 987 ② — pop. 617 600 — alt. 91 m — ✿ 069.
See : Zoo★★★ FX — Goethe's House (Goethehaus)★★ and Goethemuseum★ DEY M1 — Cathedral (Dom)★ (Tower★★, Treasure★, Choir-stalls★) EY — Tropical Garden (Palmengarten)★ CV — Senckenberg-Museum★ (Palaeontology department★★) CX M8 — Städel Museum (Städelsches Kunstinstitut) ★★ DY M 2 — Museum of Applied Arts (Museum für Kunsthandwerk)★★ EY M4 — St. Catherine's Church (Katharinenkirche) (windows★) EX A — Henninger Turm ⚛★ DZ.

🛫 Frankfurt-Niederrad, by Kennedy-Allee CDZ, 𝒫 6 66 23 17.

🚅 Rhein-Main (by ⑤ : 12 km), 𝒫 6 90 25 95.

🚢 at Neu-Isenburg (by ④ : 7 km) 𝒫 (06102) 85 75.

Exhibition Centre (Messegelände) (CY), 𝒫 7 57 50, Telex 411558.

🛈 Tourist Information, Main Station (Hauptbahnhof), 𝒫 21 23 88 49.

🛈 Tourist Information, im Römer (EY), 𝒫 21 23 87 08.

🛈 Tourist Information, in the Airport (arrival, hall B), 𝒫 69 31 53.

ADAC, Schumannstr. 4, 𝒫 7 43 00.

Wiesbaden 41 ⑤ — Bonn 178 ⑤ — Nürnberg 226 ④ — Stuttgart 204 ⑤.

The reference (F 15) at the end of the address is the postal district : Frankfurt 15

Plans on following pages

🏨 **Steigenberger Frankfurter Hof**, Bethmannstr. 33 (F 1), 𝒫 2 15 02, Telex 411806, Fax 215900, 🌫 — 📳 ✃⊃ rm 🗏 📺 — ⚙ 25/300. ⚿ ⓪ **Frankfurter Stubb** below) : **Hofgarten** *(closed Saturday)* **M** a la carte 47/79 — **Kaiserbrunnen M** a la carte 33/47 — **360 rm** 320/530 Bb — 30 apart. 1294/3544.   DY **e**
Restaurants (see **Restaurant français** and **Frankfurter Stubb** below) : **Hofgarten** *(closed Saturday)* **M** a la carte 47/79 — **Kaiserbrunnen M** a la carte 33/47 — **360 rm** 320/530 Bb — 30 apart. 1294/3544.

🏨 **Hessischer Hof**, Friedrich-Ebert-Anlage 40 (F 97), 𝒫 7 54 00, Telex 411776, Fax 7540924, « Rest. with collection of Sèvres porcelain » — 📳 🗏 📺 ⇔ 🅿 — ⚙ 25/300. ⚿ ⓪ E 𝘝𝘐𝘚𝘈. 🛇 rest   CY **p**
M a la carte 70/103 — **114 rm** 295/575 — 11 apart. 850/1545.

🏨 **Frankfurt Intercontinental**, Wilhelm-Leuschner-Str. 43 (F 1), 𝒫 2 60 50, Telex 413639, Fax 252467, ⪴ Frankfurt, Massage, ♨, 🏊, 🔲 — 📳 ✃⊃ rm 🗏 📺 ⚐ — ⚙ 25/800. ⚿ ⓪ E 𝘝𝘐𝘚𝘈. 🛇 rest   CY **a**
M a la carte 48/99 — **800 rm** 395/600 Bb — 45 apart. 1200/3500.

🏨 **Arabella Grand Hotel**, Konrad-Adenauer-Str. 7 (F 1), 𝒫 2 98 10, Telex 4175926, Fax 2981810, Massage, ♨, 🔲 — 📳 ✃⊃ rm 📺 ⚐ ⇔ — ⚙ 25/500. ⚿ ⓪ E 𝘝𝘐𝘚𝘈 🛇 rest
Restaurants (see also **Restaurant Dynasty** below): **Premiere** *(dinner only)* **M** a la carte 65/95 — **Brasserie M** 38 (buffet lunch) and a la carte 36/62 — **378 rm** 316/521 Bb — 11 apart. 846/1951.   EX **c**

🏨 **Mövenpick Parkhotel Frankfurt**, Wiesenhüttenplatz 28 (F 1), 𝒫 2 69 70, Telex 412808, Fax 26978849, ♨ — 📳 ✃⊃ rm 🗏 📺 🅿 — ⚙ 25/160. ⚿ ⓪ E 𝘝𝘐𝘚𝘈   CY **y**
Restaurants : **La Truffe** *(closed Saturday, Sunday, Bank Holidays and 4 weeks July - August)* **M** a la carte 68/97 — **Mövenpick-Restaurants M** a la carte 37/63 — **300 rm** 299/509 Bb — 4 apart. 630/2442.

🏨 **Frankfurt Marriott Hotel**, Hamburger Allee 2 (F 90), 𝒫 7 95 50, Telex 412573, Fax 79552432, ⪴ Frankfurt — 📳 ✃⊃ rm 🗏 📺 — ⚙ 25/1000. ⚿ ⓪ E 𝘝𝘐𝘚𝘈. 🛇 rest   CX **a**
M a la carte 54/100 — **591 rm** 320/547 Bb — 25 apart. 652/1252.

🏨 **Palmenhof - Restaurant Bastei**, Bockenheimer Landstr. 89 (F 1), ℰ 7 53 00 60, Fax
75300666 – 🔄 📺 🚗, 🅰🅴 ⑩ 🕿 𝗩𝗜𝗦𝗔   CX **m**
M *(closed Saturday except exhibitions, Sunday and Bank Holidays)* a la carte 50/78 – **47 rm**
150/300 Bb.

🏨 **Altea Hotel**, Voltastr. 29 (F 90), ℰ 7 92 60, Telex 413791, Fax 79261606, 🍴, 🚬s – 🔄
🔄 rm 📺 🚗, 🅰🅴 ⑩ 🕿 𝗩𝗜𝗦𝗔   by ⑤
M a la carte 43/73 – **426 rm** 170/308 Bb – 12 apart. 343/403.

🏨 **Scandic Crown Hotel**, Wiesenhüttenstr. 42 (F 16), ℰ 27 39 60, Telex 416394, Fax 27396795,
Massage, 🚬s, 🔲, 🔄 ⟻ rm 🗐 rest 📺 🚗 – 🔺 25/100. 🕸   CY **s**
Restaurants : **Savoy** – **Rhapsody** – **144 rm** Bb.

🏨 **Pullman Hotel Savigny**, Savignystr. 14 (F 1), ℰ 7 53 30, Telex 412061, Fax 7533175 – 🔄
📺 – 🔺 25/80. 🅰🅴 ⑩ 🕿 𝗩𝗜𝗦𝗔   CY **f**
M 35 (lunch) and a la carte 47/74 – **124 rm** 209/498 Bb.

🏨 **National**, Baseler Str. 50 (F 1), ℰ 27 39 40, Telex 412570, Fax 234460 – 🔄 📺 – 🔺 25/60.
🅰🅴 ⑩ 🕿 𝗩𝗜𝗦𝗔   CY **x**
M 29/38 (lunch) and a la carte 45/72 – **76 rm** 151/270 Bb.

🏨 **An der Messe** without rest, Westendstr. 104 (F 1), ℰ 74 79 79, Telex 4189009, Fax 748349
– 🔄 📺 🚗, 🅰🅴 ⑩ 🕿 𝗩𝗜𝗦𝗔   CX **e**
46 rm 180/400 Bb.

🏨 **Novotel Frankfurt-Messe**, Voltastr. 1 b (F 90), ℰ 79 30 30, Telex 412054, Fax 79303930,
🍴, 🚬s, 🔄 ⟻ rm 🗐 📺 🕿 🚿, 🚗 ❷ – 🔺 25/300. 🅰🅴 ⑩ 🕿 𝗩𝗜𝗦𝗔   CX **r**
M a la carte 41/68 – **235 rm** 190/260 Bb.

🏨 **Imperial**, Sophienstr. 40 (F 90), ℰ 7 93 00 30, Telex 4189636, Fax 79300388 – 🔄 🗐 📺
🚗, 🅰🅴 ⑩ 🕿 𝗩𝗜𝗦𝗔   CV **t**
M *(dinner only)* a la carte 40/68 – **60 rm** 240/380 Bb.

🏨 **Rhein-Main** without rest, Heidelberger Str. 3 (F 1), ℰ 25 00 35, Telex 413434, Fax 252518
– 🔄 📺 🕿 ❷. 🅰🅴 ⑩ 🕿 𝗩𝗜𝗦𝗔.   CY **b**
48 rm 180/450 Bb.

🏨 **Mozart** without rest, Parkstr. 17 (F 1), ℰ 55 08 31 – 🔄 📺 🕿. 🅰🅴 ⑩ 🕿 𝗩𝗜𝗦𝗔   CV **p**
closed 23 December - 2 January – **35 rm** 125/195 Bb.

🏨 **Turm - Hotel** without rest, Eschersheimer Landstr. 20 (F 1), ℰ 15 40 50, Fax 553578 – 🔄
📺 🕿 ❷. 🅰🅴 ⑩ 🕿 𝗩𝗜𝗦𝗔   EX **b**
closed 23 December - 2 January – **75 rm** 120/175 Bb.

🏨 **Continental**, Baseler Str. 56 (F 1), ℰ 23 03 41, Telex 412502, Fax 232914 – 🔄 📺 🕿 –
🔺 30. 🅰🅴 ⑩ 🕿 𝗩𝗜𝗦𝗔 🕸   CY **y**
M *(closed Sunday and Bank Holidays)* a la carte 34/61 🍴 – **80 rm** 140/300.

🏨 **Attaché** without rest, Kölner Str. 10 (F 1), ℰ 73 02 82, Telex 414099, Fax 7392194 – 🔄 📺
❷. 🕸 – **40 rm** Bb.   CY **u**

🏨 **Topas** without rest, Niddastr. 88 (F 1), ℰ 23 08 52, Fax 237228 – 🔄 📺 🕿. 🅰🅴 ⑩ 🕿 𝗩𝗜𝗦𝗔.
🕸 – **31 rm** 95/290 Bb.   CY **z**

🏨 **Cristall** without rest, Ottostr. 3 (F 1), ℰ 23 03 51, Telex 4170654, Fax 253368 – 🔄 📺 🕿. 🅰🅴
⑩ 𝗩𝗜𝗦𝗔 🕸   CY **c**
closed 23 December - 4 January – **30 rm** 105/290 Bb.

🏨 **Am Dom** without rest, Kannengießergasse 3 (F 1), ℰ 28 21 41, Telex 414955, Fax 283237
– 🔄 📺 🕿. 🕸   EY **s**
30 rm 100/250 Bb – 4 apart. 300.

🏨 **Falk** without rest, Falkstr. 38a (F 90), ℰ 70 80 94, Fax 708017 – 🔄 📺 🕿 ❷ – 🔺 25
closed 2 weeks July - August and 20 December - 2 January – **32 rm** 110/190.   CV **n**

🏵🏵🏵🏵 ۞ **Restaurant Français** (at Steigenberger Frankfurter Hof), Bethmannstr. 33 (F 1),
ℰ 2 15 02 – 🗐. 🅰🅴 ⑩ 🕿 𝗩𝗜𝗦𝗔. 🕸   DY **e**
closed Sunday, Monday and Bank Holidays except exhibitions and 4 weeks July - August –
M *(booking essential)* a la carte 74/124.

🏵🏵🏵🏵 ۞ **Weinhaus Brückenkeller**, Schützenstr. 6 (F 1), ℰ 28 42 38, « Old vaulted cellar with
precious antiques » – 🗐 ❷. 🅰🅴 ⑩ 🕿 𝗩𝗜𝗦𝗔   FY **a**
closed Sunday and Bank Holidays except exhibitions and 20 December - 10 January –
M *(booking essential) (dinner only)* 135/160 and a la carte 76/112
Spec. Kartoffel-Kräutersuppe mit Meeresfischen, Geschmorte Rindsbäckchen in Rotwein mit Marknockerln,
Grießknödel mit Früchten.

🏵🏵🏵 ۞ **Humperdinck**, Grüneburgweg 95 (F 1), ℰ 72 21 22 – 🅰🅴 ⑩ 🕿 𝗩𝗜𝗦𝗔. 🕸   CV **a**
closed Saturday lunch, Sunday, 2 weeks June - July and 22 December - early January – **M** a
la carte 78/106
Spec. Nantaiser Ente mit Grünkernrisotto, Hummer-Maultaschen im Safransud, Abgeflämmte Limonencreme
mit verschiedenen Saucen.

🏵🏵🏵 **Mövenpick - Baron de la Mouette**, Opernplatz 2 (F 1), ℰ 2 06 80, Fax 296135, 🍴 – 🗐.
🅰🅴 ⑩ 🕿 𝗩𝗜𝗦𝗔   DX **f**
M a la carte 46/79 – **Orangerie M** a la carte 32/61.

🏵🏵🏵 **Tse-Yang** (Chinese rest.), Kaiserstr. 67 (F 1), ℰ 23 25 41, Fax 237825 – 🅰🅴 ⑩ 🕿 𝗩𝗜𝗦𝗔. 🕸
M 18 (lunch) and a la carte 43/75.   CY **v**

🏵🏵🏵 **Dynasty** (Chinese rest.), Konrad-Adenauer-Str. 7 (at Arabella Grand Hotel) (F 1),
ℰ 29 30 41, Fax 283866 – 🅰🅴 ⑩ 🕿 𝗩𝗜𝗦𝗔. 🕸   EX **c**
M a la carte 49/70.

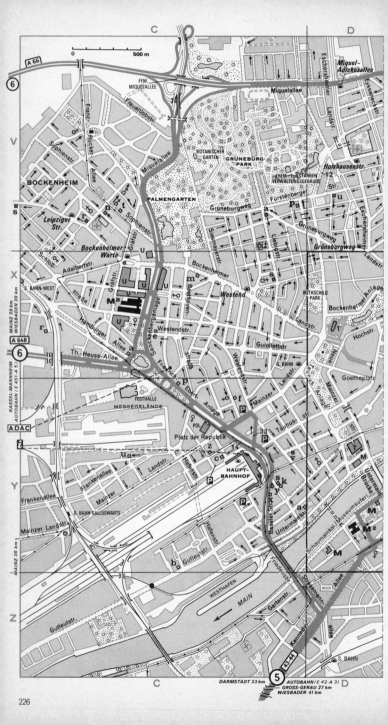

FRANKFURT AM MAIN

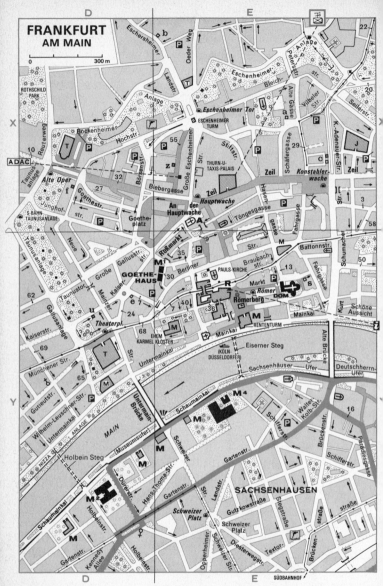

FRANKFURT AM MAIN

0   300 m

XX **Windows im Europaturm** (revolving restaurant at 218 m), Wilhelm-Eppstein-Str. 50 (F 50), 𝒫 53 30 77, Fax 533076, ⁂ Frankfurt and environs — 🍽. 🖭 ⓞ 🄴 𝘝𝘐𝘚𝘈. ⅍
dinner only, closed Sunday and Monday — **M** *(booking essential)* a la carte 67/89.
by Miquelallee CV

XX **Il Cavaliere** (Italian rest.), Berger Str. 30 (F 1), 𝒫 43 39 56 — 🍽. ⅍ FX s
M *(booking essential)*.

XX **La Femme**, Am Weingarten 5 (F 90), 𝒫 7 07 16 06 — 🖭 ⓞ 🄴 𝘝𝘐𝘚𝘈. ⅍ CV r
dinner only, closed Sunday — **M** 73/108.

XX **Kikkoman** (Japanese rest.), Friedberger Anlage 1 (Zoo-Passage) (F 1), 𝒫 4 99 00 21, Fax 447032 — 🖭 🄴 𝘝𝘐𝘚𝘈. ⅍ FX e
closed Sunday — **M** a la carte 44/80.

XX **Casa Toscana** (Italian rest.), Friedberger Anlage 14 (F 1), 𝒫 44 98 44, « Courtyard - terrace » — 🖭 ⓞ 🄴 𝘝𝘐𝘚𝘈 FX d
closed Monday — **M** a la carte 52/75.

XX **Da Franco** (Italian rest.), Fürstenbergerstr. 179 (F 1), 𝒫 55 21 30 — 🍽. 🖭 🄴 𝘝𝘐𝘚𝘈. ⅍ DV u
closed Sunday and mid July - mid August — **M** a la carte 46/79.

XX **La Galleria** (Italian rest.), Theaterplatz 2 (BFG-Haus) (F 1), 𝒫 23 56 80 — 🍽. 🖭 ⓞ 🄴 𝘝𝘐𝘚𝘈. ⅍ DY u
closed Sunday and Bank Holidays except exhibitions, Easter and Christmas — **M** *(booking essential)* a la carte 55/82.

XX **Frankfurter Stubb** (Rest. in the vaulted cellar of Hotel Steigenberger Frankfurter Hof), Bethmannstr. 33 (F 1), 𝒫 2 15 02 — 🍽. 🖭 ⓞ 🄴 𝘝𝘐𝘚𝘈. ⅍ DY e
closed Sunday and Bank Holidays except exhibitions — **M** *(booking essential)* a la carte 37/63.

XX **Börsenkeller**, Schillerstr. 11 (F 1), 𝒫 28 11 15, Fax 293144 — 🍽. 🖭 ⓞ 🄴 𝘝𝘐𝘚𝘈 EX z
closed Sunday and Bank Holidays except exhibitions — **M** a la carte 32/75.

XX **Intercity-Restaurant**, im Hauptbahnhof (1 st floor |≑|) (F 1), 𝒫 27 39 50, Fax 27395168 — 🔦 25/80. 🄴 CY
M a la carte 31/59.

X **Gasthof im Elsass**, Waldschmidtstr. 59 (F 1), 𝒫 44 38 39 FX c
dinner only, closed 22 December - 4 January — **M** a la carte 44/71.

X **Ernos Bistro** (French rest.), Liebigstr. 15 (F 1), 𝒫 72 19 97, ☆ — 🖭 ⓞ 🄴 𝘝𝘐𝘚𝘈 CX s
closed Saturday and Sunday except exhibitions and mid June - mid July — **M** *(booking essential)* a la carte 68/103.

X **Gargantua** (rest. in Bistro style), Friesengasse 3 (F 90), 𝒫 77 64 42 — 🖭 ⓞ 🄴 𝘝𝘐𝘚𝘈 ⅍
closed Saturday and Sunday except exhibitions and 3 weeks June — **M** *(booking essential)* a la carte 68/88. CV s

at Frankfurt 80-Griesheim by ⑥ :

🏫 **Ramada Caravelle**, Oeserstr. 180, 𝒫 3 90 50, Telex 416812, Fax 3808218, ⊆ₛ, 🔲 — |≑| ⇐⇒ rm 🍽 rest 📺 ☏ — 🔦 25/350
238 rm Bb.

at Frankfurt 71-Niederrad by ⑤ :

🏫 **Arabella Congress Hotel**, Lyoner Str. 44, 𝒫 6 63 30, Telex 416760, Fax 6633666, ⊆ₛ, 🔲 — |≑| 🍽 📺 ⇐⇒ ☏ — 🔦 25/500. 🖭 ⓞ 🄴 𝘝𝘐𝘚𝘈 ⅍
Restaurants (closed Saturday and Sunday): **Capriccio M** a la carte 52/77 — **Brasserie M** a la carte 38/60 — **Tölzer Stube M** a la carte 26/40 — **400 rm** 205/365 Bb — 8 apart. 440/660.

🏫 **Queens Hotel**, Isenburger Schneise 40, 𝒫 6 78 40, Telex 416717, Fax 6702634, ☆ — |≑| ⇐⇒ rm 🍽 📺 ☏ — 🔦 25/400. 🖭 ⓞ 🄴 𝘝𝘐𝘚𝘈 ⅍ rest
Restaurants: **La Fleur M** a la carte 55/88 — **Brasserie Brentano M** a la carte 40/72 — **279 rm** 232/336 Bb — 3 apart. 596/814.

🏛 **Dorint**, Hahnstr. 9, 𝒫 66 30 60, Telex 4032180, Fax 66306600, ⊆ₛ, 🔲 — |≑| 🍽 📺 ☏ ☏ — 🔦 60/200. 🖭 ⓞ 🄴 𝘝𝘐𝘚𝘈
M a la carte 38/65 — **191 rm** 190/400 Bb.

XX **Weidemann**, Kelsterbacher Str. 66, 𝒫 67 59 96, ☆ — ☏. 🖭 ⓞ 🄴 𝘝𝘐𝘚𝘈
closed Saturday lunch, Sunday and Bank Holidays — **M** *(booking essential)* a la carte 62/87.

at Frankfurt 70 - Sachsenhausen :

🏫 **Holiday Inn - Conference Center**, Mailänder Str. 1, 𝒫 6 80 20, Telex 411805, Fax 6802333, ⊆ₛ — |≑| ⇐⇒ rm 🍽 📺 ♿ ⇐⇒ ☏ — 🔦 25/400. ⅍ rest by ④
Restaurants : **Le Chef** *(dinner only, closed Sunday)* **M** a la carte 40/70 — **Kaffeemühle M** 38/41 (buffet) — **404 rm** 288/541 Bb.

🏨 **Primus** without rest, Große Rittergasse 19, 𝒫 62 30 20, Telex 4189600, Fax 621238 — |≑| 📺 ☏ ☏ — **30 rm**. FY c

XX ❀ **Bistrot 77**, Ziegelhüttenweg 1, 𝒫 61 40 40, ☆ — 🖭 ⓞ 🄴 𝘝𝘐𝘚𝘈 EZ a
closed Saturday lunch, Sunday, 15 June - 8 July and 23 December - 6 January — **M** a la carte 75/101
Spec. Perigord-Trüffel im Blätterteig (Nov.-March). Zanderfilet auf Linsen, Lammsattel mit Rosmarin (2 pers.).

X **Henninger Turm** - Drehrestaurant (|≑| DM 3,50), Hainer Weg 60, 𝒫 6 06 36 00, ⁂ Frankfurt, « Revolving rest. at 101 m » — 🍽 ☏. ⅍ FZ

at Eschborn 6236   NW : 12 km :

🏨 Novotel, Philipp-Helfmann-Str. 10, ℰ (06196) 90 10, Telex 4072842, Fax 482114, ⌂, ⊠ (heated), ⚞ – 🛗 ▤ 📺 ☎ & 🅿 – ⚐ 25/350   by A 66 CV
227 rm Bb.

at Neu-Isenburg 2-Gravenbruch 6078   SE : 11 km by ④ :

🏨 **Gravenbruch-Kempinski-Frankfurt**, ℰ (06102) 50 50, Telex 417673, Fax 505445, ⌂, « Park », Massage, ⇗, ⊠ (heated), 🔲, ⚞, ⨯ – 🛗 ▤ 📺 ⟻ 🅿 – ⚐ 25/600. ⬛ ⓞ E **VISA**. ⨯ rest
M (*see also* **Gourmet-Restaurant** below) a la carte 52/92 – **298 rm** 320/545 Bb – 30 apart. 720/1950.

XXXX **Gourmet-Restaurant** (at hotel Gravenbruch-Kempinski), ℰ (06102) 50 50 – ▤ 🅿. ⬛ ⓞ E **VISA** ⨯
dinner only, closed Saturday, Sunday and Bank Holidays except exhibitions and 4 weeks June - July – **M** (booking essential) a la carte 74/123.

near Rhein-Main airport   SW : 12 km by ⑤ (near motorway Flughafen exit) – ⊠ **6000** Frankfurt 75 – ✦ 069 :

🏨 **Sheraton**, Am Flughafen (Terminal Mitte), ℰ 6 97 70, Telex 4189294, Fax 69772209, Ⅰ6, ⇗, 🔲 – 🛗 ⨯⟻ rm ▤ 📺 & 🅿 – ⚐ 25/1000. ⬛ ⓞ E **VISA**. ⨯ rest
Restaurants : **Papillon** (remarkable wine-list) (closed Saturday lunch, Sunday and Bank Holidays) **M** a la carte 69/114 – **Kachelofen** (dinner only, closed Sunday and Monday) **M** a la carte 53/94 – **Maxwell's Bistro and Taverne** (closed Saturday and Sunday) **M** a la carte 41/75 – **1050 rm** 322/584 Bb – 30 apart.

🏨 **Steigenberger Hotel Frankfurt Airport**, Unterschweinstiege 16, ℰ 6 97 50, Telex 413112, Fax 69752505, ⇗, 🔲 – 🛗 ⨯⟻ rm ▤ 📺 🅿 – ⚐ 25/550. ⬛ ⓞ E **VISA**
M 39.(buffet) a la carte 49/75 (Italian rest.) – **430 rm** 300/510 Bb – 30 apart. 650/2800.

XXX **Rôtisserie 5 Continents**, in the Airport, Ankunft Ausland B (Besucherhalle, Ebene 3), ℰ 6 90 34 44, Fax 694730, ⇐ – ▤ – ⚐ 30. ⬛ ⓞ E **VISA**. ⨯
M a la carte 57/95.

XX **Waldrestaurant Unterschweinstiege**, Unterschweinstiege 16, ℰ 69 75 25 00, « Country house atmosphere, terrace » – ▤ 🅿. ⬛ ⓞ E **VISA**
M (booking essential) 39/buffet (lunch) and a la carte 50/79.

on the road from Neu-Isenburg to Götzenhain ④ : 13 km by A 661 and motorway-exit Dreieich :

XXX Gutsschänke Neuhof, ⊠ 6072 Dreieich-Götzenhain, ℰ (06102) 32 00 14, Telex 411377, « Country house atmosphere, terrace » – & 🅿.

at Maintal 6457   ② : 13 km :

XXX ❀ **Hessler**, Am Bootshafen 4 (Dörnigheim), ℰ (06181) 49 29 51, remarkable wine-list – 🅿. E. ⨯
closed Sunday - Monday and 3 weeks July – **M** (booking essential) 60/70 (lunch) and a la carte 88/109
Spec. Lasagne von Meeresfrüchten in Kaviarschaum, Galantine von Kaninchenrücken in Trüffelsauce, Taube in Piroggenteig.

Guldental 6531. Rheinland-Pfalz 🉑🉐 G 17 – pop. 2 600 - alt. 150 m – ✦ 06707.
Frankfurt am Main 75.

XXX ❀ **Le Val d'Or**, Hauptstr. 3, ℰ 17 07, Fax 8489 – ⓞ E
Tuesday to Friday dinner only, closed Monday, 3 weeks January and 2 weeks August – **M** (remarkable wine-list) (booking essential) 120/145 and a la carte 85/128
Spec. Kalbsbriesparfait, Frühlingsrolle von Edelfischen, Gefüllte Bresse-Taube im Mangoldblatt.

Mannheim 6800 Baden-Württemberg 🉓🉖🉗 ✦. 🉑🉒🉓 I 18 – pop. 305 000 – alt. 95 m – ✦ 0621.
Frankfurt am Main 79.

XXX ❀❀ **Da Gianni** (elegant italian rest.), R 7, 34 (Friedrichsring), ℰ 2 03 26 – ⬛ E
closed Monday, Bank Holidays and 3 weeks July – **M** (booking essential) a la carte 73/94
Spec. Meeresfrüchte in Limonenvinaigrette, Steinbutt auf Artischocken, Rinderfilet mit Trüffeln in Dolcetto.

Wertheim 6980. Baden-Württemberg 🉓🉖🉗 ✦. 🉑🉒🉓 L 17 – pop. 20 600 – alt. 142 m – ✦ 09342.
Frankfurt am Main 87.

🏨 ❀❀ **Schweizer Stuben** ⌂, at Wertheim-Bettingen (E : 10 km), Geiselbrunnweg 11, ℰ 30 70, Telex 689190, Fax 307155, ⌂, « Hotel in a park », ⇗, 🔲 (heated), ⚞, ⨯ (indoor) – 📺 🅿 – ⚐ 30. ⬛ ⓞ E **VISA**
M (booking essential) (closed lunch Sunday and Tuesday, Monday and 1 to 26 January) 158/198 and a la carte 95/145 – **33 rm** 210/395 – 11 apart. 420/990
Spec. Langustinen in Limonen-Ingwer-Sud. Gefüllter Kalbsschwanz auf Kartoffel-Lauch-Gemüse. Schokoladenüberraschung Schweizer Stuben.

HAMBURG 2000. Ⓛ Hamburg **987** ⑤ — pop. 1 600 000 — alt. 10 m — ✪ 040.

See : Jungfernstieg★ DY — Außenalster★★★ (trip by boat★★★) EX — Hagenbeck Zoo (Tierpark Hagenbeck)★★ — Television Tower (Fernsehturm)★ (🌟★★) BX — Art Gallery (Kunsthalle)★★ (19C German painting) EY **M1** — St. Michael's church (St. Michaelis)★ (tower 🌟★) BZ — Stintfang (≤★) BZ — Port (Hafen)★★ (trip by boat ★★) BZ.

🛚 Hamburg-Blankenese, In de Bargen 59 (W : 17 km), 𝒫 81 21 77 ; 🛚 Ammersbek (NE : 15 km), 𝒫 (040) 6 05 13 37 ; 🛚 Hamburg-Wendlohe (N : 14 km), 𝒫 5 50 50 14 ; 🛚 Wentorf, Golfstr. 2 (SE : 21 km), 𝒫 (040) 7 20 26 10.

✈ Hamburg-Fuhlsbüttel (N : 15 km), 𝒫 50 80.

🚗 𝒫 39 18 65 56.

Exhibition Centre (Messegelände) (BX), 𝒫 3 56 91, Telex 212609.

🛈 Tourismus-Zentrale Hamburg, Burchardstr. 14, 𝒫 30 05 10, Telex 2163036, Fax 30051253.

🛈 Tourist-Information im Bieberhaus, Hachmannplatz, 𝒫 30 05 12 45.

🛈 Tourist-Information im Hauptbahnhof (main station), 𝒫 30 05 12 30.

🛈 Tourist-Information im Flughafen (airport, terminal 3 - arrival), 𝒫 30 05 12 40.

ADAC, Amsinckstr. 39 (H 1), 𝒫 2 39 90.

Berlin 289 — Bremen 120 — Hannover 151.

The reference (H 15) at the end of the address is the postal district : Hamburg 15

Plan on following pages

near Hauptbahnhof, at St. Georg, east of the Außenalster :

🏨 **Atlantic-Hotel Kempinski** 🕭, An der Alster 72 (H 1), 𝒫 2 88 80, Telex 2163297, Fax 247129, ≤ Außenalster, Massage, ☎s, 🔲 — 🛗 🍽 rest 📺 ⇌ — 🔬 25/500. 🆎 ⑩ Ε 𝗩𝘐𝘚𝘈. 🎇 rest   EX **a**
M 52/59 (lunch) and a la carte 60/100 — **259 rm** 293/440 Bb — 13 apart. 650/1250.

🏨 **Holiday Inn Crowne Plaza**, Graumannsweg 10 (H 76), 𝒫 22 80 60, Telex 2165287, Fax 2208704, Massage, ☎s, 🔲 — 🛗 🌞⇌ rm 🍽 📺 ♿ ⇌ — 🔬 25/120. 🆎 ⑩ Ε 𝗩𝘐𝘚𝘈   FX **a**
M 42 (lunch) and a la carte 61/85 — **290 rm** 294/648 Bb.

🏨 **Europäischer Hof**, Kirchenallee 45 (H 1), 𝒫 24 82 48, Telex 2162493, Fax 24824799, ☎s, 🔲 — 🛗 🍽 rest 📺 ⇌ — 🔬 25/500. 🆎 ⑩ Ε 𝗩𝘐𝘚𝘈   FY **e**
M a la carte 35/70 — **320 rm** 194/348 Bb.

🏨 **Maritim Hotel Reichshof**, Kirchenallee 34 (H 1), 𝒫 24 83 30, Telex 2163396, Fax 24833588 — 🛗 📺 ⇌ — 🔬 25/120. 🆎 ⑩ Ε 𝗩𝘐𝘚𝘈. 🎇 rest   FY **d**
M a la carte 43/73 — **300 rm** 195/394 Bb — 6 apart. 400/480.

🏨 **Prem-Restaurant La Mer**, An der Alster 9 (H 1), 𝒫 24 54 54, Telex 2163115, Fax 2803851, « Antique furnishing, garden », ☎s — 🛗 📺 🅿. 🆎 ⑩ Ε 𝗩𝘐𝘚𝘈. 🎇 rest   FX **c**
M (Saturday and Sunday dinner only) (remarkable wine-list) 60 (lunch) and a la carte 80/120 — **52 rm** 185/339 Bb — 3 apart. 529.

🏨 **Berlin - Brasserie Miro**, Borgfelder Str. 1 (H 26), 𝒫 25 16 40, Telex 213939, Fax 25164413 — 🛗 🍽 rest 📺 ☎ ⇌ 🅿 — 🔬 30. 🆎 ⑩ Ε 𝗩𝘐𝘚𝘈. 🎇 rest
M a la carte 45/85 — **93 rm** 128/195 Bb.   by Kurt-Schumacher-Allee   FY

🏨 **Ambassador**, Heidenkampsweg 34 (H 1), 𝒫 23 00 02, Telex 2166100, Fax 230009, ☎s, 🔲 — 🛗 📺 ☎ ⇌ 🅿 — 🔬 25/150. 🆎 ⑩ Ε 𝗩𝘐𝘚𝘈. 🎇 rest   by Nordkanalstr.   FZ
M a la carte 30/63 — **124 rm** 115/360 Bb.

🏨 **St. Raphael**, Adenauer-Allee 41 (H 1), 𝒫 24 82 00, Telex 2174733, Fax 24820333, ☎s — 🛗 🌞⇌ rm 📺 ☎ 🅿 — 🔬 25/70. 🎇 rest   FY **m** ②
135 rm Bb — 15 apart..

🏨 **Senator** without rest, Lange Reihe 18 (H 1), 𝒫 24 12 03, Telex 2174002, Fax 2803717 — 🛗 🌞⇌ 📺 ☎ ⇌. 🆎 ⑩ Ε 𝗩𝘐𝘚𝘈   FY **u** ①
56 rm 142/210 Bb.

🏨 **Aussen-Alster-Hotel**, Schmilinskystr. 11 (H 1), 𝒫 24 15 57, Telex 211278, Fax 2803231, ☎s — 🛗 📺 ☎. 🆎 ⑩ Ε 𝗩𝘐𝘚𝘈   FX **e**
M (closed Saturday lunch and Sunday) a la carte 42/78 — **27 rm** 165/290 Bb.

🏨 **Bellevue**, An der Alster 14 (H 1), 𝒫 24 80 11, Telex 2162929, Fax 2803380 — 🛗 📺 ☎ ⇌ 🅿 — 🔬 25/60. 🆎 ⑩ Ε 𝗩𝘐𝘚𝘈   FX **t**
M (closed Sunday July - August) a la carte 39/68 — **80 rm** 130/220 Bb.

🏨 **Alte Wache**, Adenauer-Allee 25 (H 1), 𝒫 24 12 91, Telex 2162254 — 🛗 📺 ☎ 🅿 — 🔬 60. 🎇   FY **s**
(dinner only, residents only) — **85 rm**.

🏨 **Fürst Bismarck** without rest, Kirchenallee 49 (H 1), 𝒫 2 80 10 91, Telex 2162980, Fax 2801096 — 🛗 📺 ☎. 🆎 ⑩ Ε 𝗩𝘐𝘚𝘈   FY **x**
closed 23 to 31 December — **59 rm** 98/155.

🏨 **Kronprinz - Restaurant Schiffer Börse**, Kirchenallee 46 (H 1), 𝒫 24 32 58 (hotel) 24 52 40 (rest.), Telex 2161005, Fax 2801097 — 🛗 📺 ☎. 🆎 ⑩ Ε   FY **c**
M (mainly seafood) a la carte 35/70 — **73 rm** 110/170 Bb.

🍴 **Peter Lembcke**, Holzdamm 49 (H 1), 𝒫 24 32 90 — 🆎 ⑩ Ε 𝗩𝘐𝘚𝘈   FY **t**
closed Saturday lunch, Sunday and Bank Holidays — **M** (booking essential) a la carte 55/95.

231

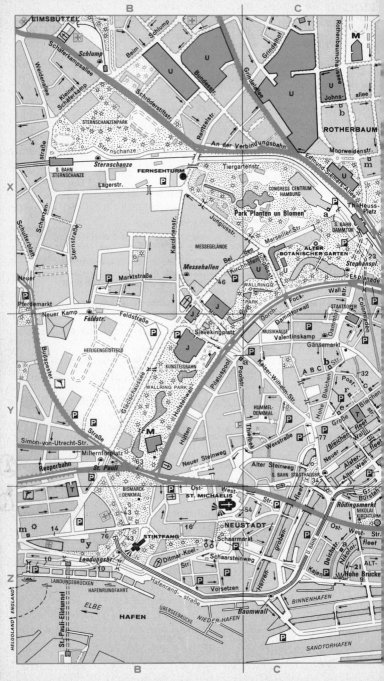

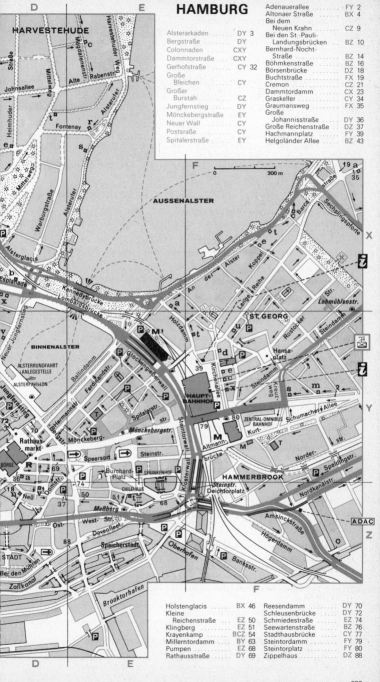

HAMBURG

HARVESTEHUDE

AUSSENALSTER

BINNENALSTER

ST. GEORG

HAUPT-BAHNHOF

HAMMERBROOK

Rathausmarkt

BÖRSE

STADT

at Binnenalster, Altstadt, Neustadt :

Vier Jahreszeiten - Restaurant Haerlin, Neuer Jungfernstieg 9 (H 36), ℰ 3 49 40, Telex 211629, Fax 3494602, ≼ Binnenalster – 🛗 ⇆ rm 📺 ⇌ – 🛦 25/70. 🝵 ⓞ 🝳 𝐕𝐈𝐒𝐀. 🛠
DY **v**
M *(closed Sunday and Bank Holidays)* 48/62 (lunch) and a la carte 69/116 – **175 rm** 355/650 – 11 apart. 850/1109.

Ramada Renaissance Hotel, Große Bleichen (H 36), ℰ 34 91 80, Fax 34918431, Massage, 🖙 – 🛗 ⇆ rm 🖩 📺 🗗 🗗 – 🛦 25/150. 🝵 ⓞ 🝳 𝐕𝐈𝐒𝐀. 🛠 rest
CY **e**
M a la carte 53/85 – **211 rm** 320/510 Bb – 5 apart. 950/2000.

Hamburg Marriott Hotel, ABC-Str. 52 (H 36), ℰ 3 50 50, Telex 2165871, Fax 35051777, 🗗, 🖙, 🖾 – 🛗 ⇆ rm 🖩 📺 🗗 ⇌ – 🛦 25/200. 🝵 ⓞ 🝳 𝐕𝐈𝐒𝐀. 🛠 rest
CY **b**
M *(mainly seafood)* a la carte 59/93 – **276 rm** 274/473 Bb – 6 apart. 598/1148.

SAS Plaza Hotel, Marseiller Str. 2 (H 36), ℰ 3 50 20, Telex 214400, Fax 35023333, ≼ Hamburg, 🖙, 🖾 – 🛗 ⇆ rm 📺 🗗 ⇌ – 🛦 25/600. 🝵 ⓞ 🝳 𝐕𝐈𝐒𝐀. 🛠 rest
CX **a**
M a la carte 35/60 – **562 rm** 235/460 Bb – 7 apart. 590/1250.

Hafen Hamburg, Seewartenstr. 9 (H 11), ℰ 31 11 30, Telex 2161319, Fax 3192736, ≼ – 🛗 ⇆ rm 📺 ☎ ⇌ 🗗 – 🛦 25/120. 🝵 ⓞ 🝳 𝐕𝐈𝐒𝐀
BZ **y**
M a la carte 47/81 – **252 rm** 100/200 Bb.

Baseler Hof, Esplanade 11 (H 36), ℰ 35 90 60, Telex 2163707, Fax 35906918 – 🛗 📺 ☎ – 🛦 25/40. 🝵 ⓞ 🝳 𝐕𝐈𝐒𝐀. 🛠
DX **x**
M a la carte 20/50 – **Wein Bistro M** a la carte 38/64 – **160 rm** 110/180.

Alster-Hof without rest, Esplanade 12 (H 36), ℰ 35 00 70, Fax 35007514 – 🛗 📺 ☎. 🝵 ⓞ 🝳 𝐕𝐈𝐒𝐀
DX **x**
closed 23 December - 1 January – **120 rm** 125/250 Bb.

Zum alten Rathaus (with entertainment-rest. Fleetenkieker), Börsenbrücke 10 (H 11), ℰ 36 75 70
DZ **n**
M *(booking essential)*.

Ratsweinkeller, Gr. Johannisstr. 2 (H 11), ℰ 36 41 53, Fax 372201, « 1896 Hanseatic rest. » – 🛦 25/400. 🝵 ⓞ 🝳
DY **R**
closed Sunday and Bank Holidays – **M** a la carte 36/76.

Cölln's Austernstuben, Brodschrangen 1 (H 11), ℰ 32 60 59 – 🝵 ⓞ 🝳 𝐕𝐈𝐒𝐀
DZ **v**
closed Saturday lunch, Sunday and Bank Holidays – **M** *(booking essential)* a la carte 80/114.

Deichgraf, Deichstr. 23 (H 11), ℰ 36 42 08, Fax 373055 – 🝵 ⓞ 🝳 𝐕𝐈𝐒𝐀
CZ **a**
closed Saturday lunch, Sunday and Bank Holidays – **M** *(booking essential)* a la carte 40/99.

il Ristorante (Italian rest.), Große Bleichen 16 (1st floor) (H 36), ℰ 34 33 35 – 🝵 ⓞ 🝳
CY **c**
M a la carte 70/88.

Mövenpick - Café des Artistes, Große Bleichen 36 (ground-floor, 🛗) (H 36), ℰ 34 10 00, Fax 3410042 – 🝵 ⓞ 🝳 𝐕𝐈𝐒𝐀
CY **r**
closed Sunday – **M** a la carte 48/77 – **Mövenpick-Restaurant M** a la carte 32/63.

Restaurant im Finnlandhaus, Esplanade 41 (12th floor, 🛗) (H 36), ℰ 34 41 33, ≼ Hamburg, Binnen- and Außenalster – 🖩
DX **b**

Dominique, Karl-Muck-Platz 11 (H 36), ℰ 34 45 11 – ⓞ
BCY **a**
closed Saturday lunch and Sunday – **M** a la carte 45/66.

Viking, Depenau 3 (at Chilehaus) (H 1), ℰ 32 71 71 – 🝵 ⓞ 🝳 𝐕𝐈𝐒𝐀
EZ **t**
closed Saturday dinner, Sunday and Bank Holidays – **M** a la carte 44/70.

al Pincio (Italian rest.), Schauenburger Str. 59 (1st floor, 🛗) (H 1), ℰ 36 52 55 – 🝵 ⓞ 🝳
DY **a**
closed Sunday, Bank Holidays and 12 July - 9 August – **M** *(booking essential)* a la carte 41/75.

at Hamburg-Alsterdorf by Grindelallee CX :

Alsterkrug-Hotel, Alsterkrugchaussee 277 (H 60), ℰ 51 30 30, Telex 2173828, Fax 51303403, 🖙 – 🛗 ⇆ rm 📺 ⇌ 🗗 – 🛦 25/60. 🛠 rest
80 rm Bb.

at Hamburg-Altona by Reeperbahn BY :

Raphael Hotel Altona, Präsident-Krahn-Str. 13 (H 50), ℰ 38 12 39, Fax 3809009, 🖙 – 🛗 📺 ☎ 🗗. 🝵 ⓞ 🝳 𝐕𝐈𝐒𝐀. 🛠 rest
closed 23 December - 2 January – **M** (dinner only, residents only) – **45 rm** 115/220 Bb.

Landhaus Scherrer, Elbchaussee 130 (H 50), ℰ 8 80 13 25, remarkable wine-list – 🗗. 🝵 ⓞ 🝳
closed Sunday and Bank Holidays – **M** *(booking essential)* a la carte 70/118 – **Bistro-Restaurant** *(lunch only)* **M** a la carte 53/85
Spec. Carpaccio vom Bonito, Roulade von Lachs und Zander im Mangoldblatt, Gefüllter Ochsenschwanz mit Burgundersauce.

Le canard, Elbchaussee 139 (H 50), ℰ 8 80 50 57, Fax 472413, ≼, �, remarkable wine-list – 🗗 ⓞ 🝳 𝐕𝐈𝐒𝐀. 🛠
closed Sunday and 4 weeks June - July – **M** *(booking essential)* a la carte 78/134
Spec. Terrine von Taube und Gänsestopfleber, Steinbutt mit Räucheraal-Sauce, Délices variés.

XXX Fischereihafen-Restaurant Hamburg (only seafood), Große Elbstr. 143 (H 50), $\mathscr{S}$ 38 18 16, $\leqslant - \textbf{P} - \textbf{M}$ *(booking essential)*.

XXX **Landhaus Zavrakis**, Elbchaussee 94 (H 50), $\mathscr{S}$ 3 90 67 26 $- \textbf{P}$. ⓘ **E** $\overline{VISA}$
dinner only, closed Monday, 2 weeks January - February and 2 weeks July - August $- \textbf{M}$ a la carte 65/100 $-$ **Bistro** *(also lunch)* **M** a la carte 43/72.

XX **La Mouette**, Neumühlen 50 (H 50), $\mathscr{S}$ 39 65 04 $-$ 🖭 ⓘ **E** $\overline{VISA}$
closed Sunday and Monday $- \textbf{M}$ *(booking essential for dinner)* a la carte 50/72.

at Hamburg-Billstedt by Nordkanalstr. FZ :

🏥 **Panorama** without rest, Billstedter Hauptstr. 44 (H 74), $\mathscr{S}$ 73 17 01, Telex 212162, Fax 7326627, 🔽 $- |\textbf{\$}|$ 🖭 🕿 ⟷ **P** $- \underline{A}$ 25/250. 🖭 ⓘ **E** $\overline{VISA}$
closed 24 December - 2 January $-$ **111 rm** 170/260 Bb $-$ 7 apart. 250/300.

at Hamburg-Blankenese W : 16 km by Reeperbahn BY :

🏨 **Strandhotel** ⑤, Strandweg 13 (H 55), $\mathscr{S}$ 86 13 44, Fax 864936, $\leqslant$, 🍴, « Villa with elegant installation, painting collection », 🕿🖪 $-$ 🖭 🕿 🖭 $-$ 🖭 **E** $\overline{VISA}$
M *(closed Sunday dinner and Monday)* a la carte 49/75 $-$ **16 rm** 148/386 Bb.

XXX **Süllberg**, Süllbergsterrasse 2 (H 55), $\mathscr{S}$ 86 16 86, Fax 869052, « Terraced garden with $\leqslant$ » $- \textbf{P} - \underline{A}$ 25/220. 🖭 ⓘ **E** $\overline{VISA}$
closed 13 January - 15 February $- \textbf{M}$ a la carte 47/81.

XX **Strandhof**, Strandweg 27 (H 55), $\mathscr{S}$ 86 52 36, Fax 867475, $\leqslant$, 🍴 $- \textbf{P}$. 🖭 ⓘ **E** $\overline{VISA}$
closed Tuesday $- \textbf{M}$ a la carte 36/74.

XX **Sagebiels Fährhaus**, Blankeneser Hauptstr. 107 (H 55), $\mathscr{S}$ 86 15 14, « Terrace with $\leqslant$ » $- \textbf{P}$.

at Hamburg-City Nord by Buchtstraße FX :

🏥 **Queens Hotel Hamburg**, Mexicoring 1 (H 60), $\mathscr{S}$ 63 29 40, Telex 2174155, Fax 6322472 $- |\textbf{\$}|$ ⟷ rm 🖭 ⟷ **P** $- \underline{A}$ 25/200. 🖭 ⓘ **E** $\overline{VISA}$
M a la carte 48/76 $-$ **185 rm** 204/288 Bb $-$ 4 apart. 332.

at Hamburg-Duvenstedt by Grindelallee CX :

XXX **Le Relais de France**, Poppenbütteler Chaussee 3 (H 65), $\mathscr{S}$ 6 07 07 50 $- \textbf{P}$. 🖭 ⓘ
dinner only, closed Sunday $- \textbf{M}$ *(booking essential)* a la carte 76/89 $-$ **Bistro** *(also lunch)* **M** a la carte 32/40.

at Hamburg-Eppendorf by Grindelallee CX :

XX ❀ **Anna e Sebastiano** (Italian rest.), Lehmweg 30 (H 20), $\mathscr{S}$ 4 22 25 95 $-$ ⓘ **E** $\overline{VISA}$. 🍴
dinner only, closed Sunday, Monday, 1 to 29 January and 3 weeks July - August $-$ **M** *(booking essential)* 90/100 and a la carte 67/77
Spec. Warmer Salat von Hummer und weißen Bohnen, Gebratene Gänsestopfleber im Nudelteig, Wolfsbarsch im Spinatblatt.

XX **Il Gabbiano** (Italian rest.), Eppendorfer Landstr. 145 (H 20), $\mathscr{S}$ 4 80 21 59 $-$ 🖭 ⓘ $\overline{VISA}$
closed Sunday $- \textbf{M}$ *(booking essential)* a la carte 50/72.

XX **Sellmer** (mainly seafood), Ludolfstr. 50 (H 20), $\mathscr{S}$ 47 30 57 $- \textbf{P}$. 🖭 ⓘ **E** $\overline{VISA}$
M a la carte 45/81.

at Hamburg-Fuhlsbüttel by Grindelallee CX :

🏨 **Airport Hotel Hamburg**, Flughafenstr. 47 (H 62), $\mathscr{S}$ 53 10 20, Telex 2166399, Fax 53102222, Massage, 🕿🖪, 🔽 $- |\textbf{\$}|$ ⟷ rm 🗏 🖭 ⟷ **P** $- \underline{A}$ 25/240. 🖭 ⓘ **E** $\overline{VISA}$
M a la carte 39/62 $-$ **158 rm** 196/389 Bb.

at Hamburg-Hamm by Nordkanalstr. FZ :

🏨 **Hamburg International**, Hammer Landstr. 200 (H 26), $\mathscr{S}$ 21 14 01, Telex 2164349, Fax 211409 $- |\textbf{\$}|$ 🖭 🕿 ⟷ **P** $- \underline{A}$ 25/40. 🖭 **E** $\overline{VISA}$
M *(closed Sunday)* a la carte 55/80 $-$ **112 rm** 110/260 Bb.

at Hamburg-Harvestehude :

🏨 **Inter-Continental**, Fontenay 10 (H 36), $\mathscr{S}$ 41 41 50, Telex 211099, Fax 41415186, $\leqslant$ Hamburg and Alster, 🍴, Massage, 🕿🖪, 🔽 $- |\textbf{\$}|$ ⟷ rm 🗏 🖭 ⟷ **P** $- \underline{A}$ 25/240. 🖭 ⓘ **E** $\overline{VISA}$. 🍴 rest   EX **r**
Restaurants : **Fontenay-Grill** *(dinner only)* **M** a la carte 62/105 $-$ **Orangerie M** a la carte 47/63 $-$ **300 rm** 281/441 Bb $-$ 16 apart. 852/1252.

🏨 **Garden Hotels Pöseldorf** ⑤ without rest, Magdalenenstr. 60 (H 13), $\mathscr{S}$ 44 99 58, Telex 212621, Fax 449958, « Elegantly furnished », � $- |\textbf{\$}|$ 🖭 🕿. 🖭 ⓘ **E** $\overline{VISA}$ EX **c**
73 rm 177/584.

🏨 **Smolka**, Isestr. 98 (H 13), $\mathscr{S}$ 47 50 57, Telex 215275, Fax 473008 $- |\textbf{\$}|$ 🖭 🕿 ⟷. 🖭 ⓘ **E** $\overline{VISA}$. 🍴 rest   by Rothenbaumchaussee CX
M *(closed Saturday dinner, Sunday and Bank Holidays)* a la carte 38/61 $-$ **38 rm** 128/280 Bb.

🏨 **Abtei** ⑤ without rest, Abteistr. 14 (H 13), $\mathscr{S}$ 44 29 05, Telex 2165645, Fax 449820, � $-$ 🖭 🕿. 🍴 $-$ **12 rm**.   by Rothenbaumchaussee CX

🏨 **Mittelweg** without rest, Mittelweg 59 (H 13), $\mathscr{S}$ 4 14 10 10, Telex 2165663, Fax 41410120 $-$ 🖭 🕿 ⟷ **P**   by Mittelweg DX
26 rm 110/224.

XXX **Die Insel - Restaurant Amadeus**, Alsterufer 35 (1st floor) (H 36), ℰ 4 10 69 55, Fax
4103713 – ⒶⒺ ⓪ Ε 𝘝𝘐𝘚𝘈   EX s
M *(booking essential) (dinner only)* a la carte 91/108.

XX La vite (Italian rest.), Heimhuder Str. 5 (H 13), ℰ 45 84 01, 斎   DX e
M *(booking essential)*.

XX **Daitokai** (Japanese rest.), Milchstr. 1 (H 13), ℰ 4 10 10 61, Fax 4102296 – ▤. ⒶⒺ ⓪ Ε 𝘝𝘐𝘚𝘈.
𝒮𝒮   by Mittelweg DX
closed Sunday – **M** *(booking essential)* a la carte 53/83.

XX **Osteria Martini** (Italian rest.), Badestr. 4 (H 13), ℰ 4 10 16 51 – ⒶⒺ ⓪ Ε 𝘝𝘐𝘚𝘈   DX t
M *(booking essential)* a la carte 39/69.

at Hamburg-Nienstedten   W : 13 km by Reeperbahn BY :

XX ✿ **Landhaus Dill**, Elbchaussee 404 (H 52), ℰ 82 84 43, Fax 828213 – ⓟ. ⒶⒺ ⓪ Ε 𝘝𝘐𝘚𝘈
dinner only Tuesday to Friday, closed Monday – **M** *(booking essential)* (also vegetarian
Menu) a la carte 60/102 – **Bistro** *(lunch only, closed Saturday, Sunday and Monday)* **M** a la
carte 51/65
Spec. Zander mit Zitronenbuttersauce, Seezungenröllchen mit Lachsmousse gefüllt, Flugentenbrust mit
Senfkörnersauce.

at Hamburg-Rotherbaum :

🏨 **Elysee** 🐾, Rothenbaumchaussee 10 (H 13), ℰ 41 41 20, Telex 212455, Fax 41412733,
Massage, ⟲⟲, 🔲 – ▐▊ ▤ ⓣⓥ ⅙ ⇔ – 🔬 25/500. ⒶⒺ ⓪ Ε 𝘝𝘐𝘚𝘈. 𝒮𝒮 rm   CX m
Restaurants : **Piazza Romana M** a la carte 50/63 – **Brasserie M** a la carte 40/55 – **299 rm**
249/368 Bb – 4 apart. 550/1150.

🏛 **Vorbach** without rest, Johnsallee 63 (H 13), ℰ 44 18 20, Telex 213054 – ▐▊ ⓣⓥ ☎ ⇔. ⒶⒺ
Ε 𝘝𝘐𝘚𝘈   CX b
106 rm 125/220.

XX **Ventana** (European-Asiatic cooking), Grindelhof 77 (H 13), ℰ 45 65 88, Fax 481719 – ⒶⒺ
⓪ Ε   by Grindelhof CX
closed Saturday lunch and Sunday – **M** *(booking essential for dinner)* a la carte 73/87.

XX ✿ **L'auberge française** (French rest.), Rutschbahn 34 (H 13), ℰ 4 10 25 32 – ⒶⒺ ⓪ Ε 𝘝𝘐𝘚𝘈.
𝒮𝒮   by Grindelhof CX
closed Saturday lunch, Sunday and July – **M** *(booking essential)* a la carte 56/85
Spec. Gebratene Gänsestopfleber in Trüffelsauce, Seeteufel in Safran-Sauce, Gratinierte Früchte mit
Kirschcreme.

XX Fernsehturm - Restaurant (revolving rest. at 132 m), Lagerstr. 2 (▐▊, DM 4,-) (H 6), ℰ 43 80 24,
❄ Hamburg – ▤ ⓟ – **M** *(booking essential)*.   BX

at Hamburg-St. Pauli :

XX Bavaria-Blick, Bernhard-Nocht-Str. 99 (7th floor, ▐▊) (H 4), ℰ 31 48 00, ≼ harbour – ▤
M *(booking essential)*.   BZ m

at Hamburg-Schnelsen   by Grindelallee CX :

🏛 Novotel, Oldesloer Str. 166 (H 61), ℰ 5 50 20 73, Telex 212923, Fax 5592020, 斎, ⍁ (heated)
– ▐▊ ⓣⓥ ☎ ⅙ ⓟ – 🔬 25/250. ⒶⒺ ⓪ Ε 𝘝𝘐𝘚𝘈. 𝒮𝒮 rest
M a la carte 34/60 – **122 rm** 165/199 Bb.

at Hamburg-Stellingen   by Schäferkampsallee BX :

🏛 **Helgoland**, Kieler Str. 177 (H 54), ℰ 85 70 01, Fax 8511445 – ▐▊ ⓣⓥ ☎ ⇔ ⓟ – 🔬 25. ▤
⓪ Ε 𝘝𝘐𝘚𝘈
(dinner only, residents only) – **109 rm** 133/228 Bb.

🏡 **Münch** without rest, Frühlingstr. 37 (H 54), ℰ 8 50 50 26, Fax 8511662, 🌺 – ⓣⓥ ☎ ⇔. ⒶⒺ
⓪ Ε 𝘝𝘐𝘚𝘈. 𝒮𝒮
13 rm 105/150.

at Hamburg-Stillhorn   by Amsinckstr. FZ :

🏨 **Forte Hotel**, Stillhorner Weg 40 (H 93), ℰ 7 52 50, Telex 217940, Fax 7525444, ⟲⟲, 🔲 – ▐▊
▤ rest ⓣⓥ ⅙ ⓟ – 🔬 25/200. ⒶⒺ ⓪ Ε 𝘝𝘐𝘚𝘈. 𝒮𝒮 rest
Restaurants : **Senator M** a la carte 45/74 – **Moorwerder Stube M** a la carte 27/40 – **148 rm**
188/468 Bb.

at Hamburg-Uhlenhorst   by Buchtstraße FX :

🏛 **Parkhotel Alster-Ruh** 🐾 without rest, Am Langenzug 6 (H 76), ℰ 22 45 77 – ⓣⓥ ☎ ⇔.
ⒶⒺ Ε
24 rm 119/315 Bb.

🏛 **Nippon** (Japanese installation and rest.), Hofweg 75 (H 76), ℰ 2 27 11 40, Telex 211081,
Fax 22711490 – ▐▊ ⓣⓥ ☎ ⇔. ⒶⒺ ⓪ Ε 𝘝𝘐𝘚𝘈. 𝒮𝒮
M *(dinner only, closed Monday)* a la carte 34/57 – **42 rm** 160/331 Bb.

at Hamburg-Veddel   by Amsinckstr. FZ :

🏛 **Carat-Hotel**, Sieldeich 9 (H 26), ℰ 78 96 60, Telex 2163354, Fax 786196, ⟲⟲ – ▐▊ ⓣⓥ ☎
⇔ ⓟ – 🔬 25/40. ⒶⒺ ⓪ Ε 𝘝𝘐𝘚𝘈
M a la carte 37/55 – **92 rm** 145/220 Bb.

HANOVER (HANNOVER) 3000. Niedersachsen 987 ⑮. 412 M 9 – pop. 500 000 – alt. 55 m – ✆ 0511.

See : Herrenhausen Gardens (Herrenhäuser Gärten)★★ (Großer Garten★★, Berggarten★) CV – Kestner-Museum★ DY M1 – Market Church (Marktkirche) (Altarpiece★★) DY A – Museum of Lower Saxony (Niedersächsisches Landesmuseum) (Prehistorical department★) EZ M2 – Museum of Arts (Kunstmuseum) (Collection Sprengel★) EZ M4.

Ⓖ Garbsen, Am Blauen See (⑥ : 14 km), ✆ (05137) 7 30 68 ; Ⓖ Isernhagen FB, Gut Lohne, ✆ (05139) 29 98.

✈ Hanover-Langenhagen (① : 11 km), ✆ 7 30 51.

🚗 ✆ 1 28 54 52.

Exhibition Center (Messegelände) (by ② and B 6), ✆ 8 90, Telex 922728.

🛈 Tourist office, Ernst-August-Platz 8, ✆ 1 68 23 19.

ADAC, Hindenburgstr. 37, ✆ 8 50 00.

Berlin 288 ② – Bremen 123 ① – Hamburg 151 ①.

Plan on following pages

🏨🏨 **Inter-Continental**, Friedrichswall 11, ✆ 3 67 70, Telex 923656, Fax 3677195 – 🛗 ⇔ rm
🍴 rest 📺 ₺ – 🚪 25/300. 🆎 ⓪ 🅴 𝚅𝙸𝚂𝙰. ℅ rest   DY **a**
Restaurants : **Prinz Taverne M** 32 (lunch) and a la carte 45/81 – **Wilhelm-Busch-Stube**
(closed Sunday dinner and Bank Holidays) **M** a la carte 25/40 – **285 rm** 265/565 Bb –
14 apart. 850/1600.

🏨🏨 **Maritim**, Hildesheimer Str. 34, ✆ 1 65 31, Telex 9230268, Fax 884846, ⇔, 🔲 – 🛗 ⇔ rm
▤ 📺 ₺ 🚗 🅿 – 🚪 25/600. 🆎 ⓪ 🅴 𝚅𝙸𝚂𝙰. ℅ rest   EZ **b**
M a la carte 50/81 – **293 rm** 205/524 Bb.

🏨🏨 **Kastens Hotel Luisenhof**, Luisenstr. 1, ✆ 3 04 40, Telex 922325, Fax 3044807 – 🛗 ▤ rest
📺 ₺ 🚗 🅿 – 🚪 25/150. 🆎 ⓪ 🅴 𝚅𝙸𝚂𝙰. ℅ rest   EX **b**
M (closed Sunday July - August) 30/50 (lunch) and a la carte 54/84 – **160 rm** 183/498 Bb –
5 apart. 450/800.

🏨🏨 ✿ **Schweizerhof Hannover - Schu's Restaurant**, Hinüberstr. 6, ✆ 3 49 50 (hotel)
3 49 52 52 (rest.), Telex 923359, Fax 3495123 – 🛗 ▤ rest 📺 🚗 – 🚪 25/160. 🆎 ⓪ 🅴 𝚅𝙸𝚂𝙰
M (closed Saturday lunch) (remarkable wine list) a la carte 77/113 – **Gourmet's Buffet M** a
la carte 45/80 – **Zirbelstube M** a la carte 31/43 – **115 rm** 235/375 Bb – 3 apart. 650   EX **d**
Spec. Lauwarmer Salat vom Ochsenschwanz, Pot au feu vom Hummer, Pochierter Heidschnuckenrücken mit
Meerrettich überbacken (season).

🏨🏨 **Congress-Hotel am Stadtpark**, Clausewitzstr. 6, ✆ 2 80 50, Telex 921263, Fax 814652,
🏤, Massage, ⇔, 🔲 – 🛗 ⇔ rm 📺 🚗 🅿 – 🚪 25/3000. 🆎 ⓪ 🅴 𝚅𝙸𝚂𝙰   by ②
M (also diet) 24/48 (lunch) and a la carte 38/78 – **252 rm** 144/368 Bb – 4 apart. 650/1200.

🏨🏨 **Grand Hotel Mussmann** without rest, Ernst-August-Platz 7, ✆ 32 79 71, Telex 922859,
Fax 324325 – 🛗 📺 – 🚪 25/50. 🆎 ⓪ 🅴 𝚅𝙸𝚂𝙰   EX **v**
100 rm 158/418 Bb.

🏨 **Königshof** without rest, Königstr. 12, ✆ 31 20 71, Telex 922306, Fax 312079 – 🛗 📺 ☎
🚗 – 🚪 30. 🆎 ⓪ 🅴 𝚅𝙸𝚂𝙰   EX **c**
84 rm 144/440 Bb.

🏨 **Plaza**, Fernroder Str. 9, ✆ 3 38 80, Telex 921513, Fax 3388488, 🏤 – 🛗 ⇔ rm ▤ 📺 ☎ –
🚪 25/200. 🆎 ⓪ 🅴 𝚅𝙸𝚂𝙰   EX **e**
M a la carte 44/59 – **102 rm** 168/396 Bb.

🏨 **Mercure**, Am Maschpark 3, ✆ 8 00 80, Telex 921575, Fax 8093704, ⇔ – 🛗 ⇔ rm ▤ rest
📺 ☎ ₺ 🚗 – 🚪 25/230. 🆎 ⓪ 🅴 𝚅𝙸𝚂𝙰   EZ **n**
M a la carte 40/71 – **141 rm** 169/515 Bb.

🏨 **Central-Hotel Kaiserhof**, Ernst-August-Platz 4, ✆ 3 68 30, Telex 922810, Fax 3683114 – 🛗
📺 ☎ – 🚪 25/100. ℅ – **81 rm** Bb.   EX **a**

🏨 **Am Funkturm - Ristorante Milano**, Hallerstr. 34, ✆ 3 39 80 (hotel) 31 70 33 (rest.),
Telex 922263 – 🛗 📺 ☎ ₺ 🅿. 🆎 ⓪ 🅴 𝚅𝙸𝚂𝙰   EV **s**
accomodation closed August – **M** a la carte 38/58 – **45 rm** 88/296.

🏨 **Am Leineschloß** without rest, Am Markte 12, ✆ 32 71 45, Telex 922010, Fax 325502 – 🛗
⇔ rm 📺 ☎ 🚗. 🆎 ⓪ 🅴 𝚅𝙸𝚂𝙰   DY **z**
81 rm 163/325 Bb.

🏨 **Loccumer Hof**, Kurt-Schumacher-Str. 16, ✆ 32 60 51, Fax 131192 – 🛗 📺 ☎ 🚗 –
🚪 35. 🆎 ⓪ 🅴 𝚅𝙸𝚂𝙰. ℅ rest   DX **s**
M (closed Saturday and Sunday for dinner) 22/36 (lunch) and a la carte 36/76 – **70 rm**
95/180 Bb.

🏨 **Intercity-Hotel**, Ernst-August-Platz 1, ✆ 32 74 61, Telex 921171, Fax 324119 – 🛗 ▤ rest
📺 ☎ – 🚪 25/100. 🆎 ⓪ 🅴   EX **r**
M a la carte 21/48 – **57 rm** 105/290 Bb.

🏨 **Körner**, Körnerstr. 24, ✆ 1 46 66, Telex 921313, Fax 18048, 🏤, 🔲 – 🛗 📺 ☎ 🚗 –
🚪 25/60. 🆎 ⓪ 🅴 𝚅𝙸𝚂𝙰   DX **e**
M a la carte 37/60 – **81 rm** 138/196 Bb.

🏨 **Vahrenwald**, Vahrenwalder Str. 205, ✆ 63 30 77, Telex 923713, Fax 673163 – 🛗 📺 ☎ 🅿.
🆎 ⓪ 🅴 𝚅𝙸𝚂𝙰   by ①
(dinner only, residents only) – **26 rm** 95/190 Bb.

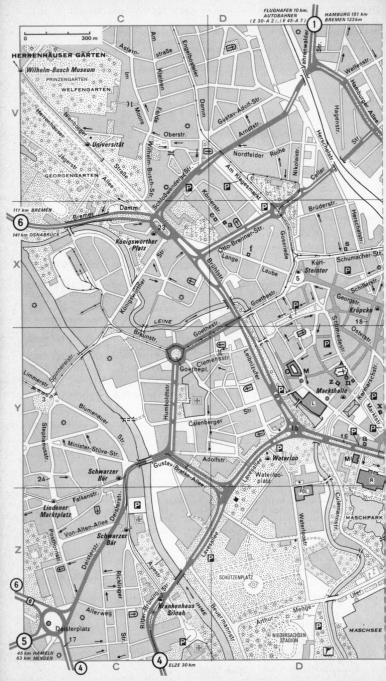

HANNOVER

BERLIN 288 km
BRAUNSCHWEIG 64 km
AUTOBAHN (E 4G/A 7)

HILDESHEIM 31 km
KASSEL 164 km

🏛 **Am Rathaus**, Friedrichswall 21, ℰ 32 62 68, Telex 923865, Fax 328868, ⇔ – 📶 📺 ☎
47 rm Bb.   EY **y**

🏛 **Vahrenwalder Hotel 181** without rest, Vahrenwalder Str. 181, ℰ 35 80 60, Fax 3505250, ⇔
– 📶 📺 ☎ 🅿   by ①
34 rm Bb.

🏛 **Alpha - Tirol** without rest, Lange Laube 20, ℰ 13 10 66, Fax 341535 – 📺 ☎ ⇐⇒ ᴬᴱ ⊙
E 𝘝𝘐𝘚𝘈   DX **f**
15 rm 98/170.

🏛 **Thüringer Hof** without rest, Osterstr. 37, ℰ 32 64 37, Telex 923994, Fax 3681793 – 📶 📺
☎ ⊙ E 𝘝𝘐𝘚𝘈   EY **e**
closed 23 December - 2 January – **55 rm** 85/250 Bb.

✗✗✗✗ ❀ **Landhaus Ammann** with rm, Hildesheimer Str. 185, ℰ 83 08 18, Telex 9230900, Fax
8437749, « Elegant installation, patio with terrace », 🌳 – 📶 📺 ₷ ⇐⇒ 🅿 – 🛂 25/100. ᴬᴱ
⊙ E 𝘝𝘐𝘚𝘈. ✛ rest   by ③
M (remarkable wine-list) 105/145 and a la carte 69/100 – **14 rm** 210/450 Bb
Spec. Salat von Nudeln mit Kaviar und Langustinen, Perlhuhnküken auf Lauch mit Trüffeln, Lammfilet mit
Rosmarinsauce und Gemüsegelee.

✗✗✗ ❀ **Romantik Hotel Georgenhof - Stern's Restaurant** 🍃 with rm, Herrenhäuser
Kirchweg 20, ℰ 70 22 44, Fax 708559, « Lower Saxony country house in a park, terrace » –
📺 ☎ 🅿. ᴬᴱ ⊙ E 𝘝𝘐𝘚𝘈. ✛ rm   by Engelbosteler Damm   CV
M (also vegetarian Menu) (remarkable wine list) 37/60 (lunch) and a la carte 71/121 – **13 rm**
140/300 Bb.
Spec. Steinbuttfilet in Champagner, Heidschnucken-Rücken (Saison), Barbarie-Ente mit Aprikosensauce.

✗✗✗ **Mövenpick - Baron de la Mouette**, Georgenstr. 35 (1st floor), ℰ 32 62 85, Fax 323160 –
▤   EX **x**

✗✗✗ **Lila Kranz**, Kirchwender Str. 23, ℰ 85 89 21, Fax 854383, 🌳 – ⊙ E 𝘝𝘐𝘚𝘈   FX **b**
closed Saturday and Sunday lunch – **M** 36/48 (lunch) and a la carte 54/79.

✗✗ **Stern's Sternchen**, Marienstr. 104, ℰ 81 73 22 – ᴬᴱ ⊙ E 𝘝𝘐𝘚𝘈   FY **b**
closed Sunday, Monday and 3 weeks July - August – **M** a la carte 56/76.

✗✗ **Das Körbchen**, Körnerstr. 3, ℰ 32 44 26   DX **a**
closed Sunday – **M** a la carte 48/71.

✗✗ **Ratskeller**, Köbelinger Str. 60 (entrance Schmiedestraße), ℰ 1 53 63 – ᴬᴱ E 𝘝𝘐𝘚𝘈   DY **n**
closed Sunday – **M** a la carte 35/65.

✗✗ **Clichy**, Weißekreuzstr. 31, ℰ 31 24 47 – ᴬᴱ E   EV **d**
closed Sunday and 10 to 31 July – **M** a la carte 60/96.

✗✗ **Mandarin-Pavillon** (Chinese rest.), Marktstr. 45 (Passage), ℰ 30 66 30 – ᴬᴱ ⊙ E 𝘝𝘐𝘚𝘈
M (also vegetarian dishes) a la carte 30/58.   DY **x**

✗ **Rôtisserie Helvetia**, Georgsplatz 11, ℰ 30 47 47, Fax 304746, 🌳 – ⊙ E 𝘝𝘐𝘚𝘈   EY **k**
M a la carte 26/55.

✗ **Tai-Pai** (Chinese rest.), Hildesheimer Str. 73, ℰ 88 52 30   EZ **a**
closed Monday – **M** a la carte 25/46.

✗ **Härke-Klause** (brewery - inn), Ständehausstr. 4, ℰ 32 11 75 – ᴬᴱ ⊙ E 𝘝𝘐𝘚𝘈   EY **b**
closed Saturday dinner, Sunday and Bank Holidays – **M** a la carte 21/46.

at Hanover 51-Bothfeld by Bödekerstr. FV :

🏛 **Residenz Hotel Halberstadt** without rest, Im Heidkampe 80, ℰ 64 01 18, 🌳 – 📺 ☎
🅿. ᴬᴱ E 𝘝𝘐𝘚𝘈
closed 20 December - 3 January – **36 rm** 95/175 Bb.

at Hanover 51-Buchholz by Bödekerstr. FV :

🏛 **Föhrenhof**, Kirchhorster Str. 22, ℰ 6 17 21, Fax 619719, 🌳 – 📶 📺 ☎ 🅿 – 🛂 30. ᴬᴱ ⊙
E 𝘝𝘐𝘚𝘈
M 25/33 (lunch) and a la carte 40/70 – **77 rm** 130/250 Bb.

✗✗ **Buchholzer Windmühle**, Pasteurallee 30, ℰ 64 91 38, Fax 6478930, 🌳 – 🅿. ✛
closed Sunday, Monday and Bank Holidays – **M** a la carte 42/75.

at Hanover 81-Döhren by ③ :

✗✗✗ **Wichmann**, Hildesheimer Str. 230, ℰ 83 16 71, Fax 8379811, « Courtyard » – E. ✛
M a la carte 57/97.

✗✗ ❀ **Etoile**, Wiehbergstr. 98, ℰ 83 55 24 – ᴬᴱ ⊙ E 𝘝𝘐𝘚𝘈
dinner only, closed Sunday, Monday and 3 weeks July - August – **M** (booking essential) a
la carte 52/77
Spec. Rote Bete-Apfel-Suppe, Lammrücken aus dem Kräutersud, Dessertteller.

at Hanover 42-Flughafen (Airport) by ① : 11 km :

🏨 **Holiday Inn**, Am Flughafen, ℰ 7 70 70, Telex 924030, Fax 737781, ⇔, 🔾 – 📶 ✛ rm ▤
📺 ₷ 🅿 – 🛂 25/160. ᴬᴱ ⊙ E 𝘝𝘐𝘚𝘈
M a la carte 46/87 – **210 rm** 256/400 Bb.

✗ **Mövenpick- Restaurant**, Abflugebene (departure), ℰ 7 30 55 09, Fax 7305709 – ▤ –
🛂 25/400. ᴬᴱ ⊙ E 𝘝𝘐𝘚𝘈
M (also vegetarian dishes) a la carte 28/56.

at *Hanover 71-Kirchrode* by ② and B 65 :

🏨 **Queens Hotel am Tiergarten** ⑤, Tiergartenstr. 117, ℰ 5 10 30, Telex 922748, Fax 526924, 🏤 – 🛗 📺 🅿 ⇔ 🅿 – 🔬 25/200. 🄰🄴 ⑩ 🄴 🆅🅸🆂🄰
M a la carte 42/65 – **108 rm** 218/412 Bb – 3 apart. 450.

at *Hanover 71-Kleefeld* by ② and B 65 :

XX **Alte Mühle**, Hermann-Löns-Park 3, ℰ 55 94 80, Fax 552680, « Converted lower Saxony farmhouse, terrace » – 💪 🄰🄴 ⑩ 🄴
closed Thursday, 28 January - 15 February and 22 July - 9 August – **M** 30/45 (lunch) and a la carte 50/79.

at *Hanover 72-Messe (near exhibition Centre)* by ② :

🏨 **Parkhotel Kronsberg**, Laatzener Str. 18 (at Exhibition Centre), ℰ 86 10 86, Telex 923448, Fax 867112, 🏤, 🈺, 🄽 – 🛗 🗏 rest 📺 ⇔ 🅿 – 🔬 25/200. 🄰🄴 ⑩ 🄴 🆅🅸🆂🄰
M a la carte 36/70 – **145 rm** 135/300 Bb.

at *Laatzen 3014* by ③ : 9 km :

🏨 **Britannia Hannover**, Karlsruher Str. 26, ℰ (0511) 8 78 20, Telex 9230392, Fax 863466, 🈺.
🎾 (covered court) – 🛗 📺 💪 🅿 – 🔬 25/80. 🄰🄴 ⑩ 🄴 🆅🅸🆂🄰
M a la carte 41/75 – **100 rm** 145/545 Bb.

🏨 **Haase**, Am Thie 4 (district Grasdorf), ℰ (0511) 82 10 41, Fax 828079 – 📺 ☎ 🅿
M a la carte 33/50 – **40 rm** 95/190 Bb.

at *Langenhagen 3012* by ① : 10 km :

🏨 **Grethe**, Walsroder Str. 151, ℰ (0511) 73 80 11, Fax 772418, 🏤, 🈺, 🄽 – 🛗 📺 ☎ 🅿 –
🔬 25/40. 🄰🄴
closed 22 July - 22 August and 22 December - 8 January – **M** (closed Saturday and Sunday) a la carte 33/57 – **51 rm** 98/210 Bb.

at *Langenhagen 6-Krähenwinkel 3012* by ① : 11 km :

🏨 Jägerhof, Walsroder Str. 251, ℰ (0511) 7 79 60, Telex 9218211, Fax 7796111, 🏤 – 📺 ☎ 🅿
– 🔬 25/70
77 rm Bb.

at *Ronnenberg-Benthe 3003* ⑤ : 10 km by B 65 :

🏨 **Benther Berg** ⑤, Vogelsangstr. 18, ℰ (05108) 6 40 60, Telex 922253, Fax 640650, 🏤, 🈺,
🄽, 🐎 – 🛗 🗏 rest 📺 ☎ 🅿 – 🔬 25/60. 🄰🄴 ⑩ 🄴 🆅🅸🆂🄰 🎿
M (Sunday and Bank Holidays lunch only) a la carte 60/82 – **64 rm** 104/220 Bb.

at *Garbsen 4-Berenbostel 3008* ⑥ : 13 km by B 6 :

🏨 **Landhaus Köhne am See** ⑤, Seeweg, ℰ (05131) 9 10 85, Fax 8367, ≼, « Garden terrace », 🈺, 🄽 (heated), 🐎, 🎿 – 📺 ☎ 🅿 🄰🄴 ⑩ 🄴
closed 15 December - 2 January – **M** a la carte 41/65 – **26 rm** 90/195 Bb.

▉▉▉▉ **LEIPZIG** 7010. 🗺 Sachsen 🄊🄉🄋 ⑲. 🄊🄉🄍 ⑰ – pop. 530 000 – alt. 88 m – ✪ 003741.

See : Old Town Hall★ (Altes Rathaus) BY – St. Thomas Church★ (Thomaskirche) BY – Old Stock Exchange★ (Alte Börse, Naschmarkt) BY E – St. Nicolas Church CY – Karl-Marx-Platz (New Gewandhaus) CY – Egyptian Museum (Ägyptisches Museum) BZ **M1** – Grassi Museum DY **M** – Georgi-Dimitroff-Museum and Museum of Fine Arts★★ (Museum der Bildenden Künste) BZ **M2**.

✈ Leipzig-Schkeuditz (NW : 15 km), ℰ 39 13 65. Interflug City Office, Sachsenplatz 1, ℰ 28 62 46.

Exhibition Grounds (Messegelände), Universitätsstr. 5 (Information Center), ℰ 29 53 36. Messeamt (Fair Office), Markt 11, ℰ 7 18 10, Telex 512294, Fax 7181575.

🛈 Leipzig-Information, Sachsenplatz 1, ℰ 7 95 90, Telex 512134.

Berlin 165 – Dresden 111 – Erfurt 126.

Plan on following pages

🏨 **Merkur**, Gerberstr. 15, ℰ 79 90, Telex 512609, Fax 7991229, 🏤, Massage, 🈺, 🄽 – 🛗 🗏
📺 💪 ⇔ 🅿 – 🔬 30/350. 🄰🄴 ⑩ 🄴 🆅🅸🆂🄰   BX **a**
M (also vegetarian dishes) a la carte 27/82 – **440 rm** 220/295 Bb – 13 apart. 410/820.

🏨 **Astoria**, Platz der Republik 2, ℰ 7 22 20, Telex 51535, Fax 7224747, Massage, 🈺 – 🛗
🗏 rest 📺 ☎ 🅿 – 🔬 30/100   CX **b**
M a la carte 30/76 – **305 rm** 145/250 Bb – 5 apart. 300/400.

🏨 **Gästehaus am Park**, Schwägrichstr. 14, ℰ 3 93 90, Telex 512301, Fax 326098, 🏤, « Park »
– 🛗 📺 ☎ 🅿 – 🔬 30/100   by Harkortstraße   BZ
M a la carte 18/44 – **35 rm** 189/309 Bb – 5 apart. 400.

🏨 **Stadt Leipzig**, Richard-Wagner-Str. 1, ℰ 28 88 14, Telex 51426, Fax 284037, 🈺 – 🛗 📺
☎ 🅿 – 🔬 25/120. 🄰🄴 ⑩ 🄴 🆅🅸🆂🄰   CY **d**
M 24/60 – **348 rm** 120/230 Bb.

🏨 **Deutschland**, Karl-Marx-Platz, ℰ 7 95 20, Telex 51559, Fax 289165 – 🛗 📺 ☎. 🄰🄴 ⑩ 🄴
🆅🅸🆂🄰 🎿   CY **f**
M a la carte 23/62 – **275 rm** 115/205 Bb – 8 apart. 295.

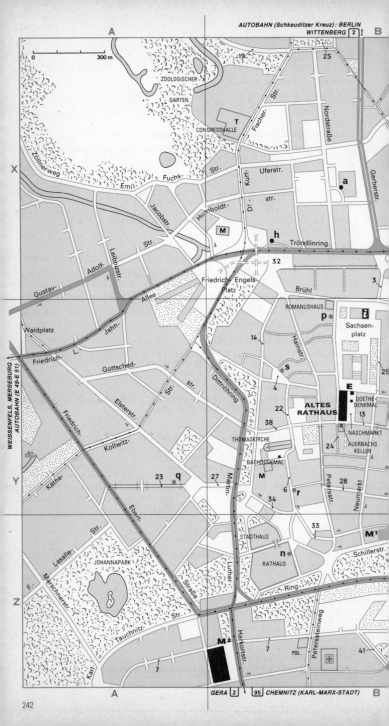

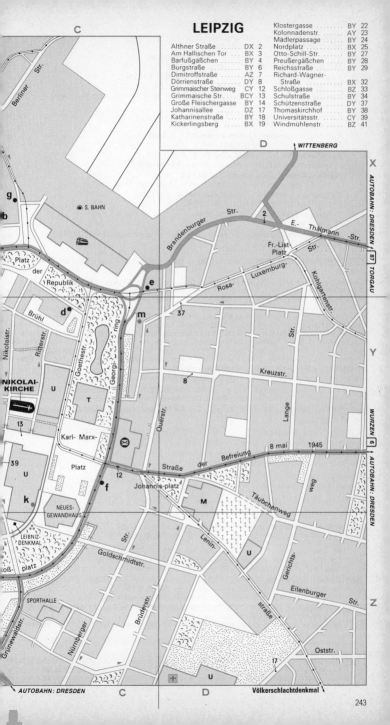

LEIPZIG

Zum Löwen, Rudolf-Breitscheid-Str. 1, ✆ 7 22 30 – |♦| ▤ rest TV ☎. AE ⓓ E VISA CX **g**
M a la carte 24/47 – **110 rm** 90/230 Bb.

International, Tröndlinring 8, ✆ 7 18 80 – |♦| TV ☎ BX **h**
M a la carte 24/65 – **85 rm** 95/205 Bb – 2 apart. 280.

Continental, Georgiring 13, ✆ 75 66 – |♦| ☎. AE ⓓ E VISA CX **e**
M a la carte 22/41 – **52 rm** 97/143 Bb.

XX **Panorama-Restaurant** (restaurant at 110 m, |♦|, 1,50 DM), Karl-Marx-Platz 9, ✆ 74 66, ≤ Leipzig – ▤ – **M** a la carte 35/61. CY **k**

XX **Falstaff**, Georgiring 9, ✆ 28 64 03 CY **m**
closed Monday – **M** a la carte 22/56.

XX **Plovdiv** (Bulgarian rest.), Katharinenstr. 17, ✆ 20 92 27 BY **p**
M *(also vegetarian dishes)* 70 and a la carte 29/64.

X **Auerbachs Keller**, Grimmaische Str. 2, ✆ 20 91 31 BY
closed Sunday lunch and Monday dinner – **M** a la carte 21/49.

X **Apels Garten** Kolonnadenstr. 2, ✆ 28 50 93, 🏡 AY **q**
closed Saturday lunch and Sunday dinner – **M** a la carte 18/42.

X **Ratskeller**, Lotter Str. 1 (New Town Hall), ✆ 7 91 35 91 BZ **n**
closed Monday dinner – **M** a la carte 13/43.

X **Thüringer Hof**, Burgstr. 19, ✆ 20 98 84 BY **r**
M a la carte 14/30.

X **Kaffeebaum** (15C historic citizen house), Kleine Fleischergasse 4, ✆ 20 04 52 BY **s**
M a la carte 19/37.

MUNICH (MÜNCHEN) 8000. L Bayern 987 ㉗, 426 ⑰, 413 R 22 – pop. 1 300 000 – alt. 520 m – ☎ 089.

See : Marienplatz★ KLY – Church of Our Lady (Frauenkirche)★★ (tower ✻★) KY – Old Pinakothek (Alte Pinakothek)★★★ KY – German Museum (Deutsches Museum)★★ LZ **M1** – The Palace (Residenz)★ (Treasury★★ Palace Theatre★) LY – Church of Asam Brothers (Asamkirche)★ KZ **A** – National Museum of Bavaria (Bayerisches Nationalmuseum)★★ HV – New Pinakothek (Neue Pinakothek)★ GU – City Historical Museum (Münchener Stadtmuseum)★ (Moorish Dancers★★) KZ **M2** – Villa Lenbach Collections (Städt. Galerie im Lenbachhaus) (Portraits by Lenbach★) KY **M5** – Antique Collections (Staatl. Antikensammlungen)★(Etruscan trinkets★) KY **M6** – Glyptothek★ KY **M7** – German Hunting Museum (Deutsches Jagdmuseum)★ KY **M8** – Olympic Park (Olympia-Park) (Olympic Tower ✻★★★) – New Town Hall (Neues Rathaus)★ LY **R** – Church of the Theatines (Theatinerkirche)★(Choir and Cupola★) LY **D** – English Garden (Englischer Garten)(view from Monopteros Temple★) HU.

Envir. : Nymphenburg★★ (castle★, park★, Amalienburg★★, Botanical Gardens★★).

⛳18 Straßlach, Tölzer Straße (S : 17 km), ✆ (08170) 4 50 ; ⛳9 München-Thalkirchen, Zentralländstr. 40, ✆ 7 23 13 04 ; ⛳18 Eichenried (NE : 24 km), Münchener Str. 55, ✆ (08123) 10 05.

✈ München-Riem (③ : 11 km) ✆ 92 11 21, City Air Terminal, Arnulfstraße (Main Station)..

🚗 ✆ 12 88 44 25.

Exhibition Centre (Messegelände) (EX), ✆ 5 10 70, Telex 5212086, Fax 5107506.

ℹ Tourist office in the Main Station, ✆ 2 39 12 56.

ℹ Tourist office in the airport München-Riem, ✆ 2 39 12 66.

ℹ Tourist-Information, town-hall, ✆ 2 39 12 72.

ADAC, Sendlinger-Tor-Platz 9, ✆ 59 39 79.

Innsbruck 162 ④ – Nürnberg 165 ② – Salzburg 140 ④ – Stuttgart 222 ⑦.

The reference (M 15) at the end of the address is the postal district : Munich 15

Plans on following pages

✿ **Vier Jahreszeiten Kempinski** 🐎, Maximilianstr. 17 (M 22), ✆ 23 03 90, Telex 523859, Fax 23039693, Massage, ≘s, 🏊 – |♦| ⇔ rm ▤ TV 🚗 – 🏛 25/350. AE ⓓ E VISA. ✱ rest LY **a**
M *(Monday and Saturday dinner only, closed August)* 85/130 and a la carte 60/100 – **Bistro Eck** (also vegetarian dishes) **M** a la carte 42/72 – **344 rm** 343/586 Bb – 25 apart. 1081/2806
Spec. Salat von Meeresfrüchten und Krustentieren, Entenbrust in der Salzkruste, Lammsattel im Kräutersud.

Rafael, Neuturmstr. 1 (M 2), ✆ 29 09 80, Telex 5213666, Fax 222539, « Roof-garden with terrace and 🏊 » – |♦| ▤ TV 🚗 – 🏛 25/100. AE ⓓ E VISA. ✱ rest LY **s**
M 45 (lunch) and a la carte 67/107 – **74 rm** 350/650 – 7 apart. 850/1850.

✿ **Königshof**, Karlsplatz 25 (M 2), ✆ 55 13 60, Telex 523616, Fax 55136113 – |♦| ▤ TV 🚗 – 🏛 30/90. AE ⓓ E VISA. ✱ rest KY **s**
M *(remarkable wine-list)* (booking essential) 108/138 and a la carte 72/104 – **106 rm** 240/384 Bb – 9 apart. 534/994
Spec. Gänseleberterrine mit Madeiragelee, Kalbsbries in Hummersauce, Soufflierte Taubenbrust auf Trüffelsauce.

Bayerischer Hof-Palais Montgelas, Promenadeplatz 6 (M 2), ✆ 2 12 00, Telex 523409, Fax 2120906, 🏡, Massage, ≘s, 🏊 – |♦| ⇔ rm TV 🚗 – 🏛 25/800. AE ⓓ E VISA KY **y**
Restaurants : **Grill** *(dinner only)* **M** a la carte 50/75 – **Trader Vic's** *(dinner only)* **M** a la carte 42/68 – **Palais Keller M** a la carte 28/50 – **442 rm** 253/515 – 45 apart. 625/1590.

🏨 **Park Hilton**, Am Tucherpark 7 (M 22), ℰ 3 84 50, Telex 5215740, Fax 38451845, 🎐, beer-garden, Massage, ⟨s⟩, 🖼 – 🛗 🗝⟩ rm ▦ 🍴 ⟸⟹ – 🔏 25/250. 🖭 ⓞ 🗲 𝗩𝗜𝗦𝗔 ⅀ rest
Restaurants : **Hilton-Grill** (also vegetarian dishes) (closed Saturday lunch, 1 week January and 3 weeks July - August) **M** a la carte 66/95 – **Tse Yang** (Chinese rest.) **M** a la carte 45/76 – **Isar-Terrassen** (also vegetarian dishes) **M** 39 (buffet) – **477 rm** 308/435 – 21 apart. 828/1628.
HU n

🏨 **Continental**, Max-Joseph-Str. 5 (M 2), ℰ 55 15 70, Telex 522603, Fax 55157500, 🎐 – 🛗 🗝⟩ rm 🚗 ⟸⟹ – 🔏 25/160. 🖭 ⓞ 🗲 𝗩𝗜𝗦𝗔 ⅀ rest
M a la carte 48/87 – **149 rm** 244/448 Bb – 18 apart. 698/998.
KY f

🏨 **Excelsior**, Schützenstr. 11 (M 2), ℰ 55 13 70, Telex 522419, Fax 55137121 – 🛗 🗹 – 🔏 30. 🖭 ⓞ 🗲 𝗩𝗜𝗦𝗔 ⅀ rest
M a la carte 55/85 – **114 rm** 195/320 Bb – 4 apart. 390.
JY z

🏨 **Regent**, Seidlstr. 2 (M 2), ℰ 55 15 90, Telex 523787, Fax 55159154, ⟨s⟩ – 🛗 ▦ rest 🗹 🚗 – 🔏 25/70 🖭 🗲
M a la carte 38/69 – **183 rm** 190/390 Bb.
JY d

🏨 **Eden-Hotel-Wolff**, Arnulfstr. 4 (M 2), ℰ 55 11 50, Telex 523564, Fax 55115555 – 🛗 🗹 ⟸⟹ – 🔏 25/250. 🖭 ⓞ 🗲 𝗩𝗜𝗦𝗔
M a la carte 30/66 – **214 rm** 150/350 Bb – 4 apart. 550.
JY p

🏨 **Arabella-Westpark-Hotel**, Garmischer Str. 2 (M 2), ℰ 5 19 60, Telex 523680, Fax 5196649, ⟨s⟩, 🖼 – 🛗 🗝⟩ rm ▦ rest 🗹 🕭 ⟸⟹ – 🔏 25/80. 🖭 ⓞ 🗲 𝗩𝗜𝗦𝗔
by ⑥
M (also vegetarian dishes) a la carte 35/63 – **258 rm** 198/358 Bb – 5 apart.

🏨 **King's Hotel** without rest, Dachauer Str. 13 (M 2), ℰ 55 18 70, Fax 5232667 – 🛗 🗝⟩ rm 🗹 🚗 – 🔏 30. 🖭 ⓞ 🗲 𝗩𝗜𝗦𝗔
closed 23 December - 1 January – **85 rm** 160/195 Bb – 8 apart. 240/540.
JY f

🏨 **Drei Löwen**, Schillerstr. 8 (M 2), ℰ 55 10 40, Telex 523867, Fax 55104905 – 🛗 🗝⟩ rm 🗹 ⟸⟹ 🅿 – 🔏 35. 🖭 ⓞ 🗲 𝗩𝗜𝗦𝗔
M a la carte 39/67 – **130 rm** 149/228 Bb.
JY e

🏨 **Trustee Parkhotel**, Parkstr. 31 (approach Gollierstraße) (M 2), ℰ 51 99 50, Telex 5218296, Fax 51995420 – 🛗 🗹 🚗 ⟸⟹ – 🔏 25. 🖭 ⓞ 🗲 𝗩𝗜𝗦𝗔
EV r
closed 24 December - 2 January – (dinner only, closed to non-residents) – **36 rm** 189/338 Bb – 7 apart. 313/428.

🏨 **Exquisit** without rest, Pettenkoferstr. 3 (M 2), ℰ 5 51 99 00, Telex 529863, Fax 55199499, ⟨s⟩ – 🛗 🗹 🕭 ⟸⟹ – 🔏 25. 🖭 ⓞ 🗲 𝗩𝗜𝗦𝗔
KZ s
50 rm 180/260 Bb – 5 apart. 340.

🏨 **Krone** without rest, Theresienhöhe 8 (M 2), ℰ 50 40 52, Telex 5213870, Fax 506706 – 🛗 🗹 🕿 🖭 ⓞ 🗲 𝗩𝗜𝗦𝗔
EV a
30 rm 150/250 Bb.

🏨 **Platzl-Restaurant Pfistermühle**, Platzl 1 (Entrance Sparkassenstraße) (M 2), ℰ 23 70 30, Telex 522910, Fax 23703800, ⟨s⟩ – 🛗 🗝⟩ rm 🗹 🕿 🕭 ⟸⟹ – 🔏 25/120. 🖭 🗲 𝗩𝗜𝗦𝗔 ⅀ rest
LY z
M (closed Sunday and 14 July - 18 August) 32 (lunch) and a la carte 46/68 – **167 rm** 175/280 Bb – 4 apart. 350.

🏨 **Arabella-Central-Hotel** without rest, Schwanthalerstr. 111 (M 2), ℰ 51 08 30, Telex 5216031, Fax 51083249, ⟨s⟩ – 🛗 🗝⟩ rm 🗹 🕿 ⟸⟹ – 🔏 30. 🖭 ⓞ 🗲 𝗩𝗜𝗦𝗔
EV s
closed 21 December - 7 January – **103 rm** 170/300 Bb.

🏨 **Erzgießerei-Europe**, Erzgießereistr. 15 (M 2), ℰ 1 26 82, Telex 5214977, Fax 1236198 – 🛗 🗹 🕿 ⟸⟹ – 🔏 70. 🖭 ⓞ 🗲 𝗩𝗜𝗦𝗔
EU a
M (closed 22 December - 6 January) a la carte 33/61 – **106 rm** 155/250 Bb.

🏨 **Mercure** without rest, Senefelder Str. 7 (M 2), ℰ 55 13 20, Telex 5218428, Fax 596444 – 🛗 🗹 🕿 🕭 – 🔏 25/80 – **167 rm** Bb.
JY r

🏨 **Hungar-Hotel**, Paul-Heyse-Str. 24 (M 2), ℰ 51 49 00, Telex 522395, Fax 51490701, 🎐 – 🛗 🗹 🕿 🕭 ⟸⟹ – 🔏 25/90. 🖭 ⓞ 🗲 𝗩𝗜𝗦𝗔
JZ r
M a la carte 35/55 – **182 rm** 170/368 Bb.

🏨 **Budapest**, Schwanthalerstr. 36 (M 2), ℰ 55 11 10, Telex 529213, Fax 55111992 – 🛗 ▦ rest 🗹 🕿 – 🔏 25/150. 🖭 ⓞ 🗲 𝗩𝗜𝗦𝗔
JY h
M (closed Sunday, July and August) a la carte 31/55 – **100 rm** 170/395 Bb.

🏨 **Germania**, Schwanthalerstr. 28 (M 2), ℰ 5 16 80, Telex 523790, Fax 598491, ⟨s⟩ – 🛗 🗝⟩ rm 🗹 🕿 – 🔏 40/60. 🖭 🗲 𝗩𝗜𝗦𝗔
JY a
M (closed Sunday) a la carte 34/65 – **100 rm** 205/355 Bb.

🏨 **Metropol**, Bayerstr. 43, (Entrance Goethestr.) (M 2), ℰ 53 07 64, Telex 522816, Fax 5328134 – 🛗 🗹 🕿 – 🔏 25/60. 🖭 ⓞ 🗲 𝗩𝗜𝗦𝗔
JY k
M a la carte 28/60 – **275 rm** 105/185.

🏨 **Concorde** without rest, Herrnstr. 38 (M 22), ℰ 22 45 15, Telex 522002, Fax 2283282 – 🛗 🗹 🕿 ⟸⟹ 🖭 ⓞ 🗲 𝗩𝗜𝗦𝗔
LZ q
closed 23 December - 1 January – **73 rm** 155/330 Bb.

🏨 **Domus** without rest, St.-Anna-Str. 31 (M 22), ℰ 22 17 04, Telex 529835, Fax 2285359 – 🛗 🗹 🕿 🖭 ⓞ 🗲 𝗩𝗜𝗦𝗔
LY b
closed 23 December - 2 January – **45 rm** 160/250 Bb.

🏨 **Austrotel München**, Arnulfstr. 2 (M 2), ℰ 5 38 60, Telex 522650, Fax 53862255, 15th floor rest. with ≤ Munich – 🛗 🗹 🕿 – 🔏 25/300
JY s
174 rm Bb.

245

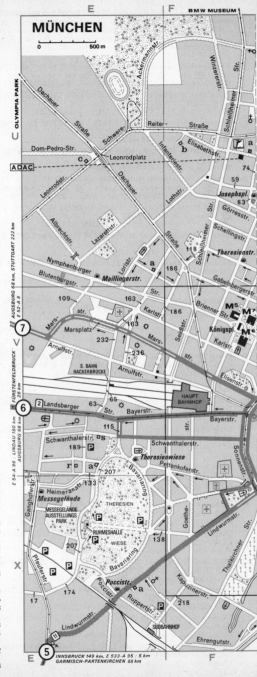

MÜNCHEN

0   500 m

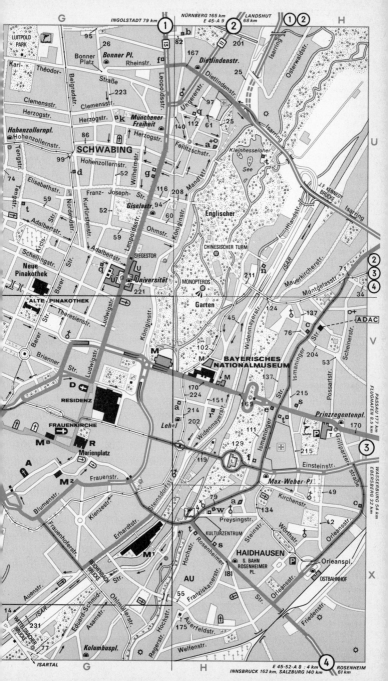

STREET INDEX TO MÜNCHEN TOWN PLANS

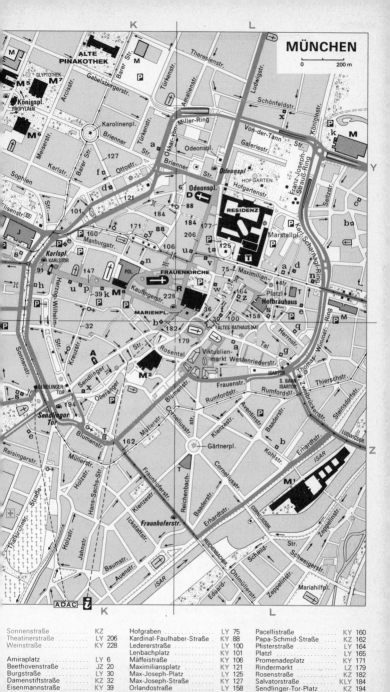

MÜNCHEN

0   200 m

STREET INDEX TO MÜNCHEN TOWN PLANS (Concluded)

Intercity-Hotel, Bayerstr. 10 (M 2), ℰ 55 85 71, Telex 523174, Fax 596229 – ≡ TV ☎ – 🔬 25/150. ⊙ E VISA — JY u
M a la carte 33/53 – **209 rm** 140/228 Bb – 4 apart. 265.

Admiral without rest, Kohlstr. 9 (M 5), ℰ 22 66 41, Telex 529111, Fax 293674, 🐾 – ≡ TV ☎ ⇔. AE ⊙ E VISA — LZ b
33 rm 180/270 Bb.

Torbräu without rest, Tal 37 (M 2), ℰ 22 50 16, Telex 522212, Fax 225019 – ≡ TV ☎ ⇔. P. AE ⊙ E VISA — LZ g
closed 23 December - 7 January – **88 rm** 160/280 – 3 apart.

Atrium without rest, Landwehrstr. 59 (M 2), ℰ 51 41 90, Telex 5212162, Fax 598491, ⬚s – ≡ ⇔ TV ☎ ⇔ – 🔬 50. AE ⊙ E VISA — JZ d
163 rm 190/240 Bb.

Apollo without rest, Mittererstr. 7 (M 2), ℰ 53 95 31, Telex 5212981, Fax 534033 – ≡ TV ☎ ⇔. AE ⊙ E VISA — JY w
closed 20 to 30 December – **74 rm** 130/165 Bb.

Europäischer Hof without rest, Bayerstr. 31 (M 2), ℰ 55 15 10, Telex 522642, Fax 55151222 – ≡ TV ☎ ⇔. AE ⊙ E VISA — JY b
160 rm 100/260 Bb.

Schlicker without rest, Tal 74 (M 2), ℰ 22 79 41, Fax 296059 – ≡ TV ☎ P. AE ⊙ E VISA — LZ a
closed 20 December - 7 January – **70 rm** 105/180 Bb.

Brack without rest, Lindwurmstr. 153 (M 2), ℰ 77 10 52, Telex 524416, Fax 7250615 – ≡ TV ☎ ⇔. AE ⊙ E VISA — EX a
50 rm 110/185 Bb.

Mark without rest, Senefelderstr. 12 (M 2), ℰ 59 28 01, Telex 522721, Fax 553954 – ≡ TV ☎ ⇔ P. AE ⊙ E VISA — JY v
91 rm 120/190.

Arcade without rest, Dachauer Str. 21 (M 2), ℰ 55 19 30, Telex 523752, Fax 55193102 – ≡ TV ☎ ⇔ – 🔬 25/80. E VISA — JY j
202 rm 120/160 Bb.

Daniel without rest, Sonnenstr. 5 (M 2), ℰ 55 49 45, Telex 523863, Fax 553420 – ≡ TV ☎. AE ⊙ E VISA — KY h
76 rm 105/250 Bb.

Adria without rest, Liebigstr. 8a (M 22), ℰ 29 30 81, Telex 5214111, Fax 227015 – ≡ TV ☎. AE ⊙ E VISA — HV a
closed 23 December - 7 January – **47 rm** 98/190.

🏠 **Andi** without rest, Landwehrstr. 33 (M 2), ℰ 59 60 67, Fax 553427 — 🛗 📺 ☎. AE ① E VISA
closed 21 December - 7 January — **30 rm** 95/140 Bb.
JZ **u**

🏠 **Müller** without rest, Fliegenstr. 4 (M 2), ℰ 26 60 63, Fax 268624 — 🛗 📺 ☎ ❷. ① E VISA
closed 23 to 31 December — **44 rm** 105/195.
KZ **e**

XXXX ✿✿✿ **Aubergine**, Maximiliansplatz 5 (M 2), ℰ 59 81 71, Fax 5236753 — ① E VISA
KY **d**
closed Sunday, Monday, Bank Holidays, first 2 weeks of August and 23 December - 7 January — **M** (booking essential) 165/225 and a la carte 95/145
Spec. Hummer mit Artischocken und Rotweinbutter, Lammcrêpinetten mit Wirsing, Warme Aprikosen-Tarte mit Amarettoeis.

XXX ✿ **Le Gourmet im Weinhaus Schwarzwälder**, Hartmannstr. 8 (1st floor) (M 2), ℰ 2 12 09 58 — AE ① E VISA
KY **n**
closed Sunday, Monday and August — **M** (booking essential) 150/180 and a la carte 75/115
Spec. Weißwurst von Meeresfrüchten, Souffliertes Seezungenfilet, Entenbrust mit Sesam-Ingwer-Sauce.

XXX ✿ **Sabitzer**, Reitmorstr. 21 (M 22), ℰ 29 85 84, Fax 3003304 — AE ① E VISA
HV **r**
dinner only, closed Sunday — **M** (booking essential) a la carte 85/110
Spec. Wildlachs auf Gänsestopflebercrème, Lamm- und Wildgerichte, Topfenmousse auf Himbeermark.

XXX **Weinhaus Schwarzwälder** (Old Munich wine restaurant), Hartmannstr. 8 (M 2), ℰ 2 12 09 79 — AE ① E VISA
KY **n**
M a la carte 34/70.

XXX **El Toula**, Sparkassenstr. 5 (M 2), ℰ 29 28 69 — ▤. AE ① E VISA
LY **f**
closed Sunday lunch, Monday, 26 May - 3 June and 28 July - 19 August — **M** (booking essential for dinner) a la carte 65/95.

XX ✿ **Boettner** (small Old Munich rest.), Theatinerstr. 8 (M 2), ℰ 22 12 10 — AE ① E VISA
closed Saturday dinner, Sunday, Bank Holidays and May — **M** (booking essential) a la carte 62/120
LY **u**
Spec. Hechtsoufflé mit Sauce Nantua, Hummereintopf ''Hartung'', Rote Grütze.

XX **Zum Bürgerhaus**, Pettenkoferstr. 1 (M 2), ℰ 59 79 09, « Bavarian farm house furniture, court terrace »
KZ **s**
closed Saturday lunch, Sunday and Bank Holidays — **M** (booking essential) 30 (lunch) and a la carte 48/76.

XX **Gasthaus Glockenbach** (former old Bavarian pub), Kapuzinerstr. 29 (M 2), ℰ 53 40 43 — E
JZ **s**
closed Sunday, Monday, Bank Holidays and 24 December - 2 January — **M** (booking essential) 45 (lunch) and a la carte 58/82.

XX **Halali**, Schönfeldstr. 22 (M 22), ℰ 28 59 09
LY **x**
closed Saturday lunch, Sunday and Bank Holidays — **M** (booking essential) 32 (lunch) and a la carte 53/78.

XX **La Belle Epoque**, Maximilianstr. 29 (M 22), ℰ 29 33 11, 🍽 — AE ① VISA
LY **n**
closed Saturday lunch, Sunday and 3 weeks August — **M** (booking essential for dinner) a la carte 48/75.

XX **Chesa Rüegg**, Wurzerstr. 18 (M 22), ℰ 29 71 14 — ▤
LY **d**
M (booking essential).

XX **Austernkeller**, Stollbergstr. 11 (M 22), ℰ 29 87 87 — AE ① E VISA 🍽
LY **e**
dinner only, closed Monday and 23 to 26 December — **M** (booking essential) a la carte 45/83.

XX **La Piazzetta**, Oskar-v.-Miller-Ring 3 (M 2), ℰ 28 29 90, 🍽, beer-garden — AE ① E VISA
closed Saturday lunch — **M** (booking essential) a la carte 51/78 — **Rosticceria M** a la carte 33/55.
KY **a**

XX **Mövenpick**, Lenbachplatz 8 (M 2), ℰ 55 78 65, Fax 5236538, 🍽 — ♨ 25/280. AE ① E VISA
KY **e**
closed Christmas — **M** a la carte 33/67.

XX **Csarda Piroschka** (Hungarian rest. with gipsy music), Prinzregentenstr. 1 (M 22), ℰ 29 54 25, Fax 293850 — ❷. AE ① E VISA
LY **k**
dinner only, closed Sunday — **M** (booking essential) a la carte 38/65.

XX **Dallmayr**, Dienerstr. 14 (1st floor) (M 2), ℰ 2 13 51 00, Fax 2135167 — AE ① E VISA
LY **w**
closed Saturday dinner and Sunday, August lunch only — **M** a la carte 43/83.

X **Goldene Stadt** (Bohemian cooking), Oberanger 44 (M 2), ℰ 26 43 82 — AE ① E VISA
M (booking essential for dinner) a la carte 26/57.
KZ **x**

X **Ratskeller**, Marienplatz 8 (M 2), ℰ 22 03 13, Fax 229195 — AE E
LY **R**
M a la carte 29/55.

Brewery - inns :

X **Spatenhaus-Bräustuben**, Residenzstr. 12 (M 2), ℰ 22 78 41, Fax 294076, 🍽, « Furnished in traditional alpine style » — ① E VISA
LY **t**
M a la carte 40/69.

X **Augustiner - Gaststätten**, Neuhauser Str. 16 (M 2), ℰ 55 19 92 57, « Beer garden » — AE ① E VISA
KY **p**
M a la carte 25/56.

X **Franziskaner Fuchs'n Stuben**, Perusastr. 5 (M 2), ℰ 2 31 81 20, Fax 23181244, 🍽 — AE ① VISA
LY **v**
M a la carte 27/58.

✗ **Zum Pschorrbräu** (with wine cellar St. Michael), Neuhauser Str. 11 (M 2), ℰ 2 60 30 01, 佘 – ⌸ ⓪ Ε   KY **k**
M a la carte 26/58.

✗ **Zum Spöckmeier**, Rosenstr. 9 (M 2), ℰ 26 80 88, 佘 – ⌸ ⓪ Ε *VISA*   KYZ **b**
closed Sunday June - August – **M** a la carte 26/55.

✗ **Spatenhofkeller**, Neuhauser Str. 26 (M 2), ℰ 26 40 10, 佘 – ⌸ Ε   KY **u**
M a la carte 21/42.

at Munich-Bogenhausen :

🏨 **Sheraton**, Arabellastr. 6 (M 81), ℰ 9 26 40, Telex 522391, Fax 916877, ≤ Munich, beer garden, Massage, 佘, ▨ – ▮ ≫ rm ▤ ▥ & ⇦ – 🛆 25/1200. ⌸ ⓪ Ε *VISA* ✲ rest
Restaurants : **Atrium M** a la carte 50/85 – **Alt Bayern Stube** *(dinner only)* **M** a la carte 37/65 – **650 rm** 255/440 Bb – 16 apart. 850/2000.   by Isarring HU

🏨 **Palace** without rest, Trogerstr. 21 (M 80), ℰ 4 70 50 91, Telex 528256, Fax 4705090, « Elegant installation with period furniture », 佘, ≋ – ▮ ▥ ⇦ – 🛆 . ⌸ ⓪ Ε *VISA*
73 rm 245/460 Bb – 6 apart.   HV **t**

🏨 **Arabella-Hotel**, Arabellastr. 5 (M 81), ℰ 9 23 20, Telex 529987, Fax 92324449, ≤ Munich, Massage, 佘, ▨ – ▮ ≫ rm ▤ rest ▥ ⇦ – 🛆 25/320. ⌸ ⓪ Ε *VISA*
M *(closed Sunday, Bank Holidays and August)* a la carte 35/69 – **478 rm** 216/372 Bb – 32 apart.   by Isarring HU

🏨 **Rothof** without rest, Denniger Str. 114 (M 81), ℰ 91 50 61, Fax 915066, ≋ – ▮ ▥ ⇦ ⌸ ⓪ Ε *VISA* ✲   by ③
37 rm 198/460 Bb.

🏨 **Prinzregent** without rest, Ismaninger Str. 42 (M 80), ℰ 41 60 50, Telex 524403, Fax 41605466, 佘 – ▮ ▥ ⇦ – 🛆 40. ⌸ ⓪ Ε *VISA*   HV **t**
closed 23 December - 7 January – **68 rm** 230/390 Bb.

🏨 **Queens Hotel München**, Effnerstr. 99 (M 81), ℰ 98 25 41, Telex 529987, Fax 983813 – ▮ ≫ rm ▤ rest ▥ ☎ ℗ ⇦ – 🛆 25/220. ⌸ ⓪ Ε *VISA*   by Isarring HU
M a la carte 39/62 – **155 rm** 206/362 Bb.

✗✗✗ **da Pippo** (Italian rest.), Mühlbaurstr. 36 (M 80), ℰ 4 70 48 48, Fax 476464, 佘 – Ε ✲
closed Saturday lunch, Sunday, Bank Holidays, 2 weeks May and 2 weeks December – **M** a la carte 46/80.   by Prinzregentenstr. HV

✗✗ **Käfer-Schänke**, Schumannstr. 1 (M 80), ℰ 4 70 63 00, 佘, « Several rooms with rustic and elegant installation » – ✲   HV **s**
M *(booking essential)*.

✗✗ **Bogenhauser Hof** (1825 former hunting lodge), Ismaninger Str. 85 (M 80), ℰ 98 55 86, Fax 9810221, « Terrace » – ⓪   HV **c**
closed Sunday and Bank Holidays – **M** *(booking essential)* a la carte 55/100.

✗✗ **Prielhof**, Oberföhringer Str. 44 (M 81), ℰ 98 53 53, 佘 – ⓪ Ε   by Herkomerplatz HU
closed Saturday lunch, Sunday, Bank Holidays and 2 weeks January – **M** *(booking essential)* 30 (lunch) and a la carte 52/75.

✗✗ **Tai Tung** (Chinese rest.), Prinzregentenstr. 60 (Villa Stuck) (M 80), ℰ 47 11 00 – ⌸ ⓪ Ε *VISA*   HV **e**
M *(also vegetarian dishes)* a la carte 38/61.

at Munich 80-Haidhausen :

🏨 **City Hilton**, Rosenheimer Str. 15, ℰ 4 80 40, Telex 529437, Fax 48044804, 佘 – ▮ ≫ rm ▤ ▥ & ⇦ – 🛆 25/180. ⌸ ⓪ Ε *VISA*   HX **s**
Restaurants: **Zum Gasteig M** a la carte 45/73 – **Löwenschänke M** a la carte 32/50 – **483 rm** 257/513 – 10 apart. 513/1200.

🏨 **Preysing**, Preysingstr. 1, ℰ 48 10 11, Telex 529044, Fax 4470998, 佘, ▨ – ▮ ▥ ▤ ⇦
closed 23 December - 6 January – **M** (see **Preysing-Keller** below) – **76 rm** 155/284 – 5 apart. 357/515.   HX **w**

🏨 **München Penta Hotel**, Hochstr. 3, ℰ 4 48 55 55, Telex 529046, Fax 4488277, Massage, 佘, ▨ – ▮ ≫ rm ▤ ▥ ⇦ – 🛆 25/400. ⌸ ⓪ Ε *VISA*   HX **t**
M 33 (buffet) and a la carte 43/76 – **583 rm** 264/373 Bb – 12 apart. 548.

✗✗✗ ❀ **Preysing-Keller**, Innere-Wiener-Str. 6, ℰ 48 10 15, « Vaulted cellar, country house furniture » – ▤   HX **w**
dinner only, closed Sunday, Bank Holidays and 23 December - 6 January – **M** *(remarkable wine list)* (booking essential) 109 and a la carte 61/82
Spec. Räucheraal-Parfait, Hasenrücken mit Walnußkruste, Barbarie Ente auf bayerische Art (2 pers.).

✗✗ **Balance**, Grillparzerstr. 1, ℰ 4 70 54 72, 佘 – ⌸ ⓪ Ε   HX **c**
closed Saturday lunch, Sunday and Bank Holidays – **M** a la carte 46/68.

✗ **Rue des Halles** (Rest. bistro-style), Steinstr. 18, ℰ 48 56 75 – Ε   HX **a**
dinner only – **M** *(booking essential)* a la carte 54/66.

at Munich 45-Harthof by Schleißheimer Str. FU :

✗✗ **Zur Gärtnerei**, Schleißheimer Str. 456, ℰ 3 13 13 73, 佘 – ℗
closed Wednesday – **M** a la carte 32/60.

at Munich 21-Laim by ⑥ :

🏨 **Transmar-Park-Hotel** without rest, Zschokkestr. 55, ℰ 57 93 60, Telex 5218609, Fax 57936100, 🔄 – 🛗 📺 ⚛ ⬅ – 🔺 30. ⅏ ⓞ 🇪 𝚅𝙸𝚂𝙰
71 rm 170/290 Bb.

at Munich 60 - Langwied by ⑦ :

🆇🆇 ❀ **Das kleine Restaurant im Gasthof Böswirth** 🦢 with rm, Waidachanger 9, ℰ 8 11 97 63 – ⬅ 🅿 ⅏ ⓞ 🇪
closed 19 May - 3 June and 23 December - 21 January – **M** (dinner only, closed Sunday, Monday and Bank Holidays) (remarkable wine list) 70/110 and a la carte 65/92 – **12 rm** 70/110
Spec. Hummer in Basilikumsud, Milchkalbsnuß in Kartoffelkruste, Topfenmousse mit Beeren.

at Munich 83-Neu Perlach by ④ :

🏨 **Orbis Hotel**, Karl-Marx-Ring 87, ℰ 6 32 70, Telex 5213357, Fax 6327407, beer-garden, 🔄, 🔲 – 🛗 ⅟⟐ rm 📺 ⚛ 🅿 – 🔺 25/130. ⅏ ⓞ 🇪 𝚅𝙸𝚂𝙰
Restaurants : **Perlacher Bürgerstuben M** a la carte 42/70 – **Hubertuskeller** (dinner only) **M** a la carte 32/50 – **Sakura** (dinner only, closed Monday) **M** a la carte 30/45 – **185 rm** 155/235 Bb – 4 apart. 315.

at Munich 40-Schwabing :

🏨 **Ramada Parkhotel**, Theodor-Dombart-Str. 4, ℰ 36 09 90, Telex 5218720, Fax 36099684, 🍴, 🔄 – 🛗 ⅟⟐ rm 📺 ⚛ – 🔺 25/60. ⅏ ⓞ 🇪 𝚅𝙸𝚂𝙰   by ②
M a la carte 35/70 – **260 rm** 235/390 Bb – 80 apart. 500/600.

🏨 **Marriott-Hotel**, Berliner Str. 93, ℰ 36 00 20, Telex 5216641, Fax 36002200, 🛁, 🔄, 🔲 – 🛗 ⅟⟐ rm 📺 ⚛ ⬅ – 🔺 25/350. ⅏ ⓞ 🇪 𝚅𝙸𝚂𝙰. ✻ rest   by ②
M a la carte 48/81 – **350 rm** 329/433 Bb – 18 apart. 483/798.

🏨 **Holiday Inn**, Leopoldstr. 194, ℰ 38 17 90, Telex 5215439, Fax 38179888, 🍴, Massage, 🔄, 🔲 – 🛗 ⅟⟐ rm 📺 ⚛ – 🔺 25/320. ⅏ ⓞ 🇪 𝚅𝙸𝚂𝙰   by ①
M 35/buffet (lunch)and a la carte 42/74 – **349 rm** 225/410 Bb – 4 apart. 600/1050.

🏨 **Residence**, Artur-Kutscher-Platz 4, ℰ 38 17 80, Telex 529788, Fax 38178951, 🍴, 🔲 – 🛗 ⅟⟐ rm 📺 ⚛ ⬅ – 🔺 25/100. ⅏ ⓞ 🇪 𝚅𝙸𝚂𝙰. ✻ rest   HU q
M a la carte 44/68 – **165 rm** 193/320.

🏨 **König Ludwig** without rest, Hohenzollernstr. 3, ℰ 33 59 95, Telex 5216607, Fax 394658 – 🛗 📺 ☎ ⬅. ⅏ ⓞ 🇪 𝚅𝙸𝚂𝙰   GU g
46 rm 169/300 Bb.

🏨 **Consul** without rest, Viktoriastr. 10, ℰ 33 40 35 – 🛗 📺 ☎ ⬅ 🅿   GU k
31 rm Bb.

🏨 **Leopold**, Leopoldstr. 119, ℰ 36 70 61, Telex 5215160, Fax 367061, 🍴 – 🛗 📺 ☎ ⬅ 🅿. ⅏ ⓞ 🇪 𝚅𝙸𝚂𝙰   GU f
closed 22 to 31 December – **M** (closed Saturday) a la carte 25/56 – **78 rm** 115/185 Bb.

🆇🆇🆇🆇 ❀❀❀ **Tantris**, Johann-Fichte-Str. 7, ℰ 36 20 61, Fax 3618469, 🍴 – 🍽 🅿. ⅏ ⓞ 🇪 𝚅𝙸𝚂𝙰. ✻   HU b
Monday and Saturday dinner only, closed Sunday, Bank Holidays, 1 week January and 18 May - 9 June – **M** (booking essential) a la carte 85/145
Spec. Lotte in Zitronensauce, Wachtelkotelett im Kartoffelmantel, Crépinettes vom Reh in Senfkörnersauce.

🆇🆇 **Romagna Antica** (Italian rest.), Elisabethstr. 52, ℰ 2 71 63 55, Fax 2711364, 🍴 – ⅟⟐. ✻
M (booking essential).   FU a

🆇🆇 **Seehaus**, Kleinhesselohe 3, ℰ 39 70 72, Fax 341803, ≤, « Lake-side setting, terrace » – 🅿. ⓞ 🇪 𝚅𝙸𝚂𝙰   HU t
M a la carte 43/72.

🆇🆇 **Walliser Stuben**, Leopoldstr. 33, ℰ 34 80 00, beer-garden – ⅏ ⓞ 🇪 𝚅𝙸𝚂𝙰   GU g
dinner only, closed Sunday and Bank Holidays – **M** a la carte 34/64.

🆇🆇 **Bistro Terrine**, Amalienstr. 89 (Amalien-Passage), ℰ 28 17 80, 🍴 – ⅏ 🇪. ✻   GU q
closed Monday lunch, Sunday, Bank Holidays, 1 to 8 January, 3 weeks June and 22 to 27 December – **M** (booking essential for dinner) 37 (lunch) and a la carte 65/90.

🆇🆇 **Daitokai** (Japanese rest), Nordendstr. 64 (entrance Kurfürstenstr.), ℰ 2 71 14 21, Fax 2718392 – 🍽. ⅏ ⓞ 🇪 𝚅𝙸𝚂𝙰. ✻   GU d
closed Sunday – **M** (booking essential) a la carte 48/76.

🆇🆇 **Restaurant 33**, Feilitzschstr. 33, ℰ 34 25 28, 🍴   HU a
dinner only – **M** (dinner only, booking essential).

🆇🆇 **Savoy** (Italian cooking), Tengstr. 20, ℰ 2 71 14 45 – ⅏ ⓞ 🇪 𝚅𝙸𝚂𝙰   GU t
closed Sunday – **M** a la carte 38/64.

🆇 **Ristorante Grazia** (Italian cooking), Ungererstr. 161, ℰ 36 69 31 – 🇪   by ②
closed Saturday and Sunday – **M** (booking essential) a la carte 45/62.

at Munich 70 - Sendling :

🏨 **Holiday Inn München - Süd**, Kistlerhofstr. 142, ℰ 78 00 20, Telex 5218645, Fax 78002672, beer garden, Massage, 🔄, 🔲 – 🛗 ⅟⟐ rm 🍽 📺 ⚛ ⬅ – 🔺 25/100. ⅏ ⓞ 🇪 𝚅𝙸𝚂𝙰. ✻ rest
M a la carte 41/67 – **320 rm** 233/406 Bb – 8 appart. 446/596.

at Munich 50-Untermenzing by ⑦ :

🏨 **Romantik-Hotel Insel Mühle**, von-Kahr-Str. 87, ℰ 8 10 10, Telex 5218292, Fax 8120571, 斎, beer garden, « Converted 16C riverside mill » – 📺 ⇔ 🅿. 🖭 ⑩ 🖃 𝚅𝙸𝚂𝙰
M *(closed Sunday and Bank Holidays)* 28 (lunch) and a la carte 51/77 – **37 rm** 150/370.

at Aschheim 8011 ③ : 13 km by Riem :

🏨 **Schreiberhof**, Erdinger Str. 2, ℰ (089) 90 00 60, Fax 90006459, 斎 – 🛗 📺 ৬ ⇔ 🅿 –
🔬 25/80. 🖭 ⑩ 🖃 𝚅𝙸𝚂𝙰
M a la carte 47/67 – **86 rm** 165/255 Bb.

🏨 **Zur Post**, Ismaninger Str. 11 (B 471), ℰ (089) 9 03 20 27, Fax 9044669, 斎 – 🛗 📺 ☎ ⇔
🅿 – 🔬 30. 🖃
M a la carte 24/46 – **55 rm** 75/150 Bb.

at Grünwald 8022 S : 13 km by Wittelsbacher Brücke GX – ✪ 089 (München) :

🏨 **Tannenhof** without rest, Marktplatz 3, ℰ 6 41 70 74, Fax 6415608, « Turn of the century house with elegant installation » – 📺 ☎ 🅿. 🖭 ⑩ 🖃 𝚅𝙸𝚂𝙰
closed 1 to 6 January – **21 rm** 120/200 Bb.

🏨 **Forsthaus Wörnbrunn** 🦌, in Grünwalder Forst (E : 1 km), ℰ 6 41 78 85, Fax 6413968, beer garden – 📺 ☎ 🅿 – 🔬 25/100. 🖭 🖃
closed 23 January - 11 February – **M** a la carte 38/72 – **17 rm** 90/195 Bb.

🏨 **Alter Wirt**, Marktplatz 1, ℰ 6 41 78 55, Fax 6414266, 斎, « Bavarian inn with cosy atmosphere » – 🛗 📺 ☎ ⇔ 🅿 – 🔬 25/70. 🖃
M a la carte 37/65 – **49 rm** 98/180 Bb.

🏨 **Schloß-Hotel Grünwald** 🦌, Zeillerstr.1, ℰ 6 41 79 35, Fax 6414771, ≼, « Terrace » –
📺 🅿. 🖭 ⑩ 🖃
closed 1 to 15 January – **M** a la carte 33/64 – **16 rm** 105/260 Bb.

STUTTGART 7000. 🏙 Baden-Württemberg 𝟜𝟙𝟛 KL 20, 𝟿𝟪𝟽 ㉟ – pop. 559 000 – alt. 245 m –
✪ 0711.

See : Site (Lage)** – Park Wilhelma DU and Killesberg-Park (Höhenpark Killesberg) ** – Television Tower (Fernsehturm)** (⁂⁑) DZ – Birkenkopf ⁂⁑ AY – Congress- and Concert Hall (Liederhalle)* BX – Old Castle (Altes Schloß) (Renaissance courtyard*) CX – Stuttgart State Gallery (Staatsgalerie)* CX M1 – Collegiate Church (Stiftskirche) (Commemorative monuments of dukes*) CX A – Württemberg Regional Museum (Württembergisches Landesmuseum) (Medieval art objects**) CX M2 – Daimler-Benz Museum* EX M – Porsche-Museum* by ⑧.

Envir. : Bad Cannstatt Spa Park (Kurpark)* E : 4 km EU.

🏌 Kornwestheim, Aldinger Str. (N : 11 km), ℰ (07141) 87 13 19 ; 🏌 Mönsheim (NW : 30 km by A 8), ℰ (07044) 69 09.

✈ Stuttgart-Echterdingen, by ③ ℰ 7 90 11, City Air Terminal, Stuttgart, Lautenschlagerstr. 14, ℰ 20 12 68.

Exhibition Centre (Messegelände Killesberg) (BU), ℰ 2 58 91, Telex 722584.

🛈 Tourist-Information, Klett-Passage (subway to the Main Station), ℰ 2 22 82 40, Telex 723854.

ADAC, Am Neckartor 2, ℰ 2 80 00.

Frankfurt am Main 204 ⑧ – Karlsruhe 88 ⑥ – München 222 ④ – Strasbourg 156 ⑥.

Plans on following pages

🏨 ✿ **Steigenberger-Hotel Graf Zeppelin** 🦌, Arnulf-Klett-Platz 7, ℰ 29 98 81, Telex 722418, Fax 292141, Massage, ≘s, 🏊 – 🛗 ⁂⇔ rm 🛗 📺 ৬ – 🔬 25/300. 🖭 ⑩ 🖃 𝚅𝙸𝚂𝙰
                                                                                                                                    CX s
M *(closed Saturday, Sunday, Bank Holidays and mid July - mid August)* (booking essential for dinner) 45/60 (lunch) and a la carte 64/98 – **Bistro Zepp 7 M** a la carte 33/53 – **280 rm** 269/480 Bb – 20 apart. 600/1650
Spec. Hummer auf Sesamkruste, Stern von Lachs, Seezunge und Jacobsmuscheln, Rehrücken im Wirsingmantel.

🏨 **Inter-Continental**, Neckarstr. 60, ℰ 2 02 00, Telex 721996, Fax 202012, ƒ₅, ≘s, 🏊 – 🛗 ⁂⇔ rm 🛗 📺 ৬ ⇔ – 🔬 25/500. 🖭 ⑩ 🖃 𝚅𝙸𝚂𝙰
                                                                                                                                    DX t
Restaurants : **Les Continents** *(closed Saturday lunch)* **M** a la carte 70/100 – **Neckarstube** *(closed Sunday)* **M** a la carte 38/60 – **277 rm** 315/490 Bb – 24 apart. 800/3500.

🏨 **Am Schloßgarten**, Schillerstr. 23, ℰ 2 02 60, Telex 722936, Fax 2026888, « Terrace with ≼ » – 🛗 🍴 rest 📺 ⇔ – 🔬 25/120. 🖭 ⑩ 🖃 𝚅𝙸𝚂𝙰. ⁂
                                                                                                                                    CX u
M a la carte 54/92 – **125 rm** 175/615 Bb.

🏨 **Royal**, Sophienstr. 35, ℰ 62 50 50, Telex 722449, Fax 628809 – 🛗 🍴 rest 📺 ⇔ 🅿 –
🔬 25/50. 🖭 ⑩ 🖃 𝚅𝙸𝚂𝙰
                                                                                                                                    BY b
M a la carte 41/72 – **90 rm** 208/415 Bb – 3 apart. 605.

🏨 **Park-Hotel**, Villastr. 21, ℰ 2 80 10, Telex 723405, Fax 284353, 斎 – 🛗 📺 ⇔ 🅿 –
🔬 25/80. 🖭 ⑩ 🖃 𝚅𝙸𝚂𝙰
                                                                                                                                    DV r
M a la carte 47/85 – **Radiostüble** *(dinner only, closed Sunday and Bank Holidays)* **M** a la carte 31/66 – **75 rm** 180/580 Bb.

🏨 **Ruff**, Friedhofstr. 21, ℰ 2 58 70, Telex 721645, Fax 2587404, ⇌, ▣ – |≋| 📺 ☎ ⇔ ℗, 🖭
⊛ ① E 💳
closed 21 December - 2 January and 28 March - 1 April – **M** (closed Sunday lunch and
Saturday) 18/29 (lunch) and a la carte 28/56 – **85 rm** 117/180 Bb.
CV a

🏨 **Rega-Hotel**, Ludwigstr. 18, ℰ 61 93 40, Telex 722701, Fax 6193477 – |≋| 📺 ☎ ⇔ –
🔥 30. 🖭 ① E 💳
M a la carte 27/59 – **60 rm** 155/195 Bb.
AX a

🏨 **Intercity-Hotel** without rest, Arnulf-Klett-Platz 2, ℰ 29 98 01, Telex 723543, Fax 2261899 –
|≋| 📺 ☎ – 🔥 25/60
112 rm Bb.
CX p

🏨 **Unger** without rest, Kronenstr. 17, ℰ 2 09 90, Telex 723995, Fax 2099100 – |≋| 📺 ☎ ⇔.
🖭 ① E 💳
closed 21 December - 6 January – **80 rm** 139/219 Bb.
CX a

🏨 **Bergmeister** without rest, Rotenbergstr. 16, ℰ 28 33 63, ⇌ – |≋| 📺 ☎ ℗. 🖭 ① E 💳
26 rm 148/210 Bb.
DX r

🏨 **Kronen-Hotel** without rest, Kronenstr. 48, ℰ 29 96 61, Telex 723632, Fax 296940, ⇌ –
📺 ☎ ⇔. 🖭 ① E
closed 20 December - 7 January – **85 rm** 105/280 Bb.
BX m

🏨 **Wörtz zur Weinsteige** ॐ, Hohenheimer Str. 30, ℰ 24 06 81, Telex 723821, Fax 6407279,
« Terrace » – 📺 ☎. 🖭 ① E 💳
closed 15 December - 15 January – **M** (closed Saturday, Sunday and Bank Holidays) a la
carte 30/72 – **25 rm** 75/240 Bb.
CY p

🏨 **Stadthotel am Wasen** without rest, Schlachthofstr. 19, ℰ 48 30 61, Telex 722030 – |≋|
📺 ☎ ⇔ ℗. 🖭 ① E 💳. ⅍
31 rm 110/150 Bb.
EVX e

🏨 **Azenberg** ॐ, Seestr. 116, ℰ 22 10 51, Fax 297426, ⇌, ▣ – |≋| 📺 ☎ ⇔ ℗. 🖭 ① E
💳
(dinner only, residents only) – **55 rm** 130/230 Bb.
AV e

🏨 **Ketterer**, Marienstr. 3, ℰ 2 03 90, Telex 722340, Fax 2039600 – |≋| 📺 ☎ ⇔. 🖭 ① E 💳
closed 21 December- 7 January – **M** (closed Friday, Saturday and 21 July - 17 August) a la
carte 32/54 – **107 rm** 127/220 Bb.
BY y

🏨 **Rieker** without rest, Friedrichstr. 3, ℰ 22 13 11 – |≋| 📺 ☎
63 rm
CX d

🏨 **Am Feuersee**, Johannesstr. 2, ℰ 62 61 03 – |≋| 📺 ☎
closed 21 December - 7 January – **M** (dinner only, closed Saturday, Sunday and Bank
Holidays) a la carte 25/50 – **38 rm** 125/170 Bb.
AY t

🏨 **Astoria** without rest, Hospitalstr. 29, ℰ 29 93 01, Telex 722783, Fax 299307 – |≋| 📺 ☎ ℗.
🖭 ① E 💳
55 rm 75/240 Bb.
BX e

XXX ⊛ **Alte Post**, Friedrichstr. 43, ℰ 29 30 79 – ① E 💳
Monday and Saturday dinner only, closed Sunday, Bank Holidays and late July - mid August
– **M** (booking essential) 58 (lunch) and a la carte 65/100
Spec. Gänseleberterrine, Gefüllter Seeteufel in Vin Jaune, Kaninchenrückenfilet im Pinienmantel.
CX e

XXX **Da Franco** (modern rest. with Italian cooking), Calwer Str. 23, ℰ 29 15 81 – ▦
BX c

XXX **Mövenpick-Rôtisserie Baron de la Mouette**, Kleiner Schloßplatz 11 (entrance
Theodor-Heuss-Str.), ℰ 2 26 89 34, Fax 2268728, ⛲ – ▦. 🖭 ① E 💳
M a la carte 45/75.
BX a

XX **Martins Stuben im Engelhorn**, Neckarstr. 119, ℰ 26 16 31, Fax 265210 – 🖭 E
closed Saturday, Sunday and Bank Holidays – **M** a la carte 38/75.
DV u

XX **Intercity-Restaurant**, Arnulf-Klett-Platz 2, ℰ 29 49 46
CX v

XX **Der Goldene Adler**, Böheimstr. 38, ℰ 6 40 17 62 – ℗. 🖭 ① E 💳
closed Monday and August – **M** a la carte 38/68.
AY e

XX **Gaisburger Pastetchen**, Hornbergstr. 24, ℰ 48 48 55
closed Saturday lunch, Sunday and Bank Holidays – **M** a la carte 57/78.
EX a

XX **Zeppelin - Stüble**, Lautenschlagerstr. 2 (at Graf Zeppelin Hotel), ℰ 22 40 13, ⛲ – ▦.
🖭 ① E 💳
M (Swabian cooking) (booking essential) a la carte 31/59.
CX s

XX **Krämer's Bürgerstuben**, Gablenberger Hauptstr. 4, ℰ 46 54 81 – 🖭 ① E 💳
closed Monday and 3 weeks July - August – **M** (booking essential) a la carte 51/78.
DX n

X **Brauereigasthof Ketterer**, Marienstr. 3b, ℰ 29 75 51
closed Sunday – **M** a la carte 21/44.
BY y

Swabian wine taverns (Weinstuben) (light meals only) :

X **Kachelofen**, Eberhardstr. 10 (entrance Töpferstraße), ℰ 24 23 78
dinner only, closed Sunday, Bank Holidays and 23 December - 9 January – **M** a la carte
33/45.
CY x

X **Weinstube am Stadtgraben**, Am Stadtgraben 6 (S 50-Bad Cannstatt), ℰ 56 70 06
closed Saturday, Sunday, Bank Holidays and 2 weeks September - October – **M** a la carte
25/37.
EU e

255

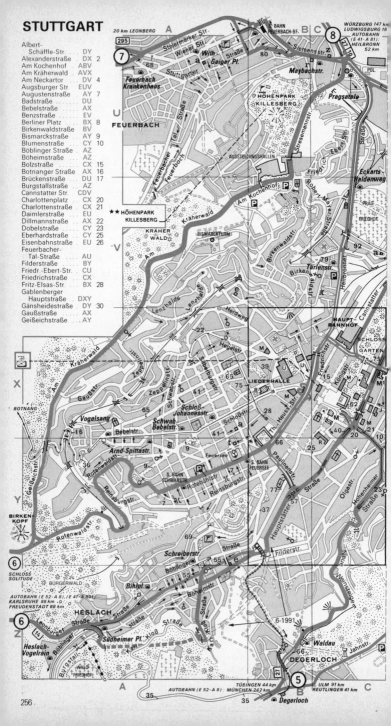

STUTTGART

**★★ HÖHENPARK
KILLESBERG**

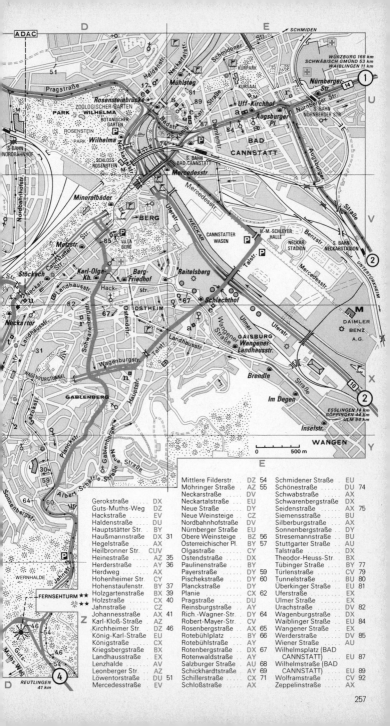

ADAC

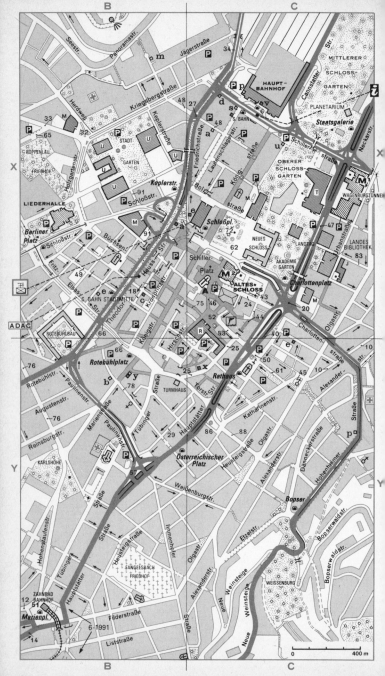

STUTTGART

✗ **Weinstube Schreinerei**, Zaisgasse 4 (S 50-Bad Cannstatt), ☎ 56 74 28, ✿ – ℗   EU s
closed Saturday dinner, Sunday and Bank Holidays – **M** a la carte 27/57.

✗ **Bäcka-Metzger**, Aachener Str. 20 (S 50-Bad Cannstatt), ☎ 54 41 08   DU e
dinner only, closed Sunday, Monday, Bank Holidays, 20 August - 10 September and 23 December - 10 January – **M** a la carte 28/42.

✗ **Weinhaus Stetter**, Rosenstr. 32, ☎ 24 01 63, remarkable wine list   CY e
closed Monday to Friday until 3 p.m., Saturday dinner, Sunday, Bank Holidays, 3 weeks July - August and 24 December - 6 January – **M** (mainly cold dishes) a la carte 12/17 ♨.

at Stuttgart 80-Büsnau by ⑥ :

🏨 **Relexa Waldhotel Schatten**, Gewandschatten 2, ☎ 6 86 70, Telex 7255557, Fax 6867999, ✿, ≦s – 📶 ⟨⟩ rm 📺 ♿ ⟨⟩ – 🔬 25/120. 🕮 ⑩ ⴹ 🆅🆂🅰 ℁ rest
Restaurants : **La Fenêtre** (dinner only, closed Sunday, Monday and 4 weeks July - August)
M a la carte 70/95 – **Kaminrestaurant M** a la carte 37/73 – **144 rm** 170/300 Bb – 9 apart. 375/490.

at Stuttgart 50 - Bad Cannstatt :

🏨 **Spahr** without rest, Waiblinger Str. 63 (B 14), ☎ 55 39 30, Telex 7254608, Fax 5539333 – 📶 📺 ☎ ⟨⟩ – 🔬 50. 🕮 ⑩ ⴹ 🆅🆂🅰   EU a
62 rm 135/230.

🏨 **Krehl's Linde**, Obere Waiblinger Str. 113, ☎ 52 75 67, Fax 548370, ✿ – 📺 ☎ ⟨⟩. 🕮 ⴹ   EU r
M (closed Sunday, Monday and 3 weeks July - August) a la carte 35/79 – **25 rm** 85/200 Bb.

✗✗ **Weinstube Pfund**, Waiblinger Str. 61a, ☎ 56 63 63, ✿, beer-garden – ℗. 🕮 ⑩ ⴹ 🆅🆂🅰
closed Saturday lunch, Sunday, Bank Holidays, 3 weeks August and 23 December - 6 January   EU a
– **M** a la carte 39/70.

at Stuttgart 70 - Degerloch :

🏨 **Waldhotel Degerloch** ❧, Guts-Muths-Weg 18, ☎ 76 50 17, Telex 7255728, Fax 767762, ✿, ≦s, ℁ – 📶 📺 ☎ ♿ ℗ – 🔬 25/100. 🕮 ⑩ ⴹ 🆅🆂🅰   by Guts-Muths-Weg DZ
M a la carte 35/68 – **50 rm** 165/230 Bb.

✗✗ **Fäßle**, Löwenstr. 51, ☎ 76 01 00   by ⑤
closed Sunday lunch, Saturday and August – **M** a la carte 40/74.

at Stuttgart 30 - Feuerbach :

🏨 **Messehotel Europe**, Siemensstr. 33, ☎ 81 48 30, Telex 7252132, Fax 8148348 – 📶 ⟨⟩ rm 🍴 📺 ⟨⟩. 🕮 ⑩ ⴹ 🆅🆂🅰 ℁ rest   BCU r
M a la carte 40/70 – **120 rm** 210/500 Bb.

🏨 **Kongresshotel Europe**, Siemensstr. 26, ☎ 81 50 91, Telex 723650, Fax 854082, ≦s – 📶 🍴 📺 ⟨⟩ – 🔬 25/130. 🕮 ⑩ ⴹ 🆅🆂🅰   CU z
M a la carte 48/75 – **150 rm** 150/350 Bb.

✗ **Anker**, Grazer Str. 42, ☎ 85 44 19 – 🕮 ⑩ ⴹ   AU a
closed Sunday dinner, Saturday, 12 July - 2 August and 23 December - 6 January – **M** (also vegetarian dishes) a la carte 32/69.

at Stuttgart 23 - Flughafen (Airport) ④ : 15 km :

🏨 **Airport Mövenpick-Hotel**, Randstraße, ☎ 7 90 70, Telex 7245677, Fax 793585, ✿, ≦s – 📶 ⟨⟩ rm 🍴 rest 📺 ♿ ℗ – 🔬 25/70. 🕮 ⑩ ⴹ 🆅🆂🅰
M a la carte 34/66 – **230 rm** 216/404 Bb.

✗✗ **top air**, Randstraße (in the airport), ☎ 79 01 21 10, Fax 7979210, ≪ – 🍴. 🕮 ⑩ ⴹ 🆅🆂🅰
M a la carte 55/84.

at Stuttgart 80 - Möhringen ⑤ : 7 km :

🏨 **Gloria - Restaurant Möhringer Hexle**, Sigmaringer Str. 59, 🖉 7 18 50, Fax 7185121, 🚗
— 📳 📺 ☎ ⇔ 🅿 — 🅰 25/50
M a la carte 25/47 — **79 rm** 113/175 Bb.

🏨 **Möhringen** without rest, Filderbahnstr. 43, 🖉 71 60 80, Fax 7160850 — 📳 📺 ☎ ⇔ 🅰
⑩ Ⓔ 𝘝𝘐𝘚𝘈
39 rm 140/250 Bb.

🏨 **Neotel** without rest, Vaihinger Str. 151, 🖉 7 80 06 35, Telex 7255179, Fax 7804314 — 📳 📺
☎ 🅿 🅰 ⑩ Ⓔ 𝘝𝘐𝘚𝘈
71 rm 147/209 Bb.

🏚 **Anker**, Vaihinger Str. 76, 🖉 71 30 31 (hotel) 71 78 09 (rest.) — 📳 ☎ ⇔
25 rm Bb.

💥💥💥 ✿ **Hirsch-Weinstuben**, Maierstr. 3, 🖉 71 13 75, remarkable wine list — 🅿 🅰 ⑩ Ⓔ 𝘝𝘐𝘚𝘈
✿
closed lunch Monday and Saturday, Sunday, Bank Holidays and Easter — **M** *(booking essential)* 52/155 and a la carte 48/85
Spec. Gänseleberterrine mit Traminergelee, Lachs vom Grill auf Burgundersauce, Kalbsleber auf Senfsabayon.

💥💥 **Landgasthof Riedsee**, Elfenstr. 120, 🖉 71 24 84, � — 🅿 🅰 ⑩ Ⓔ 𝘝𝘐𝘚𝘈
closed Sunday dinner and Monday — **M** a la carte 45/65.

at Stuttgart 50 - Mühlhausen by Neckartalstraße EU :

💥💥💥 ✿ **Öxle's Löwen**, Veitstr. 2, 🖉 53 22 26 — 🅰 Ⓔ
closed lunch Monday and Saturday, Sunday, Bank Holidays, 1 to 10 January and 2 weeks July - August — **M** *(booking essential)* 95/125 and a la carte 53/72
Spec. Variation von Hummer, Suprême von Lachs mit Brennesselpüree, Pochierte Taube mit Gänseleberravioli.

at Stuttgart 61 - Obertürkheim by ② :

🏨 **Brita Hotel - Restaurant Post**, Augsburger Str. 671, 🖉 32 02 30, Fax 32023400 — 📳
🔆 rm 🗐 rest 📺 ☎ ⇔ — 🅰 30/80. 🅰 ⑩ 𝘝𝘐𝘚𝘈, ✿ rest
M *(closed Sunday)* a la carte 37/66 — **70 rm** 102/334 Bb.

💥 **Weinstube Paule**, Augsburger Str. 643, 🖉 32 14 71 — 🅿 🅰 ⑩ Ⓔ 𝘝𝘐𝘚𝘈
closed Wednesday dinner, Thursday, last Sunday of the month, 7 to 20 February, 1 to 25 August and 24 to 30 December — **M** a la carte 32/59.

at Stuttgart 70 - Plieningen ④ : 13 km :

🏨 **Fissler-Post**, Filderhauptstr. 2, 🖉 4 58 40, Fax 4584333 — 📳 📺 ☎ ⇔ 🅿 — 🅰 25/80. 🅰
⑩ Ⓔ 𝘝𝘐𝘚𝘈
M *(also vegetarian menu)* (booking essential) 33/40 and a la carte 42/74 — **61 rm** 88/180 Bb
— 10 apart. 198.

🏨 **Traube**, Brabandtgasse 2, 🖉 45 48 33, Fax 4569567, � — ☎ 🅿
closed 23 December - 6 January and 3 weeks August — **M** *(booking essential)* (closed Saturday and Sunday) a la carte 48/96 — **22 rm** 125/280.

💥💥 **Recknagel's Nagelschmiede**, Brabandtgasse 1, 🖉 45 74 54 — 🅿
closed lunch Monday to Saturday, Tuesday and 3 weeks August — **M** a la carte 37/66.

at Stuttgart 40 - Stammheim by ⑧ :

🏨 **Novotel**, Korntaler Str. 207, 🖉 80 10 65, Telex 7252137, Fax 803673, 🚗, ⛱ (heated) — 📳
🗐 📺 ☎ ఉ 🅿 — 🅰 25/200. 🅰 Ⓔ 𝘝𝘐𝘚𝘈
M a la carte 35/58 — **117 rm** 163/201 Bb.

at Stuttgart 80-Vaihingen by ⑥ and B 14 :

🏨 **Fontana**, Vollmöllerstr. 5, 🖉 73 00, Telex 7255763, Fax 7302525, Massage, 🎣, 🚗, ⛱, �
— 📳 🔆 rm 🗐 📺 ఉ ⇔ 🅿 — 🅰 25/380. 🅰 ⑩ Ⓔ 𝘝𝘐𝘚𝘈
Restaurants : **Fontana M** a la carte 53/80 — **Bräustube M** a la carte 34/67 — **250 rm** 209/350
Bb — 5 apart. 475/1000.

near Schloß Solitude by ⑥ :

💥💥💥 **Herzog Carl Eugen**, ✉ 7000 Stuttgart, 🖉 (0711) 6 99 07 24, Fax 6990771, � — 🅿 🅰 Ⓔ
𝘝𝘐𝘚𝘈
closed Sunday, Monday and Bank Holidays — **M** a la carte 58/84 — **Schloß - Restaurant**
(also vegetarian dishes) **M** a la carte 30/53.

at Fellbach 7012 by ① : 8 km — ✪ 0711 :

🏨 **Kongresshotel**, Tainer Str. 7, 🖉 5 85 90, Telex 7254900, Fax 5859304, 🚗 — 📳 📺 ⇔ 🅿
— 🅰 30. 🅰 ⑩ Ⓔ 𝘝𝘐𝘚𝘈
M (rest. see Alt Württemberg below) — **148 rm** 175/240 Bb.

🏚 **City-Hotel** without rest, Bruckstr. 3, 🖉 58 80 14, Fax 582627 — 📺 ☎ 🅿 🅰 ⑩ Ⓔ 𝘝𝘐𝘚𝘈, ✿
closed 12 to 26 July — **26 rm** 59/125 Bb.

🏚 **Alte Kelter**, Kelterweg 7, 🖉 58 90 74 — 📺 ☎ ⇔ 🅿 🅰 Ⓔ 𝘝𝘐𝘚𝘈
(restaurant for residents only) — **20 rm** 90/140.

XX **Alt Württemberg**, Tainer Str. 7 (Schwabenlandhalle), ☞ 58 00 88 — ▤ **Ⓟ**. **AE Ⓞ E VISA**
M a la carte 47/72.

X **Weinstube Germania** with rm, Schmerstr. 6, ☞ 58 20 37 — **TV ☎**. **%**
closed mid July - mid August and 24 December - 9 January — **M** (closed Sunday, Monday and Bank Holidays) a la carte 34/58 — **8 rm** 68/125.

X **Weinkeller Häussermann** (1732 vaulted cellar), Kappelbergstr. 1, ☞ 58 77 75 — ▤. **E**
dinner only, closed Sunday, Bank Holidays and 2 weeks July - August — **M** a la carte 27/48.

at Fellbach-Schmiden 7012 by ① : 8,5 km :

🏤 **Hirsch**, Fellbacher Str. 2, ☞ (0711) 51 40 60, Fax 5181065, 😩, 🔲 — 🛗 **TV ☎** ⇔ **Ⓟ** —
🔬 25. **AE Ⓞ E VISA**
M (closed Friday and Sunday) a la carte 30/59 — **92 rm** 85/170 Bb.

🏠 **Schmidener Eintracht**, Brunnenstr. 4, ☞ (0711) 51 20 35, Fax 519915 — **TV ☎ Ⓟ**
closed 1 to 7 January — **M** (closed Saturday) a la carte 37/63 — **28 rm** 50/125 Bb.

at Korntal-Münchingen 2 7015 ⑧ : 9 km, near motorway exit S-Zuffenhausen :

🏨 Mercure, Siemensstr. 50, ☞ (07150) 1 30, Telex 723589, Fax 13266, beer garden, 😩, 🔲 —
🛗 ▤ **TV** & **Ⓟ** — 🔬 25/170
209 rm Bb — 6 apart.

at Leinfelden-Echterdingen 1 7022 by ⑤ :

🏠 **Drei Morgen** without rest, Bahnhofstr. 39, ☞ (0711) 75 10 85 — 🛗 **TV ☎** ⇔ **Ⓟ**. **AE E VISA**
25 rm 90/135 Bb.

🏠 **Stadt Leinfelden** without rest, Lessingstr. 4, ☞ (0711) 75 25 10 — **☎ Ⓟ**
20 rm 80/120.

at Leinfelden-Echterdingen 2 7022 by ⑤ :

🏤 **Filderland** without rest, Tübinger Str. 16, ☞ (0711) 7 97 89 13, Telex 7255972, Fax 7977576
— 🛗 **TV ☎** ⇔ — 🔬 25. **AE Ⓞ E VISA**
closed 24 December - 2 January — **48 rm** 120/190 Bb.

🏤 **Lamm**, Hauptstr. 98, ☞ (0711) 79 90 65, Fax 795275 — **☎ Ⓟ**. **AE Ⓞ E VISA**
M a la carte 23/49 — **26 rm** 95/130 Bb.

🏠 **Adler**, Obergasse 16, ☞ (0711) 79 35 90, 😩, 🔲 — 🛗 **TV ☎ Ⓟ** — 🔬 30
closed 24 December - 6 January — **M** (closed Saturday, Sunday and 3 weeks July - August) a la carte 27/59 — **18 rm** 100/160.

▐ Baiersbronn ▌ 7292. Baden-Württemberg **413** HI 21. **987** ㉟ — pop. 14 000 — alt. 550 m — ✿ 07442.
Stuttgart 100.

XXXX ✿✿ **Restaurant Bareiss**, Gärtenbühlweg 14 (at Kurhotel Mitteltal), ☞ 4 70, Fax 47320, ≼, remarkable wine-list — ▤ **Ⓟ**. **AE Ⓞ E VISA**
closed Monday, Tuesday, 21 May - 21 June and 25 November - 24 December — **M** (booking essential) 130/160 and a la carte 85/112
Spec. Ravioli mit Flußkrebsen, Rotbarbe in der Kartoffelkruste, Täubchen mit Perigord-Trüffel.

XXXX ✿✿ **Schwarzwaldstube** (French rest.), Tonbachstr. 237 (at Kur- and Sporthotel Traube Tonbach), ☞ 49 26 65, ≼ — **Ⓟ**. **AE Ⓞ E VISA**. **%**
closed Monday, Tuesday, 14 to 30 January and 8 to 30 July — **M** (booking essential) 120/165 and a la carte 84/120
Spec. Hausgebeizter Lachs mit Stern-Anis parfumiert, Langustinen auf Korail-Sauce, Rehkarree mit Roueneser Sauce.

▐ Öhringen ▌ 7110. Baden-Württemberg **413** L 19. **987** ㉖ — pop. 18 000 — alt. 230 m — ✿ 07941.
See : Former Collegiate Church (ehem. Stiftskirche)★ with St. Margaret's altar★.
🟢 Friedrichsruhe (N : 6 km), ☞ (07941) 6 28 01.
Stuttgart 68.

at Friedrichsruhe 7111 N : 6 km :

🏰 ✿✿ **Waldhotel und Schloß Friedrichsruhe** ❧, ☞ (07941) 6 08 70, Telex 74498, Fax 61468, 😮, deer park, « Garden, park », 😩, 🔼, 🔲, 🎾, 🟢 — 🛗 ⇔ **Ⓟ** — 🔬 25/80. **AE Ⓞ E VISA**
M (remarkable wine list) (closed Monday and Tuesday) 115/185 and a la carte 85/120 —
49 rm 165/368 — 11 apart. 388/550
Spec. Bretonischer Hummer auf marinierten Kartoffelscheiben, Steinbutt in Trüffelkruste mit zweierlei Champagnersaucen, Hohenloher Freilandpoularde.

Greece
Hellás

Athens

PRACTICAL INFORMATION

LOCAL CURRENCY

Greek Drachma : 100 Drs = 0.63 US $ (Jan. 91)

TOURIST INFORMATION

National Tourist Organisation (EOT) : 2 Kar. Servias, ☎ 322 25 45 (information) and 1 Ermou, 325 22 67. Hotel reservation : Hellenic Chamber of Hotels, 24 Stadiou, ☎ 323 69 62, Telex : 214 269. Also at East Airport ☎ 970 23 95 - Tourist Police : 7 Leoforos Singrou ☎ 171.

FOREIGN EXCHANGE

Banks are usually open on weekdays from 8am to 2pm. A branch of the National Bank of Greece is open daily from 8am to 2pm (from 9am to 1pm at weekends) at 2 Karageorgi Servias (Sindagma).

AIRLINES

OLYMPIC AIRWAYS : 96 Leoforos Singrou 117 41 Athens, ☎ 929 22 51 and 6 Othonos (Sindagma) 105 57 Athens, ☎ 961 61 61.
All following Companies are located near Sindagma Square :
AIR FRANCE : 4 Karageorgi Servias 105 62 Athens, ☎ 323 85 07.
BRITISH AIRWAYS : 10 Othonos 105 57 Athens, ☎ 325 06 01.
JAPAN AIRLINES : 4 Leoforos Amalias 105 57 Athens, ☎ 324 82 11.
LUFTHANSA : 11 Vassilissis Sofias 106 71 Athens, ☎ 771 60 02.
PAN AM : 4 Othonos 105 57 Athens, ☎ 323 52 42.
SABENA : 8 Othonos 105 57 Athens, ☎ 323 68 21.
SWISSAIR : 4 Othonos 105 57 Athens, ☎ 323 75 81.
TWA : 8 Xenofondos 105 57 Athens, ☎ 322 64 51.

TRANSPORT IN ATHENS

Taxis : may be hailed in the street even when already engaged ; it is advised to always pay by the meter. Minimum charge : 280 Drs.
Bus : good for sightseeing and practical for short distances : 50 Drs.
Metro : one single line crossing the city from North (Kifissia) to South (Piraeus).

POSTAL SERVICES

General Post Office : 100 Eolou (Omonia) with poste restante, and also at Sindagma.
Telephone (OTE) : 15 Stadiou, and 85 Patission (all services), 65 Stadiou and 50 Athinas (only for telephone calls).

SHOPPING IN ATHENS

In summer, shops are usually open from 8am to 1.30pm, and 5.30 to 8.30pm. They close on Sunday, and at 2.30pm on Monday, Wednesday and Saturday. In winter they open from 9am to 5pm on Monday and Wednesday, from 10am to 7pm on Tuesday, Thursday and Friday, from 8.30am to 3.30pm on Saturday. Department Stores in Patission and Eolou. The main shopping streets are to be found in Sindagma, Kolonaki, Monastiraki and Omonia areas. Flea Market (generally open on Sunday) and Greek Handicraft in Plaka.

TIPPING

Service is generally included in the bills but it is usual to tip employees.

SPEED LIMITS

The speed limit in built up areas is 50 km/h (31 mph) ; on motorways the maximum permitted speed is 100 km/h (62 mph) and 80 km/h (50 mph) on others roads.

SEAT BELTS

The wearing of seat belts is compulsory for drivers and front seat passengers.

BREAKDOWN SERVICE

The ELPA (Automobile and Touring Club of Greece) operate a 24 hour breakdown service : phone 104.

ATHENS

SIGHTS

Views of Athens : Lycabettos (Likavitós) ☀️ ★★★ DX — Philopappos Hill (Lófos Filo-pápou) ⇐ ★★★ AY.

ANCIENT ATHENS

Acropolis★★★ (Akrópoli) ABY — Hephaisteion★★ (Thissio) AY and Agora★ (Arhéa Ágora) AY — Theatre of Dionysos★★ (Théatro Dionissou) BY and Odeon of Herod Atticus★ (Odío Iródou Atikoú) AY — Olympieion★★ (Naós Olimpíou Diós) BY and Hadrian's Arch★ (Píli Adrianoú) BY — Roman Forum (Romaïki Ágora) : Tower of the Winds★ BY **G**.

OLD ATHENS
AND THE TURKISH PERIOD

Pláka★★ : Old Metropolitan★★ BY **A2** — Monastiráki★ (Old Bazaar) : Pandrossou Street★ BY **29**, Monastiráki Square★ BY, Kapnikaréa (Church) BY **A6**.

MODERN ATHENS

Síndagma Square★ CY : Greek guard on sentry duty — Academy, University and Library Buildings★ (Akadimía CX, Panepistímio CX, Ethnikí Vivliothíki BX) — National Garden★ (Ethnikós Kípos) CY — Stadium★ (Stádio) CDY.

MUSEUMS

National Archaeological Museum★★★ (Ethnikó Arheologikó Moussío) BX — Akrópolis Museum★★★ BY **M** — Museum of Cycladic and Ancient Greek Art★★ DY **M15** — Byzantine Museum★★ (Vizandinó Moussío) DY — Benaki Museum★★ (private collection of antiquities and traditional art) CDY — Museum of Traditional Greek Art★ BY **M2** — National Historical Museum★ BY **M7** — National Gallery and Soutzos Museum★★ (painting and sculpture) DY **M8**.

EXCURSIONS

Cape Sounion★★★ (Soúnio) SE : 71 km BY — Kessariani Monastery★★, E : 9 km DY — Daphne Monastery★★ (Dafní) NW : 10 km AX — Aigina Island★ (Égina) : Temple of Aphaia★★, 3 hours Return.

ATHENS (ATHÍNA) Attikí 🯄🯅🯀 ⑳ — Pop. 3 076 786 (Athens and Pireas area) — ⚙️ 01.

🏌️ Glifáda (near airport) ✆ 894 68 20.

✈️ S : 15 km, East Airport ✆ 969 91 11 (International Airport - All companies except Olympic Airways), West Airport ✆ 929 21 11 (Hellinikon Airport - Olympic Airways only) — East Airport Terminal : 4 Leoforos Amalias ✆ 324 20 24, West Airport Terminal : 96 Leoforos Singrou ✆ 981 12 01.

🚃 1 Karolou ✆ 522 24 91.

🅸 Tourist Information (EOT), 2 Kar. Servias ✆ 322 25 45 and East Airport ✆ 970 23 95.
ELPA (Automobile and Touring Club of Greece), 2 Messogion ✆ 779 16 15.

Igoumenitsa 581 — Pátra 215 — Thessaloniki 479.

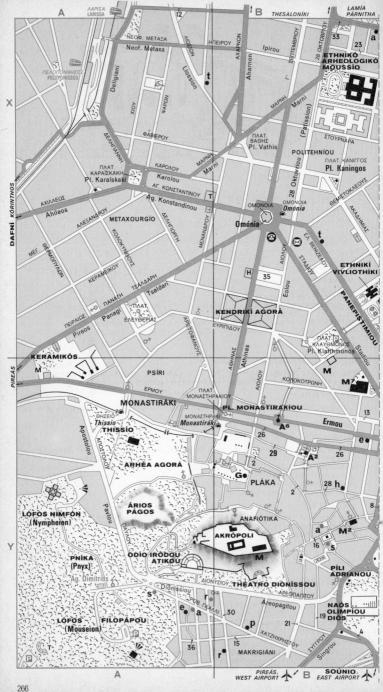

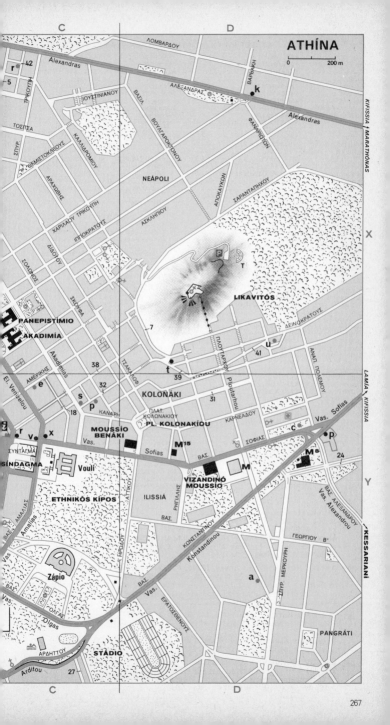

ATHÍNA

0   200 m

267

STREET INDEX TO ATHÍNA TOWN PLAN

Adrianou	ΑΔΡΙΑΝΟΥ	BY	2
Ag. Konstandinou	ΑΓ. ΚΩΝΣΤΑΝΤΙΝΟΥ	AX	
Aharnon	ΑΧΑΡΝΩΝ	BX	
Ahilleos	ΑΧΙΛΛΕΩΣ	AX	
Akadimias	ΑΚΑΔΗΜΙΑΣ	BCX	
Alexandras	ΑΛΕΞΑΝΔΡΑΣ	CDX	
Amerikis	ΑΜΕΡΙΚΗΣ	CXY	
Anapiron Polemou	ΑΝΑΠΗΡΩΝ ΠΟΛΕΜΟΥ	DXY	
Apokafkon	ΑΠΟΚΑΥΚΩΝ	DX	
Apostolou Pavlou	ΑΠΟΣΤΟΛΟΥ ΠΑΥΛΟΥ	AY	
Arahovis	ΑΡΑΧΩΒΗΣ	CX	
Arditou	ΑΡΔΗΤΤΟΥ	CY	
Aristofanous	ΑΡΙΣΤΟΦΑΝΟΥΣ	AX	
Asklipiou	ΑΣΚΛΗΠΙΟΥ	DX	
Ath. Diakou	ΑΘ. ΔΙΑΚΟΥ	BY	4
Athinas	ΑΘΗΝΑΣ	BXY	
Bouboulinas	ΜΠΟΥΜΠΟΥΛΙΝΑΣ	CX	5
Ddakalof	ΤΣΑΚΑΛΩΦ	DXY	
Deligiani	ΔΕΛΗΓΙΑΝΝΗ	AX	
Deligiorgi	ΔΕΛΗΓΙΩΡΓΗ	AX	
Didotou	ΔΙΔΟΤΟΥ	CX	
Dionissiou Areopagitou	ΔΙΟΝΥΣΙΟΥ ΑΡΕΟΠΑΓΙΤΟΥ	ABY	
El. Venizelou (Panepistimiou)	ΕΛ. ΒΕΝΙΖΕΛΟΥ (ΠΑΝΕΠΙΣΤΗΜΙΟΥ)	BCX	
Eolou	ΑΙΟΛΟΥ	BXY	
Eratosthenous	ΕΡΑΤΟΣΘΕΝΟΥΣ	DY	
Ermou	ΕΡΜΟΥ	ABY	
Evelpidos Rongakou	ΕΥΕΛΠΙΔΟΣ ΡΟΓΚΑΚΟΥ	DX	7
Fanarioton	ΦΑΝΑΡΙΩΤΩΝ	DX	
Favierou	ΦΑΒΙΕΡΟΥ	AX	
Filelinon	ΦΙΛΕΛΛΗΝΩΝ	BY	8
Hadzihristou	ΧΑΤΖΗΧΡΗΣΤΟΥ	BY	
Harilaou Trikoupi	ΧΑΡΙΛΑΟΥ ΤΡΙΚΟΥΠΗ	CX	
Hiou	ΧΙΟΥ	AX	
Ioulianou	ΙΟΥΛΙΑΝΟΥ	AX	12
Ioustinianou	ΙΟΥΣΤΙΝΙΑΝΟΥ	CX	
Ipirou	ΗΠΕΙΡΟΥ	ABX	
Ipokratous	ΙΠΠΟΚΡΑΤΟΥΣ	CX	
Irodou Atikou	ΗΡΩΔΟΥ ΑΤΤΙΚΟΥ	DY	
Kalidromiou	ΚΑΛΛΙΔΡΟΜΙΟΥ	CX	
Kanari	ΚΑΝΑΡΗ	CY	
Kar. Servias	ΚΑΡ. ΣΕΡΒΙΑΣ	BY	13
Karneadou	ΚΑΡΝΕΑΔΟΥ	DY	
Karolou	ΚΑΡΟΛΟΥ	AX	
Kavaloti	ΚΑΒΑΛΛΟΤΙ	BY	15
Keramikou	ΚΕΡΑΜΕΙΚΟΥ	AX	
Kidathineon	ΚΥΔΑΘΗΝΑΙΩΝ	BY	16
Kolokinthous	ΚΟΛΟΚΥΝΘΟΥΣ	AX	
Kolokotroni	ΚΟΛΟΚΟΤΡΩΝΗ	BY	
Kriezotou	ΚΡΙΕΖΩΤΟΥ	CY	18
Liossion	ΛΙΟΣΙΩΝ	AX	
Lomvardou	ΛΟΜΒΑΡΔΟΥ	DX	
Makri	ΜΑΚΡΗ	BY	19
Makrigiani	ΜΑΚΡΥΓΙΑΝΝΗ	BY	21
Marni	ΜΑΡΝΗ	ABX	
Meg. Alexandrou	ΜΕΓ. ΑΛΕΞΑΝΔΡΟΥ	AX	
Menandrou	ΜΕΝΑΝΔΡΟΥ	AX	
Metsovou	ΜΕΤΣΟΒΟΥ	BX	23
Mihalakopoulou	ΜΙΧΑΛΑΚΟΠΟΥΛΟΥ	DY	24
Mitropoleos	ΜΗΤΡΟΠΟΛΕΩΣ	BY	26
N. Theotoki	Ν. ΘΕΟΤΟΚΗ	CY	27
Navarhou Nikodimou	ΝΑΥΑΡΧΟΥ ΝΙΚΟΔΗΜΟΥ	BY	28
Neof. Metaxa	ΝΕΟΦ. ΜΕΤΑΞΑ	AX	
Omonia	ΟΜΟΝΟΙΑ	BX	
Pandrossou	ΠΑΝΔΡΟΣΟΥ	BY	29
Parthenonos	ΠΑΡΘΕΝΩΝΟΣ	BY	30
Patission (28 Oktovriou)	ΠΑΤΗΣΙΩΝ (28 ΟΚΤΩΒΡΙΟΥ)	BX	
Patr. Ioakim	ΠΑΤΡ. ΙΩΑΚΕΙΜ	DY	31
Pindarou	ΠΙΝΔΑΡΟΥ	CY	32
Pireos (Panagi Tsaldari)	ΠΕΙΡΑΙΩΣ (ΠΑΝΑΓΗ ΤΣΑΛΔΑΡΗ)	AX	
Pl. Anexartissias (Vathis)	ΠΛΑΤ. ΑΝΕΞΑΡΤΗΣΙΑΣ (ΒΑΘΗΣ)	BX	
Pl. Egiptou	ΠΛΑΤ. ΑΙΓΥΠΤΟΥ	BX	33
Pl. Eleftherias	ΠΛΑΤ. ΕΛΕΥΘΕΡΙΑΣ	AX	
Pl. Eth. Andistasseos (Kodzia)	ΠΛΑΤ. ΕΘΝ. ΑΝΤΙΣΤΑΣΕΩΣ (ΚΟΤΖΙΑ)	BX	35
Pl. Kaningos	ΠΛΑΤ. ΚΑΝΙΓΓΟΣ	BX	
Pl. Karaïskaki	ΠΛΑΤ. ΚΑΡΑΙΣΚΑΚΗ	AX	
Pl. Klafthmonos	ΠΛΑΤ. ΚΛΑΥΘΜΩΝΟΣ	BX	
Pl. Kolonakiou	ΠΛΑΤ. ΚΟΛΩΝΑΚΙΟΥ	DY	
Pl. Monastirakiou	ΠΛΑΤ. ΜΟΝΑΣΤΗΡΑΚΙΟΥ	ABY	
Ploutarhou	ΠΛΟΥΤΑΡΧΟΥ	DX	
Psaron	ΨΑΡΩΝ	AX	
Radzieri	ΡΑΤΖΙΕΡΗ	AY	36
Rigilis	ΡΗΓΙΛΛΗΣ	DY	
Rovertou Gali	ΡΟΒΕΡΤΟΥ ΓΚΑΛΛΙ	AY	
Sarandapihou	ΣΑΡΑΝΤΑΠΗΧΟΥ	DX	
Sindagma	ΣΥΝΤΑΓΜΑ	CY	
Singrou	ΣΥΓΓΡΟΥ	BY	
Skoufa	ΣΚΟΥΦΑ	CX	
Solonos	ΣΟΛΩΝΟΣ	CX	
Spir. Merkouri	ΣΠΥΡ. ΜΕΡΚΟΥΡΗ	DY	
Spir. Trikoupi	ΣΠΥΡ. ΤΡΙΚΟΥΠΗ	CX	
Stadiou	ΣΤΑΔΙΟΥ	BXY	
Stournara	ΣΤΟΥΡΝΑΡΑ	BX	
Themistokleous	ΘΕΜΙΣΤΟΚΛΕΟΥΣ	BCX	
Thermopilon	ΘΕΡΜΟΠΥΛΩΝ	AX	
Tossitsa	ΤΟΣΙΤΣΑ	CX	
Varvaki	ΒΑΡΒΑΚΗ	DX	
Vas. Alexandrou	ΒΑΣ. ΑΛΕΞΑΝΔΡΟΥ	DY	
Vas. Amalias	ΒΑΣ. ΑΜΑΛΙΑΣ	CY	
Vas. Georgiou B'	ΒΑΣ. ΓΕΩΡΓΙΟΥ Β'	DY	
Vas. Konstandinou	ΒΑΣ. ΚΩΝΣΤΑΝΤΙΝΟΥ	DY	
Vas. Olgas	ΒΑΣ. ΟΛΓΑΣ	CY	
Vas. Sofias	ΒΑΣ. ΣΟΦΙΑΣ	CDY	
Vassiliou Voulgaroktonou	ΒΑΣΙΛΕΙΟΥ ΒΟΥΛΓΑΡΟΚΤΟΝΟΥ	DX	
Voukourestiou	ΒΟΥΚΟΥΡΕΣΤΙΟΥ	CX	38
Xanthipou	ΞΑΝΘΙΠΠΟΥ	DXY	39
Xenokratous	ΞΕΝΟΚΡΑΤΟΥΣ	DX	41
Zaïmi	ΖΑΙΜΗ	CX	42
3 Septemvriou	Γ'ΣΕΠΤΕΜΒΡΙΟΥ	BX	

Athenaeum Inter-Continental, 89-93 Singrou, 117 45, SW : 2 ¾ km 9023 666, Telex 221554, Fax 9217 653, « Première rooftop restaurant with Athens », – rm – 2 000. by Singrou BY
M (see also **La Rotisserie** below) – **Kublai Khan** *(closed Sunday) (dinner only)* 6750 and a la carte 4500/7500 – **Première** (dinner only) a la carte 4800/6500 – 2450 – **517 rm** 34400/44800, **42 suites** 51200/78400.

Athens Hilton, 46 Vas. Sofias, 106 76, 7220 201, Telex 215808, Fax 7213 110, heated – rm – 1 700. DY **p**
M Ta Nissia *(closed July and August)* (dinner only) 5500 and a la carte – **Kellari** *(closed July and August)* (dinner only) 2145 and a la carte – **Byzantine** 4200 and a la carte – 2600 – **434 rm** 32278/42323, **19 suites** 64556/180576.

Ledra Marriott, 115 Singrou Av., 117 45, SW : 3 km 9347 711, Telex 221833, Fax 9358 603, « Rooftop terrace with and Athens » – rm – 500. by Singrou BY
M (see also **Kona Kai** below) – **Ledra Grill** *(closed Monday and June-September)* (dinner only) a la carte 5160/7750 – 2000 – **242 rm** 31000/40000, **16 suites** 75000/250000.

Le NJV Meridien, 2 Vas. Georgiou, Sintagma, 105 64, 3255 301, Telex 210568, Fax 3235 856 – rm – 100. CY **r**
M La Brasserie des Arts *(closed lunch Saturday and Sunday)* a la carte 7000/9500 – 2800 – **162 rm** 25600/41850, **15 suites** 51200/70000.

🏨🏨 **Grande Bretagne,** Vas. Georgiou, Sintagma, 105 63, 🖀 3230 251, Telex 219615, Fax 3228 034 – 🛗 ☰ 📺 ☎ – 🔬 400. 🖭 ⓪ 🔄 ꘎ ⅍
                                                                          CY **v**
M G B Corner a la carte 5600/9500 – ☲ 2800 – **330 rm** 27352/52142, **22 suites** 78377/184245.

🏨🏨 **Astir Palace,** Panepistimiou and Vas. Sofias, 106 71, 🖀 3643 112, Telex 222380, Fax 3642 825 – 🛗 ☰ 📺 ☎ – 🔬 150. 🖭 ⓪ 🔄 ꘎ ⅍
                                                                          CY **x**
M 5500 and a la carte – ☲ 2000 – **59 rm** 22500/34000, **18 suites** 50000/220000.

🏨 **Divani Palace Acropolis,** 19-25 Parthenonos, 117 42, 🖀 9222 945, Telex 218306, Fax 9214 993, « Ancient ruins of Themistocles wall in basement », ⅃ – 🛗 ☰ 📺 ☎ – 🔬 500. 🖭 ⓪ 🔄 ꘎
                                                                                BY **r**
M Aspassia 3510 and a la carte – **Roof Garden** *(summer only)* – **247 rm** ☲ 26317/33448, **6 suites** 44734.

🏨 **Holiday Inn,** 50 Mihalakopoulou, 115 28, 🖀 7248 322, Telex 218870, Fax 7248 187, ⅃ – 🛗 📺 ☎ 🚗 – 🔬 400. 🖭 ⓪ 🔄 ꘎
                                                        by Mihalakopoulou DY
M 3100 and a la carte – ☲ 2000 – **185 rm** 17722/24810, **5 suites** 39873/61138.

🏨 **Novotel Mirayia,** 4-6 Michail Voda St., 104 39, 🖀 8627 053, Telex 226264, Fax 8837 816, « Roof garden with ⅃ and ꘎ Athens » – 🛗 ☰ 📺 ☎ 🚗 – 🔬 520. 🖭 ⓪ 🔄 ꘎   AX **t**
M 2800 (lunch) and a la carte 2350/4310 – ☲ 1200 – **190 rm** 13000/15400, **5 suites** 23000/26000.

🏨 **Chandris,** 385 Singrou, 175 64, SW : 7 km 🖀 9414 824, Telex 218112, Fax 9425 082, « Summer rooftop restaurant with ⅃ and ꘎ Athens » – 🛗 ☰ 📺 ☎ – 🔬 500. 🖭 ⓪ 🔄 ꘎ ⅍
                                                            by Singrou BY
M Four Seasons *(October-May)(closed Sunday)* a la carte 2650/4680 – **Flamingo** 2200 and a la carte – **364 rm** ☲ 14000/20000, **6 suites** 50000.

🏨 **St. George Lycabettus,** 2 Kleomenous, 106 75, 🖀 7290 711, Telex 214253, Fax 7290 439, « ꘎ Athens from Grand Balcon rooftop restaurant », ⅃ – 🛗 ☰ 📺 ☎ – 🔬 120. 🖭 ⓪ 🔄 ꘎ ⅍
                                                                              DX **t**
M 2400 and a la carte – **141 rm** ☲ 13401/24164, **5 suites** 34352/48158.

🏨 **Park,** 10 Alexandras Av., 106 82, 🖀 8832 712, Telex 214748, Fax 8238 420, « Roof garden with ⅃ and ꘎ Athens » – 🛗 ☰ 📺 ☎ 🚗 – 🔬 700. 🖭 ⓪ 🔄 ꘎ ⅍
                                                                         BX **a**
M 2800 and a la carte – **126 rm** ☲ 14300/18900, **19 suites** 29300.

🏨 **Zafolia,** 87-89 Alexandras Av., 114 74, 🖀 6449 002, Telex 214468, Fax 6442 042, « Rooftop terrace with ⅃ and ≤ Athens » – 🛗 ☰ 📺 ☎ – 🔬 200. 🖭 ⓪ 🔄 ꘎
                                                                              DX **k**
M 2450 and a la carte – **183 rm** ☲ 10080/12480, **8 suites** 17160.

🏨 **Herodion,** 4 Rov. Gali, 117 42, 🖀 9236 832, Telex 219423, Fax 9235 851, « Roof garden with ≤ Acropolis » – 🛗 ☰ 📺 ☎ – 🔬 50. 🖭 ⓪ 🔄 ꘎
                                                                              BY **p**
M 2100 and a la carte – **86 rm** ☲ 14060/17986, **4 suites** 21000.

🏨 **Titania,** 52 Panepistimiou, 106 78, 🖀 3609 611, Telex 214673, Fax 3630 497, « Roof garden with ꘎ Athens » – 🛗 ☰ 📺 ☎ – 🔬 400. 🖭 ⓪ 🔄 ꘎ ⅍
                                                                          BX **t**
M 2500 and a la carte – **375 rm** ☲ 8960/11950, **21 suites** 19910/29860.

🏨 **Electra Palace,** 18 Nikodimou, 105 57, 🖀 3241 401, Group Telex 216896, Fax 3241 875, ⅃ – 🛗 ☰ 📺 ☎ 🚗 – 🔬 50. 🖭 ⓪ 🔄 ꘎
                                                                              BY **h**
M 2600 and a la carte – ☲ 1250 – **101 rm** 10600/12700, **5 suites** 17800.

🏨 **Electra,** 5 Hermou, 105 63, 🖀 3223 223, Group Telex 216896, Fax 3220 310 – 🛗 ☰ 📺 ☎. 🖭 ⓪ 🔄 ꘎
                                                                              BY **e**
M 2600 and a la carte – ☲ 1250 – **110 rm** 10600/12200.

🏠 **Acropolis View** without rest., 10 Wemster, off Rov. Gali, 117 42, 🖀 9217 303, Telex 219936, ≤ – 🛗 ☰ 🚗. 🖭 🔄 ꘎
                                                                                  AY **e**
32 rm ☲ 7400/9900.

XXXX **Mare Nostrum,** 292 Kifissias Av. (3rd floor), N. Psyhiko, 154 51, NE : 7 ½ km on Kifissia Rd 🖀 6722 891, Fax 6417 940, �, French rest. – 🛗 ☰. 🖭 ⓪ 🔄 ꘎
closed Sunday – **M** 7900 (lunch) and a la carte 9500/15500.

XXXX **La Rotisserie** (at Athenaeum Inter-Continental H.), 89-93 Singrou, 117 45, 🖀 9023 666, Telex 221554, Fax 9217 653 – 🛗 🚗. 🖭 ⓪ 🔄 ꘎
                                                                  by Singrou BY
closed Sunday, Monday and June-October – **M** (dinner only) a la carte 7800/10000.

XXX **Precieux Gastronomie,** 14 Akadimias (1st floor), 106 71, 🖀 3608 616, Fax 3608 619, French rest., « Skyscape mural by Italian artist » – 🛗 ☰ – 🔬 50. 🖭 ⓪ 🔄
                                                                            CY **s**
closed Sunday, Easter, 25 December and 1 January – **M** a la carte 7100/13200.

XXX **Athenaeum,** 8 Amerikis, International Cultural Centre, 106 71, 🖀 3631 125 – ☰. 🖭 ⓪ 🔄 ꘎
                                                                            CY **e**
closed Sunday, July-August and Bank Holidays – **M** 2300 (lunch) and a la carte 3500/6700.

XXX **Boschetto,** Evangelismos Park, off Vas. Sofias, 106 75, 🖀 7210 893, Fax 7223 598, 🌤, Italian rest., « Summerhouse in small park » – ☰. 🖭 ⓪ 🔄
                                                                            DY **c**
closed lunch November-March, Sunday and 2 weeks August – **M** 7000/8500 and a la carte.

XXX **Kona Kai** (at Ledra Marriott H.), 115 Singrou, 117 45, 🖀 9347 711, Telex 223465, Fax 9358 603, Polynesian and Japanese, (Teppan-Yaki) rest., « Pacific islands style decor » – ☰ 🚗. 🖭 ⓪ 🔄
                                                                  by Singrou BY
closed Sunday – **M** (dinner only) a la carte 5000/9500.

XX **Symbosium,** 46 Erehthiou, 117 42, ✆ 9225 321, « Conservatory in winter, ☂ in summer » – AE ⓓ VISA AY r
closed Sunday – **M** (dinner only) a la carte 4500/7800.

XX **La Brasserie,** 292 Kifissias Av. (3rd floor), N. Psyhiko, 154 51, NE : 7 ½ km on Kifissia Rd ✆ 6716 572, Fax 6417 940, ☂ – |♦| ▤. AE ⓓ E VISA
closed Sunday – **M** 3000 (lunch) and a la carte 4700/7600.

XX **Dioscuri,** 16 Dimitriou Vasiliou, N. Psyhiko, 154 51, NE : 7 km by Kifissia Rd turning at A.B. supermarket ✆ 6713 997, ☂ – ▤. AE ⓓ E VISA 7 km by Vas. Sofias DY
closed Sunday and Bank Holidays – **M** (booking essential) a la carte 3000/4500.

XX **L'Abreuvoir,** 51 Xenocratous, Kolonaki, 106 76, ✆ 7229 106, ☂, French rest. – ▤. AE ⓓ E VISA DX u
M a la carte 3400/8300.

XX **Spiros Vasilis,** 5 Lachitos, 115 21, off Vas Sofias, turn left at second set of traffic lights after Hilton H. ✆ 7237 575, Steak rest. – AE ⓓ by Vas. Sofias DY
closed Sunday, 1 week Easter, June-September and 25 December – **M** (booking essential) (dinner only) a la carte 4000/7500.

XX **Gerofinikas,** 10 Pindarou, 106 71, ✆ 3636 710 – ▤. AE ⓓ E VISA CY p
closed 16-17 April and 25 December – **M** a la carte 5000/8000.

XX **Dionysos,** 43 Rov. Gali, 117 42, ✆ 9233 182, Fax 9221 998, ≤ Acropolis, ☂ – Ⓟ. AE ⓓ E VISA AY s
M 4000/6000 and a la carte.

X **Strofi,** 25 Rov. Gali, 117 42, ✆ 9214 130, ☂, « ≤ Acropolis from rooftop terrace » – AE ⓓ E VISA AY a
closed Sunday, 3 days at Easter, 25-26 December and 31 December-1 January – **M** (dinner only) a la carte 1650/2650.

"The Tavernas".

Typical little Greek restaurants, generally very modest, where it is pleasant to spend the evening, surrounded with noisy but friendly locals, sometimes with guitar or bouzouki entertainment. These particular restaurants are usually open for dinner only.

XX **Myrtia,** 32-34 Trivonianou, 116 36, ✆ 7012 276 – ▤. AE ⓓ E VISA by N. Theotoki CY
closed Sunday, 1 week Easter, late July-late August and 25-26 December – **M** (music) (booking essential) (dinner only) 6000/8500.

X **Kostoyanis,** 37 Zaimi, 106 82, ✆ 8220 624 CX r
closed Sunday and 20 July-20 August – **M** (dinner only) a la carte 2700/3800.

X **O Anthropos,** 13 Archelaou, ✆ 7235 914, Seafood – E DY a
closed Sunday and June-September – **M** (dinner only) a la carte 3000/7000.

X **Kidathineon,** 3 Filomouson Sq., 105 58, ✆ 3234 281, ☂ – AE ⓓ E VISA BY s
closed lunch November-March except Sunday – **M** 1700/3200 and a la carte.

X **Xinos,** 4 Geronda, ✆ 3221 065 BY a
closed Saturday and Sunday – **M** (music) (booking essential) (dinner only) a la carte 1900/2400.

At Kifissia NE : 15 km by Vas Sofias DY.

🏨 **Penteliko,** 66 Diligianni, 145 62 (Kifissia), off Charilou Trikoupi follow signs to Politia ✆ 8080 311, Telex 224649, Fax 8010 314, ☂, 🏊, 🌳 – |♦| ⇔ rm ▤ TV ☎ – 🏛 350. AE ⓓ E VISA. ✻
M Vardis (dinner only) a la carte 6000/9000 – **Belle Epoque** *(closed mid June-September)* (dinner only) – ☕ 2350 – **31 rm** 35000/40100, **11 suites** 55500/95000.

at Pireas SW : 10 km by Singrou BY.

🏨 **Mistral,** 105 Vas. Pavilou, Castella, 185 33, ✆ 4117 150, Telex 212811, Fax 4122 096 – |♦| ▤ ☎ 🚗 – 🏛 250. AE E VISA. ✻
M 1850 and a la carte – ☕ 600 – **71 rm** 9000/11800, **3 suites** 20150.

XX **Aglamer,** 54-56 Akti Koumoundourou, Mikrolimano, 185 33, ✆ 4115 511, ≤, ☂, Seafood – ▤. AE ⓓ E VISA
closed 1 January – **M** a la carte 2000/5000.

X **Durambeis,** 29 Athinas Dilaveri, 185 33, ✆ 4122 092, ☂, Seafood
closed 4 days at Easter, August and 25 December – **M** a la carte 2500/8000.

X **Psaropoula,** 22 Akti Koumoundourou, Mikrolimano, 185 33, ✆ 4112 479, ≤, ☂, Seafood – AE ⓓ E VISA
M a la carte 3000/7000.

Republic

of Ireland

Dublin

PRACTICAL INFORMATION

LOCAL CURRENCY

Punt (Irish Pound) : 1 punt = 1.76 US $ (Jan. 91)

TOURIST INFORMATION

The telephone number and address of the Tourist Information office is given in the text under 🛈.

FOREIGN EXCHANGE

Banks are open 10am to 12.30pm and 1.30pm to 3pm on weekdays only.

Banks in Dublin stay open to 5pm on Thursdays and banks at Dublin and Shannon airports are open on Saturdays and Sundays.

SHOPPING IN DUBLIN

In the index of street names those printed in red are where the principal shops are found.

CAR HIRE

The international car hire companies have branches in each major city. Your hotel porter should be able to give details and help you with your arrangements.

TIPPING

Many hotels and restaurants include a service charge but where this is not the case an amount equivalent to between 10 and 15 per cent of the bill is customary. Additionally doormen, baggage porters and cloakroom attendants are generally given a gratuity.

Taxi drivers are customarily tipped between 10 and 15 per cent of the amount shown on the meter in addition to the fare.

SPEED LIMITS

The maximum permitted speed in the Republic is 55 mph (88 km/h) except where a lower speed limit is signposted.

SEAT BELTS

The wearing of seat belts is compulsory if fitted for drivers and front seat passengers. Additionaly, children under 12 are not allowed in front seats unless in a suitable safety restraint.

ANIMALS

It is forbildden to bring domestic animals (dogs, cats...) into the Republic of Ireland.

DUBLIN

SIGHTS

See : National Gallery★★★ BY — Castle (State apartments★★★ AC) BY — Christ Church Cathedral★★ (12C) BY — National Museum (Irish antiquities, Art and Industrial)★★ BY **M2** — Trinity College★ (Library★★) BY — National Museum (Zoological Collection)★ BY **M1** — Municipal Art Gallery★ BX **M3** — O'Connell Street★ (and the General Post Office) BXY — St. Stephen's Green★ BZ — St. Patrick's Cathedral (interior★) BZ — Phoenix Park (Zoological Gardens★).

Envir. : St. Doolagh's Church★ (13C) (open Saturday and Sunday, afternoon only) NE : 7 m. by L 87.

DUBLIN (BAILE ÁTHA CLIATH) Dublin 405 N 7 — pop. 528 882 — ⚙ 01.

🛆 Edmondstown, Rathfarnham ℰ 932461, S : 3 m. by N 81 — 🛆 Elm Park, Nutley House, Donnybrook ℰ 693438, S : 3 m. — 🛆 Lower Churchtown Rd, Milltown ℰ 977060, S : by T 43 — 🛆 Royal Dublin, Bull Island ℰ 336346.

✈ ℰ 379900, Telex 31266, N : 5 ½ m. by N 1 — **Terminal :** Busaras (Central Bus Station) Store St.

⛴ to Holyhead (B & I Line) 2-3 daily (3 h 30 mn - 4 h 45 mn) — to the Isle of Man : Douglas (Isle of Man Steam Packet Co.) June to September 1-6 weekly (4 h 30 mn).

🛈 14 Upper O'Connell St. ℰ 747733 — Dublin Airport ℰ 376387 — Baggot St., ℰ 747733 (weekdays only in summer).

Belfast 103 — Cork 154 — Londonderry 146.

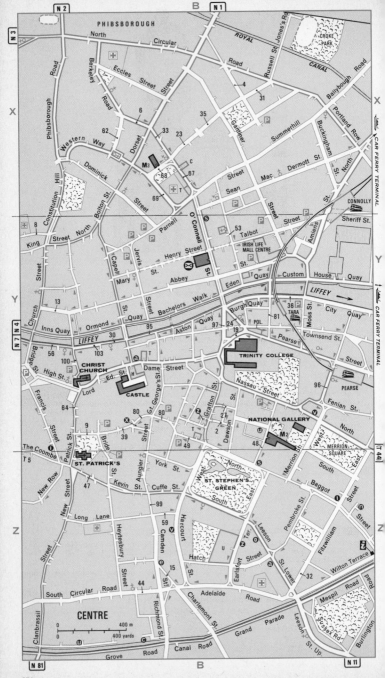

PHIBSBOROUGH

ROYAL

CROKE
PARK

North   Circular

Road

Russell St Jone's Rd

Ballybough Road

X   X

Berkeley   Eccles   Street   Street   4   31   Summerhill   Portland Row

Phibsborough Road

Western Way

6

35   Gardiner   Buckingham

Dorset   33   23

62

Dominick

Constitution Hill

M3   C

68   67

69   T

Sean   Street   Mac   Dermott   St.   North

CONNOLLY

Street

Bolton St.   O'Connell   Street   Street   Sheriff St.

Parnell

King   Street   North

8

53   Talbot   Amiens

Jervis   Henry   Street   IRISH LIFE   MALL CENTRE

Capel

Mary   Abbey   Eden   Custom   House   Quay

Church   Street

13   Street   Bachelors   Walk   Burgh Quay   LIFFEY

36   City   Quay
TARA

Inns Quay   Ormond   Quay   Aston   Quay   97   24   Townsend St.   81

N 7 N 4

LIFFEY   30   95   19   POL   Pearse   Street

56   103   Dame   Street   TRINITY COLLEGE

100   CHRIST   CHURCH

High St.   Ed. St.   H   Nassau   Street   96

Bride   St.   CASTLE   Lord   Gt. George's St.   PEARSE

Francis   Street   64   80   80   Grafton St.   NATIONAL GALLERY

9   39   Street   2   21   M2   MERRION SQUARE

The Coombe   X   49   Dawson   St.   48   West   North

T 5   ST. PATRICK'S   Bride   47   York   St.   North   South

New Row   Kevin   St.   Cuffe   St.   ST. STEPHEN'S GREEN   Baggot

Patrick St.   99   West   East

New Street   Long   Lane   Heytesbury   Street   59   Harcourt   South   Pembroke St.   Fitzwilliam

Clanbrassil Street   15   Camden   St.   V   Hatch   Leeson   St. Lower   32   Wilton Terrace

44   Adelaide   Road   Earlsfort   Street   Mespil   Road   Sussex Rd.

CENTRE   South   Circular   Road   Charlemont St.   Grand   Parade

400 m
0
400 yards

Richmond St.   Canal   Road   Leeson   St. Up.   Burlington

274

DUBLIN

Anne Street South	BY 2	Charlotte Street	BZ 15	Merchants Quay	BY 56
Dawson Street	BY	College Street	BY 19	Montague Street	BZ 59
Duke Street	BY 27	Denmark Street	BX 23	Mountjoy Street	BX 62
Grafton Street	BY	D'Olier Street	BY 24	Nicholas Street	BY 64
Henry Street	BY	Essex Quay	BY 30	Parnell Square East	BX 67
Irish Life Mall Centre	BY	Fitzgibbon Street	BX 31	Parnell	
O'Connell Street	BXY	Fitzwilliam Place	BZ 32	Square North	BX 68
		Frederick Street North	BX 33	Parnell Square West	BX 69
Belvidere Place	BX 4	Gardiner Place	BX 35	Stephen Street	BY 80
Blessington Street	BX 6	George's Quay	BY 36	Tara Street	BY 81
Brunswick Street North	BY 8	Golden Lane	BY 39	Wellington Quay	BY 95
Bull Alley	BY 9	Harrington Street	BZ 44	Westland Row	BY 96
Chancery Street	BY 13	Kevin Street Upper	BZ 47	Westmoreland Street	BY 97
		Kildare Street	BYZ 48	Wexford Street	BY 99
		King Street South	BY 49	Winetavern Street	BY 100
		Malborough Street	BY 53	Wood Quay	BY 103

Conrad, Earlsfort Terr., ℰ 765555, Fax 765424, ⌗, ⌗ – ⌗ ⌗ rm ▥ 🆃🆅 ☎ ⅙ 🅿 – 🔺 300. ⚞ 🅰🅴 ⓞ 𝗩𝗜𝗦𝗔. ⌗
BZ z
M 30.00/40.00 t. and a la carte ⅙ 7.00 – **181 rm** 120.00/150.00 t., **9 suites** 280.00/550.00 t.

Berkeley Court, Lansdowne Rd, Ballsbridge, ℰ 601711, Telex 30554, Fax 617238, ⌗, ▦ – ⌗ ▤ rest 🆃🆅 ☎ ⇐⇒ 🅿 – 🔺 250. ⚞ 🅰🅴 ⓞ 𝗩𝗜𝗦𝗔. ⌗
BY
M 14.50/19.00 t. and a la carte ⅙ 5.00 – ⌗ 7.50 – **200 rm** 115.00/145.00 t., **9 suites** 225.00/1200.00 t.

Westbury, Grafton St., ℰ 6791122, Telex 91091, Fax 6797078 – ⌗ ▤ rest 🆃🆅 ☎ 🅿 –
🔺 250. ⚞ 🅰🅴 ⓞ 𝗩𝗜𝗦𝗔. ⌗
BY z
M 14.50/19.00 t. and a la carte ⅙ 4.25 – ⌗ 7.50 – **198 rm** 115.00/145.00 t., **8 suites** 225.00/1200.00 t.

Shelbourne (T.H.F.), 27 St. Stephen's Green, ℰ 766471, Telex 93653, Fax 616006 – ⌗ 🆃🆅 ☎ ⌗ – 🔺 400. ⚞ 🅰🅴 ⓞ 𝗩𝗜𝗦𝗔
BZ s
M 18.00/22.00 t. and a la carte ⅙ 5.50 – ⌗ 9.50 – **162 rm** 105.00/185.00 t., **5 suites** 210.00/525.00 t.

Gresham, O'Connell St., ℰ 746881, Telex 32473, Fax 787175 – ⌗ ▤ rest 🆃🆅 ☎ ⅙ ⇐⇒ – 🔺 300
BY s
172 rm, **10 suites**.

Jurys, Pembroke Rd, Ballsbridge, ℰ 605000, Telex 93723, Fax 605540, ⍇ heated – ⌗ ⌗ rm ▤ rest 🆃🆅 ☎ ⅙ 🅿 – 🔺 400. ⚞ 🅰🅴 ⓞ 𝗩𝗜𝗦𝗔. ⌗
M 15.50/19.50 t. and a la carte ⅙ 5.75 – ⌗ 7.75 – **294 rm** 93.00/104.00 t., **4 suites** 300.00/500.00 t.

Annex: **Jurys (Towers)**, Pembroke Rd, Ballsbridge, ℰ 605000, Telex 93723, Fax 605540 – ⌗ ⌗ rm ☎ ⅙ 🅿. ⚞ 🅰🅴 ⓞ 𝗩𝗜𝗦𝗔. ⌗
M (see Jurys H. above) – ⌗ 7.75 – **98 rm** 135.00/165.00 t., **2 suites** 300.00/500.00 t.

Buswells, 25-26 Molesworth St., ℰ 764013, Telex 90622, Fax 762090 – ⌗ 🆃🆅 ☎ – 🔺 100. ⚞ 🅰🅴 ⓞ 𝗩𝗜𝗦𝗔
BY u
M (closed lunch Sunday and Bank Holidays and Saturday) 10.50 **st.** (lunch) and dinner a la carte ⅙ 4.50 – ⌗ 6.50 – **67 rm** 49.00/78.00 t.

Stephens Hall, 14-17 Lower Leeson St., ℰ 610585, Fax 610606 – ⌗ 🆃🆅 ☎ 🅿. ⚞ 🅰🅴 ⓞ 𝗩𝗜𝗦𝗔. ⌗
BZ o
M (closed Saturday and Sunday) (dinner only) (restricted menu) a la carte approx. 11.00 **st.** ⅙ 4.75 – ⌗ 6.00 – **37 rm** 80.00/120.00 **st.**, **34 suites** 120.00/160.00 **st.** – SB (weekends only) 140.00/200.00 **st.**

Mont Clare, Merrion Sq., ℰ 616799, Fax 615663 – ⌗ 🆃🆅 ▥ ☎ 🅿 – 🔺 150. ⚞ 🅰🅴 ⓞ 𝗩𝗜𝗦𝗔. ⌗
BY v
M 11.50/15.00 **st.** and a la carte ⅙ 4.60 – ⌗ 7.00 – **74 rm** 72.00/150.00 t. – SB (weekends only and weekdays only July and August) 85.50 **st.**

Russell Court, 21-23 Harcourt St., ℰ 784991, Fax 784066 – ⌗ 🆃🆅 ☎ – 🔺 100. ⌗   BZ v
20 rm, **1 suite**.

Longfield's, 10 Lower Fitzwilliam St., ℰ 761367, Fax 761542 – ⌗ 🆃🆅 ☎   BZ i
28 rm.

Raglan Lodge without rest., 10 Raglan Rd, off Pembroke Rd, Ballsbridge, ℰ 606697, Fax 606781, ⌗ – 🆃🆅 ☎ 🅿. ⚞ 🅰🅴 𝗩𝗜𝗦𝗔. ⌗
7 rm ⌗ 46.00/82.00 **st.**

Leeson Court, 26-27 Lower Leeson St., ℰ 763380 – ⌗ 🆃🆅 ☎   BZ a
20 rm

✿ **Patrick Guilbaud**, 46 St. James Pl., St. James' St., off Lower Baggot St., ℰ 764192, French rest. – ▤. ⚞ 🅰🅴 ⓞ 𝗩𝗜𝗦𝗔
BZ n
closed Saturday lunch, Sunday and Bank Holidays – **M** 15.50/27.00 t. and a la carte 20.50/32.50 t.
Spec. Casserole of Dublin Bay prawns and lobster with aromatic butter, Black pudding, sweetbreads and crubeens with a pepper and red wine sauce, Fillet of new season lamb with homemade pasta (spring only).

Park, 40 The Mews, Main Street, Blackrock, SE : 4 ½ m. by T 44 ℰ 886177, Fax 834365 – ⚞ 🅰🅴 ⓞ 𝗩𝗜𝗦𝗔
by T44
closed Saturday lunch, Sunday and Bank Holidays – **M** 12.00/26.50 t. ⅙ 7.50.

XXX **Le Coq Hardi,** 35 Pembroke Rd, ✆ 689070 – Ⓟ. AE VISA
closed Saturday lunch, Sunday, 2 weeks August, 2 weeks Christmas and Bank Holidays – **M** 16.00 **t.** (lunch) and a la carte 23.50/30.50 **t.** 🍾 7.50.

XX **Old Dublin,** 90-91 Francis St., ✆ **542028, Russian-Scandinavian rest.** – AE VISA
closed Saturday lunch, Sunday and Bank Holidays – **M** 11.00/20.50 **t.** 🍾 4.50. BY **i**

XX **La Vie en Rose,** 6a Upper Stephen St., ✆ **781771, French rest.** – AE VISA BY **x**
closed Sunday, Monday and Bank Holidays – **M** 12.00/22.00 **t.**

XX **Locks,** 1 Windsor Terr., Portobello, ✆ **543391** – AE VISA BZ **u**
closed Saturday lunch, Sunday, 1 week Christmas and Bank Holidays – **M** 12.95/17.50 **t.** and a la carte 🍾 5.15.

XX **Shannons,** Portobello Harbour, ✆ **782933** – Ⓟ. AE VISA BZ **c**
closed Sunday, 25 to 31 December and Bank Holidays – **M** 12.50/23.00 **t.** and a la carte 🍾 6.00.

XX **Les Frères Jacques,** 74 Dame St., ✆ **6794555, Fax 6794725** – AE VISA BY **a**
closed Saturday lunch, Sunday, Christmas, New year and Bank Holidays – **M** 13.00/20.00 **t.** and a la carte 🍾 6.50.

XX **Kapriol,** 45 Lower Camden St., ✆ **751235, Italian rest.** – AE VISA BZ **e**
closed Sunday and last 3 weeks August – **M** (dinner only) a la carte 17.00/28.00 **t.** 🍾 4.75.

XX **Osprey's,** 41-42 Shelbourne Rd, Ballsbridge, ✆ **608087** – AE VISA
closed Saturday lunch, Sunday, – **M** 10.50/22.00 **t.** and dinner a la carte 🍾 5.00.

at Dublin Airport N : 6 ½ m. by N 1 – ✉ 01 Dublin :

Dublin International (T.H.F.), ✆ **379211, Telex 32849, Fax 425874** – rm TV ☎ ♿ Ⓟ – 120. AE VISA
M 8.95/13.95 **t.** and a la carte 🍾 4.95 – ☕ 6.50 – **195 rm** 68.00/91.00 **t.** – SB (weekends only) 90.00/110.00 **st.**

Italy
Italia

PRACTICAL INFORMATION

LOCAL CURRENCY

Italian Lire : 1000 lire = 0.88 US $ (Jan. 91)

TOURIST INFORMATION

Welcome Office (Ente Provinciale per il Turismo), closed Saturday and Sunday :
— Via Parigi 5 - 00185 ROMA, ☎ 06/463748, Telex 624682
— Via Marconi 1 - 20123 MILANO, ☎ 02/809662
See also telephone number and address of other Tourist Information offices in the text of the towns under ▯.
American Express :
— Piazza di Spagna 38 - 00187 ROMA, ☎ 06/67641, Fax 678 24 56
— Via Brera 3 - 20121 MILANO, ☎ 02/85571, Fax 80 83 16

AIRLINES

ALITALIA : Via Bissolati 13 - 00187 ROMA, ☎ 06/46881
Piazzale Pastore o dell'Arte (EUR) - 00144 ROMA, ☎ 06/54441
Via Albricci 5 - 20122 MILANO, ☎ 02/62817
AIR FRANCE : Via Vittorio Veneto 93 - 00187 ROMA, ☎ 06/4818741
Piazza Cavour 2 - 20121 MILANO, ☎ 02/77381
PAN AM : Via Bissolati 46 - 00187 ROMA, ☎ 06/4773
Piazza Velasca 5 - 20122 MILANO, ☎ 02/877241
TWA : Via Barberini 59 - 00187 ROMA, ☎ 06/47241
Corso Europa 9/11 - 20122 MILANO, ☎ 02/77961

FOREIGN EXCHANGE

Money can be changed at the Banca d'Italia, other banks and authorised exchange offices (Banks close at 1.15pm and at weekends)

POSTAL SERVICES

Local post offices : open Monday to Saturday 8.00am to 2.00pm

General Post Office (open 24 hours only for telegrams) :
— Piazza San Silvestro 00187 ROMA — Piazza Cordusio 20123 MILANO

SHOPPING

In the index of street names those printed in red are where the principal shops are found. In Rome, the main shopping streets are : Via del Babuino, Via Condotti, Via Frattina, Via Vittorio Veneto ; in Milan : Via Dante, Via Manzoni, Via Monte Napoleone, Corso Vittorio Emanuele.

BREAKDOWN SERVICE

Certain garages in the centre and outskirts of towns operate a 24 hour breakdown service. If you break down the police are usually able to help by indicating the nearest one.
A free car breakdown service (a tax is levied) is operated by the A.C.I. for foreign motorists carrying the fuel card (Carta Carburante). The A.C.I. also offers telephone information in English (8am to 5pm) for road and weather conditions and tourist events : 06/4212.

TIPPING

As well as the service charge, it is the custom to tip employees. The amount can vary with the region and the service given.

SPEED LIMITS

On motorways, the maximum permitted speed is 130 km/h - 80 mph for vehicles over 1000 cc, 110 km/h - 68 mph for all other vehicles. On other roads, the speed limit is 90 km/h - 56 mph all days.

ROME

SIGHTS

Rome's most famous sights are indicated on the town plans pp. 2 to 5. For a more complete visit see the Green Guide to Italy.

ROME (ROMA) 00100 🇮🇹🇮🇹🇮🇹 ㉖ – Pop. 2 803 931 – alt. 20 – ✿ 06.

🏌 and 🏌 Parco de' Medici (closed Tuesday) ⊠ 00148 Roma SW : 4,5 km 𝒫 655 34 77.

🏌 Fioranello (closed Wednesday) at Santa Maria delle Mole ⊠ 00040 Roma SE : 19 km 𝒫 608291.

🏌 and 🏌 (closed Monday) at Olgiata ⊠ 00123 Roma NO : 19 km 𝒫 3789141.

✈ Ciampino SE : 15 km 𝒫 724241, Telex 611168 and Leonardo da Vinci di Fiumicino 𝒫 60121, Telex 620511 – Alitalia, via Bissolati 13 ⊠ 00187 𝒫 46881 and piazzale Pastore o dell'Arte (EUR) ⊠ 00144 𝒫 54442151.

🚇 Termini 𝒫 464923 – Tiburtina 𝒫 4956626.

🛈 via Parigi 5 ⊠ 00185 𝒫 463748 ; at Termini station 𝒫 465461 ; at Fiumicino Airport 𝒫 6011255.

A.C.I. via Cristoforo Colombo 261 ⊠ 00147 𝒫 5106 and via Marsala 8 ⊠ 00185 𝒫 49981, Telex 610686.

Distances from Rome are indicated in the text of the other towns listed in this Guide.

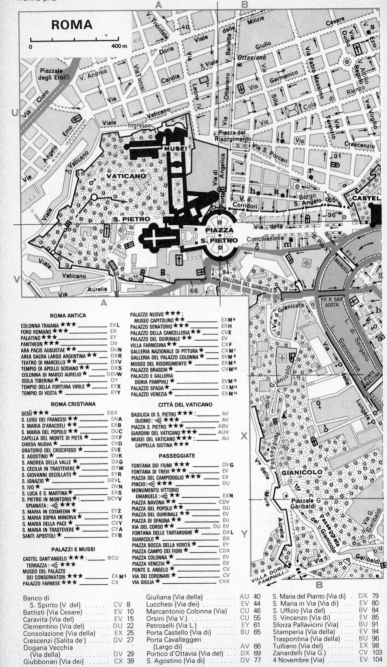

ROMA

0   400 m

ROMA ANTICA

COLONNA TRAIANA ★★★	EXL
FORO ROMANO ★★★	EX
PALATINO ★★★	EY
PANTHEON ★★★	DV
ARA PACIS AUGUSTAE ★★	DUN
AREA SACRA LARGO ARGENTINA ★★	DXR
TEATRO DI MARCELLO ★★	DXV
TEMPIO DI APOLLO SOSIANO ★★	DXS
COLONNA DI MARCO AURELIO ★	DEVW
ISOLA TIBERINA ★	DY
TEMPIO DELLA FORTUNA VIRILE ★	EYX
TEMPIO DI VESTA ★	EYY

ROMA CRISTIANA

GESÙ ★★★	DEX
S. LUIGI DEI FRANCESI ★★	DVA
S. MARIA D'ARACOELI ★★	EXB
S. MARIA DEL POPOLO ★★	DUC
CAPELLA DEL MONTE DI PIETÀ ★	DXF
CHIESA NUOVA ★	CVD
ORATORIO DEL CROCIFISSO ★	EVE
S. AGOSTINO ★	DVK
S. ANDREA DELLA VALLE ★	DXG
S. CECILIA IN TRASTEVERE ★	DYW
S. GIOVANNI DECOLLATO ★	EYR
S. IGNAZIO ★	DEVL
S. IVO ★	DVN
S. LUCA E S. MARTINA ★	EXS
S. PIETRO IN MONTORIO ★ :	BCYV
SPANATA : ◄ ★★★	
S. MARIA IN COSMEDIN ★	EYZ
S. MARIA SOPRA MINERVA ★	DVX
S. MARIA DELLA PACE ★	CVY
S. MARIA IN TRASTEVERE ★	CYA
SANTI APOSTOLI ★	EVB

PALAZZI E MUSEI

CASTEL SANT'ANGELO ★★★ :	BCU
TERRAZZA : ◄ ★★★	
MUSEO DEL PALAZZO	
DEI CONSERVATORI ★★★	EX M⁵
PALAZZO FARNESE ★★★	CX

PALAZZO NUOVO ★★★	
MUSEO CAPITOLINO ★★★	EX M⁶
PALAZZO SENATORIO ★★★	EXH
PALAZZO DELLA CANCELLERIA ★★	CVE
PALAZZO DEL QUIRINALE ★★	CXF
VILLA FARNESINA ★★	CX
GALLERIA NAZIONALE DI PITTURA ★★	CX M⁷
GALLERIA DEL PALAZZO COLONNA ★	EV M⁸
MUSEO DEL RISORGIMENTO ★	EX M⁹
PALAZZO BRASCHI ★	CVM¹⁰
PALAZZO E GALLERIA	
DORIA PAMPHILI ★	EV M¹²
PALAZZO SPADA ★	CX M¹³
PALAZZO VENEZIA ★	EX M¹⁴

CITTÀ DEL VATICANO

BASILICA DI S. PIETRO ★★★ :	AV
DUOMO : ◄ ★★★	AV
PIAZZA S. PIETRO ★★★	ABV
GIARDINI DEL VATICANO ★★★	AUV
MUSEI DEL VATICANO ★★★	AU
CAPPELLA SISTINA ★★★	

PASSEGGIATE

FONTANA DEI FIUMI ★★★	DVG
FONTANA DI TREVI ★★★	EV
PIAZZA DEL CAMPIDOGLIO ★★★	EX
PINCIO : ◄ ★★★	DU
MONUMENTO VITTORIO	
EMANUELE ★★	EX N
PIAZZA NAVONA ★★	CDV
PIAZZA DEL POPOLO ★★	DU
PIAZZA DEL QUIRINALE ★★	EU
PIAZZA DI SPAGNA ★★	EU
VIA DEL CORSO ★★	DU EV
FONTANA DELLE TARTARUGHE ★	DXL
GIANICOLO ★	BX
PIAZZA BOCCA DELLA VERITÀ ★	EY
PIAZZA CAMPO DEI FIORI ★	CDX
PIAZZA COLONNA ★	EV
PIAZZA VENEZIA ★	EX
PONTE S. ANGELO ★	CV
VIA DEI CORONARI ★	CV
VIA GIULIA ★	CVX

Banco di
S. Spirito (V. del)		CV 8
Battisti (Via Cesare)		EV 10
Caravita (Via del)		EV 15
Clementino (Via del)		DU 22
Consolazione (Via della)		EX 25
Crescenzi (Salita de')		DV 27
Dogana Vecchia		
(Via della)		DV 29
Giubbonari (Via dei)		CX 39

Giuliana (Via della)		AU 40
Lucchesi (Via dei)		EV 44
Marcantonio Colonna (Via)		CU 46
Orsini (Via V.)		CU 55
Petroselli (Via L.)		EY 61
Porta Castello (Via di)		BU 65
Porta Cavalleggeri		
(Largo di)		AV 66
Portico d'Ottavia (Via del)		DX 69
S. Agostino (Via di)		DV 77

S. Maria del Pianto (Via di)		DX 79
S. Maria in Via (Via di)		EV 80
S. Uffizio (Via del)		BV 84
S. Vincenzo (Via di)		EV 85
Sforza Pallavicini (Via)		BU 91
Stamperia (Via della)		EV 94
Traspontina (Via della)		BU 96
Tulliano (Via del)		EV 98
Zanardelli (Via G.)		CV 103
4 Novembre (Via)		EV 104

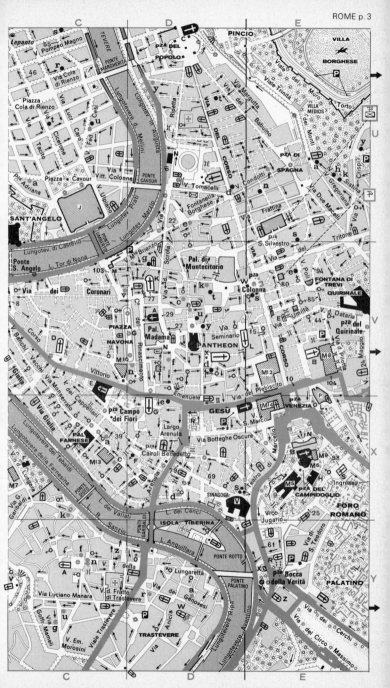

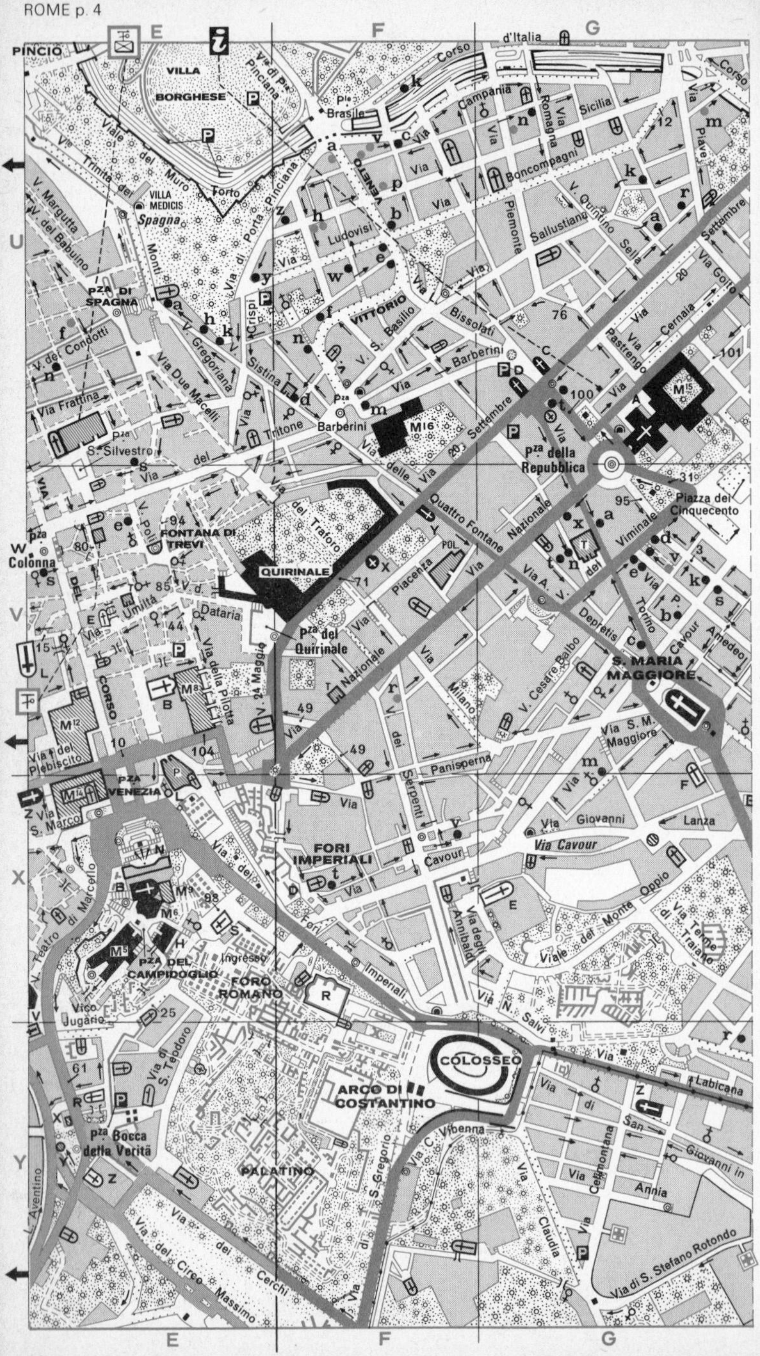

PINCIO

VILLA
BORGHESE

E

i

F

Corso

G

d'Italia

Campania

Romana

Sicilia

k

12

m

VILLA
MEDICIS

Spagna

PZA DI
SPAGNA

U

V. Marquita

IV. del Babuino

Viale del Muro Torto

Viale del

Trinita del Monti

P

P

P

Pza
Brasile

a

Via di Porta Pinciana

C

Via

Boncompagni

Via

p

b

Via

Via

Ludovisi

h

w

z

VITTORIO

V. S. Basilio

Bissolati

Piemonte

Sallustiana

n

k

Via Quintino Sella

r

a

Via

Cernia

Via

Gotilo

settembre

m

101

76

f

Via de Condotti

V. d. Croce

Via

a

h

k

Crispi

Via

Gregoriana

Sistina

i

n

Via

del

Tritone

d

Via

Barberini

Barberini

C.

Via

settembre

100

20

M15

31

Via Frattina

Pza

S. Silvestro

e

FONTANA DI
TREVI

94

Via

del Traforo

QUIRINALE

X

POL.

71

Piacenza

pza della
Repubblica

95

Piazza del
Cinquecento

x

r

n

del

Viminale

d

k

s

b

W
Colonna

pza

S

80

V. d.

Umiltà

144

E

Dataria

85

pza del
Quirinale

Via Nazionale

Via

Depretis

Via

Torino

Via Cavour

Amedeo

V

L

CORSO

Via della Pilotta

94 Mag

B

49

Nazionale

Via

Milano

V. Cesare Balbo

r

S. MARIA
MAGGIORE

M12

Via del
Plebiscito

10

104

49

Via

Panisperna

Via

Carpegna

dei

Via S. M.
Maggiore

m

F

PZA
VENEZIA

Via
S. Marco

M4

FORI
IMPERIALI

Via Cavour

Via Giovanni

Lanza

X

B

Mc

N

M6

Via dei

Via

Cavour

E

Via del Monte Oppio

Viale del Monte Oppio

Via di Tempio

PZA DEL
CAMPIDOGLIO

FORO
ROMANO

Ingresso

R

Via

Imperiali

Via N. Salvi

Via

Annia

Labicana

pza Bocca
della Verità

ARCO DI
COSTANTINO

COLOSSEO

Via

di

San

Z

Via Giovanni in

Y

z

PALATINO

Via C. Vibenna

Via di S. Gregorio

Via

Claudia

Via di S. Stefano Rotondo

Via

del

Circo

Massimo

dei

Via

Annia

E

F

G

ROMA

ROMA ANTICA

ARCO DI COSTANTINO ★★★	FY
BASILICA DI MASSENZIO ★★★	FX R
COLONNA TRAIANA ★★★	EX L
COLOSSEO ★★★	FGY
FORI IMPERIALI ★★★	FX
FORO ROMANO ★★★	EX
PALATINO ★★★	EFY
TEATRO DI MARCELLO ★★	EX V
COLONNA DI MARCO AURELIO ★	EV W
TEMPIO DELLA FORTUNA VIRILE ★	EY X
TEMPIO DI VESTA ★	EY Y

ROMA CRISTIANA

GESU ★★★	EX Z
S. GIOVANNI IN LATERANO ★★★	HY
S. MARIA MAGGIORE ★★★	GV
S. ANDREA AL QUIRINALE ★★	FV X
S. CARLO	
ALLE QUATTRO FONTANE ★★	FVY
S. CLEMENTE ★★	GYZ
S. MARIA DEGLI ANGELI ★★	GU A
S. MARIA D'ARACOELI ★★	EX B
S. MARIA DELLA VITTORIA ★★	GU C
S. SUSANNA ★★	GU D
ORATORIO DEL CROCIFISSO ★	EV E
S. IGNAZIO ★	EV L
S. GIOVANNI DECOLLATO ★	EY R
S. LUCA E S. MARTINA ★	EX S
S. MARIA IN COSMEDIN ★	EY Z
S. PIETRO IN VINCOLI ★	GX E
S. PRASSEDE ★	GVX F
SANTI APOSTOLI ★	EV B

PALAZZI E MUSEI

MUSEO NAZIONALE ROMANO ★★★	GU M15
MUSEO DEL PALAZZO	
DEI CONSERVATORI ★★★	EX M5
PALAZZO NUOVO ★★★	
MUSEO CAPITOLINO ★★★	EX M6
PALAZZO SENATORIO ★★★	EX H
PALAZZO BARBERINI ★★★	FU M16
PALAZZO DEL QUIRINALE ★★	EV
GALLERIA DEL PALAZZO COLONNA ★	EV M8
MUSEO DEL RISORGIMENTO ★	EX M9
PALAZZO E GALLERIA	
DORIA PAMPHILI ★	EV M12
PALAZZO VENEZIA ★	EX M14

PASSEGGIATE

FONTANA DI TREVI ★★★	EV
PIAZZA DEL CAMPIDOGLIO ★★★	EX
MONUMENTO VITTORIO	
EMANUELE II ★	EX N
PIAZZA DEL QUIRINALE ★★	FV
PIAZZA DI SPAGNA ★★	EU
VIA VITTORIO VENETO ★★	FU
PIAZZA COLONNA ★	EV
PIAZZA BOCCA DELLA VERITÀ ★	EY
PIAZZA DI PORTA MAGGIORE ★	JX
PIAZZA VENEZIA ★	EX
PORTA PIA ★	HU

North area Monte Mario, Stadio Olimpico, via Flaminia-Parioli, Villa Borghese, via Salaria, via Nomentana (Plans : Rome pp. 2 to 5) :

🏨 **Cavalieri Hilton** ⑤, via Cadlolo 101 ⊠ 00136 ℰ 31511, Telex 625337, Fax 31512241, ≤ town, ☆, « Terraces and park », ⊐, ⅗ – ﹩ ■ �📺 ☎ & ⇐ 🅿 – ⚘ 25-2500. 🆀 🕃 ⓪ E 𝘝𝘐𝘚𝘈, ⅗ rest   by via Trionfale   AU
M a la carte 80/100000 – ⊆ 30000 – **374 rm** 370/520000 apartments 850/2300000.

🏨 **Lord Byron** ⑤, via De Notaris 5 ⊠ 00197 ℰ 3220404, Telex 611217, Fax 3220405, ☛ – ﹩ ■ 📺 ☎. 🆀 🕃 ⓪ E 𝘝𝘐𝘚𝘈
M see rest. Relais le Jardin below – ⊆ 20000 – **50 rm** 350/500000 apartments 600/900000.
by lungotevere in Augusta   DU

🏨 **Aldrovandi Palace Hotel,** via Aldrovandi 15 ⊠ 00197 ℰ 3223993, Telex 616141, Fax 3221435, ⊐, ☛ – ﹩ ⅗ ■ 📺 ☎ & ⇐ 🅿 – ⚘ 50-350. 🆀 🕃 ⓪ E 𝘝𝘐𝘚𝘈, ⅗
M Grill Le Relais Rest. a la carte 75/110000 – **143 rm** ⊆ 380/400000 apartments 650/2000000.
by viale Trinità   EU

🏨 **Polo** without rest., piazza Gastaldi 4 ⊠ 00197 ℰ 3221041, Telex 623107, Fax 3221359 – ﹩ ■ 📺 ☎ – ⚘ 80. 🆀 🕃 ⓪ E 𝘝𝘐𝘚𝘈. ⅗   by lungotevere in Augusta   DU
66 rm ⊆ 230/325000.

🏨 **Rivoli,** via Torquato Taramelli 7 ⊠ 00197 ℰ 3224042, Telex 614615, Fax 870143 – ﹩ ■ 📺 ☎ – ⚘ 40   by lungotevere in Augusta   DU
55 rm.

🏨 **Albani** without rest., via Adda 45 ⊠ 00198 ℰ 84991, Telex 625594, Fax 8499399 – ﹩ ■ 📺 ☎ ⇐ – ⚘ 80. 🆀 🕃 ⓪ E 𝘝𝘐𝘚𝘈. ⅗   by via Piave   GU
157 rm ⊆ 250/350000 apartments 400000.

🏨 **Borromini** without rest., via Lisbona 7 ⊠ 00198 ℰ 8841321, Telex 621625, Fax 8417550 – ﹩ ■ 📺 ☎ & ⇐ – ⚘ 50-100. 🆀 🕃 ⓪ E 𝘝𝘐𝘚𝘈. ⅗   by viale Regina Margherita   JU
⊆ 19000 – **75 rm** 269/300000 apartments 440/510000.

🏨 **Degli Aranci,** via Oriani 11 ⊠ 00197 ℰ 870202, Telex 805250, ☆ – ﹩ ■ 📺 ☎ – ⚘ 50. 🆀 🕃 E 𝘝𝘐𝘚𝘈. ⅗   by lungotevere in Augusta   DU
M 45000 – **40 rm** ⊆ 169/250000.

🏨 **Clodio** without rest., via di Santa Lucia 10 ⊠ 00195 ℰ 317541, Telex 625050, Fax 3250745 – ﹩ ■ 📺 ☎. 🆀 🕃 ⓪ E 𝘝𝘐𝘚𝘈. ⅗   by via Ottaviano Barletta   BU
114 rm ⊆ 135/187000, ■ 20000.

🏨 **Panama** without rest., via Salaria 336 ⊠ 00199 ℰ 862558, Telex 620189, Fax 864454, ☛ – ﹩ 📺 ☎. 🆀 🕃 ⓪ E 𝘝𝘐𝘚𝘈   by via Piave   GU
43 rm ⊆ 120/175000.

🏮 ☼☼ **Relais le Jardin,** via De Notaris 5 ⊠ 00197 ℰ 3220404, Fax 3609541, Elegant rest. – ■. 🆀 🕃 ⓪ E 𝘝𝘐𝘚𝘈. ⅗   by lungotevere in Augusta   DU
closed Sunday – **M** (booking essential) a la carte 110/165000
Spec. Rotolino di cernia con caponatina al basilico (Summer), Fusoli al ceppo con sugo di anitra e fiori di zucchine, Filetto di maiale al miele e piselli. **Wines** Marino, Torre Ercolana.

XXX **Relais la Piscine,** via Mangili 6 ⊠ 00197 ℰ 3216126, ☆, ⊐, ☛ – ■ 🅿. 🆀 🕃 ⓪ E 𝘝𝘐𝘚𝘈   by lungotevere in Augusta   DU
closed Sunday dinner – **M** a la carte 75/110000.

XXX **Il Peristilio,** via Monte Zebio 10/d ⊠ 00195 ℰ 3223623, Fax 3223639 – ■. 🆀 ⓪ E 𝘝𝘐𝘚𝘈. ⅗   by via Marcantonio Colonna   CU
closed Monday and 5 to 26 August – **M** a la carte 40/75000 (12%).

XX **Al Fogher,** via Tevere 13/b ⊠ 00198 ℰ 8417032, Typical Venetian rest. – ■. 🆀 ⓪   by via Piave   GU
closed Saturday lunch and Sunday – **M** a la carte 43/64000.

XX **Al Ceppo,** via Panama 2 ⊠ 00198 ℰ 8419696 – ■ 🆀 🕃 ⓪ E 𝘝𝘐𝘚𝘈
closed Monday and 8 to 30 August – **M** a la carte 37/63000.
by viale Regina Margherita   JU

XX **Il Caminetto,** viale dei Parioli 89 ⊠ 00197 ℰ 803946, ☆ – ■. 🆀 🕃 ⓪ 𝘝𝘐𝘚𝘈. ⅗
closed Thursday and 12 to 18 August – **M** a la carte 36/55000.
by lungotevere in Augusta   DU

X **Delle Vittorie,** via Monte Santo 62/64 ⊠ 00195 ℰ 386847 – 🆀 🕃 ⓪ E 𝘝𝘐𝘚𝘈. ⅗
closed Sunday, 1 to 20 August and 23 December-3 January – **M** a la carte 35/53000.
by via Marcantonio Colonna   CU

Middle-western area San Pietro (Vatican City), Gianicolo, corso Vittorio Emanuele, piazza Venezia, Pantheon and Quirinale, Pincio and Villa Medici, piazza di Spagna, Palatino and Fori (Plans : Rome pp. 2 and 3) :

🏨 **Hassler,** piazza Trinità dei Monti 6 ⊠ 00187 ℰ 6792651, Telex 610208, Fax 6789991, ≤ town from roof-garden rest. – ﹩ ■ 📺 ☎. 🆀 🕃 ⓪ E 𝘝𝘐𝘚𝘈. ⅗   EU   **a**
M a la carte 102/148000 – ⊆ 24000 – **100 rm** 380/560000.

🏨 **Eden,** via Ludovisi 49 ⊠ 00187 ℰ 4743551, Telex 610567, Fax 4821584, « Roof garden rest. with ≤ town » – ﹩ ■ 📺 ☎ – ⚘ 50-100   EU   **y**
110 rm.

🏨 **D'Inghilterra,** via Bocca di Leone 14 ⊠ 00187 ℰ 672161, Telex 614552, Fax 6840828 – ﹩ ■ 📺 ☎ &. 🆀 🕃 ⓪ E 𝘝𝘐𝘚𝘈. ⅗   EU   **n**
M a la carte 45/82000 – ⊆ 22000 – **97 rm** 275/387000 apartments 430/580000.

Jolly Leonardo da Vinci, via dei Gracchi 324 ⌧ 00192 ℘ 39680, Telex 611182, Fax 3610138 – 🛗 🗏 📺 🕿 ⬛ ⟵ – 🔬 30-220. 🖭 🛐 ⓞ 🅴 𝖵𝖨𝖲𝖠. ℅ rest
CU **r**
M 45000 – **256 rm** ⇌ 235/340000 – ½ p 215/280000.

De la Ville Inter-Continental, via Sistina 69 ⌧ 00187 ℘ 67331, Telex 620836, Fax 6784213 – 🛗 🗏 📺 🕿 – 🔬 40-120. 🖭 🛐 ⓞ 🅴 𝖵𝖨𝖲𝖠. ℅
EU **h**
M a la carte 64/112000 – **189 rm** ⇌ 371/472000 apartments 590/1080000.

Visconti Palace without rest., via Cesi 37 ⌧ 00193 ℘ 3684, Telex 622489, Fax 3200551 – 🛗 🗏 📺 🕿 & ⬛ – 🔬 25-150. 🖭 🛐 ⓞ 🅴 𝖵𝖨𝖲𝖠. ℅
CU **u**
247 rm ⇌ 220/320000 apartments 400000.

Plaza without rest., via del Corso 126 ⌧ 00186 ℘ 672101, Telex 624669 – 🛗 🗏 🕿 – 🔬 50. 🖭 🛐 ⓞ 🅴 𝖵𝖨𝖲𝖠. ℅
DU **d**
⇌ 18000 – **207 rm** 200/290000 apartments 530000.

Dei Borgognoni without rest., via del Bufalo 126 ⌧ 00187 ℘ 6780041, Telex 623074, Fax 6841501 – 🛗 🗏 📺 🕿 ⬛ ⟵ – 🔬 25-60. 🖭 🛐 ⓞ 🅴 𝖵𝖨𝖲𝖠. ℅
EUV **s**
50 rm ⇌ 330/390000 apartment 550000.

Cicerone and Rest. Robià, via Cicerone 55/c ⌧ 00193 ℘ 3576, Telex 622498, Fax 6541383 – 🛗 🗏 📺 🕿 – 🔬 160. 🖭 🛐 ⓞ 🅴 𝖵𝖨𝖲𝖠. ℅
CU **t**
M a la carte 38/56000 – ⇌ 20000 – **237 rm** 220/320000 apartments 420/660000.

Atlante Star, via Vitelleschi 34 ⌧ 00193 ℘ 6879558, Telex 622355, Fax 6872300, « Roof-garden rest. with ⩻ St. Peter's Basilica » – 🛗 ⬿ 🗏 📺 🕿 – 🔬 70. 🖭 🛐 ⓞ 🅴 𝖵𝖨𝖲𝖠. ℅ rest
BU **r**
M Les Etoiles Rest. a la carte 90/120000 – **61 rm** ⇌ 395/420000 apartments 520/2250000 – ½ p 160/260000.

Delle Nazioni without rest., via Poli 7 ⌧ 00187 ℘ 6792441, Telex 614193 – 🛗 🗏 📺 🕿. 🖭 🛐 ⓞ 🅴 𝖵𝖨𝖲𝖠. ℅
EV **e**
74 rm ⇌ 225/307000 apartment 580000.

Colonna Palace without rest., piazza Montecitorio 12 ⌧ 00186 ℘ 6781341, Telex 621467, Fax 6794496 – 🛗 🗏 📺 🕿. 🖭 🛐 ⓞ 🅴 𝖵𝖨𝖲𝖠. ℅
EV **s**
105 rm ⇌ 295/400000 apartments 590000.

Giulio Cesare without rest., via degli Scipioni 287 ⌧ 00192 ℘ 3210751, Telex 613010, Fax 3211736, 🖈 – 🛗 🗏 📺 🕿 🅿 – 🔬 60. 🖭 🛐 ⓞ 🅴 𝖵𝖨𝖲𝖠. ℅
CU **s**
86 rm ⇌ 260/370000.

Nazionale, piazza Montecitorio 131 ⌧ 00186 ℘ 6789251, Telex 621427, Fax 6786677, 🍴 – 🛗 🗏 📺 🕿. 🖭 🛐 ⓞ 🅴 𝖵𝖨𝖲𝖠. ℅
DV **t**
M (closed Sunday) a la carte 32/53000 – **86 rm** ⇌ 220/350000 apartments 450/600000.

Del Sole al Pantheon without rest., piazza della Rotonda 63 ⌧ 00186 ℘ 6780441, Fax 6840689 – 🛗 🗏 📺 🕿. 🖭 🛐 ⓞ 🅴 𝖵𝖨𝖲𝖠. ℅
DV **u**
⇌ 20000 – **26 rm** 250/360000.

Columbus, via della Conciliazione 33 ⌧ 00193 ℘ 6865435, Telex 620096, Fax 6864874, « Beautiful decor in 15C style building », 🖈 – 🛗 🗏 📺 🕿 🅿 – 🔬 30-200. 🖭 🛐 ⓞ 🅴 𝖵𝖨𝖲𝖠. ℅ rest
BV **m**
M a la carte 52/73000 – **105 rm** ⇌ 155/210000 apartments 250/400000 – ½ p 155/205000.

Atlante Garden without rest., via Crescenzio 78/a ⌧ 00193 ℘ 6872361, Telex 623172, Fax 6872315 – 🛗 ⬿ 🗏 📺 🕿 – 🔬 30. 🖭 🛐 ⓞ 🅴 𝖵𝖨𝖲𝖠
BU **f**
43 rm ⇌ 250/295000.

Internazionale without rest., via Sistina 79 ⌧ 00187 ℘ 6793047, Telex 614333, Fax 6784764 – 🛗 🗏 📺 🕿. 🖭 🛐 🅴 𝖵𝖨𝖲𝖠. ℅
EU **k**
37 rm ⇌ 150/220000 apartments 500/550000.

Gerber without rest., via degli Scipioni 241 ⌧ 00192 ℘ 3216485, Fax 3217048 – 🛗 🕿. 🖭 🛐 🅴 𝖵𝖨𝖲𝖠. ℅
BU **s**
27 rm ⇌ 104/164000.

Della Torre Argentina without rest., corso Vittorio Emanuele 102 ⌧ 00186 ℘ 6548251, Telex 623281, Fax 6541641 – 🛗 🕿. 🖭 🛐 ⓞ 🅴 𝖵𝖨𝖲𝖠. ℅
DX **e**
⇌ 20000 – **32 rm** 99/140000, 🗏 25000.

Sant'Anna without rest., borgo Pio 134 ⌧ 00193 ℘ 6541602, Fax 6548717 – 🗏 📺 🕿. 🖭 🛐 ⓞ 🅴 𝖵𝖨𝖲𝖠
BU **h**
18 rm ⇌ 130/180000.

Della Conciliazione without rest., borgo Pio 165 ⌧ 00193 ℘ 6875400, Fax 6541164 – 🛗 🕿 & 🖭 🛐 ⓞ 🅴 𝖵𝖨𝖲𝖠
BU **k**
⇌ 10000 – **60 rm** 70/120000.

Senato without rest., piazza della Rotonda 73 ⌧ 00186 ℘ 6793231, Fax 6840297, ⩻ Pantheon – 🛗 🗏 📺 🕿. ℅
DV **y**
51 rm ⇌ 123/165000, 🗏 25000.

Margutta without rest., via Laurina 34 ⌧ 00187 ℘ 3614193 – 🛗 🕾. 🖭 🛐 ⓞ 🅴 𝖵𝖨𝖲𝖠 ℅
DU **t**
21 rm ⇌ 105000.

Portoghesi without rest., via dei Portoghesi 1 ⌧ 00186 ℘ 6864231, Fax 6876976 – 🛗 🗏 🕿. 🛐 🅴 𝖵𝖨𝖲𝖠
DV **g**
27 rm ⇌ 73/115000.

XXX **El Toulà**, via della Lupa 29/b ⊠ 00186 🖉 6873498, Fax 6871115, Elegant rest. – 🗐 🖭 🕃
　🕦 E 𝚅𝙸𝚂𝙰 ⚓ – closed Saturday lunch, Sunday, August and 24 to 26 December – **M**
(booking essential) a la carte 61/89000 (15%)　　　　　　　　　　　　　　　　　　DU **e**

XXX ❀ **Patrizia e Roberto del Pianeta Terra,** via Arco del Monte 95 (via dei Pettinari)
⊠ 00186 🖉 6869893, Elegant rest. – 🗐. 🖭 🕃 🕦 E 𝚅𝙸𝚂𝙰　　　　　　　　　　　　CX **c**
M closed Monday and August (dinner only) (booking essential) a la carte 70/150000 (15%)
Spec. Zuppa di lenticchie e gamberi, Orata con patate e porcini, Filetti di triglia alla purea di finocchio. Wines
Sauvignon, Vallocaia.

XXX **Passetto,** via Zanardelli 14 ⊠ 00186 🖉 6540569 – ⚓= 🗐. 🖭 🕃 🕦 E 𝚅𝙸𝚂𝙰 ⚓　　CV **v**
closed Sunday, Monday lunch and February – **M** a la carte 47/79000.

XXX **Ranieri,** via Mario de' Fiori 26 🖉 6791592 – 🗐. 🖭 🕃 🕦 E 𝚅𝙸𝚂𝙰 ⚓　　　　　EU **f**
closed Sunday – **M** (booking essential) a la carte 47/78000.

XXX **4 Colonne,** via della Posta 4 ⊠ 00186 🖉 6547152, booking essential – 🗐　　　DV **n**

XX ❀ **Quinzi Gabrieli,** via delle Coppelle 6 ⊠ 00186 🖉 6879389 – 🖭 🕦　　　　　DV **c**
closed Sunday and August – **M** (dinner only) (booking essential) (fish only)
a la carte 80/150000
Spec. Antipasti di mare, Filetti di branzino marinati, Spigola al pomodoro. Wines Riesling.

XX **Camponeschi,** piazza Farnese 50 ⊠ 00186 🖉 6874927, Fax 6865244, « Summer service
with ⧼ Farnese palace » – 🗐. 🖭 🕦 𝚅𝙸𝚂𝙰 ⚓　　　　　　　　　　　　　　　　　　CX **a**
closed Sunday – **M** (dinner only) (booking essential) a la carte 56/80000 (13%).

XX ❀ **La Rosetta,** via della Rosetta 9 ⊠ 00187 🖉 6861002, Fax 6548841, Seafood trattoria –
🗐. 🕦 𝚅𝙸𝚂𝙰　　　　　　　　　　　　　　　　　　　　　　　　　　　　　　　　　DV **e**
closed Saturday, Sunday and August – **M** (booking essential) a la carte 65/101000 (15%)
Spec. Gamberetti all'arancia marinati, Linguine ai filetti di triglia, Mazzancolle al pomodoro verde. Wines
Sauvignon, Cannonau.

XX **I Preistorici,** vicolo Orbitelli 13 ⊠ 00186 🖉 6892796, Elegant rest. – 🖭 🕃 🕦 E 𝚅𝙸𝚂𝙰
closed Sunday and August – **M** (booking essential) a la carte 35/60000.　　　　BV **b**

XX **Piperno,** Monte de' Cenci 9 ⊠ 00186 🖉 6540629, Roman rest. – 🗐　　　　　　DX **d**

XX **Piccola Roma,** via Uffici del Vicario 36 ⊠ 00186 🖉 6798606 – 🗐. 🖭 🕦 𝚅𝙸𝚂𝙰. ⚓　DV **k**
closed Sunday – **M** a la carte 30/42000.

XX **Eau Vive,** via Monterone 85 ⊠ 00186 🖉 6541095, Catholic missionaries; international
cuisine, « 16C building » – 🗐. 🖭 🕃 𝚅𝙸𝚂𝙰　　　　　　　　　　　　　　　　　　DV **f**
closed Sunday and August – **M** (booking essential for dinner) a la carte 40/67000.

X **Hostaria da Cesare,** via Crescenzio 13 ⊠ 00193 🖉 6861227, Trattoria-pizzeria with
seafood – ⚓= 🗐. 🖭 🕃 🕦 E 𝚅𝙸𝚂𝙰 ⚓　　　　　　　　　　　　　　　　　　　　CU **a**
closed Sunday dinner, Monday, Easter, August and Christmas – **M** a la carte 43/69000.

X **L'Orso 80,** via dell'Orso 33 ⊠ 00186 🖉 6864904 – 🗐. 🖭 🕃 🕦 E 𝚅𝙸𝚂𝙰 ⚓　　CDV **r**
closed Monday and 8 to 20 August – **M** a la carte 41/60000.

X **Al 59-da Giuseppe,** via Brunetti 59 ⊠ 00186 🖉 3619019, Bolognese rest. – 🗐　DU **y**

Central eastern area via Vittorio Veneto, via Nazionale, Viminale, Santa Maria Maggiore,
Colosseum, Porta Pia, via Nomentana, Stazione Termini, Porta San Giovanni (Plans : Rome
pp. 4 and 5)

🏨🏨🏨 **Le Grand Hotel,** via Vittorio Emanuele Orlando 3 ⊠ 00185 🖉 4709, Telex 610210, Fax
4747307 – 🛗 🗐 📺 🕃 🕹 – 🛦 25-500. 🖭 🕃 🕦 E 𝚅𝙸𝚂𝙰 ⚓　　　　　　　　　　GU **t**
M a la carte 95/130000 – ⊊ 23000 – **168 rm** 405/595000 apartments 893/1547000.

🏨🏨🏨 **Excelsior,** via Vittorio Veneto 125 ⊠ 00187 🖉 4708, Telex 610232, Fax 4826205 – 🛗 🗐 📺
☎ – 🛦 25-450. 🖭 🕃 🕦 E 𝚅𝙸𝚂𝙰 ⚓　　　　　　　　　　　　　　　　　　　　　FU **b**
M a la carte 86/125000 – ⊊ 27500 – **359 rm** 381/584000 apartments 833/1547000.

🏨🏨🏨 **Ambasciatori Palace,** via Vittorio Veneto 70 ⊠ 00187 🖉 47493, Telex 610241, Fax
4743601, 🏧 – 🛗 🗐 📺 ☎ 🕹 – 🛦 50-200. 🖭 🕃 🕦 E 𝚅𝙸𝚂𝙰 ⚓ rest　　　　　FU **e**
M Grill Bar ABC Rest. a la carte 61/100000 – **149 rm** ⊊ 300/400000 apartments 550/750000.

🏨🏨 **Bernini Bristol,** piazza Barberini 23 ⊠ 00187 🖉 463051, Telex 610554, Fax 4824266 – 🛗
⚓= rm 🗐 📺 ☎ – 🛦 40-120. 🖭 🕃 🕦 E 𝚅𝙸𝚂𝙰 ⚓　　　　　　　　　　　　　　FU **m**
M a la carte 65/108000 – ⊊ 20000 – **126 rm** 340/470000 apartments 536/1190000.

🏨🏨 **Holiday Inn Minerva,** piazza della Minerva 69 ⊠ 00186 🖉 6841888, Fax 6794165 – 🛗
⚓= rm 🗐 📺 🕹 – 🛦 80. 🖭 🕃 🕦 E 𝚅𝙸𝚂𝙰 ⚓ rest　　　　　　　　　　　　　DV **d**
M 90/120000 – ⊊ 30000 – **134 rm** 320/456000 apartments 800/1200000 – ½ p 406/456000.

🏨🏨 **Jolly Vittorio Veneto,** corso d'Italia 1 ⊠ 00198 🖉 8495, Telex 612293, Fax 8841104 – 🛗
🗐 📺 ☎ 🚗 – 🛦 35-450. 🖭 🕃 🕦 E 𝚅𝙸𝚂𝙰 ⚓ rest　　　　　　　　　　　　　FU **k**
M 50000 – **200 rm** ⊊ 255/375000 – ½ p 238/305000.

🏨🏨 **Quirinale,** via Nazionale 7 ⊠ 00184 🖉 4707, Telex 610332, Fax 4820099, « Rest. Summer
service in garden » – 🛗 🗐 📺 ☎ 🕹 – 🛦 250. 🖭 🕃 🕦 E 𝚅𝙸𝚂𝙰 ⚓ rest　　　　GV **x**
M 50/60000 – **186 rm** ⊊ 242/330000 apartments 450/700000 – ½ p 215/292000.

🏨🏨 **Regina Baglioni,** via Vittorio Veneto 72 ⊠ 00187 🖉 476851, Telex 620863, Fax 485483 – 🛗
⚓= rm 📺 ☎. 🖭 🕃 🕦 E 𝚅𝙸𝚂𝙰 ⚓ rest　　　　　　　　　　　　　　　　　　　FU **e**
M a la carte 65/103000 – **130 rm** ⊊ 320/450000 apartments 650/1200000.

🏨🏨 **Majestic,** via Veneto 50 ⊠ 00187 🖉 486841, Telex 622262, Fax 460984 – 🛗 🗐 📺 ☎ 🕹 –
🛦 150. 🖭 E 𝚅𝙸𝚂𝙰 ⚓　　　　　　　　　　　　　　　　　　　　　　　　　　　FU **f**
M a la carte 70/120000 – **95 rm** ⊊ 480/540000.

🏥 **Metropole,** via Principe Amedeo 3 🖂 00185 ℰ 4774, Telex 611061, Fax 4740413 – 🛗 ▤ 📺
🕿 ⅃ ⇦ – 🛦 90. 🖭 🖭 ⓪ ᴇ 𝘝𝘐𝘚𝘈. 🕉 rest   GV **e**
M a la carte 40/65000 – **268 rm** 🖵 220/270000. – ½ p 240/270000.

🏥 **Victoria,** via Campania 41 🖂 00187 ℰ 473931, Telex 610212, Fax 4941330 – 🛗 ▤ 📺 🕿. 🖭
🖭 ᴇ 𝘝𝘐𝘚𝘈. 🕉 rest   FU **c**
M (residents only) a la carte 44/71000 – **110 rm** 🖵 220/350000.

🏥 **Mediterraneo,** via Cavour 15 🖂 00184 ℰ 4884051, Fax 4744105 – 🛗 ▤ 📺 🕿 – 🛦 25-90.
🖭 🖭 ⓪ ᴇ 𝘝𝘐𝘚𝘈. 🕉   GV **k**
M (closed Saturday) 43000 – **268 rm** 🖵 232/327000 apartments 440/880000.

🏥 **Genova** without rest., via Cavour 33 🖂 00184 ℰ 476951, Telex 621599, Fax 4827580 – 🛗 ▤
📺 ⅃ 𝘝𝘐𝘚𝘈. 🕉   GV **b**
91 rm 🖵 197/294000.

🏥 **Londra e Cargill,** piazza Sallustio 18 🖂 00187 ℰ 473871, Telex 622227, Fax 4746674 – 🛗
▤ 📺 🕿 ⇦ – 🛦 25-200. 🖭 🖭 ⓪ ᴇ 𝘝𝘐𝘚𝘈. 🕉   GU **k**
M a la carte 45/70000 – 🖵 15000 – **105 rm** 250/350000 apartments 400/600000 –
½ p 200/230000.

🏥 **Forum,** via Tor de' Conti 25 🖂 00184 ℰ 6792446, Telex 622549, Fax 6786479, « Roof
garden rest. with ≤ Imperial Forums » – 🛗 ▤ 📺 🕿 ⇦ – 🛦 100. 🖭 🖭 ⓪ ᴇ 𝘝𝘐𝘚𝘈. 🕉
M (closed Sunday) a la carte 73/118000 – 🖵 25000 – **81 rm** 270/390000 apartments
550/650000.   FX **t**

🏥 **Massimo D'Azeglio,** via Cavour 18 🖂 00184 ℰ 4880646, Telex 610556, Fax 4827386 – 🛗
▤ 📺 🕿 – 🛦 200. 🖭 🖭 ⓪ ᴇ 𝘝𝘐𝘚𝘈. 🕉   GV **s**
M (closed Sunday) 43000 – **209 rm** 🖵 202/284000.

🏥 **Pullman Boston,** via Lombardia 47 🖂 00187 ℰ 473951, Telex 622247, Fax 4821019 – 🛗 ▤
📺 🕿 – 🛦 25-90   FU **z**
125 rm.

🏥 **Imperiale,** via Vittorio Veneto 24 🖂 00187 ℰ 4756351, Telex 621071 – 🛗 ▤ 📺 🕿. 🖭 🖭
⓪ ᴇ 𝘝𝘐𝘚𝘈. 🕉 rest   FU **n**
M a la carte 42/60000 – **85 rm** 🖵 270/400000 – ½ p 235/305000.

🏥 **Mondial** without rest., via Torino 127 🖂 00184 ℰ 472861, Telex 612219, Fax 4824822 – 🛗
▤ 📺 🕿 ⇦ – 🛦 25. 🖭 🖭 ⓪ ᴇ 𝘝𝘐𝘚𝘈. 🕉   GV **a**
77 rm 🖵 190/270000.

🏥 **Napoleon,** piazza Vittorio Emanuele 105 🖂 00185 ℰ 737646, Telex 611069, Fax 737646 –
🛗 ▤ 📺 🕿 – 🛦 25-60. 🖭 🖭 ⓪ ᴇ 𝘝𝘐𝘚𝘈. 🕉   HX **a**
M (dinner only) a la carte 39/56000 – **80 rm** 🖵 160/260000.

🏥 **La Residenza** without rest., via Emilia 22 🖂 00187 ℰ 4744480, Fax 485721 – 🛗 ▤ 📺 🕿
🅿. 🕉   FU **w**
27 rm 🖵 115/200000.

🏥 **Universo,** via Principe Amedeo 5 🖂 00185 ℰ 476811, Telex 610342 – 🛗 ▤ 📺 🕿 ⅃ –
🛦 25-300   GV **e**
207 rm.

🏥 **Britannia** without rest., via Napoli 64 🖂 00184 ℰ 463153, Telex 611292, Fax 462343 – 🛗 ▤
📺 🕿 🅿. 🖭 🖭 ⓪ ᴇ 𝘝𝘐𝘚𝘈   GV **t**
32 rm 🖵 146/226000.

🏨 **Commodore** without rest., via Torino 1 🖂 00184 ℰ 485656, Telex 612170, Fax 4747562 – 🛗
🖵 25000 – **60 rm** 185/270000.   GV **c**

🏨 **Marcella** without rest., via Flavia 106 🖂 00187 ℰ 4746451, Telex 621351, Fax 4815832 – 🛗
▤ 📺 🕿 🖭 🖭 ⓪ ᴇ 𝘝𝘐𝘚𝘈. 🕉   GU **r**
68 rm 🖵 140/210000.

🏨 **Regency** without rest., via Romagna 42 🖂 00187 ℰ 4819281, Telex 622321, Fax 4746850 –
🛗 ▤ 📺 ⇦. 🖭 🖭 ⓪ ᴇ 𝘝𝘐𝘚𝘈   GU **n**
51 rm 🖵 200/300000.

🏨 **Sitea** without rest., via Vittorio Emanuele Orlando 90 🖂 00185 ℰ 4827560, Telex 614163,
Fax 4817637 – 🛗 ▤ 📺 🕿. 🖭 🖭 ⓪ ᴇ 𝘝𝘐𝘚𝘈   GU **t**
37 rm 🖵 160/242000 apartment 484000.

🏨 **Edera** ⌀ without rest., via Poliziano 75 🖂 00184 ℰ 7316341, Telex 623651, Fax 899371, 🚗
– 🛗 📺 🕿 🅿. 🖭 🖭 ⓪ ᴇ 𝘝𝘐𝘚𝘈. 🕉   GY **r**
48 rm 🖵 125/185000.

🏨 **Milani** without rest., via Magenta 12 🖂 00185 ℰ 4457051, Telex 614356, Fax 4462317 – 🛗
📺 🕿. 🕉   HU **z**
77 rm 🖵 173000.

🏨 **Colosseum** without rest., via Sforza 10 🖂 00184 ℰ 4827228, Fax 4827285 – 🛗 🕿. 🖭 🖭
⓪ ᴇ 𝘝𝘐𝘚𝘈. 🕉   GVX **m**
49 rm 🖵 97/158000.

🏨 **Diana,** via Principe Amedeo 4 🖂 00185 ℰ 4827541, Telex 611198, Fax 486998 – 🛗 ▤ 📺 🕿
– 🛦 25   GV **e**
187 rm.

🏨 **Canada** without rest., via Vicenza 58 ⊠ 00185 ℰ 4957385, Telex 613037, Fax 4450749 – 📳
🖩 📺 ☎ 🅰🅴 🚷 ⓓ 🅴 *VISA* ⋘ HU **e**
83 rm ⊡ 110/162000.

🏨 **King** without rest., via Sistina 131 ⊠ 00187 ℰ 4743487, Telex 626246, Fax 491047 – 📳 🖩
📺 ☎ 🅰🅴 🚷 ⓓ 🅴 *VISA* ⋘ FU **d**
72 rm ⊡ 130/185000.

🏨 **Nord-Nuova Roma** without rest., via Amendola 3 ⊠ 00185 ℰ 4885441, Fax 4817163 – 📳
🖩 📺 ☎ 🅰🅴 🚷 ⓓ 🅴 *VISA* ⋘ GV **x**
156 rm ⊡ 142/200000.

🏨 **Medici** without rest., via Flavia 96 ⊠ 00187 ℰ 4827319, Fax 4740767 – 📳 📺 🅰🅴 🚷 ⓓ
🅴 *VISA* ⋘ GU **a**
68 rm ⊡ 92/154000.

🏨 **Centro** without rest., via Firenze 12 ⊠ 00184 ℰ 464142, Telex 612125, Fax 4957729 – 📳 🖩
📺 ☎ 🅰🅴 🚷 ⓓ 🅴 *VISA* ⋘ GV **n**
38 rm ⊡ 130/180000.

🏨 **Igea** without rest., via Principe Amedeo 97 ⊠ 00185 ℰ 4466911 – 📳 ☎ ⋘ HV **u**
⊡ 8000 – **42 rm** 65/100000.

🏨 **Duca d'Alba** without rest., via Leonina 12 ⊠ 00184 ℰ 484712, Telex 620401, Fax 4884840
– 📳 🖩 🕸 🅰🅴 🚷 ⓓ 🅴 *VISA* FX **v**
25 rm ⊡ 85/120000, 🖩 20000.

XXXX ✿ **Sans Souci**, via Sicilia 20/24 ⊠ 00187 ℰ 4823845, Fax 4821771, Elegant tavern-late
night dinners – 🖩 🅰🅴 🚷 ⓓ 🅴 *VISA* ⋘ FU **p**
closed 13 August-4 September – **M** (dinner only) (booking essential) a la carte 74/128000
(15%)
Spec. Quenelle di spigola farcita all'astaco. Risotti e soufflé. Agnello pré-salé in crosta alla salsa di timo.
Wines Sauvignon, Rubesco.

XXX **Harry's Bar**, via Vittorio Veneto 150 ⊠ 00187 ℰ 4745832, booking essential – 🖩 FU **a**

XX **Piccolo Mondo**, via Aurora 39/d ⊠ 00187 ℰ 4814595, Elegant tavern – 🖩 FU **h**

XX **Coriolano**, via Ancona 14 ⊠ 00198 ℰ 8551122 – 🖩 🅰🅴 🚷 ⓓ 🅴 *VISA* HU **g**
closed Sunday and 3 August-2 September – **M** (booking essential) a la carte 64/106000
(15%).

XX **Cesarina**, via Piemonte 109 ⊠ 00187 ℰ 460828, Bolognese rest. – 🖩 🅰🅴 🚷 ⓓ 🅴 *VISA* ⋘
closed Sunday – **M** a la carte 40/68000. GU **n**

XX **Loreto**, via Valenziani 19 ⊠ 00187 ℰ 4742454, Seafood – 🖩 🅰🅴 ⋘ GU **m**
closed Sunday and 10 to 28 August – **M** a la carte 51/76000.

XX **Andrea**, via Sardegna 28 ⊠ 00187 ℰ 4821891, Fax 4828151 – 🖩 🅰🅴 🚷 ⓓ 🅴 *VISA* FU **v**
closed Sunday, Monday lunch and August – **M** (booking essential) a la carte 52/99000.

XX **Girarrosto Toscano**, via Campania 29 ⊠ 00187 ℰ 4821899, Fax 4821899 – 🖩 🅰🅴 🚷 ⓓ
🅴 *VISA* ⋘ FU **v**
closed Wednesday – **M** a la carte 48/77000.

X **La Taverna**, via Massimo d'Azeglio 3/f ⊠ 00184 ℰ 4744305 – 🖩 🅰🅴 🚷 ⓓ 🅴 *VISA* GV **v**
closed Saturday and 1 to 26 August – **M** a la carte 25/38000.

X **Hostaria Costa Balena**, via Messina 5/7 ⊠ 00198 ℰ 8417686, Seafood trattoria – 🖩 🅰🅴
🚷 ⓓ 🅴 *VISA* ⋘ HU **b**
closed Saturday lunch, Sunday and 10 to 29 August – **M** a la carte 28/53000.

X **Crisciotti-al Boschetto**, via del Boschetto 30 ⊠ 00184 ℰ 4744770, 🍽, Rustic trattoria
– 🖩 *VISA* FV **r**
closed Saturday and August – **M** a la carte 23/39000 (10%).

X **Tempio di Bacco**, via Lombardia 36/38 ⊠ 00187 ℰ 4814625, « Little hall fresco »
🖩 FU **h**

Southern area Aventino, Porta San Paolo, Terme di Caracalla, via Appia Nuova (Plans :
Rome pp. 2 to 5) :

🏨 **Sant'Anselmo** without rest., piazza Sant'Anselmo 2 ⊠ 00153 ℰ 5743547, Telex 622812,
Fax 5783604, 🝔 – 🕸 ☎ 🚷 *VISA* ⋘ by lungotevere Aventino DY
45 rm ⊡ 115/165000.

🏨 **Villa San Pio** without rest., via di Sant'Anselmo 19 ⊠ 00153 ℰ 5755231, Fax 5783604, 🝔
– 📳 🝔 ☎ 🚷 *VISA* ⋘ by lungotevere Aventino DEY
59 rm ⊡ 115/165000.

🏨 **Domus Maximi** 🕸 without rest., via Santa Prisca 11/b ⊠ 00153 ℰ 5782565 – ☎ 🚷
23 rm ⊡ 80/133000. by via del Circo Massimo EY

XX ✿ **Checchino dal 1887**, via Monte Testaccio 30 ⊠ 00153 ℰ 5746318, 🍽, Historical Rest.
typical roman food – 🅰🅴 🚷 ⓓ 🅴 *VISA* ⋘ by lungotevere Aventino DEY
closed August, Sunday dinner and Monday July-September – **M** (booking essential)
a la carte 51/74000 (15%).
Spec. Rigatoni con la pajata, Coda alla vaccinara, Padellotto di frattaglie. **Wines** Barbera.

XX **Da Severino**, piazza Zama 5/c ⊠ 00183 ℰ 7000872 – 🖩 🅰🅴 🚷 ⓓ 🅴 *VISA* ⋘
closed Sunday dinner, Monday, 1 to 28 August and 24 to 30 December – **M**
a la carte 50/73000. by via dell'Amba Aradam HY

Trastevere area (typical district) (Plan : Rome p. 3) :

XXX ✿ **Alberto Ciarla,** piazza San Cosimato 40 ⊠ 00153 ℰ 5818668, Fax 6884377, ╬ – AE ⓞ
E VISA ⋙   CY u
   closed Sunday, 12 to 28 August and 23 December-6 January – **M** (dinner only) (booking
   essential) a la carte 75/105000
   Spec. I crudi di pesce e crostacei, Zuppa di pasta e fagioli ai frutti di mare, Panacea calda di pesci e crostacei.
   Wines Velletri bianco.

XXX **Cul de Sac 2,** vicolo dell'Atleta 21 ⊠ 00153 ℰ 5813324 – ▤. AE ⓑ ⓞ VISA   DY a
   closed Sunday dinner, Monday and August – **M** (booking essential) a la carte 60/
   70000.

XX **Corsetti-il Galeone,** piazza San Cosimato 27 ⊠ 00153 ℰ 5816311, Seafood, « Typical
   ambient » – ▤. AE ⓑ ⓞ E VISA ⋙   CY g
   closed Wednesday – **M** a la carte 35/62000.

XX **Carlo Menta,** via della Lungaretta 101 ⊠ 00153 ℰ 5803737, Seafood – ▤. AE ⓑ ⓞ E
   VISA ⋙   CY z
   closed Monday, August and January – **M** (dinner only) (booking essential) a la carte 63/78000
   (15%).

XX Sabatini a Santa Maria in Trastevere, piazza di Santa Maria in Trastevere 13 ⊠ 00153
   ℰ 582026, ╬, Roman and seafood rest. .   CY h

XX **Galeassi,** piazza di Santa Maria in Trastevere 3 ⊠ 00153 ℰ 5803775, ╬, Roman and
   seafood rest. – ▤. ⋙   CY f
   closed Monday and 20 December-20 January – **M** a la carte 44/69000.

XX **Sabatini,** vicolo Santa Maria in Trastevere 18 ⊠ 00153 ℰ 5818307, ╬, Roman and
   seafood rest.   CY n
   closed Monday – **M** a la carte 48/90000.

XX **Checco er Carettiere,** via Benedetta 10 ⊠ 00153 ℰ 5817018, ╬, Typical Roman and
   seafood rest. – ▤. AE ⓞ VISA   CX k
   closed Sunday dinner, Monday and 10 August-10 September – **M** a la carte 50/69000.

XX **Pastarellaro,** via di San Crisogono 33 ⊠ 00153 ℰ 5810871, Roman and seafood rest. –
   ▤. AE ⓑ ⓞ E VISA   DY r
   closed Tuesday and August – **M** a la carte 40/56000 (10%).

Outskirts of Rome

on national road 1 - Aurelia :

🏨 **Jolly Hotel Midas,** via Aurelia al km 8 ⊠ 00165 ℰ 6506, Telex 622821, Fax 6808457, ⌇,
   ╬, ⋇ – ▯ ▤ TV 🕿 ら 🄿 – 🔬 800. AE ⓑ ⓞ E VISA ⋙ rest   by via Aurelia AV
   M 40000 – **357 rm** ⇌ 195/290000 – ½ p 185/235000.

🏨 **Villa Pamphili,** via della Nocetta 105 ⊠ 00164 ℰ 5862, Telex 626539, Fax 6257747, ┺,
   ⇌, ⌇ (covered in winter), ╬, ⋇ – ▯ ▤ TV 🕿 ら 🄿 – 🔬 25-500. AE ⓑ ⓞ E VISA
   ⋙ rest   by via Garibaldi BY
   M a la carte 42/70000 – **254 rm** ⇌ 200/265000.

🏨 **Holiday Inn St. Peter's,** via Aurelia Antica 415 ⊠ 00165 ℰ 5872, Telex 625434, Fax
   6237190, ⇌, ⌇, ╬, ⋇ – ▯ ⇆ rm ▤ TV 🕿 ら 🄿 – 🔬 25-300. AE ⓑ ⓞ E VISA
   ⋙   by via Garibaldi BY
   M a la carte 56/85000 – ⇌ 19000 – **321 rm** 208/307000.

🏨 **MotelAgip,** via Aurelia al km 8 ⊠ 00165 ℰ 6379001, Telex 613699, Fax 6379001, ⌇ – ▯ ▤
   TV 🕿 ら 🄿 – 🔬 25-160. AE ⓑ ⓞ E VISA ⋙ rest   by via Aurelia AV
   M 32000 – **213 rm** ⇌ 135/190000 – ½ p 143/198000.

XX **La Maielletta,** via Aurelia Antica 270 ⊠ 00165 ℰ 6374957, Fax 6374957, Typical Abruzzi
   rest. – 🄿. AE ⓑ ⓞ E VISA ⋙   by via Aurelia AV
   closed Monday – **M** a la carte 37/50000.

on national road 4 - Salaria :

🏨 **Motel la Giocca and Rest. L'Elite,** via Salaria 1223 ⊠ 00138 ℰ 8804365 and rest
   ℰ 8804503, Fax 8804495, ⌇ – ▯ ▤ 🕿 ⇜ 🄿 – 🔬 30. AE ⓑ ⓞ E VISA ⋙
   M *(closed Sunday dinner, 8 to 28 August and 23 December-6 January)* a la carte 45/64000 –
   ⇌ 18000 – **50 rm** 108/153000 apartments 192/228000, ▤ 30000 – P 150/186000.
                                                                                              by via Piave GU

🏨 **Eurogarden** without rest., raccordo anulare Salaria Flaminia ⊠ 00138 ℰ 8804507, ⌇, ╬
   – ▤ TV 🕿 ら 🄿 AE ⓞ VISA. ⋙   by via Piave GU
   ⇌ 15000 – **40 rm** 160000, ▤ 10000.

on the Ancient Appian way :

XX **Cecilia Metella,** via Appia Antica 125/127 ⊠ 00179 ℰ 5136743, ╬, « Shaded garden »
   – 🄿   by via Claudia GY
   closed Monday – **M** a la carte 38/62000.

P.T.O. →

to E.U.R. Garden City :

🏨 **Sheraton,** viale del Pattinaggio ⊠ 00144 ✆ 5453, Telex 626073, Fax 5423281, 〔ś, ℐ, ℀ – ⧢ 🗏 📺 ☎ ♿ 🅿 – 🔬 25-1800. 🖭 🕃 ⓞ Ⅎ 𝘝𝘐𝘚𝘈. ℀
   M a la carte 55/110000 – **591 rm** 🚊 420000 apartments 595/1700000.
   by via di San Gregorio   FY

🏨 **Shangri Là-Corsetti,** viale Algeria 141 ⊠ 00144 ✆ 5916441, Telex 614664, Fax 5413813, ℐ heated, 🍴, ℀ – ⧢ 🗏 📺 ☎ ♿ 🅿 – 🔬 25-80. 🖭 🕃 ⓞ Ⅎ 𝘝𝘐𝘚𝘈. ℀
   M (closed 11 to 31 August) a la carte 35/62000 – 🚊 12000 – **52 rm** 180/230000 apartments 250/350000.
   by via di San Gregorio   FY

🏨 **Dei Congressi** without rest., viale Shakespeare 29 ⊠ 00144 ✆ 5926021, Telex 614140, Fax 5911903 – ⧢ 🗏 ☎ – 🔬 25-300. 🖭 🕃 ⓞ Ⅎ 𝘝𝘐𝘚𝘈. ℀
   96 rm 🚊 145/210000.
   by via di San Gregorio   FY

🍴🍴 **Vecchia America-Corsetti,** piazza Marconi 32 ⊠ 00144 ✆ 5926601, Typical rest. and ale house – 🗏 🖭 🕃 ⓞ Ⅎ 𝘝𝘐𝘚𝘈
   by via di San Gregorio   FY
   closed Tuesday – **M** a la carte 43/69000.

on the motorway to Fiumicino close to the ring-road :

🏨 **Holiday Inn-Eur Parco dei Medici,** viale Castello della Magliana 65 ⊠ 00148 ✆ 68581, Telex 613302, Fax 6857005, ℐ, 🐎, ℀ – ⧢ 🗏 📺 ☎ ♿ 🅿 – 🔬 160-800. 🖭 🕃 ⓞ Ⅎ 𝘝𝘐𝘚𝘈. ℀
   by viale Trastevere   CY
   M 60000 – 🚊 15000 – **317 rm** 210/300000 – P 135000.

FLORENCE (FIRENZE) 50100 ℗ 988 ⑮, 429 K 15 – pop. 413 069 alt. 49 – ❀ 055.

See : Cathedral★★ : east end★★, dome★★★ (⁂★★) – Campanile★★ : ⁂★★ – Baptistry★★ : doors★★★, mosaics★★★ – Cathedral Museum★★ M1 – Piazza della Signoria★★ – Loggia della Signoria★ : Perseus★★★ by B. Cellini – Palazzo Vecchio★★★ – Uffizi Gallery★★★ – Bargello Palace and Museum★★★ – San Lorenzo★★★ : Church★★, Laurentian Library★★, Medici tombs★★★ in Medici Chapels★★ – Medici Riccardi★ : frescoes by Benozzo Gozzoli★★, Luca Giordano Gallery★★ – Church of Santa Maria Novella★★ : frescoes by Ghirlandaio★★★, Crucifix by Brunelleschi★★, frescoes★★ of the Spaniards' Chapel in the Green Cloisters★ – Ponte Vecchio★ – Pitti Palace★★ : Palatine Gallery★★★, Silver Museum★★, Works by the Macchiaioli★★ in Modern Art Gallery★ – Boboli Garden★ : ⁂★★ from the Citadel Belvedere ABZ – Monastery and Museum of St. Mark★★ : works by Fra Angelico★★★ – Academy Gallery★★ : main gallery★★★ – Piazza della Santissima Annunziata★ CX : frescoes★ in the church E, portico★ with corners decorated of terracotta medallions★★ in the Foundling Hospital – Church of Santa Croce★★ – Pazzi Chapel★★ – Excursion to the hills★★ : Church of San Miniato al Monte★★ – Strozzi Palace★★ BY F – Frescoes by Masaccio★★ in the Church of Santa Maria del Carmine AY Z – Last Supper of San Salvi★★ – Orsanmichele★ : tabernacle by Orcagna★★ BCY L – La Badia CY S : campanile★, delicate relief sculpture in marble★★, tombs★, Virgin appearing to St. Bernard★ by Filippino Lippi – Sassetti Chapel★★ and the Chapel of the Annunciation★ in the Holy Trinity Church BY N – Church of the Holy Spirit★ ABY R – Last Supper of Sant'Apollonia★ CVX V – Last Supper by Ghirlandaio★ AX X – New Market Loggia★ BY Y – Buonarroti's House★ DY Z – Museums : Archaeological★ (Chimera from Arezzo★★) CX M4, Florentine House★ BY M5, Science★ CY M6, Semi-precious Stone Workshop★ CX M7.

Envir. : Medici Villas★★ : garden★ of the Villa della Pretaia, Villa di Poggio a Caiano★ by ⑥ : 17 km – Cloisters★ in the Galluzzo Carthusian Monastery S : 6 km.

🐇 Dell'Ugolino (closed Monday), to Grassina ⊠ 50015 ✆ 2301009, S : 12 km.

✈ of Peretola NW : 4 km ✆ 373498 – Alitalia, lungarno Acciaiuoli 10/12 r, ⊠ 50123 ✆ 27889.

🚩 via Manzoni 16 ⊠ 50121 ✆ 2478141 – via de' Tornabuoni 15 ⊠ 50123 ✆ 216544, Telex 572263.

A.C.I. viale Amendola 36 ⊠ 50121 ✆ 24861.

Roma 277 ③ – Bologna 105 ⑧ – Milano 298 ⑧.

Plans on following pages

🏨 **Excelsior,** piazza Ognissanti 3 ⊠ 50123 ✆ 264201, Telex 570022, Fax 210278, « Rest. with summer service on terrace with ≤ » – ⧢ 🗏 📺 ☎ ♿ – 🔬 50-350. 🖭 🕃 ⓞ Ⅎ 𝘝𝘐𝘚𝘈. ℀ rest
   M a la carte 95/141000 – 🚊 22000 – **203 rm** 370/536000 apartments 1428000.
   AY **g**

🏨 **Savoy,** piazza della Repubblica 7 ⊠ 50123 ✆ 283313, Telex 570220, Fax 284840 – ⧢ 🗏 📺 ☎ ♿ – 🔬 150. 🖭 🕃 ⓞ Ⅎ 𝘝𝘐𝘚𝘈. ℀ rest
   BY **e**
   M (dinner only) a la carte 64/104000 – **101 rm** 🚊 330/530000 apartments 850/1030000.

🏨 **Villa Medici and Rest. Lorenzo de' Medici,** via Il Prato 42 ⊠ 50123 ✆ 261331, Telex 570179, Fax 261336, 🏡, ℐ, 🐎 – ⧢ 🗏 📺 ☎ – 🔬 30-90. 🖭 🕃 ⓞ Ⅎ 𝘝𝘐𝘚𝘈
   AX **g**
   M a la carte 55/110000 – 🚊 20000 – **103 rm** 321/500000 apartments 607/893000.

🏨 **Regency and Rest. Relais le Jardin,** piazza Massimo D'Azeglio 3 ⊠ 50121 ✆ 245247, Telex 571058, Fax 2342938, 🐎 – ⧢ 🗏 📺 ☎ 🔄 🖭 🕃 ⓞ Ⅎ 𝘝𝘐𝘚𝘈. ℀ rest
   DX **c**
   M (closed Sunday) (booking essential) a la carte 70/110000 – 🚊 20000 – **38 rm** 330/480000 apartments 520/860000.

🏨 **Helvetia e Bristol,** via dei Pescioni 2 ⊠ 50123 ✆ 287814, Telex 572696, Fax 288353 – ⧢ 🗏 📺 ☎ 🖭 🕃 ⓞ Ⅎ 𝘝𝘐𝘚𝘈
   BY **f**
   M a la carte 60/97000 – 🚊 24000 – **52 rm** 322/476000 apartments 584/1131000.

🏨 **Brunelleschi,** piazza Santa Elisabetta 3 ⊠ 50122 ✆ 562068, Telex 575805, Fax 219653 – ⧢ ℀ rm 🗏 📺 ☎ – 🔬 100. 🖭 🕃 ⓞ Ⅎ 𝘝𝘐𝘚𝘈. ℀ rest
   CY **p**
   M a la carte 47/74000 – **94 rm** 🚊 245/340000 apartments 400/520000 – ½ p 180/230000.

Plaza Hotel Lucchesi, lungarno della Zecca Vecchia 38 ⊠ 50122 𝒫 264141, Telex 570302, Fax 2480921, ≤ – 🛗 ▤ ⊡ ☎ 👌 – 🔬 50-100. ◭ 🕄 ⓪ Ε 𝘷𝘪𝘴𝘢 ❀ rest　　　　DY **f**
M (residents only) (closed Sunday) a la carte 58/87000 – **97 rm** ⊑ 238/340000 apartments 450000 – ½ p 220/288000.

Grand Hotel Baglioni, piazza Unità Italiana 6 ⊠ 50123 𝒫 218441, Telex 570225, Fax 215695, « Roof garden rest. with ≤ » – 🛗 🗐 ⊡ ☎ 👌 – 🔬 25-200. ◭ 🕄 ⓪ Ε 𝘷𝘪𝘴𝘢 ❀ rest　　　　BX **e**
M a la carte 48/63000 – **195 rm** ⊑ 235/330000 apartments 450/550000.

Grand Hotel Ciga, piazza Ognissanti 1 ⊠ 50123 𝒫 278781, Telex 570055, Fax 217400 – 🛗 🗐 ⊡ ☎. ◭ 🕄 ⓪ Ε 𝘷𝘪𝘴𝘢 ❀ rest　　　　AXY **a**
M a la carte 62/97000 – ⊑ 25000 – **107 rm** 488/595000 apartments 952/1666000.

Jolly, piazza Vittorio Veneto 4/a ⊠ 50123 𝒫 2770, Telex 570191, Fax 294794, « 🍷 on panoramic terrace » – 🛗 ⇆ rm 🗐 ⊡ ☎ – 🔬 30-100. ◭ 🕄 ⓪ Ε 𝘷𝘪𝘴𝘢 ❀ rest　　AX **u**
M 55000 – **167 rm** ⊑ 220/330000 – ½ p 220/275000.

Majestic, via del Melarancio 1 ⊠ 50123 𝒫 264021, Telex 570628, Fax 268428 – 🛗 🗐 ⊡ ☎ 👌 🚗 – 🔬 80. ◭ 🕄 ⓪ Ε 𝘷𝘪𝘴𝘢 ❀ rest　　　　BX **u**
M a la carte 39/56000 – ⊑ 25000 – **103 rm** 210/280000 apartments 460000 – ½ p 175/265000.

De la Ville, piazza Antinori 1 ⊠ 50123 𝒫 261805, Telex 570518, Fax 261809 – 🛗 🗐 ⊡ ☎ 👌 – 🔬 60. ◭ 🕄 ⓪ Ε 𝘷𝘪𝘴𝘢 ❀　　　　BX **n**
M a la carte 40/50000 – **75 rm** ⊑ 232/331000 apartments 560/660000.

Berchielli without rest., piazza del Limbo 6 r ⊠ 50123 𝒫 264061, Telex 575582, Fax 218636, ≤ – 🛗 🗐 ⊡ ☎ 👌 – 🔬 80. ◭ 🕄 ⓪ Ε 𝘷𝘪𝘴𝘢. ❀　　　　BY **b**
74 rm ⊑ 215/300000 apartments 426/495000.

Bernini Palace without rest., piazza San Firenze 29 ⊠ 50122 𝒫 278621, Telex 573616, Fax 268272 – 🛗 🗐 ⊡ ☎ – 🔬 40. ◭ 🕄 ⓪ Ε 𝘷𝘪𝘴𝘢　　　　CY **x**
86 rm ⊑ 250/360000 apartments 480000.

Montebello Splendid, via Montebello 60 ⊠ 50123 𝒫 298051, Telex 574009, Fax 211867, 🌮 – 🛗 🗐 ⊡ ☎ 👌 – 🔬 100. ◭ 🕄 ⓪ Ε 𝘷𝘪𝘴𝘢 ❀ rest　　　　AX **e**
M (closed Sunday) a la carte 43/83000 – **53 rm** ⊑ 230/330000 apartment 660000 – ½ p 150/255000.

Michelangelo, via Fratelli Rosselli 2 ⊠ 50123 𝒫 278711, Telex 571113, Fax 278717 – 🛗 🗐 ⊡ ☎ 🚗 – 🔬 50-250. ◭ 🕄 ⓪ Ε 𝘷𝘪𝘴𝘢 ❀ rest　　　　AX **w**
M a la carte 50/65000 – **138 rm** ⊑ 220/280000 – ½ p 218/285000.

Anglo American, via Garibaldi 9 ⊠ 50123 𝒫 282114, Telex 570289, Fax 268513 – 🛗 🗐 ⊡ ☎ – 🔬 50-150. ◭ 🕄 🕄 Ε 𝘷𝘪𝘴𝘢 ❀ rest　　　　AX **d**
M (closed Sunday) a la carte 56/79000 – **107 rm** ⊑ 220/310000 apartments 390/450000 – ½ p 205/295000.

Gd H. Minerva, piazza Santa Maria Novella 16 ⊠ 50123 𝒫 284555, Telex 570414, Fax 268281, 🍷 – 🛗 🗐 ⊡ ☎ 👌 – 🔬 30-90. ◭ 🕄 ⓪ Ε 𝘷𝘪𝘴𝘢 ❀ rest　　　　BX **s**
M a la carte 42/63000 – ⊑ 20000 – **96 rm** 210/280000 apartments 395000.

Augustus without rest., piazzetta dell'Oro 5 ⊠ 50123 𝒫 283054, Telex 570110, Fax 268557 – 🛗 🗐 ⊡ ☎. ◭ 🕄 ⓪ Ε 𝘷𝘪𝘴𝘢. ❀　　　　BY **a**
⊑ 18000 – **67 rm** 210/240000.

Kraft, via Solferino 2 ⊠ 50123 𝒫 284273, Telex 571523, Fax 298267, « Roof garden rest. with ≤ », 🍷 – 🛗 🗐 ⊡ ☎ – 🔬 50. ◭ 🕄 ⓪ Ε 𝘷𝘪𝘴𝘢 ❀ rest　　　　AX **c**
M a la carte 45/70000 – ⊑ 25000 – **68 rm** 230/300000.

Londra, via Jacopo da Diacceto 18 ⊠ 50123 𝒫 262791, Telex 571152, Fax 210682, 🌮 – 🛗 🗐 ⊡ ☎ 👌 🚗 – 🔬 200. ◭ 🕄 ⓪ Ε 𝘷𝘪𝘴𝘢 ❀ rest　　　　AX **n**
M a la carte 49/74000 – ⊑ 20000 – **107 rm** 210/280000 – ½ p 197/267000.

Lungarno without rest., borgo Sant'Jacopo 14 ⊠ 50125 𝒫 264211, Telex 570129, Fax 268437, ≤, « Collection of modern pictures » – 🛗 🗐 ⊡ ☎ – 🔬 30. ◭ 🕄 ⓪ Ε 𝘷𝘪𝘴𝘢　BY **d**
⊑ 18000 – **66 rm** 185/260000 apartments 350/380000.

Alexander, viale Guidoni 101 ⊠ 50127 𝒫 4378951, Telex 574026, Fax 416818 – 🛗 🗐 ⊡ ☎ 👌 🅿 – 🔬 50-400. ◭ 🕄 ⓪ Ε 𝘷𝘪𝘴𝘢 ❀ rest　　　　by ⑥
M a la carte 35/56000 – **88 rm** ⊑ 217/296000 – ½ p 183/252000.

Pullman Astoria Palazzo Gaddi, via del Giglio 9 ⊠ 50123 𝒫 2398022, Telex 571070, Fax 214632 – 🛗 🗐 ⊡ ☎ – 🔬 50-130. ◭ 🕄 ⓪ Ε 𝘷𝘪𝘴𝘢 ❀ rest　　　　BX **f**
M (closed Sunday) a la carte 42/63000 – **88 rm** ⊑ 220/320000 apartment 540000 – ½ p 180/225000.

Holiday Inn and Rest. la Tegolaia, viale Europa 205 ⊠ 50126 𝒫 686841, Telex 570376, Fax 686806, 🌮, 🍷 heated – 🛗 ⇆ rm 🗐 ⊡ ☎ 👌 🅿 – 🔬 50-120. ◭ 🕄 ⓪ Ε 𝘷𝘪𝘴𝘢 ❀ rest　　　　by ③
M a la carte 45/70000 – **92 rm** ⊑ 230/360000.

Pierre without rest., via de' Lamberti 5 ⊠ 50123 𝒫 217512, Telex 573175, Fax 2396573 – 🛗 🗐 ⊡ ☎. ◭ 🕄 ⓪ Ε 𝘷𝘪𝘴𝘢　　　　BY **k**
⊑ 20000 – **39 rm** 273000.

Raffaello, viale Morgagni 19 ⊠ 50134 𝒫 439871, Telex 580035, Fax 434374 – 🛗 🗐 ⊡ ☎ 🚗 – 🔬 110. ◭ 🕄 ⓪ Ε 𝘷𝘪𝘴𝘢 ❀ rest　　　by via del Romito AV
M a la carte 35/55000 – **141 rm** ⊑ 255/275000 apartments 300/450000 – ½ p 124/244000.

FIRENZE

0   300 m

SESTO FIORENTINO

MICHELIN

★★ S. LORENZO
★★ STA MA NOVELLA

LE CASCINE

pza Vittorio Veneto

83 km PISA
AUTOSTRADA A 1

ARNO

LUNGARNO

PONTE VECCHIO

GIARDINO DI BOBOLI

VIA
CASSIA
SIENA 68 km

AUTOSTRADA
DEL SOLE (A 1)
per Superstrada:
SIENA 68 km

★ PONTE VECCHIO
★★ PALAZZO PITTI

292

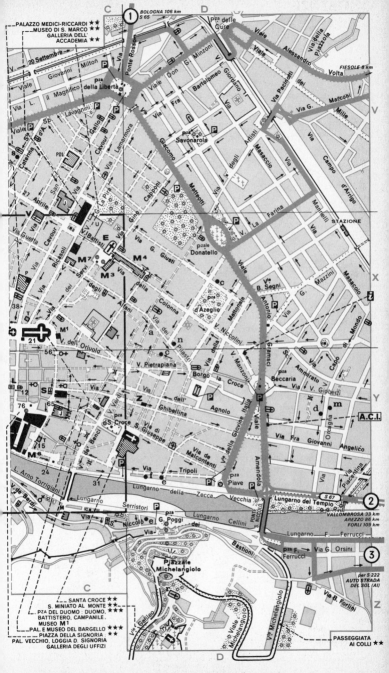

BOLOGNA 106 km
S 65

P.ta delle
Cure

FIESOLE 8 km
Volta

STAZIONE

pza
Savonarola

pza
della Libertà

pzale
Donatello

pza
d'Azeglio

V. Pietrapiana

Borgo
la Croce

Beccaria

A.C.I.

pza
S. Croce

dell'
Ghibellina

Via di
S. Giuseppe

Via de'
Malcontenti

Via
Tripoli

pza
Piave

L. Arno Torrigiani

Lungarno
della
Zecca
Vecchia

Lungarno del Tempio
S 67

VALLOMBROSA 33 km
AREZZO 86 km
FORLÌ 109 km

Serristori

Lungarno
Cellini

Lungarno F. Ferrucci

pza
G. Poggi

pza F.
Ferrucci

Via G. Orsini

Piazzale
Michelangiolo

per S 222
AUTO STRADA
DEL SOL (A1)

Viale
Michelangiolo

PASSEGGIATA
AI COLLI ★★

FIRENZE

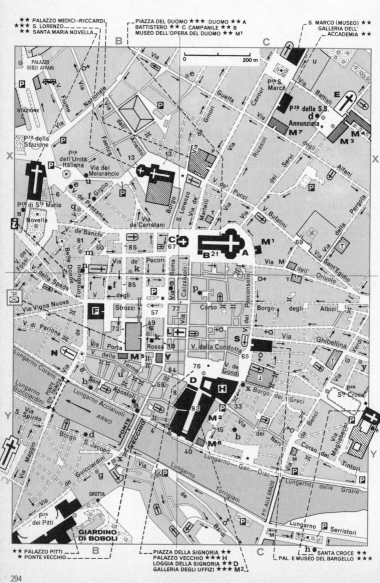

🏛 **Principe** without rest., lungarno Vespucci 34 ⊠ 50123 ℰ 284848, Telex 571400, Fax 262396, ≤, 🐾 – 🛄 ▤ 🔟 ☎. 🖭 🚯 ⓪ 🖪 *VISA*
AX **b**
⬛ 20000 – **21 rm** 220/260000.

🏛 **J e J** without rest., via di Mezzo 20 ⊠ 50121 ℰ 240951, Telex 570554, Fax 240282 – ▤ 🔟 ☎. 🖭 🚯 *VISA*
DY **c**
19 rm ⬛ 280000 apartments 280/380000.

🏛 **Continental** without rest., lungarno Acciaiuoli 2 ⊠ 50123 ℰ 282392, Telex 580525, Fax 283139, « Flowered terrace with ≤ » – 🛄 ▤ 🔟 ☎. 🖭 🚯 ⓪ 🖪 *VISA*
BY **a**
⬛ 18000 – **61 rm** 150/230000 apartments 300/420000.

🏛 **Loggiato dei Serviti** without rest., piazza SS. Annunziata 3 ⊠ 50122 ℰ 289592, Telex 575808, Fax 289595 – 🛄 ▤ 🔟 ☎. 🖭 🚯 ⓪ 🖪 *VISA*
CX **d**
29 rm ⬛ 100/160000 apartments 200/400000.

🏛 **Fleming** without rest., viale Guidoni 87 ⊠ 50127 ℰ 4379536 – 🛄 ▤ 🔟 ☎ – 🔬 35-60. 🖭 🚯 ⓪ 🖪 *VISA*
per ⑧
119 rm ⬛ 99/163000.

🏛 **Villa Azalee** without rest., viale Fratelli Rosselli 44 ⊠ 50123 ℰ 214242, Fax 268264, 🐾 – ▤ 🔟 ☎. 🖭 🚯 ⓪ 🖪 *VISA*
AVX **y**
⬛ 22000 – **25 rm** 81/120000.

🏛 **Privilege** without rest., lungarno della Zecca Vecchia 26 ⊠ 50122 ℰ 2341221, Fax 243287 – ▤ 🔟 ☎. 🖭 🚯 ⓪ 🖪 *VISA*
DY **e**
15 rm ⬛ 106/170000.

🏠 **Rapallo**, via di Santa Caterina d'Alessandria 7 ⊠ 50129 ℰ 472412, Telex 574251, Fax 268364 – 🛄 ▤ ☎ 🚗. 🖭 🚯 ⓪ 🖪 *VISA*. ⚘
CV **s**
M (residents only) a la carte 28/42000 (12%) – ⬛ 11000 – **30 rm** 81/120000 – ½ p 83/117000.

🏠 **Franchi** without rest., via Sgambati 28 ⊠ 50127 ℰ 315425, Telex 580425, Fax 315563 – 🛄 ☎ 🅿. 🖭 🚯 ⓪ 🖪 *VISA*
by ⑧
⬛ 11000 – **35 rm** 71/107000.

🏠 **Arizona** without rest., via Farini 2 ⊠ 50121 ℰ 245321, Telex 575572 – 🛄 🔟 🖳. 🖭 🚯 ⓪ 🖪 *VISA*. ⚘
DX **n**
21 rm ⬛ 92/141000.

🏠 **Fiorino** without rest., via Osteria del Guanto 6 ⊠ 50122 ℰ 210579 – ▤ 🖳
CY **b**
⬛ 9000 – **21 rm** 60/87000, ▤ 4000.

🏠 **Jane** without rest., via Orcagna 56 ⊠ 50121 ℰ 677382, Fax 677383 – 🛄 ▤ ☎. ⚘
DY **m**
⬛ 9000 – **24 rm** 60/85000, ▤ 4000.

🏠 **Orcagna** without rest., via Orcagna 57 ⊠ 50121 ℰ 669959 – 🛄 ☎. 🚯 ⓪ 🖪 *VISA*. ⚘
DY **d**
⬛ 9000 – **18 rm** 51/75000.

🏠 **San Remo** without rest., lungarno Serristori 13 ⊠ 50125 ℰ 2342823, Fax 2342269 – 🛄 ▤ 🔟 🖳. 🖭 🚯 ⓪ 🖪 *VISA*
DZ **e**
20 rm ⬛ 87/128000.

🏠 **Silla** without rest., via dei Renai 5 ⊠ 50125 ℰ 2342888, Fax 2341437 – 🛄 ▤ 🔟 ☎. 🖭 🚯 ⓪ 🖪 *VISA*
CY **h**
32 rm ⬛ 87/132000, ▤ 6000.

XXXX ✿✿ **Enoteca Pinchiorri,** via Ghibellina 87 ⊠ 50122 ℰ 242777, Fax 244983, « Summer service in a cool court yard » – ▤. 🖭 *VISA*
CY **y**
closed Sunday, Monday lunch, August and 24 to 28 December – **M** (booking essential) a la carte 90/150000 (12%)
Spec. Filetti di triglia panati al rosmarino e tartufo nero, Gnocchi di latte al limone e rucola, Sella di coniglio in arrosto e salvia fritta. Wines I Sistri, Cannaio di Montevertine.

XXXX **Sabatini**, via de' Panzani 9/a ⊠ 50123 ℰ 211559, Fax 210293, Elegant traditional decor – ▤
BX **q**

XXX **Al Lume di Candela,** via delle Terme 23 r ⊠ 50123 ℰ 294556, Fax 355481 – ▤. 🖭 🚯 ⓪ 🖪 *VISA*. ⚘
BY **u**
closed Sunday, Monday lunch and 10 to 25 August – **M** (booking essential) a la carte 50/70000 (16%).

XXX **Harry's Bar,** lungarno Vespucci 22 r ⊠ 50123 ℰ 2396700 – ▤. 🖭 *VISA*
AY **x**
closed Sunday and 15 December-5 January – **M** (booking essential) a la carte 40/66000 (16%).

XXX **Don Chisciotte**, via Ridolfi 4 r ⊠ 50129 ℰ 475430, booking essential – ▤
BV **u**

XX **Al Campidoglio,** via del Campidoglio 8 r ⊠ 50123 ℰ 287770 – ▤. 🖭 🚯 ⓪ 🖪 *VISA*. ⚘
BXY **k**
closed Thursday, 13 August-2 September and 20 to 27 December – **M** a la carte 46/64000 (12%).

XX ✿ **I 4 Amici**, via degli Orti Oricellari 29 ⊠ 50123 ℰ 215413 – ▤. 🖭 🚯 ⓪ 🖪 *VISA*. ⚘
AX **h**
closed Wednesday and August – **M** (fish only) a la carte 41/66000 (12%)
Spec. Antipasti di mare, Spaghetti alle vongole, Dentice alla paesana. Wines Vermentino.

XX **La Posta**, via de' Lamberti 20 r ⊠ 50123 ℰ 212701 – ▤. 🖭 🚯 ⓪ *VISA*
BY **s**
closed Tuesday – **M** a la carte 37/62000 (13%).

XX **La Loggia**, piazzale Michelangiolo 1 ⊠ 50125 ℰ 2342832, « Outdoor service in Summer with ≤ » – ▤ 🅿 – 🔬 100. 🖭 🚯 ⓪ 🖪 *VISA*. ⚘
DZ **r**
closed Wednesday and 10 to 25 August – **M** a la carte 40/60000 (13%).

XX **Il Biribisso,** via dell'Albero 28/r ⊠ 50123 ℰ 293180 – 🗐 🖭 🕄 ① 🗲 𝓥𝓘𝓢𝓐   AX   **t**
closed Sunday, Monday lunch and August – **M** a la carte 25/39000.

XX ❀ **Da Noi,** via Fiesolana 46 r ⊠ 50122 ℰ 242917 – 𝒮𝒦   DX   **a**
closed Sunday, Monday and August – **M** (dinner only) (booking essential) 61000 (10%)
Spec. Tagliatelle di castagne con ragù di piccione, Carrè di vitella ai porri salsa allo zabaione di vino, Terrina di
pesche salsa alla menta. **Wines** Pinot bianco, Chianti.

XX **i' Toscano,** via Guelfa 70/r ⊠ 50129 ℰ 215475 – 🗐. 🖭 🕄 ① 🗲 𝓥𝓘𝓢𝓐. 𝒮𝒦   CX   **e**
closed Tuesday and August – **M** a la carte 30/45000.

XX **13 Gobbi,** via del Porcellana 9 r ⊠ 50123 ℰ 2398769, Tuscan rest. – 🗐. 🕄 ① 🗲 𝓥𝓘𝓢𝓐
𝒮𝒦   AX   **v**
closed Sunday, Monday and 31 July-30 August – **M** a la carte 38/60000 (12%).

XX **La Sagrestia,** via Gucciardini 27/r ⊠ 50125 ℰ 210003 – 🗐. 🖭 🕄 ① 🗲 𝓥𝓘𝓢𝓐. 𝒮𝒦   BY   **g**
closed Monday – **M** a la carte 27/48000 (12%).

X **La Capannina di Sante,** piazza Ravenna ang. Ponte da Verrazzano ⊠ 50126 ℰ 688345,
≤, 🛱 – 🗐. 🖭 🕄 ① 𝓥𝓘𝓢𝓐. 𝒮𝒦   per ③
closed Sunday, Monday lunch, 10 to 20 August and 24 to 31 December – **M** (fish only)
a la carte 70/80000.

X **Il Giardino di Barbano,** piazza Indipendenza 3 r ⊠ 50129 ℰ 486752, « Summer service
in garden » – 🖭 🕄 ① 🗲 𝓥𝓘𝓢𝓐   BV   **w**
closed Wednesday – **M** a la carte 24/46000 (12%).

X **Buca Lapi,** via del Trebbio 1 r ⊠ 50123 ℰ 213768, Typical tavern – 🗐. 🖭 ① 𝓥𝓘𝓢𝓐   BX   **m**
closed Sunday and Monday lunch – **M** a la carte 36/51000 (12%).

X **Celestino,** piazza Santa Felicita 4 r ⊠ 50125 ℰ 296574 – 🗐. 🖭 🕄 ① 🗲 𝓥𝓘𝓢𝓐   BY   **x**
closed Sunday and 5 to 20 August – **M** a la carte 28/49000 (12%).

on the hills S : 3 km :

🏨 **Gd H. Villa Cora and Rest. Taverna Machiavelli** 🦢, viale Machiavelli 18 ⊠ 50125
ℰ 2298451, Telex 570604, Fax 229086, 🛱, « Floral park with 🏊 » – 🛗 🗐 📺 🕿 🅿.
🔬 50-150. 🖭 🕄 ① 🗲 𝓥𝓘𝓢𝓐. 𝒮𝒦 rest   by viale Machiavelli ABZ
M a la carte 52/76000 (15%) – 🍴 24000 – **48 rm** 339/539000 apartments 817/1024000.

🏨 **Torre di Bellosguardo** 🦢 without rest., via Roti Michelozzi 2 ⊠ 50124 ℰ 2298145,
≤ town and hills, « Park and terrace with 🏊 » – 🛗 🅿. 🖭 🕄 ① 🗲 𝓥𝓘𝓢𝓐. 𝒮𝒦   by ④
🍴 18000 – **13 rm** 210/280000 apartments 380000.

🏨 **Villa Carlotta** 🦢, via Michele di Lando 3 ⊠ 50125 ℰ 2336134, Telex 573485, Fax 2336147,
🌺 – 🛗 🗐 📺 🕿 🅿. 🖭 🕄 ① 🗲 𝓥𝓘𝓢𝓐. 𝒮𝒦 rest   AZ   **a**
M a la carte 32/62000 – **27 rm** 🍴 228/319000 – ½ p 160/275000.

🏨 **Villa Belvedere** 🦢 without rest., via Benedetto Castelli 3 ⊠ 50124 ℰ 222501, Telex
575648, Fax 223163, ≤ town and hills, « Garden-park with 🏊 », 𝒮𝒦 – 🛗 🗐 📺 🕿 ⅊ 🅿. 🖭
🕄 ① 🗲 𝓥𝓘𝓢𝓐. 𝒮𝒦   by ④
March-November – **27 rm** 🍴 155/230000.

XX **Antico Crespino,** largo Enrico Fermi 15 ⊠ 50125 ℰ 221155, ≤ – 🖭 🕄 ① 🗲 𝓥𝓘𝓢𝓐   by ④
closed Wednesday – **M** a la carte 40/69000 (13%).

at Arcetri S : 5 km – ⊠ **50125** Firenze :

X **Omero,** via Pian de' Giullari 11 r ℰ 220053, Country trattoria with ≤, « Summer service on
terrace » – ① 𝓥𝓘𝓢𝓐. 𝒮𝒦   by viale Galileo CDZ
closed Tuesday and August – **M** a la carte 28/42000 (13%).

at Galluzzo S : 6,5 km – ⊠ **50124** Firenze :

🏨 **Relais Certosa,** via Colle Ramole 2 ℰ 2047171, Telex 574332, Fax 268575, ≤, « Park-
garden », 𝒮𝒦 – 🛗 ⅍ 🗐 📺 🕿 🅿 – 🔬 30-60. 🖭 🕄 ① 🗲 𝓥𝓘𝓢𝓐. 𝒮𝒦 rest   by ④
M a la carte 45/77000 – **69 rm** 🍴 215/290000 apartments 413000 – ½ p 215000.

at Candeli – ⊠ **50010** :

🏨 **Villa La Massa and Rest. Il Verrocchio** 🦢, via La Massa 6 ℰ 666141, Telex 573555,
Fax 632579, ≤, 🛱, « House and furnishing in 18C style », 🏊, 🌺 – 🛗 🗐 📺 🕿 ⅊ 🅿 –
🔬 100. 🖭 🕄 ① 🗲 𝓥𝓘𝓢𝓐. 𝒮𝒦 rest
M *(closed Monday and Tuesday lunch November-March)* a la carte 50/70000 – 🍴 25000 –
38 rm 240/440000 apartments 700000 – ½ p 320/460000.

towards Trespiano N : 7 km :

🏨 **Villa le Rondini** 🦢, via Bolognese Vecchia 224 ⊠ 50139 Firenze ℰ 400081, Telex 575679,
Fax 268212, ≤ town, « Among the olive trees », 🏊, 🌺, 𝒮𝒦 – ⅍≈ rest 🕿 🅿 – 🔬 80-200.
🖭 🕄 ① 🗲 𝓥𝓘𝓢𝓐. 𝒮𝒦 rest
M a la carte 40/120000 – **33 rm** 🍴 97/154000 apartments 240000 – ½ p 104/137000.

If you would like a more complete selection of hotels and restaurants,
consult the **Michelin Red Guides** *for the following countries:*
Benelux, Deutschland, España Portugal, France,
Great Britain and Ireland, Italia.

MILAN (MILANO) 20100 📖 🖫🖫🖫 ③, 🖫🖫🖫 F 9 – pop. 1 449 403 alt. 122 – 😊 02.

See : Cathedral★★★ (Duomo) – Cathedral Museum★★ CV **M1** – Via and Piazza Mercanti★ CV –
La Scala Opera House★ CV – Brera Art Gallery★★★ CU – Castle of the Sforzas★★★ BU : Municipal
Art Collection★★★ – Sempione Park★ ABU – Ambrosian Library★★ BV : portraits★★★ of Gaffurio
and Isabella d'Este, Raphael's cartoons★★★ – Poldi-Pezzoli Museum★★ CU : portrait of a
woman★★★ (in profile) by Pollaiolo – Leonardo da Vinci Museum of Science and Technology★
AV **M1** : Leonardo da Vinci Gallery★★ – Church of St. Mary of Grace★ AV **A** : Leonardo da Vinci's
Last Supper★★★ – Basilica of St. Ambrose★ AV **B** : altar front★★ – Church of St. Eustorgius★
BY **B** : Portinari Chapel★★ – General Hospital★ DX **U** – Church of St. Maurice★ BV **E** – Church of
St. Lawrence Major★ BX **F** – Dome★ of the Church of St. Satiro CV **C**.

Envir. : Chiaravalle Abbey★ SE : 7 km.

🖪🅱 e 🖪🛱 (closed Monday) at Monza Park ⊠ 20052 Monza 𝒫 (039) 303081, Fax (039) 304427 by ② :
20 km;

🖪🅱 Molinetto (closed Monday) at Cernusco sul Naviglio ⊠ 20063 𝒫 (02) 9238500, by ⑤ : 14 km;

🖪🅱 Barlassina (closed Monday) at Birago di Camnago ⊠ 20030 𝒫 (0362) 560621, by ① : 26 km;

🖪🅱 (closed Monday) at Zoate di Tribiano ⊠ 20067 𝒫(02) 90632183, SE : 20 km by Strada Paullese;

🖪🛱 Le Rovedine at Noverasco di Opera ⊠ 20090 Opera 𝒫 (02) 57602730, S : 8 km by via Ripamonti.

Motor-Racing circuit at Monza Park by ② : 20 km, 𝒫 (039) 22366.

✈ Forlanini of Linate E : 8 km 𝒫 74852200 and Malpensa by ⑫ : 45 km 𝒫 74852200 – Alitalia,
corso Como 15 ⊠ 20154 𝒫 62818 and via Albricci 5 ⊠ 20122 𝒫 62817.

🚗 𝒫 6690734.

🖪 via Marconi 1 ⊠ 20123 𝒫 809662 – Central Station ⊠ 20124 𝒫 6690532.

A.C.I. corso Venezia 43 ⊠ 20121 𝒫 77451.

Roma 572 ⑦ – Genève 323 ⑫ – Genova 142 ⑨ – Torino 140 ⑫.

Plans on following pages

Northern area Piazza della Repubblica, Central Station, viale Zara, Porta Garibaldi Station,
Porta Volta, corso Sempione (Plans : Milan pp. 2 and 3) :

🏨🏨🏨 **Principe di Savoia,** piazza della Repubblica 17 ⊠ 20124 𝒫 6230, Telex 310052, Fax
6595838, 😼 – 🛊 🗏 ⯑ 🗺 🕿 ♿ 🅿 – 🔏 700. 🆎 🕦 ⑩ 🖪 𝑉𝑆𝐴 🎉 rest   DS **x**
M a la carte 80/124000 – ⯑ 25000 – **280 rm** 405/595000 apartments 833/1904000.

🏨🏨🏨 **Palace and Rest. Casanova Grill,** piazza della Repubblica 20 ⊠ 20124 𝒫 6336
and rest 𝒫29000803, Telex 311026, Fax 654485 – 🛊 🗏 🗺 🕿 ♿ 🅿 – 🔏 25-300. 🆎 🕦 ⑩ 🖪
𝑉𝑆𝐴. 🎉 rest   DS **t**
closed August – **M** (booking essential) a la carte 90/110000 – ⯑ 26500 – **210 rm** 381/548000
apartments 883/1428000.

🏨🏨🏨 **Excelsior Gallia,** piazza Duca d'Aosta 9 ⊠ 20124 𝒫 6785, Telex 311160, Fax 656306, 🖪🛱,
😼 – 🛊 🗏 ⯑ – 🔏 500. 🆎 🕦 ⑩ 🖪 𝑉𝑆𝐴. 🎉   DR **a**
M a la carte 85/136000 – ⯑ 20500 – **260 rm** 423/566000 apartments 833/1428000.

🏨🏨🏨 **Milano Hilton,** via Galvani 12 ⊠ 20124 𝒫 69831, Telex 330433, Fax 6071904 – 🛊 🗏 🗺
♿ 😼 – 🔏 250. 🆎 🕦 ⑩ 🖪 𝑉𝑆𝐴. 🎉 rest   DR **t**
M a la carte 64/107000 – ⯑ 18500 – **332 rm** 460/560000 apartments 1140/1750000.

🏨🏨🏨 **Duca di Milano,** piazza della Repubblica 13 ⊠ 20124 𝒫 6284, Telex 325026 – 🛊 🗏 🗺
– 🔏 30. 🆎 🕦 ⑩ 🖪 𝑉𝑆𝐴. 🎉 rest   DS **v**
M 75/100000 – ⯑ 28000 – **60 rm** 393/572000.

🏨🏨🏨 **Michelangelo,** via Scarlatti 33 ⊠ 20124 𝒫 6755, Telex 340330, Fax 6694232 – 🛊 ⯑ rm 🗏
🗺 🕿 😼 – 🔏 250. 🆎 🕦 ⑩ 🖪 𝑉𝑆𝐴. 🎉   DR **c**
M a la carte 85/115000 – **250 rm** ⯑ 340/470000 apartments 940000.

🏨🏨🏨 **Executive,** viale Luigi Sturzo 45 ⊠ 20154 𝒫 6294, Telex 310191, Fax 653240 – 🛊 🗏 🗺 🗺
♿ 😼 – 🔏 25-800. 🆎 🕦 🖪 𝑉𝑆𝐴. 🎉   CRS **v**
M (closed Friday) a la carte 63/95000 – **414 rm** ⯑ 390000 apartments 600000.

🏨🏨 **Anderson** without rest., piazza Luigi di Savoia 20 ⊠ 20124 𝒫 6690141, Telex 321018, Fax
6690331 – 🛊 🗏 🗺 🗺 😼 . 🆎 🕦 🖪 𝑉𝑆𝐴 🎉   DR **v**
closed August – ⯑ 18000 – **106 rm** 188/240000 apartments 310000.

🏨🏨 **Jolly Hotel Touring,** via Tarchetti 2 ⊠ 20121 𝒫 6335, Telex 320118, Fax 6592209 – 🛊 🗏
🗺 😼 – 🔏 120. 🆎 🕦 ⑩ 🖪 𝑉𝑆𝐴. 🎉   DT **v**
M 60000 – **270 rm** ⯑ 310/390000 – ½ p 255/370000.

🏨🏨 **Splendido,** viale Andrea Doria 4 ⊠ 20124 𝒫 6789, Telex 321413, Fax 656874 – 🛊 🗏 🗺 🗺
– 🔏 25-100. 🆎 🕦 🖪 𝑉𝑆𝐴. 🎉   DR **x**
M a la carte 40/55000 – **156 rm** ⯑ 240/280000 – ½ p 180/295000.

🏨🏨 **Royal** without rest., via Cardano 1 ⊠ 20124 𝒫 6709151, Telex 333167, Fax 6703024 – 🛊 ⯑
🗏 🗺 🗺 😼 – 🔏 40. 🆎 🕦 🖪 𝑉𝑆𝐴   DR **b**
closed August – ⯑ 20000 – **215 rm** 215/275000.

🏨🏨 **Atlantic** without rest., via Napo Torriani 24 ⊠ 20124 𝒫 6691941, Telex 321451, Fax 6706533
– 🛊 🗏 🗺 🗺 😼 – 🔏 25. 🆎 🕦 🖪 𝑉𝑆𝐴   DS **q**
62 rm ⯑ 200/300000.

🏨🏨 **Madison** without rest., via Gasparotto 8 ⊠ 20124 𝒫 6085991, Telex 326543, Fax 6887821 –
🛊 🗏 🗺 😼 – 🔏 100. 🆎 🕦 ⑩ 🖪 𝑉𝑆𝐴   DR **d**
92 rm ⯑ 190/280000 apartments 300/400000.

MILANO

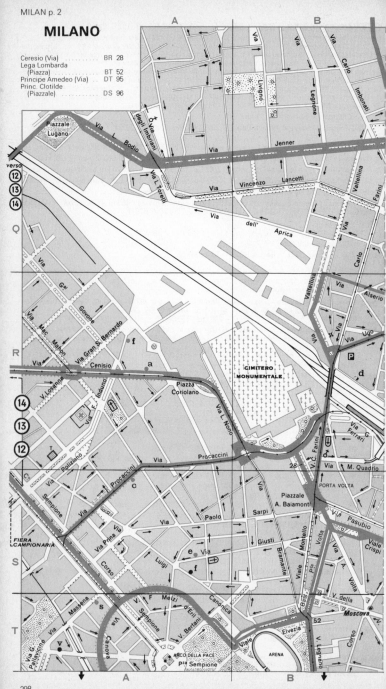

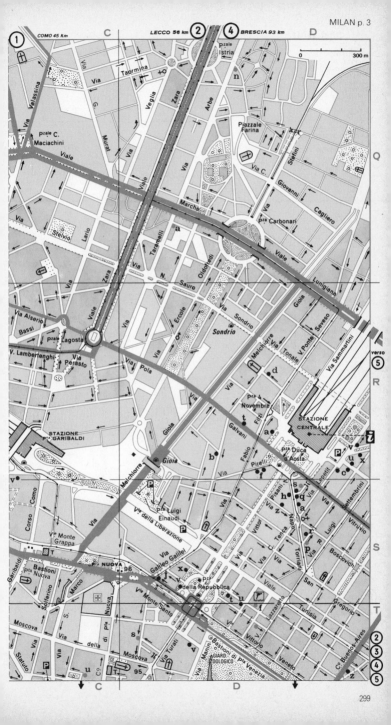

MILANO

★ PARCO SEMPIONE
★★★ CASTELLO SFORZESCO
★★ BIBLIOTECA AMBROSIANA

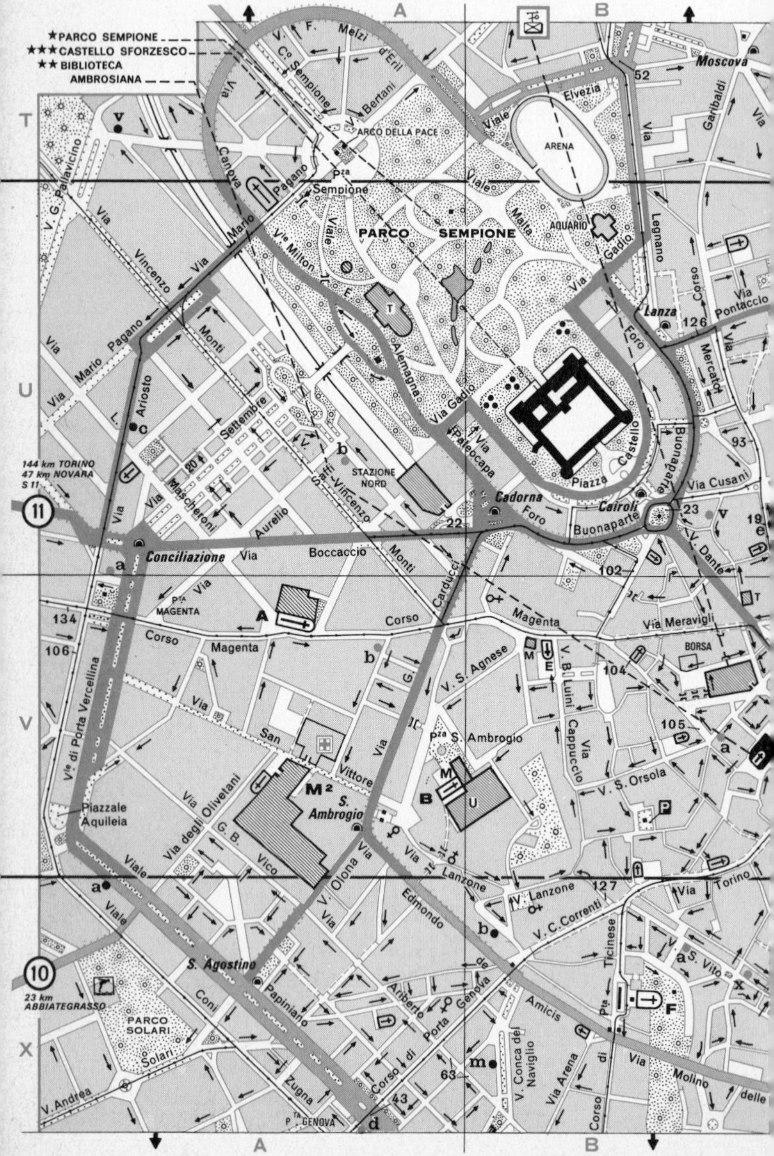

★★★ DUOMO
★★ MUSEO POLDI-PEZZOLI
★ VIA E PZA MERCANTI
★ TEATRO ALLA SCALA
★★★ PINACOTECA DI BRERA
C
D
T
U
V
X
Via della Moscova
Via Turati
Manin
GIARD. ZOOLOGICO
Bastioni di Pta Venezia
Vle Vittorio Veneto
V. Lazzaretto
Vle Tunisia
C.so Buenos-Aires
Piazza Oberdan
PTA VENEZIA
GIARDINI PUBBLICI
Via Palestro
Pza Cavour
Via Fatebenefratelli
Via Pontaccio
Via Solferino
Statuto
S. Marco
Co di Pta Nuova
Turati
Via Brera
V. Borgonuovo
Manzoni
V. Monte di Pietà
V. dell'Orso
Via Verdi
Via Senato
Corso Venezia
Palestro
A.C.I.
Viale Piave
Viale Luigi Maino
V. S. Andrea
V. Monte Napoleone
V. P. Verri
Via S. Damiano
Corso Monforte
PTA MONFORTE
Corso Matteotti
S. Babila
Via Mascagni
Cordusio
V. Mengoni
GALLERIA
Co Vitt. Emanuele II
Pza del Duomo
Europa
V. Durini
Via Corridoni
Viale Bianca Maria
Donizetti
Premuda
Via Torino
Missori
PTA VITTORIA
Co di Pta Vittoria
Via Manara
San Barnaba
V. Larga
Sforza
Via Francesco
V. Pantano
Corso di Porta Romana
Via d. Commenda
V. della Pace
Lamarmora
Viale Regina Margherita
Vle E. Caldara
Viale Monte Nero
Corso Italia
Via S. Sofia
Via S. Calimero
Armi
0
300 m

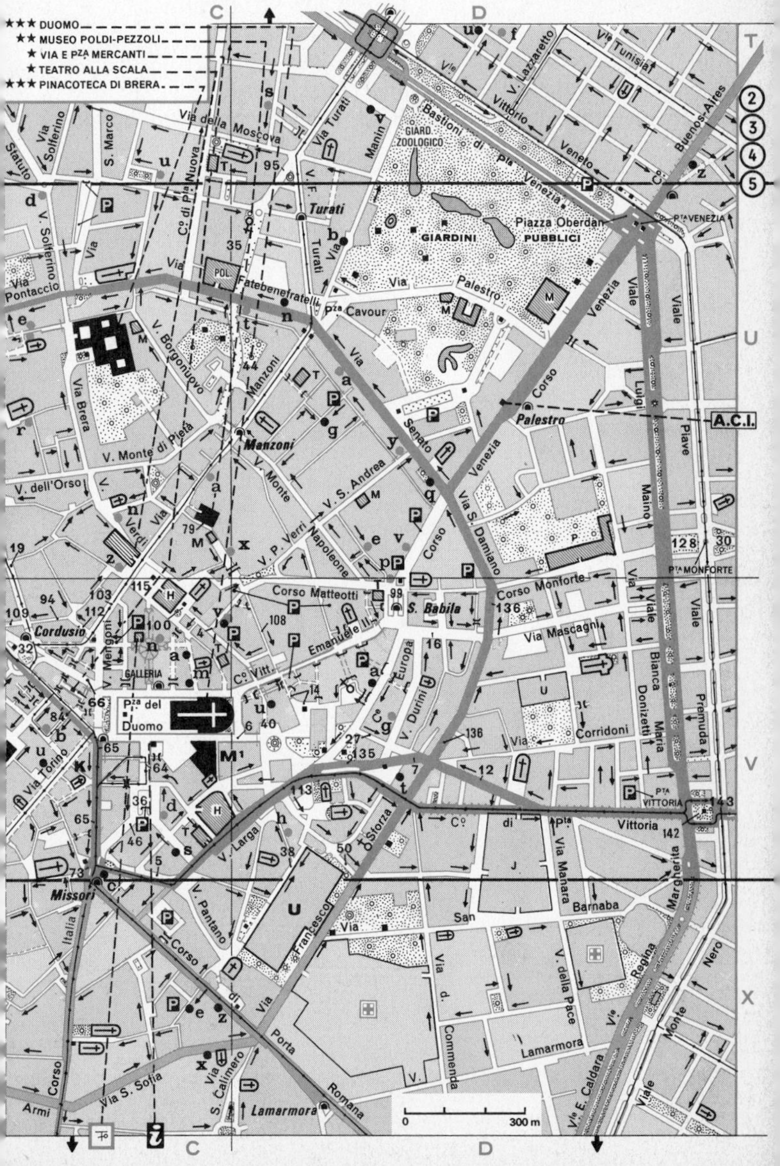

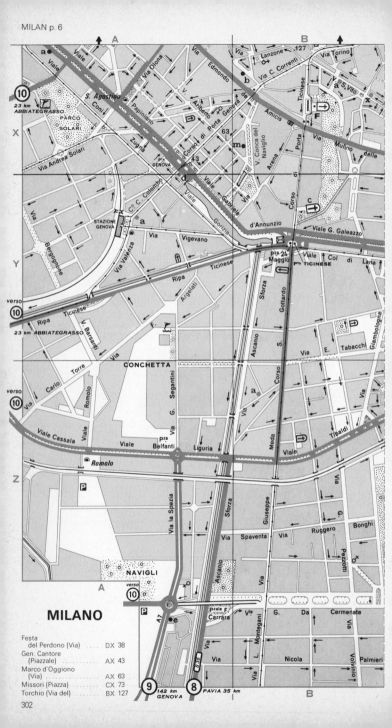

MILANO

302

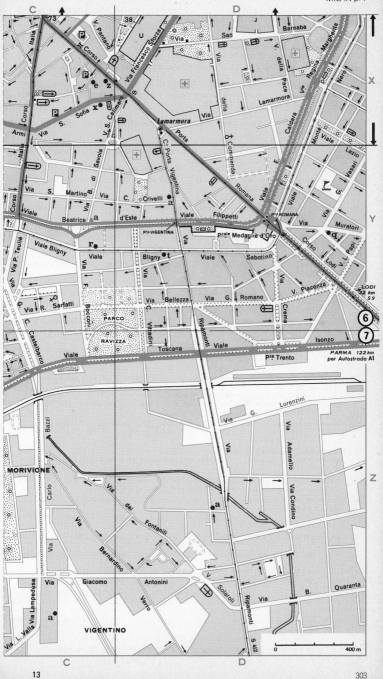

C

73

D

38

V. Pantano

U

V. Francesco Sforza

Via

San

Barnaba

J

V. della Pace

V. Regina Margherita

Nero

X

P

Corso

Italia

e

2

di

Via

della

Lamarmora

Carpara

Monte

Viale

Lazio

Vasari

S. Sofia

x

V. S. Calimero

Lamarmora

C° Porta

Porta

Commenda

Romana

Viale

di

Corso

Italia

Corso

Armi

Via

Via

Savoia

C.

Crivelli

Viale

Filippetti

P.tA ROMANA

Muratori

Via

Papi

q

Y

Viale

S. Martino

di

Via

C.

d'Este

Beatrice

a

PtA VIGENTINA

P.zale Medaglie d'Oro

Corso

Lodi

V.

Via

Via P. Teulié

Viale Bligny

r

Via

Viale

Bligny

t

Viale

Sabotino

Via

Piacenza

LODI

32 km

S 9

Via P. Teulié

Via

R. Sarfatti

G

Via

Bellezza

Via

G. Romano

Crema

V. Placenza

6

C.

Bocconi

PARCO

Vitadini

Ripamonti

Isonzo

7

Castelbarco

RAVIZZA

Toscana

Viale

Viale

P.za Trento

PARMA 122 km

per Autostrada A1

MORIVIONE

Bazzi

Via

Carlo

Via dei

Via G. Lorenzini

Via

Adamello

Via Condino

Z

Via

Fontanili

a

Via

Bernardino

Giacomo

Antonini

Verro

V. Solaroli

Ripamonti

Via

B.

Quaranta

Via

a

VIGENTINO

Via L. Valla

Via Lampedusa

S 412

0   400 m

C

D

13

303

🏨 **Berna** without rest., via Napo Torriani 18 ⊠ 20124 𝒫 6691441, Telex 334695, Fax 6693892 –
|🛗| 🗏 🔟 ☎ – ♨ 30-60. 🅰🅴 🚫 ⓪ 🅴 𝗩𝗜𝗦𝗔 🕸
DS a
� 18000 – **83 rm** 160/220000.

🏨 **Auriga** without rest., via Pirelli 7 ⊠ 20124 𝒫 66985851, Telex 350146, Fax 66980698 – |🛗| 🗏
🔟 ☎ – ♨ 25. 🅰🅴 🚫 ⓪ 🅴 𝗩𝗜𝗦𝗔 🕸
DR f
closed August – �️ 18000 – **65 rm** 175/215000.

🏨 **Windsor,** via Galilei 2 ⊠ 20124 𝒫 6346, Telex 330562, Fax 6590663 – |🛗| 🗏 🔟 ☎ 🚗 –
♨ 40
DS j
M *(closed Saturday)* 30000 – **118 rm** ⊿ 194/242000 apartments 302000 – ½ p 142/224000.

🏨 **Mediolanum** without rest., via Mauro Macchi 1 ⊠ 20124 𝒫 6705312, Telex 310448, Fax
66981921 – |🛗| 🗏 🔟 ☎ ♿. 🅰🅴 🚫 🅴 𝗩𝗜𝗦𝗔
DS r
52 rm ⊿ 174/263000.

🏨 **Bristol** without rest., via Scarlatti 32 ⊠ 20124 𝒫 6694141, Fax 6702942 – |🛗| 🗏 🔟 ☎ – ♨
50. 🅰🅴 🚫 ⓪ 🅴 𝗩𝗜𝗦𝗔
DR u
closed August – ⊿ 20000 – **71 rm** 203/270000.

🏨 **Augustus** 🐾 without rest., via Napo Torriani 29 ⊠ 20124 𝒫 66988271, Telex 333112, Fax
6703096 – |🛗| 🗏 🔟 ☎ 🚗. 🅰🅴 🚫 ⓪ 🅴 𝗩𝗜𝗦𝗔
DS h
closed 5 to 25 August and 23 December-5 January – **56 rm** ⊿ 127/188000.

🏨 **Europeo** without rest., via Canonica 38 ⊠ 20154 𝒫 3314751, Fax 33105410, 🛋 – |🛗| 🗏 🔟
☎ 🚗 – ♨ 25. 🅰🅴 🚫 🅴 𝗩𝗜𝗦𝗔
AS f
closed August – **45 rm** ⊿ 125/220000.

🏨 **Lancaster** without rest., via Abbondio Sangiorgio 16 ⊠ 20145 𝒫 315602, Fax 344649 – 🗏
🔟 ☎. 🅰🅴 🚫 🅴 𝗩𝗜𝗦𝗔
AT v
closed August – **30 rm** ⊿ 125/220000.

🏨 **New York** without rest., via Pirelli 5 ⊠ 20124 𝒫 66985551, Telex 325057, Fax 6697267 – |🛗|
🗏 🔟 ☎ – ♨ 40. 🅰🅴 🚫 ⓪ 🅴 𝗩𝗜𝗦𝗔. 🕸
DR f
closed 1 to 28 August and 24 December-5 January – ⊿ 15000 – **70 rm** 106/151000.

🏨 **Sempione,** via Finocchiaro Aprile 11 ⊠ 20124 𝒫 6570323, Telex 340498, Fax 6575379 – |🛗|
🔆 🗏 🔟 ☎. 🅰🅴 🚫 🅴 𝗩𝗜𝗦𝗔
DST u
M see rest. Piazza Repubblica below – ⊿ 18000 – **39 rm** 100/140000 – ½ p 120000.

🏨 **Florida** without rest., via Lepetit 33 ⊠ 20124 𝒫 6705921, Telex 314102, Fax 6692867 – |🛗| 🗏
🔟 ☎. 🅰🅴 🚫 ⓪ 🅴 𝗩𝗜𝗦𝗔
DR c
⊿ 20000 – **52 rm** ⊿ 96/138000.

🏨 **Bolzano** without rest., via Boscovich 21 ⊠ 20124 𝒫 6691451, Fax 6691455, 🛋 – |🛗| 🗏 🔟
☎. 🅰🅴 🚫 ⓪ 🅴 𝗩𝗜𝗦𝗔. 🕸
DS z
⊿ 15000 – **35 rm** 100/140000.

🏨 **San Carlo** without rest., via Napo Torriani 28 ⊠ 20124 𝒫 656336, Telex 314324, Fax
6703116 – |🛗| 🗏 🔟 ☎. 🅰🅴 🚫 ⓪ 🅴 𝗩𝗜𝗦𝗔
DS s
75 rm ⊿ 118/176000.

🏵️ ✿ **Alfredo-Gran San Bernardo,** via Borgese 14 ⊠ 20154 𝒫 3319000, Milanese cuisine –
🗏 🅰🅴 🚫 ⓪ 🅴 𝗩𝗜𝗦𝗔
AR f
closed Sunday and August – **M** (booking essential) a la carte 58/76000
Spec. Risotto alla milanese ed al salto, Ossobuco in cremolata, Costolette alla milanese. **Wines** Lugana,
Franciacorta rosso.

🏵️ **Gianni e Dorina,** via Pepe 38 ⊠ 20159 𝒫 606340, 🌂 – 🗏 🅰🅴 🚫 ⓪ 🅴 𝗩𝗜𝗦𝗔 🕸 BR d
closed Saturday lunch, Sunday and 25 July-15 September – **M** (booking essential)
a la carte 40/65000 (10%).

🏵️ **China Club,** via Giusti 34 ⊠ 20154 𝒫 33104309 – 🗏 AS e
closed Tuesady, August and 24 December-2 January – **M** (booking essential) a la
carte 45/70000.

🏵️ **Dall'Antonio,** via Cenisio 8 ⊠ 20154 𝒫 33101511 – 🗏. 🅰🅴 🚫 ⓪ 𝗩𝗜𝗦𝗔 🕸 AR a
closed Sunday and August – **M** (booking essential) a la carte 75/90000.

🏵️ **Ai 3 Pini,** via Tullo Morgagni 19 angolo via Arbe ⊠ 20125 𝒫 6898464, « Summer service
under a pergola » – 🅰🅴 🚫 ⓪ 🅴 𝗩𝗜𝗦𝗔 DQ n
closed Saturday, Sunday dinner, 5 to 31 August and 25 December-4 January – **M** (booking
essential) a la carte 40/60000.

🏵️ ✿ **A Riccione,** via Taramelli 70 ⊠ 20124 𝒫 6686807, Seafood – 🗏. 🅰🅴 🚫 ⓪ 🅴 𝗩𝗜𝗦𝗔 DQ a
closed Monday – **M** (booking essential) a la carte 85/105000
Spec. Pasta fresca con sugo di pesce, Paella valenciana o di solo pesce, Grigliata mista alla brace. **Wines** del
Collio.

🏵️ **Joia,** via Panfilo Castaldi 18 ⊠ 20124 𝒫 222124, Vegetarian cuisine – 🔆 🗏. 🅰🅴 🚫 ⓪ 🅴
𝗩𝗜𝗦𝗔 – *closed Saturday lunch, Sunday and 1 to 21 August* – **M** a la carte 30/60000. DT z

🏵️ **Cavallini,** via Mauro Macchi 2 ⊠ 20124 𝒫 6693174, 🌂 – 🗏. 🅰🅴 🚫 ⓪ 🅴 𝗩𝗜𝗦𝗔 🕸 DS p
closed Saturday, Sunday, 3 to 23 August and 22 December-4 January – **M** a la carte 28/53000
(12%).

🏵️ **La Buca,** via Antonio da Recanate ang. via Napo Torriani ⊠ 20124 𝒫 6693176 – 🗏 🅰🅴
⓪ 🅴 𝗩𝗜𝗦𝗔. 🕸
DS s
closed Friday dinner, Saturday, August and 25 December-6 January – **M** a la carte 40/79000.

🏵️ **La Torre del Mangia,** via Procaccini 37 ⊠ 20154 𝒫 314871 – 🗏. 🅰🅴 🚫 🅴 𝗩𝗜𝗦𝗔. 🕸 AS c
closed Sunday dinner and Monday – **M** (booking essential) a la carte 38/67000.

Le 5 Terre, via Appiani 9 ✉ 20121 ✆ 653034, Seafood – 🍽. ⅍ ⑤ ⑩ Ⅼ 𝑉𝐼𝑆𝐴   DT s
closed Saturday lunch, Sunday and 8 to 22 August – **M** a la carte 54/79000.

Piazza Repubblica, via Manunzio 11 ✉ 20124 ✆ 6552715 – 🍽. ⅍ ⑤ Ⅼ 𝑉𝐼𝑆𝐴   DT f
closed Saturday lunch, Sunday and 5 to 19 August – **M** a la carte 35/53000.

Il Verdi, piazza Mirabello 5 ✉ 20121 ✆ 6590797 – 🍽   CT u
closed Saturday lunch, Sunday, 11 to 31 August and 23 December-1 January – **M** a la carte 42/71000 (13%).

Trattoria della Pesa, viale Pasubio 10 ✉ 20154 ✆ 6555741, Old Milan typical trattoria with Lombardy specialities – 🍽   BS s
closed Sunday and August – **M** a la carte 37/58000.

Central area Duomo, Scala, Sempione Park, Sforza Castle, Public gardens, corso Venezia, via Manzoni, North Station, corso Magenta, Porta Vittoria (Plans : Milan pp. 4 and 5) :

Jolly Hotel President, largo Augusto 10 ✉ 20122 ✆ 7746, Telex 312054, Fax 783449 – 🛗
⇔⇔ rm 🍽 📺 ☎ &. – 🔬 30-100. ⅍ ⑤ ⑩ Ⅼ 𝑉𝐼𝑆𝐴. ⅍ rest   DV t
M 60000 – **220 rm** ⊊ 350/420000 – ½ p 270/410000.

Gd H. Duomo, via San Raffaele 1 ✉ 20121 ✆ 8833, Telex 312086, Fax 872752 – 🛗 🍽 📺
☎. ⅍ ⑤ ⑩ Ⅼ 𝑉𝐼𝑆𝐴. ⅍   CV m
M (residents only) a la carte 40/61000 – ⊊ 20000 – **160 rm** 260/360000 apartments 520/580000 – ½ p 240/320000.

Brunelleschi and Rest. Le Volte, via Baracchini 12 ✉ 20123 ✆ 8843, Telex 312256, Fax 870144 – 🛗 🍽 📺 ☎. ⅍ ⑤ ⑩ Ⅼ 𝑉𝐼𝑆𝐴. ⅍ rest   CV s
M *(closed Saturday, Sunday and August)* a la carte 85/105000 – **120 rm** ⊊ 340/470000 apartments 850000 – ½ p 300/400000.

Dei Cavalieri without rest., piazza Missori 1 ✉ 20123 ✆ 8857, Telex 312040, Fax 72021683
– 🛗 🍽 📺 ☎. – 🔬 40-60. ⅍ ⑤ ⑩ Ⅼ 𝑉𝐼𝑆𝐴   CVX c
177 rm ⊊ 250/295000 apartments 450/650000

Galileo without rest., corso Europa 9 ✉ 20122 ✆ 7743, Telex 322095, Fax 656319 – 🛗 🍽
📺 ☎. ⅍ ⑤ ⑩ Ⅼ 𝑉𝐼𝑆𝐴. ⅍ rest   DV a
70 rm ⊊ 340/500000 apartments 500000.

Carlton Hotel Senato, via Senato 5 ✉ 20121 ✆ 798583, Telex 331306, Fax 783300 – 🛗
🍽 📺 ☎ ⇔. ⅍ ⑤ ⑩ Ⅼ 𝑉𝐼𝑆𝐴. ⅍ rest   DU q
closed August – **M** *(closed Saturday, Sunday and 20 December-7 January)* a la carte 43/67000 – ⊊ 17500 – **79 rm** 195/250000 – ½ p 222/292000.

Manin, via Manin 7 ✉ 20121 ✆ 6596511, Telex 320385, Fax 6552160, 🌳 – 🛗 🍽 📺 ☎.
🔬 30-120. ⅍ ⑤ ⑩ Ⅼ 𝑉𝐼𝑆𝐴. ⅍ rest   DU b
closed 7 to 23 August – **M** *(closed Sunday)* a la carte 60/82000 – ⊊ 20000 – **119 rm** 195/250000 apartments 350/450000 – ½ p 190/260000.

Cavour, via Fatebenefratelli 21 ✉ 20121 ✆ 6572051, Telex 320498, Fax 6592263 – 🛗 🍽 📺
☎ &. ⅍ ⑤ ⑩ Ⅼ 𝑉𝐼𝑆𝐴. ⅍ rest   DU n
M *(closed Friday dinner, Saturday and Sunday lunch)* 50000 – ⊊ 15000 – **113 rm** 191/215000 apartments 264000 – P 188/271000.

Rosa, via Pattari 5 ✉ 20122 ✆ 8831, Telex 316067, Fax 8057964 – 🛗 🍽 📺 ☎ – 🔬 30-120.
⅍ ⑤ ⑩ Ⅼ 𝑉𝐼𝑆𝐴. ⅍   DV u
M *(closed Sunday)* a la carte 46/60000 – **166 rm** ⊊ 250/290000 – ½ p 191/310000.

De la Ville without rest., via Hoepli 6 ✉ 20121 ✆ 867651, Telex 312642, Fax 866609 – 🛗 🍽
📺 ☎. ⅍ ⑤ ⑩ Ⅼ 𝑉𝐼𝑆𝐴   CV v
104 rm ⊊ 300/380000.

Ariosto without rest., via Ariosto 22 ✉ 20145 ✆ 4817844, Fax 4980516 – 🛗 🍽 📺 ☎ &. –
🔬 40. ⅍ ⑤ ⑩ Ⅼ 𝑉𝐼𝑆𝐴   AU c
⊊ 11000 – **53 rm** 103/146000.

Manzoni without rest., via Santo Spirito 20 ✉ 20121 ✆ 76005700, Fax 784212 – 🛗 ☎ ⇔.
⅍   DU g
⊊ 16000 – **52 rm** 103/146000 apartments 210000.

Casa Svizzera without rest., via San Raffaele 3 ✉ 20121 ✆ 8692246, Telex 316064, Fax 3498190 – 🛗 🍽 📺 ☎. ⅍ ⑤ ⑩ Ⅼ 𝑉𝐼𝑆𝐴   CV a
closed 28 July-24 August – **45 rm** ⊊ 119/178000.

Gritti without rest., piazza Santa Maria Beltrade 4 ✉ 20123 ✆ 801056, Telex 350597, Fax 89010999 – 🛗 🍽 📺 ☎. ⅍ ⑤ ⑩ Ⅼ 𝑉𝐼𝑆𝐴   CV u
⊊ 15000 – **48 rm** 115/167000.

Centro without rest., via Broletto 46 ✉ 20121 ✆ 875232, Telex 332632, Fax 875578 – 🛗 🍽
📺 ☎   BU e
54 rm ⊊ 105/161000.

Savini, galleria Vittorio Emanuele II ✉ 20121 ✆ 8058343, Fax 807306, Elegant traditional decor, « Winter garden » – 🍽. ⅍ ⑤ ⑩ Ⅼ 𝑉𝐼𝑆𝐴   CV n
closed Sunday, 10 to 19 August and 23 December-3 January – **M** (booking essential) a la carte 86/141000 (15%).

St. Andrews, via Sant'Andrea 23 ✉ 20121 ✆ 793132, Elegant installation, late night dinners – 🍽. ⅍ ⑤ ⑩ Ⅼ 𝑉𝐼𝑆𝐴. ⅍   DU y
closed Sunday and August – **M** (booking essential) a la carte 80/112000 (15%).

XXX **Biffi Scala,** piazza della Scala ⌧ 20121 ✆ 866651, Fax 807306, Late night dinners – ▤. ⬚ CU z
⬚ ⬚ E ⚡VISA⚡
closed Sunday, 10 to 20 August and 25 December-6 January – **M** a la carte 65/103000 (15%).

XXX ❈ **Peck,** via Victor Hugo 4 ⌧ 20123 ✆ 876774, Fax 860408 – ▤. ⬚ ⬚ ⬚ E VISA. ✻ CV b
closed Sunday and 2 to 23 July – **M** a la carte 67/103000
Spec. Insalata ricca d'astice, Paglia e fieno alle melanzane e capperi, Filetto di branzino ai semi di finocchio.
Wines Pinot bianco.

XXX **Tino Fontana,** piazza Diaz 5 ⌧ 20123 ✆ 800390 – ▤. ⬚ ⬚ ⬚ E VISA. ✻ CV d
closed Sunday and 6 to 20 August – **M** a la carte 60/86000

XXX **Santini,** corso Venezia 3 ⌧ 20121 ✆ 782010, Fax 76014691, 🏠 – ▤ DU v
closed Sunday and 12 to 26 August – **M** a la carte 52/108000.

XXX **Don Lisander,** via Manzoni 12/a ⌧ 20121 ✆ 790130, Fax 784573, « Outdoor summer
service » – ▤ ⬚ ⬚ ⬚ E VISA CU a
closed Saturday dinner and Sunday – **M** (booking essential) a la carte 71/95000.

XXX **Orti di Leonardo,** via Aristide de' Togni 6/8 ⌧ 20123 ✆ 4983197, Fax 4983476 – ▤ ⬚. ⬚
⬚ ⬚ VISA. ✻ AV b
closed Sunday and 5 to 26 August – **M** a la carte 51/86000

XXX ❈ **Canoviano,** via Hoepli 6 ⌧ 20121 ✆ 8058472 (will change to 86460147) – ▤. ⬚ ⬚ ⬚
E VISA. ✻ CV v
closed Saturday lunch, Sunday and August – **M** (booking essential) a la carte 69/119000
Spec. Trittico di pesce al vapore, Risotto alla milanese con pistilli di zafferano, Branzino con pomodoro e timo
(Summer-Autumn). **Wines** Pinot bianco, Dolcetto.

XXX **Suntory,** via Verdi 6 ⌧ 20121 ✆ 8693022, Fax 72023282, Japanese rest. – ▤. ⬚ ⬚ E
VISA. ✻ CU n
closed Sunday and 14 to 21 August – **M** a la carte 70/110000.

XXX **Alfio-Cavour,** via Senato 31 ⌧ 20121 ✆ 780731, Fax 783446 – ▤. ⬚ ⬚ ⬚ ⬚ E VISA
✻ DU a
closed Saturday, Sunday lunch, August and 23 December-3 January – **M** a la carte 56/100000.

XXX **Boeucc,** piazza Belgioioso 2 ⌧ 20121 ✆ 790224, 🏠 – ▤. ⬚. ✻ CDU x
closed Saturday, Sunday lunch, August and 24 December-2 January – **M** (booking essential)
a la carte 53/81000.

XXX **Peppino,** via Durini 7 ⌧ 20122 ✆ 781729 – ▤. ⬚ ⬚ ⬚. ✻ DV g
closed Friday and Saturday lunch – **M** a la carte 44/70000.

XXX **Royal Dynasty,** via Bocchetto 15 a ⌧ 20123 ✆ 872106, Chinese rest. – ▤. ⬚ ⬚ ⬚ E
VISA. ✻ – *closed Monday and 14 to 21 August* – **M** a la carte 31/47000 (12%). BV a

XX Odeon, via Bergamini 11 ⌧ 20122 ✆ 58307418 – ▤ DV h

XX **Le Api,** via Bagutta 2 ⌧ 20121 ✆ 76005780, 🏠 – ▤. ⬚ ⬚ ⬚ VISA. ✻ DUV p
closed Saturday lunch and Sunday – **M** a la carte 45/64000.

XX **La Bitta,** via del Carmine 3 ⌧ 20121 ✆ 879159 – ▤. ⬚ ⬚ ⬚ E VISA. ✻ CU r
closed Saturday lunch, Sunday, August and Christmas – **M** (fish only) a la carte 51/78000.

XX **Bagutta,** via Bagutta 14 ⌧ 20121 ✆ 76002767, Fax 799613, 🏠, Artists' meeting place,
« Typical paintings and caricatures » – ⬚ ⬚ ⬚ E VISA. ✻ DU e
closed Sunday, 7 to 31 August and 23 December-5 January – **M** a la carte 60/90000.

XX **Franco il Contadino,** via Fiori Chiari 20 ⌧ 20121 ✆ 808153, Typical rest. and artists'
meeting place – ▤. ⬚ ⬚ ⬚ E VISA CU e
closed Tuesday and July – **M** a la carte 39/64000 (10%).

XX **L'Infinito,** via Leopardi 25 ⌧ 20123 ✆ 4692276 – ▤. ⬚ ⬚ ⬚ E VISA. ✻ AU b
closed Saturday lunch and Sunday – **M** a la carte 40/62000.

XX **Opera Prima,** via Rovello 3 ⌧ 20121 ✆ 865235 – ✖ ▤. ⬚ ⬚ ⬚ E VISA BU v
closed Sunday – **M** a la carte 53/92000.

XX **Rigolo,** largo Treves angolo via Solferino 11 ⌧ 20121 ✆ 8059768, Habitués' rest. – ▤. ⬚
⬚ ⬚ E VISA. ✻ CU d
closed Monday, Tuesday lunch and July – **M** a la carte 36/59000.

XX **Kota Radja,** piazzale Baracca 6 ⌧ 20123 ✆ 468850, Chinese rest. – ▤. ⬚ ⬚ ⬚ E VISA
closed Monday – **M** a la carte 26/57000 (12%). AU a

X **Trattoria dell'Angolo,** via Fiori Chiari ang via Formentini ⌧ 20121 ✆ 86460152 – ▤. ⬚
⬚ VISA CU e
closed Saturday lunch, Sunday, 6 to 25 August and 1 to 7 January – **M** a la carte 47/66000.

Southern area Porta Ticinese, Porta Romana, Genova Station, Navigli, Ravizza Park, Vigentino (Plans : Milan pp. 6 and 7)

🏨 **Pierre Milano,** via Edmondo de Amicis 32 ⌧ 20123 ✆ 72000581, Telex 333303, Fax
8052157 – 📶 ✖ rm ▤ ⬚ ✆ ⬚ ⬚ ⬚ E VISA. ✻ BX b
M *(closed August)* a la carte 65/113000 – **47 rm** ⬚ 430/640000 apartments 800/950000 –
P 420/510000.

🏨 **Quark,** via Lampedusa 11/a ⌧ 20141 ✆ 84431, Telex 353448, Fax 8464190 – 📶 ▤ ⬚ ✆ ⬚
⬚ ⬚ – ⬚ 25-1000. ⬚ ⬚ ⬚ ⬚ E VISA. ✻ CZ a
M *(closed 31 July-22 August)* (residents only) a la carte 50/80000 – **122 rm** ⬚ 275000 apartments 330/390000 – ½ p 185000.

Liberty without rest., viale Bligny 56 ✉ 20136 ℘ 55182698, Fax 55191059 – AE E VISA. – *closed 10 to 25 August* – ☕ 15000 – **52 rm** 185/260000. DY **t**

Ascot without rest., via Lentasio 3/5 ✉ 20122 ℘ 58303300, Telex 311303, Fax 58303203 – AE E VISA. CX **e**
closed August – **63 rm** ☕ 195/280000.

Lloyd without rest., corso di Porta Romana 48 ✉ 20122 ℘ 58303332, Telex 335028, Fax 58303365 – 40-80. AE E VISA CX **z**
☕ 20000 – **52 rm** 195/260000.

D'Este without rest., viale Bligny 23 ✉ 20136 ℘ 5461041, Telex 324216 – 40-80. AE E VISA. CY **r**
☕ 18000 – **54 rm** 170/250000.

Crivi's without rest., corso Porta Vigentina 46 ✉ 20122 ℘ 5463341, Telex 313255, Fax 5400637 – 60. AE E VISA DY **a**
closed August – ☕ 20000 – **85 rm** 190/260000.

Ambrosiano without rest., via Santa Sofia 9 ✉ 20122 ℘ 58306044, Fax 58305067 – AE E VISA. CX **x**
closed August and 23 December-2 January – **68 rm** ☕ 120/180000.

Sant'Ambroeus without rest., viale Papiniano 14 ✉ 20123 ℘ 48008989, Telex 313373, Fax 48008687 – 50. AE E VISA AX **a**
closed August and Christmas – ☕ 16000 – **52 rm** 103/146000.

Mediterraneo without rest., via Muratori 14 ✉ 20135 ℘ 55019151, Telex 335812, Fax 55019151 – 120. AE E VISA DY **q**
closed 1 to 21 August – ☕ 15000 – **93 rm** 103/146000.

Adriatico without rest., via Conca del Naviglio 20 ✉ 20123 ℘ 58104141, Fax 8324141 – AE E VISA BX **m**
closed 1 to 21 August – ☕ 14000 – **105 rm** 98/135000.

Dei Fiori without rest., raccordo autostrada A7 ✉ 20142 ℘ 8436441, Fax 89501096 – AE E VISA AZ **e**
55 rm ☕ 77/120000, 8000.

Garden without rest., via Rutilia 6 ✉ 20141 ℘ 537368 – DZ **a**
closed August – ☕ 3000 – **23 rm** 56/78000.

XXX **L'Ulmet,** via Disciplini ang. via Olmetto ✉ 20123 ℘ 86452718 – AE E VISA BX **x**
closed Sunday and Monday lunch – **M** (booking essential) a la carte 61/79000.

XXX **Il Punto Malatesta,** via Bianca di Savoia 19 ✉ 20122 ℘ 58300079, Fax 656047 – AE VISA. – *closed Sunday, August and 1 to 7 January* – **M** a la carte 50/70000. CY **a**

XXX **Al Genovese,** via Pavia 9/14 ang. via Conchetta ✉ 20136 ℘ 8373180, Ligurian rest. – E VISA. – *closed Sunday, Monday lunch, 10 to 25 August and 1 to 7 January* – **M** (booking essential) a la carte 59/84000 BZ **a**

XXX **San Vito da Nino,** via San Vito 5 ✉ 20123 ℘ 8377029 – VISA. BX **a**
closed Monday and August – **M** (booking essential) a la carte 60/70000 (13%).

XXX ✿ **Scaletta,** piazzale Stazione Genova 3 ✉ 20144 ℘ 58100290 – AY **a**
closed Sunday, Monday, Easter, August and 24 December-6 January – **M** (booking essential) a la carte 80/100000
Spec. Insalata di seppioline e porcini, Gnocchi alla fontina, Coniglio alla peperonata. **Wines** Villa Bucci, Castellare.

XX ✿ **Al Porto,** piazzale Generale Cantore ✉ 20123 ℘ 8321481, Seafood – AE VISA
closed Sunday, Monday lunch, August and 24 December-3 January – **M** (booking essential) a la carte 54/74000 AXY **d**
Spec. Zuppa di fagioli e scampi, Rombo chiodato al rosmarino, Orata al pepe rosa. **Wines** Ribolla, Grignolino.

Districts : Bruzzano, Niguarda, Bicocca, viale Fulvio Testi – N : by : Monza, Lecco, Erba, Venezia :

Leonardhotel, via Senigallia 6 ✉ 20161 ℘ 64071, Telex 331552, Fax 64074839, – rm – 1200. AE E VISA. by ①
M 65000 – **290 rm** ☕ 344000 apartments 654/841000.

Starhotel Tourist, viale Fulvio Testi 300 ✉ 20126 ℘ 6437777, Telex 326852, Fax 6472516 – – 30-70. AE E VISA. rest by viale Zara DQ
closed August – **M** *(closed Saturday)* a la carte 42/55000 – **81 rm** ☕ 160/200000 – ½ p 142/215000.

Districts : corso Buenos Aires, Loreto, Lambrate – NE : by : Bergamo, Brescia :

Nasco without rest., via Spallanzani 40 ✉ 20129 ℘ 29512301, Telex 333116, Fax 208679 – – 50. AE E VISA by corso Buenos Aires DT
154 rm ☕ 240/280000 apartments 325/399000.

Concorde without rest., via Petrocchi 1 ang. viale Monza ✉ 20125 ℘ 2895853, Telex 315805, Fax 656802 – AE E VISA. by corso Buenos Aires DT
closed 1 to 24 August – ☕ 20000 – **120 rm** 175/275000.

Galles without rest., via Ozanam 1 ✉ 20129 ℘ 29404250, Telex 322091, Fax 29404872 – – 25-45. AE E VISA. by corso Buenos Aires DT
97 rm ☕ 325/425000.

XX ❀ **Calajunco,** via Stoppani 5 ✉ 20129 ℰ 2046003, Aeolian rest. – 🍽. 🕃 🖲 ⓞ 🇪 *VISA* . ⌘
closed Saturday lunch, Sunday, 10 to 31 August and 23 December-4 January – **M**
a la carte 69/106000   by corso Buenos Aires   DT
Spec. Reginelle al verde mare, Involtino di triglia, Salsiccia di mare, Coppa eoliana. **Wines** Cellaro, Chardonnay.

XX **Montecatini Alto,** viale Monza 7 ✉ 20125 ℰ 2846773 – 🍽. 🕃
closed Saturday lunch, Sunday and August – **M** a la carte 32/57000 (10%).
                                                        by Corso Buenos Aires   DT

Districts : Città Studi, Monforte, corso 22 Marzo, viale Corsica – E : by : Linate Airport,
Idroscalo, strada Rivoltana :

🏨 **Zefiro** without rest., **via Gallina 12** ✉ 20129 ℰ 7384253, Fax 713811 – 🛗 🖭 🅰 – 🔬 30.
VISA . ⌘
closed August, and 23 December-3 January – ⌑ 13000 – **55 rm** 92/129000.   by corso Concordia   DU

🏨 **Vittoria** without rest., via Pietro Calvi 32 ✉ 20129 ℰ 55190196, Fax 55190246 – 🛗 🖭 🕃 ☎.
🅰🖩 🕃 ⓞ 🇪 *VISA*
18 rm ⌑ 128/198000.   by corso 22 Marzo   DV

🏛 **Città Studi** without rest., via Saldini 24 ✉ 20133 ℰ 744666, Fax 713122 – 🛗 ☎. 🅰🖩 🕃 🇪
VISA
⌑ 10000 – **45 rm** 60/88000.   by corso Concordia   DU

XXXX ❀❀❀ **Gualtiero Marchesi,** via Bonvesin de la Riva 9 ✉ 20129 ℰ 741246, Fax 7384079,
Elegant installation – 🍽. 🅰🖩 🕃 ⓞ 🇪 *VISA* . ⌘   by corso 22 Marzo   DV
closed August, holidays, Sunday, Monday lunch and Saturday in July – **M** (booking essential)
a la carte 95/140000
Spec. Raviolo aperto, Filetti di sogliola fritti in salsa agrodolce, Costoletta di vitello alla milanese con piccoli
bouquets di verdure. **Wines** Selezione di Gualtiero Marchesi.

XXXX ❜**Giannino,** via Amatore Sciesa 8 ✉ 20135 ℰ 5452948, Traditional style, « Original decoration; winter garden » – 🅿. 🅰🖩 🕃 🖲 🇪 *VISA*   by corso 22 Marzo   DV
closed Sunday and August – **M** a la carte 81/134000.

XXXX **Soti's,** via Pietro Calvi 2 ✉ 20129 ℰ 796838, Fax 796838, Elegant installation – 🍽. 🅰🖩 🕃
🖲 🇪 *VISA* . ⌘   by corso 22 Marzo   DV
closed Saturday lunch, Sunday and August – **M** (booking essential) 80000 bc (lunch only)
and a la carte 80/120000 (dinner only).

XXX ❀ **L'Ami Berton,** via Nullo 14 angolo via Goldoni ✉ 20129 ℰ 713669 – 🍽. 🅰🖩 🕃 🇪 *VISA*
⌘   · by corso 22 Marzo   DV
closed Saturday lunch, Sunday, August and Christmas – **M** (booking essential)
a la carte 75/126000
Spec. Aragostelle gratinate con zucchini, Tagliolini con fiori di zucca e gamberi (February-November), Filetto di
storione in salsa di gamberi e caviale. **Wines** Sauvignon.

XXX **La Zelata,** via Anfossi 10 ✉ 20135 ℰ 5484115 – 🍽. 🅰🖩 🖲 *VISA* . ⌘
closed Saturday lunch, Sunday and August – **M** (booking essential) a la carte 48/69000.
                                                        by corso 22 Marzo   DV

XXX **Nino Arnaldo,** via Poerio 3 ✉ 20129 ℰ 76005981 – 🍽   by corso 22 Marzo   DV
closed Saturday lunch, Sunday, August and 23 December-7 January – **M** (booking essential)
a la carte 70/110000.

Districts : Fiera Campionaria, San Siro, Porta Magenta – NW : by ⑩ and ⑪ : Novara,
Torino :

🏨🏨 **Gd H. Brun and Rest. Ascot** ⌂, via Caldera ✉ 20153 ℰ 45271 and rest. ℰ 4526279,
Telex 315370, Fax 48204746 – 🛗 🖭 🖭 ☎ ♣ ⟷ 🅿 – 🔬 500. 🅰🖩 🕃 🖲 🇪 *VISA* . ⌘   by ⑪
closed August – **M** *(closed Sunday)* a la carte 78/119000 – **330 rm** ⌑ 305/400000 apartments
500/600000.

🏨 **Gd H. Fieramilano,** viale Boezio 20 ✉ 20145 ℰ 3105, Telex 331426, Fax 314119, ⚞ – 🛗
🍽 🖭 ☎ ♣ – 🔬 60. 🅰🖩 🕃 🖲 🇪 *VISA* . ⌘ rest   by via Vincenzo Monti   AU
M 70000 – **238 rm** ⌑ 280/330000.

🏨 **Rubens** without rest., via Rubens 21 ✉ 20148 ℰ 40302, Telex 333503, Fax 48193114 – 🛗 🍽
🖭 ☎ 🅿. 🅰🖩 🕃 🖲 🇪 *VISA* . ⌘   by corso Vercelli   AV
closed 1 to 21 August – **87 rm** ⌑ 195/230000.

🏨 **Washington** without rest., via Washington 23 ✉ 20146 ℰ 4813216, Fax 4814761 – 🛗 🍽
🖭 ☎. 🅰🖩 🕃 🖲 🇪 *VISA*   by corso Vercelli   AV
⌑ 18000 – **34 rm** 195/280000.

🏨 **Capitol,** via Cimarosa 6 ✉ 20144 ℰ 4988851, Telex 316150, Fax 4694724 – 🛗 🍽 🖭 ☎ –
🔬 60. 🅰🖩 🕃 🖲 🇪 *VISA* . ⌘ rest   by corso Vercelli   AV
M *(closed August)* (dinner only) a la carte 40/60000 – **96 rm** ⌑ 208/285000 – ½ p 182/248000.

🏨 **Domenichino** without rest., via Domenichino 41 ✉ 20149 ℰ 48009692, Fax 48003953 – 🛗
🍽 🖭 ⟷ 🅿 – 🔬 50. 🅰🖩 🕃 🖲 🇪 *VISA* . ⌘   by ⑪
closed 5 to 25 August and 25 December-5 January – ⌑ 14000 – **63 rm** 102/145000 apartments
204/247000.

🏨 **Mini Hotel Portello,** without rest., via Silva 12 ✉ 20152 ℰ 4814944, Fax 4819243 – 🛗 🍽 🖭
♣ 🅿 – 🔬 60 – **48 rm**.   . by ⑩

🏨 **Green House,** without rest., viale Famagosta 50 ✉ 20142 ℰ 8132451, Telex 335261, Fax
816624 – 🛗 🍽 🖭 ☎ ⟷ – **45 rm**   by ⑩

XXX ✿✿ **Aimo e Nadia,** via Montecuccoli 6 ⊠ 20147 ℰ 416886 – ☰. ⅋⅊ ⑤ ⑩ Ε 𝑉𝐼𝑆𝐴 ⋇
closed Saturday lunch, Sunday and August – **M** (booking essential) a la carte 70/114000
Spec. Mousse di fiori di zucca e ricotta fresca, Risotto con gamberi in crema di pisellini freschi, Piccione
novello farcito ai profumi di bosco. **Wines** Riesling e Ronco rosso Oltrepo. by ⑩

XXX **Trattoria del Ruzante,** via Massena 1 ⊠ 20145 ℰ 316102 – ☰. ⅋⅊ AT **s**
closed Sunday – **M** (booking essential) a la carte 43/58000.

XXX **Raffaello,** via Monte Amiata 4 ⊠ 20149 ℰ 4814227 – ☰. ⅋⅊ ⑤ Ε 𝑉𝐼𝑆𝐴 by ⑪
closed Wednesday and 1 to 24 August – **M** a la carte 39/63000.

XX **La Corba,** via dei Gigli 14 ⊠ 20147 ℰ 4158977, « Summer service in garden » – ⅋⅊ ⑤ ⑩
Ε 𝑉𝐼𝑆𝐴 by ⑩
closed Sunday dinner, Monday and 7 to 30 August – **M** a la carte 50/69000.

XX **Ribot,** via Cremosano 41 ⊠ 20148 ℰ 33001646, « Summer service in garden » – ⅊ ⅋⅊
𝑉𝐼𝑆𝐴. ⋇ by ⑪
closed Monday and 10 to 25 August – **M** a la carte 40/60000.

Districts : Sempione-Bullona, viale Certosa – NW : by ⑫ ⑬ and ⑭ :Varese, Como, Torino,
Malpensa Airport :

🏨 **Accademia** without rest., viale Certosa 68 ⊠ 20155 ℰ 3271841, Telex 315550, Fax 33103878,
« Frescoed rooms » – ⧖ ☰ 📺 ☎ ⅊ ⅋⅊ ⑤ ⑩ Ε 𝑉𝐼𝑆𝐴 by via Cenisio AR
67 rm ⊆ 220/315000.

🏨 **Raffaello** without rest., viale Certosa 108 ⊠ 20156 ℰ 3270146, Telex 315499, Fax 3270440
– ⧖ ☰ 📺 ☎ – 🔏 180. ⅋⅊ ⑤ ⑩ Ε 𝑉𝐼𝑆𝐴 by via Cenisio AR
150 rm ⊆ 170/245000.

🏨 **Berlino** without rest., via Plana 33 ⊠ 20155 ℰ 324141, Telex 312609, Fax 324145 – ⧖ ☰ 📺
☎. ⅋⅊ ⑤ ⑩ Ε 𝑉𝐼𝑆𝐴 by via Cenisio AR
closed August and 23 December-3 January – ⊆ 20000 – **47 rm** 103/146000.

XX **La Pobbia,** via Gallarate 92 ⊠ 20151 ℰ 305641, Neo rustic rest., « Outdoor service in
summer » – 🔏 40. ⅋⅊ 𝑉𝐼𝑆𝐴. ⋇ by via Cenisio AR
closed Sunday and August – **M** a la carte 40/60000 (12%).

XX **Da Stefano il Marchigiano,** via Arimondi 1 angolo via Plana ⊠ 20155 ℰ 33001869 –
☰ by via Cenisio AR

X **Al Vöttantott,** corso Sempione 88 ⊠ 20154 ℰ 33603114 – ☰. ⅋⅊
closed Sunday and August – **M** a la carte 28/46000. by corso Sempione AS

Abbiategrasso 20081 Milano ⑨⑧⑧ ③, ⑫⑫⑧ F 8 – pop. 27 593 alt. 120 – ✪ 02.
Roma 590 – Alessandria 74 – Milano 23 – Novara 29 – Pavia 33.

at Cassinetta di Lugagnano N : 3 km – ⊠ 20080 :

XXXX ✿✿✿ **Antica Osteria del Ponte,** ℰ 9420034, Fax 9420610 – ☰ ⅊ ⅋⅊ ⑤ ⑩ 𝑉𝐼𝑆𝐴. ⋇
closed Sunday, Monday, August, January and February – **M** (booking essential)
a la carte 90/141000
Spec. Foie gras d'anatra farcito uvetta pinoli e pistacchi, Ravioli di aragosta nella sua salsa, Filetti di triglia alla
mediterranea (Spring-Summer). **Wines** Franciacorta bianco, Dolcetto di Dogliani.

Malgrate 22040 Como ⑫⑫⑧ E 10, ②①⑨ ⑨ ⑩ – pop. 4 196 alt. 224 – ✪ 0341.
Roma 623 – Bellagio 20 – Como 27 – Lecco 2 – Milano 54.

🏨 ✿✿ **Il Griso,** ℰ 283217 (will change in 202040), Fax 202248, ⟨ lago e monti, « Small park »,
🎣, ⇄, 🏊 – ⧖ ☰ 📺 ☎ ⅊ – 🔏 30. ⅋⅊ ⑤ ⑩ Ε 𝑉𝐼𝑆𝐴
closed 20 December-6 January – **M** a la carte 60/110000 – ⊆ 15000 – **41 rm** 125/160000,
☰ 10000 – ½ p 180000
Spec. Terrina di primizie con fegato grasso d'anitra (Summer), Ravioli di rane con crema di scalogno (Spring).
Stufato di scampi con fonduta di porri. **Wines** Pinot Cà del Bosco, Barbaresco.

Ranco 21020 Varese ⑫⑫⑧ E 7, ②①⑨ ⑦ – pop. 971 alt. 214 – ✪ 0331.
Roma 644 – Laveno Mombello 21 – Milano 67 – Novara 51 – Sesto Calende 12 – Varese 27.

XXX ✿✿ **Del Sole** ⟐ with rm, ℰ 976507, Fax 976620, ⟨, « Summer service under pergola »,
🎣⚬, 🚗 – 📺 ☎ ⅊ ⅋⅊ ⑤ ⑩ Ε. ⋇
closed January-11 February – **M** (booking essential) (closed Monday dinner and Tuesday)
a la carte 75/117000 (10%) – ⊆ 10000 – 7 apartments 200/220000 – ½ p 170/190000
Spec. Terrina di foie gras affumicato, Lasagne al branzino e salsa al limone , Gomitolo di salmone in fili di
patate. **Wines** Ribolla, Barbaresco.

Soriso 28018 Novara ⑫⑫⑧ E 7, ②①⑨ ⑯ – pop. 753 alt. 452 – ✪ 0322.
Roma 654 – Arona 20 – Milano 78 – Novara 40 – Torino 114 – Varese 46.

XXXX ✿✿ **Al Sorriso** with rm, ℰ 983228, Fax 983328 – 📺 ☎. ⑤ 𝑉𝐼𝑆𝐴. ⋇
closed 7 to 21 August and 10 to 31 January – **M** (booking essential) (closed Monday and
Tuesday lunch) a la carte 90/135000 – ⊆ 12000 – **8 rm** 70/98000 – ½ p 150000
Spec. Salmi di triglie con le fave (Spring), Fagottini di animelle al tartufo nero, Sandwich di porcino con fegato
d'oca e vinaigrette. **Wines** Sauvignon, Gattinara.

NAPOLI

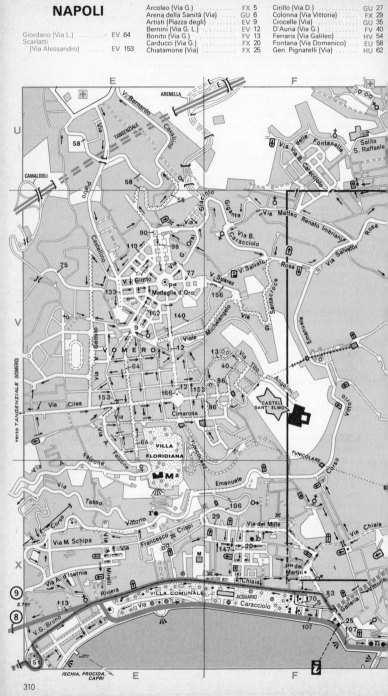

ISCHIA, PROCIDA, CAPRI

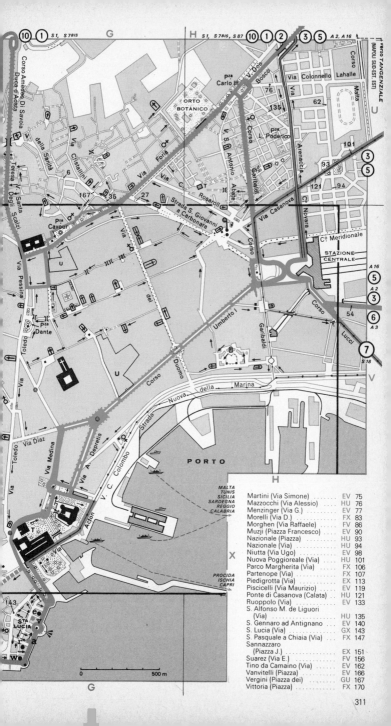

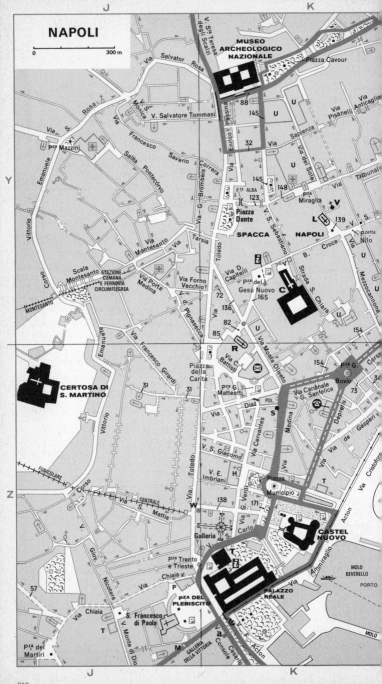

NAPOLI

0   300 m

MUSEO ARCHEOLOGICO NAZIONALE

Piazza Cavour

V. Sta Teresa degli Scalzi

Salvator Rosa

V. Salvatore Tommasi

Via S. Rosa

Via Monica

Via Francesco

Via S. Emanuele

P.za Mazzini

Via S. Francesco Saverio

Salita Pontecórvo

Via Brombeis

Correra

Enrico Pessina

Via Antcaglia

Via Pisanelli

Sapienza

Via dei Sole

Via Tribunali

P.za Miraglia

P.ta ALBA

Piazza Dante

SPACCA NAPOLI

Via Montesanto

Via Tarsia

Toledo

Via S. Sebastiano

B. Croce

P.zetta Nilo

Via Mezzocannone

Scala Montesanto
STAZIONE CUMANA E FERROVIA CIRCUMFLEGREA

Via Porta Medina

Via Forno Vecchio

Via D. Capitelli

Gesù Nuovo

Strada S. Chiara

C

Pignasecca

Via Monte Oliveto

Via Battisti

R

Piazza della Carità

P.za G. Matteotti

Via Diaz

Via Cervantes

P.za G. Bovio

Via Cardinale G. Santelice

Via Medina

Depretis

Via de' Gasperi

CERTOSA DI S. MARTINO

Via Francesco Girardi

Emanuele

Vittorio

POL

S

V. S. Giacomo

V. E. Imbriani

G. Verdi

Piazza Municipio

H

Via Acton

Via Cristoforo

FUNICOLARE

Corso Via S. Mattia

Via CENTRALE

W

Carlo

Galleria

Giov.

Nicotera

Via Toledo

P.za Trento e Trieste

Via Chiaia

P

P.za DEL PLEBISCITO

CASTEL NUOVO

PALAZZO REALE

MOLO BEVERELLO

PORTO

MOLO

P.za del Martiri

S. Francesco di Paola

V. Monte di Dio

M

GALLERIA DELLA VITTORIA

Via Cesario

Via Console

Admiraglio

88

145

32

145

148

123

139

165

72

136

82

85

154

154

73

31

31

138

171

57

312

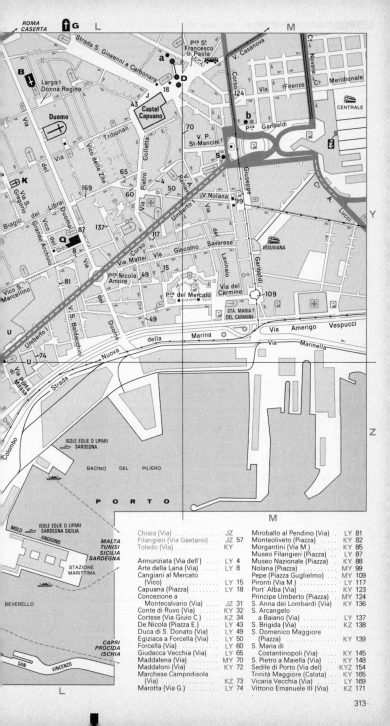

NAPLES (NAPOLI) 80100 P 988 ㉗ – pop. 1 204 149 – h.s. April-October – ☎ 081.

See : National Archaeological Museum*** KY – New Castle** KZ – Port of Santa Lucia**: ≤** of Vesuvius and bay – ≤*** at night from via Partenope of the Vomero and Posillipo FX – San Carlo Theatre* KZ **T** – Piazza del Plebiscito* JKZ – Royal Palace* KZ – Carthusian Monastery of St. Martin** JZ : ≤*** of the Bay of Naples from gallery 25.

Spacca-Napoli quarter** KY – Tomb** of King Robert the with in Church of Santa Chiara* KY **C** – Caryatids* by Tino da Camaino in Church of St. Dominic Major KY **L** – Sculptures* in Chapel of San Severo KY **V** – Arch*, Tomb* of Catherine of Austria, apse* in Church of St. Lawrence Major LY **K** – Capodimonte Palace and National Gallery**.

Mergellina*: ≤** of the bay – Villa Floridiana* EVX: ≤* – Catacombs of San Gennaro* FU **X** – Church of Santa Maria Donnaregina* LY **B** – Church of San Giovanni Carbonara* LY **G** – Capuan Gate* LMY **D** – Cuomo Palace* LY **Q** – Sculptures* in the Church of St. Anne of the Lombards KYZ **R** – Posillipo* – Marechiaro* – ≤** of the Bay from Virgiliano Park (or Rimembranza Park).

Exc : Bay of Naples*** by the coast road to Campi Flegrei** by ⑧, to Sorrento Peninsula by ⑦ – Island of Capri*** – Island of Ischia***.

⛳9 (closed Monday) in Arco Felice ✉ 80072 ✆ 8674296, by ⑧ : 19 km.

✈ Ugo Niutta of Capodichino NE : 6 km (except Sunday) ✆ 5425333 – Alitalia, via Medina 41 ✉ 80133 ✆ 5425222.

⛴ to Capri daily (1 h 15 mn) – Navigazione Libera del Golfo, molo Beverello ✉ 80133 ✆ 5520763, Telex 722661; to Capri (1 h 15 mn), Ischia (1 h 15 mn) and Procida (1 h), daily – Caremar De Luca Agency, molo Beverello ✉ 80133 ✆ 5513882; to Cagliari June-September, Tuesday, Friday and Sunday, Friday and Sunday in other months (15 h 45 mn) and Palermo daily (10 h 30 mn) – Tirrenia Navigazione, Stazione Marittima, molo Angioino ✉ 80133 ✆5512181, Telex 710030, Fax 7201441; to Ischia daily (1 h 15 mn) – Libera Navigazione Lauro, via Caracciolo 11 ✉ 80122 ✆ 991889, Telex 720354.

🚤 to Capri (45 mn), Ischia (45 mn) and Procida (35 mn) daily – Caremar De Luca Agency, molo Beverello ✉ 80133 ✆ 5513882; to Ischia daily (1 h) – Alilauro, via Caracciolo 11 ✉ 80122 ✆ 7611004, Telex 720354; to Capri daily (45 mn) and Aeolian Island May-15 September daily (5 h) and Procida-Ischia daily (45 mn) – SNAV, via Caracciolo 10 ✉ 80122 ✆ 7612348, Telex 720446, Fax 7612141.

ℹ via Partenope 10/a ✉ 80121 ✆ 7644871 – piazza del Plebiscito (Royal Palace) ✉ 80132 ✆ 418744 – Central Station ✉ 80142 ✆ 268779 - Capodichino Airport ✉ 80133 ✆ 7805761 – piazza del Gesù Nuovo 7 ✉ 80135 ✆ 5523328 - Passaggio Castel dell'Ovo ✉ 80132 ✆ 411461.

A.C.I. piazzale Tecchio 49/d ✉ 80125 ✆ 614511.

Roma 219 ③ – Bari 261 ⑤.

Plans on preceding pages

Excelsior, via Partenope 48 ✉ 80121 ✆ 417111, Telex 710043, Fax 411743, ≤ gulf, Vesuvius and Castel dell'Ovo – |♦| ▤ TV ☎ – 🏛 30-200. AE ⓢ ⓞ E VISA. ✈ GX **w**
M a la carte 80/120000 – ☕ 25000 – **114 rm** 286/429000 apartments 655/1131000.

Vesuvio, via Partenope 45 ✉ 80121 ✆ 417044, Telex 710127, Fax 417044, « Roof garden rest. with ≤ gulf and Castel dell'Ovo » – |♦| ⇆ ▤ TV ☎ – 🏛 25-250. AE ⓢ ⓞ E VISA. ✈
M a la carte 55/80000 – **170 rm** ☕ 200/290000 apartments 500/1000000, ▤ 25000 – ½ p 195/250000. FX **n**

Britannique, corso Vittorio Emanuele 133 ✉ 80121 ✆ 7614145, Telex 722281, Fax 669760, ≤, « Garden » – |♦| ▤ TV ☎ 🚗 – 🏛 25-100. AE ⓢ ⓞ E VISA. ✈ rest EX **r**
M 40000 – ☕ 11000 – **80 rm** 173/231000 apartments 273000, ▤ 11000 – ½ p 166000.

Jolly, via Medina 70 ✉ 80133 ✆ 416000, Telex 720335, Fax 5518010, « Roof garden rest. with ≤ town, gulf and Vesuvius » – |♦| ▤ TV ☎ – 🏛 250. AE ⓢ ⓞ E VISA. ✈ rest KZ **s**
M 45000 – **278 rm** ☕ 190/250000 – ½ p 170/235000.

Paradiso, via Catullo 11 ✉ 80122 ✆ 7614161, Telex 722049, Fax 7613449, ≤ gulf, town and Vesuvius, 🌴 – |♦| ▤ TV ☎ – 🏛 40-50. AE ⓢ ⓞ E VISA. ✈ by via Caracciolo FX
M *(closed 6 to 26 August)* a la carte 42/60000 – **71 rm** ☕ 150/240000 – ½ p 160/190000.

San Germano, via Beccadelli 41 ✉ 80125 ✆ 5705422, Telex 720080, Fax 5701546, « Beautiful garden-park », 🏊 – |♦| ▤ TV ☎ 🚗 Ⓟ – 🏛 220. AE ⓢ ⓞ E VISA. ✈ rest by ⑧
M (residents only) (closed Sunday) 40000 – **101 rm** ☕ 135/215000 – ½ p 130/170000.

Royal, via Partenope 38 ✉ 80121 ✆ 7644800, Telex 710167, Fax 7645707, ≤ gulf, Posillipo and Castel dell'Ovo, 🏊 – |♦| ▤ TV ☎ 🚗 – 🏛 25-200. AE ⓢ ⓞ E VISA. ✈ rest FX **n**
M a la carte 65/108000 – **273 rm** ☕ 196/293000 apartments 600000, ▤ 42000 – ½ p 220/260000.

Majestic, largo Vasto a Chiaia 68 ✉ 80121 ✆ 416500, Telex 720408, Fax 416500 – |♦| ▤ TV ☎ 🚗 – 🏛 25-100. AE ⓢ ⓞ E VISA. ✈ FX **b**
M a la carte 30/50000 – **132 rm** ☕ 140/230000 apartments 300/350000, ▤ 10000.

Miramare without rest., via Nazario Sauro 24 ✉ 80132 ✆ 427388, Fax 416775, ≤ – |♦| ▤ TV ☎. AE ⓢ ⓞ E VISA. ✈ GX **e**
closed 16 to 31 August – **30 rm** ☕ 200/280000.

Serius, viale Augusto 74 ✉ 80125 ✆ 614844 – |♦| ▤ TV ☎ 🚗. ✈ by ⑧
M a la carte 50/70000 – **69 rm** ☕ 105/150000 – ½ p 130/150000.

Cavour, piazza Garibaldi 32 ✉ 80142 ✆ 283122 – |♦| TV ☎. AE ⓢ ⓞ E VISA. ✈ MY **b**
M rest. see Cavour below – **94 rm** ☕ 96/141000 – ½ p 96/117000.

🏨 **Mexico** without rest., via Cesare Rossarol 13/15 ⊠ 80139 ℰ 266554, Fax 266330 – 🖷 📺 ☎
40 rm. LY **a**

🏨 **Palace Hotel,** piazza Garibaldi 9 ⊠ 80142 ℰ 5535978, Telex 720262, Fax 264306 – 📳 📺
☎ – 🏦 30-80. 🖭 🖸 ⓪ 🇪 𝘝𝘐𝘚𝘈. 🛠
M rest. see Cavour below – **102 rm** ⊑ 96/141000 – ½ p 96/117000. MY **s**

🏨 **Rex** without rest., via Palepoli 12 ⊠ 80132 ℰ 416388, Fax 416919 – 🖷 📺 ☎. 🖭 🖸 ⓪ 🇪
𝘝𝘐𝘚𝘈 – ⊑ 7000 – **40 rm** 87/151000, 🖷 18000. GX **r**

XXX **La Sacrestia,** via Orazio 116 ⊠ 80122 ℰ 7611051, Elegant rest., « Summer service in
garden-terrace with ≤ » – 🖷 🖭 ⓪ 𝘝𝘐𝘚𝘈. 🛠 by via Caracciolo FX
closed August, Sunday in July and Monday except July – **M** a la carte 80/100000 (14%).

XXX ❀ **La Cantinella,** via Cuma 42 ⊠ 80132 ℰ 405375, Fax 415523 – 🖷. 🖭 🖸 ⓪ 🇪 𝘝𝘐𝘚𝘈. 🛠
closed Sunday, Christmas, New Year's Day and August – **M** a la carte 45/60000 (12%).
Spec. Linguine in salsa di spinaci con scampi, Risotto alla Cantinella, Pesce in brodetto. **Wines** Greco di Tufo,
Taurasi. GX **v**

XXX **Rosolino,** via Nazario Sauro 5/7 ⊠ 80132 ℰ 415873, Fax 405457, rest. piano bar – 🖷 –
🏦 70. 🖭 🖸 ⓪ 🇪 𝘝𝘐𝘚𝘈
closed Sunday and August – **M** a la carte 54/95000. GX **a**

XX **Cavour,** piazza Garibaldi 34 ⊠ 80142 ℰ 264730 – 🖷. 🖭 🖸 ⓪ 🇪 𝘝𝘐𝘚𝘈. 🛠 MY **b**
closed Sunday – **M** a la carte 33/56000 (15%).

XX **San Carlo,** via Cesario Console 18/19 ⊠ 80132 ℰ 426057 – 🖭 🖸 ⓪ 🇪 𝘝𝘐𝘚𝘈. 🛠 KZ **a**
closed Sunday and 10 to 20 August – **M** (booking essential) a la carte 45/60000 (10%).

XX ❀ **Giuseppone a Mare,** via Ferdinando Russo 13-Capo Posillipo ⊠ 80123 ℰ 7696002,
Seaside rest. with ≤ – 🅿 🖭 🖸 ⓪ 🇪 𝘝𝘐𝘚𝘈. 🛠 by via Caracciolo FX
closed Sunday and 23 to 31 December – **M** a la carte 33/56000 (12%).
Spec. Linguine con scampi, Polipetti al pignatiello, Spigola all'acqua pazza. **Wines** Ischia bianco e rosso.

XX **Ciro a Santa Brigida,** via Santa Brigida 73 ⊠ 80132 ℰ 5524072, rest. and pizzeria – ⤜➙
🖷 🖭 ⓪ 𝘝𝘐𝘚𝘈 JZ **w**
closed Sunday and 10 to 25 August – **M** a la carte 37/61000.

XX **A' Fenestrella,** calata Ponticello a Marechiaro ⊠ 80123 ℰ 7690020, ≤, 🍽 – 🅿. 𝘝𝘐𝘚𝘈
closed Wednesday and lunch July-August – **M** a la carte 34/52000 (15%).
by via Caracciolo FX

X **Sbrescia,** rampe Sant'Antonio a Posillipo 109 ⊠ 80122 ℰ 669140, Typical Neapolitan
rest. with ≤ town and gulf – 🖭 𝘝𝘐𝘚𝘈. 🛠 by via Caracciolo FX
closed Monday and 15 to 28 August – **M** a la carte 27/45000 (12%).

Island of Capri 80073 Napoli 𝟵𝟴𝟴 ㉗ – pop. 12 666 – h.s. Easter and June-September –
✪ 081.

🏨 **Gd H. Quisisana,** via Camerelle 2 ℰ 8370788, Telex 710520, Fax 8376080, ≤ sea and
Certosa, 🍽, « Garden with ⊒ », 🖽, 🏊, 🏋, 🎾 – 📳 🖷 📺 ☎ – 🏦 25-400. 🖭 🖸 ⓪ 🇪
𝘝𝘐𝘚𝘈
Easter-October – **M** (residents only) a la carte 65/115000 – **150 rm** ⊑ 320/500000 apartments
750/1200000 – ½ p 320/360000.

🏨 **Scalinatella** ⤷ without rest., via Tragara 8 ℰ 8370633, Telex 721204, Fax 8378291, ≤ sea
and Certosa, ⊒ heated – 📳 🖷 📺 ☎. 🖭 𝘝𝘐𝘚𝘈
15 March-5 November – **28 rm** ⊑ 220/420000.

🏨 **Europa Palace,** via Capodimonte 2 ℰ 8370955, Telex 710397, Fax 8373191, ≤, 🍽, « Floral
terraces with ⊒ », 🏋 – 🖷 ☎ – 🏦 400. 🖭 🖸 ⓪ 🇪 𝘝𝘐𝘚𝘈. 🛠
April-October – **M** a la carte 60/92000 – **92 rm** ⊑ 195/360000 apartments 540/610000 –
½ p 163/225000.

🏨 **Luna** ⤷, viale Matteotti 3 ℰ 8370433, Telex 721247, Fax 8377459, ≤ sea, Faraglioni and
Certosa, 🍽, « Terraces and garden with ⊒ » – 📳 🖷 rm 📺 ☎. 🖭 🖸 ⓪ 🇪 𝘝𝘐𝘚𝘈. 🛠 rest
April-October – **M** a la carte 50/68000 – ⊑ 22000 – **44 rm** 190/290000, 🖷 9000 –
½ p 150/220000.

🏨 **La Palma and Rest. Relais la Palma,** via Vittorio Emanuele 39 ℰ 8370133, Telex
722015, Fax 8376966, 🍽, 🏋 – 📳 🖷 📺 ☎ – 🏦 25-200. 🖭 🖸 ⓪ 🇪 𝘝𝘐𝘚𝘈. 🛠 rest
M *(closed lunch 15 to 31 July)* a la carte 37/63000 – **80 rm** ⊑ 250/320000 – ½ p 105/200000.

🏨 **La Pazziella** ⤷ without rest., via Fuorlovado 36 ℰ 8370044, Fax 8370085, « Flowered
garden » – 🖷 📺 ☎. 🖭 🖸 ⓪ 🇪 𝘝𝘐𝘚𝘈
19 rm ⊑ 200/300000 apartments 350/500000.

🏨 **Punta Tragara** ⤷, via Tragara 57 ℰ 8370844, Telex 710261, Fax 8377790, ≤ Faraglioni and
coast, 🍽, « Panoramic terrace with ⊒ heated » – 🖷 📺 ☎. 🖭 🖸 ⓪ 🇪 𝘝𝘐𝘚𝘈. 🛠
22 March-22 October – **M** a la carte 58/100000 – 33 apartments ⊑ 530000.

🏨 **La Pineta** ⤷, via Tragara 6 ℰ 8370644, Telex 710011, Fax 8376445, ≤ sea and Certosa,
« Floral terraces in pine-wood », 🏋, 🏊, ⊒ – 🖷 📺 ☎. 🏦 30. 🖭 🖸 ⓪ 🇪 𝘝𝘐𝘚𝘈. 🛠
M a la carte 58/70000 – **52 rm** ⊑ 200/300000 apartments 350/400000 – ½ p 140/180000.

🏨 **Villa delle Sirene,** via Camerelle 51 ℰ 8370102, Fax 8370957, ≤, 🍽, « Lemon-grove
with ⊒ » – 📳 🖷 ☎. 🖭 🖸 ⓪ 🇪 𝘝𝘐𝘚𝘈
April-October – **M** *(closed Tuesday)* a la carte 32/45000 – **35 rm** ⊑ 220/270000, 🖷 20000 –
½ p 130/170000.

La Brunella ⌂, via Tragara 24 ℰ 8370122, Telex 721451, Fax 8370430, ≤ sea and coast, 斧, « Floral terraces », ⅃ heated – ▤ rm ⊡ ⊛ 🅴 VISA ⅗
19 March-5 November – **M** a la carte 27/52000 (12%) – **18 rm** ☲ 250000 – ½ p 150/160000.

Flora ⌂ without rest., via Serena 26 ℰ 8370211, Fax 8378949, ≤ sea and Certosa, « Floral terrace » – ▤ ☎ 🅰🅴 🅱 ⊛ 🅴 VISA ⅗
closed 9 January-14 March – ☲ 30000 – **22 rm** 124/258000, ▤ 20000.

Gatto Bianco, via Vittorio Emanuele 32 ℰ 8370446, Fax 8378060, « Summer rest. service under pergola » – 劇 ▤ rm 🅰🅴, 🅰🅴 🅱 ⊛ 🅴 VISA ⅗ rm
27 December-6 January and March-October – **M** 35/45000 – **44 rm** ☲ 105/190000, ▤ 20000 – ½ p 120/145000.

Villa Sarah ⌂ without rest., via Tiberio 3/a ℰ 8377817, ≤, « Shaded garden » – ☎. 🅰🅴. ⅗ – *Easter-October* – **20 rm** ☲ 90/150000.

San Felice without rest., via li Campi 13 ℰ 8376122, Fax 8378264, 斧, ⅃ – ▤ rm ☎. 🅰🅴 🅱 ⊛ VISA
April-October – ☲ 25000 – **30 rm** 94/140000, ▤ 25000.

Florida without rest., via Fuorlovado 34 ℰ 8370710, Fax 8370497, 斧 – ☎. 🅰🅴 🅱 ⊛ VISA
March-11 November – ☲ 13000 – **19 rm** 58/95000.

La Certosella, via Tragara 15 ℰ 8370713, Fax 8370541, ≤, « Summer service on terrace with ⅃ heated » – 🅰🅴 🅱 ⊛ VISA ⅗
May-October; closed Tuesday (except July-September) – **M** a la carte 60/94000.

La Capannina, via Le Botteghe 14 ℰ 8370732, Fax 8376990 – ▤. 🅰🅴 🅱 🅴 VISA
15 March-6 November; closed Wednesday (except August) – **M** (booking essential for dinner) a la carte 40/58000 (15%).

La Pigna, via Roma 30 ℰ 8370280, Fax 8370280, ≤ gulf of Naples, « Summer service on lemon-grove » – 🅰🅴 🅱 ⊛ 🅴 VISA
Easter-October; closed Tuesday (except July-September) – **M** a la carte 38/57000 (15%).

Casanova, via Le Botteghe 46 ℰ 8377642 – 🅰🅴 🅱 ⊛ 🅴 VISA
April-October; closed Thursday (except July-September) – **M** a la carte 35/50000 (15%).

La Tavernetta, via Lo Palazzo 23/a ℰ 8376864 – 🅰🅴 🅱 ⊛ 🅴 VISA
closed 15 January-15 February, Monday and lunch October-May (except weekend) – **M** a la carte 30/62000 (15%).

Al Grottino, via Longano 27 ℰ 8370584 – ▤. 🅰🅴 VISA
closed Tuesday, 26 January-9 March and 11 November-28 December – **M** a la carte 26/37000 (15%).

Sant'Agata sui due Golfi 80064 Napoli – alt. 391 – h.s. April-September – ✪ 081.
Roma 266 – Castellammare di Stabia 28 – ♦Napoli 57 – Salerno 56 – Sorrento 9.

✪✪**Don Alfonso 1890**, ℰ 8780026, Fax 8780026, 斧 – 🅿 🅰🅴 ⊛ VISA ⅗
closed 8 January-23 February, Sunday dinner and Monday (except Christmas, New Year's Day, Easter and 15 July-15 September) – **M** (booking essential) a la carte 52/77000 (15%)
Spec. Insalata di aragosta o astice agli agrumi, Linguine alle vongole e zucchine, Filetti di boccadoro ai cetrioli e rosmarino. Wines Biancolella, Aglianico.

PALERME (PALERMO) 90100 🄿 🞵🞵🞵 ⊛ – pop. 731 418 – ✪ 091.

See : Palace of the Normans★★: the palatine Chapel★★★, mosaics★★★ AZ – Regional Gallery of Sicily★★ in Abbatellis Palace★: Death Triumphant★★★ by Antonello da Messina CY **M1** – Piazza Bellini★★ BY : Martorana Church★★, Church of St. Cataldo★★ – Church of St. John of the Hermits★★ AZ – Capuchin Catacombs★★ – Piazza Pretoria★ BY : fountain★★ – Archaeological Museum★: metopes from the temples at Selinus★★, the Ram★★ BY **M** – Chiaramonte Palace★: magnolia fig trees★★ in Garibaldi Gardens CY – St. Lawrence Oratory★ CY **N** – Quattro Canti★ BY – Cathedral★ AZ – Villa Bonanno★ AZ – Palazzo della Zisa★ – Botanical Garden★ CDZ – Sicilian carts★ in Ethnographic Museum.

Envir. : Monreale★★★ by ② : 8 km – Monte Pellegrino★★ by ③ : 14 km.

✈ Punta Raisi by ③ : 30 km ℰ 6019333 – Alitalia, via della Libertà 29 ☒ 90139 ℰ 6019111.

⛴ to Genova Tuesday, Friday and Sunday, 25 June-15 October, Tuesday and Friday other months (23 h) and to Livorno Monday, Wednesday, Friday and Sunday (19 h) – Grandi Traghetti, via Mariano Stabile 53 ☒ 90141 ℰ 587839, Telex 910098, Fax 589629; to Napoli daily (10 h 30 mn); to Genova Monday, Wednesday, Friday and Saturday, June-September, Monday, Wednesday and Friday other months (23 h) and to Cagliari June-September, Sunday and Friday other months (12 h 30 mn) – Tirrenia Navigazione, via Roma 385 ☒ 90133 ℰ 333300, Telex 910020, Fax 6021221; to Ustica daily (2 h 20 mn) – Siremar Prestifilippo Agency, via Crispi 118 ☒ 90133 ℰ 582403.

⛴ to Ustica daily (1 h 15 mn) – Siremar Prestifilippo Agency, via Crispi 118 ☒ 90133 ℰ 582403; to Cefalù-Aeolian Island daily June-September (3 h 30 mn) – SNAV Barbaro Agency, piazza Principe di Belmonte 51 ☒ 90139 ℰ 586533 Fax 584830.

🛈 piazza Castelnuovo 34 ☒ 90141 ℰ 583847, Telex 910179 – Punta Raisi Airport ℰ 591698 – Central Station ☒ 90127 ℰ 6166000 ext. 3010.

A.C.I. via delle Alpi 6 ☒ 90144 ℰ 300471.

Messina 235 ①.

Plan on following pages

Villa Igiea Gd H. 🦢, salita Belmonte 43 ⊠ 90142 𝒫 543744, Telex 910092, Fax 547654, ≤, 🌴, « Floral terraces overlooking the sea », ⅃, ✍, ％ – ⅃ 🛏 🖭 ☎ ♿ 🅿 – 🟰 50-500. 🆎 🗓 ⓞ Ε VISA. ℅ rest   by ③
M 80000 – **117 rm** � 260/390000 apartments 560/620000 – ½ p 260000.

Astoria Palace, via Monte Pellegrino 62 ⊠ 90142 𝒫 6371820, Telex 911045, Fax 6372178, 🔲 – ⅃ 🛏 🖭 ☎ 🅿 – 🟰 30-1000. 🆎 🗓 ⓞ VISA. ℅   by via Crispi BX
M 40000 – **325 rm** � 139/198000 apartments 325000 – ½ p 160/205000.

Gd H. et des Palmes, via Roma 398 ⊠ 90139 𝒫 583933, Telex 911082, Fax 331545, « Roof-garden rest. nightly » – ⅃ 🛏 🖭 ☎ – 🟰 30-250   BX **g**
187 rm.

President, via Crispi 230 ⊠ 90139 𝒫 580733, Telex 910359, Fax 6111588, ≤, « Roof garden rest. » – ⅃ 🛏 🖭 ☎ – 🟰 30-150. 🆎 🗓 ⓞ Ε VISA. ℅   BX **e**
M a la carte 32/47000 – **129 rm** ⊏ 110/145000 – ½ p 100/125000.

Jolly, Foro Italico 22 ⊠ 90133 𝒫 6165090, Telex 910076, Fax 6161441, 🌴, ⅃, ✍ – ⅃ 🛏 🖭 ☎ 🅿 – 🟰 50-500. 🆎 🗓 ⓞ Ε VISA. ℅ rest   DY **s**
M 35000 – **273 rm** ⊏ 145/190000 – ½ p 130/180000.

Excelsior Palace, via Marchese Ugo 3 ⊠ 90141 𝒫 6256176, Telex 911149, Fax 342139 – ⅃ ✢ rest 🛏 🖭 ☎ – 🟰 50-100. 🆎 🗓 ⓞ Ε VISA. ℅ rest   AX **c**
M 35000 – **128 rm** ⊏ 120/210000 apartments 240000 – ½ p 140000.

Politeama Palace, piazza Ruggero Settimo 15 ⊠ 90139 𝒫 322777, Telex 911053, Fax 6111589 – ⅃ 🛏 🖭 ☎ – 🟰 50-130   AX **s**
102 rm.

Europa, via Agrigento 3 ⊠ 90141 𝒫 6256323, Fax 6256323 – ⅃ 🛏 🖭 ☎. 🆎 🗓 ⓞ Ε VISA. ℅   AX **r**
M (residents only) 30000 – ⊏ 15000 – **73 rm** 75/110000 – ½ p 90/110000.

Mediterraneo, via Rosolino Pilo 43 ⊠ 90139 𝒫 581133, Telex 912140, Fax 586974 – ⅃ 🛏 🖭 ☎ – 🟰 50. 🆎 🗓 ⓞ Ε VISA. ℅   BX **k**
M (residents only) 30000 – ⊏ 15000 – **105 rm** 75/110000 – ½ p 91/111000.

Ponte, via Crispi 99 ⊠ 90139 𝒫 583744, Telex 910492, Fax 581845 – ⅃ 🛏 🖭 ☎. 🆎 🗓 ⓞ Ε VISA. ℅   BX **a**
M a la carte 30/40000 – ⊏ 7000 – **137 rm** 60/88000 – ½ p 86000.

MotelAgip, viale della Regione Siciliana 2620 ⊠ 90145 𝒫 552033, Telex 911196, Fax 408198 – ⅃ 🛏 🖭 ☎ 🅿 – 🟰 🆎 🗓 ⓞ Ε VISA. ℅ rest   by ③
M 30000 – **105 rm** ⊏ 98/142000 – ½ p 110/150000.

Sausele without rest., via Vincenzo Errante 12 ⊠ 90127 𝒫 6161308 – ⅃ ✢ ➸ 🚗. 🆎 🗓 ⓞ Ε VISA   BZ **u**
⊏ 8500 – **37 rm** 39/60000.

Touring without rest., via Mariano Stabile 136 ⊠ 90139 𝒫 584444 – ⅃ 🛏 ☎. 🆎 🗓 ⓞ VISA. BX **h**
⊏ 10000 – **22 rm** 55/80000, 🛏 20000.

Villa Archirafi without rest., via Lincoln 30 ⊠ 90133 𝒫 6168827 – ⅃ ➸ 🅿. 🆎 🗓 Ε VISA   CZ **m**
⊏ 8000 – **30 rm** 36/55000.

Liguria without rest., via Mariano Stabile 128 ⊠ 90139 𝒫 581588 – ➸. 🆎 🗓 ⓞ. ℅   BX **b**
⊏ 4500 – **16 rm** 27/55000.

XXXX ۞ **Charleston,** piazzale Ungheria 30 ⊠ 90141 𝒫 321366, Fax 321347 – 🛏 🆎 🗓 ⓞ Ε VISA. ℅   AY **r**
closed Sunday and 16 June-25 September – **M** a la carte 55/80000
Spec. Risotto mediterraneo, Piccata di vitello, Desiderio del Re. **Wines** Corvo bianco e rosso.

XXXX ۞ **Gourmand's,** via della Libertà 37/e ⊠ 90139 𝒫 323431, Fax 323431 – 🛏 🆎 🗓 ⓞ Ε VISA. ℅   AX **e**
closed Sunday and 5 to 25 August – **M** a la carte 45/70000
Spec. Pesce spada affumicato, Fettuccine alla Nelson, Costolette di vitello Ducale. **Wines** Donnafugata, Cerasuolo.

XXX **L'Approdo da Renato,** via Messina Marine 224 ⊠ 90123 𝒫 6302881, 🌴 – ⓞ. ℅
closed Wednesday and 10 to 25 August – **M** (booking essential) a la carte 40/56000 (18%)   by ① DZ

XXX **Friend's Bar,** via Brunelleschi 138 ⊠ 90145 𝒫 201401   by ③

XX **Regine,** via Trapani 4/a ⊠ 90141 𝒫 586566 – 🛏. 🆎 🗓 ⓞ Ε VISA. ℅   AX **d**
closed Sunday and August – **M** a la carte 37/50000.

XX **Savoya,** via Torrearsa 22 ⊠ 90139 𝒫 582173 – 🛏. 🆎 🗓 ⓞ Ε VISA   AX **n**
closed Monday and August – **M** a la carte 35/47000.

X **A Cuccagna,** via Principe Granatelli 21/a ⊠ 90139 𝒫 587267 – 🛏. 🆎 🗓 ⓞ Ε VISA. ℅   BX **m**
closed Friday and 7 to 24 August – **M** a la carte 28/50000.

☞   *Inclusion in the Michelin Guide cannot be achieved by pulling strings or by offering favours.*

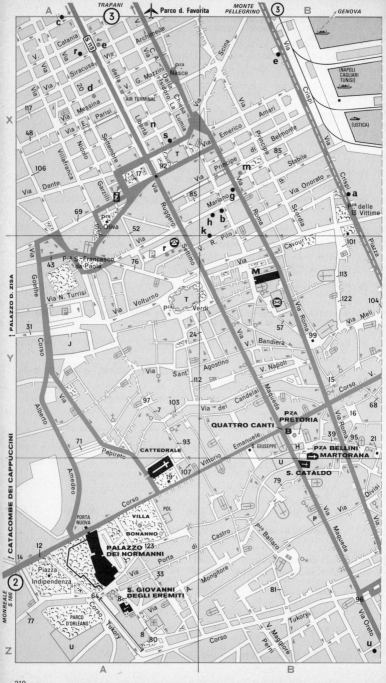

PALERMO

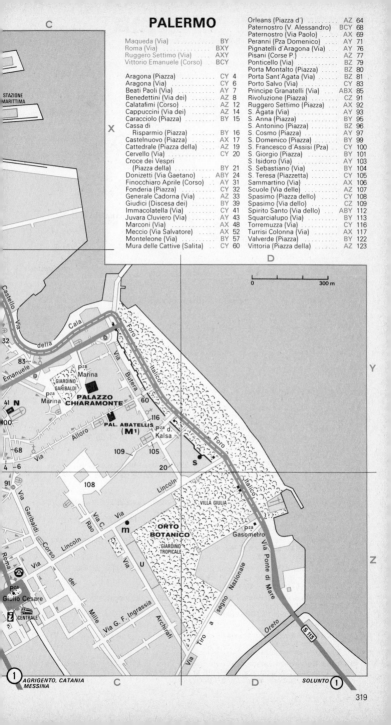

TAORMINA 98039 Messina 988 ㊲ – pop. 10 797 alt. 250 – ☏ 0942.

See : Site★★★ – Greek Theatre★★ : vu★★★ B – Public garden★★ B – ※★★ from the Square 9 Aprile A **9** – Corso Umberto★ A – Belvedere★ A – Castle★ : ≤★ A.

Exc : Etna★★★ SW for Linguaglossa.

ℹ (June-September) largo Santa Caterina (Corvaja palace) ✆ 23243, Telex 981167, Fax 24941.

Catania 52 ② – Enna 135 ② – Messina 52 ① – Palermo 255 ② – Siracusa 111 ② – Trapani 359 ②.

TAORMINA

Umberto (Corso)	A	
Cappuccini (Via)	A	2
Crocifisso (Via)	A	3
Dionisio (Via)	A	5
Duomo (Piazza)	A	6
Rotabile Castelmola	A	8
S. Antonio (Piazza)	A	9
Vittorio Emanuele (Pza)	B	10
9 Aprile (Piazza)	A	13

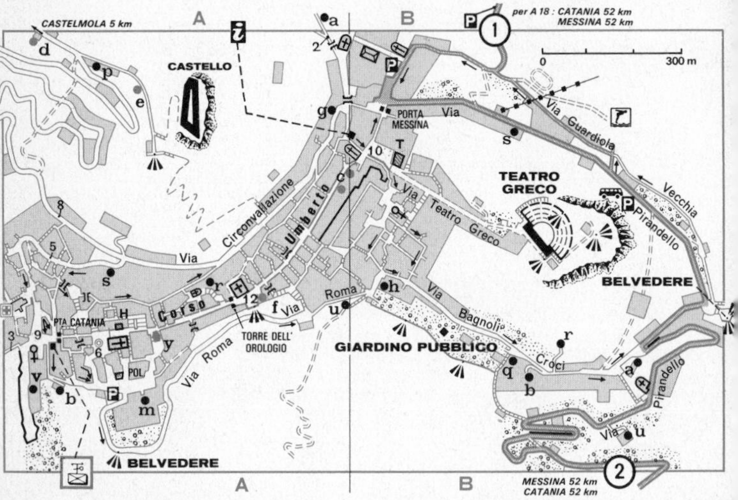

San Domenico Palace ⛴, piazza San Domenico 5 ✆ 23701, Telex 980013, Fax 625506, ⛱, « 15C Monastery with flowered garden, ≤ sea, coast and Etna », ⛱ heated – ⛻ ▤ TV ☎ – 🏠 400. AE ⓢ ⓞ E VISA. ✻ rest — A **m**
M 110000 – **101 rm** ☐ 320/560000 apartments 920/1010000 – ½ p 315/400000.

Excelsior Palace ⛴, via Toselli 8 ✆ 23975, Telex 980185, Fax 23978, ≤ sea, coast and Etna, « Small park, heated ⛱ on panoramic terrace » – ⛻ ▤ TV ☎ Ⓟ – 🏠 100. AE ⓞ VISA. ✻ rest — A **v**
M 65000 – **89 rm** ☐ 120/210000 – ½ p 180000.

Jolly Diodoro, via Bagnoli Croci 75 ✆ 23312, Telex 980028, Fax 23391, ≤ sea, coast and Etna, « ⛱ on panoramic terrace », ⛱ – ⛻ ▤ TV ☎ Ⓟ – 🏠 250. AE ⓢ ⓞ E VISA ✻ rest — B **q**
M 48000 – **102 rm** ☐ 150/210000 – ½ p 140/185000.

Bristol Park Hotel, via Bagnoli Croci 92 ✆ 23006, Telex 980005, Fax 24519, ≤ sea, coast and Etna, ⛱ – ⛻ ▤ TV ☎ 🚗. AE ⓢ ⓞ E VISA. ✻ rest — B **r**
closed 1 to 20 December and 10 January to February – **M** 40/60000 – **50 rm** ☐ 125/200000 apartments 200/230000 – ½ p 100/150000.

Vello d'Oro, via Fazzello 2 ✆ 23788, Telex 980186, « Terrace-solarium with ≤ sea and coast » – ⛻ ▤. AE ⓢ ⓞ E VISA. ✻ — A **r**
15 March-October – **M** (dinner only) 30000 – ☐ 15000 – **57 rm** 65/110000 – ½ p 95000.

Monte Tauro ⛴, via Madonna delle Grazie 3 ✆ 24402, Telex 980048, Fax 24403, ≤ sea and coast – ⛻ ▤ TV ☎ Ⓟ. AE ⓢ ⓞ E VISA. ✻ rest — AB **u**
M 40000 – **67 rm** ☐ 248000 – ½ p 130/159000.

Villa Paradiso, via Roma 2 ✆ 23922, Fax 625800, ≤ sea, coast and Etna – ⛻ ▤ TV ☎. AE ⓢ ⓞ E VISA. ✻ rest — B **h**
closed November-18 December – **M** (dinner only) 30/40000 – **33 rm** ☐ 120/200000 – ½ p 85/135000.

Villa Fiorita without rest., via Pirandello 39 ✆ 24122, ≤ sea and coast, ⛱, ⛱ – ⛻ ▤ TV ☎ 🚗. AE ⓢ E VISA. ✻ — B **s**
☐ 7500 – **24 rm** 80000.

Villa Belvedere without rest., via Bagnoli Croci 79 ✆ 23791, ≤ gardens, sea and Etna, « ⛱ on panoramic terrace », ⛱ – ⛻ ☎ Ⓟ. ⓢ E VISA — B **b**
16 March-October – **40 rm** ☐ 73/136000.

🏛 **Villa Sirina,** contrada Sirina ℰ 51776, Fax 51671, ⊥, 🐜 – 📺 🛎 🅿 📧 🖭 📼
🎇   2 km by via Crocifisso   A
closed November-20 December – **M** 30/38000 – ☷ 14000 – **15 rm** 145000 – ½ p 100/120000.

🏛 **Villa Riis** ⑤, via Rizzo 13 ℰ 24874, ⩽ sea, coast and Etna, 🏡, ⊥, 🐜 – 🛗 📺 🛎 ⑤ 🅿 📧
🖭 📼 rest   A b
March-October – **M** (dinner only) (residents only) – **30 rm** ☷ 70/134000 – ½ p 105000.

🏛 **Continental,** via Dionisio I n° 2/a ℰ 23805, Telex 981144, 🏡, « Panoramic terrace with ⩽
sea and coast », 🐜 – 🛗 📺 🖭 ⑤ 📧 🖭 📼 rest   A s
M *(closed lunch May-September)* 25/35000 – ☷ 15000 – **43 rm** 70/110000 – ½ p 75/95000.

🏛 **Sole-Castello,** Rotabile Castelmola 83 ℰ 28036, Fax 28444, ⩽ sea, coast and Etna, ⊥, 🎇
– 🛗 📺 🛎 🅿 📧 📼 🎇   A p
15 March-October – **M** (residents only) (dinner only) – **54 rm** ☷ 70/120000 – ½ p 80000.

🏠 **Andromaco** without rest., via Fontana Vecchia ℰ 23436, Fax 24985, ⩽, ⊥ – 📺 🛎 📧 🎇
16 rm ☷ 55/110000.   by via Cappuccini   A

🏠 **La Campanella** without rest., via Circonvallazione 3 ℰ 23381, ⩽ – 🎇   A g
12 rm ☷ 55/80000.

🏠 **Villa Carlotta** without rest., via Pirandello 81 ℰ 23732, Fax 23732, ⩽ sea and coast, 🐜 –
🛎 – *15 March-October* – ☷ 15000 – **21 rm** 42/73000.   B a

🏠 **Condor** without rest., via Cappuccini 25 ℰ 23124, Fax 21147, ⩽ – 🛎, ⑤ 🅿 📼   A a
☷ 7000 – **12 rm** 43/68000.

🏠 **Belsoggiorno,** via Pirandello 60 ℰ 23342, ⩽ sea and coast, 🐜 – 🅿 📧 ⑤ 🅿 📼
🎇 rest – **M** (dinner only) 25/30000 – ☷ 7000 – **19 rm** 53/86000 – ½ p 65/80000.   B u

🗙🗙🗙 **La Giara,** vico La Foresta 1 ℰ 23360, Fax 23233 – 📺 📧 ⑤ 📧 📼 🎇   A f
M (dinner only) a la carte 43/70000.

🗙🗙 **Al Castello da Ciccio,** via Madonna della Rocca ℰ 28158, « Outdoor service in summer
with ⩽ Giardini Naxos, sea and Etna » – 📧 ⑤ 📧 📼 🎇   A e
closed Wednesday – **M** a la carte 37/60000.

🗙🗙 **La Griglia,** corso Umberto 54 ℰ 23980 – 📧 ⑤ 📧 📼 🎇   A c
closed Tuesday – **M** a la carte 35/52000.

🗙🗙 **Giova Rosy Senior,** corso Umberto 38 ℰ 24411, 🏡 – 📧 ⑤ 📧 📼   A c
closed Monday (except July to September) and 8 January-14 February – **M** a la carte 35/54000
(15%).

🗙🗙 **Quattropini,** contrada Sant'Antonio ℰ 24832, ⩽, 🏡 – 🅿 📧 ⑤ 📧 📼   1 km by ①
closed Monday and 26 November-26 December – **M** a la carte 28/46000.

🗙 **La Chioccia d'Oro,** rotabile Castelmola ℰ 28066, ⩽   A d
closed Wednesday – **M** a la carte 23/33000.

🗙 **Ciclope,** corso Umberto ℰ 23263, 🏡 – 📺 📧 ⑤ 📼 🎇   A y
closed Wednesday and 10 to 31 January – **M** a la carte 29/39000.

at Capo Taormina by ② : 3 km – ⊠ 98030 Mazzarò :

🏨 **Grande Alb. Capotaormina,** ℰ 24000, Telex 980147, Fax 625467, ⩽ sea and coast, ⊥,
🐜 – 🛗 📺 🛎 ⌖ 🅿 – 🔬 150-350. 📧 ⑤ 📧 📼 🎇 rest
closed until 20 March – **M** 85000 – **207 rm** ☷ 189/278000 apartments 348000 – ½ p 226000.

at Lido di Spisone by ① : 4 km – ⊠ 98030 Mazzarò :

🏨 **Lido Méditerranée,** ℰ 24422, Telex 980175, Fax 24774, ⩽ sea, 🏡, 🐜 – 🛗 📺 🛎 🅿 ⑤
📧 📼 🎇 rest
20 March-October – **M** 60000 – **72 rm** ☷ 265000 – ½ p 170000.

at Castelmola NW : 5 km A – alt. 550 – ⊠ 98030 :

🗙 **Il Faro,** contrada Pretalia ℰ 28193, ⩽ sea and coast, 🏡 – 🅿
closed Wednesday – **M** a la carte 22/35000.

at Mazzarò by ② : 5,5 km – ⊠ 98030 :

🏨 **Mazzarò Sea Palace,** ℰ 24004, Telex 980041, Fax 24004, ⩽ small bay, 🏡, ⊥ heated,
🐜 – 🛗 📺 📼 🛎 ⌖ – 🔬 200. 📧 ⑤ 📧 📼 🎇 rest
April-October – **M** 75000 – ☷ 26000 – **81 rm** 220/380000 apartments 460/630000 –
½ p 205/265000.

🏨 **Villa Sant'Andrea,** ℰ 23125, Telex 980077, Fax 24838, ⩽ small bay, 🏡, « Shaded terraces », 🐜 – 🛗 📺 🅿 📧 ⑤ 📧 📼 🎇
M (dinner only) (booking essential) Oliviero Rest. a la carte 58/87000 – ☷ 30000 – **58 rm**
180/214000 – ½ p 160/192000.

🗙 **Il Pescatore,** ℰ 23460, ⩽ sea, cliffs and Isolabella – 🅿 📼
3 March-October; closed Monday – **M** a la carte 31/53000.

🗙 **Drago d'Oro,** ℰ 24212, Chinese rest. – ⑤ 📧 📼
closed Monday, Tuesday and Wednesday-Thursday lunch – **M** a la carte 32/45000 (15%).

🗙 **Il Delfino-da Angelo,** ℰ 23004, ⩽ small bay, 🏡 – 📧 ⑤ 📧 📼
15 March-October – **M** a la carte 26/45000.

🗙 **Da Giovanni,** ℰ 23531, ⩽ sea and Isolabella – 📧 ⑤ 📧 📼 🎇
closed Monday and 7 January-7 February – **M** a la carte 33/68000.

TURIN (TORINO) 10100 P 988 ⑫ – pop. 1 002 863 alt. 239 – ☎ 011.

See : Piazza San Carlo★★ CXY – Egyptian Museum★★, Sabauda Gallery★★ in Academy of Science CX **M** – Cathedral★ CX : relic of the Holy Shroud★★★ – Mole Antonelliana★ : ☀★★ DX – Palazzo Madama★ : museum of Ancient Art★ CX **A** – Royal Palace★ : Royal Armoury★ CDVX – Risorgimento Museum★ in Palazzo Carignano CX **M2** – Carlo Biscaretti di Ruffia Motor Museum★ – Model medieval village★ in the Valentino Park CDZ.

Envir. : Basilica of Superga★ : ≤★★★, royal tombs★ – Tour to the pass, Colle della Maddalena★: ≤★★ of the city from the route Superga-Pino Torinese, ≤★ of the city from the route Colle della Maddalena-Cavoretto.

18 and 9 I Roveri (March-November; closed Monday) at La Mandria ✉ 10070 Fiano ☎ 9235667, by ① : 18 km;

18 and 18 (closed January, February and Monday), at Fiano ✉ 10070 ☎ 9235440, by ① : 20 km;

9 (closed Monday and August), at Stupinigi ✉ 10135 ☎ 343975;

9 (closed Monday and 24 December-7 January) at Vinovo ✉ 10048 ☎ 9653880;

18 Le Fronde (closed Monday and January) at Avigliana ✉ 10051 ☎938053, W : 24 km.

✈ Turin Airport of Caselle by ① : 15 km ☎ 5778361 – Alitalia, via Lagrange 35 ✉ 10123 ☎ 57697.

🚗 ☎ 537766.

ℹ via Roma 222 (piazza C.L.N.) ✉ 10121 ☎ 535901 – Porta Nuova Railway station ✉ 10125 ☎ 531327.

A.C.I. via Giovanni Giolitti 15 ✉ 10123 ☎ 57791.

Roma 669 ⑦ – Briançon 108 ⑪ – Chambéry 209 ⑪ – Genève 252 ③ – Genova 170 ⑦ – Grenoble 224 ⑪ – Milano 140 ③ – Nice 220 ⑨.

Plans on following pages

Turin Palace Hotel, via Sacchi 8 ✉ 10128 ☎ 515511, Telex 221411, Fax 5612187 – |♦| ▤ TV ☎ ♿ 🚗 – 🏛 30-200. AE ⓢ ◑ E VISA. ✗ rest CY **u**
M *(closed 5 to 25 August)* a la carte 53/100000 – ☕ 27000 – **125 rm** 270/320000 apartments 400/550000 – ½ p 235/340000.

Jolly Principi di Piemonte, via Gobetti 15 ✉ 10123 ☎ 519693, Telex 221120, Fax 510270 – |♦| ▤ TV ☎ – 🏛 100. AE ⓢ ◑ E VISA. ✗ rest CY **z**
M 60000 – **107 rm** ☕ 264/340000 – ½ p 230/324000.

Gd H. Sitea, via Carlo Alberto 35 ✉ 10123 ☎ 5570171, Telex 220229, Fax 548090 – |♦| ▤ TV ☎ – 🏛 30-100. AE ⓢ ◑ E VISA. ✗ rest CY **t**
M a la carte 58/85000 – **116 rm** ☕ 220/295000 – ½ p 250000.

Jolly Ambasciatori, corso Vittorio Emanuele 104 ✉ 10121 ☎ 5752, Telex 221296, Fax 544978 – |♦| ▤ TV ☎ 🚗 – 🏛 25-400. AE ⓢ ◑ E VISA. ✗ rest BX **a**
M 40000 – **195 rm** ☕ 220/280000 – ½ p 180/260000.

Jolly Hotel Ligure, piazza Carlo Felice 85 ✉ 10123 ☎ 55641, Telex 220167, Fax 535438 – |♦| ▤ TV ☎ ♿ – 🏛 30-250. AE ⓢ ◑ E VISA. ✗ rest CY **b**
M 40000 – **156 rm** ☕ 235/298000 – ½ p 189/275000.

Diplomatic without rest., via Cernaia 42 ✉ 10122 ☎ 5612444, Telex 225445, Fax 540472 – |♦| ▤ TV ☎ 🚗 – 🏛 50-200. AE ⓢ ◑ E VISA BX **g**
129 rm ☕ 200/270000.

City without rest., via Juvarra 25 ✉ 10122 ☎ 540546, Telex 216228, Fax 548188 – |♦| ▤ TV ☎ – 🏛 25. AE ⓢ ◑ E VISA. ✗ BV **e**
closed August, Christmas and 1 January – **44 rm** ☕ 245/325000 apartments 380000.

Concord, via Lagrange 47 ✉ 10123 ☎ 5576756, Telex 221323, Fax 5576305 – |♦| ▤ TV ☎ ♿ 🚗 – 🏛 180. AE ⓢ ◑ E VISA. ✗ rest CY **s**
M 53000 – **139 rm** ☕ 215/270000 apartments 370000 – ½ p 176/253000.

Majestic, corso Vittorio Emanuele II n° 54 ✉ 10123 ☎ 539153, Telex 216260, Fax 534963 – |♦| ▤ TV ☎ ♿ 🚗 – 🏛 30-150. AE ⓢ ◑ E VISA. ✗ rest CY **e**
M a la carte 40/45000 – **159 rm** ☕ 265/290000 – ½ p 195/290000.

Genio without rest., corso Vittorio Emanuele II n° 47 ✉ 10125 ☎ 6505771, Telex 220308, Fax 6508264 – |♦| ▤ TV ☎ ♿ – 🏛 35. AE ⓢ ◑ E VISA CYZ **w**
75 rm ☕ 105/150000, ▤ 12000.

Royal, corso Regina Margherita 249 ✉ 10144 ☎ 748444, Telex 220259, Fax 748393, ✗ – |♦| ▤ TV ☎ 🚗 – 🏛 25-600. AE ⓢ ◑ E VISA. ✗ BV **u**
closed 1 to 28 August – **M** rest. see **La Dea** below – ☕ 15000 – **72 rm** 150/200000.

Victoria without rest., via Nino Costa 4 ✉ 10123 ☎ 553710, Telex 212580, Fax 5611806 – |♦| TV ☎. AE ⓢ ◑ VISA. ✗ CY **v**
☕ 14000 – **70 rm** 90/120000.

Stazione e Genova without rest., via Sacchi 14 ✉ 10128 ☎ 545323, Telex 224242, Fax 519896 – |♦| TV ☎ – 🏛 50. AE ⓢ ◑ E VISA. ✗ CZ **b**
40 rm ☕ 105/150000.

Alexandra without rest., lungo Dora Napoli 14 ✉ 10152 ☎ 858327, Telex 221562, Fax 2483805 – |♦| ▤ TV ☎ 🚗. AE ⓢ ◑ E VISA CV **c**
55 rm ☕ 155/200000.

🏨 **Boston** without rest., via Massena 70 ✉ 10128 ℘ 500359, Fax 599358 – 🖭 📺 ☎ 🔙. 🖭
🖾 🖪 *VISA*   BZ **c**
40 rm ⊑ 105/150000, 📇 12000.

🏨 **Luxor** without rest., corso Stati Uniti 7 ✉ 10128 ℘ 531529, Telex 225549 – 🛗 📇 📺 ☎. 🖭
🖾 🔘 🖪 *VISA*   CZ **s**
closed August – **64 rm** ⊑ 105/151000.

🏨 **President** without rest., via Cecchi 67 ✉ 10152 ℘ 859555, Telex 220417, Fax 2480465 – 🛗
📇 📺 ☎. 🖭 🖾 🔘 🖪 *VISA*   CV **s**
72 rm ⊑ 149000.

🏨 **Goya** without rest., via Principe Amedeo 41 bis ✉ 10123 ℘ 874951, Fax 874953 – 🛗 📇 📺
☎. 🖭 🖾 🔘 🖪 *VISA*   DY **n**
closed 1 to 26 August – ⊑ 12000 – **26 rm** 90/110000, 📇 10000.

🏠 **Cristallo** 🦢 without rest., corso Traiano 28/9 ✉ 10135 ℘ 618383, Fax 3171565 – 📺 ☎. 🖾
🔘 🖪 *VISA*   by ⑩
⊑ 12000 – **20 rm** 110/140000.

🏫🏫🏫🏫 **Villa Sassi-El Toulà** 🦢 with rm, strada al Traforo del Pino 47 ✉ 10132 ℘ 890556, Telex
225437, Fax 890095, 🏡, « 18C Country house in a spacious park » – 🛗 📇 rest 📺 ☎ 🅿 –
🏛 200. 🖭 🖾 🔘 🖪 *VISA*. 🛠   by ⑤
closed August – **M** (closed Sunday) a la carte 83/110000 – ⊑ 20000 – **17 rm** 240/340000
apartment 500000 – ½ p 240000.

🏫🏫🏫🏫 ❀❀ **Vecchia Lanterna,** corso Re Umberto 21 ✉ 10128 ℘ 537047, Elegant installation –
📇. 🖭 🖾 🔘 🖪 *VISA*   CY **v**
closed Saturday lunch, Sunday and 10 to 20 August – **M** (booking essential) a la carte
78/116000 (10%)
Spec. Pollarda al passito, Tortelloni di aragosta all'essenza di crostacei, Mignonette di agnello e animelle
brasate al Sauternes. **Wines** Sauvignon, Brachetto.

🏫🏫🏫🏫 **Del Cambio,** piazza Carignano 2 ✉ 10123 ℘ 546690, Elegant traditional decor, « 19C
Decoration » – 📇. 🖭 🖾 🔘 🖪 *VISA*. 🛠   CX **a**
closed Sunday and 27 July-27 August – **M** (booking essential) a la carte 59/100000
(15%).

🏫🏫🏫 **Al Saffi,** via Aurelio Saffi 2 ✉ 10138 ℘ 442213, Elegant installation – ⬅️✖ 📇. 🔘
VISA   AV **n**
closed Sunday and August – **M** (booking essential) a la carte 50/65000.

🏫🏫🏫 **Balbo,** via Andrea Doria 11 ✉ 10123 ℘ 511743 – 📇. 🖭 🖾 🔘 🖪 *VISA*. 🛠   CY **n**
closed Monday and 18 July-18 August – **M** (booking essential) a la carte 73/103000.

🏫🏫🏫 ❀ **Due Lampioni da Carlo,** via Carlo Alberto 45 ✉ 10123 ℘ 8397409, Fax 831970 – ⬅️✖
📇. 🖭 *VISA*. 🛠   CY **n**
closed Sunday and August – **M** a la carte 66/91000
Spec. Cassoulet di lumache alla piemontese (November-March), Ravioli di porcini e salsa tartufata, Scaloppa
di pescatrice alla peperonata. **Wines** Sauvignon, Barbaresco.

🏫🏫🏫 ❀ **Neuv Caval 'd Brôns,** piazza San Carlo 157 ✉ 10123 ℘ 553491 – ⬅️✖ 📇. 🖭 🖾 🔘 🖪
VISA. 🛠   CXY **v**
closed Sunday – **M** (booking essential) a la carte 65/110000
Spec. Carpaccio di pesce marinato, Tagliolini neri ai moscardini, Filetto di branzino in crosta, Sottofiletto di
Angus in salsa al cerfoglio. **Wines** Prato di Canzio, Barbaresco.

🏫🏫🏫 ❀ **La Smarrita,** corso Unione Sovietica 244 ✉ 10134 ℘ 390657 – 📇. 🖭 🖾 🔘 🖪 *VISA*
🛠   by ⑩
closed Monday and 3 to 27 August – **M** (booking essential) a la carte 50/80000
Spec. Gamberi e pinoli sulle patate (Winter), Tortelli di mozzarella e pomodorini (Autumn), Capretto allo spiedo
con salsa di menta (Spring). **Wines** Gavi, Nebbiolo.

🏫🏫 **Adriano,** via Pollenzo 39 ✉ 10141 ℘ 3358311, 🏡   AY **b**
closed Saturday and August – **M** a la carte 28/52000.

🏫🏫 **Al Bue Rosso,** corso Casale 10 ✉ 10131 ℘ 830753 – 📇. 🖭 🔘 *VISA*   DY **e**
closed Monday, Saturday lunch and August – **M** a la carte 42/68000 (10%).

🏫🏫 **Della Rocca,** via della Rocca 22/b ✉ 10123 ℘ 831814, booking essential – 📇   DY **a**

🏫🏫 **Due Mondi-da Ilio,** via San Pio V n° 3 ang. via Saluzzo ✉ 10125 ℘ 6692056 – 🖭 🖾 🖪
VISA   CZ **k**
closed Sunday and August – **M** a la carte 39/67000.

🏫🏫 **IL Porticciolo,** via Barletta 58 ✉ 10136 ℘ 321601, Seafood – ⬅️✖ 📇. 🖭 🖾 🔘 🖪 *VISA*
🛠   AZ **a**
closed Monday, Saturday lunch and August – **M** a la carte 39/76000.

🏫🏫 **Duchesse,** via Duchessa Jolanda 7 ang. via Beaumont ✉ 10138 ℘ 7495494   BX **c**
closed Sunday dinner and Monday – **M** a la carte 42/69000.

🏫 **Crocetta,** via Marco Polo 21 ✉ 10129 ℘ 582820, 🏡 – 📇. 🖭 🖾 🔘 🖪 *VISA*. 🛠   BZ **d**
closed Sunday and August – **M** a la carte 32/57000.

🏫 **Ostu Bacu,** corso Vercelli 226 ✉ 10155 ℘ 264579, Modern Piedmontese trattoria – 📇.
🖾 🔘 🖪 *VISA*   by corso Vercelli DV
closed Sunday and 25 July-25 August – **M** a la carte 30/53000.

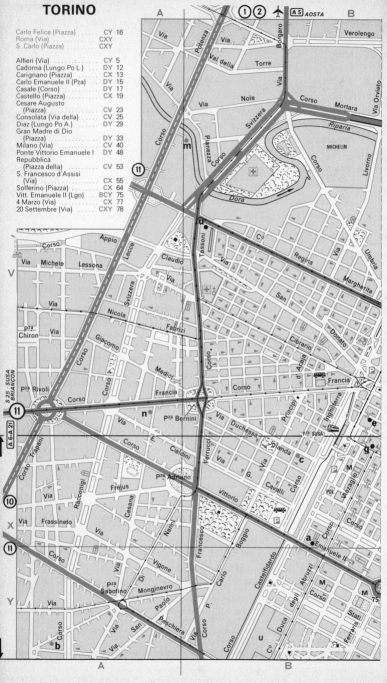

TORINO

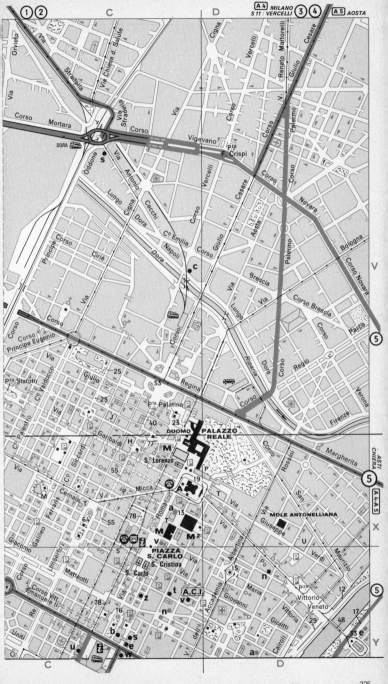

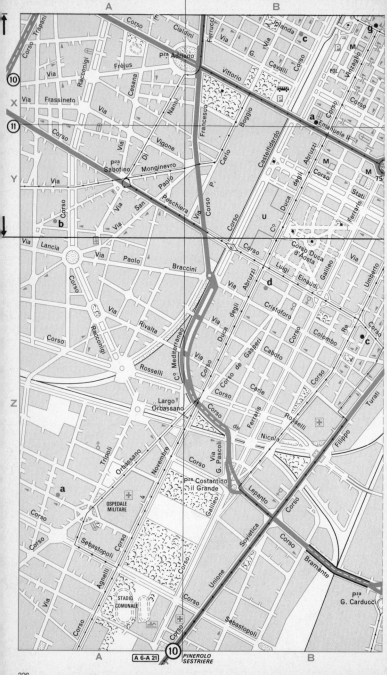

TORINO

✗ **Porta Rossa,** corso Appio Claudio 227 ⊠ 10146 𝒫 790963, 🍴 – ⚎ ⬤ 𝘝𝘐𝘚𝘈 ✗ by ⑪
closed Saturday lunch, Sunday and August – **M** (booking essential) a la carte 36/71000

✗ **C'era una volta,** corso Vittorio Emanuele II n° 41 ⊠ 10125 𝒫 655498, Typical Piedmontese
rest. – 🔲 ⚎ ⓢ ⬤ 🄴 𝘝𝘐𝘚𝘈 CZ **k**
closed Sunday and August – **M** (dinner only) (booking essential) 45000.

✗ **Anaconda,** via Angiolino 16 (corso Potenza) ⊠ 10143 𝒫 752903, Rustic trattoria, « Outdoor
service in Summer » – ❷. ⚎ ⓢ ⬤ 🄴 𝘝𝘐𝘚𝘈 BV **m**
closed Friday dinner, Saturday and August – **M** 40000 bc.

✗ **Da Giudice,** strada Valsalice 78 ⊠ 10131 𝒫 6602020, « Summer service under pergola »
– ✗⊱ ❷. ⚎ ⓢ 𝘝𝘐𝘚𝘈 ✗ by ⑤
closed Tuesday, Wednesday lunch and August – **M** a la carte 37/59000.

✗ **Trattoria della Posta,** strada Mongreno 16 ⊠ 10132 𝒫 890193, Habitués' trattoria Piedmontese cheese – 🔲. ✗ by ⑤
closed Sunday dinner, Monday and 10 July-20 August – **M** a la carte 30/45000.

Costigliole d'Asti 14055 Asti 🄦🄦🄦 ⓐ – pop. 5 938 alt. 242 – ✿ 0141.
Roma 629 – Acqui Terme 34 – Alessandria 51 – Asti 15 – Genova 108 – Milano 141 – Torino 70.

XXX ✿✿ **Guido,** piazza Umberto I n° 27 𝒫 966012 – ⓢ 🄴 𝘝𝘐𝘚𝘈
closed Sunday and holidays – **M** (dinner only) (booking essential) 100/120000
Spec. Agnolotti di Costigliole, Peperone ripieno al forno, Cardo gobbo con fonduta e tartufi. **Wines** Arneis, Barbaresco.

VENICE (VENEZIA) 30100 🄿 🄦🄦🄦 ⑤, 🄶🄶🄶 F 19 – pop. 320 990 – h.s. 15 March-October and
Christmas – ✿ 041.

See : St. Marks Square★★★ FZ :

St. Mark's Basilica★★★ GZ – Doges Palace★★★ GZ – Campanile★★ : ✳★★ FGZ F – Procuratie★★
FZ – Libreria Vecchia★ GZ – Correr Museum★ FZ **M** – Clock Tower★ FZ **K** – Bridge of Sighs★ GZ.

Grand Canal★★★ :

Rialto Bridge★ FY – Right bank : Cà d'Oro★★★ : Franchetti Gallery★★ EX – Palazzo Vendramin-
Calergi★★ BT **R** – Cà Loredan★★ EY **N** – Palazzo Grimani★★ EY **Q** – Palazzo Corner-Spinelli★★
BTU **D** – Left bank : Academy of Fine Arts★★★ BV – Palazzo Dario★★ BV **S** – Peggy Guggenheim
Collection★★ in Palazzo Venier dei Leoni BV **M2** – Palazzo Rezzonico★ AU : masterpieces by
Guardi★★, frescoes★★ by Tiepolo in Venice in the 18C★ – Palazzo Giustinian★★ AU **X** – Cà
Foscari★★ AU **Y** – Palazzo Bernardo★★ BT **Z** – Palazzo dei Camerlenghi★★ FX **A** – Palazzo
Pesaro★★ : Museum of Modern Art★ EX.

Churches :

Santa Maria della Salute★★ : Marriage at Cana★★★ by Tintoretto BV – San Giorgio Maggiore★★ :
✳★★★ from campanile★★, works by Tintoretto★★★ CV – San Zanipolo★★ : polyptych★★★ of San
Vincenzo Ferrari, ceiling★★★ of the Rosary Chapel GX – Santa Maria Gloriosa dei Frari★★ : works
by Titian★★★ AT – San Zaccaria★ : altarpiece★★ by Bellini, altarpieces★★ by Vivarini and by
Ludovico da Forlì CX – Interior decoration★★ by Veronese in the Church of San Sebastiano AU –
Paintings★ by Guardi in the Church of Angelo Raffaele AU – Ceiling★ of the Church of San
Pantaleone AT – Santa Maria dei Miracoli★ GX – Madonna and Child★ in the Church of San
Francesco della Vigna DT – Madonna and Child★ in the Church of Redentore (Giudecca Island)
AV.

Scuola di San Rocco★★★ AT – Scuola dei Carmini★ : paintings★★ by Tiepolo AU – Scuola di San
Giorgio degli Schiavoni★ : paintings★★ by Carpaccio DT – Palazzo Querini-Stampalia★ GY – Rio
dei Mendicanti★ GX – Facade★ of the Scuola di San Marco GX – Frescoes★ by Tiepolo in
Palazzo Labia AT.

The Lido★★ – Murano★★ : Glass Museum★★★, Church of Santi Maria e Donato★★ – Burano★★ -
Torcello★★ : mosaics★★★ in the Cathedral of Santa Maria Assunta★★, peristyle★★ and columns★★
inside the Church of Santa Fosca★.

🄱 (closed Monday) at Lido Alberoni ⊠ 30011 𝒫 731333, 15 mn by boat and 9 km;

🄱 and 🄱 Cà della Nave (closed Tuesday), at Martellago ⊠ 30030 𝒫 5401555, Fax 5401926, NW :
12 km.

✈ Marco Polo di Tessera, NE : 13 km 𝒫 661262 (plan : Outskirts p. 3) – Alitalia, San Marco-San
Moisé1463 ⊠ 30124 𝒫 5216222.

⛴ to Lido - San Nicolò from piazzale Roma (Tronchetto) daily (35 mn); to Punta Sabbioni from
Riva degli Schiavoni daily (40 mn); to island of Pellestrina-Santa Maria del Mare from Lido
Alberoni daily (1 h 15 mn); to islands of Murano (10 mn), Burano (40 mn) and Torcello (45 mn)
daily, from Fondamenta Nuove; to Treporti-Cavallino from Fondamenta Nuove daily (1 h 10 mn)
– Information : ACTV - Venetian Transport Union, piazzale Roma ⊠ 30124 𝒫 5287886, Telex
223487.

🄱 San Marco Ascensione 71/c ⊠ 30124 𝒫 5226356 – Santa Lucia Railway station ⊠ 30121 𝒫 715016.

A.C.I. fondamenta Santa Chiara 518/a ⊠ 30125 𝒫 719078.

Roma 528 ① – Bologna 152 ① – Milano 267 ① – Trieste 158 ①.

Plans on following pages

Cipriani ⚓, isola della Giudecca 10 ☒ 30133 ℰ 5207744, Telex 410162, Fax 5203930, ≤, 🌿, « Flower garden with heated 🏊 », ⚹, ⚯ – 📶 – ▐ 🔟 ☺ 🕭 – 🍴 100. 🖭 🖾 ⑩ 🗲 *VISA*. 🍳
M a la carte 120/170000 – **98 rm** ☲ 588/830000 apartments 1500/2550000. CV **h**

Gritti Palace, campo Santa Maria del Giglio 2467 ☒ 30124 ℰ 794611, Telex 410125, Fax 5200942, ≤ Grand Canal, « Outdoor rest. service in Summer on the Grand Canal » – ▐ 🔟 ☎ 🕭 – 🍴 🔟 *VISA*. 🍳 rest EZ **a**
M a la carte 100/130000 – **97 rm** ☲ 506/714000 apartments 1369/1845000.

Danieli, riva degli Schiavoni 4196 ☒ 30122 ℰ 5226480, Telex 410077, Fax 5200208, ≤ canal di San Marco, « Hall in a small Venetian style courtyard and in summer rest. service on panoramic terrace » – ▐ 🔟 ☎ – 🍴 70-150. 🖭 🖾 ⑩ 🗲 *VISA*. 🍳 rest GZ **a**
M a la carte 106/168000 – ☲ 27500 – **222 rm** 405/595000 apartments 1071/1785000.

Bauer Grünwald, campo San Moisè 1459 ☒ 30124 ℰ 5231520, Telex 410075, Fax 5207557, ≤ Grand Canal, 🌿, ≤⊱ rm 🔟 ☎ 🕭 – 🍴 25-180. 🖭 🖾 ⑩ 🗲 *VISA*. 🍳 rest FZ **h**
M a la carte 90/120000 – **214 rm** ☲ 320/520000 apartments 990/1300000.

Londra Palace, riva degli Schiavoni 4171 ☒ 30122 ℰ 5200533, Telex 431315, Fax 5225032, ≤ canal di San Marco – ▐ 🔟 ☎ – 🍴 200. 🖭 🖾 ⑩ 🗲 *VISA* GZ **t**
M rest. see **Les Deux Lions** below – ☲ 25000 – **69 rm** 245/385000.

Europa e Regina, calle larga 22 Marzo 2159 ☒ 30124 ℰ 5200477, Telex 410123, Fax 5231533, ≤ Grand Canal, 🌿 – ▐ 🔟 ☎ 🕭 – 🍴 30-140. 🖭 🖾 ⑩ 🗲 *VISA*. 🍳 rest FZ **d**
M 75/85000 – ☲ 24000 – **189 rm** 298/536000 apartments 833/1071000.

Monaco e Grand Canal, calle Vallaresso 1325 ☒ 30124 ℰ 5200211, Telex 410450, Fax 5200501, ≤ Grand Canal, 🌿 – ▐ 🔟 ☎ 🕭 – 🍴 40. 🖭 🖾 🗲 *VISA*. 🍳 rest FZ **e**
M Grand Canal Rest. a la carte 82/126000 – **72 rm** ☲ 270/410000 apartments 450/850000.

Metropole without rest., riva degli Schiavoni 4149 ☒ 30122 ℰ 5205044, Telex 410340, Fax 5223679, ≤ canal di San Marco, « Small epoch collection articles » – ▐ 🔟 ☎ – 🍴 40. 🖭 🖾 ⑩ 🗲 *VISA* DU **t**
63 rm ☲ 255/360000.

Luna Baglioni, calle larga dell'Ascensione 1243 ☒ 30124 ℰ 5289840, Telex 410236, Fax 5287160 – ▐ 🔟 ☎ – 🍴 30-150. 🖭 🖾 ⑩ 🗲 *VISA*. 🍳 rest FZ **p**
M 65000 – **125 rm** ☲ 265/490000 apartments 700/1200000.

Splendid-Suisse, San Marco-Mercerie 760 ☒ 30124 ℰ 5200755, Telex 410590, Fax 5286498 – ▐ 🔟 ☎ – 🍴 150. 🖭 🖾 ⑩ 🗲 *VISA*. 🍳 rest FY **n**
M a la carte 68/86000 – **157 rm** ☲ 270/380000 apartments 300/430000 – ½ p 258/355000.

Pullman Park Hotel, giardini Papadopoli ☒ 30125 ℰ 5285394, Telex 410310, Fax 5230043 – ▐ 🔟 ☎ – 🍴 60. 🖭 🖾 ⑩ 🗲 *VISA* AT **k**
M a la carte 56/86000 – **100 rm** ☲ 200/310000 apartments 350/480000.

Saturnia-International and Rest. Il Cortile, calle larga 22 Marzo 2398 ☒ 30124 ℰ 5208377, Telex 410355, Fax 5207131, 🌿, « 14C Patrician building » – ▐ 🔟 ☎ – 🍴 60. 🖭 🖾 ⑩ 🗲 *VISA*. 🍳 rest EZ **n**
M (closed Wednesday) a la carte 61/93000 – **95 rm** ☲ 235/360000 – ½ p 200/240000.

Gabrielli Sandwirth, riva degli Schiavoni 4110 ☒ 30122 ℰ 5231580, Telex 410228, Fax 5209455, ≤ canal di San Marco, « Small courtyard and garden » – ▐ 🔟 ☎. 🖭 🖾 ⑩ 🗲 *VISA*. 🍳 rest DU **b**
closed 26 November-January – **M** 38/55000 – **100 rm** ☲ 225/370000 – ½ p 120/270000.

Amadeus, lista di Spagna 227 ☒ 30121 ℰ 715300, Telex 420811, Fax 5240841 – ▐ 🔟 ☎ – 🍴 40-150. 🖭 🖾 ⑩ 🗲 *VISA*. 🍳 AT **b**
M 50/70000 – ☲ 18000 – **63 rm** 220/305000 apartments 305/350000 – ½ p 180/250000.

La Fenice et des Artistes without rest., campiello de la Fenice 1936 ☒ 30124 ℰ 5232333, Telex 411150, Fax 5203721 – ▐ 🔟 ☎. 🖾 🗲 *VISA*. 🍳 EZ **v**
61 rm ☲ 148/200000 apartments 250/300000, ▤ 15000.

Cavalletto e Doge Orseolo, calle del Cavalletto 1107 ☒ 30124 ℰ 5200955, Telex 410684, Fax 5238184, ≤ – ▐ 🔟 ☎. 🖭 🖾 🗲 *VISA*. 🍳 FZ **f**
M a la carte 55/85000 – **80 rm** ☲ 210/354000.

Concordia without rest., calle larga San Marco 367 ☒ 30124 ℰ 5206866, Telex 411069, Fax 5206775 – ▐ 🔟 ☎. 🖭 🖾 🗲 *VISA*. 🍳 GZ **r**
55 rm ☲ 200/320000.

Santa Chiara without rest., Santa Croce 548 ☒ 30125 ℰ 5206955, Telex 420690, Fax 5228799 – ▐ 🔟 ☎ 🕭. 🖾 🗲 *VISA*. 🍳 AT **c**
☲ 17000 – **28 rm** 130/166000.

Flora ⚓ without rest., calle larga 22 Marzo 2283/a ☒ 30124 ℰ 5205844, Telex 410401, Fax 5228217, « Small flowered garden » – ▐ 🔟 ☎ 🕭. 🖭 🖾 ⑩ 🗲 *VISA* EZ **t**
closed 15 November-27 January – **44 rm** ☲ 140/190000, ▤ 16000.

Rialto, riva del Ferro 5149 ☒ 30124 ℰ 5209166, Telex 420809, Fax 5238958 – ▤ 🔟 ☎. 🖭 🖾 🗲 *VISA*. 🍳 FY **v**
M (closed Thursday and November-15 March) a la carte 32/70000 (12%) – **71 rm** ☲ 154/211000 apartments 250/450000, ▤ 16000.

San Cassiano without rest., Santa Croce 2232 ☒ 30125 ℰ 5241733, Telex 420810, ≤ – ▤ 🔟 🕭. 🖭 🖾 🗲 *VISA* EX **f**
35 rm ☲ 141/191000.

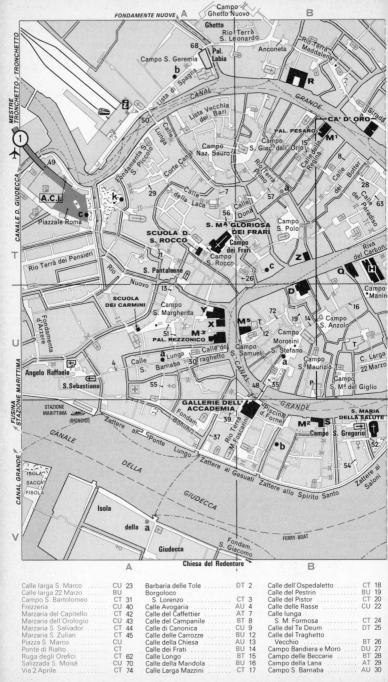

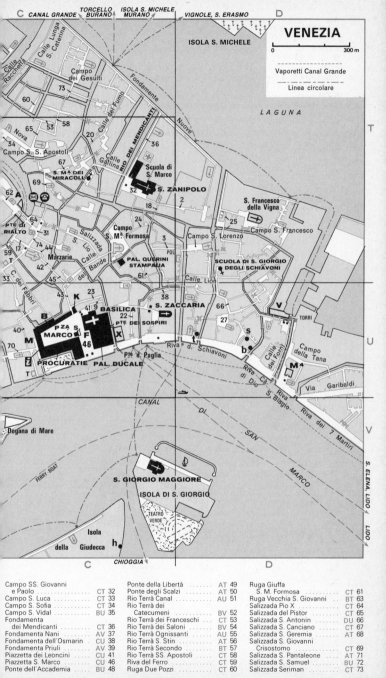

331

🏦 **Ala** without rest., campo Santa Maria del Giglio 2494 ⊠ 30124 𝒫 5208333, Telex 410275,
Fax 5206390 – 🛗 🗐 🕿 🖭 🕃 ⓔ 𝑽𝑰𝑺𝑨   EZ **e**
77 rm ⊆ 140/195000. 🍴 15000.

🏦 **Torino** without rest., calle delle Ostreghe 2356 ⊠ 30124 𝒫 5205222, Fax 5228227 – 🗐 📺
🕿 🖭 🕃 ⓞ ⓔ 𝑽𝑰𝑺𝑨   EZ **z**
20 rm ⊆ 125/190000.

🏦 **Pausania San Barnaba** without rest., Dorsoduro 2824 ⊠ 30123 𝒫 5222083, Telex 420178
– ⬚ 🗐 📺 🕿 🖭 🕃 ⓔ 𝑽𝑰𝑺𝑨   AU **a**
25 rm ⊆ 140/190000.

🏠 **San Moisè** without rest., San Marco 2058 ⊠ 30124 𝒫 5203755, Telex 420655 – 📺 🕿 🖭
🕃 ⓞ ⓔ 𝑽𝑰𝑺𝑨 ✀   EZ **b**
16 rm ⊆ 148/200000.

🏠 **Ateneo** without rest., San Marco 1876-calle Minelli ⊠ 30124 𝒫 5200588, Fax 5228550 – 🗐
📺 🕾 🖭 🕃 ⓔ 𝑽𝑰𝑺𝑨   EZ **d**
20 rm ⊆ 150/204000.

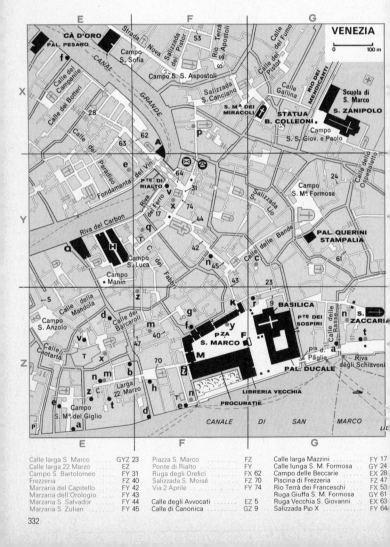

🏠 **Nuovo Teson** without rest., calle de la Pescaria 3980 ⊠ 30122 ℰ 5205555, Fax 5285335 – ⑳ ♿ 🅰 🔟 **E** **VISA**
DU **s**
closed 10 to 30 November – **30 rm** ⊋ 77/110000.

🏠 **Carpaccio** 🦢 without rest., San Polo-calle Corner 2765 ⊠ 30125 ℰ 5235946, Fax 5242134, ⪡ Grand Canal ⪢ – 🕿 🔟 **E** **VISA**
BT **c**
14 March-18 November – **17 rm** ⊋ 125/185000.

🏠 **American** without rest., San Vio 628 ⊠ 30123 ℰ 5204733, Telex 410508, Fax 5204048 – 🗐 🔟 🕿 🅰 🔟 ⓪ **E** **VISA**
BV **b**
29 rm ⊋ 145/195000.

🏠 **San Stefano** without rest., San Marco-campo San Stefano 2957 ⊠ 30124 ℰ 5200166, Fax 5224460 – 🖳 🗐 🔟 🕿 🔟 ⓪ **E** **VISA** 🛠
BU **a**
closed 7 to 31 January – **11 rm** ⊋ 85/180000, 🗐 15000.

XXXX **Caffè Quadri,** piazza San Marco 120 ⊠ 30124 ℰ 5289299, Fax 791661 – 🅰 🔟 ⓪ **E** **VISA** 🛠
FZ **y**
closed Monday – **M** a la carte 72/112000.

XXXX **Antico Martini,** campo San Fantin 1983 ⊠ 30124 ℰ 5224121, Fax 5289857 – 🗐 🅰 🔟 ⓪ **E** **VISA**
EZ **x**
closed Tuesday, Wednesday lunch, 8 January-24 March (except Carnival) and 27 November-21 December – **M** a la carte 69/113000 (15%).

XXX ❀ **Harry's Bar,** calle Vallaresso 1323 ⊠ 30124 ℰ 5285777, Fax 5208822, American bar-rest. – 🗐 🅰 🔟 ⓪ **E** **VISA**
FZ **n**
closed Monday and 4 January-15 February – **M** a la carte 91/120000 (20%)
Spec. Tagliolini alle seppie (15 July-15 October), Filetti di San Pietro al radicchio (Winter), Scampi alla Thermidor (Summer), Pasticceria della Casa. **Wines** Soave, Cabernet.

XXX **Les Deux Lions,** riva degli Schiavoni 4175 ⊠ 30122 ℰ 5200533, Fax 5225032, Elegant rest., ⪡ Summer service on the bank of the canal ⪢ – 🗐 🅰 🔟 ⓪ **E** **VISA**
GZ **t**
closed Tuesday 21 October-19 June – **M** (booking essential) a la carte 61/92000.

XXX ❀ **La Caravella,** calle larga 22 Marzo 2397 ⊠ 30124 ℰ 5208901, Typical rest. – 🗐 🅰 🔟 ⓪ **E** **VISA**
EZ **m**
closed Wednesday – **M** (booking essential) a la carte 77/110000
Spec. Bigoli in salsa, Scampi allo Champagne, Filetto di bue Caravella. **Wines** Pinot bianco, Cabernet Sauvignon.

XXX **Malamocco,** campiello del Vin 4650 ⊠ 30122 ℰ 5227438, Elegant installation – 🗐 🅰 🔟 ⓪ **E** **VISA**
GZ **n**
closed Wednesday and 3 January-3 February – **M** a la carte 48/80000 (15%).

XXX **Al Campiello,** calle dei Fuseri 4346 ⊠ 30124 ℰ 5206396, Rest.-American-bar-late night dinners – 🗐 🅰 🔟 ⓪ **E** **VISA**
FZ **z**
closed Monday and August – **M** (booking essential) a la carte 50/86000 (13%).

XXX **La Colomba,** piscina di Frezzeria 1665 ⊠ 30124 ℰ 5221175, 🏤, ⪡ Modern art picture collection ⪢ – 🗐 🅰 🔟 ⓪ **E** **VISA**
FZ **m**
closed Wednesday November-June – **M** a la carte 60/120000 (15%).

XX **Do Forni,** calle dei Specchieri 457/468 ⊠ 30124 ℰ 5237729, Telex 420832, Fax 5288132, New rustic rest. – 🗐 🅰 🔟 ⓪ **E** **VISA**
GY **c**
closed 22 November-5 December and Thursday except June-October – **M** a la carte 53/74000 (12%).

XX **Al Graspo de Ua,** calle dei Bombaseri 5094 ⊠ 30124 ℰ 5223647, Telex 420180, Typical tavern – 🗐 🅰 🔟 ⓪ **E** **VISA**
FY **x**
closed Monday, Tuesday, 25 July-10 August and 20 December-13 January – **M** a la carte 56/86000 (16%).

XX **Harry's Dolci,** Giudecca 773 ⊠ 30133 ℰ 5224844, Fax 5222322, ⪡ Outdoor Summer service on the canal della Giudecca ⪢ – 🗐 🅰 🔟 ⓪ **E** **VISA**
AV **a**
closed 7 November-7 March and Tuesday except September – **M** a la carte 42/74000 (15%).

XX **Noemi** with rm, calle dei Fabbri 909 ⊠ 30124 ℰ 5225238 and hotel ℰ 5238144 – 🗐 rest. 🅰 🔟 ⓪ **E** **VISA**
FZ **g**
M *(closed Sunday, Monday lunch and 16 December-31 January)* a la carte 47/69000 (13%) – ⊋ 9000 – **15 rm** 38/58000.

XX **Osteria da Fiore,** San Polo - calle del Scaleter 2202 ⊠ 30125 ℰ 721308 – 🗐 🅰 🔟 ⓪ **E** **VISA** 🛠
BT **a**
closed Sunday, Monday, 7 to 30 August and Christmas-6 January – **M** (fish only) (booking essential) a la carte 45/74000 (10%).

X **Madonna,** calle della Madonna 594 ⊠ 30125 ℰ 5223824, Venetian trattoria – 🗐 🅰 🔟 **E** **VISA**
EY **e**
closed Wednesday, 4 to 17 August and 24 December-31 January – **M** a la carte 27/44000 (12%).

X **Antica Carbonera,** calle Bembo 4648 ⊠ 30124 ℰ 5225479, Venetian trattoria – 🗐 🅰 🔟 ⓪ **E** **VISA**
FY **q**
closed Tuesday and 20 July-10 August – **M** a la carte 33/53000 (12%).

X **Da Bruno,** Castello-calle del Paradiso 5731 ⊠ 30122 ℰ 5221480 – ⑁⪥ 🗐 🅰 🔟 **VISA**
GY **r**
closed Tuesday, 15 to 30 July and 15 to 31 January – **M** a la carte 26/36000 (10%).

in Lido : 15 mn by boat from San Marco FZ – ⊠ **30126** Venezia Lido.

🖪 Gran Viale S. M. Elisabetta 6 🖋 5265721 :

🏨🏨 **Excelsior,** lungomare Marconi 41 🖋 5260201, Telex 410023, Fax 5267276, ≼, ⌲, ▲₀, ※,
🏠 – 🛗 🗐 🔟 🕿 🕭 ⟶ 🕭 – 🛂 40-600. 🖭 🛐 ⓞ ⋿ 𝘝𝘚𝘈. ✻ rest
March-October – **M** a la carte 90/145000 – ☲ 27500 – **218 rm** 405/536000 apartments
1131/1476000 – ½ p 420/515000.

🏨🏨 **Des Bains,** lungomare Marconi 17 🖋 5265921, Telex 410142, Fax 5260113, ≼, « Flowered
park with heated ⌲ and ※ », ▲₀ – 🛗 🗐 🔟 🕿 🕭 – 🛂 90-380. 🖭 🛐 ⓞ ⋿ 𝘝𝘚𝘈. ✻
April-October – **M** 88000 – **193 rm** ☲ 318/493000 apartment 1023000 – ½ p 334/406000.

🏨 **Quattro Fontane** 🕸, via 4 Fontane 16 🖋 5260227, Telex 411006, Fax 5260726, ⚑, ※
– 🛗 🔟 🕿 🕭 – 🛂 40. 🖭 🛐 ⋿ 𝘝𝘚𝘈. ✻ rest
21 April-15 October – **M** a la carte 63/97000 – ☲ 18000 – **68 rm** 200/300000 – ½ p 175/250000.

🏨 **Le Boulevard and Rest. Grimod,** Gran Viale S. M. Elisabetta 41 🖋 5261990, Telex
410185, Fax 5261917 – 🛗 ✣ 🗐 🔟 🕿 🕭 – 🛂 60. 🖭 🛐 ⓞ ⋿ 𝘝𝘚𝘈. ✻ rest
closed January – **M** a la carte 38/64000 – ☲ 20000 – **45 rm** 216/270000. 🗐 15000 –
½ p 180/223000.

🏨 **Villa Mabapa,** riviera San Nicolò 16 🖋 5260590, Telex 410357, Fax 5269441, « Summer
rest. in garden », ⚑ – 🛗 🗐 rm 🕿 🕭 – 🛂 60. 🖭 🛐 ⓞ ⋿ 𝘝𝘚𝘈. ✻ rest
closed until 15 March – **M** a la carte 37/51000 – **62 rm** ☲ 160/260000 – ½ p 115/155000.

🏨 **Villa Laguna,** via San Gallo 6 🖋 5260342, Fax 5268922, ≼ laguna of San Marco, 🍴 – 🛗
🗐 🔟 🕿 🕭 – 🛂 25. 🖭 🛐 ⓞ ⋿ 𝘝𝘚𝘈. ✻ rest
M a la carte 45/55000 – ☲ 19000 – **34 rm** 164/338000.

🏨 **Villa Otello** without rest., via Lepanto 12 🖋 5260048 – 🛗 ✣ ☎ 🕭
15 March-October – **34 rm** ☲ 115/165000.

🏨 **Adria Urania, Villa Nora, Villa Ada-Biasutti,** via Dandolo 29 🖋 5260120, Telex 410666,
Fax 5261259, 🍴, ⚑ – 🛗 🗐 rm 🔟 🕿 🕭 – 🛂 50. 🖭 🛐 ⓞ ⋿ 𝘝𝘚𝘈. ✻ rest
March-November – **M** 30000 – **86 rm** ☲ 190/330000 – ½ p 120/195000.

🏨 **Rigel** without rest., viale Dandolo 13 🖋 5268810, Telex 420835, Fax 5204083 – 🛗 ✣ 🗐 🕿.
🖭 🛐 ⓞ ⋿ 𝘝𝘚𝘈
February-October – **42 rm** ☲ 113/169000. 🗐 11000.

🏨 **Centrale e Byron,** via Bragadin 30 🖋 5260291, Telex 410391, Fax 5260052, ⚑ – 🛗 🗐 🕾.
🖭 🛐 𝘝𝘚𝘈. ✻ rest
March-October – **M** 25/35000 – ☲ 15000 – **36 rm** 100/140000. 🗐 10000 – ½ p 66/132000.

XX **Ai Murazzi,** località Cà Bianca 🖋 5267278, ≼ – 🛗 🕭 🖭
April-October; closed Tuesday – **M** a la carte 36/79000 (12%).

X **Trattoria da Ciccio,** via S. Gallo 241-in direction of Malamocco 🖋 5265489, 🍴 – 🕭 🛐
⋿ 𝘝𝘚𝘈
closed Tuesday and 15 to 30 November – **M** a la carte 26/42000 (12%).

in Torcello 45 mn by boat from fondamenta Nuove CT – ⊠ **30012** Burano :

XX ❀ **Locanda Cipriani,** 🖋 730150, Fax 735433, « Summer service in garden » – 🗐 🖭 🛐 ⓞ
⋿ 𝘝𝘚𝘈
19 March-10 November; closed Tuesday – **M** a la carte 69/96000 (15%)
Spec. Brodetto di pesce, Ravioloni alle erbe, Filetto di Sampietro e scampi alla Cá d' Oro. **Wines** Soave,
Cabernet.

XX **Ostaria al Ponte del Diavolo,** 🖋 730401, Fax 730250, 🍴 – 🖭 🛐 ⓞ ⋿ 𝘝𝘚𝘈
March-15 November; closed Thursday and dinner (except Saturday) – **M** a la carte 47/65000
(10%).

Norway
Norge

Oslo

PRACTICAL INFORMATION

LOCAL CURRENCY

Norwegian Kroner : 100 N-Kr = 16.88 US $ (Jan. 91)

TOURIST INFORMATION

The telephone number and address of the Tourist Information office is given in the text under 🛈.

FOREIGN EXCHANGE

In the Oslo area banks are usually open between 8.15am and 3.30pm, but in summertime, 15.5 - 31/8, they close at 3pm. Thursdays they are open till 5pm. Saturdays closed.

Most large hotels, main airports and railway stations have exchange facilities. At Fornebu Airport the bank is open from 6.30am to 10.30pm on weekdays and 7.00am to 10pm on Sundays, all the year round.

MEALS

At lunchtime, follow the custom of the country and try the typical buffets of Scandinavian specialities.

At dinner, the a la carte and the menus will offer you more conventional cooking.

SHOPPING IN OSLO

(Knitted ware - silver ware)

Your hotel porter will be able to help you and give you information.

CAR HIRE

The international car hire companies have branches in each major city. Your hotel porter should be able to give details and help you with your arrangements.

TIPPING IN NORWAY

A service charge is included in hotel and restaurant bills and it is up to the customer to give something in addition if he wants to.

The cloakroom is sometimes included in the bill, sometimes you pay a certain amount.

Taxi drivers and baggage porters have no claim to be tipped. It is up to you if you want to give a gratuity.

SPEED LIMITS

The maximum permitted speed within congested areas is 50 km/h - 31mph. Outside congested areas it is 80 km/h - 50mph. Where there are other speed limits (lower or higher) they are signposted.

SEAT BELTS

The wearing of seat belts in Norway is compulsory for drivers and passengers. All cars registered in Norway after 1/1-84 have got to have seat belts in the back seat too, and after 1/3-85 it is compulsory to use them.

ANIMALS

Very strict quarantine regulations for animals from all countries except Sweden. NO dispensations.

OSLO

OSLO Norge 985 M 7 – pop. 450 800 – ✆ 02.

🏌 Oslo Golfklubb ✆ 50 44 02.

✈ Fornebu SW : 8 km ✆ 59 67 16 – SAS : Ruseløkkveien 6 ✆ Business travel : 42 75 50 (Europe and Overseas) 42 79 00 (Domestics and Scandinavia), Vacation travel : 42 77 60 – Air Terminal : Havnegata, main railway station, seaside.

🚢 Copenhagen, Frederikshavn, Kiel : contact tourist information centre (see below).

🛈 Oslopro, Rådhusgaten 23 ✆ 33 43 86, Fax 334389, Telex 71969 and main railway station – **KNA** (Kongelig Norsk Automobilklub) Royal Norwegian Automobile Club ✆ 56 19 00 – **NAF** (Norges Automobil Forbund) ✆ 34 14 00.

Hamburg 888 – København 583 – Stockholm 522.

OSLO

BYGDØY

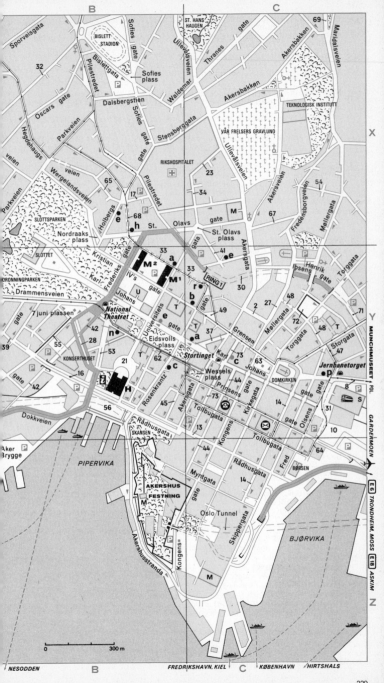

🏨🏨 **Grand,** Karl Johansgate 31, 0159 Oslo 1, ℰ 42 93 90, Telex 71683, Fax 42 12 25, ⇌, 🔲 – 📶
⇌ rm 📺 ☎ ⇌ – 🔬 300. 🗚 ⓞ 🗉 𝘝𝘐𝘚𝘈. 🛠
M (see Grand Café below) – **Etoile** 245 (dinner) and a la carte 318/402 – **Grand Grill** –
290 rm ⇌ 1400/2950, **5 suites** 2200/10000.   CY **a**

🏨🏨 **Oslo Plaza,** Sonja Henie Plass 3, 0107 Oslo 1, ℰ 17 10 00, Telex 11241, Fax 17 73 00, ⩽, 𝑓₆,
⇌, 🔲 – 📶 ⇌ rm 📺 ☎ ⅃ ⇌ – 🔬 1 000. 🗚 ⓞ 🗉 𝘝𝘐𝘚𝘈
M 192/385 and a la carte – **665 rm** ⇌ 1145/1995, **20 suites** 2200/8500.
                                                                    by Biskop Gunnerus' Gate   CY

🏨🏨 **SAS Scandinavia,** Holbergsgate 30, 0166 Oslo 1, ℰ 11 30 00, Telex 79090, Fax 11 30 17,
« Sky bar on 21st floor with ⩽ over the city », ⇌, 🔲 – 📶 ⇌ rm 📺 ☎ ⅃ ⇌ – 🔬
800. 🗚 ⓞ 🗉 𝘝𝘐𝘚𝘈   BX **e**
M (see Holberg below) – **Brasseriet** a la carte 225/295 – **487 rm** ⇌ 1495/1710, **4 suites**
3000/6800.

🏨🏨 Royal Christiania, Biskop Gunnerus gate 3, 0106 Oslo 1, ℰ 42 94 10, Telex 71342, Fax
42 46 22, 𝑓₆, ⇌, 🔲 – 📶 ⇌ rm 📺 ☎ ⅃ ⇌ – 🔬 400. 🛠   CY **p**
354 rm, 103 suites.

🏨🏨 **Continental,** Stortingsgaten 24-26, 0161 Oslo 1, ℰ 41 90 60, Telex 71012, Fax 42 96 89 – 📶
🔲 📺 ☎ ⇌ – 🔬 320. 🗚 ⓞ 🗉 𝘝𝘐𝘚𝘈. 🛠   BY **n**
closed Christmas – **M** (see Theatercaféen below) – **Annen Etage** (closed Saturday, Sunday,
Easter, 3 weeks July, Christmas and Bank Holidays) (dinner only) a la carte 316/538 – **169 rm**
⇌ 1350/1650, **8 suites** 2400/3900.

🏨🏨 **Scandic Crown,** Parkveien 68, 0254 Oslo 2, ℰ 44 69 70, Telex 71763, Fax 44 26 01, 𝑓₆, ⇌
– 📶 ⇌ rm 🔲 rest 📺 ☎ – 🔬 110. 🗚 ⓞ 🗉 𝘝𝘐𝘚𝘈. 🛠   AY **f**
closed Easter and Christmas – **M** 185/210 and a la carte – **179 rm** ⇌ 895/1350, **6 suites**.

🏨 **Bristol,** Kristian IV's des gate 7, 0130 Oslo 1, ℰ 41 58 40, Telex 71668, Fax 42 86 51 – 📶
⇌ rm 🔲 rest 📺 ☎ – 🔬 400. 🛠   CY **b**
141 rm, 4 suites.

🏨 **Gabelshus** ⤶, Gabelsgate 16, 0272 Oslo 2, ℰ 55 22 60, Telex 74073, Fax 44 27 30, « Antique
furniture, paintings » – 📶 📺 ☎ ⓟ – 🔬 60. 🗚 ⓞ 🗉 𝘝𝘐𝘚𝘈. 🛠   AY **m**
closed Easter and Christmas – **M** (bar lunch)/dinner 525 – **45 rm** ⇌ 750/1000.

🏨 **Ambassadeur** ⤶, Camilla Colletts vei 15, 0258 Oslo 2, ℰ 44 18 35, Telex 71446, Fax
44 47 91, « Distinctively themed bedrooms », ⇌, 🔲 – 📶 🔲 rest 📺 ☎ – 🔬 25. 🗚 ⓞ 🗉
𝘝𝘐𝘚𝘈. 🛠   AX **t**
closed Easter, Christmas and New Year – **M** (see Sabroso below) – **42 rm** ⇌ 1050/1270,
8 suites 1300/1500.

🏨 **Cecil** without rest., Stortingsgatan 8, 0161 Oslo 1, ℰ 42 70 00, Telex 71668, Fax 42 26 70 –
📶 ⇌ rm 🔲 📺 ☎ ⅃ ⇌. 🗚 ⓞ 🗉 𝘝𝘐𝘚𝘈. 🛠   BY **c**
closed Easter and Christmas – **112 rm** ⇌ 745/1240.

🏨 **Stefan,** Rosenkrantzgate 1, 0159 Oslo 1, ℰ 42 92 50, Telex 19809, Fax 33 70 22 – 📶 ⇌ rm
📺 ☎ ⅃ – 🔬 70   CY **r**
M (non alcoholic beverages only) – **131 rm**.

🏨 **Ritz** ⤶, Frederik Stangs Gate 3, 0272 Oslo 2, ℰ 44 39 60, Telex 19668, Fax 44 67 13 – 📶
⇌ rm 📺 ☎ ⓟ – 🔬 60. 🗚 ⓞ 🗉 𝘝𝘐𝘚𝘈   AY **e**
closed 22 December-2 January – **M** a la carte 190/280 – **52 rm** ⇌ 770/950.

🏨 **Europa** without rest., St. Olavsgate 31, 0166 Oslo 1, ℰ 20 99 90, Telex 71512, Fax 11 27 27 –
📶 ⇌ rm 📺 ☎. 🛠   BX **h**
156 rm, 2 suites.

🏨 **Savoy,** Universitetsgt. 11, 0164 Oslo 1, ℰ 20 26 55, Telex 76418, Fax 11 24 80 – 📶 📺 ☎
– 🔬 50. 🗚 ⓞ 🗉 𝘝𝘐𝘚𝘈   BY **a**
closed 22 December-2 January – **M** (closed Sunday) 115/195 and a la carte – **72 rm**
⇌ 945/1350.

🏨 **Rica Carlton,** Parkveien 78, 0254 Oslo 2, ℰ 69 61 70, Telex 71902, Fax 69 61 70 – 📶 📺 ⩩
– 🔬 50. 🗚 ⓞ 🗉 𝘝𝘐𝘚𝘈   AY **q**
M (closed Friday to Sunday and Bank Holidays) (dinner only) 220 and a la carte – **50 rm**
⇌ 850/1050.

🏨 **Munch** without rest., Munchsgt. 5, 0340 Oslo 1, ℰ 42 42 75, Telex 74096, Fax 20 64 69 – 📶
⇌ rm 📺 ☎ ⅃. 🗚 ⓞ 🗉 𝘝𝘐𝘚𝘈   CY **e**
closed Easter and Christmas – **180 rm** ⇌ 585/685.

🏨 **Norum,** Bygdøy Allé 53, 0265 Oslo 2, ℰ 44 79 90, Telex 79315, Fax 44 92 39 – 📶 🔲 rest 📺
⩩ – 🔬 50. 🗚 ⓞ 🗉 𝘝𝘐𝘚𝘈. 🛠   AX **s**
closed Christmas – **M** (closed Saturday and Sunday) (dinner only) a la carte approx. 250 –
59 rm ⇌ 860/990.

XXX **Holberg** (at SAS Scandinavia H.), Holbergsgate 30, 0166 Oslo 1, ℰ 11 30 00, Telex 79090,
Fax 11 30 17 – 🔲 ⇌. 🗚 ⓞ 🗉 𝘝𝘐𝘚𝘈   BX **e**
closed Monday, Sunday, 7 July-5 August and Bank Holidays – **M** (dinner only) 385/525 and
a la carte.

XXX ⚜ **Bagatelle** (Hellstrøm), Bygdøy Allé 3, 0257 Oslo 1, ℰ 44 63 97, Fax 55 35 92 – 🗚 ⓞ 🗉
𝘝𝘐𝘚𝘈   AY **x**
closed lunch Saturday and Monday, Sunday, Easter and Christmas – **M** 250/550 and a la
carte 425/540
Spec. Lasagne de homard au chou-fleur, Escalope de saumon au caviar, Dos de cabillaud rôti.

XXX **Kastanjen,** Bygdøy Allé 18, 0262 Oslo 2, ℰ 43 44 67 – ⒶⒺ ⓪ Ɛ 𝑽𝑰𝑺𝑨 AY **a**
closed Sunday – **M** (booking essential) dinner a la carte 205/365.

XXX **Sabroso** (at Ambassadeur H.) Camilla Colletts vei 15, 0208 Oslo 2, ℰ 55 25 31, « Elegant
decor, paintings » – ▤. ⒶⒺ ⓪ Ɛ 𝑽𝑰𝑺𝑨 AX **t**
closed Saturday, Sunday, Easter, 17 May, July, Christmas and Bank Holidays – **M** (dinner
only) a la carte approx. 349.

XX **Feinschmecker,** Balchensgate 5, Box 3165, 0265 Oslo 2, ℰ 44 17 77 – ▤. ⒶⒺ ⓪ Ɛ 𝑽𝑰𝑺𝑨
closed Easter, 17 May, 15 to 31 July, Christmas and Bank Holidays – **M** (dinner only) a la
carte 316/427. AX **n**

XX ❀ **D'Artagnan,** Øvre Slottsgate 16, 0157 Oslo 1, ℰ 41 50 62 – ▤. ⒶⒺ ⓪ Ɛ 𝑽𝑰𝑺𝑨 CY **c**
*closed Saturday except October-December, Sunday, 8 July-5 August and 21 December-6
January and Bank Holidays* – **M** (dinner only) 420/550 and a la carte 415/495
Spec. Scallops with asparagus, mousseline sauce, Home smoked arctic trout with a cream of parsley and trout
caviar, Confit of Bresse duck legs served grilled with green peppers.

XX **Det Blå Kjøkken,** Drammensveien 30, 0255 Oslo 2, ℰ 44 26 50, Fax 55 71 56 – ▤. ⒶⒺ ⓪
Ɛ 𝑽𝑰𝑺𝑨 AY **k**
closed Sunday, Easter and 23 December-3 January – **M** (dinner only) 345/495 and a la carte.

XX **Blom,** Karl Johansgate 41b, 0162 Oslo 1, ℰ 42 73 00, Fax 42 04 28, « Original heraldic
shields, collection dedicated to outstanding artists » – ▤. ⒶⒺ ⓪ Ɛ 𝑽𝑰𝑺𝑨 BY **e**
closed Sunday and 24 December-2 January – **M** 250/500 and a la carte.

XX **Theatercaféen** (at Continental H.), Stortingsgaten 24-26, 0161 Oslo 1, ℰ 41 90 60, Telex
71012, Fax 42 96 89 – ⒶⒺ ⓪ Ɛ 𝑽𝑰𝑺𝑨 BY **n**
M (buffet lunch) 72 and dinner a la carte 204/396.

X **Grand Café** (at Grand H.), Karl Johansgt. 31, 0159 Oslo 1, ℰ 42 93 90, Telex 71683, Fax
42 12 25 – ▤. ⒶⒺ ⓪ Ɛ 𝑽𝑰𝑺𝑨 CY **a**
M a la carte 127/273.

at Fornebu Airport SW : 8 km by E 18 – AY – and Snarøyveien – ✉ ✿ 02 Oslo :

🏨 **SAS Park Royal,** Forneburparken, Box 185, Oslo-N-1324, Lysaker ℰ 12 02 20, Telex 78745,
Fax 12 00 11, ≼, ☎, « Private beach and park », ⚲ – 🛗 ↤ rm ▤ 📺 ☎ & ℗ – 🏛 170.
ⒶⒺ ⓪ Ɛ 𝑽𝑰𝑺𝑨 ✺
M 145/245 and a la carte – **254 rm** ⊏ 1230/1415.

at Sandvika SW : 14 km by E 18 Exit E 68 – ✉ ✿ 02 Oslo :

🏨 Rica H. Oslofjord, Sandviksveien 184, 1301 Sandvika, ℰ 54 57 00, Telex 74345, Fax 54 27 33,
☎ – 🛗 ↤ rm ▤ 📺 ☎ & ⟷ ℗ – 🏛 250
M Orchidee – **245 rm, 3 suites**.

Portugal

Lisbon

PRACTICAL INFORMATION

LOCAL CURRENCY

Escudo : 100 Esc. = 1.03 US $ (Jan. 91)

FOREIGN EXCHANGE

Hotels, restaurants and shops do not always accept foreign currencies and the tourist is therefore advised to change cheques and currency at banks, saving banks and exchange offices - The general opening times are as follows: banks 8.30am to noon and 1 to 2.45pm (closed on Saturdays), money changers 9.30am to 6pm (usually closed on Saturday afternoons and Sundays).

SHOPPING IN LISBON

Shops and boutiques are generally open from 9am to 1pm and 3 to 7pm - In Lisbon, the main shopping streets are: Rua Augusta, Rua do Carmo, Rua Garrett (Chiado), Rua do Ouro, Rua da Prata, Av. da Roma.

TIPPING

A service charge is added to all bills in hotels, restaurants and cafés. It is usual, however, to give an additional tip for personal service ; 10 % of the fare or ticket price is also the usual amount given to taxi drivers and cinema and theatre usherettes.

SPEED LIMITS

The speed limit on motorways is 120 km/h - 74 mph, on other roads 90 km/h - 56 mph and in built up areas 60 km/h - 37 mph.

SEAT BELTS

Out of cities, it is compulsory for drivers and front seat passengers to wear seat belts.

THE FADO

The Lisbon Fado (songs) can be heard in restaurants in old parts of the town such as the Alfama, the Bairro Alto and the Mouraria. A selection of fado cabarets will be found at the end of the Lisbon restaurant list.

LISBON

SIGHTS

See : View : ★★ from the Suspension Bridge (Ponte de 25 Abril), ⚡ ★★ from Christ in Majesty (Cristo-Rei) S : 3,5 km.

CENTRE : POMBALINE LISBON

See : Rossio★ (square) GY — Avenida da Liberdade★ FX — Edward VII Park★ (Cold Greenhouse) EX — St. Rock★ (Igreja São Roque) FY **M¹** — Terreiro do Paço (square) GZ.

MEDIAEVAL LISBON

See : St. George's Castle★★ (Castelo de São Jorge) GY — Cathedral★ (Sé) GZ — Santa Luzia Belvedere★ (Miradouro de Santa Luzia) — Alfama★★ HYZ.

MANUELINE LISBON

See : Hieronymite Monastery★★ (Mosteiro dos Jerónimos : church★★, cloister★★★) — Belém Tower★★ (Torre de Belém) — Monument to the Discoveries★ (Padrão dos Descobrimentos).

MUSEUMS

Museum of Ancient Art★★ (Museu Nacional de Arte Antiga : polyptych by Nuno Gonçalves★★★) — Calouste Gulbenkian Museum★★★ (Art collection) — Azulejo Museum★ and Church of the Mother of God★★ (Igreja da Madre de Deus) — Coach Museum★★ (Museu Nacional dos Coches) — Maritime Museum★★ (Museu de Marinha).

LISBON (LISBOA) 1100 **437** P 2 — Pop. 826 140 — alt. 111 — ✪ 01.

🏌, 🏌 Estoril Golf Club W : 25 km 𝒫 268 01 76 Estoril — 🏌 Lisbon Sports Club NW : 20 km 𝒫 96 00 77 — 🏌 Club de Campo de Lisboa S : 15 km 𝒫 24 57 17 Aroeira, Fonte da Telha.

✈ Lisbon Airport N : 8 km from city centre — T.A.P., Praça Marquês de Pombal 3, ⊠ 1200, 𝒫 54 40 80 and airport 𝒫 88 91 81.

🚗 𝒫 87 75 09.

⚓ to Madeira : E.N.M., Rua de São Julião 5, ⊠ 1100, 𝒫 87 01 21, and Rocha Conde de Óbidos, ⊠ 1300.

🛈 Palácio Foz, Praça dos Restauradores 𝒫 346 63 07 and airport 𝒫 89 36 89 — A.C.P. Rua Rosa Araújo 24, ⊠ 1200, 𝒫 56 39 31, Telex 12581 — A.C.P. Av. Barbosa do Bocage 23, ⊠ 1000, 𝒫 77 54 75, Telex 14070.

Madrid 653 — Bilbao 904 — Paris 1817 — Porto 325 — Sevilla 411.

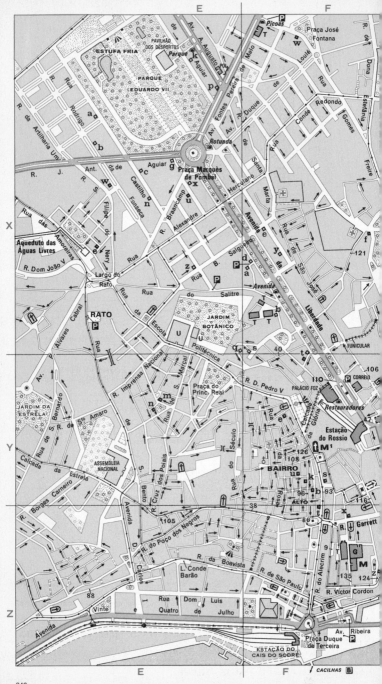

LISBOA

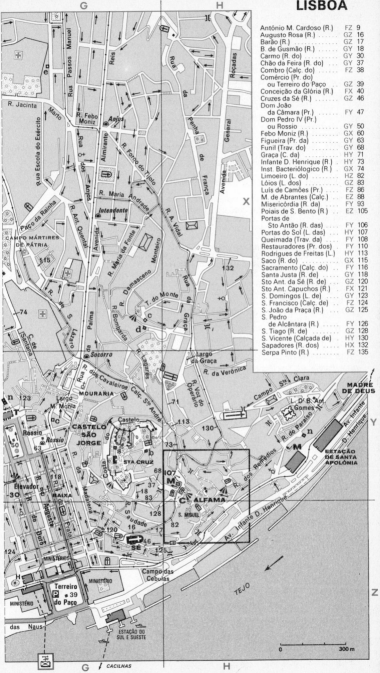

347

🏨🏨🏨 **Ritz,** Rua Rodrigo da Fonseca 88, ⊠ 1093, ℰ 69 20 20, Telex 12589, Fax 69 17 83, ≼, ⇑ –
│≉│ ▤ TV ☎ ⇔ **P** – 🄰 25/600. 🅰🄴 ⑩ 🄴 **VISA**. ✺ rest   EX **b**
M Varanda a la carte 4050/4700 - **The Grill** a la carte 6300/7400 – **310 rm** ☲ 39000/44000.

🏨🏨🏨 **Lisboa Sheraton,** Rua Latino Coelho 1, ⊠ 1000, ℰ 57 57 57, Telex 12774, Fax 54 71 64, ≼,
▟ heated – │≉│ ▤ TV ☎ & ⇔ – 🄰 25/550. 🅰🄴 ⑩ 🄴 **VISA**. ✺
M Alfama Grill *(closed Saturday and Sunday)* a la carte 4800/6100 - **Caravela** a la carte
4700/5200 – **384 rm** ☲ 35000/40000.   by Av. Fontes Pereira de Melo EFX

🏨🏨🏨 **Le Meridien Lisboa,** Rua Castilho 149, ⊠ 1000, ℰ 69 09 00, Telex 64315, Fax 69 32 31, ≼
– │≉│ ▤ TV ☎ & ⇔ – 🄰 25/480. 🅰🄴 ⑩ 🄴 **VISA**. ✺ rest   EX **a**
M 4800 - **Atlantic** *(closed Saturday and Sunday)* a la carte 5700/7100 - **Brasserie des Amis** a
la carte 4750/5500 – **331 rm** ☲ 35000/40000.

🏨🏨 **Tivoli Lisboa,** Av. da Liberdade 185, ⊠ 1200, ℰ 53 01 81, Telex 12588, Fax 57 94 61, ⇑,
« Terrace with ≼ town », ▟ heated, ✕ – │≉│ ▤ TV ☎ ⇔ – 🄰   FX **d**
M Grill Terraço and Zodíaco – **327 rm**.

🏨🏨 **Alfa Lisboa,** Av. Columbano Bordalo Pinheiro, ⊠ 1000, ℰ 726 21 21, Telex 18477, Fax
726 30 31, ≼ – │≉│ ▤ TV ☎ ⇔ – 🄰 25/250. 🅰🄴 ⑩ 🄴 **VISA**. ✺
M 2800 – Grill Pombalino and A Aldeia – **350 rm** ☲ 21000/26000.
                                                                  NW : by Av. A. Augusto Aguiar. EX

🏨🏨 **Altis,** Rua Castilho 11, ⊠ 1200, ℰ 52 24 96, Telex 13314, Fax 54 86 96, 🔲 – │≉│ ▤ TV ☎
⇔ – 🄰   EX **z**
M Girasol and Grill Dom Fernando – **307 rm**.

🏨🏨 **Continental,** Rua Laura Alves 9, ⊠ 1000, ℰ 793 50 05, Telex 65632, Fax 77 36 69 – │≉│ ▤
TV ☎ ⇔ – 🄰 25/180. 🅰🄴 ⑩ 🄴 **VISA**. ✺   N : by Av. Fontes Pereira de Melo EFX
M D. Miguel *(closed Saturday dinner)* a la carte 3800/4650 - **Coffee Shop** a la carte 3800/4650
– **220 rm** ☲ 19500/22000.

🏨🏨 **Lisboa Penta,** Av. dos Combatentes, ⊠ 1600, ℰ 726 40 54, Telex 18437, Fax 726 42 81, ≼,
▟ – │≉│ ▤ TV ☎ ⇔ **P** – 🄰 25/600. 🅰🄴 ⑩ 🄴 **VISA**. ✺ rest
M 3450 - Grill Passarola and Verde Pino – **588 rm** ☲ 17000/20700.
                                                                  NW : by Av. A. Augusto de Aguiar EX

🏨 **Holiday Inn,** Av. António José de Almeida 28 A, ⊠ 1000, ℰ 73 52 22, Telex 60330, Fax
73 66 72 – │≉│ ▤ TV ☎ ⇔ – 🄰. 🅰🄴 ⑩ 🄴 **VISA**. ✺
M 2800 – **169 rm** ☲ 21000/23000.   N : by Av. Fontes Pereira de Melo EFX

🏨 **Novotel Lisboa,** Av. José Malhoa 1642, ⊠ 1000, ℰ 726 60 22, Telex 40114, Fax 726 64 96,
≼, ▟ – │≉│ ▤ TV ☎ & ⇔ – 🄰 25/300. 🅰🄴 ⑩ 🄴 **VISA**. ✺
M 3450 – **246 rm** 11800/14300.   NW : by Av. A. Augusto de Aguiar EX

🏨 **Lisboa Plaza,** Travessa do Salitre 7, ⊠ 1200, ℰ 346 39 22, Telex 16402, Fax 37 16 30 – │≉│
▤ TV ☎. 🅰🄴 ⑩ 🄴 **VISA**. ✺   FX **b**
M 3900 – **93 rm** ☲ 22000/25000.

🏨 **Lutécia,** Av. Frei Miguel Contreiras 52, ⊠ 1700, ℰ 80 31 21, Telex 12457, Fax 80 78 18, ≼ –
│≉│ ▤ TV ☎. 🅰🄴 ⑩ 🄴 **VISA**. ✺   N : by Av. Almirante Reis GX
M 2400 – **151 rm** ☲ 15000/18000.

🏨 **Tivoli Jardim,** Rua Julio Cesar Machado 7, ⊠ 1200, ℰ 53 99 71, Telex 12172, Fax 55 65 66,
▟ heated, ✕ – │≉│ ▤ TV ☎ ☎ **P**. 🅰🄴 ⑩ 🄴 **VISA**. ✺   FX **a**
M a la carte 3050/4700 – **119 rm** ☲ 17500/21500.

🏨 **Diplomático,** Rua Castilho 74, ⊠ 1200, ℰ 56 20 41, Telex 13713, Fax 52 21 55 – │≉│ ▤ TV
☎ – 🄰   EX **c**
90 rm.

🏨 **Flórida** without rest, Rua Duque de Palmela 32, ⊠ 1200, ℰ 57 61 45, Telex 12256, Fax
54 35 84 – │≉│ ▤ TV ☎ – 🄰 25/100. 🅰🄴 ⑩ 🄴 **VISA**. ✺ rest   EX **x**
112 rm ☲ 15000/18000.

🏨 **Mundial,** Rua D. Duarte 4, ⊠ 1100, ℰ 86 31 01, Telex 12308, Fax 87 91 29, ≼ – │≉│ ▤ TV ☎
P – 🄰 25/140. 🅰🄴 ⑩ 🄴 **VISA**. ✺   GY **c**
M 3000 – **147 rm** ☲ 13800/17500.

🏨 **Fénix and Rest. el Bodegón,** Praça Marqués de Pombal 8, ⊠ 1200, ℰ 53 51 21, Telex
12170 – │≉│ ▤ TV ☎ – 🄰 25/100. 🅰🄴 ⑩ 🄴 **VISA**. ✺   EX **g**
M 2950 – **122 rm** ☲ 13500/15700.

🏨 **Dom Manuel I** without rest, Av. Duque d'Avila 189, ⊠ 1000, ℰ 57 61 60, Telex 43558, Fax
57 69 85, « Tasteful decor » – │≉│ ▤ TV ☎. 🅰🄴 ⑩ 🄴 **VISA**. ✺
64 rm ☲ 12000/14000.   N : by Av. Fontes Pereira de Melo EFX

🏨 **Lisboa** without rest, Rua Barata Salgueiro 5, ⊠ 1100, ℰ 55 41 31, Telex 60228, Fax 55 41 39
– │≉│ ▤ TV ☎ ⇔. 🅰🄴 ⑩ 🄴 **VISA**. ✺   FX **e**
61 rm ☲ 16000/19250.

🏛 **Roma,** Av. de Roma 33, ⊠ 1700, ℰ 76 77 61, Telex 16586, Fax 793 29 81, ≼, 🔲 – │≉│ ▤ ☎ –
🄰 25/230. 🅰🄴 ⑩ 🄴 **VISA**. ✺   N : by Av. Almirante Reis EX
M 2000 – **265 rm** ☲ 8000/10000.

🏛 **Eduardo VII,** Av. Fontes Pereira de Melo 5, ⊠ 1000, ℰ 53 01 41, Telex 18340, Fax 53 38 79,
≼ – │≉│ ▤ TV ☎ – 🄰 25/60. 🅰🄴 ⑩ 🄴 **VISA**. ✺   EX **p**
M 3450 – **121 rm** ☲ 13800/14400.

🏛 **Miraparque,** Av. Sidónio Pais 12, ⊠ 1000, ℰ 57 80 70, Telex 16745, Fax 57 89 20 – │≉│ ▤
☎. 🅰🄴 ⑩ 🄴 **VISA**. ✺   EX **k**
M a la carte 1900/2600 – **100 rm** ☲ 8000/9500.

🏨 **Príncipe Real,** Rua da Alegria 53, ✉ 1200, 𝒫 346 01 16, Telex 44571, Fax 52 34 92 – 📶 🗐
📺 ☎ 🄰🄴 ① E 𝘝𝘐𝘚𝘈 🛇   EX q
M 2500 – **24 rm** ⬄ 16000/19500.

🏨 **Britânia** without rest, Rua Rodrigues Sampaio 17, ✉ 1100, 𝒫 57 50 16, Telex 13733, Fax
57 58 45 – 📶 🗐 📺 ☎ 🄰🄴 ① E 𝘝𝘐𝘚𝘈 🛇   FX y
30 rm ⬄ 11300/13900.

🏨 **York House,** Rua das Janelas Verdes 32, ✉ 1200, 𝒫 396 25 44, Telex 16791, Fax 67 27 93,
🏤, « Former 16C convent, Portuguese decor » – ☎ 🄰🄴 ① E 𝘝𝘐𝘚𝘈
M a la carte 2400/3300 – **36 rm** ⬄ 15000/17000.   W : by calçada M. de Abrantes   EZ

🏨 **Residencia York House** without rest, Rua das Janelas Verdes 47, ✉ 1200, 𝒫 396 81 43,
Telex 16791, Fax 67 27 93 – 🕾. 🄰🄴 ① E 𝘝𝘐𝘚𝘈 🛇   W : by calçada M. de Abrantes   EZ
17 rm ⬄ 15000/17000.

🏨 **Botânico** without rest, Rua Mãe de Agua, ✉ 1200, 𝒫 32 03 92, Telex 16174, Fax 32 01 25 –
📶 🗐 📺 ☎ 🄰🄴 ① E 𝘝𝘐𝘚𝘈 🛇   FX s
30 rm ⬄ 10500/16000.

🏨 **Flamingo,** Rua Castilho 41, ✉ 1200, 𝒫 53 21 91, Telex 14736, Fax 352 12 16 – 📶 🗐 📺 ☎
🄰🄴 ① E 𝘝𝘐𝘚𝘈 🛇   EX n
M 2000 – **39 rm** ⬄ 10600/12600.

🏨 **Albergaria Senhora do Monte** without rest, Calçada do Monte 39, ✉ 1100, 𝒫 86 60 02,
Fax 87 77 83, ≤ São Jorge castle, town and river Tejo – 📶 🗐 ☎ 🄰🄴 ① E 𝘝𝘐𝘚𝘈 🛇   GX c
28 rm ⬄ 9000/12000.

🏩 **Fonte Luminosa** without rest, Alameda D. Afonso Enriques 70 6, ✉ 1000, 𝒫 80 48 96,
Telex 15063, Fax 80 90 03 – 📶 ☎. E 𝘝𝘐𝘚𝘈 🛇   N : by Av. Almirante Reis   GX
37 rm ⬄ 5000/6900.

🏩 **São Pedro** without rest, Rua Pascoal de Melo 130, ✉ 1000, 𝒫 57 87 65, Telex 65470 – 📶
🕾. 𝘝𝘐𝘚𝘈 🛇   N : by Av. Almirante Reis   CU
85 rm 5900/7500.

🏩 **Insulana** without rest, Rua da Assunção 52, ✉ 1100, 𝒫 342 76 25 – 📶 📺 ☎. 🄰🄴 ① E 𝘝𝘐𝘚𝘈
🛇   GY e
32 rm ⬄ 8000/10000.

🏩 **Dom João** without rest, Rua José Estevão 43, ✉ 1100, 𝒫 54 30 64 – 📶 ☎. 🄰🄴 ① E 𝘝𝘐𝘚𝘈
18 rm ⬄ 7000/10000.   GX e

🏩 **Imperador** without rest, Av. 5 de Outubro 55, ✉ 1000, 𝒫 52 48 84 – 📶 ☎. 🄰🄴 ① E 𝘝𝘐𝘚𝘈
🛇   N : by Av. Fontes Pereira de Melo EFX
43 rm ⬄ 6000/7500.

🏵🏵🏵🏵 ❀ **Tágide,** Largo da Academia Nacional de Belas Artes 18, ✉ 1200, 𝒫 32 07 20, ≤ – 🗐
🄰🄴 ① E 𝘝𝘐𝘚𝘈 🛇   FZ z
closed Saturday and Sunday – **M** a la carte 4600/8300
Spec. Crepes Santola Tágide, Bacalhao no forno à Tágide, Churrasco de cabrito con ervas aromáticas.

🏵🏵🏵🏵 **Antonio Clara - Clube de Empresários,** Av. da República 38, ✉ 1000, 𝒫 76 63 80,
Telex 62506, Fax 77 41 44, « Former old palace » – 🗐 🄿 🄰🄴 ① E 𝘝𝘐𝘚𝘈 🛇
closed Sunday – **M** a la carte 3700/5750.   N : by Av. Fontes Pereira de Melo EFX

🏵🏵🏵🏵 **Clara,** Campo dos Mártires da Patria 49, ✉ 1100, 𝒫 57 04 34, 🏤 – 🗐 🄰🄴 ① E 𝘝𝘐𝘚𝘈 🛇   FX f
closed Saturday lunch and Sunday – **M** a la carte 4400/6200.

🏵🏵🏵🏵 Aviz, Rua Serpa Pinto 12-B, ✉ 1200, 𝒫 32 83 91 – 🗐   FZ x

🏵🏵🏵🏵 **Tavares,** Rua da Misericórdia 37, ✉ 1200, 𝒫 32 11 12, Late 19C decor – 🗐 🄰🄴 ① E 𝘝𝘐𝘚𝘈
🛇   FZ t
closed Saturday – **M** a la carte 5200/6400.

🏵🏵🏵 **Gare Maritima-Michel** (Hotel Trade School), Gare Maritima de Alcantara-Alcantara Sul
𝒫 67 63 35, ≤ – 🗐. 🄰🄴 E 𝘝𝘐𝘚𝘈 🛇   W : by Av. 24 de Julho   EZ
closed Saturday lunch, Sunday, Bank Holidays and August – **M** a la carte 3950/4700.

🏵🏵🏵 **Gambrinus,** Rua das Portas de Santo Antão 25, ✉ 1100, 𝒫 32 14 66, Fax 346 50 32 – 🗐.
🄰🄴 𝘝𝘐𝘚𝘈 🛇   GY n
M a la carte 8800/11600.

🏵🏵🏵 **Escorial,** Rua das Portas de Santo Antão 47, ✉ 1100, 𝒫 346 44 29 – 🗐. 🄰🄴 ① E 𝘝𝘐𝘚𝘈
M a la carte 5850/6450.   GY n

🏵🏵🏵 ❀ **Casa da Comida,** Travessa das Amoreiras 1, ✉ 1200, 𝒫 68 53 76, « Patio with plants »
– 🗐. 🄰🄴 ① E 𝘝𝘐𝘚𝘈 🛇   EX e
closed Saturday lunch and Sunday – **M** a la carte 3800/7400
Spec. Sapateira recheada quente ou fria, Pregado com pimenta verde, Perdiz ou faisão à Covento de Alcantara..

🏵🏵🏵 **Mister Cook** with coffee shop, Av. Guerra Junqueiro 1, ✉ 1000, 𝒫 80 72 37, « Original
decor » – 🗐. 🄰🄴 ① E 𝘝𝘐𝘚𝘈 🛇   N : by Av. Fontes Pereira de Melo EFX
closed Sunday – **M** a la carte 3100/4850.

🏵🏵🏵 **Pabe,** Rua Duque de Palmela 27-A, ✉ 1200, 𝒫 53 74 84, English pub style – 🗐. 🄰🄴 ① E
𝘝𝘐𝘚𝘈 🛇   EX u
M a la carte 3400/4700.

🏵🏵🏵 **Chester,** Rua Rodrigo da Fonseca 87-D, ✉ 1200, 𝒫 65 73 47, Meat – 🗐. 🄰🄴 ① E 𝘝𝘐𝘚𝘈 🛇
closed Sunday and Bank Holidays – **M** a la carte 4600/6050.   EX w

XXX **Saraiva's,** Rua Eng. Canto Resende 3, ⊠ 1000, 🖋 53 19 87, Modern decor – 🗏. 🖭 ⓪ E
VISA. 🕸 N : by Av. Augusto de Aguiar EX
closed Saturday and Bank Holidays – **M** a la carte 4050/5850.

XXX **Bachus,** Largo da Trindade 9, ⊠ 1200, 🖋 32 28 28 – 🗏. 🖭 ⓪ E *VISA*. 🕸 FY **s**
M a la carte 6300/6800.

XXX ⊛ **Conventual,** Praça das Flores 45, ⊠ 1200, 🖋 60 91 96 – 🗏. 🖭 ⓪ E *VISA* EY **m**
closed Saturday lunch and Sunday – **M** a la carte 3130/5000
Spec. Ameijoas "Capelà da Sines". Lombo de linguado com molho marisco. Pato com champagne e pimenta
rosa.

XXX **O Faz Figura,** Rua do Paraíso 15 B, ⊠ 1100, 🖋 86 89 81, ⩽ 🗏. ⓪ E *VISA*. 🕸 HY **n**
closed Sunday – **M** a la carte 3500/4500.

XX **Via Graça,** Rua Damasceno Monteiro 9 B, ⊠ 1100, 🖋 87 08 30, ⩽ São Jorge castle, town
and river Tejo – 🗏. 🖭 ⓪ E *VISA*. 🕸 GX **d**
closed Saturday lunch, Sunday and 15 to 30 August – **M** a la carte 2900/5400.

XX **Casa do Leão,** Castelo de São Jorge, ⊠ 1100, 🖋 87 59 62, Fax 87 63 29, ⩽ – 🗏. 🖭 ⓪ E
VISA. 🕸 GY **s**
M (only lunch) a la carte 4800/9000.

XX **Santa Cruz - Michel,** Largo de Santa Cruz do Castelo 5, ⊠ 1100, 🖋 86 43 38 – 🗏. 🖭 ⓪
E *VISA* GY **b**
closed Saturday lunch, Sunday and Bank Holidays – **M** a la carte 3550/4600.

XX **São Jerónimo,** Rua dos Jerónimos 12, ⊠ 1400, 🖋 64 87 96 – 🗏. 🖭 ⓪ E *VISA*. 🕸
closed Saturday lunch and Sunday – **M** a la carte 2850/4450. W : by Av. 24 de Julho EZ

XX **Espelho d'Água,** Av. de Brasilia, ⊠ 1400, 🖋 61 73 73, ⩽, 🏛, Artificial lake side setting.
Modern decor – 🗏. 🖭 ⓪ E *VISA*. 🕸 W : 3 km by Av. 24 de Julho AZ
closed Sunday – **M** a la carte 2690/3300.

XX **Sancho,** Travessa da Glória 14, ⊠ 1200, 🖋 346 97 80 – 🗏. 🖭 E *VISA*. 🕸 FXY **t**
closed Sunday – **M** a la carte 1650/3200.

XX **Saddle Room,** Praça José Fontana 17C, ⊠ 1000, 🖋 52 31 57, Telex 64269, Fax 54 09 61,
Rustic english style decor – 🗏. 🖭 ⓪ E *VISA* FX **w**
closed Sunday – **M** a la carte 2850/4800.

XX **Adega Tia Matilde,** Rua da Beneficencia 77, ⊠ 1600, 🖋 77 21 72 – 🗏. 🖭 ⓪ E *VISA*. 🕸
closed Sunday – **M** a la carte 3500/5650. by Av. Fontes Pereira de Melo EFX

X **Xêlê Bananas,** Praça das Flores 29, ⊠ 1200, 🖋 67 05 15, Tropical style decor – 🗏. 🖭 ⓪
E *VISA* EY **n**
closed Saturday lunch and Sunday – **M** a la carte 2700/4850.

X **Sua Excelencia,** Rua do Conde 42, ⊠ 1200, 🖋 60 36 14 – 🗏. 🖭 ⓪ E *VISA*
closed Saturday, Sunday lunch, Wednesday and September – **M** a la carte 2850/5050.
W : by Av. 24 de Julho EZ

X **Chez Armand,** Rua Carlos Mardel 38, ⊠ 1900, 🖋 52 07 70, French rest-Meat – 🗏. 🖭 ⓪
E *VISA* by Av. Almirante Reis GX
closed Saturday lunch, Sunday and 14 August-8 September – **M** a la carte 2540/3490.

X **Porta Branca,** Rua do Teixeira 35, ⊠ 1200, 🖋 32 10 24 – 🗏. 🖭 ⓪ E *VISA*. 🕸 FY **e**
closed Sunday and July – **M** a la carte 3050/5000.

Typical atmosphere:

XX **Arcadas do Faia,** Rua da Barroca 56, ⊠ 1200, 🖋 32 67 42, Telex 13649, Fax 73 04 07, Fado
cabaret – 🗏. 🖭 ⓪ E *VISA*. 🕸 FY **f**
closed Sunday – **M** (dinner only) a la carte 3350/5750.

XX **Sr. Vinho,** Rua do Meio -à- Lapa 18, ⊠ 1200, 🖋 67 74 56, Telex 42222, Fado cabaret – 🗏.
🖭 ⓪ E *VISA*. 🕸 EZ **r**
closed Sunday – **M** (dinner only) a la carte 8420/13580.

XX **A Severa,** Rua das Gáveas 51, ⊠ 1200, 🖋 346 40 06, Fado cabaret in the evening – 🗏. 🖭
⓪ E *VISA*. 🕸 FY **b**
closed Thursday – **M** a la carte 4500/5300.

X **Adega Machado,** Rua do Norte 91, ⊠ 1200, 🖋 32 87 13, Fax 346 75 07, Fado cabaret –
🗏. 🖭 ⓪ E *VISA*. 🕸 FY **k**
closed Monday November-March – **M** (dinner only) a la carte 4000/5500.

Spain

España

Madrid
Barcelona
Malaga - Marbella
Sevilla
Valencia

PRACTICAL INFORMATION

LOCAL CURRENCY

Peseta : 100 ptas = 0.74 US $ (Jan. 91)

TOURIST INFORMATION

The telephone number and address of the Tourist Information offices is given in the text of the towns under 🛈.

FOREIGN EXCHANGE

Banks are usually open from 9am to 2pm (12.30pm on Saturdays).
Exchange offices in Sevilla and Valencia airports open from 9am to 2pm, in Barcelona airport from 9am to 2pm and 7 to 11pm. In Madrid and Málaga airports, offices operate a 24 hour service.

TRANSPORT

Taxis may be hailed when showing the green light or sign "Libre" on the windscreen.
Madrid, Barcelona and Valencia have a Metro (subway) network. In each station complete information and plans will be found.

SHOPPING

In the index of street names, those printed in red are where the principal shops are found.
The big stores are easy to find in town centres; they are open from 10am to 8pm.
Exclusive shops and boutiques are open from 10am to 2pm and 5 to 8pm - In Madrid they will be found in Serrano, Princesa and the Centre; in Barcelona, Passeig de Gracia, Diagonal and the Rambla de Catalunya.
Second-hand goods and antiques: El Rastro (Flea Market), Las Cortes, Serrano in Madrid; in Barcelona, Los Encantes (Flea Market), Barrio Gótico.

TIPPING

Hotel, restaurant and café bills always include service in the total charge. Nevertheless it is usual to leave the staff a small gratuity which may vary with the district and the service given. Doormen, porters and taxi-drivers are used to being tipped.

SPEED LIMITS

The maximum permitted speed on motorways is 120 km/h - 74 mph, and 90 km/h - 56 mph on other roads.

SEAT BELTS

Out of cities, the wearing of seat belts is compulsory for drivers and front seat passengers.

"TAPAS"

Bars serving "tapas" (typical Spanish food to be eaten with a glass of wine or an aperitif) will usually be found in central, busy or old quarters of towns. In Madrid, idle your way to the Calle de Cuchilleros (Plaza Mayor) or to the Calle Cardenal Cisnero (Glorieta de Bilbao).

MADRID

SIGHTS

See : The Prado Museum★★★ (Museo del Prado) NZ — Parque del Buen Retiro★★ HY — Paseo del Prado (Plaza de la Cibeles) NXYZ — Paseo de Recoletos NVX — Paseo de la Castellana NV — Puerta del Sol and Calle de Alcalá LMNY — Plaza Mayor★ KYZ — Royal Palace (Palacio Real)★★ KY — Descalzas Reales Convent★★ (Convento de las Descalzas Reales) KY **L** — San Antonio de la Florida (frescos by Goya★) DX **R**.

Other Museums : Archeological Museum★★ (Arqueológico Nacional) NV **M**22 — Lázaro Galdiano★★ HV **M**7 — The Americas Museum★ DV **M**8 — Museum of Contemporary Spanish Art★ — Army Museum (del Ejército★) NY **M**2.

Envir. : El Pardo (Palacio★) NW : 13 km by C 601.

MADRID 444 y 447 K 19 — Pop. 3 188 297 — alt. 646 — ✆ 91.

Racecourse of the Zarzuela — 🏇, 🏇 Puerta de Hierro ✆ 216 17 45 — 🏇, 🏇 Club de Campo ✆ 357 21 32 — 🏇 La Moraleja by ① : 11 km ✆ 650 07 00 — 🏇 Club Barberán by ⑥ : 10 km ✆ 218 85 05 — 🏇 Las Lomas — El Bosque by ⑥ : 18 km ✆ 616 21 70 — 🏇 Real Automóvil Club de España by ① : 28 km ✆ 652 26 00 — 🏇 Nuevo Club de Madrid, Las Matas by ⑦ : 26 km ✆ 630 08 20 — 🏇 Somosaguas W : 10 km by Casa de Campo ✆ 212 16 47.

✈ Madrid-Barajas by ② : 13 km ✆ 205 40 90 — Iberia : pl. de Cánovas 5, ✉ 28014, ✆ 585 85 85 NZ and Aviaco, Modesto Lafuente 76, ✉ 28003, ✆ 234 46 00 FV.

🚃 Atocha ✆ 228 52 37 — Chamartin ✆ 733 11 22 — Principe Pío ✆ 248 87 16.

Shipping Companies : Cía. Trasmediterránea, Pedro Muñoz Seca 2 NX, ✉ 1, ✆ 431 07 00, Telex 23189.

🛈 Princesa 1, ✉ 28008, ✆ 541 23 25, Duque de Medinaceli 2, ✉ 28014, ✆ 429 49 51 pl. Mayor 3, ✉ 28012, ✆ 266 54 77, Caballero de Gracia 7, ✉ 28013, ✆ 531 44 57 and Barajas airport ✆ 205 86 56 — R.A.C.E. José Abascal 10, ✉ 28003, ✆ 447 32 00, Telex 27341.

París (by Irún) 1310 ① — Barcelona 627 ② — Bilbao 397 ① — La Coruña 603 ⑦ — Lisboa 653 ⑥ — Málaga 548 ④ — Porto 599 ⑦ — Sevilla 550 ④ — Valencia 351 ③ — Zaragoza 322 ②.

Centre : Paseo del Prado, Puerta del Sol, Gran Vía, Alcalá, Paseo de Recoletos, Plaza Mayor, (plan pp. 6 and 7) :

🏨🏨🏨🏨 **Palace,** pl. de las Cortes 7, ⊠ 28014, ℰ 429 75 51, Telex 23903, Fax 429 82 66 – 🛗 🗐 📺 ☎ 🕭 🚗 – 🔏 25/500. 🖭 ① Ɛ 💳. 🛠 rest MY **e**
M Grill Neptuno a la carte 4550/6000 – ⌂ 1950 – **500 rm** 32300/39800.

🏨🏨🏨 **Princesa Plaza,** Princesa 40, ⊠ 28008, ℰ 542 21 00, Telex 44377, Fax 542 35 01 – 🛗 🗐 ☎ 🚗 – 🔏 25/750. 🖭 ① Ɛ 💳. 🛠 KV **c**
M 6000 – ⌂ 1500 – **406 rm** 21600/27000.

🏨🏨🏨 **Villa Real** without rest. coffee shop only, pl. de las Cortes, 10, ⊠ 28014, ℰ 420 37 67, Telex 44600, Fax 420 25 47, « Tasteful decor » – 🛗 🗐 📺 ☎ 🚗 – 🔏 25/150. 🖭 ① Ɛ 💳. 🛠 – **M** 5000 – ⌂ 1600 – **115 rm** 22000/30000. MY **c**

🏨🏨🏨 **Plaza,** pl. de España, ⊠ 28013, ℰ 247 12 00, Telex 27383, Fax 248 23 89, ≤, ⌕, ☒ – 🛗 🗐 📺 ☎ – 🔏 25/300. 🖭 ① Ɛ 💳. 🛠 KV **s**
M 3520 – ⌂ 1050 – **306 rm** 13860/17330.

🏨🏨🏨 **Tryp Ambassador,** Cuesta de Santo Domingo 5, ⊠ 28013, ℰ 541 67 00, Telex 49538, Fax 559 10 40 – 🛗 🗐 📺 ☎ – 🔏 25/280. 🖭 ① Ɛ 💳. 🛠 KX **k**
M a la carte 3800/5350 – ⌂ 1100 – **181 rm** 15200/19000.

🏨🏨 **G.H. Reina Victoria,** pl. del Angel 7, ⊠ 28012, ℰ 531 45 00, Telex 47547, Fax 522 03 07 – 🛗 🗐 ☎. 🖭 ① Ɛ 💳. 🛠 LZ **u**
M 3000 – ⌂ 1100 – **201 rm** 15200/19000.

🏨🏨 **Liabeny,** Salud 3, ⊠ 28013, ℰ 532 53 06, Telex 49024, Fax 532 74 21 – 🛗 🗐 📺 ☎ 🚗. 🖭 Ɛ 💳. 🛠 – **M** 1950 – ⌂ 800 – **220 rm** 7500/11600. LY **e**

🏨🏨 **Suecia and Rest. Bellman,** Marqués de Casa Riera 4, ⊠ 28014, ℰ 531 69 00, Telex 22313, Fax 521 71 41 – 🛗 🗐 📺 ☎ – 🔏 25/150. 🖭 ① Ɛ 💳. 🛠 MY **b**
M (closed Sunday, Saturday and August) a la carte approx. 6500 – ⌂ 1250 – **128 rm** 16900/19800.

🏨🏨 **Emperador** without rest., Gran Vía 53, ⊠ 28013, ℰ 247 28 00, Telex 46261, Fax 247 28 17, ☒ – 🛗 🗐 📺 ☎ – 🔏 25/300. 🖭 ① Ɛ 💳. 🛠 KX **n**
⌂ 800 – **232 rm** 10950/13660.

🏨🏨 **Arosa** without rest., coffee shop only, Salud 21, ⊠ 28013, ℰ 532 16 00, Telex 43618, Fax 531 31 27 – 🛗 🗐 📺 ☎ 🚗. 🖭 ① Ɛ 💳 LX **q**
⌂ 870 – **139 rm** 8880/13140.

🏨🏨 **Mayorazgo,** Flor Baja 3, ⊠ 28013, ℰ 247 26 00, Telex 45647, Fax 541 24 85 – 🛗 🗐 📺 ☎ 🚗 – 🔏 25/250. 🖭 ① Ɛ 💳. 🛠 KX **b**
M 2950 – ⌂ 800 – **200 rm** 8200/11400.

🏨🏨 **Tryp Menfis,** Gran Vía 74, ⊠ 28013, ℰ 247 09 00, Telex 48773, Fax 247 51 99 – 🛗 🗐 📺 ☎. 🖭 ① Ɛ 💳. 🛠 KV **u**
2300 – ⌂ 750 – **116 rm** 11200/14000.

🏨🏨 **Tryp Washington** without rest., Gran Vía 72, ⊠ 28013, ℰ 541 72 27, Telex 48773, Fax 247 51 99 – 🛗 🗐 📺 ☎. 🖭 ① Ɛ 💳. 🛠 KV **u**
M (at Hotel Tryp Menfis) – ⌂ 750 – **120 rm** 9600/12000.

🏨🏨 **El Coloso,** Leganitos 13, ⊠ 28013, ℰ 248 76 00, Telex 47017, Fax 247 49 68 – 🛗 🗐 📺 ☎ 🚗 – 🔏 25/175. 🖭 ① Ɛ 💳. 🛠 KX **y**
M 2500 – ⌂ 1100 – **84 rm** 12800/16000.

🏨🏨 **Regina** without rest., Alcalá 19, ⊠ 28014, ℰ 521 47 25, Telex 27500, Fax 521 47 25 – 🛗 🗐 📺 ☎. 🖭 ① 💳. 🛠 LY **v**
⌂ 500 – **142 rm** 7600/9500.

🏨 **Casón del Tormes** without rest., Río 7, ⊠ 28013, ℰ 541 97 46, Fax 541 18 52 – 🛗 🗐 📺 ☎. Ɛ 💳. 🛠 – ⌂ 470 – **61 rm** 5775/8500. KX **v**

🏨 **Mercator** without rest. coffee shop only, Atocha 123, ⊠ 28012, ℰ 429 05 00, Telex 46129 – 🛗 ☎ 🅿. 🖭 ① Ɛ 💳. 🛠 rest NZ **b**
⌂ 600 – **89 rm** 6250/8500.

🏨 **Los Condes** without rest., Los Libreros 7, ⊠ 28004, ℰ 521 54 55, Telex 42730 – 🛗 🗐 📺 ☎. 🖭 Ɛ 💳. 🛠 – ⌂ 540 – **68 rm** 5400/9150. KX **g**

🏨 **Tryp Capitol** without rest., Gran Vía 41, ⊠ 28013, ℰ 521 83 91, Telex 41499 – 🛗 🗐 📺 ☎. 🖭 ① Ɛ 💳. 🛠 KX **e**
⌂ 750 – **144 rm** 9600/12000.

🏨 **Carlos V** without rest., Maestro Vitoria 5, ⊠ 28013, ℰ 531 41 00, Telex 48547, Fax 531 37 61 – 🛗 🗐 📺 ☎. 🖭 ① Ɛ 💳. 🛠 KY **f**
⌂ 600 – **67 rm** 9000/11250.

🏨 **Atlántico** (3rd floor), without rest., Gran Vía 38, ⊠ 28013, ℰ 522 64 80, Telex 43142, Fax 531 02 10 – 🛗 🗐 ☎. 🖭 ① Ɛ 💳. 🛠 LX **e**
⌂ 600 – **62 rm** 5750/7830.

🏨 **Anaco** without rest. coffee shop only, Tres Cruces 3, ⊠ 28013, ℰ 522 46 04, Fax 531 64 84 – 🛗 🗐 📺 ☎. 🖭 ① Ɛ 💳. 🛠 LY **a**
⌂ 525 – **39 rm** 4950/7625.

🏨 **California** (1st floor), without rest., Gran Vía 38, ⊠ 28013, ℰ 522 47 03 – 🛗 ☎. 🖭 ① Ɛ 💳. 🛠 – ⌂ 300 – **26 rm** 4300/5950. LX **x**

🏨 **Alexandra** without rest., San Bernardo 29, ⊠ 28015, ℰ 542 04 00, Fax 559 28 25 – 🛗 ☎. 💳 – ⌂ 370 – **69 rm** 4980/6680. KV **z**

MADRID

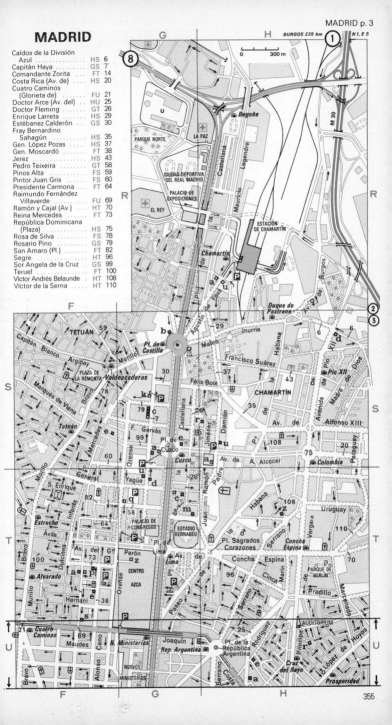

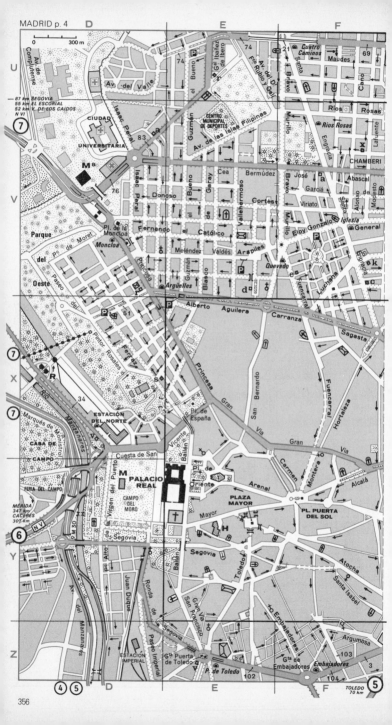

MADRID

357

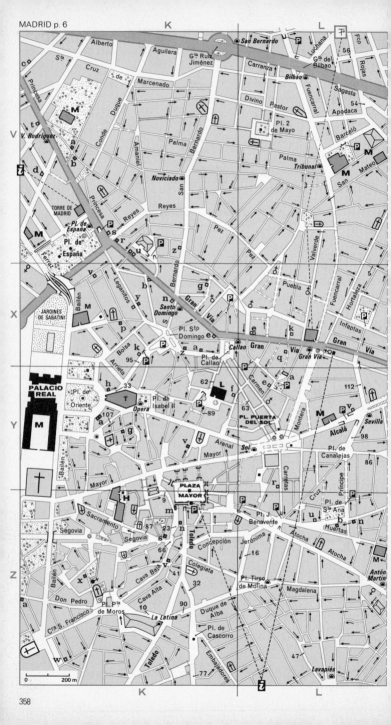

MADRID

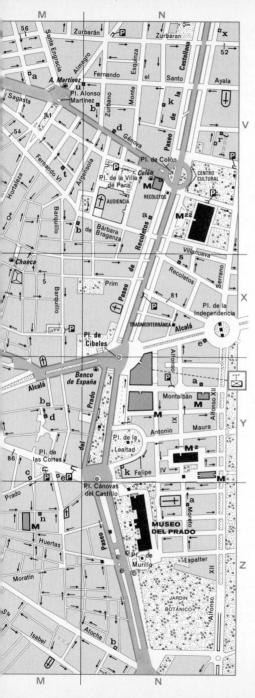

When driving through towns

use the plans

in the **Michelin Guide**

Features indicated include :

throughroutes

and by -passes ;

traffic junctions and

major squares,

new streets,

car parks,

pedestrian streets...

All this information

is revised annually.

XXXX ✿ **El Cenador del Prado,** Prado 4, ⊠ 28014, ℰ 429 15 61 – 🍴. 🅰🄴 ⊚ 🄴 *VISA*. ⋘   LZ **n**
closed Saturday lunch, Sunday and 15 days in August – **M** a la carte 5850/6950
Spec. Patatas a la importancia con almejas, Solomillo sobre hojaldre a la pera, Tarta de chocolate.

XXX ✿ **Café de Oriente,** pl. de Oriente 2, ⊠ 28013, ℰ 541 39 74, Basque and French rest.
Tasteful decor – 🍴. 🅰🄴 ⊚ 🄴 *VISA*. ⋘   KY **a**
closed Saturday lunch, Sunday, Holy Week and August – **M** a la carte 4400/6050
Spec. Terrina de poularda con foie-gras, Kokotxas de merluza al pil-pil, Paloma asada con ciruelas al Armagnac.

XXX **Jaun de Alzate,** Princesa 18, ⊠ 28008, ℰ 247 00 10, Fax 541 82 80 – 🍴. 🅰🄴 ⊚ 🄴 *VISA*. ⋘
closed Saturday lunch and 1 to 15 August – **M** a la carte 4300/5750.   KV **a**

XXX **Korynto,** Preciados 36, ⊠ 28013, ℰ 521 59 65, Seafood – 🍴. 🅰🄴 ⊚ 🄴 *VISA*. ⋘   KX **a**
M a la carte 4200/5700.

XXX **Bajamar,** Gran Via 78, ⊠ 28013, ℰ 248 48 18, Telex 22818, Fax 248 90 90, Seafood – 🍴. 🅰🄴
⊚ 🄴 *VISA*. ⋘   KV **r**
M a la carte 3260/5600.

XXX **Irizar** (1st floor), Jovellanos 3, ⊠ 28014, ℰ 531 45 69, Basque and French rest. – 🍴. 🅰🄴 ⊚
VISA. ⋘   MY **d**
closed Saturday lunch, Sunday, Bank Holidays dinner, Holy Week and 22 to 26 December –
M a la carte 3250/5150.

XXX **El Landó,** pl. Gabriel Miró 8, ⊠ 28005, ℰ 266 76 81, Tasteful decor – 🍴. 🅰🄴 ⊚ 🄴 *VISA*. ⋘
closed Sunday, Bank Holidays and August – **M** a la carte 3800/5000.   KZ **a**

XX **El Espejo,** paseo de Recoletos 31, ⊠ 28004, ℰ 308 23 47, Fax 593 22 23, « Old Parisian
café style » – 🍴. 🅰🄴 ⊚ 🄴 *VISA*. ⋘   NV **a**
M a la carte 3550/4800.

XX **Horno de Santa Teresa,** Santa Teresa 12, ⊠ 28004, ℰ 319 10 61 – 🍴. 🅰🄴 ⊚ 🄴 *VISA*. ⋘
closed Saturday, Sunday and August – **M** a la carte 3650/5350.   MV **t**

XX **Café de Oriente (Horno de Leña),** pl. de Oriente 2, ⊠ 28013, ℰ 247 15 64, Fax 247 77 07,
In a cellar – 🍴. 🅰🄴 ⊚ 🄴 *VISA*. ⋘   KY **a**
M a la carte 2400/3750.

XX **Platerías,** pl. de Santa Ana 11, ⊠ 28012, ℰ 429 70 48, Early 20C café style – 🍴. 🅰🄴 ⊚ 🄴
VISA. ⋘ – closed Sunday – **M** a la carte 3725/4975.   LZ **b**

XX **El Asador de Aranda,** Preciados 44, ⊠ 28013, ℰ 247 21 56, Roast lamb, « Castilian
decor » – 🍴. 🄴 *VISA*. ⋘   KX **z**
closed Monday dinner and 20 July-10 August – **M** a la carte 2950/3700.

XX **Casa Gallega,** Bordadores 11, ⊠ 28013, ℰ 551 90 55, Galician rest. – 🍴. 🅰🄴 ⊚ 🄴 *VISA*. ⋘
M a la carte 3300/5000.   KY **v**

XX **La Taberna de Liria,** Duque de Liria 9, ⊠ 28015, ℰ 541 45 19 – 🍴. 🅰🄴 ⊚ 🄴 *VISA*. ⋘
closed Saturday lunch, Sunday, Bank Holidays and 10 August-2 September – **M** a la
carte 3600/4300.   KV **b**

XX ✿ **Gure-Etxea,** pl. de la Paja 12, ⊠ 28005, ℰ 265 61 49, Basque rest. – 🍴. 🅰🄴 ⊚ 🄴 *VISA*. ⋘
closed Sunday and August – **M** a la carte 3675/4725   KZ **x**
Spec. Bacalao al pil-pil. Kokotxas a la guetariana. Lomo de merluza especial..

XX **El Mentidero de la Villa,** Santo Tomé 6, ⊠ 28004, ℰ 308 12 85 – 🍴. 🅰🄴 ⊚ 🄴 *VISA*. ⋘
closed Saturday lunch, Sunday and 15 to 31 August – **M** a la carte 3490/4200.   MV **b**

XX **La Opera de Madrid,** Amnistia 5, ⊠ 28013, ℰ 248 50 92 – 🍴. 🅰🄴 ⊚ 🄴 *VISA*. ⋘   KY **g**
M a la carte 2800/3900.

X **El Schotis,** Cava Baja 11, ⊠ 28005, ℰ 265 32 30 – 🍴. 🅰🄴 ⊚ 🄴 *VISA*. ⋘   KZ **v**
closed Monday and August – **M** a la carte 2700/3950.

X **Casa Paco,** Puerta Cerrada 11, ⊠ 28005, ℰ 266 31 66 – 🍴. ⋘   KZ **s**
closed Sunday and August – **M** a la carte 3450/4650.

X **El Ingenio,** Leganitos 10, ⊠ 28013, ℰ 541 91 33 – 🍴. 🅰🄴 ⊚ 🄴 *VISA*. ⋘   KX **y**
closed Sunday, Bank Holidays and August – **M** a la carte 1950/2550.

Typical atmosphere :

XX **Posada de la Villa,** Cava Baja 9, ⊠ 28005, ℰ 266 18 80, Fax 266 18 80, « Castilian decor »
– 🍴. 🅰🄴 ⊚ 🄴 *VISA*. ⋘   KZ **v**
closed Sunday dinner and 28 July-27 August – **M** a la carte 2775/4625.

XX **Botín,** Cuchilleros 17, ⊠ 28005, ℰ 266 42 17, Old Madrid decor, typical bodega – 🍴. 🅰🄴
⊚ 🄴 *VISA*   KZ **n**
M a la carte 3400/4400.

XX **Sixto Gran Mesón,** Cervantes 28, ⊠ 28014, ℰ 429 22 55, Castilian decor – 🍴. 🅰🄴 ⊚ 🄴
VISA. ⋘   MZ **n**
closed Sunday dinner – **M** a la carte 2350/3000.

XX **Café de Chinitas,** Torija 7, ⊠ 28013, ℰ 248 51 35, Flamenco cabaret – 🍴. 🅰🄴 🄴. ⋘
closed Sunday – **M** (dinner only) a la carte 5950/7000.   KX **p**

X **Las Cuevas de Luis Candelas,** Cuchilleros 1, ⊠ 28012, ℰ 266 54 28, Old Madrid decor-
Staff in bandit costume – 🍴. 🅰🄴 ⊚ 🄴 *VISA*. ⋘   KZ **m**
M a la carte 2775/4625.

X **Taberna del Alabardero,** Felipe V - 6, ⊠ 28013, ℰ 247 25 77, Fax 247 77 07, Typical
tavern – 🍴. 🅰🄴 ⊚ 🄴 *VISA*. ⋘   KY **h**
M a la carte 2860/3900.

Retiro-Salamanca-Ciudad Lineal : Castellana, Velázquez, Serrano, Goya, Príncipe de Vergara, Narváez. (plan p.5 except where otherwise stated) :

🏨🏨🏨 **Ritz,** pl. de la Lealtad 5, ⊠ 28014, ℰ 521 28 57, Telex 43986, Fax 532 87 76, 🛬 – 📳 🗏 📺
☎ – 🛗 25/280. 🖭 ⓞ 🗉 ☑️. 🕸 rest   plan p. 7   NY **k**
M 8500 – ⛷ 2300 – **158 rm** 55000/65000.

🏨🏨🏨 **Villa Magna,** paseo de la Castellana 22, ⊠ 28046, ℰ 578 20 00, Telex 27738, Fax 575 95 04
– 📳 🗏 📺 🛗 🕹 🚗 – 🛗 25/250. 🖭 ⓞ 🗉 ☑️   plan p. 7   NV **x**
M a la carte 6300/9000 – ⛷ 2250 – **182 rm** 52000/64000.

🏨🏨🏨 **Wellington,** Velázquez 8, ⊠ 28001, ℰ 575 44 00, Telex 22700, Fax 276 41 64, 🏊 – 📳 🗏 📺
☎ 🚗 – 🛗 25/300. 🖭 ⓞ 🗉 ☑️. 🕸   HX **t**
M (See rest. **El Fogón** below) – ⛷ 1750 – **258 rm** 16600/26000.

🏨🏨 **Tryp Fénix,** Hermosilla 2, ⊠ 28001, ℰ 431 67 00, Telex 45639, Fax 576 06 61 – 📳 🗏 📺
☎ – 🛗 25/100. 🖭 ⓞ 🗉 ☑️. 🕸   NV **c**
M 5000 – ⛷ 1250 – **226 rm** 18300/22900.

🏨🏨 **Sol Los Galgos and Rest. Diábolo,** Claudio Coello 139, ⊠ 28006, ℰ 562 66 00, Telex
43957, Fax 561 76 62 – 📳 🗏 📺 ☎ 🚗 – 🛗 25/300. 🖭 ⓞ 🗉 ☑️. 🕸   HV **a**
M a la carte 2750/4000 – ⛷ 1250 – **358 rm** 14600/18300.

🏨🏨 **Príncipe de Vergara,** Príncipe de Vergara 92, ⊠ 28001, ℰ 563 26 95, Telex 27064, Fax
563 72 53 – 📳 🗏 📺 ☎ 🚗 – 🛗 25/300. 🖭 ⓞ 🗉 ☑️. 🕸   HV **c**
M 3600 – ⛷ 1500 – **173 rm** 13800/19800.

🏨🏨 **Sanvy,** Goya 3, ⊠ 28001, ℰ 576 08 00, Telex 44994, Fax 575 24 43, 🏊 – 📳 🗏 📺 ☎ 🚗 –
🛗 25/120. 🖭 ⓞ 🗉 ☑️. 🕸   plan p. 7   NV **r**
M a la carte 3550/4500 – ⛷ 1500 – **141 rm** 15800/19800.

🏨🏨 **Tryp G.H. Velázquez,** Velázquez 62, ⊠ 28001, ℰ 575 28 00, Telex 22779, Fax 575 28 09 –
📳 🗏 📺 ☎ 🚗 – 🛗 25/280. 🖭 ⓞ 🗉 ☑️. 🕸   HX **s**
M 3000 – ⛷ 1500 – **144 rm** 12200/15900.

🏨🏨 **Agumar** without rest. coffee shop only, paseo Reina Cristina 7, ⊠ 28014, ℰ 552 69 00,
Telex 22814, Fax 433 60 95 – 📳 🗏 📺 ☎ 🚗. 🖭 ⓞ 🗉 ☑️. 🕸   HZ **a**
⛷ 850 – **252 rm** 10400/13000.

🏨🏨 **Novotel Madrid,** Albacete 1, ⊠ 28027, ℰ 405 46 00, Telex 41862, Fax 404 11 05, 🛬, 🏊 –
📳 🗏 📺 🛗 🕹 🚗 ❷ – 🛗 25/250. 🖭 ⓞ 🗉 ☑️   E : by M 30   JY
M 3275 – ⛷ 950 – **236 rm** 11500/14500.

🏨🏨 **Convención** without rest. coffee shop only, O'Donnell 53, ⊠ 28009, ℰ 574 84 00, Telex
23944, Fax 574 56 01 – 📳 🗏 📺 ☎ 🚗 – 🛗 25/1000. 🖭 ⓞ 🗉 ☑️. 🕸   JX **a**
⛷ 890 – **790 rm** 10450/13250.

🏨🏨 **Alcalá and rest. Basque,** Alcalá 66, ⊠ 28009, ℰ 435 10 60, Telex 48094, Fax 435 11 05 –
📳 🗏 📺 ☎ 🚗 – 🛗 25/60. 🖭 ⓞ 🗉 ☑️. 🕸   HX **w**
M (closed Sunday) a la carte 2475/3750 – ⛷ 800 – **153 rm** 10200/14900.

🏨🏨 **Pintor,** Goya 79, ⊠ 28001, ℰ 435 75 45, Telex 23281, Fax 576 81 57 – 📳 🗏 📺 ☎ 🚗 –
🛗 25/350. 🖭 🗉 ☑️. 🕸   HX **c**
M 1900 – ⛷ 975 – **176 rm** 9800/14200.

🏨🏨 **G. H. Colón,** Pez Volador 11, ⊠ 28007, ℰ 573 86 00, Telex 22984, Fax 573 08 89, 🏊, 🛬 –
🛗 25/130. 🖭 ⓞ 🗉 ☑️. 🕸   JY **x**
M 2700 – ⛷ 600 – **390 rm** 7600/11200.

🏨🏨 **Emperatriz,** López de Hoyos 4, ⊠ 28006, ℰ 563 80 88, Telex 43640, Fax 563 98 04 – 📳 🗏
📺 🛗 🕹 – 🛗 25/150. 🖭 ⓞ 🗉 ☑️. 🕸   GV **z**
M 2750 – ⛷ 950 – **170 rm** 9150/14550.

🏨 **Serrano** without rest., Marqués de Villamejor 8, ⊠ 28006, ℰ 435 52 00, Fax 435 48 49 – 📳
🗏 📺 ☎. 🖭 🗉 ☑️. 🕸   HV **b**
⛷ 750 – **34 rm** 10000/12600.

🏨 **Balboa,** Nuñez de Balboa 112, ⊠ 28006, ℰ 563 03 24, Telex 27063, Fax 262 69 80 – 📳 🗏
📺 ☎ 🚗 – 🛗 25/30. 🖭 ⓞ 🗉 ☑️. 🕸   HV **n**
M 3500 – ⛷ 1000 – **122 rm** 12400/17400.

🏨 **Sur** without rest. coffee shop only, paseo Infante Isabel 9, ⊠ 28014, ℰ 239 94 00, Telex
47494, Fax 467 09 96 – 🗏 – 🛗 25/45. 🖭 ⓞ 🗉 ☑️. 🕸   GZ **a**
⛷ 900 – **67 rm** 10200/14000.

🏨 **Abeba** without rest, Alcántara 63, ⊠ 28006, ℰ 401 16 50, Fax 402 75 91 – 📳 🗏 📺 🕾 🚗.
🖭 ⓞ 🗉 ☑️. 🕸   HV **r**
⛷ 550 – **90 hab** 7200/9350.

🏨 **Don Diego** (5th. floor), without rest., Velázquez 45, ⊠ 28001, ℰ 435 07 60 – 📳 ☎. 🖭 ☑️
⛷ 450 – **58 rm** 5500/7900.   HX **k**

XXX Bidasoa, Claudio Coello 24, ⊠ 28001, ℰ 431 20 81, Telex 42948 – 🗏   HX **h**

XXX **Club 31,** Alcalá 58, ⊠ 28014, ℰ 531 00 92 – 🗏. 🖭 ⓞ 🗉 ☑️. 🕸   plan p. 7   NX **e**
closed August – **M** a la carte 5500/7800.

XXX ❀ **El Amparo,** Callejón de Puigcerdá 8, ⊠ 28001, ℰ 431 64 56, « Original decor » – 🗏.
🖭 ☑️. 🕸   HX **h**
closed Saturday lunch, Sunday, Holy Week and August – **M** a la carte 5950/7425
Spec. Terrina de hígado fresco de pato. Kokotxas de merluza con huevas. Hojaldre de pera Williams caramelizada.

XXX **Suntory,** Castellana 36, ⌧ 28046, ℰ 577 37 33, Fax 577 75 05, Japanese rest. – 🗐 🚗. 🎟
⓪ 𝘝𝘐𝘚𝘈. ⁒ GHV **d**
closed Sunday and Bank Holidays – **M** a la carte 5000/7000.

XXX **Villa y Corte de Madrid,** Serrano 110, ⌧ 28006, ℰ 564 50 19, Fax 564 50 91, Tasteful
decor – 🗐. 🎟 ⓪ 🗉 𝘝𝘐𝘚𝘈. ⁒ HV **a**
closed Sunday and August – **M** a la carte 3425/4450.

XXX **El Gran Chambelán,** Ayala 46, ⌧ 28001, ℰ 576 40 51 – 🗐. 🎟 𝘝𝘐𝘚𝘈. ⁒ HX **r**
closed Sunday and Bank Holidays dinner – **M** a la carte 3100/3350.

XXX Belagua, Hermosilla 4, ⌧ 28001, ℰ 576 08 00, Telex 44994, Fax 275 24 43 – 🗐 NV **r**

XXX **Balzac,** Moreto 7, ⌧ 28014, ℰ 420 01 77, 🍽 – 🗐. 🎟 ⓪ 🗉 𝘝𝘐𝘚𝘈. ⁒ plan p. 9 NZ **a**
closed Saturday lunch and Sunday – **M** a la carte approx. 5500.

XXX **El Comedor,** Montalbán 9, ⌧ 28014, ℰ 531 69 68, 🍽 – 🗐. 🎟 ⓪ 🗉 𝘝𝘐𝘚𝘈. ⁒ NY **a**
closed Saturday lunch and Sunday – **M** a la carte 3350/4950.

XX **El Fogón** (at Hotel Wellington), Villanueva 34, ⌧ 28001, ℰ 575 44 00, Telex 22700, Fax
276 41 64 – 🗐. 🎟 ⓪ 🗉 𝘝𝘐𝘚𝘈. ⁒ HX **t**
M a la carte 3850/4500.

XX **Ponteareas,** Claudio Coello 96, ⌧ 28006, ℰ 575 58 73, Galician rest. – 🗐 🚗. 🎟 ⓪ 🗉
𝘝𝘐𝘚𝘈. ⁒ HV **w**
closed Sunday, Bank Holidays and August – **M** a la carte 4495/5545.

XX **Schwarzwald (Selva Negra),** O'Donnell 46, ⌧ 28009, ℰ 409 55 35, Fax 544 75 92, « Original decor » – 🗐. 🎟 ⓪ 🗉 𝘝𝘐𝘚𝘈. ⁒ JX **n**
M a la carte 3350/3650.

XX **St.-James,** Juan Bravo 26, ⌧ 28006, ℰ 275 60 10, 🍽, Rice rest. – 🗐. 🎟 HV **t**
closed Sunday – **M** a la carte 3300/4650.

XX **Al Mounia,** Recoletos 5, ⌧ 28001, ℰ 435 08 28, North African rest., « Oriental atmosphere » – 🗐. 🎟 ⓪ 🗉 𝘝𝘐𝘚𝘈. ⁒ plan p. 7 NX **s**
closed Sunday, Monday and August – **M** a la carte 3620/4100.

XX **La Fonda,** Lagasca 11, ⌧ 28001, ℰ 577 79 24, Catalonian rest. – 🗐. 🎟 ⓪ 🗉 𝘝𝘐𝘚𝘈. ⁒
closed Sunday dinner – **M** a la carte 2255/3300. HX **f**

X **Asador Velate,** Jorge Juan 91, ⌧ 28009, ℰ 435 10 24, Basque rest. – 🗐. 🎟 ⓪ 🗉 𝘝𝘐𝘚𝘈.
⁒ HJX **x**
closed Sunday and August – **M** a la carte 3350/3750.

X 🕸 **La Trainera,** Lagasca 60, ⌧ 28001, ℰ 576 05 75, Fax 575 47 17, Seafood – 🗐. 🗉 𝘝𝘐𝘚𝘈. ⁒
closed Sunday and August – **M** a la carte 3500/4800 HX **k**
Spec. Salpicón de mariscos. Pescados finos a la plancha. Mariscos cocidos a la plancha o a la americana..

X 🕸 **El Pescador,** José Ortega y Gasset 75, ⌧ 28006, ℰ 402 12 90, Seafood – 🗐. 🗉 𝘝𝘐𝘚𝘈. ⁒
closed Sunday and 5 August-10 September – **M** a la carte 3150/3775 JV **t**
Spec. Crema tres eles. Lenguado Evaristo. Bogavante a la americana.

X 🕸 **Viridiana,** Fundadores 23, ⌧ 28028, ℰ 256 77 73 – 🗐 JX **c**
closed Sunday and August – **M** a la carte 3350/4700
Spec. Lentejas estofadas con arroz salvaje al curry. Solomillo de buey a las trufas blancas de Alba. Biscuit de
vainilla al arrope de miel..

Arganzuela, Carabanchel Villaverde : Antonio López, paseo de Las Delicias, paseo de
Santa María de la Cabeza (plan p. 2 except where otherwise stated) :

🏨 **Carlton,** paseo de las Delicias 26, ⌧ 28045, ℰ 239 71 00, Telex 44571, Fax 227 85 10 – 📶
🗐 📺 ☎. 🎟 ⓪ 🗉 𝘝𝘐𝘚𝘈. ⁒ plan p. 5 GZ **n**
M 1950 – ⌷ 875 – **112 rm** 12000/15000.

🏨 **Praga** without rest, coffee shop only, Antonio López 65, ⌧ 28019, ℰ 469 06 00, Telex
22823, Fax 469 83 25 – 📶 🗐 ☎ 🚗 – 🔏 25/350. 🎟 ⓪ 🗉 𝘝𝘐𝘚𝘈. ⁒ by ⑤
⌷ 585 – **428 rm** 7100/9400.

🏨 **Aramo,** paseo Santa María de la Cabeza 73, ⌧ 28045, ℰ 473 91 11, Telex 45885, Fax
473 92 14 – 📶 🗐 📺 ☎ 🚗. 🎟 ⓪ 🗉 𝘝𝘐𝘚𝘈. ⁒ rest by ⑤
M 2200 – ⌷ 700 – **105 rm** 10000/13500.

🏨 **Puerta de Toledo,** glorieta Puerta de Toledo 4, ⌧ 28005, ℰ 474 71 00, Telex 22291, Fax
474 07 47 – 📶 🗐 ☎ 🚗. 🎟 ⓪ 🗉 𝘝𝘐𝘚𝘈. ⁒ plan p. 4 EZ **v**
M (See Puerta de Toledo below) – ⌷ 550 – **152 rm** 4800/8500.

XX **Puerta de Toledo** (at Hotel Puerta de Toledo), glorieta Puerta de Toledo 4 ℰ 474 76 75,
Telex 22291, Fax 474 07 47 – 🗐. ⓪ 🗉 𝘝𝘐𝘚𝘈. ⁒ plan p. 4 EZ **v**
closed Saturday – **M** a la carte 2700/3500.

Moncloa : Princesa, paseo del Pintor Rosales, paseo de la Florida, Casa de Campo (plan p.
4 except where otherwise stated) :

🏨🏨 **Meliá Madrid,** Princesa 27, ⌧ 28008, ℰ 541 82 00, Telex 22537, Fax 541 19 88 – 📶 🗐 📺
☎ – 🔏 25/200. 🎟 ⓪ 🗉 𝘝𝘐𝘚𝘈. ⁒ plan p. 6 KV **v**
M – ⌷ 1750 – **266 rm** 21800/27100.

🏨 **Monte Real** 🦢, Arroyofresno 17 ℰ 316 21 40, Telex 22089, Fax 316 21 40, 🍽, « Garden »,
🏊 – 📶 🗐 ☎ 🚗 🅿 – 🔏 25/200. 🎟 ⓪ 🗉 𝘝𝘐𝘚𝘈. ⁒ NW : 8 km by ⑦ and C 601
M 6720 – ⌷ 1320 – **79 rm** 18705/29680.

🏨 **Florida Norte,** paseo de la Florida 5, ⌧ 28008, ℰ 542 83 00, Telex 23675, Fax 247 78 33 –
📶 🗐 📺 ☎ 🚗. 🎟 ⓪ 𝘝𝘐𝘚𝘈. ⁒ DX **v**
M 1950 – ⌷ 700 – **399 rm** 10500/14500.

🏨 **Pullman Calatrava** without rest, Tutor 1, ⊠ 28008, 𝒫 541 98 80, Telex 43190, Fax 248 51 26
 – 🛗 ▤ 📺 ☎ ⇔. 🎫 ⓪ 𝐄 𝘝𝘐𝘚𝘈. ❄️   KV **d**
 ⊑ 890 – **98 rm** 12775/16325.

🏨 **Tirol** without rest, coffee shop only, Marqués de Urquijo 4, ⊠ 28008, 𝒫 248 19 00 – 🛗 ▤
 ☎. 𝐄 𝘝𝘐𝘚𝘈. ❄️   DV **r**
 97 rm 6315/7890.

XXX **Café Viena,** Luisa Fernanda 23, ⊠ 28008, 𝒫 248 15 91, « Old Style café » – ▤. 🎫 ⓪ 𝐄
 𝘝𝘐𝘚𝘈. ❄️ – *closed Sunday and August* – **M** a la carte approx. 3700.   DX **s**

X **Currito,** Casa de Campo - Pabellón de Vizcaya, ⊠ 28011, 𝒫 464 57 04, Fax 479 72 54, 🏠,
 Basque rest. – 🎫 ⓪ 𝘝𝘐𝘚𝘈. ❄️   by Segovia plan p. 4 DY
 M a la carte 3800/4600.

 Chamberí : San Bernardo, Fuencarral, Alberto Aguilera, Santa Engracia (plan p. 4 to 7) :

🏨 **Miguel Angel,** Miguel Angel 31, ⊠ 28010, 𝒫 442 00 22, Telex 44235, Fax 442 53 20, ⊠ –
 🛗 ▤ 📺 ☎ ⇔ – 🔬 25/300. 🎫 ⓪ 𝐄 𝘝𝘐𝘚𝘈. ❄️   GV **c**
 M 5500 – ⊑ 1500 – **278 rm** 22600/28300.

🏨 **Mindanao,** San Francisco de Sales 15, ⊠ 28003, 𝒫 549 55 00, Telex 22631, Fax 244 55 96,
 🏊, ⊠ – 🛗 ▤ 📺 ☎ ⇔ – 🔬 25/200. 🎫 ⓪ 𝐄 𝘝𝘐𝘚𝘈. ❄️   DV **v**
 M 4750 – ⊑ 1575 – **289 rm** 20000/25000.

🏨 **Castellana Inter-Continental,** paseo de la Castellana 49, ⊠ 28046, 𝒫 410 02 00, Telex
 27686, Fax 319 58 53, 🏠 – 🛗 ▤ 📺 ☎ ⇔ – 🔬 25/550. 🎫 ⓪ 𝐄 𝘝𝘐𝘚𝘈. ❄️   GV **a**
 M 4500 – ⊑ 2100 – **305 rm** 27900/35000.

🏨 **Escultor and Rest. Vanity,** Miguel Angel 3, ⊠ 28010, 𝒫 410 42 03, Telex 44285, Fax
 319 25 84 – ▤ 📺 ☎. 🎫 ⓪ 𝐄 𝘝𝘐𝘚𝘈. ❄️   GV **s**
 M *(closed Saturday lunch, Sunday, Bank Holidays and September)* 3600 – ⊑ 950 – **82 rm**
 13200/16500.

🏨 **Sol Alondras** without rest, coffee shop only, José Abascal 8, ⊠ 28003, 𝒫 447 40 00,
 Telex 49454, Fax 593 88 00 – 🛗 ▤ 📺 ☎. 🎫 ⓪ 𝐄 𝘝𝘐𝘚𝘈. ❄️   FV **a**
 ⊑ 850 – **72 rm** 11850/14800.

🏨 **Gran Versalles** without rest, Covarrubias 4, ⊠ 28010, 𝒫 447 57 00, Telex 49150, Fax
 446 39 87 – ▤ – 🔬 25/140. 🎫 ⓪ 𝐄 𝘝𝘐𝘚𝘈. ❄️   MV **a**
 ⊑ 900 – **145 rm** 13200/16500.

🏨 **Zurbano,** Zurbano 79-81, ⊠ 28003, 𝒫 441 45 00, Telex 27578, Fax 441 32 24 – 🛗 ▤ ☎
 ⇔ – 🔬 25/100. 🎫 ⓪ 𝐄 𝘝𝘐𝘚𝘈. ❄️   GV **x**
 M 3000 – ⊑ 1100 – **269 rm** 13900/17400.

🏨 **Conde Duque** without rest, pl. Conde Valle de Suchil 5, ⊠ 28015, 𝒫 447 70 00, Telex
 22058, Fax 448 35 69 – 🛗 ▤ ☎ – 🔬 25/160. 🎫 ⓪ 𝐄 𝘝𝘐𝘚𝘈   EV **d**
 ⊑ 530 – **138 rm** 11550/16500.

XXXXX ❀ **Fortuny,** Fortuny 34, ⊠ 28010, 𝒫 308 32 67, Fax 593 22 23, 🏠, « Former palace, tastefully decorated » – ▤. 🎫 ⓪ 𝐄 𝘝𝘐𝘚𝘈. ❄️   GV **n**
 closed Saturday lunch, Sunday and Bank Holidays – **M** a la carte 5600/7225
 Spec. Ensalada de bogavante al vinagre de laurel. Bacalao con almejas al estilo de la casa. Manitas de cerdo
 rellenas de hongos y trufas.

XXXX ❀ **Jockey,** Amador de los Rios 6, ⊠ 28010, 𝒫 319 24 35, Fax 319 24 35, « Tasteful decor »
 – ▤. 🎫 ⓪ 𝐄 𝘝𝘐𝘚𝘈. ❄️   NV **k**
 closed Sunday, Bank Holidays and August – **M** a la carte 6550/9600
 Spec. Ensalada de bacalao marinado, Ragout de bogavante con pasta fresca y trufa, Carre de cordero asado
 con pisto.

XXXX ❀ **Lúculo,** Génova 19, ⊠ 28004, 𝒫 319 40 29, 🏠 – ▤. 🎫 ⓪ 𝐄 𝘝𝘐𝘚𝘈. ❄️   NV **d**
 closed Saturday lunch, Sunday, 1 to 6 January, Holy Week and 10 August-2 September – **M**
 a la carte 5400/7300
 Spec. Escabeche de hígado de pato, Cocido de pescados, Rable de liebre (octubre a marzo).

XXXX ❀ **Las Cuatro Estaciones,** General Ibáñez Ibero 5, ⊠ 28003, 𝒫 553 63 05, Telex 43709,
 Fax 553 32 98, Modern decor – ▤. 🎫 ⓪ 𝐄 𝘝𝘐𝘚𝘈   EU **r**
 closed Saturday, Sunday and August-3 September – **M** a la carte 4250/5250
 Spec. Gazpacho de bogavante Las Cuatro Estaciones, Foie-gras a las uvas y Pedro Ximenez (verano) Perdiz en
 salmis con endivias a la crema (temp. caza).

XXX **Lur Maitea,** Fernando el Santo 4, ⊠ 28010, 𝒫 308 03 50, Basque rest – ▤. 🎫 ⓪ 𝐄 𝘝𝘐𝘚𝘈.
 ❄️   MNV **u**
 closed Saturday lunch, Sunday, Bank Holidays and August – **M** a la carte approx. 5500.

XXX **Annapurna,** Zurbano 5, ⊠ 28010, 𝒫 410 77 27, Indian rest – ▤. 🎫 ⓪ 𝐄 𝘝𝘐𝘚𝘈. ❄️   NV **b**
 closed Saturday lunch in Summer, Sunday and Bank Holidays – **M** a la carte 3400/4600.

XX **Aymar,** Fuencarral 138, ⊠ 28010, 𝒫 445 57 67, Seafood – ▤. 🎫 ⓪ 𝐄 𝘝𝘐𝘚𝘈. ❄️   FV **e**
 M a la carte 3200/4100.

XX **La Plaza de Chamberí,** pl. de Chamberí 10, ⊠ 28010, 𝒫 446 06 97, 🏠 – ▤. 🎫 ⓪ 𝐄
 𝘝𝘐𝘚𝘈. ❄️ – *closed Sunday and Holy Week* – **M** a la carte 3175/4100.   FV **k**

X **La Gran Tasca,** Santa Engracia 24, ⊠ 28010, 𝒫 448 77 79, Castilian decor – ▤. 🎫 ⓪ 𝐄
 𝘝𝘐𝘚𝘈. ❄️ – *closed Sunday, Bank Holidays and August* – **M** a la carte 2625/5300.   FV **c**

X **Casa Félix,** Bretón de los Herreros 39, ⊠ 28003, 𝒫 441 24 79 – ▤ 🅿. 🎫 𝐄 𝘝𝘐𝘚𝘈   FV **x**
 M a la carte 2650/4450.

Chamartín, Tetuán : Capitán Haya, Orense, Alberto Alcocer, paseo de la Habana (plan p. 3 except where otherwise stated) :

Eurobuilding, Padre Damián 23, ⊠ 28036, ℰ 457 31 00, Telex 22548, Fax 457 97 29, « Garden and terrace with 🏊 » – 🛗 ▤ 📺 ☎ 🚗 – 🏛 25/900. AE ⓓ E VISA. 🚫 HS **a**
M 3200 - **La Taberna** a la carte 4300/ 6000 - **Le Relais** (buffet) a la carte 3800/4200 – ☕ 1600 – **520 rm** 20800/26600.

Meliá Castilla, Capitán Haya 43, ⊠ 28020, ℰ 571 22 11, Telex 23142, Fax 571 22 10, 🏊 – 🛗 ▤ 📺 ☎ ♿ 🚗 – 🏛 25/800. AE ⓓ E VISA. 🚫 GS **c**
M (see **L'Albufera**, **La Fragata** and **El Hidalgo** below) – ☕ 2000 – **907 rm** 20500/25200.

Holiday Inn, pl. Carlos Trías Beltrán 4 (entrance by Orense 22-24), ⊠ 28020, ℰ 597 01 02, Telex 44709, Fax 597 02 92, 🏊 – 🛗 ▤ 📺 ☎ ♿ – 🏛 25/400. AE ⓓ E VISA. 🚫 GT **z**
M Rib Room 4500 - **La Terraza** a la carte 3500/4650 – ☕ 1600 – **313 rm** 21900/27500.

Cuzco without rest, coffee shop only, paseo de la Castellana 133, ⊠ 28046, ℰ 556 06 00, Telex 22464, Fax 556 03 72 – 🛗 ▤ 📺 ☎ 🚗 Ⓟ – 🏛 25/500. AE ⓓ E VISA. 🚫 GS **a**
☕ 1100 – **330 rm** 14400/18000.

Chamartín, Chamartín railway Station, ⊠ 28036, ℰ 733 90 11, Telex 49201, Fax 733 02 14 – 🛗 ▤ 📺 ☎ – 🏛 25/500. AE ⓓ E VISA. 🚫 HR
M (see **Cota 13** below) – ☕ 900 – **378 rm** 10700/14500.

Orense 38 without rest, coffee shop only, Pedro Teixeira 5, ⊠ 28020, ℰ 597 15 68, Fax 597 12 95 – 🛗 ▤ 📺 ☎ 🚗. AE ⓓ E VISA. 🚫 GT **q**
☕ 850 – **140 rm** 16900/20150.

Foxá 32 without rest, coffee shop only, Agustín de Foxá 32, ⊠ 28036, ℰ 733 10 60, Telex 49366, Fax 314 11 65 – 🛗 ▤ 📺 ☎ 🚗 – 🏛 25/250. AE ⓓ E VISA. 🚫 HR **u**
☕ 850 – **161 rm** 13650/16900.

Foxá 25 without rest, coffee shop only, Agustín de Foxá 25, ⊠ 28036, ℰ 323 11 19, Telex 44911, Fax 314 11 65 – 🛗 ▤ 📺 ☎ 🚗. AE ⓓ E VISA. 🚫 HR **a**
☕ 850 – **121 rm** 13650/16900.

El Gran Atlanta without rest, Comandante Zorita 34, ⊠ 28020, ℰ 253 59 00, Telex 45210, Fax 533 08 58 – 🛗 ▤ 📺 ☎ 🚗 – 🏛 25/120. AE ⓓ E VISA. 🚫 FT **p**
☕ 975 – **180 rm** 12000/16500.

Apartotel El Jardín without rest, carret. N I km 5,7 (service lane), ⊠ 28050, ℰ 202 83 36, Fax 766 86 91, 🏊, 🌳, 🎾 – 🛗 ▤ 📺 ☎ 🚗 Ⓟ. AE ⓓ E VISA. 🚫 by ①
☕ 500 – **41 rm** 14840.

Aitana without rest, coffee shop only, paseo de la Castellana 152, ⊠ 28046, ℰ 250 71 07, Telex 49186 – 🛗 ▤ 📺 ☎. AE ⓓ E VISA. 🚫 GT **c**
☕ 700 – **111 rm** 9000/13000.

Aristos and Rest. El Chaflán, av. Pío XII-34, ⊠ 28016, ℰ 457 04 50, Fax 457 10 23, 🍽 – 🛗 ▤ 📺 ☎. AE ⓓ VISA. 🚫 HS **d**
M 3900 – ☕ 550 – **24 rm** 7000/10800.

XXXXX ✿✿✿ **Zalacaín,** Alvarez de Baena 4, ⊠ 28006, ℰ 261 48 40, Fax 261 47 32, 🍽 – ▤. AE ⓓ E VISA. 🚫 plan p. 5 GV **b**
closed Saturday lunch, Sunday, Holy Week and August – **M** a la carte 7050/9000
Spec. Tosta de gambas y almejas, Lenguado al estilo de Zalacaín, Pato asado a los aromas de hongos y trufas..

XXXXX **Príncipe y Serrano,** Serrano 240, ⊠ 28016, ℰ 250 41 03, Fax 259 60 79 – ▤. AE ⓓ E VISA. 🚫 HT **a**
closed Saturday lunch, Sunday and August – **M** a la carte 4000/4700.

XXXX **El Bodegón,** Pinar 15, ⊠ 28006, ℰ 262 31 37 – ▤. AE ⓓ E VISA. 🚫 plan p. 5 GV **q**
closed Saturday lunch, Sunday, Bank Holidays and August – **M** a la carte 6050/7650.

XXXX ✿ **Príncipe de Viana,** Manuel de Falla 5, ⊠ 28036, ℰ 259 14 48, Fax 259 53 92, 🍽, Basque rest. – ▤. AE ⓓ E VISA. 🚫 GT **c**
closed Saturday lunch, Sunday, Holy Week and August – **M** a la carte 5950/7200
Spec. Menestra de verduras, Rape al Pil-Pil, Pularda fría a los vinagres.

XXX **Nicolasa,** Velázquez 150, ⊠ 28002, ℰ 261 99 85 – ▤. AE ⓓ E VISA. 🚫 HU **a**
closed Sunday and August – **M** a la carte 4900/5900.

XXX **L'Albufera,** Capitán Haya 45, ⊠ 28020, ℰ 279 63 74, Telex 23142, Fax 571 22 10, Rice rest. – AE ⓓ E VISA. 🚫 GS **c**
M a la carte 3790/ 5070.

XXX **La Fragata,** Capitán Haya 45, ⊠ 28020, ℰ 270 98 34, Telex 23142, Fax 571 22 10 – AE ⓓ E VISA – **M** a la carte 3600/4600. GS **c**

XXX **El Hidalgo,** Capitán Haya 45, ⊠ 28020, ℰ 270 68 16, Telex 23142, Fax 571 22 10, Regional rest. – ▤ Ⓟ. AE ⓓ E VISA. 🚫 GS **c**
M a la carte 2450/3070.

XXX **La Máquina,** Sor Angela de la Cruz 22, ⊠ 28020, ℰ 572 33 18, Fax 572 33 19 – ▤. AE ⓓ. 🚫 – *closed Sunday* – **M** a la carte 4600/5400. FS **e**

XXX **O'Pazo,** Reina Mercedes 20, ⊠ 28020, ℰ 534 37 48, Seafood – ▤. E VISA. 🚫 FT **p**
closed Sunday and August – **M** a la carte 3450/5150.

XXX **José Luis,** Rafael Salgado 11, ⊠ 28036, ℰ 250 02 42, Telex 41779, Fax 250 99 11 – ▤. AE ⓓ E VISA. 🚫 GT **m**
closed Sunday and August – **M** a la carte 3550/5350.

XXX ꕥ **Señorío de Bertiz,** Comandante Zorita 6, ✉ 28020, ✆ 533 27 57 – ▤. AE ⓓ E VISA. ✗
closed Saturday lunch, Sunday and August – **M** a la carte 4225/5975 FT **s**
Spec. Ensalada de bogavante aliñada a la española, Lenguado a la parrilla con salsa Bearnesa, Costillar de cordero lechal asado.

XXX **Cota 13,** Estación de Chamartín, ✉ 28036, ✆ 315 10 83, Telex 49201, Fax 733 02 14 – ▤. AE ⓓ E VISA. ✗ HR
closed Saturday, Sunday, Bank Holidays and August – **M** a la carte 4125/4850.

XXX **Bogavante,** Capitán Haya 20, ✉ 28020, ✆ 556 21 14, Seafood – ▤. AE ⓓ E VISA. ✗
closed Sunday dinner – **M** a la carte 3950/5800. GT **d**

XXX **Señorío de Alcocer,** Alberto Alcocer 1, ✉ 28036, ✆ 457 16 96 – ▤. AE ⓓ E VISA. ✗
closed Sunday, Bank Holidays and August – **M** a la carte 4500/8000. GS **e**

XXX **La Boucade,** Capitán Haya 30, ✉ 28020, ✆ 556 02 45 – ▤. AE ⓓ E VISA. ✗ GS **a**
M a la carte approx. 4000.

XXX **Gaztelubide (Goizeko Kabi),** Comandante Zorita 37, ✉ 28020, ✆ 533 01 85 – ▤. AE ⓓ E VISA. ✗ – *closed Sunday* – **M** a la carte 4750/5950. FT **a**

XXX ꕥ **Cabo Mayor,** Juan Ramón Jimenez 37, ✉ 28036, ✆ 250 87 76, Fax 458 16 21 – ▤. AE ⓓ E VISA. ✗ – *closed Sunday and Holy Week* – **M** a la carte 6500/7500 GHS **r**
Spec. Ajedrez de foie-gras con melón, Bogavante a la mantequilla de Jerez, Muslo de pularda relleno con hongos.

XXX **El Foque de Quiñones,** Suero de Quiñones 22, ✉ 28002, ✆ 519 25 72 – ▤. AE ⓓ E VISA. ✗ – *closed Sunday dinner* – **M** a la carte 4600/5650. HU **r**

XXX **Lutecia,** Corazón de María 78, ✉ 28002, ✆ 519 34 15 – ▤. AE E VISA. ✗
closed Saturday lunch, Sunday and August – **M** a la carte 2375/3200.
by López de Hoyos HU

XX **Rugantino,** Velázquez 136, ✉ 28006, ✆ 261 02 22, Italian rest. – ▤ Ⓟ. AE ⓓ E VISA. ✗
M a la carte 3480/3750. plan p. 5 HV **e**

XX **De Funy,** Serrano 213, ✉ 28016, ✆ 259 72 25, Telex 44885, Fax 250 72 54, ☂, Lebanese rest. – ▤. AE ⓓ E VISA. ✗ HT **z**
closed Monday – **M** a la carte 2800/3650.

XX **Rheinfall,** Padre Damián 44, ✉ 28036, ✆ 457 82 88, German rest., « Regional German decor » – ▤. AE ⓓ E VISA. ✗ – **M** a la carte 2400/3600. HS **u**

XX **La Tahona,** Capitán Haya 21 (Side), ✉ 28020, ✆ 555 04 41, Cordero asado, « Castilian-medieval decor ⛲ » – ▤. E VISA. ✗ GT **u**
closed Sunday dinner and August – **M** a la carte 2950/3700.

XX **Serramar,** Rosario Pino 12, ✉ 28020, ✆ 270 07 90, Seafood – ▤. AE ⓓ E VISA. ✗ GS **k**
closed Sunday – **M** a la carte 3275/4975.

XX **House of Ming,** paseo de la Castellana 74, ✉ 28046, ✆ 261 10 13, Chinese rest. – ▤. AE ⓓ E VISA. ✗ – **M** a la carte approx. 3000. GV **f**

X **El Asador de Aranda,** pl. de Castilla 3, ✉ 28046, ✆ 733 87 02, Roast lamb, Castilian decor – ▤. E VISA. ✗ GS **b**
closed Sunday dinner and 15 August-15 September – **M** a la carte 2950/3700.

on the road to the Airport : 12,5 km – ✉ 28042 Madrid – ☎ 91 :

🏨 **Diana and Rest. Asador Duque de Osuna,** Galeón 27 (Alameda de Osuna) ✆ 747 13 55, Telex 45688, Fax 747 97 97, ⛲ – ▥ ▤ 📺 ☎ – 🏟 25/220. AE ⓓ E VISA. ✗
M *(closed Sunday)* a la carte 3050/4950 – ☕ 650 – **271 rm** 10800/13500.

Environs

at El Plantío by ⑦ : 13 km – ✉ 28023 El Plantío – ☎ 91 :

XX **Los Remos,** carret. N VI : 13 km ✆ 207 72 30, Seafood, Terrace – ▤ Ⓟ. E VISA. ✗
closed Sunday, Bank Holidays dinner and 15 to 31 August – **M** a la carte 3200/4000.

at Barajas by ② : 14 km – 28042 Madrid – ☎ 91 :

🏨 **Barajas,** av. de Logroño 305 ✆ 747 77 00, Telex 22255, Fax 747 87 17, ☂, ⛲, 🌳 – ▥ ▤ 📺 ☎ Ⓟ – 🏟 25/675. AE ⓓ E VISA. ✗ rest
M 4350 – ☕ 1400 – **230 rm** 19200/24000.

🏨 **Alameda,** av. de Logroño 100 ✆ 747 48 00, Telex 43809, Fax 747 89 28, ⛲, ⛲ – ▥ ▤ 📺 ☎ 🚗 Ⓟ – 🏟 25/280. AE ⓓ E VISA. ✗ rest
M 3950 – ☕ 1050 – **145 rm** 14800/18500.

at San Sebastián de los Reyes by ① : 17 km – ✉ 28700 San Sebastián de los Reyes – ☎ 91 :

XXX **Mesón Tejas Verdes,** carret. N 1 ✆ 652 73 07, ☂, Castilian decor, 🌳 – ▤ Ⓟ. AE ⓓ E VISA. ✗
closed dinner Sunday and Bank Holidays and August – **M** a la carte 2950/4500.

Moralzarzal 28411 Madrid 444 J 18 – pop. 1 600 – ☎ 91 – ♦Madrid 42.

XXX ꕥ **El Cenador de Salvador,** av. de España 30 ✆ 857 77 22, Fax 857 77 80, ☂, « Garden terrace » – Ⓟ. AE ⓓ E VISA
closed Sunday dinner, Monday and 15 to 31 October – **M** a la carte 4900/6700
Spec. Ensalada de carabineros, Lomos de merluza al pil-pil, Becada en Salmis (October- February.

■BARCELONA■ 0800 **4️4️3️** H36 – pop. 1 754 900 – ✪ 93 – Bullring.

See : Gothic Quarter★★ (Barrio Gótico) : Cathedral★★ NR , Federic Marés Museum★★ (Museo F. Marés) NR, Provincial Council★ (Palau de la Generalitat) NR – Montjuic★ (<★) : Museum of Catalonian Art★★ (Museo de Arte de Cataluña) : Romanesque and Gothic department★★★, Ceramics Museum★ – Archeological Museum (Museo Arqueológico), Spanish Village★ (Pueblo Español), Joan Miró Foundation★ – Zoo★ (Parque Zoológico) KX – Tibidabo★ (☼★★) – Maritime Museum★★ (Drassanes i Museo Maritim) JY **M6** – Cambo Collection (Palau de la Virreina)★ LX **M7** – Picasso Museum★ MV **M8** – Church of the Holy Family★ (Sagrada Familia) JU.

🛫, 🛫 of Prat by ⑤ : 16 km 𝒫 379 02 78 – 🛫 of Sant Cugat by ⑦ : 20 km 𝒫 674 39 58 – 🛫 of Vallromanas by ④ : 25 km 𝒫 568 03 62.

🛬 Barcelona by ⑤ : 12 km 𝒫 317 10 11 – Iberia : Paseo de Gracia 30, ⊠ 08007, 𝒫 301 68 00 HV and Aviaco : aeropuerto 𝒫 379 24 58.

🚗 𝒫 410 38 65.

🚢 to the Balearic islands : Cía. Trasmediterránea, via Laietana 2, ⊠ 08003, 𝒫 319 82 12, Telex 54629 MX.

🛈 Gran Via de les Corts Catalanes 658, ⊠ 08010, 𝒫 301 74 43, Palacio de Congresos ⊠ 08004, 𝒫 423 31 01 and at Airport 𝒫 325 58 29 – R.A.C.C. Santaló 8, ⊠ 08006, 𝒫 200 33 11, Telex 53056.

Madrid 627 ⑥ – Bilbao 607 ⑥ – Lérida/Lleida 169 ⑥ – Perpignan 187 ② – Tarragona 109 ⑥ – Toulouse 388 ② – Valencia 361 ⑥ – Zaragoza 307 ⑥.

Plans on following pages

Old Town and the Gothic Quarter Ramblas, pl. S. Jaume, via Laietana, Passeig Nacional, Passeig de Colom

🏨 **Ramada Renaissance,** Ramblas 111, ⊠ 08002, 𝒫 318 62 00, Telex 54634, Fax 301 77 76 –
📶 ▤ 📺 ☎ ⟷ – 🔬 25/200. 🆎 ⓞ 🅴 𝘝𝘐𝘚𝘈. ⁑ LX **b**
M 3500 – ☲ 2000 – **207 rm** 28400/35500.

🏨 **Colón,** av. de la Catedral 7, ⊠ 08002, 𝒫 301 14 04, Telex 52654, Fax 317 29 15 – 📶 ▤ 📺
☎ – 🔬 25/200. 🆎 ⓞ 🅴 𝘝𝘐𝘚𝘈. ⁑ rest MV **e**
M 3000 – ☲ 700 – **155 rm** 11000/19000.

🏨 **Rivoli Rambla,** Rambla dels Estudis 128, ⊠ 08002, 𝒫 302 66 43, Telex 99222, Fax 317 50 53
– 📶 ▤ 📺 ☎ – 🔬 25/180. 🆎 🅴 𝘝𝘐𝘚𝘈. ⁑ LX **r**
M 3300 – ☲ 1100 – **90 rm** 17500/21000.

🏨 **Royal** without rest, coffee shop only, Rambla dels Estudis 117, ⊠ 08002, 𝒫 301 94 00,
Telex 97565, Fax 317 31 79 – 📶 ▤ 📺 ☎ ⟷. 🆎 ⓞ 🅴 𝘝𝘐𝘚𝘈. ⁑ LX **e**
☲ 1200 – **108 rm** 17500/21800.

🏨 **Gravina** without rest, coffee shop only, Gravina 12, ⊠ 08001, 𝒫 301 68 68, Telex 99370,
Fax 317 28 38 – 📶 ▤ 📺 – 🔬 25/50. 🆎 🅴 𝘝𝘐𝘚𝘈. ⁑ HX **d**
☲ 600 – **60 rm** 8900/12900.

🏨 **Montecarlo** without rest, Rambla dels Estudis 124, ⊠ 08002, 𝒫 317 58 00, Telex 93345,
Fax 317 57 50 – 📶 ▤ 📺 ☎ ⟷. 🆎 ⓞ 🅴 𝘝𝘐𝘚𝘈 LX **r**
☲ 495 – **75 rm** 6600/9900.

🏨 **Rialto** without rest, coffee shop only, Ferrán 42, ⊠ 08003, 𝒫 318 52 12, Telex 97206, Fax
315 38 19 – 📶 ▤ 📺 ☎. 🆎 ⓞ 🅴 𝘝𝘐𝘚𝘈 NR **s**
☲ 600 – **129 rm** 10895/14800.

🏨 **Metropol** without rest, Ample 31, ⊠ 08002, 𝒫 315 40 11, Fax 319 12 76 – 📶 ▤ ☎. 🆎 ⓞ
🅴 𝘝𝘐𝘚𝘈. ⁑ MY **r**
☲ 750 – **68 rm** 8000/10200.

🏨 **Regencia Colón** without rest, Sagristans 13, ⊠ 08002, 𝒫 318 98 58, Telex 98175, Fax
317 28 22 – 📶 ▤ 📺 ☎. 🆎 ⓞ 🅴 𝘝𝘐𝘚𝘈. ⁑ MV **r**
☲ 600 – **55 rm** 7500/11000.

🏨 **Gótico** without rest, Jaume I-14, ⊠ 08002, 𝒫 315 22 11, Telex 97206, Fax 315 38 19 – ▤ 📺
☎. 🆎 ⓞ 🅴 𝘝𝘐𝘚𝘈 NR **a**
☲ 600 – **70 rm** 10230/14000.

🏨 **Suizo,** pl. del Angel 12, ⊠ 08002, 𝒫 315 41 11, Telex 97206, Fax 315 38 19 – 📶 ▤ 📺 ☎.
ⓞ 🅴 𝘝𝘐𝘚𝘈. ⁑ rest NR **p**
M 2500 – ☲ 600 – **48 rm** 10895/14800.

🏨 **Lleó,** Pelai 24, ⊠ 08001, 𝒫 318 13 12, Telex 98338, Fax 412 26 57 – 📶 ▤ rm ☎. 🆎 🅴
⁑ rest HX **a**
M 1100 – ☲ 300 – **80 rm** 6000/8000.

🍴🍴🍴 ✿ **La Odisea,** Copons 7, ⊠ 08002, 𝒫 302 36 92 – ▤. 🆎 ⓞ 🅴 𝘝𝘐𝘚𝘈 MV **n**
closed Saturday lunch, Sunday and 3 August-2 September – **M** a la carte 3350/5700
Spec. Ensalada de hígado de pato al vinagre de Módena, Bullit Bartolozzi (November-April), Lubina al vapor con algas marinas al aceite de oliva..

🍴🍴 **Agut d'Avignon,** Trinitat 3, ⊠ 08002, 𝒫 302 60 34 – ▤. 🆎 ⓞ 🅴 𝘝𝘐𝘚𝘈. ⁑ MY **n**
closed Holy Week – **M** a la carte 3075/4600.

🍴🍴 **Quo Vadis,** Carmen 7, ⊠ 08001, 𝒫 302 40 72 – ▤. 🆎 ⓞ 🅴 𝘝𝘐𝘚𝘈 LX **k**
closed Sunday and August – **M** a la carte 4275/6475.

🍴🍴 **El Gran Café,** Avinyó 9, ⊠ 08002, 𝒫 318 79 86, « Early 20C style » – ▤. 🆎 ⓞ 🅴 𝘝𝘐𝘚𝘈. ⁑ MY **t**
closed Saturday lunch, Sunday and August – **M** a la carte 3500/4500.

STREET INDEX TO BARCELONA TOWN PLAN

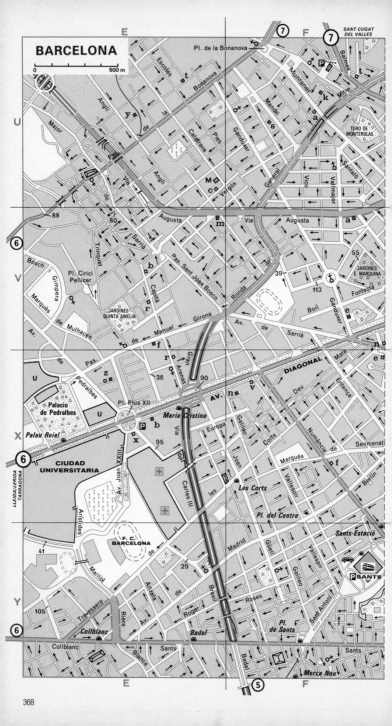

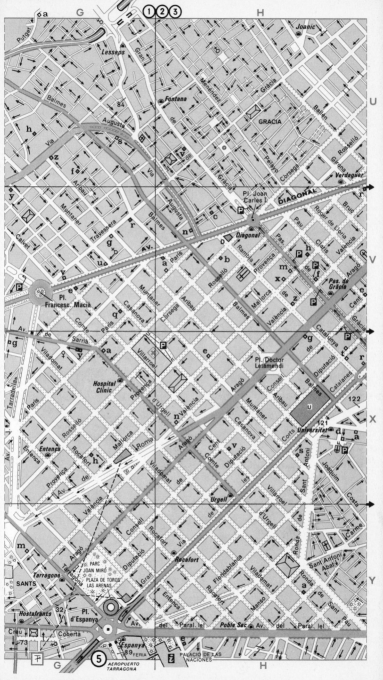

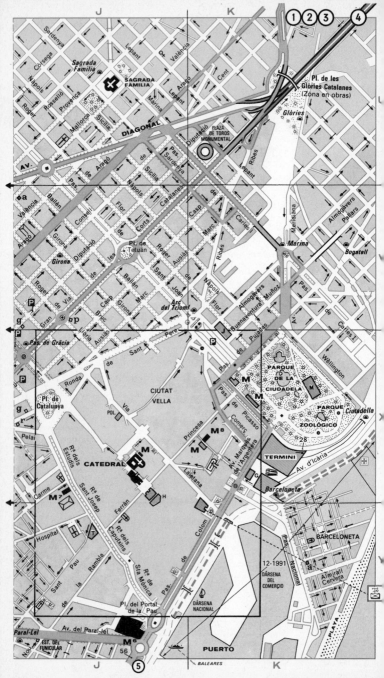

BARCELONA

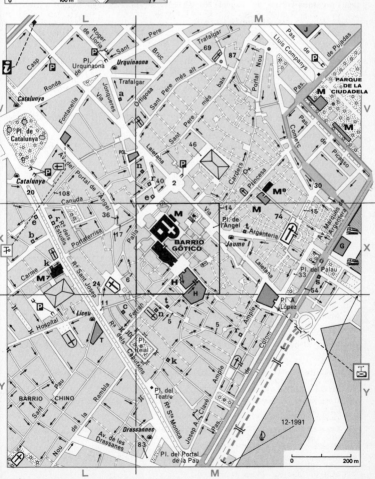

12-1991

0   200 m

XX **Brasserie Flo,** Junqueres 10, ⊠ 08003, ℰ 317 80 37 – 🗏. 🝙 ⓞ 🝔 𝘝𝘐𝘚𝘈 LV **a**
M a la carte 2515/3530.

XX **Senyor Parellada,** Argentería 37, ⊠ 08003, ℰ 315 40 10 – 🗏. 🝙 ⓞ 🝔 𝘝𝘐𝘚𝘈 ⋘ MX **t**
closed Sunday, Bank Holidays and August – **M** a la carte 2600/2850.

XX **7 Puertas,** passeig d'Isabel II - 14, ⊠ 08003, ℰ 319 30 33, Fax 319 46 62 – 🗏. 🝙 🝔 𝘝𝘐𝘚𝘈
⋘ MX **s**
M a la carte 2095/3000.

X **Can Sole,** Sant Carles 4, ⊠ 08003, ℰ 319 50 12, Seafood – 🗏. 🝙 ⓞ 🝔 𝘝𝘐𝘚𝘈 ⋘ KY **a**
closed Sunday – **M** a la carte 2250/3150.

South of Av. Diagonal pl. de Catalunya, Gran Vía de les Corts Catalanes, Passeig de
Gràcia, Balmes, Muntaner, Aragó

🏨🏨🏨 **Princesa Sofía,** pl. de Pius XII 4, ⊠ 08028, ℰ 330 71 11, Telex 51032, Fax 330 76 21, ≼, 🔲
– 🗏 🗏 📺 🖭 🕿 – 🚊 25/1200. 🝙 ⓞ 🝔 𝘝𝘐𝘚𝘈 ⋘ EX **x**
M 2200 - **Le Gourmet** *(closed August)* a la carte 3600/4950 - **L'Empordá** *(closed Saturday,
Sunday and July)* a la carte 3150/4100 – � 1600 – **496 rm** 20500/32500.

🏨🏨🏨 **Ritz,** Gran Vía de les Corts Catalanes 668, ⊠ 08010, ℰ 318 52 00, Telex 52739, Fax 318 01 48,
🍴 – 🗏 🗏 📺 🕿 – 🚊 25/350. 🝙 ⓞ 🝔 𝘝𝘐𝘚𝘈 ⋘ JV **p**
M a la carte 4400/6200 – ⊑ 2050 – **158 rm** 32800/41000.

🏨🏨 **Barcelona Hilton,** av. Diagonal 589, ⊠ 08014, ℰ 419 22 33, Telex 99623, Fax 322 52 91,
🍴 – 🗏 🕿 🕭 ⬅ – 🚊 25/800. 🝙 ⓞ 🝔 𝘝𝘐𝘚𝘈 ⋘ FX **v**
M 5100 – ⊑ 2000 – **290 rm** 28500/35000.

🏨🏨 **Meliá Barcelona Sarriá,** av. de Sarriá 50, ⊠ 08029, ℰ 410 60 60, Telex 51033, Fax
321 51 79, ≼ – 🗏 🗏 🕿 ⬅ – 🚊 🝙 ⓞ 🝔 𝘝𝘐𝘚𝘈 ⋘ FV **n**
M 5000 – ⊑ 2000 – **290 rm** 23000/28750.

🏨🏨 **Avenida Palace,** Gran Vía de les Corts Catalanes 605, ⊠ 08007, ℰ 301 96 00, Telex
54734, Fax 318 12 34 – 🗏 🗏 📺 🕿 – 🚊 25/300. 🝙 ⓞ 🝔 𝘝𝘐𝘚𝘈 HX **r**
M 4650 – ⊑ 875 – **211 rm** 19800/24700.

🏨🏨 **Majestic,** passeig de Grácia 70, ⊠ 08008, ℰ 215 45 12, Telex 52211, Fax 215 77 73, ⨯ – 🗏
📺 🕿 – 🚊 25/600. 🝙 ⓞ 🝔 𝘝𝘐𝘚𝘈 ⋘ rest HV **f**
M 3000 – ⊑ 1250 – **340 rm** 13500/22500.

🏨🏨 **Diplomatic and Rest. La Salsa,** Pau Claris 122, ⊠ 08009, ℰ 317 31 00, Telex 54701, Fax
318 65 31, ⨯ – 🗏 🗏 📺 🕿 ⬅ – 🚊 25/250. 🝙 ⓞ 🝔 𝘝𝘐𝘚𝘈 ⋘ HV **e**
M *(closed Sunday)* 5300 – ⊑ 1550 – **217 rm** 21200/26500.

🏨🏨 **Calderón,** Rambla de Catalunya 26, ⊠ 08007, ℰ 301 00 00, Telex 99529, Fax 317 31 57, ⨯,
🔲 – 🗏 🗏 📺 🕿 ⬅ – 🚊 25/200. 🝙 ⓞ 🝔 𝘝𝘐𝘚𝘈 ⋘ HX **t**
M a la carte 2100/4175 – ⊑ 1300 – **264 rm** 17600/22000.

🏨🏨 **Condes de Barcelona,** Passeig de Grácia 75, ⊠ 08008, ℰ 487 37 37, Telex 51531, Fax
216 08 35, ⨯ – 🗏 🗏 📺 🕿 – 🚊 25/300. 🝙 ⓞ 🝔 𝘝𝘐𝘚𝘈 ⋘ HV **m**
M 3000 – ⊑ 1300 – **100 rm** 15500/22000.

🏨 **St. Moritz** without rest, Diputació, 262 bis, ⊠ 08007, ℰ 412 15 00, Fax 412 12 36 – 🗏 🗏
📺 🕿 🕭 ⬅ – 🚊 25/140. 🝙 ⓞ 🝔 𝘝𝘐𝘚𝘈 ⋘ JV **g**
⊑ 1100 – **92 rm** 13750/20900.

🏨 **Cristal,** Diputació 257, ⊠ 08007, ℰ 301 66 00, Telex 54560 – 🗏 🗏 📺 ⬅ – 🚊 25/70. 🝙
ⓞ 🝔 𝘝𝘐𝘚𝘈 ⋘ HX **t**
M 2850 – ⊑ 850 – **148 rm** 11600/17000.

🏨 **Derby** without rest, coffee shop only, Loreto 21, ⊠ 08029, ℰ 322 32 15, Telex 97429, Fax
410 08 62 – 🗏 🗏 📺 🕿 ⬅ – 🚊 25/100. 🝙 ⓞ 🝔 𝘝𝘐𝘚𝘈 FX **e**
⊑ 1250 – **116 rm** 16300/20400.

🏨 **Gran Derby** without rest, Loreto 28, ⊠ 08029, ℰ 322 20 62, Telex 97429, Fax 419 68 20 – 🗏
🗏 📺 🕿 ⬅ – 🚊 25/100. 🝙 ⓞ 🝔 𝘝𝘐𝘚𝘈 GX **g**
⊑ 1250 – **38 rm** 21800.

🏨 **Alexandra,** Mallorca 251, ⊠ 08008, ℰ 487 05 05, Telex 81107, Fax 216 06 06 – 🗏 🗏 📺 🕿
⬅ – 🚊 25/100. 🝙 ⓞ 🝔 𝘝𝘐𝘚𝘈 ⋘ HV **x**
M 3500 – ⊑ 1250 – **75 rm** 17500/21800.

🏨 **Núñez Urgel,** Compte d'Urgell 232, ⊠ 08036, ℰ 322 41 53, Fax 419 01 06 – 🗏 🗏 📺 🕿
⬅ – 🚊 25/100. 🝙 ⓞ 🝔 𝘝𝘐𝘚𝘈 ⋘ rest GX **a**
M 4000 – ⊑ 900 – **120 rm** 12000/18000.

🏨 **Regente,** rambla de Catalunya 76, ⊠ 08008, ℰ 215 25 70, Telex 51939, Fax 487 32 27, ⨯ –
🗏 🗏 📺 🕿. 🝙 ⓞ 🝔 𝘝𝘐𝘚𝘈 HV **z**
M 3000 – ⊑ 900 – **78 rm** 13900/20300.

🏨 **Astoria** without rest, Paris 203, ⊠ 08036, ℰ 209 83 11, Telex 81129, Fax 202 30 08 – 🗏 🗏
📺 🕿. 🝙 ⓞ 🝔 𝘝𝘐𝘚𝘈 HV **a**
⊑ 950 – **114 rm** 10520/13150.

🏨 **Expo H.,** Mallorca 1, ⊠ 08014, ℰ 325 12 12, Telex 54147, Fax 325 11 44, ⨯ – 🗏 🗏 📺 🕿
⬅ – 🚊 25/800. 🝙 ⓞ 🝔 𝘝𝘐𝘚𝘈 ⋘ GY **m**
M 1925 – ⊑ 900 – **432 rm** 10915/19015.

🏨 **Master,** Valencia 105, ⊠ 08011, ℰ 323 62 15, Telex 81258, Fax 323 43 89 – 🗏 🗏 📺 🕿
⬅ – 🚊 25/170. 🝙 ⓞ 🝔 𝘝𝘐𝘚𝘈 ⋘ rest HX **n**
M 3500 – ⊑ 1100 – **81 rm** 15600/19600.

Numancia, Numáncia 74, ✉ 08029, ☎ 322 44 51, Fax 410 76 42 – |♦| ▤ ☎ ⇔ – 🏛 25/70. AE ⓓ E VISA. ✗ FX **f**
M 2950 – ☕ 800 – **140 rm** 10800/14900.

Dante without rest, Mallorca 181, ✉ 08036, ☎ 323 22 54, Telex 52588, Fax 323 74 72 – |♦| ▤ TV ☎ ⇔ – 🏛 25/100. AE ⓓ E VISA. ✗ HX **e**
☕ 950 – **81 rm** 13000/18000.

Duques de Bergara, Bergara 11, ✉ 08002, ☎ 301 51 51, Telex 81257, Fax 317 34 42 – |♦| ▤ ☎. AE ⓓ VISA. ✗ JX **g**
M 2100 – ☕ 1150 – **56 rm** 16900/23900.

Taber without rest, Aragó 256, ✉ 08007, ☎ 318 70 50, Telex 93452, Fax 318 70 12 – |♦| ▤ TV ☎ – 🏛 25/40. AE E VISA. ✗ HX **g**
☕ 500 – **78 rm** 5700/9000.

Regina without rest, coffee shop only, Vergara 2, ✉ 08002, ☎ 301 32 32, Telex 59380, Fax 318 23 26 – |♦| ▤ TV ☎. AE ⓓ E VISA. ✗ JX **r**
☕ 900 – **102 rm** 10180/15180.

XXXXX **Beltxenea,** Mallorca 275, ✉ 08008, ☎ 215 30 24, Fax 487 00 81, 🌳, « Garden terrace » – ▤. AE ⓓ E VISA. ✗ HV **h**
closed Saturday lunch and Sunday – **M** a la carte 4750/6200.

XXXX ✿ **La Dama,** av. Diagonal 423, ✉ 08036, ☎ 202 06 86, Fax 200 72 99 – ▤. AE ⓓ E VISA. ✗
M a la carte 3700/5825 HV **a**
Spec. Ensalada de judias verdes y mariscos La Dama, Manitas de cerdo deshuesadas y rellenas al perfume de trufas, Carro de pasteleria y de quesos artesanos.

XXX **Oliver y Hardy,** av. Diagonal 593, ✉ 08014, ☎ 419 31 81, 🌳 – ▤ Ⓟ. AE ⓓ E VISA
M a la carte 3500/5200. FX **n**

XXX **Finisterre,** av. Diagonal 469, ✉ 08036, ☎ 439 55 76 – ▤. AE ⓓ E VISA. ✗ GV **e**
closed Sunday July and August – **M** a la carte 4550/5600.

XX ✿ **Jaume de Provença,** Provença 88, ✉ 08029, ☎ 430 00 29, Modern decor – ▤. AE ⓓ E VISA. ✗ GX **h**
closed Sunday dinner, Monday, Holy Week and August-10 September – **M** a la carte 4750/6000
Spec. Pastel de esqueixada de bacalao, Lubina en escamas de patatas al estragón, Pastelitos crujientes de foie-gras y trufas al oloroso.

XX **Bel Air,** Córcega 286, ✉ 08008, ☎ 237 75 88, Rice rest. – ▤. AE ⓓ E VISA HV **b**
M a la carte 4050/5100.

XX **La Sopeta,** Muntaner 6, ✉ 08011, ☎ 323 56 32 – ▤. AE ⓓ E VISA. ✗ HX **s**
closed Sunday – **M** a la carte 2080/4050.

XX **Vinya Rosa - Magí,** av. de Sarriá 17, ✉ 08029, ☎ 430 00 03 – ▤. AE ⓓ E VISA GX **y**
closed Saturday lunch and Sunday – **M** a la carte 3800/5600.

XX **Rías de Galicia,** Lleida 7, ✉ 08004, ☎ 424 81 52, Fax 426 13 07, Seafood – ▤. AE ⓓ E VISA. ✗ HY **e**
M a la carte 3600/5300.

XX **Casa Chus,** av. Diagonal 339 Bis, ✉ 08037, ☎ 207 02 15, Seafood – ▤. AE ⓓ E VISA
closed Sunday dinner – **M** a la carte 3200/5350. HV **r**

XX **Alt Berlín,** Sabino Arana 54, ✉ 08028, ☎ 339 01 66, German rest – ▤. AE ⓓ E VISA
M a la carte 3475/4375. EX **b**

X **El Pescador,** Mallorca 314, ✉ 08037, ☎ 207 10 24, Seafood – ▤. AE ⓓ E VISA. ✗ JV **a**
closed Sunday – **M** a la carte 2800/3950.

X **Els Perols de L'Empordá,** Villarroel 88, ✉ 08011, ☎ 323 10 33, Ampurdan rest. – ▤. AE ⓓ E VISA HX **v**
closed Sunday dinner, Monday, Holy Week and 1 to 15 August – **M** a la carte 2200/3600.

X **Azpiolea,** Casanova 167, ✉ 08036, ☎ 430 90 30, Basque rest. – ▤. ⓓ E VISA. ✗ GV **q**
closed Sunday dinner and August – **M** a la carte 3000/4625.

North of Av. Diagonal vía Augusta, Capitá Arenas, ronda General Mitre, passeig de la Bonanova, av. de Pedralbes

Presidente, av. Diagonal 570, ✉ 08021, ☎ 200 21 11, Telex 52180, Fax 209 51 06, 🏊 – |♦| ▤ TV ☎ – 🏛 25/180. AE ⓓ E VISA. ✗ GV **u**
M 3750 – ☕ 1250 – **161 rm** 22000/26000.

Hesperia without rest, coffee shop only, Vergós 20, ✉ 08017, ☎ 204 55 51, Telex 98403, Fax 204 43 92 – |♦| ▤ TV ☎ ⇔ – 🏛 25/200. AE ⓓ E VISA. ✗ EU **c**
☕ 1100 – **139 rm** 19800.

Suite Hotel without rest, Muntaner 505, ✉ 08022, ☎ 212 80 12, Telex 99077, Fax 211 23 17 – |♦| ▤ TV ☎ ⇔ – 🏛 25/150. AE ⓓ VISA. ✗ FU **a**
☕ 1300 – **70 rm** 29900.

Balmoral without rest, vía Augusta 5, ✉ 08006, ☎ 217 87 00, Telex 54087, Fax 415 14 21 – |♦| ▤ TV ☎ ⇔ – 🏛 25/100. AE ⓓ E VISA. ✗ HV **n**
☕ 900 – **94 rm** 12650/19500.

🏛 **Cóndor,** via Augusta 127, ✉ 08006, ℰ 209 45 11, Telex 52925, Fax 202 27 13 – 📶 🗐 📺 ☎
↩ – 🏨 25/50. 🆎 ⓐ 🇪 *VISA*. ⚶   GU z
M a la carte approx. 2500 – ☲ 1100 – **78 rm** 14000/17500.

🏛 **Arenas** without rest, coffee shop dinner only, Capitá Arenas 20, ✉ 08034, ℰ 280 03 03,
Telex 54990, Fax 280 33 92 – 📶 🗐 📺 ☎ – 🏨 25/50. 🆎 ⓐ 🇪 *VISA*.   EX r
☲ 825 – **59 rm** 13200/16500.

🏛 **Victoria,** av. de Pedralbes 16 Bis, ✉ 08034, ℰ 204 27 54, Telex 98302, Fax 204 27 66, ⩲ –
📶 🗐 📺 ☎ ↩. 🆎 ⓐ 🇪 *VISA*. ⚶ rest   EX z
M 1200 – ☲ 1100 – **79 apartments** 16800/21000.

🏛 **Park Putxet,** Putxet 68, ✉ 08023, ℰ 212 51 58, Telex 98718, Fax 418 51 57 – 📶 🗐 📺 ☎
↩ – 🏨 25/200. 🆎 ⓐ 🇪 *VISA*. ⚶   GU a
M 1650 – ☲ 900 – **125 rm** 19900.

🏛 **Belagua,** via Augusta 89, ✉ 08006, ℰ 237 39 40, Telex 99643, Fax 415 30 62 – 📶 🗐 📺 ☎
↩. 🆎 ⓐ 🇪 *VISA*. ⚶   GU s
M 2900 – ☲ 800 – **72 rm** 11900/14900.

🏛 **Mitre** without rest, Bertrán 9, ✉ 08023, ℰ 212 11 04, Telex 98671, Fax 418 94 81 – 📶 🗐 📺
☎ ↩. 🆎 ⓐ 🇪 *VISA*   FU t
☲ 600 – **57 rm** 10800/13500.

🏛 **Condado,** Aribau 201, ✉ 08021, ℰ 200 23 11, Telex 54546, Fax 200 25 86 – 📶 🗐 ☎. 🆎
ⓐ 🇪 *VISA*. ⚶ rest   GV g
M 1700 – ☲ 650 – **88 rm** 12800/16000.

🏛 **Pedralbes** without rest, coffee shop dinner only, Fontcuberta 4, ✉ 08034, ℰ 203 71 12,
Telex 99850 – 📶 🗐 📺 ☎ ↩. 🆎 ⓐ 🇪 *VISA*. ⚶   EV b
☲ 700 – **28 rm** 10600/14500.

🏛 **Covadonga** without rest, av. Diagonal 596, ✉ 08021, ℰ 209 55 11, Telex 93394, Fax
209 58 33 – 📶 🗐 📺 ☎. 🆎 ⓐ 🇪 *VISA*. ⚶   GV v
☲ 500 – **76 rm** 6200/9800.

🏛 **Bonanova Park** without rest, Capitá Arenas, 51, ✉ 08034, ℰ 204 09 00, Telex 98671, Fax
204 50 14 – 📶 ☎. 🆎 ⓐ 🇪 *VISA*. ⚶   EV r
☲ 500 – **60 rm** 9200/11500.

XXXX ✿ **Via Veneto,** Ganduxer 10, ✉ 08021, ℰ 200 72 44, Fax 201 60 95, « Early 20C style » –
🗐. 🆎 ⓐ 🇪 *VISA*. ⚶   FV e
closed Saturday lunch, Sunday and 1 to 20 August – **M** a la carte 4040/5740
Spec. Ensalada de Cap i Pota de ternera con tomate confitado, Salmón fresco asado al aceite de nueces,
Pichón de masia asado con cebollitas doradas.

XXXX ✿ **Reno,** Tuset 27, ✉ 08006, ℰ 200 91 29, Fax 202 23 08 – 🗐. 🆎 ⓐ 🇪 *VISA*. ⚶   GV r
closed Saturday July-September – **M** a la carte 4900/6350
Spec. Ostras a las trufas sobre fondo de puerros (October-April), Filetes de lenguado Reno, Salteado de
solomillo al agridulce de cebolla.

XXX ✿✿ **Neichel,** av. de Pedralbes 16 bis, ✉ 08034, ℰ 203 84 08, Fax 205 63 69 – 🗐. 🆎 ⓐ 🇪
VISA   EX z
closed Sunday, Bank Holidays, Holy Week, August-4 September and Christmas – **M** *(booking
essential)* a la carte 5050/6250
Spec. Ensalada de gambas a la vinagreta de algas y rovellones en escabeche. Rollitos de cigalas al vinagre de
Módena. Lomo de corderito en su costra..

XXX ✿ **Botafumeiro,** Mayor de Gracia, 81, ✉ 08012, ℰ 218 42 30, Fax 415 54 04, Seafood –
🗐. 🆎 ⓐ 🇪 *VISA*. ⚶   HU v
closed Sunday dinner, Holy Week, Monday and August – **M** a la carte 3100/6200
Spec. Rodaballo asado con salsa de limón. Bogavante al vinagre de Jerez. Rollitos de lenguado con langostinos..

XXX ✿ **Eldorado Petit,** Dolors Monserdá 51, ✉ 08017, ℰ 204 51 53, Fax 280 57 02, 🌤 – 🗐. 🆎
🇪 *VISA*. ⚶   EU y
closed Sunday and 5 to 21 August – **M** a la carte 3700/6950
Spec. Nido de judias verdes y salpicón de frutos de mar, Arroz de gambas de Palamós y erizos de mar, Sesitos
de cordero en un milhojas de patatas nuevas.

XXX ✿ **Azulete,** Via Augusta 281, ✉ 08017, ℰ 203 59 43, 🌤 – 🆎 ⓐ 🇪 *VISA*   EV m
*closed Saturday lunch, Sunday, Bank Holidays, Holy Week, 3 to 18 August and 21 to 31
December* – **M** a la carte 4300/5200
Spec. Láminas de escórpora sobre ajitos tiernos rehogados, Lomo de cordero acompañado de couscous de
verduras, Buñuelos de chocolate.

XXX **El Tunel de Muntaner,** Sant Màrius 22, ✉ 08022, ℰ 212 60 74 – 🗐. 🆎 ⓐ 🇪 *VISA*   FU k
closed Saturday lunch, Sunday and August – **M** a la carte 3800/4800.

XXX **Roncesvalles,** via Augusta 201, ✉ 08021, ℰ 209 01 25, Fax 209 12 95, 🌤 – 🗐. 🆎 ⓐ 🇪
VISA. ⚶   FV a
closed Sunday dinner – **M** a la carte 3600/4900.

XX **La Petite Marmite,** Madrazo 68, ✉ 08006, ℰ 201 48 79 – 🗐. 🆎 ⓐ 🇪 *VISA*. ⚶   GU f
closed Sunday, Bank Holidays, Holy Week and August – **M** a la carte 2450/3275.

XX ✿ **Florián,** Bertrand i Serra 20, ✉ 08022, ℰ 212 46 27, Fax 418 72 30 – 🗐. ⓐ 🇪 *VISA*   FU s
closed Sunday and July – **M** a la carte 4800/5600
Spec. Trufa fresca, envuelta en tocino y asada al horno. Pasta fresca marinera con almejas. Rabo de buey al
Cabernet.

XX **El Trapío,** Esperanza 25, ⌨ 08017, ✆ 211 58 17, 🍴 – **AE ⓘ E VISA**. ⚡   EU   t
closed Sunday and Monday lunch – **M** a la carte 3340/4490.

XX **El Asador de Aranda,** av. del Tibidabo 31, ⌨ 08022, ✆ 417 01 15, 🍴, Roast lamb,
« Former palace » – **E VISA**. ⚡   by ⑦
closed Sunday dinner – **M** a la carte 3050/3500.

XX **La Balsa,** Infanta Isabel 4, ⌨ 08022, ✆ 211 50 48, 🍴 – **AE E VISA**   by ⑦
closed Sunday, Monday lunch and Holy Week – **M** (buffet dinner only in August)
a la carte 3600/4700.

XX ✿ **El Racó D'En Freixa,** Sant Elies 22, ⌨ 08006, ✆ 209 75 59 – 🍽. **AE E VISA**. ⚡   GU   h
closed dinner Bank Holidays, Monday, Holy Week and August-2 September – **M**
a la carte 2425/4850
Spec. Quenelles de setas con pétalos de tomate. Atado de lenguado relleno de cigalas con salsa americana.
Milhojas de mousse al sorbete de piña.

XX **Roig Robi,** Séneca 20, ⌨ 08006, ✆ 218 92 22, 🍴, « Terrace » – 🍽. **AE ⓘ E VISA**   HV   c
closed Sunday – **M** a la carte 3550/4850.

XX **Arcs de Sant Gervasi,** Santaló 103, ⌨ 08021, ✆ 201 92 77 – 🍽. **AE ⓘ E VISA**. ⚡   GV   y
M a la carte 2500/4025.

XX **Hostal Sant Jordi,** Travesera de Dalt 123, ⌨ 08024, ✆ 213 10 37 – 🍽. **AE ⓘ E VISA**
⚡   by Travessera de Gracia   HU
closed Sunday dinner and August – **M** a la carte 3100/4350.

X **La Masía,** Cumbre del Tibidabo, ⌨ 08023, ✆ 417 63 50, Fax 211 21 11, ≤ town, sea and
mountains – **AE ⓘ E VISA**. ⚡   by ⑦
closed Monday except Bank Holidays – **M** (lunch only in summer) a la carte 3500/4100.

Typical atmosphere:

XX **Font del Gat,** passeig Santa Madrona, Montjuic, ⌨ 08004, ✆ 424 02 24, 🍴, Regional
decor – **ⓟ. AE ⓘ E VISA**. ⚡   by Av. Reina María Cristina   GY
M a la carte 2500/3600.

X **La Cuineta,** Paradis, 4, ⌨ 08002, ✆ 315 01 11, Fax 315 07 98, « In a 17C cellar » – 🍽. **AE
ⓘ E VISA**. ⚡   NR   e
closed Monday – **M** a la carte 2875/5575.

X **Can Culleretes,** Quintana 5, ⌨ 08002, ✆ 317 64 85 – 🍽. **E VISA**   LY   c
closed Sunday dinner, Monday and 1 to 21 July – **M** a la carte 1625/2400.

X **Los Caracoles,** Escudellers 14, ⌨ 08002, ✆ 302 31 85, Fax 302 07 43, Rustic regional
decor – 🍽. **AE ⓘ E VISA**. ⚡   MY   k
M a la carte 2000/3600.

X **Pá i Trago,** Parlament 41, ⌨ 08015, ✆ 241 13 20 – 🍽. **AE E VISA**   HY   a
closed Monday and 24 June-24 July – **M** a la carte 2400/3250.

X **A la Menta,** passeig Manuel Girona 50, ⌨ 08034, ✆ 204 15 49, Tavern – 🍽. **AE ⓘ E VISA**.
⚡   EV   f
closed Sunday in summer – **M** a la carte 2900/4600.

Environs

at Esplugues de Llobregat by ⑥ – ⌨ 08950 Esplugues de Llobregat – ✿ 93 :

XXX **La Masía,** av. Paisos Catalans 58 ✆ 371 00 09, Fax 372 84 00, 🍴, « Terrace under pine
trees » – 🍽 **ⓟ. AE ⓘ E VISA**. ⚡
M a la carte 2900/4200.

X ✿ **Quirce,** Laureà Miró 202 ✆ 371 10 84, 🍴 – 🍽 **ⓟ. AE ⓘ E VISA**. ⚡
closed Sunday dinner, Monday and August – **M** a la carte 3350/4200
Spec. Mousseline de alcachofas y zanahorias. Lubina a la crema de ciboulette.Perdiz estofada con cebolla.

at Sant Just Desvern by ⑥ – ⌨ 08960 Sant Just Desvern – ✿ 93 :

🏨 **Sant Just,** Frederic Mompou 1 ✆ 473 25 17, Fax 473 24 50 – |🛗| 🍽 📺 ☎ ⟺ – 🔬 25/450.
AE ⓘ E VISA. ⚡
M 3000 – 🍷 1100 – **150 hab** 16500/19800.

on the road to Sant Cugat del Vallés by ⑦ : 11 km – ⌨ 08190 Sant Cugat del Vallés –
✿ 93 :

X **Can Cortés,** urbanización Ciudad Condal Tibidabo ✆ 674 17 04, ≤, 🍴, Exhibition of
Catalan wines, « Old masia, rustic decor », ⅃ – **ⓟ. AE ⓘ E VISA**. ⚡
closed 4 to 23 November – **M** (lunch only from Sunday to Thursday in winter)
a la carte 2100/3050.

San Celoni Barcelona 🆘🆘🆘 G37 – pop. 11 929 alt. 152 – ✿ 93.
Barcelona 49.

XX ✿✿ **El Racó de Can Fabes,** Sant Joan 6 ✆ 867 28 51, Fax 867 38 61, 🍴, Rustic decor –
🍽. **AE ⓘ E VISA**. ⚡
closed Sunday dinner, Monday 4 to 17 February and 24 june-8 July – **M** a la carte 4950/5850
Spec. Raviolis de gambas con ceps y su aceite, Escórpora a la vinagreta con cebollitas y ajo confitado, Lomo
de ciervo con manzanas salteadas (season).

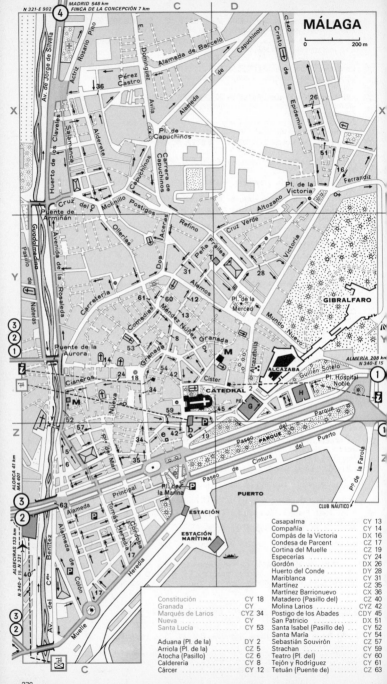

MÁLAGA

0   200 m

N 340 - E 15   ALMERÍA 208 km

ALGECIRAS 133 km   N 340 - E 15 - N 321

ALORCA 41 km   MA 401

MADRID 548 km

CLUB NÁUTICO

PUERTO

ESTACIÓN

ESTACIÓN MARÍTIMA

GIBRALFARO

ALCAZABA

CATEDRAL

PARQUE

Málaga 29000 🅐🅐🅖 V16 – pop. 503 251 – ✪ 952 – Seaside resort.

See : Cathedral★ CY – Fine Arts Museum★ (Museo de bellas Artes) DY **M** – Alcazaba★ (museum★) DY – Gibralfaro ≤★★ DY.

Envir. : Finca de la Concepción★ by ④ : 7 km – Road from Málaga to Antequera ≤★★.

🏋 Club de Campo of Málaga by ② : 9 km ✒ 38 11 20 – 🏋 of El Candado by ① : 5 km ✒ 29 46 66.

⤴ Málaga by ② : 9 km ✒ 32 20 00 – Iberia : Molina Larios 13, ✉ 29015, ✒ 21 37 31 and Aviaco : airport ✒ 31 78 58.

🚂 ✒ 31 62 49.

⛴ to Melilla : Cia Trasmediterránea, Juan Díaz 4, ✉ 29015 (CZ), ✒ 22 43 93, Telex 77042.

🛈 Larios 5, ✉ 29015, ✒ 21 34 45, av. Cervantes, ✉ 29016, ✒ 22 86 00 – R.A.C.E. Calderería 1, ✉ 29008, ✒ 21 42 60.

Madrid 548 ④ – Algeciras 133 ② – Córdoba 175 ④ – Sevilla 217 ④ – Valencia 651 ④.

Plan opposite

Centre :

🏨 **Málaga Palacio** without rest, av. Cortina del Muelle 1, ✉ 29015, ✒ 21 51 85, Telex 77021, Fax 21 51 85, ≤, 🛌, – 🛗 🖴 📺 ☎ – 🔬 25/300. 🆎 ⓘ 🄴 📮. 🛠   CZ **b**
🖙 700 – **223 rm** 9850/12600.

🏨 **Don Curro** without rest, coffee shop only, Sancha de Lara 7, ✉ 29015, ✒ 22 72 00, Telex 77366, Fax 21 59 46 – 🛗 🖴 📺 ☎. 🆎 ⓘ 🄴 📮. 🛠   CZ **e**
🖙 580 – **105 rm** 6560/9240.

suburbs :

🏯 Parador de Málaga-Gibralfaro 🗺, ✉ 29016, ✒ 22 19 03, Fax 22 19 02, « Beautiful location with ≤ bay and town » –   DY
Might close in 1991 due to refurbishment.

XXX **Café de París,** Vélez Málaga 8, ✉ 29016, ✒ 22 50 43, Fax 22 50 43 – 🖴. 🆎 ⓘ 🄴 📮
🛠   by ①
closed Sunday and 21 August-15 September – **M** a la carte 4100/5600.

XX **Antonio Martín,** paseo Marítimo 4, ✉ 29016, ✒ 22 21 13, Fax 21 10 18, ≤, �, Large terrace by the sea – 🖴. 📮. 🆎 ⓘ 🄴 📮   by ①
M a la carte 3150/4245.

X **La Taberna del Pintor,** Maestranza 6, ✉ 29016, ✒ 21 53 15, Typical decor, Meat – 🖴. 🆎 ⓘ 🄴 📮   by ⑩
M a la carte 2125/3495.

at Urbanización Cerrado de Calderón by ① – ✉ 29018 Málaga – ✪ 952 :

XXX Romara, 4,5 km,.paseo Cerrado de Calderón 3 ✒ 29 91 17, � – 🖴 📮.

XX **El Campanario de Camborio,** 6 km, paseo de la sierra 36 ✒ 29 50 51, ≤ Bay, � – 🖴 📮. 🆎 ⓘ 🄴 📮. 🛠
closed Sunday dinner and Monday – **M** a la carte 2700/4250.

at Club de Campo by ② : 9 km – ✉ 29000 Málaga – ✪ 952 :

🏨 **Parador de Málaga del Golf,** ✉ 29080 apartado 324 Málaga, ✒ 38 12 55, Fax 38 21 41, ≤, �, « Situated near the golf course », 🛌, 🛠, 🏋 – 🖴 📺 ☎ 📮 – 🔬 25/70. 🆎 ⓘ 🄴 📮
M 3100 – 🖙 950 – **60 rm** 12500.

at Urbanización Mijas Golf by N 340 SW : 30 km – ✉ 29640 Fuengirola – ✪ 952 :

🏨🏨 **Byblos Andaluz** 🗺, ✒ 47 30 50, Telex 79713, Fax 47 67 83, ≤ golf course and mountains, �, Talassotherapy facilities, « Luxury establishment in the Andalusian style situated between two golf courses », 🛌 heated, 🛌, 🌲, 🛠, 🏋 – 🛗 🖴 📺 ☎ 📮 – 🔬 40/170. 🆎 ⓘ 🄴 📮. 🛠
M (see Le Nailhac below) - El Andaluz a la carte 3400/4000 – 🖙 1800 – **144 rm** 26000/38000.

XXX ✪ **Le Nailhac,** at Hotel Byblos Andaluz ✒ 47 30 50, Telex 79713, Fax 47 67 83, 🌺 – 🖴 📮. 🆎 ⓘ 🄴 📮. 🛠
closed Wednesday – **M** (dinner only) a la carte 6000/7500
Spec. Tártar de lubina y salmón con caviar de berenjenas, Filetes de salmonete sobre copos de patata, Tarta fina de manzana y su sorbete.

Marbella Málaga 🅐🅐🅖 W 15 – pop. 67 882 – ✪ 952 – Beach.

🏋 Rio Real-Los Monteros by ① : 5 km ✒ 77 37 76 – 🏋 Nueva Andalucía by ② : 5 km ✒ 78 72 00 – 🏋 Aloha golf, urbanización Aloha by ② : 8 km ✒ 81 23 88 – 🏋 golf Las Brisas, Nueva Andalucía by ② ✒ 81 08 75 – Iberia : paseo Marítimo ✒ 77 02 84.

🛈 Miguel Cano 1 ✒ 77 14 42.

Madrid 602 ① – Algeciras 77 ② – Málaga 56 ①.

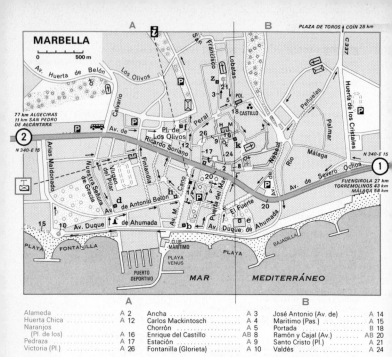

🏨 **Meliá Don Pepe and Grill La Farola** ⤫, Finca Las Merinas by ② 🖋 77 03 00, Telex 77055, Fax 77 03 00, ≤ sea and mountains, 🏠, « Subtropical plants », 🏊, 🐎, 🎾 – 📶 📺
📺 ☎ & 📠 – 🔬 25/400. 🅰🅴 ⓞ 🄴 🆅🅸🆂🅰. 🎐
M a la carte 4550/5100 – 🍴 2100 – **218 rm** 24000/31000.

🏨 **El Fuerte**, av. del Fuerte 🖋 77 15 00, Telex 77523, Fax 82 44 11, ≤, 🏠, « Garden with palmtrees », 🏊 heated, 🛀, 🎾 – 📶 📺 ☎ ⟵ 📠 – 🔬 25/600. 🅰🅴 ⓞ 🄴 🆅🅸🆂🅰. 🎐 rest
M 2600 – 🍴 900 – **263 rm** 8150/13000. AB e

🏨 **San Cristóbal**, Ramón y Cajal 3 🖋 77 12 50, Telex 77712, Fax 86 20 44 – 📶 🖶 ☎. 🄴 🆅🅸🆂🅰. 🎐 rest A t
March-December – **M** 1225 – 🍴 350 – **97 rm** 4425/6500.

🏨 **Lima** without rest, av. Antonio Belón 2 🖋 77 05 00, Fax 86 30 91 – 📶 ☎. 🅰🅴 ⓞ 🄴 🆅🅸🆂🅰.
🍴 400 – **64 rm** 4000/5950. A h

🍴🍴🍴 ⊛ **La Fonda**, pl. Santo Cristo 10 🖋 77 25 12, 🏠, « Andalusian Patio » – 🅰🅴 ⓞ 🄴 🆅🅸🆂🅰. 🎐
closed Sunday except August – **M** (dinner only) a la carte 4625/5370 A z
Spec. Crepes de aguacates y gambas, Dorada al estilo Fonda, Emince de hígado de ternera al vinagre de manzana.

🍴🍴🍴 Calycanto, av. Cánovas del Castillo 9 🖋 77 20 59, 🏠, « Original decor » – 📶 by ②

🍴🍴 **Santiago**, av. Duque de Ahumada 5 🖋 77 43 39, Fax 824503, 🏠, Seafood – 📶. 🅰🅴 ⓞ 🄴 🆅🅸🆂🅰. 🎐 A b
M a la carte 3500/4750.

🍴🍴 **Los Naranjos**, pl. de Los Naranjos 🖋 77 18 19, 🏠 – 🅰🅴 ⓞ 🄴 🆅🅸🆂🅰. 🎐 AB k
closed 20 November-20 February – **M** a la carte 2700/4350.

🍴 **Mamma Angela**, Virgen del Pilar 26 🖋 77 68 99, 🏠, Italian rest. – 📶. 🎐 A d
closed Tuesday and 30 December-February – **M** a la carte 2200/2350.

on the road to Cádiz – ✉ 29600 Marbella – ☎ 952 :

🏨 **Marbella Club** ⤫, by ② : 3 km 🖋 77 13 00, Telex 77319, Fax 82 98 84, 🏠, « Elegant decor; garden », 🏊 heated, 🎾 – 📶 📺 ☎ 📠 – 🔬 25/200. 🅰🅴 ⓞ 🄴 🆅🅸🆂🅰. 🎐
M 5900 – 🍴 1750 – **100 rm** 26640/38060.

🏨 **Puente Romano** ⤫, by ② : 3,5 km 🖋 77 01 00, Telex 77399, Fax 77 57 66, 🏠, « Elegant Andalusian complex in beautiful garden », 🏊 heated, 🎾 – 📶 📺 ☎ 📠 – 🔬 25/160. 🅰🅴 ⓞ 🄴 🆅🅸🆂🅰. 🎐 rest
M 4600 – 🍴 1500 – **220 rm** 24000/30000.

Coral Beach, by ② : 5 km ℰ 82 45 00, Telex 79816, Fax 82 82 57, 🏊, 🎾 – 📶 📺 ☎ ♿
⇔ 🅿 – 🕍 25/300. 🖭 ⓘ 🗲 𝓥𝓘𝓢𝓐
March-October – **M** 3700 – ☑ 1300 – **170 rm** 17200/22400.

Andalucía Plaza, urb. Nueva Andalucia by ② : 7,5 km, ⊠ 29660 Nueva Andalucia,
ℰ 81 20 00, Telex 77086, Fax 81 47 92, 🌴, 🏊, 🏊, 🎾, ⚹ – 📶 📺 ☎ 🅿 – 🕍 25/800. 🖭
ⓘ 🗲 𝓥𝓘𝓢𝓐
M 3350 – ☑ 900 – **415 rm** 10815/13175.

Marbella Dinamar Club 24, by ② : 6 km, ⊠ 29660 Nueva Andalucia, ℰ 81 05 00, Telex
77656, Fax 81 23 46, ≼, 🌴, « Garden with 🏊 », 🏊, ⚹ – 📶 ☎ 🅿 – 🕍 25/150. 🖭 ⓘ 🗲
𝓥𝓘𝓢𝓐 𝓢𝓧
M 3000 – ☑ 1000 – **117 rm** 12200/15000.

Guadalpín, by ② : 1,5 km ℰ 77 11 00, 🌴, 🏊, 🎾 – ☎ 🅿 – **110 rm**.

Las Fuentes del Rodeo, by ② : 8 km, ⊠ 29660 Nueva Andalucia, ℰ 81 40 17, Telex
77340, Fax 81 15 01, 🌴, « Garden », 🏊, ⚹ – ☎ 🅿. 🖭 ⓘ 🗲 𝓥𝓘𝓢𝓐 𝓢𝓧 rest
M 2500 – ☑ 650 – **85 rm** 4700/9000.

Nagüeles without rest, by ② : 3,5 km ℰ 77 16 88 – 🅿. 𝓢𝓧
March-15 October – ☑ 325 – **17 rm** 2150/3550.

La Meridiana, by ② : 3,5 km and detour 1 km - camino de la Cruz-urb Lomas del Virrey
ℰ 77 61 90, ≼, 🌴, « Terrace garden », 🏊 – 🅿. 🖭 ⓘ 🗲 𝓥𝓘𝓢𝓐
closed Monday and 10 January-11 February – **M** a la carte 4800/6600.

on the road to Málaga – ⊠ 29600 Marbella – ✆ 952 :

Los Monteros 🍃, by ① : 5,5 km ℰ 77 17 00, Telex 77059, Fax 82 58 46, ≼, 🌴, « Subtropical garden », 🏊, 🏊, 🛥 – 📶 ☎ 🅿 – 🕍 25/50. 🖭 ⓘ 🗲 𝓥𝓘𝓢𝓐
M (see rest. El Corzo below) – ☑ 1600 – **170 rm** 36000/41300.

Don Carlos 🍃, by ① : 10 km ℰ 83 11 40, Telex 77481, Fax 83 34 29, ≼, 🌴, « Large
garden », 🏊 heated, ⚹ – 📶 📺 ☎ 🅿 – 🕍 25/1200. 🖭 ⓘ 🗲 𝓥𝓘𝓢𝓐. 𝓢𝓧
M a la carte 4450/6500 – ☑ 1250 – **238 rm** 20100/25500.

Estrella del Mar 🍃, by ① : 9 km ℰ 83 12 75, Telex 79669, Fax 83 35 40, 🌴, 🏊, 🎾, ⚹ –
📶 📶 rest ☎ 🅿. 🖭 𝓥𝓘𝓢𝓐 𝓢𝓧 rest
March-November – **M** 2000 – ☑ 700 – **98 rm** 5800/9000.

Artola without rest, by ① : 12,5 km ℰ 83 13 90, Telex 79678, Fax 83 04 50, ≼, « On a golf
course », 🏊, 🎾, 🛥 – 🔙 ☎ 🅿. 🖭 🗲 𝓥𝓘𝓢𝓐 𝓢𝓧 rest
☑ 600 – **31 rm** 6500/8750.

El Corzo, at Hotel Los Monteros, by ① : 5,5 km ℰ 77 17 00, Telex 77059, Fax 82 58 46,
🌴 – 📶 🅿. 🖭 ⓘ 🗲 𝓥𝓘𝓢𝓐. 𝓢𝓧
M (dinner only) a la carte 4900 a 6000
Spec. Ensalada de aguacates con cangrejos salsa de albahaca, Hígado de oca al vino de Oporto, Papaya con
fresas y frambuesas salsa de menta.

La Hacienda, by ① : 11,5 km and detour 1,5 km ℰ 83 11 16, Fax 83 33 28, 🌴, « Rustic
decor-Patio » – 🅿. 🖭 ⓘ 🗲 𝓥𝓘𝓢𝓐. 𝓢𝓧
closed Monday lunch in August, Monday and Tuesday the rest of the year and 15 November-
20 December – **M** a la carte 5325/5925.

Los Altos de Marbella, by ① : 5 km and detour 3 km ℰ 77 12 16, ≼ mountains, sea and
Marbella, 🌴, Swiss rest. – 🅿. 🖭 🗲 𝓥𝓘𝓢𝓐 𝓢𝓧
closed Monday – **M** a la carte 2900/3900.

at Puerto Banús W : 8 km – ⊠ 29660 Nueva Andalucia – ✆ 952 :

Taberna del Alabardero, muelle Benabola ℰ 81 27 94, 🌴 – 📶. 🖭 ⓘ 🗲 𝓥𝓘𝓢𝓐. 𝓢𝓧
closed February and Sunday except in Summer – **M** a la carte 3650/5200.

Michel's, muelle Ribera 48 ℰ 81 55 59, 🌴 – 📶. 🖭 ⓘ 🗲 𝓥𝓘𝓢𝓐
closed February – **M** carta 3450 a 4700.

Cipriano, Edificio Levante - local 4 and 5 ℰ 81 10 77, 🌴, Seafood – 📶. 🖭 ⓘ 🗲 𝓥𝓘𝓢𝓐
M a la carte 3150/5250.

SEVILLA 4100 🅿 🟦🟦🟦 T 11 12 – pop. 653 833 alt. 12 – ✆ 954.

See : Cathedral★★★ CV – Giralda★★★ (≼★★) CV – Alcazar★★★ (gardens★★, Admiral's Apart-
ments : Virgin of the Navigators altarpiece★) CX – Maria Luisa Park★★ – Fine Arts Museum★★
AU **M1** – Santa Cruz Quarter★ CV – Pilate's House★★ (casa de Pilatos : azulejos★★) DV **R** –
Archeological Museum (Roman department★).

Envir. : Itálica ≼★ 9 km.

🛢 and Racecourse Club Pineda : 3 km ℰ 461 14 00.

✈ Sevilla - San Pablo : 14 km ℰ 451 06 77 – Iberia : Almirante Lobo 2, ⊠ 41001 ℰ 421 88 00.
🚄 ℰ 422 03 70.

🛈 ⊠ 41012, ℰ 423 44 65 – R.A.C.E. (R.A.C. de Andalucía) av. Eduardo Dato 22, ⊠ 41002, ℰ 463 13 50.
Madrid 550 – La Coruña 950 – Lisboa 417 – Málaga 217 – Valencia 682.

Plan ou following pages

Alfonso XIII, San Fernando 2, ✉ 41004, ☎ 422 28 50, Telex 72725, Fax 421 60 33, « Magnificient Andalousian building », – ▯ ▤ TV ☎ – P – 25/500. AE ⓓ VISA. CX **c**
M 5750 – ☐ 2150 – **149 rm** 24000/32800.

Sol Lebreros, Luis Morales 2, ✉ 41005, ☎ 457 94 00, Telex 72772, Fax 457 23 09, – ▯ ▤ TV ☎ – P – . AE ⓓ E VISA.
☐ 1200 – **439 rm** 24400/30500.
by Luis Montoto DV

Meliá Sevilla, av. de la Borbolla 3, ✉ 41004, ☎ 442 26 11, Telex 73094, Fax 442 16 08, – ▯ ▤ TV ☎ ♿ – 25/100. AE ⓓ E VISA.
by Av. de Portugal DX
☐ 1200 – **366 rm** 24400/30500.

Porta Coeli, av. Eduardo Dato 49, ✉ 41018, ☎ 457 00 40, Telex 72913, Fax 457 85 80, – ▯ ▤ TV ☎ – by E. Dato DV
(see rest. **Florencia** below) – **243 rm**.

Sol Macarena, San Juan de Ribera 2, ✉ 41009, ☎ 437 58 00, Telex 72815, Fax 438 18 03, – ▯ ▤ TV ☎ – 25/700. AE ⓓ E VISA.
☐ 1200 – **327 rm** 24400/30500. CDT **a**

Tryp Colón, Canalejas 1, ✉ 41001, ☎ 422 29 00, Telex 72726, Fax 422 09 38 – ▯ ▤ TV ☎ ♿ – 25/80. AE ⓓ E VISA.
M 4700 – ☐ 1500 – **218 rm** 24800/31000.
AV **b**

Inglaterra, pl. Nueva 7, ✉ 41001, ☎ 422 49 70, Telex 72244, Fax 456 13 36 – ▯ ▤ TV ☎ . AE ⓓ E VISA. rest BV **a**
M 2750 – ☐ 600 – **116 rm** 16000/20000.

Pasarela without rest, av. de la Borbolla 11, ✉ 41004, ☎ 441 55 11, Telex 72486, Fax 442 07 29 – ▯ ▤ TV ☎. AE ⓓ E VISA.
☐ 750 – **82 rm** 11500/17500.
by Av. de Portugal DX

G. H. Lar, pl. Carmen Benítez 3, ✉ 41003, ☎ 441 03 61, Telex 72816, Fax 441 04 52 – ▯ ▤ TV ☎ – 25/250. AE ⓓ E VISA
DV **v**
M 2200 – ☐ 800 – **137 rm** 10300/15000.

Husa Sevilla, Pagés del Corro 90, ✉ 41010, ☎ 434 24 12, Fax 434 27 07 – ▯ ▤ ☎ – 25/220. AE E VISA. AX **a**
M 2900 – ☐ 980 – **128 rm** 9900/15400.

Becquer without rest, Reyes Católicos 4, ✉ 41001, ☎ 422 89 00, Telex 72884, Fax 421 44 00 – ▯ ▤ ☎ . AE ⓓ E VISA. AV **s**
☐ 450 – **120 rm** 6000/8500.

Doña María without rest, Don Remondo 19, ✉ 41004, ☎ 422 49 90, « Elegant classic decor-terrace with ≤ Giralda », – ▯ ▤ TV ☎ – 25/40. AE ⓓ E VISA. CV **b**
☐ 700 – **61 rm** 12100/18700.

Monte Triana without rest, Clara de Jesús Montero 24, ✉ 41010, ☎ 434 31 11, Fax 434 33 28 – ▤ – 25/50. AE E VISA
W : by Puente Isabel II AX
☐ 500 – **117 rm** 5500/9000.

Alcazar without rest, Menéndez Pelayo 10, ✉ 41004, ☎ 441 20 11, Telex 72360, Fax 442 16 59 – ▯ ▤ TV ☎ . AE ⓓ E VISA
DX **u**
☐ 400 – **100 rm** 6800/9000.

Resid. and Rest. Fernando III, San José 21, ✉ 41004, ☎ 421 77 08, Telex 72491, – ▯ ▤ ☎ – 25/250. AE ⓓ VISA. rest
M 2500 – ☐ 550 – **157 rm** 7985/9980. CV **z**

SEVILLA

Francos	CV	59
Sierpes	BUV	
Tetuán	BV	144
Alemanes	CV	5
Almirante Apodaca	CU	6
Almirante Lobo	BX	8
Caballerizas	CV	16
Cabeza Rey Don Pedro	CV	18
Campana	BU	20
Carmona (Carretera de)	DT	27
Concordia (Pl.)	BU	32
Demetrio de los Rios	DVX	41
Fray Ceferino González	CX	61
García de Vinuesa	BV	62
Gerona	CU	66
Jerez (Puerta de)	CX	72
Julio César	AV	74
Martín Villa	BU	90

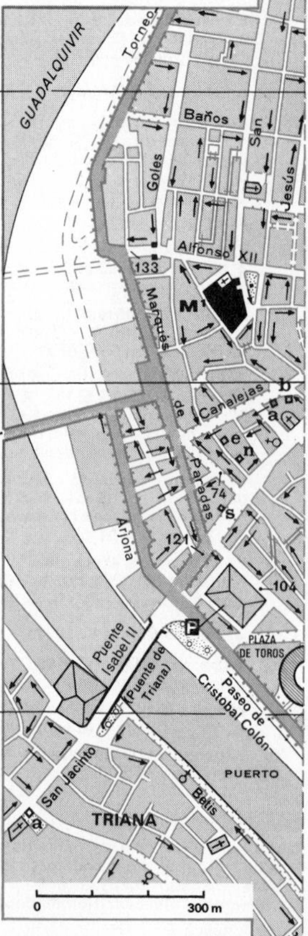

Mateos Gago	CV	92
O'Donnell	BU	98
Pastor y Landero	AV	104
Peñuelas	DU	107
Reyes Católicos	AV	121
Rioja	BV	123
San Laureano	AU	133
Santa María la Blanca	DV	139
Santo Tomás	CX	141
Triunfo (Pl. del)	CX	147
Velázquez	BU	148

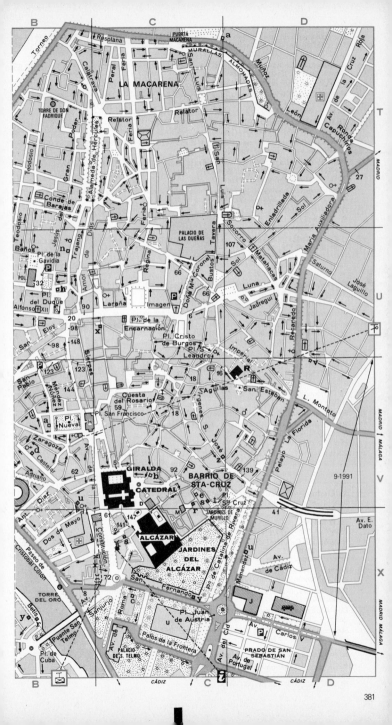

América without rest, coffee shop only, Jesús del Gran Poder 2, ⊠ 41002, ℰ 422 09 51, Telex 72709, Fax 421 06 26 – 🛗 🗏 📺 ☎. 🖭 ⓪ 🖻 𝚅𝙸𝚂𝙰. ⅏
BU **h**
⌦ 450 – **100 rm** 9000/15000.

Hispalis, av. de Andalucia 52, ⊠ 41006, ℰ 452 94 33, Telex 73208, Fax 467 53 13 – 🛗 🗏 📺 ☎ ⟷ 🅿 – 🔬 25/40. 🖭 🖻 𝚅𝙸𝚂𝙰. ⅏
by Luis Montoto DV
M 1225 – ⌦ 850 – **68 rm** 18000/23000.

Monte Carmelo without rest, Turia 7, ⊠ 41011, ℰ 427 90 00, Telex 73195, Fax 427 10 04 – 🛗 🗏 ☎ ⟷. 🖭 🖻 𝚅𝙸𝚂𝙰. ⅏
SW : by pl. de Cuba BX
⌦ 500 – **68 rm** 5500/9000.

La Rábida, Castelar 24, ⊠ 41001, ℰ 422 09 60, Telex 73062, 🍽 – 🛗 🗏 rm 📺 ☎. ⅏ rest
M 1500 – ⌦ 300 – **100 rm** 4000/6500.
BV **d**

Venecia without rest, Trajano 31, ⊠ 41002, ℰ 438 11 61, Fax 490 19 55 – 🛗 🗏 📺 ☎ ⟷.
🖭 𝚅𝙸𝚂𝙰. ⅏ – ⌦ 375 – **24 rm** 8500/4800.
BU **n**

Murillo and apart. Murillo without rest, Lope de Rueda 7 y 9, ⊠ 41004, ℰ 421 60 95, Fax 421 96 16 – 🛗 🗏 ☎. 🖭 🖻 𝚅𝙸𝚂𝙰. ⅏
CV **e**
⌦ 300 – **61 rm** 5300/9000 – **14 apartments**.

Montecarlo, Gravina 51, ⊠ 41001, ℰ 421 75 03, Telex 72729 – 🛗 ☎. 🖭 ⓪ 🖻 𝚅𝙸𝚂𝙰. ⅏
M 1650 – ⌦ 400 – **25 rm** 6300/9700.
AV **e**

Reyes Católicos without rest, Gravina 57, ⊠ 41001, ℰ 421 12 00, Fax 421 63 12 – 🛗 🗏 ☎. 🖭 ⓪ 🖻 𝚅𝙸𝚂𝙰. ⅏
AV **n**
⌦ 400 – **26 rm** 9000/14000.

XXX ❀ **Egaña Oriza,** San Fernando 41, ⊠ 41004, ℰ 422 72 11, Fax 421 04 29, « Winter garden » – 🗏. 🖭 ⓪ 🖻 𝚅𝙸𝚂𝙰. ⅏
CX **y**
closed Saturday lunch, Sunday and August – **M** a la carte 4500/6000
Spec. Tosta de foie gras gratinada con cebollitas a la miel. Lomo de merluza con kokotxas en salsa verde. Becada flambeada al armagnac.

XXX **Florencia,** av. Eduardo Dato 49, ⊠ 41018, ℰ 457 00 40, Telex 72913, Fax 457 85 80, Tasteful decor – 🗏. 🖭 ⓪ 🖻 𝚅𝙸𝚂𝙰. ⅏
by Av. E. Dato DX
closed August – **M** a la carte 3150/4400.

XXX **Maitres,** av. República Argentina 54, ⊠ 41011, ℰ 445 68 80 – 🗏
by pl. de Cuba BX

XXX **El Burladero,** Canalejas 1, ⊠ 41001, ℰ 422 29 00, Telex 72726, Fax 422 09 38, Bullfighting decor – 🗏. 🖭 ⓪ 🖻 𝚅𝙸𝚂𝙰. ⅏
AV **a**
closed August – **M** a la carte 3400/4900.

XXX **San Marco,** Cuna 6, ⊠ 41004, ℰ 421 24 40 – 🗏
CU **x**

XXX **Pello Roteta,** Farmacéutico Murillo Herrera 10, ⊠ 41010, ℰ 427 84 17, Basque rest – 🗏. 🖭 ⓪ 🖻 𝚅𝙸𝚂𝙰. ⅏
by Luis Montoto DV
closed Sunday and 15 August-15 September – **M** a la carte 3500/5500.

XXX **La Dehesa,** Luis Morales 2, ⊠ 41005, ℰ 457 94 00, Telex 72772, Typical Andalusian decor, Grill – 🗏
by Luis Montoto DV

XXX **Rincón de Curro,** Virgen de Luján 45, ⊠ 41011, ℰ 445 02 38 – 🗏
by pl. de Cuba BX

XXX **Río Grande,** Betis, ⊠ 41010, ℰ 427 39 56, Fax 427 98 46, ≤, 🍽, « Large terraces on riverside » – 🗏. 🖭 ⓪ 🖻 𝚅𝙸𝚂𝙰. ⅏
BX **r**
M a la carte 3000/3550.

XXX **Ox's,** Betis 61, ⊠ 41010, ℰ 427 95 85, Basque rest – 🗏. 🖭 ⓪ 🖻 𝚅𝙸𝚂𝙰. ⅏
BX **y**
closed Sunday dinner and August – **M** a la carte 3500/4950.

XX **Jamaica,** Jamaica 16, ⊠ 41012, ℰ 461 12 44, Fax 461 10 50 – 🗏. 🖭 ⓪ 🖻 𝚅𝙸𝚂𝙰. ⅏
closed Sunday dinner – **M** a la carte 2550/3100.
by Av. del Cid CX

XX **La Encina,** Virgen de Aguas Santas 6 acceso E, ⊠ 41011, ℰ 445 93 22 – 🗏. 🖭 ⓪ 🖻 𝚅𝙸𝚂𝙰. ⅏
closed Sunday, Bank Holidays and 10 August-10 September – **M** a la carte 2650/3700. by ③

XX **La Albahaca,** pl. Santa Cruz 12, ⊠ 41004, ℰ 422 07 14, « Former manor house » – 🗏. 🖭 ⓪ 🖻 𝚅𝙸𝚂𝙰. ⅏
CV **s**
closed Sunday – **M** a la carte 3200/4000.

XX **Rincón de Casana,** Santo Domingo de la Calzada 13, ⊠ 41018, ℰ 457 27 97, Regional decor – 🗏. 🖭 ⓪ 🖻 𝚅𝙸𝚂𝙰. ⅏
by Av. E. Dato DX
closed Sunday in Summer – **M** a la carte 3000/3825.

XX **La Isla,** Arfe 25, ⊠ 41001, ℰ 421 26 31 – 🗏. 🖭 ⓪ 🖻 𝚅𝙸𝚂𝙰. ⅏
BV **u**
closed Monday and 15 August-15 September – **M** a la carte 3000/5450.

X **Rías Baixas,** av. Ciudad Jardin 6, ⊠ 41005, ℰ 463 43 16, Seafood – 🗏. 🖭 ⓪ 🖻 𝚅𝙸𝚂𝙰. ⅏
closed Monday and 16 to 31 August – **M** a la carte 2925/3925.
by Av. E. Dato DX

X **Los Alcázares,** Miguel de Mañara 10, ⊠ 41004, ℰ 421 31 03, Fax 456 18 29, 🍽, Regional decor – 🗏. 🖭 🖻 𝚅𝙸𝚂𝙰. ⅏ – *closed Sunday* – **M** a la carte 2500/3100.
CX **s**

X **Hostería del Laurel,** pl. de los Venerables 5, ⊠ 41004, ℰ 422 02 95, Typical decor – 🗏. 🖭 ⓪ 🖻 𝚅𝙸𝚂𝙰. ⅏ – **M** a la carte approx. 2850.
CV **r**

at Alcalá de Guadaira SE : 14 km by N 334 – ⊠ 41500 – ❀ 954 :

Oromana ⟲, av. de Portugal ℰ 470 08 04, ≤, 🍽, « Andalusian style construction surroundel by pinetrees », ⊼ – 🗏 📺 🅿 – 🔬 25/180. 🖭 ⓪ 🖻 𝚅𝙸𝚂𝙰. ⅏
M 2800 – ⌦ 575 – **29 rm** 7000/9000.

VALENCIA 46000 **44** N 28 29 – pop. 751 734 – alt. 13 – ✪ 96.

See : Fine Arts Museum★★ (Museo Provincial de Bellas Artes) FX **M3** – Cathedral★ (Miguelete★)
EX **A** – Palacio de la Generalidad★ (ceilings★) EX **D** – Lonja★ (silkhall★, Maritime consulate hall :
ceiling★)EX **E** – Corpus Christi Collegiate Church★ (Colegio del Patriarca) EY **N** – Ceramics
Museum★ (Museo Nacional de Cerámica) EY **M1** – Serranos Towers★ EX **V** – Santo Domingo
Monastery (Royal Chapel★) FY **S**.

🛧 of Manises by ④ : 12 km ✆ 379 08 50 – 🛱 Club Escorpión NW : 19 km by Liria Road
✆ 160 12 11 – 🛱 El Saler, Parador Luis Vives by ② : 15 km ✆ 161 11 86.

🛧 Valencia - Manises Airport by ④ : 9,5 km ✆ 154 60 15 – Iberia : Paz 14, ⊠ 46003,
✆ 351 44 95.

🚗 ✆ 351 00 43.

🚢 To the Balearic and Canary Islands : Cia. Trasmediterránea, av. Manuel Soto Ingeniero 15,
⊠ 46024, ✆ 367 07 04, Telex 62648.

🛈 pl. del Ayuntamiento 1, ⊠ 46002, ✆ 351 04 17, Paz 48, ⊠ 46003, ✆ 352 28 97, and Airport, ✆ 370 95 00 –
R.A.C.E. (R.A.C. de Valencia) av. Jacinto Benavente 25, ⊠ 46005, ✆ 374 94 05.

Madrid 351 ④ – Albacete 183 ③ – Alicante (by coast) 174 ③ – Barcelona 361 ① – Bilbao 606 ① – Castellón de
la Plana 75 ① – Málaga 654 ③ – Sevilla 682 ④ – Zaragoza 330 ①.

Plan on following pages

🏨 **Meliá Valencia**, av. Baleares 2, ⊠ 46023, ✆ 360 73 00, Telex 64252, Fax 360 89 21, ⩢ – 🛗
■ 📺 ☎ – 🔏 25/250. 🆎 ⓘ E 🆅🆂🅰 by Puente Aragón   FZ
M 3500 – � 1250 – **314 rm** 13500/18000.

🏨 **Astoria Palace**, pl. Rodrigo Botet 5, ⊠ 46002, ✆ 352 67 37, Telex 62733, Fax 352 80 78 –
🛗 ■ 📺 ☎ – 🔏 25/500. 🆎 ⓘ E 🆅🆂🅰   EY **p**
M 3200 – ⊠ 900 – **207 rm** 15800/19800.

🏨 **Reina Victoria**, Barcas 4, ⊠ 46002, ✆ 352 04 87, Telex 64755, Fax 352 04 87 – 🛗 ■ 📺
☎ – 🔏 25/50. 🆎 ⓘ E 🆅🆂🅰   EY **s**
M 3150 – ⊠ 775 – **97 rm** 10500/17200.

🏨 **Dimar** without rest, coffee shop only, Gran Vía Marqués del Turia 80, ⊠ 46005, ✆
334 18 07, Telex 62952, Fax 373 09 26 – 🛗 ■ 📺 ☎ 🚗 – 🔏 25/80. 🆎 ⓘ E 🆅🆂🅰 🛠   FZ **q**
⊠ 800 – **95 rm** 9000/12500.

🏨 **Expo H.** without rest, coffee shop only, av. Pio XII-4, ⊠ 46009, ✆ 347 09 09, Telex 63212,
Fax 348 31 81, ⩢ – 🛗 ■ 📺 ☎ – 🔏 25/500. 🆎 ⓘ E 🆅🆂🅰 🛠   by Cuart   DX
⊠ 800 – **396 rm** 9360/17550.

🏨 **Inglés**, Marqués de Dos Aguas 6, ⊠ 46002, ✆ 351 64 26, Telex 62228, Fax 394 02 51 – 🛗
■ 📺 ☎. 🆎 ⓘ E 🆅🆂🅰 🛠   EY **m**
M 1500 – ⊠ 450 – **62 rm** 5500/6500.

🏨 **Renasa** without rest, coffee shop only, av. Cataluña 5, ⊠ 46010, ✆ 369 24 50, Fax 393 18 24
– 🛗 ■ 📺 ☎. 🆎 ⓘ E 🆅🆂🅰   by ①
⊠ 500 – **73 rm** 5260/8500.

🏨 **Llar** without rest, Colón 46, ⊠ 46004, ✆ 352 84 60 – 🛗 ■ ☎. 🆎 ⓘ E 🆅🆂🅰   EZ **u**
⊠ 350 – **50 rm** 5000/7000.

🏨 **Sorolla** without rest, no ⊠, Convento de Santa Clara 5, ⊠ 46002, ✆ 352 33 92, Fax
352 14 65 – 🛗 ■ ⊛. 🆎 E 🆅🆂🅰 🛠 – **50 rm** 4900/7000.   EZ **z**

🏨 **Continental** without rest, Correos 8, ⊠ 46002, ✆ 351 09 26, Fax 351 09 26 – 🛗 ■ ☎. 🆎 E
🆅🆂🅰 🛠 – ⊠ 400 – **43 rm** 4200/6850.   EY **h**

XXX **Eladio**, Chiva 40, ⊠ 46018, ✆ 384 22 44 – ■. 🆎 ⓘ E 🆅🆂🅰 🛠   by Cuart   DX
closed Sunday and August – **M** a la carte 3950/6750.

XXX **Oscar Torrijos**, Dr. Sumsi 4, ⊠ 46005, ✆ 373 29 49 – ■. 🆎 ⓘ E 🆅🆂🅰 🛠   EZ
closed Sunday and August – **M** a la carte 3400/ 4500.   by Av. Antiguo R. de Valencia

XXX **La Hacienda**, Navarro Reverter 12, ⊠ 46004, ✆ 373 18 59 – ■. 🆎 ⓘ E 🆅🆂🅰 🛠   FY **y**
closed Saturday lunch, Sunday and Holy Week – **M** a la carte 3300/5900.

XXX **Ma Cuina**, Gran Vía Germanías 49, ⊠ 46006, ✆ 341 77 99 – ■ 🚗. 🆎 ⓘ E 🆅🆂🅰 🛠   DZ **n**
closed Saturday lunch, Sunday and 24 March-2 April – **M** a la carte 3650/5550.

XXX **Versalles**, Dolores Alcayde 14 ✆ 342 37 38, Fax 341 54 54, �, « In a villa » – ■. 🆎 ⓘ E
🆅🆂🅰 🛠   by San Vicente Mártir   DZ
closed Sunday and 15 August-15 September – **M** a la carte 3450/4050.

XXX ✿ **Galbis**, Marvá 28, ⊠ 46007, ✆ 325 88 13 – ■. 🆎 🆅🆂🅰 🛠   DZ **f**
closed Saturday lunch, Sunday and 28 July-August – **M** a la carte 3250/3700
Spec. Lubina en alli pebre. Fritada de cabrito con ajos tiernos. Arroz caldoso de la Ribera Alta..

XXX **La Reserva**, Juan de Austria 30, ⊠ 46002, ✆ 352 58 02 – ■   FY **e**

XXX **La Oca Dorada**, Puerta del Mar 6, ⊠ 46004, ✆ 352 22 57 – ■   FY **f**

XXX **Lionel**, Pizarro 9, ⊠ 46004, ✆ 351 65 66 – ■   EZ **b**

XXX **Comodoro**, Transits 3, ⊠ 46002, ✆ 351 38 15 – ■. 🆎 ⓘ E 🆅🆂🅰 🛠   EY **r**
closed Saturday lunch, Sunday, Bank Holidays and August – **M** a la carte 2400/3500.

XX **El Gourmet**, Taquígrafo Martí 3, ⊠ 46005, ✆ 374 50 71 – ■. 🆎 E 🆅🆂🅰 🛠   FZ **b**
closed Sunday, Holy Week and August – **M** a la carte 2450/3050.

XX **El Gastrónomo**, av. Primado Reig 149, ⊠ 46020, ✆ 369 70 36 – ■. 🆎 E 🆅🆂🅰 🛠
closed Sunday, dinner Bank Holidays, Holy Week and August – **M** a la carte 2450/3400.
by Puente del Real   FX

383

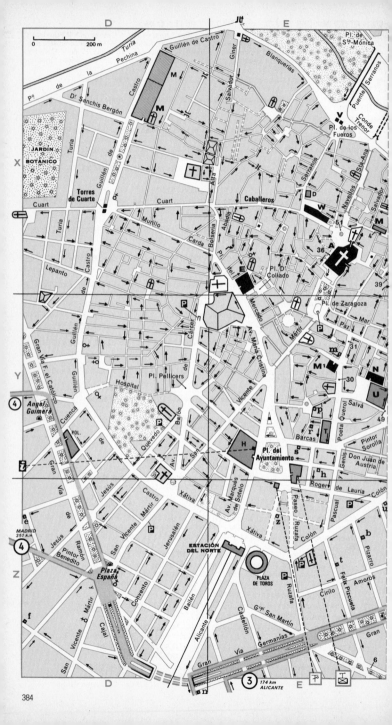

VALENCIA
STREET INDEX

XX **Civera,** Lérida 11, ✉ 46009, 𝒞 347 59 17, Seafood – 🗐. 𝔸𝔼 ⓞ 𝐄 𝕍𝕀𝕊𝔸. ✗
  closed Monday and August – **M** a la carte approx. 7000.   by Pl. de Santa Mónica EX

XX **Mey Mey,** Historiador Diago 19, ✉ 46007, 𝒞 326 07 47, Chinese rest – 🗐. 𝔸𝔼 𝕍𝕀𝕊𝔸. ✗
  closed Holy Week and 15 to 30 August – **M** a la carte 1400/2090.   DZ **e**

XX **Asador de Aranda,** Félix Pizcueta 9, ✉ 46004, 𝒞 352 97 91, Roast lamb – 🗐. 𝐄 𝕍𝕀𝕊𝔸. ✗
  closed Saturday lunch and Sunday dinner – **M** a la carte 2500/2900.   EZ **t**

X **Eguzki,** av. Baleares, 1, ✉ 46023, 𝒞 369 90 60, Basque rest – 🗐. 𝐄 𝕍𝕀𝕊𝔸. ✗
  closed Saturday and August – **M** a la carte 3100/4250.   by Puente Aragón FZ

X **Palace Fesol,** Hernán Cortés 7, ✉ 46004, 𝒞 352 93 23, « Regional decor » – 🗐. 𝔸𝔼 ⓞ 𝐄
  𝕍𝕀𝕊𝔸. ✗   FZ **s**
  closed Sunday dinner and Monday – **M** a la carte 2200/3100.

  by road C 234 NW : 8,5 km – ✉ 46035 Valencia – ✪ 96 :

🏨 **Feria,** the Exhibition Centre 𝒞 364 44 11, Telex 61079, Fax 364 54 83 – 🛗 🗐 📺 ☎ ⟵ –
  🔏 25/60. 𝔸𝔼 ⓞ 𝐄 𝕍𝕀𝕊𝔸. ✗ rest
  ⊡ 750 – **136 rm** 19500/21000.

  at El Saler by ② : 8 km – ✉ 46012 Valencia – ✪ 96 :

🏨 **Sidi Saler** ⟡, SE : 3 km 𝒞 161 04 11, Telex 64208, Fax 161 08 38, ≤, ⊐, ◩, ☞, ✗ – 🛗 🗐
  📺 ☎ ⓟ – 🔏 25/300. 𝔸𝔼 ⓞ 𝐄 𝕍𝕀𝕊𝔸. ✗ rest
  M a la carte 3100/4600 – ⊡ 1200 – **276 rm** 15300/22300.

🏨 **Parador Luis Vives** ⟡, SE : 7 km 𝒞 161 11 86, Telex 61069, Fax 162 70 16, ≤, « In the
  middle of the golf course », ⊐, ✗, ⌀ – 🛗 🗐 📺 ☎ ⓟ – 🔏 25/300. 𝔸𝔼 ⓞ 𝐄 𝕍𝕀𝕊𝔸. ✗
  M 3100 – ⊡ 950 – **58 rm** 13000.

  at Manises on the road to the Airport by ④ : 9,5 km – ✉ 46940 Manises – ✪ 96 :

🏨 **Sol Azafata,** 𝒞 154 61 00, Telex 61451, Fax 153 20 19 – 🛗 🗐 📺 ☎ ⟵ ⓟ – 🔏 25/300.
  𝔸𝔼 ⓞ 𝐄 𝕍𝕀𝕊𝔸. ✗ rest
  ⊡ 800 – **130 rm** 12000/15000.

  at Puçol N : 25 km by motorway A 7 – ✉ 46760 Puçol – ✪ 96 :

🏨 **Monte Picayo** ⟡, urbanización Monte Picayo 𝒞 142 01 00, Telex 62087, Fax 142 21 68,
  🍴, « On a hillside with ≤ orange-groves, Puçol and sea », ⊐, ☞, ✗ – 🛗 🗐 📺 ☎ ⓟ –
  🔏 25/600. 𝔸𝔼 ⓞ 𝐄 𝕍𝕀𝕊𝔸. ✗
  M 3300 – ⊡ 1150 – **82 rm** 14800/18500.

Sweden
Sverige

Stockholm
Gothenburg

PRACTICAL INFORMATION

LOCAL CURRENCY

Swedish Kronor : 100 SEK = 17.67 US $ (Jan. 91)

TOURIST INFORMATION

In Stockholm, the Tourist Centre is situated in the Sweden House, entrance from Kungsträdgården at Hamngatan. Open Mon-Fri 9am-5pm. Sat. and Sun. 9am-2pm. Telephone weekdays 08/789 20 00, weekends to Excursion Shop and Tourist Centre 08/789 24 28 or 789 24 29. For Gothenburg, see information in the text of the town under 🛈.

FOREIGN EXCHANGE

Banks are open between 9.00am and 3.00pm on weekdays only. Some banks in the centre of the city are usually open weekdays 9am to 5.30pm. Most large hotels have exchange facilities, and Arlanda airport has banking facilities between 7am to 10pm seven days a week.

MEALS

At lunchtime, follow the custom of the country and try the typical buffets of Scandinavian specialities.

At dinner, the a la carte and the menus will offer you more conventional cooking.

SHOPPING

In the index of street names, those printed in red are where the principal shops are found.

The main shopping streets in the centre of Stockholm are: Hamngatan, Biblioteksgatan, Drottninggatan.

In the Old Town mainly Västerlånggatan.

THEATRE BOOKINGS

Your hotel porter will be able to make your arrangements or direct you to Theatre Booking Agents.

CAR HIRE

The international car hire companies have branches in Stockholm, Gothenburg, Arlanda and Landvetter airports. Your hotel porter should be able to give details and help you with your arrangements.

TIPPING

Hotels and restaurants normally include a service charge of 15 per cent. Doormen, baggage porters etc. are generally given a gratuity.

Taxi drivers are customarily tipped about 10 per cent of the amount shown on the meter in addition to the fare.

SPEED LIMITS - SEAT BELTS

The maximum permitted speed on motorways and dual carriageways is 110 km/h - 68 mph and 90 km/h - 56 mph on other roads except where a lower speed limit is signposted.

The wearing of seat belts is compulsory for drivers and passengers.

STOCKHOLM

SIGHTS

See : Old Town★★★ (Gamla Stan) : Stortorget★★, AZ, Köpmangatan★★ AZ **35**, Österlånggatan★★ AZ ; Royal Warship Vasa★★★ (Wasavarvet) DY ; Skansen Open-Air Museum★★★ DY.
Royal Palace★★ (Kungliga Slottet) AZ ; Changing of the Guard★★ ; Apartments★★, Royal Armoury★★, Treasury★ ; Museum★ ; Great Church★★ (Storkyrkan) AZ ; Riddarholmen Church★★ (Riddarholmskyrkan) AZ ; Town Hall★★ (Stadshuset) BYH : ☀★★★, Djurgården DYZ : Waldemarsudde House★★, Rosendal Palace★, Thiel Gallery★ ; Gröna Lunds Tivoli★ DZ.
Kaknäs TV Tower★ (Kaknäs Tornet) ☀★★★ DY ; Gustav Adolf Square★ (Gustav Adolfs Torg) CY **16** ; Kings Gardens★ (Kungsträdgården) CY ; Riddarhouse★ (Riddarhuset) AZ ; German Church★ (Tyska Kyrkan) AZ ; Fjällgatan★ DZ ; Sergels Torg CY **54** – Hötorget★ CY **20**.

Museums : Museum of National Antiquities★★★ (Historiska Museet) DY ; National Art Gallery★★ (National Museet) DY **M1** ; Nordic Museum★★ (Nordiska Museet) DY **M2** ; Museum of Far Eastern Antiquities★★ (Ostasiastiska Museet) DY **M3** ; Museum of Modern Art (Moderna Museet) DYZ **M4** ; National Maritime Museum★★ (Sjöhistoriska Museet) DY ; Halwyl Museum★ (Halwylska Museet) CY **M5** ; City Museum★ (Stads Museet) CZ **M6** ; Strindberg Museum★ BX **M7** ; Museum of Medieval Stockholm★ (Stockholms Medeltidsmuseum) CY **M8**.

Outskirts : Drottningholm Palace★★ (Drottningholms Slott) W : 12 km BY ; Apartments★★, Gardens★★, Court Theatre★, Chinese Pavilion★ ; Tours by boat★★ (in summer) : Under the Bridges★★ ; Archipelago★★ (Vaxholm, Möja, Sandhamn, Utö), Mälarenlake★ (Gripsholm, Skokloster) ; Haga Park and Pavilion of Gustav III★ (N : 4 km) BX ; Millesgården★ (E : 4 km) DX.

STOCKHOLM Sverige 985 M 15 – pop. 667 862 Greater Stockholm 1 466 862 – ✆ 08.

🏌 Svenska Golfförbundet ✆ 753 02 65.

✈ Stockholm-Arlanda N : 41 km ✆ (08) 797 60 00 – SAS : Flygcity, Klarabergsviadukten 72 ✆ 020/91 01 50 – Air Terminal : opposite main railway station.

🚐 Motorail for Southern Europe : SJ Travel Agency, Vasagatan 22 ✆ 14 89 15.

⛴ To Finland : contact Silja Line ✆ 22 21 40 or Viking Line ✆ 714 56 00 – Excursions by boat : contact Stockholm Information Service (see below).

🛈 Stockholm Information Service, Tourist Centre, Sverigehuset, Hamngatan 27 ✆ 789 20 00 – Motormännens Riksförbund ✆ 782 38 00 – Kungl. Automobilklubben (Royal Automobile Club) ✆ 660 00 55.

Hamburg 935 – København 630 – Oslo 522.

STOCKHOLM

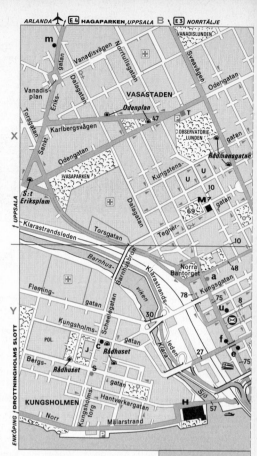

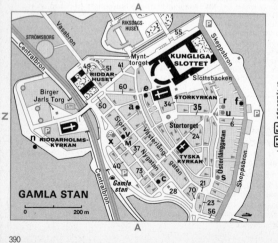

GAMLA STAN

0   200 m

RIDDARFJÄRDEN

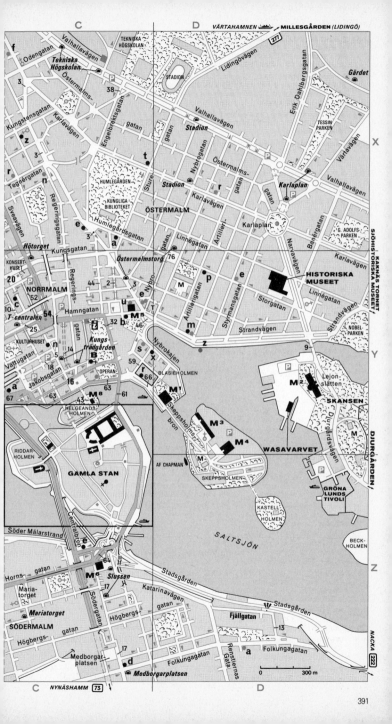

Grand H., Södra Blasieholmshamnen 8, Box 16424, S-103 27, ℰ 22 10 20, Telex 19500, Fax 21 86 88, ⩽, 🖨 – ⧫ ᐳⵗ rm 🔟 ☎ – 🚗 400. 🖭 ⓪ 🗲 🎟   CY r
M Verandan 145/290 and a la carte – (see also **Franska Matsalen** below) - **299 rm** ⌑ 1380/2800, **19 suites** 3810/15340.

Sheraton-Stockholm, Tegelbacken 6, Box 289, S-101 23, ℰ 14 26 00, Telex 17750, Fax 21 70 26, ⩽, – ⧫ ᐳⵗ rm 🔟 ☎ ᕀ, 🚗 – 🚗 500. 🖭 ⓪ 🗲 🎟   CY a
M Premiere (closed Saturday lunch and Sunday) 300/450 and a la carte – Bistro – **445 rm** ⌑ 1250/1950, **15 suites**.

SAS Royal Viking, Vasagatan 1, Box 234, S-101 23, ℰ 14 10 00, Telex 13900, Fax 10 81 80, 🖨, 🔃 – ⧫ ᐳⵗ rm 🔟 ☎ ᕀ, 🚗 – 🚗 140. 🖭 ⓪ 🗲 🎟. 🛠   BY f
M Royal Room 370 and a la carte – **315 rm** ⌑ 1780/2140, **4 suites** 3900/5360.

Sergel Plaza, Brunkebergstorg 9, Box 16411, S-103 27, ℰ 22 66 00, Telex 16700, Fax 21 50 70, 🖨 – ⧫ ᐳⵗ rm 🔟 ☎ 🚗 – 🚗 200. 🖭 ⓪ 🗲 🎟   CY n
M Anna Rella 243/430 and a la carte – **394 rm** ⌑ 1195/1910, **12 suites** 2350/5800.

Scandic Crown, Guldgränd 8, Box 15270, S-104 65, ℰ 702 25 00, Telex 11019, Fax 642 83 58, 🖨, 🔃 – ⧫ ᐳⵗ rm 🔟 ☎ ᕀ, 🚗 – 🚗 285. 🖭 ⓪ 🗲 🎟   CZ e
M La Couronne d'or 200/250 and a la carte – **246 rm** ⌑ 1190/1560, **18 suites** 2050/3400.

SAS Strand, Nybrokajen 9, Box 16396, S-103 27, ℰ 678 78 00, Telex 10504, Fax 611 24 36, ⩽, 🖨 – ⧫ ᐳⵗ rm 🔟 ☎ – 🚗 25. 🖭 ⓪ 🗲 🎟. 🛠   CDY x
M 125/390 and a la carte – **119 rm** ⌑ 1550/2300, **18 suites** 2600/5500.

Amaranten, Kungsholmsgatan 31, S-104 20, ℰ 654 10 60, Telex 17498, Fax 652 62 48, 🖨, 🔃 – ⧫ ᐳⵗ rm 🔟 ☎ ᕀ 🚗 – 🚗 170. 🖭 ⓪ 🗲 🎟. 🛠   BY c
M 350/375 and a la carte – **404 rm** ⌑ 1095/1535, **6 suites** 2200/4500.

Continental, Klara Vattugränd 4, corner of Vasagatan, S-101 22, ℰ 24 40 20, Telex 10100, Fax 11 36 95 – ⧫ ᐳⵗ rm 🔟 ☎ 🚗 – 🚗 70. 🖭 ⓪ 🗲 🎟   BY e
M 155/255 and a la carte – **219 rm** ⌑ 1290/2210, **1 suite** 3000.

Stockholm Plaza, Birger Jarlsgatan 29, Box 7707, S-103 95, ℰ 14 51 20, Telex 13982, Fax 10 34 92, 🖨 – ⧫ ᐳⵗ rm 🔟 ☎ ᕀ, 🚗 – 🚗 45. 🖭 ⓪ 🗲 🎟   CX e
closed 22 to 27 December – **M** (closed Saturday lunch and Sunday) a la carte approx. 265 –
147 rm ⌑ 1250/1450, **8 suites** 1850/2850.

Diplomat, Strandvägen 7c, Box 14059, S-104 40, ℰ 663 58 00, Telex 17119, Fax 783 66 34, ⩽, 🖨 – ⧫ ᐳⵗ ☎ 🖭 ⓪ 🗲 🎟   DY m
closed 3 days at Christmas – **M** (closed Saturday dinner and Sunday) 110/175 and a la carte
– **127 rm** ⌑ 1250/1990, **3 suites** 2750/5150.

Anglais, Humlegårdsgatan 23, Box 5178, S-102 44, ℰ 614 16 00, Telex 19475, Fax 611 09 72
– ⧫ ᐳⵗ rm 🔟 ☎ 🚗 – 🚗 250. 🖭 ⓪ 🗲 🎟   CX a
closed 20 to 30 December – **M** 230/350 and a la carte – **162 rm** ⌑ 1145/1820, **9 suites**
3380.

Globe, Arenaslingan 7, Box 10004, S-121 26, S : 1 ½ km by Rd 73 ℰ 725 90 00, Telex 12630,
Fax 649 08 80, 🖨 – ⧫ ᐳⵗ rm 🔟 ☎ ᕀ, 🚗 – 🚗 220. 🖭 ⓪ 🗲 🎟. 🛠   CZ
M 185/345 and a la carte – **281 rm** ⌑ 1040/1545, **9 suites** 2675/4800.

Palace, S : t Eriksgatan 115, Box 21034, S-100 31, ℰ 24 12 20, Telex 19877, Fax 30 23 29, 🖨
– ⧫ ᐳⵗ rm 🔟 ☎ 🚗 – 🚗 130. 🖭 ⓪ 🗲 🎟   BX m
closed Christmas-New Year – **M** (closed Sunday) (buffet lunch) 65 and a la carte approx.
210 – **213 rm** ⌑ 950/1350, **5 suites** 1500/1800.

Berns, Näckströmsgatan 8, Berzelii Park, S-111 47, ℰ 614 07 00, Telex 12132, Fax 611 51 75
– ⧫ ᐳⵗ rm 🔟 ☎ 🖭 ⓪ 🗲 🎟   CY b
closed 23 to 30 December – **M** Röda Rummet (closed Sunday lunch, 23 June, 24-25 December
and 1 January) 139 and a la carte – **59 rm** ⌑ 1350/1975, **3 suites** 2800/4000.

Park, Karlavägen 43, S-102 45, ℰ 22 96 20, Telex 10666, Fax 21 62 68, 🖨 – ⧫ ᐳⵗ rm 🔟
☎ ᕀ, 🚗 – 🚗 120   CX t
193 rm, **9 suites**.

City, Slöjdgatan 7, Hötorget, Box 1132, S-111 81, ℰ 22 22 40, Telex 12487, Fax 20 82 24, 🖨
– ⧫ ᐳⵗ rm 🔟 ☎ – 🚗 70. 🖭 ⓪ 🗲 🎟. 🛠   CY c
closed 20 December-1 January – **M** (closed Sunday dinner) (unlicensed) 150/180 and a la
carte – **300 rm** ⌑ 925/1050.

Malmen, Götgatan 49 - 51, Box 4069, S-102 61, ℰ 22 60 80, Telex 19489, Fax 641 11 48, 🖨
– ⧫ ᐳⵗ rm 🔟 ☎ ᕀ, 🚗 – 🚗 100. 🖭 ⓪ 🗲 🎟   CZ d
closed 20 December-2 January – **M** (closed Sunday except summer) 135/180 and a la carte
– **278 rm** ⌑ 1040/1450, **2 suites** 2000/2500.

Birger Jarl without rest. (unlicensed), Tulegatan 8, Box 19016, S-104 32, ℰ 15 10 20, Telex
11843, Fax 673 73 66, 🖨 – ⧫ ᐳⵗ rm 🔟 ☎ 🚗 – 🚗 175. 🖭 ⓪ 🗲 🎟   CX z
closed 20 December-2 January – **229 rm** ⌑ 900/1260, **6 suites** 1400/1550.

Wellington without rest., Storgatan 6, S-114 51, ℰ 667 09 10, Telex 17963, Fax 667 12 54,
🖨 – ⧫ ᐳⵗ rm 🔟 ☎ 🖭 ⓪ 🗲 🎟   DY p
closed 21 December-2 January – **50 rm** ⌑ 970/1400, **1 suite** 1600/1800.

Freys, Bryggargatan 12b, Box 70439, S-107 25, ℰ 20 13 00, Telex 16750, Fax 24 22 24 – ⧫
ᐳⵗ rm 🔟 ☎ ᕀ, 🖭 ⓪ 🗲 🎟   BY u
M (closed Sunday lunch) 150/95 – **99 rm** ⌑ 870/990.

XXXXX **Operakällaren,** (at Opera House), **Operahuset, Box 1616, S-111 86,** ✆ **24 27 00, Fax 20 95 92,** « **Opulent classical decor** » CY

XXXXX **Franska Matsalen** (at Grand H.), **Södra Blasieholmshamnen 8, Box 16424, S-103 27,** ✆ **22 10 20, Telex 19500, Fax 21 86 88,** ≤ – AE ⓓ E VISA CY **r**
closed Saturday lunch and Sunday – **M** 198/695 and a la carte.

XXX ✿ **L'Escargot, 1st. floor, Scheelegatan 8, S-112 23,** ✆ **53 05 77, Fax 53 60 05** – ▤. AE ⓓ E VISA BY **s**
closed Sunday and 8 July-4 August – **M** (dinner only) 395/560 and a la carte 372/452
Spec. Escargots au beurre Roquefort, Assiette de poissons et crustacés avec fenouil, tomates et sauce basilic, Duo aux deux chocolats.

XXX ✿ **Michel** (Settergren), **Karlavägen 73, S-114 49,** ✆ **662 22 62** – AE ⓓ E VISA DX **r**
closed Saturday lunch, Sunday, midsummer, Christmas, New Year, Easter and Bank Holidays – **M** 225/725 and a la carte 405/745
Spec. Cured salmon with crème fraîche spiced with bleak roe and red onion, Duck livers with fresh beetroot and port sauce, White chocolate mousse with thin leaves of dark chocolate, raspberry sauce.

XX ✿ **Paul and Norbert** (Lang), **Strandvägen 9, S-114 56,** ✆ **663 81 83** – AE ⓓ E VISA DY **m**
closed Saturday, Sunday, July, 24 December-8 January, Easter and Bank Holidays – **M** (booking essential) 200/940 and a la carte 465/545
Spec. Roe deer tartar marinated in vodka, Baked fillet of blackcock in savoy cabbage with a port wine sauce, Armagnac marinated prune soufflé with mace ice cream.

XX **Coq Blanc, Regeringsgatan 111, S-111 39,** ✆ **11 61 53, Fax 10 76 35** – ▤. AE ⓓ E VISA
closed Saturday lunch, Monday dinner, Sunday, 21 June-5 August and Bank Holidays – **M** 350/450 and a la carte. CX **n**

XX **Wärdshuset Stallmästaregården,** Norrtull, S-113 47, N : 2 km (at beginning of E 4) ✆ **24 39 11, Fax 31 50 16,** ≤, 斎, « **17C inn, waterside setting** », 舟 – **P**. AE ⓓ E VISA
M 325 and a la carte 290/440. by Sveavägen BX

XX **Riche,** Birger Jarlsgatan 4, S-114 34, ✆ **10 70 22** – ▤. AE ⓓ E VISA CY **e**
closed Sunday and July – **M** 200/225 and a la carte.

XX **Teatergrillen,** Nybrogatan 3, S-114 34, ✆ **611 70 44, Fax 611 05 13,** « **Theatre atmosphere** » – ▤. AE ⓓ E VISA CY **e**
closed Sunday and July – **M** 200/225 and a la carte.

XX **Den Gyldene Freden,** Österlånggatan 51, S-103 17, ✆ **24 97 60, Fax 21 38 70** – AE ⓓ E VISA AZ **s**
closed Sunday – **M** (dinner only) 320/420 and a la carte.

XX **Clas På Hörnet** with rm, **Surbrunnsgatan 20, S-113 48,** ✆ **16 51 30, Fax 612 53 15,** « **18C atmosphere** » – 閣 TV ☎. AE ⓓ E VISA. ✻ CX **f**
closed 24 to 26 December – **M** *(closed lunch Saturday and Sunday)* 185/350 and a la carte – **10 rm** ⊇ 1065/1560.

XX **Gourmet,** Tegnérgatan 10, S-113 58, ✆ **31 43 98, Fax 32 93 67** – ▤. AE ⓓ E VISA CX **r**
closed Saturday lunch, Sunday, 1 July-11 August and Bank Holidays – **M** 280/580 and a la carte.

XX **Nils Emil,** Folkungagatan 122, S-116 30, ✆ **640 72 09** – ▤. AE ⓓ E VISA DZ **a**
closed Saturday lunch, Sunday, 21 June-29 July and Bank Holidays – **M** (booking essential) 170 (lunch) and a la carte 285/440.

XX **La Brochette,** Storgatan 27, S-114 55, ✆ **662 20 00, Fax 622 37 75,** 斎 – ▤. AE ⓓ E VISA
closed Sunday – **M Ma Cave** ✆ 60 25 28 (basement, with cellar) 200/250 and a la carte – **Brasserie** *(ground floor).* DY **e**

X ✿ **Wedholms Fisk** (Wedholm), **Nybrokajen 17,** ✆ **10 48 74** – AE ⓓ E VISA CY **s**
closed Sunday, 6 July-6 August and Bank Holidays – **M** (lunch) 130 and a la carte 195/465
Spec. Tartar of salmon and salmon roe with crème fraîche, Grilled turbot with Dijon hollandaise sauce, Fricassé of sole, turbot, lobster, and scallops with a champagne sauce.

X ✿ **KB,** Smålandsgatan 7, S-111 46, ✆ **679 60 32, Fax 791 22 24** – AE ⓓ E VISA CY **u**
closed Saturday lunch, Sunday and late June-mid August – **M** 98/350 and a la carte 195/435
Spec. Marinated fillets of Baltic herring in dill sauce, Roast lamb with artichoke bottom and morel mushrooms, Almond basket with arctic raspberry sorbet.

X **Greitz,** Vasagatan 50, S- 111 20, ✆ **23 48 20, Fax 24 20 93** – AE ⓓ E VISA BY **a**
closed Saturday lunch, Sunday and Bank Holidays – **M** 275 and a la carte.

Gamla Stan (Old Stockholm) :

🏨 **Reisen,** Skeppsbron 12-14, S-111 30, ✆ **22 32 60, Telex 17494, Fax 20 15 59,** ≤, « **Original maritime decor** », ≦s, ⊠ – 閣 ⇆ rm ▤ rest TV ☎ – 🏃 60. AE ⓓ E VISA AZ **f**
closed 22 December-2 January – **M** *(closed lunch July)* 250/590 and a la carte – **110 rm** ⊇ 1300/2750, **3 suites** 3900/4500.

🏨 **Victory,** Lilla Nygatan 5, S-111 28, ✆ **14 30 90, Telex 14050, Fax 20 21 77,** « **Swedish rural furnishings, maritime antiques** », ≦s – 閣 ⇆ rm ▤ TV ☎ – 🏃 90. AE ⓓ E VISA. ✻
closed 20 to 29 December – **M** (see **Leijontornet** below) – **44 rm** ⊇ 1715/2300, **4 suites** 3265/5900. AZ **v**

🏨 **Lady Hamilton** without rest., **Storkyrkobrinken 5, S-111 28,** ✆ **23 46 80, Telex 10434, Fax 11 11 48,** « **Swedish rural antiques** », ≦s – 閣 TV ☎. AE ⓓ E VISA. ✻ AZ **e**
closed 20 December-2 January – **34 rm** ⊇ 1480/1845.

🏨 **Mälardrottningen,** Riddarholmen, S-111 28, 𝒫 24 36 00, Telex 15864, Fax 24 36 76, ⩽, « Formerly Barbara Hutton's yacht », 🕿 – 🖭 🔟 🕿 – ⚿ 20. 🖭 ⒶⒺ ⓞ 🇪 𝑉𝐼𝑆𝐴　　　　　　 AZ **n**
  closed 21 December-7 January – **M** (closed Sunday in winter) 75/200 and a la carte – **58 rm**
  (cabins) ⌓ 750/1050, **1 suite**.

🏨 **Gamla Stan** without rest., Lilla Nygatan 25, S-111 28, 𝒫 24 44 50, Telex 13896, Fax 21 64 83
  – |🕭| ⁓ rm 🔟 🕿 – ⚿ 25. 🖭 ⒶⒺ ⓞ 🇪 𝑉𝐼𝑆𝐴 – closed Christmas – **51 rm** ⌓ 915/1590.　　 AZ **c**

🏠 **Lord Nelson** without rest., Västerlånggatan 22, S-111 29, 𝒫 23 23 90, Telex 10434, Fax
  10 10 89, « Ship style installation, maritime antiques », 🕿 – |🕭| 🔟 🕿. 🖭 ⓞ 🇪 𝑉𝐼𝑆𝐴. ⌘
  closed 17 December-2 January – **31 rm** ⌓ 1025/1480.　　　　　　　　　　　　 AZ **a**

XXX ⊛ **Eriks** (Lallerstedt), Österlånggatan 17, S-111 31, 𝒫 23 85 00, Fax 796 60 69, Seafood –
  ▤. 🖭 ⓞ 🇪 𝑉𝐼𝑆𝐴　　　　　　　　　　　　　　　　　　　　　　　　　　　　　　 AZ **u**
  closed Sunday, July and Christmas-New Year – **M** a la carte 421/593
  Spec. Marinated Baltic herring, Ragout of salmon, scallops, mushrooms, peppers and potatoes, Fudge pie
  with whipped cream.

XX ⊛ **Leijontornet** (at Victory H.), Lilla Nygatan 5, S-111 28, 𝒫 14 23 55, Telex 14050, Fax
  20 21 77, 🏠, « Remains of a 14C fortification tower in the dining room » – 🖭 ⓞ 🇪 𝑉𝐼𝑆𝐴
  closed Saturday lunch, Sunday, July and Bank Holidays – **M** 300/580 and (dinner) a la carte
  330/570　　　　　　　　　　　　　　　　　　　　　　　　　　　　　　　　　　 AZ **v**
  Spec. Scallops with cress mousse and oyster sauce, Breast of grouse with savoy cabbage and port wine sauce,
  White chocolate mousse with coffee cream.

XX **Källaren Aurora,** Munkbron 11, S-111 28, 𝒫 21 93 59, Fax 11 16 22, « In the cellars of a
  17C house » – ▤. 🖭 ⓞ 🇪 𝑉𝐼𝑆𝐴　　　　　　　　　　　　　　　　　　　　　　　 AZ **x**
  closed Sunday and Bank Holidays – **M** (dinner only) 385/475 and a la carte.

XX **Fem Små Hus,** Nygränd 10, S-111 30, 𝒫 10 87 75, Fax 14 96 95, « 17C Cellars, antiques »
  – ▤. 🖭 ⓞ 🇪 𝑉𝐼𝑆𝐴 – **M** 145/360 and a la carte.　　　　　　　　　　　　　 AZ **r**

to the E :

at Djurgården E : 3 km by Strandvägen DY – ✉ ⊛ 08 Stockholm :

XXX ⊛ **Villa Källhagen** ⌘ with rm, Djurgårdsbrunnsvägen 10, S-115 27, 𝒫 667 60 63, Fax
  667 60 43, ⩽, « Waterside setting, garden », 🕿 – |🕭| ⁓ rm 🖭 🔟 🕿 ② – ⚿ 40
  19 rm, 1 suite.

to the NW :

at Solna 5 km by Sveavägen – BX – and E4 – ✉ Solna – ⊛ 08 Stockholm :

XXX ⊛ **Ulriksdals Wärdshus** (Krücken), 171 71 Solna, Exit E 18/E 3 from E4 𝒫 85 08 15, Fax
  85 08 58, ⩽, « Former inn in Royal Park », ⌘ – ②. 🖭 ⓞ 🇪 𝑉𝐼𝑆𝐴
  closed Sunday, 24 to 26 December and Bank Holidays – **M** 460 (dinner) and a la carte
  490/570
  Spec. Papillon d'avocat, oeufs d'ablette, Gelinotte aux raisins, Melon en surprise.

XX **Finsmakaren,** Råsundavägen 9, 171 52 Solna, 𝒫 27 67 71 – 🖭 ⓞ 🇪 𝑉𝐼𝑆𝐴
  closed Saturday, Sunday, 1 July-8 August, 21 December-10 January and Bank Holidays –
  M 405/460 and a la carte.

at Sollentuna 15 km by Sveavägen – BX – and E4 – ✉ Sollentuna – ⊛ 08 Stockholm :

XX **Edsbacka Krog,** Sollentunavägen 220, 191 47, 𝒫 96 33 00, Fax 92 80 55, « 17C inn » – ②.
  🖭 ⓞ 🇪 𝑉𝐼𝑆𝐴 – closed Saturday lunch, Monday dinner, Sunday, 7 July-5 August and Bank
  Holidays – **M** 275/500 and a la carte.

at Arlanda Airport 40 km by Sveavägen – BX – and E4 – ⊛ 0760 Arlanda :

🏨 **SAS Arlandia,** 190 45 Stockholm - Arlanda 𝒫 618 00, Telex 13018, Fax 619 70, 🏠, 🕿,
  🅽, ⚿ ⁓ rm 🖭 🔟 🕿 ⌕ ② – ⚿ 250. 🖭 ⓞ 🇪 𝑉𝐼𝑆𝐴
  M (buffet lunch) 195 and dinner a la carte 240/380 – **337 rm** ⌓ 1195/1595, **8 suites** 1700.

■GOTHENBURG■ (GÖTEBORG) Sverige 🏙🏙🏙 0 8 – pop. 429 339 – ⊛ 031.

See : Art Gallery★★★ (Konstmuseum) CX **M1** – Castle Park★★★ (Slottsskogen) AX – Botanical
Gardens★★ (Botaniska Trädgården) AX – East India House★★ (Ostindiska Huset) BU **M2** – Liseberg
Amusement Park★★ (Lisebergs Nöjespark) DX – Natural History Museum★★ (Naturhistoriska
Museet) AX – Röhss Museum of Arts and Crafts★★ (Röhsska Konstslöjdmuseet) BV **M3** – Älvsborg
Bridge★ (Älvsborgsbron) AV – Kungsportsavenyn★ CVX **22** – Maritime Centre★ (Maritim Centrum)
(Viking★) BT – Maritime Museum★ (Sjöfartsmuseet) AV – New Älvsborg Fortress★ (Nya Älvsborgs
Fästning) AU – Götaplatsen (Carl Milles, Poseidon★★) CX – Seaman's Tower (Sjöman-
stornet) (✳★★) AV – Masthugg Church (Masthuggskyrkran) (inside★) AV.

Envir. : Northern and southern archipelago★ (Hönö, Öckerö, Vrångö) – Kungsbacka: Tjolöholms
Castle★, S : 40 km by E6.

🇮🇸 Albatross, Lillbagsvägen Hisings Backa, R 15 𝒫 55 04 40 – 🇮🇸 Delsjö, Kallebäck, H 7 𝒫 40 69 59
– 🇮🇸 Göteborgs, Golfbanevägen, Hovås, R 23 𝒫 28 24 44.

✈ Scandinavian Airlines System : Norra Hamngatan 20-22 𝒫 94 20 00/63 85 00 Landvetter
Airport : 𝒫 94 10 00 – ⚓ To Denmark : contact Stena Line A/B, Telex 20886, Fax 24 10 38 – To
continent : contact Scandinavian Seaways 𝒫 65 06 00, Telex 21724.

🄱 Basargatan 10 (vid Kungsportsplatsen), F 5 𝒫 10 07 40 – Kungsportsplatsen 2 𝒫 17 11 70.

Copenhague 279 – Oslo 322 – Stockholm 500.

Plan on following pages

Sheraton Göteborg, Södra Hamngatan 59-65, Box 288, S-401 24, ℰ 80 60 00, Telex 28250, Fax 15 98 88, ⇌, 🔲 ఈ⚬ rm 🔳 📺 ☎ 𝄢 ⇐⇒ – 🛗 450. 🖭 ⓞ ᴇ 𝘝𝘐𝘚𝘈. ⅏   BU **b**
closed mid June-mid August, Christmas and New Year – **M Madeleine** *(closed Saturday and sunday)* (dinner only) 265/545 and a la carte – **Frascati** *(closed Saturday lunch)* 175/195 and a la carte 207/319 – **325 rm** ⊑ 1650/1850, **17 suites** 2190/6700.

Park Avenue, Kungsportsavenyn 36-38, Box 53 233, S-400 16, ℰ 17 65 20, Telex 2320, Fax 16 95 68, ≼, ⇌, 🔲 – 🛗 🍽 rest 📺 ☎ – 🔏 600. 🖭 ⓞ ᴇ 𝘝𝘐𝘚𝘈   CX **f**
M Belle Avenue a la carte 320/485 – **Harlequin** – **301 rm** ⊑ 1340/2035, **17 suites** 1800/3400.

Scandic Crown, Polhemsplatsen 3, S-411 11, ℰ 80 09 00, Fax 15 45 88, ⇌ – 🛗 ఈ⚬ rm 🔳 📺 ☎ ఈ ⊕ – 🔏 200. 🖭 ⓞ ᴇ 𝘝𝘐𝘚𝘈   CU **d**
closed 23 to 27 December – **M Primary** – **Kåsören** 58 (lunch) and a la carte 191/363 – **315 rm** ⊑ 980/1125, **5 suites** 1700/2700.

Gothia, Mässans Gata, Box 5184, S-402 26, ℰ 40 93 00, Telex 21941, Fax 18 98 04, ≼, ⇌ – 🛗 📺 ☎ ఈ   DX **k**
M Grandeur – **Gallery** – **298 rm**, **2 suites**.

Europa, Köpmansgatan 38, Box 264, S-401 24, ℰ 80 12 80, Telex 21374, Fax 15 47 55, ⇌, 🔲 – 🛗 ఈ⚬ rm 🔳 📺 ☎ ⊕ – 🔏 50. 🖭 ⊑ 1160/1515, **5 suites** 2250/4250.   BU **a**
M 154/245 and a la carte – **475 rm**

Scandinavia, Kustgatan 10, Box 12123, S-402 42, ℰ 42 70 00, Telex 21522, Fax 12 29 65, ≼, ⇌, 🔲 – 🛗 ఈ⚬ rm 📺 ☎ ⇐⇒ – 🔏 120   by E 3   AV
317 rm, **6 suites**.

Opalen, Engelbrektsgatan 73, Box 5106, S-402 23, ℰ 81 03 00, Telex 2215, Fax 18 76 22, ≼ – 🛗 ఈ⚬ rm 📺 ☎ ⇐⇒ ⊕ – 🔏 180. 🖭 ⓞ ᴇ 𝘝𝘐𝘚𝘈   DV **u**
M 153/270 and a la carte – **235 rm** ⊑ 1070/1405, **2 suites** 1500/2900.

Rubinen, Kunsportsavenyn 24, Box 53097, S-400 14, ℰ 81 08 00, Telex 20837, Fax 16 75 86 – 🛗 ఈ⚬ rm 📺 ☎ ఈ ⊕ – 🔏 40. 🖭 ⓞ ᴇ 𝘝𝘐𝘚𝘈   CV **c**
M 200/300 and a la carte – **177 rm** ⊑ 1085/1385, **8 suites** 1670/2570.

Panorama, Eklandagatan 51-53, Box 24037, S-400 22, ℰ 81 08 80, Telex 27716, Fax 81 42 37, ≼, ⇌ – 🛗 ఈ⚬ rm 🔳 📺 ☎ ఈ ⊕ – 🔏 100. 🖭 ⓞ ᴇ 𝘝𝘐𝘚𝘈   DX **s**
closed 20 December-7 January – **M** *(closed lunch Saturday and Sunday)* 165/240 and a la carte – **340 rm** ⊑ 990/1390.

Riverton, Stora Badhusgatan 26, Box 2547, S-403 17, ℰ 10 12 00, Telex 21590, Fax 13 08 66, ≼, ⇌ – 🛗 ఈ⚬ rm 📺 ☎ ఈ ⊕ – 🔏 300. 🖭 ⓞ ᴇ 𝘝𝘐𝘚𝘈. ⅏   AU **c**
closed 21 to 26 December – **M** *(closed Sunday)* (dinner only) 100/210 and a la carte – **177 rm** ⊑ 1120/1445.

Victors, Skeppsbroplatsen 1, S-411 18, ℰ 17 41 80, Telex 20076, Fax 13 96 10, ≼, ⇌ – 🛗 📺 ☎ – 🔏 30. 🖭 ⓞ ᴇ 𝘝𝘐𝘚𝘈   AU **b**
closed 29 March-2 April, 1 July-5 August and 20 December-7 January – **M** *(closed 14 December)* a la carte approx. 485 – **31 rm** ⊑ 950/1150, **9 suites** 1395/1695.

Windsor, Kungsportsavenyn 6-8, S-411 36, ℰ 17 65 40, Telex 21014, Fax 11 34 39, ⇌ – 🛗 ఈ⚬ rm 🔳 📺 ☎ ⊕ – 🔏 35. 🖭 ⓞ ᴇ 𝘝𝘐𝘚𝘈   CV **e**
closed 20 December-2 January – **M** (see **Brasserie Lipp** below) – **91 rm** ⊑ 940/1490.

Tidbloms, Olskroksgatan 23, Box 6162, S-400 60, NE : 3 km ℰ 19 20 70, Telex 27369, Fax 19 78 35, ⇌ – ఈ⚬ rm 📺 ☎ ఈ ⊕ – 🔏 50. 🖭 ⓞ ᴇ 𝘝𝘐𝘚𝘈   by Redbergsvägen   DT
closed 20 December-8 January – **M** *(closed Sunday dinner and Saturday)* 250/300 – **42 rm** ⊑ 940/1080.

Novotel, Klippan 1, S-414 51, SW : 3,5 km ℰ 14 90 00, Telex 28181, Fax 42 22 32, ≼, ⇌ – 🛗 ఈ⚬ rm 📺 ☎ ఈ ⊕ – 🔏 250. 🖭 ⓞ ᴇ 𝘝𝘐𝘚𝘈   by E 3   AV
M 150/200 and a la carte – ⊑ 52 – **146 rm** ⊑ 955/1085, **4 suites** 1475.

Liseberg Heden, Sten Sturegatan, S-411 38, ℰ 20 02 80, Telex 27450, Fax 16 52 83 – 🛗 ఈ⚬ rm 📺 ☎ ఈ ⊕ – 🔏 80. 🖭 ⓞ ᴇ 𝘝𝘐𝘚𝘈   CV **b**
closed 20 December-6 January – **M** *(closed lunch Saturday and Sunday)* 150 and a la carte 235/305 – **159 rm** ⊑ 870/1500.

Ekoxen without rest., Norra Hamngatan 38, S-411 06, ℰ 80 50 80, Telex 21993, Fax 11 33 76, ⇌ – 🛗 ఈ⚬ 📺 ☎. 🖭 ⓞ ᴇ 𝘝𝘐𝘚𝘈   BU **c**
74 rm ⊑ -/1095, **1 suite** 2150.

Kung Karl without rest., Nils Ericssongatan 23, Box 428, S-401 26, ℰ 80 58 35, Telex 21908, Fax 80 58 17, ⇌ – 🛗 ఈ⚬ 📺 ⊜. 🖭 ⓞ ᴇ 𝘝𝘐𝘚𝘈. ⅏   BU **e**
70 rm ⊑ 720/980.

Poseidon without rest., Storgatan 33, S-411 38, ℰ 10 05 50, Telex 27663, Fax 13 83 91, ⇌ – 🛗 ఈ⚬ 📺 ☎ ⇐⇒. 🖭 ⓞ ᴇ 𝘝𝘐𝘚𝘈. ⅏   BV **a**
closed 21 to 23 June and 22 to 27 December – **49 rm** ⊑ 890/1070.

Klang without rest., Stora Badhusgatan 28b, S-411 21, ℰ 17 40 50, Fax 17 40 58 – 🛗 ఈ⚬ 📺 ☎. 🖭 ⓞ ᴇ 𝘝𝘐𝘚𝘈. ⅏   AV **f**
closed 22 December-3 January – **50 rm** ⊑ 550/900.

XXX **Johanna,** Södra Hamngatan 47, S-411 06, ℰ 15 20 50   BU **f**

XXX ❀ **The Place** (Wagner), Arkivgatan 7, S-411 34, ℰ 16 03 33, Fax 16 78 54 – 🖭 ⓞ ᴇ 𝘝𝘐𝘚𝘈
closed Sunday and 22 December-2 January – **M** (dinner only) 650 and a la carte 345/495
Spec. Smoked breast of pigeon with a luke warm salad of beetroot and truffles. Supreme of chicken with goose liver in savoy cabbage and a lemon sauce. Fresh figs in baklava pastry with Cognac sauce.   CX **d**

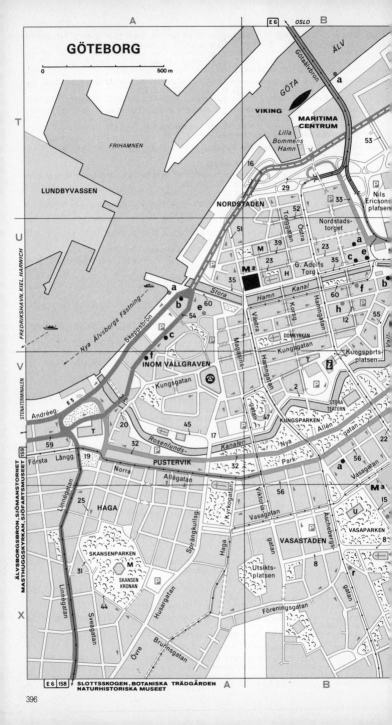

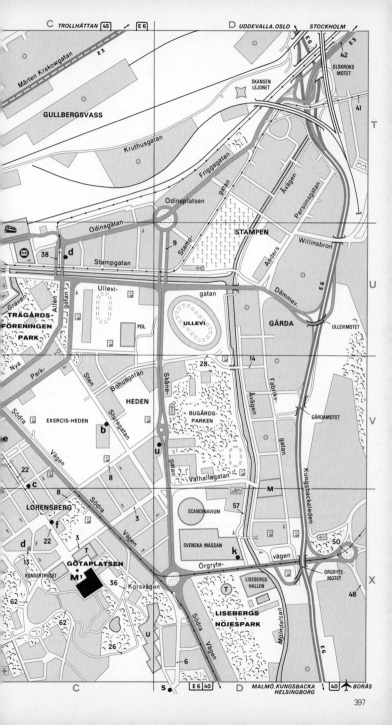

STREET INDEX TO GÖTEBORG TOWN PLAN

✕✕✕ Westra Piren, at Eriksberg, Docks (on Pier No 4), S-402 79, NW : 3 km by Götaälvbron BT
✆ 51 95 55, Fax 23 99 40, 佘, « Dockside setting, overlooking the harbour » – ℿ ① ℇ 𝑉𝐼𝑆𝐴
closed July-5 August – **M** (booking essential) 255/520 and a la carte – **Brasserie** a la carte
approx. 260.

✕✕ Le Chablis, Aschebergsgatan 22, S-411 27, *✆* 20 35 45, Fax 20 82 01, seafood – ℿ ① ℇ
𝑉𝐼𝑆𝐴 BX r
closed 15 July-5 August, Christmas and New Year – **M** (dinner only) 475 and a la carte.

✕✕ S/S Marieholm, Skeppsbroplatsen, Stenpiren, S-403 20, *✆* 13 88 80, Fax 13 65 70, ≤,
seafood, « Converted Ship » – ℿ ① ℇ 𝑉𝐼𝑆𝐴 AU a
closed Saturday and Sunday – **M** 175/395 and a la carte.

✕✕ Fiskekrogen, Lilla Torget 1, S-411 18, *✆* 11 21 84, Fax 74 04 83, seafood – ℿ ① ℇ 𝑉𝐼𝑆𝐴
closed Sunday and Bank Holidays – **M** 250 and a la carte 190/320. AU e

✕✕ Sjömagasinet, Klippans Kulturreservat, S-414 51, SW : 3,5 km *✆* 24 65 10, Fax 24 55 39,
≤, seafood, « Former East India company warehouse » – ℗. ℿ ① ℇ 𝑉𝐼𝑆𝐴 by E 3 AV
closed Sunday – **M** 300/400 and a la carte.

✕✕ ✪ 28 ✝ (Lyxell), Götabergsgatan 28, S-411 34, *✆* 20 21 61, Fax 20 21 61, « Cellar » – ℿ ① ℇ
𝑉𝐼𝑆𝐴 BX n
*closed Saturday lunch, Sunday, 29 March-1 April, 20 June-4 August, 22 December-6 January
and Bank Holidays* – **M** 85/238 and a la carte 270/450
Spec. Grilled fillet of sole with mushrooms, eel paté and a red wine sauce. Fillet of roe deer with a cheese
sauce, apple chutney and hazelnut timbale. Fillet of lamb with a small sausage, onion marmelade and morel
sauce.

✕✕ Stallgården, Kyrkogatan 33, S-404 25, *✆* 13 03 16, « Interior courtyard » BU h

✕ Eriksbergsfärjan, Gullbergskajen, Plats 212, S-411 04, *✆* 15 35 05, ≤ – ℿ ① ℇ 𝑉𝐼𝑆𝐴
closed dinner Monday, Thursday and Friday and Saturday – **M** 155 (dinner) and a la carte
210/335. BT a

✕ Brasserie Lipp (at Windsor H.), Kungsportsavenyn 6-8, S-411 36, *✆* 11 50 58, Telex 21014,
Fax 11 34 39, 佘, « French brasserie style » – ℿ ① ℇ 𝑉𝐼𝑆𝐴 CV e
closed Sunday (15 September-15 April), Christmas and New Year – **M** 195 and a la carte
200/350.

at Landvetter Airport E : 30 km – ✉ **S-438 02** Landvetter.

🏨 Landvetter Airport Hotel, Box 2103, ✉ S-438 02, *✆* 94 64 10, Telex 28733, Fax 94 64 70 – 🛗
‰ rm 📺 ☎ & ℗ – 🔏 20. ℿ ① ℇ 𝑉𝐼𝑆𝐴. ✵ by Rd 40 DX
closed Christmas – **M** *(closed lunch Saturday and Sunday)* – **38 rm** ⇆ 830/950, **6 suites**
1250.

Switzerland
Suisse
Schweiz
Svizzera

Basle
Geneva
Zürich

PRACTICAL INFORMATION

LOCAL CURRENCY

Swiss Franc : 100 F = 77.61 US $ (Jan. 91)

LANGUAGES SPOKEN

German, French and Italian are usually spoken in all administrative departments, shops, hotels and restaurants.

AIRLINES

A large number of international airlines operate out of the main Swiss airports. For general information ring the number given after the airport symbol and name in the text of each town.

POSTAL SERVICES

In large towns, post offices are open from 7.30am to noon and 1.45pm to 6.30pm, and Saturdays untill 11am. The telephone system is fully automatic.

SHOPPING

Department stores are generally open from 8.30am to 6pm, except on Saturdays when they close at 4 or 5pm.

In the index of street names, those printed in red are where the principal shops are found.

TIPPING

In hotels, restaurants and cafés the service charge is generally included in the prices.

SPEED LIMITS – MOTORWAYS

The speed limit on motorways is 120 km/h - 74 mph, on other roads 80 km/h - 50 mph, and in built up areas 50 km/h - 31 mph.

Driving on Swiss motorways is subject to the purchase of a single rate vignette (one per car) obtainable from frontier posts, tourist offices and post offices.

SEAT BELTS

The wearing of seat belts is compulsory in all Swiss cantons for front seat passengers.

BASLE (BASEL) 4000 Switzerland 🔲 🔲 ④ — pop. 180 463 h. alt. 273 — ✿ Basle and environs from France 19-41-61 from Switzerland 061.

See : Cathedral (Munster)★★ : ≤★ CY — Zoological Garden★★★ AZ — The Port (Hafen)※★, Exposition★ CX — Fish Market Fountain★ (Fischmarktbrunnen)BY — Old Streets★ BY — Oberer Rheinweg ≤★ CY — Museums : Fine Arts★★★ (Kunstmuseum) CY, Historical★ (Historisches Museum)CY, Ethnographic (Museum für Völkerkunde) ★ CY M1 — Haus zum Kirschgarten★ CZ, Antiquities (Antikenmuseum)★ CY — ※★ from Bruderholz Water Tower 3,5 km by ⑥.

🏌 private ℰ 89 68 50 91 at Hagenthal-le-Bas (68-France) SW : 10 km.

✈ Basle-Mulhouse ℰ 325 31 11 at Basle (Switzerland) by Zollfreie Strasse 8 km and at Saint-Louis (68-France) ℰ 89 69 00 00.

🚄 Office de Tourisme Blumenrain 2/Schifflände ℰ 25 50 50 (from April 1991 ℰ 261 50 50), Telex 963318 and at Railway Station (Bahnhof) (Mars-Sept.) ℰ 22 36 84 — A.C. Suisse, Birsigstr. 4 ℰ 23 39 33 — T.C.S., Petrihof, Steinentorstr. 13ℰ 23 19 55.

Paris 554 ⑧ — Bern 95 ⑤ — Freiburg 71 ① — Lyon 401 ⑧ — Mulhouse 35 ⑧ — Strasbourg 145 ①.

Plan on following pages

🏨 **Trois Rois,** Blumenrain 8 ⊠ 4001 ℰ 261 52 52, Telex 962937, Fax 261 21 53, ≤, 🍴 — 🛗 📺 ⚏ 📺 ⚙ 🛗 🖢 80. 🖭 ⓘ ᕮ 𝘝𝘐𝘚𝘈 ※ rest BY **a**
Rôtisserie des Rois **M** 48/89 🍴 — Rhy-Deck **M** 15/35 🍴 — ⚌ 25 — **89 rm** 200/440, 8 apartments.

🏨 **Plaza** Ⓜ, Riehenring 45 ⊠ 4058 ℰ 692 33 33, Telex 964439, Fax 691 56 33, 🔲 — 🛗 ⟨≠⟩ rm 📺 📺 ⚙ 🖢 ᕮ ⊶ — 🖢 50. 🖭 ⓘ ᕮ 𝘝𝘐𝘚𝘈 ※ rest DX **r**
Rôtisserie Plaza *(closed Sunday)* **M** a la carte 65/98 🍴 — **Grand Café M** a la carte 25/50 🍴 — **240 rm** ⚌ 240/380, 3 apartments.

🏨 **International** Ⓜ, Steinentorstrasse 25 ⊠ 4001 ℰ 281 75 85, Telex 962370, Fax 281 76 27, ⛲ — 🛗 ⟨≠⟩ rm 📺 rm 📺 ⚙ ᕮ — 🖢 230. 🖭 ⓘ ᕮ 𝘝𝘐𝘚𝘈 BZ **b**
Steinenpick **M** a la carte 40/80 🍴 — **Rôt. Charolaise M** a la carte 50/85 🍴 — **210 rm** ⚌ 190/375, 5 apartments.

🏨 **Euler,** Centralbahnplatz 14 ⊠ 4002 ℰ 23 45 00, Telex 962215, Fax 22 50 00 — 🛗 ▤ rest 📺 ⚙ ⚏ ᕮ ⊶ — 🖢 160. 🖭 ⓘ ᕮ 𝘝𝘐𝘚𝘈 ※ rest CZ **a**
M a la carte 80/115 🍴 — ⚌ 16,50 — **55 rm** 225/395, 9 apartments 480/690.

🏨 **Hilton** Ⓜ, Aeschengraben 31 ⊠ 4002 ℰ 271 66 22, Telex 965555, Fax 271 52 20, 🔲 — 🛗 ⟨≠⟩ rm ▤ 📺 ⚙ 🖢 ᕮ — 🖢 50 - 300. 🖭 ⓘ ᕮ 𝘝𝘐𝘚𝘈 ※ rest CZ **d**
M 13/39 🍴 — ⚌ 19,50 — **217 rm** 185/310, 10 apartments.

🏨 ✿ **Europe et rest. Quatre Saisons** Ⓜ, Clarastrasse 43 ⊠ 4005 ℰ 691 80 80, Telex 964103, Fax 691 82 01 — 🛗 ⟨≠⟩ rm ▤ 📺 ⚙ ᕮ ⊶ — 🖢 40 - 100. 🖭 ⓘ ᕮ 𝘝𝘐𝘚𝘈 ※ rest CX **k**
M *(closed Sunday)* 75/155 🍴 — **170 rm** ⚌ 135/250
Spec. Crème d'artichauts et olives noires au carpaccio d'agneau, Blanc de turbot "Vaudoise", Pojarski de lapin à la truffe noire. **Wines** Maispracher.

🏨 **Schweizerhof,** Centralbahnplatz 1 ⊠ 4002 ℰ 271 28 33, Telex 962373, Fax 271 29 19, 🍴 — 🛗 ▤ 📺 ⚙ ⚏ — 🖢 100. 🖭 ⓘ ᕮ 𝘝𝘐𝘚𝘈 CZ **n**
M a la carte 60/100 — **75 rm** ⚌ 140/250.

🏨 **Mérian,** Rheingasse 2 ⊠ 4058 ℰ 681 00 00, Telex 964389, Fax 681 11 01, ≤, 🍴 — 🛗 📺 ⚙ ᕮ — 🖢 25 - 100. 🖭 ⓘ ᕮ 𝘝𝘐𝘚𝘈 CY **b**
M 25/45 🍴 — ⚌ 15 — **63 rm** 160/215.

🏨 **Basel,** Münzgasse 12 ⊠ 4051 ℰ 25 24 23, Telex 964199, Fax 25 25 95 — 🛗 ▤ rest 📺 ⚙ ᕮ 𝘝𝘐𝘚𝘈 BY **x**
M a la carte 65/115 — **71 rm** ⚌ 145/280.

🏨 **Métropol** without rest, Elisabethenanlage 5 ⊠ 4002 ℰ 22 77 21, Telex 962268, Fax 22 78 82 — 🛗 📺 ⚙ — 🖢 40 - 120. 🖭 ⓘ ᕮ 𝘝𝘐𝘚𝘈 CZ **a**
46 rm ⚌ 145/195.

🏨 **Krafft am Rhein** ⛵, Rheingasse 12 ⊠ 4058 ℰ 691 88 77, Telex 964360, Fax 691 09 07, ≤, 🍴 — 🛗 📺 ⚙ ᕮ 𝘝𝘐𝘚𝘈 CY **z**
M 13/45 🍴 — **52 rm** ⚌ 90/240 — ½ P 95/155.

🏨 **Muenchnerhof,** Riehenring 75 ⊠ 4058 ℰ 691 77 80, Telex 964476, Fax 691 14 90 — 🛗 📺 ⚙ 🖢 ᕮ 𝘝𝘐𝘚𝘈 CX **u**
M 12/60 🍴 — ⚌ 8,50 — **40 rm** 50/240.

🍴 ✿✿ **Stucki,** Bruderholzallee 42 ⊠ 4059 ℰ 35 82 22, Fax 35 82 03, 🍴, « Flowered garden » — ⚙. 🖭 ⓘ ᕮ 𝘝𝘐𝘚𝘈 by ⑥
closed 29 July-19 August, Sunday and Monday — **M** 95/155 and a la carte
Spec. Boudin noir aux reinettes (November-February), Côte de veau double "crémolata", Crêpe soufflée aux baies. **Wines** Pinot noir de Pratteln.

🍴 **Zum Schützenhaus,** Schützenmattstrasse 56 ⊠ 4051 ℰ 272 67 60, Fax 272 65 86, 🍴, « Converted 16C hunting lodge » — ⚙. 🖭 ⓘ ᕮ 𝘝𝘐𝘚𝘈 AY **e**
closed Sunday and Bank Holidays — **Garten Saal M** a la carte 75/120 — **Brasserie Le Schluuch M** carte approx. 70.

🍴 **Donati,** St-Johannsvorstadt 48 ⊠ 4056 ℰ 322 09 19, 🍴, Italian rest. BX **p**
closed 10 July-3 August, Monday and Tuesday — **M** a la carte 70/100 🍴.

🍴 **St Alban Eck,** St Alban Vorstadt 60 ⊠ 4052 ℰ 22 03 20 — 🖭 ⓘ ᕮ 𝘝𝘐𝘚𝘈 CDY **t**
closed 20 July-12 August, 21 December-6 January, Saturday and Sunday — **M** a la carte 65/95 🍴.

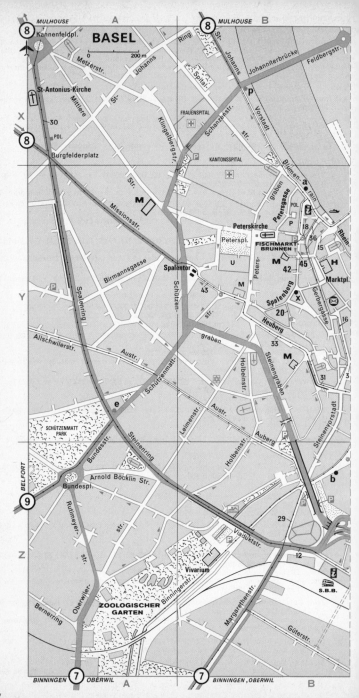

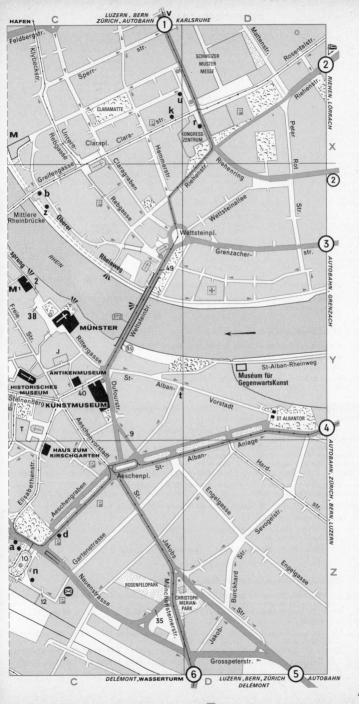

STREET INDEX TO BASEL TOWN PLAN

Aeschenvorstadt	CYZ	
Barfüsserpl.	BY	3
Centralbahnpl.	CZ	10
Clarapl.	CX	
Eisengasse	BY	15
Falknerstr.	BY	16
Freie Str.	CY	
Gerbergasse	BY	
Greifengasse	CY	
Marktpl.	BY	
Steinenvorstadt	BY	
Aeschengraben	CZ	
Aeschenpl.	CZ	
Allschwilerstr.	AY	
Arnold Böcklin-Str.	AZ	
Auberg	BYZ	
Augustinergasse	CY	2
Austr.	ABY	
Bernerring	AZ	
Birmannsgasse	AY	
Blumenrain	BY	
Brunngässlein	CY	9
Bundespl.	AZ	
Bundesstr.	AYZ	
Burgfelderpl.	AX	
Centralbahnstr.	CZ	12
Claragraben	CY	
Clarastr.	CX	
Dufourstr.	CY	
Elisabethenstr.	CZ	
Engelgasse	DZ	
Feldbergstr.	BCX	
Fischmarktpl.	BY	18
Gemsberg	BY	20
Grenzacherstr.	DY	
Grosspeterstr.	DZ	
Güterstr.	BZ	
Hammerstr.	CXY	
Hardstr.	DZ	
Heuberg	BY	
Holbeinstr.	BYZ	
Innere-Margarethenstr.	BZ	29
Jacob Burckhardt-Str.	DZ	
Johanniterbrücke	BX	
Kannenfeldpl.	AX	
Kannenfeldstr.	AX	30
Klingelbergstr.	AX	
Kohlenberg	BY	31
Leimenstr.	BY	
Leonhardsgraben	BY	33
Lindenhofstr.	CZ	35
Margarethenstr.	BZ	
Marktgasse	BY	36
Mattenstr.	DX	
Metzerstr.	AX	
Missionsstr.	AY	
Mittlere-Rheinbrücke	CY	
Mittlere-Str.	AXY	
Münchensteinerstr.	CZ	
Münsterpl.	CY	38
Nauenstr.	CZ	
Oberer-Rheinweg	CY	
Oberwilerstr.	AZ	
Peter Rot-Str.	DXY	
Petersgasse	BY	
Petersgraben	BY	
Peterspl.	BY	
Rebgasse	CY	
Rheinsprung	BCY	
Riehenring	DY	
Riehenstr.	DY	
Rittergasse	CY	
Rosentalstr.	DX	
Rutimeyerstr.	AZ	
St-Alban-Anlage	CDZ	
St-Alban-Graben	CY	40
St-Alban-Vorstadt	CDY	
St-Jakobs-Str.	CDZ	
St-Johanns-Ring	ABX	
St-Johanns-Vorstadt	BX	
Schanzenstr.	BX	
Schneidergasse	BY	42
Schützengraben	ABY	
Schützenmattstr.	ABY	
Sevogelstr.	DZ	
Spalenberg	BY	
Spalenring	AY	
Spalenvorstadt	BY	43
Sperrstr.	CX	
Spitalstr.	BX	
Stadthausgasse	BY	45
Steinenberg	CY	
Steinengraben	BY	
Steinenring	AYZ	
Untere-Rebgasse	CX	
Viaduktstr.	BZ	
Wettsteinallee	DY	
Wettsteinbrücke	CY	
Wettsteinpl.	CDY	
Wettsteinstr.	CY	49

at Binningen by ⑧ : 8 km : – ✉ **4102** Binningen :

XXX **Schloss Binningen,** Schlossgasse 5 ℰ 47 20 55, Fax 47 06 35, 斋, « 16C mansion, elegantly decorated, garden » – **P**. AE ① E VISA
closed 21 July-12 August, Sunday and Monday – **M** 88/120 ₰.

at the Basle-Mulhouse airport : by ⑧ : 8 km :

XX **Airport rest,** 5th floor in the airport, ← – ▤. AE ① E VISA.

Swiss Side, ✉ 4030 Bâle ℰ 325 32 32, Fax 325 39 19 – AE ① E VISA
M 54 ₰.

French Side, ✉ 68300 St-Louis ℰ 89 69 77 48, Fax 89 69 15 19 – AE ① E VISA
M (in FF) 173 ₰.

GENEVA Switzerland **74**, **217** ⑪ – pop. 239 517 h. Greater Geneva 613 102 alt. 375 – Casino – ✪ Geneva, environs:from France 19-41-22, from Switzerland 022.

See : The Shores of the lake ←*** – Parks** : Mon Repos, la Perle du Lac and Villa Barton – Botanical Garden* : alpine rock-garden** – Cathedral* : ✵** FY **F** – Reformation Monument* FYZ **D** – Palais des Nations* ←** – Parc de la Grange* GY – Parc des Eaux-Vives* – Nave* of Church of Christ the King – Woodwork* in the Historical Museum of the Swiss Abroad – Museums : Art and History*** GZ, Ariana**, Natural History** GZ, Petit Palais – Modern Art Museum* GZ **M1** - Baur Collection* (in 19C mansion) GZ **M2,** Old Musical Instruments* GZ **M3.**

Exc. : by boat on the lake. Rens. Cie Gén. de Nav., Jardin Anglais ℰ 21 25 21 – Mouettes genevoises, 8 quai du Mont-Blanc ℰ 32 29 44 – Swiss Boat, 4 quai du Mont-Blanc ℰ 736 79 35.

18 at Cologny ℰ 735 75 40 ; 18 Country Club de Bossey ℰ 50 43 75 25, by road to Troinex.

✈ Genève-Cointrin ℰ 799 31 11.

i Office de Tourisme gare Cornavin ℰ 738 52 00, Telex 412679 - A.C. Suisse, 21 r. de la Fontenette ℰ 42 22 33 - T.C. Suisse, 9 r. P.-Fatio ℰ 737 12 12.

Paris 538 ⑦ – Bern 154 ② – Bourg-en-B. 101 ⑦ – Lausanne 63 ② – Lyon 151 ⑦ – Torino 252 ⑥.

Plan on following pages

Right Bank (Cornavin Railway Station - Les Quais) :

Richemond, Brunswick garden ✉ 1211 ℰ 731 14 00, Telex 412560, Fax 731 67 09, ←, 斋 – |¢| ▤ rm TV ☎ ⇔ – 🔬 250. AE ① E VISA FY **u**
M see **Le Gentilhomme** below - **Le Jardin M** a la carte 45/80 ₰ – ☕ 25 – **68 rm** 360/530, 31 apartments 800.

Rhône, quai Turrettini ✉ 1201 ℰ 731 98 31, Telex 22213, Fax 732 45 58, ←, 斋 – |¢| ⚡ rm ▤ TV ☎ ♿ ⇔ – 🔬 40 - 150. AE ① E VISA. ✱ rest EY **r**
M (see also **Le Neptune** below) a la carte 70/110 ₰ – ☕ 23 – **220 rm** 220/560, 8 apartments.

Les Bergues, 33 quai Bergues ✉ 1201 ℰ 731 50 50, Telex 412540, Fax 732 19 89, ←, 斋 – |¢| ▤ rm TV ☎ ♿ – 🔬 40 - 350. AE ① E VISA FY **k**
M see **Amphitryon** below - **Le Pavillon M** 35/50 ₰ – ☕ 23 – **123 rm** 270/500, 10 apartments.

🏨🏨🏨 **Noga Hilton** Ⓜ, 19 quai Mt-Blanc ✉ 1201 ✆ 731 98 11, Telex 412337, Fax 738 64 32, ≤, 🌇, ▨ – ▮ ✿➤ rm ▤ rm ☎ ὀ 👌 ⇌ 🛦 850. 🆎 ⑩ ⏃ rest   GY y
M see **Le Cygne** below – **La Grignotière M** a la carte 55/75 – **Le Bistroquai M** 16 ♨ – ⇌ 25 –
377 rm 315/525, 36 apartments.

🏨🏨🏨 **Beau Rivage**, 13 quai Mt-Blanc ✉ 1201 ✆ 731 02 21, Telex 412539, Fax 738 98 47, ≤, 🌇
– ▮ ▤ ☎ ← 🛦 30 - 350. 🆎 ⑩ ⏃ 𝘝𝘐𝘚𝘈   FY d
M see Le Chat Botté below - **Le Quai 13** ✆ 731 31 82 **M** a la carte 50/75 ♨ – ⇌ 21 – **97 rm**
290/600, 7 apartments.

🏨🏨🏨 **Président** Ⓜ, 17 quai Wilson ✉ 1211 ✆ 731 10 00, Telex 412328, Fax 731 22 06, ≤ lake –
▮ ✿➤ rm ▤ rm ▤ ☎ 👌 ← – 🛦 25 - 80. 🆎 ⑩ ⏃ 𝘝𝘐𝘚𝘈. ❄ rest   GX d
M (lunch only) 28/45 ♨ – ⇌ 25 – **152 rm** 225/355, 28 apartments.

🏨🏨🏨 **Paix**, 11 quai Mt-Blanc ✉ 1201 ✆ 732 61 50, Telex 412554, Fax 738 87 94, ≤ – ▮ ▤ ▤ ☎
– 🛦 70. 🆎 ⑩ ⏃ 𝘝𝘐𝘚𝘈   FY s
M 36/52 ♨ – ⇌ 21 – **86 rm** 210/470, 14 apartments.

🏨🏨🏨 **Ramada Renaissance** Ⓜ, 19 r. Zurich ✉ 1201 ✆ 731 02 41, Telex 412557, Fax 738 75 14
– ▮ ✿➤ rm ▤ rm ☎ ὀ 👌 ← – 🛦 150. 🆎 ⑩ ⏃ 𝘝𝘐𝘚𝘈   FX s
La Cortille M 30/55 – **Café Ragueneau M** 30/55 – ⇌ 22 – **219 rm** 235/335, 7 apartments – P
½ P 208/246.

🏨🏨 **Bristol** Ⓜ, 10 quai Mt-Blanc ✉ 1201 ✆ 732 38 00, Telex 412544, Fax 738 90 39, ƒ6 – ▮
▤ rest ▤ ☎ 🛦 30 - 100. 🆎 ⑩ ⏃ 𝘝𝘐𝘚𝘈   FY w
M a la carte 60/105 ♨ – ⇌ 23 – **100 rm** 225/330, 5 apartments 530.

🏨🏨 **Pullman Rotary** Ⓜ, 18 r. Cendrier ✉ 1201 ✆ 731 52 00, Telex 412704, Fax 731 91 69, 🌇
– ▮ ▤ ▤ ☎ 🆎 ⑩ ⏃ 𝘝𝘐𝘚𝘈. ❄   FY t
M (closed Saturday and Sunday) 40/60 – ⇌ 18 – **84 rm** 220/270, 10 duplex 460.

🏨🏨 **Warwick** Ⓜ, 14 r. Lausanne ✉ 1201 ✆ 731 62 50, Telex 412731, Fax 738 99 35 – ▮ ✿➤ rm
▤ ▤ ☎ – 🛦 25 - 300. 🆎 ⑩ ⏃ 𝘝𝘐𝘚𝘈. ❄ rest   FY n
Les 4 Saisons (closed 22 July-18 August, Saturday, Sunday and Bank Holidays) **M** 65/100 –
⇌ 19 – **169 rm** 255/330.

🏨🏨 **Rex**, 44 av. Wendt ✉ 1203 ✆ 45 71 50, Telex 415890, Fax 44 04 20, 🌇 – ▮ ▤ rest ▤ ☎ –
🛦 40. 🆎 ⑩ ⏃   DX e
Le Régent (closed August, Saturday and Sunday) **M** 27/82 – **74 rm** ⇌ 160/310.

🏨🏨 **Berne**, 26 r. Berne ✉ 1201 ✆ 731 60 00, Telex 412542, Fax 731 11 73 – ▮ ▤ ▤ ☎ – 🛦
30 - 100. 🆎 ⑩ ⏃ 𝘝𝘐𝘚𝘈. ❄ rest   FY x
M 14/32 ♨ – **84 rm** ⇌ 180/250, 4 apartments – ½ P 122/142.

🏨🏨 **Cornavin** without rest, 33 bd James Fazy ✉ 1211 ✆ 732 21 00, Telex 412548, Fax 732 88 43
– ▮ ▤ ▤ ☎. 🆎 ⑩ ⏃ 𝘝𝘐𝘚𝘈   EY t
125 rm ⇌ 125/260.

🏨🏨 **Ambassador**, 21 quai Bergues ✉ 1201 ✆ 731 72 00, Telex 412533, Fax 738 90 80, 🌇 – ▮
rm ▤ ▤ ☎ – 🛦 40. 🆎 ⑩ ⏃   FY p
M 40/50 ♨ – ⇌ 12 – **86 rm** 115/245.

🏨🏨 **Carlton**, 22 r. Amat ✉ 1202 ✆ 731 68 50, Telex 412546, Fax 732 82 47 – ▮ kitchenette ▤
☎ ←. 🆎 ⑩ ⏃   FX a
M (closed Saturday and Sunday) a la carte 30/45 ♨ – **123 rm** ⇌ 155/270.

🏨 **Grand Pré** without rest, 35 r. Gd Pré ✉ 1202 ✆ 733 91 50, Telex 414210, Fax 734 76 91 – ▮
✿➤ ▤ ☎ – 🛦 30. 🆎 ⑩ ⏃ 𝘝𝘐𝘚𝘈   EX s
80 rm ⇌ 165/245.

🏨 **Midi** Ⓜ, pl. Chevelu ✉ 1201 ✆ 731 78 00, Telex 412552, Fax 731 00 20, 🌇 – ▮ ▤ rest ▤
☎. 🆎 ⑩ ⏃ 𝘝𝘐𝘚𝘈   FY r
M (closed Sunday) 22 ♨ – **85 rm** ⇌ 135/190.

XXXX **Le Gentilhomme** -Hôtel Richemond, Brunswick garden ✉ 1211 ✆ 731 14 00, Telex 412560,
Fax 731 67 09 – ▤ 🆎 ⑩ ⏃ 𝘝𝘐𝘚𝘈   FY u
M (dinner only) 98/135.

XXXX ❀ **Le Chat Botté** - Hôtel Beau Rivage, 13 quai Mt-Blanc ✉ 1201 ✆ 731 65 32, Telex 412539,
Fax 738 98 47 – ▤ 🆎 ⑩ ⏃ 𝘝𝘐𝘚𝘈   FY d
closed 23 March-7 April, 21 December-6 January, Saturday, Sunday and Bank Holidays –
M 85/115 and a la carte 80/110
Spec. Pétales de tomates au caviar d'aubergines, Rouelles de homard à la mousseline d'artichaut, Suprême de
volaille à la vapeur de thym. **Wines** Peissy, Féchy.

XXXX ❀ **Le Cygne** -Hôtel Noga Hilton, 19 quai Mt-Blanc ✉ 1201 ✆ 731 98 11, Telex 412337, Fax
738 64 32, ≤ – ▤ 🆎 ⑩ ⏃ 𝘝𝘐𝘚𝘈. ❄   GY y
M 130/150
Spec. Bar cuit à la fumée de bois et vinaigrette de truffe, Grouse d'Ecosse (August-December), Gratinée de
poularde au beurre de truffe. **Wines** Dardagny.

XXXX **Amphitryon** -Hôtel Les Bergues, 33 quai Bergues ✉ 1201 ✆ 731 50 50 – ▤ 🆎 ⑩ ⏃ 𝘝𝘐𝘚𝘈. ❄
closed Saturday and Sunday – **M** 65/80.   FY k

XXX **Le Neptune** - Hôtel du Rhône, quai Turrettini ✉ 1201 ✆ 731 98 31, Telex 22213, Fax
732 45 58, 🌇 – ▤ 🆎 ⑩ ⏃ 𝘝𝘐𝘚𝘈.   EY r
closed Saturday, Sunday and Bank Holidays – **M** a la carte 95/120.

X **Boeuf Rouge**, 17 r. A. Vincent ✉ 1201 ✆ 732 75 37, lyonnaise cuisine   FY z
closed Saturday and Sunday – **M** 22/55 ♨.

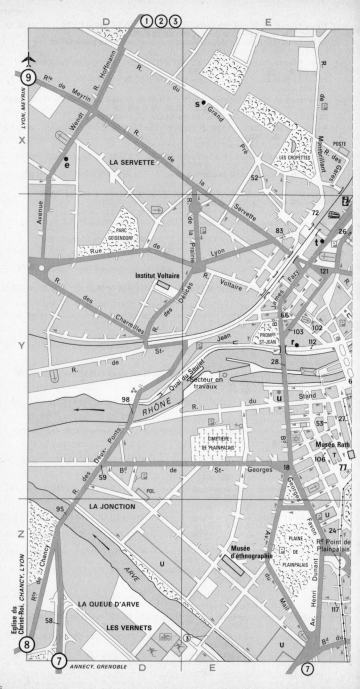

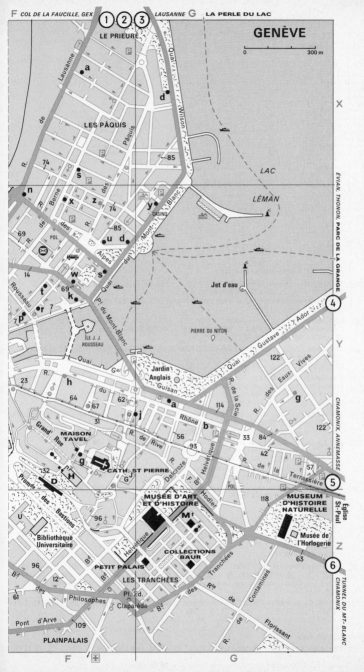

STREET INDEX TO GENEVE TOWN PLAN

Left Bank (Commercial Centre) :

Métropole, 34 quai Gén. Guisan ⊠ 1204 ℰ 21 13 44, Telex 421550, Fax 21 13 50, 🏤 – 🛗
🔲 📺 ☎ – 🔬 50 - 200. 🆎 ⓞ 🇪 𝑉𝐼𝑆𝐴 🛏 rest　　　　　　　　　　　　　GY **a**
M see **L'Arlequin** below - **Le Grand Quai M** a la carte 55/95 – **121 rm** ☲ 230/550, 6 apartments 800/900.

La Cigogne, 17 pl. Longemalle ⊠ 1204 ℰ 21 42 42, Telex 421748, Fax 21 40 65, « Tastefully decorated and furnished » – 🛗 📺 ☎ – 🔬 25. 🆎 ⓞ 🇪 𝑉𝐼𝑆𝐴 🛏 rest　　　　　　FGY **j**
M 65/95 – **45 rm** ☲ 228/395, 5 apartments 720.

Armures 🅼 🦶, 1 r. Puits-St-Pierre ⊠ 1204 ℰ 28 91 72, Telex 421129, Fax 28 98 46 – 🛗 🔲
📺 ☎. 🆎 ⓞ 🇪 𝑉𝐼𝑆𝐴　　　　　　　　　　　　　　　　　　　　　　　　　FY **g**
M a la carte 45/65 ⚖ – **28 rm** ☲ 210/410, 4 apartments 420.

Parc des Eaux-Vives, 82 quai G. Ador ⊠ 1207 ℰ 735 41 40, Fax 786 87 65, « Pleasant setting in extensive park, attractive view » – 🅿. 🆎 ⓞ 🇪 𝑉𝐼𝑆𝐴　　　　　　　　by ④
closed 1 January-15 February, Sunday dinner from 1 November-30 April and Monday –
M 78/130 ⚖.

L'Arlequin - Hôtel Métropole, 34 quai Gén. Guisan ⊠ 1204 ℰ 21 13 44, Telex 421550, Fax 21 13 50 – 🔲. 🆎 ⓞ 🇪 𝑉𝐼𝑆𝐴. 🛏　　　　　　　　　　　　　　　　　　GY **a**
closed August, Saturday and Sunday – **M** 90/110.

Le Béarn (Goddard), 4 quai Poste ⊠ 1204 ℰ 21 00 28 – 🔲. ⓞ 🇪 𝑉𝐼𝑆𝐴　　　　EY **u**
closed 20 July-26 August, 16 to 23 February, Saturday (except dinner from October-April) and Sunday – **M** 95/140 and a la carte
Spec. Ravioli de saumon et huître en nage glacée, Soufflé de truffe (15 December-15 February), Oursin fourré de coquille Saint-Jacques. **Wines** Dardagny, Côtes de Russin.

Baron de la Mouette (Mövenpick Fusterie), 40 r. Rhône ⊠ 1204 ℰ 21 88 55, Fax 28 93 22, 🏤 – 🔲. 🆎 ⓞ 🇪 𝑉𝐼𝑆𝐴　　　　　　　　　　　　　　　　　　　　FY **h**
M a la carte 55/95 ⚖.

Environs

to the N :

Palais des Nations :

Intercontinental 🅼, 7 petit Saconnex ⊠ 1211 ℰ 734 60 91, Telex 412921, Fax 734 28 64, ≤, 🏤, 🎿 – 🛗 🔲 📺 ☎ 🚗 🅿 – 🔬 25 - 600. 🆎 ⓞ 🇪 𝑉𝐼𝑆𝐴. 🛏 rest　　　by ①
M see **Les Continents** below - **La Pergola M** a la carte 50/75 ⚖ – ☲ 19 – **353 rm** 300/400, 64 apartments.

Les Continents - Hôtel Intercontinental, 7 petit Saconnex ⊠ 1211 ℰ 734 60 91, Telex 412921, Fax 734 28 64 – 🔲 🅿. 🆎 ⓞ 🇪 𝑉𝐼𝑆𝐴　　　　　　　　　　　　by ①
closed Sunday lunch and Saturday – **M** a la carte 71/120
Spec. Foie gras de canard poêlé, Carpaccio de saumon et tartare de dorade, Homard braisé au jus d'olives et ravioli de cèpes.

Perle du Lac, 128 r. Lausanne ⊠ 1202 ℰ 731 79 35, Fax 731 49 79, ≤, 🏤 – 🆎 ⓞ 🇪 𝑉𝐼𝑆𝐴
🛏　　　　　　　　　　　　　　　　　　　　　　　　　　　by quai Wilson　GX
closed 22 December-22 January and Monday – **M** 95/130.

at Palais des Expositions : 5 km – ⊠ 1218 Grand Saconnex :

🏨🏨 **Holiday Inn Crowne Plaza** Ⓜ, 26 voie Moëns ℰ 791 00 11, Telex 415695, Fax 798 92 73, 🔲 – 🛗 ✜✜ 🔳 📺 ☎ ⚐ ⇐⇒ – 🔬 40 - 160. 🆔 ⓞ Ε 𝖵𝖨𝖲𝖠
M a la carte 50/90 🍴 – � 20 – **288 rm** 220/330, 17 apartments.

at Bellevue by ③ and road to Lausanne : 6 km – ⊠ 1293 Bellevue :

🏨🏨🏨 **La Réserve** Ⓜ ⌘, 301 rte Lausanne ℰ 774 17 41, Telex 419117, Fax 774 25 71, ≤, 🌤, « Set in a park near the lake, marina », 🔼, 🔲, 🎾 – 🛗 🔳 📺 ☎ ⚐ ⇐⇒ ⚐ – 🔬 80. 🆔 ⓞ Ε 𝖵𝖨𝖲𝖠
M see **Tsé Fung** below – ⊑ 25 – **114 rm** 250/450, 9 apartments.

𝖷𝖷𝖷 **Tsé Fung** - Hôtel La Réserve, 301 rte Lausanne ℰ 774 17 41, Telex 419117, Fax 774 25 71, 🌤, Chinese rest. – 🔳 ⚐. 🆔 ⓞ Ε 𝖵𝖨𝖲𝖠
M 75/125.

at Genthod by ③ and road to Lausanne : 7 km – ⊠ 1294 Genthod :

𝖷𝖷 ✿ **Rest. du Château de Genthod** (Leisibach), 1 rte Rennex ℰ 774 19 72, 🌤 – Ε 𝖵𝖨𝖲𝖠
closed 12 to 18 August, 20 December-10 January, Sunday and Monday – M 42/65
Spec. Mousse de foie de poularde aux pignons, Terrine de brochet au basilic (February-June and October-15 December), Noisettes de chevreuil Saint-Hubert (season). **Wines** Côtes de Russin, Féchy.

to the E by road to Evian :

at Cologny by ④ : 3,5 km – ⊠ 1223 Cologny :

𝖷𝖷𝖷𝖷 ✿✿ **Aub. du Lion d'Or** (Large), au Village ℰ 736 44 32, ≤, 🌤, « Overlooking the lake and Geneva » – ⚐. 🆔 ⓞ Ε 𝖵𝖨𝖲𝖠
closed 25 March to 2 April, 20 December-20 January, Saturday and Sunday – M 120/160 and a la carte 🍴
Spec. Rosette de lotte maraîchère, Daurade royale grillée à l'ail, Chariot de pâtisseries. **Wines** Lully, Pinot noir du Valais.

to the S :

at Petit-Lancy by ⑧ : 3 km – ⊠ 1213 Petit Lancy :

🏨🏨 ✿ **Host. de la Vendée,** 28 chemin Vendée ℰ 792 04 11, Telex 421304, Fax 792 05 46, 🌤 – 🛗 📺 ☎ ⚐ – 🔬 80. 🆔 ⓞ Ε 𝖵𝖨𝖲𝖠
closed 23 December-6 January – M *(closed Saturday lunch, Sunday)* 48/105 🍴 – **33 rm** ⊑ 140/245 – ½ P 143/163
Spec. Feuilleté de légumes et ris de veau au Sauternes, Papillote de filets de rougets "Provençale", Soufflé chaud à la vanille (May-September). **Wines** Pinot gris, Pinot noir.

at Grand-Lancy by ⑦ : 3 km – ⊠ 1212 Lancy :

𝖷𝖷𝖷 ✿ **Marignac** (Pelletier), 32 av. E. Lance ℰ 794 04 24, 🌤, park – 🔳 ⚐ Ε 𝖵𝖨𝖲𝖠
closed 4 to 20 August, Saturday lunch, Monday lunch and Sunday – M 75/110
Spec. Saumon cru mariné et son tartare, Escalopes de foie gras poêlées sur purée de pommes. **Wines** Côtes de Russin, Lully.

to the W :

at Peney-Dessus by road to Peney : 10 km – ⊠ 1242 Staigny :

𝖷𝖷𝖷 ✿ **Aub. de Châteauvieux** ⌘ with rm, ℰ 753 15 11, Fax 753 19 24, ≤, 🌤, « Old manor farmhouse », 🍃 – 📺 ☎ ⚐ – 🔬 30. ⓞ Ε 𝖵𝖨𝖲𝖠
closed 28 July-12 August and 22 December-7 January – M *(closed Sunday and Monday)* 85/98 – **19 rm** ⊑ 115/185
Spec. Pavé de saumon croustillant et fin ragoût de supions, Râble de lapereau en casserole, Chariot de pâtisseries.

at Cointrin by road to Lyon : 4 km – ⊠ 1216 Cointrin :

🏨🏨 **Mövenpick Radisson** Ⓜ, 20 rte Pré Bois ℰ 798 75 75, Telex 415701, Fax 791 02 84 – 🛗 ✜✜ 🔳 📺 ⚐ ⇐⇒ – 🔬 270. 🆔 ⓞ Ε 𝖵𝖨𝖲𝖠
M a la carte 50/80 - **Kikkoman** M 58/75 – ⊑ 20 – **350 rm** 210/330, 14 apartments.

🏨🏨 **Penta** Ⓜ, 75 av. L. Casaï ℰ 798 47 00, Telex 415571, Fax 798 77 58, 🌤 – 🛗 ✜✜ 🔳 📺 ☎ ⚐ – 🔬 700. 🆔 ⓞ Ε 𝖵𝖨𝖲𝖠. 🍴 rest
La Récolte M a la carte 55/85 – ⊑ 21 – **308 rm** 180/260 – ½ P 240/260.

𝖷𝖷 **Rôt. Plein Ciel,** (at the airport) ℰ 717 76 76, Telex 415775, Fax 798 77 68, ≤ – 🔳. 🆔 ⓞ Ε 𝖵𝖨𝖲𝖠
M 59/65.

Do not mix up :

Comfort of hotels : 🏨🏨🏨🏨 ... 🏠
Comfort of restaurants : 𝖷𝖷𝖷𝖷𝖷 ... 𝖷
Quality of the cuisine : ✿✿✿, ✿✿, ✿

ZÜRICH 8001 ④②⑦ ⑥ ②①⑥ ⑱ – pop. 380 000 - alt. 409 m – ✦ 01.

See : The Quays★★ BYZ – Fraumünster cloisters★ (Alter Kreuzgang des Fraumünsters) BZ **D** –
View of the town from the Zürichhorn Gardens★ V – Church of SS. Felix and Regula★ U **E** –
Church of Zürich-Altstetten★ U **F** – Zoological Gardens★ (Zoo Dolder) U – Museums : Swiss
National Museum★★★ (Schweizerisches Landesmuseum) BY – Fine Arts Museum★★ (Kunsthaus)
CZ – Rietberg Museum★★ V **M2** – Buhrle Collection★★ (Sammlung Buhrle) V **M3**.

✈ Kloten ℰ 812 71 11.

🛈 Offizielles Verkehrsbüro, Bahnhofplatz 15 ⊠ 8023 ℰ 211 40 00, Telex 813 744 – A.C.S. Forchstrasse 95
⊠ 8032 ℰ 55 15 00 – T.C.S. Alfred-Escher-Strasse 38 ⊠ 8002 ℰ 201 25 36.

Basle 109 ⑥ – Bern 125 ⑥ – Geneva 278 ⑥ – Innsbruck 288 ① – Milan 304 ⑤.

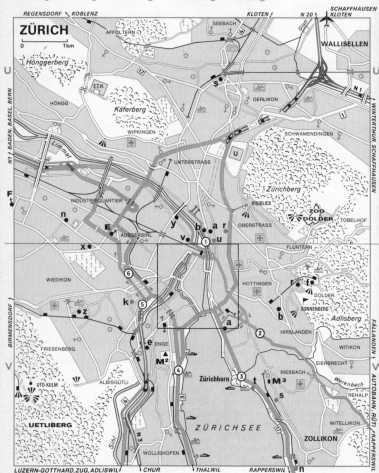

On the right bank of river Limmat (University, Fine Arts Museum) :

🏨 **Dolder Grand Hotel and rest. La Rotonde** ⌂, Kurhausstr. 65, ⊠ 8032, ℰ 251 62 31,
Telex 816416, Fax 251 88 29, ≤ Zürich and lake, 🍴, ⤳, ⌂, park, ✼ – 🛗 🗏 rest 📺 ☎ 🚗
🅿 – 🔬 200. 🆎 ⓞ 🗉 𝒱𝐼𝑆𝐴. ✼ rest
M 64/70 and a la carte 65/120 – **165 rm** ⊇ 290/470, **11 suites** 1150/2200.
V **f**

🏨 **Eden au Lac**, Utoquai 45, ⊠ 8023, ℰ 261 94 04, Telex 816339, Fax 261 94 09, ≤, ⇔ – 🛗
🗏 📺 🅿 – 🔬 25. 🆎 ⓞ 🗉 𝒱𝐼𝑆𝐴
M 95 and a la carte – **54 rm** ⊇ 250/450, **3 suites** 800.
V **a**

🏨 Zurich Ⓜ, Neumühlequai 42, ⊠ 8001, ℰ 363 63 63, Telex 817587, Fax 363 60 15, ≤, ⇔, 🗐
– 🛗 🗏 📺 ☎ 🕭 🚗 – 🔬 400 – **M** Tourne Broche – **301 rm**, **11 suites**.
U **b**

410

Waldhaus Dolder ⑤, Kurhausstr. 20, ☒ 8030, ℘ 251 93 60, Telex 816460, Fax 251 00 29, ≼ Zürich and lake, 舒, ☎, ☒, ┠, ℁ – ▯ ⅍ rest ▤ rest ▥ ☎ ⇌ ⇎ ℗ – 🖾 40. 巫 ⓞ 🖪 ᴠɪ𝘀𝘈
V r
M 40/50 and a la carte – ☲ 12 – **97 rm** 180/380, **3 suites** 400/650.

Pullman Continental H., Stampfenbachstr. 60, ☒ 8035, ℘ 363 33 63, Telex 817089, Fax 363 33 18 – 🖪 ▤ ▥ ☎ ⇌ ℗ – 🖾 80. 巫 ⓞ 🖪 ᴠɪ𝘀𝘈
U a
M Diff *(closed sunday)* 85 and dinner a la carte – **Coq d'Or** 45/95 and a la carte – **180 rm** ☲ 240/650.

Central Plaza ▥ ⑤, Central 1, ☒ 8001, ℘ 251 55 55, Telex 817152, Fax 251 85 35 – 🖪 ▤ ▥ ☎ – 🖾 150. 巫 ⓞ 🖪 ᴠɪ𝘀𝘈
BY z
M Cascade *(closed Saturday and Sunday)* 29,50/56 and a la carte – **99 rm** ☲ 250/330, **4 suites** 450.

Europe without rest., Dufourstr. 4, ☒ 8008, ℘ 47 10 30, Telex 816461, Fax 251 03 67 – 🖪 ▤ ▥ ☎
CZ e
39 rm, 3 suites.

Opera without rest., Dufourstr. 5, ☒ 8008, ℘ 251 90 90, Telex 816480, Fax 251 90 01 – 🖪 ▤ ▥ ☎. 巫 ⓞ 🖪 ᴠɪ𝘀𝘈
CZ b
68 rm ☲ 190/290.

Ambassador, Falkenstr. 6, ☒ 8008, ℘ 261 76 00, Telex 816508, Fax 251 23 94 – 🖪 ▤ ▥ ☎. 巫 ⓞ 🖪 ᴠɪ𝘀𝘈
CZ a
M 21 (lunch) and a la carte approx. 72,50 – **45 rm** ☲ 190/290.

Zürcherhof, Zähringerstr. 21, ☒ 8025, ℘ 47 10 40, Telex 816490, Fax 262 04 84 – 🖪 ▤ rest ▥ ☎. 巫 ⓞ 🖪 ᴠɪ𝘀𝘈
CY q
M *(closed Saturday and Sunday)* 18,50/36 and a la carte – **35 rm** ☲ 100/220.

Rütli ▥ without rest., Zähringerstr. 43, ☒ 8001, ℘ 251 54 26, Telex 816037 – 🖪 ▥ ☎. ℁
59 rm.
CY a

Chesa Rustica, Limmatquai 70, ☒ 8001, ℘ 251 92 91, Telex 817651, Fax 261 01 79 – 🖪 ▥ ☎
23 rm.
BY r

Helmhaus without rest., Schiffländeplatz 30, ☒ 8001, ℘ 251 88 10, Telex 816525, Fax 251 04 30 – 🖪 ▥ ☎. 巫 ⓞ 🖪 ᴠɪ𝘀𝘈. ℁
BCZ s
closed 1 October-28 February – **25 rm** ☲ 137/208.

Eos ⑤ without rest., Carmenstrasse 18, ☒ 8032, ℘ 47 10 60, Telex 812074, Fax 47 23 94, 舒 – 🖪 ☎
V b
24 rm.

XXX ❀ **Agnès Amberg,** Hottingerstr. 5, ☒ 8032, ℘ 251 26 26, Fax 252 50 62 – 巫 ⓞ 🖪 ᴠɪ𝘀𝘈
closed lunch Monday and Saturday, Sunday, 3 weeks july- August and 24 December-7 January – **M** 43/175 and a la carte approx. 96
CY d
Spec. Caramelized terrine of goose liver, Lobster in carrot juice with exotic spices, Pigeon on a pear purée with olive sauce and corn pancake.

XXX **Haus Zum Rüden,** Limmatquai 42 (1st floor), ☒ 8001, ℘ 261 95 66, Fax 261 18 04, Former 13C guildhall – 🖪 ▤. 巫 ⓞ 🖪 ᴠɪ𝘀𝘈
BY m
M 55/140 and a la carte.

XX **Wirtschaft Flühgass,** Zollikerstr. 214, Riesbach, ☒ 8008, ℘ 53 12 15, Fax 55 75 32, « 16C inn » – ℗. 巫 ⓞ 🖪 ᴠɪ𝘀𝘈
V s
closed Saturday, Sunday and 6 July-7 August – **M** (booking essential) 60/120 and a la carte.

XX Kronenhalle, Rämistrasse 4, ☒ 8001, ℘ 251 02 56, Typical atmosphere, paintings – ▤
CZ r

XX **Jacky's Stapferstube,** Culmannstr. 45, ☒ 8033, ℘ 361 37 48, Veal and beef specialities – ▤ ℗. 巫 ⓞ 🖪 ᴠɪ𝘀𝘈
U r
closed Sunday, Monday and 13 July-13 August – **M** 35 (lunch) and a la carte 74/100.

XX **Casa Ferlin,** Stampfenbachstr. 38, ☒ 8006, ℘ 362 35 09, Italian rest. – ▤ 巫 ⓞ 🖪 ᴠɪ𝘀𝘈
U u
closed Saturday, Sunday and mid July-mid August – **M** a la carte 60,50/81,50.

On the left bank of River Limmat (Main railway station, Business centre) :

Baur au Lac, Talstr. 1, ☒ 8022, ℘ 221 16 50, Telex 813567, Fax 211 81 39, « Lakeside setting, park » –▯🖪 ▤ ▥ ☎ ⇌ ℗ – 🖾 150. 巫 ⓞ 🖪 ᴠɪ𝘀𝘈
BZ a
M Le Pavillon 55/69 and a la carte 54/143 – **Le Grill** – **139 rm** ☲ 290/480, **16 suites** 950/1700.

Savoy Hotel Baur en Ville ▥, Paradeplatz, ☒ 8001, ℘ 211 53 60, Telex 812845, Fax 221 14 67 – 🖪 ▤ ▥ ☎ ⇌ – 🖾 135. 巫 ⓞ 🖪 ᴠɪ𝘀𝘈. ℁
BZ e
M Orsini (Italian rest.) 52/85 and a la carte – **Savoy Grill** 56/95 and a la carte – **104 rm** ☲ 350/650, **8 suites** 950/1100.

Atlantis Sheraton ▥ ⑤, Döltschiweg 234, ☒ 8055, ℘ 463 00 00, Telex 813338, Fax 463 03 88, ≼, 舒, ☒, park – 🖪 ⅍ rm ▥ ☎ ⇌ ℗ – 🖾 200. 巫 ⓞ 🖪 ᴠɪ𝘀𝘈
V z
M a la carte 60/80 – **157 rm** ☲ 330/410, **4 suites** 450/1200.

Annexe Guesthouse, ℘ 463 00 00 – 🖪 ⅍ rm ▥ ☎. 巫 ⓞ 🖪 ᴠɪ𝘀𝘈
61 rm ☲ 198/218.

Schweizerhof, Bahnhofplatz 7, ☒ 8023, ℘ 211 86 40, Telex 813754, Fax 211 35 05 – 🖪 ▤ ▥ ☎ – 🖾 80
BY a
114 rm, 1 suite.

ZÜRICH

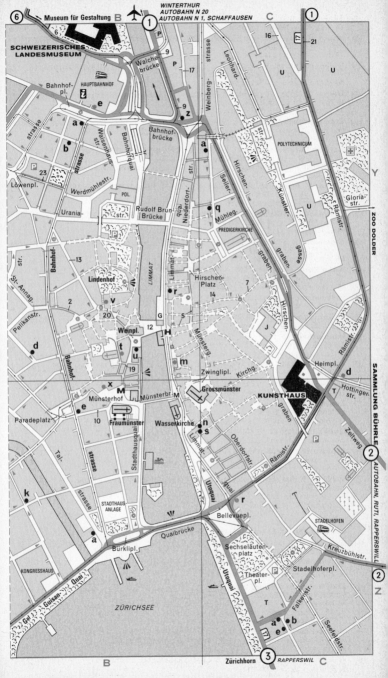

🏨 St. Gothard, Bahnhofstr. 87, ⊠ 8023, ℰ 211 55 00, Telex 812420, Fax 211 24 19 – 📶 🗏 📺
☎ – 🔏 40 – **128 rm, 7 suites.**
BY **b**

🏨 Ascot Ⓜ, Tessinerplatz 9, ⊠ 8002, ℰ 201 18 00, Telex 815454, Fax 202 72 10 – 📶 🗏 📺 ☎
🖤 – 🔏 50. 🖭 ⑩ 🖪 ⅥⅥⅩ
M 78 (dinner) and a la carte 41/74 – **73 rm** ⊐ 240/450.
AZ **a**

🏨 Splügenschloss, Splügenstr. 2, ⊠ 8002, ℰ 201 08 00, Telex 815553, Fax 201 42 86 – 📶
🖤🖤 rm 🗏 📺 ☎ 🅟 – 🔏 20. 🖭 ⑩ 🖪 ⅥⅩⅩ. 🖤 rest
M 95 and a la carte – **54 rm** ⊐ 240/400. **1 suite** 450/550.
AZ **e**

🏨 Neues Schloss, Stockerstr. 17, ⊠ 8022, ℰ 201 65 50, Telex 815560, Fax 201 64 18 – 📶 📺
☎ 🅟 – 🔏 25. 🖭 ⑩ 🖪 ⅥⅩⅩ. 🖤 rest
M (closed Sunday to non-residents) 57/90 and a la carte – **58 rm** ⊐ 200/600.
AZ **m**

🏨 Zum Storchen, Weinplatz 2, ⊠ 8022, ℰ 211 55 10, Telex 813354, Fax 211 64 51, ⩽ Limmat
and town, 🍴, « Limmat-side setting » – 📶 📺 ☎ – 🔏 40. 🖭 ⑩ 🖪 ⅥⅩⅩ
M a la carte 49,50/74 – **79 rm** ⊐ 190/800.
BY **u**

🏨 Carlton Elite Bahnhofstr. 41, ⊠ 8001, ℰ 211 65 60, Telex 812781, Fax 211 30 19, 🍴 – 📶
🗏 rest 📺 ☎ – 🔏 200. 🖭 ⑩ 🖪 ⅥⅩⅩ. 🖤
M Locanda (closed Sunday) a la carte 49/65 – **Bundnerstube** (Swiss spec.) – ⊐ 15 Bb –
72 rm 155/340.
BY **d**

🏨 Stoller Ⓜ, Badenerstr. 357, ⊠ 8040, ℰ 492 65 00, Telex 822460, Fax 492 65 01, 🍴 – 📶 📺
☎ 🖤 – 🔏 50. 🖭 ⑩ 🖪 ⅥⅩⅩ
M 25 (lunch) and a la carte 39/66 – **78 rm** ⊐ 180/280 Bb.
V **x**

🏨 Glärnischhof, Claridenstr. 30, ⊠ 8022, ℰ 202 47 47, Telex 815366, Fax 201 01 64 – 📶
🗏 rest 📺 ☎ 🅟 – 🔏 40. 🖭 ⑩ 🖪 ⅥⅩⅩ
M La Rotisserie 39/42 and a la carte – **70 rm** ⊐ 190/480.
BZ **k**

🏨 Glockenhof, Sihlstr. 31, ⊠ 8023, ℰ 211 56 50, Telex 812466, Fax 211 56 60, 🍴 – 📶
🗏 rest 📺 ☎. 🖭 ⑩ 🖪 ⅥⅩⅩ
M 12,50/33 and a la carte – **106 rm** ⊐ 170/254.
AY **e**

🏨 Nova Park, Badenerstr. 420, ⊠ 8040, ℰ 491 22 22, Telex 822822, Fax 491 22 20, 🍴, 🚗,
🔲 – 📶 🖤🖤 rm 🗏 rest 📺 ☎ 🖤 🅟 – 🔏 600. 🖭 🖪 ⅥⅩⅩ. 🖤 rest
M a la carte 32,50/73 – ⊐ 19 – **354 rm** 240/285. **9 suites** 275/350.
U **n**

🏨 Engematthof 🖤, Engimattstr. 14, ⊠ 8002, ℰ 201 25 04, Telex 817273, Fax 201 25 16, 🍴,
🍴 – 📶 📺 ☎ 🅟 – 🔏 20. 🖤 – **79 rm.**
V **e**

🏨 Trümpy, Limmatstr. 5, ⊠ 8031, ℰ 271 54 00, Telex 822980, Fax 272 19 30, 🍴 – 📶 📺 ☎ –
🔏 60. 🖭 ⑩ 🖪 ⅥⅩⅩ. 🖤 – **M** 18 and a la carte 26/57 – **71 rm** ⊐ 150/220.
U **v**

🏨 Limmathaus without rest., Limmatstr. 118, ⊠ 8031, ℰ 271 52 40, Telex 823161, Fax
272 86 76 – 📶 ☎ – 🔏 1 000. 🖭 ⑩ 🖪 ⅥⅩⅩ
M 24,50 (lunch) and a la carte – **56 rm** ⊐ 120/220.
U **y**

XXX Au Premier, Bahnhofplatz, Bahnhofbuffet, ⊠ 8023, ℰ 211 15 10, Telex 812552, Fax 212
04 25
BY **e**

XX Baron de la Mouette (Mövenpick Dreikönigshaus), Beethovenstr. 32, ⊠ 8002, ℰ 202 09 10,
Telex 815856, Fax 202 73 74 – 🗏
AZ **r**

XX Zunfthaus zur Waag, Münsterhof 8, ⊠ 8001, ℰ 211 07 30, Fax 212 01 69, Former hatters
guildhall – 🖭 ⑩ 🖪 ⅥⅩⅩ
M (booking essential) 35/44,80 and a la carte.
BZ **x**

XX Nouvelle, Erlachstr. 46, ⊠ 8003, ℰ 462 63 63, Fax 462 81 55 – 🗏. 🖭 ⑩ 🖪 ⅥⅩⅩ
closed Saturday lunch and Sunday – **M** 110/120 a la carte.
V **k**

XX Rotisserie Lindenhofkeller, Pfalzgasse 4, ⊠ 8001, ℰ 211 70 71, 🍴 – 🗏. 🖭 ⑩ 🖪 ⅥⅩⅩ
🖤 – closed Saturday, Sunday, 24 August-15 September and 16 to 24 February – **M** a la
carte 46/117
BY **v**

XX Veltliner Keller, Schlüsselgasse 8, ⊠ 8022, ℰ 221 32 28, Fax 212 20 94, « 14C house » –
🖭 ⑩ 🖪 ⅥⅩⅩ
closed Saturday, Sunday, 13 July-8 August and 21 December-5 January – **M** 58 and a la
carte 62/79.
BY **t**

Environs North

at Zurich-Oerlikon : by ① – ⊠ 8050 Zurich-Oerlikon :

🏨 International Ⓜ, Am Marktplatz, ⊠ 8050, ℰ 311 43 41, Telex 823251, Fax 312 44 68, ⩽, 🚗,
🔲 – 📶 🖤🖤 rm 🗏 📺 ☎ 🖤 – 🔏 700. 🖤
M Panorama Grill – **335 rm. 11 suites.**
U **s**

at Zürich-Kloten (Airport) : 10 km by ① :

🏨 Zürich Kloten Airport Hilton Ⓜ 🖤, Hohenbühlstr. 10, ⊠ 8058, ℰ 810 31 31, Telex
825428, Fax 810 93 66, 🍴, 🚗 – 📶 🖤🖤 rm 🗏 📺 ☎ 🖤 🅟 – 🔏 180. 🖭 ⑩ 🖪 ⅥⅩⅩ. 🖤 rest
M Harvest Grill (closed Saturday Lunch) 46/76 and a la carte – **Taverne** (closed Saturday
lunch, Sunday, Easter, Christmas and New Year) 36 and a la carte – ⊐ 21,50 – **278 rm**
255/360. **8 suites** 545/640.

🏨 Novotel Zurich Airport Ⓜ, Talackerstr. 21 ⊠ 8152 Glattbrugg, ℰ 810 31 11, Telex 828770,
Fax 810 81 85, 🍴 – 📶 🖤🖤 rm 🗏 📺 ☎ 🖤 – 🔏 320. 🖭 ⑩ 🖪 ⅥⅩⅩ
M a la carte 49/76 – ⊐ 16 – **257 rm** 140/300.

🏨 Welcome Inn, Holbergstr. 1 (at Kloten), ⊠ 8302 Kloten, ℰ 814 07 27, Telex 825527, 🍴 –
📶 ☎ 🖤 – 🔏 20 – **96 rm.**

at Unterengstringen : 7 km by ① – ⊠ **8103** Unterengstringen :

XXX **Witschi's,** Zurcherstr. 55, ⊠ 8103, ✆ 750 44 60, Fax 750 19 68, 斎, Elegant installation – ⟵, AE ⓞ E *VISA*
closed Sunday, Monday, 25 June-15 July and 24 December-14 January – **M** 68/180 and a la carte.

at Dielsdorf : NW : 15,5 km by ① and B 17 – ⊠ **8157** Dielsdorf :

XX **Bienengarten** with rm., Regensbergerstr. 9, ✆ 853 12 17, Fax 853 24 41, 斎, Modern paintings, 🐎 – 🛗 TV ☎ Ⓟ AE ⓞ E *VISA*
closed Saturday lunch and 25 July-12 August – **M** 70/90 (dinner) and a la carte 40/90 –
8 rm ⏦ 160/320.

at Nürensdorf : 17 km by ① – ⊠ **8309** Nürensdorf :

XXX ❀ Gasthof Zum Bären Ⓜ with rm, ✆ 836 42 12, 斎 – 🛗 TV ☎ ⟵ Ⓟ
14 rm.

Environs South

at Küsnacht : 6 km by ③ – ⊠ **8700** Küsnacht :

🏛 Ermitage, Seestr. 80, ⊠ 8700, ✆ 910 52 22, Telex 825707, Fax 910 52 44, ≼, « Attractive lakeside setting, terrace and garden » – 🛗 TV ☎ Ⓟ
25 rm.

XXX ❀❀ **Petermann's Kunststube** (Petermann), Seestr. 160, ⊠ 8700, ✆ 910 07 15, Fax 910 04 95 – 🍽 Ⓟ AE ⓞ E *VISA*. ⌀
closed Sunday, Monday, 3 weeks late August and 2 weeks late January – **M** 65/175 and a la carte 76/98
Spec. Pigeon farci aux abats, Loup de mer a l'huile vièrge et son soufflé d'artichaut, Les délices au chocolat amer.

at Rüschlikon : 9 km by ④ – ⊠ **8803** Rüschlikon :

🏛 Belvoir Ⓜ ⌀, Säumerstr. 37, ⊠ 8803, ✆ 724 02 02, Telex 826522, ≼ lake, 斎 – 🛗 🍽 rest TV ☎ ⟵ ⟵ Ⓟ – 🏔 150. ⌀ rest
25 rm.

at Gattikon : 13,5 km by ⑤ – ⊠ **8136** Gattikon-Thalwil :

XX ❀ **Sihlhalde,** Sihlhaldenstr. 70, ⊠ 8136, ✆ 720 09 27, 斎 – Ⓟ. E
closed Sunday, Monday and 20 July-10 August – **M** 50/70 and a la carte approx. 40.

at Wädenswil : 22 km by ④ – ⊠ **8820** Wädenswil :

XX **Eichmühle,** by N3, exit Richterswill, ✆ 780 34 44, ≼, 斎 – Ⓟ. AE E *VISA*
closed Sunday and Monday – **M** 130 (dinner) and a la carte 74/89.

United Kingdom

London
Birmingham
Edinburgh
Glasgow
Leeds
Liverpool
Manchester

PRACTICAL INFORMATION

LOCAL CURRENCY

Pound Sterling : £ 1 = 1.91 US $ (Jan. 91)

TOURIST INFORMATION

Tourist Information offices exist in each city included in the Guide. The telephone number and address is given in each text under 🖪.

FOREIGN EXCHANGE

Banks are open between 9.30am and 3pm on weekdays only. Most large hotels have exchange facilities, and Heathrow and Gatwick Airports have 24-hour banking facilities.

SHOPPING

In London : Oxford St./Regent St. (department stores, exclusive shops) Bond St. (exclusive shops, antiques)
Knightsbridge area (department stores, exclusive shops, boutiques)
For other towns see the index of street names : those printed in red are where the principal shops are found.

THEATRE BOOKINGS IN LONDON

Your hotel porter will be able to make your arrangements or direct you to Theatre Booking Agents.
In addition there is a kiosk in Leicester Square selling tickets for the same day's performances at half price plus booking fee. It is open 12-6.30pm.

CAR HIRE

The international car hire companies have branches in each major city. Your hotel porter should be able to give details and help you with your arrangements.

TIPPING

Many hotels and restaurants include a service charge but where this is not the case an amount equivalent to between 10 and 15 per cent of the bill is customary. Additionally doormen, baggage porters and cloakroom attendants are generally given a gratuity.
Taxi drivers are customarily tipped between 10 and 15 per cent of the amount shown on the meter in addition to the fare.

SPEED LIMITS

The maximum permitted speed on motorways and dual carriageways is 70 mph (113 km/h.) and 60 mph (97 km/h.) on other roads except where a lower speed limit is signposted.

SEAT BELTS

The wearing of seat belts in the United Kingdom is compulsory for drivers, front seat passengers and children under 14 in the rear where seat belts are fitted. It is illegal for front seat passengers to carry children on their lap.

ANIMALS

It is forbidden to bring domestic animals (dogs, cats…) into the United Kingdom.

LONDON

LONDON (Greater) 404 folds ④ to ④ — pop. 7 566 620 — ✪ 071 or 081.

✈ Heathrow, ✆ (081) 759 4321, Telex 934892 — **Terminal :** Airbus (A1) from Victoria, Airbus (A2) from Paddington — Underground (Piccadilly line) frequent service daily.

✈ Gatwick, ✆ 0293 (Crawley) 28822 and ✆ 081 (London) 668 4211, Telex 877725, by A 23 and M 23 — **Terminal :** Coach service from Victoria Coach Station (Flightline 777, hourly service) — Railink (Gatwick Express) from Victoria (24 h service).

✈ London City Airport, ✆ (071) 589 55 99, Telex 264731.

✈ Stansted, at Bishop's Stortford, ✆ 0279 (Bishop's Stortford) 680800, Telex 818708, NE : 34 m. off M 11 and A 120.

British Airways, Victoria Air Terminal : 115 Buckingham Palace Rd., SW1, ✆ (071) 834 9411, p. 16 BX.

🚃 Euston and Paddington ✆ 0345 090700.

🛈 London Tourist Board and Convention Bureau. Telephone Information Services, ✆ (071) 730 3488.
British Travel Centre, 12 Regent St., Piccadilly Circus, SW1, ✆ (071) 730 3400.
National Tourist Information Centre, Victoria Station Forecourt, SW1, ✆ (071) 730 3488.

SIGHTS

HISTORIC BUILDINGS AND MONUMENTS

Palace of Westminster*** p. 10 LY — Tower of London*** p. 11 PVX — Banqueting House** p. 10 LX — Buckingham Palace** p. 16 BVX — Kensington Palace** p. 8 FX — Lincoln's Inn** p. 17 EV — London Bridge** p. 11 PVX — Royal Hospital Chelsea** p. 15 FU — St. James's Palace** p. 13 EP — South Bank Arts Centre** p. 10 MX — The Temple** p. 6 MV — Tower Bridge** p. 11 PX — Albert Memorial* p. 14 CQ — Apsley House* p. 12 BP — George Inn*, Southwark p. 11 PX — Guildhall* p. 7 OU — Dr Johnson's House* p. 6 NUV A — Leighton House* p. 8 EY — The Monument* (⁂*) p. 7 PV G — Royal Opera Arcade* p. 13 FGN — Staple Inn* p. 6 MU Y — Theatre Royal* (Haymarket) p. 13 GM.

CHURCHES

The City Churches

St. Paul's Cathedral*** p. 7 NOV — St. Bartholomew the Great** p. 7 OU K — St. Mary-at-Hill** p. 7 PV B — Temple Church** p. 6 MV — All Hallows-by-the-Tower (font cover**, brasses*) p. 7 PV Y — St. Bride* (steeple**) p. 7 NV J — St. Giles Cripplegate* p. 7 OU N — St. Helen Bishopsgate* (monuments**) p. 7 PUV R — St. James Garlickhythe (tower and spire*, sword rests*) p. 7 OV R — St. Margaret Lothbury* p. 7 PU S — St. Margaret Pattens (woodwork*) p. 7 PV N — St. Mary Abchurch* p. 7 PV X — St. Mary-le-Bow (tower and steeple**) p. 7 OV G — St. Michael Paternoster Royal (tower and spire*) p. 7 OV D — St. Olave* p. 7 PV S.

Other Churches

Westminster Abbey*** p. 10 LY — Southwark Cathedral** p. 11 PX — Queen's Chapel* p. 13 EP — St. Clement Danes* p. 17 EX — St. James's* p. 13 EM — St. Margaret's* p. 10 LY A — St. Martin in-the-Fields* p. 17 DY — St. Paul's* (Covent Garden) p. 17 DX — Westminster Roman Catholic Cathedral* p. 10 KY B.

STREETS — SQUARES — PARKS

The City*** p. 7 NV — Regent's Park*** (Terraces**, Zoo***) p. 5 HIT — Bedford Square** p. 6 KLU — Belgrave Square** p. 16 AVX — Burlington Arcade** p. 13 DM — Hyde Park** p. 9 GHVX — The Mall** p. 13 FP — Piccadilly** p. 13 EM — St. James's Park** p. 10 KXY — Trafalgar Square** p. 17 DY — Whitehall** (Horse Guards)* p. 10 LX — Barbican* p. 7 OU — Bloomsbury* p. 6 LMU — Bond Street* pp. 12-13 CK-DM — Charing Cross* p. 17 DY — Cheyne Walk* p. 9 GHZ — Jermyn Street* p. 13 EN — Piccadilly Arcade* p. 13 DEN — Queen Anne's Gate* p. 10 KY — Regent Street* p. 13 EM — St. James's Square* p. 13 FN — St. James's Street* p. 13 EN — Shepherd Market* p. 12 CN — Strand* p. 17 DY — Victoria Embankment* p. 17 DEXY — Waterloo Place* p. 13 FN.

MUSEUMS

British Museum*** p. 6 LU — National Gallery*** p. 13 GM — Science Museum*** p. 14 CR — Tate Gallery*** p. 10 LZ — Victoria and Albert Museum*** p. 15 DR — Courtauld Institute Galleries** p. 6 KLU M — Museum of London** p. 7 OU M — National Portrait Gallery** p. 13 GM — Natural History Museum** p. 14 CS — Queen's Gallery** p. 16 BV — Wallace Collection** p. 12 AH — Imperial War Museum* p. 10 NY — London Transport Museum* p. 17 DX — Madame Tussaud's* p. 5 IU M — Sir John Soane's Museum* p. 6 MU M — Wellington Museum* p. 12 BP.

■ ## ALPHABETICAL LIST OF AREAS INCLUDED

LONDON CENTRE

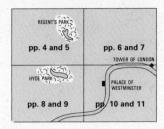

STREET INDEX TO LONDON CENTRE TOWN PLANS

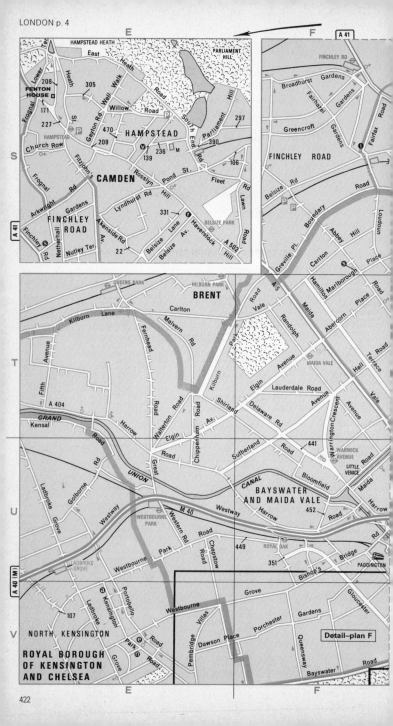

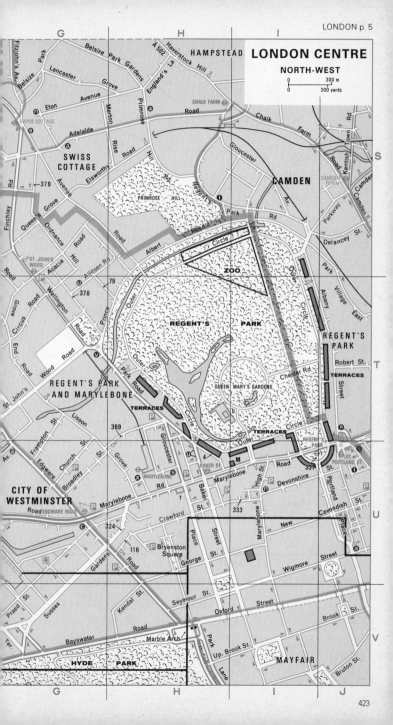

LONDON CENTRE

NORTH-EAST

425

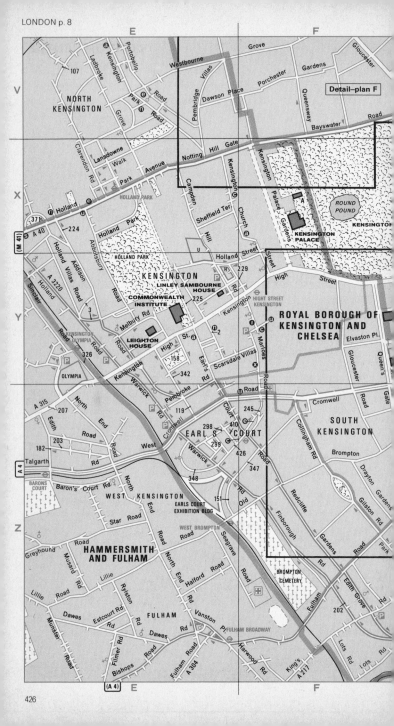

LONDON CENTRE
SOUTH-WEST

0 — 300 m
0 — 300 yards

G H I J

Praed St.
Sussex
Ter.
Bayswater
Kendal St.
Seymour St.
Oxford
Marble Arch
Park
Road
Up. Brook
Lane
MAYFAIR
Bruton St.
Berkeley St.

V

HYDE PARK
THE LONG WATER
CITY OF WESTMINSTER
Park
South
Audley
St.
Curzon
St.
Piccadilly

X

GARDENS
Serpentine
THE SERPENTINE
Road
Lane
GREEN PARK
Constitution
Hill

HYDE PARK AND KNIGHTSBRIDGE

Kensington
Road
Knightsbridge
HYDE PARK
CORNER
Grosvenor Pl.
BUCKINGHAM
PALACE

Exhibition
Road
Brompton
Road
Sloane
Street
Belgrave
Square
Chapel St.
Detail–plan D
BELGRAVIA

Y

Road
Walton
Street
Pont
Street
Cadogan
Street
Lyall
St.
Street
VICTORIA

Pelham Street
Sloane
Square
King's
Road
Ebury
Belgrave

Detail–plan C

Road
Onslow Gdns
Sydney
Cale
Street
Avenue
Pimlico
Buckingham Palace Rd
Warwick Way
Sutherland
St.
Gloucester

Fulham
Old
Church
King's
Smith Street
Hospital
Road
Chelsea Bridge
Ebury Bridge Rd
156
Lupus

Z

Beaufort
Street
Oakley
Street
Royal
Chelsea
Embankment
Bridge
Chelsea
Bridge
Grosvenor

Walk
Cheyne
Walk
Cheyne Walk
Albert
Bridge
The
Parade
Carriage
Drive
75
Queenstown
Road

Battersea
Bridge
Mon.–Fri.
Tidal traffic
flow
Albert
Bridge
75
BATTERSEA PARK
East

Parkgate
Rd.
Battersea Bridge Rd.
WANDSWORTH
361
19

G H I J

427

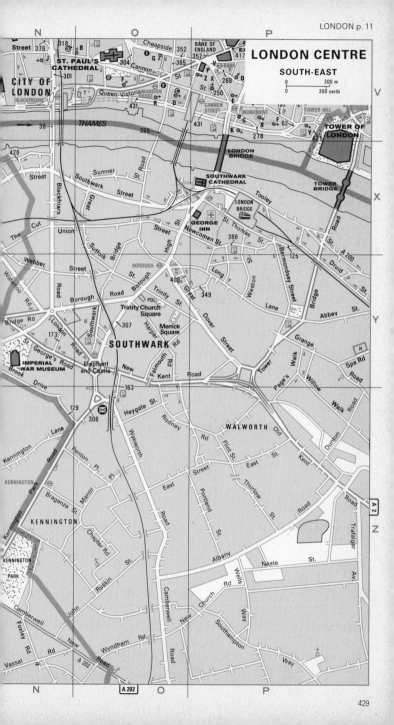

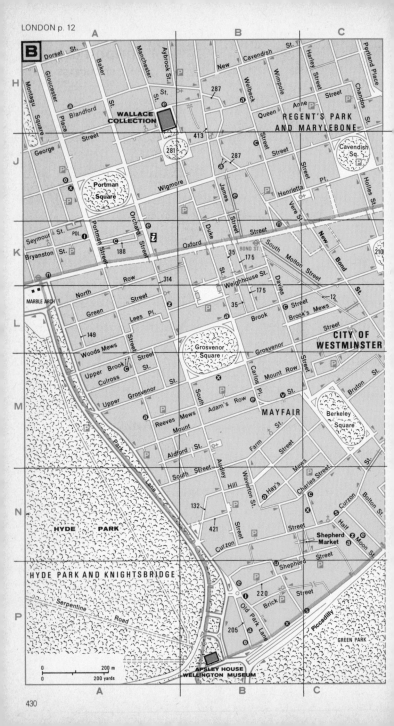

Oxford Street is closed to private traffic, Mondays to Saturdays :
from 7 am to 7 pm between Portman Street and St. Giles Circus

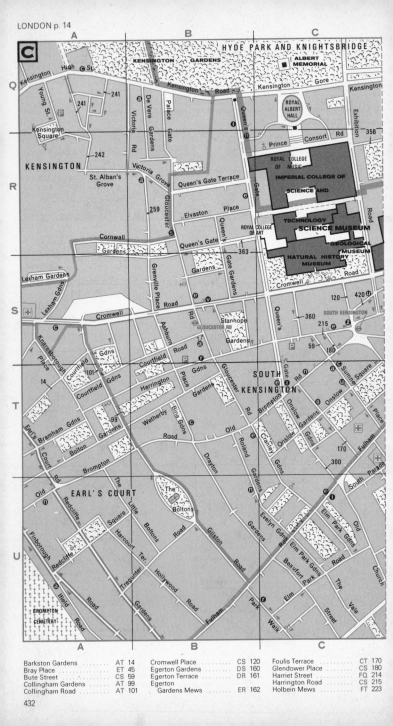

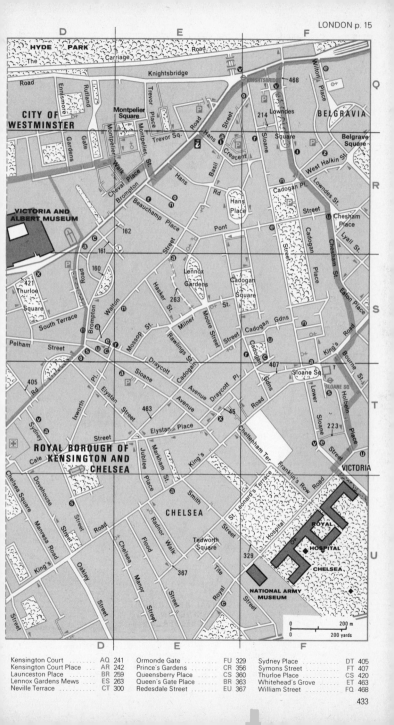

HYDE PARK

The Carriage Road

Knightsbridge

CITY OF WESTMINSTER

Montpelier Square

Trevor Sq.

Rutland Gate

Ennismore Gardens

Montpelier Walk

Montpelier St.

Cheval Place

Brompton

Beauchamp Place

Road

Knightsbridge

KNIGHTSBRIDGE — 468

Lowndes Square

214

Sloane Street

Hans Crescent

Basil St.

BELGRAVIA

Belgrave Square

West Halkin St.

Lowndes St.

Chesham Place

Lyall St.

VICTORIA AND ALBERT MUSEUM

162

161

421 Thurloe Square

160

South Terrace

Pelham Street

Brompton Road

Walton

Hasker St.

263

Mossop St.

Milner

Moore Street

Rawlings St.

Draycott

Cadogan

Hans Rd

Pont Street

Hans Place

Lennox Gardens

Cadogan Square

St.

Cadogan Gdns

Cadogan Place

Cadogan Street

Cadogan

Chesham St.

Eaton Place

King's Road

Bourne St.

407

Sloane Sq.

SLOANE SQ

Lower Sloane

Holbein Place

223

VICTORIA

405 Rd

Ixworth

Sydney

Cale

Elystan Street

Pl.

Sloane Avenue

463

Draycott Avenue

Elystan Place

Markham St.

Jubilee Place

45

King's

Draycott Pl.

Road

Cheltenham Ter

Leonard's Terrace

Franklin's Row

ROYAL BOROUGH OF KENSINGTON AND CHELSEA

CHELSEA

Chelsea Square

Dovehouse Street

Manresa Road

Oakley

King's

Road

Radnor Walk

Flood Street

Chelsea Manor Street

Smith Street

Teadworth Square

367

Tite Street

St. Leonard's Terrace

Royal Hospital Road

329

Street

ROYAL HOSPITAL CHELSEA

NATIONAL ARMY MUSEUM

VICTORIA

0   200 m
0   200 yards

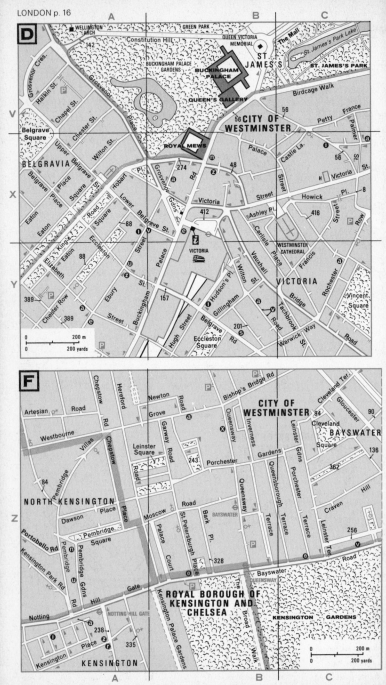

D

WELLINGTON ARCH

GREEN PARK

QUEEN VICTORIA MEMORIAL

Constitution Hill

142

The Mall

ST. JAMES'S PARK LAKE

BUCKINGHAM PALACE GARDENS

BUCKINGHAM PALACE

ST. JAMES'S

ST. JAMES'S PARK

Birdcage Walk

Grosvenor Cres.

Halkin St.

Chapel St.

Grosvenor Place

QUEEN'S GALLERY

56 CITY OF WESTMINSTER

56

Petty France

Palmer St.

V

Belgrave Square

Chester St.

Wilton St.

ROYAL MEWS

274

Palace

Castle La.

56

Victoria St.

BELGRAVIA

Upper Belgrave

Grosvenor Gdns.

48

Street

H

8

Belgrave Place

Hobart Pl.

Rd.

Howick

416

Row

X

Eaton Square

Lower Belgrave St.

Victoria

412

Ashley Pl.

Street

Pl.

Street

Eaton Place

Road

88

Street

Carlisle Place

WESTMINSTER CATHEDRAL

Francis

King's

Eccleston

VICTORIA

412

Vauxhall

Rochester

Elizabeth

88

Palace

VICTORIA

Wilton

Vincent Square

Y

389

Chester Row

Ebury

Street

St.

157

Buckingham

Hudson's Pl.

Gillingham

Bridge

Tachbrook

Vincent Square

389

Street

Hugh Street

Belgrave Rd

Eccleston Square

201

Warwick Way

Road

| 0 | 200 m |
| 0 | 200 yards |

F

Artesian Road

Chepstow

Hereford

Newton

Road

Grove

Bishop's Bridge Rd

Queensway

CITY OF WESTMINSTER

84

Cleveland Terr.

Gloucester

90

Westbourne

Chepstow Rd.

Villas

Chepstow Place

Leinster Square

Garway Road

Porchester

Inverness

Leinster Gdns

Cleveland Square

BAYSWATER

136

Z

NORTH KENSINGTON

84

Dawson Place

Road

243

Gardens

Queensborough Terrace

Porchester Terrace

362

Pembridge Square

Moscow Road

St.Petersburgh Place

Bark

BAYSWATER

Queensway

Terrace

Craven Hill

256

Portobello Rd

Kensington Park Rd

Pembridge

Pembridge Gdns

Pembridge Square

Palace Court

328

Bayswater

QUEENSWAY

Road

V

Notting

Rd

Hill

Gate

NOTTING HILL GATE

Kensington Palace Gdns

The Broad Walk

ROYAL BOROUGH OF KENSINGTON AND CHELSEA

KENSINGTON GARDENS

238

335

KENSINGTON

Place

| 0 | 200 m |
| 0 | 200 yards |

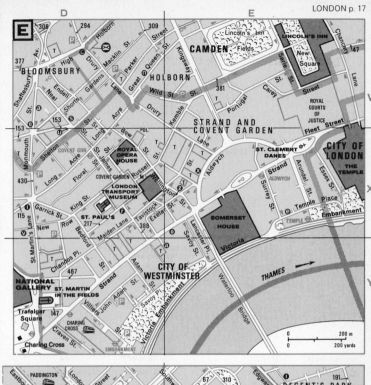

■ STARRED ESTABLISHMENTS IN LONDON

🏵🏵🏵

	Area	Page
XXXX **Le Gavroche**	Mayfair	32

🏵🏵

	Area	Page
XXXX **La Tante Claire**	Chelsea	26
XXXX **Chez Nico**	Regent's Park and Marylebonne	34
XXX **Harvay's**	Wandsworth	30

🏵

	Area	Page			Area	Page
⌂ **Connaught**	Mayfair	31		XXX **Cavalier's**	Battersea	30
⌂ **Capital**	Chelsea	25		XXX **L'Arlequin**	Battersea	30
XXXXX **Oak Room**	Mayfair	32		XXX **Suntory**	St. James's	35
XXXX **Four Seasons**	Mayfair	32		XX **Sutherlands**	Soho	35

■ FURTHER ESTABLISHMENTS WHICH MERIT YOUR ATTENTION

XXX **Keat's**	Hampstead	24		XX **Hilaire**	South Kensington	29
XXX **Turner's**	Chelsea	26		XX **Le Caprice**	St. James's	35
XXX **Bibendum**		26		X **Vijay**	Kilburn	23
XXX **Dynasty II**		26		X **Chinon**	Shepherd's Bush	25
XXX **Red Fort**	Soho	35		X **Kensington Place**	Kensington	28
XXX **Zen Central**	Mayfair	32		X **Al San Vicenzo**	Cheam	30

■ RESTAURANTS CLASSIFIED ACCORDING TO TYPE

SEAFOOD

KENSINGTON & CHELSEA (Royal Borough of)

Chelsea		XX	**Poissonnerie de l'Avenue**	p. 26
–		XX	**Suquet (Le)**	p. 27
Earl's Court		XX	**Croisette (La)**	p. 27
–		XX	**Tiger Lee**	p. 27
Mayfair		XX	**La Seppia**	p. 33

WESTMINSTER (City of)

Soho		XX	**L'Hippocampe**	p. 35
Strand & Covent Garden		XX	**Sheekey's**	p. 36
Victoria		XX	**Hoizin**	p. 37

CHINESE

CAMDEN

Bloomsbury		XX	**Poons of Russell Square**	p. 23

KENSINGTON & CHELSEA (Royal Borough of)

Chelsea		XXX	**Zen**	p. 26
–		XX	**Good Earth**	p. 27
–		XX	**Good Earth**	p. 27
–		XX	**Magic Dragon**	p. 27
Earl's Court		XX	**Tiger Lee**	p. 27
Kensington		XX	**I Ching**	p. 28
–		XX	**Sailing Junk**	p. 28
–		XX	**Shanghai**	p. 28

WESTMINSTER (City of)

Bayswater & Maida Vale		XX	**Poons**	p. 30
–		XX	**Hsing**	p. 30
Mayfair		XXX	**Princess Garden**	p. 32
–		XXX	**Zen Central**	p. 32
–		XXX	**Emperess Garden**	p. 32
Soho		XX	**Ming**	p. 35
–		XX	**Gallery Rendez-Vous**	p. 35
Victoria		XXX	**Inn of Happiness**	p. 36
–		XX	**Hoizin**	p. 37
–		XX	**Hunan**	p. 37
–		XX	**Ken Lo's Memories of China**	p. 37
–		XX	**Kym's**	p. 37

ENGLISH

KENSINGTON & CHELSEA (Royal Borough of),

Chelsea		XX	**English Garden**	p. 26

WESTMINSTER (City of)

Mayfair		XXX	**Jason's Court**	p. 34
St. James's		XX	**Green's**	p. 35
Soho		XXX	**Lindsay House**	p. 35
Strand & Covent Garden		XXX	**Simson's-in-the-Strand**	p. 36
Victoria		XX	**Green's**	p. 37
–		X	**Tate Gallery Rest.**	p. 37

FRENCH

HUNGARIAN

INDIAN & PAKISTANI

ITALIAN	ISLINGTON			
	Finsbury	XX	**Brivati's**	p. 25
	KENSINGTON & CHELSEA (Royal Borough of)			
	Chelsea	XX	**Beccofino**	p. 27
	–	XX	**Eleven Park Walk**	p. 27
	–	XX	**La Finezza**	p. 26
	–	XX	**Mario**	p. 26
	–	XX	**Ponte Nuovo**	p. 27
	–	XX	**Toto**	p. 27
	–	XX	**Waterfront**	p. 26
	–	XX	**Salotto**	p. 26
	Earl's Court	XX	**Primula (La)**	p. 27
	Kensington	XX	**Paesana (La)**	p. 28
	–	XX	**Topo d'Oro**	p. 28
	SUTTON			
	Cheam	X	**Al San Vicenzo**	p. 30
	WESTMINSTER (City of)			
	Bayswater & Maida Vale	XX	**San Marino**	p. 30
	Regent's Park & Marylebonne	XX	**Fontana Amorosa**	p. 34
	–	XX	**Loggia (La)**	p. 34
	Strand & Covent Garden	XX	**Orso**	p. 36
	Victoria	XXX	**Incontro**	p. 36
	–	XXX	**Santini**	p. 36
	–	XX	**Amico (L')**	p. 37
	–	XX	**Gran Paradiso**	p. 37

JAPANESE	CAMDEN			
	Hampstead	XXX	**Benihana**	p. 24
	CITY OF LONDON			
	City of London	XX	**Miyama**	p. 25
	KENSINGTON & CHELSEA (Royal Borough of)			
	Kensington	XX	**Hiroko**	p. 28
	WESTMINSTER (City of)			
	Mayfair	XX	**Miyama**	p. 33
	–	XX	**Shogun**	p. 33
	Regent's Park & Marylebonne	XX	**Asuka**	p. 34
	–	XX	**Masako**	p. 34
	–	XX	**Mon**	p. 34
	St. James's	XXX	✿ **Suntory**	p. 35

KOREAN	WESTMINSTER (City of)			
	Soho	XX	**Kaya**	p. 35

LEBANESE	KENSINGTON & CHELSEA (Royal Borough of)			
	Kensington	XX	**Phoenicia**	p. 28

ORIENTAL	KENSINGTON & CHELSEA (Royal Borough of)			
	Chelsea	XX	**Dynasty II**	p. 26
	WESTMINSTER (City of)			
	Mayfair	XX	**Ho-Ho**	p. 32

SPANISH	WESTMINSTER (City of)			
	Regent's Park	XX	**Tino's**	p. 34

SWEDISH	ISLINGTON			
	Canonbury	X	**Anna's Place**	p. 25

THAI	KENSINGTON & CHELSEA (Royal Borough of)			
	South Kensington	XX	**Tui**	p. 29

Greater London *is divided, for administrative purposes, into 32 boroughs plus the City; these sub-divide naturally into minor areas, usually grouped around former villages or quarters, which often maintain a distinctive character.*

🕭 *of Greater London: 071 or 081 except special cases.*

LONDON AIRPORTS

Heathrow Middx. W : 17 m. by A 4, M 4 – **Underground** Piccadilly line direct – **404** ⓐ – 🕭 081.

✈ ℰ 759 4321, Telex 934892.

🏨 **Sheraton Skyline,** Bath Rd, Hayes, UB3 5BP, ℰ 759 2535, Telex 934254, Fax 750 9150, « Exotic indoor garden with 🔲 », ⇔, 🔲 – 🛗 ✻ rm 🔟 🏧 🐧 🅿 – 🔬 500. 🔼 🆎 ⓞ 𝘝𝘐𝘚𝘈 ⋙
M 21.50/34.00 **t.** and a la carte ᐧ 6.50 – ⌁ 9.50 – **347 rm** 120.00/150.00 s., **5 suites** 345.00/785.00 **s.**

🏨 **Excelsior** (T.H.F.), Bath Rd, West Drayton, UB7 0DU, ℰ 759 6611, Telex 24525, Fax 759 3421, *ℓ₅*, ⇔, 🔲 – 🛗 ✻ rm 🔟 🏧 🐧 🅿 – 🔬 700. 🔼 🆎 ⓞ 𝘝𝘐𝘚𝘈
M *(closed Saturday lunch)* 13.95 **st.** and a la carte ᐧ 4.35 – ⌁ 8.75 – **830 rm** 110.00/135.00 **st.**, **7 suites** 200.00/225.00 **st.**

🏨 **Holiday Inn,** Stockley Rd, West Drayton, UB7 9NA, ℰ 0895 (West Drayton) 445555, Telex 934518, Fax 445122, ⇔, 🔲, 🟦, ⋘, squash – 🛗 ✻ rm 🔟 🏧 🐧 🅿 – 🔬 100. 🔼 🆎 ⓞ 𝘝𝘐𝘚𝘈
M 15.00 **st.** and a la carte ᐧ 5.00 – ⌁ 8.50 – **374 rm** 104.00/124.00 **st.**, **6 suites** 450.00/510.00 **st.** – SB (weekends only) 150.00/300.00 **st.**

🏨 **Post House** (T.H.F.), Sipson Rd, West Drayton, UB7 0JU, ℰ 759 2323, Telex 934280, Fax 897 8659, *ℓ₅*, ⇔ – 🛗 ✻ rm 🔟 🏧 🅿 – 🔬 200. 🔼 🆎 ⓞ 𝘝𝘐𝘚𝘈
M (carving rest.) 13.95/16.00 **st.** and a la carte ᐧ 4.35 – ⌁ 7.00 – **565 rm** 85.00/180.00 **st.** – SB (weekends only) 91.90 **st.**

🏨 **Sheraton Heathrow,** Colnbrook by-pass, West Drayton, UB7 0HJ, ℰ 759 2424, Telex 934331, Fax 759 2091, 🔲, ✻ – 🛗 ✻ rm 🔟 🏧 🐧 🅿 – 🔬 70. 🔼 🆎 ⓞ 𝘝𝘐𝘚𝘈 ⋙
M 12.00/30.00 **t.** and a la carte ᐧ 6.00 – ⌁ 8.75 – **439 rm** 135.00/160.00 s., **1 suite** 253.00 **s.**

🏨 **Heathrow Penta,** Bath Rd, Hounslow, TW6 2AQ, ℰ 897 6363, Telex 934660, Fax 897 1113, ⟨, *ℓ₅*, ⇔ – 🛗 ✻ rm 🔟 🏧 🐧 🅿 – 🔬 600. 🔼 🆎 ⓞ 𝘝𝘐𝘚𝘈 ⋙
M *(closed lunch Saturday and Sunday)* 14.50/15.70 **st.** and a la carte ᐧ 5.30 – ⌁ 8.80 – **629 rm** 95.00/107.00 **st.**, **6 suites** 167.00/385.00 **st.**

🏨 **Skyway,** 140 Bath Rd, Hayes, UB3 5AW, ℰ 759 6311, Telex 23935, Fax 759 4559, 🔲 heated – 🛗 🗒 rest 🔟 🏧 🅿 – 🔬 250
444 rm, 2 suites.

🏨 **Heathrow Park** (Mt. Charlotte Thistle), Bath Rd, Longford, West Drayton, UB7 0EQ, ℰ 759 2400, Telex 934093, Fax 759 5278 – 🗒 rm 🔟 🏧 🅿 – 🔬 700. 🔼 🆎 ⓞ 𝘝𝘐𝘚𝘈
M *(closed Sunday dinner)* (carving lunch)/dinner 13.50 **st.** and a la carte – **306 rm** 75.00/105.00 **st.**

🏨 **Ariel** (T.H.F.), Bath Rd, Hayes, UB3 5AJ, ℰ 759 2552, Telex 21777, Fax 564 9265 – 🛗 ✻ rm 🔟 🏧 🅿 🔼 🆎 ⓞ 𝘝𝘐𝘚𝘈
M *(closed Saturday lunch)* 13.50/14.50 **st.** and a la carte ᐧ 3.60 – ⌁ 7.75 – **177 rm** 90.00/100.00 **st.**

Gatwick West Sussex S : 28 m. by A 23 and M 23 – **Train** from Victoria : Gatwick Express **404** T 30 – ✉ West Sussex – 🕭 0293 Gatwick.

✈ ℰ 28822 (general information) 31299 (flight information) and ℰ 081 (London) 668 42111.
🛈 International Arrivals Concourse ℰ 560108.

🏨 **London Gatwick Airport Hilton,** Gatwick Airport, RH6 0LL, ℰ 518080, Telex 877021, Fax 28980, *ℓ₅*, ⇔, 🔲 – 🛗 ✻ rm 🔟 🏧 🐧 🅿 – 🔬 450. 🔼 🆎 ⓞ 𝘝𝘐𝘚𝘈
M 13.50/22.90 **st.** and a la carte ᐧ 6.95 – ⌁ 9.95 – **549 rm** 115.00/125.00 **st.**, **3 suites** 185.00/295.00 **st.**

🏨 **Gatwick Penta,** Povey Cross Rd, ✉ Horley (Surrey), RH6 0BE, ℰ 820169, Telex 87440, Fax 820259, ⇔, 🔲, squash – 🛗 ✻ rm 🔟 🏧 🐧 🅿 – 🔬 150. 🔼 🆎 ⓞ 𝘝𝘐𝘚𝘈
M *(closed Saturday lunch)* 13.00/16.25 **st.** and a la carte ᐧ 4.40 – ⌁ 7.75 – **256 rm** 95.00/110.00 **st.**, **4 suites** 205.00/220.00 **st.** – SB (weekends only) 281.50 **st.**

🏨 **Post House** (T.H.F.), Povey Cross Rd, ✉ Horley (Surrey), RH6 0BA, ℰ 771621, Telex 877351, Fax 771054, 🔲, – 🛗 ✻ rm 🔟 🏧 🅿 – 🔬 100. 🔼 🆎 ⓞ 𝘝𝘐𝘚𝘈
M *(closed Saturday lunch)* 10.50/14.50 **st.** and a la carte ᐧ 4.35 – ⌁ 8.00 – **216 rm** 80.00/90.00 **st.**

BRENT

Kilburn – ✉ NW6 – ☎ 071.

✗ **Vijay,** 49 Willesden Lane, NW6 7RF, ✆ 328 1087, South Indian rest. – ▤. 🅰 🄰🄴 ⑩ 𝗩𝗜𝗦𝗔
M a la carte 7.50/8.00 **t.**

CAMDEN Except where otherwise stated see pp. 4-7.

Bloomsbury – ✉ NW1/W1/WC1 – ☎ 071.

🛈 35 Woburn Pl. WC1 ✆ 580 4599.

🏨🏨🏨 **Russell** (T.H.F.), Russell Sq., WC1B 5BE, ✆ 837 6470, Telex 24615, Fax 837 2857 – 🛗 ⇖ rm
📺 ☎ – 🔬 450. 🅰 🄰🄴 ⑩ 𝗩𝗜𝗦𝗔 ⌖   LU o
M (carving rest.) 14.50 **t.** and a la carte 🍷 6.95 – ⇌ 9.95 – **317 rm** 107.00/130.00 **st.**, **3 suites**
141.00/216.00 **st.** – SB (weekends only) 127.00/145.00 **st.**

🏨🏨 **Mountbatten,** 20 Monmouth St., WC2H 9HD, ✆ 836 4300, Telex 298087, Fax 240 3540 –
🛗 ⇖ rm ▤ rest 📺 ☎ – 🔬 75. 🅰 🄰🄴 ⑩ 𝗩𝗜𝗦𝗔   p. 17 DV o
M (closed Saturday lunch) 18.50/22.50 **st.** and dinner a la carte 🍷 5.00 – ⇌ 11.00 – **121 rm**
136.00/161.00 **st.**, **6 suites** 350.00 **st.** – SB (weekends only) 201.00 **st.**

🏨🏨 Marlborough, Bloomsbury St., WC1B 3QD, ✆ 636 5601, Telex 298274 – 🛗 ⇖ ▤ rest 📺 ☎
🔬 – 🔬 300   LU i
167 rm, **2 suites**.

🏨🏨 **Grafton,** 130 Tottenham Court Rd, W1P 9HP, ✆ 388 4131, Telex 297234, Fax 387 7394 – 🛗
▤ rest 📺 ☎ – 🔬 100. 🅰 🄰🄴 ⑩ 𝗩𝗜𝗦𝗔   KU n
M (closed Saturday lunch) 18.50 **st.** and a la carte 🍷 5.75 – ⇌ 9.00 – **232 rm** 94.00/124.00 **st.**,
4 suites 175.00/220.00 **st**

🏨🏨 **Kenilworth,** 97 Great Russell St., WC1B 3LB, ✆ 637 3477, Telex 25842, Fax 631 3133 – 🛗
▤ rest 📺 ☎ – 🔬 150. 🅰 🄰🄴 ⑩ 𝗩𝗜𝗦𝗔 ⌖   LU a
M 13.00 **st.** and a la carte – ⇌ 9.00 – **192 rm** 99.00/135.00 **st.**

🏨 **Kingsley** (Mt. Charlotte Thistle), Bloomsbury Way, WC1A 2SD, ✆ 242 5881, Telex 21157,
Fax 831 0225 – 🛗 ⇖ rm 📺 ☎ – 🔬 80. 🅰 🄰🄴 ⑩ 𝗩𝗜𝗦𝗔   LU r
M 13.00 **t.** and a la carte 🍷 3.95 – ⇌ 7.75 – **143 rm** 77.50/97.50 **st.**, **2 suites** 200.00 **st.** –
SB (weekends only) 107.00 **st.**

🏨 **Bloomsbury Crest** (T.H.F.), Coram St., WC1N 1HT, ✆ 837 1200, Telex 22113, Fax 837 5374
– 🛗 ⇖ rm ▤ rest 📺 ☎. 🅰 🄰🄴 ⑩ 𝗩𝗜𝗦𝗔   LT c
M 16.50/18.50 **s.** and a la carte 🍷 5.95 – ⇌ 9.25 – **282 rm** 104.00/119.00 **st.**, **2 suites**
215.00/275.00 **st.** – SB (weekends only) 101.00/113.00 **st.**

🏨 **Bloomsbury Park** (Mt. Charlotte Thistle), 126 Southampton Row, WC1B 5AD, ✆ 430 0434,
Telex 25757, Fax 242 0665 – 🛗 📺 ☎. 🅰 🄰🄴 ⑩ 𝗩𝗜𝗦𝗔   LU u
M (closed Friday dinner, Saturday and Sunday) 12.50 **st.** (dinner) and a la carte 14.25/20.80 **st.**
🍷 4.00 – ⇌ 7.25 – **95 rm** 72.50/100.00 **st.**

✗✗ **Jamdani,** 34 Charlotte St., W1P 1HJ, ✆ 636 1178, Indian rest. – ⇖ ▤. 🅰 🄰🄴 ⑩ 𝗩𝗜𝗦𝗔
closed Sunday and 25-26 December – M a la carte 15.50/20.00 **t.**   KU e

✗✗ **Neal Street,** 26 Neal St., WC2 9PH, ✆ 836 8368 – 🅰 🄰🄴 𝗩𝗜𝗦𝗔   p. 17 DV s
closed Saturday, Sunday, Christmas-New Year and Bank Holidays – M a la carte 20.50/36.00 **t.**
🍷 6.50.

✗✗ **Poons of Russell Square,** 50 Woburn Pl., WC1H 0JE, ✆ 580 1188, Chinese rest. – ▤.
🅰 🄰🄴 ⑩ 𝗩𝗜𝗦𝗔   LU x
closed 25-26 December and Bank Holidays – M a la carte 9.50/18.25 **t.**

✗✗ **Heals** 1st floor, Heal's Department Store, 196 Tottenham Rd, W1P 9LD,
✆ 636 1666 (ext: 5513), Fax 631 3091 – ▤. 🅰 🄰🄴 𝗩𝗜𝗦𝗔   KU z
closed Sunday and Bank Holidays – M (lunch only) 25.75 **t.** 🍷 4.50.

✗✗ **Mon Plaisir,** 21 Monmouth St., WC2H 9DD, ✆ 836 7243, French rest. – 🅰 🄰🄴 ⑩
𝗩𝗜𝗦𝗔   p. 17 DV a
closed Saturday lunch and Sunday – M 12.95 **t.** and a la carte 14.00/19.10 **t.** 🍷 4.90.

✗ **Smith's,** 33 Shelton St., WC2 9HT, ✆ 379 0310 – 🅰 🄰🄴 ⑩ 𝗩𝗜𝗦𝗔   p. 17 DVX u
closed Saturday lunch except September-22 December, 23 December-1 January and Bank
Holidays – M a la carte 12.35/24.20 **st.** 🍷 5.80.

✗ **Auntie's,** 126 Cleveland St., W1P 5DN, ✆ 387 1548 – 🅰 🄰🄴 ⑩ 𝗩𝗜𝗦𝗔   JU s
closed Saturday lunch, Sunday, 3 weeks August and Christmas – M approx. 18.50 **t.** 🍷 8.00.

Camden Town – ✉ NW1 – ☎ 071.

✗ **La Bougie,** 7 Murray St., NW1 9RE, ✆ 485 6400, Bistro   KS a
closed Saturday lunch, Monday, last 2 weeks August, 25 December-2 January and Bank
Holidays – M a la carte 12.75/14.50 **t.** 🍷 3.00.

Finchley Road – ✉ NW3/NW6 – ☎ 071.

🏨 **Charles Bernard,** 5-7 Frognal, NW3 6AL, ✆ 794 0101, Telex 23560, Fax 794 0100 – 🛗 📺
☎ 🅿. 🅰 🄰🄴 ⑩ 𝗩𝗜𝗦𝗔 ⌖   ES s
M (bar lunch)/dinner a la carte 9.00/15.75 **st.** 🍷 3.50 – **57 rm** ⇌ 52.00/88.00 **st.**

Hampstead – ⊠ NW3 – ☎ 071.

🏠 **Clive** (Hilton), Primrose Hill Rd, NW3 3NA, ☎ 586 2233, Telex 22759, Fax 586 1659 – 🛗 📺 ☎ 🅿 – 🕍 350. 🔼 🖭 ⓪ 𝒱𝐼𝒮𝒜
HS **a**
M *(closed lunch Saturday and Bank Holidays)* 15.50/17.50 **st.** ⓙ 4.50 – � 8.50 – **93 rm** 82.00/100.00 **st.**, **3 suites** 115.00/120.00 **st.** – SB (weekends only) 106.00/112.00 **st.**

🏠 **Swiss Cottage,** 4 Adamson Rd, NW3 3HP, ☎ 722 2281, Telex 297232, Fax 483 4588, « Antique furniture collection » – 🛗 📺 𝒱𝐼𝒮𝒜 ⓙ 40. 🔼 🖭 𝒱𝐼𝒮𝒜 ⟩⟩
GS **n**
M 12.80/20.65 **t.** and a la carte ⓙ 4.95 – **62 rm** ⊒ 65.00/105.00 **t.**, **2 suites** 115.00/125.00 **t.** – SB (weekends only) 75.00/90.00 **st.**

🏠 **Post House** (T.H.F.), 215 Haverstock Hill, NW3 4RB, ☎ 794 8121, Telex 262494, Fax 435 5586 – 🛗 ⟩⟨ rm 📺 ☎ 🅿 – 🕍 30. 🔼 🖭 ⓪ 𝒱𝐼𝒮𝒜
ES **r**
M 12.00/14.75 **st.** and a la carte – ⊒ 6.25 – **140 rm** 83.00/100.00 **st.** – SB (weekends only) 98.00/110.00 **st.**

🍴🍴🍴 **Keats,** 3a Downshire Hill, NW3 1NR, ☎ 435 3544 – 🔼 🖭 𝒱𝐼𝒮𝒜
ES **v**
closed Sunday, Monday, 3 weeks August and Bank Holidays – **M** 18.50/28.00 **st.** and a la carte ⓙ 6.00.

🍴🍴🍴 **Benihana,** 100 Avenue Rd, NW3 3HF, ☎ 586 9508, Fax 586 6740, Japanese Teppan-Yaki rest. – 🍽, 🔼 🖭 ⓪ 𝒱𝐼𝒮𝒜
GS **o**
M a la carte 16.40/46.95 **t.**

Holborn – ⊠ WC2 – ☎ 071.

🏨 **Drury Lane Moat House** (Q.M.H.), 10 Drury Lane, High Holborn, WC2B 5RE, ☎ 836 6666, Telex 8811395, Fax 831 1548 – ⟩⟨ rm 🍽 rm 📺 ☎ – 🕍 100. 🔼 🖭 ⓪ 𝒱𝐼𝒮𝒜
p. 17 DV **c**
closed Christmas – **M** 15.00/20.00 **st.** and a la carte ⓙ 5.00 – ⊒ 8.95 – **151 rm** 109.00/153.50 **st.**, **2 suites** 175.00/250.00 **st.** – SB (weekends only) 104.00/115.00 **st.**

🍴🍴🍴 L'Opera, 32 Great Queen St., WC2B 5AA, ☎ 405 9020
p. 17 DV **n**

Kentish Town – ⊠ NW5 – ☎ 071.

🍴🍴 **Bengal Lancer,** 253 Kentish Rd, NW5 2JT, ☎ 485 6688, Fax 482 4523 – 🍽. 🔼 🖭 ⓪ 𝒱𝐼𝒮𝒜
JS **c**
closed Saturday lunch and 25-26 December – **M** 12.00 **t.** (dinner) and a la carte 10.50/23.50 **t.** ⓙ 3.50.

Regent's Park – ⊠ NW1 – ☎ 071.

🏨 **White House** (Rank), Albany St., NW1 3UP, ☎ 387 1200, Telex 24111, Fax 388 0091, 🅵🅶, ⟺🅢 – ⟩⟨ rm 🍽 📺 ☎ & 🅿 – 🕍 100. 🔼 🖭 ⓪ 𝒱𝐼𝒮𝒜 ⟩⟩
JT **o**
M 18.50 **st.** and a la carte ⓙ 4.50 – ⊒ 10.00 – **561 rm** 105.00/135.00 **st.**, **15 suites** 180.00/300.00 **st.**

🍴🍴 **Odette's,** 130 Regent's Park Rd, NW1 8XL, ☎ 586 5486 – 🔼 🖭 ⓪ 𝒱𝐼𝒮𝒜
HS **i**
closed Saturday lunch, Sunday, last 2 weeks August and Bank Holidays – **M** a la carte 19.70/25.50 **t.** ⓙ 5.95.

Swiss Cottage – ⊠ NW3 – ☎ 071.

🏨 **Holiday Inn,** 128 King Henry's Rd, NW3 3ST, ☎ 722 7711, Telex 267396, Fax 586 5822, 🅵🅶, ⟺🅢, 🔲 – 🛗 ⟩⟨ rm 🍽 📺 ☎ & 🅿 – 🕍 400. 🔼 🖭 ⓪ 𝒱𝐼𝒮𝒜
GS **a**
M 17.00/18.50 **st.** and a la carte ⓙ 6.50 – ⊒ 10.25 – **298 rm** 139.00/160.00 **t.**, **4 suites** 350.00/600.00 **t.**

🍴🍴 **Peter's,** 65 Fairfax Rd, NW6 4EE, ☎ 624 5804 – 🔼 🖭 ⓪ 𝒱𝐼𝒮𝒜
FS **i**
closed Saturday lunch and 26-27 December – **M** 13.95 **t.** (lunch) and a la carte 19.20/22.70 **t.** ⓙ 4.50.

CITY OF LONDON – ☎ 071 Except where otherwise stated see p. 7.

🍴🍴 **Candlewick Room,** 45 Old Broad St., EC2N 1HT, ☎ 628 7929 – 🔼 🖭 ⓪ 𝒱𝐼𝒮𝒜
PU **n**
closed Saturday, Sunday, 25 December and Bank Holidays – **M** (lunch only) 23.95 **t.** and a la carte ⓙ 4.95.

🍴🍴 **Le Poulbot** (basement), 45 Cheapside, EC2V 6AR, ☎ 236 4379, French rest. – 🍽. 🔼 ⓪ 𝒱𝐼𝒮𝒜
OV **i**
closed Saturday, Sunday, Christmas and Bank Holidays – **M** (lunch only) 28.50 **st.** ⓙ 5.20.

🍴🍴 **Corney and Barrow,** 109 Old Broad St., EC2N 1AP, ☎ 638 9308 – 🍽. 🔼 🖭 𝒱𝐼𝒮𝒜
PU **c**
closed Saturday, Sunday and Bank Holidays – **M** (lunch only) 24.95 **t.** and a la carte ⓙ 11.75 .

🍴🍴 **Corney and Barrow,** 118 Moorgate, EC2M 6UR, ☎ 628 2898 – 🍽. 🔼 🖭 ⓪ 𝒱𝐼𝒮𝒜
PU **o**
closed Saturday, Sunday and Bank Holidays – **M** (lunch only) a la carte 23.85/27.85 **t.** ⓙ 7.00.

🍴🍴 **Corney and Barrow,** 44 Cannon St., EC4N 6JJ, ☎ 248 1700 – 🍽. 🔼 🖭 ⓪ 𝒱𝐼𝒮𝒜
OV **r**
closed Saturday, Sunday and Bank Holidays – **M** (lunch only) a la carte 19.85/24.40 **t.** ⓙ 7.00.

🍴🍴 **Le Sous Sol,** 32 Old Bailey, EC4M 7HS, ☎ 236 7931 – 🍽. 🔼 🖭 𝒱𝐼𝒮𝒜
NV **a**
closed Saturday, Sunday and Bank Holidays – **M** (lunch only) 22.50 **st.** ⓙ 4.95.

XX **Shares,** 12-13 Lime St., EC3M 7AA, 𝒫 623 1843 – 🔼 AE ⓪ VISA   PV **s**
closed Saturday, Sunday and Bank Holidays – **M** (lunch only) 28.50 **t.**

XX **Miyama,** 17 Godliman St., EC4V 5BD, 𝒫 489 1937, Japanese rest. – 🍽. 🔼 AE ⓪ VISA   OV **e**
closed Saturday, Sunday and Bank Holidays – **M** 16.00/38.00 **t.** and a la carte ≬ 4.00.

X **Bubb's,** 329 Central Market, Farringdon St., EC1A 9NB, 𝒫 236 2435, French rest.   NU **a**
closed Saturday, Sunday, 2 weeks August, 1 week Christmas and Bank Holidays –
M (booking essential) (lunch only) a la carte 17.50/24.05 **t.** ≬ 4.50.

X **Whittington's,** 21 College Hill, EC4R 2RP, 𝒫 248 5855 – 🍽. 🔼 AE ⓪ VISA   OV **c**
closed Saturday, Sunday and Bank Holidays – **M** (lunch only) a la carte 15.95/22.20 **t.** ≬ 3.75.

HAMMERSMITH AND FULHAM p.8.

Shepherd's Bush – ✉ W12/W14 – ✆ 071.

X **Chinon,** 25 Richmond Way, W14, 𝒫 602 5968 – 🍽. 🔼 VISA
closed Saturday lunch, Sunday, Monday, Easter, 2 weeks August and Bank Holidays –
M a la carte 23.00/30.50 **t.**

ISLINGTON pp. 4-7.

Canonbury – ✉ N1 – ✆ 071.

X **Anna's Place,** 90 Mildmay Park, N1 4PR, 𝒫 249 9379, Swedish rest.
closed Sunday, Monday, 2 weeks Easter, August and 2 weeks Christmas – **M** (booking essential) a la carte 12.00/16.40 **t.**

Finsbury – ✉ WC1/EC1/EC2 – ✆ 071.

XX Brivati's, 71-73 St. John St., EC1, 𝒫 253 4109, Italian rest.   NU **r**

XX Café Rouge, 2c Cherry Tree Walk, Whitecross St., EC1Y 0NX, 𝒫 588 0710   OU **e**

Islington – ✉ N1 – ✆ 071.

XX **Frederick's,** Camden Passage, N1 8EG, 𝒫 359 2888, Fax 359 5173, « Conservatory and
walled garden » – 🍽. 🔼 AE ⓪ VISA   NS **a**
closed Sunday, 25 December, 29 March and Bank Holidays – **M** 10.95 **st.** (lunch) a la
carte 15.25/18.80 **t.** ≬ 4.50.

KENSINGTON and CHELSEA (Royal Borough of).

Chelsea – ✉ SW1/SW3/SW10 – ✆ 071 – Except where otherwise stated see pp. 14
and 15.

🏨🏨 **Hyatt Carlton Tower,** 2 Cadogan Pl., SW1X 9PY, 𝒫 235 5411, Telex 21944, Fax 245 6570,
≼, ſ♠, ≘s, ☆, ⹀ – ᵇ ⁀ rm 🍽 ⓥ ☎ ⌕ – 🕍 250. 🔼 AE ⓪ VISA   FR **n**
M Chelsea Room 26.50/70.00 **t.** and a la carte ≬ 6.00 – **Rib Room** 23.50/50.00 **t.** (lunch)
and a la carte ≬ 6.75 – **194 rm** 210.00. **30 suites** 320.00/1500.00.

🏨🏨 **Conrad Chelsea Harbour,** Chelsea Harbour, SW1D 0XG, 𝒫 823 3000, Telex 919222, Fax
351 6525, ≼, ſ♠, ≘s, 🔳 – ᵇ ⁀ rm 🍽 ⓥ ☎ ⌕ 🅟 – 🕍 180. 🔼 AE ⓪ VISA
M 15.00 **t.** (lunch) and a la carte 16.75/45.50 **t.** – 🖵 11.50 – . **160 suites** 205.00/1000.00.

🏨🏨 **Sheraton Park Tower,** 101 Knightsbridge, SW1X 7RN, 𝒫 235 8050, Telex 917222, Fax
235 8231 – ᵇ ⁀ rm 🍽 ⓥ ☎ ⌕ 🅟 – 🕍 80. 🔼 AE ⓪ VISA ⹀   FQ **v**
M a la carte 28.00/35.25 **t.** ≬ 9.00 – 🖵 9.25 – **273 rm** 180.00/240.00 **s.,** **22 suites** 365.00/
980.00 **s.**

🏨🏨 ❀ **Capital,** 22-24 Basil St., SW3 1AT, 𝒫 589 5171, Telex 919042, Fax 225 0011 – ᵇ 🍽 ⓥ ☎.
🔼 AE ⓪ VISA ⹀   ER **a**
M 18.50/30.00 **st.** and a la carte 36.00/40.50 – 🖵 8.75 – **48 rm** 150.00/265.00 **st.**
Spec. Beignets de foie gras, endive salad, apple and Calvados coulis, Confit of veal sweetbreads cooked in
goose fat with a garlic soubise, Tarte Tatin, Calvados sorbet crème anglaise.

🏨🏨 **Draycott,** 24-26 Cadogan Gdns, SW3 2RP, 𝒫 730 6466, Telex 914947, Fax 730 0236 – ᵇ ⓥ
☎   FS **c**
M (room service only) – **26 rm.**

🏨🏨 **Basil Street,** 8 Basil St., SW3 1AH, 𝒫 581 3311, Telex 28379, Fax 581 3693 – ᵇ ⓥ ☎ –
🕍 55. 🔼 AE ⓪ VISA   FQ **o**
M 15.50 **t.** (lunch) and a la carte 22.00/26.00 **t.** ≬ 4.95 – 🖵 9.00 – **91 rm** 103.00/133.00 **st.,**
1 suite 207.00 **st.**

🏨🏨 **Fenja** without rest., 69 Cadogan Gdns, SW3 2RB, 𝒫 589 7333, Telex 934272, Fax 581 4958 –
ᵇ ⓥ ☎. 🔼 VISA ⹀   FS **r**
🖵 9.50 – **13 rm** 95.00/190.00 **t.**

🏨🏨 Cadogan, 75 Sloane St., SW1X 9SG, 𝒫 235 7141, Telex 267893, Fax 245 0994 – ᵇ ⁀ rm ⓥ
☎ ⌕ 🕍 40   FR **e**
64 rm, 5 suites.

🏨🏨 **Chelsea,** 17-25 Sloane St., SW1X 9NU, 𝒫 235 4377, Telex 919111, Fax 235 3705 – ᵇ
⁀ rm 🍽 ⓥ ☎ – 🕍 120. 🔼 AE ⓪ VISA ⹀   FR **r**
M a la carte 14.10/31.20 **st.** ≬ 4.90 – 🖵 9.75 – **218 rm** 140.80/184.80 **st.,** **7 suites** 302.50 **st.**

🏨 **Beaufort,** 33 Beaufort Gdns, SW3 1PP, ℰ 584 5252, Telex 929200, Fax 589 2834, « English floral watercolour collection » – ៛ 父 rm 🔟 ☎. 🔼 ﷾ ⑩ 𝘝𝘐𝘚𝘈. 💝
ER n
closed 23 December-2 January – **M** (room service only) – **28 rm** ⌷ (room service included) 150.00/250.00 **st.** – SB (weekends only) 144.00/225.00 **st.**

🏨 **Royal Court** (Q.M.H.), Sloane Sq., SW1W 8EG, ℰ 730 9191, Telex 296818, Fax 824 8381 –
᐀ ▤ rest 🔟 ☎ – 🔬 40. 🔼 ﷾ ⑩ 𝘝𝘐𝘚𝘈. 💝
FST a
M *(closed Saturday lunch)* 14.50/19.50 **st.** and a la carte – ⌷ 8.50 – **102 rm** 120.00/150.00 **st.**

🏨 **Eleven Cadogan Gardens** without rest., 11 Cadogan Gardens, SW3 2RJ, ℰ 730 3426, Fax 730 5217 – ᐀ ☎
FS u
56 rm, 5 suites.

🏨 **L'Hotel** without rest., 28 Basil St., SW3 1AT, ℰ 589 6286, Telex 919042, Fax 225 0011 – ᐀ 🔟 ☎. 🔼 ﷾ 𝘝𝘐𝘚𝘈. 💝
ER i
12 rm ⌷ 110.00/145.00 **t.**

🏨 **Stone House in London** without rest., 16 Sydney St., SW3, ℰ 0435 (Rushlake Green) 830553 – 🔟 ☎. 💝
DT a
3 rm.

🏠 **Claverley** without rest., 13-14 Beaufort Gdns, SW3 1PS, ℰ 589 8541, Fax 584 3410 – ᐀ 父 🔟 ☎. 🔼 𝘝𝘐𝘚𝘈. 💝
ER o
32 rm ⌷ 65.00/170.00 **t.**

🏠 **Willett** without rest., 32 Sloane Gdns, SW1W 8DJ, ℰ 824 8415, Telex 926678, Fax 824 8415 – 🔟 ☎. 🔼 ﷾ ⑩ 𝘝𝘐𝘚𝘈. 💝
FT s
18 rm ⌷ 59.95/79.95.

🏠 **Wilbraham,** 1-5 Wilbraham Pl., Sloane St., SW1X 9AE, ℰ 730 8296 – ᐀ ☎. 💝
FS n
M *(closed Saturday lunch and Sunday)* (restricted menu) approx. 14.85 **t.** ᐟ 2.95 – ⌷ 5.50 – **53 rm** 36.50/72.00.

XXXX ✿✿ **La Tante Claire** (Koffmann), 68-69 Royal Hospital Rd, SW3 4HP, ℰ 352 6045, Fax 352 3257, French rest. – ▤. 🔼 ﷾ ⑩ 𝘝𝘐𝘚𝘈
EU c
closed Saturday, Sunday, 10 days Easter, 3 weeks August and Christmas-New Year – **M** 21.50 **st.** (lunch) and a la carte 44.50/50.00 **st.** ᐟ 7.80
Spec. Coquilles St. Jacques poêlées à l'encre de seiche, Confit de saumon sauvage à la graisse d'oie, Côte de veau poêlée à l'estragon.

XXX **Waltons,** 121 Walton St., SW3 2HP, ℰ 584 0204 – ▤. 🔼 ﷾ ⑩ 𝘝𝘐𝘚𝘈
DS a
closed 25 and 26 December – **M** 14.75/19.75 **t.** and a la carte ᐟ 4.50.

XXX **Turners,** 87-89 Walton St., SW3 2HP, ℰ 584 6711 – ▤. 🔼 ﷾ ⑩ 𝘝𝘐𝘚𝘈
ES n
closed Saturday lunch, 24 to 31 December and Bank Holidays – **M** 17.50/26.50 **st.** and a la carte ᐟ 6.50.

XXX **Bibendum,** Michelin House, 81 Fulham Rd, SW3 6RD, ℰ 581 5817, Fax 823 7925 – ▤. 🔼 𝘝𝘐𝘚𝘈
DS s
closed 24 to 28 December – **M** 24.50 **t.** (lunch) and dinner a la carte 34.00/45.00 **t.** ᐟ 5.25.

XXX **Dynasty II,** Chelsea Wharf, 15 Lots Rd, SW10 0QJ, ℰ 351 1020, ◁, Oriental Cuisine, « Riverside setting » – ▤ 🅿. 🔼 ﷾ ⑩ 𝘝𝘐𝘚𝘈
p. 9 GZ n
closed Easter and 25-26 December – **M** 18.00/30.00 **t.** and a la carte 18.00/28.00 **t.**

XXX **Zen,** Chelsea Cloisters, Sloane Av., SW3 3DW, ℰ 589 1781, Chinese rest. – ▤. 🔼 ﷾ ⑩ 𝘝𝘐𝘚𝘈
ET a
M 13.50/38.00 **t.** and a la carte.

XX **Daphne's,** 110-112 Draycott Av., SW3 3AE, ℰ 589 4257 – ▤. 🔼 ﷾ ⑩ 𝘝𝘐𝘚𝘈
DS e
closed Saturday lunch, Sunday and Bank Holidays – **M** a la carte 19.50/25.00 **t.** ᐟ 4.50.

XX **Salotto,** 257-259 Fulham Rd, SW3 6HY, ℰ 351 1383, Italian rest. – 🔼 ﷾ ⑩ 𝘝𝘐𝘚𝘈
CU i
M a la carte approx. 18.25 **t.** ᐟ 3.95.

XX **La Finezza,** 62-64 Lower Sloane St., SW1N 8BP, ℰ 730 8639, Italian rest. – ▤. 🔼 ﷾ ⑩ 𝘝𝘐𝘚𝘈
FT v
closed Sunday and Bank Holidays – **M** a la carte 22.00/33.00 **t.** ᐟ 4.00.

XX **English Garden,** 10 Lincoln St., SW3 2TS, ℰ 584 7272, English rest. – ▤. 🔼 ﷾ ⑩ 𝘝𝘐𝘚𝘈
ET x
closed 25 and 26 December – **M** 14.75 **t.** (lunch) and a la carte 21.00/28.50 **t.** ᐟ 4.00.

XX **Gavvers,** 61-63 Lower Sloane St., SW1W 8DH, ℰ 730 5983, French rest. – ▤. 🔼 ﷾ 𝘝𝘐𝘚𝘈
FT e
closed Saturday lunch, Sunday and Bank Holidays – **M** 13.50/27.50 **st.** ᐟ 5.20.

XX **Waterfront,** Harbour Yard, Chelsea Harbour, SW10 0QJ, ℰ 352 4562, Fax 351 6576, Italian rest – ▤. 🔼 ﷾ 𝘝𝘐𝘚𝘈
closed Sunday dinner, Easter, 25-26 December, 1 January and Bank Holidays – **M** 16.50 **t.** and a la carte ᐟ 3.75.

XX **Mario,** 260-262a Brompton Rd, SW3 2AS, ℰ 584 1724, Italian rest. – 🔼 ﷾ ⑩ 𝘝𝘐𝘚𝘈
DS n
closed Bank Holidays – **M** 16.50 **t.** (lunch) and a la carte 22.40/29.00 **t.** ᐟ 4.75.

XX **Poissonnerie de l'Avenue,** 82 Sloane Av., SW3 3DZ, ℰ 589 2457, Fax 581 3360, French, Seafood rest. – ▤
DS u
closed Sunday, 23 December-3 January, 29 March-2 April and Bank Holidays – **M** a la carte 15.35/23.85 **t.** ᐟ 4.50.

XX **Les Trois Plats,** 4 Sydney St., SW3 6PP, ℰ 352 3433, French rest. – ▤. 🔼 ﷾ ⑩ 𝘝𝘐𝘚𝘈
DT v
closed Sunday, Monday and Bank Holidays – **M** 12.00/22.00 **st.** and a la carte ᐟ 5.20.

XX **St. Quentin,** 243 Brompton Rd, SW3 2EP, ℰ 589 8005, Fax 584 6064, French rest. – ▤. ◪ ◪ ◎ **VISA** DR **a**
M 11.90/14.90 **t.** and a la carte.

XX **Eleven Park Walk,** 11 Park Walk, SW10 LOPZ, ℰ 352 3449, Italian rest. – ▤. ◪ ◪ **VISA** CU **r**
closed Sunday and Bank Holidays – **M** 13.50/20.50 **t.** and a la carte ▯ 3.50.

XX **Magic Dragon,** 99-103 Fulham Rd, SW3 6RH, ℰ 225 2244, Fax 929 5690, Chinese rest. – ▤. ◪ ◪ ◎ **VISA** DS **o**
closed Bank Holidays – **M** 9.50/34.00 **st.** and a la carte.

XX **Good Earth,** 233 Brompton Rd, SW3 2EP, ℰ 584 3658, Fax 823 8769, Chinese rest. – ▤. ◪ ◪ ◎ **VISA** DR **c**
closed 24 to 27 December – **M** 15.50/22.50 **t.** and a la carte ▯ 3.25.

XX Good Earth, 91 King's Rd, SW3 4PA, ℰ 352 9231, Chinese rest. – ▤ EU **a**

XX **Nakano,** 11 Beauchamp Pl., SW3 1NQ, ℰ 581 3837, Japanese rest. – ▤. ◪ ◪ ◎ **VISA** ER **r**
closed Sunday lunch, Monday, Easter, last 2 weeks August and Christmas-New Year – **M** a la carte 21.00/33.00 **t.**

XX **Toto,** Walton House, Walton St., SW3 2JH, ℰ 589 0075, Italian rest. – ◪ ◪ **VISA** ES **a**
closed 3 days at Easter and 4 days at Christmas – **M** a la carte 21.00/29.00 **st.** ▯ 4.50.

XX **Ponte Nuovo,** 126 Fulham Rd, SW3 6HU, ℰ 370 6656, Italian rest. – ◪ ◪ ◎ **VISA** CU **e**
closed Bank Holidays – **M** a la carte 17.50/26.00 **t.** ▯ 4.50.

XX **Beccofino,** 100 Draycott Av., SW3 3AD, ℰ 584 3600, Italian rest. – ◪ ◪ **VISA** ES **r**
closed Sunday and Bank Holidays – **M** a la carte 12.30/19.00 **t.** ▯ 3.50.

XX **Le Suquet,** 104 Draycott Av., SW3 3AE, ℰ 581 1785, French, seafood rest. – ◪ ◪ ◎ **VISA** DS **c**
M a la carte 18.50/26.50 **t.**

XX **Dan's,** 119 Sydney St., SW3 6NR, ℰ 352 2718, Fax 352 3265 – ◪ ◪ ◎ **VISA** DU **s**
closed Saturday lunch and Sunday – **M** 19.00 **t.** (dinner) and a la carte.

Earl's Court – ✉ SW5/SW10 – ✆ 071 – Except where otherwise stated see pp. 14 and 15.

🏠 **Rushmore** without rest., 11 Trebovir Rd, SW5 9LS, ℰ 370 3839, Fax 370 0274 – ▣ ☎ ℗. ◪ ◪ **VISA** ✂ p. 8 EZ **c**
22 rm � 42.00/78.00 **st.**

🏠 **Amsterdam** without rest., 7 Trebovir Rd, SW5 9LS, ℰ 370 2814, Fax 244 7608 – ▤ ▣ ☎. ◪ ◪ **VISA** ✂ p. 8 EZ **c**
20 rm ⊐ 38.00/65.00 **st.**

XX **Tiger Lee,** 251 Old Brompton Rd, SW5 9HP, ℰ 370 3176, Chinese, seafood rest. – ▤. ◪ ◪ ◎ **VISA** AU **n**
closed 25 and 26 December – **M** (dinner only) a la carte 19.00/31.50 **t.**

XX **La Croisette,** 168 Ifield Rd, SW10 9AF, ℰ 373 3694, French, seafood rest. – ◪ ◪ ◎ **VISA** AU **a**
closed Tuesday lunch, Monday and Christmas – **M** 25.00 **t.** and a la carte.

XX **La Primula,** 12 Kenway Rd, SW5 0RR, ℰ 370 5958, Italian rest. – ◪ ◪ ◎ **VISA** p. 8 FZ **e**
M 18.50 **t.** and a la carte ▯ 5.50.

Kensington – ✉ SW7/W8/W11/W14 – ✆ 071 – Except where otherwise stated see pp. 8-11.

🏨 **Royal Garden** (Rank), Kensington High St., W8 4PT, ℰ 937 8000, Telex 263151, Fax 938 4532, ≤ – ▤ ✇ rm ▤ ▣ ☎ ℗ – 🔬 900. ◪ ◪ ◎ **VISA** ✂ p. 14 AQ **c**
M Royal Roof (closed Saturday lunch and Sunday) (Dancing Saturday night) 22.00/32.00 **st.** and a la carte – ⊐ 10.75 – **381 rm** 135.00/185.00 **st.**, **17 suites** 400.00/950.00 **st.**

🏨 **Halcyon,** 81 Holland Park, W11 3RZ, ℰ 727 7288, Telex 266721, Fax 229 8516 – ▤ ▤ ▣ ☎. ◪ ◪ ◎ **VISA** ✂ EX **u**
M Kingfisher (closed Saturday lunch, Sunday and Bank Holidays except Christmas and New Year) a la carte 19.25/29.50 **st.** ▯ 5.00 – ⊐ 12.25 – **41 rm** 165.00/250.00 **st.**, **3 suites** 375.00/550.00 **st.** – SB (October-March) (weekends only) 375.00 **st.**

🏨 **London Tara,** Scarsdale Pl., W8 5SR, ℰ 937 7211, Telex 918834, Fax 937 7100 – ▤ ✇ rm ▤ ▣ ☎ ♿ ℗ – 🔬 500. ◪ ◪ ◎ **VISA** ✂ FY **u**
M 12.20 **t.** and a la carte ▯ 6.00 – ⊐ 8.40 – **823 rm** 93.00/130.00 **st.**, **8 suites** 220.00/330.00 **st.** – SB (weekends only) 206.00 **st.**

🏨 **London Kensington Hilton,** 179-199 Holland Park Av., W11 4UL, ℰ 603 3355, Telex 919763, Fax 602 9397 – ▤ ✇ rm ▤ ▣ ☎ ♿ ℗ – 🔬 200. ◪ ◪ ◎ **VISA** EX **s**
M 25.00/35.00 **st.** and a la carte ▯ 6.25 – ⊐ 12.50 – **606 rm** 110.00/350.00 **st.** – SB (weekends only) 252.00/300.00 **st.**

🏨 **Kensington Palace Thistle** (Mt. Charlotte Thistle), De Vere Gdns, W8 5AF, ℰ 937 8121, Telex 262422, Fax 937 2816 – ▤ ✇ rm ▤ ▣ ☎ – 🔬 160. ◪ ◪ ◎ **VISA** ✂ p. 14 BQ **x**
M 17.50 **st.** and a la carte – ⊐ 8.25 – **297 rm** 90.00/140.00 **st.**, **1 suite.**

🏨 **Kensington Close** (T.H.F.), Wrights Lane, W8 5SP, ℰ 937 8170, Telex 23914, Fax 937 8289, 🛋, ⌘, 🏊, 🏋, squash – ▤ ✇ rm ▤ rest ▣ ☎ ℗ – 🔬 200. ◪ ◪ ◎ **VISA** FY **c**
M a la carte 13.00/18.25 **st.** ▯ 4.50 – ⊐ 8.50 – **524 rm** 90.00/105.00 **st.**

XXX La Ruelle, 14 Wright's Lane, W8 6TF, ℰ 937 8525, French rest.   FY i

XX   **Clarke's,** 124 Kensington Church St., W8 4BH, ℰ 221 9225, Fax 229 4564 – ▤. 🅰 VISA
     closed Saturday, Sunday, 4 days at Easter, 3 weeks August-September, 1 week Christmas-
     New Year and Bank Holidays – **M** 20.00/30.00 **st.**   EX c

XX   **Shanghai,** 38c Kensington Church St., W8 4BX, ℰ 938 2501, Chinese rest. – ▤. 🅰 AE ⓞ
     VISA   FX a
     M 15.50/21.50 **t.** and a la carte ⓙ 3.95.

XX   **Launceston Place,** 1a Launceston Pl., W8 5RL, ℰ 937 6912, Fax 376 0581 – ▤. 🅰 VISA
     closed Saturday lunch and Sunday dinner – **M** 13.75 **t.** and a la carte ⓙ 3.95.   p. 14 BR a

XX   **Boyd's,** 135 Kensington Church St., W8 7LP, ℰ 727 5452 – 🅰 AE VISA   p. 16 AZ r
     closed Saturday, Sunday, 1 week Christmas and Bank Holidays – **M** 17.50/27.00 **t.**

XX   La Pomme d'Amour, 128 Holland Park Av., W11 4UE, ℰ 229 8532, French rest. – ▤   EX e

XX   **Phoenicia,** 11-13 Abingdon Rd, W8, ℰ 937 0120, Lebanese rest. – ▤. 🅰 AE ⓞ VISA
     closed 25 and 26 December – **M** 12.70/23.70 **t.** and a la carte ⓙ 4.00.   EY n

XX   **Hiroko** (at London Kensington Hilton H.), 179-199 Holland Park Av., W11 4UL, ℰ 603 5003,
     Japanese rest. – ℗. 🅰 VISA   EX s
     closed Monday lunch – **M** 19.00/32.00 **t.** and a la carte ⓙ 6.70.

XX   Sailing Junk, 59 Marloes Rd, W8 6LE, ℰ 937 5833, Chinese rest. – ▤   FY x

XX   **La Paesana,** 50 Uxbridge St., W8 7TA, ℰ 229 4332, Italian rest. – ▤. AE ⓞ VISA
     closed Sunday – **M** a la carte 11.55/13.30 **t.**   p. 16 AZ i

XX   Topo D'oro, 39 Uxbridge St., W8, ℰ 727 5813, Italian rest. –   p. 16 AZ a

XX   I Ching, 40 Earls Court Rd, W8 6EJ, ℰ 937 0409, Chinese rest. – ▤   EY a

X   **Kensington Place,** 201 Kensington Church St., W8 7LX, ℰ 727 3184, Fax 229 2025 – ▤.
     🅰 VISA   p. 16 AZ z
     closed 3 days August Bank Holidays and 24 to 27 December – **M** 12.50 **t.** (lunch) and a la
     carte 14.75/26.50 **t.** ⓙ 3.75.

North Kensington – ✉ W2/W10/W11 – ☎ 071 – Except where otherwise stated see
pp. 4-7.

🏛   **Abbey Court** without rest., 20 Pembridge Gdns, W2 4DU, ℰ 221 7518, Telex 262167, Fax
     792 0858, « Tastefully furnished Victorian town house » – 📺 ☎. 🅰 AE ⓞ VISA. ⅍
     ⌑ 7.50 – **22 rm** 80.00/165.00 **t.**   p. 16 AZ u

🏠   **Portobello,** 22 Stanley Gdns, W11 2NG, ℰ 727 2777, Telex 268349, Fax 792 9641, « Attrac-
     tively furnished town house in victorian terrace » – ▤ 📺 ☎. 🅰 AE ⓞ VISA. ⅍   EV n
     closed 22 December-2 January – **M** (residents only) 15.00/20.00 **st.** and a la carte ⓙ 6.50 –
     ⌑ 6.75 – **24 rm** 60.00/85.00 **st.**, **1 suite** 150.00 **st.**

🏠   **Pembridge Court,** 34 Pembridge Gdns, W2 4DX, ℰ 229 9977, Telex 298363, Fax 727 4982
     – ▤⑂ rest ▤ rest 📺 ☎. 🅰 AE ⓞ VISA   p. 16 AZ n
     M *(closed Sunday and Bank Holidays)* (dinner only) a la carte 13.50/17.50 **t.** ⓙ 3.60 – **25 rm**
     ⌑ 69.00/130.00 **st.**

XXX **Leith's,** 92 Kensington Park Rd, W11 2PN, ℰ 229 4481 – ▤. 🅰 AE ⓞ VISA   EV e
     closed 25-26 August and 24 to 27 December – **M** (dinner only) 21.50/42.50 **st.** ⓙ 6.75.

XX   **Chez Moi,** 1 Addison Av., Holland Park, W11 4QS, ℰ 603 8267, French rest. – 🅰 AE ⓞ
     VISA   EX n
     closed Saturday lunch, Sunday, Christmas-New Year and Bank Holidays – **M** 13.50 **t.** (lunch)
     and a la carte 17.25/24.50 **t.** ⓙ 3.50.

XX   **Monsieur Thompsons,** 29 Kensington Park Rd, W11 2ELI, ℰ 727 9957, French rest. – 🅰
     AE ⓞ VISA   EV a
     closed Sunday and 25 December-3 January – **M** 18.50/20.00 **t.** (dinner) and a la carte
     17.50/25.50 **t.** ⓙ 3.50.

South Kensington – ✉ SW5/SW7/W8 – ☎ 071 – pp.14 and 15.

🏛🏛 **Blakes,** 33 Roland Gdns, SW7 3PF, ℰ 370 6701, Telex 8813500, Fax 373 0442, « Oriental
     antique furnishings » – ▤ 📺 ☎. 🅰 AE ⓞ VISA. ⅍   BU n
     M *(closed 25 and 26 December)* 28.50 **st.** (lunch) and a la carte 51.25/57.20 **t.** ⓙ 7.00 –
     14.00 – **42 rm** 125.00/185.00 **st.**, **10 suites** 220.00/600.00 **st.**

🏛🏛 **Pelham,** 15 Cromwell Place, SW7 2LA, ℰ 589 8288, Telex 8814714, Fax 584 8444, « Taste-
     fully furnished Victorian town house » – ▤ ▤ 📺 ☎. 🅰 AE VISA. ⅍   CS z
     M 12.00/15.00 **t.** and a la carte ⓙ 8.50 – **35 rm** 130.00/155.00 **t.**, **2 suites** 250.00 **t.**

🏛🏛 **Norfolk** (Q.M.H.), 2-10 Harrington Rd, SW7 3ER, ℰ 589 8191, Telex 268852, Fax 581 1874,
     🎵, 🈺 – ▤ ▤ rest 📺 ☎ – 🔏 60. 🅰 AE ⓞ VISA. ⅍   CS e
     M (see **Brasserie de la Paix** below) – ⌑ 8.50 – **93 rm** 110.00/140.00 **st.**, **3 suites** 160.00/
     180.00 **st.** – SA 124.00/141.00 **st.**

🏛🏛 **Gloucester** (Rank), 4-18 Harrington Gdns, SW7 4LH, ℰ 373 6030, Telex 917505, Fax 373 0409
     – ▤ ⅍ rm ▤ 📺 ☎ ℗ – 🔏 400. 🅰 AE ⓞ VISA. ⅍   BS r
     M 18.25/19.25 **st.** and a la carte – ⌑ 10.50 – **544 rm** 122.00/172.00 **st.**, **6 suites** 335.00/
     695.00 **st.**

🏨🏨 **Swallow International,** Cromwell Rd, SW5 0TH, ℰ 973 1000, Telex 27260, Fax 244 8194, ⅃₅, ☎, ⬜ – 📶 ⤢ rm ▤ rest 📺 ☎ ℗ – 🔏 200. ◪ ㏜ ⓪ *VISA* ⬩ AS **c**
M 11.75/13.95 **st.** and a la carte ⅃ 4.95 – ⌥ 5.45 – **415 rm** 93.50/110.00 **st.,** **1 suite** 165.00/275.00 st.

🏨🏨 **Rembrandt,** 11 Thurloe Pl., SW7 2RS, ℰ 589 8100, Telex 295828, Fax 225 3363, ⅃₅, ☎, ⬜ – 📶 ⤢ rm ▤ rest 📺 ☎ – 🔏 120. ◪ ㏜ ⓪ *VISA* ⬩ DS **x**
M 14.95 **st.** and a la carte – ⌥ 8.75 – **200 rm** 90.00/110.00 **st.** – SB (weekends only) 106.90 st.

🏨 **Gore,** 189-190 Queen's Gate, SW7 5EX, ℰ 584 6601, Telex 296244, Fax 589 8127 – 📶 📺 ☎. ◪ ㏜ ⓪ *VISA* ⬩ BR **n**
M (see One Ninety Queen's Gate below) – ⌥ 9.00 – **54 rm** 83.00/155.00 **st.**

🏨 **Regency,** 100 Queen's Gate, SW7 5AG, ℰ 370 4595, Telex 267594, Fax 370 5555, ⅃₅, ☎ – 📶 ⤢ rm ▤ rest 📺 ☎ – 🔏 100. ◪ ㏜ ⓪ *VISA* ⬩ CT **e**
M 16.50/30.00 **st.** and a la carte ⅃ 5.00 – ⌥ 12.00 – **205 rm** 99.00/115.00 **st., 5 suites** 180.00/225.00 **st.** – SB (weekends only) 179.00/215.00 **st.**

🏨 **John Howard,** 4 Queen's Gate, SW7 5EH, ℰ 581 3011, Telex 8813397, Fax 589 8403 – 📶 ▤ 📺 ☎. ◪ ㏜ ⓪ *VISA* ⬩ BQ **i**
M 16.50 **st.** and a la carte ⅃ 9.50 – **52 rm** 85.00/250.00 **st.** – SB (weekends only) 132.00 **st.**

🏨 **Vanderbilt,** 68-86 Cromwell Rd, SW7 5BT, ℰ 589 2424, Telex 946944, Fax 225 2293 – 📶 ▤ rest 📺 ☎ – 🔏 120. ◪ ㏜ ⓪ *VISA* ⬩ BS **v**
M 11.50/12.50 **st.** and a la carte – ⌥ 8.00 – **223 rm** 90.00/250.00 **st.** – SB (weekends only) 110.00/132.00 **st.**

🏨 **Baileys,** 140 Gloucester Rd, SW7 4HQ, ℰ 373 6000, Telex 264221, Fax 370 3760 – 📶 📺 ☎ – 🔏 70. ◪ ㏜ ⓪ *VISA* ⬩ – **M** (closed lunch Saturday and Sunday) 14.25 **st.** and a la carte – ⌥ 8.25 – **162 rm** 90.00/150.00 **st.** BS **a**

🏨 **Onslow,** 109-113 Queen's Gate, SW7 5LR, ℰ 589 6300, Telex 262180, Fax 581 1492 – 📶 ▤ rest 📺 ☎ – 🔏 80. ◪ ㏜ ⓪ *VISA* ⬩ CT **i**
M 15.00 **st.** and a la carte ⅃ 6.00 – ⌥ 8.50 – **173 rm** 95.00/120.00 **st.** – SB (weekends only) 80.00/110.00 **st.**

🏨 **Cranley Gardens** without rest. 8 Cranley Gardens, SW7 3DB, ℰ 373 3222, Telex 894489, Fax 373 7944 – 📺 ☎. ◪ ㏜ ⓪ *VISA* BT **e**
⌥ 4.50 – **85 rm** 63.00/109.00 **st.**

🏨 **Embassy House** 31-33 Queens Gate, SW7 5JA, ℰ 584 7222, Telex 914893 – 📶 📺 ☎. ◪ ㏜ ⓪ *VISA* ⬩ BR **e**
M (closed lunch Saturday, Sunday and Bank Holidays) (buffet lunch)/dinner 14.50 **st.** and la carte ⅃ 4.10 – ⌥ 4.50 – **68 rm** 68.00/87.00 **st., 1 suite** 230.00/255.00 **st.**

🏨 **Kensington Plaza,** 61 Gloucester Rd, SW7 4PE, ℰ 584 8100, Telex 8950993, Fax 823 9175 – 📶 📺 ☎ – 🔏 50. ◪ ㏜ ⓪ *VISA* ⬩ BS **e**
M (Indian rest.) 20.00/25.00 **st.** and a la carte ⅃ 6.00 – ⌥ 7.00 – **51 rm** 60.00/110.00 **st.** – SB (weekends only) 94.00/116.00 **st.**

🏠 **Cranley** without rest., 10-12 Bina Gardens, SW5 0LA, ℰ 373 0123, Fax 373 9497, « Tasteful decor, antiques » – 📶 ⤢ rm 📺 ☎. ◪ ㏜ ⓪ *VISA* ⬩ BT **c**
⌥ 5.45 – **31 rm** 97.50/155.00 **st., 1 suite** 200.00/250.00 **st.**

🏠 **Cranley Place** without rest., 1 Cranley Pl., SW7 3AB, ℰ 589 7944, Fax 225 3931, « Tasteful decor » – 📺 ☎ – **10 rm.** CT **o**

🏠 **Alexander** without rest., 9 Sumner Pl., SW7 3EE, ℰ 581 1591, Telex 917133, Fax 581 0824, « Attractively furnished Victorian town houses », ⌂ – 📶 📺 ☎. ◪ ㏜ ⓪ *VISA* ⬩ CT **a**
37 rm ⌥ 89.00/104.00, **1 suite** 182.00.

🏠 **Number Sixteen** without rest., 14-17 Sumner Pl., SW7 3EG, ℰ 589 5232, Telex 266638, Fax 584 8615, « Attractively furnished Victorian town houses », ⌂ – 📶 📺 ☎. ◪ ㏜ ⓪ *VISA* ⬩ – **36 rm** ⌥ 95.00/165.00 **t.** CT **c**

🏠 **Aster House** without rest., 3 Sumner Pl., SW7 3EE, ℰ 581 5888, Fax 584 4925, ⌂ – 📺 ☎. ◪ ㏜ *VISA* ⬩ – **12 rm** ⌥ 50.00/95.00 **st.** CT **u**

XXX **One Ninety Queen's Gate** (at Gore H.), 190 Queen's Gate, SW7 5EU, ℰ 581 5666, Fax 581 8261 – ▤. ◪ ㏜ ⓪ *VISA* BR **n**
closed Saturday lunch and Sunday – **M** 22.50/32.50 **t.** and a la carte ⅃ 5.50.

XXX **Bombay Brasserie,** Courtfield Close, 140 Gloucester Rd, SW7 4QH, ℰ 370 4040, Indian rest., « Raj- style decor, conservatory garden » – ◪ *VISA* BS **a**
closed 26 and 27 December – **M** (Buffet lunch) 12.95 **t.** and dinner a la carte approx. 15.25 **t.** ⅃ 4.25.

XX **Hilaire,** 68 Old Brompton Rd, SW7 3LQ, ℰ 584 8993 – ▤. ◪ ㏜ ⓪ *VISA* CT **n**
closed Saturday lunch, Sunday dinner, 1 week Christmas, 1 week Easter, 2 weeks August and Bank Holidays – **M** (booking essential) 18.00/34.00 **t.** and a la carte.

XX **Brasserie De La Paix** (at Norfolk H.), 10 Harrington Rd, SW7 3ER, ℰ 589 8191, Telex 268852, Fax 581 1874 – ▤. ◪ ㏜ ⓪ *VISA* CS **e**
closed Saturday lunch – **M** 14.50/16.75 **t.** and a la carte ⅃ 5.75.

XX **Tui,** 19 Exhibition Rd, SW7 2HE, ℰ 584 8359, Fax 352 8343, Thai rest. – ◪ ㏜ ⓪ *VISA* CS **u**
closed Bank Holidays – **M** a la carte 15.35/18.50 **t.** ⅃ 3.75.

XX **Delhi Brasserie,** 134 Cromwell Rd, SW7 4HA, ℰ 370 7617, Indian rest. – ▤. ◪ ㏜ ⓪ *VISA* – closed 25 and 26 December – **M** 12.95 **t.** and a la carte. p. 8 EFZ **u**

XX **Memories of India,** 18 Gloucester Rd, SW7 4RB, ℰ 589 6450, Telex 265196, Fax 581 5980, Indian rest. – ◪ ㏜ ⓪ *VISA* – **M** 14.50 **st.** and a la carte. BR **s**

MERTON

Wimbledon – ⌧ SW19 – ☎ 081.

🏨 **Cannizaro House** (Mt. Charlotte Thistle) ⤳, West Side, Wimbledon Common, SW19 4UF, ℰ 879 1464, Telex 9413837, Fax 879 7338, ≼, « 18C country house overlooking Cannizaro Park », 🌳 – ▯ TV ☎ ℗ – 🔬 50. ◪ ▣ ⓪ VISA
M 16.50 **st.** and a la carte – ⊄ 8.00 – **47 rm** 85.00/140.00 **st.**

SUTTON

Cheam – ⌧ Surrey – ☎ 081.

✕ **Al San Vincenzo,** 52 Upper Mulgrave Rd, SM2 7AJ, ℰ 661 9763, Italian rest. – ◪ VISA
closed Saturday lunch, Sunday, Monday, 5 days at Easter, 2 weeks August and 1 week Christmas-New Year – **M** (booking essential) 23.00 **t.** ⱬ 4.75.

WANDSWORTH

Battersea – ⌧ SW8/SW11 – ☎ 071.

✕✕✕ ❀ **Cavaliers'** (Cavalier), 129 Queenstown Rd, SW8 3RH, ℰ 720 6960 – ◪ ▣ ⓪ VISA
closed Sunday, Monday, and 2 weeks at Christmas – **M** 16.50/33.00 **t.** ⱬ 4.50
Spec. Terrine de foie gras, muscat jelly, Nage of shellfish with cabbage, "Miniatures".

✕✕✕ ❀ **L'Arlequin** (Delteil), 123 Queenstown Rd, SW8 3RH, ℰ 622 0555, Fax 498 0715, French rest. – ▤. ◪ ▣ ⓪ VISA – *closed Saturday, Sunday, 3 weeks August and 1 week at Christmas* – **M** (booking essential) 19.50 **st.** (lunch) and a la carte approx. 50.00 **st.** ⱬ 6.00
Spec. Petits choux farcis à l'ancienne, Pistou aux coquilles St. Jacques, Assiette gourmande.

✕✕ **Le Chausson,** Ransome's Dock, 35-37 Parkgate Rd, SW11 4NP, ℰ 223 1611, French rest.
– ▤ ℗. ◪ ▣ ⓪ VISA   p. 9 HZ **e**
closed Saturday lunch, Sunday and August – **M** 18.00/29.00 **t.** ⱬ 4.50.

Wandsworth – ⌧ SW17 – ☎ 081.

✕✕✕ ❀❀ **Harvey's** (White), 2 Bellevue Rd, SW17 7EG, ℰ 672 0114 – ▤. ◪ VISA
closed Monday, Sunday, first 2 weeks August, 2 weeks Christmas and Bank Holidays –
M (booking essential) 22.00/42.00 **t.**
Spec. Vinaigrette de poireaux et homard aux truffes, Loup de mer au caviar, Feuillantine de framboise et sa crème légère.

WESTMINSTER (City of)

Bayswater and Maida Vale – ⌧ W2/W9 – ☎ 071 – Except where otherwise stated see pp. 16 and 17.

🏨 **Royal Lancaster** (Rank), Lancaster Terr., W2 2TY, ℰ 262 6737, Telex 24822, Fax 724 3191,
≼ – ▯ ⌁ rm ▤ TV ☎ ℗ – 🔬 1 400. ◪ ▣ ⓪ VISA ⌘   DZ **e**
M 18.50/21.50 **st.** and a la carte ⱬ 6.50 – ⊄ 11.00 – **398 rm** 140.00/190.00 **st.**, **20 suites** 395.00/1050.00 **st.**

🏨 **Whites** (Mt. Charlotte Thistle), Bayswater Rd, 90-92 Lancaster Gate, W2 3NR, ℰ 262 2711,
Telex 24771, Fax 262 2147 – ▯ ▤ TV ☎ ℗. ◪ ▣ ⓪ VISA ⌘   CZ **v**
M 19.50/21.50 **t.** and a la carte ⱬ 6.40 – ⊄ 9.50 – **52 rm** 130.00/260.00 **st.**, **2 suites** 315.00 **st.**

🏨 **London Metropole,** Edgware Rd, W2 1JU, ℰ 402 4141, Telex 23711, Fax 724 8866, ≼ – ▯ ▤
TV ☎ ℗ – 🔬 220 – **567 rm**, **4 suites**.   p. 5 GU **c**

🏨 **Plaza on Hyde Park** (Hilton), Lancaster Gate, W2 3NA, ℰ 262 5022, Telex 8954372, Fax
724 8666 – ▯ ⌁ rm TV ☎ – 🔬 50. ◪ ▣ ⓪ VISA   DZ **r**
M 13.75 **t.** (dinner) and a la carte 9.15/23.90 **t.** ⱬ 4.20 – ⊄ 8.75 – **402 rm** 73.00/140.00 **st.** –
SB (weekends only) 108.00 **st.**

🏨 **London Embassy,** 150 Bayswater Rd, W2 4RT, ℰ 229 1212, Telex 27727, Fax 229 2623 –
▯ ⌁ rm TV ☎ ℗ – 🔬 70. ◪ ▣ ⓪ VISA   EZ **o**
M (carving rest.) 12.00 **st.** and a la carte ⱬ 4.15 – ⊄ 8.00 – **192 rm** 95.00/130.00 **st.**, **1 suite**
170.00 **st.** – SB (weekends only) 104.00/124.00 **st.**

🏨 **Hospitality Inn** (Mt. Charlotte Thistle), 104 Bayswater Rd, W2 3HL, ℰ 262 4461, Telex
22667, Fax 706 4560 – ▯ ⌁ rm ▤ TV ☎ ℗ – 🔬 40. ◪ ▣ ⓪ VISA   CZ **o**
M 8.50/16.00 **st.** and a la carte – ⊄ 7.50 – **175 rm** 75.00/150.00 **st.**, **1 suite**.

🏨 **Mornington** without rest., 12 Lancaster Gate, W2 3LG, ℰ 262 7361, Telex 24281, Fax
706 1028, ⌂ – ▯ TV ☎. ◪ ▣ ⓪ VISA   DZ **s**
closed 21 December-2 January – ⊄ 3.50 – **68 rm** 71.00/92.00 **st.**

✕✕✕ **Bombay Palace,** 50 Connaught St., Hyde Park Sq., W2 2AA, ℰ 723 8855, North Indian
rest. – ◪ ▣ ⓪ VISA – **M** 18.00/25.00 **st.** and a la carte.   EZ **o**

✕✕ Poons, Whiteleys, Queensway, W2 4YN, ℰ 792 2884, Chinese rest. – ▤   BZ **x**

✕✕ **San Marino,** 26 Sussex Pl., W2 2TH, ℰ 723 8395, Italian rest. – ◪ ▣ ⓪ VISA   DZ **u**
closed Bank Holidays – **M** a la carte 15.60/19.80 **t.** ⱬ 4.90.

✕✕ **Hsing,** 451 Edgware Rd, W2 1TH, ℰ 402 0904, Chinese rest. – ◪ ▣ ⓪ VISA   p. 5 GU **a**
M a la carte 12.50/18.00 **t.**

✕✕ Monsoon, 57 Westbourne Grove, W2 4UA, ℰ 221 9396, Indian rest.   BZ **a**

Belgravia – ⊠ SW1 – ✆ 071 – Except where otherwise stated see pp. 14 and 15.

🏨🏨 **Berkeley**, Wilton Pl., SW1X 7RL, ℰ 235 6000, Telex 919252, Fax 235 4330, 🖦, ≘s, 🔲 – 🕴
🔳 🎴 ⟁, ⚠ ④ VISA ℀
FQ **e**
M Restaurant (closed Saturday) a la carte 25.50/43.00 **st.** 👖 4.80 – **Buttery** (closed Sunday) a
la carte 17.25/32.75 **st.** 👖 4.80 – **133 rm** 150.00/270.00 **st.**, **27 suites** 430.00/490.00 **st.**

🏨🏨 Belgravia-Sheraton, 20 Chesham Pl., SW1X 8HQ, ℰ 235 6040, Telex 919020, Fax 259 6243 –
🕴 ℀ rm 🔳 🎴 ☎
FR **u**
82 rm, 7 suites

🏨🏨 **Lowndes**, 21 Lowndes St., SW1X 9ES, ℰ 235 6020, Telex 919065, Fax 235 1154 – 🕴 ℀ rm
🔳 rest 🎴 ☎, ⟁ ⚠ ④ VISA ℀
FR **i**
M 21.50 **t.** and a la carte 👖 5.20 – **74 rm** 135.00/155.00 **s.**, **5 suites** 200.00/225.00 **s.**

✗✗ **Motcombs**, 26 Motcomb St., SW1X 8JU, ℰ 235 6382 – ⟁ ⚠ ④ VISA
FR **z**
closed Saturday lunch, Sunday and Bank Holidays – **M** a la carte 14.90/26.00 **t.**

Hyde Park and Knightsbridge – ⊠ SW1/SW7 – ✆ 071 – pp. 14 and 15.

🗺 Harrods, Knightsbridge, SW1 ℰ 730 3488.

🏨🏨 **Hyde Park** (T.H.F.), 66 Knightsbridge, SW1Y 7LA, ℰ 235 2000, Telex 262057, Fax 235 4552,
≼ – 🕴 ℀ rm 🔳 🎴 ☎ – 🔬 230. ⟁ ⚠ ④ VISA ℀
EQ **v**
M 26.00/45.00 **st.** and a la carte 👖 8.00 – ⌷ 14.50 – **167 rm** 199.00/265.00 **st.**, **19 suites**
475.00/1250.00 **st.**

Mayfair – ⊠ W1 – ✆ 071 – pp. 12 and 13.

🏨🏨 **Claridge's**, Brook St., W1A 2JQ, ℰ 629 8860, Telex 21872, Fax 499 2210 – 🕴 🔳 🎴 ☎ ⟁.
⟁ ⚠ ④ VISA ℀
BL **c**
M a la carte 28.00/58.00 **st.** and a la carte 👖 4.10 – **Causerie** (closed Saturday) 14.50/26.00 **st.**
and a la carte 20.50/39.50 **st.** – ⌷ 13.50 – **133 rm** 185.00/285.00 **st.**, **57 suites** 475.00 **st.**

🏨🏨 **Inn on the Park**, Hamilton Pl., Park Lane, W1A 1AZ, ℰ 499 0888, Telex 22771, Fax 493 1895
– 🕴 🔳 🎴 ☎ ⟁ – 🔬 250. ⟁ ⚠ ④ VISA ℀
BP **a**
M – **Lanes** 29.20 **st.** (lunch)/dinner a la carte 29.50/35.00 **st.** – (see also **Four Seasons** rest.
below) – ⌷ 12.50 – **209 rm** 190.00/235.00 **s.**, **19 suites** 470.00/780.00 **s.**

🏨🏨 **Le Meridien Londres**, Piccadilly, W1V 0BH, ℰ 734 8000, Telex 25795, Fax 437 3574, 🖦,
🔲, squash – 🕴 🔳 🎴 ⟁ ⟁ – 🔬 200. ⟁ ⚠ ④ VISA ℀
EM **a**
M (see also **Oak Room** below) – ⌷ 10.25 – **244 rm** 175.00/220.00 **s.**, **40 suites** 240.00/
550.00 **s.**

🏨🏨 **Grosvenor House** (T.H.F.), Park Lane, W1A 3AA, ℰ 499 6363, Telex 24871, Fax 493 3341,
🖦, ≘s, 🔲 – 🕴 ℀ rm 🔳 🎴 ☎ ⟁ 🅿 – 🔬 2000. ⟁ ⚠ ④ VISA ℀
AM **a**
M 19.50/25.00 **st.** – (see also **90 Park Lane** below) – ⌷ 12.00 – **381 rm** 205.00/225.00 **st.**,
73 suites 357.00/1700.00 **st.**

🏨🏨 ✿ **Connaught**, 16 Carlos Pl., W1Y 6AL, ℰ 499 7070 – 🕴 🔳 rest 🎴 ☎. ⟁. ℀
BM **e**
M (booking essential) – **66 rm, 24 suites**
Spec. Pâté de turbot froid au homard, sauce pudeur, Rendez-vous du pêcheur, sauce légère au parfum
d'Armorique, Salmis de canard strasbourgeoise en surprise.

🏨🏨 **Fortyseven Park Street**, 47 Park St., W1Y 4EB, ℰ 491 7282, Telex 22116, Fax 491 7281 –
🕴 🔳 🎴 ☎
AM **c**
M (see **Le Gavroche** below) – **52 suites** 275.00/400.00 **s.**

🏨🏨 **Inter-Continental**, 1 Hamilton Pl., Hyde Park Corner, W1V 0QY, ℰ 409 3131, Telex
25853, Fax 409 7460, 🖦, ≘s – 🕴 ℀ rm 🔳 🎴 ☎ ⟁ ⟑ – 🔬 700. ⟁ ⚠ ④ VISA
BP **o**
M (see **Le Soufflé** below) – ⌷ 12.50 – **438 rm** 165.00/210.00, **29 suites** 270.00/1300.00.

🏨🏨 **Park Lane**, Piccadilly, W1Y 8BX, ℰ 499 6321, Telex 21533, Fax 499 1965, 🖦 – 🕴 ℀ rm 🎴
☎ 🅿 – 🔬 600. ⟁ ⚠ ④ VISA ℀
BP **x**
M 15.00/19.00 **st.** and a la carte 👖 5.00 – ⌷ 9.95 – **266 rm** 159.95/199.95 **st.**, **54 suites**
230.00/350.00.

🏨🏨 **Brown's** (T.H.F.), 29-34 Albemarle St., W1A 4SW, ℰ 493 6020, Telex 28686, Fax 493 9381 –
🕴 ℀ rm 🔳 rest 🎴 ☎ – 🔬 65. ⟁ ⚠ ④ VISA ℀
DM **e**
M 25.75/29.95 **st.** and a la carte 👖 7.00 – ⌷ 11.75 – **127 rm** 155.00/195.00 **st.**, **6 suites**
230.00/390.00 **st.**

🏨🏨 **Londonderry**, Park Lane, W1Y 8AP, ℰ 493 7292, Telex 263292, Fax 495 1395 – 🕴 ℀ rm 🔳
🎴 ☎ ⟑ – 🔬 400. ⟁ ⚠ ④ VISA ℀
BP **i**
120 rm 160.00/200.00 **st.**, **10 suites** 235.00/550.00 **st.**

🏨🏨 **Britannia** (Inter-Con.), Grosvenor Sq., W1A 3AN, ℰ 629 9400, Telex 23941, Fax 629 7736 –
🕴 ℀ rm 🔳 🎴 ☎ – 🔬 80. ⟁ ⚠ ④ VISA
BM **x**
M (closed Saturday lunch and Sunday) 25.50 **t.** and a la carte 👖 5.75 – (see also **Shogun**
below) – ⌷ 10.50 – **314 rm** 125.00/210.00 **s.**, **12 suites** 375.00 **s.**

🏨🏨 **London Hilton on Park Lane**, 22 Park Lane, W1A 2HH, ℰ 493 8000, Telex 24873, Fax
493 4957, ≼ London, 🕴 ℀ rm 🔳 🎴 ☎ ⟁ – 🔬 1000. ⟁ ⚠ ④ VISA ℀
BP **e**
M 11.50 **st.** and a la carte 👖 6.50 – ⌷ 12.50 – **394 rm** 165.00/260.00 **s.**, **54 suites** 300.00/1500.00 **s.**

🏨🏨 **May Fair** (Inter-Con.), Stratton St., W1A 2AN, ℰ 629 7777, Telex 262526, Fax 629 1459, 🖦,
≘s, 🔲 – 🕴 ℀ rm 🔳 🎴 ☎ ⟁ – 🔬 270. ⟁ ⚠ ④ VISA
DN **z**
M (see **Le Chateau** below) – ⌷ 12.00 – **251 rm** 195.00/240.00 **st.**, **24 suites** 300.00/1400.00 **st.**

449

Westbury (T.H.F.), Conduit St., W1A 4UH, ℰ 629 7755, Telex 24378, Fax 495 1163 – 劇
↔ rm ▤ ▥ ☎ ❷ – 🔬 110. 🔼 🖭 ① 𝓥𝓘𝓢𝓐. ※
DM **a**
M 20.00/24.00 **st.** and a la carte ⅙ 7.50 – ☲ 11.50 – **228 rm** 160.00/190.00 **st.**, **15 suites** 250.00/550.00 **st.**

Marriott, Duke St., Grosvenor Sq., W1A 4AW, ℰ 493 1232, Telex 268101, Fax 491 3201 –
劇 ▤ ▥ ☎ ♿ – 🔬 375. 🔼 🖭 ① 𝓥𝓘𝓢𝓐. ※
BL **a**
M (closed Saturday lunch) 26.00 **t.** (lunch) and a la carte 12.25/19.25 **t.** ⅙ 6.25 – ☲ 9.50 – **206 rm** 170.00/205.00, **17 suites** 260.00/460.00.

Athenaeum (Rank), 116 Piccadilly, W1V 0BJ, ℰ 499 3464, Telex 261589, Fax 493 1860 – 劇 ↔ rm ▤ ▥ ☎ – 🔬 50. 🔼 🖭 ① 𝓥𝓘𝓢𝓐. ※
CP **s**
M 21.50/28.00 **st.** and a la carte ⅙ 7.75 – ☲ 11.00 – **106 rm** 160.00/188.00 **st.**, **6 suites** 230.00/270.00 **st.**

Washington, Curzon St., W1 8DT, ℰ 499 7000, Telex 24540, Fax 495 6172 – 劇 ↔ rm ▤ ▥ ☎ – 🔬 80. 🔼 🖭 ① 𝓥𝓘𝓢𝓐. ※
CN **s**
M 17.00 **st.** ⅙ 6.25 – ☲ 10.25 – **169 rm** 138.00/168.00 **st.**, **4 suites** 178.00/375.00 **st.** – SB (weekends only) 296.00 **st.**

Chesterfield, 35 Charles St., W1X 8LX, ℰ 491 2622, Telex 269394, Fax 491 4793 – 劇 ▥ ☎ – 🔬 100. 🔼 🖭 ① 𝓥𝓘𝓢𝓐. ※
CN **c**
M 18.50/22.00 **t.** and a la carte ⅙ 5.75 – ☲ 8.75 – **109 rm** 105.00/175.00 **st.**, **4 suites** 235.00/300.00 **st.**

Holiday Inn, 3 Berkeley St., W1X 6NE, ℰ 493 8282, Telex 24561, Fax 629 2827 – 劇 ↔ rm ▤ ▥ ☎ – 🔬 50. 🔼 🖭 ① 𝓥𝓘𝓢𝓐
DN **r**
M 17.25/23.00 **st.** and a la carte ⅙ 5.00 – ☲ 10.25 – **178 rm** 149.00/195.00 **st.**, **8 suites** 290.00/450.00 **st.** – SB (weekends only) 158.00/219.00 **st.**

Green Park, Half Moon St., W1Y 8BP, ℰ 629 7522, Telex 28856, Fax 491 8971 – 劇 ↔ rm ▤ rest ▥ ☎ – 🔬 70. 🔼 🖭 ① 𝓥𝓘𝓢𝓐. ※
CN **a**
M 17.00 **t.** and a la carte ⅙ 5.00 – ☲ 9.00 – **160 rm** 102.00/140.00 **st.**

Hilton Mews at Park Lane without rest., 2 Stanhope Row, W1Y 7HE, ℰ 493 7222, Telex 24665, Fax 629 9423 – 劇 ↔ ▤ ▥ ☎ – 🔬 50. 🔼 🖭 ① 𝓥𝓘𝓢𝓐
BP **u**
70 rm ☲ 130.00/175.00 **st.**, **1 suite** 350.00/450.00 **st.**

Flemings, 7-12 Half Moon St., W1 7RA, ℰ 499 2964, Telex 27510, Fax 629 4023 – 劇 ▥ ☎. ※
CN **z**
137 rm.

XXXXX ✿ **Oak Room** (at Le Meridien Londres H.), Piccadilly, W1V 0BH, ℰ 734 8000, Telex 25795, Fax 437 3574, French rest. – ▤. 🔼 🖭 ① 𝓥𝓘𝓢𝓐
EM **a**
closed Saturday lunch, Sunday and Bank Holidays – **M** 21.00/43.00 **t.** and a la carte 28.00/37.50 **t.** ⅙ 6.50
Spec. Gazpacho de langoustines à la crème de courgettes, Bar légèrement fumé à la Crème de caviar, Dos de jeune lapin aux champignons et au romarin.

XXXXX **90 Park Lane** (T.H.F.), (at Grosvenor House H.), Park Lane, W1V 7RD, ℰ 499 6363, Telex 24871, Fax 493 3341 – ▤. 🔼 🖭 ① 𝓥𝓘𝓢𝓐
AM **a**
closed Saturday lunch and Sunday – **M** 25.00/45.00 **st.** and a la carte.

XXXX ✿✿✿ **Le Gavroche** (Roux), 43 Upper Brook St., W1P 1PF, ℰ 408 0881, Fax 409 0939, French rest. – ▤. 🔼 🖭 ① 𝓥𝓘𝓢𝓐
AM **c**
closed Saturday, Sunday, 22 December-2 January and Bank Holidays – **M** (booking essential) 30.00/60.00 **st.** and a la carte 41.10/77.20 **st.** ⅙ 10.50
Spec. Soufflé suissesse, Assiette du boucher, Sablé aux fraises.

XXXX **Le Soufflé** (at Inter-Continental H.), 1 Hamilton Pl., Hyde Park Corner, W1V 0QY, ℰ 409 3131, Telex 25853, Fax 493 3476 – ▤ ⇔. 🔼 🖭 ① 𝓥𝓘𝓢𝓐
BP **o**
M 24.00/40.00 **t.** and a la carte 35.50/42.50 **t.** ⅙ 7.00.

XXXX ✿ **Four Seasons** (at Inn on the Park H.) Hamilton Pl., Park Lane, W1A 1AZ, ℰ 499 0888, Telex 22771, Fax 493 1895, French rest. – ▤ ⇔. 🔼 🖭 ① 𝓥𝓘𝓢𝓐
BP **a**
M 25.00/40.00 **st.** and a la carte 33.25/46.50 **st.**
Spec. Coquilles Saint-Jacques grillées et grecque de légumes, Poulet de Bresse rôti au jus, sa cuisse cuite à la vapeur, Nougat glacé, salade de fruits au gingembre.

XXXX **Le Chateau** (Inter-Con.), (at Mayfair H.) Stratton St., W1A 2AN, ℰ 629 7777, Telex 262526, Fax 629 1459, French rest. – ▤. 🔼 🖭 ① 𝓥𝓘𝓢𝓐
DN **z**
closed Sunday – **M** 21.50/32.50 **t.** and a la carte ⅙ 9.00.

XXX **Princess Garden**, 8-10 North Audley St., W1Y 1WF, ℰ 493 3223, Fax 938 4694, Chinese (Peking) rest. – ▤. 🔼 🖭 ① 𝓥𝓘𝓢𝓐
AL **z**
M 25.00 **t.** (lunch) and a la carte 20.00/30.00 **t.** ⅙ 6.00.

XXX **Empress Garden**, 15-16 Berteley St., W1X 5AE, ℰ 493 1381, Chinese (Peking) rest. – ▤. 🔼 🖭 ① 𝓥𝓘𝓢𝓐
DN **i**
M 15.00/30.00 **t.** and a la carte ⅙ 5.00.

XXX **Zen Central**, 20 Queen St., W1X 7PJ, ℰ 629 8089, Chinese rest. – ▤ ❷. 🔼 🖭 ① 𝓥𝓘𝓢𝓐
CN **x**
M a la carte approx. 15.50 **t.**

XX **Greenhouse**, 27a Hay's Mews, W1X 7RJ, ℰ 499 3331
BN **a**

XX **Copper Chimney**, 13 Heddon St., W1R 7LF, ℰ 439 2004, Indian rest. – ▤
EM **e**

XX **Ho-Ho**, 29 Maddox St., W1 9LD, ℰ 493 1228, Oriental cuisine – ▤. 🔼 🖭 ① 𝓥𝓘𝓢𝓐
DL **x**
closed Sunday and Bank Holidays – **M** 22.00 **t.** (dinner) and a la carte 14.70/22.00 **t.**

XX **Langan's Brasserie,** Stratton St., W1X 5FD, ☏ 491 8822 – 🖸 AE ⓞ VISA DN e
closed Saturday lunch, Sunday, Easter, Christmas and Bank Holidays – **M** (booking essential)
a la carte 16.90/28.95 **t**. ▯ 5.00.

XX **Shogun,** (at Britannia H.), Adams Row, W1Y 5DE, ☏ 493 1255, Japanese rest. – 🖸 AE ⓞ
VISA BM x
closed Monday – **M** (dinner only) 28.00 **t**. and a la carte.

XX **La Seppia,** 8a Mount St., ☏ 499 3385, Italian, Seafood rest. – 🖸 AE ⓞ VISA BM v
closed Saturday, Sunday, last 3 weeks August, 10 days at Christmas and Bank Holidays –
M 18.50/24.50 **t**. and a la carte ▯ 5.00.

XX **Miyama,** 38 Clarges St., W1Y 7PJ, ☏ 499 2443, Japanese rest. – 🍽. 🖸 AE ⓞ VISA CN e
closed Saturday dinner and Sunday – **M** 12.00/32.00 **t**. and a la carte ▯ 6.00.

Regent's Park and Marylebone – ✉ NW1/NW6/NW8/W1 – ☎ 071 – Except where
otherwise stated see pp. 12 and 13.

🛈 Selfridges, Oxford St., W1 ☏ 730 3488.

🏨🏨 **Churchill,** 30 Portman Sq., W1A 4ZX, ☏ 486 5800, Telex 264831, Fax 486 1255, ✂ – 🛗 🖃
📺 🅿 ♿ 🅿 – 🔺 200. 🖸 AE ⓞ VISA AJ x
M a la carte 30.00/50.00 **t**. ▯ 5.00 – ☲ 13.50 – **403 rm** 185.00/200.00 **st**., **49 suites**
300.00/995.00 **st**.

🏨🏨 **Portman Inter-Continental,** 22 Portman Sq., W1H 9FL, ☏ 486 5844, Telex 261526, Fax
935 0537, ✂ – 🛗 ⇆ rm 📺 ☎ ♿ 🅿 – 🔺 370. 🖸 AE ⓞ VISA. ✂ AJ o
M 19.50/28.50 **t**. and a la carte ▯ 7.50 – ☲ 11.50 – **262 rm** 144.90/166.75 **st**., **10 suites**
402.50/690.00 **st**.

🏨🏨 **Selfridge** (Mt. Charlotte Thistle), 400 Orchard St., W1H 0JS, ☏ 408 2080, Telex 22361, Fax
629 8849 – 🛗 ⇆ rm 📺 ☎ – 🔺 220. 🖸 AE ⓞ VISA. ✂ AK e
M 17.00 **t**. and a la carte – ☲ 9.25 – **294 rm** 124.00/170.00 **st**., **2 suites**.

🏨 **Berkshire,** 350 Oxford St., W1N 0BY, ☏ 629 7474, Telex 22270, Fax 629 8156 – 🛗 ⇆ rm
🖃 📺 ☎. 🖸 AE ⓞ VISA BK n
M 19.75 **st**. (lunch) .and a la carte ▯ 5.00 – ☲ 11.50 – **144 rm** 142.00/190.00 **st**., **3 suites**
385.00 **st**.

🏨 **Clifton Ford,** 47 Welbeck St., W1M 8DN, ☏ 486 6600, Telex 22569, Fax 486 7492 – 🛗
🖃 rest 📺 ☎ – 🔺 80. 🖸 AE ⓞ VISA BH a
M 13.00 **st**. (lunch) and dinner a la carte 13.00/23.00 **st**. ▯ 5.00 – ☲ 10.50 – **214 rm**
120.00/175.00, **4 suites** 350.00/750.00.

🏨 **Holiday Inn,** 134 George St., W1H 6DN, ☏ 723 1277, Telex 27983, Fax 402 0666, 🛴, ⇌.
🔲 – 🛗 ⇆ rm 🖃 📺 ☎ ♿ 🅿 – 🔺 120. 🖸 AE ⓞ VISA p. 17 EZ i
M 14.50/25.00 **st**. and a la carte ▯ 6.00 – ☲ 10.25 – **239 rm** 136.00/152.00 **st**., **2 suites**
395.00/495.00 **st**.

🏨 **Ramada H. London,** W1A 3BE, ☏ 636 1629, Fax 580 3972 – 🛗 🖃 rest 📺 ☎ ♿ – 🔺 300.
🖸 AE ⓞ VISA EJ r
M. 18.75/21.00 **st**. and a la carte ▯ 5.50 – ☲ 9.75 – **232 rm** 100.00/165.00 **st**., **3 suites**
300.00 **st**.

🏨 **London Regents Park Hilton,** 18 Lodge Rd, NW8 7JT, ☏ 722 7722, Telex 23101, Fax
483 2408 – 🛗 🖃 📺 ☎ 🅿 – 🔺 150. 🖸 AE ⓞ VISA p. 5 GT v
M *(closed Saturday lunch)* (carving rest.) 15.95 **t**. and a la carte ▯ 5.00 – ☲ 9.95 – **374 rm**
124.00/164.00 **st**., **3 suites** 175.00/185.00 **st**.

🏨 Montcalm, Great Cumberland Pl., W1A 2LF, ☏ 402 4288, Telex 28710, Fax 724 9180 – 🛗
🖃 rm 📺 ☎. ✂ p. 17 EZ x
102 rm, 12 suites.

🏨 **St. George's** (T.H.F.), Langham Pl., W1N 8QS, ☏ 580 0111, Telex 27274, Fax 436 7997, ⇐ –
🛗 ⇆ rm 🖃 rest 📺 ☎ – 🔺 40. 🖸 AE ⓞ VISA p. 5 JU a
M 18.50 **st**. and a la carte ▯ 6.60 – ☲ 10.50 – **83 rm** 110.00/140.00 **st**., **3 suites** 250.00/
275.00 **st**.

🏨 **Regent Crest** (T.H.F.), Carburton St., W1P 8EE, ☏ 388 2300, Telex 22453, Fax 387 2806 –
🛗 rest 📺 ☎ 🅿 – 🔺 500. 🖸 AE ⓞ VISA ✂ p. 5 JU i
M 15.00 **st**. and a la carte ▯ 4.00 – ☲ 9.95 – **312 rm** 104.00/134.00 **st**., **5 suites** 220.00/
300.00 **st**.

🏨 **Dorset Square,** 39-40 Dorset Sq., NW1 6QN, ☏ 723 7874, Telex 263964, Fax 724 3328,
« Attractively furnished Regency town house » – 🛗 🖃 📺 ☎. 🖸 AE VISA. ✂ p. 5 HU s
M 16.50 **t**. and a la carte ▯ 4.50 – ☲ 9.00 – **37 rm** 80.00/155.00 **st**.

🏨 **Durrants,** 26-32 George St., W1H 6BJ, ☏ 935 8131, Telex 894919, Fax 487 3510, « Converted
Georgian houses with Regency facade » – 🛗 📺 ☎ – 🔺 50. 🖸 AE ⓞ AH e
M 24.00/34.00 **st**. and a la carte ▯ 4.50 – ☲ 8.00 – **93 rm** 55.00/110.00 **st**., **3 suites**
140.00/180.00 **st**.

🏨 Mostyn, Bryanston St., W1H 0DE, ☏ 935 2361, Telex 27656, Fax 487 2759 – 🛗 ☎ – 🔺 180
119 rm, 3 suites. AK i

🏨 Londoner, Welbeck St., W1M 8HS, ☏ 935 4442, Telex 894630, Fax 487 3782 – 🛗 📺 ☎ –
🔺 90 BJ c
144 rm.

451

🏛 **Rathbone,** Rathbone St., W1P 1AJ, ℰ 636 2001, Telex 28728, Fax 636 3882 – 🛗 🗏 rest 📺
☎   p. 6 KU **x**
M 12.50/38.00 **st.** and a la carte 🍴 5.60 – ♎ 8.50 – **72 rm** 105.00/180.00 **st.**

🏛 Savoy Court, W1H 0EH, ℰ 408 0130, Telex 8955515, Fax 493 2070 – 🛗 📺 ☎. ✑   AK **c**
97 rm

🏛 **Harewood,** Harewood Row, NW1 6SE, ℰ 262 2707, Telex 297225, Fax 262 2975 – 🛗
🗏 rest 📺 ☎ – 🔬 60. 🆔 ⅢⅡ ⓪ 𝘝𝘐𝘚𝘈 ✑   p. 5 HU **x**
M *(closed lunch Saturday and Sunday)* 12.75/14.25 **st.** and a la carte 🍴 7.95 – **93 rm**
85.00/105.00 **st.** – SB (weekends only) 106.50/118.00 **st.**

XXXX ✿✿ **Chez Nico** (Ladenis), 35 Great Portland St., W1N 5DD, ℰ 436 8846, French rest. – 🗏.
🆔 ⓪ 𝘝𝘐𝘚𝘈   DJ **c**
*closed Bank Holiday lunch, Saturday, Sunday, 4 days at Easter, 3 weeks August and 10 days
at Christmas* – **M** (booking essential) 46.00/61.00 **st.** 🍴 10.0
Spec. Grillade coquille St. Jacques à l'ail confit et aux nouilles, Jarret de veau braisé "Jardinière", Tarte au
citron.

XXX **Jason's Court,** Jason's Court, 76 Wigmore St., W1H 9DQ, ℰ 224 2992, English rest. –
🗏. 🆔 ⅢⅡ ⓪ 𝘝𝘐𝘚𝘈   BJ **a**
closed Saturday, Sunday, 10 to 27 August, 25 December-2 January and Bank Holidays –
M 20.00 **t.** (lunch) and a la carte 23.00/31.00 **t.** 🍴 4.25.

XXX **Rue St. Jacques,** 5 Charlotte St., W1P 1HD, ℰ 637 0222, French rest. – 🗏. 🆔 ⅢⅡ ⓪
𝘝𝘐𝘚𝘈   p. 6 KU **c**
closed Saturday lunch, Sunday, Easter, Christmas-New Year and Bank Holidays –
M 23.00/33.00 **t.**

XXX **Odins,** 27 Devonshire St., W1N 1RJ, ℰ 935 7296 – 🆔 ⅢⅡ ⓪ 𝘝𝘐𝘚𝘈   p. 5 IU **n**
closed Saturday lunch, Sunday, Easter, Christmas and Bank Holidays – **M** a la carte
24.45/31.50 **t.**

XXX **Martin's,** 239 Baker St., NW1 6XE, ℰ 935 3130 – 🗏. 🆔 ⅢⅡ ⓪ 𝘝𝘐𝘚𝘈   p. 5 HU **u**
closed Saturday lunch, Sunday, Easter, Christmas and Bank Holidays – **M** 17.50/21.00 **t.**
🍴 5.00.

XX Gaylord, 79-81 Mortimer St., W1N 7TB, ℰ 580 3615, Indian and Pakistani rest. – 🗏
                                                                                            p. 6 KU **o**

XX **Masako,** 6-8 St. Christopher's Pl., W1M 5HB, ℰ 935 1579, Japanese rest. – 🆔 ⅢⅡ ⓪ 𝘝𝘐𝘚𝘈
closed Sunday – **M** 18.00/32.00 **t.** and a la carte.   BJ **e**

XX **Mon,** (at Cumberland H.), Marble Arch, W1A 4RF, ℰ 262 6528, Japanese rest. – 🗏. 🆔 ⅢⅡ
⓪ 𝘝𝘐𝘚𝘈   AK **n**
M a la carte approx. 16.50 🍴 5.00.

XX **La Loggia,** 68 Edgware Rd, W2 2EG, ℰ 723 0554, Italian rest. – 🗏. 🆔 ⅢⅡ ⓪ 𝘝𝘐𝘚𝘈
closed Sunday – **M** a la carte 15.20/26.20 **t.** 🍴 4.00.   p. 17 EZ **y**

XX **Asuka,** Berkeley Arcade, 209a Baker St., NW1 6AB, ℰ 486 5026, Fax 2621456, Japanese
rest. – 🆔 ⅢⅡ ⓪ 𝘝𝘐𝘚𝘈   p. 5 HU **u**
closed Saturday lunch, Sunday, 1 week at Christmas and Bank Holidays – **M** a la carte
23.90/41.00 **st.**

XX **Le P'tit Montmartre,** 15 Marylebone Lane, W1M 5FE, ℰ 935 9226, French rest. – 🗏. 🆔
ⅢⅡ ⓪ 𝘝𝘐𝘚𝘈   BJ **a**
closed Saturday lunch, Sunday, 4 days Easter, 4 days Christmas and Bank Holidays – **M** a la
carte 22.20/27.45 **t.** 🍴 4.50.

XX **Tino's,** 128 Allitsen Rd, NW8 7AU, ℰ 586 6264 – 🆔 ⅢⅡ 𝘝𝘐𝘚𝘈   p. 5 GT **u**
closed 29 March, 25 December and 1 January – **M** 20.00/32.00 **st.** and a la carte 🍴 4.50.

XX **Fontana Amorosa,** 1 Blenheim Terr., NW8 0EH, ℰ 328 5014, Italian rest. – 🆔 ⅢⅡ ⓪
𝘝𝘐𝘚𝘈   p. 4 FS **s**
closed Monday lunch, Sunday and mid August-mid September – **M** a la carte 15.00/26.00 **t.**

XX **Stepen Bull,** 5-7 Blandford St., W1H 3AA, ℰ 486 9696 – 🆔 𝘝𝘐𝘚𝘈   AH **a**
closed Saturday lunch, Sunday, 23 December-3 January and Bank Holidays – **M** a la carte
17.75/25.00 **t.** 🍴 5.00.

St. James's – ✉ W1/SW1/WC2 – ☎ 071 – pp. 12 and 13.

🏛🏛🏛 **Ritz,** Piccadilly, W1V 9DG, ℰ 493 8181, Telex 267200, Fax 493 2687, « Elegant restaurant in
Louis XV style » – 🛗 🗏 📺 ☎. 🆔 ⅢⅡ ⓪ 𝘝𝘐𝘚𝘈. ✑   DN **a**
M 23.50/39.50 **st.** and a la carte 🍴 5.75 – ♎ 12.50 – **111 rm** 185.00/255.00 **st.**, **17 suites**
490.00/880.00 **st.**

🏛🏛 **Dukes** ✑, 35 St. James's Pl., SW1A 1NY, ℰ 491 4840, Telex 28283, Fax 493 1264 – 🛗
🗏 rest 📺 ☎. 🆔 ⅢⅡ ⓪ 𝘝𝘐𝘚𝘈. ✑   EP **x**
M *(closed Saturday lunch)* 25.00 **t.** (lunch) and a la carte 31.50/41.00 **t.** 🍴 5.50 – ♎ 11.00 –
36 rm 165.00/194.00 **t.**, **26 suites** 310.00/590.00 **t.**

🏛 **22 Jermyn St.,** 22 Jermyn St., SW1Y 6HL, ℰ 734 2353, Fax 734 0750 – 🛗 ✕⇔ rm 📺 ☎.
🆔 ⓪ 𝘝𝘐𝘚𝘈   FM **c**
M (room service only) – ♎ 12.00 – **5 rm** -/150.00 **st.**, **13 suites** 210.00/260.00 **st.**

🏛 Stafford ✑, 16-18 St. James's Pl., SW1A 1NJ, ℰ 493 0111, Telex 28602, Fax 493 7121 – 🛗
🗏 rest 📺 ☎ – 🔬 40   DN **u**
56 rm, **6 suites**.

🏛️ **Cavendish** (T.H.F.), 81 Jermyn St., SW1Y 6JF, ℰ 930 2111, Telex 263187, Fax 839 2125 – 📶
⤢🚇 rm 📺 🅿 – 🔔 90. 🔺 🆎 ⓪
M *(closed Saturday lunch and Sunday)* a la carte 14.00/21.95 **st.** – **254 rm** ⤢ 135.00/185.00 **st.** EN v
– SB (weekends only) 130.00/150.00 **st.**

🏛️ **Hospitality Inn Piccadilly** (Mt. Charlotte Thistle), 31-39 Coventry St., W1V 8EL,
ℰ 930 4033, Telex 8950058, Fax 925 2586 – 📶 📺 ☎. 🔺 🆎 ⓪ 🆅🆂🅰 ✂ FGM a
M *(dinner only)* 18.50 **t.** ₰ 4.25 – ⤢ 8.75 – **92 rm** 102.50/112.50 **t.**

🏛️ **Royal Trafalgar Thistle** (Mt. Charlotte Thistle), Whitcomb St., WC2H 7HG, ℰ 930 4477,
Telex 298564, Fax 925 2149 – 📶 ⤢ rm 📺 ☎. 🔺 🆎 ⓪ 🆅🆂🅰 GM r
M 12.50 **st.** and a la carte ₰ 5.00 – ⤢ 8.95 – **108 rm** 87.00/115.00 **st.**

XXX ❀ **Suntory**, 72-73 St. James's St., SW1A 1PH, ℰ 409 0201, Fax 499 7993, Japanese rest. –
▤. 🔺 🆎 ⓪ 🆅🆂🅰 – *closed Sunday, 27 December-4 January and Bank Holidays* – **M** 54.00
st. and a la carte 28.00/54.50 **st.** ₰ 5.00
Spec. Teppan-yaki, Shabu-Shabu, Sashimi EP z

XX **Le Caprice**, Arlington House, Arlington St., SW1A 1RT, ℰ 629 2239, Fax 493 9040 – ▤. 🔺
🆎 ⓪ 🆅🆂🅰 – *closed 24 December-2 January* – M a la carte 18.25/23.25 **t.** ₰ 5.50. DN c

XX **Green's**, 36 Duke St., St. James's, SW1Y 6DF, ℰ 930 4566, Fax 930 1383, English rest. –
🔺 🆎 🆅🆂🅰 EN n
closed Sunday dinner, Christmas, New Year and Bank Holidays – **M** a la carte 19.00/24.00 **t.**

Soho – ✉ W1/WC2 – ❀ 071 – pp. 12 and 13.

🏛️ **Hampshire**, Leicester Sq., WC2H 7LH, ℰ 839 9399, Telex 914848, Fax 930 8122 – 📶 ▤ 📺
☎ – 🔔 90. 🔺 🆎 ⓪ 🆅🆂🅰 – **M** 17.50/35.00 **st.** and a la carte ₰ 10.5 – ⤢ 12.00 – **118 rm**
165.00/195.00 **st.**, **5 suites** 250.00/650.00 **st.** GM s

XXX **Lindsay House**, 21 Romilly St., W1V 5TG, ℰ 439 0450, English rest. – ▤. 🔺 🆎 ⓪ 🆅🆂🅰
closed 25 and 26 December – **M** 14.75 **t.** (lunch) and a la carte 24.25/34.00 **t.** ₰ 4.50. GL i

XXX **Red Fort**, 77 Dean St., W1V 5HA, ℰ 437 2525, Indian rest. – ▤. 🔺 🆎 ⓪ 🆅🆂🅰 FJK k
closed 25 and 26 December – **M** a la carte 15.90/25.20 **st.**

XX **La Bastide**, 50 Greek St., W1V 5LQ, ℰ 734 3300 – 🔺 🆎 ⓪ 🆅🆂🅰 GK v
closed Saturday lunch, Sunday, Christmas-New Year and Bank Holidays – **M** 19.50/21.00 **t.**
and a la carte ₰ 6.50.

XX **Au Jardin des Gourmets**, 5 Greek St., Soho Sq., W1V 5LA, ℰ 437 1816, Fax 437 0043,
French rest. – ▤. 🔺 🆎 ⓪ 🆅🆂🅰 – *closed Saturday lunch, Sunday, Easter, Christmas and
Bank Holidays* – **M** 16.50 **t.** and a la carte ₰ 3.50 GJ a

XX **L'Escargot**, 48 Greek St., W1V 5LQ, ℰ 437 2679, Fax 437 0790 – 🔺 🆎 🆅🆂🅰 GK e
closed Saturday lunch, Sunday, Easter, Christmas and Bank Holidays – **M** a la carte
21.20/27.95 **t.** ₰ 4.30.

XX **Burts**, 42 Dean St., W1V 5AP, ℰ 734 3339 – 🔺 🆎 ⓪ 🆅🆂🅰 FK n
closed Saturday lunch, Sunday and Bank Holidays – **M** a la carte 18.55/25.85 **t.** ₰ 5.00.

XX ❀ **Sutherlands**, 45 Lexington St., W1R 3LG, ℰ 434 3401, Fax 287 2997 – ▤. 🔺 🆅🆂🅰 EK u
closed Saturday lunch, Sunday and Bank Holidays – **M** 27.50/29.50 **t.** ₰ 4.95
Spec. Sutherlands shellfish terrine, Breast of duck in a rich Armagnac sauce with duck liver, apples and
prunes, Chocolate tear filled with white chocolate and orange truffle.

XX **L'Hippocampe**, 63 Frith St., W1V 5TA, ℰ 734 4545, French Seafood rest. – ▤. 🔺 🆎 🆅🆂🅰
closed Saturday lunch, Sunday, 24 December-4 January and Bank Holiday Saturdays – **M** a
la carte 21.00/30.00 **t.** FK z

XX **Gay Hussar**, 2 Greek St., W1V 6NB, ℰ 437 0973, Hungarian rest. – ▤. 🆎 GJ c
closed Sunday and Bank Holidays – **M** 14.00 **t.** (lunch) and a la carte 16.60/24.10 **st.** ₰ 5.60.

XX **Ming**, 35-36 Greek St., W1V 5LN, ℰ 734 2721, Chinese rest. – 🔺 🆎 ⓪ 🆅🆂🅰 GK c
closed Sunday and 25-26 December – **M** 12.00/20.00 **t.** and a la carte ₰ 6.00.

XX **Gopal's**, 12 Bateman St., W1V 5TD, ℰ 434 0840, Indian rest. – 🔺 🆎 ⓪ 🆅🆂🅰 GK e
closed 25 and 26 December – **M** 8.50/9.50 **t.** and a la carte ₰ 3.90.

XX **Chesa** (Swiss Centre), 2 New Coventry St., W1V 3HG, ℰ 734 1291 – ▤ GM n

XX **Kaya**, 22-25 Dean St., W1V 5AL, ℰ 437 6630, Korean rest. – ▤ FJ i

XX **Gallery Rendezvous**, 53-55 Beak St., W1R 3LF, ℰ 734 0455, Chinese (Peking) rest. – ▤.
🔺 🆎 ⓪ 🆅🆂🅰 – **M** 16.50/32.00 **t.** and a la carte ₰ 4.45. EL a

---

Strand and Covent Garden – ✉ WC2 – ❀ 071 – p. 17.

🏛️ **Savoy**, Strand, WC2R 0EU, ℰ 836 4343, Telex 24234, Fax 240 6040 – 📶 ⤢ rm ▤ 📺 ☎
⤢ – 🔔 450. 🔺 🆎 ⓪ 🆅🆂🅰 ✂ DEY a
M Grill 29.00 **t.** (dinner) and a la carte ₰ 5.15 – **River** 26.00/43.25 **st.** and a la carte ₰ 5.15 –
⤢ 16.50 – **152 rm** 170.00/260.00 **st.**, **49 suites** 280.00/600.00 **st.**

🏛️ **Howard**, 12 Temple Pl., WC2R 2PR, ℰ 836 3555, Telex 268047, Fax 379 4547 – 📶 ▤ 📺 ☎
⤢ – 🔔 120. 🔺 🆎 ⓪ 🆅🆂🅰 EX e
M a la carte 26.25/59.50 **st.** ₰ 8.70 – ⤢ 13.50 – **135 rm** 195.00/220.00 **st.**, **2 suites**
239.00/449.00 **st.**

🏛️ **Waldorf** (T.H.F.), Aldwych, WC2B 4DD, ℰ 836 2400, Telex 24574, Fax 836 7244 – 📶 ⤢ rm
▤ rest 📺 ☎ – 🔔 300. 🔺 🆎 ⓪ 🆅🆂🅰 ✂ EX x
M 17.00/25.00 **st.** and a la carte ₰ 6.75 – ⤢ 11.00 – **291 rm** 145.00/170.00 **st.**, **19 suites**
250.00/475.00 **st.**

XXXX **Boulestin,** 1a Henrietta St., WC2E 8PS, ☎ 836 7061, Fax 836 1283, French rest. – ▤. 🔼 AE
① VISA DX **r**
    closed Saturday lunch, Sunday, 1 week Christmas and Bank Holidays – **M** 22.50 **st.** (lunch)
and a la carte 28.75/37.50 **st.** 🛢 6.00.

XXX **Ivy,** 1 West St., WC2H 9NE, ☎ 836 4751, Fax 497 3644 – 🔼 AE ① VISA p. 13 GK **z**
    closed 25 and 26 December – **M** a la carte 18.75/28.00 **t.** 🛢 5.50.

XXX **Simpson's-in-the-Strand,** 100 Strand, WC2R 0EW, ☎ 836 9112, Fax 836 9112, English
rest. – ▤. 🔼 AE ① VISA EX **o**
    closed Sunday and Bank Holidays – **M** 17.50 **t.** and a la carte 🛢 4.95.

XX **Orso,** 27 Wellington St., WC2E 7DA, ☎ 240 5269, Fax 497 2148, Italian rest. – ▤ EX **z**
    closed 25 and 26 December – **M** (booking essential) a la carte 13.50/22.00 **t.** 🛢 4.25.

XX **Sheekey's,** 28-32 St. Martin's Court, WC2N 4AL, ☎ 240 2565, Seafood – ▤. 🔼 AE ①
VISA DX **v**
    closed Saturday lunch, Sunday and Bank Holidays – **M** a la carte 20.20/26.80 **t.** 🛢 4.50.

XX **Chez Solange,** 35 Cranbourn St., WC2H 7AD, ☎ 836 0542, French rest. – ▤. 🔼 AE ①
VISA DX **i**
    closed Sunday and Bank Holidays – **M** 14.50 **t.** and a la carte 🛢 5.50.

    Victoria – ✉ SW1 – ☎ 071 – Except where otherwise stated see p. 16.

🛈 Victoria Station Forecourt ☎ 730 3488.

🏨 **St. James Court,** Buckingham Gate, SW1E 6AF, ☎ 834 6655, Telex 938075, Fax 630 7587,
🛢, 🝔s – 🛎 ←→ rm ▤ rest ▦ ☎ – 🔬 180. 🔼 AE ① VISA ⁂ CX **i**
M (see **Auberge de Provence** and **Inn of Happiness** below) – ⌷ 12.00 – **373 rm** 130.00/170.00,
18 suites 200.00/500.00.

🏨 **Royal Horseguards Thistle** (Mt. Charlotte Thistle), 2 Whitehall Court, SW1A 2EJ,
☎ 839 3400, Telex 917096, Fax 925 2263 – 🛎 ←→ rm ▤ rest ▦ ☎ – 🔬 60. 🔼 AE ① VISA
⁂ p. 10 LX **a**
M 16.00/20.00 **t.** and a la carte 🛢 5.00 – ⌷ 8.95 – **373 rm** 93.00/170.00 **st.**, **3 suites**.

🏨 **Stakis St Ermin's,** 2 Caxton St., SW1H 0QW, ☎ 222 7888, Telex 917731, Fax 222 6914 –
🛎 ←→ rm ▤ rest ▦ ☎ – 🔬 150. 🔼 AE ① VISA CX **a**
M (carving rest.) 14.50/15.50 **t.** and a la carte – ⌷ 7.50 – **282 rm** 108.00/163.00 **t.**, **8 suites**
240.00 **t.** – SB 84.00/185.000 **st.**

🏨 **Goring,** 15 Beeston Pl., Grosvenor Gdns, SW1W 0JW, ☎ 834 8211, Telex 919166, Fax
834 4393 – 🛎 ▦ ☎ – 🔬 50. 🔼 AE ① VISA ⁂ BX **a**
M 17.50/23.00 **t.** and a la carte 🛢 6.00 – ⌷ 10.50 – **82 rm** 115.00/165.00 **st.**, **4 suites**
210.00 **st.**

🏨 **Grosvenor** (Mt. Charlotte Thistle), 101 Buckingham Palace Rd, SW1W 0SJ, ☎ 834 9494,
Telex 916006, Fax 630 1978 – 🛎 ←→ rm ▦ ☎ – 🔬 150. 🔼 AE ① VISA ⁂ BX **e**
M (carving rest.) 14.95 **st.** and a la carte 🛢 4.15 – ⌷ 8.50 – **363 rm** 89.50/110.00 **st.**, **3 suites**
215.00/295.00 **st.**

🏨 **Royal Westminster Thistle** (Mt. Charlotte Thistle), 49 Buckingham Palace Rd, SW1W
0QT, ☎ 834 1821, Telex 916821, Fax 931 7542 – 🛎 ←→ rm ▤ ▦ ☎ – 🔬 150. 🔼 AE ① VISA
⁂ BX **z**
M 16.00 **st.** and a la carte 🛢 5.00 – ⌷ 9.25 – **134 rm** 105.00/155.00 **st.**

🏨 **Rubens,** 39-41 Buckingham Palace Rd, SW1W 0PS, ☎ 834 6600, Telex 916577, Fax 828 5401
– 🛎 ←→ rm ▤ rest ▦ ☎ – 🔬 60. 🔼 AE ① VISA ⁂ BX **n**
M 13.75/16.50 **st.** and a la carte 🛢 6.50 – ⌷ 8.75 – **189 rm** 90.00/325.00 **t.**

🏨 **Scandic Crown,** 2 Bridge Pl., SW1V 1QA, ☎ 834 8123, Telex 914973, Fax 828 1099, 🝔s, 🔼
– 🛎 ←→ rm ▦ ☎ ₺ – 🔬 200. 🔼 AE ① VISA ⁂ BY **i**
M *(closed Saturday lunch and Sunday)* 15.75 **t.** (lunch) and a la carte approx. 16.45 **t.** 🛢 4.75
– ⌷ 9.00 – **205 rm** 105.00/135.00 **st.**, **5 suites** 215.00 **st.**

🏨 **Winchester** without rest., 17 Belgrave Rd, SW1V 1RB, ☎ 828 2972, Fax 828 5191 – ▦. ⁂
    closed 23 to 30 December – **18 rm** ⌷ –/62.00 BY **s**

🏨 **Ebury Court,** 26 Ebury St., SW1W 0LU, ☎ 730 8147 – 🛎 ☎. 🔼 ① VISA AX **r**
    closed 2 weeks Christmas-New Year – **M** 12.25/16.40 **st.** and a la carte 🛢 3.00 – **39 rm**
⌷ 50.00/130.00 **st.**

XXX **Inn of Happiness,** (at St. James Court H.) Buckingham Gate, SW1E 6AF, ☎ 834 6655, Telex
938075, Fax 630 7587, Chinese rest. – ▤ CX **i**

XXX **Auberge de Provence,** (at St. James Court H.) Buckingham Gate, SW1E 6AF, ☎ 834 6655,
Telex 938075, Fax 630 7587, French rest. – ▤ CX **i**
    closed Saturday lunch, Sunday, Easter and Bank Holidays – **M** 19.50 **t.** (lunch) and a la carte
28.50/37.75 **t.**

XXX **Santini,** 29 Ebury St., SW1W 0NZ, ☎ 730 4094, Fax 7300544, Italian rest. – ▤. 🔼 AE ①
VISA ABX **v**
    closed Saturday and Sunday lunch and Bank Holidays – **M** 16.50 **t.** (lunch) and a la carte
28.20/40.50 **t.**

XXX **L'Incontro,** 87 Pimlico Rd, SW1W 8PH, ☎ 730 6327, Fax 730 5062, Italian rest. – ▤
    closed Sunday lunch and Bank Holidays – **M** 14.50 **t.** (lunch) and a la carte 28.35/39.30 **t.**
p. 15 FT **u**

XX **Green's,** Marsham Court, Marsham St., SW1P 4JY, ✆ 834 9552, English rest. – ▤. 🄰 AE
⓪ VISA
p. 10   LZ **z**
closed Sunday lunch, Saturday, Christmas-New Year and Bank Holidays – **M** (booking
essential) a la carte 19.00/24.00 **t.**

XX **Ken Lo's Memories of China,** 67-69 Ebury St., SW1W 0NZ, ✆ 730 7734, Chinese rest.
– ▤. 🄰 AE ⓪ VISA
AY **u**
closed Sunday and Bank Holidays – **M** a la carte 17.00/56.00 **t.** 🛊 4.00.

XX **Mijanou,** 143 Ebury St., SW1W 9QN, ✆ 730 4099, Fax 823 6402 – ⋙ 🄰 ▤. 🄰 AE ⓪ VISA
closed Saturday, Sunday, 1 week at Easter, 3 weeks August, 2 weeks at Christmas and Bank
Holidays 16.50/36.00 **t.** 🛊 6.00.
AY **e**

XX **Very Simply Nico,** 48a Rochester Row, SW1P 1JU, ✆ 630 8061 – 🄰 VISA
CY **A**
closed lunch Saturday and Bank Holidays, Sunday, 4 days at Easter, 3 weeks August and 10
days at Christmas – **M** 21.00/25.00 **st.**

XX **Kym's,** 70-71 Wilton Rd, SW1V 1DE, ✆ 828 8931, Chinese(Szechuan, Hunan) rest. – ▤.
🄰 AE VISA
BY **v**
M a la carte 9.40/15.50 **t.** 🛊 3.50.

XX **Hoizin,** 72-73 Wilton Rd, SW1V 1DE, ✆ 630 5108, Chinese (Canton) Seafood rest. – ▤.
🄰 AE ⓪ VISA
BY **v**
M 13.00/25.00 **t.** and a la carte 🛊 5.30.

XX **Pomegranates,** 94 Grosvenor Rd, SW1V 3LG, ✆ 828 6560 – 🄰 AE ⓪ VISA   p. 10   KZ **A**
closed Saturday lunch, Sunday, Easter, Christmas and New Year – **M** 16.00/28.00 **t.** 🛊 5.60.

XX **Hunan,** 51 Pimlico Rd, SW1W 8NE, ✆ 730 5712, Chinese (Hunan) rest. – 🄰 AE VISA
closed Bank Holidays – **M** a la carte 10.90/21.60 **t.** 🛊 4.00.
p. 9   IZ **a**

XX **Eatons,** 49 Elizabeth St., SW1W 9PP, ✆ 730 0074 – 🄰 AE ⓪ VISA
AY **a**
closed Saturday, Sunday and Bank Holidays – **M** a la carte 16.95/20.00 **s.** 🛊 4.20.

XX **Ciboure,** 21 Eccleston St., SW1W 9LX, ✆ 730 2505, French rest. – ▤. 🄰 AE ⓪ VISA
closed Saturday, Sunday, 10 August-4 September and Bank Holidays – **M** 15.00/19.50 **t.** and
a la carte.
AY **z**

XX **L'Amico,** 44 Horseferry Rd, SW1P 2AF, ✆ 222 4680, Italian rest. – ▤. 🄰 AE ⓪ VISA
closed Saturday, Sunday and 2 weeks August – **M** (booking essential) a la carte
16.30/25.90 **st.** 🛊 4.00.
p. 10   LY **e**

XX **Gran Paradiso,** 52 Wilton Rd, SW1V 1DE, ✆ 828 5818, Italian rest. – 🄰 AE ⓪ VISA
closed Saturday lunch, Sunday and last 2 weeks August – **M** 16.00/20.00 **t.** and a la carte
🛊 2.80.
BY **a**

X **Tate Gallery Rest.,** Tate Gallery, Millbank, SW1P 4RG, ✆ 834 6754, English rest., « Rex
Whistler murals » – ▤. 🄰 VISA
p. 10   LZ **c**
closed Sunday, 29 March, 1 May, 24 to 26 December and 1 January – **M** (lunch only)
(booking essential) a la carte 14.85/18.90 **t.** 🛊 4.75.

Bray-on-Thames Berks W : 34 m. by M 4 (junction 8-9) and A 308 – 𝟰𝟬𝟰 R 29 – pop. 9 427
– ✉ ✿ 0628 Maidenhead

XXXX ✿✿✿ **Waterside Inn** (Roux), Ferry Rd, SL6 2AT, ✆ 20691, Fax 784710, French rest.,
« ≤ Thames-side setting », 🍽 – ▤ **P.** 🄰 AE ⓪ VISA
X **a**
closed Tuesday lunch, Sunday dinner 20 October-Easter, Monday and 26 December-
8 February – **M** 25.50/49.50 **st.** and a la carte 39.30/54.00 **st.** 🛊 10.00
Spec. Blanc de poulet fermier en gelée aux champignons sauvages et pistaches, Caneton croisé Challandais
aux clous de girofle et au miel (2 persons), Soufflé chaud aux framboises.

Reading

at **Shinfield** Berks. W : 43 m. on A 327 𝟰𝟬𝟯 𝟰𝟬𝟰 Q 29 – pop. 194 727 – ✿ 0734.

XXX ✿✿ **L'Ortolan** (Burton-Race). The Old Vicarage, Church Lane, RG2 9BY, ✆ 883783, Fax
885391, French rest., 🍽 – **P.** 🄰 AE ⓪ VISA
closed Sunday dinner, Monday, last 2 weeks February and last 2 weeks August –
M 27.00/50.00 **t.**
Spec. Lasagne de homard à l'huile de truffe, Pigeonneau soubise au coulis de cresson, Assiette chocolatière.

Oxford

at **Great Milton** Oxon NW : 49 m. by M 40 (junction 7) and A 329 – 𝟰𝟬𝟯 𝟰𝟬𝟰 Q 28 – ✉
✿ 0844 Great Milton :

🏚 ✿✿ **Le Manoir aux Quat'Saisons** (Blanc) 🔊, Church St., OX9 7PD, ✆ 278881, Telex
837552, Fax 278847, ≤, « 15C and 16C manor house », 🏊 heated, 🌳, park, 🎾 – ▤ rest 📺
🕿 ☎ 🕘 – 🅰 40. 🄰 AE ⓪ VISA
closed 23 December-18 January – **M** 56.00 **st.** and a la carte 59.50/68.00 **st.** – 🖙 12.00 –
14 rm –/250.00 **st.**, **5 suites** 300.00/350.00 **st.**
Spec. Tiàn d'aubergines et tomates au vinaigre Balsamique, Croustillant de rouget de roche et son jus parfumé
aux langues d'oursins, Le café crème.

If you find you cannot take up a hotel booking you have made,
please let the hotel know immediately.

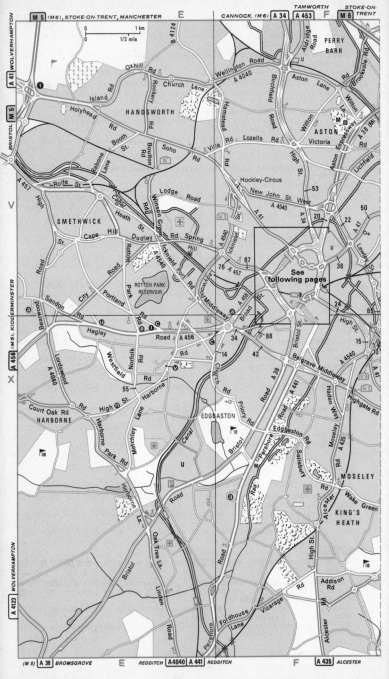

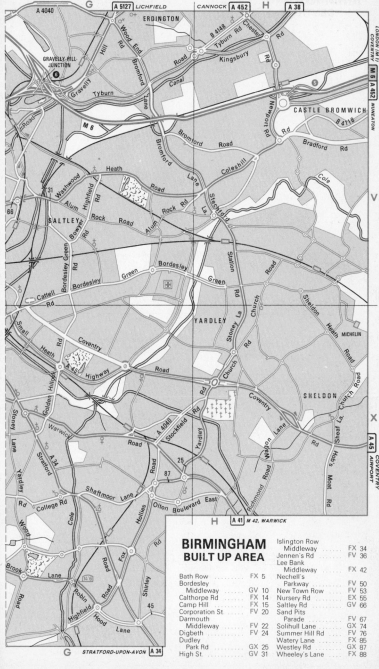

BIRMINGHAM
BUILT UP AREA

BIRMINGHAM
CENTRE

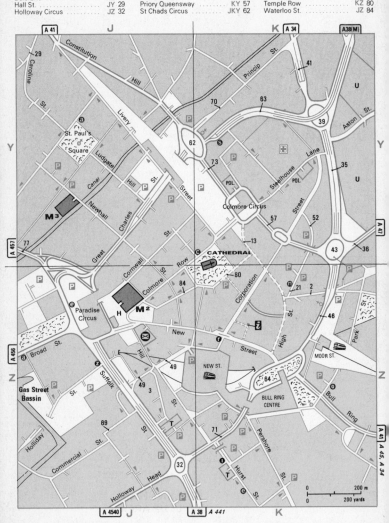

GREEN TOURIST GUIDES

Picturesque scenery, buildings

Attractive route

Touring programmes

Plans of towns and buildings.

🏛 **Howard,** 32-36 Gt. King St., EH3 6QH, 𝒫 557 3500, Fax 557 6515, « Georgian town houses »
– 🛗 📺 🕿 & 🅿 – 🔬 35. 🆎 🆎 ⑩ 𝘝𝘐𝘚𝘈. 🦾 DY **s**
M No 36 *(closed Saturday lunch)* 14.75/30.00 **t.** and a la carte 🛴 5.00 – **16 rm** ⊇ 95.00/250.00 **t.**
– SB (weekends only) (except August and Christmas) 85.00/120.00 **st.**

🏛 **Dalmahoy H. Golf & Country Club** 🏌, Kirknewtown, EH27 8EB, SW : 7 m. on A 71
𝒫 333 1845, Telex 772205, Fax 335 3203, ≤, ♨, ≘s, 🏊, ⅂ß, ☞, park, ✳ , squash – 🛗
↔ rm 📺 rest 📺 🕿 & 🅿 – 🔬 260. 🆎 🆎 ⑩ 𝘝𝘐𝘚𝘈. 🦾
M 12.50/18.50 **t.** and a la carte 🛴 5.75 – **114 rm** ⊇ 93.00/108.00 **t.**, **1 suite** 115.00/150.00 **t.** –
SB 110.00/140.00 **st.**

🏛 **Hilton National,** Bells Mills, 69 Belford Rd, EH4 3DG, 𝒫 332 2545, Telex 727979, Fax
332 3805 – 🛗 ↔ rm 📺 🕿 & 🅿 – 🔬 120. 🆎 🆎 ⑩ 𝘝𝘐𝘚𝘈 CY **i**
M *(closed Saturday lunch)* a la carte 14.00/26.00 **st.** 🛴 4.50 – ⊇ 8.50 – **143 rm** 90.00/120.00 **st.**,
1 suite 175.00 **st.** – SB (weekends only) 80.00/85.00 **st.**

🏛 Capital Moat House (Q.M.H.), Clermiston RD, EH12 6UG, 𝒫 334 3391, Telex 728284, Fax
334 9712, ⅂ß, ≘s, 🏊 – 🛗 ↔ rm 📺 🕿 & 🅿 – 🔬 400 by A8 CZ
99 rm.

🏛 Roxburghe, 38 Charlotte Sq., EH2 4HG, 𝒫 225 3921, Telex 727054, Fax 220 2518 – 🛗 📺 🕿
& – 🔬 200 DY **o**
73 rm, **2 suites**.

🏛 **Royal Scott** (Swallow), 111 Glasgow Rd, EH12 8NF, W : 4 ½ m. on A 8 𝒫 334 9191, Telex
727197, Fax 316 4507, ⅂ß, ≘s, 🏊 – 🛗 ↔ rm 📺 🕿 🅿 – 🔬 250. 🆎 🆎 ⑩ 𝘝𝘐𝘚𝘈
M 15.00/16.00 **st.** and a la carte 🛴 4.50 – **254 rm** ⊇ 82.00/110.00 **st.**, **4 suites** 150.00 **st.** –
SB (weekends only) 95.00 **st.** by A 8 CZ

🏨 Royal Terrace, 18 Royal Terrace, EH7 5AQ, 𝒫 557 3222, Telex 727182, Fax 557 5334, ⅂ß, ≘s,
☞ – 🛗 ↔ rm 📺 🕿 – 🔬 60
97 rm, **1 suites**.

🏨 **King James Thistle** (Mt. Charlotte Thistle), 107 Leith St., EH1 3SW, 𝒫 556 0111, Telex
727200, Fax 557 5333 – 🛗 ↔ rm 📺 🕿 🅿 – 🔬 250. 🆎 🆎 ⑩ 𝘝𝘐𝘚𝘈 EY **u**
M 9.50/14.50 **st.** and a la carte – ⊇ 7.75 – **142 rm** 65.00/115.00 **st.**, **5 suites** – SB 105.00 **st.**

🏨 **Bruntsfield,** 6974 Bruntsfield Pl., EH10 4HH, 𝒫 229 1393, Telex 727897, Fax 229 5634 – 🛗
📺 🕿 🅿 – 🔬 25. 🆎 🆎 ⑩ 𝘝𝘐𝘚𝘈 DZ **e**
M 8.50/16.50 **st.** and a la carte 🛴 3.75 – ⊇ 5.50 – **52 rm** 65.00/120.00 **st.**

🏨 **Ellersly House,** 4 Ellersly Rd, EH12 6HZ, 𝒫 337 6888, Fax 313 2543, ☞ – 🛗 ↔ rm 📺 🕿
🅿 – 🔬 45. 🆎 🆎 ⑩ 𝘝𝘐𝘚𝘈 by A8 CZ
M 8.75/14.25 **st.** and a la carte 🛴 4.75 – ⊇ 7.50 – **54 rm** 75.00/87.00 **st.** – SB 64.00/
90.00 **st.**

🏨 Crest (Holiday Inn), Queens Ferry Rd, EH4 3HL, 𝒫 332 2442, Telex 72541, Fax 332 3408, ≤ –
🛗 ↔ rm 📺 rest 📺 🕿 🅿 – 🔬 200. 🦾 by A90 CY
118 rm, **1 suite**.

🏨 **Barnton Thistle** (Mt. Charlotte Thistle), 562 Queensferry Rd, EH4 6AS, 𝒫 339 1144, Telex
727928, Fax 339 5521, ≘s – 🛗 ↔ rm 📺 🕿 🅿 – 🔬 100. 🆎 🆎 ⑩ 𝘝𝘐𝘚𝘈 by A90 CY
M 9.00 **t.** (lunch) and a la carte 12.00/25.00 **t.** – ⊇ 7.75 – **47 rm** 65.00/95.00 **st.**, **3 suites** –
SB 99.00 **st.**

🏨 **Stakis Grosvenor,** Grosvenor St., EH12 5EF, 𝒫 226 6001, Telex 72445, Fax 220 2387 – 🛗
↔ rm 📺 🕿 & – 🔬 160. 🆎 🆎 ⑩ 𝘝𝘐𝘚𝘈 CZ **a**
M (grill rest.) 13.50 and a la carte – ⊇ 7.25 – **135 rm** 77.00/109.50 **t.**, **1 suite** 135.50 **t.** –
SB 82.00/162.00 **st.**

🏨 **Post House** (T.H.F.), Corstorphine Rd, EH12 6UA, 𝒫 334 0390, Telex 727103, Fax 334 9237
– 🛗 ↔ rm 📺 🕿 🅿 – 🔬 130. 🆎 🆎 ⑩ 𝘝𝘐𝘚𝘈 by A8 CY
M 9.00/15.00 **st.** and a la carte 🛴 4.65 – ⊇ 7.50 – **206 rm** 68.00/80.00 **st.**, **1 suite**.

🏨 Mount Royal, 53 Princes St., EH2 2DG, 𝒫 225 7161, Telex 727641, Fax 220 4671 – 🛗 📺 🕿 –
🔬 50 DY **a**
158 rm, **1 suite**.

🏨 **Lady Nairne** (B.C.B.), 228 Willowbrae Rd, EH8 7NG, 𝒫 661 3396, Fax 652 2789 – 🛗 📺 🕿
🅿 – 🔬 120. 🆎 🆎 ⑩ 𝘝𝘐𝘚𝘈. 🦾 by A1 EY
M 8.00/15.00 **st.** – **33 rm** ⊇ 48.00/64.50 **st.**

🍴🍴🍴🍴 **Pompadour** (at Caledonian) Princes St., EH1 2AB, 𝒫 225 2433 – 🅿. 🆎 🆎 ⑩ 𝘝𝘐𝘚𝘈 CY **n**
M 15.75/51.00 **st.** and a la carte 🛴 6.75.

🍴🍴 **Vintners Room,** The Vaults, 87 Giles St., Leith, EH6 6BZ, 𝒫 554 6767 – ↔. 🆎 🆎
𝘝𝘐𝘚𝘈 by A900 EY
closed Sunday and 2 weeks Christmas – **M** 11.00 **t.** (lunch) and a la carte 17.00/22.00 **t.**
🛴 4.50.

🍴🍴 **Martins,** 70 Rose St., North Lane, EH2 3DX, 𝒫 225 3106 – ↔. 🆎 🆎 ⑩ 𝘝𝘐𝘚𝘈 DY **n**
closed Saturday lunch, Sunday, Monday and 22 December-21 January – **M** (booking essential) 15.00 **t.** (lunch) and a la carte 19.15/25.25 **t.** 🛴 5.00.

🍴🍴 **L'Auberge,** 56 St. Mary's St., EH1 1SX, 𝒫 556 5888, French rest. – 🆎 🆎 ⑩ 𝘝𝘐𝘚𝘈 EYZ **c**
closed 25-26 December and 1-2 January – **M** 12.00/33.00 **t.** and a la carte 🛴 7.00.

XX **Raffaelli,** 10-11 Randolph Pl., EH3 7TA, ✆ 225 6060, Fax 225 8830, Italian rest. – 🔼 AE ⓞ
VISA   CY c
closed Saturday lunch, Sunday, 25-26 December and 1-2 January – **M** a la carte 13.10/22.50 t.
⋔ 4.30.

XX **Lancer's Brasserie,** 5 Hamilton Pl., Stockbridge, EH3 5BA, ✆ 332 3444, North Indian
rest. – 🔼 AE ⓞ VISA   CY r
M a la carte 8.70/18.10 t.

XX **Umberto,** 29-33 Dublin St., EH3 6NL, ✆ 556 2231, Italian rest. – 🔼 AE ⓞ VISA   EY e
closed lunch Saturday and Sunday and Sunday dinner in winter – **M** 7.95 t. (lunch) and a la
carte 9.90/18.75 t. ⋔ 4.15.

XX **Merchants,** 17 Merchants St., (under bridge), EH1 2QD, ✆ 225 4009 – 🔼 AE ⓞ VISA
closed Sunday, 25-26 December and 1 January – **M** (booking essential) 15.00/25.00 t. and a
la carte ⋔ 3.50.   EZ x

XX **Indian Cavalry Club,** 3 Atholl Pl., EH3 8HP, ✆ 228 3282, Indian rest. – 🔼 AE ⓞ VISA
M 5.95/13.95 t. and a la carte ⋔ 4.00.   CZ c

XX **Debbretts,** 33-36 Castle Terr., EH1 2EL, ✆ 229 1181 – 🔼 AE ⓞ VISA   DZ a
closed Sunday lunch, Sunday dinner except August, 25-26 December and 1-2 January –
M 10.50/22.50 t. and a la carte 16.40/23.35 t. ⋔ 5.75.

XX **Cosmo,** 58a North Castle St., EH2 3LU, ✆ 226 6743, Italian rest. – 🔼 VISA   DY r
closed Saturday lunch, Sunday and Monday – **M** a la carte 13.80/21.00 t. ⋔ 3.90.

XX Premier Mandarin, 8b Abercromby Pl., EH3 6LB, ✆ 556 2321, Chinese rest.   EY x

GLASGOW Lanark. (Strathclyde) 401 402 H 16 – pop. 754 586 – ✪ 041.

See : Site*** – Burrell Collection*** – Cathedral*** DYZ – Tolbooth Steeple* DZ A – Hunte-
rian Art Gallery** (Whistler Collection*** Mackintosh wing***) CY M2 Art Gallery and Museum
Kelvingrove** CY – City Chambers* DZ C – Glasgow School of Art* CY B – Museum of
Transport** (Scottish cars***, Clyde Room of Ship Models***) M3 – Pollok House* (Spanish
paintings**).

Envir. : Trossachs*** N : by A 739 and A 81 – Loch Lomond** NW : by A 82 – Clyde Estuary*
(Dumbarton Castle, Site*, Hill House*, Helensburgh) by A 82 – Bothwell Castle* and David
Livingstone Centre (Museum*) SE : 9 m. by A 724.

🛆 Linn Park, Simshill Rd ✆ 637 5871, S : 4 m. – 🛆 Lethamhill, Cumbernauld Rd ✆ 770 6220 –
🛆 Knightswood, Lincoln Av. ✆ 959 2131, W : 4 m. – 🛆 Kings Park, Croftpark Av., S : 4 m. by
B 766 – 🛆 Alexandra Park, Alexandra Par. ✆ 556 3211.

Access to Oban by helicopter.

✈ Glasgow Airport : ✆ 887 1111 W : 8 m. by M 8 – Terminal : Coach service from Glasgow
Central and Queen Street main line Railway Stations and from Anderston Cross and Buchanan
Bus Stations.

✈ see also Prestwick.

🛈 35-39 St. Vincent Pl. ✆ 227 4880 – Inchinnon Rd ✆ 848 4440.

Edinburgh 46 – Manchester 221.

Plan on following pages

🏨 **Holiday Inn,** 500 Argyle St., Anderston, G3 8RR, ✆ 226 5577, Telex 776355, Fax 221 9202,
🛆, ⇋, 🔼, squash – 🕴 ❦ rm 🔳 🔟 ☎ & Ⓟ – 🔏 700. 🔼 AE ⓞ VISA   CZ a
M (buffet meals) 17.90 **st.** and a la carte ⋔ 7.65 – 🖵 9.85 – **293 rm** 99.00/140.00 st., **5 suites**
200.00/230.00 st.

🏨 **Forte Albany** (T.H.F.), Bothwell St., G2 7EN, ✆ 248 2656, Telex 77440, Fax 221 8986, ⇋ –
🕴 ❦ rm 🔳 🔟 ☎ Ⓟ – 🔏 1 000. 🔼 AE ⓞ VISA   CZ z
M 12.50 **st.** and a la carte ⋔ 3.95 – 🖵 8.50 – **251 rm** 95.00/105.00 st., **3 suites** 210.00/
250.00 st. – SB (weekends only) 104.00/124.00 st.

🏨 **One Devonshire Gardens,** 1 Devonshire Gdns, G12 OUX, ✆ 339 2001, Fax 337 1663,
« Opulent interior design » – 🔟 ☎. 🔼 AE ⓞ VISA ❦
M *(closed Saturday lunch)* 19.29/39.50 t. and a la carte – 🖵 6.50 – **16 rm** 105.00/150.00 t.,
2 suites 175.00 t.

🏨 Moat House International, Congress Rd, G3 8QT, ✆ 204 0733, Telex 776244, Fax 221 2022,
⇋, 🛆, ⇋, 🔼 – 🕴 ❦ rm 🔳 🔟 ☎ & Ⓟ – 🔏 800   CZ r
285 rm, 15 suites.

🏨 **Hospitality Inn** (Mt. Charlotte Thistle), 36 Cambridge St., G2 3HN, ✆ 332 3311, Telex
777334, Fax 332 4050 – 🕴 🔟 ☎ & Ⓟ – 🔏 1 500. 🔼 AE ⓞ VISA   DY z
M 13.75/16.50 **st.** and a la carte – 🖵 8.50 – **313 rm** 80.00/105.00 st., **3 suites** 180.00 st. –
SB 75.00/85.00 st.

🏨 Stakis Grosvenor, Grosvenor Terr., Great Western Rd, G12 0TA, ✆ 339 8811, Telex 776247,
Fax 334 0710 – 🕴 ❦ 🔟 ☎ Ⓟ – 🔏 250. 🔼 AE ⓞ VISA   CY r
🖵 7.50 – **93 rm** 84.50/109.50 t., **2 suites** 156.00 t. – SB 82.00/136.00 st.

🏨 **Copthorne,** George Sq., G2 1DS, ✆ 332 6711, Telex 778147, Fax 332 4264 – 🕴 ❦ 🔟 ☎ –
🔏 100. 🔼 AE ⓞ VISA ❦   DZ n
M *(closed lunch Saturday, Sunday, and Bank Holiday Mondays)* (carving rest.) 14.00/
15.00 **st.** and a la carte ⋔ 4.95 – 🖵 7.90 – **135 rm** 84.00/96.00 st., **5 suites** 115.00/140.00 st.

🏨 **White House** without rest., 12 Cleveden Cres., G12 0PA, ✆ 339 9375, Telex 777582, Fax 337 1430 – 📺 ☎ – 🏛 25. ✀
20 rm. 11 suites.

🏨 **Swallow**, 517 Paisley Rd West, G51 1RW, ✆ 427 3146, Telex 778795, Fax 427 4059, ⌧, 🔲 – 🛆 ⌧ rm ▤ rest 📺 ☎ 🅿 – 🏛 250
119 rm.

🏨 **Tinto Firs Thistle** (Mt. Charlotte Thistle), 470 Kilmarnock Rd, G43 2BB, ✆ 637 2353, Telex 778329, Fax 633 1340 – 📺 ☎ 🅿 – 🏛 60. 🔼 🅰🅴 ⓞ 𝖵𝖨𝖲𝖠
M 8.00/12.50 **st.** and a la carte – ⌧ 7.75 – **25 rm** 65.00/85.00 **st.. 2 suites** – SB 90.00 **st.**

🏨 **Kelvin Park Lorne** (Q.M.H.), 923 Sauchiehall St., G3 7TE, ✆ 334 4891, Telex 778935, Fax 337 1659 – 🛆 📺 ☎ 🅿 – 🏛 175. 🔼 🅰🅴 ⓞ 𝖵𝖨𝖲𝖠   CY **a**
M *(closed Saturday lunch)* 9.95/14.25 **st.** and a la carte ♦ 4.95 – ⌧ 6.50 – **99 rm** 65.00/130.00 **st.**

🏨 **Crest** (T.H.F.), 377 Argyle St., G2 8LL, ✆ 248 2355, Telex 779652, Fax 221 1014 – 🛆 ⌧ rm 📺 ☎ 🅿 – 🏛 80. 🔼 🅰🅴 ⓞ 𝖵𝖨𝖲𝖠 ✀   CZ **x**
M *(closed lunch Saturday, Sunday, Monday and Bank Holidays)* 9.25/15.95 **t.** and a la carte – ⌧ 7.95 – **121 rm** 60.00/90.00 **st.**

🏨 **Stakis Ingram,** 201 Ingram St., G1 1DQ, ✆ 248 4401, Telex 776470, Fax 226 5149 – 🛆 ⌧ rm 📺 ☎ – 🏛 200. 🔼 🅰🅴 ⓞ 𝖵𝖨𝖲𝖠   DZ **c**
M 8.50/12.95 **t.** – ⌧ 7.50 – **90 rm** 69.00/91.00 **t.** – SB 70.00/114.00 **st.**

🏨 **Jury's Pond** (Stakis), 2-4 Shelley Rd, off Great Western Rd, G12 0XP, ✆ 334 8161, Telex 776573, Fax 334 3846, ⌧, ⌧, 🔲 – 🛆 ⌧ rm 📺 ☎ 🅿 – 🏛 50
137 rm.

XXX **North Rotunda,** (2nd floor) 28 Tunnel St., G3 8HL, ✆ 204 1238, Fax 226 4264, French rest. – 🅿 🔼 🅰🅴 ⓞ 𝖵𝖨𝖲𝖠   CZ **u**
closed Saturday lunch, Sunday, 25-26 December, 1-2 January and Bank Holiday Mondays –
M 10.75/19.00 **t.** and a la carte ♦ 4.95.

XXX Killermont House, 2022 Maryhill Rd, Maryhill Park, G20 0AB, ✆ 946 5412, ☞ – 🅿.

XXX **Fountain,** 2 Woodside Cres., G3 7UL, ✆ 332 6396 – 🔼 𝖵𝖨𝖲𝖠   CY **c**
closed Saturday lunch and Sunday – **M** 9.00/13.95 **t.** and a la carte.

XX **Buttery,** 652 Argyle St., G3 8UF, ✆ 221 8188, Fax 204 4639 – 🅿 🔼 🅰🅴 ⓞ 𝖵𝖨𝖲𝖠   CZ **e**
closed Saturday lunch, Sunday and Bank Holidays – **M** 12.50 **st.** (lunch) and a la carte 17.55/26.00 **t.**

XX **Rogano,** 11 Exchange Pl., G1 3AN, ✆ 248 4055, Fax 248 2608, Seafood, « Art deco » – 🔼 🅰🅴 𝖵𝖨𝖲𝖠   DZ **i**
closed Sunday and Bank Holidays – **M** a la carte 22.95/27.95 **t.**

XX Cafe India, 171 North St., G3 7DL, ✆ 248 4074, Indian rest. – 🅿   CY **e**

XX Ho Wong, 82 York St., G2 3LE, ✆ 221 3550, Chinese (Peking) rest. – ▤   CZ **v**

XX Amber Royale, 336 Argyle St., G2 8LY, ✆ 221 2550, Chinese rest. – ▤   CZ **o**

X **Ubiquitous Chip,** 12 Ashton Lane, off Byres Rd, G12 8SJ, ✆ 334 5007 – 🔼 🅰🅴 ⓞ 𝖵𝖨𝖲𝖠
closed 25 and 31 December-1 January – **M** a la carte 14.70/22.80 **t.**

at Glasgow Airport Renfrew. (Strathclyde) W : 8 m. by M 8 – ✉ ✪ 041 Glasgow :

🏨 **Excelsior** (T.H.F.), Abbotsinch, PA3 2TR, ✆ 887 1212, Telex 777733, Fax 887 3738 – 🛆 ⌧ rm ▤ 📺 ☎ 🅿 – 🏛 400. 🔼 🅰🅴 ⓞ 𝖵𝖨𝖲𝖠 ✀
M (carving rest.) 13.50 **st.** and a la carte ♦ 7.00 – ⌧ 9.00 – **283 rm** 80.00/90.00 **st.. 5 suites** 120.00 **st.** – SB (weekends only) (except Easter, Christmas and New Year) 80.00/100.00 **st.**

When in Europe never be without :

Michelin **Main Road** Maps ;

Michelin Sectional Maps ;

Michelin Red Guides :

**Benelux, Deutschland, España Portugal, France,
Great Britain and Ireland, Italia**

(Hotels and restaurants listed with symbols ; preliminary pages in English)

Michelin Green Guides :

**Austria, England : The West Country, Germany, Greece, Italy,
London, Netherlands, Portugal, Rome, Scotland, Spain, Switzerland,
Brittany, Burgundy, Châteaux of the Loire, Dordogne,
French Riviera, Ile-de-France, Normandy Cotentin,
Normandy Seine Valley, Paris, Provence**

(Sights and touring programmes described fully in English ; town plans).

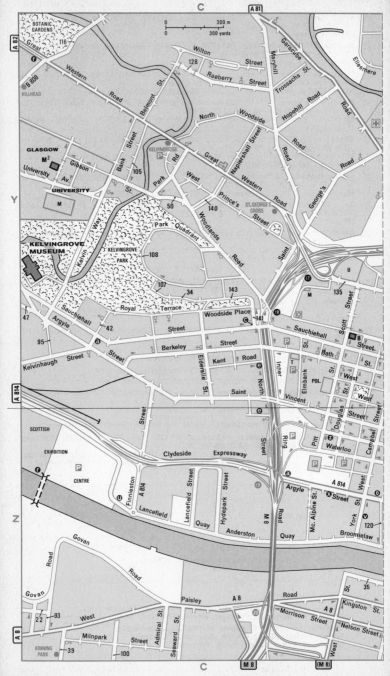

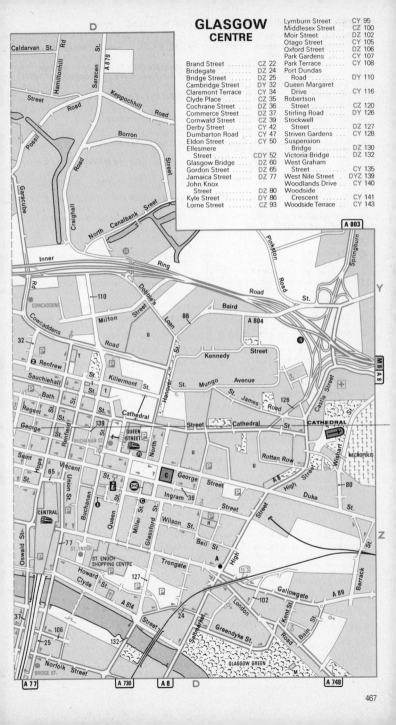

GLASGOW
CENTRE

467

LEEDS West Yorks. **402** P 22 – pop. 445 242 – ECD : Wednesday – ✆ 0532.

See : Site★ – City Art Gallery★ DZ M.

Envir. : Temple Newsam House★ 17C (interior★★) *AC*, E : 4 m. – Kirkstall Abbey★ (ruins 12C) *AC*, NW : 3 m.

🏌, 🏌 The Temple Newsam, Temple Newsam Rd, Halton ✆ 645624, E : 3 m. – 🏌 Gotts Park, Armley Ridge Rd, ✆ 638232, W : 2 m. – 🏌 Middleton Park, Town St., Middleton ✆ 700449, S : 3 m. – 🏌 Roundhay, Park Lane ✆ 662695.

✈ Leeds and Bradford Airport : ✆ 509696, Telex 557868 NW : 8 m. by A 65 and A 658.

🛈 19 Wellington St. ✆ 462454.

London 204 – Liverpool 75 – Manchester 43 – Newcastle-upon-Tyne 95 – Nottingham 74.

Plan opposite

🏨 **Leeds Hilton,** Neville St., LS1 4BX, ✆ 442000, Telex 557143, Fax 433577 – 🕴 ⇔ rm 🗏 📺 DZ **r**
   ☎ & 🄿 – 🛗 400. 🕾 🖭 ⓞ *VISA*
   M 11.50/15.50 **t.** and a la carte ⚱ 4.70 – ☲ 11.75 – **225 rm** 95.00/110.00 **st.**, **3 suites** 135.00/155.00 **st.**

🏨 **Queens** (T.H.F.), City Sq., LS1 1PL, ✆ 431323, Telex 55161, Fax 425154 – 🕴 ⇔ rm 📺 ☎ & DZ **a**
   – 🛗 600. 🕾 🖭 ⓞ *VISA*
   M 12.00/15.00 **st.** and a la carte ⚱ 4.00 – ☲ 9.00 – **183 rm** 90.00/100.00 **st.**, **5 suites** 150.00/200.00 **st.** – SB (except Christmas) 80.00 **st.**

🏤 **Golden Lion** (Mt. Charlotte Thistle), Lower Briggate, LS1 4AE, ✆ 436454, Fax 429327 – 🕴 DZ **v**
   📺 ☎ – 🛗 80. 🕾 🖭 ⓞ *VISA*
   M *(closed Sunday lunch)* 11.25 **st.** (dinner) and a la carte 13.25/17.95 **t.** – **89 rm** ☲ 60.00/70.00 **st.** – SB (weekends only) 67.00 **st.**

🏤 **Merrion** (Mt. Charlotte Thistle), Merrion Centre, 17 Wade Lane, LS2 8NH, ✆ 439191, Telex 55459, Fax 423527 – 🕴 📺 ☎ 🄿 – 🛗 80. 🕾 🖭 ⓞ *VISA* DZ **x**
   M 12.25 **t.** and a la carte ⚱ 4.10 – ☲ 7.25 – **120 rm** 70.95/76.40 **t.** – SB 82.50/166.10 **st.**

XXX **Mandalay,** 8 Harrison St., LS1 6PA, ✆ 446453, Indian rest. – 🗏. 🕾 🖭 ⓞ *VISA* DZ **e**
   closed Sunday lunch, 25-26 December and 1 January – **M** 12.50 **t.** and a la carte.

   at Seacroft NE : 5 ½ m. at junction of A 64 and A 6120 – ✉ ✆ 0532 Leeds :

🏤 **Stakis Windmill,** Ring Rd, LS14 5QP, ✆ 732323, Telex 55452, Fax 323018 – 🕴 🗏 rest 📺
   ☎ 🄿 – 🛗 300. 🕾 🖭 ⓞ *VISA*
   M 7.95/13.95 **t.** – ☲ 7.50 – **99 rm** 70.00/92.00 **t.** – SB 74.00/110.00 **st.**

   at Garforth E : 6 m. at Junction of A 63 and A 642 – ✉ ✆ 0532 Leeds :

🏤 Hilton National, Wakefield Rd, LS25 1LH, ✆ 866556, Telex 556324, Fax 868326, 🖾 – ⇔ rm
   📺 ☎ & 🄿 – 🛗
   141 rm

   at Horsforth NW : 5 m. by A 65 off A 6120 – ✉ ✆ 0532 Leeds :

XXX **Low Hall,** Calverley Lane, LS18 5EF, ✆ 588221, « Elizabethan manor », 🐴 – 🄿. 🕾 *VISA*
   closed Saturday lunch, Sunday and Monday – **M** 11.50/19.50 **t.** and a la carte.

   at Bramhope NW : 8 m. on A 660 – ✉ ✆ 0532 Leeds :

🏤 **Post House** (T.H.F.), Leeds Rd, LS16 9JJ, ✆ 842911, Telex 556367, Fax 843451, ≼, ⇋, 🖾,
   🐴 – 🕴 ⇔ rm 📺 ☎ 🄿 – 🛗 180. 🕾 🖭 ⓞ *VISA*
   M 19.95 **st.** and a la carte – ☲ 7.60 – **126 rm** 85.00/100.00 **st.**, **1 suite** 150.00 **st.** – SB (weekends only) 90.00/104.00 **st.**

🏤 **Parkway,** Otley Rd, LS16 8AG, S : 2 m. on A 660 ✆ 672551, Fax 674410, ⇋, 🖾, 🐴, ⚹
   – 🕴 📺 ☎ & 🄿 – 🛗 250. 🕾 🖭 ⓞ *VISA*. ✼
   M 10.95/14.00 **st.** and a la carte ⚱ 4.95 – ☲ 7.50 – **103 rm** 79.00/120.00 **st.** – SB (weekends only) 36.00/41.00 **st.**

Ilkley West Yorks. NW : 16 m. by A 660 on A 65 – **402** O 22 – pop. 13 060 – ✆ 0943.

XXX ✿ **Box Tree,** 35-37 Church St., LS29 9DR, ✆ 608484, « Ornate decor » – 🕾 🖭 ⓞ *VISA*
   closed Sunday dinner, Monday, 25-26 December and 1 January – **M** (booking essential) (dinner only and Sunday lunch)/dinner 18.50/30.00 **st.** and a la carte approx. 30.00 **st.** ⚱ 5.95
   Spec. Dodine of duck, shallot and thyme marmalade, Fillet of sea bass with scallops and champagne, Timbale of strawberries.

Michelin Green Guides in English

Austria	Italy	New York City
Canada	London	Portugal
England : The West Country	Mexico	Rome
Germany	Netherlands	Scotland
Greece	New England	Spain
		Switzerland

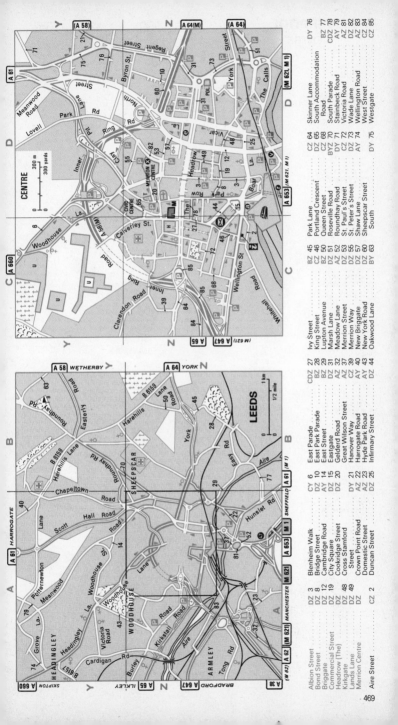

LIVERPOOL
CENTRE

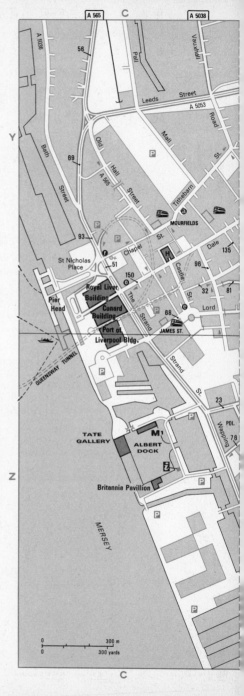

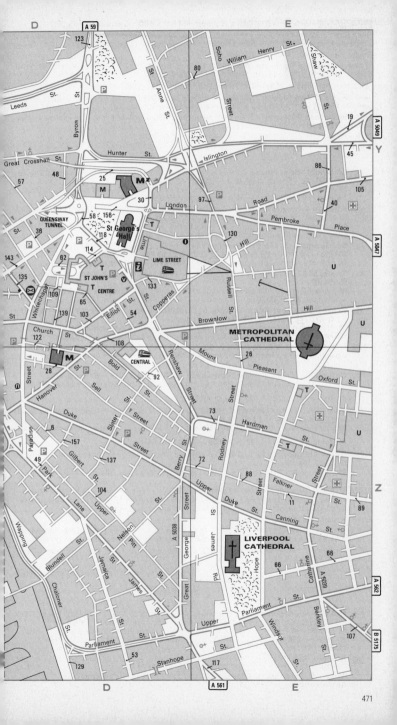

LIVERPOOL Merseyside **402 403** L 23 – pop. 538 809 – ECD : Wednesday – ✪ 051.

See : Site★ – Walker Art Gallery★★ DY **M2** – Liverpool Cathedral★★ – Metropolitan Cathedral of Christ the King★★ (1967) EYZ – Albert Dock★ CZ – Tate Gallery Liverpool★ CZ.

Envir. : Speke Hall★ (16C) *AC*, SE : 8 m. by A 561.

🖪 Dunnings Bridge Rd, Bootle 𝒫 928 1371 N : 5 m. by A 5036 – 🖪 Allerton Park 𝒫 428 8510, S : 5 m. by B 5180 – 🖪 Childwall, Naylor's Rd, Gateacre 𝒫 487 0654, E : 7 m. by B 5178.

✈ Liverpool Airport 𝒫 486 8877, Telex 629323, SE : 6 m. by A 561 – **Terminal :** Pier Head.

⚓ to Ireland (Dun Laoghaire)(Sealink) 1 daily – to Belfast (Belfast Ferries) 1 daily (9 h) – to Douglas (Isle of Man Steam Packet Co.) 2-4 weekly (summer only) (4 h).

⚓ to Birkenhead (Merseyside Transport) frequent services daily (7-8 mn) – to Wallasey (Merseyside Transport) frequent services daily (7-8 mn).

🛈 29 Lime St. 𝒫 709 3631 – Atlantic Pavilion, Albert Dock 𝒫 708 8854.

London 219 – Birmingham 103 – Leeds 75 – Manchester 35.

Plan on preceding pages

🏨 **Liverpool Moat House** (Q.M.H.), Paradise St., L1 8JD, 𝒫 709 0181, Telex 627270, Fax 709 2706, ⛴, 🔲 – 🛗 📺 🅿 ♿ – 🔬 400. ◫ ◫ ⑩ 𝖵𝖨𝖲𝖠   DZ **n**
M *(closed Saturday lunch)* 14.00/17.25 **st.** and a la carte ₰ 7.45 – **244 rm** ⊆ 77.50/99.00 t., **7 suites** 180.00/230.00 t. – SB (weekends only) 87.00/118.00 st.

🏨 **Atlantic Tower** (Mt. Charlotte Thistle), 30 Chapel St., L3 9RE, 𝒫 227 4444, Telex 627070, Fax 236 3973, ⇐ – 🛗 ▤ 📺 🅿 🖂 – 🔬 120. ◫ ◫ ⑩ 𝖵𝖨𝖲𝖠   CY **r**
M *(closed Saturday lunch)* 14.50/14.95 **t.** and a la carte ₰ 4.40 – ⊆ 6.95 – **216 rm** 67.50/75.00 st., **10 suites** 125.00/150.00 st. – SB 72.00 st.

🏨 **St. George's** (T.H.F.), St. John's Precinct, Lime St., L1 1NQ, 𝒫 709 7090, Telex 627630, Fax 709 0137 – 🛗 ⇔ rm 📺 ▤ 🅿 – 🔬 200. ◫ ◫ ⑩ 𝖵𝖨𝖲𝖠   DY **v**
M 10.45 **st.** and a la carte ₰ 3.75 – ⊆ 7.60 – **153 rm** 60.00/81.00 st., **2 suites** 87.00/95.00 st.

🏨 **Trials**, 56-62 Castle St., L2 7LQ, 𝒫 227 1021, Telex 626125, Fax 236 0110 – 🛗 📺 ☎ 🅿. ◫ ◫ ⑩ 𝖵𝖨𝖲𝖠 ✄   CY **e**
M *(closed Saturday lunch and Sunday)* 10.95 **t.** (lunch)/dinner a la carte 12.70/20.35 t. ₰ 6.95 – ⊆ 7.50 – **20 rm** 98.00/150.00 t.

🏨 **Crest** (T.H.F.), Lord Nelson St., L3 5QB, 𝒫 709 7050, Telex 627954, Fax 709 2193 – 🛗 ⇔ rm 📺 ☎ 🅿 – 🔬 500. ◫ ◫ ⑩ 𝖵𝖨𝖲𝖠   DY **i**
M *(closed lunch Saturday and Sunday)* 8.00/15.00 **st.** and a la carte ₰ 6.50 – ⊆ 7.95 – **155 rm** 64.00/76.00 st., **1 suite** 80.00/95.00 st. – SB (weekends only) 74.00/82.00 st.

XXX **L'Oriel**, Oriel Chambers, 14 Water Street, L2 8TD, 𝒫 236 5025 – ◫ ◫ ⑩ 𝖵𝖨𝖲𝖠   CY **o**
closed 25-26 December and 1 January – **M** *(closed lunch Saturday, Sunday and Bank Holidays)* 12.25/14.25 **t.** and a la carte ₰ 4.10.

XXX **Churchill's**, Churchill House, Tithebarn St., L2 2PB, 𝒫 227 3877 – ◫ ◫ ⑩ 𝖵𝖨𝖲𝖠   CY **a**
closed Saturday lunch, Sunday and Bank Holidays – **M** 12.00/14.00 **t.** and a la carte.

at Bootle N : 5 m. by A 565 – ✉ ✪ 051 Liverpool :

🏨 **Park** (De Vere), Park Lane West, L30 3SU, on A 5036 𝒫 525 7555, Telex 629772, Fax 525 2481 – 🛗 📺 ☎ 🅿 – 🔬 50. ◫ ◫ ⑩ 𝖵𝖨𝖲𝖠
M 6.00/9.95 **t.** and a la carte ₰ 3.50 – **58 rm** ⊆ 49.50/62.00 t. – SB (weekends only) 60.00 **st.**

at Huyton E : 7 m. by M 62 on A 5058 – ✉ ✪ 051 Liverpool :

🏨 **Derby Lodge**, Roby Rd, L36 4HD, 𝒫 480 4440, Telex 629371, Fax 480 8132, ☞ – 📺 ☎ 🅿. ◫ ◫ 𝖵𝖨𝖲𝖠 ✄
M *(closed Saturday lunch)* 10.50/12.00 **st.** and a la carte ₰ 3.70 – **19 rm** ⊆ 70.00/84.00 t.

MANCHESTER Greater Manchester **402 403 404** N 23 – pop. 437 612 – ECD : Wednesday – ✪ 061 – See : Site★ – Town Hall★ (19C) DYZ **H** - City Art Gallery★ DZ – Whitworth Art Gallery★ – Cathedral 15C (chancel★) DY **B** – John Ryland's Library (manuscripts★) CY **A**.

Envir. : Heaton Hall★ (18C) *AC*, N : 5 m.

🖪 Heaton Park, 𝒫 798 0295, N : by A 576 – 🖪 Fairfield Golf and Sailing, Booth Rd, Audenshaw, 𝒫 370 1641, E : by A 635 – 🖪 Houldsworth, Wingate House, Higher Levenshulme 𝒫 224 5055.

✈ Manchester International Airport 𝒫 (061) 489 3000 (British Airways) Tele – **Terminal :** Coach service from Victoria Station.

🛈 Town Hall Extension, Lloyd St. 𝒫 234 3157/8 – Manchester International Airport, International Arrivals Hall 𝒫 436 3344.

London 202 – Birmingham 86 – Glasgow 221 – Leeds 43 – Liverpool 35 – Nottingham 72.

Plan opposite

🏨 **Holiday Inn Crowne Plaza Midland**, 16 Peter St., M60 2DS, 𝒫 236 3333, Telex 667550, Fax 228 2241, ⛴, 🔲, squash – 🛗 ⇔ rm ▤ 📺 ☎ ♿ – 🔬 300. ◫ ◫ ⑩ 𝖵𝖨𝖲𝖠 ✄   DZ **x**
M French rest. 14.95/27.50 **t.** and a la carte – **Trafford Room** (carving rest.) 14.95 st. – ⊆ 8.95 – **296 rm** 95.00/112.00 st., **7 suites** 185.00/375.00 st. – SB (weekends only) 113.90/138.00 **st.**

🏨 **Ramada Renaissance**, Blackfriars St., Deansgate, M3 2EQ, 𝒫 835 2555, Telex 669699, Fax 835 3077 – 🛗 ⇔ rm ▤ rest 📺 ☎ 🅿 – 🔬 400. ◫ ◫ ⑩ 𝖵𝖨𝖲𝖠   CY **v**
M 14.50/27.00 **st.** and a la carte – **200 rm** ⊆ 95.00/110.00 t., **5 suites** 145.00/250.00 t. – SB (weekends only) 138.50/142.50 **st.**

Piccadilly, Piccadilly Plaza, M60 1QR, ℰ 236 8414, Telex 668765, Fax 228 1568, ≤, ≘s, ⬛ – 🛗 ⚡ rm ▤ rest 📺 ☎ 🅿 – 🛗 700. ⬛ 🅰🅴 ⑩ 𝓥𝓘𝓢𝓐. 🍽 DY **s**
M 11.50/17.50 **t.** and a la carte ≬ 4.00 – 🖃 8.75 – **264 rm** 95.00/115.00 **st.. 9 suites** 210.00/220.00 **st.** – SB (weekends only) 99.00/105.00 **st.**

Copthorne Manchester, Clippers Quay, Salford Quays, M5 3DL, ℰ 873 7321, Telex 669090, Fax 873 7318, ≘s, ⬛ – 🛗 ⚡ rm ▤ rest 📺 ☎ 🕭 🅿 – 🛗 75. ⬛ 🅰🅴 ⑩ 𝓥𝓘𝓢𝓐. 🍽
M 13.50/28.25 **st.** and a la carte ≬ 4.75 – 🖃 8.25 – **166 rm** 75.00/100.00 **st.**

Portland Thistle (Mt. Charlotte Thistle), Portland St., Piccadilly Gdns, M1 6DP, ℰ 228 3400, Telex 669157, Fax 228 6347, ≘s, ⬛ – 🛗 ⚡ rm ▤ rest 📺 ☎ 🅿 – 🛗 300. ⬛ 🅰🅴 ⑩ 𝓥𝓘𝓢𝓐
M 12.00/14.00 **st.** – **205 rm** 79.00/105.00 **st..** **3 suites** – SB 85.00 **st.** DY **a**

Isola Bella, Dolefield, Crown Sq., M3 3EN, ℰ 831 7099, Italian rest. – ⬛ 🅰🅴 𝓥𝓘𝓢𝓐 CY **e**
closed Sunday and Bank Holidays – **M** a la carte 14.20/30.20 **st.** ≬ 5.00.

Giulio's Terrazza, 14 Nicholas St., M1 4FE, ℰ 236 4033, Italian rest. – ⬛ 🅰🅴 ⑩ 𝓥𝓘𝓢𝓐 DZ **r**
closed Sunday and Bank Holidays – **M** 9.50 **t.** and a la carte 19.35/28.35 **t.** ≬ 4.50.

MANCHESTER
CENTRE

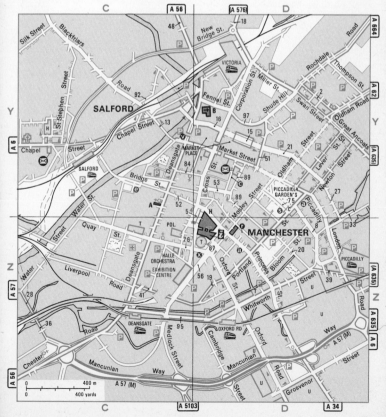

XX **Gaylord,** Amethyst House, Marriott's Court, Spring Gdns, M2 1EA, 𝒫 832 6037, Indian
rest. – 🍽. 🔼 ⅍ꜰ ① 𝑉𝐼𝑆𝐴   DY **c**
closed 25 December and 1 January – **M** a la carte 6.85/9.50 **t.** ⬧ 4.25.

X **Yang Sing,** 34 Princess St., M1 4JY, 𝒫 236 2200, Fax 236 5934, Chinese (Canton) rest. –
🔼 ⅍ꜰ 𝑉𝐼𝑆𝐴   DZ **a**
closed 25 December – **M** (booking essential) a la carte approx. 12.00 **t.**

at Manchester Airport S : 9 m. by A 5103 off M 56 – ✉ ✿ 061 Manchester :

🏢 **Manchester Airport Hilton,** Outwood Lane, Ringway, M22 5WP, 𝒫 436 4404, Telex
668361, Fax 436 1521 – ⬧ ↔ rm 📺 ☎ ⅍ 🅟 – ⅍ 130. 🔼 ⅍ꜰ ① 𝑉𝐼𝑆𝐴
M a la carte 15.50/31.75 ⬧ 6.25 – ☞ 10.25 – **223 rm** 97.50/140.00 **st.** – SB (weekends
only) 245.00 **st.**

🏢 **Excelsior** (T.H.F.), Ringway Rd, Wythenshawe, M22 5NS, 𝒫 437 5811, Telex 668721, Fax
436 2340, ⬧⬧, ⅃ heated – ⬧ ↔ rm 🍽 📺 ☎ ⅍ 🅟 – ⅍ 200. 🔼 ⅍ꜰ ① 𝑉𝐼𝑆𝐴
M 11.50/16.50 **st.** and a la carte ⬧ 5.25 – ☞ 8.50 – **300 rm** 95.00/110.00 **st.**, **4 suites**
170.00/270.00 **st.** – SB (weekends only) 90.00/100.00 **st.**

XXX **Moss Nook,** Ringwood Rd, Moss Nook, M22 5NA, 𝒫 437 4778 – 🅟. 🔼 ⅍ꜰ ① 𝑉𝐼𝑆𝐴
closed Saturday lunch, Sunday, Monday, 25 December-10 January and Bank Holidays –
M 16.50/24.00 **st.** and a la carte ⬧ 6.50.

at Worsley W : 7 ¼ m. by A 57 and M 602 off M 62 East – ✉ ✿ 061 Manchester :

🏢 **Novotel Manchester West,** Worsley Brow, at Junction 13 of M 62, M28 4YA, 𝒫 799 3535,
Telex 699586, Fax 703 8207, ⅃ heated – ⬧ ↔ rm 🍽 📺 ☎ ⅍ 🅟 – ⅍ 200. 🔼 ⅍ꜰ ① 𝑉𝐼𝑆𝐴
M 11.50/12.50 **st.** and a la carte ⬧ 3.85 – ☞ 6.50 – **119 rm** 58.00/116.00 **st.**

INTERNATIONAL DIALLING CODES — **INDICATIFS TÉLÉPHONIQUES INTERNATIONAUX** — **INTERNATIONALE TELEFON-VORWAHLNUMMERN** — 国際電話国別番号

from \ to	Ⓐ	Ⓑ	ⒸⒽ	Ⓓ	ⒹⓀ	Ⓔ	Ⓕ	ⒼⒷ	Ⓘ	ⒾⓇⓁ	Ⓙ	Ⓛ	Ⓝ	ⓃⓁ	Ⓟ	Ⓢ	ⓈⒻ	ⓊⓈⒶ
AUSTRIA	–	0032	05	06	0045	0034	0033	0044	040	00353	0081	00352	0047	0031	00351	0046	00358	001
BELGIUM	0043	–	0041	0049	0045	0034	0033	0044	0039	00353	0081	00352	0047	0031	00351	0046	00358	001
DENMARK	00943	00932	00941	00949	–	00934	00933	00944	00939	009353	00981	009352	00947	00931	009351	00946	009358	0091
FINLAND	99043	99032	99041	99049	99045	99034	99033	99044	99039	990353	99081	990352	99047	99031	990351	990046	–	9901
FRANCE	1943	1932	1941	1949	1945	1934	–	1944	1939	19353	1981	19352	1947	1931	19351	1946	19358	191
GERMANY	0043	0032	0041	–	0045	0034	0033	0044	0039	00353	0081	00352	0047	0031	00351	0046	00358	001
GREECE	0043	0032	0041	0049	0045	0034	0033	0044	0039	00353	0081	00352	0047	0031	00351	0046	00358	001
IRELAND	1643	1632	1641	1649	1645	1634	1633	1644	1639	–	1681	16352	1647	1631	16351	1646	16358	161
ITALY	0043	0032	0041	0049	0045	0034	0033	0044	–	00353	0081	00352	0047	0031	00351	0046	00358	001
JAPAN	00143	00132	00141	00149	00145	00134	00133	00144	00139	001353	–	001352	00147	00131	001351	00146	001358	0011
LUXEMBOURG	0043	0032	0041	0049	0045	0034	0033	0044	0039	00353	0081	–	0047	0031	00351	0046	00358	001
NORWAY	09543	09532	09541	09549	09545	09534	09533	09544	09539	095353	09581	095352	–	09531	095351	09546	095358	0951
NEDERLAND	0943	0932	0941	0949	0945	0934	0933	0944	0939	09353	0981	09352	0947	–	09351	0946	09358	091
PORTUGAL	0743	0732	0741	0749	0745	0734	0733	0744	0739	07353	0781	07352	0747	0731	–	0746	07358	071
SPAIN	0743	0732	0741	0749	0745	–	0733	0744	0739	07353	0781	07352	0747	0731	07351	0746	07358	071
SWEDEN	00943	00932	00941	00949	00945	00934	00933	00944	00939	009353	00981	009352	00947	00931	009351	–	009358	0091
SWITZERLAND	0043	0032	–	0049	0045	0034	0033	0044	0039	00353	0081	00352	0047	0031	00351	0046	00358	001
UNITED KINGDOM	01043	01032	01041	01049	01045	01034	01033	–	01039	010353	01081	010352	01047	01031	010351	01046	010358	0101
USA	01143	01132	01141	01149	01145	01134	01133	01144	01139	011353	01181	011352	01147	01131	011351	01146	011358	–

CALENDAR OF MAIN TRADE FAIRS AND OTHER INTERNATIONAL EVENTS

AUSTRIA
Vienna	Wiener Festwochen	May-June
Salzburg	Salzburg Festival (Festspiele)	23 March to 1 April
		26 July to 31 August

BENELUX
Amsterdam	Holland Festival	June
Bruges	Ascension Day Procession	Ascension
Brussels	Guild Procession (Ommegang)	first Thursday of July
	Holiday and Leisure Activities International Show	16 to 24 March
	Belgian Antique Dealers Fair	end Jan./beginning Feb.
	Eurantica (Antiques Show)	20 to 28 April

DENMARK
Copenhagen	Scandinavian Furniture Fair	24 to 28 April
	Future Fashion Fair	14 to 17 February
		22 to 25 August

FINLAND
Helsinki	Nordic Fashion Fair	January
	Finnish Boot and Shoe Fair	28 and 29 Sept.
	International Horse Show	18 to 20 October

FRANCE
Paris	Paris Fair	27 April to 9 May
Cannes	International Film Festival	9 to 20 May
Lyons	Lyons Fair	6 to 15 April
Marseilles	Marseilles Fair	27 Sept. to 7 Oct.

GERMANY
Berlin	Berlin Fair (Grüne Woche)	25 Jan. to 3 February
Frankfurt	International Fair	16 to 20 February
		24 to 28 August
	IAA International Motor Show	12 to 22 September
	Frankfurt Book Fair	9 to 14 October
Hanover	Hanover Fair	13 to 20 March
		10 to 17 April
Leipzig	Leipzig Fair (Spring)	17 to 23 March
	» » (Autumn)	1 to 7 September
	International Book Fair	24 to 29 April
Munich	Beer Festival (Oktoberfest)	21 Sept. to 6 Oct.

GREECE
Athens	Athens Festival	From June to end Sept.
Salonica	International Fair	September

IRELAND
Dublin	Dublin Horse Show	6 to 10 Aug.

ITALY
Milan	Fashion Fair (Milanovendemoda)	7 to 11 February
Palermo	Mediterranean Fair	25 May to 9 June
Turin	Motor Show	8 to 12 April

NORWAY
Oslo	Nor-Shipping	11 to 14 June
	Fashion Week	31 Aug. to 3 Sept.

PORTUGAL

| Lisbon | International Fair | 15 to 19 May |

SPAIN

Madrid	Expo-Ocio	16 to 24 March
Barcelona	International Fair	27 May to 1 June
Sevilla	April Fair	16 to 21 April
Valencia	International Fair	26 Dec. to 3 Jan.
	Fallas	12 to 19 March

SWEDEN

Stockholm	Computer and Office Fair	23 to 27 Sept.
	International Technical Fair	21 to 26 October
	Stockholm Water Festival	9 to 18 August
Gothenburg	International Boat Show	31 Jan. to 9 Feb 92
	Book and Library Fair	9 to 13 Sept.

SWITZERLAND

| Geneva | Motor Show | March 92 |
| Zurich | Boat Show | February 92 |

UNITED KINGDOM

London	London International Boat Show	2 to 12 January 92
Birmingham	International Antique Fair	9 to 15 April
Edinburgh	Arts Festival	11 to 31 August
	Edinburgh Science Festival	1 to 14 April

MANUFACTURE FRANÇAISE DES PNEUMATIQUES MICHELIN

Société en commandite par actions au capital de 2 000 000 000 de francs.

Place des Carmes-Déchaux - 63 Clermont-Ferrand (France)

R.C.S. Clermont-Fd B 855 200 507

© Michelin et Cie, Propriétaires-Éditeurs 1991

Dépôt légal 4-91 - ISBN 2 06 007 019 - 8

Printed in France 3-91-45

Impression : KAPP LAHURE JOMBART, Évreux n° 1324